Brand Library & Art Center
1601 West Mountain Street
Glendale CA 91201
818.548.2051
www.BrandLibrary.org

The Grove Dictionary of

Musical Instruments

Volume Five

The Grove Dictionary of
Musical Instruments

Second Edition

Volume Five

Tibia – Zygmuntowicz, Samuel

Edited by
Laurence Libin

OXFORD
UNIVERSITY PRESS

OXFORD
UNIVERSITY PRESS

Oxford University Press is a department of the University of Oxford.
It furthers the University's objective of excellence in research, scholarship,
and education by publishing worldwide.

Oxford   New York
Auckland   Cape Town   Dar es Salaam   Hong Kong   Karachi
Kuala Lumpur   Madrid   Melbourne   Mexico City   Nairobi
New Delhi   Shanghai   Taipei   Toronto

With offices in
Argentina   Austria   Brazil   Chile   Czech Republic   France   Greece
Guatemala   Hungary   Italy   Japan   Poland   Portugal   Singapore
South Korea   Switzerland   Thailand   Turkey   Ukraine   Vietnam

Oxford and Grove are registered trade marks of Oxford University Press
in the UK and certain other countries.

Published in the United States of America by
Oxford University Press
198 Madison Avenue, New York, NY 10016

The first edition was published as *The New Grove Dictionary of Musical Instruments*
Edited by Stanley Sadie (Macmillan, 1984).

Library of Congress Cataloging-in-Publication Data

The Grove dictionary of musical instruments / edited by Laurence Libin. Second edition.
volumes cm
Includes bibliographical references and index.
Previous edition published under title: New Grove dictionary of musical instruments.
ISBN 978–0–19–974339–1 (set: alk. paper) — ISBN 978–0–19–935030–8
(v.1 : alk. paper) — ISBN 978–0–19–935031–5 (v.2 : alk. paper) — ISBN 978–0–19–935032–2
(v.3 : alk. paper) — ISBN 978–0–19–935033–9 (v.4 : alk. paper) — ISBN 978–0–19–935034–6
(v.5 : alk. paper) 1. Musical instruments—Dictionaries. I. Libin, Laurence, editor.
ML102.I5N48 2014
784.1903—dc23   2013020197

1 3 5 7 9 8 6 4 2

Printed in the United States of America
on acid-free paper

Contents

General Abbreviations

A	alto, contralto [voice]	ASOL	American Symphony Orchestra League
a	alto [instrument]	Assn	Association
AA	Associate of the Arts	attrib(s).	attribution(s), attributed to; ascription(s), ascribed to
AAS	Associates in Arts and Sciences		
AB	Alberta; Bachelor of Arts	Aug	August
ABC	American Broadcasting Company; Australian Broadcasting Commission	aut.	autumn
		AZ	Arizona
Abt.	Abteilung [section]	aztl	*azione teatrale*
ACA	American Composers Alliance		
acc.	accompaniment, accompanied by	B	bass [voice], bassus
accdn	accordion	B	Brainard catalogue [Tartini], Benton catalogue [Pleyel]
addl	additional		
addn(s)	addition(s)	b	bass [instrument]
ad lib	ad libitum	*b*	born
AFM	American Federation of Musicians	BA	Bachelor of Arts
AFRS	Armed Forces Radio Service	bal(s)	ballad opera(s)
AFR&TS	Armed Forces Radio & Television Service	bap.	baptized
aft(s)	afterpiece(s)	Bar	baritone [voice]
Ag	Agnus Dei	bar	baritone [instrument]
AGMA	American Guild of Musical Artists	B-Bar	bass-baritone
AIDS	Acquired Immune Deficiency Syndrome	BBC	British Broadcasting Corporation
AK	Alaska	BC	British Columbia
AL	Alabama	bc	basso continuo
all(s)	alleluia(s)	BCE	before Common Era [BC]
AM	Master of Arts	Bd.	Band [volume]
a.m.	ante meridiem [before noon]	BEd	Bachelor of Education
AMC	American Music Center	Beds.	Bedfordshire
Amer.	American	Berks.	Berkshire
amp	amplified	Berwicks.	Berwickshire
AMS	American Musicological Society	BFA	Bachelor of Fine Arts
Anh.	Anhang [appendix]	BFE	British Forum for Ethnomusicology
anon.	anonymous(ly)	bk(s)	book(s)
ant(s)	antiphon(s)	BLitt	Bachelor of Letters/Literature
appx(s)	appendix(es)	blq(s)	burlesque(s)
AR	Arkansas	blt(s)	burletta(s)
arr(s).	arrangement(s), arranged by/for	BM	Bachelor of Music
ARSC	Association for Recorded Sound Collections	BME,	
a-s	all-sung	BMEd	Bachelor of Music Education
AS	American Samoa	BMI	Broadcast Music Inc.
ASCAP	American Society of Composers, Authors and Publishers	BMus	Bachelor of Music

bn	bassoon		c/o	care of
BRD	Federal Republic of Germany (Bundesre-publik Deutschland [West Germany])		CO	Colorado
			Co.	Company; County
Bros.	Brothers		Cod.	Codex
BRTN	Belgische Radio en Televisie Nederlands		coll.	collected by
Bs	Benedictus		collab.	in collaboration with
BS, BSc	Bachelor of Science		colln	collection
BSM	Bachelor of Sacred Music		col(s).	column(s)
Bte	Benedicite		com	*componimento*
Bucks.	Buckinghamshire		comm(s)	communion(s)
Bulg.	Bulgarian		comp.	compiler, compiled by
bur.	buried		comp(s).	composer(s), composed (by)
BVM	Blessed Virgin Mary		conc(s).	concerto(s)
BWV	Bach-Werke-Verzeichnis [Schmieder, catalogue of J.S. Bach's works]		cond(s).	conductor(s), conducted by
			cont	continuo
			contrib(s).	contribution(s)
			Corp.	Corporation
C	contralto		c.p.s.	cycles per second
c	circa [about]		cptr(s)	computer(s)
c	cent(s)		Cr	Credo, Creed
CA	California		CRI	Composers Recordings, Inc.
Cambs.	Cambridgeshire		CSc	Candidate of Historical Sciences
Can.	Canadian		CT	Connecticut
CanD	Cantate Domino		Ct	Contratenor, countertenor
cant(s).	cantata(s)		CUNY	City University of New York
cap.	capacity		CVO	Commander of the Royal Victorian Order
carn.	Carnival		Cz.	Czech
cb	contrabass [instrument]			
CBC	Canadian Broadcasting Corporation			
CBE	Commander of the Order of the British Empire		D	Deutsch catalogue [Schubert]; Dounias catalogue [Tartini]
CBS	Columbia Broadcasting System		d.	denarius, denarii [penny, pence]
CBSO	City of Birmingham Symphony Orchestra		*d*	died
CCNY	City College of New York		DA	Doctor of Arts
CD(s)	compact disc(s)		Dan.	Danish
CE	Common Era [AD]		db	double bass
CeBeDeM	Centre Belge de Documentation Musicale		DBE	Dame Commander of the Order of the British Empire
cel	celesta			
CEMA	Council for the Encouragement of Music and the Arts		dbn	double bassoon
			DC	District of Columbia
cf	confer [compare]		Dc	Discantus
c.f.	cantus firmus		DD	Doctor of Divinity
CFE	Composers Facsimile Edition		DDR	German Democratic Republic (Deutsche Demokratische Republik [East Germany])
CG	Covent Garden, London			
CH	Companion of Honour		DE	Delaware
chap(s).	chapter(s)		Dec	December
chbr	chamber		ded(s).	dedication(s), dedicated to
Chin.	Chinese		DeM	Deus misereatur
chit	chitarrone		Den.	Denmark
choreog(s).	choreography, choreographer(s), choreographed by		Dept(s)	Department(s)
			Derbys.	Derbyshire
Cie	Compagnie		DFA	Doctor of Fine Arts
cimb	cimbalom		dg	*dramma giocoso*
CIMCIM	International Committee for Museums and Collections of Musical Instruments		dir(s).	director(s), directed by
			diss.	dissertation
cl	clarinet		dl	*drame lyrique*
clvd	clavichord		DLitt	Doctor of Letters/Literature
cm	centimetre(s); *comédie en musique*		DM	Doctor of Music
CM	Northern Mariana Islands (US Trust Territory of the Pacific)		dm	*dramma per musica*
			DMA	Doctor of Musical Arts
cmda	*comédie mêlée d'ariettes*		DME, DMEd	Doctor of Musical Education
CNRS	Centre National de la Recherche Scientifique			

DMus	Doctor of Music		GEMA	Gesellschaft für Musikalische Aufführungs- und Mechanische Vervielfaltingungsrechte
DMusEd	Doctor of Music Education			
DPhil	Doctor of Philosophy		Ger.	German
Dr	Doctor		Gk.	Greek
DRC	Democratic Republic of the Congo		Gl	Gloria
DSc	Doctor of Science/Historical Sciences		Glam.	Glamorgan
DSM	Doctor of Sacred Music		glock	glockenspiel
Dut.	Dutch		Glos.	Gloucestershire
			GmbH	Gesellschaft mit Beschränkter Haftung [limited-liability company]
E.	East, Eastern		grad(s)	gradual(s)
EBU	European Broadcasting Union		GSM	Guildhall School of Music, London (to 1934)
EdD	Doctor of Education		GSMD	Guildhall School of Music and Drama, London (1935–)
edn(s)	edition(s)			
ed(s).	editor(s), edited (by)		GU	Guam
EdS	Education Specialist		gui	guitar
EEC	European Economic Community			
e.g.	exempli gratia [for example]			
el-ac	electro-acoustic		H	Hoboken catalogue [Haydn]; Helm catalogue [C.P.E. Bach]
elec	electric, electronic			
EMI	Electrical and Musical Industries		Hants.	Hampshire
Eng.	English		Heb.	Hebrew
eng hn	english horn		Herts.	Hertfordshire
ENO	English National Opera		HI	Hawaii
ens	ensemble		hmn	harmonium
ENSA	Entertainments National Service Association		HMS	His/Her Majesty's Ship
EP	extended-play (record)		HMV	His Master's Voice
esp.	especially		hn	horn
etc.	et cetera		Hon.	Honorary; Honourable
EU	European Union		hp	harp
ex., exx.	example, examples		hpd	harpsichord
			HRH	His/Her Royal Highness
			Hung.	Hungarian
f	forte		Hunts.	Huntingdonshire
facs.	facsimile(s)		Hz	Hertz [c.p.s.]
fa(s)	farsa(s)			
fasc(s).	fascicle(s)			
Feb	February		IA	Iowa
ff	fortissimo		IAML	International Association of Music Libraries
f, ff	following page, following pages		IAWM	International Alliance for Women in Music
f., ff.	folio, folios		ibid.	ibidem [in the same place]
fff	fortississimo		ICTM	International Council for Traditional Music
fig(s).	figure(s) [illustration(s)]		ID	Idaho
FL	Florida		i.e.	id est [that is]
fl	flute		IFMC	International Folk Music Council
fl	floruit [he/she flourished]		IL	Illinois
Flem.	Flemish		ILWC	International League of Women Composers
fp	fortepiano [dynamic marking]		IMC	International Music Council
Fr.	French		IMS	International Musicological Society
frag(s).	fragment(s)		IN	Indiana
FRAM	Fellow of the Royal Academy of Music, London		Inc.	Incorporated
FRCM	Fellow of the Royal College of Music, London		inc.	incomplete
FRCO	Fellow of the Royal College of Organists, London		incid	incidental
FRS	Fellow of the Royal Society, London		incl.	includes, including
fs	full score		inst(s)	instrument(s), instrumental
			intl	international
			int(s)	intermezzo(s), introit(s)
GA	Georgia		IPEM	Instituut voor Psychoakoestiek en Elektronische Muziek, Ghent
Gael.	Gaelic			
GEDOK	Gemeinschaft Deutscher Organisationen von Künstlerinnen und Kunstfreundinnen		IRCAM	Institut de Recherche et Coordination Acoustique/Musique

ISAM	Institute for Studies in American Music	Mag	Magnificat
ISCM	International Society for Contemporary Music	MALS	Master of Arts in Library Sciences
ISDN	Integrated Services Digital Network	mand	mandolin
ISM	Incorporated Society of Musicians	mar	marimba
ISME	International Society for Music Education	MAT	Master of Arts and Teaching
It.	Italian	MB	Bachelor of Music; Manitoba
		MBE	Member of the Order of the British Empire
		MD	Maryland
Jan	January	ME	Maine
Jap.	Japanese	MEd	Master of Education
Jb	Jahrbuch [yearbook]	mel	*melodramma, mélodrame*
JD	Doctor of Jurisprudence	mels	*melodramma serio*
Jg.	Jahrgang [year of publication/volume]	melss	*melodramma semiserio*
Jr.	Junior	Met	Metropolitan Opera House, New York
jr	junior	Mez	mezzo-soprano
Jub	Jubilate	*mf*	mezzo-forte
		MFA	Master of Fine Arts
		MGM	Metro-Goldwyn-Mayer
K	Kirkpatrick catalogue [D. Scarlatti]; Köchel catalogue [Mozart: no. after '/' is from 6th edn; also Fux]	MHz	megahertz [megacycles]
		MI	Michigan
		mic	microphone
kbd	keyboard	Middx	Middlesex
KBE	Knight Commander of the Order of the British Empire	MIDI	Musical Instrument Digital Interface
		MIMO	Musical Instrument Museums Online
KCVO	Knight Commander of the Royal Victorian Order	MIT	Massachusetts Institute of Technology
		MLA	Music Library Association
kg	kilogram(s)	MLitt	Master of Letters/Literature
Kgl	Königlich(e, er, es) [Royal]	Mlle, Mlles	Mademoiselle, Mesdemoiselles
kHz	kilohertz [1000 c.p.s.]	MM	Master of Music
km	kilometre(s)	M.M.	Metronome Maelzel
KS	Kansas	mm	millimetre(s)
KY	Kentucky	MMA	Master of Musical Arts
Ky	Kyrie	MME, MMEd	Master of Music Education
		Mme, Mmes	Madame, Mesdames
L.	no. of song in R.W. Linker: *A Bibliography of Old French Lyrics* (University, MS, 1979)	M, MM.	Monsieur, Messieurs
		MMT	Master of Music in Teaching
L	Longo catalogue [A. Scarlatti]	MMus	Master of Music
LA	Louisiana	MN	Minnesota
Lanarks.	Lanarkshire	MO	Missouri
Lancs.	Lancashire	mod	modulator
Lat.	Latin	Mon.	Monmouthshire
Leics.	Leicestershire	movt(s)	movement(s)
LH	left hand	*mp*	mezzo-piano
lib(s)	libretto(s)	MPhil	Master of Philosophy
Lincs.	Lincolnshire	MP(s)	Member(s) of Parliament
Lith.	Lithuanian	Mr	Mister
lit(s)	litany (litanies)	Mrs	Mistress; Messieurs
LittD	Doctor of Letters/Literature	MS	Master of Science(s); Mississippi
LLB	Bachelor of Laws	MSc	Master of Science(s)
LLD	Doctor of Laws	MSLS	Master of Science in Library and Information Science
loc. cit.	loco citato [in the place cited]		
LP	long-playing record	MSM	Master of Sacred Music
LPO	London Philharmonic Orchestra	MS(S)	manuscript(s)
LSO	London Symphony Orchestra	MT	Montana
Ltd	Limited	Mt	Mount
Ltée	Limitée	MTNA	Music Teachers National Association
		mt(s)	music-theatre piece(s)
m	metre(s)	MusB, MusBac	Bachelor of Music
MA	Massachusetts; Master of Arts		

muscm(s)	musical comedy (comedies)		opt.	optional
MusD,			OR	Oregon
MusDoc	Doctor of Music		orat(s)	oratorio(s)
musl(s)	musical(s)		orch	orchestra(tion), orchestral
MusM	Master of Music		orchd	orchestrated (by)
			org	organ
			orig.	original(ly)
N.	North, Northern		ORTF	Office de Radiodiffusion-Télévision
nar(s)	narrator(s)			Française
NB	New Brunswick		os	*opera seria*
NBC	National Broadcasting Company		oss	*opera semiseria*
NC	North Carolina		OUP	Oxford University Press
ND	North Dakota		ov(s).	overture(s)
n.d.	no date of publication		Oxon.	Oxfordshire
NDR	Norddeutscher Rundfunk			
NE	Nebraska			
NEA	National Endowment for the Arts		P	Pincherle catalogue [Vivaldi]
NEH	National Endowment for the Humanities		p.	*pars*
NET	National Educational Television		*p*	piano [dynamic marking]
NF	Newfoundland and Labrador		PA	Pennsylvania
NH	New Hampshire		p.a.	per annum [annually]
NHK	Nippon Hōsō Kyōkai [Japanese broadcasting		pan(s)	pantomime(s)
	system]		PBS	Public Broadcasting System
NJ	New Jersey		PC	no. of chanson in A. Pillet and H. Carstens:
NM	New Mexico			*Bibliographie der Troubadours* (Halle,
n(n).	footnote(s)			1933)
Nor.	Norwegian		PE	Prince Edward Island
Northants.	Northamptonshire		perc	percussion
no(s).	number(s)		perf(s).	performance(s), performed (by)
Notts.	Nottinghamshire		pf	piano [instrument]
Nov	November		pfmr(s)	performer(s)
n.p.	no place of publication		PhB	Bachelor of Philosophy
NPR	National Public Radio		PhD	Doctor of Philosophy
n.pub.	no publisher		PhDEd	Doctor of Philosophy in Education
nr	near		pic	piccolo
NRK	Norsk Rikskringkasting [Norwegian broad-		pl(s).	plate(s); plural
	casting system]		p.m.	post meridiem [after noon]
NS	Nova Scotia		PO	Philharmonic Orchestra
NSW	New South Wales		Pol.	Polish
NT	North West Territories		pop.	population
Nunc	Nunc dimittis		Port.	Portuguese
NV	Nevada		posth.	posthumous(ly)
NY	New York [State]		POW(s)	prisoner(s) of war
NZ	New Zealand		*pp*	pianissimo
			p., pp.	page, pages
			ppp	pianississimo
ob	*opera buffa*; oboe		PQ	Province of Quebec
obbl	obbligato		PR	Puerto Rico
OBE	Officer of the Order of the British Empire		pr.	printed
obl	*opéra-ballet*		prep pf	prepared piano
OC	Opéra-Comique, Paris [the company]		PRO	Public Record Office, London
oc	*opéra comique* [genre]		prol(s)	prologue(s)
Oct	October		PRS	Performing Right Society
off(s)	offertory (offertories)		pseud(s).	pseudonym(s)
OH	Ohio		Ps(s)	Psalm(s)
OK	Oklahoma		ps(s)	psalm(s)
OM	Order of Merit		ptbk(s)	partbook(s)
ON	Ontario		pt(s)	part(s)
op. cit.	opere citato [in the work cited]		pubd	published
op., opp.	opus, opera [plural of opus]		pubn(s)	publication(s)
op(s).	opera(s)		PWM	Polskie Wydawnictwo Muzyczne

QC	Queen's Counsel
qnt(s)	quintet(s)
qt(s)	quartet(s)
R	[in signature] editorial revision
R	photographic reprint [edn of score or early printed source]
R.	no. of chanson in G. Raynaud, *Bibliographie des chansonniers français des XIIIe et XIVe siècles* (Paris, 1884)
R	Ryom catalogue [Vivaldi]
r	recto
R	response
RAAF	Royal Australian Air Force
RAF	Royal Air Force
RAI	Radio Audizioni Italiane
RAM	Royal Academy of Music, London
RCA	Radio Corporation of America
RCM	Royal College of Music, London
rec	recorder
rec.	recorded [in discographic context]
recit(s)	recitative(s)
red(s).	reduction(s), reduced for
reorchd	reorchestrated (by)
repr.	reprinted
re(s)	response(s) [type of piece]
resp(s)	respond(s)
Rev.	Reverend
rev(s).	revision(s); revised (by/for)
RH	right hand
RI	Rhode Island
RIAS	Radio im Amerikanischen Sektor
RIdIM	Répertoire International d'Iconographie Musicale
RILM	Répertoire International de Littérature Musicale
RIPM	Répertoire International de la Presse Musicale
RISM	Répertoire International des Sources Musicales
RKO	Radio-Keith-Orpheum
RMCM	Royal Manchester College of Music
rms	root mean square
RNCM	Royal Northern College of Music, Manchester
RO	Radio Orchestra
Rom.	Romanian
r.p.m.	revolutions per minute
RPO	Royal Philharmonic Orchestra
RSFSR	Russian Soviet Federated Socialist Republic
RSO	Radio Symphony Orchestra
RTÉ	Radio Telefís Éireann
RTF	Radiodiffusion-Télévision Française
Rt Hon.	Right Honourable
RTVB	Radio-Télévision Belge de la Communauté Française
Russ.	Russian
RV	Ryom catalogue [Vivaldi]
S	San, Santa, Santo, São [Saint]; soprano [voice]
S	sound recording
S.	South, Southern

s	soprano [instrument]
s.	solidus, solidi [shilling, shillings]
SACEM	Société d'Auteurs, Compositeurs et Editeurs de Musique
San	Sanctus
sax	saxophone
SC	South Carolina
SD	South Dakota
sd	*scherzo drammatico*
SDR	Süddeutscher Rundfunk
SEM	Society for Ethnomusicology
Sept	September
seq(s)	sequence(s)
ser.	series
Serb.	Serbian
ser(s)	serenata(s)
sf, *sfz*	sforzando, sforzato
SFSR	Soviet Federated Socialist Republic
sing.	singular
SJ	Societas Jesu [Society of Jesus]
SK	Saskatchewan
SMT	Society for Music Theory
SO	Symphony Orchestra
SOCAN	Society of Composers, Authors and Music Publishers of Canada
Sp.	Spanish
spkr(s)	speaker(s)
Spl	Singspiel
SPNM	Society for the Promotion of New Music
spr.	spring
sq	square
Sr.	Senior
sr	senior
SS	Saints (It., Sp.); Santissima, Santissimo [Most Holy]
SS	steamship
SSR	Soviet Socialist Republic
Staffs.	Staffordshire
STB	Bachelor of Sacred Theology
Ste	Sainte
str	string(s)
St(s)	Saint(s)/Holy, Sankt, Sint, Szent
sum.	summer
SUNY	State University of New York
Sup	superius
suppl(s).	supplement(s), supplementary
Swed.	Swedish
SWF	Südwestfunk
sym(s).	symphony (symphonies), symphonic
synth	synthesizer, synthesized
T	tenor [voice]
t	tenor [instrument]
tc	*tragicommedia*
td(s)	*tonadilla(s)*
TeD	Te Deum
ThM	Master of Theology
timp	timpani
tm	*tragédie en musique*
TN	Tennessee

tpt	trumpet
Tr	treble [voice]
trad.	traditional
trans.	translation, translated by
transcr(s).	transcription(s), transcribed by/for
trbn	trombone
tr(s)	tract(s); treble [instrument]
TV	television
TWV	Menke catalogue [Telemann]
TX	Texas
U.	University
UCLA	University of California at Los Angeles
UHF	ultra-high frequency
UK	United Kingdom of Great Britain and Northern Ireland
Ukr.	Ukrainian
unacc.	unaccompanied
unattrib.	unattributed
UNESCO	United Nations Educational, Scientific and Cultural Organization
UNICEF	United Nations International Children's Emergency Fund
unorchd	unorchestrated
unperf.	unperformed
unpubd	unpublished
UP	University Press
US	United States [adjective]
USA	United States of America
USO	United Service Organisations
USSR	Union of Soviet Socialist Republics
UT	Utah
v	verso
v.	versus
V	versicle
VA	Virginia
va	viola
vc	cello
vcle(s)	versicle(s)
VEB	Volkseigener Betrieb [people's own industry]
Ven	Venite

VHF	very high frequency
VI	Virgin Islands
vib	vibraphone
viz	videlicet [namely]
vle	violone
vn	violin
vol(s).	volume(s)
vs	vocal score, piano-vocal score
VT	Vermont
v, vv	voice, voices
v., vv.	verse, verses
W.	West, Western
WA	Washington [State]
Warwicks.	Warwickshire
WDR	Westdeutscher Rundfunk
WI	Wisconsin
Wilts.	Wiltshire
wint.	winter
WNO	Welsh National Opera
WOO	Werke ohne Opuszahl
Worcs.	Worcestershire
WPA	Works Progress Administration
WQ	Wotquenne catalogue [C.P.E. Bach]
WV	West Virginia
ww	woodwind
WY	Wyoming
xyl	xylophone
YMCA	Young Men's Christian Association
Yorks.	Yorkshire
YT	Yukon Territory
YWCA	Young Women's Christian Association
YYS	(Zhongguo yishu yanjiuyuan) Yinyue yanjiusuo and variants [Music Research Institute (of the Chinese Academy of Arts)]
Z	Zimmermann catalogue [Purcell]
zargc	*zarzuela género chico*
zar(s)	zarzuela(s)

Bibliographical Abbreviations

19CM	*19th Century Music*
ACAB	*American Composers Alliance Bulletin*
AcM	*Acta musicologica*
ADB	*Allgemeine deutsche Biographie* (Leipzig, 1875–1912)
AdlerHM	G. Adler, ed.: *Handbuch der Musikgeschichte* (Frankfurt, 1924, 2/1930/R)
AfM	*African Music*
AH	*Analecta hymnica medii aevi*
AllacciD	L. Allacci: *Drammaturgia*
AllenH	W.C. Allen: *Hendersonia: the Music of Fletcher Henderson and his Musicians: a Bio-discography* (Highland Park, NJ, 1973)
AM	*Antiphonale monasticum pro diurnis horis* (Tournai, 1934)
AmbrosGM	A.W. Ambros: *Geschichte der Musik* (Leipzig, 1862–82/R)
AMe	*Algemene muziekencyclopedie*
AMeS	*Algemene muziekencyclopedie suppl.*
AMf	*Archiv für Musikforschung*
AMI	*L'arte musicale in Italia*
AMMM	*Archivium musices metropolitanum mediolanense*
AMP	*Antiquitates musicae in Polonia*
AMw	*Archiv für Musikwissenschaft*
AMZ	*Allgemeine musikalische Zeitung* (1798–1848, 1863–5, 1866–82)
AMz	*Allgemeine (deutsche) Musik-Zeitung/ Musikzeitung* (1874–1943)
ANB	*American National Biography Online* (<http://www.anb.org>)
Anderson2	E.R. Anderson: *Contemporary American Composers: a Biographical Dictionary*
AnM	*Anuario musical*
AnMc	*Analecta musicologica*
AnnM	*Annales musicologiques*
AnthonyFB	J.R. Anthony: *French Baroque Music from Beaujoyeulx to Rameau* (London, 1973, 3/1997)

AntMI	*Antiquae musicae italicae*
AÖAW	*Anzeiger der Österreichischen Akademie der Wissenschaften, philosophisch-historische Klasse* (1948–)
ApelG	W. Apel: *Geschichte der Orgel- und Klaviermusik bis 1700* (Kassel, 1967; Eng. trans., rev., 1972)
AR	*Antiphonale sacrosanctae romanae ecclesiae pro diurnis horis* (Paris, Tournai, and Rome, 1949)
ARJS	*Annual Review of Jazz Studies*
ARSCJ	*Association for Recorded Sound Collections Journal*
AS	W.H. Frere, ed.: *Antiphonale sarisburiense* (London, 1901–25/R)
AshbeeR	A. Ashbee: *Records of English Court Music* (Snodland/Aldershot, 1986–95)
AsM	*Asian Music*
AudaM	A. Auda: *La musique et les musiciens de l'ancien pays de Liège*
AusDB	*Australian Dictionary of Biography* (Melbourne, 1966–96)
Baker5[–9]	*Baker's Biographical Dictionary of Musicians* (New York, 1958–2001)
BalliettA (1986)	W. Balliett: *American Musicians: Fifty-six Portraits in Jazz* (New York, and Oxford, England, 1986)
BalliettA (1996)	W. Balliett: *American Musicians II: Seventy-two Portraits in Jazz* (New York, and Oxford, England, 1996)
BAMS	*Bulletin of the American Musicological Society*
BDA	*A Biographical Dictionary of Actors, Actresses, Musicians, Dancers, Managers & Other Stage Personnel in London, 1660-1800* (Carbondale, IL, 1973–93)
BDECM	A. Ashbee and D. Lasocki, eds.: *A Biographical Dictionary of English Court Musicians, 1485-1714* (Aldershot, 1998)

BDRSC	A. Ho and D. Feofanov, eds.: *Biographical Dictionary of Russian/Soviet Composers*
BeckEP	J.H. Beck: *Encyclopedia of Percussion*
BeJb	*Beethoven-Jahrbuch*
BenoitMC	M. Benoit: *Musiques de cour: chapelle, chambre, écurie, 1661-1733* (Paris, 1971)
BenzingB	J. Benzing: *Die Buchdrucker des 16. und 17. Jahrhunderts* (Wiesbaden, 1963, 2/1982)
BerliozM	H. Berlioz: *Mémoires* (Paris, 1870; ed. and trans. D. Cairns, 1969, 2/1970); ed. P. Citron (Paris, 1969, 2/1991)
BertolottiM	A. Bertolotti: *Musici alla corte dei Gonzaga in Mantova dal secolo XV al XVIII* (Milan, 1890/R)
BHcF	*Bulletin du Hot Club de France*
BicknellH	S. Bicknell: *The History of the English Organ* (Cambridge, 1996)
BJb	*Bach-Jahrbuch*
BladesPI	J. Blades: *Percussion Instruments and their History* (London, 1970, 2/1974)
BlumeEK	F. Blume: *Die evangelische Kirchenmusik* (Potsdam, 1931–4/R, enlarged 2/1965 as *Geschichte der evangelischen Kirchenmusik*; Eng. trans., enlarged, 1974, as *Protestant Church Music: a History*)
BMB	*Bibliotheca musica bononiensis* (Bologna, 1967–)
BMw	*Beiträge zur Musikwissenschaft*
BNB	*Biographie nationale [belge]* (Brussels, 1866–1986)
BoalchM	D.H. Boalch: *Makers of the Harpsichord and Clavichord 1440 to 1840*
BoetticherOL	W. Boetticher: *Orlando di Lasso und seine Zeit* (Kassel, 1958)
BooneT	O. Boone: *Les tambours du Congo belge et du Ruanda-Urundi* (Tervuren, 1951)
BooneX	O. Boone: *Les xylophones du Congo belge* (Tervuren, 1936)
BoydenH	D.D. Boyden: *A History of Violin Playing from its Origins to 1761* (London, 1965)
BPM	*Black Perspective in Music*
BrenetC	M. Brenet: *Les concerts en France sous l'ancien régime* (Paris, 1900/R)
BrenetM	M. Brenet: *Les musiciens de la Sainte-Chapelle du Palais* (Paris, 1910/R)
BrookB	B.S. Brook, ed.: *The Breitkopf Thematic Catalogue, 1762-1787* (New York, 1966)
BrookSF	B.S. Brook: *La symphonie française dans la seconde moitié du XVIIIe siècle* (Paris, 1962)
BrownI	H.M. Brown: *Instrumental Music Printed Before 1600: a Bibliography* (Cambridge, MA, 1965)
Brown-Stratton BMB	J.D. Brown and S.S. Stratton: *British Musical Biography*
BSIM	*Bulletin français de la S.I.M.* [also *Mercure musical* and other titles]
BUCEM	E.B. Schnapper, ed.: *British Union-Catalogue of Early Music* (London, 1957)
BurneyFI	C. Burney: *The Present State of Music in France and Italy* (London, 1771, 2/1773)
BurneyGN	C. Burney: *The Present State of Music in Germany, the Netherlands, and the United Provinces* (London, 1773, 2/1775)
BurneyH	C. Burney: *A General History of Music from the Earliest Ages to the Present Period* (London, 1776–89); ed. F. Mercer (London, 1935/R) [p. nos. refer to this edn]
BWQ	*Brass and Woodwind Quarterly*
CaffiS	F. Caffi: *Storia della musica sacra nella già cappella ducale di San Marco in Venezia dal 1318 al 1797* (Venice, 1854–5/R); ed. E. Surian (Florence, 1987)
CaM	*Catalogus musicus* (Kassel, 1963–)
CampbellGC	M. Campbell: *The Great Cellists*
CampbellGV	M. Campbell: *The Great Violinists*
CAO	*Corpus antiphonalium officii* (Rome, 1963–79)
CarrJ	I. Carr, D. Fairweather, and B. Priestley: *Jazz: the Rough Guide* (London, 1995, rev. and enlarged 2/2000)
CBY	*Current Biography Yearbook* (1955–)
CC	B. Morton and P. Collins, eds.: *Contemporary Composers*
CeBeDeM directory	*CeBeDeM et ses compositeurs affiliés*, ed. D. von Volborth-Danys (Brussels, 1977–80)
CEKM	*Corpus of Early Keyboard Music*
CEMF	*Corpus of Early Music* (in Facsimile) (Brussels, 1970–72)
ChartersJ	S.B. Charters: *Jazz: New Orleans, 1885-1957: an Index to the Negro Musicians of New Orleans* (Belleville, NJ, 1958, rev. 2/1963/R1983 as *Jazz: New Orleans, 1885-1963: an Index to the Negro Musicians of New Orleans*)
ChiltonB	J. Chilton: *Who's Who of British Jazz* (London and New York, 1997)
ChiltonW	J. Chilton: *Who's Who of Jazz: Storyville to Swing Street* (London, 1970, rev. and enlarged 4/1985)
CHM	*Collectanea historiae musicae* (1953–66)
Choron-FayolleD	A.-E. Choron and F.J.M. Fayolle: *Dictionnaire historique des musiciens*
CI	*Crescendo International*
CK	*Contemporary Keyboard*
ClinkscaleMP	M.N. Clinkscale: *Makers of the Piano*
CM	*Le choeur des muses*
CMc	*Current Musicology*
CMI	*I classici musicali italiani* (Milan, 1941–56)
CMM	*Corpus mensurabilis musicae*
ČMm	*Časopis Moravského musea* [muzea, 1977–]
CMR	*Contemporary Music Review*
CMz	*Cercetări de muzicologie*

CohenE	A.I. Cohen: *International Encyclopedia of Women Composers*
CohenWE	Y.W. Cohen: *Werden und Entwicklung der Musik in Israel* (Kassel, 1976)
COJ	*Cambridge Opera Journal*
ConnorBG	D.R. Connor: *BG off the Record: a Bio-discography of Benny Goodman* (Fairless Hills, PA, 1958, rev. and enlarged [4]/1988 as *Benny Goodman: Listen to his Legacy*, addns and corrections, 1996, as *Benny Goodman: Wrappin' it up*)
CooverMA	J.B. Coover: *Music at Auction: Puttick and Simpson* (Warren, MI, 1988)
Cousse makerS	C.-E.-H. de Coussemaker: *Scriptorum de musica medii aevi nova series* (Paris, 1864–76/R, 2/1908, ed. U. Moser)
CroceN	B. Croce: *I teatri di Napoli* (Naples, 1891/R, 5/1966)
ČSHS	*Československý hudební slovník*
CSM	*Corpus scriptorum de musica* (Rome, later Stuttgart, 1950–)
CSPD	*Calendar of State Papers* (Domestic) (London, 1856–1972)
Cw	*Das Chorwerk*
DAB	*Dictionary of American Biography* (New York, 1928–37, suppls., 1944–)
DAM	*Dansk aarbog for musikforskning*
Day-Murrie ESB	C.L. Day and E.B. Murrie: *English Song-Books* (London, 1940)
DB	*Down Beat*
DBF	*Dictionnaire de biographie française* (Paris, 1933–)
DBI	*Dizionario biografico degli italiani* (Rome, 1960–)
DBL	*Dansk biografisk leksikon* (Copenhagen, 1887–1905)
DBL2	*Dansk biografisk leksikon* (Copenhagen, 2/1933–45)
DBL3	*Dansk biografisk leksikon* (Copenhagen, 3/1979–84)
DBNM	*Darmstädter Beiträge zur neuen Musik*
DBP	E. Vieira, ed.: *Diccionário biográphico de musicos portuguezes* (Lisbon, 1900)
DČHP	*Dějiny české hudby v příkladech* (Prague, 1958)
DDT	*Denkmäler deutscher Tonkunst*
DEMF	A. Devriès and F. Lesure: *Dictionnaire des éditeurs de musique français*
DEUMM	*Dizionario enciclopedico universale della musica e dei musicisti*
Deutsch-MPN	O.E. Deutsch: *Music Publishers' Numbers* (London, 1946)
DF	*Discographical Forum*
DHM	*Documenta historica musicae*
Dichter-ShapiroSM	H. Dichter and E. Shapiro: *Early American Sheet Music*
DJbM	*Deutsches Jahrbuch der Musikwissenschaft*
DlabačžKL	G.J. Dlabacž: *Allgemeines historisches Künstler-Lexikon*
DM	*Documenta musicologica* (Kassel, 1951–)
DMt	*Dansk musiktidsskrift*
DMV	*Drammaturgia musicale veneta* (Milan, 1983–)
DNB	*Dictionary of National Biography* (Oxford, 1885–1901, suppls., 1901–96)
DoddI	G. Dodd, ed.: *Thematic Index of Music for Viols* (London, 1980–)
DTB	*Denkmäler der Tonkunst in Bayern*
DTÖ	*Denkmäler der Tonkunst in Österreich*
DugganIMI	M.K. Duggan: *Italian Music Incunabula: Printers and Type* (Berkeley, 1991)
DVLG	*Deutsche Vierteljahrsschrift für Literaturwissenschaft und Geistesgeschichte* (1923–)
ECCS	*The Eighteenth-Century Continuo Sonata*
ECFC	*The Eighteenth-Century French Cantata*
EDM	*Das Erbe deutscher Musik*
EECM	*Early English Church Music*
EG	*Etudes grégoriennes*
EI	*The Encyclopaedia of Islam* (Leiden, 1928–38, 2/1960–)
EinsteinIM	A. Einstein: *The Italian Madrigal* (Princeton, NJ, 1949/R)
EIT	*Yezhegodnik imperatorskikh teatrov*
EitnerQ	R. Eitner: *Biographisch-bibliographisches Quellen-Lexikon*
EitnerS	R. Eitner: *Bibliographie der Musik-Sammelwerke des XVI. und XVII. Jahrhunderts* (Berlin, 1877/R)
EKM	*Early Keyboard Music*
EL	*The English School of Lutenist Songwriters*, rev. as *The English Lute-Songs*
EM	*The English Madrigal School*, rev. as *The English Madrigalists*
EMc	*Early Music*
EMC1	*Encyclopedia of Music in Canada* (Toronto, 1981)
EMC2	*Encyclopedia of Music in Canada* (Toronto, 2/1992)
EMDC	A. Lavignac and L. de La Laurencie, eds.: *Encyclopédie de la musique et dictionnaire du Conservatoire*
EMH	*Early Music History*
EMN	*Exempla musica neerlandica*
EMS	see *EM*
EMuz	*Encyklopedia muzyczne*
ERO	*Early Romantic Opera*
ES	*English Song 1600-1675* (New York, 1986–9)
ES	*Enciclopedia dello spettacolo*
ESLS	see *EL*
EthM	*Ethnomusicology*
EthM Newsletter	*Ethno[-]musicology Newsletter*
EwenD	D. Ewen: *American Composers: a Biographical Dictionary*
FAM	*Fontes artis musicae*
FasquelleE	*Encyclopédie de la musique*
FCVR	*Florilège du concert vocal de la Renaissance*

Feather '60s	L. Feather: *The Encyclopedia of Jazz in the Sixties* (New York, 1966/R1986)
FeatherE	L. Feather: *The Encyclopedia of Jazz* (New York, 1955, rev. and enlarged 2/1960/R1984)
Feather-Gitler '70s	L. Feather and I. Gitler: *The Encyclopedia of Jazz in the Seventies* (New York, 1976/R1987)
Feather-Gitler BEJ	L. Feather and I. Gitler: *The Biographical Encyclopedia of Jazz* (New York, and Oxford, England, 1999)
FellererG	K.G. Fellerer: *Geschichte der katholischen Kirchenmusik* (Düsseldorf, 1939, enlarged 2/1949; Eng. trans., 1961/R)
FellererP	K.G. Fellerer: *Der Palestrinastil und seine Bedeutung in der vokalen Kirchenmusik des 18. Jahrhunderts* (Augsburg, 1929/R)
FenlonMM	I. Fenlon: *Music and Patronage in Sixteenth-Century Mantua* (Cambridge, 1980–82)
FétisB	F.-J. Fétis: *Biographie universelle des musiciens*
FétisBS	F.-J. Fétis: *Biographie universelle des musiciens suppl.*
FisherMP	W.A. Fisher: *One Hundred and Fifty Years of Music Publishing in the United States* (Boston, 1933)
FiskeETM	R. Fiske: *English Theatre Music in the Eighteenth Century* (London, 1973, 2/1986)
FlorimoN	F. Florimo: *La scuola musicale di Napoli e i suoi conservatorii* (Naples, 1880–83/R)
Fn	*Footnote*
FO	*French Opera in the 17th and 18th Centuries* (New York, 1983–)
FortuneISS	N. Fortune: *Italian Secular Song from 1600 to 1635: the Origins and Development of Accompanied Monody* (diss., U. of Cambridge, 1954)
Friedlaender DL	M. Friedlaender: *Das deutsche Lied im 18. Jahrhundert* (Stuttgart and Berlin, 1902/R)
FriedwaldB	W. Friedwald: *A Biographical Guide to the Great Jazz and Pop Singers* (New York, 2010)
FrotscherG	G. Frotscher: *Geschichte des Orgelspiels und der Orgelkomposition* (Berlin, 1935–6/R, music suppl. 1966)
FuldWFM	J.J. Fuld: *The Book of World-Famous Music*
FullerPG	S. Fuller: *The Pandora Guide to Women Composers: Britain and the United States (1629–Present)*
FürstenauG	M. Fürstenau: *Zur Geschichte der Musik und des Theaters am Hofe zu Dresden* (Dresden, 1861–2/R)
GänzlBMT	K. Gänzl: *The British Musical Theatre* (London, 1986)
GänzlEMT	K. Gänzl and A. Lamb: *Encyclopedia of Musical Theatre*
GaspariC	G. Gaspari: *Catalogo della Biblioteca del Liceo musicale di Bologna*, i–iv (Bologna, 1890–1905/R); v, ed. U. Sesini (Bologna, 1943/R)
GerberL	E.L. Gerber: *Historisch-biographisches Lexikon der Tonkünstler*
GerberNL	E.L. Gerber: *Neues historisch-biographisches Lexikon der Tonkünstler*
GerbertS	M. Gerbert: *Scriptores ecclesiastici de musica sacra potissimum* (St Blasien, 1784/R, 3/1931)
GEWM	*The Garland Encyclopedia of World Music*
GfMKB	*Gesellschaft für Musikforschung: Kongress-Bericht* [1950–]
GiacomoC	S. di Giacomo: *I quattro antichi conservatorii musicali di Napoli* (Milan, 1924–8)
GLMT	*Greek and Latin Music Theory* (Lincoln, NE, 1984–)
GMB	*Geschichte der Musik in Beispielen*
GMM	*Gazzetta musicale di Milano*
GMO	*Grove Music Online*
GOB	*German Opera 1770-1800*, ed. T. Bauman (New York, 1985–6)
GöhlerV	A. Göhler: *Verzeichnis der in den Frankfurter und Leipziger Messkatalogen der Jahre 1564 bis 1759 angezeigten Musikalien* (Leipzig, 1902/R)
GoldJL	R.S. Gold: *A Jazz Lexicon: an A-Z Dictionary of Jazz Terms* (New York, 1964, rev. 2/1975 as *Jazz Talk*)
GoovaertsH	A. Goovaerts: *Histoire et bibliographie de la typographie musicale dans les Pays-Bas* (Antwerp, 1880/R)
GP	*Guitar Player*
GR	*Graduale sacrosanctae romanae ecclesiae* (Tournai, 1938)
GrayF	J. Gray: *Fire Music: a Bibliography of the New Jazz, 1959-1990* (New York, 1991)
Grove1[-5]	G. Grove, ed.: *A Dictionary of Music and Musicians*
Grove6	*The New Grove Dictionary of Music and Musicians*
Grove7	S. Sadie and J. Tyrell, eds.: *The New Grove Dictionary of Music and Musicians* (2/London, 2001)
GroveA	*The New Grove Dictionary of American Music*
GroveI	*The New Grove Dictionary of Musical Instruments*
GroveJ	*The New Grove Dictionary of Jazz*
GroveJ2	*The New Grove Dictionary of Jazz* (2/2002)
GroveJapan	*The New Grove Dictionary of Music and Musicians*, Jap. trans.
GroveO	*The New Grove Dictionary of Opera*
GroveW	*The New Grove Dictionary of Women Composers*
GS	W.H. Frere, ed.: *Graduale sarisburiense* (London, 1894/R)
GSJ	*Galpin Society Journal*

GSL	K.J. Kutsch and L. Riemann: *Grosses Sängerlexikon*
GV	R. Celletti: *Le grandi voci: dizionario critico-biografico dei cantanti*
HAM	*Historical Anthology of Music*
Harrison-MMB	F.Ll. Harrison: *Music in Medieval Britain* (London, 1958, 4/1980)
HawkinsH	J. Hawkins: *A General History of the Science and Practice of Music* (London, 1776)
HBSJ	*Historical Brass Society Journal*
HDM	W. Apel: *Harvard Dictionary of Music*
HiFi	*High Fidelity*
HiFi/MusAm	*High Fidelity/Musical America Edition*
HJb	*Händel-Jahrbuch*
HJbMw	*Hamburger Jahrbuch für Musikwissenschaft*
HM	*Hortus musicus*
HMC	*Historical Manuscripts Commission* [Publications]
HMT	*Handwörterbuch der musikalischen Terminologie*
HMw	*Handbuch der Musikwissenschaft* (Potsdam, 1927–34)
HMYB	*Hinrichsen's Musical Year Book*
HoneggerD	M. Honegger: *Dictionnaire de la musique*
HopkinsonD	C. Hopkinson: *A Dictionary of Parisian Music Publishers 1700-1950*
Hopkins-RimbaultO	E.J. Hopkins and E.F. Rimbault: *The Organ: its History and Construction* (London, 1855, 3/1887/R)
HPM	*Harvard Publications in Music*
HR	*Hudební revue*
HRo	*Hudební rozhledy*
Humphries-SmithMP	C. Humphries and W.C. Smith: *Music Publishing in the British Isles*
HV	*Hudební věda*
IAJRCJ	*International Association of Jazz Record Collectors Journal*
ICSC	*The Italian Cantata in the Seventeenth Century* (New York, 1985–6)
IIM	*Italian Instrumental Music of the Sixteenth and Early Seventeenth Centuries*
IIM	*Izvestiya na Instituta za muzika*
IM	*International Musician*
IMa	*Instituta et monumenta*
IMi	*Istituzioni e monumenti dell'arte musicale italiana* (Milan, 1931–9, new ser., 1956–64)
IMSCR	*International Musicological Society: Congress Report* [1930–]
IMusSCR	*International Musical Society: Congress Report* [II–IV, 1906–11]
IO	*The Italian Oratorio 1650-1800*
IOB	*Italian Opera 1640-1770*, ed. H.M. Brown
IOG	*Italian Opera 1810-1840*, ed. P. Gossett
IRASM	*International Review of the Aesthetics and Sociology of Music*
IRMAS	*International Review of Music Aesthetics and Sociology*
IRMO	S.L. Ginzburg: *Istoriya russkoy muzïki v notnïkh obraztsakh* (Leningrad, 1940–52, 2/1968–70)
ISS	*Italian Secular Song 1606-1636* (New York, 1986)
IZ	*Instrumentenbau-Zeitschrift*
JAMIS	*Journal of the American Musical Instrument Society*
JAMS	*Journal of the American Musicological Society*
JASA	*Journal of the Acoustical Society of America*
JazzM	*Jazz Monthly*
J&B	*Jazz & Blues*
JB	*Jazz Beat*
JBIOS	*Journal of the British Institute of Organ Studies*
JbLH	*Jahrbuch für Liturgik und Hymnologie*
JbMP	*Jahrbuch der Musikbibliothek Peters*
JbO	*Jahrbuch für Opernforschung*
JbSIM	*Jahrbuch des Staatlichen Instituts für Musikforschung Preussischer Kulturbesitz*
JCAS	*Journal of the Catgut Acoustical Society*
JEFDSS	*Journal of the English Folk Dance and Song Society*
Jf	*Jazzforschung/Jazz Research*
JF [intl edn]	*Jazz Forum* [international edition]
JF [Pol. Edn]	*Jazz Forum* [Polish edition]
JFSS	*Journal of the Folk-Song Society*
Jh	*Jazz hot, Jazz-hot*
JIFMC	*Journal of the International Folk Music Council*
JJ	*Jazz Journal*
JJI	*Jazz Journal International*
JJS	*Journal of Jazz Studies*
JLSA	*Journal of the Lute Society of America*
Jm	*Jazz magazine* (Paris)
JM	*Journal of Musicology*
JMR	*Journal of Musicological Research*
JMT	*Journal of Music Theory*
JoãoIL	[João IV:] *Primeira parte do index da livraria de musica do muyto alto, e poderoso Rey Dom João o IV. nosso senhor* (Lisbon, 1649); ed. J. de Vasconcellos (Oporto, 1874–6)
Johansson-FMP	C. Johansson: *French Music Publishers' Catalogues* (Stockholm, 1955)
JohanssonH	C. Johansson: *J.J. & B. Hummel: Music Publishing and Thematic Catalogues* (Stockholm, 1972)
J&P	*Jazz and Pop*
JP	*Jazz-Podium*
JPMMS	*Journal of the Plainsong and Mediaeval Music Society*
JR	*Jazz Review*
JRBM	*Journal of Renaissance and Baroque Music*
JRMA	*Journal of the Royal Musical Association*
JRME	*Journal of Research in Music Education*
JSAM	*Journal of the Society for American Music*
JSN	*Jazz Spotlite News*
JT	*Jazz Times* (Washington, 1980–)

JVdGSA	*Journal of the Viola da Gamba Society of America*
KdG	*Komponisten der Gegenwart*, ed. H.-W. Heister and W.-W. Sparrer
KermanEM	J. Kerman: *The Elizabethan Madrigal: a Comparative Study* (New York, 1962)
KidsonBMP	F. Kidson: *British Music Publishers, Printers and Engravers*
KingMP	A.H. King: *Four Hundred Years of Music Printing* (London, 1964)
KirbyMISA	P.R. Kirby: *The Musical Instruments of the Native Races of South Africa* (London, 1934, 2/1965)
KJb	*Kirchenmusikalisches Jahrbuch*
KM	*Kwartalnik muzyczny*
KöchelKHM	L. von Köchel: *Die kaiserliche Hof-Musikkapelle in Wien von 1543 bis 1867* (Vienna, 1869/R)
KretzschmarG	H. Kretzschmar: *Geschichte des neuen deutschen Liedes* (Leipzig, 1911/R)
KrummelEMP	D.W. Krummel: *English Music Printing* (London, 1975)
LaborD	*Diccionario de la música Labor*
La BordeE	J.-B. de La Borde: *Essai sur la musique ancienne et moderne D*
LabordeMP	L.E.S.J. de Laborde: *Musiciens de Paris, 1535-1792*
LafontaineKM	H.C. de Lafontaine: *The King's Musick* (London, 1909/R)
La Laurenc-ieEF	L. de La Laurencie: *L'école française de violon de Lully à Viotti* (Paris, 1922–4/R)
LAMR	*Latin American Music Review*
LaMusicaD	*La musica: dizionario*
LaMusicaE	*La musica: enciclopedia storica*
LangwillI7	see *Waterhouse-LangwillI*
LaurentyA	J.S. Laurenty: *Systématique des aerophones de l'Afrique centrale* (Tervuren, 1974)
LaurentyC	J.S. Laurenty: *Les chordophones du Congo belge et du Ruanda Urundi* (Tervuren, 1960)
LaurentyS	J.S. Laurenty: *Les sanza du Congo* (Tervuren, 1962)
LaurentyTF	J.S. Laurenty: *Les tambours à fente de l'Afrique centrale* (Tervuren, 1968)
LedeburTLB	C. von Ledebur: *Tonkünstler-Lexicon Berlin's* (Berlin, 1861/R)
Le HurayMR	P. Le Huray: *Music and the Reformation in England, 1549-1660* (London, 1967, 2/1978)
LipowskyBL	F.J. Lipowsky: *Baierisches Musik-Lexikon*
LM	*Lucrări de muzicologie*
LockwoodMRF	L. Lockwood: *Music in Renaissance Ferrara* (Oxford, 1984)
LoewenbergA	A. Loewenberg: *Annals of Opera, 1597-1940*
LPS	*The London Pianoforte School 1766-1860*
LS	*The London Stage, 1660-1800* (Carbondale, IL, 1960–68)
LSJ	*Lute Society Journal*
LU	*Liber usualis missae et officii pro dominicis et festis duplicibus cum cantu gregoriano* (Solesmes, 1896, and later edns incl. Tournai, 1963)
LütgendorffGL	W.L. von Lütgendorff: *Die Geigen- und Lauten-macher vom Mittelalter bis zur Gegenwart*
LZMÖ	*Lexikon zeitgenössischer Musik aus Österreich* (Vienna, 1997)
MA	*Musical Antiquary*
MAB	*Musica antiqua bohemica*
MAk	*Muzïkal'naya akademiya*
MAM	*Musik alter Meister*
MAMF	*Maîtres anciens de la musique française*
MAMS	*Monumenta artis musicae Sloveniae*
MAn	*Music Analysis*
MAP	*Musica antiqua polonica*
MAS	*Musical Antiquarian Society* [Publications]
MatthesonGEP	J. Mattheson: *Grundlage einer Ehren-Pforte* (Hamburg, 1740); ed. Max Schneider (Berlin, 1910/R)
MB	*Musica britannica*
MC	*Musica da camera*
McCarthyB	A. McCarthy: *Big Band Jazz* (London, 1974)
McCarthyJR	A. McCarthy: *Jazz on Record* (London, 1968)
MCL	H. Mendel and A. Reissmann, eds.: *Musikalisches Conversations-Lexikon* (Berlin, 1870–80, 3/1890–91/R)
MD	*Musica disciplina*
ME	*Muzïkal'naya entsiklopediya*
MEJ	*Music Educators Journal*
MEM	*Mestres de l'Escolania de Montserrat*
MersenneHU	M. Mersenne: *Harmonie universelle*
MeyerECM	E.H. Meyer: *English Chamber Music* (London, 1946/R, rev. 3/1982 with D. Poulton as *Early English Chamber Music*)
MeyerMS	E.H. Meyer: *Die mehrstimmige Spielmusik des 17. Jahrhunderts* (Kassel, 1934)
MF	*Music in Facsimile* (New York, 1983–91)
Mf	*Die Musikforschung*
MG	*Musik und Gesellschaft*
MGG1	*Die Musik in Geschichte und Gegenwart*
MGG2	*Die Musik in Geschichte und Gegenwart*
MGH	*Monumenta Germaniae historica*
MH	*Música hispana*
MischiatiI	O. Mischiati: *Indici, cataloghi e avvisi degli editori e librai musicali italiani* (Florence, 1984)
MISM	*Mitteilungen der Internationalen Stiftung Mozarteum*
MJb	*Mozart-Jahrbuch* [Salzburg, 1950–]
ML	*Music & Letters*
MLE	*Music for London Entertainment 1660-1800*
MLMI	*Monumenta lyrica medii aevi italica*
MM	*Modern Music*
MMA	*Miscellanea musicologica* [Australia]
MMB	*Monumenta musicae byzantinae*
MMBel	*Monumenta musicae belgicae*
MMC	*Miscellanea musicologica* [Czechoslovakia]

MME	Monumentos de la música española
MMFTR	Monuments de la musique française au temps de la Renaissance
MMg	Monatshefte für Musikgeschichte
MMI	Monumenti di musica italiana
MMMA	Monumenta monodica medii aevi
MMN	Monumenta musica neerlandica
MMP	Monumenta musicae in Polonia
MMR	Monthly Musical Record
MMRF	Les maîtres musiciens de la Renaissance française
MMS	Monumenta musicae svecicae
MNAN	Music of the New American Nation
MO	Musical Opinion
MooserA	R.-A. Mooser: Annales de la musique et des musiciens en Russie au XVIIIme siècle
MoserGV	A. Moser: Geschichte des Violinspiels (Berlin, 1923, rev. 2/1966–7 by H.J. Nösselt)
MQ	Musical Quarterly
MR	Music Review
MRM	Monuments of Renaissance Music
MRS	Musiche rinascimentali siciliane
MS	Muzïkal'nïy sovremennik
MSD	Musicological Studies and Documents
MT	Musical Times
MusAm	Musical America
MVH	Musica viva historica
MVSSP	Musiche vocali e strumentali sacre e profane
Mw	Das Musikwerk
MZ	Muzikološki zbornik
NA	Note d'archivio per la storia musicale
NBeJb	Neues Beethoven-Jahrbuch
NBL	Norsk biografisk leksikon (Oslo, 1923–83)
NDB	Neue deutsche Biographie (Berlin, 1953–)
Neighbour-TysonPN	O.W. Neighbour and A. Tyson: English Music Publishers' Plate Numbers (London, 1965)
NericiS	L. Nerici: Storia della musica in Lucca (Lucca, 1879/R)
NewcombMF	A. Newcomb: The Madrigal at Ferrara, 1579-1597 (Princeton, NJ, 1980)
NewmanSBE	W.S. Newman: The Sonata in the Baroque Era (Chapel Hill, NC, 1959, 4/1983)
NewmanSCE	W.S. Newman: The Sonata in the Classic Era (Chapel Hill, NC, 1963, 3/1983)
NewmanSSB	W.S. Newman: The Sonata since Beethoven (Chapel Hill, NC, 1969, 3/1983)
NicollH	A. Nicoll: The History of English Drama, 1660-1900 (Cambridge, 1952–9)
NM	Nagels Musik-Archiv
NMÅ	Norsk musikkgranskning årbok
NNBW	Nieuw Nederlandsch biografisch woordenboek (Leiden, 1911–37)
NÖB	Neue österreichische Biographie (Vienna, 1923–35)
NOHM	The New Oxford History of Music (Oxford, 1954–90)
NRMI	Nuova rivista musicale italiana
NZM	Neue Zeitschrift für Musik
OHM	The Oxford History of Music (Oxford, 1901–5, 2/1929–38)
OM	Opus musicum
ÖMz	Österreichische Musikzeitschrift
ON	Opera News
OQ	Opera Quarterly
OW	Opernwelt
PalMus	Paléographie musicale
PAMS	Papers of the American Musicological Society
PÄMw	Publikation älterer praktischer und theoretischer Musikwerke
PazdírekH	B. Pazdírek: Universal-Handbuch der Musikliteratur aller Zeiten und Völker (Vienna, 1904–10/R)
PBC	Publicaciones del departamento de música
PEM	C. Dahlhaus and S. Döhring, eds.: Pipers Enzyklopädie des Musiktheaters (Munich and Zürich, 1986–97)
PG	Patrologiae cursus completus, ii: Series graeca, ed. J.-P. Migne (Paris, 1857–1912)
PGfM	see PÄMw
PierreH	C. Pierre: Histoire du Concert spirituel 1725-1790 (Paris, 1975)
PIISM	Pubblicazioni dell'Istituto italiano per la storia della musica
PirroHM	A. Pirro: Histoire de la musique de la fin du XIVe
PirrottaDO	N. Pirrotta and E. Povoledo: Li due Orfei: da Poliziano a Monteverdi (Turin, 1969, enlarged 2/1975; Eng. trans., 1982, as Music and Theatre from Poliziano to Monteverdi)
PitoniN	G.O. Pitoni: Notitia de contrapuntisti e de compositori di musica (MS, c1725, I-Rvat C.G.I/1–2); ed. C. Ruini (Florence, 1988)
Pj	Le point du jazz
PL	Patrologiae cursus completus, i: Series latina, ed. J.-P. Migne
PM	Portugaliae musica
PMA	Proceedings of the Musical Association
PMFC	Polyphonic Music of the Fourteenth Century
PMM	Plainsong and Medieval Music
PNM	Perspectives of New Music
PraetoriusSM	M. Praetorius: Syntagma musicum, i (Wittenberg and Wolfenbüttel, 1614–15, 2/1615/R); ii (Wolfenbüttel, 1618, 2/1619/R; Eng. trans., 1986, 2/1991); iii (Wolfenbüttel, 1618, 2/1619/R)
PraetoriusTI	M. Praetorius: Theatrum instrumentorum [pt ii/2 of PraetoriusSM]
PRM	Polski rocznik muzykologiczny
PRMA	Proceedings of the Royal Musical Association
Przywecka-SameckaDM	M. Przywecka-Samecka: Drukarstwo muzyczne w Polsce do końca XVIII wieku (Kraków, 1969)

PSB	*Polskich słownik biograficzny* (Kraków, 1935)
PSFM	*Publications [Société française de musicologie]*
Quaderni della RAM	*Quaderni della Rassegna musicale*
Rad JAZU	*Rad Jugoslavenske akademije znanosti i umjetnosti*
RaM	*Rassegna musicale*
RBM	*Revue belge de musicologie*
RdM	*Revue de musicologie*
RdMc	*Revista de musicología*
ReclamsJ	C. Bohländer and K.H. Holler: *Reclams Jazzführer* (Stuttgart, Germany, 1970, rev. and enlarged 2/1977)
ReeseMMA	G. Reese: *Music in the Middle Ages* (New York, 1940)
ReeseMR	G. Reese: *Music in the Renaissance* (New York, 1954, 2/1959)
RefardtHBM	E. Refardt: *Historisch-biographisches Musikerlexikon der Schweiz*
ReM	*Revue musicale*
RFS	*Romantic French Song 1830-1870*
RGMP	*Revue et gazette musicale de Paris*
RHCM	*Revue d'histoire et de critique musicales*
RicciTB	C. Ricci: *I teatri di Bologna nei secoli XVII e XVIII: storia aneddotica* (Bologna, 1888/R)
RicordiE	C. Sartori and R. Allorto: *Enciclopedia della musica*
RiemannG	H. Riemann: *Geschichte der Musiktheorie im IX.-XIX. Jahrbundert* (Berlin, 2/1921/R; Eng. trans. of pts i–ii, 1962/R, and pt iii, 1977)
RiemannL11	*Hugo Riemanns Musiklexikon* (11/1929)
RiemannL12	*Hugo Riemanns Musiklexikon* (12/1959–75)
RIM	*Rivista italiana di musicologia*
RIMS	*Rivista internazionale di musica sacra*
RM	*Ruch muzyczny*
RMARC	*R.M.A. [Royal Musical Association] Research Chronicle*
RMC	*Revista musical chilena*
RMF	*Renaissance Music in Facsimile* (New York, 1986–8)
RMFC	*Recherches sur la musique française classique*
RMG	*Russkaya muzïkal'naya gazeta*
RMI	*Rivista musicale italiana*
RMS	*Renaissance Manuscript Studies* (Stuttgart, 1975–)
RN	*Renaissance News*
RosaM	C. de Rosa, Marchese di Villarosa: *Memorie dei compositori di musica del regno di Napoli* (Naples, 1840)
RRAM	*Recent Researches in American Music*
RRMBE	*Recent Researches in the Music of the Baroque Era*
RRMCE	*Recent Researches in the Music of the Classical Era*
RRMMA	*Recent Researches in the Music of the Middle Ages and Early Renaissance*
RRMNETC	*Recent Researches in the Music of the Nineteenth and Early Twentieth Centuries*
RRMR	*Recent Researches in the Music of the Renaissance*
RS	*Rolling Stone*
SachsH	C. Sachs: *The History of Musical Instruments* (New York, 1940)
SainsburyD	J.H. Sainsbury: *A Dictionary of Musicians*
SartoriB	C. Sartori: *Bibliografia della musica strumentale italiana stampata in Italia fino al 1700* (Florence, 1952–68)
SartoriD	C. Sartori: *Dizionario degli editori musicali italiani*
SartoriL	C. Sartori: *I libretti italiani a stampa dalle origini al 1800* (Cuneo, 1990–94)
SBL	*Svenskt biografiskt lexikon* (Stockholm, 1918–)
SCC	*The Sixteenth-Century Chanson*
ScheringGIK	A. Schering: *Geschichte des Instrumental-Konzerts* (Leipzig, 1905, 2/1927/R)
ScheringGO	A. Schering: *Geschichte des Oratoriums* (Leipzig, 1911/R)
SchillingE	G. Schilling: *Encyclopädie der gesammten musikalischen Wissenschaften, oder Universal-Lexicon der Tonkunst*
SČHK	*Slovník české hudební kultury* (Prague, 1997)
SchmidlD	C. Schmidl: *Dizionario universale dei musicisti*
SchmidlDS	C. Schmidl: *Dizionario universale dei musicisti suppl.*
SchmitzG	E. Schmitz: *Geschichte der weltlichen Solokantate* (Leipzig, 1914, 2/1955)
SchullerEJ	G. Schuller: *Early Jazz* (New York, 1968/R)
SchullerSE	G. Schuller: *The Swing Era* (New York, 1989)
SchwarzGM	B. Schwarz: *Great Masters of the Violin*
SCISM	*Seventeenth-Century Italian Sacred Music*
SCKM	*Seventeenth-Century Keyboard Music* (New York, 1987–8)
SCMA	*Smith College Music Archives*
SCMad	*Sixteenth-Century Madrigal*
SCMot	*Sixteenth-Century Motet*
SeegerL	H. Seeger: *Musiklexikon*
SEM	*Series of Early Music* [University of California]
SennMT	W. Senn: *Musik und Theater am Hof zu Innsbruck* (Innsbruck, 1954)
SH	*Slovenská hudba*
SheridanCB	C. Sheridan: *Count Basie: a Bio-discography* (Westport, CT, and London, 1986)
SIMG	*Sammelbände der Internationalen Musik-Gesellschaft*
SJ	*Swing Journal*
SKM	*Sovetskiye kompozitorï i muzïkovedï* (Moscow, 1978–89)
SL	*Second Line*
SM	see *SMH*
SMA	*Studies in Music* [Australia]
SMC	*Studies in Music from the University of Western Ontario* [Canada]
SMd	*Schweizerische Musikdenkmäler*
SMH	*Studia musicologica Academiae scientiarum hungaricae*
SmitherHO	H. Smither: *A History of the Oratorio* (Chapel Hill, NC, 1977–)
SML	*Schweizer Musikerlexikon*

SMM	*Summa musicae medii aevi*
SMN	*Studia musicologica norvegica*
SMP	*Słownik muzyków polskich*
SMSC	*Solo Motets from the Seventeenth Century* (New York, 1987–8)
SMw	*Studien zur Musikwissenschaft*
SMz	*Schweizerische Musikzeitung/Revue musicale suisse*
SOB	*Süddeutsche Orgelmeister des Barock*
SOI	L. Bianconi and G. Pestelli, eds.: *Storia dell'opera italiana* (Turin, 1987–; Eng. trans., 1998–)
SolertiMBD	A. Solerti: *Musica, ballo e drammatica alla corte medicea dal 1600 al 1637* (Florence, 1905/R)
SouthernB	E. Southern: *Biographical Dictionary of Afro-American and African Musicians*
SovM	*Sovetskaya muzïka*
SpataroC	B.J. Blackburn, E.E. Lowinsky and C.A. Miller: *A Correspondence of Renaissance Musicians* (Oxford, 1991)
SPFFBU	*Sborník prací filosofické [filozofické] fakulty brněnské university [univerzity]*
SpinkES	I. Spink: *English Song: Dowland to Purcell* (London, 1974, repr. 1986 with corrections)
StevensonRB	R. Stevenson: *Renaissance and Baroque Musical Sources in the Americas* (Washington DC, 1970)
StevensonSCM	R. Stevenson: *Spanish Cathedral Music in the Golden Age* (Berkeley, 1961/R)
StevensonSM	R. Stevenson: *Spanish Music in the Age of Columbus* (The Hague, 1960/R)
StiegerO	F. Stieger: *Opernlexikon*
STMf	*Svensk tidskrift för musikforskning*
StrohmM	R. Strohm: *Music in Late Medieval Bruges* (Oxford, 1985)
StrohmR	R. Strohm: *The Rise of European Music* (Cambridge, 1993)
StrunkSR1	O. Strunk: *Source Readings in Music History* (New York, 1950/R)
StrunkSR2	O. Strunk: *Source Readings in Music History* (New York, rev. 2/1998 by L. Treitler)
SubiráHME	J. Subirá: *Historia de la música española ehispanoamericana*
Sv	*Storyville*
TCM	*Tudor Church Music*
TCMS	*Three Centuries of Music in Score* (New York, 1988–90)
Thompson1[-11]	O. Thompson: *The International Cyclopedia of Music and Musicians*, 1st-11th edns
TM	*Thesauri musici*
TraceyCSA	H. Tracey: *Catalogue of the Sound of Africa Series* (Roodeport, 1973)
TSM	*Tesoro sacro musical*
TuckerDE	M. Tucker, ed.: *The Duke Ellington Reader* (New York, and Oxford, England, 1993)
TVNM	*Tijdschrift van de Vereniging voor Nederlandse muziekgeschiedenis* [and earlier variants]

UVNM	*Uitgave van oudere Noord-Nederlandsche Meesterwerken*
Vander StraetenMPB	E. Vander Straeten: *La musique aux Pays-Bas avantle XIXe siècle*
VannesD	R. Vannes, with A. Souris: *Dictionnaire des musiciens (compositeurs)*
VannesE	R. Vannes: *Essai d'un dictionnaire universel des luthiers*
VintonD	J. Vinton: *Dictionary of Contemporary Music*
VirdungMG	S. Virdung: *Musica getutscht* (Basle, 1511/R)
VMw	*Vierteljahrsschrift für Musikwissenschaft*
VogelB	E. Vogel: *Bibliothek der gedruckten weltlichen Vocalmusik Italiens, aus den Jahren 1500 bis 1700* (Berlin, 1892/R)
VV	*Village Voice*
WalterG	F. Walter: *Geschichte des Theaters und der Musik am kurpfalzischen Hofe* (Leipzig, 1898/R)
WaltherML	J.G. Walther: *Musicalisches Lexicon, oder Musicalische Bibliothec*
Waterhouse-LangwillI	W. Waterhouse: *The New Langwill Index: a Dictionary of Musical Wind-Instrument Makers and Inventors*
WDMP	*Wydawnictwo dawnej muzyki polskiej*
WE	*The Wellesley Edition*
WECIS	*Wellesley Edition Cantata Index Series* (Wellesley, MA, 1964–72)
WeinmannWM	A. Weinmann: *Wiener Musikverleger und Musikalienhändler von Mozarts Zeit bis gegen 1860* (Vienna, 1956)
WickesIBJ, i	J. Wickes: *Innovations in British Jazz, i: 1900-1980* (Chelmsford, England, 1999)
WilliamsNH	P. Williams: *A New History of the Organ: from the Greeks to the Present Day* (London, 1980)
WinterfeldEK	C. von Winterfeld: *Der evangelische Kirchengesang und sein Verhältniss zur Kunst des Tonsatzes* (Leipzig, 1843–7/R)
WolfeMEP	R.J. Wolfe: *Early American Music Engraving and Printing* (Urbana, IL, 1980)
WolfH	J. Wolf: *Handbuch der Notationskunde* (Leipzig, 1913–19/R)
WurzbachL	C. von Wurzbach: *Biographisches Lexikon des Kaiserthums Oesterreich* (Vienna, 1856–91)
YIAMR	*Yearbook, Inter-American Institute for Musical Research, later Yearbook for Inter-American Musical Research*
YIFMC	*Yearbook of the International Folk Music Council*
YoungHI	P.T. Young: *4900 Historical Woodwind Instruments* (London, 1993) [enlarged 2nd edn of *Twenty Five Hundred Historical Woodwind Instruments* (New York, 1982)]

YTM	*Yearbook for Traditional Music*	*ŹHMP*	*Źródła do historii muzyki polskiej*
ZahnM	J. Zahn: *Die Melodien der deutschen evangelischen Kirchenlieder* (Gütersloh, 1889–93/R)	*ZI*	*Zeitschrift für Instrumentenbau*
		ZIMG	*Zeitschrift der Internationalen Musik-Gesellschaft*
ZDADL	*Zeitschrift für deutsches Altertum und deutsche Literatur* (1876–)	*ZL*	*Zenei lexikon*
		ZMw	*Zeitschrift für Musikwissenschaft*
ZfM	*Zeitschrift für Musik*	*ZT*	*Zenetudományi tanulmányok*

Library Sigla

A-SPL	St Paul, Benediktinerstift St Paul im Lavanttal
A-ST	Stams, Zisterzienserstift, Musikarchiv
A-STEp	Steyr, Stadtpfarre
A-Sca	Salzburg, Carolino Augusteum: Salzburger Museum für Kunst und Kulturgeschichte, Bibliothek
A-Sd	Salzburg, Dom, Konsistorialarchiv, Dommusikarchiv
A-Sk	Salzburg, Kapitelbibliothek
A-Sl	Salzburg, Landesarchiv
A-Sm	Salzburg, Internationale Stiftung Mozarteum, Bibliotheca Mozartiana
A-Smi	Salzburg, Universität Salzburg, Institut für Musikwissenschaft, Bibliothek
A-Sn	Salzburg, Nonnberg (Benediktiner-Frauenstift), Bibliothek
A-Sp	Salzburg, Bibliothek des Priesterseminars
A-Ssp	Salzburg, Erzabtei St Peter, Musikarchiv
A-Sst	Salzburg, Bundesstaatliche Studienbibliothek [in *A-Su*]
A-Su	Salzburg, Universitätsbibliothek
A-TU	Tulln, Pfarrkirche St Stephan
A-VOR	Vorau, Stift
A-WAIp	Waidhofen (Ybbs), Stadtpfarre
A-WIL	Wilhering, Zisterzienserstift, Bibliothek und Musikarchiv
A-Wa	Vienna, St Augustin, Musikarchiv
A-Waf	Vienna, Pfarrarchiv Altlerchenfeld
A-Wdo	Vienna, Zentralarchiv des Deutschen Orden
A-Wdp	Vienna, Bibliothek der Dominikanerprovinz
A-Wdtö	Vienna, Gesellschaft zur Herausgabe von Denkmälern der Tonkunst in Österreich
A-Wgm	Vienna, Gesellschaft der Musikfreunde
A-Wh	Vienna, Pfarrarchiv Hernals
A-Whh	Vienna, Haus-, Hof- und Staatsarchiv
A-Whk	Vienna, Hofburgkapelle [in *A-Wn*]
A-Wk	Vienna, St Karl Borromäus
A-Wkm	Vienna, Kunsthistorisches Museum
A-Wlic	Vienna, Pfarrkirche Wien-Lichtental
A-Wm	Vienna, Minoritenkonvent
A-Wmi	Vienna, Institut für Musikwissenschaft der Universität
A-Wn	Vienna, Österreichische Nationalbibliothek, Musiksammlung
A-Wp	Vienna, Musikarchiv, Piaristenkirche Maria Treu
A-Ws	Vienna, Schottenabtei, Musikarchiv
A-Wsa	Vienna, Stadtarchiv
A-Wsfl	Vienna, Schottenfeld, Pfarrarchiv St Laurenz
A-Wsp	Vienna, St Peter, Musikarchiv
A-Wst	Vienna, Stadt- und Landesbibliothek, Musik-sammlung
A-Wu	Vienna, Universitätsbibliothek
A-Wwessely	Vienna, Othmar Wessely, private collection
A-Z	Zwettl, Zisterzienserstift, Stiftsbibliothek

BELARUS

BY-MI	Minsk, Biblioteka Belorusskoj Gosudarstvennoj Konservatorii

BELGIUM

B-Aa	Antwerp, Stadsarchief
B-Aac	Antwerp, Archief en Museum voor het Vla-amse Culturleven
B-Ac	Antwerp, Koninklijk Vlaams Muziekconservatorium
B-Ak	Antwerp, Onze-Lieve-Vrouw-Kathedraal, Archief
B-Amp	Antwerp, Museum Plantin-Moretus
B-As	Antwerp, Stadsbibliotheek
B-Asj	Antwerp, Collegiale en Parochiale Kerk St-Jacob, Bibliotheek en Archief
B-BRc	Bruges, Stedelijk Muziekconservatorium, Bibliotheek
B-BRs	Bruges, Stadsbibliotheek
B-Ba	Brussels, Archives de la Ville
B-Bc	Brussels, Conservatoire Royal, Bibliothèque, Koninklijk Conservatorium, Bibliotheek
B-Bcdm	Brussels, Centre Belge de Documentation Musicale [CeBeDeM]
B-Bg	Brussels, Cathédrale St-Michel et Ste-Gudule [in *B-Bc* and *B-Br*]
B-Bmichotte	Brussels, Michotte private collection [in *B-Bc*]
B-Br	Brussels, Bibliothèque Royale Albert 1er/ Koninlijke Bibliotheek Albert I, Section de la Musique
B-Brtb	Brussels, Radiodiffusion-Télévision Belge
B-Bsp	Brussels, Société Philharmonique
B-D	Diest, St Sulpitiuskerk
B-Gc	Ghent, Koninklijk Muziekconservatorium, Bibliotheek
B-Gcd	Ghent, Culturele Dienst Province Oost-Vlaanderen
B-Geb	Ghent, St Baafsarchief
B-Gu	Ghent, Universiteit, Centrale Bibliotheek, Handskriftenzaal
B-LVu	Leuven, Katholieke Universiteit van Leuven
B-La	Liège, Archives de l'État, Fonds de la Cathédrale St Lambert
B-Lc	Liège, Conservatoire Royal de Musique, Bibliothèque
B-Lg	Liège, Musée Grétry
B-Lu	Liège, Université de Liège, Bibliothèque
B-MA	Morlanwelz-Mariemont, Musée de Mariemont, Bibliothèque
B-MEa	Mechelen, Archief en Stadsbibliotheek
B-Tc	Tournai, Chapitre de la Cathédrale, Archives
B-Tv	Tournai, Bibliothèque de la Ville

BRAZIL

BR-Rem	Rio de Janeiro, Universidade Federal do Rio de Janeiro, Escola de Música, Biblioteca Alberto Nepomuceno
BR-Rn	Rio de Janeiro, Fundação Biblioteca Nacional, Divisão de Música e Arquivo Sonoro

CANADA

CDN-CaQMG	Canada, Montreal, Quebec, Concordia University, Sir George Williams Campus

CDN-Cu	Calgary, University of Calgary, Library
CDN-E	Edmonton (AB), University of Alberta
CDN-HNu	Hamilton (ON), McMaster University, Mills Memorial Library, Music Section
CDN-Lu	London (ON), University of Western Ontario, Music Library
CDN-Mc	Montreal, Conservatoire de Musique, Centre de Documentation
CDN-Mcm	Montreal, Centre de Musique Canadienne
CDN-Mm	Montreal, McGill University, Faculty and Conservatorium of Music Library
CDN-Mn	Montreal, Bibliothèque Nationale
CDN-On	Ottawa, National Library of Canada, Music Division
CDN-Qmu	Quebec, Monastère des Ursulines, Archives
CDN-Qsl	Quebec, Musée de l'Amérique Française
CDN-Qul	Quebec, Université Laval, Bibliothèque des Sciences Humaines et Sociales
CDN-Tcm	Toronto, Canadian Music Centre
CDN-Tu	Toronto, University of Toronto, Faculty of Music Library
CDN-VIu	Victoria, University of Victoria
CDN-Vcm	Vancouver, Canadian Music Centre

COLOMBIA

CO-B	Bogotá, Archivo de la Catedral

CROATIA

HR-Dsmb	Dubrovnik, Franjevački Samostan Male Braće, Knjižnica
HR-KIf	Kloštar Ivanić, Franjevački Samostan
HR-OMf	Omiš, Franjevački Samostan
HR-R	Rab, Župna Crkva
HR-SMm	Samobor, Samoborski Muzej
HR-Sk	Split, Glazbeni Arhiv Katedrale Sv. Dujma
HR-Vu	Varaždin, Uršulinski Samostan
HR-ZAzk	Zadar, Znanstvena Knjižnica
HR-Zaa	Zagreb, Hrvatska Akademija Znanosti i Umjetnosti, Arhiv
HR-Zh	Zagreb, Hrvatski Glazbeni Zavod, Knjižnica i Arhiv
HR-Zha	Zagreb, Zbirka Don Nikole Udina-Algarotti [on loan to *HR-Zh*]
HR-Zhk	Zagreb, Arhiv Hrvatsko Pjevačko Društvo Kolo [in *HR-Zh*]
HR-Zs	Zagreb, Glazbeni Arhiv Nadbiskupskog Bogoslovnog Sjemeništa
HR-Zu	Zagreb, Nacionalna i Sveučilišna Knjižnica, Zbirka Muzikalija i Audiomaterijala

CUBA

C-HABn	Havana, Biblioteca Nacional José Martí

CZECH REPUBLIC

CZ-BER	Beroun, Statní Okresní Archiv
CZ-BROb	Broumov, Knihovna Benediktinů [in *CZ-HK*]
CZ-Bam	Brno, Archiv města Brna
CZ-Bb	Brno, Klášter Milosrdných Bratří [in *CZ-Bm*]
CZ-Bm	Brno, Moravské Zemské Muzeum, Oddělení Dějin Hudby
CZ-Bsa	Brno, Státní Oblastní Archiv
CZ-Bu	Brno, Moravská Zemská Knihovna, Hudební Oddělení

CZ-CH	Cheb, Okresní Archiv
CZ-CHRm	Chrudim, Okresní Muzeum
CZ-D	Dačice, Knihovna Františkánů [in *CZ-Bu*]
CZ-H	Hronov, Muzeum
CZ-HK	Hradec Králové, Státní Vědecká Knihovna
CZ-HKm	Hradec Králové, Muzeum Východńich Čech
CZ-HR	Hradiště u Znojma, Knihovna Křižovníků [in *CZ-Bu*]
CZ-JIa	Jindřichův Hradec, Státní Oblastní Archív Třeboňi
CZ-K	Český Krumlov, Státní Oblastní Archiv v Třeboni, Hudební Sbírka
CZ-KA	Kadaň, Děkansky Kostel
CZ-KL	Klatovy, Státní Oblastní Archiv v Plzni, Pobočka Klatovy
CZ-KR	Kroměříž, Knihovna Arcibiskupského Zámku
CZ-KRA	Králíky, Kostel Sv. Michala [in *CZ-UO*]
CZ-KRa	Kroměříž, Arcibiskupský zámek, hudební sbírka
CZ-KRm	Kroměříž, Umeleckohistorické muzeum
CZ-KU	Kutná Hora, Okresní Muzeum [in *CZ-Pnm*]
CZ-LIT	Litoměřice, Státní Oblastní Archiv
CZ-LIa	Česká Lípa, Okresní Archív
CZ-LO	Loukov, Farní Kostel
CZ-LUa	Louny, Okresní Archív
CZ-ME	Mělník, Okresní Muzeum [on loan to *CZ-Pnm*]
CZ-MH	Mnichovo Hradiště, Vlastivědné Muzeum
CZ-MHa	Mnichovo Hradiště, Státní Oblatní Archiv v Praze - Pobočka v Mnichovoě Hradiští
CZ-MT	Moravská Třebová, Knihovna Františ-kánů [in *CZ-Bu*]
CZ-NR	Nová Řše, Klášter Premonstrátů, Knihovna a Hudební Sbírka
CZ-OLa	Olomouc, Zemeský Archiv Opava, Pracoviště Olomouc
CZ-OP	Opava, Slezské Muzeum
CZ-OS	Ostrava, Česky Rozhlas, Hudební Archiv
CZ-OSE	Osek, Knihovna Cisterciáků [in *CZ-Pnm*]
CZ-PLa	Plzeň, Městský Archiv
CZ-PLm	Plzeň, Západočeské Muzeum, Umělec-koprůmyslové Oddělení
CZ-POa	Poděbrady, Okresní Archiv Nymburk, Pobočka Poděbrady
CZ-POm	Poděbrady, Muzeum
CZ-Pa	Prague, Státní Ústřední Archiv
CZ-Pak	Prague, Pražská Metropolitní Kapitula
CZ-Pdobrovského	Prague, Národní Muzeum, Dobrovského (Nostická) Knihovna
CZ-Pk	Prague, Konservatoř, Archiv a Knihovna
CZ-Pkřiž	Praha, Rytířský řád křižovníků s červenou hvězdou, hudební sbírka
CZ-Pn	Prague, Knihovna Národního Muzea

CZ-Pnd	Prague, Národní Divadlo, Hudební Archiv
CZ-Pnm	Prague, Národní Muzeum
CZ-Pr	Prague, Česky Rozhlas, Archívní a Programové Fondy, Fond Hudebnin
CZ-Ps	Prague, Památník Národního Písemnictví, Knihovna
CZ-Psj	Prague, Kostel Sv. Jakuba, Farní Rad
CZ-Pst	Prague, Knihovna Kláštera Premonstrátů (Strahovská Knihovna) [in CZ-Pnm]
CZ-Pu	Prague, Národní Knihovna, Hudenbí Oddělení
CZ-Puk	Prague, Karlova Univerzita, Filozofická Fakulta, Ústav Hudební Vědy, Knihovna
CZ-R	Rajhrad, Knihovna Benediktinského Kláštera [in CZ-Bm]
CZ-RO	Rokycany, Okresní Muzeum
CZ-ROk	Rokycany, Děkansky Úřad, Kostel
CZ-SE	Semily, Okresní Archiv v Semilech se Sídlem v Bystré nad Jizerou
CZ-SO	Sokolov, Okresní Archiv se Sídlem Jindřchovice, Zámek
CZ-TC	Třebíč, Městsky Archiv
CZ-TU	Turnov, Muzeum, Hudební Sbírka [in CZ-SE]
CZ-VB	Vyšší Brod, Knihovna Cisterciáckého Kláštera
CZ-Z	Žatec, Muzeum
CZ-ZI	Žitenice, Státní Oblastní Archiv v Litoměřicích
CZ-ZL	Zlonice, Památník Antonína Dvořáka

DENMARK

DK-A	Århus, Statsbiblioteket
DK-Ch	Christiansfeld, Brødremenigheden (Herrnhutgemeinde)
DK-Kar	Copenhagen, Det Arnamagnaeanske Institut
DK-Kc	Copenhagen, Carl Claudius Musikhistoriske Samling
DK-Kk	Copenhagen, Kongelige Bibliotek
DK-Kmk	Copenhagen, Kongelige Danske Musikkonservatorium
DK-Ku	Copenhagen, Det Kongelige Bibliotek Fiolstraede
DK-Kv	Copenhagen, Københavns Universitét, Musikvidenskabeligt Institut, Bibliotek
DK-Ol	Odense, Landsarkivet for Fyen
DK-Ou	Odense, Universitetsbibliotek, Musikafdelingen
DK-Sa	Sorø, Sorø Akademi, Biblioteket
DK-Tv	Tåsinge, Valdemars Slot

EGYPT

ET-Cn	Cairo, National Library (Dar al-Kutub)
ET-MSsc	Mount Sinai, St Catherine's Monastery

ESTONIA

EV-TALg	Tallinn, National Library of Estonia

FINLAND

FIN-A	Turku, Åbo Akademi, Sibelius Museum, Bibliotek ja Arkiv
FIN-FiHJ	Finland, Helsinki, Jazz & Pop Arkisto [Archive]
FIN-Hy	Helsinki, Helsingin Yliopiston Kirjasto/Helsinki University Library/Suomen Kansalliskikjasto
FIN-Hyf	Helsinki, Helsingin Yliopiston Kirjasto, Department of Finnish Music

FRANCE

F-A	Avignon, Médiathèque Ceccano
F-AB	Abbeville, Bibliothèque Nationale
F-AG	Agen, Archives Départementales de Lot-et-Garonne
F-AI	Albi, Bibliothèque Municipale
F-AIXc	Aix-en-Provence, Bibliothèque du Conservatoire
F-AIXm	Aix-en-Provence, Bibliothèque Méjanes
F-AIXmc	Aix-en-Provence, Bibliothèque de la Maîtrise de la Cathédrale
F-AL	Alençon, Bibliothèque Municipale
F-AM	Amiens, Bibliothèque Municipale
F-AN	Angers, Bibliothèque Municipale
F-APT	Apt, Basilique Ste Anne
F-AS	Arras, Médiathèque Municipale
F-ASOlang	Asnières-sur-Oise, Collection François Lang
F-AUT	Autun, Bibliothèque Municipale
F-AVR	Avranches, Bibliothèque Nationale
F-Ac	Avignon, Bibliothèque du Conservatoire
F-B	Besançon, Bibliothèque Municipale
F-BE	Beauvais, Bibliothèque Municipale
F-BG	Bourg-en-Bresse, Bibliothèque Municipale
F-BO	Bordeaux, Bibliothèque Municipale
F-BS	Bourges, Bibliothèque Municipale
F-Ba	Besançon, Bibliothèque de l'Archevêché
F-C	Carpentras, Bibliothèque Municipale (Inguimbertine)
F-CA	Cambrai, Médiathèque Municipale
F-CAc	Cambrai, Cathédrale
F-CC	Carcassonne, Bibliothèque Municipale
F-CF	Clermont-Ferrand, Bibliothèque Municipale et Interuniversitaire, Département Patrimoine
F-CH	Chantilly, Musée Condé
F-CHRm	Chartres, Bibliothèque Municipale
F-CHd	Chantilly, Musée Dobrie
F-CLO	Clermont-de-l'Oise, Bibliothèque
F-CO	Colmar, Bibliothèque de la Ville
F-COM	Compiègne, Bibliothèque Municipale
F-CSM	Châlons-en-Champagne, Bibliothèque Municipale
F-DI	Dieppe, Fonds Anciens et Local, Médiathèque Jean Renoir
F-DO	Dôle, Bibliothèque Municipale
F-DOU	Douai, Bibliothèque Nationale
F-Dc	Dijon, Conservatoire Jean-Philippe Rameau, Bibliothèque
F-Dm	Dijon, Bibliothèque Municipale
F-E	Epinal, Bibliothèque Nationale
F-EMc	Embrun, Trésor de la Cathédrale
F-EV	Evreux, Bibliothèque Municipale
F-F	Foix, Bibliothèque Municipale
F-G	Grenoble, Bibliothèque Municipale
F-LA	Laon, Bibliothèque Municipale
F-LG	Limoges, Bibliothèque Francophone Municipale
F-LH	Le Havre, Bibliothèque Municipale
F-LM	Le Mans, Bibliothèque Municipale Classée, Médiathèque Louis Aragon
F-LYc	Lyons, Conservatoire National de Musique

F-LYm	Lyons, Bibliothèque Municipale
F-Lad	Lille, Archives Départementales du Nord
F-Lc	Lille, Bibliothèque du Conservatoire
F-Lm	Lille, Bibliothèque Municipale Jean Levy
F-MD	Montbéliard, Bibliothèque Municipale
F-ME	Metz, Médiathèque
F-MH	Mulhouse, Bibliothèque Municipale
F-ML	Moulins, Bibliothèque Municipale
F-MO	Montpellier, Bibliothèque de l'Université
F-MON	Montauban, Bibliothèque Municipale Antonin Perbosc
F-MOf	Montpellier, Bibliothèque Inter-Universitaire, Section Médecine
F-Mc	Marseilles, Conservatoire de Musique et de Déclamation
F-NAc	Nancy, Bibliothèque du Conservatoire
F-Nm	Nantes, Bibliothèque Municipale, Médiathèque
F-O	Orléans, Médiathèque
F-Pa	Paris, Bibliothèque de l'Arsenal
F-Pan	Paris, Archives Nationales
F-Pc	Paris, Conservatoire [in F-Pn]
F-Pcf	Paris, Bibliothèque de la Comédie Française
F-Pcnrs	Paris, Centre National de la Recherche Scientifique, Bibliothèque
F-Pd	Paris, Centre de Documentation de la Musique Contemporaire
F-Pe	Paris, Schola Cantorum
F-Peb	Paris, Ecole Normale Supérieure des Beaux-Arts, Bibliothèque
F-Pgm	Paris, Gustav Mahler, Bibliothèque Musicale
F-Phanson	Paris, Collection Hanson
F-Pi	Paris, Bibliothèque de l'Institut de France
F-Pim	Paris, Bibliothèque Pierre Aubry
F-Pm	Paris, Bibliothèque Mazarine
F-Pmeyer	Paris, André Meyer, private collection
F-Pn	Paris, Bibliothèque Nationale de France
F-Po	Paris, Bibliothèque-Musée de l'Opéra
F-Ppincherle	Paris, Marc Pincherle, private collection
F-Ppo	Paris, Bibliothèque Polonaise de Paris
F-Prothschild	Paris, Germaine, Baronne Edouard de Rothschild, private collection
F-Prt	Paris, Radio France, Documentation Musicale
F-Ps	Paris, Bibliothèque de la Sorbonne
F-Psal	Paris, Editions Salabert
F-Pse	Paris, Société des Auteurs, Compositeurs et Editeurs de Musique
F-Psg	Paris, Bibliothèque Ste-Geneviève
F-Pshp	Paris, Société d'Histoire du Protestantisme Français, Bibliothèque
F-Pthibault	Paris, Geneviève Thibault, private collection [in F-Pn]
F-R	Rouen, Bibliothèque Municipale
F-RS	Reims, Bibliothèque Municipale
F-RSc	Reims, Maîtrise de la Cathédrale
F-Rc	Rouen, Bibliothèque du Conservatoire
F-SDI	St Dié, Bibliothèque Municipale
F-SERc	Serrant, Château
F-SEm	Sens, Bibliothèque Municipale

F-SO	Solesmes, Abbaye de St-Pierre
F-SOM	St Omer, Bibliothèque Municipale
F-SQ	St Quentin, Bibliothèque Municipale
F-Sc	Strasbourg, Bibliothèque du Conservatoire
F-Sgs	Strasbourg, Union Sainte Cécile, Bibliothéque Musicale du Grand Séminaire
F-Sim	Strasbourg, Université des Sciences Humaines, Institut de Musicologie
F-Sm	Strasbourg, Bibliothèque Municipale
F-Sn	Strasbourg, Bibliothèque Nationale et Universitaire
F-Ssp	Strasbourg, Bibliothèque du Séminaire Pro-testant
F-T	Troyes, Bibliothèque Municipale
F-TLm	Toulouse, Bibliothèque Municipale
F-TOm	Tours, Bibliothèque Municipale
F-V	Versailles, Bibliothèque
F-VA	Vannes, Bibliothèque Municipale
F-VAL	Valenciennes, Bibliothèque Municipale
F-VN	Verdun, Bibliothèque Municipale

GERMANY

D-AAm	Aachen, Domarchiv (Stiftsarchiv)
D-AAst	Aachen, Öffentliche Bibliothek, Musikbibliothek
D-AB	Amorbach, Fürstlich Leiningische Bibliothek
D-ABG	Annaberg-Buchholz, Kirchenbibliothek St Annen
D-ABGa	Annaberg-Buchholz, Kantoreiarchiv St Annen
D-AG	Augustusburg, Evangelisch-Lutherisches Pfarramt der Stadtkirche St Petri, Musiksammlung
D-AIC	Aichach, Stadtpfarrkirche [on loan to D-FS]
D-ALa	Altenburg, Thüringisches Hauptstaadtsarchiv Weimar, Aussenstelle Altenburg
D-AM	Amberg, Staatliche Bibliothek
D-AN	Ansbach, Staatliche Bibliothek
D-ANsv	Ansbach, Sing- und Orchesterverein (Ansbacher Kantorei), Archiv [in D-AN]
D-ARk	Arnstadt, Evangelisch-Lutherisches Pfarramt, Bibliothek
D-ARsk	Arnstadt, Stadt- und Kreisbibliothek
D-ASh	Aschaffenburg, Schloss Johannisburg, Hofbibliothek
D-ASsb	Aschaffenburg, Schloss Johannisburg, Stiftsbibliothek
D-Aa	Augsburg, Kantoreiarchiv St Annen
D-Aab	Augsburg, Archiv des Bistums Augsburg
D-Af	Augsburg, Fuggersche Domänenkanzlei, Bibliothek
D-Ahk	Augsburg, Heilig-Kreuz-Kirche, Dominikaner-kloster, Biliothek [in D-Asa]
D-As	Augsburg, Staats- und Stadtbibliothek
D-Asa	Augsburg, Stadtarchiv
D-Au	Augsburg, Universität Augsburg, Universitätsbibliothek
D-AÖhk	Altötting, Kapuziner-Kloster St Konrad, Bibliothek
D-BAL	Ballenstedt, Stadtbibliothek
D-BAR	Bartenstein, Fürst zu Hohenlohe-Barten-steinsches Archiv [on loan to D-NEhz]

D-BAUd	Bautzen, Domstift und Bischöfliches Ordinariat, Bibliothek und Archiv
D-BAUk	Bautzen, Stadtbibliothek
D-BAUm	Bautzen, Stadtmuseum
D-BAa	Bamberg, Staatsarchiv
D-BAs	Bamberg, Staatsbibliothek
D-BB	Benediktbeuern, Pfarrkirche, Bibliothek
D-BDH	Bad Homburg vor der Höhe, Stadtbibliothek
D-BDS	Bad Schwalbach, Evangelisches Pfarrarchiv
D-BDk	Brandenburg, Dom St Peter und Paul, Domstiftsarchiv und -bibliothek
D-BE	Bad Berleburg, Fürstlich Sayn-Wittgenstein-Berleburgsche Bibliothek
D-BEU	Beuron, Bibliothek der Benediktiner-Erzabtei
D-BFb	Burgsteinfurt, Fürst zu Bentheimsche Musikaliensammlung [on loan to D-MÜu]
D-BG	Beuerberg, Stiftskirche
D-BGD	Berchtesgaden, Stiftkirche, Bibliothek [on loan to D-FS]
D-BH	Bayreuth, Stadtbücherei
D-BIB	Bibra, Pfarrarchiv
D-BIT	Bitterfeld, Kreis-Museum
D-BKÖs	Bad Köstritz, Forschungs- und Gedenkstätte Heinrich-Schütz-Haus
D-BMs	Bremen, Staats- und Universitätsbibliothek
D-BNba	Bonn, Beethoven-Haus, Beethoven-Archiv
D-BNms	Bonn, Musikwissenschaftliches Seminar der Rheinischen Friedrich-Wilhelm-Universität
D-BNsa	Bonn, Stadtarchiv und Wissenschaftliche Stadtbibliothek
D-BNu	Bonn, Universitäts- und Landesbibliothek
D-BO	Bollstedt, Evangelische Kirchengemeinde, Pfarrarchiv
D-BOCHmi	Bochum, Ruhr-Universität, Fakultät für Geschichtswissenschaft, Musikwissenschaftliches Institut
D-BS	Brunswick, Stadtarchiv und Stadtbibliothek
D-BUCH	Buchen (Odenwald), Bezirksmuseum, Kraus-Sammlung
D-Ba	Berlin, Amerika-Gedenkbibliothek, Musikabteilung [in D-Bz]
D-Bda	Berlin, Akademie der Künste, Stiftung Archiv
D-Bdhm	Berlin, Hochschule für Musik Hanns Eisler
D-Bga	Berlin, Geheimes Staatsarchiv, Stiftung Preussischer Kulturbesitz
D-Bgk	Berlin, Bibliothek zum Grauen Kloster [in D-Bs]
D-Bhbk	Berlin, Staatliche Hochschule für Bildende Kunst, Bibliothek
D-Bhm	Berlin, Hochschule der Künste, Hochschulbibliothek, Abteilung Musik und Darstellende Kunst
D-Bim	Berlin, Staatliches Institut für Musikforschung, Bibliothek
D-Bk	Berlin, Staatliche Museen Preussischer Kulturbesitz, Kunstbibliothek
D-Bkk	Berlin, Staatliche Museen Preussischer Kulturbesitz, Kupferstichkabinett
D-Br	Berlin, Deutsches, Rundfunkarchiv Frankfurt am Main - Berlin, Historische Archive, Bibliothek
D-Bs	Berlin, Stadtbibliothek, Musikbibliothek [in D-Bz]
D-Bsb	Berlin, Staatsbibliothek zu Berlin Preussischer Kulturbesitz
D-Bsommer	Berlin, Sommer private collection
D-Bsp	Berlin, Evangelische Kirche Berlin-Brandenburg, Sprachenkonvikt, Bibliothek
D-Bst	Berlin, Stadtbücherei Wilmersdorf, Hauptstelle
D-CEbm	Celle, Bomann-Museum, Museum für Volkskunde Landes- und Stadtgeschichte
D-CR	Crimmitschau, Stadtkirche St Laurentius, Notenarchiv
D-CZ	Clausthal-Zellerfeld, Kirchenbibliothek [in D-CZu]
D-CZu	Clausthal-Zellerfeld, Technische Universität, Universitätsbibliothek
D-Cl	Coburg, Landesbibliothek, Musiksammlung
D-Cs	Coburg, Staatsarchiv
D-Cv	Coburg, Kunstsammlung der Veste Coburg, Bibliothek
D-DB	Dettelbach, Franziskanerkloster, Bibliothek
D-DDS (JI)	Germany, Darmstadt, Jazz-Institut Darmstadt
D-DEl	Dessau, Anhaltische Landesbücherei
D-DEsa	Dessau, Stadtarchiv
D-DGs	Duisburg, Stadtbibliothek, Musikbibliothek
D-DI	Dillingen an der Donau, Kreis- und Studienbibliothek
D-DL	Delitzsch, Museum, Bibliothek
D-DM	Dortmund, Stadt- und Landesbibliothek, Musikabteilung
D-DO	Donaueschingen, Fürstlich Fürstenbergische Hofbibliothek
D-DS	Darmstadt, Hessische Landes- und Hochschulbibliothek, Musikabteilung
D-DSim	Darmstadt, Internationales Musikinstitut, Informationszentrum für Zeitgenössische Musik, Bibliothek
D-DSsa	Darmstadt, Hessisches Staatsarchiv
D-DT	Detmold, Lippische Landesbibliothek, Musikabteilung
D-DTF	Dietfurt, Franziskanerkloster [in D-Ma]
D-DWc	Donauwörth, Cassianeum
D-Dhm	Dresden, Hochschule für Musik Carl Maria von Weber, Bibliothek [in D-Dl]
D-Dl	Dresden, Sächsische Landesbibliothek - Staats- und Universitäts-Bibliothek, Musikabteilung
D-Dla	Dresden, Sächsisches Hauptstaatsarchiv
D-Dmb	Dresden, Städtische Bibliotheken, Haupt- und Musikbibliothek [in D-Dl]
D-Ds	Dresden, Sächsische Staatsoper, Notenbibliothek [in D-Dl]
D-DÜha	Dietfurt, Nordrhein-Westfälisches Hauptstaatsarchiv
D-DÜk	Düsseldorf, Goethe-Museum, Bibliothek

D-DÜl	Düsseldorf, Universitätss- und Landesbibliothek, Heinrich Heine Universität
D-EB	Ebrach, Katholisches Pfarramt, Bibliothek
D-EC	Eckartsberga, Pfarrarchiv
D-EF	Erfurt, Stadt- und Regionalbibliothek, Abteilung Wissenschaftliche Sondersammlungen
D-EIa	Eisenach, Stadtarchiv, Bibliothek
D-EIb	Eisenach, Bachmuseum
D-EN	Engelberg, Franziskanerkloster, Bibliothek
D-ERP	Landesberg am Lech-Erpfting, Katholische Pfarrkirche [on loan to *D-Aab*]
D-ERu	Erlangen, Universitätsbibliothek
D-EW	Ellwangen (Jagst), Stiftskirche
D-Ed	Eichstätt, Dom [in *D-Eu*]
D-Es	Eichstätt, Staats- und Seminarbibliothek [in *D-Eu*]
D-Eu	Eichstätt, Katholische Universität, Universitätsbibliothek
D-Ew	Eichstätt, Benediktinerinnen-Abtei St Walburg, Bibliothek
D-F	Frankfurt, Stadt- und Universitätsbibliothek
D-FBa	Freiberg (Lower Saxony), Stadtarchiv
D-FBo	Freiberg (Lower Saxony), Geschwister-Scholl-Gymnasium, Andreas-Möller-Bibliothek
D-FLa	Flensburg, Stadtarchiv
D-FLs	Flensburg, Landeszentralbibliothek Schleswig-Holstein
D-FRIts	Friedberg, Bibliothek des Theologischen Seminars der Evangelischen Kirche in Hessen und Nassau
D-FRu	Freiburg, Albert-Ludwigs-Universität, Universitätsbibliothek, Abteilung Handschriften, Alte Drucke und Rara
D-FRva	Freiburg, Deutsches Volksliedarchiv
D-FS	Freising, Erzbistum München und Freising, Dombibliothek
D-FUl	Fulda, Hessische Landesbibliothek
D-FW	Frauenchiemsee, Benediktinerinnenabtei Frauenwörth, Archiv
D-Ff	Frankfurt, Freies Deutsches Hochstift, Frankfurter Goethe-Museum, Bibliothek
D-Frl	Frankfurt, Musikverlag Robert Lienau
D-Fsa	Frankfurt, Stadtarchiv
D-FÜS	Füssen, Katholisches Stadtpfarramt St Mang
D-GBR	Grossbreitenbach (nr Arnstadt), Pfarramt, Archiv
D-GD	Goch-Gaesdonck, Collegium Augustinianum
D-GI	Giessen, Justus-Liebig-Universität, Bibliothek
D-GLAU	Glauchau, St Georgen, Musikarchiv
D-GM	Grimma, Göschenhaus-Seume-Gedenkstätte
D-GMl	Grimma, Landesschule [in *D-Dl*]
D-GOL	Goldbach (nr Gotha), Pfarrbibliothek
D-GOa	Gotha, Augustinerkirche, Notenbibliothek
D-GOl	Gotha, Forschungs- und Landesbibliothek, Musiksammlung
D-GRH	Gerolzhofen, Katholische Pfarrei [on loan to *D-WÜd*]
D-GRu	Greifswald, Universitätsbibliothek
D-GZsa	Greiz, Thüringisches Staatsarchiv Rudolstadt, Aussenstelle Greiz
D-Ga	Göttingen, Staatliches Archivlager
D-Gb	Göttingen, Johann-Sebastian-Bach-Institut
D-Gms	Göttingen, Musikwissenschaftliches Seminar der Georg-August-Universität
D-Gs	Göttingen, Niedersächsische Staats- und Universitätsbibliothek
D-GÖs	Görlitz, Oberlausitzische Bibliothek der Wissenschaften bei den Städtischen Sammlungen
D-GÜ	Güstrow, Museum der Stadt
D-HAR	Hartha (Kurort), Kantoreiarchiv
D-HAf	Halle, Hauptbibliothek und Archiv der Franck-eschen Stiftungen
D-HAh	Halle, Händel-Haus
D-HAmi	Halle, Martin-Luther-Universität, Universitäts- und Landesbibliothek Sachsen-Anhalt, Institut für Musikwissenschaft, Bibliothek
D-HAmk	Halle, Marktkirche Unser Lieben Frauen, Marienbibliothek
D-HAu	Halle, Martin-Luther-Universität, Universitäts- und Landesbibliothek Sachsen-Anhalt
D-HB	Heilbronn, Stadtarchiv
D-HER	Herrnhut, Evangelische Brüder-Unität, Archiv
D-HEms	Heidelberg, Musikwissenschaftliches Seminar der Rupert-Karls-Universität
D-HEu	Heidelberg, Ruprecht-Karls-Universität, Universitätsbibliothek, Abteilung Handschriften und Alte Drucke
D-HGm	Havelberg, Prignitz-Museum, Bibliothek
D-HL	Haltenbergstetten, Schloss (über Niederstetten, Baden-Württemburg), Fürst zu Hohenlohe-Jagstberg'sche Bibliothek [in *D-Mbs*]
D-HOE	Hohenstein-Ernstthal, Kantoreiarchiv der Chri-stophorikirche
D-HR	Harburg (nr Donauwörth), Fürstlich Oettingen-Wallerstein'sche Bibliothek Schloss Harburg [in *D-Au*]
D-HRD	Arnsberg-Herdringen, Schlossbibliothek (Bibliotheca Fürstenbergiana) [in *D-Au*]
D-HSj	Helmstedt, Ehemalige Universitätsbibliothek
D-HSk	Helmstedt, Kantorat St Stephani [in *D-W*]
D-HVkm	Hanover, Bibliothek des Kestner-Museums
D-HVl	Hanover, Niedersächsische Landesbibliothek
D-HVs	Hanover, Stadtbibliothek, Musikbibliothek
D-HVsa	Hanover, Staatsarchiv
D-Ha	Hamburg, Staatsarchiv
D-Hkm	Hamburg, Kunstgewerbemuseum, Bibliothek
D-Hmb	Hamburg, Öffentlichen Bücherhallen, Musikbücherei
D-Hs	Hamburg, Staats- und Universitätsbibliothek Carl von Ossietzky, Musiksammlung
D-IN	Markt Indersdorf, Katholisches Pfarramt, Bibliothek [on loan to *D-FS*]
D-ISL	Iserlohn, Evangelische Kirchengemeinde, Varnhagen-Bibliothek
D-JE	Jever, Marien-Gymnasium, Bibliothek
D-Jmb	Jena, Ernst-Abbe-Bücherei und Lesehalle der Carl-Zeiss-Stiftung, Musikbibliothek
D-Jmi	Jena, Friedrich-Schiller-Universität, Sektion Literatur- und Kunstwissenschaften, Bibliothek des ehem. Musikwissenschaftlichen Instituts [in *D-Ju*]
D-Ju	Jena, Friedrich-Schiller-Universität, Thüringer Universitäts- und Landesbibliothek

D-KA	Karlsruhe, Badische Landesbibliothek
D-KAsp	Karlsruhe, Pfarramt St Peter
D-KAu	Karlsruhe, Universitätsbibliothek
D-KBs	Koblenz, Stadtbibliothek
D-KFp	Kaufbeuren, Protestantisches Kirchenarchiv
D-KIl	Kiel, Schleswig-Holsteinische Landesbibliothek
D-KIu	Kiel, Universitätsbibliothek
D-KMs	Kamenz, Stadtarchiv
D-KNa	Cologne, Historisches Archiv der Stadt
D-KNd	Cologne, Kölner Dom, Erzbischöfliche Diözesan- und Dombibliothek
D-KNh	Cologne, Staatliche Hochschule für Musik, Bibliothek
D-KNmi	Cologne, Musikwissenschaftliches Institut der Universität
D-KNu	Cologne, Universitäts- und Stadtbibliothek
D-KPs	Kempten, Stadtbücherei
D-KPsl	Kempten, Stadtpfarrkirche St Lorenz, Musikarchiv
D-KR	Kleinröhrsdorf (nr Bischofswerda), Pfarrkirchenbibliothek
D-KZa	Konstanz, Stadtarchiv
D-Kdma	Kassel, Deutsches Musikgeschichtliches Archiv
D-Kl	Kassel, Gesamthochschul-Bibliothek, Landesbibliothek und Murhardsche Bibliothek, Musiksammlung
D-Km	Kassel, Musikakademie, Bibliothek
D-Ksp	Kassel, Louis Spohr-Gedenk- und Forschungsstätte, Archiv
D-LA	Landshut, Historischer Verein für Niederbayern, Bibliothek
D-LB	Langenburg, Fürstlich Hohenlohe-Langen-burg'sche Schlossbibliothek [on loan to D-NEhz]
D-LDB	Landsberg am Lech, Stadtpfarrkirche
D-LDN	Landau an der Isar, Pfarrkirchenstiftung St. Maria (Dpt. in: D-Po)
D-LEb	Leipzig, Bach-Archiv
D-LEbh	Leipzig, Breitkopf & Härtel, Verlagsarchiv
D-LEdb	Leipzig, Deutsche Bücherei, Musikaliensammlung
D-LEm	Leipzig, Leipziger Städtische Bibliotheken, Musikbibliothek
D-LEmi	Leipzig, Universität, Zweigbibliothek Musikwissenschaft und Musikpädagogik [in D-LEu]
D-LEsm	Leipzig, Stadtgeschichtliches Museum, Bibliothek, Musik- und Theatergeschichtliche Sammlungen
D-LEst	Leipzig, Stadtbibliothek [in D-LEu and D-LEm]
D-LEt	Leipzig, Thomanerchor, Bibliothek [in D-LEb]
D-LEu	Leipzig, Karl-Marx-Universität, Universitäts-bibliothek, Bibliotheca Albertina
D-LFN	Laufen, Stiftsarchiv
D-LI	Lindau, Stadtbibliothek
D-LIM	Limbach am Main, Pfarrkirche Maria Limbach
D-LST	Lichtenstein, Stadtkirche St Laurentius, Kantoreiarchiv
D-LUC	Luckau, Stadtkirche St Nikolai, Kantoreiarchiv
D-Lm	Lüneburg, Michaelisschule
D-Lr	Lüneburg, Ratsbücherei, Musikabteilung
D-LÜh	Lübeck, Bibliothek der Hansestadt, Musikabteilung
D-MAl	Magdeburg, Landeshauptarchiv Sachsen-Anhalt [in D-WERa]
D-MAs	Magdeburg, Stadtbibliothek Wilhelm Weitling, Musikabteilung
D-MBGk	Miltenberg, Katholische Pfarrei
D-ME	Meissen, Stadt- und Kreisbibliothek
D-MEIk	Meiningen, Bibliothek der Evangelisch-Lutherischen Kirchengemeinde
D-MEIl	Meiningen, Thüringisches Staatsarchiv
D-MEIr	Meiningen, Meininger Museen, Abteilung Musikgeschichte/Max-Reger-Archiv
D-MERa	Merseburg, Domstift, Stiftsarchiv
D-MG	Marburg, Westdeutsche Bibliothek [in D-Bsb]
D-MGB	Mönchen-Gladbach, Bibliothek Wissenschaft und Weisheit, Johannes-Duns-Skotus-Akademie der Kölnischen Ordens-Provinz der Franziskaner
D-MGmi	Marburg, Musikwissenschaftliches Institut der Philipps-Universität, Abteilung Hessisches Musikarchiv
D-MGs	Marburg, Staatsarchiv und Archivschule
D-MGu	Marburg, Philipps-Universität, Universitätsbibliothek
D-MH	Mannheim, Wissenschaftliche Stadtbibliothek
D-MHrm	Mannheim, Städtisches Reiss-Museum
D-MHst	Mannheim, Stadtbücherei, Musikbücherei
D-MLHb	Mühlhausen, Blasiuskirche, Pfarrarchiv Divi Blasii [on loan to D-MLHm]
D-MLHm	Mühlhausen, Marienkirche
D-MLHr	Mühlhausen, Stadtarchiv
D-MMm	Memmingen, Evangelisch-Lutherisches Pfarramt St Martin, Bibliothek
D-MR	Marienberg, Kirchenbibliothek
D-MT	Metten, Abtei, Bibliothek
D-MY	Mylau, Kirchenbibliothek
D-MZmi	Mainz, Musikwissenschaftliches Institut der Johannes-Gutenberg-Universität
D-MZp	Mainz, Bischöfliches Priesterseminar, Bibliothek
D-MZs	Mainz, Stadtbibliothek
D-MZsch	Mainz, Musikverlag B. Schott's Söhne, Verlagsarchiv
D-MZu	Mainz, Johannes-Gutenberg-Universität, Universitätsbibliothek, Musikabteilung
D-Ma	Munich, Franziskanerkloster St Anna, Bibliothek
D-Mb	Munich, Benediktinerabtei St Bonifaz, Bibliothek
D-Mbm	Munich, Bibliothek des Metropolitankapitels
D-Mbn	Munich, Bayerisches Nationalmuseum, Bibliothek
D-Mbs	Munich, Bayerische Staatsbibliothek
D-Mf	Munich, Frauenkirche [on loan to D-FS]
D-Mh	Munich, Staatliche Hochschule für Musik, Bibliothek
D-Mhsa	Munich, Bayerisches Hauptstaatsarchiv
D-Mk	Munich, Theatinerkirche St Kajetan
D-Mm	Munich, Bibliothek St Michael
D-Mmb	Munich, Münchner Stadtbibliothek, Musikbibliothek
D-Mo	Munich, Opernarchiv
D-Msa	Munich, Staatsarchiv
D-Mth	Munich, Theatermuseum der Clara-Ziegler-Stiftung

D-URS	Ursberg, St Josef-Kongregation, Orden der Franziskanerinnen
D-Us	Ulm, Stadtbibliothek
D-Usch	Ulm, Von Schermar'sche Familienstiftung, Bibliothek
D-W	Wolfenbüttel, Herzog August Bibliothek, Handschriftensammlung
D-WA	Waldheim, Stadtkirche St Nikolai, Bibliothek
D-WAB	Waldenburg, St Bartholomäus, Kantoreiarchiv
D-WD	Wiesentheid, Musiksammlung des Grafen von Schönborn-Wiesentheid
D-WERhb	Wernigerode, Harzmuseum, Harzbücherei
D-WEY	Weyarn, Pfarrkirche, Bibliothek [on loan to D-FS]
D-WF	Weissenfels, Schuh- und Stadtmuseum Weissenfels (mit Heinrich-Schütz-Gedenkstätte) [on loan to D-BKÖs]
D-WFe	Weissenfels, Ephoralbibliothek
D-WFmk	Weissenfels, Marienkirche, Pfarrarchiv [in D-HAmk]
D-WGH	Waigolshausen, Katholische Pfarrei [on loan to D-WÜd]
D-WGl	Wittenberg, Lutherhalle, Reformationsgeschichtliches Museum
D-WH	Bad Windsheim, Stadtbibliothek
D-WINtj	Winhöring, Gräflich Toerring-Jettenbachsche Bibliothek [on loan to D-Mbs]
D-WIl	Wiesbaden, Hessische Landesbibliothek
D-WO	Worms, Stadtbibliothek und Öffentliche Büchereien
D-WRdn	Weimar, Deutsches Nationaltheater und Staatskappelle, Archiv
D-WRgm	Weimar, Goethe-National-Museum (Goethes Wohnhaus)
D-WRgs	Weimar, Stiftung Weimarer Klassik, Goethe-Schiller-Archiv
D-WRh	Weimar, Hochschule für Musik Franz Liszt
D-WRiv	Weimar, Hochschule für Musik Franz Liszt, Institut für Volksmusikforschung
D-WRl	Weimar, Thüringisches Hauptstaatsarchiv Weimar
D-WRtl	Weimar, Thüringische Landesbibliothek, Musiksammlung [in D-WRz]
D-WRz	Weimar, Stiftung Weimarer Klassik, Herzogin Anna Amalia Bibliothek
D-WS	Wasserburg am Inn, Chorarchiv St Jakob, Pfarramt [on loan to D-FS]
D-Wa	Wolfenbüttel, Niedersächsisches Staatsarchiv
D-WÜd	Würzburg, Diözesanarchiv
D-WÜst	Würzburg, Staatsarchiv
D-WÜu	Würzburg, Bayerische Julius-Maximilians-Universität, Universitätsbibliothek
D-Z	Zwickau, Ratsschulbibliothek, Wissenschaftliche Bibliothek
D-ZE	Zerbst, Stadtarchiv
D-ZEo	Zerbst, Gymnasium Francisceum, Bibliothek
D-ZGh	Zörbig, Heimatmuseum
D-ZI	Zittau, Christian-Weise-Bibliothek, Altbestand [in D-Dl]
D-ZL	Zeil, Fürstlich Waldburg-Zeil'sches Archiv
D-ZZs	Zeitz, Stiftsbibliothek
D-Zsa	Zwickau, Stadtarchiv
D-Zsch	Zwickau, Robert-Schumann-Haus

GREAT BRITAIN

GB-A	Aberdeen, University, Queen Mother Library
GB-AB	Aberystwyth, Llyfryell Genedlaethol Cymru/National Library of Wales
GB-ABu	Aberystwyth, University College of Wales
GB-ALb	Aldeburgh, Britten-Pears Library
GB-AM	Ampleforth, Abbey and College Library, St Lawrence Abbey
GB-AR	Arundel Castle, Archive
GB-BA	Bath, Municipal Library
GB-BEL	Belton (Lincs.), Belton House
GB-BEV	Beverley, East Yorkshire County Record Office
GB-BEcr	Bedford, Bedfordshire County Record Office
GB-BO	Bournemouth, Central Library
GB-BRp	Bristol, Central Library
GB-BRu	Bristol, University of Bristol Library
GB-Bp	Birmingham, Public Libraries
GB-Bu	Birmingham, Birmingham University
GB-CA	Canterbury, Cathedral Library
GB-CDp	Cardiff, Public Libraries, Central Library
GB-CDu	Cardiff, University of Wales/Prifysgol Cymru
GB-CF	Chelmsford, Essex County Record Office
GB-CH	Chichester, Diocesan Record Office
GB-CHc	Chichester, Cathedral
GB-CL	Carlisle, Cathedral Library
GB-Ccc	Cambridge, Corpus Christi College, Parker Library
GB-Ccl	Cambridge, Central Library
GB-Cclc	Cambridge, Clare College Archives
GB-Ce	Cambridge, Emmanuel College
GB-Cfm	Cambridge, Fitzwilliam Museum, Dept of Manuscripts and Printed Books
GB-Cgc	Cambridge, Gonville and Caius College
GB-Cjc	Cambridge, St John's College
GB-Ckc	Cambridge, King's College, Rowe Music Library
GB-Cmc	Cambridge, Magdalene College, Pepys Library
GB-Cp	Cambridge, Peterhouse College Library
GB-Cpc	Cambridge, Pembroke College Library
GB-Cpl	Cambridge, Pendlebury Library of Music
GB-Cssc	Cambridge, Sidney Sussex College
GB-Ctc	Cambridge, Trinity College, Library
GB-Cu	Cambridge, University Library
GB-DRc	Durham, Cathedral Church, Dean and Chapter Library
GB-DRu	Durham, University Library
GB-DU	Dundee, Central Library
GB-EL	Ely, Cathedral Library [in GB-Cu]
GB-EXcl	Exeter, Cathedral Library
GB-En	Edinburgh, National Library of Scotland, Music Dept
GB-Ep	Edinburgh, City Libraries, Music Library
GB-Er	Edinburgh, Reid Music Library of the University of Edinburgh
GB-Es	Edinburgh, Signet Library
GB-Eu	Edinburgh, University Library, Main Library
GB-GL	Gloucester, Cathedral Library
GB-GLr	Gloucester, Record Office
GB-Ge	Glasgow, Euing Music Library
GB-Gm	Glasgow, Mitchell Library, Arts Dept
GB-Gsma	Glasgow, Scottish Music Archive
GB-Gu	Glasgow, University Library

GB-H	Hereford, Cathedral Library
GB-HAdolmetsch	Haslemere, Carl Dolmetsch, private collection
GB-HFr	Hertford, Hertfordshire Record Office
GB-Ir	Ipswich, Suffolk Record Office
GB-KNt	Knutsford, Tatton Park (National Trust)
GB-LA	Lancaster, District Central Library
GB-LEbc	Leeds, University of Leeds, Brotherton Library
GB-LEc	Leeds, Leeds Central Library, Music and Audio Dept
GB-LF	Lichfield, Cathedral Library
GB-Lfom	London, Foundling Museum: Gerald Coke, private collection
GB-LI	Lincoln, Cathedral Library
GB-Lnsa	Great Britain, London, National Sound Archive of the British Library
GB-LVp	Liverpool, Libraries and Information Services, Humanities Reference Library
GB-LVu	Liverpool, University, Music Department
GB-Lam	London, Royal Academy of Music, Library
GB-Lbbc	London, British Broadcasting Corporation, Music Library
GB-Lbc	London, British Council Music Library
GB-Lbl	London, British Library
GB-Lcm	London, Royal College of Music, Library
GB-Lcml	London, Central Music Library
GB-Lco	London, Royal College of Organists
GB-Lcs	London, English Folk Dance and Song Society, Vaughan Williams Memorial Library
GB-Ldc	London, Dulwich College Library
GB-Lfm	London, Faber Music
GB-Lgc	London, Guildhall Library
GB-Lk	London, King's Music Library [in GB-Lbl]
GB-Lkc	London, King's College Library
GB-Llp	London, Lambeth Palace Library
GB-Lmic	London, British Music Information Centre
GB-Lmt	London, Minet Library
GB-Lpro	London, Public Record Office
GB-Lrcp	London, Royal College of Physicians
GB-Lsp	London, St Paul's Cathedral Library
GB-Lspencer	London, Woodford Green: Robert Spencer, private collection
GB-Lst	London, Savoy Theatre Collection
GB-Lu	London, University of London Library, Music Collection
GB-Lue	London, Universal Edition
GB-Lv	London, Victoria and Albert Museum, Theatre Museum
GB-Lwa	London, Westminster Abbey Library
GB-Lwcm	London, Westminster Central Music Library
GB-MA	Maidstone, Kent County Record Office
GB-Mch	Manchester, Chetham's Library
GB-Mp	Manchester, Central Library, Henry Watson Music Library
GB-Mr	Manchester, John Rylands Library, Deansgate
GB-NH	Northampton, Record Office

GB-NO	Nottingham, University of Nottingham, Department of Music
GB-NTp	Newcastle upon Tyne, Public Libraries
GB-NW	Norwich, Central Library
GB-NWhamond	Norwich, Anthony Hamond, private collection
GB-NWr	Norwich, Record Office
GB-Oas	Oxford, All Souls College Library
GB-Ob	Oxford, Bodleian Library
GB-Oc	Oxford, Coke Collection
GB-Occc	Oxford, Corpus Christi College Library
GB-Och	Oxford, Christ Church Library
GB-Ojc	Oxford, St John's College Library
GB-Olc	Oxford, Lincoln College Library
GB-Omc	Oxford, Magdalen College Library
GB-Onc	Oxford, New College Library
GB-Ouf	Oxford, Faculty of Music Library
GB-Owc	Oxford, Worcester College
GB-P	Perth, Sandeman Public Library
GB-PB	Peterborough, Cathedral Library
GB-PM	Parkminster, St Hugh's Charterhouse
GB-R	Reading, University, Music Library
GB-SA	St Andrews, University of St Andrews Library
GB-SB	Salisbury, Cathedral Library
GB-SC	Sutton Coldfield, Oscott College, Old Library
GB-SH	Sherborne, Sherborne School Library
GB-SHR	Shrewsbury, Salop Record Office
GB-SHRs	Shrewsbury, Library of Shrewsbury School
GB-SOp	Southampton, Public Library
GB-SRfa	Studley Royal, Fountains Abbey [in GB-LEc]
GB-STb	Stratford-on-Avon, Shakespeare's Birthplace Trust Library
GB-STm	Stratford-on-Avon, Shakespeare Memorial Library
GB-T	Tenbury Wells, St Michael's College Library [in GB-Ob]
GB-W	Wells, Cathedral Library
GB-WA	Whalley, Stonyhurst College Library
GB-WB	Wimborne, Minster Chain Library
GB-WC	Winchester, Chapter Library
GB-WCc	Winchester, Winchester College, Warden and Fellows' Library
GB-WCr	Winchester, Hampshire Record Office
GB-WMl	Warminster, Longleat House Old Library
GB-WO	Worcester, Cathedral Library
GB-WOr	Worcester, Record Office
GB-WRch	Windsor, St George's Chapel Library
GB-WRec	Windsor, Eton College, College Library
GB-Y	York, Minster Library
GB-Ybi	York, Borthwick Institute of Historical Research

GREECE

GR-AOd	Mt Athos, Mone Dionysiou
GR-AOdo	Mt Athos, Mone Dohiariou
GR-AOh	Mt Athos, Mone Hilandariou
GR-AOi	Mt Athos, Mone ton Iveron
GR-AOk	Mt Athos, Mone Koutloumousi
GR-AOml	Mt Athos, Mone Megistis Lávras
GR-AOpk	Mt Athos, Mone Pantokrátoros

GR-AOva	Mt Athos, Vatopedi Monastery
GR-Aels	Athens, Ethniki Lyriki Skini
GR-Akounadis	Athens, Panayis Kounadis, private collection
GR-Aleotsakos	Athens, George Leotsakos, private collection
GR-Am	Athens, Mousseio ke Kendro Meletis Ellinikou Theatrou
GR-An	Athens, Ethnikē Bibliotēkē tēs Hellados
GR-THpi	Thessaloniki, Patriarhikó Idryma Paterikon Meleton, Vivliotheke

GUATEMALA

GCA-Gc	Guatemala City, Cathedral, Archivo Capitular

HUNGARY

H-BA	Bártfá, St Aegidius [in H-Bn]
H-Ba	Budapest, Magyar Tudományos Akadémia Könytára
H-Bami	Budapest, Magyar Tudományos Akadémia Zenetudományi Intézet, Könyvtár
H-Bb	Budapest, Bartók Béla Zeneművészeti Szakközépiskola, Könyvtár [in H-Bl]
H-Bl	Budapest, Liszt Ferenc Zeneművészeti Főiskola, Könyvtár
H-Bn	Budapest, Országos Széchényi Könyvtár
H-Bo	Budapest, Állami Operaház
H-Br	Budapest, Ráday Gyűjtemény
H-Bs	Budapest, Központi Szemináriumi Könyvtár
H-Bu	Budapest, Eötvös Loránd Tudományegyetem, Egyetemi Könyvtár
H-Efko	Esztergom, Főszékesegyházi Kottatár
H-Efkö	Esztergom, Főszékesegyházi Könyvtár
H-GYm	Gyula, Múzeum
H-Gc	Győr, Püspöki Papnevelő Intézet Könyvtára
H-Gk	Győr, Káptalan Magánlevéltár Kottatára
H-K	Kalocsa, Érseki Könyvtár
H-KE	Keszthely, Helikon Kastélymúzeum, Könyvtár
H-P	Pécs, Székesegyházi Kottatár
H-PH	Pannonhalma, Főapátság, Könyvtár
H-SFm	Székesfehérvár, István Király Múzeum
H-Se	Sopron, Evangélikus Egyházközség Könyvtára
H-VEs	Veszprém, Székesegyházi Kottatár

IRELAND

IRL-C	Cork, Boole Library, University College
IRL-Da	Dublin, Royal Irish Academy Library
IRL-Dam	Dublin, Royal Irish Academy of Music, Monteagle Library
IRL-Dc	Dublin, Contemporary Music Centre
IRL-Dcb	Dublin, Chester Beatty Library
IRL-Dcc	Dublin, Christ Church Cathedral, Library
IRL-Dm	Dublin, Archbishop Marsh's Library
IRL-Dmh	Dublin, Mercer's Hospital [in IRL-Dtc]
IRL-Dn	Dublin, National Library of Ireland
IRL-Dpc	Dublin, St Patrick's Cathedral
IRL-Dtc	Dublin, Trinity College Library, University of Dublin
IRL-Duc	Dublin, University College

ISRAEL

IL-J	Jerusalem, Jewish National and University Library, Music Dept
IL-Jgp	Jerusalem, Greek Orthodox Patriarchate, Library (Hierosolymitike Bibliotheke)
IL-Jp	Jerusalem, Patriarchal Library
IL-Ta	Tel-Aviv, American for Music Library in Israel, Felicja Blumental Music Center and Library
IL-Tmi	Tel-Aviv, Israel Music Institute

ITALY

I-ALTsm	Altamura, Associazione Amici della Musica Saverio Mercadante, Biblioteca
I-AN	Ancona, Biblioteca Comunale Luciano Benincasa
I-AO	Aosta, Seminario Maggiore
I-AOc	Aosta, Cattedrale, Biblioteca Capitolare
I-AP	Ascoli Piceno, Biblioteca Comunale Giulio Gabrielli
I-APa	Ascoli Piceno, Archivio di Stato
I-AT	Atri, Basilica Cattedrale di S Maria Assunta, Bib-lioteca Capitolare e Museo
I-Ac	Assisi, Biblioteca Comunale [in I-Af]
I-Ad	Assisi, Cattedrale S Rufino, Biblioteca dell'Archivio Capitolare
I-Af	Assisi, Sacro Convento di S Francesco, Biblioteca-Centro di Documentazione Francescana
I-BAR	Barletta, Biblioteca Comunale Sabino Loffredo
I-BAca	Bari, Biblioteca Capitolare
I-BAcp	Bari, Conservatorio di Musica Niccolò Piccinni, Biblioteca
I-BAn	Bari, Biblioteca Nazionale Sagarriga Visconti-Volpi
I-BDG	Bassano del Grappa, Biblioteca Archivo Museo (Biblioteca Civica)
I-BE	Belluno, Biblioteche Lolliniana e Gregoriana
I-BGc	Bergamo, Biblioteca Civica Angelo Mai
I-BGi	Bergamo, Civico Istituto Musicale Gaetano Donizetti, Biblioteca
I-BI	Bitonto, Biblioteca Comunale E. Bogadeo (ex Vitale Giordano)
I-BRc	Brescia, Conservatorio Statale di Musica A. Venturi, Biblioteca
I-BRd	Brescia, Archivio e Biblioteca Capitolari
I-BRq	Brescia, Biblioteca Civica Queriniana
I-BRs	Brescia, Seminario Vescovile Diocasano, Archivio Musicale
I-BRsmg	Brescia, Chiesa della Madonna delle Grazie (S Maria), Archivio
I-BV	Benevento, Biblioteca Capitolare
I-BZa	Bolzano, Archivio di Stato, Biblioteca
I-BZf	Bolzano, Convento dei Minori Francescani, Biblioteca
I-BZtoggenburg	Bolzano, Count Toggenburg, private collection
I-Baf	Bologna, Accademia Filarmonica, Archivio

I-Bam	Bologna, Collezioni d'Arte e di Storia della Casa di Risparmio (Biblioteca Ambrosini)	*I-COc*	Como, Biblioteca Comunale
I-Bas	Bologna, Archivio di Stato, Biblioteca	*I-COd*	Como, Duomo, Archivio Musicale
I-Bc	Bologna, Civico Museo Bibliografico Musicale	*I-CRE*	Crema, Biblioteca Comunale
I-Bca	Bologna, Biblioteca Comunale dell'Archiginnasio	*I-CRas*	Cremona, Archivio di Stato
		I-CRd	Cremona, Biblioteca Capitolare [in *I-CRsd*]
I-Bl	Bologna, Conservatorio Statale di Musica G.B. Martini, Biblioteca	*I-CRg*	Cremona, Biblioteca Statale
		I-CRsd	Cremona, Archivio Storico Diocesano
I-Bof	Bologna, Congregazione dell'Oratorio (Padri Filippini), Biblioteca	*I-CT*	Cortona, Biblioteca Comunale e dell'Accademia Etrusca
I-Bpm	Bologna, Università degli Studi, Facoltà di Magistero, Cattedra di Storia della Musica, Biblioteca	*I-DO*	Domodossola, Biblioteca e Archivio dei Rosminiani di Monte Calvario [in *I-ST*]
		I-E	Enna, Biblioteca e Discoteca Comunale
I-Bsf	Bologna, Convento di S Francesco, Biblioteca	*I-FA*	Fabriano, Biblioteca Comunale
		I-FAN	Fano, Biblioteca Comunale Federiciana
I-Bsm	Bologna, Biblioteca del Convento di S Maria dei Servi e della Cappella Musicale Arcivescovile	*I-FAd*	Fabriano, Duomo (S Venanzio), Biblioteca Capitolare
		I-FBR	Fossombrone, Biblioteca Civica Passionei
I-Bsp	Bologna, Basilica di S Petronio, Archivio Musicale	*I-FELc*	Feltre, Museo Civico, Biblioteca
		I-FEM	Finale Emilia, Biblioteca Comunale
I-Bu	Bologna, Biblioteca Universitaria, sezione Musicale	*I-FERaa*	Fermo, Archivio Storico Arcivescovile con Archivio della Pietà
I-CARc	Castell'Arquato, Archivio Capitolare (Parrocchiale)	*I-FERas*	Fermo, Archivio di Stato di Ascoli Piceno, sezione di Fermo
I-CARcc	Castell'Arquato, Chiesa Collegiata dell'Assunta, Archivio Musicale	*I-FERc*	Fermo, Biblioteca Comunale
		I-FERd	Fermo, Metropolitana (Duomo), Archivio Capitolare [in *I-FERaa*]
I-CAS	Cascia, Monastero di S Rita, Archivio		
I-CATa	Catania, Archivio di Stato	*I-FERvitali*	Fermo, Gualberto Vitali-Rosati, private collection
I-CATc	Catania, Biblioteche Riunite Civica e Antonio Ursino Recupero		
		I-FEc	Ferrara, Biblioteca Comunale Ariostea
I-CATm	Catania, Museo Civico Belliniano, Biblioteca	*I-FEd*	Ferrara, Duomo, Archivio Capitolare
I-CATus	Catania, Università degli Studi di Catania, Facoltà di Lettere e Filosofia, Dipartimento di Scienze Storiche, Storia della Musica, Biblioteca	*I-FOLc*	Foligno, Biblioteca Comunale
		I-FOLd	Foligno, Duomo, Archivio
		I-FOc	Forlì, Biblioteca Comunale Aurelio Saffi
I-CAcon	Cagliari, Conservatorio di Musica Giovanni Pierluigi da Palestrina, Biblioteca	*I-FRa*	Fara in Sabina, Monumento Nazionale di Farfa, Biblioteca
I-CC	Città di Castello, Duomo, Archivio Capitolare [in *I-CCsg*]	*I-FZac*	Faenza, Basilica Cattedrale, Archivio Capitolare
I-CCc	Città di Castello, Biblioteca Comunale Giosuè Carducci	*I-FZc*	Faenza, Biblioteca Comunale Manfrediana, Raccolte Musicali
I-CCsg	Città di Castello, Biblioteca Stori Guerri e Archivi Storico	*I-Fa*	Florence, Ss Annunziata, Archivio
		I-Fas	Florence, Archivio di Stato, Biblioteca
I-CDO	Codogno, Biblioteca Civica Luigi Ricca	*I-Fbecherini*	Florence, Becherini private collection
I-CEc	Cesena, Biblioteca Comunale Malatestiana	*I-Fc*	Florence, Conservatorio Statale di Musica Luigi Cherubini
I-CF	Cividale del Friuli, Duomo (Parrocchia di S Maria Assunta), Archivio Capitolare	*I-Fd*	Florence, Opera del Duomo (S Maria del Fiore), Biblioteca e Archivio
I-CFVd	Castelfranco Veneto, Duomo, Archivio	*I-Ffabbri*	Florence, Mario Fabbri, private collection
I-CFm	Cividale del Friuli, Museo Archeologico Nazionale, Biblioteca	*I-Fl*	Florence, Biblioteca Medicea Laurenziana
		I-Fm	Florence, Biblioteca Marucelliana
I-CHTd	Chieti, Biblioteca della Curia Arcivescovile e Archivio Capitolare	*I-Fn*	Florence, Biblioteca Nazionale Centrale, Dipartimento Musica
I-CHc	Chioggia, Biblioteca Comunale Cristoforo Sabbadino	*I-Folschki*	Florence, Olschki private collection
		I-Fr	Florence, Biblioteca Riccardiana
I-CHf	Chioggia, Archivio dei Padri Filippini [in *I-CHc*]	*I-Fs*	Florence, Seminario Arcivescovile Maggiore, Biblioteca
I-CMac	Casale Monferrato, Duomo di Sant'Evasio, Archivio Capitolare	*I-Fsa*	Florence, Biblioteca Domenicana di S Maria Novella
I-CMbc	Casale Monferrato, Biblioteca Civica Giovanni Canna	*I-Fsl*	Florence, Parrocchia di S Lorenzo, Biblioteca
I-CMs	Casale Monferrato, Seminario Vescovile, Biblioteca	*I-Fsm*	Florence, Convento di S Marco, Biblioteca
		I-GO	Gorizia, Seminario Teologico Centrale, Biblioteca
I-CORc	Correggio, Biblioteca Comunale		

I-GR	Grottaferrata, Biblioteca del Monumento Nazionale
I-GUBd	Gubbio, Biblioteca Vescovile Fonti e Archivio Diocesano (con Archivio del Capitolo della Cattedrale)
I-Gc	Genoa, Biblioteca Civica Berio
I-Gim	Genoa, Civico Istituto Mazziniano, Biblioteca
I-Gl	Genoa, Conservatorio di Musica Nicolò Paganini, Biblioteca
I-Gremondini	Genoa, P.C. Remondini, private collection
I-Gsl	Genoa, S Lorenzo (Duomo), Archivio Capitolare
I-Gu	Genoa, Biblioteca Universitaria
I-I	Imola, Biblioteca Comunale
I-IBborromeo	Isola Bella, Borromeo private collection
I-IE	Iesi, Biblioteca Comunale
I-IV	Ivrea, Cattedrale, Biblioteca Capitolare
I-LA	L'Aquila, Biblioteca Provinciale Salvatore Tommasi
I-LANc	Lanciano, Biblioteca Diocesano (con Archivio della Cattedrale)
I-LT	Loreto, Santuario della S Casa, Archivio Storico
I-LU	Lugo, Biblioteca Comunale Fabrizio Trisi
I-LUi	Lugo, Istituto Musicale Pareggiato G.L. Malerbi
I-La	Lucca, Archivio di Stato
I-Las	Lucca, Biblioteca-Archivio Storico Comunale
I-Lc	Lucca, Biblioteca Capitolare Feliniana e Biblioteca Arcivescovile
I-Lg	Lucca, Biblioteca Statale
I-Li	Lucca, Istituto Musicale L. Boccherini, Biblioteca
I-Ls	Lucca, Seminario Arcivescovile, Biblioteca
I-MAC	Macerata, Biblioteca Comunale Mozzi-Borgetti
I-MAa	Mantua, Archivio di Stato
I-MAad	Mantua, Archivio Storico Diocesano
I-MAav	Mantua, Accademia Nazionale Virgiliana di Scienze, Lettere ed Arti, Archivio Musicale
I-MAc	Mantua, Biblioteca Comunale
I-MC	Montecassino, Monumento Nazionale di Montecassino, Biblioteca
I-MDAegidi	Montefiore dell'Aso, Francesco Egidi, private collection
I-ME	Messina, Biblioteca Regionale Universitaria
I-MEs	Messina, Biblioteca Painiana (del Seminario Arcivescovile S Pio X)
I-MOd	Modena, Duomo, Biblioteca e Archivio Capitolare
I-MOe	Modena, Biblioteca Estense e Universitaria
I-MOs	Modena, Archivio di Stato [in *I-MOe*]
I-MTc	Montecatini Terme, Biblioteca Comunale
I-MTventuri	Montecatini Terme, Antonio Venturi, private collection [in *I-MTc*]
I-MZ	Monza, Parrocchia di S Giovanni Battista, Biblioteca Capitolare
I-Ma	Milan, Biblioteca Ambrosiana
I-Malfieri	Milan, Familglia Trecani degli Alfieri, private collection
I-Mas	Milan, Archivio di Stato
I-Mb	Milan, Biblioteca Nazionale Braidense
I-Mc	Milan, Conservatorio di Musica Giuseppe Verdi, Biblioteca
I-Mcap	Milan, Archivio Capitolare di S Ambrogio, Biblioteca
I-Mcom	Milan, Biblioteca Comunale Sormani
I-Md	Milan, Capitolo Metropolitano, Biblioteca e Archivio
I-Mgallini	Milan, Natale Gallini, private collection
I-Mr	Milan, Biblioteca della Casa Ricordi
I-Ms	Milan, Biblioteca Teatrale Livia Simoni
I-Msartori	Milan, Claudio Sartori, private collection [in *I-Mc*]
I-Msc	Milan, Chiesa di S Maria presso S Celso, Archivio
I-Mt	Milan, Biblioteca Trivulziana e Archivio Storico Civico
I-Mu	Milan, Università degli Studi di Milano, Facoltà di Giurisprudenza, Biblioteca
I-Muc	Milan, Università Cattolica del Sacro Cuore, Biblioteca
I-NON	Nonantola, Seminario Abbaziale, Biblioteca
I-NOVd	Novara, S Maria (Duomo), Biblioteca Capitolare
I-NOVg	Novara, Seminario Teologico e Filosofico di S Gaudenzio, Biblioteca
I-NOVi	Novara, Istituto Civico Musicale Brera, Biblioteca
I-NT	Noto, Biblioteca Comunale Principe di Villadorata
I-Na	Naples, Archivio di Stato
I-Nc	Naples, Conservatorio di Musica S Pietro a Majella, Biblioteca
I-Nf	Naples, Biblioteca Oratoriana dei Gerolamini (Filippini)
I-Ng	Naples, Monastero di S Gregorio Armeno, Archivio
I-Nlp	Naples, Biblioteca Lucchesi Palli [in *I-Nn*]
I-Nn	Naples, Biblioteca Nazionale Vittorio Emanuele III
I-OFma	Offida, Parrocchia di Maria Ss Assunta, Archivio
I-OS	Ostiglia, Opera Pia G. Greggiati Biblioteca Musicale
I-Od	Orvieto, Opera del Duomo, Biblioteca
I-PAVc	Pavia, Chiesa di S Maria del Carmine, Archivio
I-PAVs	Pavia, Seminario Vescovile, Biblioteca
I-PAVu	Pavia, Biblioteca Universitaria
I-PAac	Parma, Duomo, Archivio Capitolare con Archivio della Fabbriceria
I-PAas	Parma, Archivio di Stato
I-PAc	Parma, Biblioteca Palatina, sezione Musicale
I-PAcom	Parma, Biblioteca Comunale
I-PAp	Parma, Biblioteca Nazionale Palatina
I-PAt	Parma, Archivio Storico del Teatro Regio [in *I-PAcom*]
I-PCc	Piacenza, Biblioteca Comunale Passerini Landi
I-PCcon	Piacenza, Conservatorio di Musica G. Nicolini, Biblioteca
I-PCd	Piacenza, Duomo, Biblioteca e Archivio Capitolare
I-PCsa	Piacenza, Basilica di S Antonino, Biblioteca e Archivio Capitolari
I-PEA	Pescia, Biblioteca Comunale Carlo Magnani
I-PESc	Pesaro, Conservatorio di Musica G. Rossini, Biblioteca

I-PESd	Pesaro, Duomo, Archivio Capitolare [in *I-PESdi*]
I-PESdi	Pesaro, Biblioteca Diocesana
I-PESo	Pesaro, Ente Olivieri, Biblioteca e Musei Oliveriana
I-PESr	Pesaro, Fondazione G. Rossini, Biblioteca
I-PEas	Perugia, Archivio di Stato
I-PEc	Perugia, Biblioteca Comunale Augusta
I-PEd	Perugia, Biblioteca Domincini
I-PEl	Perugia, Conservatorio di Musica Francesco Morlacchi, Biblioteca
I-PEsf	Perugia, Congregazione dell' Oratorio di S Filippo Neri, Biblioteca e Archivio
I-PEsl	Perugia, Duomo (S Lorenzo), Archivio
I-PEsp	Perugia, Basilica Benedettina di S Pietro, Archivo e Museo della Badia
I-PIa	Pisa, Archivio di Stato
I-PIp	Pisa, Opera della Primaziale Pisana, Archivio Musicale
I-PIraffaelli	Pisa, Raffaelli private collection
I-PIst	Pisa, Chiesa dei Cavalieri di S Stefano, Archivio
I-PIt	Pisa, Teatro Verdi
I-PIu	Pisa, Biblioteca Universitaria
I-PLa	Palermo, Archivio di Stato
I-PLcom	Palermo, Biblioteca Comunale
I-PLcon	Palermo, Conservatorio di Musica Vincenzo Bellini, Biblioteca
I-PLi	Palermo, Università degli Studi, Facoltà di Lettere e Filosofia, Istituto di Storia della Musica, Biblioteca
I-PLn	Palermo, Biblioteca Centrale della Regione Sicilia tex (Nazionale)
I-PLpagano	Palermo, Roberto Pagano, private collection
I-PO	Potenza, Biblioteca Provinciale
I-PR	Prato, Archivio Storico Diocesano, Biblioteca (con Archivio del Duomo)
I-PS	Pistoia, Basilica di S Zeno, Archivio Capitolare
I-PSc	Pistoia, Biblioteca Comunale Forteguerriana
I-PSrospigliosi	Pistoia, Rospigliosi private collection
I-Pas	Padua, Archivio di Stato
I-Pc	Padua, Duomo, Biblioteca Capitolare, Curia Vescovile
I-Pca	Padua, Basilica del Santo, Biblioteca Antoniana
I-Pci	Padua, Biblioteca Civica
I-Pl	Padua, Conservatorio Cesare Pollini
I-Ps	Padua, Seminario Vescovile, Biblioteca
I-Pu	Padua, Biblioteca Universitaria
I-RA	Ravenna, Duomo (Basilica Ursiana), Archivio Capitolare [in *I-RAs*]
I-RAc	Ravenna, Biblioteca Comunale Classense
I-RAs	Ravenna, Seminario Arcivescovile dei Ss Angeli Custodi, Biblioteca
I-REm	Reggio nell'Emilia, Biblioteca Panizzi
I-REsp	Reggio nell'Emilia, Basilica di S Prospero, Archivio Capitolare
I-RI	Rieti, Biblioteca Diocesana, sezione dell'Archivio Musicale del Duomo
I-RIM	Rimini, Biblioteca Civica Gambalunga
I-RPTd	Ripatransone, Duomo, Archivio
I-RVE	Rovereto, Biblioteca Civica Girolamo Tartarotti
I-RVI	Rovigo, Accademia dei Concordi, Biblioteca
I-Ra	Rome, Biblioteca Angelica
I-Raf	Rome, Accademia Filarmonica Romana
I-Ras	Rome, Archivio di Stato, Biblioteca
I-Rbompiani	Rome, Bompiani private collection
I-Rc	Rome, Biblioteca Casanatense, sezione Musica
I-Rcg	Rome, Curia Generalizia dei Padre Gesuiti, Biblioteca
I-Rchg	Rome, Chiesa del Gesù, Archivio
I-Rcsg	Rome, Congregazione dell'Oratorio di S Girolamo della Carità, Archivio [in *I-Ras*]
I-Rdp	Rome, Archivio Doria Pamphili
I-Rf	Rome, Congregazione dell'Oratorio S Filippo Neri
I-Ria	Rome, Istituto di Archeologia e Storia dell'Arte, Biblioteca
I-Ribimus	Rome, Istituto di Bibliografia Musicale, Biblioteca [in *I-Rn*]
I-Rig	Rome, Istituto Storico Germanico di Roma, sezione Storia della Musica, Biblioteca
I-Rims	Rome, Pontificio Istituto di Musica Sacra, Biblioteca
I-Rli	Rome, Accademia Nazionale dei Lincei e Corsiniana, Biblioteca
I-Rlib	Rome, Basilica Liberiana, Archivio
I-Rmalvezzi	Rome, Lionello Malvezzi, private collection
I-Rmassimo	Rome, Massimo princes, private collection
I-Rn	Rome, Biblioteca Nazionale Centrale Vittorio Emanuele II
I-Rp	Rome, Biblioteca Pasqualini [in *I-Rsc*]
I-Rps	Rome, Chiesa di S Pantaleo (Padri Scolipi), Archivio
I-Rrai	Rome, RAI-Radiotelevisione Italiana, Archivio Musica
I-Rrostirolla	Rome, Giancarlo Rostirolla, private collection [in *I-Fn* and *I-Ribimus*]
I-Rsc	Rome, Conservatorio di Musica S Cecilia
I-Rscg	Rome, Abbazia di S Croce in Gerusalemme, Biblioteca
I-Rsg	Rome, Basilica di S Giovanni in Laterano, Archivio Musicale
I-Rslf	Rome, Chiesa di S Luigi dei Francesi, Archivio
I-Rsm	Rome, Basilica di S Maria Maggiore, Archivio Capitolare [in *I-Rvat*]
I-Rsmm	Rome, S Maria di Monserrato, Archivio
I-Rsmt	Rome, Basilica di S Maria in Trastevere, Archivio Capitolare [in *I-Rvic*]
I-Rsp	Rome, Chiesa di S Spirito in Sassia, Archivio
I-Rss	Rome, Curia Generalizia dei Domenicani (S Sabina), Biblioteca
I-Ru	Rome, Biblioteca Universitaria Alessandrina
I-Rv	Rome, Biblioteca Vallicelliana
I-Rvat	Rome, Biblioteca Apostolica Vaticana
I-Rvic	Rome, Vicariato, Archivio
I-SA	Savona, Biblioteca Civica Anton Giulio Barrili
I-SAa	Savona, Seminario Vescovile, Biblioteca
I-SE	Senigallia, Biblioteca Comunale Antonelliana
I-SO	Sant'Oreste, Collegiata di S Lorenzo sul Monte Soratte, Biblioteca
I-SPE	Spello, Collegiata di S Maria Maggiore, Archivio

I-SPEbc	Spello, Biblioteca Comunale Giacomo Prampolini
I-SPc	Spoleto, Biblioteca Comunale Giosuè Carducci
I-SPd	Spoleto, Biblioteca Capitolare (Duomo di S Lorenzo)
I-ST	Stresa, Biblioteca Rosminiana
I-STE	Vipiteno, Convento dei Cappuccini (Kapuzinerkloster), Biblioteca
I-Sac	Siena, Accademia Musicale Chigiana, Biblioteca
I-Sas	Siena, Archivio di Stato
I-Sc	Siena, Biblioteca Comunale degli Intronati
I-Sco	Siena, Convento dell'Osservanza, Biblioteca
I-Sd	Siena, Opera del Duomo, Archivio Musicale
I-Smo	Asciano (nr Siena), Abbazia Benedettina di Monte Oliveto Maggiore, Biblioteca
I-TAc	Taranto, Biblioteca Civica Pietro Acclavio
I-TE	Terni, Istituto Musicale Pareggiato Giulio Briccialdi, Biblioteca
I-TEd	Terni, Duomo, Archivio Capitolare
I-TLp	Torre del Lago Puccini, Museo di Casa Puccini
I-TOL	Tolentino, Biblioteca Comunale Filelfica
I-TRE	Tremezzo, Count Gian Ludovico Sola-Cabiati, private collection
I-TRP	Trapani, Biblioteca Fardelliana
I-TRa	Trent, Archivio di Stato
I-TRbc	Trent, Castello del Buon Consiglio, Biblioteca [in *I-TRmp*]
I-TRc	Trent, Biblioteca Comunale
I-TRcap	Trent, Biblioteca Capitolare con Annesso Archivio
I-TRfeininger	Trent, Biblioteca Musicale Laurence K.J. Feininger [in *I-TRmp*]
I-TRmd	Trent, Museo Diocesano, Biblioteca
I-TRmp	Trent, Castello del Buonconsiglio: Monumenti e Collezioni Provinciali, Biblioteca
I-TRmr	Trent, Museo Trentino del Risorgimento e della Lotta per la Libertà, Biblioteca
I-TSci	Trieste, Biblioteca Comunale Attilio Hortis
I-TScon	Trieste, Conservatorio di Musica Giuseppe Tartini, Biblioteca
I-TSmt	Trieste, Civico Museo Teatrale di Fondazione Carlo Schmidl, Biblioteca
I-TVco	Treviso, Biblioteca Comunale
I-TVd	Treviso, Biblioteca Capitolare della Cattedrale
I-Ta	Turin, Archivio di Stato
I-Tci	Turin, Civica Biblioteca Musicale Andrea della Corte
I-Tco	Turin, Conservatorio di Musica Giuseppe Verdi, Biblioteca
I-Td	Turin, Cattedrale Metropolitana di S Giovanni Battista, Archivio Capitolare, Fondo Musicale della Cappella dei Cantori del Duomo e della Cappella Regia Sabauda
I-Tf	Turin, Accademia Filarmonica, Archivio
I-Tfanan	Turin, Giorgio Fanan, private collection

I-Tn	Turin, Biblioteca Nazionale Universitaria, sezione Musicale
I-Tr	Turin, Biblioteca Reale
I-Trt	Turin, RAI - Radiotelevisione Italiana, Biblioteca
I-UD	Udine, Duomo, Archivio Capitolare [in *I-UDs*]
I-UDa	Udine, Archivio di Stato
I-UDc	Udine, Biblioteca Comunale Vincenzo Joppi
I-UDs	Udine, Seminario Arcivescovile, Biblioteca
I-URBcap	Urbania, Biblioteca Capitolare [in *I-URBdi*]
I-URBdi	Urbania, Biblioteca Diocesana
I-Us	Urbino, Cappella del Ss Sacramento (Duomo), Archivio
I-VCd	Vercelli, Biblioteca Capitolare
I-VEaf	Verona, Accademia Filarmonica, Biblioteca e Archivio
I-VEas	Verona, Archivio di Stato
I-VEc	Verona, Biblioteca Civica
I-VEcap	Verona, Biblioteca Capitolare
I-VEss	Verona, Chiesa di S Stefano, Archivio
I-VIGsa	Vigévano, Biblioteca del Capitolo della Cattedrale
I-VIb	Vicenza, Biblioteca Civica Bertoliana
I-VId	Vicenza, Biblioteca Capitolare
I-VIs	Vicenza, Seminario Vescovile, Biblioteca
I-VRNs	Chiusi della Verna, Santuario della Verna, Biblioteca
I-Vas	Venice, Archivio di Stato
I-Vc	Venice, Conservatorio di Musica Benedetto Marcello, Biblioteca
I-Vcg	Venice, Casa di Goldoni, Biblioteca
I-Vgc	Venice, Fondazione Giorgio Cini, Istituto per le Lettere, il Teatro ed il Melodramma, Biblioteca
I-Vlevi	Venice, Fondazione Ugo e Olga Levi, Biblioteca
I-Vmarcello	Venice, Andrighetti Marcello, private collection
I-Vmc	Venice, Museo Civico Correr, Biblioteca d'Arte e Storia Veneziana
I-Vnm	Venice, Biblioteca Nazionale Marciana
I-Vqs	Venice, Fondazione Querini-Stampalia, Biblioteca
I-Vs	Venice, Seminario Patriarcale, Archivio
I-Vsf	Venice, Biblioteca S Francesco della Vigna
I-Vsm	Venice, Procuratoria di S Marco [in *I-Vlevi*]
I-Vsmc	Venice, S Maria della Consolazione detta Della Fava
I-Vt	Venice, Teatro La Fenice, Archivio Storico-Musicale

JAPAN

J-Tma	Tokyo, Musashino Ongaku Daigaku, Ioshokan
J-Tn	Tokyo, Nanki Ongaku Bunko

LATVIA

LV-J	Jelgava, Muzei
LV-R	Riga, Latvijas Mūzikas Akademijas Biblioteka

LITHUANIA

LT-V	Vilnius, Lietuvos Muzikos Akademijos Biblioteka
LT-Va	Vilnius, Lietuvos Moksly Akademijos Biblioteka

P-Ln	Lisbon, Biblioteca Nacional, Centro de Estudos Musicológicos
P-Lt	Lisbon, Teatro Nacional de S Carlos
P-Mp	Mafra, Palácio Nacional, Biblioteca
P-Pm	Porto, Biblioteca Pública Municipal
P-VV	Vila Viçosa, Fundaçao da Casa de Brangança, Biblioteca do Paço Ducal, Arquivo Musical
P-Va	Viseu, Arquivo Distrital
P-Vs	Viseu, Arquivo da Sé

ROMANIA

RO-BRm	Braşov, Biblioteca Judeteana
RO-Ba	Bucharest, Academiei Române, Biblioteca
RO-Cu	Cluj-Napoca, Universitatea Babes Bolyai, Biblioteca Centrală Universitară Lucian Blaga
RO-J	Iaşi, Biblioteca Centrală Universitară Mihai Eminescu, Departmentul Colecţii Speciale
RO-Sa	Sibiu, Direcţia Judeţeană a Arhivelor Naţionale
RO-Sb	Sibiu, Muzeul Naţional Bruckenthal, Biblioteca

RUSSIAN FEDERATION

RUS-KA	Kaliningrad, Oblastnaya Universal'naya Nauchnaya Biblioteka
RUS-KAg	Kaliningrad, Gosudarstvennaya Biblioteka
RUS-KAu	Kaliningrad, Nauchnaya Biblioteka Kalingradskogo Gosudarstvennogo Universiteta
RUS-Mcl	Moscow, Rossiyskiy Gosudarstvennïy Arkhiv Literaturï i Iskusstva (RGALI)
RUS-Mcm	Moscow, Gosudarstvennïy Tsentral'nïy Muzey Musïkal'noy Kul'turï imeni M.I. Glinki
RUS-Mim	Moscow, Gosudarstvennïy Istoricheskïy Muzey
RUS-Mk	Moscow, Moskovskaya Gosudarstvennaya Konservatoriya im. P.I. Chaykovskogo, Nauchnaya Muzikal'naya Biblioteka imeni S.I. Taneyeva
RUS-Mm	Moscow, Gosudarstvennaya Publichnaya Istoricheskaya Biblioteka
RUS-Mrg	Moscow, Rossiyskaya Gosudarstvennaya Biblioteka
RUS-Mt	Moscow, Gosudarstvennïy Tsentral'nïy Teatral'nïy Musey im. A. Bakhrushina
RUS-SPan	St Petersburg, Rossiyskaya Akademiya Nauk, Biblioteka
RUS-SPia	St Petersburg, Gosudarstvennïy Tsentral'nïy Istoricheskïy Arkhiv
RUS-SPil	St Petersburg, Biblioteka Instituta Russkoy Literaturï Rossiyskoy Akademii Nauk (Pushkinskiy Dom)
RUS-SPit	St Petersburg, Rossiyskiy Institut Istorii Iskusstv
RUS-SPk	St Petersburg, Biblioteka Gosudarstvennoy Konservatorii im. N.A. Rimskogo-Korsakova
RUS-SPph	St Petersburg, Gosurdarstvennaya Filarmoniya im D.D. Shostakovicha
RUS-SPsc	St Petersburg, Rossiyskaya Natsional'naya Biblioteka
RUS-SPtob	St Petersburg, Gosudarstvennïy Akademichesky Mariinsky Teatr, Tsentral'naya Muzïkal'naya Biblioteka

SERBIA

YU-Bn	Belgrade, Narodna Biblioteka Srbije, Odelenje Posebnih Fondova

SLOVAKIA

SK-BRa	Bratislava, Štátny Oblastny Archív
SK-BRhs	Bratislava, Knižnica Hudobného Seminára Filozofickej Fakulty Univerzity Komenského
SK-BRm	Bratislava, Archív Mesta Bratislavy
SK-BRmp	Bratislava, Miestne Pracovisko Matice Slovenskej [in *SK-Mms*]
SK-BRnm	Bratislava, Slovenské Národné Múzeum, Hudobné Múzeum
SK-BRsa	Bratislava, Slovenský Národný Archív
SK-BRsav	Bratislava, Ústav Hudobnej Vedy Slovenská Akadémia Vied
SK-BRu	Bratislava, Univerzitná Knižnica, Narodné Knižničné Centrum, Hudobńy Kabinet
SK-BSk	Banská Štiavnica, Farský Rímsko-Katolícky Kostol, Archív Chóru
SK-J	Júr pri Bratislave, Okresny Archív, Bratislava-Vidiek [in *SK-MO*]
SK-KRE	Kremnica, Štátny Okresny Archív Žiar nad Hronom
SK-Le	Levoča, Evanjelická a.v. Cirkevná Knižnica
SK-MO	Modra, Štátny Okresny Archív Pezinok
SK-Mms	Martin, Matica Slovenská
SK-Mnm	Martin, Slovenské Národné Múzeum, Archív
SK-NM	Nové Mesto nad Váhom, Rímskokatolícky Farsky Kostol
SK-TN	Trenčín, Štátny Okresny Archív
SK-TR	Trnava, Štátny Okresny Archív

SLOVENIA

SI-Lf	Ljubljana, Frančiškanski Samostan, Knjižnica
SI-Ln	Ljubljana, Narodna in Univerzitetna Knjižnica, Glavni Knjižni Fond
SI-Lna	Ljubljana, Nadškofijski Arhiv
SI-Lng	Ljubljana, Narodna in Univerzitetna Knjižnica, Glasbena Zbirka
SI-Lnr	Ljubljana, Narodna in Univerzitetna Knjižnica, Rokopisna Zbirka
SI-Ls	Ljubljana, Katedral, Glazbeni Arhiv
SI-Nf	Novo Mesto, Frančiškanski Samostan, Knjižnica
SI-Nk	Novo Mesto, Kolegiatni Kapitelj, Knjižnica
SI-Pk	Ptuj, Knjižnica Ivana Potrča

SOUTH AFRICA

ZA-Csa	Cape Town, South African Library

SPAIN

E-AL	Alquézar, Colegiata
E-ALB	Albarracín, Catedral, Archivo
E-AR	Aránzazu, Archivo Musical del Monasterio de Aránzazu
E-AS	Astorga, Catedral
E-Ac	Avila, S Apostólica Iglesia Catedral de el Salvador, Archivo Catedralicio
E-Asa	Avila, Monasterio de S Ana
E-BA	Badajoz, Catedral, Archivo Capitular
E-BUa	Burgos, Catedral, Archivo
E-BUlh	Burgos, Cistercian Monasterio de Las Huelgas
E-Bac	Barcelona, Archivo de la Corona de Aragón/Arixiu de la Corona d'Aragó
E-Bbc	Barcelona, Biblioteca de Catalunya, Seccíon de Música

E-Bc	Barcelona, S.E. Catedra Basiclica, Arixiu
E-Bcd	Barcelona, Centro de Documentació Musical de la Generalitat de Catalunya 'El Jardi Dels Tarongers'
E-Bih	Barcelona, Arixiu Históric de la Ciutat
E-Bim	Barcelona, Consejo Superior de Investigaciones Científicas, Departamento de Musicología, Biblioteca
E-Bit	Barcelona, Institut del Teatre, Centre d'Investigació, Documentació i Difusió
E-Boc	Barcelona, Orfeó Catalá, Biblioteca
E-Bu	Barcelona, Universitat Autónoma
E-C	Córdoba, S Iglesia Catedral, Archivo de Música
E-CA	Calahorra, Catedral
E-CAL	Calatayud, Colegiata de S María
E-CU	Cuenca, Catedral, Archivo Capitular
E-CUi	Cuenca, Instituto de Música Religiosa
E-CZ	Cádiz, Archivo Capitular
E-E	San Lorenzo de El Escorial, Monasterio, Real Biblioteca
E-G	Gerona, Catedral, Archivo/Arxiu Capitular
E-GRc	Granada, Catedral Metropolitana, Archivo Capitular [in *E-GRcr*]
E-GRcr	Granada, Capilla Real, Archivo de Música
E-GRmf	Granada, Archivo Manuel de Falla
E-GU	Guadalupe, Real Monasterio de S María, Archivo de Música
E-Gp	Gerona, Biblioteca Pública
E-H	Huesca, Catedral
E-J	Jaca, Catedral, Archivo Musical
E-JA	Jaén, Catedral, Archivo Capitular
E-JEc	Jerez de la Frontera, Colegiata
E-L	León, Catedral, Archivo Histórico
E-LEc	Lérida, Catedral
E-LPA	Las Palmas de Gran Canaria, Catedral de Canarias
E-Lc	León, Real Basilica de S Isidoro
E-MA	Málaga, Catedral, Archivo Capitular
E-MO	Montserrat, Abadía
E-MON	Mondoñedo, Catedral, Archivo
E-Mah	Madrid, Archivo Histórico Nacional
E-Mba	Madrid, Archivo de Música, Real Academia de Bellas Artes de S Fernando
E-Mc	Madrid, Real Conservatorio Superior de Música, Biblioteca
E-Mca	Madrid, Casa de Alba
E-Mcns	Madrid, Congregación de Nuestra Señora
E-Md	Madrid, Centro de Documentación Musical del Ministerio de Cultura
E-Mdr	Madrid, Convento de las Descalzas Reales
E-Mm	Madrid, Biblioteca Histórica Municipal
E-Mmc	Madrid, Casa Ducal de Medinaceli, Biblioteca
E-Mn	Madrid, Biblioteca Nacional
E-Mp	Madrid, Patrimonio Nacional
E-Msa	Madrid, Sociedad General de Autores y Editores
E-OL	Olot, Biblioteca Popular
E-ORI	Orihuela, Catedral, Archivo
E-OV	Oviedo, Catedral Metropolitana, Archivo
E-P	Plasencia, Catedral, Archivo de Música
E-PAL	Palencia, Catedral de S Antolín, Archivo de Música
E-PAMc	Pamplona, Catedral, Archivo

E-PAS	Pastrana, Museo Parroquial
E-PAc	Palma de Mallorca, Catedral, Archivo
E-PAp	Palma de Mallorca, Biblioteca Provincial
E-RO	Roncesvalles, Monasterio S María, Biblioteca
E-SA	Salamanca, Catedral, Archivo Catedralicio
E-SAN	Santander, Biblioteca de la Universidad Menéndez, Sección de Música
E-SAc	Salamanca, Conservatorio Superior de Música de Salamanca, Biblioteca
E-SAu	Salamanca, Biblioteca Universitaria
E-SC	Santiago de Compostela, Catedral Metropolitana
E-SCu	Santiago de Compostela, Biblioteca de la Universidad
E-SD	Santo Domingo de la Calzada, Catedral Archivo
E-SE	Segovia, Catedral, Archivo Capitular
E-SEG	Segorbe, Archivo de la Catedral
E-SI	Silos, Abadía de S Domingo, Archivo
E-SU	Seo de Urgel, Catedral
E-Sc	Seville, Institución Colombina
E-TAc	Tarragona, Catedral
E-TE	Teruel, Catedral, Archivo Capitular
E-TO	Tortosa, Catedral
E-TUY	Tuy, Catedral
E-TZ	Tarazona, Catedral, Archivo Capitular
E-Tc	Toledo, Catedral, Archivo y Biblioteca Capítulares
E-Tp	Toledo, Biblioteca Pública Provincial y Museo de la S Cruz
E-V	Valladolid, Catedral Metropolitana, Archivo de Música
E-VAa	Valencia, Archivo Municipal
E-VAc	Valencia, Catedral Metropolitana, Archivo y Biblioteca, Archivo de Música
E-VAcp	Valencia, Real Colegio: Seminario de Corpus Christi, Archivo Musical del Patriarca
E-VAu	Valencia, Biblioteca Universitaria
E-VI	Vich, Museu Episcopal
E-Vp	Valladolid, Parroquia de Santiago
E-ZAc	Zamora, Catedral
E-Zac	Zaragoza, Catedrale de La Seo y Basílica del Pilar, Archivo de Música de las Catedrales
E-Zcc	Zaragoza, Colegio de las Escuelas Pías de S José de Calasanz, Biblioteca
E-Zs	Zaragoza, La Seo, Biblioteca Capitular [in *E-Zac*]
E-Zvp	Zaragoza, Iglesia Metropolitana [in *E-Zac*]

SWEDEN

S-A	Arvika, Ingesunds Musikhögskola
S-B	Bålsta, Skoklosters Slott
S-Gu	Göteborg, Universitetsbiblioteket
S-Hfryklund	Helsingborg, Daniel Fryklund, private collection [in *S-Skma*]
S-HÄ	Härnösand, Länsmuseet-Murberget
S-HÖ	Höör, Biblioteket
S-J	Jönköping, Per Brahegymnasiet
S-K	Kalmar, Stadsbibliotek, Stifts- och Gymnasiebiblioteket
S-Klm	Kalmar, Länsmuseet
S-L	Lund, Universitet, Universitetsbiblioteket, Handskriftsavdelningen

S-LB	Leufsta Bruk, De Geer private collection [in S-Uu]
S-LI	Linköping, Linköpings Stadsbibliotek, Stiftsbiblioteket
S-N	Norrköping, Stadsbiblioteket
S-Ssv	Sweden, Stockholm, Svenskt Visarchiv, Central-institution för Vis och Folkmusikforskning
S-STr	Strängnäs, Roggebiblioteket
S-Sdt	Stockholm, Drottningholms Teatermuseum
S-Sfo	Stockholm, Frimurare Orden, Biblioteket
S-Sic	Stockholm, Svensk Musik
S-Sk	Stockholm, Kungliga Biblioteket: Sveriges Nationalbibliotek
S-Skma	Stockholm, Statens Musikbibliotek
S-Sm	Stockholm, Musikmuseet, Arkiv
S-Smf	Stockholm, Stiftelsen Musikkulturens Främjande
S-Sn	Stockholm, Nordiska Museet, Arkivet
S-Ssr	Stockholm, Sveriges Radio Förvaltning, Musikbiblioteket
S-St	Stockholm, Kung. Teatern [in S-Skma]
S-Sva	Stockholm, Svenskt Visarkiv
S-Uu	Uppsala, Universitetsbiblioteket
S-V	Västerås, Stadsbibliotek, Stiftsavdelningen
S-Vll	Visby, Landsarkivet
S-VX	Växjö, Landsbiblioteket

SWITZERLAND

CH-A	Aarau, Aargauische Kantonsbibliothek
CH-BEb	Berne, Burgerbibliothek/Bibliothèque de la Bourgeoisie
CH-BEl	Berne, Schweizerische Landesbibliothek/ Bibliothèque Nationale Suisse/ Biblioteca Nazionale Svizzera/Biblioteca Naziunala Svizra
CH-BEsu	Berne, Stadt- und Universitätsbibliothek
CH-BM	Beromünster, Musikbibliothek des Stifts
CH-BU	Burgdorf, Stadtbibliothek
CH-Bab	Basle, Archiv der Evangelischen Brüdersozietät
CH-Bps	Basle, Paul Sacher Stiftung, Bibliothek
CH-Bu	Basle, Universität Basel, Öffentliche Bibliothek, Musikabteilung
CH-CHW (Jda)	Switzerland, Wallbach, Jazzdocumentation Archive
CH-CObodmer	Cologny-Geneva, Fondation Martin Bodmer, Bibliotheca Bodmeriana
CH-D	Disentis, Stift, Musikbibliothek
CH-E	Einsiedeln, Benedikterkloster, Musikbibliothek
CH-EN	Engelberg, Kloster, Musikbibliothek
CH-FF	Frauenfeld, Thurgauische Kantonsbibliothek
CH-Fcu	Fribourg, Bibliothèque Cantonale et Universitaire
CH-Gc	Geneva, Conservatoire de Musique, Bibliothèque

CH-Gpu	Geneva, Bibliothèque Publique et Universitaire
CH-LAac	Lausanne, Archives Cantonales Vaudoises
CH-LAcu	Lausanne, Bibliothèque Cantonale et Universitaire
CH-LU	Lugano, Biblioteca Cantonale
CH-Lmg	Lucerne, Allgemeine Musikalische Gesellschaft
CH-Lz	Lucerne, Zentralbibliothek
CH-MSbk	Mariastein, Benediktinerkloster
CH-MÜ	Müstair, Frauenkloster St Johann
CH-N	Neuchâtel, Bibliothèque Publique et Universitaire
CH-OB	Oberbüren, Kloster Glattburg
CH-P	Porrentruy, Bibliothèque Cantonale Jurasienne (incl. Bibliothèque du Lycée Cantonal)
CH-R	Rheinfelden, Christkatholisches Pfarramt
CH-S	Sion, Bibliothèque Cantonale du Valais
CH-SAM	Samedan, Biblioteca Fundaziun Planta
CH-SAf	Sarnen, Benediktinerinnen-Abtei St Andreas
CH-SGd	St Gallen, Domchorarchiv
CH-SGs	St Gallen, Stiftsbibliothek, Handschriftenabteilung
CH-SGv	St Gallen, Kantonsbibliothek (Vadiana)
CH-SH	Schaffhausen, Stadtbibliothek
CH-SO	Solothurn, Zentralbibliothek, Musiksammlung
CH-SObo	Solothurn, Bischöfliches Ordinariat der Diözese Basel, Diözesanarchiv des Bistums Basel
CH-W	Winterthur, Stadtbibliothek
CH-ZGm	Zug, Pfarrarchiv St Michael
CH-Zi	Zürich, Israelitische Kultusgemeinde
CH-Zma	Zürich, Schweizerisches Musik-Archiv [in S-Nf]
CH-Zz	Zürich, Zentralbibliothek

THE NETHERLANDS

NL-At	Amsterdam, Toonkunst-Bibliotheek
NL-Au	Amsterdam, Universiteitsbibliotheek
NL-DEta	Delden, Huisarchief Twickel
NL-DHa	The Hague, Koninklijk Huisarchief
NL-DHgm	The Hague, Haags Gemeentemuseum, Muziekafdeling
NL-DHk	The Hague, Koninklijke Bibliotheek
NL-E	Enkhuizen, Archief Collegium Musicum
NL-L	Leiden, Gemeentearchief
NL-LE	Leeuwarden, Provinciale Bibliotheek van Friesland
NL-Lml	Leiden, Museum Lakenhal
NL-Lt	Leiden, Bibliotheca Thysiana [in S-Lu]
NL-Lu	Leiden, Rijksuniversiteit, Bibliotheek
NL-R	Rotterdam, Gemeentebibliotheek
NL-SH	's-Hertogenbosch, Illustre Lieve Vrouwe Broederschap
NL-Uim	Utrecht, Letterenbibliotheek, Universiteit
NL-Uu	Utrecht, Universiteit Utrecht, Universiteitsbibliotheek

TURKEY

TR-Ino	Istanbul, Nuruosmania Kütüphanesi
TR-Itks	Istanbul, Topkapi Sarayi Müzesi
TR-Iü	Istanbul, Üniversite Kütüphanesi

UKRAINE

UA-Kan	Kiev, Natsional'na Akademiya Nauk Ukraïni, Natsional'na Biblioteka Ukraïni im V.I. Vernads'kyy

UA-Km	Kiev, Spilka Kompozytoriv Ukrainy, Centr. 'Muz. Inform'
UA-LV	L'viv, Biblioteka Vyshchoho Muzychnoho Instytutu im. M. Lyssenka

UNITED STATES OF AMERICA

US-AAu	Ann Arbor, University of Michigan, Music Library
US-AB	Albany (NY), New York State Library
US-AKu	Akron (OH), University of Akron, Bierce Library
US-ATS	Athens (GA), University of Georgia Libraries
US-ATet	Atlanta (GA), Emory University, Pitts Theology Library
US-ATu	Atlanta (GA), Emory University Library
US-AU	Aurora (NY), Wells College Library
US-AUS	Austin, University of Texas at Austin, The Harry Ransom Humanities Research Center
US-AUSm	Austin, University of Texas at Austin, Fine Arts Library
US-AtaT	Talladega, AL, Talladega College
US-BAR	Baraboo (WI), Circus World Museum Library
US-BAep	Baltimore, Enoch Pratt Free Library
US-BAhs	Baltimore, Maryland Historical Society Library
US-BApi	Baltimore, Arthur Friedheim Library, Johns Hopkins University
US-BAu	Baltimore, Johns Hopkins University Libraries
US-BAue	Baltimore, Milton S. Eisenhower Library, Johns Hopkins University
US-BAw	Baltimore, Walters Art Gallery Library
US-BER	Berea (OH), Riemenschneider Bach Institute Library
US-BETm	Bethlehem (PA), Moravian Archives
US-BEm	Berkeley, University of California at Berkeley, Music Library
US-BL	Bloomington (IN), Indiana University Library
US-BLl	Bloomington (IN), Indiana University, Lilly Library
US-BLu	Bloomington (IN), Indiana University, Cook Music Library
US-BO	Boulder (CO), University of Colorado at Boulder, Music Library
US-BU	Buffalo (NY), Buffalo and Erie County Public Library
US-Ba	Boston, Athenaeum Library
US-Bc	Boston, New England Conservatory of Music, Harriet M. Spaulding Library
US-Bfa	Boston, Museum of Fine Arts
US-Bgm	Boston, Isabella Stewart Gardner Museum, Library
US-Bh	Boston, Harvard Musical Association, Library
US-Bhs	Boston, Massachusetts Historical Society Library
US-Bp	Boston, Public Library, Music Department
US-Bu	Boston, Boston University, Mugar Memorial Library, Department of Special Collections
US-CA	Cambridge (MA), Harvard University, Harvard College Library
US-CAe	Cambridge (MA), Harvard University, Eda Kuhn Loeb Music Library
US-CAh	Cambridge (MA), Harvard University, Houghton Library

US-CAt	Cambridge (MA), Harvard University Library, Theatre Collection
US-CAward	Cambridge (MA), John Milton Ward, private collection [on loan to *US-CA*]
US-CF	Cedar Falls (IA), University of Northern Iowa, Library
US-CHAhs	Charleston (SC), The South Carolina Historical Society
US-CHH	Chapel Hill (NC), University of North Carolina at Chapel Hill
US-CHua	Charlottesville (VA), University of Virginia, Alderman Library
US-CHum	Charlottesville (VA), University of Virginia, Music Library
US-CIhc	Cincinnati, Hebrew Union College Library: Jewish Institute of Religion, Klau Library
US-CIp	Cincinnati, Public Library
US-CIu	Cincinnati, University of Cincinnati College – Conservatory of Music, Music Library
US-CLAc	Claremont (CA), Claremont College Libraries
US-CLU	Los Angeles (CA), University of California, Los Angeles
US-CLp	Cleveland, Public Library, Fine Arts Department
US-CLwr	Cleveland, Western Reserve University, Freiberger Library and Music House Library
US-COhs	Columbus (OH), Ohio Historical Society Library
US-COu	Columbus (OH), Ohio State University, Music Library
US-CP	College Park (MD), University of Maryland, McKeldin Library
US-CR	Cedar Rapids (IA), Iowa Masonic Library
US-Cn	Chicago, Newberry Library
US-Cp	Chicago, Chicago Public Library, Music Information Center
US-CtY	New Haven (CT), Yale University
US-Cu	Chicago, University, Joseph Regenstein Library, Music Collection
US-DAVu	Davis (CA), University of California at Davis, Peter J. Shields Library
US-DAu	Dallas, Southern Methodist University, Music Library
US-DLC	Washington, DC, Library of Congress
US-DMu	Durham (NC), Duke University Libraries
US-DN	Denton (TX), University of North Texas, Music Library
US-DO	Dover (NH), Public Library
US-DSI (JOHP)	Washington, DC, Smithsonian Institution: Jazz Oral History Program
US-Dp	Detroit, Public Library, Main Library, Music and Performing Arts Department
US-E	Evanston (IL), Garrett Biblical Institute
US-EDu	Edwardsville (IL), Southern Illinois University
US-EU	Eugene (OR), University of Oregon
US-Eu	Evanston (IL), Northwestern University
US-FAy	Farmington (CT), Yale University, Lewis Walpole Library

US-FW	Fort Worth (TX), Southwestern Baptist Theological Seminary
US-G	Gainesville (FL), University of Florida Library, Music Library
US-GB	Gettysburg (PA), Lutheran Theological Seminary
US-GR	Granville (OH), Denison University Library
US-GRB	Greensboro (NC), University of North Carolina at Greensboro, Walter C. Jackson Library
US-HA	Hanover (NH), Dartmouth College, Baker Library
US-HG	Harrisburg (PA), Pennsylvania State Library
US-HO	Hopkinton (NH), New Hampshire Antiquarian Society
US-Hhc	Hartford (CT), Hartt College of Music Library, The University of Hartford
US-Hm	Hartford (CT), Case Memorial Library, Hartford Seminary Foundation [in *US-ATet*]
US-Hs	Hartford (CT), Connecticut State Library
US-Hw	Hartford (CT), Trinity College, Watkinson Library
US-I	Ithaca (NY), Cornell University
US-ICJic	Chicago, IL, Jazz Institute of Chicago
US-ICU	Chicago, IL, University of Chicago
US-IDt	Independence (MO), Harry S. Truman Library
US-IO	Iowa City (IA), University of Iowa, Rita Benton Music Library
US-InUAtm	Bloomington (IN), Indiana University Archives of Traditional Music
US-K	Kent (OH), Kent State University, Music Library
US-KC	Kansas City (MO), University of Missouri: Kansas City, Miller Nichols Library
US-KCm	Kansas City (MO), Kansas City Museum, Library and Archives
US-KN	Knoxville (TN), University of Tennessee, Knoxville, Music Library
US-LAcs	Los Angeles, California State University, John F. Kennedy Memorial Library
US-LApiatigorsky	Los Angeles, Gregor Piatigorsky, private collection [in *US-STEdrachman*]
US-LAs	Los Angeles, The Arnold Schoenberg Institute Archives
US-LAuc	Los Angeles, University of California at Los Angeles, William Andrews Clark Memorial Library
US-LAum	Los Angeles, University of California at Los Angeles, Music Library
US-LAur	Los Angeles, University of California at Los Angeles, Special Collections Dept, University Research Library
US-LAusc	Los Angeles, University of Southern California, School of Music Library
US-LBH	Long Beach (CA), California State University
US-LEX	Lexington (KY), University of Kentucky, Margaret I. King Library
US-LNT	New Orleans (LA), Tulane University [transcripts of interviews held at *US-LNT* were published on microfilm as New York Times Oral History Program: New Orleans Jazz Oral History Collection (1978–9)]
US-LOu	Louisville, University of Louisville, Dwight Anderson Music Library
US-LT	Latrobe (PA), St Vincent College Library
US-Lu	Lawrence (KS), University of Kansas Libraries
US-M	Milwaukee, Public Library, Art and Music Department
US-MAhs	Madison (WI), Wisconsin Historical Society
US-MAu	Madison (WI), University of Wisconsin
US-MB	Middlebury (VT), Middlebury College, Christian A. Johnson Memorial Music Library
US-MED	Medford (MA), Tufts University Library
US-MG	Montgomery (AL), Alabama State Department of Archives and History Library
US-MT	Morristown (NJ), National Historical Park Museum
US-Mc	Milwaukee, Wisconsin Conservatory of Music Library
US-MoKmh	Kansas City (MO), Kansas City Museum of History
US-MoUSt	St. Louis (MO), University of Missouri
US-NA	Nashville (TN), Fisk University Library
US-NAu	Nashville (TN), Vanderbilt University Library
US-NBu	New Brunswick (NJ), Rutgers - The State University of New Jersey, Music Library, Mabel Smith Douglass Library
US-NCH (HCJA)	Clinton (NY), Hamilton College: Hamilton College Jazz Archive
US-NEij	Newark (NJ), Rutgers – The State University of New Jersey, Rutgers Institute of Jazz Studies Library
US-NH	New Haven (CT), Yale University, Irving S. Gilmore Music Library
US-NHoh	New Haven (CT), Yale University, Oral History Archive
US-NHub	New Haven (CT), Yale University, Beinecke Rare Book and Manuscript Library
US-NNC	New York (NY), Columbia University
US-NNSc	New York (NY), Schomburg Collection, New York Public Library
US-NNSc (HBC)	New York (NY), Schomburg Collection, New York Public Library, Hatch-Billops Collection

US-NNSc (*LAJOHP*)	New York (NY), Schomburg Collection, New York Public Library, Louis Armstrong Jazz Oral History Project
US-NO	Normal (IL), Illinois State University, Milner Library, Humanities/Fine Arts Division
US-NORsm	New Orleans, Louisiana State Museum Library
US-NORtu	New Orleans, Tulane University, Howard Tilton Memorial Library
US-NYamc	New York, American Music Center Library
US-NYbroude	New York, Broude private collection
US-NYcc	New York, City College Library, Music Library
US-NYcu	New York, Columbia University, Gabe M. Wiener Music & Arts Library
US-NYcub	New York, Columbia University, Rare Book and Manuscript Library of Butler Memorial Library
US-NYgo	New York, University, Gould Memorial Library [in *US-NYu*]
US-NYgr	New York, The Grolier Club Library
US-NYgs	New York, G. Schirmer, Inc.
US-NYhs	New York, New York Historical Society Library
US-NYhsa	New York, Hispanic Society of America, Library
US-NYj	New York, The Juilliard School, Lila Acheson Wallace Library
US-NYkallir	New York, Rudolf F. Kallir, private collection
US-NYlehman	New York, Robert O. Lehman, private collection [in *US-NYpm*]
US-NYlibin	New York, Laurence Libin, private collection
US-NYma	New York, Mannes College of Music, Clara Damrosch Mannes Memorial Library
US-NYp	New York, Public Library at Lincoln Center, Music Division
US-NYpl	New York, Public Library, Center for the Humanities
US-NYpm	New York, Pierpont Morgan Library
US-NYpsc	New York, New York Public Library, Scho-mburg Center for Research in Black Culture in Harlem
US-NYq	New York, Queens College of the City University, Paul Klapper Library, Music Library
US-NYu	New York, University Bobst Library
US-NYw	New York, Wildenstein Collection
US-NYyellin	New York, Victor Yellin, private collection
US-Nf	Northampton (MA), Forbes Library
US-NjR	Newark (NJ), Rutgers, the State University of New Jersey
US-NjR (*JOHP*)	Newark (NJ), Rutgers, the State University of New Jersey: Jazz Oral History Project

US-Nsc	Northampton (MA), Smith College, Werner Josten Library
US-OAm	Oakland (CA), Mills College, Margaret Prall Music Library
US-OB	Oberlin (OH), Oberlin College Conservatory of Music, Conservatory Library
US-OX	Oxford (OH), Miami University, Amos Music Library
US-PHci	Philadelphia, Curtis Institute of Music, Library
US-PHf	Philadelphia, Free Library of Philadelphia, Music Dept
US-PHff	Philadelphia, Free Library of Philadelphia, Edwin A. Fleisher Collection of Orchestral Music
US-PHgc	Philadelphia, Gratz College
US-PHhs	Philadelphia, Historical Society of Pennsylvania Library
US-PHlc	Philadelphia, Library Company of Philadelphia
US-PHmf	Philadelphia, Musical Fund Society [on loan to *US-PHf*]
US-PHphs	Philadelphia, The Presbyterian Historical Society Library [in *US-PHlc*]
US-PHps	Philadelphia, American Philosophical Society Library
US-PHu	Philadelphia, University of Pennsylvania, Van Pelt-Dietrich Library Center
US-PO	Poughkeepsie (NY), Vassar College, George Sherman Dickinson Music Library
US-PROhs	Providence (RI), Rhode Island Historical Society Library
US-PROu	Providence (RI), Brown University
US-PRV	Provo (UT), Brigham Young University
US-PRs	Princeton (NJ), Theological Seminary, Speer Library
US-PRu	Princeton (NJ), Princeton University, Firestone Memorial Library
US-PRw	Princeton (NJ), Westminster Choir College
US-Pc	Pittsburgh, Carnegie Library, Music and Art Dept
US-Ps	Pittsburgh, Theological Seminary, Clifford E. Barbour Library
US-Pu	Pittsburgh, University of Pittsburgh
US-Puf	Pittsburgh, University of Pittsburgh, Foster Hall Collection, Stephen Foster Memorial
US-R	Rochester (NY), Sibley Music Library, University of Rochester, Eastman School of Music
US-SA	Salem (MA), Peabody and Essex Museums, James Duncan Phillips Library
US-SBm	Santa Barbara (CA), Mission Santa Barbara
US-SFp	San Francisco, Public Library, Fine Arts Department, Music Division
US-SFs	San Francisco, Sutro Library
US-SFsc	San Francisco, San Francisco State University, Frank V. de Bellis Collection
US-SJb	San Jose (CA), Ira F. Brilliant Center for Beethoven Studies, San José State University

US-SL	St Louis, St Louis University, Pius XII Memorial Library
US-SLC	Salt Lake City, University of Utah Library
US-SLug	St Louis, Washington University, Gaylord Music Library
US-SM	San Marino (CA), Huntington Library
US-SPma	Spokane (WA), Moldenhauer Archives
US-SR	San Rafael (CA), American Music Research Center, Dominican College
US-STEdrach-mann	Stevenson (MD), Mrs Jephta Drachman, private collection; Mrs P.C. Drachman, private collection
US-STO	Stony Brook (NY), State University of New York at Stony Brook, Frank Melville Jr Memorial Library
US-STu	Palo Alto (CA), University, Memorial Library of Music, Department of Special Collections of the Cecil H. Green Library
US-SY	Syracuse (NY), University Music Library
US-SYkrasner	Syracuse (NY), Louis Krasner, private collection [in *US-CAh* and *US-SY*]
US-Su	Seattle, University of Washington, Music Library
US-TA	Tallahassee (FL), Florida State University, Robert Manning Strozier Library
US-TNF	Nashville (TN), Fisk University
US-TxU	Austin (TX), University of Texas
US-U	Urbana (IL), University of Illinois, Music Library
US-Uplamenac	Urbana (IL), Dragan Plamenac, private collection [in *US-NH*]
US-V	Villanova (PA), Villanova University, Falvey Memorial Library
US-WB	Wilkes-Barre (PA), Wilkes College Library
US-WC	Waco (TX), Baylor University, Music Library
US-WGc	Williamsburg (VA), College of William and Mary, Earl Gregg Swenn Library
US-WI	Williamstown (MA), Williams College Library
US-WOa	Worcester (MA), American Antiquarian Society Library
US-WS	Winston-Salem (NC), Moravian Music Foundation, Peter Memorial Library
US-Wc	Washington, DC, Library of Congress, Music Division
US-Wca	Washington, Cathedral Library
US-Wcf	Washington, Library of Congress, American Folklife Center and the Archive of Folk Culture
US-Wcg	Washington, General Collections, Library of Congress
US-Wcm	Washington, Library of Congress, Motion Picture, Broadcasting and Recorded Sound Division
US-Wcu	Washington, Catholic University of America, Music Library
US-Wdo	Washington, Dumbarton Oaks
US-Wgu	Washington, Georgetown University Libraries
US-Whu	Washington, Howard University, College of Fine Arts Library
US-Ws	Washington, Folger Shakespeare Library
US-Y	York (PA), Historical Society of York County, Library and Archives

Collection Sigla

The system of instrument collection sigla in this dictionary has been devised by Arnold Myers and is used by permission. It parallels the RISM system of library sigla used by *Grove*. The structure, length, and level of mnemonic value are the same, but to avoid confusion between the two systems, sigla for instrument collections are differently punctuated. The first and second elements of the sigla use the same national and city codes as RISM's, but separated by a period (stop) rather than a hyphen. The third element of the codes (designating specific collections) is in some cases the same as RISM's, for example where an institution operates both a library and a museum, but the same siglum is not used for different institutions in RISM and instrument collection sigla. Where a collection has named sub-collections but the sub-collections have no separate ownership, management, or inventory numbering system, only the whole collection is allocated a siglum. Further details on major collections can be found in COLLECTIONS.

The sigla listed below include all those used in this dictionary. Further sigla are being created, and the evolving list is maintained on the website of the International Committee of Musical Instrument Museums and Collections (CIMCIM; <http://cimcim.icom.museum>). In the case of future changes of collection name or ownership, cross-references from the old sigla will be made, thus ensuring the necessary permanence of sigla. Requests for additional sigla should be made to the contact given in the list of sigla on the CIMCIM website.

Place names are given in the English-language forms with references to local language form(s).

A.BA.h	Austria	Bad Aussee	Heimatmuseum
A.G.dm	Austria	Graz	Diözesanmuseum
A.G.hm	Austria	Graz	Hochschule für Musik und Darstellende Kunst, Institut für Aufführungspraxis
A.G.lj	Austria	Graz	Universalmuseum Joanneum
A.GÖ.s	Austria	Göttweig	Musikarchiv Stift Göttweig
A.I.a	Austria	Innsbruck	Schloss Ambras, Kunsthistorische Sammlungen
A.I.mf	Austria	Innsbruck	Tiroler Landesmuseum Ferdinandeum
A.I.mh	Austria	Innsbruck	Musikhochschule, Institut für Aufführungspraxis
A.K.e	Austria	Klagenfurt	Eboardmuseum
A.K.lk	Austria	Klagenfurt	Landesmuseum Kärnten
A.KR.sk	Austria	Kremsmünster	Musikinstrumentenmuseum Schloss Kremsegg
A.LI.m	Austria	Linz	Oberösterreichisches Landesmuseum
A.S.ca	Austria	Salzburg	Salzburger Museum Carolino Augusteum
A.W.gm	Austria	Vienna [Wien]	Gesellschaft der Musikfreunde
A.W.hh	Austria	Vienna [Wien]	Haydn House [Haydnhaus]
A.W.km	Austria	Vienna [Wien]	Kunsthistorisches Museum (Sammlung alter Musikinstrumente)
A.W.mf	Austria	Vienna [Wien]	Österreichisches Museum für Völkerkunde
A.W.nb	Austria	Vienna [Wien]	Österreichisches Nationalbank
A.W.ömv	Austria	Vienna [Wien]	Österreichisches Museum für Volkskunde
A.W.t	Austria	Vienna [Wien]	Technisches Museum für Industrie und Gewerbe
ANG.D.m	Angola	Dundo	Museu do Dundo
ANG.L.a	Angola	Luanda	Museu Nacional de Antropologia

AUS.BR.qm	Australia	Brisbane	Queensland Museum
AUS.NL.uwa	Australia	Nedlands	University of Western Australia, Department of Music
AUS.S.am	Australia	Sydney	Australia Museum
AUS.S.phm	Australia	Sydney	Powerhouse Museum
AZ.B.sm	Azerbaijan	Baku	State Museum of Azerbaijani Musical Culture
B.A.em	Belgium	Antwerp [Anvers, Antwerpen]	Etnografisch Museum
B.A.mp	Belgium	Antwerp [Anvers, Antwerpen]	Museum Plantin-Moretus
B.A.mv	Belgium	Antwerp [Anvers, Antwerpen]	Museum Vleeshuis
B.A.v	Belgium	Antwerp [Anvers, Antwerpen]	Volkskundemuseum
B.B.bw	Belgium	Brussels [Bruxelles]	Bibliotheca Wittockiana
B.B.mim	Belgium	Brussels [Bruxelles]	Musée des Instruments de Musique
B.B.mra	Belgium	Brussels [Bruxelles]	Royal Museum of the Armed Forces and of Military History [Musée Royal de l'Armée et d'Histoire Militaire]
B.BR.gm	Belgium	Bruges [Brugge]	Gruuthusemuseum
B.G.b	Belgium	Ghent [Gent]	Bylokemuseum
B.G.sek	Belgium	Ghent [Gent]	Seminarie voor Etnische Kuns
B.GO.o	Belgium	Gooik	Cultural Center for Traditional Music [Ontmoetingscentrum 'De Cam']
B.KW.hm	Belgium	Klein-Willebroek	Harmonium Art Museum
B.L.w	Belgium	Liège	Musée de la Vie Wallonne
B.T.rmca	Belgium	Tervuren	Royal Museum for Central Africa [Koninklijk Museum voor Midden-Afrika]
BF.G.mp	Burkina Faso	Gaoua	Musée Provincial du Poni
BF.O.m	Burkina Faso	Ouagadougou	Musée de la Musique
BG.B.oim	Bulgaria	Blagoevgrad	Regional Historical Museum [Okrazen Istoriceski Muzej]
BG.H.oim	Bulgaria	Haskovo	Regional Historical Museum [Okrazen Istoriceski Muzej]
BG.SO.im	Bulgaria	Sofia	Institut za Muzika
BG.SO.nem	Bulgaria	Sofia	National Ethnographic Museum of the Bulgarian Academy of Sciences [Nacionalen Etnografski Muzej na Balgarskata Akademija na Naukite]
BOL.LP.mn	Bolivia	La Paz	Museo Nacional
BR.B.mg	Brazil	Belém	Museu Paraense Emílio Goeldi
BR.R.mh	Brazil	Rio de Janeiro	National Historical Museum of Brazil [Museu Histórico Nacional]
BR.R.mi	Brazil	Rio de Janeiro	Museu do Índio
BR.R.mn	Brazil	Rio de Janeiro	Universidade Federal do Rio de Janeiro, Museu Nacional
BR.SP.mf	Brazil	São Paulo	Museu do Folclore
BR.SP.mp	Brazil	São Paulo	Museu Paulista da Universidade de São Paulo
C.HAB.c	Cuba	Havana	Centro de Información y Documentación de la Música Cubana 'Odilio Urfé'
C.HAB.m	Cuba	Havana	Museo Nacional de la Música
CAM.B.m	Cameroon	Bamenda	Musée de Bamenda
CAM.F.pr	Cameroon	Foumban	Musée du Palais Royal
CAM.Y.mdm	Cameroon	Yaoundé	Musée de la Danse et de la Musique
CDN.A.meredith	Canada	Arva, ON	Henry Meredith, private collection
CDN.C.g	Canada	Calgary, AB	Glenbow-Alberta Institute, Glenbow Museum
CDN.C.n	Canada	Calgary, AB	National Music Centre (formerly Cantos Music Foundation)
CDN.E.m	Canada	Edmonton, AB	Provincial Museum and Archives of Alberta
CDN.HU.mcc	Canada	Hull, PQ	Canadian Museum of Civilization [Musée canadien des civilisations]
CDN.HV.maf	Canada	Hauteville, PQ	Musée de l'Amérique Française

CDN.KIT.dhc	Canada	Kitchener, ON	Doon Heritage Crossroads (formerly Doon Pioneer Village)
CDN.M.rm	Canada	Montreal, QC [Montréal]	McGill University, Redpath Museum
CDN.MIN.scm	Canada	Minesing, ON	Simcoe County Museum
CDN.O.mst	Canada	Ottawa, ON	National Museum of Science and Technology
CDN.O.nm	Canada	Ottawa, ON	National Museum of Man, Canadian Centre for Folk Culture Studies
CDN.REV.nm	Canada	Revelstoke, BC	Revelstoke Nickelodeon Museum
CDN.SJ.m	Canada	St John, NB	New Brunswick Museum
CDN.T.m	Canada	Toronto, ON	Royal Ontario Museum
CDN.V.m	Canada	Vancouver, BC	Vancouver Museum
CDN.V.um	Canada	Vancouver, BC	University of British Columbia Museum of Anthropology
CDN.VI.rbcm	Canada	Victoria, BC	Royal British Columbia Museum
CDN.Y.csm	Canada	Yarmouth, NS	Yarmouth County Society Museum
CH.AF.lm	Switzerland	Affoltern am Albis	Swiss National Museum [Schweizerisches Landesmuseum] Collections Centre
CH.AP.mm	Switzerland	Appenzell	Retonios Mechanisches Musik- und Zaubermuseum
CH.AU.baud	Switzerland	L'Auberson	Musée Baud
CH.B.hm	Switzerland	Basle [Basel]	Musikmuseum, Historisches Museum Basel
CH.B.mi	Switzerland	Basle [Basel]	Universität Basel, Musikwissenschaftliches Institut
CH.B.mk	Switzerland	Basle [Basel]	Museum of Cultures [Museum der Kulturen, formerly Museum für Völkerkunde und Schweiz]
CH.BE.burri	Switzerland	Berne [Bern]	Burri family private collection
CH.BE.hm	Switzerland	Berne [Bern]	Bernisches Historisches Museum
CH.BIN.bopp	Switzerland	Binningen	Joseph Bopp Sammlung
CH.BR.gb	Switzerland	Brienz, Berne	Kantonale Geigenbauschule
CH.BU.s	Switzerland	Burgdorf	Schloss Burgdorf
CH.C.rm	Switzerland	Chur	Rätisches Museum
CH.CH.cellier	Switzerland	Chexbres	Marcel Cellier collection
CH.E.k	Switzerland	Einsiedeln	Kloster Einsiedeln, Hillel String Collection
CH.EK.ae	Switzerland	Ebnat-Kappel	Heimatmuseum der Albert Edelmann-Stiftung
CH.FF.m	Switzerland	Frauenfeld	Museum des Kantons Thurgau
CH.G.m	Switzerland	Geneva [Genève]	Musée d'Art et d'Histoire
CH.G.me	Switzerland	Geneva [Genève]	Musée d'Ethnographie
CH.L.hm	Switzerland	Lucerne [Luzern]	Handharmonikamuseum Utenberg
CH.L.wm	Switzerland	Lucerne [Luzern]	Richard Wagner Museum, Tribschen
CH.LI.hm	Switzerland	Liestal	Harmonium & Organ Museum Liestal
CH.LL.mh	Switzerland	Le Locle	Musée d'Horlogerie
CH.LM.-habisreitinger	Switzerland	Lustmüle	Rolf H.A. Habisreitinger collection
CH.LS.mm	Switzerland	Lichtensteig	Fredys Mechanisches Musikmuseum
CH.N.me	Switzerland	Neuchâtel	Musée d'Ethnographie
CH.R.fm	Switzerland	Rheinfelden	Fricktaler Museum
CH.RI.jaccottet	Switzerland	Rivaz, Vaud	Christiane Jaccottet collection
CH.ROC.mso	Switzerland	Roche	Musée Suisse de l'Orgue
CH.SG.hm	Switzerland	St Gallen	Historisches Museum
CH.SON.mv	Switzerland	Sonogno	Museo di Val Verzasca
CH.STE.brechbühl	Switzerland	Steffisburg	Heinrich Brechbühl collection
CH.SUM.hirsbrunner	Switzerland	Sumiswald	Hirsbrunner private collection
CH.UT.sl	Switzerland	Utzensdorf	Schloss Landshut
CH.W.meier	Switzerland	Winterthur	Walter M. Meier collection
CH.WÄ.mma	Switzerland	Wädenswil	Music of Man Archive
CH.WLS.patt	Switzerland	Willisau	Christian Patt collection
CH.Z.am	Switzerland	Zürich	Altstetten Museum
CH.Z.m	Switzerland	Zürich	Schweizerisches Landesmuseum
CH.Z.mb	Switzerland	Zürich	Museum Bellerive
CH.Z.mr	Switzerland	Zürich	Museum Rietberg
CH.Z.vm	Switzerland	Zürich	Völkerkundemuseum der Universität Zürich
CH.ZOL.mangold	Switzerland	Zollikon	Karl Mangold collection
CI.A.csh	Ivory Coast	Abidjan	Musée du Centre des Sciences Humaines

CL.C.nm	Sri Lanka	Colombo	National Museum of Sri Lanka
CN.B.aa	China	Beijing	Chinese Academy of Arts, Music Research Institute [Zhongguo Yinyue Yanjiusuo]
CN.B.cpn	China	Beijing	Cultural Palace of Nationalities
CN.B.gbt	China	Beijing	Great Bell Temple, Ancient Bell Museum
CN.B.pm	China	Beijing	Palace Museum
CN.CH.hm	China	Changsa	Hunan Provincial Museum
CN.GUL.om	China	Gulangyu	Gulangyu Organ Museum
CN.GUL.pm	China	Gulangyu	Gulangyu Piano Museum
CN.HK.u	China	Hong Kong	University Museum and Art Gallery
CN.K.ym	China	Kunming	Yunnan Provincial Museum
CN.SH.pm	China	Shenyang	Palace Museum
CN.UR.xum	China	Urumxi	Xinjiang Uygur Autonomous Region Museum
CN.WU.hm	China	Wuhan	Hubei Provincial Museum
CO.B.cu	Colombia	Bogotá	Conservatorio de Música Ciudad Universitaría, Museo Organológico Folklórico Musical
CO.B.ia	Colombia	Bogotá	Instituto Colombiano de Antropología, Museo Arqueológico y Etnológico
CO.B.pe	Colombia	Bogotá	José Ignacio Perdomo Escobar Collection
CO.I.u	Colombia	Ibagué (Tolima)	Universidad de Ibagué, Museo de Instrumentos Musicales, incl. Alfonso Viña Calderón and Mundo Sonoro collections
CO.M.u	Colombia	Medellín	Museo Universitario
CO.VL.laa	Colombia	Villa de Leyva (Boyacá)	Museo Luis A. Acuña
CZ.B.m	Czech Republic	Brno	Moravian Regional Museum [Moravský Zemský Muzeum]
CZ.B.tm	Czech Republic	Brno	Technical Museum [Technické Muzeum]
CZ.KRAS.s	Czech Republic	Kraslice [formerly Graslitz]	Secondary School for Musical Instrument Making [Strední Prumyslová Skola Výroby Hudebních Nástroju v Kraslicích]
CZ.LE.vm	Czech Republic	Lesany	Military Technical Museum [Vojenské Technické Muzeum]
CZ.OP.sm	Czech Republic	Opava	Silesia Regional Museum [Slezské Zemské Muzeum]
CZ.P.lp	Czech Republic	Prague [Praha]	Lobkowicz Palace
CZ.P.nm	Czech Republic	Prague [Praha]	National Museum (including Museum of Czech Music) [Narodni Muzeum v Praze, Muzeum Czeské Hudby]
CZ.P.ntm	Czech Republic	Prague [Praha]	National Technical Museum [Národní Technické Muzeum [National Technical Museum]
D.A.sk	Germany	Augsburg	Städtische Kunstsammlungen Augsburg, Maximilianmuseum
D.A.u	Germany	Augsburg	Zentralbibliothek der Universität Augsburg
D.APO.gm	Germany	Apolda	Glockenmuseum
D.B.äm	Germany	Berlin	Ägyptisches Museum
D.B.ch	Germany	Berlin	Schloss Charlottenburg
D.B.em	Germany	Berlin	Ethnologisches Museum, Staatliche Museen zu Berlin (formerly Museum für Völkerkunde)
D.B.im	Germany	Berlin	Musikinstrumenten Museum, Staatliches Institut für Musikforschung
D.B.km	Germany	Berlin	Kunstgewerbemuseum
D.B.udk	Germany	Berlin	Berlin University of the Arts [Universität der Künste Berlin] (formerly Hochschule für Musik und Darstellende Kunst)
D.BAB.f	Germany	Babenhausen	Fugger Museum
D.BDB.mm	Germany	Baden-Baden	Museum für Mechanische Musikinstrumente
D.BDSA.t	Germany	Bad Säckingen	Trompeten Museum
D.BDW.ff	Germany	Bad Windsheim	Fränkisches Freilandmuseum
D.BEUL.willms	Germany	Beulardstein	Wolfgang Willms collection
D.BIEB.h	Germany	Biebrich	Heckel Museum
D.BKB.km	Germany	Blankenburg	Instrumentenmuseum Michaelstein der Stiftung Kloster Michaelstein
D.BKZ.st	Germany	Bad Krozingen	Sammlung alter Tasteninstrumente

D.BM.üm	Germany	Bremen	Übersee-Museum
D.BN.ba	Germany	Bonn	Beethoven Haus
D.BOCH.m	Germany	Bochum	Museum Bochum (Musikinstrumentensammlung Grumbt)
D.BORG.o	Germany	Borgentreich	Orgelmuseum
D.BS.bl	Germany	Brunswick [Braunschweig]	Braunschweigisches Landesmuseum
D.BS.mm	Germany	Brunswick [Braunschweig]	Museum der Mechanischen Musik
D.BS.sm	Germany	Brunswick [Braunschweig]	Städtisches Museum
D.BUCHH.bartels	Germany	Buchholtz	Uwe Bartels private collection
D.BUTZ.m	Germany	Butzbach	Butzbach Museum
D.CE.bm	Germany	Celle	Bomann Museum
D.CRA.hm	Germany	Crailsheim	Heimatmuseum
D.D.km	Germany	Dresden	Museum of Decorative Arts [Kunstgewerbemuseum, formerly Museum für Kunsthandwerk]
D.D.mps	Germany	Dresden	Mathematisch-Physikalischer Salon des Zwingers
D.DEG.sm	Germany	Deggendorf	Stadtmuseum
D.DS.hl	Germany	Darmstadt and Kassel	Hessisches Landesmuseum
D.EBG.j	Germany	Albstadt	Musikhistorische Sammlung Jehle, Stauffenberg-Schloss, Lautlingen
D.EI.b	Germany	Eisenach	Bachhaus
D.ER.gm	Germany	Erlangen	Geigenbaumuseum, Bubenreuth
D.ER.mv	Germany	Erlangen	Museum für Völkerkunde
D.ER.u	Germany	Erlangen	Musikinstrumentensammlung, Universität Erlangen-Nürnberg
D.EU.s	Germany	Eutin	Schloss Eutin
D.F.dm	Germany	Frankfurt	Dreieichmuseum
D.F.fosshag	Germany	Frankfurt	Bengt Fosshag collection
D.F.hm	Germany	Frankfurt	Historisches Museum der Stadt Frankfurt-am-Main
D.F.mw	Germany	Frankfurt	Museum der Weltkulturen
D.F.spohr	Germany	Frankfurt	Peter Spohr collection
D.FBL.burseg	Germany	Föhrden-Barl	Rolf Burseg collection
D.FF.mv	Germany	Frankfurt an de Oder	Museum Viadrina (Reka-Sammlung historischer Musikinstrumente)
D.FR.am	Germany	Freiburg	Augustinermuseum
D.FUL.mm	Germany	Fuldatal	Mechanisches Musik-Museum
D.FÜS.sm	Germany	Füssen	Museum der Stadt Füssen
D.G.iv	Germany	Göttingen	Ethnographische Sammlung, Instituts für Völkerkunde der Georg-August-Universität Göttingen
D.G.ms	Germany	Göttingen	Musikinstrumentensammlung des Musikwissenschaftlichen Seminars, Georg-August-Universität Göttingen
D.GARB.irle	Germany	Garbsen	Rolf Irle collection
D.GL.mim	Germany	Goslar	Musikinstrumenten-Museum Walter Erdmann
D.GO.rv	Germany	Gotha	Museum für Regionalgeschichte und Volkskunde
D.H.hein	Germany	Hamburg	Manfred Hein Collection
D.H.km	Germany	Hamburg	Museum für Kunst und Gewerbe Hamburg
D.H.mg	Germany	Hamburg	Museum für Hamburgische Geschichte
D.H.mv	Germany	Hamburg	Museum für Völkerkunde
D.HA.h	Germany	Halle	Händel-Haus
D.HANN.si	Germany	Hanover [Hannover]	Schuhknecht Musikwissenschaftliches Museum für Selbstspielende Instrumente
D.HE.vm	Germany	Heidelberg	Völkerkunde-Museum der J. und E. von Portheim-Stiftung
D.HRS.hm	Germany	Hersbruck	Deutsches Hirtenmuseum
D.ING.ba	Germany	Ingolstadt	Bayerisches Armeemuseum
D.KI.mv	Germany	Kiel	Museum für Völkerkunde, Christian-Albrechts Universität zu Kiel
D.KIS.ns	Germany	Kisslegg	Neues Schloss
D.KN.mi	Germany	Cologne [Köln]	Musikwissenschaftliches Institut der Universität zu Köln
D.KN.rjm	Germany	Cologne [Köln]	Rautenstrauch-Joest-Museum Kulturen der Welt
D.KN.s	Germany	Cologne [Köln]	Stadtmuseum

D.KÜR.ba	Germany	Kürnbach	Blasmusikverband Baden-Württemberg, Musikakademie
D.LE.mv	Germany	Leipzig	Museum für Völkerkunde (Grassi Museum)
D.LE.u	Germany	Leipzig	Musikinstrumenten-Museum der Universität Leipzig (Grassi Museum)
D.LI.kalina	Germany	Lindau	F.W. Kalina collection
D.LIN.mm	Germany	Linz am Rhein	Musik Museum
D.LIS.mim	Germany	Lissberg	Musikinstrumenten-Museum Lissberg
D.LÜ.mk	Germany	Lübeck	Museum für Kunst und Kulturgeschichte der Hansestadt Lübeck, St. Annen Museum
D.M.bn	Germany	Munich [München]	Bayerisches Nationalmuseum
D.M.dm	Germany	Munich [München]	Deutsches Museum
D.M.goldgruber	Germany	Munich [München]	Maximilian Goldgruber private collection
D.M.mv	Germany	Munich [München]	Staatliches Museum für Völkerkunde
D.M.sm	Germany	Munich [München]	Stadtmuseum
D.MEI.sm	Germany	Meinigen	Staatliche Museum, Musikgeschichtliche Abteilung
D.MH.lm	Germany	Mannheim	Landesmuseum für Technik und Arbeit
D.MK.mim	Germany	Markneukirchen	Musikinstrumenten Museum
D.MR.s	Germany	Marienburg, Lower Saxony	Schloss der Prinzessin Ortrud von Hannover
D.MTW.gm	Germany	Mittenwald	Geigenbau- und Heimatmuseum
D.MÜ.e	Germany	Münster	Erbdrostenhof
D.N.gnm	Germany	Nuremberg [Nürnberg]	Germanisches Nationalmuseum
D.NEUW.k	Germany	Neuwied	Kreusmuseum
D.P.o	Germany	Passau	Oberhausmuseum
D.R.hm	Germany	Regensburg	Historisches Museum der Stadt Regensburg
D.RÜD.sm	Germany	Rüdesheim am Rhein	Siegfrieds Mechanisches Musikkabinett
D.S.lm	Germany	Stuttgart	Linden-Museum
D.S.lw	Germany	Stuttgart	Landesmuseum Württemberg, Musikinstrumentensammlung im Fruchtkasten
D.S.schmid	Germany	Stuttgart	Martin Schmid private collection
D.SH.m	Germany	Sondershausen	Schlossmuseum Sondershausen
D.SI.hm	Germany	Sigmaringen	Fürstlich-Hohenzollernsches Museum
D.SIE.gdhm	Germany	Siegen	Glocken-Museum Eiserfeld
D.SIH.atm	Germany	Sinsheim	Auto und Technik Museum
D.TRO.hm	Germany	Trossingen	Harmonikamuseum
D.UH.reil	Germany	Uhingen	Thomas Reil collection
D.WAK.em	Germany	Waldkirch, Freiburg	Elztalmuseum
D.WAS.m	Germany	Wasserburg	Museum Wasserburg, Kunst- und Kulturgeschichte Sammlungen
D.Z.sch	Germany	Zwickau	Robert-Schumann-Haus
DK.A.k	Denmark	Århus	The Old Town Museum [Købstadmuseet 'Den gamle by']
DK.AU.l	Denmark	Auning	Danish Agricultural Museum [Dansk Landbrugsmuseum]
DK.K.m	Denmark	Copenhagen [København]	National Museum of Denmark (Musikmuseet – Musikhistorisk Museum & Carl Claudius Samling)
DK.K.rs	Denmark	Copenhagen [København]	Rosenborg Castle [Rosenborg Slot]
DK.KO.kh	Denmark	Kolding	Koldinghus
DK.NF.fm	Denmark	Nykøbing Falster	Falsters Minder Museum
DY.PN.me	Benin	Porto-Novo	Musée Ethnographique 'Alexandre Senou Adande'
DZ.A.mb	Algeria	Algiers	Musée du Bardo
E.A.mp	Spain	Avila	Museo Provincial de Avila
E.B.ma	Spain	Barcelona	Museu d'Arts, Industries i Tradicions Populars
E.B.mi	Spain	Barcelona	Museu de la Música
E.BI.ma	Spain	Bilbao	Euskal Arkeologia, Etnografia eta Kondaira Museoa (Museo Arqueologico, Etnografico e Historico Vaso)
E.CM.sancho	Spain	Carbonero el Mayor, Segovia	Lorenzo Sancho collection
E.GI.m	Spain	Gijón	Museu de la Gaita
E.M.a	Spain	Madrid	Biblioteca Musical del Ayuntamiento
E.M.c	Spain	Madrid	Real Conservatorio Superior de Música de Madrid

E.M.hazen	Spain	Madrid	Félix Hazen collection
E.M.ma	Spain	Madrid	Museo de América
E.M.mad	Spain	Madrid	Museo Nacional de Artes Decorativas
E.M.man	Spain	Madrid	Museu Arqueológico Nacional
E.M.mm	Spain	Madrid	Museu Municipal
E.M.mna	Spain	Madrid	Museo Nacional de Antropología
E.M.mr	Spain	Madrid	Museo Romántico
E.M.nieto	Spain	Madrid	López Nieto collection
E.M.p	Spain	Madrid	Royal Palace of Madrid [Palacio Real de Madrid]
E.M.uam	Spain	Madrid	Museo de Artes y Tradiciones Populares, Universidad Autónoma de Madrid
E.OR.eg	Spain	Orense	Escola de Gaitas
E.PAM.oe	Spain	Pamplona	Ortzadar Euskal Folklore Taldea
E.S.ma	Spain	Seville [Sevilla]	Museum of Fine Arts [Museo de Bellas Artes de Sevilla]
E.U.jd	Spain	Urueña, Valladolid	Centro Etnográfico Joaquín Díaz, Diputación Provincial de Valladolid
EAK.N.nm	Kenya	Nairobi	National Museum of Kenya
EAK.N.u	Kenya	Nairobi	University of Nairobi, Institute of African Studies
EAT.D.nm	Tanzania	Dar Es Salaam	National Museum of Tanzania
EAT.Z.so	Tanzania	Zanzibar	Sankt Ottilien Missionary Station
EAU.K.um	Uganda	Kampala	Uganda Museum
EC.C.ap	Ecuador	Cuenca	Museo de las Artes Populares de America
EC.Q.t	Ecuador	Quito	Museo de Instrumentos Musicales Pablo Traversari (Pablo Traversari Musical Instrument Museum)
ET.C.am	Egypt	Cairo	National Arabic Music Institute (The Cairo Opera House Theatres) Museum of Musical Instruments
ET.C.em	Egypt	Cairo	Egyptian Museum
ETH.AA.u	Ethiopia	Addis Ababa	Addis Ababa University, Department of Ethnography and Ancient Arts, Institute of Ethiopian Studies
EV.TA.em	Estonia	Tartu	State Ethnographic Museum of Estonia
EV.TAL.tm	Estonia	Tallinn	Museum for Music and Theater [Eesti Teatri-ja Muusikamuuseum]
F.A.mc	France	Avignon	Musée Calvet
F.ANG.mm	France	Angoulême	Musée Municipal
F.AR.ma	France	Arles	Museon Arlaten
F.BA.mb	France	Bayonne	Musée Basque
F.BG.mb	France	Bourg-en-Bresse	Musée de Brou
F.BLB.wirsta	France	Bourg-la-Reine	Aristide Wirsta collection
F.BO.ma	France	Bordeaux	Musée d'Aquitaine
F.BO.u	France	Bordeaux	Université de Bordeaux, Musée d'Ethnographie
F.CAN.mc	France	Cannes	Musée de la Castre et de la Mer
F.CE.mi	France	Céret	Musée des instruments (Músic)
F.CHAU.prunieres	France	Chaumontel	René Prunières private collection
F.CHR.mba	France	Chartres	Musée des Beaux-Arts
F.EC.mr	France	Ecouen	Musée National de la Renaissance
F.GI.mc	France	Gien	Musée International de la Chasse
F.IV.camboulive	France	Ivry-la-Bataille	François Camboulive private collection
F.JE.av	France	Jenzat	Les Amis de la Vielle de Jenzat, Centre de Recherche sur les Musiques Traditionnelles
F.L.hc	France	Lille	Musée Regional de l'Hospice Comtesse (collection of Joseph and Pierre Hel, violin makers)
F.LAI.ma	France	L'Aigle	Musée Marcel Angot
F.LAI.mim	France	L'Aigle	Musée des Instruments de Musique
F.LC.v	France	La Couture Boussey	Musée des Instruments à Vent (Musée Jacques Hotteterre)
F.LGE.mm	France	Les Gets	Musée de la Musique Mécanique
F.LOU.mp	France	Lourdes	Musée Pyrénéen
F.LT.dudon	France	Le Thoronet	Jacques Dudon collection
F.LY.ma	France	Lyons	Musée Africain
F.LY.mad	France	Lyons	Musée des Arts Décoratifs

F.LY.montbel	France	Lyons	Eric Montbel collection
F.M.cm	France	Marseilles [Marseille]	Musée des Civilisations de l'Europe et de la Méditerranée
F.M.gl	France	Marseilles [Marseille]	Musée Grobet-Labadie
F.MAC.mu	France	Macon	Musée des Ursulines
F.MD.c	France	Montebéliard	Musée du Château
F.MIR.ml	France	Mirecourt	Museé de la Lutherie et de l'Archeterie Françaises
F.MLN.mmp	France	Montluçon	Musée des Musiques Populaires
F.N.db	France	Nantes	Musée du Château des Ducs de Bretagne
F.NA.mh	France	Nancy	Musée Historique Lorrain
F.NI.pl	France	Nice	Musée du Palais Lascaris
F.P.ad	France	Paris	Musée des Arts Décoratifs
F.P.caron	France	Paris	Nelly Caron collection
F.P.cm	France	Paris	Cité de la Musique, Musée de la Musique
F.P.guillou	France	Paris	Yannick Guillou collection
F.P.kampmann	France	Paris	Bruno Kampmann private collection
F.P.ma	France	Paris	Musée de l'Armée
F.P.mam	France	Paris	Musée des Arts et Métiers
F.P.ml	France	Paris	Musée du Louvre
F.P.qb	France	Paris	Musée du Quai Branly
F.P.puyana	France	Paris	Rafael Puyana private collection
F.P.rf	France	Paris	Musée de Radio-France
F.PE.m	France	Périgueux	Musée du Périgord
F.PER.cp	France	Perpignan	Musée Catalan des Arts et Traditions Populaires la Casa Pairal
F.RE.mah	France	Rennes	Musée d'Art et d'Histoire
F.ROE.ma	France	Rouen	Musée des Antiquites
F.S.mad	France	Strasbourg	Musée des Arts Décoratifs
F.SG.m	France	Saint Germain-en-Laye	Musée
F.SMAX.p	France	Sainte Maxime	Musée du Phonographie et de la Musique Mécanique
F.SMIC.b	France	Saint Michel-sur-Orge	Baschet collection
F.TL.d	France	Toulouse	Musée Dupuy
F.TU.pa	France	Tulle	Pôle de l'Accordéon
F.V.m	France	Versailles	Musée et Domaine National de Versailles et de Trianon, Château
F.VAR.ag	France	Varzy	Musée Auguste Grasset
FIN.H.nm	Finland	Helsinki	National Museum of Finland [Suomen kansallismuseo]
FIN.K.k	Finland	Kaustinen	Kansanmusiikki Instituutti
FIN.T.ål	Finland	Turku	Provincial Museum of Turku [Åbo Landskapsmuseum]
FIN.T.moisio	Finland	Turku	Heikki Moisio private collection
FIN.T.s	Finland	Turku	Sibelius Museum
FIN.V.mm	Finland	Varkaus	Mechanical Music Museum
FJI.S.m	Fiji	Suva, Viti Levu	Fiji Museum
G.L.mat	Gabon	Libreville	Musée des Arts et Traditions du Gabon
GB.A.u	UK	Aberdeen	Marischal Museum, University of Aberdeen
GB.AY.w	UK	Aylesbury	Waddeston Manor
GB.B.c	UK	Birmingham	Conservatoire
GB.B.cm	UK	Birmingham	City Museum and Art Gallery
GB.B.mag	UK	Birmingham	Museums and Art Gallery
GB.BA.h	UK	Bath	Holburne Museum
GB.BAR.b	UK	Barnard Castle	The Bowes Museum
GB.BAT.b	UK	Batley	Bagshaw Museum
GB.BET.colt	UK	Bethersden	Colt Clavier Collection
GB.BEX.steele-perkins	UK	Bexhill	Crispian Steele-Perkins, private collection
GB.BO.rc	UK	Bournemouth	Russell-Cotes Art Gallery and Museum
GB.BN.mag	UK	Brighton	Museum and Art Gallery
GB.BR.m	UK	Bristol	City of Bristol Museum and Art Gallery

GB.BR.mobbs	UK	Bristol	Mobbs Keyboard Collection (parts of the collection formerly in Bristol are now at *NZ.GB.mobbs*, *GB.L.am*, and *GB.E.u*)
GB.BR.sm	UK	Bristol	EMIS Synthesizer Museum
GB.BRE.m	UK	Brentford	The Musical Museum (formerly the British Piano Museum)
GB.BRO.s	UK	Broadway	Snowshill Manor (Charles Paget Wade Collection)
GB.BT.u	UK	Belfast	Ulster Museum and Botanic Gardens
GB.BU.m	UK	Bury St Edmunds	Moyse's Hall Museum
GB.BUC.ch	UK	Buckingham, Middle Claydon	Claydon House
GB.C.fm	UK	Cambridge	Fitzwilliam Museum, University of Cambridge
GB.C.ua	UK	Cambridge	University Museum of Archaeology and Anthropology, University of Cambridge
GB.CAS.prowse	UK	Castle Douglas	Martin Prowse private collection
GB.CD.nhm	UK	Cardiff	National History Museum (formerly Museum of Welsh Life, St Fagans)
GB.CH.m	UK	Chichester	Mechanical Music and Doll Collection
GB.CHL.h	UK	Cheltenham	Gustav Holst Birthplace Museum
GB.CHL.m	UK	Cheltenham	Art Gallery and Museums (Department of Applied Art)
GB.CHL.- waterhouse	UK	Cheltenham	William Waterhouse collection
GB.CR.m	UK	Chester	Grosvenor Museum (Local History Department)
GB.CL.m	UK	Carlisle	Museum & Art Gallery
GB.COL.m	UK	Colchester	Colchester Museums (Social History Department)
GB.DO.m	UK	Douglas, Isle of Man	Manx Museum and National Trust
GB.DU.m	UK	Dundee	Art Galleries and Museums Department, McManus Galleries (City Museum)
GB.E.chick	UK	Edinburgh	John Chick (private collection)
GB.E.n	UK	Edinburgh	National Museums of Scotland (including Royal Museum of Scotland)
GB.E.u	UK	Edinburgh	Edinburgh University Collection of Historic Musical Instruments
GB.EC.h	UK	East Clandon	Hatchlands Park (Alec Cobbe Collection)
GB.EX.m	UK	Exeter	Royal Albert Memorial Museum (Department of Decorative Arts)
GB.G.c	UK	Glasgow	College of Piping
GB.G.h	UK	Glasgow	Hunterian Museum and Art Gallery, University of Glasgow
GB.G.mag	UK	Glasgow	Museums and Art Galleries
GB.G.p	UK	Glasgow	The Piping Centre (including the National Piping Museum)
GB.G.rcs	UK	Glasgow	Royal Conservatoire of Scotland (including the John Webb collection)
GB.GL.m	UK	Gloucester	Gloucester Folk Museum
GB.GO.f	UK	Goudhurst	Finchcocks (Richard Burnett Collection of Historical Keyboard Instruments)
GB.HAL.m	UK	Halifax	Calderdale Museums & Arts
GB.HF.m	UK	Hertford	Hertford Museum
GB.HO.m	UK	Hove	Hove Museum and Art Gallery
GB.HUM.m	UK	Huddersfield	Tolson Memorial Museum
GB.I.m	UK	Ipswich	Colchester and Ipswich Museums
GB.K.m	UK	Keighley	Cliffe Castle Museum, Bradford Art Galleries and Museums Service
GB.KE.m	UK	Keswick	Keswick Museum and Art Gallery
GB.KID.m	UK	Kidderminster	Hereford and Worcester County Museum, Hartlebury Castle
GB.KIL.d	UK	Kilmarnock	Dean Castle, Kilmarnock and Louden District Museums
GN.KT.u	UK	Kingston upon Thames	School of Music, Kingston University
GB.L.am	UK	London	The Royal Academy of Music, York Gate Collections
GB.L.bm	UK	London	British Museum
GB.L.cm	UK	London	The Royal College of Music Museum of Instruments
GB.L.fh	UK	London	Fenton House, Hampstead
GB.L.hm	UK	London	Horniman Museum

GB.L.ml	UK	London	Museum of London
GB.L.msm	UK	London	Royal Military School of Music, Kneller Hall
GB.L.nms	UK	London	National Museum of Science and Industry (The Science Museum)
GB.L.ra	UK	London	Royal Armouries, and the Jewel House, Tower of London
GB.L.soas	UK	London	School of Oriental and African Studies, Centre of Music Studies
GB.L.v	UK	London	Victoria & Albert Museum
GB.L.wc	UK	London	The Wallace Collection
GB.LB.pierce	UK	Lisbellaw	Richard Pierce collection
GB.LE.a	UK	Leeds	Abbey House Museum, Kirkstall
GB.LE.m	UK	Leeds	Leeds City Museum (Department of Ethnography)
GB.LEI.u	UK	Leicester	Charles Moore Collection of Musical Instruments, University of Leicester
GB.LEW.m	UK	Lewes	Anne of Cleves House Museum, MacDermott Collection of Sussex Church Music and Instruments
GB.LEW.sai	UK	Lewes	Sussex Archaeological Institute
GB.LIS.corin	UK	Liskeard	Paul Corin's Magnificent Music Machines
GB.LV.m	UK	Liverpool	National Museums Liverpool
GB.M.cm	UK	Manchester	Royal Northern College of Music
GB.M.u	UK	Manchester	Manchester Museum, University of Manchester
GB.MA.m	UK	Maidstone	Museum and Art Gallery
GB.MOR.bm	UK	Morpeth	Chantry Bagpipe Museum
GB.MT.m	UK	Merthyr Tydfil	Museum and Art Gallery, Cyfarthfa Castle
GB.NEW.m	UK	Newark	Newark Museum
GB.NH.m	UK	Northampton	Central Museum and Art Gallery (Social History Department)
GB.NOR.harding	UK	Northleach	Keith Harding's World of Mechanical Music
GB.NT.u	UK	Newcastle upon Tyne	University of Newcastle upon Tyne, Hancock Museum
GB.NW.cm	UK	Norwich	Norfolk County Council Museums Service (St Peter Hungate Church Museum and Strangers Hall Museum)
GB.O.montagu	UK	Oxford	Jeremy Montagu private collection
GB.O.prm	UK	Oxford	Pitt Rivers Museum, University of Oxford
GB.O.ua	UK	Oxford	Ashmolean Museum, University of Oxford
GB.O.ub	UK	Oxford	Bate Collection, University of Oxford
GB.PO.mr	UK	Portsmouth	The Mary Rose
GB.RIC.hh	UK	Richmond-upon-Thames	Ham House
GB.RO.m	UK	Rochester	Guildhall Museum
GB.SAF.m	UK	Saffron Walden	Saffron Walden Museum
GB.SAI.o	UK	St Albans	Organ Museum
GB.SEV.kh	UK	Sevenoaks	Knole House
GB.SHE.m	UK	Sheffield	City Museum
GB.SHI.v	UK	Shipley	Victorian Reed Organ & Harmonium Museum
GB.SK.m	UK	Skipton	Craven Museum
GB.SPA.e	UK	Spalding	Museum of Entertainment (incorporating Rutland Cottage Music and Fairground Museum)
GB.SN.m	UK	Swindon	Museum and Art Gallery
GB.SN.webb *[discontinued]*	UK	Swindon	John Webb private collection (now Royal Conservatoire of Scotland, Glasgow)
GB.STH.jm	UK	St Helier	Jersey Museum
GB.STR.m	UK	Stroud	Stroud District (Cowle) Museum
GB.TA.m	UK	Taunton	Somerset County Museum (Taunton Castle)
GB.TOR.m	UK	Torquay	Torquay Museum
GB.TOT.dc	UK	Totnes, Devon	Dartington College of Arts
GB.WAR.m	UK	Warrington	Museum & Art Gallery
GB.WC.m	UK	Winchester	Winchester Museums
GB.WI.m	UK	Wigan	Museum of Wigan Life (The Rimmer Collection)
GB.WW.c	UK	Warwick	Warwick Castle Ltd
GB.WW.m	UK	Warwick	Warwickshire Museum Service
GB.Y.m	UK	York	Castle Museum
GCA.G.mae	Guatemala	Guatemala	Museo Nacional de Arqueologia y Etnologia

GE.T.gf	Georgia	Tbilisi	State Museum of Georgian Folk Songs and Musical Instruments
GE.T.tm	Georgia	Tbilisi	Georgian State Museum of Theatre, Music, Cinema and Choreography
GH.A.nm	Ghana	Accra	Ghana National Museum
GH.L.u	Ghana	Legon	University of Ghana, Institute of African Studies
GR.A.a	Greece	Athens [Athenai]	Academy of Athens, Research Center of Greek Folklore
GR.A.mpi	Greece	Athens [Athenai]	Museum of Popular Instruments
GR.A.-Papageorgiou	Greece	Athens [Athenai]	Nicolas Papageorgiou collection
GR.NA.pff	Greece	Nafplion	Peloponnesian Folklore Foundation
H.B.birinyi	Hungary	Budapest	András and József Birinyi collection
H.B.im	Hungary	Budapest	Museum of Applied Arts [Iparmüvészeti Múzeum]
H.B.l	Hungary	Budapest	Franz Liszt Academy of Music [Liszt Ferenc Zenemüvészeti Föiskola]
H.B.mmh	Hungary	Budapest	Hungarian Academy of Sciences, Research Centre for the Humanities, Institute of Musicology, Museum of Music History [Magyar Tudományos Akadémia, Zenetörténeti Múzeum]
H.B.mnm	Hungary	Budapest	Hungarian National Museum, Collection of Musical Instruments [Magyar Nemzeti Múzeum Hangszergyüjteménye]
H.B.nm	Hungary	Budapest	Hungarian Ethnographic Museum, Music Collection [Magyar Néprajzi Múzeum Gyüjteménye]
H.B.semmelweis	Hungary	Budapest	Tibor Semmelweis collection
H.EGG.km	Hungary	Eggenburg	Krahuletz Museum
H.KEC.leskowsky	Hungary	Kecskemét	Leskowsky Collection of Musical Instruments [Leskowsky Hangszergyüjtemény]
H.S.m	Hungary	Sopron	Museum of Sopron [Soproni Múzeum]
HR.S.em	Croatia	Split [Splitu]	Ethnographical Museum [Etnografski Muzej u Splitu]
HR.Z.em	Croatia	Zagreb	Ethnographical Museum [Etnografski Muzej]
HR.Z.mg	Croatia	Zagreb	Museum of the City of Zagreb [Muzej Grada Zagreba]
HR.Z.mu	Croatia	Zagreb	Museum of Art and Handicrafts [Muzej za Umjetnost i Obrt]
HR.Z.zif	Croatia	Zagreb	Institute of Folklore Research [Zavod za Istrazivanje Folklora]
I.A.c	Italy	Assisi	Biblioteca Comunale
I.A.f	Italy	Assisi	Convento di San Francesco
I.B.af	Italy	Bologna	Accademia Filarmonica
I.B.c	Italy	Bologna	Museo Internazionale della Musica (Civico Museo Bibliografico Musicale)
I.B.mm	Italy	Bologna	Museo Civico Medievale
I.B.sc	Italy	Bologna	San Colombano (Tagliavini Collection)
I.BA.me	Italy	Bari	Museo Etnografico Africa-Mozambico
I.BG.m	Italy	Bergamo	Museo Donizettiano
I.BR.mc	Italy	Brescia	Museo Chitarristico degli Strumenti Musicali e della Liuteria Bresciana (the Virginio Cattaneo Collection)
I.BRU.mm	Italy	Brugherio, Lombardy	Museo Miscellaneo [Fermo] Galbiati
I.BSC.giulini	Italy	Briosco	Villa Medici Giulini, Fernanda Giulini collection
I.CR.ms	Italy	Cremona	Museo Stradivariano
I.CR.pc	Italy	Cremona	Palazzo Comunale, 'I Violini del Palazzo Comunale di Cremona'
I.CR.pl	Italy	Cremona	Museo della Scuola Internazionale di Liuteria (formerly Isituto Professionale Internazionale per l'Artigianato Liutario e del Legno 'Antonio Stradivari')
I.CR.sf	Italy	Cremona	Società Filodrammatica Cremonese
I.CAF.mf	Italy	Castelfidardo	Civico Museum Internazionale della Fisarmonica
I.F.abc	Italy	Florence [Firenze]	Accademia Bartolomeo Cristofori Amici del Fortepiano

I.F.ga	Italy	Florence [Firenze]	Galleria dell'Academia (Collezione del Conservatorio Luigi Cherubini)
I.F.mba	Italy	Florence [Firenze]	Bardini Museum [Museo Stefano Bardini]
I.F.msn	Italy	Florence [Firenze]	Università degli Studi, Museo di Storia Naturale, Sezione Anthropologia ed Ethnologia
I.FAE.mt	Italy	Faenza	Museo Teatrale and Biblioteca Comunale
I.FO.mr	Italy	Forli	Museo Romagnolo del Teatro Angelo Masini
I.G.mao	Italy	Genoa [Genova]	Museo d'Arte Orientale Edoardo Chiossone
I.IB.borromeo	Italy	Isola Bella, Lago Maggiore	Palazzo Borromeo
I.I.pms	Italy	Imola	Palazzo Monsignani-Sassatelli
I.M.msm	Italy	Milan [Milano]	Museo degli Strumenti Musicali, Civiche Raccolte di Arte Applicate, Castello Sforzesco
I.M.mst	Italy	Milan [Milano]	Museo Nazionale della Scienza e della Tecnologia 'Leonardo da Vinci'
I.M.ts	Italy	Milan [Milano]	Teatro alla Scala
I.MA.pa	Italy	Mantua [Mantova]	Museo di Palazzo d'Arco
I.MAL.mc	Italy	Magliano Alfieri	Museo Civico
I.MO.m	Italy	Modena	Museo Civico di Storia e Arte Medievale e Moderna
I.MRO.cp	Italy	Merano	Castello Principesco
I.N.c	Italy	Naples [Napoli]	Conservatorio di Musica San Pietro a Majella
I.N.ma	Italy	Naples [Napoli]	Naples National Archaeological Museum [Museo Archeologico Nazionale di Napoli]
I.N.ms	Italy	Naples [Napoli]	Museo Storico Musicale
I.NOV.mc	Italy	Novara, Piemonte	Museo Civico, Sezione Teatrale e Sezione Etnografico
I.PA.mc	Italy	Parma	Conservatorio di Musica 'Arrigo Boito'
I.PES.fr	Italy	Pesaro	Tempietto Rossiniano della Fondazione Rossini
I.PI.carreras	Italy	Pisa	Francesco Carreras collection
I.PL.me	Italy	Palermo	Museo Etnografico Siciliano Pitré
I.PLM.mc	Italy	Palmi	Museo Calabrese di Etnografia e Folklore Raffaele Corso
I.PS.mc	Italy	Pistoia	Museo Clemente Rospigliosi
I.QS.msq	Italy	Quarna Sotto	Museo Etnografico e dello Strumento a Fiato (Associazione Museo di Storia Quarnese)
I.R.an	Italy	Rome [Roma]	Accademia nazionale di Santa Cecilia
I.R.mat	Italy	Rome [Roma]	Museo Nazionale delle Arti e Tradizioni Popolari
I.R.mpe	Italy	Rome [Roma]	Museo Preistorico Etnografico 'Luigi Pigorini'
I.R.ms	Italy	Rome [Roma]	Museo Nazionale degli Strumenti Musicali
I.R.mv	Italy	Rome [Roma]	Musei Vaticani
I.RIM.mce	Italy	Rimini	Museo delle Culture Extra-Europee Dinz Rialto
I.S.ac	Italy	Siena	Accademia Musicale Chigiana
I.SCP.mz	Italy	Scapoli	Museo della Zampogna
I.S.cm	Italy	Siena	Civico museo, Palazzo pubblico
I.SVO.mm	Italy	Savio	Museo Marini
I.T.ma	Italy	Turin [Torino]	Museo Civico di Arte Antica a Palazzo Madama
I.T.mn	Italy	Turin [Torino]	Museo Civico di Numismatica, Etnografia, Arti Orientali
I.TS.con	Italy	Trieste	Conservatorio 'Giuseppe Tartini'
I.TS.mt	Italy	Trieste	Museo Civico Teatrale 'Carlo Schmidl'
I.V.c	Italy	Venice [Venezia]	Conservatorio di Musica 'Benedetto Marcello', Museo Strumentale Musicali
I.V.ip	Italy	Venice [Venezia]	Istituto Provenciale per l'Infanzia Santa Maria della Pietà
I.V.mao	Italy	Venice [Venezia]	Museo d'Arte Orientale
I.V.mc	Italy	Venice [Venezia]	Museu Civico Correr
I.VE.af	Italy	Verona	Accademia Filarmonica
I.VE.cap	Italy	Verona	Museo della Biblioteca Capitolare
I.VE.mc	Italy	Verona	Museo Civico di Castelvecchio
IL.B.mb	Israel	Be'er Sheba'	Museum of Bedouin Culture
IL.H.ml	Israel	Haifa	Museum of Music and Ethnology and Amli Library [Muzé'on ve-Sifriyyah le-Musiqah]
IL.HE.zeldis	Israel	Herzliyya	Leon and Luisa Zeldis collection
IL.J.fm	Israel	Jerusalem	Franciscanum Museum
IL.J.im	Israel	Jerusalem	Israel Museum
IL.J.ra	Israel	Jerusalem	Rubin Academy of Music
IL.T.a	Israel	Tel Aviv	Felicja Blumental Music Center (formerly AMLI Central Library for Music and Dance)

IL.T.weinstein	Israel	Tel Aviv	Amnon Weinstein [violin-maker] collection
IND.AH.mm	India	Ahmedabad, Gujarat	Maharaja Museum and Picture Gallery
IND.AM.sgs	India	Amreli, Gujarat	Shri Girdharbhai Sangranalaya, Children's Museum
IND.AR.am	India	Alwar	Government Archaeological and Art Museum
IND.BHU.osm	India	Bhubaneswar	Orissa State Museum
IND.BO.c	India	Baroda, Gujarat	College of Indian Music, Dance and Dramatics
IND.BO.m	India	Baroda, Gujarat	Museum and Picture Gallery
IND.BOL.rb	India	Bolpur, West Bengal	Rabindra-Bhavana
IND.C.am	India	Calcutta	University of Calcutta, Asutosh Museum of Indian Art
IND.C.cm	India	Calcutta	Central Museum, Calcutta
IND.C.cri	India	Calcutta	Cultural Research Institute
IND.C.icm	India	Calcutta	Government Industrial and Commercial Museum
IND.C.im	India	Calcutta	Indian Museum
IND.C.mp	India	Calcutta	Marbel Palace Art Gallery and Zoo
IND.C.rbm	India	Calcutta	Rabindra Bharati Museum
IND.CH.sm	India	Chhindwara	Madhya Pradesh State Tribal Museum
IND.D.u	India	Delhi	University of Delhi, Anthropology Museum
IND.DH.lw	India	Dharampur, Gujarat	Lady Wilson Museum
IND.G.mm	India	Gwalior, Madhya Pradesh	Municipal Museum
IND.G.sg	India	Gwalior, Madhya Pradesh	Sarod Ghar, Museum of Musical Heritage
IND.GAU.sm	India	Gauhati, Assam	Assam State Museum, Musical Instrument and Ethnographic Sections
IND.GAU.ua	India	Gauhati, Assam	Gauhati University, Anthropological Museum
IND.GAU.uc	India	Gauhati, Assam	Gauhati University, Commercial Museum
IND.GOA.sm	India	Goa	State Museum
IND.J.msm	India	Jaipur	Maharaja Sawai Man Singh II Museum
IND.L.sm	India	Lucknow, Uttar Pradesh	State Museum
IND.M.pa	India	Mumbai	National Centre for the Performing Arts
IND.M.pwm	India	Mumbai	Prince of Wales Museum of Western India
IND.MA.gm	India	Madras	Government Museum and National Art Gallery
IND.MA.sv	India	Madras	Sangita Vadyalaya
IND.MU.hp	India	Murshidabad, West Bengal	Hazarduary Palace Museum
IND.MY.maa	India	Mysore, Karnataka	Museum of Art and Archaeology, University of Mysore
IND.NA.cm	India	Nagpur, [AMaharashtra	Central Museum
IND.ND.hm	India	New Delhi	National Handicrafts & Handlooms Museum
IND.ND.nm	India	New Delhi	National Museum, Gallery of Musical Instruments
IND.ND.sna	India	New Delhi	National Academy of Music, Dance and Drama [Sangeet Natak Akademi]
IND.PA.sm	India	Patiala, Punjab	Sheesh Mahal Art Gallery
IND.PU.dkm	India	Pune	Raja Dinkar Kelkar Museum
IND.PU.twm	India	Pune	Tribal Welfare Museum
IND.PUD.gm	India	Pudukkottai, Tamil Nadu	Government Museum
IND.RA.wm	India	Rajkot, Gujarat	Watson Museum
IND.SH.sm	India	Shillong	Meghalaya State Museum
IND.UD.fm	India	Udaipur	Folklore Museum
IND.VA.bkm	India	Varanasi, Uttar Pradesh	Bharat Kala Museum, Benaras Hindu University
IR.KE.hg	Iran	Kernan	Harandi Garden Museum, Musical Instrument Collection [Majmoe saaz-haye musiqi-ye bagh muzeye]
IR.T.bm	Iran	Teheran	Cultural Institute of Bonyad Museums [Arshiv va khazaneye musiqi-ye Moasseseye farhangi-ye muse-haye bonyad]
IR.T.mm	Iran	Teheran	The Music Museum of Iran [Muse-ye Musiqi-ye Iran]

IR.T.sb	Iran	Teheran	Master Saba's House/Music Museum [Khaneh muze-ye ostad abolhassan-e Saba]
IR.TA.qm	Iran	Tabriz	Qajar Museum, musical instrument hall [Talar-e saaz-e muse-ye qajar]
IRL.D.nm	Republic of Ireland	Dublin	National Museum of Ireland
J.FU.keiji	Japan	Fuchu	Azechi Keiji collection
J.H.mmi	Japan	Hamamatsu	Hamamatsu Museum of Musical Instruments
J.HIG.ot	Japan	Higashi-Kurume, Tokyo	Oikawa Takao, Kofu-Taimukan
J.K.bm	Japan	Kyoto	Sen'oku Hakkokan Museum [Sen'oku Hakkokan Hakubutsukan]
J.K.pm	Japan	Kyoto	Kyoto Prefectural Museum [Kyoto-Kenritsu Sogo Shiryokan]
J.K.u	Japan	Kyoto	Umenomiya Shrine
J.MA.pm	Japan	Matsue, Shimane	Shimane Prefectural Museum [Shimane-Kenritsu Hakubutsukan]
J.MAT.at	Japan	Matsuto, Ishikawa	Asano Taiko Saishi Co., Ltd [Taiko-no-Sato Shiryo-kan]
J.NA.as	Japan	Nagoya	Atsuta Shrine Treasure House [Atsuta Jinja Homotsuden]
J.NA.tm	Japan	Nagoya	Tokugawa Art Museum [Tokugawa Bijutsukan]
J.NR.kt	Japan	Nara	Kasuga Taisha Shrine Treasure House [Kasuga Taisha Jinja Homotsuden]
J.NR.s	Japan	Nara	Shōsōin Treasury [Shosoin Homotsuden]
J.NR.tu	Japan	Nara	Tenri University, Sankokan Museum
J.O.cm	Japan	Osaka	Osaka College of Music, Museum of Musical Instruments [Osaka Ongaku Daigaku Fuzoku Gakki Hakubutsukan]
J.O.me	Japan	Osaka	National Museum of Ethnology [Kokuritsu Minzokugaku Hakubutsukan
J.S.nm	Japan	Sakura	National Museum of Japanese History, Folklore Research Department
J.SH.i	Japan	Shimane	Izumo Taisha Homotsuden [shrine]
J.SH.m	Japan	Shimane	Mizuho Museum of Musical Instruments
J.SHI.a	Japan	Shimonoseki, Yamaguchi	Akama Shrine Treasure House [Akama Jinja Homotsuden]
J.T.ca	Japan	Tokyo	Min-On Music Music Museum [Minshu Ongaku Kyokai Toshokan]
J.T.k	Japan	Tokyo	Kunitachi College of Music
J.T.mam	Japan	Tokyo	Musashino Academia Musicae, Museum of Musical Instruments [Musashino Ongaku Daigaku]
J.T.mus	Japan	Tokyo	Miyamoto Unosuke Shoten, Drum Museum
J.T.nm	Japan	Tokyo	National Museum [Kokuritsu Hakubutsukan]
J.T.o	Japan	Tokyo	Museum of Musical Boxes [Orugoru no Chiisana Hakubutsukan]
J.T.sk	Japan	Tokyo	Suntory Ltd, Schambach-Kaston collection
J.T.tsumura	Japan	Tokyo	Akira Tsumura collection
J.T.u	Japan	Tokyo	Tokyo National University of Fine Arts and Music, Faculty of Music [Tokyo Geijutsu Daigaku]
J.T.uu	Japan	Tokyo	Ueno Gakuen University, Institute for the Study of Musical Instruments
J.T.wu	Japan	Tokyo	Tsubouchi Memorial Theatre Museum, Waseda University [Waseda Daigaku Tsubouchi Hakase Kinen Engeki Hakubutsukan]
J.Uw.dm	Japan	Uwajima, Ehime	Uwajima Date Museum [Uwajima-Shiritsu Date Hakubutsukan]
J.YA.b	Japan	Yamanashi	Hall of Halls
JA.K.ij	Jamaica	Kingston	Institute of Jamaica
K.PP.mn	Cambodia	Phnom Penh	Musée National de Phnom Penh
KS.B.bm	Kyrgyzstan	Bishkek	State Historical Museum of Kyrgyzstan
KZ.A.bbs	Kazakhstan	Almaty	Bolat Shamgalievitch Saribaev Museum

KZ.A.sm	Kazakhstan	Almaty	State Museum of the Traditional Musical Instruments of Kazakhstan
LT.V.nm	Lithuania	Vilnius	National Museum of Lithuanian History and Ethnography [Lietuvos TSR istorijos it etnografijos musiejus]
LV.R.em	Latvia	Riga	Latvian Open-Air Ethnographic Museum
LV.R.bm	Latvia	Riga	Museum of the History of Riga and Navigation
M.MD.pf	Malta	Mdina	Palazza Falson
MA.R.mo	Morocco	Rabat	Musée des Oudâias
MA.T.c	Morocco	Tétouan	Conservatoire de Musique
MAL.KK.jm	Malaysia	Kota Kinabalu, Sabah	Sabah Jabatan Muzium dan Arkib Negeri Sabah
MAL.KL.nm	Malaysia	Kuala Lumpur	National Museum [Muzium Negara]
MAL.KU.sm	Malaysia	Kuching	Sarawak Museum
MAL.ME.m	Malaysia	Melaka	Muzium Melaka, Muzium Budada
MAL.PE.lm	Malaysia	Pecan, Pahang	State Museum of Pahang [Lembaga Muzium, Negeri Pahang]
MAL.PE.sab	Malaysia	Pecan, Pahang	Koleski Muzium Sultan Abu Bakar
MD.KI.me	Moldova	Chişinău	Moldavian Museum of Ethnography [Muzeul Etnografic al Moldovei]
MEX.C.aa	Mexico	Cozumel	Alejandro Alcocer Museum
MEX.M.arias	Mexico	Mexico City [Ciudad de México]	Juan Guillermo Contreras Arias collection
MEX.M.iim	Mexico	Mexico City [Ciudad de México]	Instituto de Investigaciones Musicales, Consejo Nacional para la Cultura y las Artes
MEX.M.lm	Mexico	Mexico City [Ciudad de México]	Laboratoria Museográfico, Universidad Iberoamericana
MEX.M.ma	Mexico	Mexico City [Ciudad de México]	Museo Nacional de Antropología
MEX.M.mai	Mexico	Mexico City [Ciudad de México]	Museo Nacional de Artes e Industrias Populares
MEX.M.mh	Mexico	Mexico City [Ciudad de México]	Museo Nacional de Historia, Castillo de Chapúltepec
MK.S.am	Macedonia	Skopje	Archaeological Museum of Macedonia [Arheoloski Muzej na Makadonije]
N.A.aam	Norway	Arendal	Aust-Agder Kulturhistoriske senter
N.B.bm	Norway	Bergen	Bymuseet i Bergen
N.B.u	Norway	Bergen	University Museum [Universitetsmuseet i Bergen]
N.D.m	Norway	Drammen	Drammens Museum Fylkesmuseum for Buskerud
N.EG.df	Norway	Egersund	Dalane folkemuseum
N.EL.gm	Norway	Elverum	Glomdalsmuseet
N.F.vm	Norway	Fagernes	Valdresmusea (Valdres folkemuseum and Bagn Bygdesamling)
N.GJ.mm	Norway	Gjøvik	Mjøsmuseet
N.HAL.hs	Norway	Halden	Halden historiske samlinger
N.HAM.hm	Norway	Hamar	Hedmarksmuseet
N.HAR.stm	Norway	Harstad	Sør-Troms museum
N.HAU.hm	Norway	Haugesund	Administration center for Haugalandmuseene (Karmsund, Bokn and Vikedal museums)
N.JA.rm	Norway	Jaren	Administration center for Randsfjordsmuseene (Hadeland folkemuseum and Lands museum)
N.KSN.nm	Norway	Kristiansund N	Nordmøre museum
N.KSS.vam	Norway	Kristiansand S	Vest-Agder-museet
N.L.ss	Norway	Lillehammer	Maihaugen (De Sandvigske Samlinger)
N.MO.rm	Norway	Molde	Romsdalsmuseet
N.NE.hm	Norway	Nesbyen	Hallingdal museum
N.O.em	Norway	Oslo	University of Oslo, Ethnographic Museum [Etnografisk museum]
N.O.fm	Norway	Oslo	Forsvarsmuseet

N.O.k	Norway	Oslo	Norges Musikkhøgskole, Oslo, the Trygve Lindemans and Olav Gurvins collections
N.O.nf	Norway	Oslo	Norsk Folkemuseum
N.O.nt	Norway	Oslo	Norwegian Museum of Science and Technology [Norsk Teknisk Museum]
N.RY.sm	Norway	Rysstad	Setesdalsmuseet
N.S.m	Norway	Stavanger	Stavanger Museum
N.SA.msf	Norway	Sandane	Administration center for Musea i Sogn og Fjordane (De heibergske samlinger, Sunnfjord museum, Nordfjord folkemuseum, and Kystmuseet i Sogn og Fjordane)
N.SAN.jm	Norway	Sandnes	Jaermuseet
N.SAR.øm	Norway	Sarpsborg	Administration center for Østfoldsmuseet (Borgarsyssel museum and Folkenborg museum)
N.SIG.kk	Norway	Sigdal	Kunstnerdalen kulturmuseum
N.SK.tm	Norway	Skien	Telemark museum (incl. Bø and Berg-Kragerø museum)
N.T.aksdal	Norway	Trondheim	Bjørn Aksdal collection
N.T.ntnu	Norway	Trondheim	Norwegian University of Science and Technology (NTNU)
N.T.r	Norway	Trondheim	Ringve Museum (part of Museene i Sør-Trøndelag)
N.T.rh	Norway	Trondheim	Rockheim – The national museum of pop and rock music (part of Museene i Sør-Trøndelag)
N.T.tfs	Norway	Trondheim	Trøndelag folkemuseum–Sverresborg (part of Museene i Sør-Trøndelag)
N.TØ.vm	Norway	Tønsberg	Administration center for Vestfoldsmuseene (Slottsfjellsmuseet, Tønsberg, Larvik museum, Sandefjordmuseene)
N.TY.nm	Norway	Tynset	Administration center for Nordøsterdalsmuseet
N.UT.hm	Norway	Utne	Administration center for Hardanger og Voss museum
NL.A.bruggen	Netherlands	Amsterdam	Frans Bruggen collection
NL.A.frank	Netherlands	Amsterdam	J.D. Frank flute collection
NL.A.hasselaar	Netherlands	Amsterdam	Rien Hasselaar collection
NL.A.laquestra	Netherlands	Amsterdam	Willy Langestraat/Laquestra collection
NL.A.oostrom	Netherlands	Amsterdam	Leo van Oostrom collection
NL.A.tm	Netherlands	Amsterdam	Tropenmuseum
NL.A.vries	Netherlands	Amsterdam	Han de Vries collection
NL.AS.bm	Netherlands	Asten	Nationaal Beiaardmuseum
NL.BC.hm	Netherlands	Barger-Compascuum	Harmonium Museum Nederland
NL.BD.am	Netherlands	Berg-en-Dal	Afrika Museum
NL.BE.klm	Netherlands	Bennekom	Kijk en Luistermuseum
NL.DF.km	Netherlands	Delft	Volkenkundig Museum Nusantara
NL.DH.gm	Netherlands	The Hague [Den Haag]	Gemeentemuseum
NL.DH.schepel	Netherlands	Voorburg, Den Haag	Louise Schepel private collection
NL.EL.om	Netherlands	Elburg	Gemeentemuseum Nederlands Orgelmuseum
NL.EZ.huysser	Netherlands	Egmond-aan-Zee	Johan A.L.M. Huysser collection
NL.G.m	Netherlands	Groningen	Groningermuseum voor Stad en Lande
NL.H.tm	Netherlands	Haarlem	Teylers Museum
NL.HE.dm	Netherlands	Helmond	Draaiorgelmuseum, Helmondse Muziekhal
NL.KA.olthof	Netherlands	Kampen	Wim Olthof private collection
NL.L.ro	Netherlands	Leiden	National Museum of Antiquities [Rijksmuseum van Oudheden]
NL.L.rv	Netherlands	Leiden	National Museum of Ethnology [Rijksmuseum voor Volkenkunde]
NL.LE.nm	Netherlands	Leeuwarden	Fries Natuurmuseum
NL.MON. stuttenburgh	Netherlands	Monnickendam	Stuttenburgh collection
NL.N.vm	Netherlands	Nijmegen	Volkenkundig Museum
NL.O.dk	Netherlands	Oudkerk	Muziekmuseum 'de Klinze'
NL.R.mv	Netherlands	Rotterdam	Museum voor Volkenkunde
NL.SP.vester	Netherlands	Spaarndam	Frans Vester collection
NL.U.ehrenfeld	Netherlands	Utrecht	Ehrenfeld Flute Collection, private collection
NL.U.ms	Netherlands	Utrecht	Nationaal Museum van Speelklok tot Pierement

NL.U.stam	Netherlands	Utrecht	Otto Stam collection
NL.U.u	Netherlands	Utrecht	University of Utrecht
NL.VL.ts	Netherlands	Vlaardingen	Muziek Informatie- en Documentatiecentrum Ton Stolk
NL.ZA.veer	Netherlands	Zaandam	Gerrit and Ineke van der Veer collection
NZ.A.im	New Zealand	Auckland	Auckland Institute and Museum
NZ.A.smith	New Zealand	Auckland	David L. Smith collection
NZ.D.m	New Zealand	Dunedin	Otago Museum
NZ.GB.mobbs	New Zealand	Golden Bay	Mobbs Keyboard Collection
NZ.OS.om	New Zealand	Oamaru	New Zealand Organ Museum
NZ.W.nm	New Zealand	Wellington	National Art Gallery and Museum of New Zealand
NZ.W.u	New Zealand	Wellington	Victoria University of Wellington, School of Music, Ethnomusicology Section
P.AL.mao	Portugal	Alcains	Museu de Artes e Ofícios
P.CV.s	Portugal	Castelo de Vide	Old Synagogue
P.C.uma	Portugal	Coimbra	Universidade de Coimbra, Museu e Laboratório Antropológico
P.L.c	Portugal	Lisbon [Lisboa]	Conservatório Nacional
P.L.mc	Portugal	Lisbon [Lisboa]	National Coach Museum [Museu Nacional dos Coches]
P.L.me	Portugal	Lisbon [Lisboa]	Museu Etnográfico do Ultramar, Sociedade de Geográfia de Lisboa
P.L.mm	Portugal	Lisbon [Lisboa]	Museu da Música
P.L.msr	Portugal	Lisbon [Lisboa]	Museu de São Roque, Santa Casa da Misericórdia de Lisboa
P.PD.u	Portugal	Ponta Delgada, Azores	Centro de Estudos Etnológicos, Universidade dos Açores
P.PG.scm	Portugal	Pedrógão Grande	Santa Casa da Misericórdia
P.Q.m	Portugal	Queluz	Museu do Palácio Nacional de Queluz
P.SEIA.mb	Portugal	Seia	Museu do Brinquedo de Seia
PE.L.maa	Peru	Lima	Museo Nacional de Antropologia y Arqueologia
PF.P.m	French Polynesia	Papeete, Tahiti	Musée de Papeete
PF.PU.m	French Polynesia	Punaauia, Tahiti	Musée de Tahiti et des Iles
PK.K.nm	Pakistan	Karachi	National Museum of Pakistan
PK.L.m	Pakistan	Lahore	Lahore Museum
PK.SS.am	Pakistan	Saidu Sharif	Swat Archaeological Museum
PL.B.fp	Poland	Bydgoszcz	Filharmonia Pomorska
PL.BI.rm	Poland	Biecz	Regional Museum [Muzeum Regionalne]
PL.CZ.jg	Poland	Czestochowa	Monastery of Jasna Góra
PL.GD.nm	Poland	Gdańsk	National Museum [Muzeum Narodowe]
PL.K.em	Poland	Kraków	Ethnographical Museum [Muzeum Etnograficzne]
PL.K.mn	Poland	Kraków	National Museum [Muzeum Narodowe we Kraków]
PL.LZ.mae	Poland	Łódź	Museum of Archaeology and Ethnography [Muzeum Archeologiczne i Etnograficzne]
PL.OPA.mhp	Poland	Opatówek	Industrial History Museum [Muzeum Historii Przemyslu]
PL.P.mim	Poland	Poznań	Musical Instruments Museum [Muzeum Instrumentów Muzycznych]
PL.PRZ.mnzp	Poland	Przemysl	National Museum [Muzeum Narodowe Ziemi Przemyskiej]
PL.RZ.mo	Poland	Rzeszów	Muzeum Okregowe [District Museum]
PL.SZYD.m	Poland	Szydlowiec	Museum of Popular Musical Instruments [Muzeum Ludowych Instrumentów Muzycznych]
PL.W.kil	Poland	Warsaw	Ministry of Culture Collection of Bowed Instruments supervised by Polish Artists and Violin Makers Association [Kolekcja Instrumentsw Lutniczych, Zwiazek Polskich Artystsw Lutniksw]
PL.W.map	Poland	Warsaw	Asia and Pacific Museum [Muzeum Azji i Pacyfiku]
PL.W.mn	Poland	Warsaw	National Museum [Muzeum Narodowe]
PL.W.pm	Poland	Warsaw	National Ethnographical Museum [Panstwowe Muzeum Etnograficzne]

PL.W.tmn	Poland	Warsaw	Technical Museum [Muzeum Techniki Not, Dzial Mechanizmów Grajacych]
PL.W.um	Poland	Warsaw	The Fryderyk Chopin University of Music [Uniwersytet Muzyczny Fryderyka Chopina]
PL.WR.em	Poland	Wrocław	Ethnographical Museum [Muzeum Etnograficzne, Oddzial Muzeum Narodowego we Wrocławiu]
PL.WR.mn	Poland	Wrocław	National Museum [Muzeum Narodowe we Wrocławiu]
PL.Z.mt	Poland	Zakopane	Tatra Museum and Tytusa Chalubinski Memorial [Muzeum Tatrzanskie im Tytusa Chalubinskiego]
PNG.B.nm	Papua New Guinea	Boroko	National Museum of Papua New Guinea
PNG.PM.pm	Papua New Guinea	Port Moresby	Papua and New Guinea Public Museum and Art Gallery
PY.A.me	Paraguay	Asunción	Museo Etnográfico 'Andrés Barbero'
RA.AT.msg	Argentina	Atamisqui	Museo de la Sacha Guitarra
RA.BA.c	Argentina	Buenos Aires	Teatro Colón
RA.BA.inm	Argentina	Buenos Aires	Instituto Nacional de Musicologia 'Carlos Vega', Museo de Instrumentos Indigenas y Folclorico
RA.BA.mah	Argentina	Buenos Aires	Museo de Arte Hispanoamericano 'Isaac Fernández Blanco'
RA.BA.mnh	Argentina	Buenos Aires	Museo Nacional del Hombre
RA.LP.mcn	Argentina	La Plata	Museo de Ciencias Naturales de la Plata
RA.LP.mim	Argentina	La Plata	Museo Instrumentos Musicales 'Emilio Azzarini'
RA.SSJ.mcd	Argentina	San Salvador de Jujuy	Museo 'Carlos Darwin'
RCA.B.mbb	Central African Republic	Bangui	Musée Barthélémy Boganda
RCB.B.mn	Congo	Brazzaville	Musée National Congolais
RCH.S.mc	Chile	Santiago de Chile	Museo Chileno de Arte Precolombino
RCH.V.mo	Chile	Valparaíso	Museo Organológico
RG.N.mr	Guinea	Nzerékoré	Musée Regional de Nzerékoré
RI.DE.mb	Indonesia	Denpasar, Bali	Museum Bali
RI.J.nm	Indonesia	Jakarta, Java	National Museum
RI.J.wm	Indonesia	Jakarta, Java	Wayang Museum
RI.ME.mn	Indonesia	Medan, North Sumatra	Museum Negeri Sumatera Utara
RI.RE.i	Indonesia	Rengat, Riau	Indragiri Royal Family
RI.SSI.p	Indonesia	Siak Sri Indrapura, Riau	Palace
RI.SU.r	Indonesia	Surakarta, Java	Radyapostaka [Great Library]
RI.YO.pd	Indonesia	Yogyakarta	Monument Pangeran Diponegoro
RM.A.u	Madagascar	Antananarivo	Musée d'Art et d'Archéologie de l'Université de Madagascar
RMM.B.nm	Mali	Bamako	Musée National du Mali
RN.N.cfpm	Niger	Niamey	Centre de Formation et de Promotion Musicale 'El Hadj Taya' (CFPM)
RN.N.nm	Niger	Niamey	Musée national du Niger
RO.B.cmt	Romania	Bucharest [Bucuresti]	Complex Dul Muzeal Timis
RO.B.ma	Romania	Bucharest [Bucuresti]	Minovici Museum of Popular Art [Muzeul de Arta populara 'Minovici']
RO.B.mm	Romania	Bucharest [Bucuresti]	Romanian Music Museum [Muzeul Muzicii Romanesti]
RO.B.ms	Romania	Bucharest [Bucuresti]	Village and Folk Art Museum Romania [Muzeul Satului si de Arta Populara Romania]
RO.C.me	Romania	Cluj-Napoca	Muzeul Etnografic al Transilvaniei [Transylvanian Museum of Ethnography]
RO.C.mi	Romania	Cluj-Napoca	Museum of the History of Transylvania [Muzeul de Istorie al Transilvaniei]

RO.J.mp	Romania	Iaşi	Polytechnic Museum, Sound Recording and Reproduction Section [Sectia Inregistrarea si Reproducerea Sunetului, Muzeum Politehnic]
ROK.S.cmi	Republic of Korea	Seoul	National Classical Music Institute [Kunip Kugak-Won]
RP.B.nm	Philippines	Butuan City	National Museum
RP.BON.m	Philippines	Bontoc, Luzon	Bontoc Museum
RP.CE.u	Philippines	Cebu City	University of San Carlos Museum
RP.CO.u	Philippines	Cagayan de Oro	Xavier University, Museo de Oro
RP.M.im	Philippines	Manila	Intramuros Administration Museum
RP.M.mai	Philippines	Manila	Philippine Women's University, College of Music and Fine Arts, Museum of Asian Instruments
RP.M.nm	Philippines	Manila	National Museum of the Philippines
RP.M.ust	Philippines	Manila	University of Santo Tomás, Museum of Arts and Sciences
RP.MA.ak	Philippines	Marawi	Aga Khan Museum, Mindanao State University
RP.PA.ro	Philippines	Pasay City	Ramon Obusan Folkloric Center
RP.Q.u	Philippines	Quezon City	University Museum of Anthropology
RP.ZA.em	Philippines	Zamboanga	Western Mindanao State University, Ethnological Museum
RU.G.mn	Burundi	Gitega	Musée National de Gitega
RUS.KL.c	Russia	Klin	Tchaikovsky House Museum
RUS.M.bs	Russia	Moscow [Moskva]	State Collection of Antique Bowed String Instruments
RUS.M.cm	Russia	Moscow [Moskva]	Glinka State Central Museum of Musical Culture
RUS.M.im	Russia	Moscow [Moskva]	State Historical Museum [Gosudarstvennïy Istoricheskiy Muzey]
RUS.M.mram	Russia	Moscow [Moskva]	Mirek Russian Accordion Museum
RUS.N.k	Russia	Novgorod	Cultural History Museum, Kremlin
RUS.PA.p	Russia	Pavlovsk	Palace of Paul I
RUS.SP.hmm	Russia	St Petersburg [Sankt Peterburg]	Historical Military Museum [Voyenno-Istoricheskiy Muzey Artillerii]
RUS.SP.m	Russia	St Petersburg [Sankt Peterburg]	St Petersburg State Museum of Theatre and Music, Museum of Musical Instruments
RUS.SP.ma	Russia	St Petersburg [Sankt Peterburg]	Anthropology and Ethnography Museum of Peter the Great [Muzey Antropologii i Étnografii imeni Petra I]
RUS.SP.me	Russia	St Petersburg [Sankt Peterburg]	Russian Museum of Ethnography [Gosudarstvennïy Muzey Étnografii Narodov Rossiyskoy Federatsii]
RWA.B.mn	Rwanda	Butare	Musée National
S.BOS.m	Sweden	Borås	Borås Museum
S.ES.km	Sweden	Eskilstuna	Eskilstuna Konstmuseum
S.F.dm	Sweden	Falun	Dalarnas Museum
S.G.vkm	Sweden	Göteborg [Gothenburg]	Världskulturmuseet (formerly Göteborgs Etnografiska Museum, S.G.em)
S.G.sm	Sweden	Göteborg [Gothenburg]	Göteborgs Stadsmuseum (Historiska Museum)
S.GÄ.lm	Sweden	Gävle	Länsmuseet i Gävleborgs län
S.H.m	Sweden	Helsingborg	Hälsingborgs Museum
S.HU.hm	Sweden	Hudiksvall	Hälsinglands Museum
S.K.lm	Sweden	Kalmar	Kalmar Läns Museum
S.KK.ln	Sweden	Karlskrona	Blekinge Läns Museum
S.KR.lm	Sweden	Kristianstad	Kristianstads Länsmuseum
S.L.km	Sweden	Lund	Kulturhistoriska Museet
S.LB.h	Sweden	Leufsta Bruk [Löstabruk]	Manor House [Herrgård]
S.LI.lm	Sweden	Linköping	Östergötlands Länsmuseum
S.LK.m	Sweden	Landskrona	Landskrona Museum
S.LU.nm	Sweden	Luleå	Norrbottens museum
S.Ö.lm	Sweden	Örebro	Örebro Löns Museum
S.ÖS.lm	Sweden	Östersund	Jömtlands Löns Museum
S.S.am	Sweden	Stockholm	Armémuseum
S.S.e	Sweden	Stockholm	Swedish Ethnographical Museum (Etnografiska Museet)

S.S.fm [discontinued]	Sweden	Stockholm	Folkens Museum (now Världskulturmuseerna: Etnografiska Museet; Medelhavsmuseet; Östasiatiska Museet, *S.S.vkm*)
S.S.lm	Sweden	Stockholm	Stockholms Leksaksmuseum
S.S.m	Sweden	Stockholm	Music Museum (Musik- & Teatremuseet)
S.S.mf	Sweden	Stockholm	Stiftelsen Musikkulturens Främjande (The Nydahl Collection)
S.S.sm	Sweden	Stockholm	Statens Sjöhistoriska Museum
S.S.vkm	Sweden	Stockholm	Världskulturmuseerna: Etnografiska Museet; Medelhavsmuseet; Östasiatiska Museet (former Folkens Museum, *S.S.fm*)
S.SK.vm	Sweden	Skara	Skaraborgs Länsmuseum
S.SKE.m	Sweden	Skellefteä	Skellefteä Museum
S.SO.kh	Sweden	Norrala, Söderhamn	Klaverens Hus
S.U.um	Sweden	Uppsala	Upplandsmuseet
S.VÄ.lm	Sweden	Vänersborg	Älvsborgs Länsmuseum
SD.L.nm	Swaziland	Lobamba	Swaziland National Museum
SGP.S.nm	Singapore	Singapore	National Museum (formerly the Raffles Museum)
SI.L.em	Slovenia	Ljubljana	Slovenian Ethnographical Museum [Slovenski Etnografski Muzej]
SI.L.nm	Slovenia	Ljubljana	National Museum of Slovenia [Narodni muzej Slovenije]
SI.L.terlep	Slovenia	Ljubljana	Mira in Matije Terlep collection
SI.M.pm	Slovenia	Maribor	Regional Museum [Pokrajinski Muzej]
SI.N.dm	Slovenia	Novo Mesto	Dolenjski Museum [Dolenjski Muzej]
SI.P.pm	Slovenia	Ptuj	Provincial Museum Ptuj, Musical Instrument Collection [Pokrajinski muzej Ptuj, Zbirka glasbil]
SK.BB.m	Slovak Republic	Banská Bystrica	Literary and Music Museum [Literárne a Hudobné Múzeum]
SK.BR.mm	Slovak Republic	Bratislava	City Museum [Mestské múzeum]
SK.BR.nm	Slovak Republic	Bratislava	Slovak National Museum, Music Division [Slovenské národné múzeum, Hudobné Oddelenie]
SK.M.nm	Slovak Republic	Martin	Slovak National Museum: Ethnographical Collections [Slovenské národné múzeum, Etnograficky Ústav]
SN.D.ma	Senegal	Dakar	Musée d'Archéologie
SRB.B.em	Serbia	Belgrade [Beograd]	Ethnographical Museum [Etnografski Muzej]
SRB.B.mi	Serbia	Belgrade [Beograd]	Institute of Musicology of the Serbian Academy of Sciences and Arts
SRB.B.mu	Serbia	Belgrade [Beograd]	University of Arts in Belgrade, African Museum [Muzej Africke, Univerzitet Umetnosti u Beogradu]
SRB.B.uam	Serbia	Belgrade [Beograd]	University of Arts in Belgrade, Faculty of Musical Art [Fakultet Muzicke, Univerzitet Umetnosti u Beogradu]
T.B.nm	Thailand	Bangkok	National Museum [Phipitapan Haeng Chart]
TA.D.m	Tajikistan	Dushanabe	Muzei Muttachidai Respublíkawii Tá richi Kischwazschinosi was San'ati Taswiri
TCH.A.mn	Chad	Abéché	Musée National Abéché
TN.B.mn	Tunisia	Le Bardo	Musée National du Bardo
TN.C.atp	Tunisia	Carthage	Centre des Arts et Traditions Populaires, Fonds d'Instruments de Musique
TN.SS.m	Tunisia	Sidi ben-Saïd	Museum of Music
TN.T.c	Tunisia	Tunis	Musée du Conservatoire
TR.A.em	Turkey	Ankara	Ethnographical Museum [Etnografya Müzesi]
TR.I.ak	Turkey	Istanbul	Aynalikavak Pavillion [Aynalikavak Kasri]
TR.I.am	Turkey	Istanbul	Military Museum [Askerî Müzesi]
TR.I.tks	Turkey	Istanbul	Topkapi Palace Museum [Topkapi Sarayi Müzesi]
TR.IZ.m	Turkey	Izmir	Müziksev
TR.K.me	Turkey	Konya	Mevlâna Museum [Mevlâna Müzesi]
TR.K.mm	Turkey	Konya	Müze Müdürlügü

TW.T.as	Taiwan	Taipei	Academia Sinica, Institute of History and Philology, Exhibition Rooms
UA.K.gusac	Ukraine	Kiev	Raisa Dmitriyevna Gusac collection
UA.LV.m	Ukraine	L'viv	Historical Museum [L'vivskij Istoričeskij Muzej]
US.AA.s	USA	Ann Arbor, MI	Stearns Collection of Musical Instruments, University of Michigan
US.ALB.mm	USA	Albuquerque, NM	University of New Mexico, Maxwell Museum of Anthropology
US.AMB.oe	USA	Ambridge, PA	Old Economy Village
US.ASH.frederick	USA	Ashburnham, MA	Frederick Historic Piano Collection
US.B.bso	USA	Boston, MA	Boston Symphony Orchestra Collection of Historic Instruments
US.B.c	USA	Boston, MA	New England Conservatory of Music
US.B.germann	USA	Boston, MA	Sheridan Germann, private collection
US.B.mfa	USA	Boston, MA	Museum of Fine Arts
US.B.ne	USA	Boston, MA	Historic New England (formerly Society for the Preservation of New England Antiquities)
US.BA.hs	USA	Baltimore, MD	Maryland Historical Society
US.BAH.sanfillipo	USA	Barrington Hills, IL	Plum Tree Farm, Sanfillipo Foundation collection
US.BAK.kcm	USA	Bakersfield, CA	Kern County Museum
US.BE.lanier	USA	Berkeley, CA	Jaron Lanier, private collection
US.BE.m	USA	Berkeley, CA	University of California at Berkeley, Department of Music
US.BE.u	USA	Berkeley, CA	University of California, Phoebe A. Hearst Museum of Anthropology
US.BEK.am	USA	Berea, KY	Berea College Appalachian Museum
US.BEL.lm	USA	Beloit, WI	Beloit College, Logan Museum of Anthropology
US.BEN.m	USA	Bennington, VT	Bennington Museum
US.BET.m	USA	Bethlehem, PA	Moravian Museum of Bethlehem
US.BIS.hs	USA	Bismarck, ND	Museum of the State Historical Society of North Dakota
US.BL.mm	USA	Bloomington, IN	Indiana University, Mathers Museum of World Cultures
US.BLH.cis	USA	Bloomfield Hills, MI	Cranbrook Institute of Science
US.BOG.km	USA	Bowling Green, KY	Kentucky Museum, Western Kentucky University
US.BOI.hs	USA	Boise, ID	Idaho State Historical Society
US.BOO.asu	USA	Boone, NC	Hayes School of Music, Appalachian State University
US.BRB.eo	USA	Brattleboro, VT	Estey Organ Museum
US.BRO.mpi	USA	Browning, MT	Museum of the Plains Indian and Crafts Center
US.BRS.leone	USA	Brookside, NJ	Mark Leone, private collection
US.BUR.fm	USA	Burlington, VT	Robert Hull Fleming Museum, University of Vermont
US.BV.wm	USA	Bartlesville, OK	Woolaroc Museum, Frank Phillips Foundation
US.C.fm	USA	Chicago, IL	Field Museum of Natural History
US.C.oi	USA	Chicago, IL	University of Chicago, Oriental Institute Museum
US.CA.hu	USA	Cambridge, MA	Harvard University Department of Music
US.CA.pm	USA	Cambridge, MA	Harvard University, Peabody Museum of Archaeology and Ethnology
US.CBD.u	USA	Carbondale, IL	Southern Illinois University Museum
US.CD.hs	USA	Concord, NH	New Hampshire Historical Society Museum
US.CEN.flint	USA	Centreville, DE	Karen Gebhart Flint, private collection
US.CH.j	USA	Charlottesville, VA	Thomas Jefferson Memorial Association
US.CHA.m	USA	Charleston, SC	Charleston Museum
US.CI.am	USA	Cincinnati, OH	Cincinnati Art Museum
US.CL.hs	USA	Cleveland, OH	Western Reserve Historical Society Museum
US.CL.rr	USA	Cleveland, OH	Rock and Roll Hall of Fame and Museum
US.CLB.namm	USA	Carlsbad, CA	Museum of Making Music, National Association of Music Merchants (NAMM)
US.CLD.dbm	USA	Clarksdale, MS	Delta Blues Museum
US.CM.eric	USA	Costa Mesa, CA	Christian and Kathleen Eric, private collection
US.COR.mg	USA	Corning, NY	Corning Museum of Glass
US.CS.m	USA	Colorado Springs, CO	Colorado Springs Museum
US.D.cm	USA	Detroit, MI	Children's Museum
US.D.ia	USA	Detroit, MI	Detroit Institute of Arts
US.DB.hf	USA	Dearborn, MI	Henry Ford Museum and Greenfield Village
US.DE.mnh	USA	Denver, CO	Denver Museum of Natural History
US.DEC.nam	USA	Decorah, IA	Vesterheim Norwegian-American Museum

US.DK.niu	USA	De Kalb, IL	Northern Illinois University World Music Instrument Collection
US.DM.u	USA	Durham, NC	Duke University Musical Instrument Collections
US.DVP.pm	USA	Davenport, IA	Putnam Museum of History and Natural Science
US.ED.uam	USA	Edwardsville, IL	University Art Museum, Southern Illinois University
US.ELM.hc	USA	Elmira, NY	Chemung County Historical Centre
US.FAY.-cholthitchanta	USA	Fayetteville, AR	Nophachai Cholthitchanta, private collection
US.FL.m	USA	Flagstaff, AR	Museum of Northern Arizona
US.FRA.db	USA	Franklin, PA	DeBence Antique Music World
US.GE.elrod	USA	Germantown, MD	John H. Elrod Memorial Collection, private collection
US.GRI.c	USA	Grinnell, IA	Grinnell College, Musical Instrument Collection
US.H.hs	USA	Hartford, CT	Connecticut Historical Society Museum
US.HAN.hs	USA	Hanover, MI	Hanover-Horton Area Historical Society
US.HAR.fm	USA	Harvard, MA	Fruitlands Museums
US.HOM.dudgeon	USA	Homer, NY	Ralph and Virginia Dudgeon, private collection
US.HON.bm	USA	Honolulu, HI	The Bishop Museum (formerly the Bernice Pauahi Bishop Museum)
US.HON.u	USA	Honolulu, HI	University of Hawaii, Music Department
US.HOP.pm	USA	Hopkinton, MA	The Piano Museum
US.HOU.mns	USA	Houston, TX	Houston Museum of Natural Science, Anthropology Department
US.HUN.ppm	USA	Hunter, NY	Piano Performance Museum, Catskill Mountain Foundation
US.IN.m	USA	Indianapolis, IN	Indiana State Museum
US.IN.pas	USA	Indianapolis, IN	Percussive Arts Society Museum
US.IO.u	USA	Iowa City, IA	University of Iowa
US.IVO.cfd	USA	Ivoryton, CT	The Company of Fifers and Drummers
US.J.chaney	USA	Jacksonville, AL	E. Lee Chaney, private collection
US.K.u	USA	Kent, OH	Hugh A. Glauser School of Music, Center for the Study of World Musics, Kent State University
US.KA.ptg	USA	Kansas City, KS	Piano Technicians Guild Foundation, Jack Wyatt Museum
US.KAL.vm	USA	Kalamazoo, MI	Kalamazoo Valley Museum
US.LA.dm	USA	Los Angeles, CA	University of California, Department of Musicology
US.LA.fm	USA	Los Angeles, CA	University of California, Fowler Museum of Cultural History
US.LA.sm	USA	Los Angeles, CA	Southwest Museum
US.LA.udm	USA	Los Angeles, CA	University of California (UCLA), Department of Ethnomusicology
US.LA.usc	USA	Los Angeles, CA	University of Southern California, Albert Gale and Leonardo De Lorenzo collections
US.LA.wt	USA	Los Angeles, CA	Watts Towers Arts Center
US.LB.u	USA	Lewisburg, PA	Bucknell University, Department of Music, Harold E. Cook Collection
US.LI.sm	USA	Lincoln, NE	University of Nebraska, State Museum, Anthropology Division
US.LIT.m	USA	Lititz, PA	Lititz Moravian Congregation Archives and Museum
US.LM.hm	USA	Le Mars, IA	Plymouth County Historical Museum, Parkinson (Truesdell) Collection of Historical Musical Instruments
US.M.m	USA	Milwaukee, WI	Public Museum
US.MAN.u	USA	Manoa, HI	University of Hawaii, Manoa, Music Department
US.MC.u	USA	Montclair, NJ	Montclair State University
US.MEM.ppm	USA	Memphis, TN	Memphis Pink Palace Museum
US.MH.hs	USA	Manhattan, KS	Riley County Historical Society and Museum
US.MI.wu	USA	Middletown, CT	Wesleyan University, Collection of Musical Instruments
US.MIN.pv	USA	Minden, NE	Harold Warp Pioneer Village
US.MON.hm	USA	Monroe, MI	Monroe County Historical Museum
US.MT.m	USA	Morristown, NJ	Morris Museum
US.NA.cm	USA	Nashville, TN	Country Music Hall of Fame
US.NA.csm	USA	Nashville, TN	Cumberland Science Museum
US.NA.mh	USA	Nashville, TN	Musicians Hall of Fame and Museum
US.NAS.sm	USA	Nashua, NH	New England Synthesizer Museum
US.NAZ.cfm	USA	Nazareth, PA	C.F. Martin Guitar Museum

US.NAZ.m	USA	Nazareth, PA	Moravian Historical Society
US.NC.sigal	USA	Newton Centre, MA	Marlowe Sigal private collection
US.NE.m	USA	Newark, NJ	Newark Museum
US.NH.pm	USA	New Haven, CT	Yale University, Peabody Museum of Natural History, Department of Anthropology
US.NH.y	USA	New Haven, CT	Yale University Collection of Musical Instruments
US.NN.km	USA	North Newton, KS	Kauffman Museum
US.NOR.sm	USA	New Orleans, LA	Louisiana State Museum, Music Collection
US.NRS.ma	USA	Norris, TN	Museum of Appalachia
US.NY.amnh	USA	New York, NY	The American Museum of Natural History
US.NY.mc	USA	New York, NY	Museum of the City of New York
US.NY.mma	USA	New York, NY	Metropolitan Museum of Art
US.OA.phm	USA	Oakland, CA	Pardee Home Museum
US.OB.caldwell	USA	Oberlin, OH	Caldwell Collection of Viols, private collection
US.OB.k	USA	Oberlin, OH	Oberlin College, Conservatory of Music, Roderic C. Knight Collection
US.OB.s	USA	Oberlin, OH	Oberlin College, Conservatory of Music, Selch Collection of American Music History
US.OK.abm	USA	Oklahoma City, OK	American Banjo Museum
US.OK.cwm	USA	Oklahoma City, OK	National Cowboy & Western Heritage Museum
US.OK.hs	USA	Oklahoma City, OK	Oklahoma Historical Society Museum
US.OK.payne	USA	Oklahoma City, OK	Richard W. Payne, private collection
US.ON.im	USA	Onchiota, NY	Six Nations Indian Museum
US.OR.ap	USA	Orlando, FL	Audio Playground Keyboard Museum
US.OR.hm	USA	Orlando, FL	International Harp Museum
US.ORO.hm	USA	Orono, ME	University of Maine, Hudson Museum
US.P.cm	USA	Pittsburgh, PA	Carnegie Museum of Natural History, Division of Anthropology
US.P.dt	USA	Pittsburgh, PA	Tamburitzan National Folk Arts Center
US.P.hhc	USA	Pittsburgh, PA	Senator John Heinz History Center
US.PA.pease	USA	Palmer, MA	Pease Collection of Historical Instruments
US.PB.bm	USA	Pine Bluff, AR	Band Museum
US.PD.hs	USA	Portland, ME	Maine Historical Society Museum
US.PH.ism	USA	Philadelphia, PA	Independence Seaport Museum
US.PH.maa	USA	Philadelphia, PA	University of Pennsylvania, Museum of Archaeology and Anthropology
US.PH.pma	USA	Philadelphia, PA	Philadelphia Museum of Art
US.PHO.hm	USA	Phoenix, AZ	Heard Museum of Native Cultures and Art
US.PHO.mim	USA	Phoenix, AZ	Musical Instrument Museum
US.PL.am	USA	Portland, OR	Portland Art Museum, Rasmussen Collection of Northwest Coast Indian Art
US.PL.hs	USA	Portland, OR	Oregon Historical Society Museum
US.PO.vc	USA	Poughkeepsie, NY	Vassar College Music Department
US.POT.csm	USA	Potsdam, NY	State University College, Crane School of Music
US.PRO.hs	USA	Providence, RI	Rhode Island Historical Society Museum
US.PRV.ma	USA	Provo, UT	Brigham Young University, Museum of Art
US.R.mp	USA	Rochester, NY	National Museum of Play (formerly the Strong Museum)
US.R.valenza	USA	Rochester, NY	Helen R. and Charles R. Valenza, private flute collection
US.RH.welch	USA	Rolling Hills, CA	Kermit Welch, private collection
US.RID.eldredge	USA	Ridgewood, NJ	Niles Eldredge, private collection
US.RL.wilson	USA	Red Lion, PA	Charles W. Wilson, private collection
US.RO.tm [dispersed]	USA	Rockford, IL	Time Museum [closed 1999]
US.RW.hs	USA	Red Wing, MN	Goodhue County Historical Society Museum
US.S.am	USA	Seattle, WA	Seattle Art Museum
US.S.bm	USA	Seattle, WA	University of Washington, Thomas Burke Memorial Washington State Museum
US.S.em	USA	Seattle, WA	Experience Music Project
US.S.mhi	USA	Seattle, WA	Museum of History and Industry, Historical Society of Seattle and King County
US.S.spu	USA	Seattle, WA	Seattle Pacific University, School of Fine and Performing Arts
US.S.uw	USA	Seattle, WA	University of Washington, Ethnomusicology Division
US.SA.ei	USA	Salem, MA	Peabody Essex Museum (formerly Essex Institute)

US.SAN.bmm	USA	Santa Ana, CA	Bowers Memorial Museum
US.SAR.rm	USA	Sarasota, FL	Ringling Museum of Art
US.SB.hs	USA	Santa Barbara, CA	Santa Barbara Historical Society Museum
US.SB.uc	USA	Santa Barbara, CA	University of California at Santa Barbara, Department of Music
US.SD.mm	USA	San Diego, CA	San Diego Museum of Man
US.SF.fam	USA	San Francisco, CA	Fine Arts Museums of San Francisco
US.SFE.mai	USA	Santa Fe, NM	Wheelwright Museum of the American Indian (formerly Museum of Navajo Ceremonial Art)
US.SFE.mia	USA	Santa Fe, NM	Museum of Indian Arts and Culture, Laboratory of Anthropology
US.SHB.m	USA	Shelburne, VT	Shelburne Museum
US.SJB.fm	USA	St Johnsbury, VT	Fairbanks Museum of Natural Science and Planetarium
US.SI.sjm	USA	Sitka, AK	Sheldon Jackson Museum
US.SJO.m	USA	St Joseph, MO	St Joseph Museum
US.SL.-hartenberger	USA	St Louis, MO	Aurelia W. Hartenberger, private collection
US.SLC.mch	USA	Salt Lake City, UT	Church of Jesus Christ of Latter-Day Saints, Museum of Church History and Art
US.SPA.hs	USA	St Paul, MN	Minnesota Historical Society Museum
US.SPA.sc	USA	St Paul, MN	The Schubert Club Museum of Musical Instruments
US.ST.u	USA	Stanford, CA	Stanford University Department of Music, Harry R. Lange Historical Collection of Instruments
US.STB.v	USA	Sturbridge, MA	Old Sturbridge Village
US.STG.otm	USA	Sterling, CO	Overland Trail Museum
US.SU.hs	USA	Superior, WI	Douglas County Historical Society
US.TA.ua	USA	Tallahassee, FL	Florida State University, Department of Anthropology
US.TA.ucm	USA	Tallahassee, FL	Florida State University, College of Music
US.TAR.miner	USA	Tarzana, CA	Gregg Miner, private collection
US.TC.asm	USA	Tucson, AZ	University of Arizona, Arizona State Museum
US.TL.richards	USA	Toluca Lake, CA	Emil Richards, private collection
US.TO.hs	USA	Topeka, KS	Kansas State Historical Society and Kansas Museum of History
US.TU.gm	USA	Tulsa, OK	Gilcrease Museum, Anthropology Department
US.TU.pma	USA	Tulsa, OK	Philbrook Museum of Art, Native American Collection
US.U.u	USA	Urbana-Champaign, IL	University of Illinois, Sousa Archives and Center for American Music
US.V.n	USA	Vermillion, SD	National Music Museum, University of South Dakota
US.W.c	USA	Washington, DC	Library of Congress (Music Division)
US.W.dar	USA	Washington, DC	Daughters of the American Revolution (DAR) Museum
US.W.nmai	USA	Washington, DC and New York City	Smithsonian Institution (National Museum of the American Indian)
US.W.nmnh	USA	Washington, DC	Smithsonian Institution (National Museum of Natural History), Department of Anthropology
US.W.nps	USA	Washington, DC	National Park Service, US Department of the Interior
US.W.si	USA	Washington, DC	Smithsonian Institution (National Museum of American History)
US.WAR.ucm	USA	Warrensburg, MO	University of Central Missouri, Music Division
US.WG.aa	USA	Williamsburg, VA	Abby Aldrich Rockefeller Folk Art Museum
US.WG.cw	USA	Williamsburg, VA	Colonial Williamsburg Foundation, DeWitt Wallace Decorative Arts Museum
US.WI.c	USA	Williamstown, MA	Williams College, Department of Music
US.WIC.hensley	USA	Wichita, KS	Flutes of the World, Betty Austin Hensley Collection
US.WIC.u	USA	Wichita, KS	Wichita State University, Thurlow Lieurance Indian Flutes
US.WIL.howe	USA	Wilbraham, MA	Robert S. Howe, private collection
US.WIS.wh	USA	Wiscasset, ME	The Musical Wonder House
US.WS.whs	USA	Winston-Salem, NC	Wachovia Historical Society (collection administered by Old Salem Museums & Gardens)
US.Y.ht	USA	York, PA	York County Heritage Trust (formerly Historical Society of York County)
USB.S.m	Uzbekistan	Samarkand	Museum of Uzbek History, Culture and Arts
USB.T.aam	Uzbekistan	Tashkent	Applied Arts Museum of Uzbekistan

USB.T.hm	Uzbekistan	Tashkent	Tashkent Historical Museum of the People of Uzbekistan
USB.T.ma	Uzbekistan	Tashkent	Uzbek State Museum of Art
USB.T.sel	Uzbekistan	Tashkent	Scientific Experimental Laboratory for the Sphere of Research, Reconstruction and Improvement of the Musical Instruments by the State Conservatory 'M. Ashrafi'
UY.M.mhn	Uruguay	Montevideo	Museo Histórico Nacional
UY.M.mr	Uruguay	Montevideo	Museo Romántico
VE.C.fe	Venezuela	Caracas	Fundación de Etnomusicologíma y Folklore (Fundef)
VN.S.nm	Vietnam	Saigon	National Museum of Vietnam
WAG.B.nm	Gambia	Banjul	National Museum
WAN.B.nm	Nigeria	Benin City	National Museum
WAN.J.m	Nigeria	Jos	Jos Museum (formerly the National Museum)
WAN.L.ncm	Nigeria	Lagos	National Commission for Museums and Monuments
WAN.L.nm	Nigeria	Lagos	Nigerian Museum
Z.L.m	Zambia	Livingstone	Livingstone Museum
Z.M.mmm	Zambia	Mbala	Moto-Moto Museum
ZA.C.m	South Africa	Cape Town	IZIKO Museums of Cape Town (formerly South African Cultural History Museum)
ZA.C.u	South Africa	Rondebosch, Cape Town	University of Cape Town (Kirby Collection)
ZA.EL.m	South Africa	East London	East London Museum
ZA.G.ilam	South Africa	Grahamstown	International Library of African Music (ILAM), Rhodes University
ZA.J.am	South Africa	Johannesburg	Africana Museum
ZA.J.steafel	South Africa	Johannesburg	Harold Steafel collection
ZA.J.uw	South Africa	Johannesburg	University of the Witwatersrand
ZRE.B.dac	Democratic Republic of the Congo	Bukavu	Département d'Anthropologie Culturelle
ZRE.K.mn	Democratic Republic of the Congo	Kinshasa	Institut des Musée Nationaux du Congo (IMNC)
ZW.H.qvm	Zimbabwe	Harare	Ethnography Department, Queen Victoria Museum

Volume Five

Tibia – Zygmuntowicz, Samuel

T

[continued]

Tibia. Roman wind instrument; representative of double-tube reed aerophones (commonly called double pipes) of the ancient Near East (Summerian *imbubu/ebubu*, Egyptian *ma·t*) and Mediterranean (Greek *aulos*).

1. Cultural background. 2. Terminology. 3. Sources. 4. Construction. 5. Social context.

1. Cultural background. The Latin term *tibia* (plural *tibiae*) applies to Roman double pipes from the Republic (509 bce–27 bce) to the Imperial Period (27 bce–476 ce). The instrument is commonly considered a version of the Greek *aulos* and often the terms *aulos* and *tibia* are used as synonyms. However, Romans might have adopted double pipes from the Etruscans. Moreover, during the late Republic and the Empire, musicians of different provenance introduced to Rome their own types of double-tube reed aerophones; for example, Syrian female slaves (*ambubaiae*) played double pipes (*ambubah*) in Roman streets and taverns. A sign of the multicultural origin of many double-pipe players in Rome is a law of 115 bce (Cassiodorus, *Chronica* A. U. 639) allowing only Latin pipers to perform there.

2. Terminology. *Tibia* ('shinbone') refers to the bone commonly used to make the instrument. Written sources employ many terms for different types of tibia. The most important terminological difference is between *tibiae pares* (with two pipes of equal length), and *tibiae impares* (with pipes of unequal length). The terms *tibiae Sarranae* (Tyrian tibia), *tibiae Lydiae* (Lydian tibia), and *tibiae geminae* (twin tibia) might indicate variants of *tibiae pares*. A term related to *tibiae impares* is *tibiae phrygiae* (Phrygian tibia), also referred to as *tibia berecyntia* (Berecynthian tibia, after a Phrygian mountain sacred to Cybele). Another important distinction is between *tibia dextra* and *tibia sinistra*, interpreted respectively as the right- and left-hand pipes of the *tibiae impares*. Nevertheless, the terminology is often ambiguous. Related terms are: *tibicen* (pl.: *tibicine*), a male player of a tibia; *tibicina* (pl.: *tibicinae*), a female player of a tibia; *tibia multifora,* an instrument with many fingerholes; and *ligula* or *lingula* ('little tongue'), the reed of a tibia.

3. Sources. Information about the tibia is provided by archaeological, iconographic, and written sources. Tibiae have been unearthed in many former Roman territories, e.g. Italy (Pompeii and its vicinity); United Kingdom (London); Netherlands (Mook); Sudan (Meroë); and Near East (the so-called Reading Aulos). In addition, museums preserve numerous double pipes (complete or fragmentary) of Roman provenance that have not yet been researched and published.

Tibiae appear in numerous ancient depictions, mostly from Italy but also from other regions of Roman expansion, e.g. Germany, France, Luxemburg, Tunisia, and Turkey. In many cases iconography provides a realistic impression of the instrument. Among the most valuable sculptural depictions are those of the priest of Cybele with a tibia on a relief in the Palazzo dei Conservatori (Rome, 2nd century ce), and a Maenad with a tibia on a marble sarcophagus in the Catacombs of Praetextatus (Rome, mid-3rd century ce). Construction details are also visible in many Roman mosaics (e.g. the Dionysus mosaic from Cologne, *c*220 ce; the Monnus mosaic from Trier, *c*250 ce) and paintings (e.g. from Pompeii and Ephesus).

Greek and Roman writers, e.g. Cicero, Horace, Livy, Ovid, Plutarch, Pollux, Varro, and Virgil, frequently mention the tibia. Later references appear in Johannes Tinctoris (*De inventione et usu musicae*, *c*1487, Naples), Bartolinus Casparus (*De tibiis veterum et earum antiquo usu*, Rome 1677, Amsterdam 1679), and Filippo Bonnani (*Gabinetto armonico*, Rome 1722, 1723, 1776), among other writings.

4. Construction. The instrument has two cylindrical tubes, each provided with a reed, double reeds being indicated by iconographic sources. It developed gradually in size and complexity from a simple instrument

1

with three or four fingerholes in each pipe (Varro, *De lingua latina*) to a long tibia with highly evolved construction. Iconographic sources from the Republic show simple instruments having two pipes of equal length, occasionally with a small bell at the distal end. It has been suggested that the instrument developed suddenly during the late Republic, when many Greek musicians moved to Italy and inspired Roman instrument builders by their virtuosity. As a result of this intercultural encounter, an elaborated tibia type evolved. Its complex construction is revealed by archaeological finds, e.g. from Meroë (*c*15 bce, *US.B.mfa*), Pompeii, and its vicinity (mid-1st century ce, *I.N.ma*). Numerous tibia fragments were found in Meroë, but their bad condition precludes comprehensive restoration; it is estimated that these fragments formed part of 12 to 16 instruments of various types, with and without mechanisms. Among the Pompeian discoveries, four almost complete pipes are preserved; nine further pipes were found in a *villa rustica* in Civita near Pompeii. The Civita, Meroë, and Pompeii finds show similar construction details consisting of the following main parts: (1) a reed insert in the form of a pirouette; (2) a bulb (called also 'olive' because of its shape); (3) a long main tube consisting of several sections with circular, oval, or oblong (Meroë) fingerholes; and (4) occasionally a small bell (Civita, Meroë). Among the Meroë finds, three bore sizes are present: 7, 9, and 10 mm. The bore diameter of the Civita and Pompeii pipes is about 8 mm.

The archaeological finds reveal the presence of rotary rings (called also 'rotary sleeves', 'rotating collars'), a mechanism for temporarily closing and opening fingerholes, invented by the 5th-century bce Greek musician Pronomus (Athenaeus, *Deipnosofistae* 631e). The mechanism has three concentric elements: (1) a core tube of bone or ivory with fingerholes; (2) a bronze sheath permanently affixed to the tube, perforated to match its holes; and (3) bronze or silver rings that rotate around the sheath, each provided with (usually) one fingerhole matching the hole in the tube and sheath. A small knob attached to the ring probably eased its rotation to expose or cover a fingerhole, presumably to simplify playing in different modes. Apart from this elaborated type, probably used by professional virtuosi, simple bone tibiae were still played during the Imperial period, e.g. the 1st century ce example from the Roman cemetery in Mook.

The Phrygian tibia, a variant of the instrument, is known from iconographic and written sources and characterized by a large horn-shaped bell attached to one of the tubes, presumably to amplify its sound. Very often the Phrygian tibia appears with funnel- and spike-shaped projections presumably for acoustic purposes. Some depictions also straight pipes with attached devices.

5. Social context. The tibia played a prominent role in Roman society, accompanying a vast variety of activities. Evidence of its great popularity is the archaic Law of the Twelve Tables from 451 bce, according to which more than ten pipers were forbidden to play at a funeral (Cicero, *De leg.* ii. 59; Ovid, *Fasti* vi.651). Because of their importance *tibicines* enjoyed high status and received special privileges. They were organized in the *collegium tibicinum romanorum*, and pipers appear first in the list of trade guilds into which the people of Rome were traditionally divided by the king Numa (Plutarch, *Numa* 17). Some ancient writers (Livy ix.30.5–10; Ovid, *Fasti* vi.651; Plutarch, *Quaestiones Romomanae* 55; and Valerius Maximus 2.5.4) relate a legend of the tibicines' strike from 311 or 309 bce. They left Rome after prohibition of their time-honoured privilege of feasting in the temple of Jupiter, and went to Tibur (present Tivoli) near Rome. As no sacred rite was complete without their accompaniment, the Senate was forced to get the tibicines back to Rome as soon as possible. Their former privileges were restored, and in addition they were permitted to parade through the city three days every year dressed in special garb and playing their instruments. Plutarch links the story with the mid-June festival called the *Quinquatrus minores*.

The tibia was also indispensable in the theatre. According to Livy, at the beginning of the 4th-century bce Etruscan actors in Rome performed simple stage plays and danced to the music of the tibia (Livy, vii.2). The comedies of Plautus (*c*254–185 bce) and Terence (*c*190–159 bce) include many scenes that were performed to the accompaniment of the *tibicen*, a slave musician who also composed the melodies. The production notices to Terence's plays include the names of four different types of tibiae used in this accompaniment. In later theatrical performances the tibia also formed part of an orchestra (with panpipes, cymbals, and stringed instruments), in which the tibia player kept time with his foot by means of a percussion instrument called the *scabellum*; this practice occurred also in other contexts.

Another important function of the tibia was its ritual usage. It was heard at wedding processions and funerals, and at a sacrifice its piercing tone could cover up any sound of the animal victim. The Phrygian tibia together with *cymbala* (cymbals) and *tympana* (small frame drum) played a significant role in two popular ecstatic cults in Rome: those of Dionysus/Bacchus and of the Asiatic Magna Mater Cybele (Great Mother), introduced to Rome in 204 bce during the second Punic War. The Phrygian tibia might have come to Rome with the Cybele cult. The tibia also accompanied victory celebrations, formal meals, and was played in concerts in the houses of the rich.

BIBLIOGRAPHY

E.H. Zeydel: 'A Strike of the Tibicines', *The Classical Weekly*, vol.15/7 (28 Nov 1921), 51

G. Fleischhauer: *Etrurien und Rom, Musikgeschichte in Bildern*, vol.2/5 (Leipzig, 1964, 2/1978)

H. Becker: *Zur Entwicklungsgeschichte der antiken und mittelalterlichen Rohrblattinstrumente* (Hamburg, 1966)

J.G. Landels: 'A Newly Discovered Aulos', *The Annual of the British School at Athens*, vol.60 (1968), 231–8

J. Rimmer: 'The Tibiae pares of Mook', *GSJ*, vol.29 (1976), 42–6

R. Meucci: 'Aulos, tibia e doppio flauto: antichistica e folklore musicale', *NRMI*, vol.20/4 (1986), 626–32

G. Lawson and A. Wradle: 'A Roman Pipe from London', *LAMAS Transactions of the London & Middlesex Archaeological Society*, vol.39 (1998), 35–6

S. Hagel: 'The Pompeii Auloi: Improved Data and a Hitherto Unknown Mechanism', *Klänge der Vergangenheit: Die Interpretation von musikarchäologischen Artefakten im Kontext*, ed. R. Eichmann, F. Jianjun, L.-C. Koch (Leidorf, 2012), 103–14

T. Moore: 'Chapter I: *Tibiae* and *tibicines*', *Music in Roman Comedy* (Cambridge, 2012)

O. Sutkowska: 'One of Nine *Tibiae* from a *Villa Rustica* in the Vesuvian Area Re-Discovered', *Klänge der Vergangenheit: Die Interpretation von musikarchäologischen Artefakten im Kontext*, ed. R. Eichmann, F. Jianjun, L.-C. Koch (Leidorf, 2012), 115–26

OLGA SUTKOWSKA

Tickell, Kenneth (*b* Orrell, Lancashire, England, 25 Aug 1956). English organ builder. After studying music at the University of Hull, where he was also organ scholar, Tickell trained with Grant, Degens, and Bradbeer Ltd, eventually establishing his own workshop in 1982; since 1996 he has been based in Northampton. To date, his firm has built 76 instruments including both large and chamber instruments. Although early projects were influenced by post-war 'classical' trends, his 21st-century instruments stress 19th-century English sounds alongside Continental features. Significant instruments showing this style include St Barnabas, Dulwich (1997; three manuals, 35 stops), Worcester Cathedral (2008; four manuals, 57 stops), Lincoln's Inn (2009; three manuals, 40 stops), and Keble College, Oxford (2011; four manuals, 43 stops). At Lincoln's Inn, the Swell division contains slotted diapasons reminiscent of 19th-century French techniques, a departure for Tickell. The Keble instrument shows the influence of Hill, not least in the Great chorus and its Gamba; a departure is the Choir division with its stress on solo colours. Tickell's instruments generally have tracker key action and electric stop action, with the exception of Worcester Cathedral which has electric key action. As in several English cathedral organs, the Worcester instrument is divided on both sides of the Quire, and the console is detached.

NICHOLAS STEFANO PROZZILLO

Tidinit. Half-spike plucked lute of the Moors of Mauritania. It has a wooden boat-shaped, slightly waisted resonator, 40 to 50 cm long, to which is laced or nailed a soundtable of cowhide. A wooden stick serving as the neck enters the resonator at one end, through the skin, and continues as far as a hole in the soundtable. At this point the lower end of the neck can be seen to be forked; at its upper end it has a short copper tube. The four strings, nowadays usually of nylon though traditionally of twisted hair, run from the fork over a bridge at the edge of the hole and fasten to sliding metal rings on the neck. Metal vibrators with rings are attached either to the end of the neck or are placed on the soundtable.

The tidinit is played exclusively by men and is now often electronically amplified. It is usually plucked with the fingers of the right hand, while the fingers of the left stop the strings, and the right thumb taps rhythmically on the soundtable. The middle strings are used for the melody; the outer strings are shorter and left free to vibrate sympathetically. The lute is used alone to accompany one or two male singers; to accompany women singing it is used alone or with other instruments (another tidinit, the *ardin* harp, the *t'bol* drum, and the calabash plosive aerophone *daghumma*). See M. Guignard: *Musique, honneur et plaisir au Sahara: étude psychosociologique et musicologique dans la société maure* (Paris, 1975).

K.A. GOURLAY

Tidir. Percussion idiophone of the Tolai people, Papua New Guinea. It exists in two forms: a lath of bamboo 15 cm long and 5 cm wide, laid across the thumb and index finger of the half-closed left hand and struck with a short stick; and a bamboo tube 4 cm in diameter and 12 cm long, closed by a node at the top and open at the bottom, with a 10-cm slot cut into the side from the open end. It is gripped around the top by the thumb and forefinger, and the beating stick is held loosely between the fourth and little fingers of the same hand. The player gently and rhythmically flicks his wrist in a circular motion away from the body, causing the stick to bounce against the side of the bamboo in a reiterated triplet pattern. The first form is used in lieu of drums to accompany ceremonial songs; the second as a *tinbuk* substitute to attract the affection of a woman. Similar instruments to the first form are the Lihir *keleng* and Lak *telek*.

MICHAEL WEBB

Tieffenbrucker [Dieffopruchar, Dieffoprukhar, Duiffoprugcar, Thiphobrucar, Fraburgadi]. German family of string instrument makers. They originated in the small village of Tieffenbruck, near Rosshaupten in Bavaria, in the region of Füssen. The family split into two branches, one of which settled in Lyons and soon became naturalized French, specializing in viols and other bowed instruments. The larger branch emigrated to Italy and became established principally in Venice and Padua, making mainly lutes. Tangled family relationships make a satisfactory reconstruction of the family tree impossible: some Tieffenbruckers might have shared only the place of origin, not a close family relationship.

Ulrich [Odorico, Rigo] Tieffenbrucker (i) (*d* before 1560), probably the earliest and one of the least-known members of the family, is said to have worked in Venice and Bologna. Toffolo and Cervelli attribute to him a lute inventoried in 1759 in The Hague, which bore the label 'Ulrich Duiffoprugar Lutario A. 1521'. His children established the Venetian branch of the family.

Gaspar Tieffenbrucker [Duiffoprugcar] the elder (*b* Tieffenbruck, Germany, 1514; *d* ?Lyons, France, 1571), probably a close relative or even a son of Ulrich, was the most famous member of the French branch of the family; his name appears on labels in a number of French variants, of which 'Duiffoprugcar' is perhaps the most common. He settled in Lyons in 1533 and acquired French nationality in 1558. In 1564 his house and workshop were demolished to make way for the building of fortifications for the city, and he was unable to get any compensation, a blow from which he never fully recovered. There is an engraved portrait of him by Woeiriot dated 1565. His eldest son, Gaspar Tieffenbrucker (ii) (*fl* late 16th century), moved to Paris after the death of his father; he married the sister of the Parisian instrument maker Jacques Delamotte, and his workshop was established in the rue Pot-de-Feu in 1582. Johann [Jean] Tieffenbrucker (*fl* late 16th century), another son of Gaspar (i), took over the business after his father's death and seems to have remained in Lyons until at least 1585, when he had settled the outstanding debts.

The other principal members of the family were all of the Italian branch. The sons of Ulrich (i) were Magno Tieffenbrucker [Dieffoprukhar, Dieffopruchar] (i) (*d* 1560), Ulrich [Odorico, Rigo] Tieffenbrucker (ii) (*d* c1573), and Jacob Tieffenbrucker [Jacomo] (*d* after 1573). Not much is known about Jacob: he was apparently working in Genoa about 1564, but Venetian documents mention a 'Jacomo di Rigo lauter' in the late 1560s. Ulrich (ii) is described as 'lute maker' in a 1567 Venetian document, but he might have given up his craft, since by 1573 he is called simply 'a merchant'. Magno (i) married in 1529 and had three sons, Magno (ii) (*d* 1576/7), Moisé [Moyses] (*d* 1581), and Abraam (*d* after 1575). After their father's death Magno (ii) and Moisé took over the shop, which had been willed to their mother. Abraam (the black sheep of the family) left in 1561: in 1568, heavily in debt to his brothers, he agreed to a settlement that cut him out of the family business. In 1575 Abraam was accused of heresy by the Inquisition. At the time witnesses stated that he travelled regularly to 'French lands', carrying several hundred ducats' worth of lutes: this might indicate that the French and Italian branches kept in contact. Magno (ii) and Moisé parted amicably in 1571, setting up separate shops. Moisé retained the family shop (at the sign of the 'Black Eagle'), and remained in the family house with his mother. The only son of the three brothers known to have survived into adulthood was Paolo (Paulin), son of Magno (ii), who rented a fairly expensive house with a workshop attached, from 1577 to 1591. Another Magno (iii) worked in Venice from 1589 to 1629: in the past he has been confused with Magno the younger. This third Magno called himself 'son of Rigo' and thus he might have been a cousin of Magno (ii). An archlute by the third Magno (now in *A.W.km*) has been extensively copied in modern times.

Other members of the family include Leonardo the elder (*fl* early 16th century), who lived and worked in Padua; Leonardo the younger (*fl* late 16th century), probably the son of Leonardo the elder, who also worked in Padua before moving to Venice about 1590 and who is said by Baron (1727) to have been the teacher of Michael Hartung; Johann Tieffenbrucker, who was apparently working in Venice in 1592; and Michael (*d* c1585) who is mentioned as a lute maker in the Rosshaupten archives in 1554 and 1573.

Wendelin Tieffenbrucker has created many problems for biographers, in part because of the appearance of his name in different forms, including 'Wendelio Venere'. Instruments with his name bear dates spanning an unusually long period, from 1551 to 1611, and have fuelled speculations that this name might have been shared by several members of the family. Archival discoveries by Peter Király (1994) have shown conclusively that 'Venere' was simply a nickname, and that three lute makers of the family, all working in Padua, produced lutes using this name on the label. Wendelin was a son of one of the Leonardos (probably the elder), and he signed his last lute in 1587: after 1591 the labels bearing his name were altered to remove the patronymic, and by this date Wendelin—who had been at least 50 years old in 1576—had probably died. His activity was continued in the 1590s by his nephew, Christoforo Heberle [Eberle] (*b* c1546; *d* before 1621), whose son Wendelin Heberle (1576–1643) took over the lute-making shop and the nickname of his great-uncle. Such a continuous use of nicknames through several generations of a family was not uncommon in the Renaissance. The initials 'WE', found on some instruments, and the source of considerable speculation in the past, are likely to refer to 'Wendelin Eberle'. Paduan documents also record the death of a lute maker by the name of 'Giorgio Venere' in 1624, at the age of 34. He might be a member of the same family.

A Jachomo Tieffenbrucker seems to have worked in Milan in the 17th century. Moises Tieffenbrucker is known to have worked in Venice in the 18th century, and was apparently the last maker to bear the family name.

Several instruments by members of the family survive in major instrument collections in Europe and North America, most dating from the late 16th century or early 17th. The list includes lutes, archlutes, theorbos, and chitarroni, some with later modifications. Many of those instruments, especially those attributable to Magno (ii), are of the highest quality and must have been commissioned by wealthy patrons. An example of Magno's craftsmanship is the lute now in the Castello Sforzesco in Milan, made of ivory and ebony and richly decorated, that was commissioned by the Duke of Mantua.

BIBLIOGRAPHY

E.G. Baron: *Historisch-theoretisch und practische Untersuchung des Instruments der Lauten* (Nuremberg, 1727/*R*; Eng. trans., 1976, as *Study of the Lute*)

L. Cervelli: 'Brevi noti sui liutai tedeschi attivi in Italia dal secolo XVI° al XVIII°', *AnMc*, bd.5 (1968), 299–337

F. Hellwig: 'Makers' Marks in Plucked Instruments of the 16th and 17th Centuries', *GSJ*, vol.24 (1971), 22–32

R. Bletschacher: *Die Lauten- und Geigenmacher des Füssenes Landes* (Hofheim am Taunus, 1978)

S. Toffolo and M.P. Pedani: 'Una famiglia di liutai tedeschi a Venezia: i Tieffenbrucker', *Il Fronimo*, no.51 (1985), 56–62

S. Toffolo: *Antichi strumenti veneziani 1500–1800: Quattro secoli di liuteria e cembalaria* (Venice, 1987)

G.M. Ongaro: 'The Tieffenbruckers and the Business of Lute-Making in Sixteenth-Century Venice', *GSJ*, vol.44 (1991), 46–54

P. Király: 'Some New Facts about Vendelio Venere', *The Lute*, vol.34 (1994), 26–32

IAN HARWOOD/GIULIO ONGARO

Tielke, Joachim (*b* Königsberg, Germany [modern Kaliningrad, Russia], 14 Oct 1641; *d* Hamburg, Germany, 19 Sept 1719). German luthier and instrument dealer. He was trained in instrument making in a Königsberg workshop where his elder brother Gottfried Tielke (i) probably also worked. He studied medicine and philosophy in Leiden University 1663–4. In 1667 he moved to Hamburg, where he married a daughter of the instrument maker Christoffer Fleischer (*fl c*1622–57) and worked first for his brother-in-law Hans Christoffer Fleischer (1638–*c*1692) before setting up his own establishment. He became a citizen of Hamburg in 1669. One source of information on Tielke's life is a congratulatory work compiled by his friends on the occasion of his golden wedding anniversary (it survives in a modern copy, before *c*1939, *D-Hkm*). He was well known in Hamburg musical circles, since he and his wife were godparents to the children of several musicians. His eldest son, Gottfried Tielke (ii) (1668–after 1719) was a prominent viol player and a member of the Hofkapelle at Kassel (1700–20).

Instruments from Tielke's workshop—which must have employed numerous specialized artisans—were much sought after by royalty and nobility in his lifetime. A surprisingly large number survive, about 180 in all: various kinds of lutes, guitars, citterns, pochettes, barytons, violins, violas d'amore, and especially viols. At least some pochettes bearing his name are evidently the work of the Paris luthier Jacques Regnault (*c*1630–after 1701), indicating Tielke's activity as a dealer in instruments made by others as well as his own. Tielke's versatility is uncommon in makers of his time; instruments from his own workshop are very fine musically and often lavishly decorated with bas-relief, carving, and intarsia of precious and exotic materials, the designs derived from engravings (by artists such as Niklaus Manuel Deutsch, Adrian Muntinck, and Bernard Picart), 16th- and 17th-century emblem books, and contemporary embroidery patterns. The workshop evidently did not continue after his death.

Gottfried (i) (bap. 30 Nov 1639; *d* Legitten (modern Turgenevo) in the district of Labiau (Polessk), Russia, 28 Dec 1682 or 6 Jan 1683) was ordained a Lutheran pastor in 1667 but continued to make and repair bowed and plucked string instruments, as he had done since the early 1660s. Instruments bearing his name but dated after 1682 hint that his workshop might have continued after his death.

BIBLIOGRAPHY

G. Hellwig: *Joachim Tielke, ein Hamburger Lauten- und Violenmacher der Barockzeit* (Frankfurt, 1980)

A. Pilipczuk: 'Dekorative Verwertung alchimistischer und astrologischer Bildelemente auf Joachim Tielkes Gitarre von 1703', *Jb des Museums für Kunst und Gewerbe Hamburg*, vol.2 (1983), 27–40

A. Pilipczuk: 'Joachim Tielke, Instrument-Maker and Merchant of Hamburg: Recent Findings about his Education and Professional Life', *GSJ*, vol.61 (2008), 129–46

B. Hellwig and F. Hellwig: *Joachim Tielke: Kunstvolle Musikinstrumente des Barock* (Berlin, Munich, 2011)

IAN HARWOOD/ALEXANDER PILIPCZUK/R

Tiememen. Trumpet of the Fali people of Cameroon. It is a narrow wooden tube, covered with strips of cowhide, ending in a bell. The whole instrument is approximately 165 cm long and is associated with the chief.

Tiepore. Large musical bow of the Yowabu people of Benin. It measures 1 to 1.3 metres long and has a half-calabash resonator which rests on the player's chest. The string is plucked by his right hand and stopped by a rectangular plaque in his left. The tiepore provides rhythmic and some melodic accompaniment to singing.

Tìêu. Cylindrical end-blown flute of Vietnam, derived from the Chinese *xiao*. It is made of bamboo or bronze and has five fingerholes and a thumbhole.

Tiểu cổ. Small double-headed drum of Vietnam.

Tifigim. Notched flute of the Fali people of Cameroon. It is made from antelope horn, blown from the wider end, and has three or four fingerholes and a range of one and a half octaves. Although mainly used as a solo instrument for personal enjoyment, it is sometimes played with a second flute of the same type.

Tigoto. Globular vessel flute of the Fali people of Cameroon. It is made from the shell of the giant African land snail *Achantina mauritania*, and has a blow-hole and two fingerholes, producing three to five notes.

Tĭgrĭk. Single-string spike fiddle of the Nivkhi people of Siberia. The small cylindrical body, with a skin belly and a small piece of stick as a bridge, is pierced by a long neck with a dorsal peg. It resembles the *ducheke* of the Nanai, the Buryat *khuchir*, and the Mongolian *khuuchir*.

Ṭikārā. Term used in Bengal (eastern India and Bangladesh) and Orissa (eastern India) for the kettledrum. The Orissa ṭikārā is a paired (treble and bass) earthenware kettledrum with the skins braced with ropes and a tuning paste applied to the lower drum. They accompany the martial *paik* and other dances. The Bengali ṭikārā is a single kettledrum that beats time for boat races in East Bengal (Bangladesh) and often accompanies the *śahnāī* (oboe). It is smaller than the similar *kāṙā* of Bengal. See K.S. Kothari: *Indian Folk Musical Instruments* (New Delhi, 1968).

ALASTAIR DICK

Tilincă [telincă]. Harmonic flute of Romania and Moldova. It has a metal or wooden tube 60 to 80 cm long with no fingerholes. Two types are known: *tilincă cu dop*, blown through a stopper or duct (*dop*) at one end, and the *tilincă fără dop*, which is open at both ends and has a bevelled rim (*rost*) against which the player blows. The player holds the tilincă obliquely and obtains a large number of notes from the harmonic series by varying breath pressure and opening or closing the distal end with the forefinger. The tilincă produces three kinds of higher harmonics: when the end of the tube is open; when the end of the tube is closed with the forefinger; and when the end of the tube is partially closed with the forefinger (ex.1). The complete scale encompasses the totality of these harmonics. The lowest pitch, produced by closing the end of the tube, is very difficult to obtain. The instrument is rare but still

Ex.1.

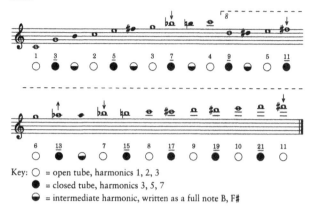

Key: ○ = open tube, harmonics 1, 2, 3
● = closed tube, harmonics 3, 5, 7
◐ = intermediate harmonic, written as a full note B, F♯

encountered in northern Transylvania, Bukovina, and northern Moldova. In 1949, Mihai Lăcătuş, a peasant from Bukovina who played the tilincă, became such a sensation that the instrument was revived. See T. Alexandru: *Instrumentele Muzicale ale Poporului Romín* (Bucharest, 1956), 52–5.

TIBERIU ALEXANDRU/PAPANA OVIDIU/R

Timbales [tymbales]. Generally adopted name for a pair of single-headed, cylindrical drums primarily associated with Latin American dance bands. They are usually teamed with one or two cowbells; the player's rhythmic patterns also involve hitting the sides of the drums. Their metal bodies are usually about 18 cm deep with diameters between 33 and 36 cm, though instruments as small in diameter as 20 cm and as large as 38 cm can be found. While timbales are usually considered to be unpitched, their screw-tensioned heads, invariably of plastic, produce definable notes, normally tuned at a convenient interval. Many 20th-century composers have scored for them; Malcolm Lipkin's *Interplay* (1975) for recorder, harpsichord, viola da gamba, and percussion uses six timbales tuned to *G*, *B♭*, *B*, *c*, *d♭*, and *e♭* instead of timpani. In French terminology, 'timbale' signifies kettledrum and 'timbales' (or occasionally 'tymbales') timpani; 'timbale mécanique' refers to a kettledrum with pedal-operated tuning (for details of Adolphe Sax's *timbale-trompette* (1855) and *timbales chromatiques* (1857), *see* Timpani).

JAMES BLADES/JAMES HOLLAND/JEREMY MONTAGU

Timbre (Lat. *tonus*). In common parlance, a term for the distinctive character of a musical sound, exclusive of pitch and loudness. The terms 'timbre' and 'tone' or 'tone colour' are often used imprecisely and interchangeably. Timbre is the quality that allows a listener to identify an instrument or a particular voice by its sound; the American National Standards Institute (ANSI S1.1–1994 (R1999)) defines timbre as 'that attribute of auditory sensation in terms of which a listener can judge that two sounds, similarly presented and having the same loudness and pitch, are dissimilar'. Scientifically, timbre usually refers to quantitative measures of noise components along with the amplitude (loudness) and distribution of the partials of a tone, their onset, development, duration, and degree of inharmonicity. Attempts to quantify aspects of timbre recognition have used various plottings of attributes into continuous multidimensional 'timbral spaces'. In addition to developing measures for descriptive words such as 'warm', these timbral space distribution methods have been used in synthesizing instrumental sounds and for composition of music using timbres that are changed during the performance.

ANNE BEETEM ACKER

Timbrel. 16th-century and later term for the frame drum. In the 14th century (e.g. Wycliffe's translation of the Bible) it appears more often as timbre or tymbre. In either form it was the most common English translation of the Hebrew *tof*.

JEREMY MONTAGU

Timbrh. Large lamellaphone of the Vute people of east-central Cameroon. Up to 20 tongues are attached to a large upright wooden box resonator, though older instruments in museums have resonators of raffia. The tongues are made of the hard stems of the raffia leaf and are tuned by moving their position on the bridge and by attaching lumps of black wax to their undersides. Characteristically, a needle, also cut from raffia leaf, is attached with wax to the upper surface of each tongue. As the tongue is plucked, the needle buzzes sympathetically, prolonging and amplifying the sound. The instrument is tuned to a pentatonic scale of paired octaves and in present-day practice the tongues are plucked by alternate thumbs. Each thumb strikes two tongues an octave apart and these paired simultaneous octaves alternate with each other. The timbrh is used in ensembles of three or four instruments of different sizes, with a flat rattle.

GERHARD KUBIK

Timiatwos. Term on the Banks and Torres Islands for the only membranophone in the southern part of Melanesia, including the southern Solomon Islands, Vanuatu, New Caledonia, and the Melanesian parts of Fiji. The trunk of a sago palm (*Metroxylon warburgii*) about 45 to 70 cm in diameter is cut to the length of a man's outstretched arms, from fingertip to fingertip, and hollowed, leaving the harder wall of the trunk with a thickness of about 2 to 3 cm and both ends open. At one end three triangles are cut out to form three legs about 60 cm long. A liana surrounds the upper open end of the drum, over which the head is attached. The head is made of several layers of large leaves and sometimes a pandanus mat cover. Informants relate that the timiatwos originates from the island of Vanua Lava. Waterfalls are characteristic of this island and it is said that the sound of the timiatwos characterizes the voice of the waterfall spirit; thus in order to learn how to play the drum it is necessary to listen to the sound of a waterfall. However, the name of the drum comes from *timiat* ('spirit') and *-wos* (a reference to the action of striking).

RAYMOND AMMANN

Timila [thimala]. Double-headed hourglass drum of Kerala, southern India. The wooden body has the form of a greatly elongated hourglass and measures about 60 cm long. The heads, of cow- or calfskin, are mounted on two bamboo hoops and braced by a cord of thin strips of the same material, in W-lacing. The cord is then wrapped once or more times around the middle of the instrument; it allows the drum to be tuned to a definite pitch and, further, vibrates when the head is beaten. The instrument is held diagonally by a fabric strap which the player passes over his left shoulder, and is beaten with bare hands on one head. It is played by members of the Marar community and used in temple music, notably in the *pañcavādyam* ensemble.

BIBLIOGRAPHY

S. Krishnaswami: *Musical Instruments of India* (Delhi, 2/1967), 99 only

C.S. Reck and D. Reck: 'Drums of India: a Pictorial Selection', *AsM*, vol.13/2 (1981), 39–54, pl.4

PRIBISLAV PITOËFF

Timki. Kettledrum of Chhattisgarh, central India. It consists of a hemispherical body covered with oxhide held in place by an interlacing of thongs. This type of drum, which is also found under the name of *turuburi*, is used by the boys of the Muria and Maria hill tribes to accompany their dancing. The dancer carries the drum hung around his neck and beats the head with sticks. The drums, whose bodies are made from pottery, wood, or metal, measure from 20 cm to more than a metre in diameter; they are mostly found throughout tribal India under different names, such as *turam* and *turburi*, or *kundi* and *kundiri*.

BIBLIOGRAPHY

W. Kaufmann: 'The Musical Instruments of the Hill Maria, Jhoria, and Bastar Muria Gond Tribes', *EthM*, vol.5/1 (1961), 1–9

B.C. Deva: *Musical Instruments of India: their History and Development* (Calcutta, 1978)

GENEVIÈVE DOURNON

Timpán [tiompán]. Middle Irish term (Middle English *timpe*) for what was most likely a species of lyre. The Latin word 'tympanum', usually referring to a drum in Continental Latin, was used in certain contexts by medieval insular writers, e.g. Osbern (1090) in his biography of St Dunstan, and Gerald of Wales in his *Topographia Hibernie* (1187), to denote a string instrument. 'Tiompan' is used in modern Irish, but only in a general sense to refer to any musical instrument.

An instrument called *timpán* is mentioned in Irish literature between the 8th century and the 17th. It is generally described as having a body of willow (sometimes ornamented with metal) and three metal strings of which one, according to some references, functioned as a melody string, and the others as a drone. In its early period at least, it was plucked with a long fingernail or plectrum. This is evident from a gloss in a Brehon Law Tract in which it is stipulated that a timpán player who suffered the loss of a nail as the result of a blow was entitled to a 'wing-nail' or quill plectrum in compensation. At some later stage this instrument was also played with a bow, according to 11th-century literary sources.

The sound of a timpán has been described as sweet-stringed, light, pure, and melancholy. It was played by both travelling and resident musicians and was used on occasion to accompany performances of epic and praise poetry at the Irish courts, a timpán player sometimes substituting for the higher-status player of a *crot(t)* or *cruit(t)*. The timpán was also played by women in their separate quarters while engaged in needlework or during their leisure time. Eight performers and two individual patrons are named in annalistic references encompassing of the early 13th century to the late 15th. The decline of the timpán (like that of the Irish harp) seems to have coincided with increasing anglicization of Ireland in the 16th century and also, as elsewhere in Europe, with the rise in popularity of the fiddle.

Clearly identifying the timpán is hampered by a lack of surviving material evidence or systematic technical descriptions. A *cruit* was an instrument used by professional court musicians with the most senior status: in its earlier period the term referred to a lyre, and subsequently to a harp (the Latin term *cithara* and the Anglo-Saxon *hearpe* also had this dual meaning). Because a timpán player was second in rank to a *cruit* player, and because of its small size and number of strings, it is likely that at an earlier stage in its history the timpán was a particular type of small lyre, rather than necessarily being distinct from the *cruit* in a strict organological sense.

The clearly identifiable lyres depicted on early 10th-century Irish high crosses and 12th-century ecclesiastical metalwork (and in a number of north British manuscripts and stone carvings of the 8th–10th centuries) seem to represent varieties of insular models observed from practice. Most are shown as relatively large instruments with apparently six strings, consistent with material evidence from 6th- and 7th-century England, Scandinavia, Germany, and Viking settlements in Russia, as well as with Continental literary accounts of the use of a six-stringed lyre (*cithara*) to accompany chant singers in rehearsal. However, a three-stringed lyre in the hands of a cleric on the 12th-century metal Shrine of the Stowe Missal is at least suggestive of the existence of a smaller sibling.

It is not possible to say precisely how and over what period harps began to replace lyres as the dominant court instrument in medieval Europe. Frame harps appear to have been established at least by 1000 ce, though iconographic evidence suggests that the process may have begun considerably earlier than that. How and when the terminology was adapted to changing circumstances remains a matter for speculation, and may well not have been consistent. Nor is it possible to establish whether the development of the bow was adopted by all timpán players or whether plucked instruments continued in use. Two pieces of evidence do link the bow with 11th- and 12th-century Ireland, in addition to the literary references mentioned above. An early 11th-century bow was excavated from one of the sites of a Viking settlement in Dublin. Although it is not possible to establish the type of instrument on which it was used, it appears to have been manufactured locally, and is the oldest bow so far found in Europe. A 12th-century carving of a figure bowing a six-stringed lyre survives in a church wall at Lough Currane, Co. Kerry.

BIBLIOGRAPHY

A. Buckley: 'What was the Tiompán? A Study in Ethnohistorical Organology: Evidence in Irish Literature', *Jb für musikalische Volks- und Völkerkunde*, vol.9 (1977), 53–88

M. Huglo: 'L'organum à Landévennec au IXe siècle', *Etudes celtiques*, vol.23 (1986), 187–92

A. Buckley: 'A Viking Bow from 11th-Century Dublin', *Archaeologia musicalis*, vol.1 (1987), 10–11

A. Buckley: 'Musical Instruments in Ireland from the Ninth to the Fourteenth Centuries: a Review of the Organological Evidence', *Irish Musical Studies, i: Musicology in Ireland*, ed. G. Gillen and H. White (Blackrock, 1990), 13–57

A. Buckley: 'Music-Related Imagery on Early Christian Insular Sculpture: Identification, Context, Function', *Imago musicae*, vol.8 (1991), 135–99

ANN BUCKLEY

Timpani (It.; Fr. *timbales*; Ger. *Pauken*). European kettledrums. Timpani are the most important percussion instruments of the orchestra, mainly because they produce notes of definite pitch and so can take part in the harmony of a composition. They are tuned precisely, each to a given note, according to the composer's directions, and these notes can be altered as required during a performance (typically for a change of key) by tightening or slackening the drumhead by means of screws or other mechanisms.

1. Construction. 2. Technique. 3. To *c*1600. 4. From *c*1600 to 1800. 5. From 1800. 6. Performance technique.

1. Construction. Each drum consists of a large bowl-shaped resonating shell, or kettle, usually of copper or brass (rarely silver or wood in the past; nowadays sometimes fibreglass), with a drumhead of specially prepared calf- or goatskin or of plastic covering the open top. The head is mounted (lapped) on a wooden 'flesh hoop', over which is fitted a metal ring (counter-hoop), which serves, on many types of timpani, as a means of tightening or slackening the drumhead.

Timpani are divided into two distinct types: 'hand-screw' drums, including cable or chain models, and 'machine' drums. The latter include three main types: lever- or crank-operated, with a single master screw; rotating, in which the entire kettle turns on a threaded screw; and pedal-tuned drums. In all three the counter-hoop is lowered or raised in a single operation. Hand-screw drums (which are supported either on a four-leg stand or on three adjustable legs, which project through sockets at the base of the shell and can be retracted inside the drum when not in use) have threaded bolts, each with its own T-shaped handle (or, before *c*1800, with square-head bolts turned by a key) fitted around the counter-hoop. These engage with brackets on the shell. The counter-hoop conveys pressure to the flesh hoop, on which the head is mounted. The screws are turned one or, usually, two at a time, the latter preferably on opposing sides of the instrument in order to stretch the head as evenly as possible. Correct tuning is not obtained by a given number of turns on the handles, or by a prescribed 'travel' of the pedal; the amount of pressure is variable, and is governed by the condition and thickness of the head, the size of the kettle and, in the case of skin, by atmospheric conditions.

The main factors determining the pitch of a kettledrum are the diameter of the bowl and the tension of the head. The depth and contour of the bowl, which can vary considerably from maker to maker, also influence the sound. Many German and some other timpani of *c*1600–1900 enclose a *Schalltrichter*, a device of copper or brass shaped like a trumpet bell or goblet with hollow stem, soldered vertically above the airhole at the base of the bowl; it improves the sound but by what means is uncertain. The acoustics of vibrating membranes and bowls have been considerably studied but remain controversial. However, investigators generally agree that the bowl magnifies certain overtones in the harmonic series, rendering the note musical, and that a shallow bowl tends to clarify the principal note of the drum, while a deep one increases the resonance and emphasizes lower harmonics. The deeper the bowl, however, the greater the tendency for pitch to flatten on impact. Most modern makers prescribe that the depth of the bowl should equal one half of its diameter. Some bowls are semicircular, others parabolic or with sloping (cambered) sides. No final formula has been agreed upon, and a wide range of types is encountered. Tonal differences are compensated for in part by the timpanist, who can, for example, adjust the striking position to suit the depth of the bowl: reasonably close to the rim for a deeper bowl, and a little nearer the centre for a shallower one. While the sound produced by timpani with an inner device for tuning is arguably inferior, modern machine timpani with well-engineered outer mechanisms and bowl suspension suffer no appreciable loss of tone.

To avoid the necessity of playing a wide range of notes on each timpanum (i.e. to avoid too taut or too slack a head) and to confine each drum to its ideal compass (middle register), a minimum of three timpani is required for orchestral purposes. The diameters of the once-ubiquitous 'symphonic set of three' hand-screw drums are approximately 61 cm, 66 cm, and 74 cm, covering a compass of an octave and a major 3rd: E♭ to B♭; G to d; and c to g. Modern pedal timpani range from about 51 cm to 81.5 cm, giving a range from D to b♭. The diameters of a standard pair of timpani are about 66 cm and 71 cm (formerly in England, about 62 cm and 70 cm), covering a range of more than an octave. It is not unusual for a timpanist to supplement a standard pair of machine drums with a larger and a smaller hand-screw drum. However, a modern symphony orchestra can have a set of five or more pedal timpani to accomodate any musical requirements, such as unusually high or low notes or two or more timpanists playing at the same time.

A further important factor governing the tone quality of a kettledrum is the material, texture, and condition of the head. Until the introduction (*c*1950) of the plastic head—made of a form of polyethylene terephthalate—timpani heads were usually of goat- or calfskin. The best quality skins are those prepared from hides of young animals in prime condition when slaughtered. Thereafter the hide is treated to preserve the skin during the process of unhairing, after which it is strengthened by immersion in a lime solution and stretched on a frame, the 'spine' orientated vertically. It is then scraped by hand or equalized by machinery to a thickness of from 0.125 to 0.175 mm. To mount a vellum head properly, it must first be soaked in cold water until pliable and then lapped completely around the flesh hoop. The lapped head is then placed on the bowl and the counter-hoop adjusted to draw the head slightly down over the rim, giving it a 'collar' to compensate for shrinkage in the head as it dries, thus ensuring the head is sufficiently slack for the lower notes.

Opinions remain divided regarding the relative tonal qualities of natural skin and plastic heads. Traditionalists argue that skin heads produce truer and more 'musical' notes, and prefer calf- or goatskin, especially in historically informed performances and recordings of early music. However, all agree that under extreme atmospheric conditions plastic is preferable. Animal skin is particularly susceptible to humidity, moisture causing the membrane to expand and consequently to produce flatter notes. Indeed, in a damp atmosphere high notes might be unobtainable, for the tension required to reach them can split the skin. Conversely, a cold, dry atmosphere may cause the skin to shrink so much that high notes are sharp and low notes cannot be reached because there is no slack. Consequently, many players using natural skins install heating or moisture-carrying units, fitted inside at the bottom of the kettles. Plastic heads have a noticeably different tone quality, with less resonance and elasticity; notes played on them decay faster and produce more sound, or noise, at low frequencies, thus causing uneven dynamics.

2. Technique. Timpani are played with a pair of drumsticks varying in design, texture, and mass according to the work being played, the instructions of the composer and the choice of the performer. To meet modern demands, a timpanist is equipped with a variety of mallets ranging from those with large ends of soft felt to those with small ends of wood. Increasingly, with the use of plastic heads and the penchant for greater volume of sound, players use harder sticks to increase the necessary 'bounce'. The length and thickness of the shaft, which is of hickory or similar straight-grained wood, bamboo, or cane, vary according to the player's choice and to national tradition; German players, for example, favour bamboo shafts over the metal or hardwood preferred by Americans. The heads of the mallets vary from elliptical to pear-shaped, and in size, weight, and texture, depending on the tone desired. The beating end of a normal timpani mallet consists of an inner core of hard felt, cork, or soft wood, which is covered with one or two layers of white piano-damper felt sliced into discs of varying thickness (the thicker the softer); the discs are formed into a small bag closed up with drawn threads and fitting the core exactly. The mallets are held identically in each hand, with the shaft nearly parallel to the drumhead and gripped firmly between the tip of the thumb and the fingers, the precise distance from the end of the shaft being governed by the length and weight of the mallet. In normal playing, the third and fourth fingers, which are clear of the shaft, act as a cushion. In 'finger rolls', used for soft passages, these fingers help to produce the 'bounce'. In England and the USA especially, the mallets are usually gripped between the thumb and the first joint of the index finger, the thumb positioned on top, while on the Continent, particularly in Germany, the second joint of the index finger is used and the thumb positioned to the side. Alternatively, the mallets can be held between thumb and first three fingers.

In timpani playing alternate beating is the general rule, which applies particularly to the roll, consisting of a succession of single strokes of equal power. The speed of the roll is related in part to the tension of the drumhead, a greater speed being required to keep the head vibrating when tensioned to a high note. Conversely, a slower roll is used on large drums with more slack to avoid a 'belting' sound. In orchestral performance a pair of timpani is placed side by side, the playing areas adjacent, while three or more drums are placed in an arc. The height and tilt of the drums are adjusted to suit the performer. The majority of Dutch, German, central European, and Russian timpanists position the large drum(s) to the right. This tradition may go back to cavalry drums: the mounted cavalry drummer counterbalanced the combined weight of the ceremonial sword worn at his left and the smaller drum by placing the larger, heavier instrument on his right. Most American, British, Italian, and French players position the large drum(s) to the left, following the layout of keyboard instruments. Today, with the almost universal use of pedal timpani, the instruments are usually played from a seated position, especially when tuning during a piece is required.

The essentials of an orchestral timpanist are an accurate sense of pitch, an unerring sense of rhythm, a fluent technique, including the ability to produce a fine tone, and the ability to count during extensive periods of rest or while retuning. The first requirement in tuning a kettledrum is the immediate recognition of the true pitch of its nominal or principal note. This note is one octave above the fundamental. Certain upper harmonics tend to register more strongly than the principal note until the ear becomes accustomed to the pitch of the drum. Tone can confuse pitch perception, particularly because tone changes across the drumhead, the brighter tone being mistaken for sharpness in pitch, while the duller-sounding places can sound flat. In the initial tuning of a hand-tuned drum the opposite pairs of handles are turned simultaneously in succession to ensure that pressure is applied to the head as evenly as possible. The head is then 'trued': the pitch corrected by turning each handle individually. In machine drums, once the head has been 'trued' all successive retunings raising or lowering the counter-hoop can be accomplished by merely turning the lever or adjusting the pedal. The pitch of the drum is tested by flipping the drumhead at the playing spot with the fleshy end of the middle finger, with a light touch of the mallet, or by gently tapping it with a fingernail.

Tuning timpani in a silent, empty concert hall, or while the orchestra is tuning up, is one thing; but changing the pitch of several drums while the orchestra is playing in a foreign key is far more challenging. Being able to 'hear' the proper notes in one's head thus becomes essential, as does a sense of relative pitch—the ability to ascertain precisely the interval between the 'old' and the 'new' note. Tuning in this situation is helped by knowing when another instrument in the orchestra will be playing the desired note; indeed, a timpanist often adds such cues to his or her part. Although the modern timpanist is obliged to cope with considerably more changes of pitch than were earlier players, the tuning gauges fitted to pedal timpani (controlled by the 'travel' of the pedal or the movement of the counterhoop) allow rapid retuning to be accomplished with relative ease. In some cases, as when playing and tuning at the same time, the timpanist must rely on these pitch indicators almost exclusively.

To produce the best possible tone the mallet must spring immediately from the head after the blow has been delivered. The head is occasionally struck at varying distances from the rim, near the rim for a particularly soft tone, towards the centre for a 'thick' tone—the least resonant sound being produced towards the centre. A drum with a skin head will have a 'playing spot' where the sound is most resonant. The player may commence a crescendo roll near the rim of the drum, and with the increasing rise and fall of the sticks move them towards the 'playing spot', reversing direction in a diminuendo roll. The careful player will ensure that the best register of each drum is used for the more important or solo passages, the positioning of such notes often requiring rapid changes on pedal-tuned timpani.

The foundation of timpani technique is a fluent hand-to-hand performance, the drums wherever possible being played with strokes from alternate hands. The double beat on the left or right hand is used only when necessary, perhaps to avoid a difficult crossover beat. In rapid tempo certain crossover beats are not practicable: there is the possibility of the mallets fouling each other (or the rim), or the danger of the drum being struck away from the correct playing spot. In a fast crossover beat between two drums some distance apart the impetus of the movement can result in an unintended *sforzando*. In such circumstances the timpanist uses a double stroke, often in the form of a 'paradiddle', the first two beats being struck by alternate sticks and the last two by one alone. To prevent notes ringing on beyond their time value and where the composer calls for *sec* effects, the vibrations are checked by 'damping'. In damping, the head is touched lightly with the flattened second, third, and fourth fingers (the mallet being held between the thumb and forefinger). Where the speed of a series of short notes renders this method of damping impracticable, a small piece of felt is placed on the head. The practice of damping or 'muting' the kettledrum is frequently met

in orchestral scores. It is indicated by the words *coperti* (It.), *couvertes* or *voilé* (Fr.), or *Dämpfer* (Ger.). *Naturale* (or *scoperti*) is used when the muted effect is to cease. Composers utilize this effect for clarifying certain passages, or to obtain a funereal effect, a tradition of long standing. In contrast to the 'shortening' or deadening of certain notes, two drums may occasionally be tuned to the same note and struck simultaneously to provide greater sonority and brilliance. Striking one drum with both mallets simultaneously is equally rare but effective; it is indicated by giving the written note two tails.

3. To *c*1600. The invention of the kettledrum goes back to remotest antiquity. Hollow tree trunks, tortoiseshells, and clay bowls covered with hide were among the musical instruments of ancient cultures. Possible evidence for the early use of a kettledrum (shaped like a goblet) comes from a Mesopotamian plaque of the early 2nd millennium bce, but it has been suggested that this instrument (*lilis*) might have had a metal head and thus is a bronze drum. A table of instructions found in Uruk (Erech) and dating from about 300 bce provides directions for making a *lilis*; at that time it was a large bowl-shaped instrument with either a head or a cover made from the skin of a bull. In the Egyptian New Kingdom (1550 bce–1070 bce) small kettledrums and vase-shaped drums had appeared, possibly imitations of Sumerian instruments, and probably made of clay, wood, or metal. They were struck by the hands and played, like most other Egyptian instruments of the time, by women. Plutarch (*c*50–*c*120 ce) mentions an instrument called the *rhoptron*, which the Parthians used as a war drum; it sounded like thunder mixed with the bellowing of beasts (*Life of Crassus*). The *rhoptron* (also known as the *tumpanon*) was made of hollowed lengths of pine or fir with a single mouth covered with oxhide. Early references suggest that the early kettledrum was used mainly in rituals or ceremonies, for signalling (rallying troops, for example), or to supply the rhythmic underpinning for dancing: there is no evidence that the drums were tuned to specific notes.

Use of a pair of kettledrums of different sizes (one presumably giving a higher tone than the other) appeared early in African, Indian, Persian, Islamic, and Mongolian cultures. Nakers (small, thong-tightened kettledrums) were adopted in Europe for martial music in consort with trumpets during the 13th-century crusades. Epic poems such as the *Chanson de Roland* (*c*1130) mention nakers, associated above all with the raucous long trumpet (*buisine*, or *cor sarrazinois*) of Muslim armies. Large kettledrums, hemispherical or egg-shaped, measuring approximately 50 cm and 60 cm in diameter, and played mounted on camel or horse by Muslims (especially the Ottoman Turks) and Mongols, had reached the West by the 15th century, and inspired European use of cavalry kettledrums. In the earliest known report, mounted kettledrums appeared in the magnificent entourage of a Hungarian envoy to France in 1457. Virdung (*Musica getutscht*, 1511) wrote disapprovingly of big army kettledrums of copper, which he called *tympana*, likening them to 'rumbling barrels'. A century later, Praetorius (*Syntagma musicum*, ii) called them 'great rattletraps', probably on account of their indistinct tone. Kettledrums spread throughout Europe primarily by way of princely courts in German-speaking lands. Following Eastern custom, they were paired with trumpets—usually six trumpets to a pair of drums—and soon appropriated as a symbol of rank and power. The nobility made possession of timpani an exclusive prerogative of emperors, kings, dukes, electors, and others of high rank. By the 16th century timpani were found in elite military regiments and at the principal courts throughout Europe. Christoph Demartius alludes to them in his *Tympanum militare, Ungarische Heerdrummel und Feldgeschrey* (1600). Mounted kettledrums attracted the interest of Henry VIII, who tried to obtain kettledrums 'in the Hungarian Fashion' and the hire of skilled performers. In the Holy Roman Empire various imperial decrees led in 1623 to establishment of the Imperial Guild of Trumpeters and Kettledrummers. As a guild member, the timpanist held officer's rank, kept himself apart from ordinary musicians and was sworn to guard the secrets of his art. Very large kettledrums mounted on a carriage were known in England towards the close of the 17th century; notable examples include the kettledrums in 'Marlborough's train of 1702' (the great kettledrums of the artillery) and those in the Rotunda Museum, Woolwich, London (96 cm and 101 cm). Paintings of battle scenes often depict a pair of military kettledrums off to one side; such instruments were highly prized as trophies.

During the 16th and 17th centuries timpani evolved from a field instrument—used for parades and outdoor ceremonies and on manoeuvres, and providing an improvised rhythmic music based on the lowest trumpet voice—to a supplemental instrument in the orchestra. Improvisation and conspicuous display gave way over time to more formalized playing, ultimately from written music, for banquets, grand balls, and other events of state. Drafted only as required, these instruments (often together with trumpets) were lent for other large-scale performances, such as operas, oratorios, *Te Deums*, and festive liturgical services, especially at the imperial court in Vienna.

The earliest illustrations indicate various systems of laced and tensioned heads, similar to the bracing of nakers and larger Arabic kettledrums. This method of applying pressure to the head was still used in the 16th century; Mersenne (*Harmonie universelle*) depicted laced kettledrums as late as 1636–7 (fig.1a). However, screw-tensioning was adopted in Germany by the start of the 16th century (fig.1b).

For several centuries the construction of timpani remained virtually unchanged except for gradual enlargement. Timpani of this sort are shown in Hans Burgkmair's *Der Weisskunig* (*c*1514–18) and in illustrations (by Burgkmair and others) for *Maximilian's Triumphal Procession* (*c*1516–18). Henceforth, numerous representations show kettledrums with threaded tuning bolts, or 'side screws', distributed around the rim in varying numbers and used to apply pressure directly to a flesh hoop or indirectly by means of a metal counterhoop. Tuning was accomplished by fitting a separate

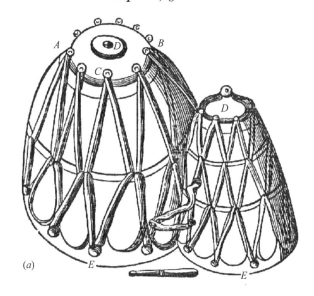

Fig.1: *(a) Lace-tensioned kettledrums: woodcut from Mersenne's 'Harmonie universelle' (1636–7); (b) screw-tensioned kettledrums: woodcut from Praetorius's 'Syntagma musicum' (2/1619)*

key over the square heads of the bolts and turning them in succession. A few illustrations show screws with a ring at the top, through which a short rod was inserted and then twisted. In any case, tuning was laborious and time-consuming. The diameters of the kettles varied. Arbeau (*Orchesographie*) refers to a width of 76 cm, while both Virdung and Mersenne give measurements equivalent to 60–63 cm. The *Heerpauken* illustrated by Praetorius in his *Syntagma musicum* are smaller—44.5 cm and 52 cm. Contemporary examples found in museums vary in diameter from approximately 58 cm to 64 cm.

Early kettledrum mallets were fashioned from ivory or wood and came in various lengths and styles with round, oval, or curved ends. Mallets intended for the cavalry drummer had wrist straps, helpful with the flamboyant style of playing then in vogue, as well as grooves around the shank to provide a secure grip. All the countless illustrations depict a standard grip with all fingers being used, never the snare drum position with the palm turned upwards. The musicianship demanded of a mounted drummer included a sound knowledge of the repertory of beating patterns—learned through long apprenticeship—as well as a good sense of rhythm and ability to follow the trumpeters in their music. Display was an important part of the timpanist's art, and he was expected to create impressive patterns with his arms while playing. Lacking concrete evidence, it is assumed that these early drums functioned much as their Near Eastern prototypes, the large and small ones each producing a different, if indistinct, pitch to aid rhythmic clarity. Later, tuning in 4ths—a plan derived from trumpet technique—became general. Precise tuning became necessary when timpani began to participate in 'composed' ensemble music.

4. From *c*1600 to 1800. From the beginning of the 17th century one finds a growing number of references to kettledrums being used in a variety of contexts. For example, the stage directions of English masques, such as Jonson's *The Golden Age Restored* (1616) cite the instrument. The earliest known written part (a brief extract) is an *Auffzüge für 2 Clarinde [und] Heerpaucken* (*c*1650) by Nikolaus Hasse. Two works by Malachias Siebenhaar consisting of sacred vocal music with instrumental accompaniment, *Des Kirchen Jesu Christi köstlicher Seelen Schmuck* (1661) and *Suaviloquium Dei Sionis mysticum* (1667), call for *Heerpaucken*. Both outdoor carousel and indoor polychoral liturgical music came to include parts for one or two pairs of timpani: for example, Schmelzer's *Arie per il balletto a cavallo* (1667) for the court of Emperor Leopold I in Vienna; and the so-called *Salzburger Festmesse*, thought to have been written about 1682 by Heinrich Biber, includes among its 53 parts two antiphonal wind bands, each with a pair of drums—surely one of the first examples of music for four timpani. The true introduction of timpani into the orchestra took place about 1670. Lully made full and interesting use of them in his operas, beginning with *Thésée* (1675); the drums were tuned in 4ths with the dominant below the tonic. The Moravian composer Vejvanovský scored for kettledrums (*tamburini*) in two serenades (XIV/98, 1680; XIV/45, 1691). In XIV/98 they are tuned in 5ths, with the dominant (*g*) above the tonic (*c*), a tuning employed also by Schmelzer and others because of the higher compass of the smaller cavalry timpani then in use. By the close of the 17th century kettledrums were firmly established as orchestral instruments, their improvisatory role restricted to ceremonial field music. Marc-Antoine Charpentier's *Te Deum* (*c*1690) contains a majestic timpani part. Purcell gave them what is considered their first solo passage in the Symphony to Act 4 of his opera *The Fairy Queen* (1692). He also included timpani in the Ode for St Cecilia's Day (1692) and *The Indian Queen* (1695).

In the first decades of the 18th century numerous festive and ceremonial compositions including timpani were written for the French court: for example, Lalande's *Symphonies pour les soupez du roy* and Mouret's Suite no.1 (*c*1729). Fux's opera *Costanza e Fortezza* (1723), written for the Austrian imperial court, called for two players, each with two drums. Pictorial evidence demonstrates

that timpani were widely used in both sacred and secular music. Their tuning was generally restricted to the trumpeter's keys of D and C, and they were tuned in 4ths: in the former to *A* and *d*, in the latter to *G* and *c*. In rare instances they were tuned in the key of G, the dominant above the tonic; Bach wrote for this tuning in several cantatas. In the cantata *Lobe den Herrn* (formerly attributed to J.S. Bach as bwv143), in the key of B♭, the unknown composer called for drums with the dominant (*F*) below the tonic, reaching the very limit of the larger drum's compass. In general Bach treated the drums as transposing instruments, writing their parts in C in the bass clef with the actual notes indicated at the start of the work. The pitch of the drums (never more than a pair) remained unchanged throughout an entire work. When the key changed the drums were silent, awaiting the return of the original key. While Bach usually employed timpani to support the brass or full choir, on rare occasions he gave them a solo part: the secular cantatas *Vereinigte Zwietracht der wechselnden Saiten* (1726) and *Tönet ihr Pauken!* (1733). The opening solo from the latter was borrowed for the Christmas Oratorio (1734–5), where the timpani herald the choir's motif of rejoicing. Kettledrums are used to dramatic advantage in the B Minor Mass (*c*1747–9). In several instances Bach indicates a roll, but even without such an indication custom dictated that cadential whole notes were to be executed in this way.

Boyce, Handel, and Telemann followed the same tradition: the parts were chiefly rhythmical, the instruments generally played in consort with trumpets as well as in major choral sections, and their pitch did not change during a work. Handel adhered rigidly to the interval of a 4th between a pair of drums; the only exception is *Il Parnasso in festa* (1734) in which he used drums tuned to *G* and *D* in the key of B♭. He was especially fond of 'double tonguing' (e.g. a series of semiquavers *d–d–A–A*, *d–d–A–A*; the term was borrowed from the trumpeter's art); it is found for instance in *Semele* (1744) and the Ode to St Cecilia ('The double, double, double beat of the thundering drum', in 'The Trumpet's loud clangour').

Similar florid writing occurs in the overture to the *Music for the Royal Fireworks*, where Handel prescribes 'Tymp 3 per parte', and the 'Hallelujah chorus' of *Messiah*. For his oratorios Handel constantly requested (and was granted) use of the huge artillery train drums, also known as the Tower Drums. These instruments, said to have been destroyed in a fire in 1841, are thought to have measured 76 cm and 96.5 cm. Drums of this size would have been played an octave lower than written.

After the middle of the 18th century decided advances occurred in the use of orchestral timpani. Francesco Barsanti called for two drums tuned to three different keys in successive movements of his Concerto Grosso (1743). Christoph Graupner's Sinfonietta (1749) features six timpani, in *F*, *G*, *A*, *B♭*, *c*, and *d*, while J.M. Molter's Sinfonia no.99 (*c*1750) uses five, tuned *F*, *G*, *A*, *B♭*, and *c*. The most soloistic of these works is a Sinfonia for eight obbligato timpani and orchestra (?*c*1785), formerly attributed to Hertel but now thought to be by Johann

Carl Fischer, in which the drums span an octave from *G* to *g* and play a daunting virtuoso cadenza. These, however, were considered showpieces and did not enter the standard concert repertory. Uncommon tunings appear in works by Salieri, whose treatment of timpani could well have influenced his pupil Beethoven. In his overture to *La secchia rapita* (1772) Salieri wrote for three drums; in *La grotta di Trofonio* (1785) he called for two, unusually tuned a diminished 5th apart (*C* and *G♭*), and in *Tarare* (1787) for two a minor 3rd apart. Further unusual tunings are found in F.L. Gassmann's opera *Issipile* (1758), where a small drum in *a* is used, and in Sacchini's opera *Oedipe à Colone* (1786), scored for four drums tuned *B♭*, *F*, *b♭*, *f* (an early use of octaves). J.F. Reichardt's 'Battle' Symphony (1781) calls for drums in *E* (a first), *G*, *B*, and *c*; his *Cantus lugubris in obitum Friderici Magni* (1786) features stepwise tuning in *G*, *A♭*, *c*, *d♭*, and *d*. Georg Druschetzky wrote several concertos, including some with six and eight timpani, as well as a concert piece for violin and orchestra ('Ungarica', 1799) with seven.

Haydn, an occasional timpanist, graced many of his symphonies and choral works with finely written and innovative parts for the timpani. The solo roll (on *e♭*) that opens Symphony no.103 (1795) was an effect new to the orchestra and gave the work its name: *Paukenwirbel*, or 'Drum Roll'. The *Missa in tempore belli*, or 'Paukenmesse' (1796) includes a wonderfully dramatic solo, while *The Creation* (1796–8) has seven changes of tuning. Symphony no.94 (1791) might possibly contain the first authenticated change of pitch within a movement (in the fourth movement, from *G* to *A* and back). In Symphony no.102 (1794) he prescribed covered kettledrums ('con sordini') with muted trumpets, an effect used earlier by Mozart and termed 'coperti' in *Idomeneo* (1781) and *Die Zauberflöte* (1791). (This effect was also applied to military kettledrums in funeral processions.)

Mozart, too, made superb use of timpani, particularly in his operas, where they always underline and enhance the dramatic impact. With one exception he confined the tuning of the drums (a pair) to the interval of a 4th, with the tonic as usual above the dominant. This interval is so consistently observed that timpani are omitted from works in the keys of G and A, where, because of the compass of the drums, the interval of a 5th with the dominant above the tonic would be necessary. The exception is his Divertimento (1776) for two flutes, six trumpets, and four timpani tuned *G*, *A*, *c*, and *d*, written for the *Reitschule* in Vienna.

5. From 1800. Beethoven liberated timpani from their purely rhythmic function, in which they were wedded to the trumpets, as well as from the conventional tuning in 4ths and 5ths. He not only made use of other, more unusual, intervals, but occasionally called for dramatic solo passages or chords (used by J.-P.-G. Martini in *Sapho*, 1794). In *Fidelio* (1805) he employed a pair a diminished 5th apart (*A* and *e♭*) in the dungeon scene for truly chilling effect. In the Scherzo of the Seventh Symphony (1811–12) the drums are a minor 6th apart (*A* and *f*), and in the Eighth (1812) and Ninth Symphonies

(1822–4) they are tuned in octaves (*F* and *f*). The final cadence of the Leonore Overture no.3 features a solo roll, a true innovation as the drums carry the harmony. The four solo notes that open the Violin Concerto (1806) provide an example of Beethoven's pioneering writing for timpani, in which the sound of the drums becomes part of the orchestral texture; the repeated rhythmic figures during the transition from Scherzo to Finale in the Fifth Symphony (1807–8) and accompanying the piano solo during the Finale of the 'Emperor' Concerto (1809) are further examples. While the composer remained conservative in calling for only two drums, he chose with consummate care the particular drum to be used at any given moment. He was equally careful in the manner by which he indicated the true roll: always with the tremolo sign. Where Beethoven wrote a note with its stem struck through three times (frequently used today to denote a roll) he intended, like other composers of his period, that the demisemiquavers be strictly observed. Neither Beethoven nor his predecessors specified a particular type of mallet, although at that time leather- or wool-covered mallets were coming into use alongside traditional wooden ones. Dalayrac, in *Lina, ou Le mystère* (1807), seems to have been the first operatic composer to call for *baguettes garnies* in a score; he was followed by Spontini in *Fernand Cortez* two years later.

By the end of the 18th century conventional tunings on the standard pair of timpani seemed unduly restrictive. Operas, with their frequent changes of key, presented a special problem. Shortly before the turn of the century a French maker of military band instruments, Rolles, invented the 'T' handle to replace the system of square-topped tensioning bolts turned with a separate key; the new handles, one to each bolt, allowed somewhat more rapid tuning. However, the range and the number of notes available at any one time were still limited. While some 19th-century composers, such as Schubert, Rossini, Donizetti, and Adam, let dissonances stand or eliminated the drums when their pitches did not fit the harmony, others reacted against these limitations and began to incorporate changes of pitch during a piece or movement and often to add other notes as well, both of which required a third drum. Vogler, in *Samori* (1804), and his student Weber, in the revised overture to *Peter Schmoll* (1807) and the overture *Der Beherrscher der Geister* (1811), were among the earliest to call for three drums. Other composers followed: Auber in *La muette de Portici* (1828), Lachner in his Third Symphony (1834), and Halévy in *Charles VI* (1843). Four timpanists, each playing a pair of drums, were called for in Reicha's *Die Harmonie der Sphären* (before 1826), and in Meyerbeer's *Robert le diable* (1831) four drums were given a melodic solo. Chélard's *Die Hermansschlacht* (1835) also required four timpani. Spohr, in *Des Heilands letzte Stunden* (1834–5), used two players, each executing rolls variously on three drums, to depict the moment of crucifixion. In the third movement of his *Historische Sinfonie* (no.6, 1840) he wrote for an orchestra like Beethoven's, but added a third drum to the previous pair. The 1830s brought a general call for more timpani. Berlioz observed that composers had 'long complained' of the limitations of timpani and he took note of the 'audacious innovation' of three drums newly installed at the Paris Opéra by its timpanist, Charles Poussard. Fétis (1836) and Kastner (1837) suggested adding a third or even a fourth drum to the orchestra to free composers from such restraints. In England Thomas Chipp used three drums when playing with his various London orchestras. (However, the practice continued of transposing an octave down for high notes above a drum's normal compass and an octave up for very low notes, especially when only a pair of instruments was available.) About this time other European orchestras began acquiring three and even four timpani, all machine drums capable of rapid tuning. The instruments now came in varying sizes, with French and English drums larger than German ones. Berlioz deplored those in the Berlin orchestra, considering that they produced an insufficient volume of sound, while Mendelssohn complained about the booming sound of those at the Paris Conservatoire.

During the early 19th century new types of mallet became available. As the loud, brittle sound produced by hard mallets was now often considered inappropriate for orchestral music, an additional pair covered with softer material such as chamois, flannel (introduced *c*1800), or, later, hat felt was introduced. During the 1820s sponge-headed mallets appeared; they are thought to have first been used by Jean Schneitzhoeffer, timpanist at the Paris Opéra. They soon became preferred for producing a more blended sound, especially for rolls. Berlioz called for their 'velvety' sound in *Huit scènes de Faust* (1828–9), *Symphonie fantastique* (1830), and *Harold en Italie* (1834); he introduced them to German orchestras during his tour as conductor (1842), and they were popularized there by the Leipzig timpanist Ernst Pfundt. Kastner (1845) wrote that three types of mallet were 'indispensible': wooden-ended for dry and loud passages; leather- or cloth-covered for ordinary playing; and sponge-headed for a soft sound. By the 1840s piano felt began to be used for timpani mallets. This material, first applied to piano hammers by J.H. Pape in 1826, was much thicker and more refined than hat felt and came in sheets that could be sliced to any thickness. Felt mallets were soon being used by Poussard at the Opéra and by other French timpanists. Carl Gollmick in Frankfurt acquired a pair as did Pfundt in Leipzig. English orchestras retained wooden mallets for several more decades (it was the loud, thudding, bass-drum-like sound produced by these mallets that the visiting Mendelssohn so objected to), and Victor de Pontigny claimed to have introduced felt mallets there in the 1860s.

Berlioz, among his other innovations in orchestration, extended the timpani's dramatic possibilities. He was tremendously impressed with the orchestral effects in Meyerbeer's *Robert le diable* and *Les Huguenots* (1836), the latter including a roll for two timpanists. In his *Grand traité d'instrumentation* he argued that two players, each with a pair of drums, could provide a wider selection of notes and greater flexibility than

had been previously available: while one timpanist was playing, the other could be re-tuning, or both could play together, sometimes with extra percussionists to produce chords. In the manuscript of his *Grande messe des morts* (1837) he called for 32 drums played by 20 timpanists, but he compromised in the printed score, reducing his demands to 16 drums and ten players. Berlioz was the first symphonic composer to call for both sponge- and wooden-headed mallets in a single work: they are used for, respectively, the rumble of thunder (played by four timpanists) and the March to the Scaffold in *Symphonie fantastique*.

About the middle of the century skins changed also, from the thick, unyielding *Kalkfell* that favours overtones over the fundamental, to the thinner, translucent *Glasfell*, chemically treated to create a more refined, focussed, and 'pure' sound. With more refined, thinner heads and with mallets covered with a variety of materials, timpani had, by mid-century, become less dry, percussive and invariably loud, and more responsive to dynamic changes in the music.

During the 19th century numerous inventors in almost every country, often working hand-in-hand with mechanics, locksmiths, and metalworkers, developed mechanisms for rapidly changing the pitch of a drum. Some of the new 'machine drums' had tuning mechanisms on the exterior, like an armature, while others contained a device inside the kettle. The most successful were tuned either by means of a single master-screw or lever, by rotating the kettle, or by using the foot to manipulate a gear wheel or pedal device. In 1812 Gerhard Cramer, court timpanist in Munich, invented the first tuning device with lever and crown gears: the movement of the lever was transferred through an axle and crown gear to a central screw, which raised and lowered (by means of an armature) the hoop on which the head was lapped. Johann Stumpff of Amsterdam introduced a rotary-tuned kettledrum (patented 1821), on which tension on the head was varied by rotating the bowl. The most significant of these early efforts was a machine drum operated by a hand-controlled screw crank connected to a rocker arm that raised or lowered an armature attached by rods to the counter-hoop, thus altering the head's tension. Designed by Johann Einbigler in 1836, it was the prototype for many later designs and attracted the favourable attention of several composers, including Mendelssohn (*AMZ*, xxxviii (1836), 495–6). Cornelius Ward of London patented two different mechanisms in 1837. The first used a cable, pulleys, and turnbuckles activated by a handle projecting from inside the kettle. The second and far superior mechanism employed pairs of racked (toothed) levers, or bars. By turning a notched pinion between them, corresponding motion was transferred to the rim, tightening or relaxing the head. Ward's new machine drums were first tried 1836–7 at Covent Garden and in the Philharmonic concerts and gained the attention of Wagner, then conducting in Dresden. About 1840 August Knocke, a Munich gunsmith, brought out a drum with an elaborate gear train that raised or lowered the head. The player tuned by using one foot to turn a notched wheel. In spite of their rather cumbersome mechanism, Knocke's drums were adopted by several German orchestras; one pair was used for rehearsals by the Staatsoper in Munich until 1963.

There were also less successful tuning devices. The Parisian instrument-maker Darche invented (before 1845) a drum involving several pedals operating on a series of internal concentric rings, each reducing in succession the head's circumference when pressed up against it, and thus raising the pitch. Carlo Boracchi, timpanist at La Scala, invented a mechanism consisting of a lever at the base of the drum which, when pushed to the right or left, turned a central screw raising or lowering the head (1842). For Adolphe Sax's *timbales chromatiques* (patented 1857), the normal bowl was replaced by a shallow frame to which the head was mounted. Henry Distin (London, 1856), Max Puschmann (Chemnitz, 1880), and George Potter (Aldershot, 1884) developed machine drums with exterior rod tensioning; Köhler & Sons (London, 1862) and Louis Jena (Reudnitz, nr Leipzig, 1877) used interior levers and screws or cams. None of these inventions endured: technical shortcomings or materials lacking the necessary tensile strength caused them all to be superseded.

The final stage in the evolution of machine drums was reached with the 'Dresden' model of Carl Pittrich (1881), which had a pedal tuning device (*Stimmvorrichtung*) that could either be attached to a drum of the Einbigler type or incorporated into a new instrument during manufacture. The device was made of strong steel and used mechanical couplings to convert the semicircular motion of the pedal into the motion of a base plate, to which struts leading to the counterhoop were attached. Accuracy was aided by a tuning gauge. This mechanism was far more reliable, rapid, and powerful than other types, enabling the timpanist to tune precisely, even while playing, and offering composers additional freedom in writing for the instrument. Pittrich's genius extended to marketing: since his new mechanism could be installed on existing drums, older lever-operated timpani could be converted rather than discarded. The way was led by Otto Lange, timpanist in the Dresden court orchestra, who had pedals attached to his pair of drums as soon as they become available. The Leipzig Gewandhaus Orchestra acquired a pair of new timpani with this mechanism in the mid-1880s, and in time such instruments were adopted by virtually every major orchestra in Europe.

Among other 19th-century inventions were the Votivtimpani introduced by V.F. Červený of Hradec Králové in 1876 and improved by him in 1882. The body of each one was a freely suspended resonating chamber in the form of a truncated cone with four to six tuning handles.

In Germany writing for the timpani was influenced by both the availability of three or four drums in the orchestra and the innovation of machine (or rapid) tuning. Mendelssohn tried out the Einbigler lever timpani in Frankfurt, and a set of three was acquired for the Leipzig Gewandhaus Orchestra during his tenure as conductor (his timpanist there was the excellent Pfundt). Mendelssohn's *St Paul* (1836) requires three drums. In the final version of *Die erste Walpurgisnacht* (1843), written after the Leipzig orchestra acquired the Einbigler machine drums, he added notes demanding rapid tuning: in *Elijah* (1846) he included several changes of pitch that had to be made in a few seconds. Schumann was also influenced by Pfundt, a cousin by marriage, and on his advice wrote for three timpani instead of two in his First Symphony (1841). His Symphony no.4 (1841, rev. 1851) calls for several changes of pitch during the first movement: A and d to A♭ and d♭ to B and e and back to A and d. In *Genoveva* (1847–8) re-tunings must be accomplished rapidly, in under one minute each. Liszt called for four drums in his symphonic poem *Festklänge* (1853), as well as in the last movement of his *Faust-Symphonie* (1854–7), in which at one point the drums are tuned stepwise to B♭, B, c, and c♯. Wagner used two players, each with a pair of machine drums, throughout the *Ring* (1869–76), adding richness to the score by often having both timpanists, with their four available notes, playing together or having one re-tune while the other was playing. His masterly solo rhythmic passages underline the emotional content of the scores.

In his use of percussion, Mahler followed the model of Berlioz and Wagner. His symphonies usually require two timpanists, each with three drums, and the parts are often melodic rather than merely rhythmic. For the First Symphony (1884–8) he appears to have had machine drums in mind, but without the pedal mechanism: during a roll on low F in the first movement he directed that a second percussionist lower the drum to E. However, in discussing an upcoming performance of his Symphony no.7 (1904–5) in 1908, Mahler wrote that 'the timpanist must have very good pedal-tuned drums'. The Rondo burleska of his Ninth Symphony (1908–9) contains a rapidly descending scale-wise pattern on one drum; the succession of pitches is: f, A, e, A, d, A, c, A. Richard Strauss, a master of atmospheric and dramatic orchestration, raised demands on the player to a new level. He took for granted the availability of four pedal drums, and often required the performer to tune while playing, count measures in changing time signatures and watch the conductor all at the same time. His innovations commenced with *Till Eulenspiegel* (1894–5) and peaked in his operas *Salome* (1905) and *Elektra* (1909), the former including descending and ascending scales and passages of semiquavers so rapid that the composer asked for the drums to be 'rearranged' so that the player could alternately strike the two closest instruments followed by the two outside ones. In Salome's dance, often performed separately as a concert piece, Strauss indicated which notes could be omitted if pedal timpani were unavailable.

Russian composers also made full use of timpani, often writing very high notes. Glinka's *Ruslan and Lyudmila* (1837–42) includes an effective solo for three drums (A, d, and g—the third an unusually high note). Rimsky-Korsakov also used a drum tuned to g, in his *Russian Easter Festival Overture* (1888), while in his opera-ballet *Mlada* (1889–90) he called for two or three timpanists, the latter at one point with a *piccolo timpano* (approximately 46 cm) tuned to *d'*. Tchaikovsky consistently scored for three drums, often with unusual tunings; he occasionally called for four timpani, as in the Polonaise and Waltz in *Yevgeny Onegin* (1877–8). Stravinsky, who wrote very complex, rhythmically demanding parts for the instrument, required two drummers plus an occasional third in *The Rite of Spring* (1911–13). At one point five drums, including one tuned to *b*, are struck simultaneously. In *Renard* (1915–16), he called for a glissando.

Mechanical developments during the 20th century took place mainly in the USA, where few of the heavy 'Dresden' pedal drums were available. Timpanists there often had to supply their own instruments, and consequently, portability and quick assembly were prerequisites. In the period 1911–13 W.F. Ludwig and his brother-in-law, R.C. Danly, designed the first American pedal timpani, with a hydraulic foot pump that operated an expandable rubber tube that pressed up against the skin and a calibrated pressure gauge for tuning. However, the tendency of the tube to burst under pressure prompted them to abandon this approach, and in the period 1917–20 they designed an improved model that relied on flexible cables and a self-locking clutch-and-pawl mechanism. Sets of three (76 cm, 71 cm, and 64 cm) were purchased by the Chicago SO, the Detroit SO, and the Philadelphia Orchestra. Ludwig's pioneering efforts culminated in the 'balanced action' mechanism (1923–5), which utilized a compression spring to hold the pedal in place, and a rod linkage inside the kettle attached to the tuning screws. Cecil Strupe, factory superintendent of the Leedy Drum Company, introduced a ratchet and pawl clutch for locking the pedal in place (patented 1923). The copper bowls of Leedy's drums were formed in a hydraulic press rather than hammered over wooden molds. Such timpani were exported to Britain during the 1920s and served as the model for the first English machine drums, manufactured by the Premier Drum Company.

In Europe a unique type of lever timpani was invented in the early 1900s by Hans Schnellar, timpanist in the Concertgebouw and later the Vienna Philharmonic orchestras. He produced several models, including portable *Reisepauken*, all based on a screw operating on a rocker-arm to raise or lower the kettle against the flesh hoop. A unique pair, based on the same principle, is still used by the Concertgebouw in Amsterdam. The shape of Schnellar's instruments (the kettles were all the same depth, whatever their diameter) gave them a unique, 'tubby' sound. In the 1980s Günter Ringer of Berlin produced an updated model of the 'Dresden' pedal timpani featuring a 'cambered' shape, hand-hammered copper kettles, and improved pedal mechanism. In the early 21st century these instruments were used in major orchestras throughout the world; in the USA they were manufactured by Ludwig Industries.

By the early 20th century pedal timpani were in use in virtually all major orchestras, except in Britain, where the pair of 'Dresden' timpani acquired by Sir Henry Wood in 1905 remained the only ones until 1930. Composers soon began to exploit the instruments further. Among the earliest and clearest examples of the use of pedal timpani are the chromatic runs in d'Indy's Second Symphony (1902–3) and *Jour d'étéà la montagne* (1905), where the composer, a former timpanist, specified *timbales chromatiques*. Credit for first use of a glissando might be due to Walford Davies, who, in his *Conversations* for piano and orchestra (1914) included this effect as well as chromatic passages. Carl Nielsen's Fourth Symphony (1914–16) includes a passage for two timpanists, playing a minor 3rd apart and rising chromatically from *F* and *A* to *d♯* and *f♯* respectively. Bartók employed the glissando frequently, for example in his *Cantata profana* (1930), *Music for Strings, Percussion, and Celesta* (1936), and the Sonata for two pianos and percussion (1937) as well as in his *Concerto for Orchestra* (1943–5). Roy Harris's Symphony no.7 (1952) and Panufnik's *Sinfonia sacra* (1963) call for glissandos; in the latter a solo descending from *e* to *E* and, later, rising back up again, is played with wooden mallets. Numerous composers favoured two timpani parts of two or three drums each: Wolf-Ferrari's *La vita nuova* (1901), Loeffler's *La mort de Tintagiles* (1900), Delius's *Song of the High Hills* (1911–12), Sibelius's *The Oceanides* (1914), and Holst's *The Planets* (1914–16). Requests for chords and for extremely high notes requiring piccolo timpani became increasingly common. Milhaud, for example, used *d'* and *f♯'* in *La création du monde* (1923) and Ravel's *L'enfant et les sortilèges* (1920–25) calls for a *d'*. Slavic composers, Janáček in particular, were fond of these sonorities. His *Sinfonietta* (1926) uses small timpani tuned to *g♭*, *a♭*, and *b♭*. Ives, Copland, Piston, Schuman, and Hartmann also favoured high drums tuned to *g* or *a* as well as low ones tuned to *E*. However, large timpani tuned to very low notes were not new: Wagner had required an *E* in *Parsifal* (1882) and Mahler a *D* in his Second Symphony (1888–94). Strauss wrote for three low drums in *Die Frau ohne Schatten* (1914–17), where the 'Keikobad' motif at one point is played by timpani in *E♭*, *F♭*, and *A♭*. English composers favoured the deep, resonant quality of big drums; they are used, for example, in Elgar's *Sea Pictures* (1897–9), Vaughan Williams's *Sea Symphony* (1903–9), and Britten's *Peter Grimes* (1944–5). Elsewhere, Casella's *Italia* (1909), Busoni's *Rondò arlecchinesco* (1915), and Hartmann's Seventh Symphony (1959) call for a low drum tuned to *E*, while Berg's *Wozzeck* (1917–22) uses timpani in *C* and *D*. In rare cases *timpani bassi* are requested. Stokowski, in his arrangement of Bach's *Komm, süsser Tod*, required a drum in *C* and in the *Toccata and Fugue* one in *D* (a 90 cm drum was made especially for the Philadelphia Orchestra by Ludwig). Harsányi's *Suite pour orchestre* (1927) even required the note *B'*.

Composers also began to call for unusual tone colours and special effects. Elgar, in his 'Enigma' *Variations* (1898–9), had asked for a roll played with side-drum sticks, although it became the custom, with his approval, to perform this tremolo with two coins. Stanford's *Songs of the Fleet* (1910) required a fingertip roll, and Holst's *The Perfect Fool* (1918–22) called for alternating a felt and a wooden mallet. Havergal Brian's daringly orchestrated 'Gothic' symphony (1919–27) requires some 100 musicians, including two timpanists each with three drums on stage, and four other players offstage to accompany the four spatially separated brass choirs in the *Te Deum* movement. Ottmar Gerster's *Capricietto* (1932) for four timpani and orchestra requires superb technique and considerable virtuosity. Timpani have a prominent role in Poulenc's Concerto for organ, strings, and timpani (1938), and in Martin's Concerto for seven wind instruments, timpani, percussion, and strings (1949). Henze's Symphony no.3 (1949–50) has an extremely complex timpani part, while Britten's *Nocturne* for tenor solo, seven obbligato instruments, and string orchestra (1958) has ascending and descending chromatic passages between E and $g\sharp$, planned carefully so that each drum restarts on the note on which it had halted previously. Bliss, in his *Meditations on a Theme of John Blow* (1955) asked that a cymbal be placed on one drumhead and struck with a glockenspiel mallet, while in Britten's *Death in Venice* (1973) the drums are hit with a bundle of twigs. Challenging timpani parts occur in Tippett's First Symphony (1944–5) and *King Priam* (1962), Copland's Third Symphony (1944–6), and Carter's *Concerto for Orchestra* (1968–9).

Works for unaccompanied timpani include Daniel Jones's Sonata for three unaccompanied kettledrums (1947), Carter's *Eight Pieces for Four Timpani* (1950–66) and *Variations for Orchestra* (1955, rev. 1966), Ridout's Sonatina for timpani (1967), and Graham Whettam's Suite for four timpani (1982). Concertos for timpani and orchestra include Donatoni's *Concertino* for strings, brass, and timpani (1952), with effects such as hitting the centre of the drumhead, Werner Thärichen's (1954), demanding consummate performing skill, Harold Farberman's (1962), and William Kraft's (1983), notable for its four-note chords and the unusual sonority created by playing with the hands while wearing leather driving gloves with felt or moleskin patches glued to their fingertips. Each drummer in the *Concert Fantasy for Two Timpanists and Orchestra* by Philip Glass (2000) has seven drums; the piece includes playing with different kinds of sticks, dragging a mallet across a drumhead and placing the palm of the hand on the skin for added effect. Arguably the most challenging and virtuosic if not unique piece in today's repertory is Kraft's Second Concerto, which calls for a 'battery' of drums: six conventional pedal timpani as well as nine specially made small drums tuned to fixed pitches and mounted in a semicircular super-structure above the player, providing a total range from e' to C.

6. Performance technique. Before the advent of written parts in the mid-17th century, the kettledrummer always performed *ad lib*, his music based upon the lowest trumpet part of the military ensemble of trumpets and drums. Kettledrummers developed a repertory of stock formulae that were elaborations of basic note patterns; these were used for field and ceremonial music, occasionally in other genres. Best known by their German term *Schlagmanieren*, they ranged from quaver, semiquaver, and demisemiquaver figures to special rolls and crossover beatings. They were embellishments in that they were selected from a repertory of formulas, but improvisations in that the experienced performer was left much to his own judgment concerning what to use and when. Both Eisel (1738) and Altenburg (1795), the latter writing after the high point of this practice, but before it had disappeared, outlined the basic formulas (14 or so) that an apprentice drummer had to perfect and commit to memory. With the development of the orchestra, the acceptance of timpani into it and the advent of written parts for them, a new, orchestral style of playing emerged; as composers incorporated many of these patterns into their scores it became less necessary for orchestral performers to play *ad lib*. Numerous *Schlagmanieren* are embedded in the music of Bach and Handel. But although the practice of improvising *Schlagmanieren* seems to have died out in France by the mid-19th century (Kastner reported in 1845 that Poussard, timpanist at the Paris Opéra, did not recognize any of them), it remained alive elsewhere, even in the orchestra. According to Carlo Boracchi, timpanist at La Scala, Milan, many of these stock formulas were still being used in Italy in 1845. It was in Germany above all that such elaborations continued; Pfundt wrote (1849) that he employed many of them, as well as varieties of rolls and beating patterns, in playing music of Meyerbeer and Rossini, for example. However, in 1862 Fechner claimed that 'today timpanists employ only a few of these, simply playing the music the way it is written'.

Until the 19th century mallets were gripped firmly between the thumb and the other four fingers, which were wrapped around it. However, in order to provide more of a recoil (far superior for rolls) and thus a clearer tone, the mallet came to be held between the thumb and the second joint of the index finger, the principal movement coming from the wrist rather than the forearm. In Germany especially the thumb was turned inwards, providing more power and a faster roll. At first, timpani were hit at or near the centre of the head. But the loud, dull thuds proved inappropriate for indoor orchestral playing, which required a precise, well-modulated tone. Haydn, while surely not the first to have objected to the former sound, has been credited with having demonstrated to the conductor George Smart in 1794 how to hold the mallets and strike the drum (obliquely rather than straight on and, probably, nearer to the rim) to create a 'bounce' and thus a better sound. With hard mallets, dynamics were controlled by the amount of pressure and the distance from the rim (softer passages were played very close to the edge). To add volume to a series of *forte* notes the timpanist hit the drum with both mallets, one striking about 7–10 cm closer to the centre, for greater resonance. These techniques were never notated, but were mentioned in contemporary manuals.

By the late 20th century the method of holding the mallets had changed, especially in the UK and North America. In those places the mallets are usually held between the thumb and the first, rather than the second, joint of the index finger, with the thumb on top of the mallet rather than facing inwards, as on the Continent. It has been argued that 'flicking' the mallet with the tip of the finger produces a more instantaneous 'bounce' and therefore a clearer tone. However, this thumb position places the wrist in an awkward position for rapid flexing up and down, and most modern timpanists who have adopted it cannot alternate their strokes so quickly as those using the so-called 'Continental' method.

Before the 20th century there were several types of rolls. In the so-called simple roll the drum was struck with the right and left mallets in rapid alternation. For the double roll the first stroke of each beat was played on the drum tuned to the tonic, with succeeding strokes played on the drum tuned to the dominant or subdominant, the pattern repeating itself until the final, accented stroke on the tonic. By the 1840s this technique had been modified so that one mallet rolled on the tonic drum while the other passed back and forth quickly between the two instruments. For the equally impressive 'bolt of lightning' roll, a fist stroke on the tonic drum was followed by a continuous roll on the other, ending with a final stroke on the tonic again. During the first half of the 19th century rolls were often played using the side-drum technique: two strokes with one mallet followed by two of the other (r, r, l, l, r, r, etc.). By the 1840s both methods existed side by side; Pfundt claimed that the alternating method was superior in tone quality, but noted that in long rolls with changing dynamics it was quite acceptable to rest one hand in soft passages by playing with a single mallet using the rebound, or repeated stroke, technique. He further advised using the rebound technique to eliminate cross-beating, as when playing triplets involving two strokes on one drum followed by one stroke on the other. By the time Fechner wrote his treatise on kettledrums (1862) the side-drum method had all but disappeared, due in part to the general use of sponge-headed mallets providing more 'bounce' and capable of faster rolls.

Cadences, particularly final ones, had always provided the timpanist with an opportunity for playing loud rolls and for conspicuous display. This was especially true during the Baroque, when the mounted kettledrummer was expected to end with a flourish, demonstrating his elegance and skill. In describing just such a procedure, Speer (1697) printed what amounts to a virtual cadenza for the instrument, adding that the drummer should execute a long roll until the trumpeters had played their final note, after which he should perform improvised figures on both drums, concluding with a strong final stroke on the tonic. During the 18th century these solo flourishes disappeared except in field music, but a vestige of the practice remained: the timpanist always rolled the final note of a cadence and ended with a loud single stroke. When a drum part concluded with a crotchet or a minim, with nothing more in the measure although the rest of the orchestra continued to the end, the timpanist filled up the measure with notes coinciding with the rhythm or else with a roll. The speed of the roll (as opposed to the rhythmically

articulated tremolo) was governed by both the duration of the note (the longer the faster) and by the musical context: the more spirited, lively, and heroic the music, the faster the roll, and conversely, the slower or more stately, the slower the roll.

Exploitation of various tone colours and effects characterizes the use of timpani in much modern music: for example, glissando passages, stepwise progressions, hitting a drum in the centre, using a different type of mallet in each hand, or playing with wire brushes or coins. There seems to have been a fundamental shift, particularly in North America, away from the concept of timpani as an ensemble instrument, supporting or underpinning the music, towards the idea that timpani are essentially a solo instrument. Indeed, many timpanists add notes to their parts at will, ignoring earlier performing practices. Whereas before the middle of the 20th century timpani blended into the orchestral texture (a fact made abundantly clear in early recordings), by the end of the century the instruments sounded more forward, louder, and more 'percussive'. There has also been a corresponding change away from larger and softer mallets to smaller, harder ones, in part to achieve a proper rebound on the more resistant plastic heads, in part to match the generally louder dynamic level. In short, earlier practice was less obtrusive, whereas that of the end of the century was more conspicuous. It is almost as though timpani have come full circle, and are again considered a virtuoso and display instrument, as they were some 300 years ago.

BIBLIOGRAPHY

M. Mersenne: *Harmonie universelle* (Paris, 1636), vol.3, book 7

D. Speer: *Grund-richtiger ... Unterricht der musikalischen Kunst* (Ulm, 1687, enlarged 2/1697/R), 105–8

J.P. Eisel: *Musicus autodidaktos: oder, Der sich selbst informirende Musicus* (Erfurt, 1738/R), 67–8

J.E. Altenburg: *Versuch einer Anleitung zur heroisch-musikalischen Trompeter- und Pauker-Kunst* (Halle, 1795/R; Eng. trans., 1974)

J. Fröhlich: *Systematischer Unterricht zum Erlernen und Behandeln der Singkunst uberhaupt: so wie des Gesanges in offentlichen Schulen und der vorzüglichsten Orchester-Instrumente* (Würzburg, 1822–9), vol.2, 489–519

J.G. Kastner: *Traité général d'instrumentation* (Paris, 1837, 2/1844)

C.A. Boracchi: *Manuale del timpanista* (Milan, 1842)

E.G.B. Pfundt: 'Maschinen-Pauken für grosses Orchester', *ZfM*, vol.19 (1843), 143f

H. Berlioz: *Grand traité d'instrumentation et d'orchestration modernes* (Paris, 1843, 2/1855/R; Eng. trans., 1856, rev. 2/1882/R by J. Bennett), 214

J.G. Kastner: *Méthode complète et raisonné de timbales* (Paris, 1845)

C. Reinhardt: *Der Paukenschlag: eine Anl[eitung], wie man ohne Hilfe eines Lehrers die Pauken schlagen lernen kann* (Erfurt, 1849)

E.G.B. Pfundt: *Die Pauken: ein Anleitung dieses Instrument zu erlernen* (Leipzig, 1849)

P. Pieranzovini: *Metodo teorico-prattico per timpani* (Milan, c1860)

G. Fechner: *Die Pauken und Trommeln in ihren neueren und vorzüglicheren Konstruktionen* (Weimar, 1862)

V. de Pontigny: 'On Kettledrums', *PMA*, vol.2 (1875–6), 48–57

A. Deutsch: *Pauken-Schule zum Selbstunterricht geeignet/Tutor for the Kettle-Drum Adapted for Self-Tuition* (Leipzig, 1894)

E.G.B. Pfundt: *Paukenschule, neu bearbeitet und durch eine Schule der kleinen Trommel vermehrt von Hermann Schmidt 3* (Leipzig, 1894)

O. Seele: *Pauken-Schule zum Selbst-unterricht* (Leipzig, 1895)

H. Knauer: 'Die Pauken', *Musik-Instrumentenkunde in Wort und Bild*, ed. E. Teuchert and E.W. Haupt, vol.3 (Leipzig, 1911), 165–71

J. Baggers: 'Les timbales, le tambour et les instruments à percussion', *EMDC*, II/iii (1927), 1684–94

P.R. Kirby: *The Kettle-Drums* (Oxford, 1930)

O. Kristufek: *The Ludwig Tympani Instructor* (Chicago, 1930)

F. Kruger, *Pauken- und kleine Trommel-Schule* (Berlin, 1942)

S. Goodman: *Modern Method for Tympani* (New York, 1948)

H.G. Farmer: *Handel's Kettledrums and Other Papers on Military Music* (London, 1950/R, 2/1960)

L. Torrebruno: *Il timpano. Technica dello strumento ad uso dei compositori, dei direttore d'orchestra e degli esecutori* (Milan, 1954)

C. Titcomb: 'Baroque Court and Military Trumpets and Kettledrums', *GSJ*, vol.9 (1956), 56–81

A. Shivas: *The Art of Tympanist and Drummer* (London, 1957)

H.C. Hardy and J.E. Ancell: 'Comparison of the Acoustical Performance of Calfskin and Plastic Drumheads', *JASA*, vol.33/10 (1961), 1391–5

Percussive Notes (1962–) [journal of the Percussive Arts Society]

Percussionist (1963–)

G. Avgerinos: *Lexikon der Pauke* (Frankfurt, 1964)

H.W. Taylor: *The Art and Science of the Timpani* (London, 1964)

C. Caskel: 'Trommeln und Pauken: Der neuere Zeit', *Die Musik in Geschichte und Gegenwart*, vol.13 (Kassel, 1966), 752–63

W. Kotónski: *Schlaginstrumente im modernen Orchester* (Mainz, 1968)

K. Peinkofer and F. Tannigel: *Handbuch des Schlagzeugs, Praxis und Technik* (Mainz, 1969)

J. Blades: *Percussion Instruments and their History* (London, 1970, 2/1974)

R.M. Longyear: 'Altenburg's Observations (1795) on the Timpani', *Percussionist*, vol.7 (1970), 90–93

D. Charlton: 'Salieri's Timpani', *MT*, vol.112/1544 (1971), 961–2

D.L. Smithers: 'The Hapsburg Imperial *Trompeter* and *Heerpaucker* Privileges of 1653', *GSJ*, vol.24 (1971), 84–95

E.A. Bowles: 'Eastern Influences on the Use of Trumpets and Drums during the Middle Ages', *AnM*, vol.27 (1972), 3–28

R.M. Longyear: 'Ferdinand Knauer's Percussion Enterprise', *GSJ*, vol.27 (1974), 2–8

J. Blades and J. Montagu: *Early Percussion Instruments from the Middle Ages to the Baroque* (London, 1976)

E.A. Bowles: 'On Using the Proper Tympani in the Performance of Baroque Music', *JAMIS*, vol.2 (1976), 56–68

G. Facchini: *Il Timpano: il suo evoluzione storica e technologica dale origini ad oggi, con guida per la fabbricazione delle bachette, discotraphica, lessico e letterature timpanistica*, 2 (Padua, 1977)

H. Tobischek: *Die Pauke: ihr spiel- und bautechnische Entwicklung in der Neuzeit* (Tutzing, 1977)

N. Benvenga: 'August Knocke's Timpani', *Percussive Notes*, vol.16 (1978), 3f

J. Holland: *Percussion* (London, 1978)

N. Benvenga: *Timpani and the Timpanist's Art: Musical and Technical Development in the 19th and 20th Centuries* (Göteborg, 1979)

G.S. Goodall: 'Early 19th Century French Timpani Practices: an Explication and Analysis of Jean George Kastner's *Méthode complète et raisonné de timbales*' (thesis, U. of California, Los Angeles, 1979)

H. Powley: 'Two Little-Known 19th-Century Timpani Tutors: Suggestions toward More Authentic Performance Practices', *Liberal Arts Review*, vol.7 (1979), 76–91

E.A. Bowles: 'Nineteenth-Century Innovations in the Use and Construction of the Timpani', *JAMIS*, vols.5–6 (1979–80), 74–143

T.D. Rossing, C.A. Anderson, and RI Mills: 'Acoustics of Timpani', *Percussionist*, vol.19 (1982), 18–30

T.D. Rossing: 'The Physics of Kettledrums', *Scientific American*, vol.247/5 (1982), 172–8

M.H. Schmid: 'Pauken in der Münchner Mussen', *Bericht über des 7. Symposium zur Fragen des Musikinstrumentenbaus* (Blankenburg, 1987), 18–49

S.L. Barnhart: *The Development of Timpani and their Repertory in Western Europe during the Seventeenth and Eighteenth Centuries* (diss., U. of Kansas, 1989)

E.A. Bowles: 'The Double, Double, Double Beat of the Thundering Drum: the Timpani in Early Music', *EMc*, vol.19/3 (1991), 419–35

O. Biba and W. Schuster: 'Das Schlagwerk', *Klang und Komponist: Ein Symposium der Wiener Philharmoniker* (Tutzing, 1992), 164–7

E.A. Bowles: 'The Kettledrum', *Encyclopedia of Percussion*, ed. J.H. Beck (New York, 1995), 201–26

P. Kogan: 'Henry Dennecke, Jr', *Percussive Notes*, vol.33 (1995), 56–64

L.S. McCausland: 'The Plastic Drumhead in History and Development', *Encyclopedia of Percussion*, ed. J. Beck (New York, 1995), 277–80

J.B. Strain: 'Published Writings on Methods for Percussion', *Encyclopedia of Percussion*, ed. J. Beck (New York, 1995), 185–9

H. Buchta: *Pauken und Paukenspiel im Europa des 17.–19. Jahrhunderts* (Heidelberg, 1996)

J.W. Cooper: 'Percussion and Timpani', *A Performer's Guide to Seventeenth-Century Music*, ed. S. Carter and J. Kite-Powell (New York, 1998)

R. Meucci: 'I timpani e gli strumenti a percussione nell'ottocento italiano', *Studi Verdiana*, vol.13 (1998), 183–254

J.K. Page: 'Brass and Percussion Instruments and Players in Vienna, 1740–1760, According to the Wiener Diarium', *Historic Brass Journal*, vol.10 (1998), 21–56

L.A. Spivak: 'Kettledrums: a European Change in Attitude, 1500–1799', *Percussive Notes*, vol.17 (1998), 54–9 and vol.18 (1999), 57–61

A. Lidner: *Die Hoftrompeter und Hofpauker im 18. und 19. Jahrhundert* (Tutzing, 2000)

E.A. Bowles: *The Timpani: a History in Pictures and Documents* (Hillsdale, 2002)

J. Montagu: *Timpani and Percussion* (New Haven, 2002)

B. Harms: 'The World of Historical Timpani', *Early Music America*, vol.14/2 (2008), 28–36

J. Atwood: 'Dresdner Apparatenbau Timpani: the Original Design', *Percussive Notes*, vol.47 (2009), 10–15

E.A. Bowles: *The Timpani: More Pictures and Documents* (Hillsdale, 2009)

B.E.H. Schmuhl, ed.: *Perkussionsinstrumente in der Kunstmusik vom 16. bis zur Mitte des 19. Jahrhunderts. Michaelsteiner Konferenzberichte 75* (Augsburg, 2010)

JAMES BLADES (1–4)/EDMUND A. BOWLES (1–5)/R

Tinan. Term for a large slit drum on Vao, a small island northeast of Malakula, Vanuatu. The name means 'mother'. In the local slit drum ensemble used at ritual pig killings, the next smaller drum is called *tarine* and another slightly smaller one is called *gheluvghe*. If enough men are available to strike the drums and enough pigs are available to be ritually killed, a fourth upright drum, the size of the *tarine,* is set up; this drum is called *petur*. In northeastern Malakula the same largest slit drums, which are decorated, stand vertically and are struck with one beater held by both hands. The smaller drums, which are undecorated, lie on the ground around the standing drums and are beaten with two sticks. The largest horizontal drum is called *ru-rurghen*; the smallest, portable horizontal drums, of which several exist in a Malakula ensemble, are called *sarune*. In all cases, the sticks for beating the drums are called *masan*. These slit drum ensembles were the largest in Vanuatu but nowadays so many drums are seldom played together. The drums are arranged on one side of the dancing ground and accompany dances as well as the ceremonial pig killing. See J. Layard: *Stone Men of Malekula* (London, 1942), 346 only.

RAYMOND AMMANN

Tinbuk. Two-bar xylophone of the Tolai people, Papua New Guinea. A man plays the tinbuk while seated on the ground, with the bars across his legs or laid across banana trunk sections. The bars are 75 to 100 cm long, 10 cm wide at the middle, narrowing to 2.5 cm at the ends; the undersides are hollowed into a shallow trough. Unequal in length and tuned less than a tone apart, they sometimes feature magical painted markings. The tinbuk is used to attract the affections of a woman. The player strikes the bars alternately with two short wooden beaters, executing rapid rolls, single and double hits, and triplets, while quickening and relaxing the tempo. Similar instruments are reported from southern New Ireland and Tami Island.

MICHAEL WEBB

Tinctoris, Johannes [Le Taintenier, Jehan] (*b* Braine-l'Alleud, nr Nivelles, *c*1430–35; *d* ?9 Feb 1511). Franco-Flemish theorist and composer. He was one of the most significant and influential writers on music of his day, as well as a wide-ranging practictioner as composer, singer, and instrumentalist. 12 Latin treatises by Tinctoris survive in whole or part; most are undated. The three principal manuscript sources comprise a copy now in Brussels, made probably at the Neapolitan court in the 1480s, which contains all the surviving treatises except for *De inventione*; and two deluxe library copies also made at the Neapolitan court—one in Valencia about 1483–5, and the other, now in Bologna, made in the 1490s.

Tinctoris's smaller treatises, mostly written by 1475, offer a meticulous introduction to the elements of musical pitch (*Expositio manus*, *c*1472–3), note values and mensural notation. Only two treatises, in whole or part, were printed during Tinctoris's lifetime. The *Terminorum musicae diffinitorium*, a glossary of musical terms, was originally compiled before 1475. As an early example of the genre it holds considerable interest; by and large it summarizes material covered in more detail in the other writings, though some of the wording suggests ways in which the author's thought evolved. The glossary was printed, with a few revisions, in Treviso about 1495.

In the early 1480s Tinctoris embarked on his most ambitious writing, *De inventione et usu musice*, a large-scale treatment of the origins and evolution of music, its theological and metaphysical roots and ramifications, and a broad survey of vocal and instrumental practice. This work has considerable interest for organology, although it can be argued that his discussion of the viol and rebec was not intended to present objective facts, but rather to mirror his personal experiences of these instruments. The complete version of *De inventione* is lost, but its size was comparable with the rest of Tinctoris's theoretical work put together. A single copy of extracts from the work has survived, printed probably in Naples by Matthias Moravus about 1481–3. A different selection of otherwise unknown chapters survives in a Cambrai manuscript whose existence suggests that the complete treatise was in circulation in northern Europe by the 1490s.

Tinctoris's reputation was high throughout Europe during his lifetime. The impact of his thinking on contemporaries and succeeding generations, however, was mostly indirect, through his influence on Gaffurius; it would undoubtedly have been greater if more of his writings had, like Gaffurius's, been committed to print. Tinctoris's work remained highly regarded after his death and was eagerly discussed. German theorists, especially, maintained an interest in his writings into the mid-16th century. His reputation in modern times dates largely from the assiduous patriotic attempts to revive and publish his writings in France and Belgium in the 19th century, culminating eventually in Coussemaker's edition of 1875–6.

For discussion of the entire scope of Tinctoris's work, and related bibliography, see GMO.

BIBLIOGRAPHY
A. Baines: 'Fifteenth-Century Instruments in Johannes Tinctoris's *De inventione et usu musicae*', *GSJ*, vol.3 (1950), 19–26
C.A. Miller: 'Early Gaffuriana: New Answers to Old Questions', *MQ*, vol.26/3 (1970), 367–88
I. Woodfield: *The Early History of the Viol* (Cambridge, 1984), 78–9

RONALD WOODLEY/R

Tindé [tende]. Small kettledrum of the Tuareg people of Niger. It consists of a goatskin stretched over a coffee-grinding mortar and fastened with a securing ring. The tindé is played by women to accompany their songs.

Tindeche. Ankle bells used by bowl-lyre players of the Marach people of Kenya.

Tingklik. Xylophone of Bali. It consists of several bamboo tubes of the *grantang* type hung horizontally in a frame. The tingklik is most often played alone or in pairs and is used primarily for private entertainment or hotel background music. Most typically the instrument has 11 tubes encompassing two octaves of the *slendro* tuning system, although five-tone *pelog* versions are also known. The musicians, using rubber-tipped wooden mallets, play the core melody with their left hand in the lower register, while the right hand plays interlocking figurations. The term *tingklik* also refers to other types of Balinese xylophones, including modern instruments with wooden bars tuned to Western diatonic and chromatic scales as are found in Denpasar and Ubud. See C. McPhee: *Music in Bali* (New Haven and London, 1966/*R*1976).

ANDREW C. MCGRAW

Ting-ting-shags. Small cymbals of Tibet, resembling crotales or antique cymbals. Two of these thick bronze cymbals, 5 or 6 cm in diameter, are often linked by a metal chain and held with the convex part upwards.

Ting-ting-shags, small cymbals, Tibet. (Aurelia W. Hartenberger, EdD)

They are sounded by brushing the rims delicately against each other with a horizontal movement. When only one cymbal is used, it is tapped with a piece of wood or horn. The use of ting-ting-shags is confined to certain Buddhist ceremonies, such as confession. They appear in pictures as symbols of offerings in sound to the deities. See M. Helffer: *Mchod-rol. Les instruments de la musique tibétaine* (Paris, 1994).

MIREILLE HELFFER

Tinguely, Jean (*b* Fribourg, Switzerland, 22 May 1925; *d* Bern, 30 Aug 1991). Swiss sculptor. He was active chiefly in or near Paris from 1952. His work is concerned with movement, and he was one of the pioneers of kinetic art in the mid-1950s. Most of his sculptures since 1954 incorporate electric motors and were constructed largely from junk and everyday materials. As a boy, about 1938, he built a percussion machine consisting of about two dozen water-wheels of different sizes, turned by a stream, which caused small hammers to strike tin cans. All his machines have strong personalities, quirky and unpredictable, and often are humorous, sometimes threatening. At first (1954–5) they were operated, like surrealistic clockwork, by handmade wire cog-wheels; these were soon replaced by various types of continuous belt drive, which, from the beginning of his found-object and auto-destructive period in 1960, involved discarded bicycle and pram wheels and, in the larger sculptures, a range of wooden and metal wheels from old industrial machinery.

In Tinguely's mature work the first sounds were tinklings incidental to the jerky operation of the cog-wheels, but from 1955 words related to 'sound' began to appear in his titles, as in *Relief méta-mécanique sonore*; this piece involves the striking of tin cans, a wooden box, bottles, and a bicycle bell by means of a cog-wheel mechanism. His first two drawing machines, which were constructed in the same year (on a principle that he later patented), produced similar sounds; these were often compared with *musique concrète*, which was becoming known in Paris at that time. In *Mes étoiles: concert pour sept tableaux* (1957) drumming sounds are made by mechanisms like those used in *Relief*. Tinguely's best-known and most notorious work, *Hommage à New York* (1960), took half an hour to destroy itself outside the city's Museum of Modern Art; it included an old upright piano (only three notes of which were played), a washing-machine drum, and a klaxon mounted on a small cart that 'escaped' after 20 minutes. Between 1960 and 1963 a series of sculptures based on scrap materials created a variety of sounds, such as that of a golf ball relentlessly striking a plinth in *Mautz II* (1963).

From 1962 Tinguely created more than a dozen radio sculptures in which a motor randomly operates the tuning control of an 'exploded' radio set to produce an instantaneous sound collage. The idea of the cart was greatly expanded during the 1960s into more sculptural, menacing, black, clanking machines, which travel along rails, sometimes dragging chains; these include *Hannibal I* and *Hannibal II* (1962, 1967, respectively)

and the Méta series (from 1968). Tinguely's later work is more colourful and larger: several huge, complex machines, such as the Méta-harmonie series (1977–80), incorporate conventional musical instruments and make elaborate use of sound.

The Museum Tinguely in Basel is devoted to his work and related documentation.

BIBLIOGRAPHY
C. Tomkins: 'A Profile of Jean Tinguely: Beyond the Machine', *New Yorker* (10 Feb 1962); rev. in *The Bride and the Bachelors* (New York, 1965); Eng. edn as *Ahead of the Game: Four Versions of Avant-garde* (London, 1965)
K.G. Pontus Hultén: *Jean Tinguely: Méta* (Berlin, 1972; Eng. trans., 1975)
Tinguely im Kunstmuseum Basel (Basel, 1976) [exhibition catalogue]
C. Bischofberger: *Tinguely: Catalogue Raisonné Sculptures and Reliefs 1954–1968 Werkkatalog Skulpturen und Reliefs* (Zurich, 1982)
R. Calvocoressi: *Tinguely* (London, 1982) [Tate Gallery exhibition catalogue]

HUGH DAVIES

Tính tầu [đàn tính]. Spike lute of the Tày, Thái, and Nùng peoples of northern Vietnam. It has a half-gourd (*tầu*) soundbox 15 to 25 cm in diameter, with pierced soundholes and a plain wooden soundtable. The neck, tapering towards the top, is about 80 cm long and unfretted, with lateral tuning pegs, and terminates in a back-curved ornamentally carved head. Small bells are sometimes attached. Among the Tày and Thái peoples it has two silk strings, among the Nùng it has three. Other sizes of *tính tầu* are made.

The instrument is said to have been introduced to court music ensembles in the 16th century. It was suppressed during the mid-20th century but revived in the 1980s. It is popularly played by men and women to accompany folk songs and dances and at celebrations, and again in rituals where it is believed to take on magical and sacred powers. Various taboos are then associated with it. See Y. La Cong: 'Dan tinh: the marvelous and sacred musical instrument of the Tay people', *Asian Ethnology*, vol. 67/2 (2008), 271–86.

TRÂN QUANG HAI/NGUYEN THUYET PHONG/R

Tini [punu]. Tin-can idiophone of Tahiti and the Cook Islands. It is an ordinary bread-bin or four-gallon kerosene tin beaten with two sticks. It has been part of the Cook Island percussion ensemble (*pakau tarekareka*) since at least 1900 and is valued for its distinctive 'bright' tone. The player alternates his sticks in a rapid single-stroke roll, incorporating accents played by the dominant hand against the main pulse. The tini often takes the lead in cueing in the other players. Other island groups that make musical use of the bread-bin or kerosene tin include Futuna, Samoa, Tokelau, Tonga, the Tuamotus, and Uvea. At least one and possibly two of the three dances it accompanies in Tonga were introduced from Uvea. During the 1960s the tini was displaced by the *fa'atete* drum in percussion ensembles accompanying dance. See W. Laird: *Drums and Drumming in the Cook Islands* (diss., U. of Auckland, 1982).

MERVYN MCLEAN

Tinimini [tinimuni, ting-ting]. Onomatopoeic term used by the Newari people of Nepal for a struck metallophone in the shape of a triangle.

Tini-tokere [tini-pate]. Small high-pitched slit drum of Aitutaki, Cook Islands, played with two sticks; it is known as *tini-pate* in Rarotonga. It was adopted from Tahiti in 1959 or 1960 and has since been steadily displacing the *tini* because of complaints from tour operators and other expatriates that the latter is 'untraditional'. The name *ka'ara* is sometimes applied to it because of the two-stick technique. See W. Laird: *Drums and Drumming in the Cook Islands* (diss., U. of Auckland, 1982).

MERVYN MCLEAN

Tin whistle [Irish whistle]. Popular form of duct flute, inexpensive and easy to play, and mostly used for traditional music. It has six fingerholes; the mouthpiece either has an inset wooden block or is made entirely of plastic. It has a typical compass of two octaves and three notes. It is usually made in the key of D, but whistles in other keys are also produced. It is essentially a diatonic instrument, although accidentals can be obtained by partially covering the fingerholes. The name 'tin whistle' is largely a misnomer. The Clarke Pennywhistle and the Sweetone are among the few brands actually made of tinplate in recent decades. In the late 1970s the Shaw Co. (who originally made bagpipes) began making copies of the Clarke Pennywhistle using nickel silver instead of tinplate. Both the Clarke and Shaw instruments have wooden blocks and conical bores. Several other widely sold makes have cylindrical bores and are produced in a variety of other materials (commonly drawn brass tubing) and with plastic mouthpieces; these are often erroneously called pennywhistles or tin whistles, but most are called whistles or flageolets. 19th-century types were often made of brass tubing with lead blocks, and many types have had folded seams. The conical types have a robust tone as well as the initial bite called 'chiff' by organ builders. The conical shape of the bore gives a flute-like quality, especially in the lower octave. Cylindrical instruments have a lighter, relatively clear tone.

The whistle's popularity owes much to its use in Irish traditional music. Irish players have incorporated traditional pipers' ornaments (cuts, rolls, etc.) into their playing to give it its characteristic style. A recent low whistle, pitched in D, has a particularly warm tonal quality, which is especially effective for playing slow airs. Whistle playing has been taken up internationally by those who enjoy Irish music. Its popularity in the USA is probably due to the influx of Irish immigrants during and after the potato famine; Clarke Pennywhistles were being sold in Ireland in the 19th century and would certainly have been taken by emigrants to the USA. The whistle has also been adopted in parts of Africa, especially by players of *kwela* music.

NORMAN DANNATT/R

Tinya [ttinya]. Double-headed frame drum used by many Andean peoples from Argentina to Colombia. Pre-Contact vases of the Yunca culture from Trujillo and Chimbote in Peru depict the tinya as a shallow cylindrical or square drum. The 16th-century Quechua used the term *ttinya* for any hand-drum, and also, at first, for the Spanish guitar and *vihuela*. Nowadays the Quechua call it *pomatinya* as the head is made from the skin of a puma. It is about 35 cm in diameter and 15 cm deep. It is played with the *pipo* (cane flute) or *antaras* to accompany *tinya palla* (an Andean ladies' dance). See R. Stevenson: 'Ancient Peruvian Instruments', *GSJ*, vol.12 (1959), 17–43.

Tiorbino (i). Small, uncommon theorbo or tiorba tuned an octave higher than the standard instrument, but retaining the theorbo's single strings, re-entrant tuning in A, and unfretted contrabass strings. It was used during the 17th century as a solo and continuo instrument. Nine duos in the *Capricci a due stromenti cioe Tiorba e Tiorbino* (Modena, 1622) of Bellerofonte Castaldi (1580–1649) are the only known compositions specifically for the tiorbino, which Castaldi referred to as 'mia invenzion[e] novella'. Castaldi writes of the tiorbino's 'six strings ... and contrabasses' ('*sei corde ... e contrabassi*'); the single rather than double courses are clearly visible in Castaldi's engravings of the instrument reproduced in *Capricci*. In its dedication, Castaldi calls the tiorbino the 'son' of the lute and tiorba, hence the masculine *tiorbino* rather than feminine *tiorbina*. Castaldi's account of its conception and the fact that his is the only known music for the tiorbino strongly suggest that he was its inventor.

Two instruments identified by Pohlmann as tiorbini are one by Johannes Hieber and Andreas Pfanzelt (Padua, 1628; *CH.G.m*) and an anonymous undated instrument (*GB.L.v*). The former has a fretted string length of 49 cm with the second pegbox for the unfretted contrabasses extending 76 cm and a body 32.8 cm long; the respective dimensions of the anonymous tiorbino are 45, 64, and 33 cm. A short single-strung *liuto attiorbato* tuned re-entrantly in A can also serve as a tiorbino. Modern makers of the tiorbino include Paolo Busato (Padua), Ivo Magherini (Dekani, Slovenia), and Stephen Barber and Sandi Harris (London).

'Tiorbino' might also refer to a harpsichord register that imitates its sound.

BIBLIOGRAPHY
E. Pohlmann: *Laute, Theorbe, Chitarrone: die Instrumente, ihre Musik und Literatur von 1500 bis zur Gegenwart* (Bremen, 1968, enlarged 5/1982)
B. Castaldi: *Capricci* (1622), *Recent Researches of Music in the Baroque Era*, vols.142 and 143, ed. D. Dolata (Middleton, WI, 2006)
DAVID DOLATA

Tiorbino (ii). Obscure type of Italian spinet, presumably strung with gut rather than wire. Only recently identified as a distinctive instrument and probably obsolete after the mid-18th century, it is known chiefly from documentary evidence dating from 1671 to 1733 and an anonymous, apparently Neapolitan example dated 1707 (*I.M.ts*). This small triangular instrument, enclosed in a separate outer case, has a 45-note compass (bass short octave) with two sets of strings at high pitch and traces of a mechanism for changing registration. The keyframe slides in and out of the inner case, and pedal pull-down wires could be connected to the lowest eight keys. Harpsichord makers mentioned in archival sources in connection with the tiorbino include the Neapolitans Giovanni Natale Boccalari (active 1679–1717), Andrea Basso (1659–1742), Gaetano Carotenuto (1682–1709), Giuseppe de Martino (1690–1720), and Salvatore Sanchez (1687–1724), as well as Angelo Faenza, Gaspare Sabbatino, Francesco Andreassi and Fabrizio Mucciardi, the Sicilian Carlo Grimaldi, and the Roman Giovanni Pietro Polizzino. See G. O'Brien and F. Nocerino: 'The Tiorbino: an Unrecognised Instrument Type Built by Harpsichord Makers with Possible Evidence for a Surviving Instrument', *GSJ*, vol.57 (2005), 184–208.

LAURENCE LIBIN

Tiparu. Bullroarer of the Toaripi people, Gulf province, Papua New Guinea. It was used for initiations and represented a malignant deity said to reside on Yule Island. See A.C. Haddon: 'Migration of Cultures in British New Guinea', *Journal of the Anthropological Institute of Great Britain and Ireland*, vol.l (1920), 237–80, 263.

Tiple. The Spanish word for 'treble' or 'soprano', often applied to specific instruments.

(1) A small guitar of Spain and Latin America. In Spain, including the Balearic and Canary Islands, the tiple (also known as *timple* or *guitarillo)* has four or five strings. It was possibly a precursor of the early Colombian tiple, which had four single gut strings. Nowadays the Colombian tiple is smaller than a guitar, with four courses of three metal strings each, tuned to the same notes as the four upper strings of a guitar, but with the middle string of the three lowest courses tuned an octave lower. The Colombian model is typically about 90 cm long overall, with body about 40 cm long and fingerboard 36 cm long with 18 frets. The soundtable and back are made from pine or cedar (*Cedrela odorata*), the fingerboard and frets of *nogal* (*Juglans neotropica*, Andean walnut); other woods used include *comino* (*Aniba* sp.) and *chuguacá* or *encenillo* (a type of oak).

The Venezuelan tiple, also called *guitarro segundo*, is a smaller verison of the Colombian one. The Peruvian tiple has four courses of one or two strings each. In Guatemala the tiple, a five-string instrument, is sometimes included in the *zarabanda* (string ensemble). In Puerto Rico the tiple is of the same general type as the *cuatro*, with three to five single strings; many different tunings are generally accepted. There are five Puerto Rican variants: *tiple grande de Ponce* (body 60 cm long; five strings); *tiplón* or *tiple con macho* (60 cm; with fifth peg on fingerboard); *tiple doliente* (40 cm; five strings; the most common); *tiple requinto costanero* (40 cm; three strings); and *tiple requinto de la montaña* (30 cm; three strings). Variants are also found in Cuba, the Dominican Republic, Uruguay, and Argentina. The Portuguese *braguinha* and *rajão* are related instruments.

See G. Abadia Moreles: *Instrumentos Musicales Folklore Colombiano* (Bogatá, 1991).

(2) The treble shawm of the Catalonian *cobla* ensemble, also called *tible*, with a normal range of *d′* to *g″*. See A. Baines: 'Shawms of the Sardana Coblas', *GSJ*, vol.5 (1952), 9–16.

JOHN M. SCHECHTER/J. RICHARD HAEFER

Tippani. Pair of bamboo percussion sticks of Gujarat, India. The sticks, which measure 175 cm long, are affixed to small wooden blocks at their lower end and are used by the Koli community in the tippani dance, to tap out the rhythmic beat on the floor.

Tiqin. Generic term for Chinese string instruments, especially fiddles (*ti:* 'to hold in the hand'; *qin:* 'string instrument'). Three chief applications of the term should be noted: a rarely heard two-string fiddle closely resembling the *banhu*; a four-string fiddle of the Qing dynasty (1644–1911) in Mongolian; and, in present usage, the Western violin family: *xiao tiqin* (violin), *jong tiqin* (viola), *da tiqin* (cello), and *beida tiqin* (double bass).

Tira. Whistle, with two fingerholes, of the Gan people of Burkina Faso. A set of three is used with rhythm instruments to accompany dancing.

Tirāyu. Flute of the Santal people of East India (Bengal, Bihar, Orissa). Two types are found, side-blown and end-blown. The transverse type is of bamboo, about 70 cm long and with an interior diameter of about 2 cm. About 19 cm from the left end the tube is closed by a natural node. Just below this is the mouthhole, and about 23 cm from there the first of six fingerholes, each about 3 cm apart. The flute is often decorated with brass bindings and feathers inserted in the left end. This type is perhaps typical of the Orissan Santal people, and resembles the *rutu* of the neighbouring Muṇḍāri people; the transverse flute *tirio* of the Uraon is identical. The tirāyu of the Santal of Bihar and Bengal, however, is end-blown, although of similar dimensions. The nonfunctional section closed by a node is at the bottom of the tube, and the six fingerholes are above this. The open upper end of the tube is held close against the lips, somewhat obliquely. It resembles the *murlī* of the Mundāri and Uraon peoples.

The tirāyu is of great importance in Santali music and culture. As often elsewhere, the instrument is reserved for males and has strong sexual symbolism. It is played by young boys while grazing the cattle (at which age, before they learn to plough, they are also taught to make the flute) and by men at dances and festivals, together with the drums *tumdak', tāmāk,* and *deger*, and sometimes also the *banam* (fiddle); the same ensemble plays at the annual summer hunt and the punitive *bitlaha* (outcasting ceremony).

BIBLIOGRAPHY
W.G. Archer: *The Hill of Flutes* (London, 1974)
B.C. Deva: 'The Santals and their Musical Instruments', *Jb für musikalische Volks- und Volkerkunde*, vol.8 (Cologne, 1977), 36–46
B.C. Deva: *Musical Instruments of India* (Calcutta, 1978)

ALASTAIR DICK

Tirucinnam [sricūrṇam]. Straight brass trumpet of Tamil Nadu, South India. It is about 75 cm long and has a slender cylindrical pipe terminating in a bell, with a prominent boss covering the joint. It is usually played in pairs by one player, one from each side of the player's mouth. There is no special mouthpiece. The name means 'sacred trumpet' (*cinnam* denoting wind instruments) and it is played in temples by mendicants. See P. Sambamoorthy: *Catalogue of Musical Instruments Exhibited by the Government Museum, Madras* (Madras, 3/1962), 20–21, pl. 3:8.

ALASTAIR DICK

Tischner, Johann August (*b* Zeisdorf, Saxony, Germany, 18 Aug 1774; *d* St Petersburg, Russia, 26 July 1852). German piano manufacturer, active in Russia. He was documented as a master at least since 1812, and St Petersburg directories show the business between 1823 and 1849 at Demidov Lane (today Grivtsova Lane); the historic building still exists, called the 'House of Tischner'. Johann August's sons liquidated the firm after his death. The only known information about the firm's output is that in 1825, when the factory burned, it held about 50 almost finished pianos (the factory was reconstructed). The firm had employed a number of Finnish workers since its founding.

Surviving Tischner grand pianos are remarkably similar to contemporary English grands, even in their metal bracing. They were reportedly favoured by the composer and pianist John Field during his time in Russia. A *C′–g″″* grand used by Glinka from 1824 to 1856 is in the Museum of Musical Instruments, St Petersburg; another grand is in the Blue Reception room of Monplaisir in Petrodvorets, and a *C′–a″″* grand is in a private collection in the USA. Tischner's pianos are as elegantly finished as any Western European piano of the time, with particularly fine cabinetry. The high reputation of Tischner's pianos inspired fraudulent imitations by other makers, prompting him to publish a public warning in 1819. At the 1829 exhibition where a Tischner piano won a Great Silver Medal, the judge wrote: 'The grand by Tischner should be put in the first rank … the instrument is excellent'. Tischner is said to have received an imperial patent from the tsar. See P. Zimin: *History of the Piano and its Predecessors* (Moscow, 1968).

HOWARD SCHOTT/ELEONORA TSVETKOVA,
ALEXANDER GALEMBO

Tita'a kohe [tita'apu, tioro, utete]. Jew's harp of the Marquesas Islands. It is made from a piece of bamboo about 2 cm wide and 23 to 25 cm long, with a rectangular notch cut in one end. A separate, thin tongue of bamboo cortex is held firmly behind the notch as the player holds the notch to the mouth with the left hand and vibrates the tongue rapidly with the index finger of the right hand. The mouth cavity amplifies the resultant sound, and players can change the shape of the cavity to approximate vowel sounds. Among an elderly generation of Marquesans, this instrument was used for intimate conversations and was considered a 'speaking instrument'. Reportedly it was used as a toy by boys and young men. It is still in use. A similar bamboo jew's harp is called *tītāpu* in Tahiti. See J. Moulin: '*KAPUTUHE*: Exploring Word-Based Performance on Marquesan Musical Instruments', *GSJ*, vol.55 (2002), 130–60.

JANE FREEMAN MOULIN

Titapu. Mouth bow of Rapa, Austral Islands. It was made by stretching one or more strings on a stick, one end of which was held in the mouth to resonate the instrument. A specimen seen by J.F.G. Stokes (*Material Culture of Rapa*; MS, *US.HON.bm*, 10) was more than 60 cm long. At one end a small piece of wood had been inserted to lift the string from die stick. The name was applied also to the bamboo jew's harp.

The term can also denote a bamboo jew's harp of Rarotonga (Cook Islands) and Hiva Oa (Marquesas Islands).

BIBLIOGRAPHY

K. Steinen: *Die Marquesaner und ihre Kunst* (Berlin, 1928), 59 only
S. Savage: *A Dictionary of the Maori Language of Rarotongo* (Wellington, 1962), 388 only

MERVYN MCLEAN

Titz [Tetz]. German family of organ builders. Heinrich Titz (*d* 4 May 1759), Wilhelm Titz (*d* 19 Nov 1775), and Wilhelm's son Johannes Henricus Titz (*b* Korschenbroich, 3 March 1745; *d* Grefrath, 11 Jan 1826) worked mainly in the Lower Rhine region (Neuss, Viersen), particularly in the Kempen-Krefeld district (Brüggen, Ürdem, St Hubert), but they also worked in Belgium (Munsterbilsen) and the Netherlands (Osch). Their organs followed the characteristic Baroque style of the Lower Rhine, represented by such builders as J.E. Teschemacher, J.C. and J.G. Kleine, and C. Roetzel. Their basic stop list consisted of an 8′ Hohlpfeife, 4′ Oktave, 4′ Hohlflöte, 2′ Superoktave, Sesquialtera II, Cornett III, Mixtur III, and 8′ Trompete, sometimes supplemented by 16′ Bordun, 8′ Prinzipal, 2⅔′ Nasard, Zimbel II, and 8′ Vox humana. String, harmonic, and undulating stops were later introduced. The organ at Brüggen still contains some of Heinrich Titz's pipework.

No relationship has been discovered between the German family and the Austrian organ and harmonium manufacturer Peter Titz (1823–73), an apprentice of Jacob Deutschmann, who worked under his own name in Vienna from 1852; his highly regarded workshop continued under the direction of his son-in-law Teofil Kotykiewicz (1849–1920) and Kotykiewicz's sons until well into the 20th century. The prominent Hungarian organ builder József Angster studied with Peter Titz before going to work for Cavaillé-Coll in 1863.

BIBLIOGRAPHY

K. Dreimüller: 'Beiträge zur niederrheinischen Orgelgeschichte', *Beiträge zur rheinischen Musikgeschichte*, vol.14 (1956), 17–51
H. Hulverscheidt: 'Die rheinische Orgellandschaft', *Acta organologica*, vol.1 (1967), 63–8
H. Hulverscheidt: 'Die Orgelbauer des Bergischen Landes vom 17. bis zum 19. Jahrhundert', *Acta organologica*, vol.2 (1968), 13–33

HANS KLOTZ/R

Tjetje. Generic term for rattles and friction membranophones among the Southern Sotho people of Lesotho and South Africa. It is applied, for example, to the *morutlhoana* and *setjoli*.

Tl'apadlo. Idiophone of eastern Slovakia. It is made from the bark removed from logs during the building of a house. Children beat the ground with it to drive out evil so that the wood can safely be used in the house. A similar noisemaker was noted by Hornbostel in North Australia. See E.M. von Hornbostel: 'The Music of the Feugians', *Ethnos*, vol.13/3–4 (July, 1948), 61–102.

IVAN MAČAK

T'ling flo'. Xylophone of the Mnong people of central Vietnam. Four horizontal logs are suspended by two rattan ropes from a fifth log fastened to a tree trunk. The other ends of the ropes are affixed to the ground by two stakes. The four logs are struck by two players, one with two mallets, the other with one.

TRÂN QUANG HAI/R

T'mbuk. Common term in medieval Armenia for folk drums of various types.

Toa ('turtle'). Friction idiophone of the forest-dwelling Moré people of eastern Bolivia. It is a small gourd with a circular opening cut on the top side and a small hole in the base. The top opening is covered with beeswax or natural resin which, when hardened, is rubbed with the thumbs or palm of the hand, or sometimes against the moistened inner side of the upper arm. The resulting sound, which is thought to affect rainfall, is said to resemble that of a turtle, hence the name *toá*. See E. Cavour Aramayo: *Instrumentos Musicales de Bolivia* (La Paz, 1994).

Toacă. Percussion beam of Romania, used in the Orthodox church. It serves to announce the time of Mass or other offices. It consists of a thick plank of wood or a metal plaque hung by two large chains from a beam, and is struck by two hammers (*ciocane, sing, ciocan*). The toacă can also be portable; in this type, the plank is long and narrow with a thinner middle section, where it is held by one hand. The player beats the toacă with a small wooden hammer, encircling the church three times. In certain places in the west of the country (Oltenia, the Banat), the toacă is also used in folk contexts.

TIBERIU ALEXANDRU

Tobă [dobă, dubăj]. Double-headed drum of Romania, usually made by craftsmen. It is used in certain instrumental ensembles, including fanfares and jazz bands. The large one (*tobă mare*), a bass drum, is normally fitted on the side with a cymbal (*cinel* or *talger*) which is struck with a metallic object (nail, penknife, etc., not with another cymbal as it is more generally elsewhere). One of the heads is beaten with a thick wooden stick called *mai* ('mallet'). The tobă might be coupled with a smaller drum (*tobă mică,* or *darabană*), sometimes placed on the ground beside it. The large single-headed drums used in masked processions on New Year's day are also called *tobă*.

TIBERIU ALEXANDRU

Tobin, Richard (*b* Ireland, 1766; *d* Shoreditch, London, England, 1 Dec 1847). Irish violin maker. He might have been apprenticed to Thomas Perry (*c*1745–1818) in Dublin, then worked briefly in Cork and Waterford before coming to London, possibly through contact with Vincenzo Panormo during one of the latter's trips to Ireland. Tobin's first known London instrument is dated 1810, but he had probably left Ireland soon after 1800 and settled in St Leonard's Street, Finsbury Square, before moving to 9 West Street, Soho, by 1823. His work is very similar to that of Henry Lockey Hill, for whom he worked, and follows a refined Stradivari pattern using location pins in the plates—a technique possibly picked up from Panormo. He also supplied John Betts, Thomas Dodd, and others with instruments either varnished or 'in the white'. Though a skilled craftsman and accounted the finest among British scroll carvers, Tobin appears not to have been successful in business and died in the Shoreditch workhouse. See J. Milnes (ed.): *The British Violin* (Oxford, 2000).

ANDREW FAIRFAX

Tobol [ţabl, tobl]. Kettledrum of the Tuareg people of West Africa. It is a shallow, wide drum with a camel-skin head. It has lost its traditional associations and is played nowadays by groups of women to accompany singing. In its known history among the Tuareg of Ahaggar, the tobol was originally a large hide-covered calabash used to summon people to hear a chief's commands. Its association with authority became so established that piercing the drum was the greatest possible insult to a chief and its capture by an enemy was the greatest blow to his prestige. A chronicle dated 1758 concerning the Tuareg of Air refers to an official, known as *tambari*, whose function was to beat the tobol on the installation of high officials. In the mid-19th century the German traveller Heinrich Barth described the *tobl* of the Tuareg of Timbuktu as a great drum used to give the call to battle. Somewhat later a Tuareg drum of this type, referred to as *ettebel*, was described as having a laced skin, being struck with two flexible beaters, and measuring 38 cm in height and 52 cm in diameter.

BIBLIOGRAPHY

H. Barth: *Travels and Discoveries in North and Central Africa* (London, 1857/R1967)
H.R. Palmer: *The Bornu Sahara and Sudan* (London, 1936)
H. Lhotó: *Les Touareg du Hoggar* (Paris, 1955)
M. Bovis and M. Gast: *Collection ethnographiques: Touareg Ahaggar* (Paris, 1959)

K.A. GOURLAY

Toda. Bamboo idiochord tube zither of the central Sikka region of Flores, Indonesia. The instrument is about 35 cm long and 5 cm in diameter, and has one string, as with the Balinese *guntang*. It is played in the *letor* bamboo ensemble where one musician plays three instruments, a second musician plays two, and a third plays a single instrument. Musicians strike the zithers with thin, unpadded sticks, performing complex rhythmic interlocking patterns. They are accompanied by a single performer playing two bamboo stamping tubes (*boku*), 40 to 50 cm long, one tuned slightly higher than the other. The tubes are closed by a node at the bottom and played by hitting them against the ground in alternation. In some instances a cracked piece of young bamboo, called a *waning ana*, may be added to this ensemble, and is struck on the beat with a wooden stick.

A similar ensemble involving four toda zithers is found in the Nage region to the east and is called the *todagu* ensemble. Four musicians play the toda, one each, and two drums (*laba toda*) are added to the ensemble. The *laba toda* are approximately 20 cm in diameter, stand upright, and are played by a single musician with thin, unpadded wooden sticks. The *todagu* ensemble was traditionally played to accompany the *jedhe* dance and when specific trees were to be felled; the music was thought to chase away the spirits of the trees.

The term can also denote a bamboo slit drum of the Nage area of Flores, Indonesia.

ANDREW C. MCGRAW

Todini, Michele (bap. Saluzzo, Piedmont, Italy, 24 May 1616; *d* Rome, Italy, 3 May 1690). Italian inventor, maker, and player of musical instruments. He moved to Rome about 1636, and from 1650 to 1652 he was known as *guardiano degli strumentisti* for the Congregazione di Santa Cecilia, a prestigious post later held by Carlo Mannelli, Arcangelo Corelli, and Giovanni Lulier. Todini was a trombone player and organist with the Musici del Campidoglio, for whom he was *decano* from at least 1676 to 1684. He also played various bowed instruments in numerous public performances, and claimed to have built and introduced the 'contrabasso di viola' to Rome about 1646. He had no children, and thus was not the father of Pietro Todini, a harpsichord maker mentioned in 1675.

Todini is best known for the famous 'Galleria armonica e matematica', which he began to assemble in 1650 in his home near the Pantheon (via dell'Arco della Ciambella). According to his own description, the 'harmonic machines' were divided between two rooms. The first room held the 'greater machine', whose seven instruments (harpsichord, three types of spinet, organ, violin, and *lira ad arco*) could be played alone or in various combinations by means of a single controlling keyboard; this is depicted in Kircher's *Phonurgia nova*, although, according to Todini, in a completely fanciful manner. The second room housed wooden statues of Galatea and Polyphemus, the latter represented as playing a 'sordellina' or 'musetta' whose mechanism was activated by the keyboard of a harpsichord enclosed in a case magnificently decorated with mythological imagery and largely gilded. The group was carved by Jacob Reiff; the makers of the instruments are unknown. The 'mathematical machines' were two ingenious clocks, each encased in a sculpture.

After 1690 the Galleria was transferred to the palace of the Verospi marquises (now the Palazzo del Credito Italiano) in the via del Corso, where it continued to attract many visitors. In 1761 Sigismondo Antonio Manci, from Trento, in his manuscript diary describes the 'greater machine' as 'the marvel of the world': a friar, at the main keyboard, demonstrated in an astounding way the different combinations of instruments before a group of tourists. However, by 1770 it had fallen into neglect. The machine was broken up and sold in 1796. Only the Galatea and Polyphemus group is known after that time; it remained in Rome in disuse until at least 1859. Having been acquired by the Viscount of Sartriges, the French ambassador to the Holy See, it was then moved to Paris, and finally to the Metropolitan Museum of Art, New York. The present statue of Galatea does not match the statue described in Todini's *Dichiaratione* (1676) or the 1672 archival documents; it is also questionable whether the mechanism of the sordellina ever actually worked. The large harpsichord has been much altered. A 19th-century terracotta model of the group is preserved in Rome (*I.R.ms*). See M. Todini: *Dichiaratione della galleria armonica eretta in Roma* (Rome, 1676, repr. with an introduction by P. Barbieri, Lucca, 1988).

PATRIZIO BARBIERI

Tō'ere [tō'are]. (1) Single-headed cylindrical drum of Tahiti. Before contact with Europeans it was beaten to mark the start and finish of a human sacrifice. About 30 cm in diameter, it was distinguishable from the larger *pahu*.

(2) Wooden slit drum (*takere* in Puamau) based on Tahitian models, used throughout French Polynesia to accompany secular dancing. The size has varied, with modern drums being generally about 80 cm tall and 20 cm in diameter. Marquesan examples range from about 63 to 76 cm long and are beaten with one stick. Rosewood (*mi'o*; *Thespesia populnea*) is favoured for making these instruments. Slit drums are documented in the region as early as the 1770s and identified by name in the early 1800s as *pa rā'au* and two types of *'īhara*: *'īhara tamanu* ('wooden slit drum') and *'īhara 'ohe* ('bamboo slit drum'); the name change to *tō'ere* occurred probably during the early 20th century. This slit drum is one of the instruments in the ensemble used to accompany dance, where it plays the main rhythmic pattern. The *tō'ere kava*, a small wooden slit drum of Tahiti, is used as an optional instrument to expand the texture of the drum ensemble. Set on a wooden stand, it is played with one or two sticks.

BIBLIOGRAPHY

D. Oliver: *Return to Tahiti: Bligh's Second Breadfruit Voyage* (Honolulu, 1988), 107

J.F. Moulin: 'Music of the Southern Marquesas Islands', *Occasional Papers on Pacific Ethnomusicology*, vol.3 (1994)

JANE FREEMAN MOULIN

Toeto [tuto]. Hide drum of the Cambeba (Omagua) people of Brazil and Peru.

Toe-yoe. Four-string fiddle of the Shan in northern Thailand and the Shan State in Myanmar; reportedly it has a metal bell that serves as a sound modifier. Neither the name nor the instrument has been verified, but possibly the name refers to Stroh violin replicas produced nowadays in Thailand.

Tof [toph] (Heb.; pl. *tuppim*). Apparently the only word used in the Bible for a drum of any kind. A common English translation has been 'tymbre' and later 'timbrel' (occasionally also 'tabret'). Ethnographic parallels as well as archaeological iconographic evidence (Bayer, 1963, group B.I) suggest that circular frame drums about 30 cm in diameter or less, akin to the Western tambourine though without the jingles, might have been the *tuppim* played by Miriam and her companions after the crossing of the Reed [Red] Sea (*Exodus* xv.20). The tof, like the Arab *duff,* was frequently, though not exclusively, played by women and was used to accompany singing and dancing.

BIBLIOGRAPHY
B. Bayer: *The Material Relics of Music in Ancient Palestine and its Environs: an Archaeological Inventory* (Tel-Aviv, 1963, 2/1964)
J. Montagu: *Musical Instruments of the Bible* (Lanham, MD, 2002), 16–19

JEREMY MONTAGU

T'ogo. Obsolete barrel drum of Korea (*t'o*: 'earth'; *go*: 'drum'), considered to be of Chinese origin. It had a ceramic body and animal-skin heads. It is first mentioned in Korea in an illustrated source of 1415, citing an early 12th-century Chinese treatise, Chen Yang's *Yueshu* ('Treatise on Music'). In 1430 the theorist Pak Yŏn proposed that new t'ogo be constructed and played in the courtyard ensemble (*hŏn'ga*) at the Sacrifice to the Spirit of Agriculture (*Sŏnnong*), rather than the drum *nogo* usually used in sacrifices to human spirits. Although Pak's proposal was approved at the time and still supported by an official publication of 1474, the standard treatise *Akhak kwebŏm* (1493) indicates that the *nogo* was reinstated by the end of the century.

BIBLIOGRAPHY
Sejong sillok (Annals of King Sejong] (1454, repr. 1603), 47.12*b* and 128.19*b*
Kukcho orye sŏrye [Rubrics for the Five Rites of the nation (1474/R1979), 1.78*a*–79*a*, 1.94*a*–95*a*
Sŏng Hyŏn, ed.: *Akhak kwebŏm* [Guide to the study of music] (Seoul, 1493/R1975), 2.3*a*

ROBERT C. PROVINE

Tohun. Water drum of the Mahi people of Benin. Two inverted half-calabashes of different sizes, hence producing different pitches, float in a larger vessel filled with water. They are struck by one musician. The tohun is used for funeral music as part of an instrumental group that includes a gourd percussion vessel (*go*).

Tōi. Idioglot bamboo jew's harp of Laos and northeastern Thailand.

Tok. Obsolete Korean stamping tube, considered to be of Chinese origin. As described in the treatise *Akhak kwebŏm* (1493), it was a brightly decorated tube of bamboo 178.7 cm long, closed at the top but with two holes in the side 26.6 cm from the top. The player held the tube vertically with both hands and pounded it against the ground. The tok was used only as part of the *mumu* ('military dance') ensemble in ritual music (*aak*). With the *ŭng* (idiophone), *a* and *sang* (drums), it was played after the regular sounding of the large drum *chin'go*— that is, after every four-note phrase of the very slow melody. See Sŏng Hyŏn, ed.: *Akhak kwebŏm* [Guide to the study of music] (Seoul, 1493/R1975), 6.27*b* only.

ROBERT C. PROVINE

Ṭokā [tokka]. Sprung bamboo clappers of Assam, northeastern India. They are made from a thick bamboo tube 30 cm to 90 cm long and slit down almost the entire length, similar in appearance to a pair of tongs, leaving the base intact as a handle. The clappers are played by beating the slit halves against the palm of one hand, or shaking them so that they rattle against each other. They might originally have been used as noisemakers in elephant hunts, but nowadays their main function is to give a simple rhythmic accompaniment to music and dance.

Ṭokāri. Variable tension chordophone ('plucked drum') of Assam, northeast India. It is a type of *ānandalaharī*, similar to the *khamak*, or *gopīyantra*, of Bengal and Orissa. It is used in *tokārigīt*, a type of religious song similar to that of the Bauls of Bengal, who also use the *gopīyantra*. See S. Ray: *Music of Eastern India* (Calcutta, 1973).

ALASTAIR DICK

Tōkere. Wood or bone clappers of the Māori people of New Zealand (Aotearoa). H.W. Williams (*A Dictionary of the Maori Language* [Wellington, 1971]) reports they were used, a pair in each hand, as castanets. There is no corroboration of their existence in travel accounts or other early literature, but they are made and used nowadays. Flintoff describes how a trial pair was fashioned, and immediately recognized by one elder who performed a song using them. See B. Flintoff: *Taonga Pūoro, Singing Treasures: the Musical Instruments of the Māori* (Nelson, NZ, 2004), 84.

MERVYN MCLEAN/TEURIKORE BIDDLE

Tōki. Side-blown free reed aerophone of the Jörai peoples of central Vietnam. The Bahnar people call it *tölut*. It consists of a buffalo horn open at both ends so that the tip can be used as a fingerhole. The reed is set into a wooden mouthpiece attached with wax at the middle of the concave side. It is a military instrument.

Tolali [tulani]. End-blown flute of the Ilongot people of Nueva Vizcaya, northern Luzon, Philippines. A small segment of bamboo tied around the head of the bamboo tube forms an external duct that channels breath to the sharp-edged blowing hole. Similar types of flute in Luzon are called *bulungudyung*, *taliwatiw* (Ayta Magkunana), and *pitu* (Ilokano). In Visayas-Mindanao, these flutes are called *tulale*, *tulali* (Subanun, Bukidnon-Aklan, Ilonggo), *yangyang* (Bukidnon), and *lantoy* (Manobo Cotabato). The *tolali* has also been identified as a nose flute with three or four fingerholes. In the 17th century the terms 'tolali' and 'lantoy' were reportedly being applied to the recorder, introduced by Spaniards. See D.R.M. Irving: *Colonial Counterpoint: Music in Early Modern Manilla* (Oxford, 2010).

ARSENIO NICOLAS/R

Tola waghe. Slit-reed (retreating reed) aerophone of Nias, Indonesia, made from a rice stalk. It is closed with a node at one end, and near the node the stalk is pinched so that it bulges. The bulge, with a vertical slit cut into it that dilates under breath pressure, is blown inside the player's mouth to produce a penetrating sound. See J. Kunst: *Music in Nias* (Leiden, 1939), 58 only.

JEREMY MONTAGU

Tolbecque, Auguste (*b* Paris, France, 30 March 1830; *d* Niort, Deux Sèvres, France, 8 March 1919). Cellist, composer, and instrument maker, member of a family of musicians from Belgium, active in France. He studied at the Paris Conservatoire, winning the cello *premier prix* in 1849. He played in the orchestra of the Grand Théâtre of Marseilles and taught at the conservatory there from 1865 to 1871, then returned to Paris and performed with the Société des Concerts du Conservatoire, the Maurin Quartet, and the Lamoureux Quartet; he also played the viol. He left Paris for Niort, having studied instrument making with Victor Rambaux, and established a workshop in which he restored old instruments and made copies of medieval ones. His large instrument collection was purchased by the Belgian government for the Brussels Conservatory in 1879; a second collection and a fine library were dispersed in 1922. Tolbecque also attempted to revive the Componium, a mechanical instrument designed to improvise upon a given theme. He composed an *opéra comique*, *Après la valse* (performed at Niort in 1894), and numerous works for the cello. He edited *Monde musical* and wrote useful books on early instruments. See J.B. Rutledge: 'Late 19th-Century Viol Revivals', *EMc*, vol.19/3 (1991), 409–18.

WRITINGS

La gymnastique du violoncelle (Paris, 1875)
Quelques considérations sur la lutherie (Paris, 1890) |
Souvenirs d'un musicien en province (Niort, 1896)
Notice historique sur les instruments à cordes et à archet (Paris, 1898)
L'art du luthier (Niort, 1903/R)

ELISABETH BERNARD/R

Tólero [toleró]. End-blown flute of the Guaymí (Ngäbe) people of Panama and Costa Rica. It was made traditionally from a leg bone of a deer or jaguar, but nowadays is made of cane, about 35 cm long. It is played in a girls' puberty ceremony and a stylized male fighting game.

Another flute used by the Guaymí is the *dru nöra*, a double duct flute of cane with two tubes tuned a 5th apart. Wax is used to form the duct and to hold the two tubes together. The *dru mugata* is a globular vessel

flute formed entirely of a sphere of beeswax with two or three fingerholes and a blow hole. The flutes are often played together with the *ton*, a calabash rattle with a spiked wooden handle, and the *caja*, a short double-headed drum of *cedro* or balsa with a head of boar's hide, or the *gnelé* friction idiophone, a tortoiseshell covered with beeswax and rubbed by the hand.

J. RICHARD HAEFER

Töliö. Mouth organ, with three holes and a single pipe, of the Bahnar people of central Vietnam.

Tololoche. String bass of northern Mexico. It is a local version of the European double bass but usually is somewhat smaller, hence more readily portable. It has four (sometimes three) strings tuned in 4ths, and is plucked rather than bowed. In popular music it has been largely replaced by the electric bass, but it is still used in traditional ensembles. Cheap examples, commercially produced, are made of plywood with a flat top.

Tom [to:m]. Lamellaphone of Ethiopia. The only lamellaphone in Ethiopia and associated with dark-skinned Nilotic peoples, it came from the Democratic Republic of the Congo through Sudan and is played by the Anuak and Nuer (who call it also *weujangue*) in the Gambela region and by the Surma in southern Ethiopia. The rectangular or trapezoidal wooden soundbox is 18 to 60 cm long and bears eight to 12 slender metal tongues tuned to a pentatonic or heptatonic scale. Half-steps occur only in the Nuer scales. Surma and Nuer toms have small rattling rings on some tongues. The Anuak tom has a slip of wood tied to the bridge; it is used to strike the soundbox for the *aksak* rhythm. Although rare and intimate today, and played only by men, toms formerly accompanied songs and dances, alternating with solo phrases. Originally the tom repertory was played on a five-string arched harp (called *thor* by the Nuer); this music, based on two-voice ostinati with variations, was transferred to the tom long ago.

BIBLIOGRAPHY

Musical Instruments of Ethiopia. Catalogue of the Collection of the Ethiopian Museum of the Institute of Ethiopian Studies (Addis Ababa, 1999)
C. Lacombe: *Les archives sonores de l'Institute of Ethiopian Studies: dépouillement, inventaire; analyse des bandes de piano à pouces de la région de Gambela, Ethiopie* (thesis, St Etienne U., 2006)

CLAIRE LACOMBE

Tomba. Hourglass drum of the Mandinka people of Sierra Leone. It is struck with two curved beaters.

Tomkison, Thomas (*b* c1764; *d* London, England, 4 Nov 1853). English piano manufacturer. The son of a London jeweler, Thomas worked in Dean Street (no.55, renumbered as 77 about 1819) from December 1798 to June 1851, and married Mary Dolling at St Anne's, Soho, on 28 June 1800. He was apprenticed on 9 April 1778 to Barker Simpson of the Cooks' Company and took over the bankrupt piano-making business of James Henry Houston in 1799. Tomkison was appointed Piano Forte

Maker in Ordinary to King George II on 9 April 1813, though earlier Royal Kalendars show him as Maker to the Prince of Wales's (and later the Prince Regent's) Household. He used the royal warrant on nameboards under succeeding monarchs.

Tomkison's early squares had five octaves, extended to five and a half octaves in the early 1800s, and to six octaves available from about 1821. There is evidence of experimental damper systems amongst the early squares, and he offered four rather than six legs for squares as early as about 1816, before Broadwood and other English makers. Tomkison made an exceptional six-and-a-half-octave square about 1824 (Catriona Hall, Tasmania), and occasionally used highly decorative metal string plates of complex design on later squares.

Tomkison experimented in casework design for English grands, adding French-inspired elements after 1815, such as three legs rather than four and a projecting keyboard with drop-down locking flap (the 'French front'). A superb example is the lavishly brass-inlaid rosewood six-octave grand, serial number 1329, made for King George IV at a cost of £236.5.0 (in *GB.BET. colt*). A Nash painting shows it in the Brighton Pavilion. He began introducing iron tension bars and metal bracing into his grands and squares in the 1820s. Contemporary advertisements show that he was still producing pianos in the late 1840s.

Tomkison stamped his instruments with a serial number and 'T TOMKISON' inside the case. He employed separate and seemingly continuous sets of serial numbers for the different types of pianos, likely numbering more than 11,200 squares (of which more than 100 survive), 2,400 grands, and 1,300 cabinet pianos. Dates are occasionally written on the side of a key or on the inner case wall. A number of Tomkison grands (*GB.L.v, D.LE.u, S.S.mf, AUS.S.phm, IRL.D.nm*, and elsewhere) survive, as do representative squares (*US.W.si, US.WG. cw, GB.Y.m, GB.CHS.m*, and elsewhere). A rare five-and-a-half-octave cabinet piano (no.235) is in the Musée des Instruments de Musique, Brussels.

No workshop records from Tomkison's business are known, but clients on the Continent included Prince Louis Ferdinand of Prussia (who took delivery of two grands in 1804) and George Onslow (whose 1824 grand is at the chateau of Lavoûte-Polignac in the Auvergne). Tomkison's export business included the USA and Australia, and his pianos were recommended as particularly suitable for tropical climates.

Tomkison aspired to be a patron for young musicians and artists. When the Royal Academy of Music was founded, Tomkison provided a grand and a square for the entrance examination in 1823. He also recommended students for admission to the Academy, the best known of whom was Charles Dickens's sister Fanny. In addition to his reputation as one of the finest English piano makers, he was esteemed as a discerning collector of paintings, with a distinguished collection of Old Masters and works by contemporaries such as John Linnell, one of whose canvases he acquired in 1820 in exchange for a piano valued at 42 guineas.

BIBLIOGRAPHY
C.F. Colt and A. Miall: *The Early Piano* (London, 1981)
Tomkison page on Friends of Square pianos website (<www.friendsof-squarepianos.co.uk/Tomkison.html>)

TIM HARDING, NORMAN MACSWEEN

Tompong [thumping]. External duct flute of the Subanun peoples in Mindanao, southern Philippines. A slip of wood attached with beeswax over a V-shaped notch in the edge of one end of the bamboo tube directs the airstream. The flute has five or six fingerholes. It is played mostly by women for personal entertainment in the morning or evening, or while watching over rice fields, but is occasionally played in ensemble with other instruments.

Tom-tom. Name loosely applied in the Western world to certain African and Eastern drums, but now generally applied to cylindrical rod-tensioned drums with wooden shells used in Western jazz and pop bands. Tom-toms are essential to the modem jazz drummer, who uses them in sets of three or more. They can be single- or double-headed and range from 25 to 46 cm in diameter. The heads, which are mounted on a hoop, are of plastic, less often of calfskin. The drums are normally mounted on stands or a framework; in the 1930s and 40s they were often affixed to the rim of the bass drum, one on each side, often along with a floor-tom raised on adjustable feet. In most cases side-drum sticks are used, particularly in jazz where tom-toms are often combined with snare drum and cymbals and pedal bass drum.

An older type was the Chinese tom-tom, a barrel-shaped drum from 12 to 90 cm tall, with a thick vellum head nailed on, often decorated with Chinese characters, dragons, etc.; the head diameter was usually between 25 and 45 cm. These were used in early drum sets as the forerunner of the modern Western tom-tom. They have a distinctive sound, rather 'darker' or 'flatter' than that of the later instrument.

Concert toms are single-headed drums, usually used in a set of eight; the heads range from 15 to 41 cm in diameter. They are easily transported, as the six smallest drums can be packed into the two largest. Sets ranging up to two chromatic octaves have also been made. They have been largely superseded by the more easily tuned Rototoms, which resemble tunable drum heads: the counter-hoop of each drum (seven sizes are available with head diameters ranging from 15 to 46 cm) is connected by a light frame to a central spindle, and pitch is raised or lowered by turning the drumhead clockwise or counterclockwise. Wood tom-toms have heads of wood. Kolberg Percussion makes four sizes, from 25 to 30 cm in diameter. As these have a drum-shell resonator, their sound is darker and less 'sharp' than that of a woodblock.

Timbales [tymbales] are smaller, single-headed drums, usually paired, which are primarily associated with the Latin American dance band, where they are usually teamed with one or two cowbells; the player's rhythmic patterns also involve hitting the drum shell.

Timbale shells are usually of metal, about 18 cm tall with diameters between 20 and 38 cm. While timbales used in the late 20th century were usually unpitched, their screw-tensioned heads, invariably of plastic, produce definable notes, normally tuned at a convenient interval, usually a 4th or 5th. Malcolm Lipkin's *Interplay* (1975) for recorder, harpsichord, viola da gamba, and percussion uses six timbales tuned to *G, B♭, B, c, d♭* and *e♭* instead of timpani. In French terminology, *timbale* signifies kettledrum and *timbales* (or occasionally *tymbales*) signifies timpani; *timbale mécanique* refers to a kettledrum with pedal-operated tuning (*see* Timpani, §1; details of Adolphe Sax's *timbale-trompette* (1855) and *timbales chromatiques* (1857) are given in §4).

Smaller still are the bongos [bongo drums], a pair of Afro-Cuban single-headed drums with conical or cylindrical hardwood shells about 18 and 15 cm in diameter. They are one of the two main drum types of Cuba, smaller than the *tumbadora*. Originally made from hollowed logs, nowadays their thick shells are often made of glued staves. The shells, joined side by side, are of the same height but of different diameters. The heads (often goatskin or plastic) are nailed or, in the tunable version, screw-tensioned, in which case the drums are tuned to clear high-sounding notes at least a 4th apart. In general, bongos are played with bare hands, the fingers striking the heads like drumsticks.

Created in Cuba about 1900 for the needs of small ensembles, bongos remain integral to Latin American dance bands, rumba bands, and jazz and pop bands. In these situations the player usually positions the larger drum to the right, a common practice in drumming. Great virtuosity is possible, the player obtaining subtle effects of tone control, including glissandos, by pressure from the fingertips, flat fingers, and heel of the palm.

Among many composers who have included bongos in their scores are Edgard Varèse (*Ionisation*, 1929–31); Carl Orff (*Astutuli*, 1953); and Pierre Boulez (*Le marteau sans maître*, 1953–5, rev. 1957, and a set of four in *Figures–Doubles–Prismes*, 1963). With the development of 'concert toms', composers began to use them in place of similar-sounding bongos.

Tom-toms appear regularly in orchestral and chamber music: John Cage used 12 in *She Is Asleep* (1943); in *Agon* (1957) Igor Stravinsky wrote for three tom-toms (or timpani tuned to *e♭, b♭* and *g♭*); Benjamin Britten called for three tom-toms, four Chinese tom-toms, and a Roto-tom tuned to *c′* in *Death in Venice* (1973); Michael Tippett used two octaves of Roto-toms tuned *c–c″* in *Byzantium* (1990); Hans Werner Henze used six tom-toms in *Appassionatamente* (1993–4); and Harrison Birtwistle called for seven conventional tom-toms, seven high tom-toms, and four very low ones in *The Mask of Orpheus* (1973–84). Andrzej Panufnik's *Sinfonia di Sfere* (1975) requires 12 unpitched drums (i.e. tom-toms) arranged in three groups.

JAMES BLADES/JAMES HOLLAND/JEREMY MONTAGU

Tondji m'dom. Single-headed, sacred drum of the Fali people of Cameroon. It is the 'male' drum, paired with the smaller 'female' *nondji m'dom*. The tondji m'dom is a cylindrical drum, about 256 cm long and 26 cm in diameter. It has three feet, a 'pad' projecting above with phallic significance, and a head affixed by four wooden pegs and a securing ring. The *nondji m'dom*, also cylindrical, is 96 cm long and 35 cm in diameter. It has four legs and its head is affixed by five wooden pegs and a securing ring. Both drums are beaten by hand and classed by the Fali as *ni wuta* (instruments of death). See J.-G. Gauthien: *Les Fali (Hon et Tsalo)* (Oosterhut, 1969).

Tondu. Plucked spike lute of eastern Flores, Indonesia. Its resonator is half a coconut shell with a soundtable made from betel-nut leaf, wood, or cardboard sewn on with fibre cord through holes in the top edge of the shell. A long flat lath of bamboo passes through the shell to form the neck and spike. A single gut or fibre string is tied to the ends of this lath, tightly enough to form a bow, with the taut string pressing against the soundtable. Immediately below the resonator, a movable loop of fibre is tied around the string and the bamboo lath, with which the player can alter the pitch while plucking the string segment above the resonator. The instrument's total length is about 45 to 57 cm. See J. Kunst: *Music in Flores* (Leiden, 1942), 130–31, fig.10B.

MARGARET J. KARTOMI/ANDREW C. MCGRAW

Tone (i) (from Lat. *tonus* and Gk. *tonos*; Fr. *ton*; Ger. *Ganzton*; It. *tono*). Interval equal to the sum of two semitones and hence referred to as a 'whole tone', usually perceived as a major 2nd; in equal temperament, the sixth part of an octave. It and the semitone are the intervals by which conjunct motion in a part or voice is generated. In the Pythagorean tuning system the whole tone is the excess of two pure 5ths over an octave (reckoned from *c*, the interval *c′–d′*), a ratio of 9:8, or 203.9 cents (a cent is a logarithmic unit equal to 1/1200 of an octave; an equal-tempered whole tone is by definition 200 cents). In just intonation, however, there are two sizes of a whole tone: the major tone, which is the same size as the Pythagorean whole tone, and the minor tone, which is the difference between a major tone and a pure major 3rd—that is, a ratio of 10:9, or 182.4 cents. Yet in any regular meantone temperament, as in equal temperament and Pythagorean intonation, the whole tone is always precisely half the major 3rd.

WILLIAM DRABKIN

Tone (ii). Any steady sound, especially one used in making measurements, as in, for example, 'pure tone' (a single frequency), 'test tone', 'standard tone', 'combination tone', etc. 'Straight tone' generally means a sound without vibrato.

WILLIAM DRABKIN/R

Tone (iii) [tone colour]. Quality of a musical sound. An oboe might be described as producing a 'reedy' tone and a flute a 'mellow' tone, but such descriptive terms (as also 'warm', 'harsh', 'brilliant', 'dull', 'plaintive', 'strident', 'hollow', etc.) are subjective and imprecise. A fundamental aspect of the perception of tone is timbre, characterized by the relative amplitudes of the fundamental and its partials, the elements of a note's attack and ending, and the relative ways in which the amplitudes of the partials grow and decay (together called the 'envelope'). The terms 'timbre' and 'tone' are often used imprecisely and interchangeably. Tonal perception is also influenced by pitch, noise or broadband components, loudness, location, vibrato or lack of it, sympathetic vibrations, incidental noises, room acoustics, and other factors including, for the player, tactile feedback from the instrument being played. The listener's hearing acuity also determines perception of tone—e.g. through diminished sensitivity to high pitches as a consequence of aging or ear injury. Psychological factors, especially experience, are crucial in forming a hearer's response to tone—e.g. whether or not it is pleasing. In many instruments performers can directly control tone but in some such as the organ, the tonal palette is predetermined by the maker. Regulating an instrument's tone during manufacture or maintenance is often called 'voicing'. Tone production is a fundamental aspect of singing.

LAURENCE LIBIN

Tonette [flutophone, song flute]. Elongated plastic vessel flute, with a (usually integral) duct mouthpiece. It was developed for the American school market during the 1930s and 40s as a 'pre-band' instrument for introductory music classes, and was manufactured and distributed by companies that specialized in musical instruments or novelties rather than by general toy companies. The Swanson Tonette, Fitchhorn Song Flute, and Thompson Flutophone were the most prominent of these low-cost instruments, which offer the simplified fingering of the ocarina but superficially resemble the recorder. Although their use in schools has largely been supplanted by better-sounding plastic recorders, the Song Flute and Flutophone continue to be produced in the 21st century.

All three models have seven fingerholes and a thumbhole, and encompass a major 9th in a C major scale without cross-fingering. Accidentals are available using cross-fingerings, but due to the irregular shape of the resonance chamber, overblowing for an upper octave produces poor tones and is not intended. The lower ends of the Tonette and the Flutophone are closed, thus all the air entering when all the fingerholes are closed emerges from the windway, similarly to an ocarina. The designs have precedent in other end-blown ocarinas such as the metal Ocariflute of Charles Mathieu, Paris, about the turn of the 20th century, but no definitive evidence shows that they were derived from or influenced by his designs.

The earliest American design was the Swanson Tonette, patented in 1938 by Ziegner Swanson (1880–1963) of DeKalb, Illinois. Distributed by the Chicago Musical Instrument Co., it was manufactured using Tenite, a cellulosic thermoplastic made by Eastman Chemical Company's Tennessee Eastman division.

The Fitchhorn Song Flute was invented by Elver J. Fitchhorn, a former french horn player with the John Phillip Sousa band and later educational director for C.G. Conn Ltd. Fitchhorn's design (1939, design patent 115,616) was for a one-piece molded instrument that has a very small opening at the lower end. His Song Flute Company, of Evanston, Illinois, manufactured the flutes for several decades. Nowadays they are made by Conn-Selmer as the Conn Song Flute.

The Flutophone was designed in 1944 by Josephus Thompson of Covington, Ohio. In addition to a removable/adjustable mouthpiece (also found on the Tonette), the Flutophone boasts superior intonation and has a recorder-like double fingerhole near the distal end for playing $c'/c\sharp'$. The instrument has been manufactured in several colours, most commonly white with a contrasting red or blue mouthpiece. Nowadays it is marketed by Trophy Music Co., a division of Grover Musical Products, Inc. of Cleveland, Ohio.

DWIGHT NEWTON

Tonewheel. Disc, usually of metal, plastic, or glass, on which are inscribed or drawn waveforms, or a cylinder or disc with a toothed or profiled rim. Originally used for producing an audio frequency for radio receivers, the wheel or cylinder rotates as part of an electromechanical system, producing regular fluctuations in the current corresponding to the frequency represented by the waveform or profile. The fluctuations are amplified and heard through a loudspeaker. Hammond organ tonewheels are about 5 cm in diameter. The frequency produced depends upon the rotation speed, as well as the waveform or profile. While tonewheels are generally designed to produce a pure sine wave, 'harmonic leakage' from adjacent tonewheels can produce harmonics that can be considered either objectionable or part of the timbre.

ANNE BEETEM ACKER

Tongali [enongol]. Bamboo nose flute of the Kalinga people, northern Luzon, Philippines. It is also known as *inonggol, inung-ngol, innung-ngor* (Kalinga), or *ungiyung* (Ifugao). It is generally played in the sleeping quarters of young girls. Some examples are carved with fine geometrical figures throughout the whole length of the tube. Names are given for each figure, consisting of webs of triangles, squares, octagons, rectangles, and parallel lines, representing a centipede, snake, bamboo plaited wall, fish, star, or tattoo. These designs are similar to tattoos on arms and torsos, signifying status and prestige earned by sponsoring village communal feasts and for men, in the more remote past, success in headhunting raids. A rare gigantic type is called *lantuy* among the Cuyunin and Batak peoples of Palawan and the Hanunuo in Mindoro; its tube is much larger in diameter than those found in northern Luzon, and has two fingerholes bored in the lower half of the tube.

Nose flutes tend to have even distances between the toneholes. Most have three fingerholes and one thumbhole. In some flutes, all the holes are bored on only one side. The first hole to be bored is approximately midway along the length, usually but not always the thumb-hole. To locate this centre, the tube is balanced on a finger. Boring the midhole produces an approximate octave. The three other holes are measured in relation to this middle one, with three fingers' width between the holes, and are bored mostly towards the distal end so that either one fingerhole is above and two are below the thumbhole or all three are below, producing hemitonic and anhemitonic gapped scales less than an octave in range. In a few examples, an alternation of three and two finger-widths creates unequal distances between the holes. Flutes with two-plus-one holes exist in Luzon and with four-plus-one holes in Mindanao.

For a system of tuning and boring holes for flutes in the southern Philippines, see *palěndag*.

ARSENIO NICOLAS/R

Tongatong. Bamboo stamping tubes of the northern highland areas of the Philippines, among the Kalinga and the Tinggguian peoples. Kalinga players use an ensemble of six graduated tubes, with one end closed at the internode which is stamped on the floor or on a wooden board, and the other end open. The tube is held with one hand, and the other hand manipulates the open end of the tube, which controls the quality of sound and the pitch the tube produces. The open end can be closed with the palm, or damped with a slight grip on the rim. In older rituals these were used for shamanistic rites, and current styles imitate the music of flat gongs. Similar bamboo stamping tube ensembles are found among the Orang Asli in West Malaysia; in Bali and Java, Indonesia; among several groups along the borders of mainland Southeast Asia and south China; and in a few islands in Oceania.

ARSENIO NICOLAS

Tonghu. Whistle of the Bali people in the Uele region, Democratic Republic of the Congo. The spindle-shaped wooden body is about 13 cm long. See J.-S. Laurenty: *Systématique des aérophones de l'Afrique centrale* (Tervuren, Belgium, 1974), 183 only.

Tongkungon. Idiochord tube zither of Sabah, Malaysia; in Sarawak it is called *satong* (*satung*). It is a bamboo tube about 60 cm long and 10 cm in diameter, closed at both ends by nodes. The cortex of the tube is cut longitudinally into four to eight 'strings', each one raised and tuned by inserting bridges at both ends. A slit along three-quarters of the length of the body provides the soundhole. The tongkungon is generally played by one person, but up to four players, each sounding one or two strings, can also play it to imitate gong music. Among the Lotud Dusun people, the tube can encompass three nodes with the top carved in the shape of a crocodile's mouth. Three of the strings play the parts of specific gongs in the hanging gong ensemble of this community, while the fourth string plays the drum part. In the Tambunan area of Sabah the tongkungon may be accompanied by a struck zither (*takobung*) made of a piece of bamboo with a portion of one side cut away to form a relatively flat upper surface from which three

strings are cut and supported with movable bridges. The strings are struck with a light strip of bamboo. A similar struck zither with two strings is called *tongkibong*, also in the Tambunan area of Sabah.

BIBLIOGRAPHY
P. Matusky and S.B.Tan: *The Music of Malaysia, the Classical, Folk and Syncretic Traditions* (London, 2004), 302–5
J. Pugh-Kitingan: *Selected Papers on Music in Sabah* (Kota Kinabalu, Sabah, 2004), 36–7

PATRICIA MATUSKY

To n'go. Cylindro-conical drum with two laced heads, of the Ngbandi people, Democratic Republic of the Congo. See O. Boone: *Les tambours du Congo belge et du Ruanda-Urundi* (Tervuren, 1951), 30, 68.

Tongoli. Eight-string bow harp of the Dhola people of Mbale district, Uganda, held horizontally.

T'ongso [t'ungae, t'ungso]. End-blown bamboo notched flute of Korea, related to the Japanese *dôshô* and the Chinese *dongxiao*. Two types are now extant, both 60 to 65 cm long. One, in the National Classical Music Institute in Seoul, has five fingerholes and a thumbhole; the other, used in the Pukch'ông masked dance-play from northeast Korea, has four fingerholes and a thumbhole and, above the first fingerhole, a hole covered with a buzzing reed membrane (like the Korean flute *taegŭm*). The historical t'ongso described in the treatise *Akhak kwebŏm* (1493) was 60 cm long and had both the membrane (mirliton) hole and the six fingerholes, plus two unstopped vent holes near the lower end of the tube.

The Institute's t'ongso is capable of the range $d\flat$ to f''', wider than that of either the folk instrument or the 15th-century instrument. The t'ongso was originally used in *tangak* ('Chinese music') at the royal court but now only the folk instrument survives in performance, and then marginally, in the masked dance-play.

BIBLIOGRAPHY
Sŏng Hyŏn, ed.: *Akhak kwebŏm* [Guide to the study of music] (Seoul, 1493/R1975), 7.12b–13a
Chang Sa-hun: *Han'guk akki taegwan* [Korean musical instruments] (Seoul, 1969), 32 ff

ROBERT C. PROVINE

Tongtong. Wooden slit drum of the Tanah Merah and Lake Sentani areas of eastern Irian Jaya (west New Guinea). See J. Kunst: *Music in New Guinea* (The Hague, 1967), 128 only.

Tongue-clicking. Technique for producing sound by pressing the tip of the tongue against the superior alveolar ridge with the mouth open and bringing the tongue down, thus creating a click. Pitch can be varied by adjusting the length of the phonatory tube by pursing the lips, by lifting the palate, and by making other small opening and closing adjustments in the mouth. Recognizable tunes can be clicked. Dynamics can also vary, principally due to the amount of pressure in the tongue tip and the forcefulness with which it is pulled away from the alveolar ridge. Tongue clicks occur in many African languages, Mongolian shamanism, and various pop, jazz, and scat styles associated, for example, with singers such as Al Jarreau, Janet Lawson, and Miriam Makeba. Karlheinz Stockhausen called for tongue-clicking in *Refrain* (1959).

Some beat boxers use a different technique, where one side of the tongue is tightened and the other side is loose while air is expelled from the mouth. It is usually microphone-dependent to be sufficiently audible. Another type of click can be made by tightening one side of the tongue and pressing it against the side of the palate and then releasing it quickly.

SALLY SANFORD

Tonguing. In playing mouth-blown wind instruments, the technique used for beginning (and sometimes ending) notes, except those which are slurred. With reed instruments the tip of the tongue is placed against the reed, then drawn quickly back to release the air stream. In playing cup-mouthpiece instruments and members of the flute family the tip of the tongue is generally placed against the palate behind the upper teeth, then drawn back as if forming the consonant 't' or 'd' with some suitable vowel. Such a movement is often termed a 'tongue stroke' (Fr. *coup de langue*; Ger. *Zungenstoss*). For playing rapid notes, pairs of syllables are generally employed, alternating an articulation of the air stream near the teeth ('te') with one created by the back of the tongue on the soft palate as in pronouncing 'ke' or 'ge'; this gives the pattern *te-ke te-ke* (known as 'double tonguing'). For triplets the patterns *te-te-ke te-te-ke* or *te-ke-te te-ke-te* are normally used ('triple tonguing'). Flutter-tonguing, a common device in 20th- and 21st-century music, is essentially a protracted rolling of the tip of the tongue, as in an Italian 'r', or for reed-instrument players, a rolling of the soft palate.

The representation of tonguing patterns as combinations of syllables has a long history with important implications for both instrumental technique and performance practice. The earliest extant written sources on tonguing, dating from the 16th century, reveal an already highly developed system, presumably continuing a rich oral tradition.

Until the mid-17th century, most sources on tonguing were instruction books on the art of improvising diminutions, since the technique of diminunition (the ultimate expression of instrumental virtuosity) created the greatest need for rapid tonguing. The tonguing tradition as described in 16th- and 17th-century sources (notably Italian ones) demonstrated great variety and subtlety. Types of double tonguing were employed not only for speed but also for expression, and additionally in imitation of vocal *gorgie*, the characteristic throat articulation used by singers to execute rapid diminutions. Most theorists, including Ganassi (*Opera intitulata Fontegara*, 1535), Girolamo Cardano (*De musica*, c1546), Girolamo Dalla Casa (*Il vero modo di diminuir*, 1584), Riccardo Rognoni (*Passaggi per potersi essercitare nel diminuire*, 1592), and Francesco Rognoni Taeggio (*Selva di varii passaggi*, 1620), distinguished between single tonguing (*te te te* or *de de de*), to be used for notes slower than quavers, and three kinds of double or compound tonguings, called *lingue*, to be used for faster notes. These *lingue* were classified according to their articulative and expressive qualities: hard and sharp (*te-che te-che*); intermediate (*te-re te-re*); and smooth (*le-re le-re*). (Note that the pronunciation of consonants in the original languages of the sources is important for understanding how the syllables were executed. The *r* in these sources was a single stroke of a rolled 'r' in which the tip of the tongue brushes quickly against the ridge of the teeth, also known as the 'alveolar ridge'; the *ch* is equivalent to the English 'k'.) Of these compound tonguings the third type, *le-re le-re*, was considered the best for diminutions, since it most closely imitated the human voice, and was thus known as the *lingua di gorgia*. It was also termed *lingua roversa* (reversed tonguing), indicating that, when executed rapidly, it was somehow transformed or 'reversed'. The exact nature of this 'reversal' is unclear but may have involved shifting the *l* from the first syllable of the pair *le-re* to the second syllable, a similar movement to Quantz's double tongue of the 18th century (see below). The tonguing considered the least suitable for diminutions was the first one, *te-che te-che*, since it was considered too 'harsh' and 'crude' to be 'vocal'. The intermediate tonguing, *te-re te-re*, was deemed to be good for diminutions of moderate speed, as it was moderate in character and easy to control. These compound tonguings were applied to all notes faster than crotchets. In the case of quavers, while the use of compound tonguings was not strictly necessary for speed, they aided in producing a slight inequality of stress considered desirable for tasteful playing. This is presumably why an alternation of hard and soft consonants (*te-re te-re*) was preferred to two hard ones (*te-che te-che*).

Until the 18th century, nearly all notes in wind playing were tongued, the only important exception being the two alternating notes of a type of trill called the *tremolo*. Even cadential trills (*groppi*) were still generally tongued in the early 17th century. Rognoni Taeggio (1620) gave the first indication that *groppi* could sometimes be slurred as well. His brief musical example with tonguing syllables below the notes is virtually the only example from before 1700 of syllables applied to actual music rather than mere tonguing exercises. It reveals that, although string players had begun to slur passages of up to 12 semiquavers, wind players continued to articulate them using compound tonguings, particularly the *lingua roversa*. The decline of the diminution tradition is represented in the work of the cornettist Bartolomeo Bismantova (*Compendio musicale*, MS, 1677, *I-REm*, Reggiani E.41). He mentioned only two types of compound tonguings, of which the 'hard' tonguing, *te-che*, was 'no longer in use' although, curiously, sometimes used to 'good effect … in the *stile cantabile*'. To these traditional tonguings he added three-letter syllables, *ter-ler* and *der-ler*, without relating them to the *lingua roversa*, as well as slurred notes (*note legate*). Finally, he considered that the cornett required a sharper basic tonguing (*te*) than did the recorder (*de*).

The French woodwind methods of the late 17th and early 18th centuries, such as Etienne Loulié's *Méthode pour apprendre à jouer de la flûte douce* (MS, c1685, F-Pn, fr.n.a.6355), J.-P. Freillon Poncein's *La véritable manière d'apprendre à jouer en perfection du haut-bois, de la flûte et du flageolet* (1700), and Jacques Hotteterre's *Principes de la flûte traversière* (1707), used only two tonguing syllables, *tu* and *ru*, in which the *t* is pronounced behind the upper front teeth and the *r* rolled from the teeth up to the alveolar ridge. These syllables probably helped players mimic French song, which in turn was influenced by poetic structure. Hotteterre recommended *tu* for longer notes and most quavers; conjunct quavers and all semiquavers intermixed *ru* in three ways: *tu | ru* for *notes inégales* (ex.1*a*); *tu ru | tu* for dotted notes and crotchet-quaver-quaver-crotchet or quaver-semiquaver-semiquaver-quaver patterns (ex.1*b*) and *tu ru tu/tu* (ex.1*a*) to conclude a phrase. He considered slurring (*coulez*) to be an ornament; yet 12 years later, the preludes and *traits* (capricious exercises) in his *L'art de préluder sur la flûte traversière* (1719), influenced by the Italian violin style, featured a great deal of slurring over long groups of smaller note-values. Although the slurring of trills was by then universal, he still allowed the two-note termination to be tongued. As the Italian style made further inroads into French music, *tu* and *ru* were abandoned; Michel Corrette (*Méthode pour apprendre aisément à jouer de la flûte traversière*, c1739) considered them 'an absurdity which serves only to perplex the student'.

Subsequent 18th-century flute methods advocated two different approaches to tonguing. The first approach retained the use of syllables. The influential German flutist Quantz (*Versuch einer Anweisung die Flöte traversiere zu spielen*, 1752) varied the single tongue stroke, giving a choice of two syllables, *ti* and *di*: with *ti*, for playing leaping quavers, 'the tongue immediately springs back to the palate'; with *di*, for playing conjunct quavers and longer notes, the air stream 'is not kept from sustaining the tone'. For dotted notes and moderately quick passage work, he changed the subtle French mixture of *tu* and *ru* into 'the word *tiri*' and its *legato* counterpart *diri*, thus varying the consonant, bringing the tongue higher in the mouth, and creating regular patterns of syllables. He also introduced the double tongue *did'll* for 'the very quickest passage work'.

Tromlitz (*Ausführlicher und gründlicher Unterricht die Flöte zu spielen*, 1791) modified the vowel to *a*; he also incorporated *a* into patterns that would otherwise have been shown by slurs: *ta-a-ra-a-da-a-ra-a, ta-a-da-ra-a-da, tad-llad'l-lad'llad'll, tad'llda-rad'llda*, and so on. The second method, which eventually dominated in the 19th and 20th centuries, rejected the use of syllables except in double tonguing. Antoine Mahaut (*Nieuwe manier om binnen korten tijd op de dwarsfluit te leeren speelen/Nouvelle méthode pour apprendre en peu de temps à jouer de la flûte traversière*, 2/c1759) followed Corrette's example in freely intermixing tongued and slurred notes along with accent marks and staccato dots and wedges. Mahaut's musical example featured what was to become the standard classical two-slurred-two-tongued pattern alongside slurred pairs of notes both on and across the beat. For double tonguing he used the Quantzian *di-del*. De Lusse (*L'art de la flûte traversière*, c1760) advocated a new double tongue, *loul-loul*. François Devienne (*Nouvelle méthode théorique et pratique pour la flûte*, 1794) mentioned something similar, 'beating the tongue on the palate', but preferred a further pattern, *dougue dougue*, similar to the old Italian compound tonguing *te-che te-che*, rejecting *tourou* or *turu* as 'mumbling'. A similar tonguing to *dougue* had been an apparently continuous tradition among trumpeters, from Fantini's *teghe* (*Modo per imparare a sonare di tromba*, 1638) through Speer's *dikedank* and *dikedikedank* (*Ungarischer oder dacianischer Simplicissimus*, 1683) to Altenburg's *kitikiton* and *tikitikiton* (*Versuch einer Anleitung zur heroisch-musikalischen Trompeter-und Pauker-Kunst*, 1795) and beyond. John Gunn (*The Art of Playing the German-Flute on New Principles*, c1793) noted the Quantzian *diddle*, but for evenness of articulation preferred a new 'staccato' double tonguing, *teddy* or *tiddy* (which he considered a development of Quantz's *tiri*).

Even in the 19th century the modern double tongue did not take precedence immediately. Louis Drouet (*Drouët's Method of Flute Playing*, London, 1830) reported that he was still encountering *tutel, tatel* (the Netherlands), *tetel, titel, totel, tutel, take, teke*, and so on (northern Europe), and *dougue* (France), but no double tongue in Italy, Spain, and southern France; he himself preferred *deureu* or *doru*. The Quantzian double tongue was mentioned as late as 1844 by A.B. Fürstenau (*Die Kunst des Flöten-Spiels*, Leipzig, 1909), who himself used exclusively single tonguing.

BIBLIOGRAPHY

M. Castellani and E.Durante: *Del portar della lingua negli instrumenti di fiato* (Florence, 1979)

P. Ranum: '*Tu–ru–tu* and *tu–ru–tu–tu*: Toward an Understanding of Hotteterre's Tonguing Syllables', *The Recorder in the Seventeenth Century: Utrecht 1993*, 217–54

P. Ranum: 'French Articulations: a Mirror of French Song', *Traverso*, vol.20/3 (1998), 1–3

BRUCE DICKEY, DAVID LASOCKI

Ex.1.

(a)

tu ru tu ru tu ru tu   ru tu ru tu ru tu ru tu

(b)

tu   tu ru tu   tu ru tu   tu ru tu

tu tu tu ru tu tu ru tu tu ru tu

Tonkori. Five-string plucked zither of the Ainu people of northern Japan. The name, supposedly onomatopoeic, is found among the Sakhalin Ainu (now resident in Hokkaido); the Hokkaido Ainu, among whom the instrument is rare, call it *ka* ('string'). Most specimens are about 120 cm long, 10 cm wide, and 5 cm deep, although smaller versions were made for playing while standing. The narrow, boat-shaped body consists of a hollowed shell covered by a thin flat soundboard, both usually of fir or yew. The pegbox perhaps shows the influence of the Japanese *shamisen*, but this cannot be substantiated because the early history of the tonkori is unknown. Two bridges run across the soundboard, much as on the *koto*, but there are no individual movable tuning-bridges. *Shamisen* strings are generally used today, replacing the earlier deer sinew, twisted whale tendon, and so on.

The player holds the instrument nearly vertically, or diagonally with the pegbox resting on the left shoulder; if he plays sitting the point can rest on the ground or on the thigh. The strings are plucked with both hands. The basic pitch of each string is never altered, as the short melodies are repeated over and over with slight variations. The range is an octave or less.

A striking feature of the tonkori is its tuning system. The many different documented tunings are all nonconsecutive (re-entrant): the pitches of successive strings tend to rise and fall alternately, generally by 4ths and 5ths. (A common tuning pattern is $a'-d'-g'-c'-f$.) This feature recalls the Japanese *wagon*, which also often had five strings until the 7th century, as well as the Korean *kŏmun'go*, but again any connection must be conjectural.

Although the tonkori was once used in ritual and to accompany song and dance, the slim modern repertory consists only of solo semi-improvised instrumental pieces of an imitative nature: 'swimming bird', 'fox sneaks into the storehouse', 'ghost's footfalls', and so on. The former ritual function is hinted at by the coloured cords that often dangle from the pegbox (as in the Ainu shamanistic drum *kacho*) and by the practice of inserting a small ball through the star-shaped soundhole in order to give the tonkori its soul.

The Orok people of Sakhalin, the Ainu's long-time neighbours, had an instrument called *tonkur*, but it was a single-string fiddle resembling the Chinese *jinghu*. The Manchu word *tenggeri* ('stringed instrument') is a likely cognate.

BIBLIOGRAPHY
Nihon Hoso Kyokai [Japan Broadcasting Corporation], ed.: *Ainu dento ongaku* [Traditional Ainu music] (Tokyo, 1965), 517 only
'Tonkori', *Ongaku daijiten* [Encyclopedia of music] (Tokyo, 1981)
K. Tanimoto: *Ainu-e o kiku* [Listening to Ainu images] (Sapporo, 2000)
DAVID W. HUGHES

Tonkur. Single-string fiddle of the Orok people of Sakhalin, Russia. It resembles the Chinese *jinghu*.

Tononi. Italian family of violin makers. Giovanni Tononi (*d* 1713) worked in Bologna at a time when there was a great demand for violins in northern Italian cities. He took as his model the work of the Amati family and showed himself to be a careful, competent workman, in some respects foreshadowing the Venetians. His soundholes appear long and elegant, but his scrolls are meanly cut. The varnish is usually superb and glowing orange-red in colour, and the tonal qualities generally excellent.

His son, Carlo Tononi (*d* after 8 March 1730), was a more important maker. Carlo Tononi's instruments or those made under his direction are closely related to his father's but show certain improvements. The scarcity of original dated labels makes it difficult to follow his progress, but at least two or three makers were involved in the instruments' manufacture. There are many violins, an occasional cello, and quite a number of violas, all apparently modelled on the unique Amati contralto viola of 1615. Carlo Tononi moved to Venice, probably between 1715 and 1720, and his violins labelled from there in the 1720s are in most respects different in character from those of the Bolognese period. His role in their construction is a matter for conjecture: certainly he appears to have had assistance at times, though not recognizably from his well-known Venetian colleagues. He introduced a harder, less attractive varnish than that used in Bologna, and elsewhere in Venice, but some of his violins are fine concert instruments.

BIBLIOGRAPHY
S. Toffolo: *Antichi strumenti veneziani 1500–1800: quattro secoli di liuteria e cembalaria* (Venice, 1987)
Les violons: lutherie venitienne, peintures et dessins, Hôtel de Ville, Paris, 21 March–7 May 1995 (Paris, 1995) [exhibition catalogue]
CHARLES BEARE

Töpfer, Johann Gottlob (*b* Niederroßla, Thuringia, Germany, 4 Dec 1791; *d* Weimar, Germany, 8 June 1870). German organist, composer, and organ theorist. He studied first with the cantor of Niederroßla and later in Weimar with Destouches, Riemann, and A.E. Müller. He is credited with having proposed, in 1833, the first 'scientific' method of organ pipe scaling in which the cross-sectional area of a flue pipe is related to its length. He then derived a standard, rational progression in which the pipe diameter halves on every 17th inclusive note of the chromatic scale proceeding upwards (i.e. eight whole tones above), yielding an octave ratio of 1:1.682. This ratio applied to a pipe diameter of 155.5 mm at 8′ C gives so-called Normal scale (*Normalmensur*). Variations are described by such terms as 'halving on the 16th' (1:1.631) or 'halving on the 18th' (1:1.741), etc. This simple mathematical method of scaling (which in fact might have been used previously) was widely but not universally adopted by organ factories in Germany, England, France, and America. Töpfer's other scientific descriptions of organ-building techniques (with tables and technical details for wind chambers, pallets, bellows, action, etc.) and formulas for calculating wind consumption and the height of the pipe mouth cut-up, were immensely useful to new builders. See H.-C. Tacke: *Johann Gottlob Töpfer: Leben, Werk, Wirksamkeit* (Kassel, 2002).

WRITINGS
(selective list)
Die Theorie und Praxis des Orgelbaues (Weimar, 1833)
Anleitung zur Erhaltung und Stimmung der Orgel (Jena, 1840)

Die Scheiblersche Stimmmethode leicht fasslich erklärt (Erfurt, 1842)
Die Orgel, Zweck und Beschaffenheit ihrer Teile (Erfurt, 1843)
Lehrbuch der Orgelbaukunst (Weimar, 1855–64)

LAURENCE LIBIN

Topshuur [tobshuur]. Two-string plucked lute of western Mongolia. Topshuur bodies vary in shape according to ethnic and family traditions; those of the Bait, Dörbet, and Hoton peoples can be small and round, shaped like a cup or bowl, rectangular, or trapezoidal. Some Altai Urianghais, Baits, and Torguts make a necked bowl topshuur. Altai Urianghais fashion their instruments from juniper in the shape of the wooden *tsatsal* ladle used to offer milk aspersions to the spirits of nature. The instrument is often named after the shape of its pegbox or soundtable. If the body is shaped like a milk ladle, it is called a *shanagan topshuur*, but if it is in the shape of a *tsatsal* ladle, it is called a *tsatsal topshuur*. Among Dörbets, Zakchins, and Torguts a spike bowl lute is played; among Baits, Dörbets, Altai Urianghais, and Zakchins a spike box lute, similar in construction to the two-string spike fiddle *igil*, might also be used.

The strings of both the topshuur and the *ikil* are tuned to an interval of a 4th. When the topshuur is strung with horsehair, as on the Tuva *toshpulur* and the Altai *topshur* (both related to the Khakass *komïs*), the thinner string should be twisted clockwise, the thicker counterclockwise; they are tuned a 4th apart and plucked with thumb and forefinger or strummed. The instrument can easily be converted into a bowed instrument by untwisting the strings and increasing the number of hairs. Gut strings have also been used, and nowadays nylon strings with mechanical tuners are used. Among the Baits and Dörbets, strings are made from sheep intestines which, after being cleaned and washed several times, are stretched and twisted clockwise and counterclockwise, then dried. The topshuur has been made with both lateral and frontal pegs. The narrow unfretted or fretted neck is often surmounted by a carved animal head, usually a horse's but nowadays also a swan's. Although the soundtable may be covered with the skin of goat or camel, or wood with soundholes, traditionally the skin of 'hot-nosed' animals was preferred—i.e. those with a kinship relation to humans, such as horses and sheep. The skin should be as thin as possible and is therefore often taken from the groin of an animal.

A legend of the origin of the topshuur explains its use to accompany epics prior to hunting. A hunter's unaccompanied performance of the epic prelude *Altain Magtaal* ('Praise-Song of the Altai') was interrupted when one of the many tiny spirit-masters of the Altai mountains, who were sitting all over him including on his face, fell from the tip of his nose onto his top lip. The diviner and hunting companion who witnessed this made an instrument to help the performer keep a steady rhythm and not spoil the spirits' entertainment (thereby causing dire consequences for the hunt), even in the face of such mishaps.

The topshuur was traditionally kept in a place of honour within the bard's tent and was allowed to be touched only by him. On the day before the epic performance, the host carried the topshuur in a special box to his home, where its presence was thought to repel danger.

The instrument has a repertory of tunes called *tsohilt*, comparable to the *huur* repertory (*tatlaga*). These descriptive pieces imitate animals and nature and are sometimes used to accompany the *biy* dance.

BIBLIOGRAPHY
S. Dulam: 'Conte, chant et instruments de musique: quelques légendes d'origine mongoles', *Etudes mongoles*, vol.18 (1987), 33–44
D. Nansalmaa: 'Oyuny soyol' [Spiritual culture], *Halhyn Ugsaatny Züi XIX–XX Zuuny Zaag Üe* [Khalkha ethnography in the late 19th and early 20th centuries], ed. S. Badamhatan (Ulaanbaatar, 1987), 334–57
C.A. Pegg: *Mongolian Music, Dance, and Oral Narrative* (Seattle, 2001) [with CD]

CAROLE PEGG/R

Töpu. End- or side-blown Triton conch horn of Santa Cruz, Solomon Islands. See G. Koch: *Die materielle Kultur der Santa Cruz Inseln* (Berlin, 1971), 174 only.

Tōr [toor]. Large round or oval wooden percussion block of the Yos Sudarso Bay (Humboldt Bay) and Lake Sentani areas of eastern Papua, Indonesia. The block was dropped from the roof to the floor of the men's cult house (*mau*) to make the uninitiated believe that a spirit had entered the house. The tōr was also dropped for each pig as it was brought to the threshold of the house to offer the spirits. Simultaneously, an ensemble of end-blown secret flutes played and the initiates stamped the floor. See P. Wirz: 'Beitrag zur Ethnologie der Sentanier (Holländisch Neuguinea)', *Nova Guinea*, vol.16 (1928), 334–5.

MARGARET J. KARTOMI/DON NILES

Torban [teorban]. Plucked lute of Ukraine. It resembles the theorbo in having a set of unfretted bass strings (typically four or six) off the fingerboard, extending to a separate pegbox, but it also has 12 to 14 unfretted treble strings (*prystrunky*) off the fingerboard on the opposite side, tuned by pegs inserted into the shoulder of the pear-shaped, ribbed soundbox. The torban also resembles the *kobza*, which however lacks the unfretted bass strings and their separate pegbox. The torban's invention has been credited speculatively to a monk, Tuliglowski, from Jasna Gora, about 1735–40, but the term was used earlier, indiscriminately, for any type of lute-like instrument. The torban proper was occasionally encountered in 19th-century Lithuania, Poland, and Russia. Because of its complexity and cost it was considered an instrument of the upper classes, and it attracted some virtuoso players and a small independent repertory in Eastern Europe before falling out of fashion during the Russian Revolution. Some 40 old torbans are preserved in museums, with a group of 14 in St Petersburg (*RUS.SP.m*); only three makers have been identified. In the late 20th century some imitations were constructed, but based on the design of the *bandura*, an unfretted psaltery. See L. Cherkasky: *Ukrainski narodni muzychni instrumenty* (Kiev, 2003).

LAURENCE LIBIN

Tori. Side-blown bronze trumpet of Madhya Pradesh (Bastar district), central India. The curved shape of the instrument is reminiscent of, or imitates, that of the *akum*, but the mouth hole is on the side. It is about 34 cm long, finely wrought, with tiny pellet bells hanging from the longer side. The bronze trumpet is used especially among the young Muria of the *ghotul* (a so-cio-religious institution), purchased from the Ghasia, a Hindi community of metal-casters who use the lost-wax technique. According to some authors, tori might be related to the Sanskrit word *turya* ('instrument'), which is clearly found in the Pali or Malayalam word *turyam*. Other trumpet names probably derive from this, such as *turi* (Orissa, Uttar Pradesh), *tur hi* (Bihar), and *tutari* (Maharashtra). Although the shapes, dimensions, and uses are different, these trumpets are made from a common material (bronze or brass) and have the same conical bore.

BIBLIOGRAPHY
W. Kaufmann: 'The Musical Instruments of the Hill Maria, Jhoria and Bastar Muria Gond Tribes', *EthM*, vol.5/1 (1961), 1–9
K.S. Kothari: *Indian Folk Musical Instruments* (New Delhi, 1968)
B.C. Deva: *Musical Instruments of India: their History and Development* (Calcutta, 1978)
GENEVIÈVE DOURNON

Tormento, el (Sp.: 'the storm'). Scraper of northern Chile. The top surface of a rectangular box about 30 by 20 cm and 15 cm deep consists of several slats of wood. Inside the box are several rows of metal beverage caps, strung on cords as rattles. Sometimes the lower panel of the box is omitted.

The box rests on a folding wooden frame about 35 cm tall, or can be placed on the performer's knees or held by a strap around the performer's neck. It is played by scraping the slats with one's fingers wearing thimbles, with bare hand, or with sticks. It is used to accompany the *cueca* (the official national dance of Chile), *tonadas*, and other central and northern Chilean dances. When played in a *fonda*, *chingana*, or *ramada* (eating or dancing venues), a larger version (about 50 to 60 cm long) is suspended from the rafters.

Tornavoz. Fitting applied to certain guitars to enhance the tone. It is a slightly conical tube of thin brass or another metal, inserted beneath the soundtable surrounding the soundhole, and widening toward (but not touching) the back of the instrument. Around the open back end, the tube is sometimes perforated to facilitate air flow. The tornavoz appears to lower the Helmholtz frequency of the soundbox and helps to focus the bass tone particularly. It is said to have been invented by Antonio de Torres (1817–92), but the term was used as early as 1841 by Antonio Xemena, probably for a device of different form. The Torres type was used by some makers into the 1930s and has occasionally been applied to modern guitars. Francisco Tárrega owned a Torres guitar with a tornavoz that he considered one of his best instruments.

Tornel Torres, Tadeo (*b* Alhama de Murcia, Spain, 1729; *d* Alhama de Murcia, *c*1790). Spanish keyboard instrument maker. In 1770, Tornel was a musician in the convent of Corpus Christi in Murcia. He sold a harpsichord in 1774 to the Orihuela cathedral for 220 *libras* (about 3430 *rs*). In 1778 he was accepted as a member of the Real Sociedad Económica de Amigos del País (Royal Economic Society of Friends of the Country), a private society that publicized Enlightenment ideas and recent advances in philosophy and science. Tornel built the only extant claviorgan combining harpsichord and piano actions with organ pipes (Museo Arqueológico, Murcia). A printed label on its soundboard reads 'D TADEUS TORNEL/me Fecit in Civitate/Murciense Año 1777/20' with the number 20 handwritten. The case of solid walnut has a double-curved bentside and seven baluster legs joined by a stretcher at the bottom and a moulded frame at the top. The keyboard compass is $G'–g'''$. The organ register (probably a set of stopped 8′ wooden pipes, now missing) operated in the treble only. Four pedals controlled the registers, apparently thus: first, to engage a harp stop; second, to simultaneously disengage the treble piano hammers and engage the flute; third, to disengage the dampers; and fourth, to disengage all the hammers and engage the harpsichord plectra. Two knee levers, operated laterally, allowed the player to pump the organ bellows. The hammer action is very similar to that of Zumpe. In 1878 the instrument was described and reported to have belonged to one Manuel Higinio. According to the same document, the flutes were removed by the sons of a Sr Cañizares to build another instrument, which remained unfinished.

The other known instrument by Tornel is a square piano (1784) numbered 28, with range $G'/A'–f'''$, formerly owned by the convent of Santa Clara in Hellín and nowadays in a private collection in Calasparra, Murcia.

BIBLIOGRAPHY
E. Máximo García: 'Tadeo Tornel, 'ymbentor de ynstrumentos de música', *Imafronte*, vol.15 (2000), 167–81
M. Latcham: 'The Instrument of Many Colours Made by Tadeo Tornel in Murcia, 1777', *Domenico Scarlatti in Spain*, ed. L. Morales (Almería, 2009), 241–97
LUISA MORALES

Torototela. Bowed monochord or stick zither of northeastern Italy. It consists of a *minugia* (thick catgut string) stretched along a *percia* (long straight stick) and near the lower end passing over an *apssìa* (inflated pig bladder or balloon) that serves as a resonator. The string is tuned by a long peg inserted at the top of the stick, and is fingered against the stick or touched lightly to produce harmonics, but mostly it sounds a rhythmic drone. It is played in folk ensembles, often to accompany singing—for instance, at carnivals or marriages.

Torowa. Gourd vessel rattle of the Ashanti people of Ghana. It has been added as a rhythmic device to *kete* drum ensembles.

Torres Jurado, Antonio de (*b* La Cañada de San Urbano, nr Almería, Spain, 13 June 1817; *d* Almería, 19 Nov

1892). Spanish guitar maker. About 1835 he became a carpenter in Vera. In 1845 he moved to Seville, where he started making guitars in earnest around 1850; his earliest surviving one is dated 1854. By 1858 one of his guitars had received a bronze medal in Seville. An instrument he built in 1859 was used by Miguel Llobet Soles for many years. Francisco Tárrega's first guitar is reported to have been a Torres of 1864, and Tárrega later owned two more. One of these (1862; *E.B.mi*) has ribs and back of papier mâché, possibly intended to demonstrate that these parts are not so important acoustically as had been believed. Another instrument, of 1865, has a six-piece back of cypress, a wood used for Torres's less expensive guitars. In the later 1860s Torres returned to Almería and opened a china shop, but by 1875 he was once again building fine, full-size guitars noted for their volume and resonance. From 1883 until his death he made about a dozen instruments a year, among them several 11-string guitars. Although Torres was credited for a time with the almost single-handed invention of the modern classical guitar, evidence now suggests that he merely incorporated extant refinements, in particular the fan-bracing of the table, into a larger and more resonant design. An instrument of 1864 in the Godia Sales collection, Barcelona, has a domed soundtable, an open lower harmonic bar with extended outer struts, and a *tornavoz* fitted inside around the soundhole, all features of Torres's concert guitars. Characteristic of most of his instruments, the top of the headstock has three lobes, the central one larger and taller than the others. The use and promotion of his guitars by the leading Spanish virtuosos of his day assured his reputation at a moment when the modern instrument, with an attractive new Spanish repertory, was beginning to be noticed in Spain and beyond.

BIBLIOGRAPHY

T. Evans: 'L'apport de Torrès à l'évolution de la guitare classique d'aujourd'hui: carrière et facture', *La facture instrumentale européenne*, Musée instrumental du Conservatoire national supérieur de musique de Paris, 6 Nov 1985–1 March 1986 (Paris, 1985) [exhibition catalogue], 231–9

P. Abondance: 'Torres: mythe ou réalité?', *Cahiers de la guitare*, no.24 (1987), 16–18

J.L. Romanillos: *Antonio de Torres, Guitar Maker: his Life and Work* (Shaftesbury, 1987)

M. Hecker: 'Don Antonio de Torres', *Instrumentenbau-Zeitschfirt*, vol.46/12 (1992), 12–15

THOMAS F. HECK/R

Tortuga. Turtle shell idiophone of Mesoamerica, used since pre-Contact times. A fresco in Structure 1 of the Bonampak ruins in Chiapas, Mexico, depicts a Mayan procession accompanied by musical instruments including the turtle shell, which continues to be used in religious processions nowadays. Tortugas are struck with mallets or sticks on the plastron side.

In Guatemala, indigenous and Ladino or mestizo (mixed-descent) people use the tortuga. Among the Maya, they accompany dances alongside other instruments. For instance, an ensemble comprising *tortuga*, trumpet, and *tun* slit drum accompanies the dance *Baile*

del Tz'unum (dance of the hummingbird), an origins dance from Aguacatán, Huehuetenango. The Q'anjob'al-Mayan word for *tun*, *akte'* (wooden turtle), suggests that the *tun* might have replaced the tortuga in some Mayan performances such as the *Kanhal Che'* (dance of the horse), from Jacaltenango, Huehuetenango.

Among Ladinos tortguas feature prominently in the *posada*, the procession representing Mary and Joseph searching for lodging. As the procession marches, tortugas sound a rhythmic pattern. Although the tortuga has no definite pitch, the pattern uses two types of strokes, the higher-sounding one striking the shell towards its edge and the lower one striking towards the centre (ex.1). Guatemalans onomatopoeically refer to the lower sound with the syllables *tu* and *cu* and to the higher pitch with the syllable *te*, so the pattern of the *posadas* is known as *tu-cu te-cu-tu* (spoken in rhythm). Composers have used variations of the tortuga *posada* pattern as the basis for compositions for marimba that celebrate Christmas.

ANDRÉS AMADO

Torupill. Bagpipe of Estonia. It usually consists of a bag of seal stomach, bladder, or dog or goat skin, a cylindrical chanter (*sõrmiline*) of juniper or pine wood with five or six fingerholes and single cane reed (*piuk*), and one or two (rarely three) bass drones. The instrument was known in Estonia probably from the 14th century and is documented from the 16th. It was played at festivities and to rouse field workers. It survived on the islands and in the coastal regions into the early 20th century, and by the 1980s had been revived by folk music ensembles and music schools.

Toshpulur. Two-string plucked lute of the Tuva people of Siberia, related to the nearby Altai *topshuur* and Khakass *komïs*.

Toubi [doubi]. Cylindrical double-headed drum of Greece. It resembles the *daouli* but is smaller and shallower. Its sizes vary, some being shallower than the diameter and others deeper. It has two gut snares, one on each head, either over the heads or within the body. The heads can be either braced with cords or nailed to the body. It is usually hung from the left shoulder, but can be held under the armpit, slung over the left thigh, or suspended from the left arm above the wrist, like a *tabor*. It is played on one head with the hands or with two short wooden sticks, one of which might have the upper end cut as a fork so that it can be used to push the thongs around the bracing cords up or down and so tune the drum. The toubi is essentially an instrument of the Aegean Islands, where it accompanies the *tsambouna* (bagpipe) or the *lyra* (short-necked fiddle), but can also accompany songs and dances by itself. Children play it while performing Christmas carols and, during the Turkish occupation, it was used to call people to church. That its use dates back to Byzantine times is shown by its presence in 14th- and 15th-century accounts of the life of Belisarius. See F. Anoyanakis: *Greek Popular Musical Instruments* (Athens, 1979), 131–2.

JEREMY MONTAGU

Touch. Term referring (1) to characteristics of an instrument (usually a keyboard type) that relate to the interaction with the player's fingers, and (2) to different methods of depressing and releasing the keys. Haptics includes the scientific study of touch. This discussion concerns keyboard instruments.

(1) Factors involved with keyboard touch generally include key surface materials, balance points, dimensions, and layout; flexibility and mass of action parts; friction, vibration, and lost motion; and psycho-physiological attributes. In addition, different types of instruments have inherent influential characteristics, some of which are discussed below. Common terms describing keyboard touch include *shallow*, *deep*, *heavy*, *light*, *fast*, *responsive*, *stiff*, and *uneven*. *Shallow* or *deep* refers to the depth of key descent, while *heavy* or *light* refers to force (touchweight) on the key needed to obtain a desired sound. Touchweight includes *downweight*, the minimum weight that will cause the key to descend, and *upweight*, the maximum weight a depressed key will lift upon being released. Touchweight alone is insufficient to characterize keyboard touch. The timing and pattern of forces fed back from the action during a keystroke also affect the player's sense of touch.

Clavichord touch is influenced by key mass, striking distance, string tension, stiffness of the listing (damping cloth), and presence or absence of a pressure bar. The clavichord's mechanism, with only one moving part (the key itself) and a limited range of motion, is very sensitive.

Harpsichord touch is primarily characterized by the resistance encountered by the plectrum when plucking the string. Another significant influence is coupling of keyboards, as when lower manual keys lift the coupled upper manual keys as well as both manuals' jacks. The number of registers engaged determines the number of plucks initiated by a single key depression. Thus, harpsichord touch is also affected by the number and order of plucks (such as 4′ then back 8′ then front 8′) and their timing (*stagger*). Other factors include string tension; material, length, stiffness, and shape of plectra; weight of the jacks; position of plectra relative to strings; and compression of action padding.

Organ touch is mainly concerned with the keys opening pallet or pneumatic valves or controlling electric switches. Mechanical-action touch can vary dramatically depending upon the type and distance of connection from key to pallet. Its salient characteristic is *pluck* (not to be confused with the harpsichord's pluck), a point of resistance during key depression when the air pressure difference across the pallet abruptly drops as the pallet begins to open. The number of registers drawn, wind pressure, pallet spring strength, action mass and inertia, keyboard coupling, and whether keys are balanced or

suspended are among many factors affecting mechanical-action touch. Artificial pluck on electric-action organ keyboards attempts to replicate the touch of mechanical actions.

Carillon touch depends largely upon the connections between the keys and the bell clappers, as well as the weight of the clappers and the distance they travel. The keys are wooden levers about 60 cm long, hinged at the distal end and descending deeply at the front. A vertical wire connects each key to a transmission system that transfers key motion to a horizontal wire that pulls the clapper for the associated bell. The length of these wires affects touch due to the amount of lost motion sensed and the distance between clapper and bell. When the keyboard is very far from the bells, the mass of the long wires affects the speed of clapper response to key motion. Compressibility of the keybed is another important factor. Countersprings and counterweights balance the weight of heavy clappers for large bells, reducing the touchweight. On large carillons, one to two octaves of pedals can sound the largest bells.

Piano touch has changed significantly along with the evolution of the piano. Early pianos typically have light, fast, relatively simple actions with a shallow key dip compared to modern instruments. Some early pianos have no escapement mechanism and very light, unpadded hammers. From the mid-18th century until the 20th, several types of actions were commonly employed, each with different touch characteristics. Early Viennese-type actions are noted for their responsiveness, relatively shallow keydip, direct control of loudness, placement and duration of notes, and minimal aftertouch (the distance the key continues to descend after hammer escapement). The touch of early English actions, while still light and shallow by modern standards, is different from contemporary Viennese-type actions due to differences in internal events felt from the action, as well as generally deeper keydip. The Erard repetition action of 1828 introduced a third kind of touch; some contemporary players considered Erard's mechanically complex action less responsive and less amenable to subtle control. Piano actions based on Erard's predominated during the 20th century and remain standard. As pianos grew larger and string tensions increased, hammers, dampers, and other action parts became heavier, increasing downweight dramatically, from as low as 10 grams for early pianos up to 65 grams for modern grand pianos.

Factors influencing the touch of modern pianos include amount of aftertouch, hammer weight and density, shank flexibility, balance point location, weighting of key levers, weight and timing of dampers, type of wippen and wippen springs, bushing and cushioning materials, tightness of centre pins, knuckle diameter, and other characteristics affecting the friction and timing of component collisions during key travel. Upright and grand piano touches differ significantly due to different action geometries. In particular, upright actions generally lack repetition levers and so have difficulty repeating notes very quickly. Short uprights generally have lighter downweights than modern grands. The touchweight of 18th- and 19th-century pianos can differ markedly from bass to treble due to such factors as varying key lengths, balance points, and hammer sizes across the compass, with no attempt at static balance from key to key.

The touch of electronic keyboards and digital pianos varies greatly. Inexpensive electronic keyboards and most synthesizers have lightweight plastic keys that are mounted on soft rubber pads and offer the player no feedback. Most electronic keyboards have spring-loaded keys. Some electronic and digital keyboards are touch-sensitive (or equivalently, velocity-sensitive). Inexpensive touch-sensitive keyboards sense only the relative pressure of touch. In better instruments, two sensors are used to detect the velocity of key depression, with faster descent indicating louder sound. In some digital pianos, harder blows produce timbre changes, as in acoustic pianos. Some electronic keyboards allow a key to be restruck before it returns completely to its resting position, allowing for faster repetition. 'Weighted response' keys have weights and springs to give a 'hammer action' feel. Some expensive electronic keyboards use actual piano hammers of graduated weights in the action to simulate more closely the touch of acoustic pianos.

The feature called 'aftertouch', introduced to higher-grade synthesizers (e.g. the CS-80) in the late 1970s, allows sound to be modulated after a key has been depressed, depending on the pressure with which the key is held down. Fade and return, vibrato, echo, and so on, can be added by means of aftertouch.

(2) With regard to performance on keyboard instruments, a term used to describe different methods of depressing and releasing the keys. Pedagogues and performers discourse at length upon touch and its relationship to technique and tone quality. Kullak (1855) wrote that touch is the art of producing sound on a keyboard instrument not just beautifully, but also correctly according to the demands of the particular instrument. At the simplest level, the term is used in describing styles of articulation such as *legato*, *staccato*, *detaché*, *tenuto*, and *marcato*. In addition, touch can refer to a performer's method of employing the shoulder, upper arm, elbow, lower arm, wrist, hand, and fingers to control how sound is produced. Many persons believe skillful touch can control tone quality, but this is a matter of dispute. Different types of keyboard instruments and actions require different approaches to touch. For example, producing a trill on a harpsichord requires a different sort of touch than on a grand piano.

The clavichord is highly responsive to touch but requires great finger control, as the tangent remains in contact with the strings for the duration of the tone. After depressing the key, the performer can increase or decrease pressure to alter the pitch, or to add portamento or vibrato. For 'good touch', clavichord keys are depressed solely by the fleshy part of the fingertips with the hand well curved (Sancta Maria, 1565). This shape gives strength in sustaining the notes. The attack must be firm and unhesitant to avoid 'chucking' of the tangent on the string. Pressure must be maintained, yet

motions must be fluid and tension in the hand avoided. C.P.E. Bach recommended that every keyboard player study the clavichord as it develops touch sensitivity and finger control in a way taught by no other keyboard instrument, enhancing the player's delicacy and nuance of touch on other instruments.

Basic touch on the harpsichord is primarily concerned with the timing of the pluck and release. Secondarily, the player can control the speed of the jack return and therefore the damping of the string as the key is released. The player cannot control loudness by finger pressure except in harpsichords with soft, pliable plectra. Harpsichordists generally employ the fingers alone, with relaxed wrists and lightly supporting arms. Playing at the extreme fronts of the keys gives the benefit of maximum leverage. Troeger describes three basic modes of touch: from just above the surface of the keys; from the surface—that is with the fingertips in contact with the keys without pressing them; and with the fingers slightly depressing the keys so that the plectra are in contact with the strings before plucking occurs. Finger strokes tend to be of two types: up and down, and 'chicken scratching' or 'squeezing the keys', where instead of the finger rising when releasing the key, the fingertip is drawn towards the player.

Organ touch can be extremely variable, depending on the type of instrument and registration being used. With a mechanical action, the player must focus on the initial resistance of the key as the pallet begins to open and the subsequent lessening of pressure as the key descends farther. Effective touch on a mechanical action can require strong fingers, flexible hands, and in some cases the use of arm weight at the beginning of a keystroke. Many organists believe they can control pipe speech transients by varying their touch on mechanical actions, but this view is highly controversial. In electric and most electropneumatic actions, all keys in all registrations offer equal resistance, and the player cannot influence the beginning or ending of a note except by timing.

The carillon is played with closed hands, but its linked mechanical action gives the performer close control of dynamics and phrasing. Pressed touch, where the key is pressed to the keybed, gives precise control of loudness and timing and is used for relatively slower music. With struck touch, the key is quickly struck from the top, so it is difficult to control the precise loudness and timing of notes, but it is possible to play much faster. Performers use a wide range of touches between these two extremes for expressive playing. In addition, the player is able to adjust slightly the length of the wire linkage before performance to change the touch response.

Piano touch has been much discussed throughout the history of the piano. Its dynamic flexibility and change of timbre at different dynamic levels mean that the player's touch can significantly affect the sound. It is commonly believed that the pianist can influence tone quality through touch even at a steady dynamic level, although the performer cannot control the hammer/string interaction once the hammer has been thrown free. Different pianists and pedagogues utilize quite different approaches to touch, and these approaches evolved along with piano design. Early pianos, with light, fast actions and shallow keydip, encouraged a touch influenced by clavichord and harpsichord techniques, employing little arm weight. Kalkbrenner (1785–1849) stressed keeping the fingers close over the keys and using only the power and pressure of the finger. According to Chopin, each finger had different capabilities, and each finger produced different sounds. He felt that 'to play entirely from the wrist, as Kalkbrenner advocates, is incorrect' (Eigeldinger). Liszt advocated a fluid, adaptive approach to touch, free of tension, with limber hands neither curved nor flat, but pliable. He emphasized never playing from the shoulders and arms.

As pianos grew more powerful, their actions required significantly more force. In response to this trend, different schools of touch developed. Lebert and Stark of the Stuttgart Royal Conservatory advocated a stiff, percussive style of playing. The fingers were to be held well above the keys, and were to strike and return to position very rapidly. This so-called percussion touch was extended to utilize the wrist or elbow as a hinge for playing rapid 6ths or octaves or for bravura passages. Tobias Matthay (1858–1945) published an exhaustive but unscientific study of physiology and touch, emphasizing the use of balanced arm weight and precisely judged key acceleration to influence tone. Debussy taught that pianists must choose their touch according to the desired tone colour. He described ways of playing to achieve the sound of bells. Tones were to be sustained with the pedal, not the fingers. He taught a special form of pianissimo production, the *carrezando* touch, produced by depressing the key not directly from above but from an oblique, slanting angle.

Whether touch can actually control piano tone is a topic of ongoing debate. In 1925, after exhaustive scientific study, Otto Ortmann concluded that touch can control only pitch, duration, and intensity. His work seemed to have been confirmed by Hart, Fuller, and Lusby, who believed the sole factor affecting piano tone is the velocity at the end of the stroke, not the velocity during the stroke (timbre is changed by hammer impact velocity). However, it has been shown that the timing of percussive components of keystrokes can change the perception of tone. In particular, pressed touch causes less percussive noise than striking a key. Alba and Inouye discuss how the key's impact on the keybed might affect soundboard vibration. Research by Anders Askenfelt in the 1980s discussing the possible effects of hammer mode vibrations on touch and tone was inconclusive. Formal study in this area continues.

BIBLIOGRAPHY

T. de Sancta Maria: *Libro llamado Arte de tañer fantasía* (Valladolid, 1565/*R*); Eng. trans., ed. A.C. Howell and W.E. Hultberg (Pittsburgh, 1991)

C.P.E. Bach: *Versuch über die wahre Art das Clavier zu spielen*, vol.1 (Berlin, 1753/*R*, 3/1787/*R*); vol.2 (Berlin, 1762/*R*, 2/1797/*R*); Eng. trans. (1949, 2/1951)

A. Kullak: *Die Kunst des Anschlags* (Leipzig, 1855; Eng. trans., 1882)

T. Matthay: *The Act of Touch in all its Diversity, an Analysis and Synthesis of Pianoforte Tone-Production* (London, 1903)

O. Ortmann: *The Physical Basis of Piano Touch and Tone* (London and New York, 1925)

M. Dumesnil: *How to Play and Teach Debussy* (New York, 1932)

H. C. Hart, M.W. Fuller, and W.S.Lusby: 'A Precision Study of Piano Touch and Tone', *Journal of the Acoustical Society of America*, vol.6 (1934–5), 80–94

R. Alba and A.T. Inouye: 'Piano Tone Color and Touch', *Piano Quarterly* (1979), no.107, pp.36–9

R. Troeger: *Technique and Interpretation on the Harpsichord and Clavichord* (Bloomington, IN, 1987)

A. Askenfelt and E.Jansson: 'From Touch to String Vibrations, 1: Timing in the Grand Piano Action', *Journal of the Acoustical Society of America*, vol.88 (1990), 52–63; '2: The Motion of the Key and Hammer', *Journal of the Acoustical Society of America*, vol.90 (1991), 2383–93; '3: String Motion and Spectra', *Journal of the Acoustical Society of America*, vol.93 (1993), 2181–96

J. J. Eigeldinger, ed.: *Frédéric Chopin: Esquisses pour une méthode de piano* (Paris, 1993) [incl. facs.]

G.W. Kornhoof and A.J. van der Walt: 'The Influence of Touch on Piano Sound', *Proceedings of Stockholm Music Acoustics Conference 1993*, 318–24

A. Galembo: 'Perception of Musical Instrument by Performer and Listener (with Application to the Piano)', *Proceedings of International Workshop on Human Supervision and Control in Engineering and Music, Kassel, 2001*, 257–66

W. Goebl, R. Bresin, and A. Galembo: 'Once Again: the Perception of Piano Touch and Tone. Can Touch Audibly Change Piano Sound Independently of Intensity?', *Proceedings of the International Symposium on Musical Acoustics, Nara, 2004*, 332–335.

W. Goebl, R. Bresin, and A. Galembo: 'Touch and Temporal Behavior of Grand Piano Actions', *Journal of the Acoustical Society of America*, vol.118/2 (2005), 1154–65

R. Gerig: *Famous Pianists and Their Technique* (Bloomington, IN, 2007)

ANNE BEETEM ACKER

Touch instruments [touch-sensitive instruments]. Electronic instruments that respond to the location and sometimes the degree of pressure of the user's fingers. Touch instruments, or touch instrument applications, are based upon software implemented on electronic visual displays, also known as touchscreens. Touchscreens detect the position of finger or stylus contact with the display area. Examples include Bebot, a touch synthesizer first released in 2008 by Russell Black for Normalware that features four-finger multi-touch polyphony and user-definable behaviour including sound-generation methods, delays, and either continuous pitch changes or various discrete scales. Pitch is determined by the horizontal position of the finger on the screen, while timbre or loudness is controlled by the vertical position. The touch instrument applications Pianist and Guitarist introduced by MooCowMusic Ltd in 2008, function as wireless MIDI digital instrument simulators, with keyboards, guitar necks, or tablature displayed on touchscreens that are played with the fingers.

Some touchscreens can also detect the degree of pressure, such as a screen made by Touchco Inc. used for the Linnstrument introduced in 2010 by Roger Linn. On this polyphonic instrument, finger pressure determines note volume, strike velocity determines the volume of percussive sounds, finger left/right position determines pitch, and the forward/back position determines note timbre. The screen can display a variety of typical instrument interfaces such as keyboards or guitar frets, or can display a hexagonal pattern programmed to respond in different ways.

The term 'touch-sensitive' is sometimes used to describe instruments more correctly identified as 'pressure-sensitive' or 'velocity-sensitive'. In pressure-sensitive devices, the control voltage varies with the degree of pressure applied to a key or touch-plate. Some keyboards of this type recognize discrete levels of pressure, while others produce a signal that varies continuously with changing pressure. In 'velocity-sensitive' keyboards, the control voltage varies with the speed at which the key is depressed.

ANNE BEETEM ACKER

Toulouhou. Whirled friction drum of the French Pyrenees. The name is a Gascon word for 'hornet'. The cylindrical body is made from a folded strip of bark or an open tin box, the top of which is covered with a piece of bladder or sheepskin; a lock of horsehair or a length of cord is threaded through the membrane and attached to a handle made from a stick with which the toulouhou is whirled in the air. The sound has become associated with death. Until 1956 at least, children played the instrument in village streets to announce church services during Holy Week, and it was heard even inside the church during Tenebrae on Good Friday. See C. Marcel-Dubois: 'Le toulouhou des Pyrénées centrales, usage rituel et parentés d'un tambour à friction tournoyant', *Les congrès et colloques de l'Université de Liège*, vol.19 (1960), 55–89.

CLAUDIE MARCEL-DUBOIS

Toumbeleki. Greek term for *darabukka*. This single-headed goblet drum is made of clay or brass with a goatskin head, which can be either glued to the shell or tied with light cord. Small pellet bells might be suspended within the drum or tied around the outside. It is found almost exclusively in Macedonia and Thrace and the islands of the eastern Aegean, and is used to accompany all the principal melodic instruments. In northern Greece it is used particularly to accompany the *gaida* (bagpipe) or other instruments. Playing technique can be elaborate, with different tone colours elicited from different areas of the head, and the pitch can be varied by pressure on the head. The toumbeleki is also played by Greek refugees from Turkey. It is sometimes called *taraboúka*, *darbuka*, or *darabuka*. See F. Anoyanakis: *Greek Popular Musical Instruments* (Athens, 1979), 114–15.

JEREMY MONTAGU

Tourin, Peter (*b* Fairfield, OH, 20 Feb 1945). American luthier and computer software engineer, active in Jericho Center, Vermont (formerly in Duxbury, Vermont). Born into a musical family, he is a bluegrass fiddler as well as a viol player. He graduated from the University of Michigan with a B.S. degree in psychology in 1967, became interested in early music while spending his junior year studying in Munich, and trained as an instrument builder in the workshops of Frank Hubbard (harpsichords) in Waltham, Massachusetts, and J. Donald Warnock (viols) in Princeton, Massachusetts. He made his first viol in 1974 and before ceasing production in the early 1990s had made about 125 copies of historical instruments, based mainly on measurements taken from examples in European and American museums. He also built some harpsichords and plucked fretted instruments. Tourin is noted for initiating a valuable database of historical viols, continued by Thomas G. MacCracken. Apprentices trained in Tourin's shop include the violin and viol maker Warren Ellison and the bowmaker Harry F. Grabenstein, who continue work in Tourin's Jericho Center shop.

Tournay, Jean (*b* Sombreffe, Belgium, 13 April 1940). Belgian clavichord and harpsichord maker and scholar. He studied piano and organ as a child and discovered the harpsichord while in secondary school at Floreffe. In 1971 he was named winner of the Fondation de la Vocation. After spending two years in the workshop of Rainer Schütze at Heidelberg, he set up his studio in Noville-les-Bois, and under the influence of Koen Vermeij, began to turn his attention to clavichords about 1989. His last harpsichord was made in 1993/4 after which he solely produced clavichords at a rate of about two per year. He studied instruments at museums internationally and copied examples by Ruckers, Delin, and Dulcken. His fretted clavichords are inspired by the sketch and manuscript by David Tannenberg and his unfretted clavichords by Friederici. In 1993 Tournay was a founding member of the German Clavichord Society (Deutsche Clavichord Societät) along with Lothar Bemmann, and served as its first president. In Tournay's retirement, his instrument production declined after 2005 to very few by 2012. His harpsichord apprentices included Emile Jobin, Jean François Chaudeurge, Christopher Jones, Ambrosius Pfaff, Nadja Finze, and Ella Extermann, while Martin Kather apprenticed both for clavichord and harpsichord construction. The harpsichord maker Michel De Mayer (*d* 2012) worked for a time in Tournay's workshop.

WRITINGS
(*selective list*)
'Apropos d'Albertus Delin, 1712–1771: petite contribution à l'histoire du clavecin', *La facture de clavecin du XVe au XVIIIe siècle: Actes du colloque international de Louvain 1976*, ed. P. Mercier and M. Kaufmann (Louvain-la-Neuve, 1980), 140–231
Archives Dulcken, vol.1 (Brussels, 2/1987)
'The Double Orientation in Harpsichord Building in the Low Countries in the 18th Century', *The Harpsichord and its Repertoire: Proceedings of the International Harpsichord Symposium, Utrecht 1990*, ed. P. Dirksen (Utrecht, 1992), 21–46
'Comments on German clavichord sources', *De Clavicordio, Proceedings of the International Clavichord Symposium, Magnano 1993*, ed. B. Brauchli, S. Brauchli, A. Galazzo (Piemonte, 1994), 99–103
'Les Clavicordes des Freres Schiedmayer', *Het Clavichord*, vol.9/1 (Apr 1996)
'Chronique Française IV', *Het Clavichord*, vol.9/2 (Aug 1996), 34
'Chronique Française V', *Het Clavichord*, vol.9/3 (Dec 1996), 54–56
'Notes & Propos sur le Clavicorde', *Clavichord International*, vol.1/1 (May 1997), 8–10
'Notes & Propos sur le Clavicorde 2', *Clavichord International*, vol.1/2 (Nov 1997), 41–43
'Chronique Française V', *Clavichord International*, vol.2/1 (May 1998), 10–11

'Chronique Française VI', *Clavichord International*, vol.2/2 (Nov 1998), 42–43

'Chronique Française VII', *Clavichord International*, vol.3/2 (Nov 1999), 51–53

'Notes et Propos sur le clavichord', *La Table Ronde* (Paris, 2009)
MARTIN KATHER

Tournebout (Fr.: 'turned end'). (1) French name for the crumhorn, used by Mersenne (1636–7) and subsequent writers including Diderot (1765), whose engraving of a *tournebout* is copied from Mersenne. The word is found only in theoretical sources.

(2) Name given to a number of instruments superficially similar to the crumhorn, found in some museum collections. These rather crude instruments lack a windcap, have a very wide, slightly conical bore with seven widely spaced fingerholes (the lowest doubled) and two vent holes, and are made in two longitudinal halves covered in black leather. Although once thought to be authentic examples of the French 17th-century *cromorne*, their close similarity to the *pifia ricoperta in pelle* illustrated in Leopoldo Franciolini's catalogues indicates that they are late 19th-century creations based on Diderot's engraving of a crumhorn (*tournebout*).

BIBLIOGRAPHY

M. Mersenne: *Harmonie universelle* (Paris, 1636–7/R; Eng. trans. of the books on instruments, 1957)

D. Diderot, ed.: *Encyclopédie*, vol.16 (Neufchâtel, 1765)

E. Ripin: *The Instrument Catalogs of Leopoldo Franciolini* (Hackensack, NJ, 1974)

R. Weber: 'Tournebout—Pifia—Bladderpipe (*Platerspiel*)', *GSJ*, vol.30 (1977), 64–9

C. Karp: 'Tournebout—Pifia—Bladderpipe', *GSJ*, vol.31 (1978), 147–9

B.R. Boydell: *The Crumhorn and Other Renaissance Windcap Instruments* (Buren, 1982)
BARRA R. BOYDELL/R

Tournier organ. Electronic organ developed in France up to 1938 by Marcel Tournier, a French musician and director of practical work at the School of Physics and Chemistry in Paris. It had three manuals, each with a range of about five octaves, and a pedalboard. The sounds were generated by beat-frequency quartz oscillators, a principle found in monophonic instruments such as the ondes martenot and theremin but rarely in polyphonic instruments. Unlike the builders of some other electronic organs of the late 1930s, Tournier took care to emulate the sound qualities of pipe organs, such as that resulting from the conflict between the natural harmonic series produced in individual pipes and the equal temperament of the tuning.

Tournier (who should not be confused with the contemporary harpist and composer of the same name) was also the co-inventor with Gabriel Gaveau, about 1927, of the Canto, an electromagnetic device for use with a piano; it fitted inside the piano and transmitted the vibrations of its strings to a set of tuned reeds, which vibrated in sympathy. Earlier, Tournier's work on scientific and military applications of soundwaves contributed to the development of active sonar by Paul Langevin. See R. Viallard: 'La synthèse des timbres dans l'orgue électrique Tournier', *La nature*, vol.67 (1939), 71–4.

HUGH DAVIES/R

Tourte. French family of bowmakers and luthiers. It comprised Nicolas Pierre Tourte and his sons Nicolas Léonard and François Xavier, and perhaps Charles Tourte, son of Nicolas Léonard. In addition, at least two channelled (*canalé*) bows dating from about 1750–60 exist bearing the brand-stamp 'A.TOURTE'.

(1) Nicolas Pierre Tourte [père] (*d* Paris, France, 1764). Described in legal documents as a luthier, he was probably the maker of a known violin bearing the label 'Pierre Tourte, Paris 1747'. Oral tradition holds that Tourte *père* was a bowmaker whose shop was the training ground for his sons.

(2) (Nicolas) Léonard Tourte [l'aîné] (*b* Paris, France, 20 Jan 1746; *d* Paris, 11 Sept 1817 or 11 Sept 1807). Bowmaker, son of (1) Nicolas Pierre Tourte. He perhaps deserves at least equal credit with his illustrious younger brother for the development of the modern bow. From about 1770 he made Cramer-type bows (and perhaps others as well). Among the Cramer-type bows a few are known which, in addition to his brand-stamp of 'TOURTE·L', bear the second brand-stamp 'AUX 15 VINGT', indicating that he had a *dépendance* (including a work space) at that institution, a hospice for the blind and those with seeing disorders. His privileges there had probably ended by 1780, and from about that time he produced bows in various styles and from different types of wood. Some of these were almost certainly intended for string instruments other than those of the standard orchestral string family.

A church parish document from 1803 (another dates from 1821, after his death) describes Léonard as an 'artiste', the term perhaps indicating that he was active as a musician. Bows with his brand-stamp also emanate from this time and perhaps for some few years afterwards. Throughout his career his bows have round sticks, and their frogs are usually 'open-trenched', less so in the later works. Collaboration with another maker or makers is suggested by certain features in the making of some bows, most markedly in the frogs of the later bows. Léonard Tourte used pernambuco wood of excellent quality in many of his Cramer-type bows and in some late bows. Otherwise he availed himself, perhaps experimentally, of various species of hardwood, for the frogs as well as for the sticks. He seems to have begun using ebony for frogs only in his later work.

(3) François Xavier Tourte [le jeune] (*b* Paris, France, 1747 or 1748; *d* Paris, 25 April 1835). Bowmaker, son of (1) Nicolas Pierre Tourte. He has often been called the Stradivari of the bow. Fétis stated that he was apprenticed at watchmaking for eight years before entering fully fledged into bowmaking. This is supported by the lack of bows that can be positively attributed to him during the time (*c*1770–80) when his brother Léonard produced Cramer-type (and perhaps other) bows. On the other hand, an argument can be made for his participation in the creation of some of these bows, specifically the extremely well-made ones. Although François Tourte did not normally brand his bows, a few from the early 1800s bearing the brand-stamp 'TOURTE' have in recent years been attributed to him. This brand-stamp is identical with that of his brother (minus the '·L'), and it is reasonable to conclude that the initial had been simply filed away. The existence of a cello bow bearing the 'TOURTE·L' and known to be a mature work (c1815) of François strongly suggests a partnership or collaboration of the two brothers during Léonard's last years.

That François Xavier Tourte was well established as the pre-eminent bowmaker by the early 1800s is born out by L'Abbé Sibire, who wrote in *La chélonomie, ou Le parfait luthier* (1806) that 'the famous Tourte (le jeune)' had begun perfecting the bow 20 years earlier. Although Sibire's writings occasionally border on the fantastic, the notion that François's development as a bowmaker was independent of Léonard's and other bowmakers from an early stage cannot be dismissed entirely.

Attempts have been made in the past to assign Tourte's work to one of three or, more recently, two chronological periods. Both of these proposed divisions, however, fail to take account of his earliest work, which has still not been clearly defined. The first of the two periods covers the 'transitional' and the early 'modern' bows, whereas the ensuing 25 to 30 years encompass a prodigiously rich and varied output which in artistry and invention dwarfed Tourte's contemporaries and the bowmakers who followed him.

The transitional and early modern bows have round sticks of pernambuco, often of the finest quality, this latter usually of a dark chocolate brown colour. They are in general slightly shorter than those that are termed Tourte's mature work. Their heads are rather gentle in contour and fairly rounded (when viewed in profile), but many possess the tension and statuesque qualities so evident in his mature and late work. Violin-bow heads of this early work usually have silver headplates. The frogs are rather long, often short in height, with a narrow ferrule and full-length pearl slides; most have plain sides. The rare open-trenched frog is mated with an ivory button, but otherwise the buttons are of silver on ivory, and the earliest buttons of the three-piece form are also found.

Probably about 1800 Tourte began making octagonal sticks as well as round ones. The former would come to dominate his production. The facets of these sticks were often left off the plane, and some resultant chatter is seen. The length of violin bowsticks was settled, for the most part, at about 72.5 cm (excluding the button); variants tend to be longer, up to about 73.1 cm. The heads are somewhat bolder and more angular, anticipating the great 'hatchet' heads which would soon follow. There is little evidence, however, of a constant evolution of the models of the heads, Tourte creating as his inspiration took him. The heads also begin to exhibit the individual working mannerisms that connoisseurs look for to establish authenticity. These include the 'travelling', almost meandering, ridge down the head's front; the angular disruptions to the curve of the back of the head (when seen in profile); and the remarkably

individual chamfers, which are usually quite exposed. The violin-bow heads now have ivory headplates as a rule, but the cello bows are found more often than not with silver headplates. The latter are mostly octagonal and the most common model of head is the 'hatchet' with a distinctly inclined front. Other cello bows have heads akin to violin bow models and, very rarely, 'swan heads'.

The frogs of the violin bows made after the transitional and early modern bows are not so long and, as well, are taller and commonly have a mother-of-pearl eye in each side. The dimensional changes reflect Tourte's continuing quest to refine the playing characteristics of his bows. At the same time there is a satisfying stylistic congruency both in the elements of the frogs and in the frogs' relationship to the head. The mountings now have heelplates as well as ferrules, and most of the small heelplates (adjacent to the pearl slide) have three pins. The frogs of the cello bows are usually rather tall, with rounded heels and sometimes, rounded ferrules. An occasional cello frog will feature the 'Parisian eye' (a smaller mother-of-pearl eye encircled by a silver ring) and these are certainly some of the earliest bows fashioned with this detail.

Buttons are always in three-piece form, normally with two pins in each ring, with those from the earliest part of this so-called second period diverging strongly one from another in their silver-ebony-silver proportions. The silver parts of the frog and button are of thicker gauge than was used by Tourte's successors and in most of the work of his contemporaries.

Viola bows, rarely encountered, are similar to violin bows in models and lengths of sticks, and their frogs have square heels.

At some point during his mature years of bowmaking, Tourte began to make the occasional frog of tortoiseshell and gold. The buttons complementing these frogs have mother-of-pearl facets between the gold rings. The precision of this work is held in high esteem by today's makers.

Tourte's only known working address was 10 quai de l'Ecole, where he remained until his move in 1833 to 38 rue Dauphine. In all likelihood the change of address marked his retirement from bowmaking, as he was listed in the professional register, Bottin's *Almanach du commerce de Paris* up to 1833. Oral tradition holds that in 1824 Tourte made a few bows into which he inserted a small parchment label stating that the bow had been made by him in 1824 at the age of 77.

Bowmaking was without question raised by Tourte to the status of a fine art. His genius lay in crafting tools that not only made an invaluable contribution to string musicians and their music but were in themselves works of art, veritable sculptures in pernambuco.

BIBLIOGRAPHY

L'Abbé Sibire: *La chélonomie, ou Le parfait luthier* (Paris, 1806, repr. 1823/R, rev. 1885 by L. de Pratis)

F.-J. Fétis: *Antoine Stradivari, luthier célèbre* (Paris, 1856; Eng. trans., 1864/R)

J. Roda: *Bows for Musical Instruments of the Violin Family* (Chicago, 1959)

E. Vatelot: *Les archets français* (Paris, 1976, 2/1977) [in Fr., Ger. and Eng.]

B. Millant and J.F. Raffin: *L'Archet* (Paris, 2000)

T. Wilder, ed.: *The Conservation, Restoration, and Repair of Stringed Instruments and Their Bows* (Montreal, 2010)

PAUL CHILDS

Towa. Large gourd vessel rattle of the Baule people of the Ivory Coast. It has an external net strung with cowrie shells or pearls and is used mainly on ceremonial occasions to mark the appearance of masked dancers. It especially evokes the most powerful divinities who protect Baule villages. It also accompanies war songs.

Towa is also the name used by the Agni-Bona and Agni-Diabe peoples for a calabash rattle with a handle, containing seeds or gravel. The Abron call this calabash rattle *touwa*, *sèssègo*, or *sèssèdjigo*. Among these peoples, it is used by women to accompany funeral and rejoicing dances. *Tobaha* is the vernacular name of a tin rattle with a handle, used by the Ehotile people; it is played by men to accompany the funeral and rejoicing dance called *kpandan*. One player shakes two of these rattles. See K. Aka: *Traditions musicales chez les Akan lagunaires de Côte d'Ivoire: cas des Abbey, Abidji, Éhotilé et M'batto* (Tervuren, 2011).

KONIN AKA

Townsend, Gabriel (*b* c1604; *d* London?, c1662). English virginal maker. He apprenticed with Thomas White, becoming a freeman of the Joiners' Company in London in 1624/1625, and a master in 1657/1658. His apprentices included Stephen Keene and John Player. Townsend probably died by 1662 as Keene was admitted free of the Joiners' Company through sponsorship by Player rather than their master Townsend. One instrument by Townsend survives (1641, *B.B.mim*), a typical English rectangular virginal with coffered lid, made for Elizabeth (Stuart) of Bohemia, daughter of James I and sister of King Charles I. It bears the Plantagenet arms under the initials 'E.R.' in the repeated pattern in the embossed gilded papers in the keywell and above the soundboard. As is typical of English virginals, it is plain on the outside and richly decorated inside. The interior lid painting depicts Orpheus (who bears a striking resemblance to Charles I) with his lyre, charming the beasts and trees. The keyboard cover painting shows ships at sea and a courtly group on an island. See D.H. Boalch: *Makers of the Harpsichord and Clavichord 1440–1840* (Oxford, 3/1995).

ANNE BEETEM ACKER

Toxocatl. Sucked trumpet of Nahua people of the states of Mexico, Puebla, and Tlaxaca, Mexico. It is made from a hollow piece of wood some 2 metres long. The distal end is inserted into the small end of a cow's horn that forms a bell, and a 10-cm length of cane about 1 cm in diameter is inserted into the proximal end, forming a mouthpiece. The mouthpiece is held to the side of the mouth and the sound is produced by aspiration. It is played with the *caja* drum or the *redoblante* snare drum for communal dances.

J. RICHARD HAEFER

Toy instruments. This term is used both of simplified or scaled-down versions of conventional instruments, mostly wind and percussion, and of special instruments and sound devices made by and for children. Toy instruments, often made from local plant and animal materials and stones, have existed since the earliest times, and the knowledge of the construction and use of such homemade instruments still to some extent forms part of children's private lore.

1. To 1990. 2. After 1900.

1. To 1900. A number of toy instruments from the second half of the 18th century have become well known because they were used as a concertante group, with a chamber orchestra, in several anonymous 'toy symphonies' composed at Berchtesgaden near Salzburg (a manufacturing centre for toy instruments at that time); these works include a cassation, three movements from which are better known as the Toy Symphony attributed to, among others, Leopold Mozart and Michael Haydn. The instruments themselves—cuckoo and quail calls, small duct flutes, wooden trumpet, toy bugle and french horn, ratchets, rattle, triangle and drum—are now in the Museum Carolino Augusteum in Salzburg. Toy instruments similar to most of these continue to be made, and have been featured in many subsequent toy symphonies, including those by A.J. Romberg, Ignaz Lachner, Carl Reinecke, Malcolm Arnold, and Joseph Horovitz.

In the second half of the 19th century toy instruments began to be mass-produced, including glockenspiels and pianos, zithers and autoharps, violins, drums, bugles, mouth organs, kazoos, bells, jew's harps, musical boxes, frog-shaped clickers, and birdcalls (blown, rubbed, whirled, or operated by clockwork). At this time, too, sounding elements, such as small bells and squeakers (consisting of a reed operated by a miniature bellows), were first added to dolls and other toys; a squeaker was even incorporated into a Victorian Christmas card. Dolls were also made to speak. One of the first persons to succeed in this was J.N. Maelzel (inventor of the Panharmonicon mechanical orchestra and perfecter of the metronome), who about 1822 in Paris produced a doll with a bellows-operated set of reeds that said 'Bonjour papa' and 'Bonjour maman'. Animals, such as dogs and lions, were also given voices, which were similarly activated by pulling a cord; the children's book *Le livre d'images parlantes* incorporated the cord-operated voices of the elephant, ass, cow, goat, cuckoo, and cockerel. (A related but simpler mechanism, in which a small bellows forces air past a reed and along a convoluted tube, is now used in the small cardboard cylinders that, when shaken or inverted, imitate the sounds of sheep, monkeys, cats, and cows.) One of the earliest commercial applications of Thomas Edison's cylinder phonograph of 1877 was in talking dolls (from 1887); small plastic gramophone discs continued to be used in dolls until the end of the 20th century, but were superseded by microchips.

Elaborate musical automata, such as the figures (often life-size) devised by the engineers Hero of Alexandria (*fl* 62 ce), al-Jazari (13th century), and Vaucanson (18th century), have long been the toys of wealthy people. With the mass-production of clockwork devices from the beginning of the 19th century, wind-up musical clockwork toys such as drummers, guitarists, violinists (often animals—monkeys were particular favourites), and singing birds became popular.

2. After 1900. The mass-production of toys of all sorts greatly increased in the 20th century. They were and are still frequently made of plastic and largely manufactured in East Asia; among the commonest are single and double duct flutes, ocarinas, nose flutes, swanee whistles, sirens, whistles (including edible sweet ones), and water-filled nightingale calls; free-reed wind instruments include various sorts of mouth organ, such as the end-blown, two-octave, keyed Melodica (made by Hohner) and the similar Pianica made by Yamaha; and devices containing a single reed of metal or plastic, such as the party toys in which a paper tube unfurls like a chameleon's tongue and instruments in which the reed is housed in a nonfunctional imitation trumpet, horn, or saxophone. The kazoo is found in various forms and is sometimes used in children's marching bands and, formerly, in workingmen's bands. Some toy instruments continue to be made of metal, including the hand-cranked musical box, cymbals, the triangle, the sistro, and a miniature nail violin with a suspended beater, housed inside a plastic animal or other shape, which is sounded by rocking the toy on its curved base. A tin drum features in Günter Grass's eponymous novel *Die Blechtrommel* (1959). In spite of the popularity of plastics, many toy instruments are still made of traditional materials such as wood, bamboo, paper, and string—for example, duct and notched flutes, panpipes, swanee whistles, pop-guns, whirled drums with cog-operated beaters, tambourines, and ratchets. Crude versions of folk instruments are made for sale to tourists; these include many of the types already mentioned as well as ceramic drums, barrel drums, pipes of different sorts, nightingale calls such as the South American 'silbador' pot, ocarinas, maracas, and wind chimes made from bamboo, seashells, and metal tubes. A true folk instrument, the string drum, can still be seen in European street markets, where it is usually demonstrated as producing the clucking of a chicken; under the name 'Waldteufel' it is used in street celebrations at Carnival time in Germany. Whistling cups and bowls, such as the miniature Japanese *saké* cups with a whistle that functions when the drinker inhales, are found in various parts of the world. In East Asia small soundmakers are often attached to kites.

An unexpectedly popular toy, introduced about 1970, is the whirler tube (it seems to have no standard commercial name; Peter Schickele uses one under the title 'lasso d'amore' in one of his P.D.Q. Bach compositions). A length (approximately 90 cm) of coloured corrugated plastic tubing (probably derived from the conduit used since the 1960s to carry bunches of electrical wiring) is whirled around the player's head, producing increasingly higher overtones the faster it is whirled. Many composers and improvisers, including David Bedford, Mauricio Kagel (*Der Schall*, 1968), and Sarah Hopkins (as the 'whirly'), have made use of this instrument, and a New York ensemble has played melodies on a collection of them, each member contributing a very limited number of pitches in the manner of handbell players. Similar tubing has also formed part of the Corrugahorns of Frank Crawford and Richard Waters. The toy piano has been featured in John Cage's *Suite for Toy Piano* (1948) and *Music for Amplified Toy Pianos* (1960), and is included in works by George Crumb, Renaud Gagneux, Mauricio Kagel, Louis Roquin, Zygmunt Krauze, Leonid Aleksandrovich, Leonid Hrabovsky, and others, and compact discs with specially commissioned—primarily solo—works have been released in the USA (Margaret Leng-Tan) and in Germany (Bernd Wiesemann). Improvisers, notably Steve Beresford and Pascal Comelade, have specialized in performing on a wide range of toy instruments. Toy instruments figure prominently in several compositions by Peter Maxwell Davies and single works by Lejaren Hiller, Mauricio Kagel, John Beckwith, David Borden, Keith Humble, Anthony Gilbert, Dubravko Detoni, and H.K. Gruber (*Frankenstein!!*, 1976–7); Joe Jones often incorporated toy instruments played by electric motors in his work. Tom Jenkins has built special humming tops, and very large tops, constructed by Floris Guntenaar and Rob Van de Poel, are used in Peter Schat's composition *To You* (1972). Susan Rawcliffe, Sharon Rowell, and others have made many ceramic wind instruments, including pipes, flutes, whistles, and ocarinas (including double and triple versions), often in ornate shapes and with unusual tunings.

Since about 1970 innumerable electronic toy instruments have appeared, starting with the Stylophone (1968). This and several later instruments, including one model of Michel Waisvisz's Kraakdoos, the Suzuki Omnichord, Mattel's Optigan, Synsonics Drums, Synsonics Rhythm Maker and Magical Musical Thing, and many Bontempi, Casio, and Yamaha keyboard instruments (some of which have narrow keys for small hands and incorporate musical ear-training games) have also been used in concerts of rock and contemporary music. The Gmebogosse is a synthesizer designed for use by small groups of children. Electronic sounds, of the kind that are increasingly heard in all kinds of machines from digital watches to electronic games, are also incorporated into toys, such as imitation plastic guitars with push buttons along the neck instead of strings. Smallest of all are the diatonic Echo Piano and the chromatic Rhythm Pocket Piano, manufactured anonymously in East Asia, which have even been incorporated into song books for younger children and are now available in mobile phone app versions. Since the 1980s the increasing complexity of the electronic circuitry contained within microchips and the corresponding reduction in power requirements (often needing only a single miniature 'button' battery as developed for pocket calculators and digital watches) meant that they could be incorporated in ever smaller toys and everyday objects, even such slim items as birthday and Christmas cards; originally restricted to sound synthesis, by the early 1990s cheap chips could store several sampled sounds, giving many toys their own voices, while some books for small children have incorporated a panel of up to a dozen or more pictorial touch plates that individually triggered appropriate sounds. From 1999 even small toy figures have been enabled to 'speak' by using a handheld receiver that also supplies power to the circuitry.

Many sound sculptors and inventors of new instruments have received enthusiastic responses from children to exhibitions and demonstrations of their work. This has led some of them—for instance, the Baschet brothers, Michael Waisvisz, and Akio Suzuki—to invent musical toys or simple instruments or to design special versions of existing instruments for children. Several artist-designed toys have been marketed, especially by the Exploratorium in San Francisco, including Robert Deissler's Zube Tube or Power Tube (containing a long resonant spring) and Reinhold Marxhausen's nail-violin-like Stardust. Bill and Mary Buchen, Hugh Davies, Max Eastley, Peter Phillips, and others have run sessions at which children and adults can invent and build their own instruments. Educational instruments, used mostly by children, have been designed by Carl Orff, a team including Davide Mosconi, and the Baschet brothers, among others. The group Echo City has specialized in building instruments for childrens' playgrounds.

A few instrument makers have used their inventions for therapy with emotionally disturbed, handicapped, and underprivileged children, and in tactile exhibitions for the blind: several Baschet instruments have been used since 1967 by the National Theater for the Deaf in the USA; in Vancouver, John Grayson constructed the permanent Environment of Musical Sculpture for Exceptional Children; and some 140 of Alfons van Legelo's foot-operated pentatonic Dance Chimes have been installed in public places worldwide since the mid-1970s, including for mentally handicapped children. The small Kraakdoos synthesizer and various Japanese electronic keyboard instruments have also been therapeutically effective.

The computer-interfaced Music Toys developed by Tod Machover and the MIT Media Lab are designed to be used by anyone. His Beatbugs are handheld percussive instruments that allow the creation, manipulation, and sharing of rhythmic motives that can be connected for collaborative music. Shapers use capacitive sensing and conductive embroidery to measure squeezing gestures that control musical contour, timbre, density, and structure. Many books of instructions for building simple instruments have been published, a large number of them intended for use by children in school. Only a small selection of those available are listed in the bibliography below, but they have been chosen in many cases because they cover less common, often non-Western instruments.

BIBLIOGRAPHY

M. Kagel, ed.: *Kinderinstrumente* (Cologne, 1972)

J. Grayson, ed.: *Environments of Musical Sculpture You Can Build* (Vancouver, 1976), 12–17, 166–207

M. Hillier: *Automata & Mechanical Toys: an Illustrated History* (London, 1976)

D. Sawyer: *Vibrations: Making Unorthodox Musical Instruments* (Cambridge, 1977, 2/1980)

T. Wishart and others: *Sun 2: a Creative Philosophy* (London, 1977)

C. Armengaud: *La musique verte: appeaux, sifflets, crécelles* (Le Puy, 1979, 2/1981/R, 3/1984 as *Musique vertes*)

R. Banek and J.Scoville: *Sound Designs: a Handbook of Musical Instrument Building* (Berkeley, CA, 1980, 2/1995)

B. Hopkin: *Making Simple Musical Instruments* (Asheville, NC, 1995)

B. Hopkin: 'Sound–Making Mechanisms in Contemporary Children's Toys', *Experimental Musical Instruments*, vol.11/1 (1995), 8–13

M. Leng-Tan: 'Toy Pianos no Longer Toys!', *Piano & Keyboard*, no.189 (1997); rev. in *Experimental Musical Instruments*, vol.14/1 (1998), 16–20

G. Summit and J.Widess: *Making Gourd Musical Instruments* (New York, 1999)

P.M. Parker: *The 2009 World Forecasts of Toy Musical Instruments and Apparatus Export Supplies* (San Diego, CA, 2009)

HUGH DAVIES/R

Toy piano (Fr. *piano jouet*; Ger. *Spielzeugklavier*; It. *pianino-giocattolo*). Small keyboard instrument manufactured as a child's plaything, with a usual compass of two diatonic octaves to three chromatic octaves. Its mechanism resembles that of the full-sized keyboard glockenspiel without dampers, a family of instruments among the earliest members of which were the Stahlklavier, built by Troiger in Dessau in 1792, and Franz Schuster's Adiaphonon (Vienna, *c*1818), and which also includes the celesta; it may also be regarded as being related to certain struck tuning-fork instruments developed from the mid-19th century onwards. The toy piano was first produced commercially in Germany in the mid-19th century. Albert Schoenhut (*b* Württemberg, Germany, 1842; *d* Philadelphia, PA, 1912), a German immigrant who came from a family of toy makers, founded a company in Philadelphia in 1872 (incorporated 1897) to manufacture toys; on 18 September 1900 he patented (no.658,284) an improved toy piano mechanism resembling that of the English single-action piano. At his death he left the factory, which produced a wide range of other toys, to his six sons. In 1984, Frank Trinca purchased the Schoenhut Company, selling it to his brother and sister in-law Len and Renee Trinca in 1996; they moved the company to St Augustine, Florida, in 2000.

Until the 1950s toy pianos were usually 'uprights', with 15 to 22 keys ('white' notes only), in sizes up to 60 by 60 by 30 cm. Later, most instruments were made in East Germany, China, and Japan, and the majority were 'grand pianos' (typically 30 cm wide and 26 cm deep). Paradoxically these are normally the simpler, cheaper models (the appearance has nothing to do with the sound production), usually having only 15 to 20 white keys, while the few larger 'uprights' often have 30 keys, which include functioning black keys. The action is extremely simple: when a key is hit a small felt-covered or plastic hammer, attached to the rear of the key with resilient material, strikes a metal plate or rod that is usually fixed at one end. The tuning is very approximate in the cheaper models, and the pitch rarely corresponds with that of conventional instruments. Consistently staying at the higher end of the market, in 2012 Schoenhut was offering an 18-key 'Mini Grand', 30-key 'Baby Grand', and a three-octave, 37-key 'Concert Grand' piano, all with the typical hammer action. In addition, the firm makes a 44-key and 49-key 'String Baby Grand' and a 44-key 'String Upright', these models having normal-width (although shorter) keys, strings, hammers, and dampers similar those on full-size pianos. Schoenhut lists 28 professional performers and composers using its pianos.

Much less common, Michelsonne toy pianos, created by Victor Michel (1904–83), were manufactured in Paris from 1939 to 1970, when a fire destroyed the factory and the patents were sold to Bontempi. Michelsonne pianos are noted for their distinctively beautiful tone and are especially favoured by French toy-piano performers. Michelsonne made chromatic uprights with 13, 16, 20, 25, 30, 37, or 49 keys and chromatic grands with 25, 30, or 37 keys.

With the decreasing cost and size of digital circuitry and computer chips, digital, computer, and handheld-device toy pianos have flourished. Many electronic toy instruments incorporate piano-type keyboards, some including features such as karaoke capability and animal sounds. Another form of toy piano features a roll-up keyboard playable by hands or feet. iPads, mobile phones, and other handheld devices offer popular toy piano apps including Toy Piano by Andreas Lindahl, Vintage Toy Piano by Holderness Media, and Tiny Tunes Toy Piano.

Despite their shortcomings and limited range, toy pianos—often those with only 'white' notes—have been used by a number of contemporary composers and performers. The first was John Cage who, in 1948, wrote the solo *Suite for Toy Piano*, a masterpiece of economy, the five movements of which use, respectively, only five, seven, nine, nine, and five notes; he composed for an unspecified number of toy pianos in *Music for Amplified Toy Pianos* (1960). The instrument is also used in works by George Crumb (*Ancient Voices of Children*, 1970), Renaud Gagneux, Joe Jones, Mauricio Kagel, and Louis Roquin. The four British composers (John White, Christopher Hobbs, Alec Hill, and Hugh Shrapnel) who formed the Promenade Theatre Orchestra in 1969, composed and played music for four toy pianos, sometimes in combination with four small reed organs. The British improviser Steve Beresford has performed pieces for toy piano alone and others for as many as ten different models, some of which have appeared on recordings of improvised and rock music. In the *Peanuts* comic strip by Charles M. Schulz, the character of Schroeder plays sonatas by Beethoven and other difficult works on a toy grand piano with the black keys apparently only painted on the white keys. See M. Leng-Tan: 'Toy Pianos no Longer Toys!', *Piano & Keyboard*, no.189 (1997); rev. in *Experimental Musical Instruments*, vol.14/1 (1998), 16–20.

HUGH DAVIES/ANNE BEETEM ACKER

Toy stop [toy counter]. Colloquial term used to refer to the various 'sound effects' stops on cinema organs (e.g. sleigh bells, Chinese block, snare drum, klaxon, marimba, etc.). In the 20th century the term also came to be applied to the accessory stops of Renaissance and Baroque organs, such as birdcalls (*Vogelgesang*), drums (*Pauke*), *Zimbelstern*, *Glockenspiel*, etc.

Traccola. Various noisemakers of Italy. They are wooden boards struck by a beater or hammer during Holy Week, particularly from Thursday to Saturday, when the church bells are silent. The first Italian treatise that describes the different types of such noisemakers is the *Gabinetto Armonico* by Filippo Bonanni (Rome, 1722). Nowadays their use is much reduced, but persists in certain contexts, where they not only announce the services but also have a magical connotation. Four variants are:

(1) *Traccola a maniglie* (also called *battola, matracca, scarabatla, tabërna, tocca tocca*): a wooden board with one or more hinged iron handles or wooden tablets at the sides that strike the board when it is rotated along its axis.

(2) *Traccola a martelli oscillanti* (also called *crepitacolo, tocca tocca, trich trach*): a board on which one (rarely two) small wooden hammer is pivoted. The hammer strikes the board when it is oscillated (held by a handle at its centre, opposite the point where the hammer is pivoted).

(3) *Traccola a martelli flessibili* (also called *matracca, tocca tocca, trich trach*): a board, often the bottom of a wooden box, struck by a series of hammers moved by a camshaft, which is rotated by a crank. This instrument is often combined with one or more ratchets.

(4) *Raganella* (ratchets) (also called *cantaraña, scarabatla, ṡghirlacia, trich trach, zirrë zirrë*). The three main types are: rotating ratchets, where the body of the instrument, holding the tongue, rotates around the handle, which holds the cogwheel; fixed ratchets, where the cogwheel is turned by a crank; fixed ratchets combined with a *traccola a martelli*: the axle that turns the cogwheel also activates one or more wooden hammers that strike the bottom of the instrument. Ratchets used during Holy Week are usually made of wood whereas for other uses they are sometimes made of cane. Toy ratchets are made of metal or plastic. See F. Guizzi: *Gli strumenti della musica popolare in Italia* (Lucca, 2002).

FEBO GUIZZI

Tracker. Flexible strip, usually of wood, exerting a pulling action (cf Dutch *trekken*) (as opposed to a sticker); as such it is part of the mechanism or action connecting the key of an organ with its pallet or valve. The term itself has an uncertain history, being presumably used by builders long before theorists; James Talbot (MS, *c*1695, *GB-Och*, Music 1187) used 'trigger' and 'ribs'; 'trigger', with the dialect 'tricker', seem to have been current throughout the 18th century.

'Tracker organ' is a relatively recent term used loosely to denote an organ with mechanical action. It seems to have originated as a derogatory usage at a time when the advantages of pneumatic or electric action were being extolled, or the supposed shortcomings of historical organs exposed (*see* G.A. Audsley, *The Art of Organ Building*, 1905).

PETER WILLIAMS/MARTIN RENSHAW

Trae farang (Thai: 'Western trumpet'). Thai metal trumpet. Of varying size, it was modelled after the European natural trumpet introduced during the Ayutthaya period (1677–1767) and popularized during the 19th century by visiting military bands. It is now obsolete and known mostly from historical paintings.

TERRY E. MILLER

Trae ngawn. Curved trumpet of Thailand. It is about 50 cm long, made of silver-plated metal in two parts, one tapering to the mouthpiece and the other widening to a bell. A cord is tied between the mouthpiece and the base of the bell. With the *trae farang* (trumpet) and the *sang* (conch horn), the trae ngawn was used in royal ceremonies and military processions; all three instruments are now obsolete.

TERRY E. MILLER

Tragalegua (Sp.: 'fast walker'). Double-headed drum of Cuba, with V-laced heads. It is the mid-size drum of the Carabalí drum ensemble, of African origin; the largest is the *quitapesar* ('take away worry'), and the smallest, *redoble* ('drum roll'). It is said that during the Ten Years War (1868–78) the Carabalí people hid guns and ammunition in their tragaleguas. See A.H. Hearn: *Cuba: Religion, Social Capital, and Development* (Durham, NC, 2008).

Trampeli [Trampel]. German family of organ builders. It consisted of Johann Paul (*b* Oberlauterbach, 16 Jan 1708; *d* Adorf, 7 Sept 1764), described as 'kunsterfahrner Orgelbaumeister und Instrumentmacher', his sons Johann Gottlob (*b* Adorf, 22 Nov 1742; *d* Adorf, 18 March 1812) and Christian Wilhelm (*b* Adorf, 16 March 1748; *d* Adorf, 26 Feb 1803), and the son of the last-named, Friedrich Wilhelm (*b* Adorf, 23 Feb 1790; *d* Adorf, 2 Nov 1832). The 'i' was added to the family's surname by Johann Paul's sons. It appears that about 1734 Johann Paul took over the workshop of Adam Heinrich Gruber, the distinguished organ builder and organist, at Adorf (the birthplace of J.C. Kerll); he built about 50 organs there but none survives. The most important member of the family was Johann Gottlob, an intimidating person of uneven temper. He and his brother built or rebuilt about 100 organs (54 of them by 1796), including those for the Nikolaikirche, Leipzig (1790–94; his largest, with three manuals, 49 stops), and the Reinoldikirche, Dortmund (1805; three manuals, 40 stops). Others survive at Plauen-Oberlosa (1784–8); Hohndorf, near Elsterberg (1788); and Rothenkirchen, Vogtland (1798–1800). Christian Wilhelm worked entirely in partnership with his brother, and was regarded as 'a first-class mechanic' ('vollkommener Meister des Regierwerks'). Friedrich Wilhelm's work included the large organs in the Stadtkirche at

Weimar (1812–13 rebuild; three manuals, 44 stops) and St Johannis at Plauen (1815; two manuals, 31 stops). Organs of his survive at Auma, Thuringia (1816–18); Windischleuba, near Altenburg (1821); and Landwüst, Vogtland (1822).

The Trampeli family were the dominant organ builders of their time in Saxony. It is thought that they owed their special knowledge of organ building to a manuscript with which they became familiar while working on the Silbermann organ at Reichenbach; in any case it is clear that they modelled their instruments on those of Gottfried Silbermann. Friedrich Wilhelm's work at Plauen and Weimar was strongly criticized (the latter, for instance, by Mendelssohn, who remarked on its weakness; the organ was again rebuilt, by Schulz, in 1825), but it is reasonable to suppose that this criticism arose only because the wind supply of Trampeli organs was still designed for the older, contrapuntal style of playing, not for the harmonic style of the subsequent period, with its thicker textures. In any case, the Trampelis were highly regarded by their contemporaries, and this opinion is confirmed by the quality of their surviving instruments.

BIBLIOGRAPHY

P. Rubardt: 'Trampel(i)', *Die Musik in Geschichte und Gegenwart*, ed. F. Blume, vol.13 (Kassel, 1966), 620–1

E. Flade: *Der Orgelbauer Gottfried Silbermann* (Leipzig, 1926, 2/1953)

U. Dähnert: *Historische Orgeln in Sachsen: ein Orgelinventar* (Frankfurt, 1980, 2/Leipzig, 1983)

F. Friedrich: *Orgelbau in Sachsen: Bibliographie* (Kleinblittersdorf, 1995)

F. Friedrich: 'Die Trampeli–Orgel zu Windischleuba', *Altenburger Geschichts- und Hauskalender*, vol.5 (1996), 146–7

HANS KLOTZ/FELIX FRIEDRICH/R

Transposing instruments. Instruments for which the music is not notated at the actual pitch of the sound, but is transposed upwards or downwards by some specific musical interval. Transposition is traditionally reckoned relative to the pitch C; an instrument 'in C' is nontransposing (or transposing by an exact number of octaves), and an instrument 'in F', for example, sounds F when C is notated. The intention is to maintain the relationship between notation and execution (fingering, etc.) among instruments of a similar kind but of different pitches. The music is therefore written in a transposition whereby a player can read it in the same manner for each instrument in the group.

1. Strings and organ. 2. Woodwind. 3. Brass. (i) Horn. (ii) Trumpet. (iii) Bass trumpet. (iv) Cornet. (v) Other band instruments.

1. Strings and organ. During the Renaissance and Baroque eras, before the modern concepts of absolute pitch and a universal standard of performing pitch had developed, some instruments—particularly harpsichords and organs—were capable of rendering the same piece of music at two or (occasionally) more pitch levels without altering its relation to the pattern of the keyboard. In one sense these may be called transposing instruments, but not in the specific modern sense of departing from a standard relation between notation and pitch level. Rather, their purpose was evidently to

allow the performer a choice between options of equal status, no one pitch level being deemed the 'real' one by which the others were judged 'transpositions'. Even so, on an instrument not tuned in equal temperament this would have been, at best, a stopgap measure, as the pitch relationships at the second level would have differed from those at the first unless (as was frequently the case) extra strings or pipes were provided.

Transposing instruments in the common sense of the term have not been common among bowed instruments, although the double bass sounds an octave below the written notes (in order to sound an octave below the cello when both read from the same part). The violino piccolo, usually tuned a 4th above the violin, is likely to have its part written a 4th below the actual sound so that the player may read the part as though written for the normal violin (e.g. in the cantata *Es ist ein grosser Gewinn* by Johann Michael Bach, Altbachisches Archiv, ii). In some music of the late 18th and 19th centuries cello parts written in the treble clef are to be read an octave lower. On fretted instruments a capo tasto permits music to be transposed upwards by one or more semitones without altered fingering.

2. Woodwind. Typical woodwind transposition is illustrated by the english horn, which is generally played by a musician whose primary instrument is the oboe. The english horn is pitched a 5th below the oboe, so that each fingering produces on the english horn a sound a 5th lower than that given by the same fingering on the oboe. The english horn part is therefore notated a 5th higher than it will sound so that the player can read it with oboe fingering. This practice was introduced early in the 18th century but did not become standard until later in the century. Bach, for example, wrote for the oboe da caccia (a curved tenor oboe with an open bell) in a C clef at sounding pitch, as had been the practice with the straight tenor oboe (*taille*) at the end of the 17th century (for further information on the notation of tenor oboe parts, *see* Oboe). In some works by Bach the woodwind parts are written in a different key from the organ part in order to allow lower-pitched woodwind instruments to play with a higher-pitched organ; this is not strictly a matter of transposition, as neither pitch level was standard.

Clarinet transpositions are reckoned against the model of clarinet on which the fingering (in the principal register for classical music, i.e. the upper register) matches that of the oboe in the actual pitches produced. This is the 'clarinet in C', so termed because it sounds at written pitch. The Bb clarinet, a longer instrument, sounds a major 2nd lower when played with the same fingerings; its music is accordingly notated a major 2nd higher than it is intended to sound. Music for the A clarinet is written a minor 3rd higher than the sound. Clarinet parts must be headed 'in Bb' or 'in A' (etc.) so that the player can select the correct instrument. Where there exist two instruments pitched an octave apart, conventional nomenclature prevents ambiguity: 'clarinet in Eb' is understood as the small clarinet pitched a minor 3rd above the C clarinet (the part notated a

minor 3rd below the sound) while 'alto clarinet in Eb' denotes an instrument pitched a major 6th below the C clarinet (the part written at this interval above the sound). The bass clarinet is normally understood as being 'in Bb' (or occasionally 'in A'), and the part is written a major 9th (or minor 10th) above the actual sound. Wagner, however, wishing to assist the conductor by making the part look more 'bass', notated it an octave lower—that is a major 2nd or minor 3rd above the sound, causing the parts to lie mainly in the bass clef. Various composers have followed this practice, though it obliges the player to become accustomed to an otherwise unfamiliar octave transposition and so interferes with the basic purpose of transposing instruments. The basset-horn pitched in F is usually notated a 5th above the sound, but passages involving the lowest notes are frequently written an octave lower in the bass clef (as in traditional notation for the horn), thus appearing on paper a 4th below the actual pitch. In the late 18th century Bb clarinet parts were sometimes notated in the tenor clef an octave below sounding pitch; such parts could be easily played by imagining the clef to be the treble and adjusting the key signature.

Under the influence of clarinet nomenclature ('in Bb', etc.) members of the oboe and flute families have often been described in similar terms. The english horn is 'in F', and the non-transposing instrument of the family, the oboe, is said to be 'in C'. The oboe d'amore is 'in A' (notated a minor 3rd above the sound); bass oboes and the bass heckelphone are 'in (low) C' (written an octave higher). Flute transpositions are reckoned against the ordinary flute (usually in C): the piccolo is notated an octave below its sound, the 'alto flute in G' (in some scores 'bass flute in G') a 4th above. The tierce flute (*Terzflöte*) often found in older music, especially military, is pitched a minor 3rd above the ordinary flute, with the parts written at this interval below the sound; it is therefore a 'flute in Eb', and is so described on the Continent. In Britain, however, it was long a traditional practice to describe the ordinary flute as 'in D' because in its early days D was its lowest note (similarly, the pitches of recorders are often given in terms of the lowest actual note, with the treble recorder, which in the USA is called 'alto', thus being said to be 'in F'). By this terminology the piccolo is 'in D' (rather than C), and the tierce flute is in F and in Britain called 'F flute'. Although this did not affect the interval of transposition when writing the parts, it can confuse score-reading of British band music. Similarly, a semitone-transposing flute may be known as 'in Db' or 'in Eb'. The correct transposition can be found by inspecting the whole score, except where doubt arises over the octave. This also applies to early 18th-century scores with transposed parts for *flauti piccoli*, and so on, as in Handel's *Water Music*, where these parts are written a 4th above the violins for small recorders pitched a 5th above the treble recorder and fingered as the latter (ex.1).

Saxophone transpositions are similar to those of the clarinet, being reckoned against a 'soprano saxophone in C'. Parts for all saxophones are notated in treble clef at the interval above the actual sound that is

Ex.1.

notated   read as   sounding

equal to the interval by which the instrument is pitched below the soprano 'in C'. Thus the 'E♭ alto saxophone' is written a major 6th higher; the 'B♭ tenor', a major 9th higher; and the 'E♭ baritone', an octave and a major 6th higher (with these last two a score-reader may prefer to imagine tenor and bass clefs, respectively, and adjust the key signature accordingly). Sarrusophones are treated in the same way, apart from the 'contrabass in C', for which parts are written in the bass clef sounding an octave lower (as are contrabassoon parts). Among other bassoons a few transposed parts exist for small instruments from the 18th century; *see* H.J. Hedlund, 'Ensemble Music for Small Bassoons', *GSJ*, vol.11 (1958), 78–84.

3. Brass. For most brass instruments the basic convention is to write the notes of the harmonic series (in the case of valve instruments the 'open notes'—that is those produced without lowering a valve) always in the key of C, whatever key the instrument actually sounds in. This practice arose in Germany in the 17th century with trumpet parts (the associated timpani sounds always being correspondingly written C and G) but became standard only during the course of the 18th (it had been used regularly from the beginning of that century for the horn, which from the first was played in a considerable number of tonalities). As technique on a natural brass instrument was based on producing the correct harmonics one after another, the player required a notation that expressed harmonics rather than absolute musical pitches. The notation fixed in C provided this and has remained in use even with valved instruments. Two distinct schemes of C notation eventually arose: the original scheme for the trumpet (still used with the horn), in which middle C (*c'*) denotes the 4th harmonic; and a later scheme, used for bugles, cornets, modern trumpets, and brass band instruments, in which middle C denotes the 2nd harmonic. For example, in the earliest days of the B♭ valve trumpet in Germany its parts were notated a minor 7th below the sound (written *c'* sounding *b♭'*, the 4th harmonic); but later parts have been notated a tone above the sound (written *c'* sounding *b♭*, the 2nd harmonic of the same instrument). Octave ambiguity occurs among parts in the older notation written for trumpets or horns in times when these instruments were used with crooks that put them into the tonality required. The most familiar case is that of horn parts from the Classical period marked simply 'in B♭' because this can be understood either as 'B♭ alto' (sounding a major 2nd lower) or 'B♭ basso' (sounding a major 9th lower). In such instances the correct solution must be found by inspecting the tessitura of the parts (those with many high notes probably being 'basso') or the score as a whole; even so the correct alternative cannot always be decided with certainty.

For score-reading purposes, the following particulars about brass instruments may be helpful:

(i) Horn. For parts in 'C alto' there is no transposition, but those in 'C basso' (implied by 'in C', unqualified) sound an octave lower; parts in 'B♭ alto' sound a major 2nd lower, in 'B♭ basso' a major 9th lower; those 'in A' sound a minor 3rd lower, and so on down to D♭ sounding a major 7th lower, except for parts in 'A♭ basso' (e.g. in Verdi), which sound a major 10th lower. Traditionally, passages written in the bass clef sound higher than written, instead of lower (e.g. *c* written in the bass clef sounds the same as *c'* written in the treble clef, etc.). There was a move during the 20th century to abolish this irrational system and use the bass clef in continuation of the treble as in other music. But, quite apart from tenacity of tradition, it would be impractical to reprint the existing body of horn music—scores as well as parts—to comply. An instruction is often printed to indicate the reformed bass-clef notation; otherwise it has to be discovered by context. Some 18th-century works use the bass clef as a visual trick: parts for horns in E♭ (in Germany 'ex Dis') are notated in bass clef an octave lower than the actual sound with the key signature of E♭, and as E♭ falls in the bass clef where C falls in the treble clef, the player reads the part by imagining the treble clef. Similarly, D and F horn parts occasionally appear in alto and mezzo-soprano clefs, respectively (but in the correct octave), the player again imagining the treble clef.

(ii) Trumpet. For parts 'in C', there is no transposition; those 'in B♭' sound a major 2nd lower, 'in A' a minor 3rd lower, 'in A♭' generally a major 3rd lower (in some early 19th-century scores, however, parts 'in A♭' sound a minor 6th higher through use of the older notation of harmonics). Beginning with parts 'in G', trumpets (including the modern small trumpets from 'in D' up to 'in G') sound higher than written: those 'in G' sound a 5th higher, and so on down to D♭ sounding a semitone higher. Parts written expressly for A or B♭ 'piccolo' trumpets also sound higher.

(iii) Bass trumpet. Parts 'in E' sound a minor 6th lower, and so on down to 'in B♭' sounding a major 9th lower (in some early 19th-century military music, parts 'in B♭' sound only a major 2nd lower than notated).

(iv) Cornet. For parts 'in C' there is no transposition; those 'in B♭' sound a major 2nd lower (as do the bugle and flugelhorn in B♭), 'in A' a minor 3rd lower and so on down to 'in E♭' sounding a major 6th lower (as in the fifth movement of Berlioz's *Symphonie fantastique*). Parts for 'soprano cornet', however, sound higher than written, so that 'in E♭' is a minor 3rd higher (in some early brass band compositions, 'in E♭' or 'in D' should be read higher than written, though 'soprano' is not stated).

(v) Other band instruments. Parts for the E♭ tenor horn (American 'alto horn'), E♭ mellophone, and so on sound a major 6th lower than notated. The B♭ baritone and

euphonium, when written in treble clef, sound a major 9th lower (as does the tenor or B♭ trombone in brass band parts), but in the bass clef there is no transposition. Parts written in the treble clef for the E♭ bass (tuba) sound an octave and a major 6th lower, and B♭ contrabass (BB♭ bass) two octaves and a major 2nd lower.

A number of 20th-century composers, notably Arnold Schoenberg, advocated the abolition of transposed notations, and in scores of atonal music all the parts are often written at sounding pitch (usually with an instruction to that effect). Clarinettists find no difficulty in reading complex parts 'in C', and trumpeters are so accustomed to transposing and re-transposing (e.g. to play parts for trumpet 'in B♭' on C trumpets of their own choice) that writing for trumpet 'in C', at sounding pitch, is in many ways the most convenient for the players. If horn parts are written at pitch, there is need for constant shifting from the treble clef to the bass, confusing the visual flow of the part. A C clef would be apt, but totally strange to most players. Standard notation for modern horn, therefore, continues to be 'in F', sounding a 5th lower than written.

ANTHONY C. BAINES/JANET K. PAGE

Transposing keyboard. Keyboard that enables the performer readily to play music in a different key from that in which it is written, generally for the purpose of enabling the music to sound at a different pitch (usually to accommodate a keyboard accompaniment to the fixed or preferred pitch of other instruments or singers) or permit the playing of music in a 'difficult' key while using the fingering of an 'easy' key. This can be accomplished in two principal ways. In one, the keyboard slides sideways relative to the jacks, hammers, stickers, strings, etc. of the instrument of which it is a part. In the other method, there are two keyboards that are displaced from each other by a certain fixed interval.

The latter method is known principally from the standard two-manual harpsichords made by the Ruckers family in the late 16th century and the first half of the 17th. In these, the upper keyboard sounds at normal pitch, while the lower keyboard, which plays the same strings as the upper keyboard, is positioned so that it sounds a 4th lower. The lower-manual *f'''* key, for example, is aligned with the upper-manual *c'''* key and acts on the same strings. A harpsichord by Joannes Ruckers, 1612 (*GB.L.fb*) might originally have had a different arrangement, with the two keyboards a whole tone apart. Although there is no known evidence of organs with transposing keyboards like those in Ruckers harpsichords, there are occasional accounts of organs with separate keyboards each with their own pipework at a different pitch from the main instrument. In 1513 a second small organ, tuned a whole tone higher, was appended to the main organ in the Church of St Jacobi, Innsbruck; the organ in the Hohenstiftskirche, Halberstadt, made by Heinrich Herbst in 1718, had two divisions with separate keyboards placed to the side, one tuned to 'Chorton' (choir pitch), presumably about a semitone below modern pitch, the other at 'Cammerton'

(chamber pitch), presumably two or three semitones lower. Somewhat more frequently, in Germany during the 17th and 18th centuries, organs tuned to choir pitch would include, on one of the regular manuals, one or more stops at chamber pitch.

Transposing instruments with shifting keyboards have generally been more common than those with fixed keyboards. The earliest surviving examples include a harpsichord by Hans Müller of Leipzig (1537; *I.R.ms*) and a chamber organ by Michael Strobel (1559; Schloss Churburg, Sluderno, Italy). In both instruments the keyboard can be shifted by a whole tone, a transposition that Arnolt Schlick (*Spiegel der Orgelmacher und Organisten*, 1511) stated was particularly useful on the organ and which, he said, was possible on two instruments that he knew.

The utility of transposing keyboards was limited when unequal temperaments were prevalent. The Strobel organ, for example, is tuned in ¼-comma meantone temperament, and when the keyboard is shifted to the right from its 'home' position the pattern of usable keys is also shifted. Thus, for example, the A and C♯ keys play a pure 3rd in the lower position of the keyboard but when shifted up they play pipes tuned in the home position to B and E♭, a dissonant diminished 4th. The problem was less severe in harpsichords, in which the tuning could easily be adjusted. Even so, the Ruckers provided doubled strings for the note which on the upper keyboard is played by the E♭ key and on the lower keyboard by the G♯ key, so that the former could be tuned pure to the upper-manual G key and the latter pure to the lower-manual E key. Otherwise, the lower-manual interval E–G♯ would sound a diminished 4th— i.e. the interval played by the upper-manual B and E♭ keys. Other problems are inherent in transposing keyboards with short octave tunings in the bass. In the Strobel organ, the pipes follow the standard *C/E* short-octave arrangement for the keyboard in the lower position, but this is disrupted when the keyboard is shifted upwards. In Ruckers harpsichords the strings follow the short-octave arrangement of the lower-manual keys, and the rear portions of three of the bass key levers in upper manual are cranked to the left to reach the appropriate strings. Eventually, both of these problems were obviated when equal (or nearly equal) temperaments were used and when keyboards with chromatic bass compasses were made.

During the 17th and 18th centuries instruments with shifting keyboards were made occasionally. Extant examples include an early 18th-century Thuringian harpsichord (*D.El.b*) with a keyboard shifting over the interval of a minor 3rd, presumably from deep chamber pitch (about a whole tone below modern pitch) to choir pitch, and two grand pianos made in the 1740s by Gottfried Silbermann, with keyboards shifting a semitone. Burney (1771) described two transposing instruments that he saw in 1770: a square piano, made in Berlin, in which, 'by drawing out the keys the hammers are transferred to different strings', and a harpsichord with a shifting keyboard made in Spain for Farinelli. A 'false keyboard' that could be installed over the functional key levers of an instrument was patented in Great Britain in 1801 by Edward Ryley with the express purpose of permitting 'any piece of music wrote in the natural key of C … [to be] transposed throughout all the keys of music without the aid of flats or sharps' and making possible 'a new mode of playing, which requires the aid of one major and one minor key'. A square piano made by Broadwood in 1808 (private collection, USA) possesses this mechanism. A separate false keyboard that could be applied to any piano was invented in France by August Wolff in 1873. Although the radically reformed keyboard patented by Paul von Jankó in 1882 does not shift, its keys are arranged so that the player's hands can shift over it and perform in any key without changing fingerings.

During the 20th century, several pianos with shifting keyboards (including one by Weser Bros., New York, 1940, now in *US.W.si*) were made for the American songwriter Irving Berlin, who could play only in the key of F♯. Many modern harpsichords are equipped with shifting keyboards allowing them to play at 'modern' (a' = 440) pitch and at 'Baroque pitch' a semitone below; sometime a third position is provided. Electronic keyboard instruments and electronic playback systems applied to pianos or other instruments are often provided with a switch or other mechanism to allow automatic transposition to any key.

Distinct from the foregoing instruments, which transpose by the intervals of conventional Western harmony, are certain microtonal instruments, which may be considered to 'transpose' by increments smaller than a semitone. Among these was a 'clavicymbalum universale' with 19 keys in the octave, made in Vienna about 1590 and described by Michael Praetorius (*Syntagma musicum*, vol.2, 1618, 2/1619), which, presumably by means of a sliding keyboard, could be set to any of seven pitch levels within the interval of a major 3rd. In the late 19th and early 20th centuries some quarter-tone pianos and reed organs were made with two conventional keyboards tuned a ¼-tone apart.

BIBLIOGRAPHY

C. Burney: *The Present State of Music in France and Italy* (London, 1771, 2/1773)

R.E.M. Harding: *The Piano-Forte: its History Traced to the Great Exhibition of 1851* (Cambridge, 1933/*R*, 2/1978/*R*), 277–80

S. Marcuse: *Musical Instruments: a Comprehensive Dictionary* (New York, 1964/*R*), 529–30

G. O'Brien: *Ruckers: a Harpsichord and Virginal Building Tradition* (Cambridge, 1990)

J. Koster: 'Pitch and Transposition Before the Ruckers', *Kielinstrumente aus der Werkstatt Ruckers: Halle 1996*, 73–94

N. Meeùs: 'The Musical Purpose of Transposing Harpsichords', *Kielinstrumente aus der Werkstatt Ruckers: Halle 1996*, 63–72

J.H. van der Meer: 'Types of Transposing Harpsichords, Mainly Outside the Netherlands', *Kielinstrumente aus der Werkstatt Ruckers: Halle 1996*, 95–103

EDWIN M. RIPIN/JOHN KOSTER/R

Transverse flute (Fr. *flûte traversière*; Ger. *Querflöte*; It. *flauto traverso*, or simply *traverso* or *traversa*). Older name for the flute, used to distinguish it from the recorder, which is end-blown rather than side-blown. Transverse flutes from earlier periods are often known nowadays by the name *traverso* (short for *flauto traverso*), a term used by some modern revivalists to distinguish them from the modern instrument. The English term 'traverso' is apparently borrowed from the modern Dutch school of Baroque flute playing; like the term 'piccolo', the Italian word was originally an adjective qualifying *flauto*. The feminine form of the noun, *traversa*, was used by Bach, Handel, and others. See A. Powell: 'Traverso or Traversa?', *Fellowship of Makers and Researchers of Historical Instruments Quarterly*, no.57 (1989), 19–22.

ARDAL POWELL/R

Transverse grand piano (Ger. *Querflügel, Querhammerflügel, Querpianoforte, Traversflügel*). Unusual small piano of the late 18th century, shaped like a bentside spinet, with the wrestpins directly behind the keyboard as on a grand but with the strings running at a diagonal and the spine at an acute angle to the keyboard. The model was supposedly invented by Joseph Brodmann. Examples include one by Christian Gottlob Hubert (in *D.N.gnm*) and one attributed to either Brodmann or Ferdinand Hofmann (in *A.W.t*).

Trantzschel [Tranzschel, Tranzelle]. German or Bohemian brass instrument makers, of unknown relationship, active in St Petersburg and Kiev. The earliest known is Johann Anton Gottlieb (1787–1865). Ivan Ivanovich, described as a '3rd guild merchant' at 19, 11th Line of Basil Island, St Petersburg, was an imperial court musical instrument maker; he was at 33, Italianskaia street in 1837. Surviving instruments include a natural trumpet in F from about 1841 (at *RUS.SP.m*). L.G. Trantzschel is the name of an instrument maker from Kiev, found on a keyed bugle in the Glinka State Central Museum of Musical Culture in Moscow. See V.V. Koshelev: 'Trumpets, Cornets, Trombones, and Horns in the St. Petersburg Museum of Musical Instruments: A Checklist', *Perspectives in Early Brass Scholarship*, ed. S. Carter (Stuyvesant, NY, 1995), 223–37.

PAUL NIEMISTÖ

Traps. Possibly a contraction of 'trappings', commonly denoting accessory equipment of a drummer. Traps include woodblocks, cowbells, and other novelty percussion instruments, as well as other sound-effect devices such as mock train whistles, bird calls, and siren. Cinema organs often include percussion traps operated from the console. The term 'trapwork' commonly refers to mechanical contrivances, such as the lever systems connected to piano pedals.

Träskofiol. Clog fiddle of Sweden. The resonator is made from a clog carved in one piece (like the Dutch clog). The upper part is covered by a flat top with f-holes. String holder, neck, strings, and other parts, bought or homemade, are added. The träskofiol is played supported against the chest; it is tuned slightly higher than a violin, which accentuates its light, nasal, and brittle tone. The träskofiol can be traced back to the late 18th century in Skåne, and probably served as a substitute violin for children and young people. Since the beginning of the 20th century it has acquired the status of an independent instrument peculiar to the region. The corresponding clog fiddle of the Low Countries is called *klompviool*. See B. Hjelmstrom-Dahl: *Träskofiolen i Skåne* (Stockholm, 1967).

BIRGIT KJELLSTRÖM

Trasuntino. Name of two apparently unrelated 16th-century Italian harpsichord makers active in Venice: Alessandro (*b* Bergamo, Italy, *c*1485; *d* *c*1545) and Vito [Guido, Giulio, Vido] (*b* Treviso, Italy, 1526; *d* after 1606). Although several spellings of the surname are known, original inscriptions give 'Trasuntini', or 'Trasuntinis'. A virginal by Bruneto Pontoni (1532) bears the faked inscription 'Gio. Francesco Trazentinus', and a 'Bernardinus de Trasuntinis' is known only from an inscription, probably not original, on a harpsichord. Vito's family name was Frassonio, but he used Alessandro's surname, probably on account of the reputation attached to it. L. Fioravanti (*Dello specchio di scientia universale* [Venice, 1564]) stated that 'Guido Trasuntino' was 'in the art of making *arpicordi*, harpsichords, organs and regals, a man of such learning and experience that everyone marvels on hearing his instruments, since the sound and harmony surpasses that of all others'.

No organs by Alessandro or Vito are known, but R. Lunelli (*Der Orgelbau in Italien* [Mainz, 1956]) records repairs made by them and that Vito was called upon to judge the work of other builders. Only three harpsichords can be firmly identified as by Alessandro, from 1530, 1531, and 1538, but two others and a virginal might have been made by him. Several instruments, including clavichords, have faked inscriptions of Alessandro's. Vito's extant work comprises three authenticated harpsichords, of 1560, 1572, and 1591, the last having a chromatic keyboard with 19 notes in the octave and compass *C–c'''*. An archicembalo (1606) by Vito, called 'clavemusicum omnitonum' in its inscription, was built with 31 notes in each octave, similar to the harpsichord in Nicola Vicentino's *L'antica musica* (Rome, 1555). Another harpsichord can be ascribed to Vito (*D.HA.b*), but others (1571, 1574) have doubtful inscriptions. Two virginals (*CZ.P.nm, D.B.im*) can also be linked to Vito's workshop. Most Trasuntino harpsichords have the typical 16th-century Venetian specification of 1 × 8' and 1 × 4', with a compass of *C/E–f'''*. They were strung with iron wire at about *a'* = 415 Hz, although Vito's 1560 harpsichord was pitched a whole tone higher.

BIBLIOGRAPHY

D. Wraight: 'Principles and Practice in Stringing Italian Keyboard Instruments', *Early Keyboard Journal*, vol.18 (2000), 235 only

N. Mitchell: 'The 1531 Trasuntino Harpsichord in a Universal European Pitch System', *Harpsichord & Fortepiano*, vol.9 (2001), 7–13

P. Bavington: 'Two Trasuntino harpsichord copies', *Early Music*, vol.32/2 (May 2004), 345–6

DENZIL WRAIGHT

Trautonium. Monophonic electronic instrument, the name of which is derived from that of its inventor, Friedrich Trautwein. It was first exhibited in Berlin in 1930, and a number of composers wrote for it: Hindemith learned to play the instrument and in 1931 wrote a concertino for Trautonium and string orchestra; other solo works with orchestra were composed by Harald Genzmer (two concertos), Hermann Ambrosius, Julius Weismann, and Oskar Sala. Sometimes it was used as a replacement for other electronic instruments that were not available—for example in the *Japanische Festmusik* by Richard Strauss. Sala (*b* Greiz, Germany, 18 July 1910; *d* Berlin, 27 Feb 2002) became the Trautonium's sole virtuoso and, besides assisting Trautwein in the development of a domestic version (manufactured by Telefunken in 1933), he constructed his own radio (1937) and concert (1940) Trautoniums, and the Mixtur-Trautonium (1949–52), all of which had two ribbon controller fingerboards and featured subharmonic timbres. In 1952–3 Trautwein produced a simpler, two-manual version known as the Elektronische Monochord. The Mixtur-Trautonium was first used in compositions by Carl Orff, Paul Dessau, Jürg Baur, Sala, and others, including a concerto by Genzmer (1952), and in 1958 it became the permanent mainstay of Sala's electronic music studio (which produced the music for Alfred Hitchcock's film *The Birds*, among others). A digital Mixtur-Trautonium was designed and built in the early 1980s as a series of student projects at the Fachhochschule der Deutschen Bundespost, Berlin. Digital synthesizer 'Trautonium' modules are available from several firms including Native Instruments and Doepfer.

The Trautonium fingerboard consists of a resistance wire, stretched over a metal rail and coupled to an oscillator. The performer, on pressing the wire against the rail, completes the circuit and the oscillator is heard through the instrument's loudspeaker. The position of the finger on the wire determines the resistance controlling the oscillator's frequency and thus the pitch of the note. The three-octave range of the fingerboard can be transposed by means of a switch. A set of filters varies the timbre, and nonharmonic partials (Trautwein called them *Hallformanten*) can also be added by selective filtering to produce a distinctive and unusual timbre. A pedal controls loudness.

BIBLIOGRAPHY

F. Trautwein: *Elektrische Musik* (Berlin, 1930)

T.L. Rhea: 'The Evolution of Electronic Musical Instruments in the United States', *The Art of Electronic Music*, ed. T. Darter and G. Armbruster (New York, 1984), 39–40

K. Ebbeke: 'Paul Hindemith und das Trautonium', *Hindemith-Jb*, vol.11 (1983), 77–113

O. Sala: 'My Fascinating Instrument', *Neue Musiktechnologie: Osnabrück 1991*, 75–93

P. Donhauser: *Elektrische Klangmaschinen* (Vienna, 2007)

RICHARD ORTON/HUGH DAVIES/PETER DONHAUSER

Trautwein, Friedrich (Adolf) (*b* Würzburg, Germany, 11 Aug 1888; *d* Düsseldorf, 20 Dec 1956). German engineer and acoustician. He studied electrical engineering (1906–8) and law (1908–11), and received the doctorate from Karlsruhe (1921) before working in the radio industry. In 1929 he was appointed lecturer at the Rundfunkversuchsstelle and in 1935 professor of musical acoustics at the Berlin Musikhochschule. His experiments in electronic music resulted in several instruments, including an amplified harpsichord (1936, in collaboration with Hanns Neupert), electronic bells, and, most importantly, the Trautonium, developed in 1930 and used by, among others, Paul Hindemith, Bernard Höffer, Harald Genzmer, and Julius Weismann, all of whom wrote concertos for it, and Carl Orff and Richard Strauss. In the late 1940s Trautwein worked in Paris in aviation research; in 1950 he set up a school of sound engineering in Düsseldorf which in 1952 became part of the Robert Schumann Conservatory. He published a Trautonium method (*Trautoniumschule*, 1934) and many articles on acoustics and electronic music in technical and musical periodicals.

BIBLIOGRAPHY

F. Winckel: 'Friedrich Trautwein', *Musica*, vol.11 (1957), 93–4

F.K. Prieberg: *Musica ex machina* (Berlin, 1960), 223 ff

P. Donhauser: *Elektrische Klangmaschinen* (Vienna, 2007)

CLIVE GREATED/R

Travale. In tambourine playing, a term (now obsolete) instructing the performer to produce a roll or drone effect by drawing a wetted thumb over the head in a circular motion. The 'double travale' is twice as fast as the 'single travale'.

Traxdorf, Heinrich (*fl* Mainz, Germany, *c*1440–44). German organ builder. He built three organs in Nuremberg between 1440 and 1443: the large organ for St Sebaldus (the modified case was destroyed in 1945) and two (medium and small) for the Frauenkirche. In 1444 he made an organ with *Rückpositiv* and 'lödiges' Positive (probably with tin pipes) for St Peter, Salzburg. Traxdorf's organs consist of one manual, Positive or *Rückpositiv* and Pedal. Traxdorf was one of the first to depart from the gothic *Blockwerk* organ by dividing the chests and separating the front stops into Flute (Principal) and Octave (Quoika termed this the 'Nuremberg type'). The apparent range of the manual was *B* to *d″* and that of the Pedal *A* to *b♭*.

BIBLIOGRAPHY

M. Praetorius: *Syntagma musicum*, vol.1 (Wittenberg and Wolfenbüttel, 1614–5, 2/1615/*R*); vol.2 (Wolfenbüttel, 1618, 2/1619/*R*; Eng. trans., 1986, 2/1991); vol.3 (Wolfenbüttel, 1618, 2/1619/*R*)

G. Pietzsch: 'Orgelbauer, Organisten und Orgelspiel in Deutschland bis zum Ende des 16. Jahrhunderts', *Die Musikforschung*, vol.12 (1959), 25 ff

K. Bormann: *Die gotische Orgel zu Halberstadt* (Berlin, 1966)

R. Quoika: *Vom Blockwerk zur Registerorgel: zur Geschichte der Orgelgotik 1200–1520* (Kassel, 1966)

H. Fischer and T. Wohnhaas: 'Zur Geschichte der Traxdorf–Orgel', *600 Jahre Ostchor St Sebald, Nürnberg, 1379–1979*, ed. H. Baier (Neustadt an der Aisch, 1979), 117–27

HERMANN FISCHER

Treat, James Elbert (*b* New Haven, CT, 1837; *d* Boston, MA, 26 May 1915). American organ builder. He was the son of a carpenter and distantly related to Barzillai Treat (1780–1845), a minor organ builder in Bristol, Connecticut. He worked for William A. Johnson and Henry Erben, as well as for George Woods, a reed-organ maker whom he left in 1875 to found the short-lived reed-organ firm of Treat & Richardson with John P. Richardson. He returned to organ building in 1876, working for Hutchings, Plaisted & Co. of Boston. He was in Philadelphia about 1880, involved with someone who was experimenting with electric action, possibly Henry Schmoele, who patented an electropneumatic action in 1873. In 1886 Treat was engaged by Edward F. Searles of Methuen, Massachusetts, to run his Methuen Organ Co.; one of the first organs built under his direction (1888) was a three-manual instrument for the music room of Searles's estate in Great Barrington, Massachusetts. Searles transferred ownership of the former Methuen Woolen Co. building, where the manufactory was located, to Treat in 1892; the U.S. Tubular Bell Co. (also owned by Searles) and the D.M. Bruce Co. (maker of metal organ pipes) were located in the same building. The Methuen Organ Co. produced several distinguished instruments, including one given by Searles to Grace Cathedral in San Francisco (1894). In 1895 Treat deeded the factory back to Searles and returned to Boston. John H. Ingraham, who had been his superintendent, took charge of the firm and supervised the rebuilding of the former Boston Music Hall organ for Searles's private Serlo Organ Hall in 1905–9. In 1907 Treat formed a short-lived partnership with James Cole, and at the time of his death he was employed by Ernest M. Skinner. His patents included ones for a pneumatic action (1879), an organette (1882), and improvements in tubular bells (1892).

BIBLIOGRAPHY

J. Lewis: *Mr Searles and the Organ* (Richmond, VA, 2010)

B. Owen: *The Great Organ at Methuen* (Richmond, VA, 2011)

BARBARA OWEN/R

Treble (Old Fr., from Lat. *triplus*: 'threefold'). High voice, especially of a boy or (less commonly) girl; a high vocal or instrumental part. As a musical term the word dates back at least to the early 14th century in England; it was also known in Burgundy by the middle of the century. In the 14th and 15th centuries it referred to the top voice of three-part polyphony or, in some four-part compositions, to the second highest part (in which case the fourth part was a 'quatreble'). 'Treble' remained in use after 1500 alongside such Latin terms as 'superius', 'cantus', and 'descantus'. In his translation (1609) of Ornithoparchus's *Musicae activae micrologus* (1517) John Dowland studiously held to the original Latin 'discantus', but in one instance discarded it for 'treble'; similarly Morley used 'cantus' and 'descant' in the first two sections of his *Plaine and Easie Introduction* (1597) but gradually adopted 'treble' in the third.

Since the 18th century 'soprano' has gradually displaced 'treble', except in reference to children's voices and to certain older instruments such as the treble viol and the treble recorder. The G (or violin) clef has long been called the 'treble clef' in the English language; Morley, for example, spoke of it as 'the clef which is commonly used in the treble or highest part'.

BIBLIOGRAPHY
S. Kenney: '"English Discant" and Discant in England', *Musical Quarterly*, vol.45 (1959), 26–48
H.H. Carter: *A Dictionary of Middle English Musical Terms* (Bloomington, IN, 1961/*R*)

OWEN JANDER

Trebs, Heinrich Nikolaus (*b* Frankenhausen, Germany, 10 Aug 1678; *d* Weimar, Germany, bur. 18 Aug 1748). German organ builder. The son of a carpenter, he learned his trade from Christian Rothe in Salzungen about 1698 and went to Weimar in 1709, perhaps at J.S. Bach's request; he became court organ builder there in 1712. When his eldest son, Johann Gottfried, was baptized on 26 Nov 1713, the godfathers were Bach and the composer and lexicographer J.G. Walther. Trebs built organs for Taubach, near Mellingen (1710; one manual with eight stops, pedal with three; specification by Bach); the Schlosskirche, Weimar (1714, during Bach's tenure; two manuals, 24 stops, a rebuild; repaired and rebuilt again 1719–20 and 1726); and the Jacobikirche, Weimar (1721; two manuals, 18 stops). He built a large organ for Bad Berka, near Weimar, between 1742 and 1743, also in collaboration with Bach and with the help of his son Christian Wilhelm Trebs and Johann Christian Immanuel Schweinefleisch; it had 13 stops in the *Hauptwerk*, 9 in the *Oberwerk*, and 6 in the Pedal. Christian Wilhelm inherited his father's court privilege.

BIBLIOGRAPHY
P. Rubardt: 'Zwei originale Orgeldispositionen J.S. Bachs', *Festschrift Heinrich Besseler zum 60. Geburtstag* (Leipzig, 1961), 495
G. Stauffer and E.May, eds.: *J.S. Bach as Organist: his Instruments, Music, and Performance Practices* (Bloomington, IN, 1986)

ULRICH DÄHNERT/R

Tréculas [tabuinhas, castanholas]. Clappers of Portugal. It is a set of small wooden boards, usually rectangular, perforated at one end and strung together with a space between each so that they strike together when shaken. The size, wood type, and number of the boards (commonly five to 20) vary greatly. This instrument has a strong tradition in the north of Portugal, where hardwood is favoured, but its use is widespread for children's entertainment and in folk music groups.

PATRÍCIA LOPES BASTOS

Trek tre. Clappers of the Jörai people of central Vietnam. Two seashells are fitted along a slit bamboo stick and a child, with another bamboo stick in one hand, strikes the shells with an up-and-down movement, the sound resembling that of small cymbals.

TRÂN QUANG HAI

Trembel [trombel]. Double-headed drum of the Kanembu, Kotoko, and other Islamic peoples of Chad. It has a cylindrical wooden body, 25 to 30 cm long and about 30 cm in diameter. The cowhide heads are laced in a Y pattern; one of them is fitted with two snares and is never hit. When played the drum is held vertically on a shoulder strap and the upper head is struck with two straight sticks. The trembel is an instrument with exclusively masculine connotations, in contrast to the instrument with which it is always associated, the *ganga* drum. A professional musician plays the trembel and among the Kotoko it is part of the sultan's orchestra.

MONIQUE BRANDILY

Tremolo (It.: 'quivering', 'trembling'). Word *tremolo* has had several different meanings but is now most strictly used to denote a rapid reiteration of a single note or chord without regard to measured time values. Early name-forms include the German *Schwärmer* (W.C. Printz, 1689) and *Rauscher* (D.G. Türk, 1789) and the Italian *bombo*. *Tremolo*, or *tremulant*, is also used for an accessory organ stop. In the 18th century the word *tremolo* was often used to signify vibrato (sometimes denoted with a wavy line). In modern usage some singers distinguish between vibrato, indicating a fluctuation in pitch, and tremolo, meaning a fluctuation in dynamics.

DAVID FALLOWS/R

Tres. Type of short-necked plucked lute with three courses of strings, found in Cuba, the Dominican Republic, and Puerto Rico. In Cuba, where it was developed, it normally has the body shape of a *bandurria* (but sometimes has a vase-shaped outline), occasionally with a cutaway upper treble bout, with three bichord courses (plain and wound steel), and 10 to 15 frets on the fretboard. Tunings include *g–c′–e′* with bichords tuned in unison or in octaves; other tunings are also common, and occasionally trichords are used. It is played in ensembles to accompany song and dance. Folk examples have been made from various materials such as codfish boxes. Also, nylon-strung guitars are often converted and restrung to make the *guitarras-tres*, with the greater tension of the tres's metal strings borne by a tailpiece rather than by the bridge.

In the Dominican Republic, the tres, also with three bichord courses (the first and third tuned in octaves, the second in unison), is primarily a melodic instrument. The Puerto Rican tres was probably adapted from the Cuban instrument; however, it has the shape of a *cuatro* and nowadays three trichord (formerly single) courses, variously tuned.

JOHN M. SCHECHTER/R

Treshchotka [treskotukha]. Russian idiophone.
(1) Set of 20 to 22 small wooden plates threaded on to a double cord or small thong; they knock against each other when the instrument is flexed between the hands. It is used in central regions by women to accompany ritual wedding songs.
(2) Cog rattle, used as a hunting instrument and a children's toy.

Tretzscher, Matthias (*b* Lichtenstadt, Bohemia [now Hrožnětín, Czech Republic], 23 March 1626; *d* Kulmbach, Upper Franconia, Germany, 9 April 1686). German organ builder. He was the son of Paul Tretzscher (*d* 1633) and Susanne Schott, who in 1636 married the organ builder Jakob Schedlich of Joachimsthal. In 1641 Matthias Tretzscher was apprenticed to his stepbrother,

Andreas Schedlich; subsequently he worked in Nuremberg for 21 months with David Schedlich, a relative of Hans Leo Hassler. He returned to Joachimsthal in 1644, to work under Jakob Schedlich (his stepfather), who made him a journeyman in 1647. On Maundy Thursday 1650 Tretzscher had to leave Joachimsthal because of his religious beliefs, and between 1651 and 1652 was organist in Marienberg, in the Ore mountains. In 1653 he built an organ in Bayreuth (Stadtkirche) in collaboration with Christoph Donati. In the same year he moved to Kulmbach where he became organ builder at the court of the Margrave of Brandenburg; in 1654 he became a citizen there, in 1674 an alderman, and in 1684 a churchwarden.

Tretzscher's organs are similar to those of his teacher, Schedlich, though they differed from Schedlich's in having the stops distributed between Great and Choir in the same manner as those of Esaias Beck. Tretzscher became the most important organ builder of the 17th century in Franconia. He made more than 60 organs and taught many organ builders in Franconia and Saxony, including Christoph Donati, Tobias Dressel, Hans Gruber, Hans Purrucker, and D.F. Streit. The magnificent cases of Tretzscher's organs came mostly from the Kulmbach workshop of J. Brenck (Brenk) and H.G. Schlehendorf. His most important organs, built between 1653 and 1686, include those at Bayreuth; Heilsbronn (monastery); Kulmbach (St Peter's); Schweinfurt (St Johannis); Strasbourg Cathedral, Coburg (Moritzkirche); Cheb (St Nicholas); Kaisheim (monastery); Bamberg (St Michael's); Maria Bildhausen Abbey; and Münsterschwarzach Abbey.

BIBLIOGRAPHY

J.C. Laurus: *Sanfftes Ruh-Bettlein* (Bayreuth, 1686) [funeral oration]

H. Hofner: 'Der ostfränkische Orgelbau', *Archiv für Geschichte von Oberfranken*, vol.52 (1972), 5–116

H. Fischer and T. Wohnhaas: 'Matthias Tretzscher', *Lebensbilder zur Geschichte der böhmischen Länder*, vol.4, ed. F. Seibt (Munich, 1981), 71–90

H. Fischer and T. Wohnhaas, eds.: *Lexicon süddeutscher Orgelbauer* (Wilhelmshaven, 1994)

HANS KLOTZ/HERMANN FISCHER

Triangle (Fr. *triangle*; Ger. *Triangel*; It. *acciarino, triangolo*). Idiophone (percussion stick) made from a steel rod bent to form an equilateral or isosceles triangle open at one angle. It is struck with a steel beater which can be tapered for a heavier or lighter stroke, or with a drumstick. Its many high dissonant partials obscure the fundamental note, so that its theoretically indeterminate pitch appears to match the prevailing tonality of the orchestra; but poorly made triangles often seem to clash with that tonality. If all corners of the triangle were closed it would have a definite pitch.

The medieval triangle was closely allied to the ancient sistrum, with rings being strung on its low side. It was generally represented in this form. The shape varied considerably: equilateral with closed or open ends (as shown by Praetorius, 2/1619, and Mersenne, 1636–7); trapeziform; or resembling a medieval stirrup (hence the German *Stegereif* and the Italian *staffa*).

Triangle for medieval music, with beater. Historical reproduction by a Dorset blacksmith, Mr Swanwick. Trapezoidal shape with no gap in the frame made of square section steel rod, with 6 rings on the frame. (Jeremy Montagu Collection, Oxford)

A 10th-century manuscript mentions a triangle without rings. Triangles without rings also appear in King Wenceslaus IV's Bible (late 14th century) and in a 15th-century window in the Beauchamp Chapel, St Mary's, Warwick. The Warwick specimen appears remarkably modern, except that at the top angle the bar is twisted into a loop through which the thumb of the performer (an angel) passes. The medieval triangle (and its beater) is often depicted as larger than the modern instrument. It was frequently illustrated in the hands of angels, who sing as they play. It was also played in secular music, and appears occasionally (with and without rings) as an accompaniment to the pipe. This use continued throughout the Middle Ages and the Renaissance.

In 1710 the triangle was reported in the Hamburg Opera, and in 1717 two triangles were purchased for the Dresden Opera. It appeared in an overture by J.F. Fasch, about the middle of the 18th century. It was employed by Mozart (*Die Entführung aus dem Serail*, 1782), Haydn ('Military' Symphony, 1794), and Beethoven (Ninth Symphony, 1823), who used it to evoke janissary music. The triangle intended by these composers might not have had rings, though these did not finally disappear until the middle of the 19th century, by which time the instrument had become a permanent member of the orchestra.

Until the end of the 18th century the orchestral triangle mainly provided rhythm. In 1853 it was given a solo by Liszt in his Piano Concerto in E♭, causing considerable consternation. Wagner's varied use of the instrument includes the tremolo, for example in *Die Meistersinger* (overture), repeated demisemiquavers in *Die Walküre*, and the economical single stroke at the end of the second act of *Siegfried*. Grieg used a triangle roll to add a silvery touch to the chord announcing Anitra's Dance (*Peer Gynt*). In the cadenza of Rimsky-Korsakov's Spanish Capriccio, the harp is joined by a *pianissimo* tremolo on the triangle.

The normal orchestral triangle measures about 15 to 18 cm on one side, but different sizes and shapes are available. Some composers request triangles of graduated sizes. William Russell's Fugue for Eight Percussion Instruments (1933) requires muffled triangles measuring about 10, 15, and 25 cm. Orff specified three triangles in *Aruigonae*, as did Messiaen in *Eclairs sur l'Au-delà* (1988–92) and *Concert à quatre* (1990–92, completed by Y. Loriod, H. Holliger, G. Benjamin). Unusual uses include Walton's *Façade* (1921–2, rev. 1942) where the triangle strikes a cymbal.

The triangle is normally suspended by a loop of thin gut or nylon that passes around the bar or through a small hole in the upper corner, or it may be suspended from a 'bulldog' paper clip. This allows the instrument to be held in the hand, or attached to a music stand or convenient part of a drum outfit when the use of two beaters is preferable, or during rests. A triangle of good-quality hardened steel, properly suspended and correctly played, can produce many varied tones. For normal orchestral purposes it is struck on the outer side, the open or lower end of its closed side being preferred for quiet strokes. The inside of the lower side is used for *fortissississimo* strokes. For the tremolo the beater is placed in either the top or bottom closed corner, and the two sides are struck in rapid alternation, the crescendo being effected by gradually moving the beater over a larger area. Beaters of varying weight are used, including a steel knitting needle to ensure a quiet tremolo. The sound is terminated by gripping the instrument with the fingers of the non-playing hand (or the other if more convenient).

The triangle is not easy to play. Composers allot it complicated rhythms and grace notes, for example in the 11th variation of Elgar's 'Enigma' Variations, where it depicts the tinkle of the medal on the collar of the bulldog Dan, and in Respighi's *Trittico botticelliano* (1927). For grace notes and repeated quavers and semiquavers, and so on, two beaters are used, or one beater strikes two inner sides with a back-and-forth movement. The triangle is notated on a single line or upper part of the staff.

Triangles are also used in folk music ensembles, for example in Cajun *zydeco* music (USA) and in central and southern Italy, where it is known as *acciarino* (*azzarinu*). *Acciaio* (steel) literally means the steel tool that is struck with a flint to light a fire. In Sardinia *su triángulu* is played with the *tumbarinu* (double-headed cylindrical drum); the *organetto* (accordion); the *pipiolu*, *pipaiolu*, or *sulittu* (duct flutes of different areas of Sardinia); and the jew's harp. In Campania and Calabria it is often made by the Roma blacksmiths who also make and sell jew's harps. In genre paintings of the 17th and 18th centuries it is depicted as the instrument of beggars, while in Neapolitan Nativity scenes it appears as an instrument of wandering ensembles.

The latter use is widely attested in the 19th and 20th centuries, particularly by the Viggianesi ensembles (with the harp of Viggiano and other instruments), or to accompany the hurdy-gurdy or violin. In wandering ensembles, the triangle is usually played by a child.

The Lithuanian *trikampis* is made from iron and struck with an iron hammer to give a high, clear, and continuous sound. This triangle has been used in village bands since the 19th century; village blacksmiths sometimes make it from the teeth of an old horse-rake.

BIBLIOGRAPHY
C.-M. Widor: *The Technique of the Modern Orchestra* (Paris, 1904, 5/1925; Eng. trans., 1906, rev. 2/1946)
J. Blades: *Percussion Instruments and their History* (London, 1970, rev. 3/1984, 4/1992, 5/2005)
F. Guizzi: *Gli strumenti della musica popolare in Italia* (Lucca, 1983/R)
JAMES BLADES/JAMES HOLLAND/JEREMY MONTAGU,
FEBO GUIZZI

Triccaballacca. Percussion idiophone of Neapolitan origin, widely used in folk music of southern Italy. Three wooden mallets are set side by side in a wooden frame, the central mallet stationary and the others pivoted to swing against it when the frame is shaken.

Trichet, Pierre (*b* Bordeaux, France, 1586–7; *d* Bordeaux, before 1649). French author, theorist, collector, and lawyer. By profession a lawyer in the Parliament of Bordeaux, he made use of the humanistic education he had received from his uncle, Jean d'Avril, by publishing during his lifetime two tragedies, a book on witchcraft, and two volumes of epigrams. He was also a collector of books, printed portraits, medals, naturalia, ethnographic objects, and mathematical and musical instruments; an inventory of the entire collection was printed in his *Synopsis rerum variarum* and translated in his *Dénombrement*. About 1630, or perhaps earlier, he began work on his *Traité des instruments de musique*. It was not published during his lifetime, possibly because he was not able to perfect it before he died. In his *Traité* Trichet divided musical instruments into three classes: wind instruments, string instruments, and percussion. For each instrument he first explained the etymology of its name, gave a brief history of its origins and then described its use. The variety of source material upon which he drew reveals the wide range of his reading; he cited not only ancient authors but also contemporary historians, poets, travellers, and men of science. To the dense series of references both ancient and modern he sometimes added trenchant and sensible observations drawn from his own experience (for example, he heard the 'Sourdeline' played by Langlois in Bordeaux in 1626). His treatise is neither so complete and systematic nor so useful to modern scholars and performers as the two best-known books of the time on musical instruments, those by Praetorius and Mersenne, with the latter of whom he corresponded. The *Traité* is the work of a provincial antiquarian and scholar; nevertheless it sometimes supplies information not otherwise available.

WRITINGS
(*selective list*)

Synopsis rerum variarum (Bordeaux, 1631)

Dénombrement de diverses et curieuses choses du Cabinet de Pierre Trichect Bourdelois (Bordeaux, 1635)

Traité des instruments de musique (*F-Psg* 1070); ed. F. Lesure, *AnnM*, iii (1955), 283–387; iv (1956), 175–248; edn pubd separately (Neuilly-sur-Seine, 1957/*R*; Eng. trans., 1973)

BIBLIOGRAPHY

R. Dezeimeris: *Pierre Trichet, un bibliophile bordelais au XVIIe siècle* (Bordeaux, 1878)

C. de Waard, ed.: *Correspondance du P. Marin Mersenne*, vol.3 (Paris, 1945, 2/1969); v (Paris, 1959)

F. Lesure: 'Pierre Trichet's *Traité des instruments de musique*: Supplement', *GSJ*, vol.15 (1962), 70–81; vol.16 (1963), 73–84

E.M. Ripin: 'The French Harpsichord before 1650', *GSJ*, vol.20 (1967), 43–7

A. Schnapper: *Le géant, la licorne et la tulipe* (Paris, 1988), 111–4, 226–8

HOWARD MAYER BROWN/FLORENCE GÉTREAU

Trideksnis. Rattle of Latvia. It consists of a metal (usually iron) rod on a wooden handle, on which are hung several rows of small jingling brass plates. The similar *čagana* is a metal hammer with jingles attached to the handle. Both instruments were formerly used only at weddings, mainly by women singers, who emphasized the rhythm of ritual songs by banging them on a table. Nowadays they also accompany songs and dances. Similar rattles named *eglīte*, *ērkulis*, *puškainis*, or *kāzu puķe* ('wedding flower') were made from wood hung with small rattling objects such as pieces of straw, quill, or jingles and decorated with ribbons, feathers, and buttons; they were also used exclusively at weddings. The *trumulis*, found mainly around Ventspils, resembled the trideksnis, with the addition of a metal ball on a chain attached to the top; it was used only at wedding rituals by young men, who would beat it against the walls and beams of the house to emphasise the rhythms of their songs. See Ī. Priedīte: *Ko spēlēja sendienās* [What Was Played in the Past] (Riga, 1983).

Triebert. French family of woodwind instrument makers. Their firm (written as Triébert after 1878) defined the characteristics of the modern French oboe. They were official providers of oboes and bassoons to the Paris and Brussels conservatoires and the French military. They also met the needs of celebrated players, notably the oboists Vogt, Barret, and Lavigne and the bassoonist Cokken, and worked closely with Theobold Boehm. Their instruments are noted for excellent workmanship and innovative bore designs and key mechanisms.

The company was established by Georges-Louis Guillaume [Georg Ludwig Wilhelm] Triebert (*b* Storndorf bei Alsfeld, Hesse, Germany, 24 Feb 1770; *d* Paris, France, 5 June 1848). Initially trained as a cabinetmaker, perhaps in Laubach, by 1804 Triebert had walked to Paris, where he entered the workshop of the woodwind maker Winnen. By 1810 he had become a *maître-facteur* and opened a business specializing in oboe manufacture. In 1811 he was granted French citizenship and in 1834 the jury at the Paris Exhibition declared his oboes superior to all others exhibited.

Guillaume's eldest son, Charles-Louis Triebert (*b* Paris, France, 31 Oct 1810; *d* Gravelle, Seine, France, 18 July 1867) was a performer and advised his younger brother, Frédéric Triebert (*b* Paris, France, 8 May 1813; *d* Paris, France, 19 March 1878) who, after studying metal engraving from 1826 to 1830, played oboe at the Opéra-Comique from 1839, then in 1842 took over his father's business. Applying new technologies and materials—innovations adopted from Boehms's flute designs, nickel-silver keywork, and exotic timbers (predominantly South American rosewoods of the genus *Dalbergia*)—Frédéric developed a series of progressive designs praised for continuing the traditional French tonal aesthetic. The firm's 1862 catalogue (*Nouveau Prix-Courant*) documents Triebert's six oboe designs (or *systèmes*) that have been used to define prevalent mechanism systems on 19th-century oboes. In particular, *système 6* was the basis of the Conservatoire oboe, still in wide use. Triebert modified designs to suit different pitch standards, including Old Philharmonic Pitch ($a' = 456$ Hz) and *diapason normal* (435 Hz), the latter coming into effect by French law in 1859. The following year Triebert was commissioned to make double-reed instruments for the Paris Opéra at diapason normal. Frédéric Triebert entered his work in international expositions from 1827 to 1870, and consistently received awards. His oboes were most appreciated in France, Belgium, and England (where a number of French players promoted his work); elswhere they were far less prevalent, possibly because he adhered to a French tonal aesthetic.

Although known primarily as an oboe maker, Frédéric Triebert also made flutes, musettes, english horns, baritone oboes, and other woodwinds, patented a *clarinette multiphonique* that incorporated A, B♭, and C keys in one instrument, and made metal clarinet mouthpieces with screw ligature and adjustable lay. He made significant contributions to traditional bassoon design with advice from the players Jancourt and Cokken. He corresponded with Theobold Boehm and, assisted by the bassoonist and maker Angelo Gaëtan Philippe Marzoli, he undertook a thorough realization of Boehm's design for bassoon.

At its height, the Triebert firm employed a workforce of ten. In addition to new instruments, the business also sold accessories including reeds and reed-making tools such as gouging machines for oboe and bassoon cane. They dealt in second-hand instruments and offered perhaps the most extensive stock of oboe music, fingering charts, methods, and so on available in Europe during the 19th century. Frédéric established at least two business partnerships, with Marzoli (1853–62) and Hilaire Martin (1868–72); both deteriorated and terminated prematurely. About 1864 he established a long-standing relationship with Cécile Anne Charlotte Dehais, the firm's reed maker, naming her his sole heir (his marriage certificate in 1845 had stipulated that his wife would not inherit the business). After his death, a dispute arose between Dehais and her daughter by Frédéric on the one hand, and on the other his wife and son (Auguste-) Raoul Triébert (*b*

Paris, France, 1845; *d* after 1895; an oboist at the Paris Opéra); the business was sold at public auction in order to meet outstanding debts. Detailed inventories compiled by the prominent Parisian woodwind instrument builders Jerôme Thibouville-Lamy and Joseph Alexis Tournier provide valuable information regarding the workshop. Dehais won the auction, but the business proved difficult to maintain, and ownership passed to the firm's key-maker Felix Paris. In 1881, bankruptcy forced sale of the business and trademark (registered sometime between 1862–66) to Gautrot *aîné,* which was itself taken over in 1883 by Couesnon, who continued making oboes stamped 'Triébert' (with accent) up to 1934, François Lorée, since 1867 the Triebert foreman, in 1881 started his own company, which continued more faithfully in the Triebert tradition and remains the pre-eminent manufacturer of Conservatoire-system oboes.

BIBLIOGRAPHY

K. Ventzke: 'Zur Biographie der Oboenbauer Triebert in Paris (1810–1878)', *Tibia,* vol.10/1 (1985), 277–9

T. Giannini: 'Frédéric Triébert (1813–1878), Designer of the Modern Oboe: Newly Found Archival Documents Featuring the Inventory and Auction of his Musical Instrument Enterprise', *Liber amicorum Isabelle Cazeaux: Symbols, Parallels and Discoveries in her Honor,* ed. P.-A. Bempéchat (Hillsdale, NY, 2005), 49–90

D. Watel: 'Les becs de clarinette à table mobile: Une invention de Frédéric Triébert,' *Larigot: Bulletin de l'Association des Collectionneurs d'Instruments à Vent,* vol.38 (2006), 10–13

R. Howe: 'Nineteenth-Century French Oboe Making Revealed: a Translation and Analysis of the Triebert et Cie "1855" Nouveau Prix-Courant', *GSJ,* vol.64 (2011), 79–116

G. Burgess: 'New Triebert Discoveries: Observations and Comments on Re-reading the Surviving Documents,' *GSJ,* vol.65 (2012), 93–111

GEOFFREY BURGESS

Triflauto (It.). Designation for an instrument, known only from a stage direction in Peri's *Euridice* (Florence, 1600): 'Tirsi Viene in scena sonando la presente Zinfonia con un Triflauto, e canta la seguente stanza'. The score at this point comprises a ritornello on three staves, all with soprano clefs. The top two parts (*e′–e″*) are written predominantly in parallel 3rds, while the lowest is a drone alternating between only four notes.

The direction might simply refer to a stage prop, perhaps an instrument comparable to the *flauto harmonico* or *armonia di flauto.* The latter was a kind of recorder with five pipes (four of which served only as a drone) made by Manfredo Settala about 1650; the only surviving example is in the Civico Museo Bibliografico Musicale, Bologna. The music could have been played on recorders, as prescribed by Francesca Caccini for a very similar ritornello in her opera *La liberazione di Ruggiero* (Florence, 1625). In another very similar scene, inscribed 'al modo antico', in Emilio de' Cavalieri's *Rappresantatione di Anima, e di Corpo* (Rome, 1600), recorders are expressly directed to be used solely as substitutes if *sordelline* are unavailable; the latter are meant to imitate 'tibie all'antica'. Mersenne described the keyed *sordellina* (a complex bellows-blown bagpipe), and they are also listed in contemporary Medici inventories, so it is possible that the term *triflauto* is an abbreviation denoting 'sordellina con tre flauti'.

BIBLIOGRAPHY

F. Puglisi: 'Signior Settala's "armonia di flauti"', *EMc,* vol.9/3 (1981), 320–24

R. Weber: 'Die Flauto harmonico: ein seltenes Instrument und sein Erbauer', *Tibia,* vol.17/1 (1992), 20–26

MARTIN KIRNBAUER

Trigōnon (Gk.: 'three-cornered'). Term for the Greek harp. It is the least ambiguous of the names used for this instrument, the other terms for which include *pēktis, magadis, sambuca,* and psaltery. Associating any of these terms with a specific type of harp is difficult, as there seems to have been no consistency of usage among the Greeks themselves. Indeed, as Maas and Snyder have suggested, the term *trigōnon,* which originated only in the 5th century bce, might have been coined as a generic term 'for various instruments that bore foreign names and were still relatively unfamiliar to Athenian (if not Eastern) Greeks'.

The Greek harp, which generally took the form of an angular harp as opposed to the arched harp of the Egyptians, appears in three types. By far the most common is the open 'vertical angular' harp. The neck of the instrument is the horizontal member, resting on the knee of the seated player. The resonator is the vertical member, rising at an angle away from the body of the player to about the height of the head, where it frequently hooks forwards. Sometimes it grows thicker towards the top, thus affording greater resonance to the longer strings. Harps are generally depicted with considerably more strings than lyres and kitharas; a range of at least two octaves was probably not uncommon. The strings extended vertically, with the shorter strings closer to the body of the player. They were probably tuned similarly to those of the lyra and kithara; representations of the harp show protuberances on the post which may represent *kollopes.* The second type of Greek harp is a less common variant of the first—the so-called frame harp, which has a supporting forepillar extending from the ends of the resonator and neck. The third type is the comparatively rare 'spindle' harp, an instrument with a resonator that is wider in the middle and narrower at the ends; the resonator of this type is usually depicted away from the player.

Players of Greek harps are generally depicted as females, both amateur and professional. They play the instruments by plucking them with the thumb and forefingers of both hands, usually with the left hand extending further outwards to the longer strings. That harps were played by plucking with the fingers (*psallein*) as opposed to 'striking' (*kruein*) with the plectrum gave rise to the later term for the harp *psaltērion.* Similarly derived is the term *psaltria,* a female harpist, although this term came to be used for female string players in general.

The angular harp was known to the pre-Greek inhabitants of the Cyclades, as attested by a number of marble statuettes dating from the period about 2800 bce–2300 bce that depict a male figure playing a frame harp. There is, however, no more evidence of harps in the Aegean area until the appearance of several references to the instrument in the poetry of 6th-century bce Eastern Greek authors such as Alcaeus, Anacreon, and Sappho. These writers generally use the term *pēktis* and associate it with Lydia. Harps came to be mentioned in Athens in the 5th century bce and are pictured with some frequency in Attic vase paintings of the second half of the century, but not nearly so often as lyres and kitharas. Harps of the period retained their foreign associations and are among the instruments that Plato and Aristotle excluded from their ideal states.

BIBLIOGRAPHY

R. Herbig: 'Griechische Harfen', *Mitteilungen des Deutschen archäologischen Instituts, Athenische Abteilung*, vol.54 (1929), 164–93

M. Maas and J.M. Snyder: *Stringed Instruments of Ancient Greece* (New Haven, CT, 1989), 147–55, 181–5

M.L. West: *Ancient Greek Music* (Oxford, 1992), 70–78

T.J. Mathiesen: *Apollo's Lyre: Greek Music and Music Theory in Antiquity and the Middle Ages* (Lincoln, NE, 1999), 275–80

JAMES W. MCKINNON

Trîmbiţă. Generic term in Romania for trumpet. It is applied specifically to the *bucium* (alphorn) of northern Transylvania and Bukovina, usually made of sheet-iron.

Trimitas (pl. *trimitai*). Trumpet of Lithuania. It has been known in a great variety of forms and sizes, including the modern valved instrument, and under different names. Trimitai were often described and depicted in ancient chronicles, books by foreign travellers and in heraldry from the 12th century onwards. They were used for various purposes: as magic and ritual instruments they were played at funerals, weddings, calendar and agricultural festivals; as signal and ceremonial instruments in pastures and forests; and for pure music-making.

ARVYDAS KARAŠKA

Trimpin, Gerhard (*b* Istein, now part of Efringen-Kirchen, Germany, 26 Nov 1951). German instrument inventor, kinetic sculptor, sound artist, and composer, known as Trimpin. His father was a brass and woodwind player, and Trimpin played with old instruments as a child but developed an allergy to metals that precluded performing on brass instruments. Instead he experimented with making new devices using old radios and parts of discarded instruments. He studied music and art at the University of Berlin from 1975 to 1979. From 1976 to 1979 he was a musician for the Theater Zentrifuge in Berlin, and designed sets for the San Quentin Drama Workshop under the direction of Rick Cluchey and Samuel Beckett. In 1979 he left Berlin for Seattle and began independent research in sound sculpture design, combining music composition and kinetics with computer technology. From 1985 to 1987 he taught at the Sweelinck Conservatory in Amsterdam, and in 2010 began collaborating with Stanford University's Center for Computer Research in Music and Acoustics (CCRMA) to create a multimedia installation, 'The Gurs Zyklus'.

Using found materials and components he fabricates himself, Trimpin creates sculptures and machines that elicit sounds from nature or modify or elaborate sounds created by conventional instruments. Using MIDI technology, he has developed means of controlling orchestral instruments so that they can exceed the limits of human performance. For example, a microtonal bass clarinet is blown by the player while a computer operates numerous added keys. He installed a six-story-tall, computer-operated microtonal xylophone in an Amsterdam theatre stairwell, and developed magnetically suspended iron bells with a very long sound decay. Falling water features in works such as a fountain in which drops fall in rhythmically timed patterns. A dance piece involved small bellows in the dancers' shoes and under their arms that sounded duck calls and other effects. However, Trimpin rarely uses electronic sounds because of the limitations of loudspeakers.

Trimpin has been strongly influenced by the Swiss sculptor Jean Tinguely (1925–91), and by the work of experimental jazz musicians such as Anthony Braxton and George Lewis, the composers Harry Partch and James Tenney, and the player-piano composer Conlon Nancarrow, whose work Trimpin converted to MIDI files for computer reproduction. He has occasionally produced works that pay homage to the musicians and composers he admires, such as *Tenney* for Tenney, *Stereo Trombone* in honour of Lewis, and *Conloninpurple*, a tribute to Nancarrow. He has created instruments and compositions for Ton de Leeuw, Merce Cunningham, and the Kronos Quartet.

Some of Trimpin's sound sculptures are activated by passersby; other devices are robotic. Among his permanent installations are *Derringhochdrei* at the Phaeno Science Center in Wolfsburg, Germany, *Magnitude in C Sharp* at the St Paul (Minnesota) Science Museum, *Sound Arch* in Ojai, California, *Klompen* at the Nora Eccles Harrison Museum of Art in Logan, Utah, and *Liquid Percussion* at the Museum Technorama in Winterthur, Switzerland. *If VI Was IX*, a 40-foot-tall tower comprising more than 530 musical instruments including 30 mechanical guitars that tune themselves automatically, is on permanent display in the EMP Museum in Seattle. In 2008 Trimpin received an honorary doctorate from the California Institute of the Arts. His numerous grants and awards include a John Simon Guggenheim Fellowship and a MacArthur Fellowship.

WORKS
(*selective list*)

Suspended Sound Illusions, 1991; Liquid Percussion, 1991; Phfft, 1992; D.R.A.M.A. ohno, 1992; Hydraulis, 1994; Fire Organ, 1994; Singing Textiles, 1995; Flow Motion, 1996; Conloninpurple, 1996; Leonardo's Boombox, 1998; Magnitude in C♯, 1999; If VI Was IX, 1999; On: Matter, Monekys, and the King, 2000; derringhochdrei, 2002; Sheng High, 2004; 4 Cast, 2006; Liquid Letters, 2007; Soundarch, 2010; The Gurs Zyklus, 2010.

BIBLIOGRAPHY

M. Fürst-Heidtmann: 'Visible Sound, der Klangkünstler und Instrumenten–Erfinder Trimpin', *NZM* (Jan–Feb 2008), 20

A. Focke, ed.: *Trimpin: Contraptions for Art and Sound* (Seattle and London, 2011)

S. Leitman: 'Trimpin: an Interview', *Computer Music Journal* vol.35/4 (2011), 12–27

SUZANNE BEAL

Triple clarinet. Aerophone consisting of three pipes, often made of cane and glued and/or tied together, each of whose air columns is set in vibration by a single beating reed, normally idioglot. Commonly one pipe sounds a drone. The best-known example of a triple clarinet (less widespread than the double clarinet) is the *launeddas*, of southern Sardinia.

Tripous [tripod]. Triple kithara said by the historian Artemon of Cassandrea (*fl* 2nd century bce), probably following Aristotle's pupil Dicaearchus (*fl* c326 bce–296 bce), to have been invented in the 5th century bce by the music theorist Pythagoras of Zacynthus (Athenaeus, xiv, 637b–f). It had a revolving base, and a touch of the performer's foot made the Dorian, Phrygian, or Lydian mode instantly available. Whether or not the instrument (or indeed its inventor, said by Aristoxenus to have headed a school of theorists) actually existed, Artemon's account of it has importance for modal theory and organology. Sachs pointed out the most obvious inference: the idea of such a multiple instrument can be based only on the assumption that even at this early period modes differed radically from one another. Light is also thrown on the disputed question of the function of the left hand in lyre playing: placing the left hand somehow within the upper part of the tripod remains inexplicable unless it is seen in relation to a standard technique whereby the fingers of this hand damped strings rather than plucked them.

Artemon's description of the tripous inspired Giovanni Battista Doni (1594–1647) to design and build the 'lyra Barberina' or 'amphicord'. He had already written a treatise on ancient Greek music, and his lyra had multiple sets of strings on which all the modes and their transpositions could be played.

BIBLIOGRAPHY

C. Sachs: *The Rise of Music in the Ancient World: East and West* (New York, 1943), 237

W.D. Anderson: 'Musical Developments in the School of Aristotle', *RMARC*, vol.16 (1980), 78–98

P. Barbieri: 'Gli strumenti poliarmonici di G.B. Doni e il ripristino dell'antica musica greca (c1630–50)', *AnMc*, vol.30 (1998), 79–114; rev. and trans. as 'Doni's Polyharmonic Instruments and the New Music Inspired by Greek Theory, c1590–1650', in P. Barbieri, *Enharmonic Instruments and Music (1470–1900)* (Latina, 2008), 221–76

WARREN ANDERSON/THOMAS J. MATHIESEN/R

Trişcă. Small or medium-sized duct flute of Romania and Moldavia. It is often about 30 cm long and like the larger *fluier cu dop*, has six fingerholes. The duct, usually at the rear, is formed by a stopper called *dop*. While many examples are left plain, others are stained, with elaborate decoration incised through the stain to the white wood below, or decorated with metal bands between the fingerholes. The trişcă is found in most of Transylvania, Bukovina, and northern Moldavia. In central Moldavia the term 'trişcă' also means the small *fluier moldovenesc or fluieraş*.

Tristan Schalmei. Woodwind instrument with some of the characteristics of the musette group, designed by the maker Wilhelm Heckel in an attempt to produce the particular timbre imagined by Wagner for the shepherd's rustic pipe in Act 3 of *Tristan und Isolde*. The sound that Wagner had in mind has in all probability been most nearly realized with the Holztrompete; the *tárogató*, english horn and other instruments have also been used. As originally constructed the Tristan Schalmei had a sharply conical bore terminating in a very wide bell with an in-curved rim after the fashion of many folk instruments. Its fundamental was *f'*. The tube was perforated by six plain fingerholes of which the uppermost was provided with a simple 'half-hole' mechanism. The instrument is apparently no longer in use.

PHILIP BATE

Tritonicon [Tritonikon]. Wide-bore, double-reed, contrabass instrument of brass. Conceived for military use by Franz Schölnast & Sohn of Pressburg, it was manufactured for the first time in 1839. Obviously inspired by Johann Stehle's Harmonie-Bass, it resembles the ophicleide in its two-tube configuration, and like both it is equipped with mostly closed-standing keys. Its 15 keys give a scale from D' to f, overblown without the aid of octave keys. Other makers using the same basic design and name included Ferdinand Hell (by 1845) and Václav František Červený (by 1853). In 1856 Červený constructed a four-tube model (three tubes plus lead pipe) linked by metal elbows, its height reduced from 157 cm to 107 cm. He also raised the tessitura from D' to $E\flat'$; this instrument, named Kontrafagott [in] E♭, was also built by August Heinrich Rott´s Sohn. Mahillon used the three-tube tritonicon as a model for his *contrebasse à anche*, introduced in 1868. In 1876 Červený built a similar instrument, pitched a 4th lower, which he advertised as Subkontrafagott [in] B♭. See T. Kiefer: 'Tiefstimmige Doppelrohrblattinstrumente von der Harmoniemusik bis in das Blasorchester des 19. Jahrhunderts', *Wissenschaftliches Jahrbuch der Tiroler Landesmuseen 2010*, ed. W. Meighörner (Innsbruck, 2010), 47–99.

THOMAS KIEFER

Trivalī [trikulyā]. Medieval hourglass drum of India. It is described as about 48 cm long and 14 cm in diameter at the faces; the middle 'can be grasped by the fist'. The heads are stretched on iron hoops in which are seven holes; they are laced with a central cross-lacing over which is a decorated fringe. The drum is hung on a shoulder strap and played with both hands. The *trikulyā* was a shorter variant (about 40 cm), but it was about 2 cm wider at the faces. See Śarṅgadeva: *Saṅgītaratnākara (13th century)*, ed. S. Subrahmanya Sastri, vol.3 (Madras, 1951).

ALASTAIR DICK

Tro [dra, tror]. Generic term for bowed lutes of Cambodia. There are six types of *tro* in common Khmer practice. They are *tro khmer* or *tro ksai bey* (three-string spike fiddle), *tro chhe*, *tro so tauch*, *tro so thom*, *tro ou*, and *tro ou chambieng* (two-string fiddles). At the Royal University of Fine Arts in Phnom Penh there are two other types of *tro*, called *tro kandal* (medium-sized two-string fiddle) and *tro thomm* (large-sized two-string fiddle), but these are used only in academic experiments within the university. The *tro khmer*, the only Khmer three-string fiddle, resembles the Thai *saw sam sai*. The *tro ou* is similar to the Lao and Thai *saw u* and the Vietnamese *đàn gao*.

The origin of the *tro khmer* is unknown. Some assert a Malayo-Indonesian origin, because it resembles the *rebab*. However, Khmer oral history maintains that the *tro khmer* has existed among the Khmer people for a long time. It is used in the *arak* (spirit-worship) and *kar* (wedding) ensembles. The bow is held stationary, the hairs being held taut by the fingers; the instrument is pivoted so that the strings rub against the bow. The melody is played on the treble string; the bass strings provide a drone. The Khmer two-string fiddles are believed to be modifications of the Chaozhou Chinese two-string fiddle (*tou xian*), which was used in the *hi* theatre ensemble brought to Cambodia about the turn of the 20th century. A *tro* has a range of approximately one octave when played in the usual finger position (first position), but the range can be extended through use of higher positions.

The resonator of the *tro khmer* is made of a thin-walled half coconut shell covered with snake or lizardskin. The three strings are made of silk or nylon. A detached bow, with bow hair made of horsehair, sugar-palm fibres, or nylon threads, is used. The resonators of the *tro chhe* and *tro so tauch* are made of bamboo or jackfruit wood, or, rarely, of ivory or buffalo horn, covered with snake- or lizardskin. The bow hairs (of horsehair, pineapple fibres, or thin nylon threads) of these instruments pass between the two metal strings. The timbre, especially of the *tro chhe*, tends to be quite nasal. The *tro so* has a large thick soundbox and produces a deeper sound. *Tro so thomm* has a resonator made of tortoiseshell, bamboo, or jackfruitwood, covered with snake- or lizardskin, and also possesses two metal strings. The two types of *tro ou* are distinguished by the shape of their resonators; the *tro ou* is made of a nearly whole coconut shell, whereas the *tro ou chambieng* is made of half a coconut shell (*chambieng*: 'half'). They are similar to the Lao and Thai *saw u* and the Vietnamese *đàn gao*. The strings of both types of *tro ou* are made of gut, silk, metal, or nylon.

The varieties of two-string tro are used in the *arak*, *kar*, *mohori* (entertainment), *ayai* (vocal genre), *yike* (folk theatre), and *basak* (theatre of Chinese origin) ensembles, sometimes solo or to accompany a vocalist.

BIBLIOGRAPHY
Sal Pich: *Brief Survey of Khmer Music* (Phnom Penh, 1970)
Sam-Ang Sam and P.S. Campbell: *Silent Temples, Songful Hearts: Traditional Music of Cambodia* (Danbury, CT, 1S991)
K. Dorivan and others: *Traditional Musical Instruments of Cambodia* (Phnom Penh, 1994)

SAM-ANG SAM/TERRY E. MILLER

Troïne. Bark aerophone used by shepherds in central France, reportedly a kind of horn or signal instrument. The term formerly applied to a medieval instrument.

Tromba marina [It.: 'trumpet marine'; Fr. *trompette marine*; Ger. *Trumscheit, Nonnengeige, Marien Trompet,* *Trompetengeige*]. Bowed monochord equipped with a vibrating bridge, in common use from the 15th century until the mid-18th. In its fully developed form the instrument is capable of sounding all of the pitches of the harmonic series up to the 16th partial. Analysis of the tone of the tromba marina shows an extremely complex waveform whose partials are in the audible range up to about 14,000 Hz (the 25th partial). Comparison of its tone with that of a modern brass trumpet shows that the partials of the latter drop off sharply after the 10th or 11th partial. The use of a straight mute, however, heightens the upper partials of the trumpet so that it begins to show the same configurations as the tromba marina for the first six or seven partials.

1. Historical development. 2. Construction. 3. Makers. 4. Performance.

1. Historical development. The history of the tromba marina may be divided into two overlapping periods: the first extending from 1450 to 1650, the second from 1550 until the late 19th century. During the first half of the 15th century a vibrating bridge was added to the drone string of the dichord (another monochord derivative stemming from the late 12th century) as a means of enhancing the tone or increasing the volume. At this time the dichord was common in two forms: a long instrument of approximately 2 metres which was played with its lower end resting on the ground and a shorter instrument held against the breast with its open end projecting into the air. The instrument with the vibrating bridge eventually became known as a *Trumscheit* and existed concurrently with the dichord until the mid-16th century when the latter disappeared.

When playing the shorter instrument it was more convenient to bow it close to the nut while supporting the body with the left hand. Although earlier representations show this string used only as a drone, the performers probably discovered that other pitches could be produced by touching the string at the nodal points, and in his *Dodecachordon* of 1547 Glarean described the sounding of trumpet blasts. Supporting the instrument with the hand, however, precludes any manual dexterity, and the short string places the upper partials so close together that their performance is impractical.

Users of the longer instrument did not encounter these problems. In the late 16th and early 17th centuries the technique was evolved to make the tromba marina a more satisfying musical instrument. Mersenne, describing the full range of available pitches, remarked in 1636: 'I do not doubt that it would be played perfectly if one should employ as much time as is done in playing the viol or the lute'. Although Mersenne, Praetorius, and other 17th-century writers mentioned only instruments with a long pyramidal body, a newer style with a more pleasing tone had been invented in the late 16th century. Apparently of German origin, the earliest of these newer instruments, of which examples still exist, might date from the third quarter of the 16th century.

By the third quarter of the 17th century public knowledge of the name 'tromba marina' was such that composers could use the instrument to reinforce a seafaring image. The origin of the 'marine' part of the name is not known, although in earlier times it was attributed to its use by sailors as an instrument or as a signalling device on ships—hypotheses for which there is no substantiation. Nor is there any proof of its derivation from 'Mary' or the name of the 15th-century trumpeter Marin (or Maurin). Similarly, Sachs's tracing of it to the Polish *tub maryna* is erroneous, as are the implications fostered by Martin Vogel's derivation of the name from the Hebrew. Nonetheless, in German-speaking countries the instrument had some real association with convents; according to Rühlmann it was still in use in Marienthal (Saxony) in 1885. Of the 70 examples surviving in museums in these areas, at least 35 were acquired from local cloisters.

For some 75 years (from about 1650 until about 1725) the tromba marina seems to have been a popular instrument. Besides the hundreds of examples constructed during this time, more than 300 pieces, including some *concerts*, sonatas, and suites, were composed for the instrument (for discussion of its repertory, see *GMO*). Also surviving are 56 arrangements from the works of Lully. Public performances were numerous, for example the programme attended by Pepys at Charing Cross in 1667, the frequently cited quartet performance offered at the Fleece tavern in 1675 (not 1674, as has been so widely printed), as well as a river performance mentioned in the *Mercure galant* of 1677. The tromba marina was often used in Swiss collegia, and instruction was given on it in some Scandinavian schools. Numerous scientific papers on the instrument were prepared in the decade preceding 1700 in both England and France. In the latter country tromba marina players were part of both the royal establishment in Paris (from 1679 until 1767—there were five listed in 1760 alone, all doubling on the cromorne) and the orchestra of the Archbishop of Lyons (1715–21). Even as late as 1752 trombas marina were sought for purchase through newspaper advertisements (Nuremberg, *Frag- und Anzeige-Nachrichten*, 1752, no.94).

In spite of its wide acceptance, critics of the instrument were plentiful. The harsh remarks of Virdung and Agricola, and Sebastian Brant's characterization of it as a fool's device, were, however, directed at the older form of the instrument. 17th-century critics, aware of its popularity, were more subtle, often referring only to the way it attracted animals, or was preferred by the bourgeoisie. By the mid-18th century its decline was apparent: Dom Caffiaux described its sound as insufferable; J.R. Wettstein ungraciously satirized it in an ink drawing of a Basle music society (*c*1792); and to Berlioz, writing in 1859, the tromba marina was 'a triton's conch, capable of frightening asses'.

2. Construction. In its most popular form the tromba marina averages 190 to 200 cm in length and consists of a hollow, open-ended resonator with an attached solid neck. The neck ends in a pegbox surmounted with a head, shield, or scroll, and has as a tuning device a peg or machine head. The form of the latter, depending on the age of the instrument, is: a vertical screw, turned by means of a knob on the end of the instrument (oldest form); a ratchet and pawl, sometimes in combination with a peg; or a worm gear. Only rarely is the tuning device mounted in the lower end of the instrument. The belly is usually of pine, and the staves, of which there are most often five or seven, are of pine, maple, or a similar hardwood. The belly is braced internally with several lateral slats or ribs, and the staves are reinforced with cloth, paper, or, not infrequently, strips of old parchment.

Other, less common features include the *guidon*, used to adjust the distance of the free foot of the vibrating bridge from the belly; a rose or soundhole, used mainly for decoration; sympathetic strings; inlays of hard material under the vibrating bridge; or other acoustical treatment. The *guidon*, a feature found on perhaps a third of the instruments, is an essential adjunct to facile performance. One end of a thin string is attached either to the bridge or to the main string below the bridge. The other end is fastened to a peg in this area or guided to one on the upper body or neck of the instrument. Mersenne, illustrating another approach to the problem of adjusting the bridge, wrote:

> It is very difficult to fit this bridge so that it trembles as it must, for if one errs only slightly, the quivering becomes too strong and disagreeable or too weak. Thus one is often many hours in finding the point of perfection that one desires.

The *guidon* was used at least as early as 1660. Sympathetic strings are rarely found even though they are frequently described as an integral part of later instruments. Interior sympathetic strings were first mentioned by Randel Holme in 1680; however, sympathetic strings do appear on the outside of the instrument pictured by Praetorius (*Theatrum instrumentorum*, 1620).

Glarean mentioned the use of nails or ebony on the foot of the vibrating bridge as a means of increasing the volume. Although one finds a few 18th-century instruments so equipped, the practice was seldom followed because it emphasized the brittleness of the tone. More commonly the entire vibrating bridge area was inlaid with hardwood, but this may have been as much to prevent excessive wear as to enhance the tone; many old instruments show signs of having had several bridge sites. The 16th-century practice of coating the interior back and sides of the instrument with ground glass serves to restrict the vibrations of these areas; this allows the belly to vibrate more freely and greatly reduces the attendant noise level.

3. Makers. More than 180 examples are preserved in museums. Of this number, five are 16th-century instruments. There seem to be no extant examples of the triangular-shaped instruments in either size, although several museums exhibit 18th-century versions or later reproductions based on pictures or early descriptions. Makers are known for about one-fifth of the instruments. In the following list the number of known instruments for each maker is indicated either by multiple dates or by a number placed after a single date.

P. Alletsee, Munich (1732, 1737); J. Berger, Landshut (c1685); Johann Balthasar Berler (Bieler), ?Switzerland (1689); Robert Brenner, England (1765, advertisement); Nicolas Duclos, Barcelona (1763); Thomas Eberle, Naples (1773, copy after Praetorius); Johann Ulrich Fischer, Landshut and Munich (1720, 3; 1722, 2; c1725; 1728, 2); Goutenoire, France (early 18th century); Frederick Hintz, England (18th century, advertisement); Matthias II Hornsteiner, Mittenwald (1790, 2); Rudolf Hoss, Munich (c1700, 1701); F. Houyet, Namur (1680); R. Imbert, France (1715, Prin's favourite builder); Jacobs (1702); G.A. Janke, Saxony (1682, 2); E. Lewis, London (c1700); MFSB (?Andreas Ferdinand Mayr), Salzburg (c1720, 3); J. Ott, Füssen (1727, c1732); Claude Pierray, Paris (1730, 1750); Sebastian Renault, Paris (c1760, 2); Pieter Rombouts, Amsterdam (1730); Seraillac, France (early 18th century); Gemiano Sighnolfi, Nonantola (1773); Johan[n] [S]tassar, Switzerland (1674); L. Tobi, ?Germany (1702); Tywersus, ?Lorraine (16th or 17th century, 2); IBST (1702); J. Weiss, Salzburg (1702); Gregori Ferdinand Wenger, Augsburg (c1713, 4).

4. Performance.

A skilled performer is capable of producing a variety of effects. It is possible, for example, to alternate the trumpet-like timbre with the normal sound of the harmonics, or to expand the usual playing range, by means of auxiliary pitches, to two full octaves. For the most part melodies use the 6th, and 8th to 13th partials; however, there are many instances, frequently in duets, where auxiliary pitches are required adjacent to the 4th, 5th, 6th, and 7th partials. These pitches (ex.1) speak best when approached diatonically, as they always are in the music. When this is taken into account there is no justification for the frequently held opinion that trumpets marine of several sizes were used for duets or ensembles.

Tonal variety is achieved in tromba marina music in ternary forms by allowing the ensemble to play the alternating sections in another key. Beyond this, temporary modulations to the subdominant are made by using the flat 14th partial. The 7th partial, an octave lower, is never used. The dominant can be implied by using the second and fifth scale steps, or more strikingly the sharp 11th partial. For example, in the key of C the *f″* is used as both an *f♮″* and an *f♯″*. In many pieces the tonality is actually shifted to the dominant key by using this pitch as a leading note.

The music is liberally ornamented, usually with a small cross or an occasional simple appoggiatura. Since all of the pitches were traditionally stopped with the thumb or one finger, even short trills can be technically demanding. Regarding the difficulty of the instrument, Mersenne noted that 'one meets few men who play it well, because the thumb or another finger must run with a certain measure and speed … which is not easy to imitate'. Prin's only remarks about ornamentation concern the trill, about which he said: 'with practice one will master it, provided that one does not become discouraged'.

Ex.1: Range and auxiliary pitches.

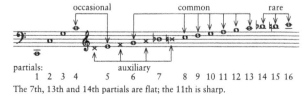

partials:
1 2 3 4   5   6   7   8 9 10 11 12 13 14 15 16

The 7th, 13th and 14th partials are flat; the 11th is sharp.

BIBLIOGRAPHY
L. Vallas: 'J.-B. Prin et sa méthode de trompette marine', *Revue musicale de Lyon*, vol.9 (1911–12), 78–87
J. Pulver: 'The Tromba Marina or Trumscheidt', *The Strad*, vol.25 (1914–15), 15–17, 56–7
D. Fryklund: 'Studier över marintrumpeten', *STMf*, vol.1(1919), 40–57
T. Norlind: 'Bidrag till marintrumpetens historia', *STMf*, vol.4 (1922), 97–101
P. Garnault: *La trompette marine* (Nice, 1926)
W. Schuh: 'Das Trumscheidt in der schweizerischen Barockmusik', *Neue Zürcher Zeitung* (8–9 Aug 1929)
F.W. Galpin: 'Monsieur Prin and his Trompette Marine', *ML*, vol.14 (1933), 18–29
C. Adkins: 'New Discoveries in the Development of the Trumpet Marine', *IMSCR XI: Copenhagen 1972*, 221–7
M. Vogel: 'Zur Etymologie von "tromba marina"', *IMSCR XI: Copenhagen 1972*, 696–701
J. Sehnal: 'Hudební inventár stráznickych piaristu z roku 1675', *Casopis moravského muzea*, vol.69 (1984), 117–28
E. Kullmer: *Mitschwingende Saiten: Musikinstrumente mit Resonanzaiten* (Bonn, 1986)
C. Adkins and A. Dickinson: *A Trumpet by any Other Name: a History of the Trumpet Marine* (Buren, 1991)

CECIL ADKINS

Trombe (Fr.). (1) *Basse trompette*.

(2) A wooden box (string drum) with a gut string stretched over a bridge on the top, used as a substitute for timpani to accompany the *tromba marina*. The bridge divides the string unequally, sounding tonic and dominant pitches when the string is struck by beaters.

JEREMY MONTAGU

Trombita [trąbita, trębita, trembita]. Cylindrical wooden trumpet of the Silesian, Żywiec Beskid, and some other regions of south Poland. It is straight, up to 4 metres long, with a short conical bell, and is made of pine. Like other highland alphorns it is covered with bark to seal the bore. Some types have separate wooden mouthpieces. The trombita is used by shepherds, sometimes with the bell end of the tube lashed to a post or tree to hold it off the ground. The Ukrainian *trembyta* is equivalent. Other wooden trumpets of Poland include the *bazuna* and *ligawka*.

Trombone (Fr., It. *trombone*; Ger. *Posaune*). Brass lip-reed aerophone with a predominantly cylindrical bore. The most common trombones are the tenor and bass counterparts of the trumpet. Though valve trombones have been popular in many contexts since the 19th century, the most ubiquitous form of the instrument is characterized by a telescopic slide with which the player varies the length of the tube; hence the term 'slide trombone' (Fr. *trombone à coulisse*, Ger. *Zugposaune*, It. *trombone a tiro*; Fr. and Eng. up to the 18th century, *saqueboute*, sackbut). Before the 19th century the term *tuba ductilis* was widely used as the Latin expression for the instrument. Both the Italian and German names for trombone are derived from terms for trumpet: *trombone* (large trumpet) from the Italian *tromba* (trumpet), and *Posaune* from *Buzûne*, derived in turn from the French *buisine* (straight trumpet). The etymology of *saqueboute*, which gave rise to the term 'sackbut', is discussed below.

The early history of the trombone was misunderstood in Britain and in the English language more generally until the early 20th century. Burney appears to have believed it to be an entirely new instrument when players of the 'Sacbut—or Double Trumpet' were sought for the 1784 Handel Commemoration, and some 19th-century antiquarians believed its origins lay in deep antiquity. The source of the latter misconception is the appearance of the word 'sackbut' in the Old Testament (*Daniel* iii.3, 5, 7 and 10); Francis W. Galpin's important paper 'The Sackbut: its Evolution and History' (1906–7) showed this to be no more than a translator's error. He correctly explained that the trombone, with a double, U-shaped slide, can be dated no earlier than the 15th century, though neither he nor any subsequent scholar has been able to establish exactly when and where it first appeared.

The instrument has always been called *trombone* in Italy and *Posaune* in German-speaking countries. Other commonly used names have a less certain origin, but most seem to be a combination of two elements: *sac* (by Galpin's suggestion from the Spanish word *sacar*, a word with several different meanings, the most likely in this context being 'to draw' in the sense of pulling); and *bu* (meaning to thrust or push). The scholarly consensus is that, irrespective of the origin of these segments of the word, it is in the French term *saquebote* that the origin of several similar words is found, including *sacabuche* (Spanish) and *sackbut* (English), each of which appeared in several different spellings between the 15th and 17th centuries. In England for example, 'sagbut', 'shakbush' and 'shagbut' were at least as common as 'sackbut', the word routinely employed in modern times to denote an early trombone. The 'sac-but' group of words is important however, because from the time they began to be applied to a musical instrument they seem to contain something of a description of how it was played: by extending and contracting a movable slide. The same could not be said of *trombone* and *Posaune*, as they could have meant no more than a large form of the trumpet. Also meaning trombone in the 16th century was 'dracht trumpet' (spelled 'draught' and 'draucht' in some sources). 'Dracht trumpet' occurs in Scottish sources from the late 15th century. In describing a wedding reception of 1538, Robert Lindsay distinguished between the 'weir trumpattis' and the 'draught trumpattis' (*The History and Cronicles of Scotland*, ed. Ae.J.G. Mackay (Edinburgh, 1899), vol.1, 379), implying that the latter was different from the former and that it had some sort of slide. At this late date it was probably a double slide instrument—a form of trombone.

Tuba ductilis seems to have been the commonly accepted Latin expression for the trombone from the 16th century. For example, an early 16th-century warrant in the Scottish Privy Seal Records, which registered the appointment of a 'draucht trumpet' player Julian Drummond, specifies his office as that of 'tuba ductilis'. Elyot's Latin-English dictionary (*Bibliotheca Eliotae*, 1538) translated *tuba ductilis* as 'a brazen trumpet', but elsewhere the phrase was consistently associated with the trombone. Praetorius used it, as did Roger North and Giles Schondonch, the author of 'The Custom Book

of St Omer', an early 17th-century manual describing practices at the English Jesuit school at Saint-Omer, France, (MS, *c*1609, Stonyhurst College, Lancs. Arch. CII 19). It is this source that provides what is probably the least unambiguous explanation: 'Tuba ductilis (vulgo Sacbottum)'.

I. Slide trombone. 1. Introduction. 2. Alto and soprano trombones. 3. Tenor trombone. 4. Bass trombone. 5. Contrabass trombone. II. Valve trombone. III. Trombone mutes. IV. History to 1900. IV. Performance technique before the 20th century. VI. Later design developments. VII. Jazz and advanced techniques.

I. Slide trombone.

1. Introduction. The structure of a slide trombone is ingenious and relatively simple, and its basic format has changed little since the 15th century. The two parallel inner tubes of the slide are connected at their upper ends by a cross-stay. The mouthpiece is inserted into the top of one tube; the bell joint fits into the top of the other, this tube being either tapered externally to achieve a tight fit, or attached to the bell section by means of a threaded collar (the 'bell lock'). Over the stationary inner tubes runs the slide proper (the outer slide), which consists of two tubes joined at the bottom by a U-shaped tube (the 'slide bow'). From the 19th century this bow has been fitted with a 'water key' for releasing the condensed moisture from the player's breath. At the top of the outer slide is a second cross-stay, with which the player moves the slide.

Friction is minimized by a slight thickening of the walls of the lowest 120 mm of the inner tubes which provide running surfaces for the outer slide. Formerly these short sleeves (known as 'stockings') were of a different metal (such as phosphor bronze) from that of the slide; in modern manufacture they are formed integrally with the inner tubes, and are of chromium-plated nickel silver. When the slide is fully retracted the outer slide comes up against buffers, either of a soft material such as cork, or, on more modern instruments, short compression springs; these 'touch springs' allow for some flexibility in the tuning of notes played in the closed position. The bore of the modern instrument is cylindrical for about half its length (more with the slide extended); the cylindrical section is usually between 12.5 mm and 14.0 mm in diameter, but in bass trombones it sometimes exceeds 14 mm. A wide variety of bore sizes is produced by modern manufacturers; particular bore sizes are favoured for different styles of music: for example, jazz trombonists tend to play instruments with a narrower bore than do most orchestral players. The bore expands to a markedly flaring bell, with a terminal diameter ranging from about 20 cm on a tenor trombone to about 25 cm or more on a bass. The U-bend of the bell section (the 'bell bow') is usually fitted with a telescopic tuning-slide and might also include a weight to help balance the whole instrument in the player's (usually) left hand.

In each position of the slide, a series of resonances approximating to a harmonic series is available to the player. Since the late 18th century, slide technique has been based on seven positions that lower the pitch of all members of this series progressively by semitones (Table 1); the 1st (highest) position is with the slide fully retracted, the 7th (lowest) with it fully extended. The distance between adjacent positions increases slightly as the slide is extended. On the tenor trombone, for instance, from 1st to 2nd position is about 8 cm, from 6th to 7th position about 12 cm. A slide allowing the pitch to be lowered by six semitones gives a complete chromatic compass from the 7th position E on the tenor trombone in B♭, upwards for some three octaves, more or less, depending on the skill and needs of the player.

The second leg (leading to the joint with the bell section) of the trombone's slide is sometimes of slightly wider diameter than the first (leading from the mouthpiece receiver); such a model is termed 'dual bore'. In any case, the high proportion of cylindrical tube, even with the slide retracted, acoustically determines the tonal character of the trombone. In order to bring the modes of vibration of the air column into a usefully close approximation to a harmonic series, there has to be a significantly high 'horn function', given by a flaring bore profile, over the final 30 cm or so of the bell. Even so, the frequencies of the lowest one or two modes are markedly lower than the nominal frequencies of the corresponding notes available to the player: one can only sound the lowest ('pedal') and next lowest resonances in tune because of the presence of an extensive series of strong higher modes allowing a 'co-operative regime'. Compared with other brass instruments of comparable tube length and tessitura, such as the euphonium, the strong higher modes of vibration (resulting from the more cylindrical bore) and the greater acoustical energy trapped in the instrument by the flaring bell of the trombone give the instrument a more brilliant character, especially when played loudly. The energy levels in a trombone can be so high that they display non-linear (shock-wave) characteristics; this characteristic is responsible for the strident, brassy effect that can occur when the trombone is played at maximum volume.

Various mouthpiece designs have been used for the trombone. Few early mouthpieces have survived, so general conclusions are difficult to draw with any confidence. Perhaps the most important extant specimen is that inscribed with the mark of the Schnitzer family, who made trombones in Nuremberg in the 16th century. This mouthpiece is important because it accompanies an extant instrument, which carries the same mark and is dated 1581. Like the representations of mouthpieces in treatises such as Mersenne's *Harmonie universelle* (1636–7), which it resembles, it suggests that mouthpieces tended to have flat rims, shallow cups and sharp, well-defined apertures.

Praetorius's mouthpieces for trumpet and trombone, as illustrated in the second volume of his *Syntagma Musicum* (*Organographia*, 1618), show them to be the same size, but elsewhere and later, trombone mouthpieces are shown to be larger than those of the trumpet. The 19th-century French trombone mouthpiece was a large version of the horn mouthpiece, with a deep funnel-shaped cup. The modern mouthpiece is of intermediate cup shape with a larger cup volume to match the larger bore of modern instruments. Many different mouthpiece designs exist, and the choice of mouthpiece is extremely personal to each player.

Though trombones are commonly referred to by their nominal pitch names ('B♭ trombone' and so on), the trombone is not usually a transposing instrument. An exception is found in the British-style brass band, in which the tenor instruments have sometimes been notated in the treble clef a major 9th higher than sounded. Otherwise, trombone parts are written in alto, tenor, or bass clef as appropriate, and exceptionally in the treble clef.

2. Alto and soprano trombones. Alto trombones in E♭ or F are illustrated in early treatises, and several early examples survive. Less frequent is unambiguous evidence of their actual use. The deployment of the instrument was not standardized throughout Europe, and many parts often assumed to have been played on the alto instrument were more probably played on the tenor. The range of the parts marked 'alto' can usually be covered by the tenor instrument. In 18th and 19th century orchestras use of the alto was sufficiently variable for modern performers (especially period instrument performers) to need to consider the contextual historical evidence carefully before electing to use the instrument. High alto parts are easier to play on the alto trombone than the tenor. Modern professional orchestral players often use the alto instrument for the 'alto' line when there is a musical need for it (typically for 18th- and early 19th-century sacred works and the symphonies of composers such as Schumann and Brahms).

The soprano trombone, usually in B♭ an octave above the tenor, appeared in the 17th century, the period from which the earliest specimens survive. It was used in Germany to play the treble part in chorales, and this tradition has survived in some Moravian church trombone choirs. In the 20th century several manufacturers made soprano trombones as doubling instruments for jazz cornet players, or as a novelty, but the instrument has never been widely used.

3. Tenor trombone. The tenor trombone has always been the most common of the family; in 16th-century Germany, for instance, it was often termed *gemeine* ('ordinary'), and the deeper-pitched instruments were described by reference to their pitch interval below the tenor (*Quartposaune*, etc.). Table 1 shows how the scale is made on the tenor trombone. Early tenor instruments usually had a nominal pitch in A, later B♭ or occasionally C. Modern tenor instruments have a nominal pitch in B♭. The lowest, fundamental note in each position (the 'pedal'), though some such notes are shown in theoretical works by writers such as Speer and Majer in the 17th century, were not written for until Berlioz. Pedal notes were included in compositions more frequently in more modernist idioms in the 20th century.

Although the trombone is understood in modern times as having seven slide positions, fine adjustment of

Table 1

Slide Position:	1st	2nd	3rd	4th	5th	6th	7th
12	f''	e''					
11		$e\flat''$			*etc*		
10	d''	$c\sharp''$					
9	c''	b'	$b\flat'$	a'	$a\flat'$	g'	$f\sharp'$
8	$b\flat'$	a'	$a\flat'$	g'	$g\flat'$	f'	e'
7	g'	$g\flat'$	f'	e'	$e\flat'$	d'	
6	f'	e'	$e\flat'$	d'	$d\flat'$	c'	b
5	d'	$c\sharp'$	c'	b	$b\flat$	a	$g\sharp$
4	$b\flat$	a	$a\flat$	g	$g\flat$	f	e
3	f	e	$e\flat$	d	$d\flat$	c	B
2	$B\flat$	A	$A\flat$	G	$G\flat$	F	E
1	$B\flat'$	A'	$A\flat'$	G'	$(G\flat')$	$(F\flat')$	(E')

(Left bracket label: Natural harmonics)

each is needed to produce good intonation, and intermediate positions are used to obtain microtones, which have been notated in works such as Iannis Xenakis's *Phlegra* (1975). In the higher part of the range, alternative positions of the slide are used to avoid long shifts in fast passages or to obtain and to facilitate smooth slurs. Alternative positions are also often needed for the first or last note of long glissandos.

Many modern tenor trombones are fitted with a thumb-operated F valve which in modern parlance is called a 'trigger' or 'plug'. The B♭/F instrument provides a greater utility for tenor trombone players by increasing the number of available low notes and offering the possibility of further options for alternative positions. The development of the B♭/F instrument is explained in more detail below.

4. Bass trombone. As with the alto trombone, a distinction has to be made between the bass line and the bass instrument. While bass trombones have been illustrated since the early 17th century and many early instruments survive, their deployment was highly variable in different periods and places. Notwithstanding such considerations, true bass instruments have been used to provide a deeper range of notes and a broader timbre from the trombone section.

The F bass trombone formerly used in Germany and central Europe barely survived into the 20th century. In Britain, however, the G bass trombone, pitched a minor 3rd below the B♭ instrument, was used in every orchestra and band from about 1815 up to the 1950s and for some time later in brass bands. Its lowest note, apart from pedals, is $C\sharp$; in the orchestra a D valve was also used. Because of the length of the slide extensions, a short handle fitted to the stay of the outer slide was necessary on F and G trombones so that the player could reach the more distant positions.

The B♭/F trombone was introduced in 1839 by the Leipzig maker Christian Friedrich Sattler; in Paris, Halary and Sax followed with similar instruments. It was at first regarded as a 'tenor-bass trombone', capable of covering the compasses of both bass and tenor, rather than a replacement for the true bass in F. With the valve operated, the slide has only six positions, and the scale of the trombone is thus extended down to C, the lowest note in bass trombone parts in the classical period. The F valve also provides further alternative positions to avoid awkward shifts: for example, the semitone from $B\flat$ to B, respectively 1st to 7th position, can be played by a movement from 1st to 2nd position (with the valve deployed for the B). B' is missing altogether as the instrument lacks the 7th position. Composers such as Bartók and Stravinsky, who have included this B' in important works, have obliged players to use an extended tuning-slide in the valve loop, putting the instrument into E, or alternatively to use a bass trombone with two valves. Many modern bass trombones have a second thumb-valve lowering the basic pitch by a 2nd or a 3rd, which gives further alternative positions as well as a complete compass down to E' or lower so that the instrument can also play contrabass trombone parts such as those in Richard Wagner's *Der Ring des Nibelungen*. If the second valve is placed in the loop of the first valve it is termed 'dependent'; if it is in the main tubing it is termed 'independent'.

During the second half of the 19th century it became common in German orchestras for the second and third players to use B♭/F trombones (if they did not use valve trombones) with a wider-bore instrument of the same pitch for the third part, while the first trombone player used the B♭ instrument. This practice has become common in modern times. For some repertory, the second or even the first player

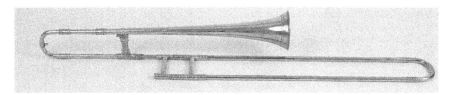

Renaissance tenor trombone. Anton Schnitzer, Nuremberg, 1594. (Edinburgh University Collection of Historic Musical Instruments (2695))

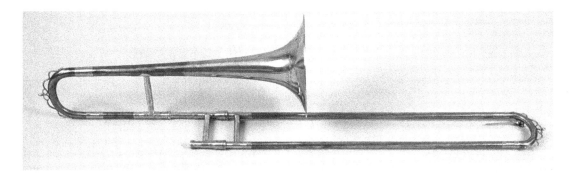

German tenor trombone in B♭. Schopper, Leipzig, c1910. (Edinburgh University Collection of Historic Musical Instruments (3207))

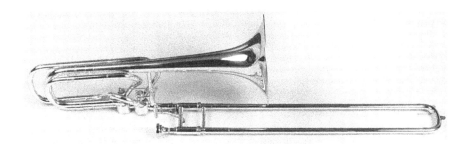

Modern bass trombone in B♭ with two independent valves. Michael Rath, Huddersfield, 1999. (Edinburgh University Collection of Historic Musical Instruments (5877))

in a section of three will prefer a B♭/F instrument, although where a valve is less useful many players prefer to use the B♭ trombone, which is lighter and usually freer-blowing.

Several new improvements have been introduced for the trombone thumb valve and the way the valve engages with the instrument. The resistance players sometimes felt when blowing through the depressed conventional rotary valve led at the end of the 20th century to the introduction of valve designs with gentler bends in the windways. Such valves are of necessity bulky, and some incorporate valve designs tried and abandoned in the 19th century, but they do provide a good response whether or not the valve is deployed.

5. Contrabass trombone. For a long time many opera houses possessed a true contrabass trombone in 18′ B♭″, provided with a double slide consisting of two parallel slides connected in series (by two U-bows at the base and one at the top), but moved as one. As each shift on such an instrument requires half the movement necessary with a normal slide, the shifts are the same as those of the ordinary B♭ trombone. Double slides were also fitted to some G and F bass trombones.

In 1881 Verdi asked the Pelitti company of Milan to produce the instrument that became known as the *trombone contrabasso Verdi*, a bell-front contrabass valve trombone in B♭″. He scored for this instrument in *Otello* (1887) and *Falstaff* (1893), where it is called *trombone basso*. It was the first trombone used for what has often been called the 'cimbasso' line; that term, however, should not be applied to any valve or slide trombone made before 1881. Cimbasso, when it means a trombone, denotes a four-valve contrabass in 18′ B♭″. An instrument of this kind is required for the lowest trombone parts in the late works of Verdi and the operas of Puccini. It is also used in larger Italian wind bands.

A contrabass in 12′ F′ or E♭′ with two valves has been used in Germany, particularly a model introduced by

Ernst Dehmel of Berlin in 1921 and used at the Bayreuth Festival of 1924; this was modified by Hans Kunitz in 1959 as the 'Cimbasso' model, in which one valve lowers the instrument to 16′ C′, the other to D′, and both together lower the pitch to 18′ B♭″.

II. Valve trombone.

Although Heinrich Stölzel, co-inventor of the valve, had considered its application to the trombone, the first known application of valves to the trombone was probably by the Berlin maker Joseph Casper Gabler (1818). Christian Friedrich Sattler's double piston valve was introduced 1821 and continued to be used until the second half of the 20th century as the *trombone Belge*. Other developments were produced during the 1820s in Vienna by other makers, and it was there that the earliest instruction manual for valve trombone appeared: that of Andreas Nemetz (after 1830), who illustrates his book with drawings of an instrument made by Johann Tobias Uhlmann.

Made in alto, tenor, and bass pitches, valve trombones reached a peak of popularity in the second half of the 19th century, and the extent of this popularity has been largely underestimated. They were ubiquitous in the military bands of many countries and the instrument of choice in several symphony and opera orchestras, including the Vienna court opera orchestra, which used valve trombones exclusively between about 1835 and 1883. The writing of trombone parts in many Italian and central European orchestral and operatic works displays the valve instrument idiom. Most valve trombones have kept the basic shape of the slide trombone, although in 'short' models the length is considerably reduced. From about 1840 instruments intended for mounted and marching bands were produced in various upright (tuba) and circular (helicon) designs. Among these was the *Armeeposaune* (Ger.: 'army trombone') invented by V.F. Červený of Hradek Králové in 1867; it had rotary valves and came in several sizes, from alto in F to contrabass in B♭.

Tenor and bass instruments are frequently fitted with a fourth valve that, as on other four-valved brass instruments, lowers the pitch by a 4th; but as the three primary valves remain tuned to the B♭ pitch, the fourth valve often introduces intonation difficulties. A valve arrangement that offers better intonation is Sax's system of six independent pistons, used for many years in Belgium. Each valve controls a loop giving a total tube length equal to a given shift on a slide; when operated, a valve diverts the windway through its own loop, cutting off all those below it. The main windway leads through all the valves to a terminal loop and back through the valves to the bell. The first valve corresponds to the 1st position, the sixth to the 6th position; without any valve operated the instrument gives the notes of the 7th position. No combinations of valves are required (unless an extra valve is fitted to serve as the fourth valve of a normal valved instrument).

Valve trombones were ubiquitous in the USA at the turn of the 20th century. Photographs of early American bands and orchestras frequently show them, and this includes images of New Orleans jazz bands; for example, in the famous photograph of the Buddy Bolden jazz band, Willie Cornish the trombonist is seen holding a short-model valve trombone. The ubiquity of the valve instrument is also documented in sources such as the oral history interviews conducted with some of the earliest jazz performers. It was the relatively late introduction of slide instruments into New Orleans (about 1910–12) that encouraged the tailgate style in which slide glissando is exhibited so prominently. In the 20th century the most celebrated examples of valve trombone playing have been those of jazz musicians such as Juan Tizol of the Duke Ellington Orchestra and Bob Brookmeyer.

III. Trombone mutes.

Trombone mutes were used from at least the early 18th century. The most commonly used model in modern times is the straight mute (often with a curved profile rather than a truncated cone)—this is the default mute for parts marked *con sordino* without further qualification. Most other mutes originate in the jazz world; these include the 'harmon' (or wah-wah) mute and the cup mute, which fit into the bell. Other mutes are loosely attached, handheld, or attached to a music stand; these include, respectively, the bucket, the plunger, and the 'derby' or hat mutes.

IV. History to 1900.

Most scholars believe that the immediate precursor of the trombone was the instrument referred to in modern times as the 'Renaissance slide trumpet'. This instrument had a single telescopic slide, which enabled the player to produce notes approximating to those of a harmonic series on each of three or four semitone-adjacent slide positions. No such instruments survive, but the case for their existence—based primarily on iconographic sources, but also on some documentary and musical evidence—seems compelling. Although no direct relationship between the slide trumpet and the trombone has been established, a progression from the former to the latter is probable since both instruments seem to have been prevalent in the same regions—Germany, the Low Countries, and Italy. It is likely that Germany, where there were established centres of brass instrument making by the mid-15th century, was the source of the design and manufacturing techniques of these instruments. From northern Europe the trombone spread to other regions. By the end of the 15th century German and Flemish players were prominent in several parts of Europe. The first named trombone players associated with the English court, for example, were Hans Broen and Hans Nagle, the latter having originated in Leipzig.

The earliest image of a trombone appears in Filippino Lippi's fresco *The Assumption of the Virgin* (1488–93) in the Basilica of Santa Maria sopra Minerva, Rome. From that time to the end of the 16th century—to the extent that sources allow such generalities to be drawn—most instruments were broadly similar. A drawing of a trombone in Virdung's *Musica getutscht* (1511) shows characteristics typical of other representations and of surviving specimens. The earliest surviving trombone, by Erasmus Schnitzer of Nuremberg, is dated 1551. While several early trombones are no longer in their original state, a comparison of the morphology of extant instruments presents a fairly consistent picture: the instruments have a narrow internal bore diameter (Nuremberg tenor sackbut bore diameters range from 9.2 mm to 10.4 mm); the tubing is cylindrical apart from the length between the final bend (in the bell section); and the bell end, which flares gently, expands to a significantly smaller final bell diameter than that of the modern trombone. H.G. Fischer (1984) compared the measurements of 22 such instruments and found that, though there was some inconsistency, the tube bore of most was about 10 mm in diameter, and the bell diameters were seldom more than 10.5 cm. Another feature common to such instruments is the thinness of the metal walls. The bore of early trombones closely matched that of contemporary trumpets. The inner tubes of the slides had a consistent external diameter: they did not have the 'stockings' mentioned earlier. There was no water key, neither were there tuning slides.

The drawings of trombones in Praetorius's *Theatrum instrumentorum* (1620) are the earliest that provide any reliable and accurate iconographical detail, and the information is broadly consistent with what can be observed in specimens of the period (though it is unlikely that any trombone dating from before the 18th century is completely intact). The instruments described by Praetorius had most of the principal features that were to characterize all trombones until the 19th century. Crooks and other devices for tuning and changing pitch were already in use at the start of the 17th century. A reference in the 1541 letters of the Nuremberg maker Georg Neuschel to an order that included two 'bogen' for the 'Quintposane' has been taken, probably correctly, to mean that crooks were already being used on trombones at this early date. Praetorius's drawings show *Krumbbügel auf ein ganz Ton* for the tenor instrument, and the bass instruments have a tuning slide on the bend of the bell section operated by a long rod extending forward. This would have been used to change the overall pitch of the instrument rather than for moving from one note to another. Other means of changing the overall pitch were a coiled crook fitted between the bell section and the slide section (Mersenne (1636–7) illustrates an instrument crooked down a 4th in this way), and straight extensions at the same point formed by one or more tapered 'bits'.

The earliest surviving instruments have loose-fitting stays held together by metal clasps, sometimes ornate and sometimes lined with leather, on both the bell and slide sections. From the second half of the 17th century, makers fitted tubular stays on the slide section, making the right hand grip of the slide more comfortable and flexible. The slide-stays on some instruments were in two parts, one fitted rigidly to each leg of the slide, joined telescopically in the middle; such a device would also have helped facilitate an easy slide action. Illustrations of 17th- and 18th-century trombone players show differences in the way that the instrument was held, but

an engraving by J.C. Weigel (*Musicalisches Theatrum*, c1722) shows the player holding the instrument in a similar way to the position used nowadays. The handle fitted to bass instruments to enable players to reach lower positions appears on many specimens. Two 17th-century English depictions of trombonists (a drawing of a waits band attributed to Marcellus Lauron the elder (*GB-Cmc*) and an anonymous painting of a trombonist on a 17th-century organ case) show the players holding such handles as they play. Given that it is unlikely that tenor instruments required such a device, it suggests that it was the bass instrument that lasted longest in England in the 17th century; this is also borne out by documentary sources.

Trombones were made in several sizes, but as has already been pointed out, the frequency with which the more extreme sizes were deployed is a matter of debate. Praetorius's description of the names and pitches of different sizes is open to interpretation, but he gives for the alto, tenor, bass, and contra/double bass trombones the following nominal pitches:

Table 2

Alto	(Alt oder Discant Posaun)	D or E
Tenor	(Gemeine rechte Posaun)	A
Bass	(Quart-Posaun or Quint-Posaun)	E and D
Double bass	(Octav-Posaun)	A (an octave lower than the tenor)

V. Performance technique before the 20th century.

The basic mechanics of the early trombone were broadly similar to those of the modern instrument, but the performance idiom was probably markedly different from that which began to develop in the late 18th century. Developments to its design and its idiom have been influenced by the contexts in which it has been employed and other pragmatic considerations such as the performance spaces in which it has been routinely used. The narrow bore, small bell, and high proportion of cylindrical tubing of early instruments facilitated a richer sound at low dynamics than is produced by the modern instrument. There have been several developments to modern instruments, but the most important trends have been towards larger bore sizes and an attempt by manufacturers to design instruments that produce a similar timbre irrespective of the part of the range or the dynamic in which they are played.

The earliest source to provide explicit, diagrammatic evidence about trombone slide positions is Aurelio Virgiliano's unpublished *Il dolcimelo* (c1600). Virgiliano's drawings are consistent with other sources up to the end of the 18th century in showing that trombone players recognized four slide positions rather than the seven used by modern players. The first of the four was likely to have been sounded not with the slide completely closed, but with it slightly extended, allowing the player to sharpen notes to bring them in tune. As there was no secondary tuning slide on early instruments, the main slide (perhaps assisted by some embouchure adjustment) was also used to adjust the overall pitch of the instrument. The recognition of only four slide positions is consistent with the view that early players thought in diatonic rather than chromatic terms: while the seven modern positions are a semitone apart, the four associated with the early trombone were diatonic, with the additional semitones treated as adjustments between them. We do not know exactly when this way of thinking changed so that players thought in more chromatic terms, but the earliest known source to illustrate this modern understanding of the trombone as having seven positions is Braun's *Gamme et méthode pour les trombonnes* (c1793–7).

The best modern reproductions of early instruments replicate not only the measurements of early specimens, but also their manufacturing processes. Such instruments provide an insight into the world of early players. They show that early trombones were versatile: not only could they be played in a number of different settings, but they were able to produce a variable timbre. When blown loudly, the sound is brassy and strident. The abundant references to trombones being combined with shawms and trumpets for declamatory fanfares and other loud outdoor music suggest that they were often heard in this mode. Mersenne commented that this type of trombone playing was 'deemed vicious and unsuitable for concerts' and he was probably correct. However, good historical reproductions also prove that early trombones were easy to play quietly; they could produce a restrained, clearly focused sound, capable of subtle articulations and inflections that would easily match articulations in the vocal lines that they often accompanied. This mode of expression was the most common in the 16th and 17th centuries. The sound is also well matched with that of the cornett: a partnership between these two instruments was established by the early part of the 16th century and continued until the closing decades of the 17th. The two instruments were superbly suited; they had wide and complementary pitch compasses, and broad dynamic and expressive ranges. They were natural accompanists for choral music, and players of them were employed in ecclesiastical foundations across Europe. While trombonists were employed with cornett players in court, church, and civic ensembles, single instruments were also used in broken consorts. Praetorius's observation that the English had a predilection for a single quiet trombone ('*eine stille Posaune*') in consort music is confirmed by other sources, and many pictorial representations show trombones in the company of various wind and string instruments. Praetorius and Mersenne recognized the trombone as one of the instruments on which it was appropriate to play diminutions and other decorations. Because many 16th- and 17th-century trombonists also played other instruments, it is likely that the majority were not only technically capable of playing such embellishments, but had a fine sense of what was tasteful and appropriate. Some were famous for their virtuosity:

Praetorius wrote of 'the famed Phileno of Munich', and the Italian Lorenzo da Lucca was said to have had 'in his playing a certain grace and lightness with a manner so pleasing' as to leave his listeners 'dumbstruck' (Haar, 1988, p.64).

Although trombones were used by European courts and ecclesiastical foundations from the middle of the 15th century, their migration to other musical centres was not simultaneous. The earliest recorded use of trombones in England does not occur until 1495, and regular wages were not allocated to trombonists until some time later. The first record of the use of a trombone by an English civic authority appears in 1526, when the Court of Aldermen of the City of London sanctioned the purchase of an instrument for their waits: the fact that the scribe needed three attempts to write the word 'sagbut' might indicate that the instrument was not a familiar sight outside court even at that time. In Spain, trumpets, shawms, and trombones (*trompetas, é chirimias, é sacabuches*) were employed to play at the baptism of Prince Juan, the son of Ferdinand and Isabella, in 1478, but it was not until well into the 16th century that trombonists were given regular employment at Seville Cathedral. However, from the opening decades of the 16th century until the closing years of the 17th, the trombone was one of the most prominent professional instruments in those European centres that had a flourishing music culture.

Few labelled trombone parts appear in 16th-century musical sources, but contextual evidence is so plentiful that it is easy to deduce the types of circumstance in which the instruments were used. Trombonists were regular members of *Stadtpfeifer*, *piffari*, waits and other town groups, and of church ensembles. However, regional differences did occur. For example, in England, where there were up to 12 trombonists in receipt of wages from the court in the 16th century (the arrival of the Bassano family swelled the numbers in the 1530s), there is no evidence of them being used for liturgical music before the second half of that century, and even though the ensemble of cornetts and sackbuts was ubiquitous in Europe, only two English sources—John Adson's *Courtly Masquing Ayres* (1621) and Matthew Locke's *Music 'ffor His Majesty's Sagbutts and Cornetts'* (1661)—specify this ensemble alone. However, other pieces such as Charles Coleman's *5 Partt things ffor the Cornetts* (1661) provide compelling evidence that this grouping might have been widely used in England. In the late 16th century and the 17th it became more common for a group of trombones to be used in ensembles to produce a heterogeneous block of sonority. Some of the *cori spezzati* effects that Andrea and Giovanni Gabrieli specified in Venice seem to exploit this feature, and similar sonorities dominate the trombone writing of Heinrich Schütz.

It is probably from this type of ensemble sonority rather than the sound of the single instrument that the symbolic association of trombones with mortality, the underworld and other dark features of the emotional spectrum derives; even though it is difficult to determine the exact point from which such meanings originate, it is certain that this symbolism was well understood by the start of the 17th century. Monteverdi's dramatic use of a large trombone ensemble in *Orfeo* might have followed an established convention, and similar passages are found, for example, in the music for the Florentine *intermedii* performed for the Medici wedding celebrations of 1589. This symbolism seems to have also been understood elsewhere: a stage direction for the first performance in London of Beaumont and Fletcher's *The Mad Lover* (1616) calls for 'A dead march within, of Drums and Sagbuts' and the same meaning has been conveyed in much later repertories.

Towards the end of the 17th century, the trombone began to fall out of use in many European centres. The evidence for this descent is unambiguous: records show a decline and then a halt in payments to players who had regularly received them. The same sources often also show that players who had long been associated with the trombone were transferred to other instruments. In England the decline was particularly complete: not a shred of evidence suggests that there was a single native-born trombone player in the country for the entire 18th century, and inventories of goods at Canterbury Cathedral in 1752 and 1761 refer to a chest in which were kept 'two brass Sackbuts not us'd for a grete number of years past'. Trombones were used for the first performances of Handel's *Israel in Egypt* and *Saul* in 1739, but they were played by visiting German performers. Their use a few years later at a benefit for the trumpeter Valentine Snow was deemed sufficiently unusual to be featured in advertisements. When they were reintroduced for the 1784 Handel Commemoration, a member of the audience annotated his programme with the observation that they looked something like 'bassoons with an end like a large speaking trumpet'.

There are several reasons why the popularity of the instrument declined. The most obvious is a change in taste which favoured more homogeneous sonorities, particularly after the fashion of the string band of the French court. Another is the decline in the practice of doubling vocal lines with cornetts and trombones, since this was a primary function of the instrument. In Austria, however, the practice of doubling vocal lines with trombones survived for much of the 18th century; indeed, as late as 1790 Albrechtsberger complained of 'trombones written in unison with alto, tenor or bass voice'. It was in Austria and Germany, especially in Vienna, that the trombone survived as a church and theatre instrument. It is no accident that it was here, in the hands of composers such as Gluck and Mozart, that the earliest developments of the modern idiom occurred.

In the mid-18th century the trombone was still used principally in church music (particularly for doubling the lower voices) and in small ensembles: it did not become a part of the orchestra until the late 18th century. The instrument also maintained its symbolic association with the underworld and the supernatural. The routine use of a trio of trombones appears to date from the beginning of the modern phase of trombone usage in the late 18th century, when it was increasingly used in opera and sacred music orchestras. When linked to the tradition of doubling choral parts, the trio could consist of alto, tenor, and bass instruments; in other cases, scores often specified alto, tenor, and bass trombones, and used those clefs, even if players used two tenors and a bass or three tenors. Gluck wrote for a trio of alto, tenor, and bass (in the oracle scene of *Alceste*, for example), as did Gossec, who also scored for a single trombone joined to a bass part. Mozart used trombones only in his operas and sacred works; his dramatic use of the instrument is particularly well exemplified in *Don Giovanni* and *Die Zauberflöte*.

The greater use of the trombone in the 19th century is the result of the burgeoning of military bands from about 1800 and brass bands somewhat later. Romantic composers considered the instrument capable of expressing a broad range of emotional situations; Berlioz said the instrument possessed 'both nobleness and grandeur' and had 'all the deep and powerful accents of high musical poetry, from the religious accent, calm and imposing ... to wild clamours of the orgy'.

Berlioz included an impressive solo in his *Symphonie funèbre et triomphale,* but this was not the first appearance of the trombone as a solo instrument. A small repertory for solo trombone survives from the 17th century, including a piece called 'La Hieronyma' (*Musicali melodiae,* 1621) by G.M. Cesare (himself a trombonist), and another by Francesco Rognoni Taeggio, who includes in his book of divisions, *Selva de varii passaggi* (1620), a piece with the rubric 'per il violone over trombone alla bastarda'. Somewhat paradoxically, as the instrument fell out of favour elsewhere, a more extensive tradition of solo writing developed in Austria in the 18th century. Apart from a repertory of solo pieces, solo obbligato passages were written in oratorios. While there were no precedents for the soloistic virtuosity that was to develop in the 20th century, several 19th-century players made reputations as soloists, including C.T. Queisser and F.A. Belcke in Germany, and A.G. Dieppo in France. Performers with closer links to art music were seldom prominent as soloists in the first half of the 20th century, but band soloists such as Arthur Pryor, who was a star soloist with the Sousa band (formed in 1892), won justified celebrity. From very late in the 19th century several American players made a good living in burlesque houses playing 'smear solos' (light, often comic pieces featuring abundant glissandos), and such pieces were incorporated into the programmes of the Sousa band.

VI. Later design developments.

From the early years of the 19th century, when the instrument became far more popular and more widely distributed, distinct models and styles developed. In Germany the bore increased from an average (for the tenor) of 11 mm about 1800, to 13 or even 14 mm by about 1840. The flare of the bell was increased in acuity and was continued to a termination of wide diameter. This enlargement of the trombone's bore and bell size (and increase in power) is usually credited to the

Leipzig maker C.F. Sattler, and its adoption in Wagner's orchestra during his period at Dresden. The tubular slide-stays, consisting of two sections, one end of each fixed to the limb of the slide and the other ends resting one inside the other in a loose fit to provide flexibility, have been continued on some German trombones until the present day. German trombones of the late 19th century and the early 20th often carried a traditional embellishment of a pair of snakes disporting themselves on the bell bow.

In France subtle changes were made to the bell flare to create an instrument capable of playing louder without greatly increasing the bore of the slide, which remained at about 11.4 mm. This model seems to have been developed by François Riedloker towards the end of the 18th century and later modified by Courtois and others. Braun described the bass as the principal member of the family, merely providing position charts for the tenor and the alto. While his alto is an instrument in E♭, the tenor is distinguished from the bass only by its use of the tenor clef and its avoidance of the lowest notes: both parts were taken by trombones in 9′ B♭′, presumably with a larger mouthpiece for the bass. The true bass and alto sizes were a rarity in France in the 19th century; the tenor was sometimes pitched in C.

The diversity of instrument designs and playing styles apparent in the earlier 20th century gradually gave way to an increasing uniformity in the second half. Wide-bored instruments in German countries, much narrower-bored instruments in England and elsewhere, and the resilient preference for the valve trombone in some countries were evidence of such diversity. This was matched by equally distinctive playing styles that are easily recognizable in recordings of the period. The forces for uniformity were similar to those that have been commonly used to explain the phenomenon of globalization: increasing awareness of performance styles and instruments through improved communications, greater access to international trade in musical instruments, and the increased international mobility of performers. The most important influence in the development of trombones and the way they are played has been the rise of the USA as a major centre for the design and production of trombones, with firms such as Vincent Bach and particularly C.G. Conn being of tremendous importance. The larger-bored instruments manufactured by such companies matched the new aesthetic of larger orchestras performing in larger concert halls. It was not long after the end of World War II that this influence became pervasive in Europe. In 1950 the trombone players in British orchestras played narrow-bore tenor instruments with a G trombone in the bass—usually manufactured by Boosey, Hawkes, or Besson. By about 1960 almost every professional British orchestral player used an American instrument, with the wide-bored Conn model 8H and its B♭/F equivalent the 88H being the most favoured. Even the relatively narrower-bored US instruments designed for use in jazz and light music were increasingly used by European players because their quality was superior.

VII. Jazz and advanced techniques.

Players from the USA also had an important influence on Europe in the 20th century, but the most important aspect of American culture that made a fundamental impact on the trombone was the advent of jazz. As well as initiating a new style of playing and new types of virtuosity, jazz players triggered a fundamental shift in much broader aspects of the idiom of the instrument. Playing techniques that might have had their origins in improvisation, instinct, and imitation exemplified new directions for the way the instrument might be played in the future.

Whereas early jazz bands typically had just one trombone player, the big band era (c1925–1950) saw the numbers in each band increase, usually to a section of three or four. The celebrity of the trombone sections of these bands—especially that of Duke Ellington—advanced the idea of a trombone sectional sound even as individual brilliance was being widely exhibited. It was not just the technical facility of jazz trombonists that made an impact, but also the various modes of expression they exploited. The ballad style of Tommy Dorsey had no real precedents in trombone lyricism, and the advent of bebop in the hands of players such as J.J. Johnson led to an entirely new species of virtuosity on the instrument. It was the jazz style that kept the medium and narrow and medium-bore species of the instrument buoyant as symphony and opera orchestras and even many military band players were taking up much wider-bored models.

Jazz trombonists have continuously explored the expressive potential of irregular articulations, glissandos, microtones, the use of a wide variety of mutes, and (particularly the German virtuoso Albert Mangelsdorff) multiphonics of up to four distinct pitches. All this revealed a greater range of expressive timbres than was usually employed even by modern symphonic composers. Vibrato—always a technical possibility—has become part of the trombone soloist's style; it can be made with the slide or by different blowing techniques. Slide technique has become more flexible, and the instrument's range has been extended at both ends, making the feasible range of the tenor trombone from $E′$, the lowest pedal note, to $g″$ or above.

In the second half of the 20th century many of the innovations of jazz players were harnessed and further developed by modernist composers to establish a new identity for the trombone as a solo instrument. Especially influential were works such as Luciano Berio's *Sequenza V* (1966), written for the American trombonist Stuart Dempster, as was the emergence of virtuoso soloists such as Vinko Globokar and Christian Lindberg.

BIBLIOGRAPHY

M. Praetorius: *Syntagma musicum*, vol.2 (Wolfenbüttel, 1618, 2/1619/R; Eng. trans., 1986, 2/1991); vol.3 (Wolfenbüttel, 1618, 2/1619/R)

M. Praetorius: *Theatrum instrumentorum* (Wolfenbüttel, 1620/R; Eng. trans., 1986, 2/1991)

M. Mersenne: *Harmonie universelle* (Paris, 1636–7/R; Eng. trans. of the books on instruments, 1957)

D. Speer: *Grund-richtiger ... Unterricht der musicalischen Kunst* (Ulm, 1687, enlarged 2/1697/*R*)

A. Braun: *Gamme et méthode pour les trombonnes alto, tenor et basse* (Paris, *c*1795)

H. Berlioz: *Grand traité d'instrumentation et d'orchestration modernes* (Paris, 1843, 2/1855/*R*; Eng. trans. and ed., H. Macdonald 2002)

F.W. Galpin: 'The Sackbut: its Evolution and History, Illustrated by an Instrument of the Sixteenth Century', *PMA*, vol.33 (1906–7), 1–25

A. Baines: 'Fifteenth–Century Instruments in Tinctoris's *De inventione et usu musicae*', *GSJ*, vol.3 (1950), 19–26

D. Wick: *Trombone Technique* (London, 1971, 2/1984)

R.L. Pratt and J.M. Bowsher: 'The Subjective Assessment of Trombone Quality', *Journal of Sound and Vibration*, vol.57/3 (1978), 425–35

S. Dempster: *The Modern Trombone* (Berkeley, 1979)

R.L. Pratt and J.M. Bowsher: 'The Objective Assessment of Trombone Quality', *Journal of Sound and Vibration*, vol.65/4 (1979), 521–47

H. Heyde: *Trompeten, Posaunen, Tuben*, Katalog: Musikinstrumenten-Museum der Karl-Marx-Universität Leipzig, vol.3 (Leipzig, 1980)

H.G. Fischer: *The Renaissance Sackbut and its Use Today* (New York, 1984)

T. Herbert: *The Trombone in Britain before 1800* (diss., Open U., 1984)

J. Haar: 'Cosimo Bartoli on Music', *EMH*, vol.8 (1988), 37–79

K. Polk: 'The Trombone, the Slide Trumpet and the Ensemble Tradition of the Early Renaissance', *EMc*, vol.17/3 (1989), 389–97

T. Herbert: 'The Sackbut in England in the 17th and 18th Centuries', *EMc*, vol.18 (1990), 609–16

K. Polk: *German Instrumental Music of the Late Middle Ages: Players, Patrons and Performance Practice* (Cambridge, 1992)

T. Herbert: 'The Sackbut and Pre–Reformation English Church Music', *HBSJ*, vol.5 (1993), 146–58

H. Weiner: 'André Braun's *Gamme et méthode pour les trombonnes*: the Earliest Modern Trombone Method Rediscovered', *HBSJ*, vol.5 (1993), 288–308

K. Dietrich: *Duke's Bone: Ellington's Great Trombonists* (Rottenburg am Neckar, 1995)

H. Weiner: 'Andreas Nemetz's *Neueste Posaun-schule*: an Early Viennese Trombone Method', *HBSJ*, vol.7 (1995), 12–35

A. Hirschberg and others: 'Shock Waves in Trombones', *JASA*, vol.99/3 (1996), 1754–8

H. Myers: 'Praetorius' Pitch', *Perspectives in Brass Scholarship: Amherst MA, 1995*, ed. S. Carter (Stuyvesant, NY, 1997)

K. Dietrich: *Jazz Bones* (Rottenburg am Neckar, 2005)

H.W. Myers: 'Evidence of the Emerging Trombone in the Late Fifteenth Century: What Iconography May Be Trying to Tell Us', *HBSJ*, vol.17 (2005), 7–35

H. Weiner: 'When is an Alto Trombone an Alto Trombone? When is a Bass Trombone a Bass Trombone?—The Makeup of the Trombone Section in Eighteenth– and Early Nineteenth–Century Orchestras', *HBSJ*, vol.17 (2005), 37–79

T. Herbert: *The Trombone* (London and New Haven, 2006)

T. Herbert: 'Trombone glissando a case study in continuity and change in brass instrument performance idioms', *HBSJ*, vol.22 (2010)

S. Carter: *The Trombone in the Renaissance* (Hillsdale, NY, 2012)

ANTHONY C. BAINES/TREVOR HERBERT AND ARNOLD MYERS

Tromlitz, Johann George (*b* Reinsdorf, nr Artern, Germany, 8 Nov 1725; *d* Leipzig, Germany, 4 Feb 1805). German flutist, teacher, and flute maker. In 1750 he received the degree of Imperial Public Notary at Leipzig University. About this time he began to make flutes. In 1754 he became principal flutist of the Grosses Conzert, a forerunner of the Gewandhaus orchestra. His career, interrupted by the disbanding of the orchestra during the Seven Years War, included solo tours as far afield as St Petersburg. J.F. Reichardt's accounts of his own travels (published 1774–6) took note of Tromlitz and only three other Leipzig virtuosos. Tromlitz left the orchestra in 1776 and devoted himself to teaching, writing, composition, and flute making. He recorded his ideas and teaching methods in several texts which shed much light on late 18th-century flute playing and performing practice. His *Kurze Abhandlung vom Flötenspielen* (1786) announced his rejection of merely average standards of performing and instrument making; this was to become a constant theme of his. He introduced the elements at the core of his ideal: clarity of articulation and expression; perfect intonation in a system having both large (5-comma) and small (4-comma) semitones, for which the E♭ and D♯ keys invented by J.J. Quantz in 1726 were essential; the appropriate choice of music for the hall and audience; and the total technical control and emotional involvement of the performer.

These themes were developed in the 1791 *Ausführlicher und gründlicher Unterricht die Flöte zu spielen*. This monumental work, the most comprehensive of the 18th-century flute tutors, was designed to give complete instruction without the aid of a teacher. It covered in detail all aspects of flute playing: intonation, articulation, flute maintenance, posture and breathing, dynamics, ornaments, musical style, cadenzas, and the flute's construction. The two chapters on articulation, for single and double tonguing, were at the time the most thorough written treatment of the subject for any instrument. Each subject was reduced to a set of well-thought-out rules and richly illustrated with examples. Though Tromlitz advocated a methodical approach to playing, his view was that once correctness had become second nature the performer's personal taste should be given free rein, especially in articulation and ornamentation.

In 1800 *Über die Flöten mit mehrern Klappen* was published as a supplement to the 1791 tutor. It gave a detailed and methodical explanation of the use of the keys on a flute of Tromlitz's own design, which had taken as its point of departure the three keys (B♭, G♯, and F) added to the instrument by London makers as early as the 1750s. Tromlitz first announced flutes with added keys in 1781. Between 1783 and 1785 he developed the essential points of his new design, a *c″* thumb key and a duplicate key for F, the latter invented in 1783 by the father of the virtuoso F.L. Dülan. Tromlitz's flute of 1785 employed these two keys as well as the B♭, G♯, and short F keys. By 1796 the system had been completed by applying a second lever, for the right index finger, to the B♭ key controlled by the left thumb. Tromlitz's original contributions were the 'long' B♭, and the *c″/b♭′* arrangement for the left thumb, which was to be adopted by Theobald Boehm in 1832 in preference to several other possibilities developed in the meantime including a *c″* key for the right index finger. A *c′* foot joint was available, but Tromlitz discouraged its use because of its detrimental effect on the flute's tone. The instrument was voiced and tuned using specialized and innovative tooling to maximize its focussed, even tone. The eight-keyed Tromlitz flute, like the two-keyed one, was intended to play scrupulously in tune in all 24 keys with a full set of major and minor semitones, even when accompanied by an equal-tempered keyboard. A critique of the Tromlitz flute, reflecting the belief that equal temperament was the better tuning system for melody instruments, was published anonymously by

H.W.T. Pottgiesser in 1803. Towards the end of his life Tromlitz began the invention of a chromatic flute with only one key, probably still with a conical bore, a design in which he no longer insisted on separate enharmonic fingerings. He discontinued this experiment because he felt he would not live to see it to fruition, or to see players accept its unfamiliar fingering patterns. More important than any mechanical detail Tromlitz invented was his philosophy that the way to improving the flute lay in completely rethinking its design along unified lines, not in the incremental refinement of existing models.

Contemporary accounts of Tromlitz's playing are uniformly positive, stressing his perfect intonation, brilliance and precision, and strong, trumpet-like tone. He was reputed to have been one of the first in Germany to practise a bravura style of concerto playing and to espouse the strong and cutting tone best suited to this style. Tromlitz's compositions (listed in F. Vester: *Flute Music of the 18th Century* (Monteux, 1985), 495) are not considered of much importance today, except for the light they shed on his musical taste. His obituary states that he had pupils from all regions. Despite his influence as a performer and teacher and his achievements as a flute maker, Tromlitz's effect on his world was overshadowed by that of major commercial instrument makers of the time. Though some players prized his flutes, and such makers as F.G.A. Kirst (Potsdam) and J.H.W. Grenser (Dresden) imitated aspects of his work, his contributions were not widely understood until after his death, when they were an important catalyst for many of the elaborate key systems of the early 19th century, including those of Boehm.

WRITINGS
(*selective list*)
Kurze Abhandlung vom Flötenspielen (Leipzig, 1786)
Ausführlicher und gründlicher Unterricht die Flöte zu spielen (Leipzig, 1791/*R*; Eng. trans., ed. A. Powell, 1991, as *The Virtuoso Flute-Player*)
An das musikalische Publikum (Leipzig, 1796/*R*)
Über die Flöten mit mehrern Klappen (Leipzig, 1800/*R*; Eng. trans., ed. A. Powell, 1996, as *The Keyed Flute by Johann George Tromlitz*)
Fingerordnung für meine Flöten zu 3, 5 und 7 Mittelstück und 1, 2, 3, 4, 5 und 6 Klappen, nebst dem Gebrauch des Register und abgetheilte Propfschraube (Leipzig, n.d.)

BIBLIOGRAPHY
F. Demmler: *Johann George Tromlitz* (Berlin, 1961/*R*)
E. Hadidian: *Johann Georg Tromlitz's Flute Treatise: Evidences of Late Eighteenth Century Performance Practice* (diss., Stanford U., 1979)
L.B. Hartig: *Johann George Tromlitz's 'Unterricht die Flöte zu spielen'* (diss., Michigan State U., 1981)
M. Castellani: '"Über den schönen Ton auf der Flöte": Il bel suono del flauto traverso secondo Johann George Tromlitz', *Recercare*, vol.2 (1990), 95–119
J. Bowers: 'Tromlitz on Playing the Flute: a Résumé', *Performance Practice Review*, vol.7/1 (1994), 65–77
A. Powell: 'Mozart und die Tromlitz–Flöte', *Tibia*, vol.26/3 (2001), 549–56

ARDAL POWELL

Trompe (Fr.). French term for a trumpet or horn, recorded from the 12th century. The Spanish equivalent is

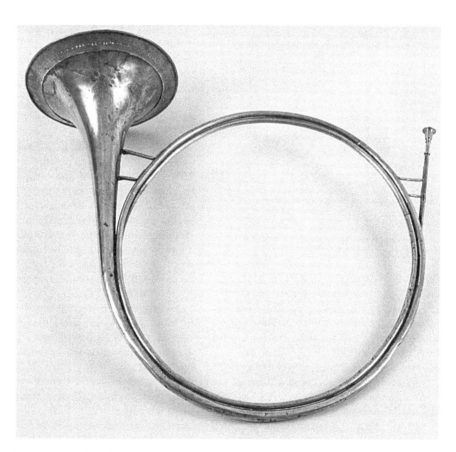

Trompe. Trompe Dauphine [hunting horn] in 14′ D, Le Brun, Paris, 1721. (Edinburgh University Collection of Historic Musical Instruments (2161))

trompa. At first the trompe was a long straight trumpet used as a signal and ceremonial instrument. In 1606 Nicot described it as made of brass. By the late 17th century the term was being used for an instrument with a single coil. It was sometimes used to denote a hunting horn (*trompe de chasse*), to distinguish it from the orchestral horn (*cor*).

The term was also used (as were *trompe de Béarn* and *trompa*) for the jew's harp.

Trompeta. Spanish term for trumpet. More particularly, it denotes a valveless brass signal trumpet, consisting of mouthpiece, tube, and bell. Like the *corneta*, it was traditionally used to attract attention, particularly by *pregoneros* (town criers). The straight form is the *añafil*, and the highest-pitched trompeta is the *clarín*. In Cuba, the *trompeta china* (also called *corneta china*) is the Chinese *suona*, used mainly in carnival music.

JOHN M. SCHECHTER/R

Trompetica china [cornet china]. Type of oboe, introduced to Cuba by Chinese immigrants. According to Ortiz its different sizes are termed *dettoi*, *sona* (from the Chinese *suona*), or *taide*. It produces five different pitches with a penetrating timbre. The player uses circular breathing. The instrument was used in Chinese theatrical performances and in 1910 was supposedly brought by Cuban soldiers to Santiago de Cuba, where it joined *conga* ensembles; since about the 1920s it has been used in certain Havana carnival retinues. See F. Ortiz: *Los instrumentos de la música afrocubana* (Havana, 1952–5), vol.5, 338–9.

JOHN M. SCHECHTER/R

Trompette des ménèstrels (Fr.: 'trumpet of the minstrels'). Term employed in areas under Franco-Burgundian influence during the 15th century for the brass instrument (probably a slide trumpet) and player associated with the alta ensemble of two or three shawms and trumpet or sackbut, by contrast with the *trompette de guerre*, or natural trumpet.

PETER DOWNEY

Trompong. Balinese gong chime. It consists of several horizontally mounted tuned bronze gongs, from 12 to 30 cm in diameter, used to perform a semi-improvised version of the melody (*lagu*) in several forms of Balinese gamelan, principally the *gamelan gong gede* (where ten gongs are used), *gamelan semar pegulingan*, *gamelan gong kebyar* (ten gongs), and *gamelan semara dana*. Usually the trompong is played by a single musician holding two padded wooden mallets (*panggul*). The *gamelan gong gede* may include two *trompong*: the larger *trompong pangarep* (*gede*) and the smaller *trompong barangan* tuned an octave higher. In the ancient and rare seven-tone *gamelan luang* (*saron*) the trompong is also called *bonang* and is arranged as a double row of gongs played by two musicians facing each other. In the *gamelan gong kebyar* the *trompong* is typically reserved for arrangements of the *gong gede* and *semar pegulingan* repertory, although

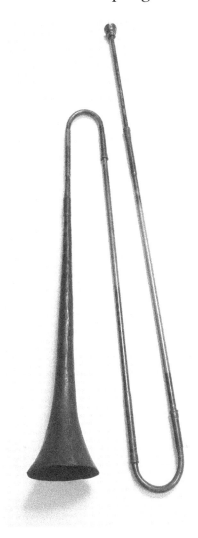

Trompette des ménèstrels. A reconstruction of the medieval form, by Peter Holmes, London. The mouthpiece shank extends all the way down the mouthyard. (Jeremy Montagu Collection, Oxford)

there are works specific to this ensemble, such as *Kebyar Trompong* and *Palawakia,* in which dancers play the instrument. In some villages in the east of Bali the *trompong* is called *seketi*. See C. McPhee: *Music in Bali: a Study in Form and Instrumental Organization in Balinese Orchestral Music* (New Haven and London, 1966/R1976).

ANDREW C. MCGRAW

Trompong beruk [trompong misi bruk]. Rare xylophone of Bali. It has bars of wood or bamboo suspended over individual resonators made of coconut shell (*beruk*). The instrument typically has eight bars tuned to either the *slendro* or *pelog* tuning system, although *slendro* appears to be the more common. It is played by a single player with two unpadded wooden mallets in the manner of the more common bronze *trompong* gong chime found in the *gamelan gong gede* and *gamelan semar pegulingan* ensembles. The trompong beruk is most often played privately by farmers guarding their fields, although it is occasionally combined with instruments of the *angklung* ensemble. It is found only in a few villages, principally Abang, of the eastern province of Karangasem. See C. McPhee: *Music in Bali: a Study in Form and Instrumental Organization in Balinese Orchestral Music* (New Haven and London, 1966/*R*1976).

ANDREW C. MCGRAW

Tronci. Italian family of organ builders and, latterly, cymbal makers. Antonio [Anton Maria] Tronci (*b* 19 June 1704; *d* 16 April 1791) and his brother Filippo (i) (*b* 18 March 1717; *d* 22 March 1788) opened an organ workshop in Pistoia about 1750, having worked as apprentices and then associates of Giovan Francesco detto Domenico Cacioli in Lucca. The organ of S Maria delle Grazie, Pistoia (1755), is one of their masterpieces. They were succeeded by Antonio's sons, Luigi (i) (*b* ?1755; *d* 23 Oct 1803) and Benedetto (*b* 24 Dec 1756; *d* 4 March 1821), whose most important work is the spectacular organ at S Pietro Maggiore, Pistoia (*c*1815). A small organ of theirs, built in 1793, originally in the Villa Rucellai, Campi Bisenzio near Florence, and which had been preserved completely intact, was restored and placed in Pistoia Cathedral (1997). It has a single manual of 47 keys (*C–c'''*; short bass octave) and eight pull-down pedals plus two accessory pedals (*Timpano* and *Usignoli*: 'Nightingale'). Benedetto's nephew, Filippo Tronci (ii) (*b* 12 July 1795; *d* 25 April 1847), inherited the firm, building organs at Montepulciano Cathedral (1840) and S Bartolomeo in Pantano, Pistoia (1844), both with brilliant Cornetto IV stops in the treble and Cornettone II in the bass. Filippo's two sons, Luigi (ii) (*b* 23 Aug 1823; *d* 3 Jan 1911) and Cesare (*b* 6 June 1827; *d* 10 Dec 1874), took over after his death. Many good organs built by them are preserved in their original state. Another Filippo (iii) (*b* 27 Feb 1849; *d* 7 July 1918) was the last organ builder of the family. By 1877 the Tronci firm had built 359 instruments.

In 1883 the Agati and Tronci workshops merged, and Filippo (ii) became the sole proprietor of Agati–Tronci. Three of his most important organs are in Lucca province: at Capezzano Pianore (1895), Corsánico (near Viaréggio; 1899), and Capánnori (1904); and he exported organs to Corsica, Buenos Aires (Teatro Colón), and Jerusalem (Church of the Holy Sepulchre).

The typical Tronci organ is very rich in colourful 'da concerto' stops (flutes, cornettos, and reeds), together with the traditional Italian Ripieno. This is due to the influence of both the monumental five-manual organ at S Stefano dei Cavalieri, Pisa, built in 1737 by Azzolino Bernardino Della Ciaia with the assistance, among others, of the young Antonio and Filippo Tronci. Also influential was the organ in Spirito Santo, Pistoia (1664), by Willem Hermans.

During the later 19th century, the Tronci family turned to producing tubular bells and bronze gongs for orchestral and theatre use; Mascagni, Puccini, and Verdi were reportedly among their patrons. In 1931 the family firm joined with other percussion instrument manufacturers to found the Unione Fabbricanti Italiani Piatti (UFIP; Union of Italian Cymbal Makers). In 2010 a member of the Tronci family was the director of UFIP, whose cymbals are used by many jazz and rock percussionists. The Luigi Tronci Foundation preserves and displays instruments and documents illustrating the music history of Pistoia.

BIBLIOGRAPHY
F. Baggiani: 'Le origini della scuola organaria pistoiese', *Bollettino storico pistoiese*, vol.95 (1993), 53–74
G. Biagetti: 'L'organo Tronci di Capannori', *Informazione organistica*, vol.5/3 (1993), 20–8
R. Berutto: 'Un capolavoro Agati–Tronci: l'"organaccio buono" di Capezzano Pianore', *Informazione organistica*, vol.6/3 (1994), 23–5; vol.7/1 (1995), 25–8
U. Pineschi: 'In S Pier Maggiore il più grande organo a tre manuali e due pedaliere', *Informazione organistica*, vol.6/1–2 (1994), 50–5

UMBERTO PINESCHI/R

Tröndlin, Johann Nepomuk (*b* Freiburg im Breisgau, Germany, 31 May 1790; *d* Leipzig, Germany, 7 April 1862). German piano maker. He reportedly studied piano making in southern Germany but fled to Vienna to escape military conscription; in Vienna he worked as a cabinetmaker and as an apprentice to one or more piano makers, likely including Matthäus Andreas Stein, whose work Tröndlin's resembles. From 1821 to 1824 he headed the instrument manufacturing division of Breitkopf & Härtel in Leipzig, being responsible for piano tuning and quality control. In April 1824 he established his own successful firm, producing Viennese-type pianos with ranges from six to six and one-half octaves; the business, which seems to have produced about 40 to 60 instruments annually, was sold in 1855 and closed about 1864. Clara Schumann and Felix Mendelssohn played Tröndlin's pianos, and until 1860 they were used in Leipzig's Gewandhaus. A restored Biedermeier-style grand of about 1830 is in the Frederick Historic Piano Collection, Ashburnham, Massachusetts, and a slightly later one is owned by the pianist Jos van Immerseel. More than ten others are in museum and private collections; one in the Museum of Musical Instruments at the University of Leipzig was pictured on the reverse of the 100 DM note before the introduction of the euro.

Trống. Generic Vietnamese term for 'drum'. The *trống bà bóng*, *trống bát cấu*, *trống bát nhã*, *trống cái*, *trống chiến*, *trống cơm*, *trống nhạc*, and *trống quân* are all barrel drums. The *trống bà bóng* is a double-headed barrel drum of southern Vietnam, 25 cm in diameter and 8 cm deep, which is beaten with a stick. The *trống bát cấu* has a single head made of buffalo hide and is set in a tripod. It is struck with two sticks, and is used in the *hát bội* (traditional theatre) and for processional music. The Chinese *bangu* is a related instrument. The double-headed *trống bát nhã* is beaten with two sticks to accompany Buddhist chanting. The *trống cái*, a double-headed drum played in pairs, is used in the *đại nhạc* court orchestra and the *nhạc ngũ âm* ('five sound') ensemble. Also known as *trống tràn* ('battle drum'), the *trống chiến* is used in traditional theatre. It is double-headed and beaten with two sticks.

The *trống cơm* is a horizontal double-headed barrel drum. The body, carved out of a single piece of jackwood, is elongated, bulging sharply in the middle. The drum, called 'rice drum' in Vietnam, has laced heads and the body is covered with thongs. The right head is larger than the left and is covered with three layers of hide, each of a different type; the left head is covered with two layers. Tuning paste is used on both ends. The drum is played with the hands and fingers and forms part of the *nhạc ngũ âm* ensemble of southern Vietnam. It is also used in the court orchestra (*đại nhạc*). The *trống nhạc* is a pair of shallow double-headed barrel drums. One has a tighter skin than the other and is known as the 'female' or 'military drum' (*trống cái, trống võ*). The other is known as the 'male' or 'civilian drum' (*trống đực, trống văn*). The drums are used in the *đại nhạc* court orchestra or in the *nhạc ngũ âm* ensemble in southern Vietnam. Another pair of double-headed barrel drums, used in the *đại nhạc* ensemble, is the *trống quân*.

Other Vietnamese drums are the *trống bộc, trống chầu, trống dê, trống giăng, trống lệnh*, and *trống mãnh*. The *trống bộc* is a single-headed open drum struck with one or two sticks. The *trống giăng*, also single-headed, is played in the *phường bát âm* ensemble. The *trống mãnh*, a small single-headed drum (*mãnh*: 'thin'), is 21 cm in diameter and 5.5 cm deep, and is struck with one or two sticks.

The *trống chầu* is a small double-headed cylindrical drum. The height of the wooden body and the diameter of the head are identical (14 cm). The drum is beaten with a wooden stick 30 cm long, using set rhythmic formulae, to praise professional singers of the *hát à đào* style of northern Vietnam. The *trống dê*, a small double-headed cylindrical drum beaten with two sticks, is used in *hát chèo*, folk music theatre. Another small double-headed cylindrical drum, the *trống lệnh*, is 21 cm in diameter and 12 cm deep, and has a handle. The drum is beaten with a wooden stick in processional music.

Trống also denotes other instruments that are struck, including the ground zither *trống quân* which provides the rhythmic accompaniment in folksong (and gave its name to the folksong type *trống quân*, 'alternate song', well known in North Vietnam), and the *trống đồng*, the bronze drum. This, known from the Dong Son culture, is believed to have first been used during the Hung Kingdom (2897–258 bce), both as a musical instrument and as a cult object. More than 200 *trống đồng* have been found in the Red River Delta. Although obsolete among the Viet people, it is still played by some of the highlanders of northern Vietnam, where it is also known as *lo*.

TRÂN QUANG HAI/NGUYEN THUYET PHONG

Trống quân. Ground zither of northern Vietnam, used to provide the rhythmic accompaniment in folksong. It is also used as a name for the folksong type *trống quân* (alternate song) well known in North Vietnam.

Trost, Tobias Heinrich Gottfried (*b* c1679–81; *d* Altenburg, Germany, bur. 15 Aug 1759). German organ builder. He was a pupil of his father, the organ builder Johann Tobias Gottfried Trost (1651–1721), himself a pupil of Christian Förner. In 1704 T.H.G. Trost married in Tonna (Gräfentonna), where he then had his workshop. In 1705 he completed his first independent instrument. In 1718 he moved to Mockern, and in 1722 to Altenburg, where in 1723 after protracted rivalry with the elder J.J. Donati he was awarded the exclusive position of organ builder to the Duchy of Saxe-Gotha-Altenburg, on the strength of a testimonial from Gottfried Silbermann. He held this post until his death. Due to his court position he was able to undertake only two major projects, the organs in Waltershausen (1724–30; completed about 1755 probably by Johann Heinrich Ruppert and restored to its 1730 state by Orgelbau Waltershausen, 1994–98) and Altenburg (1735–9). The Altenburg instrument was appraised by Silbermann, J.S. Bach, and J.A. Scheibe (1739) and found excellent. It was this instrument that J.L. Krebs used as court organist from 1756 to 1780.

Trost was the most important Thuringian organ builder of the 18th century. His instruments show an unusual modernity in conception, aimed at *Empfindsamkeit* and the *galant* styles in organ music. Typical markers of this include copious foundation and string stops, mixtures with Tierce ranks, and few mutations. J.F. Agricola, who in his youth witnessed the building of Trost's Altenburg organ, drew attention to the characteristic use of 8′ flue stops. In the form and dimension of his pipes Trost went to extremes: for instance, the 8′ Viola di Gamba is very narrow-scaled in order to imitate the original string tone. He also favoured special construction methods in some ranks, employing unusual materials, as in the double Flaute douce, the Unda maris, and the Fugara 4′. The flute stops range up to 2′ pitch and are prominent in the disposition of the instruments. The larger organs tend to have Pedal stops borrowed and extended from the *Hauptwerk*. To facilitate this, Trost developed a wind coupler (*Hauptwerk* to Pedal), which is operated by non-return valves and a wind overflow. Both the exterior and interior construction of Trost's instruments reflect the aesthetic ideals of the Enlightenment, with sumptuously fashioned consoles and embellished technical workings. Of his 30 or so instruments, only five remain to some extent complete. Because he used expensive materials, Trost never became wealthy as did Silbermann. His contemporaries admired his work, though he was often criticized for his treatment of schedules and deadlines. Among his pupils were Adam Gottlob Casparini, Johann Jacob Graichen, Johann Nikolaus Ritter, and Johann Christian Immanuel Schweinefleisch.

BIBLIOGRAPHY

F. Friedrich: *Der Orgelbauer Heinrich Gottfried Trost: Leben—Werk—Leistung* (Leipzig, 1989)

F. Friedrich: *Die Orgelbauer Johann Tobias Gottfried Trost und Tobias Gottfried Heinrich Trost: Bibliographie zu Leben und Werk* (Kleinblittersdorf, 1993)

G. Stauffer and E.May: *J.S. Bach as Organist: his Instruments, Music, and Performance Practices* (Bloomington, IN, 1998/R2000)

FELIX FRIEDRICH/R

Trough zither. Chordophone in which the strings are stretched across a wooden trough which serves as

Trough zither, enanga, probably Kabale, Kigezi District, Uganda, c1970. (Edinburgh University Collection of Historic Musical Instruments (2763))

resonator; there can be an additional gourd resonator. Its distribution is confined mainly to East and Central Africa, especially Rwanda, Burundi and bordering areas of Tanzania, and the Democratic Republic of the Congo.

Trstenke [trstenice, orglice, piščalke, glasilke]. Panpipe of Slovenia. It is made of 5 to 21 or more canes (*trstike*) of graduated length, staggered symmetrically in a flat row with the longest in the centre. Exceptional examples spanning two octaves measure about 50 cm wide. Pictorial evidence for the type appears on a 5th-century bce situla from Vače. A pastoral instrument capable of surprising melodic suppleness, the trstenke is played alone or with the transverse flute *žvegla*, or in ensembles. Traditionally, the canes (*Phragmites communis*) are gathered in marshy areas from January to April, dried for a year, then cut to length, cleaned, plugged with pine resin, tuned, and assembled. Franc Laporšek (*d* 1998), a noted maker and player, transmitted the craft from his father to his successors, including the ethnomusicologist Drago Kunej, who has helped to popularize the trstenke again. The instrument is most common in eastern Slovene territory (Štajerska region). See Z. Kumer: *Ljudska glasbila in godci na Slovenskem* [Folk Music and Musicians in Slovenia] (Ljubljana, 1983).

DARJA KOTER

Tru [tlu, trou] Side-blown ivory horn of the Dan people of the Ivory Coast. Five or six of different sizes are played in hocket style with goblet drums in an ensemble whose musical motifs are associated with verbal texts, proverbs, or names. The ensemble once belonged exclusively to chieftains and played court music in their honour. It was also played to encourage warriors going into battle or to greet them on their victorious return. Some tru are made from antelope horns and are played to rally workers for agricultural work or to produce a sacred mask voice. See H. Zemp: *Musique Dan: La musique dans la pensée et la vie sociale d'une société africaine* (Paris, 1971).

KONIN AKA

Truba [berestyanka, duda]. Trumpet of Belarus and Finland. The bore is cylindrical, sometimes widening

slightly at the end, while the external shape is conical and curving slightly to one side. It is used with or without a mouthpiece. It can be made of various kinds of wood, tree roots, or from tin-plate. The *truba* in Belarus was mentioned in manuscripts of the 12th century (e.g. the *Tale of Igor's Campaign*). Over many centuries it was used in calendar rituals and in pastoral, hunting, and military contexts. In the 20th and 21st centuries it was widespread throughout Belarus and used by shepherds for signalling. The *truba* with a valve mechanism is used in several folk ensembles (with the *bayan* and *buben*).

The Finnish and Ingrian truba is hollowed from wood and covered with strips of birch or other tree bark. It has five fingerholes and a thumbhole. It can have a cowhorn bell. The truba was a typical shepherd's instrument but was also used to accompany dance.

INNA D. NAZINA, ILKKA KOLEHMAINEN

Trubka ('tube'). Czech and Slovak term for a trumpet or bugle. It also denotes a simple oboe of Slovakia, made of bark or corn stalks and played by children.

Truchado, Raymundo (*fl* c1600–70). Spanish Dominican friar and instrument maker, from Ciempozuelos, near Madrid. He was possibly related to the organ builder Mateo de Avila (*b* Ciempozuelos, 1581), whose first wife was named Paula Truchado, and to the later organ builder José Manuel Truchado (*fl* 1736–51). Known as a learned and able musician, Raymundo Truchado designed and built the *lyra celi* (or *lyra coeli*), the only extant historical instrument of the Geigenwerk type and the earliest known Spanish stringed keyboard instrument from before about 1710. It was evidently modelled after Hans Haiden's *Geigenwerke* and was reportedly used at least as late as 1784 in the Cathedral of Toledo during Holy Week when organ playing was proscribed. The much-altered instrument (in *B.B.mim* since 1902) bears the authentic inscription 'FRAY RAYMVNDO TRVCHADO: INVENTOR: 1625'. Its remarkably short legs might not be original, nor are its lid painting and numerous parts (including the soundboard, parts of the case, and elements of the action), but its basic form and mechanism seem to have been preserved. Its four rosined friction wheels are turned by a hand crank.

BIBLIOGRAPHY
M. Awouters: 'An Early Keyboard by Raymundo Truchado: an Authentic Inscription, a Doubtful Instrument?', *Cincos Siglos de Música de Tecla Española/Five Centuries of Spanish Keyboard Music*, ed. L. Morales (Garrucha, Almeria, 2007), 219–30
C. Bordas Ibáñez: 'La Collection Barbieri de Madrid', *Musique-Images-Instruments*, vol.9 (2007), 28–51

Trúc sinh. Xylophone of Vietnam.

Trumpet (Fr. *trompette*; Ger. *Trompete*; It. *tromba*). Lip-vibrated aerophone (labrosome). The term is used not only for the modern Western instrument and its ancestors, but also generically to denote some or all of the lip-vibrated wind instruments, depending on the system of classification. In this article a distinction between trumpets and horns is not maintained.

1. Terminology and systems of classification. 2. Geographic distribution and construction. 3. Use and function. 4. The Western trumpet. (i) Sizes and types. (ii) History to 1500. (iii) 1500–1820. (iv) Since 1820.

1. Terminology and systems of classification. In the Hornbostel-Sachs classification system (1914), the term 'trumpet' is applied to any instrument in which 'the airstream passes through the player's vibrating lips, so gaining intermittent access to the air column which is to be made to vibrate'. This category is then divided into two subgroups; natural trumpets ('without extra devices to alter pitch') and chromatic trumpets ('with extra devices to modify the pitch'). Further subdivisions are made on the basis of body shape (conch shell or tubular) and method of playing (side-blown or end-blown) in the case of natural trumpets, and of pitch-alteration method (fingerholes, slides, or valves) and shape of tubing (conical or cylindrical) in the case of chromatic trumpets.

Despite its apparent inclusivity, this system has serious shortcomings when dealing with non-Western trumpets. Although non-Western trumpets are found with fingerholes (for example, the *bās* of Madhya Pradesh), most chromatic trumpets are Western, leaving the rest of the world's trumpets categorized as 'natural'. Excluding conch horns, a relatively small and distinctive subgroup, leaves an enormous variety of instruments in the 'tubular' category. Geneviève Dournon's 1992 modification of the system with subdivisions based on structure, shape, and material permits greater distinction between non-Western instruments. Useful as these classification systems are, they do not address issues of distribution and function. In many cultures trumpets have important functions that are symbolic or practical as well as, or instead of, musical.

2. Geographic distribution and construction. General observations regarding distribution are based on uneven geographical coverage and rarely take into account the variant names of instruments or the frequency with which particular specimens occur. Furthermore, early studies—many of which are still consulted because the ground has never been revisited or the instruments have become obsolete—range from firsthand research to studies based on secondary sources and museum collections. However, it can be broadly observed that trumpets are widespread in Africa and Europe, perhaps somewhat less so in Asia, and infrequently found in the Americas.

Patterns emerge of geographic distribution by material type. Some patterns are a matter of common sense: it is hardly surprising that most trumpets made from gourd or ivory are found in Africa. Exceptions, when they occur, are instructive: the medieval *oliphant*, for example, a short, thick end-blown trumpet finely carved from an elephant tusk, was probably a Middle Eastern instrument introduced to Europe during the Crusades. Instruments made from perishable materials such as tree bark depend upon suitable climate and flora. In Scandinavia and Eastern Europe, spiral bark shavings are bound firmly into conical tubes, which can range in length from the Yugoslavian *borija*, made from willow or ash bark (about 50 cm), to the now-obsolete Latvian *tāšu taure*, made from birch bark (up to 150 cm). In the hotter, more humid climate of the Amazonian rainforest, giant trumpets—up to 4 metres long—are made from tightly coiled bark attached to supporting sticks that run along one or both sides to prevent sagging.

In other cases, distribution is so widespread that patterns are less easy to discern. For example, trumpets made from animal horn are most commonly found in Africa and rarely in the Middle East (with the exception of the Jewish ram's horn *shofar*), somewhat more often elsewhere in Asia and almost never in Oceania. In Africa, where animal-horn trumpets are more often side-blown than end-blown, the rarity of a particular type of horn increases its value. For example, in Uganda, cow horns are only used when game horns or ivory tusks are unavailable or unaffordable. Wherever they occur, a horn, once selected, is boiled or otherwise softened and the interior is scraped out. Depending on the playing style, an aperture is created by sawing off the tip of the horn or by cutting a mouthhole, usually at the point where the solid tip of the horn ends and the bore of the tube begins. Many African side-blown animal horns also have a small fingerhole in the tip to give an extra pitch.

Occasionally distribution patterns are surprising. While isolated examples of bamboo trumpets can be found in Africa and South America, there are fewer in the bamboo-rich areas of East and Southeast Asia. Here cultural ambivalence toward lip-vibrated instruments overrides the regional abundance of raw material. An unusual exception is the bamboo 'brass brand' tradition of Sulawesi. Introduced to European brass bands by 19th-century Dutch missionaries but lacking the materials to reproduce instruments, local craftsmen began to make bamboo copies during the mid-1920s. Although they soon graduated to zinc replicas, there are some pockets, notably the Sangir Islands north of Minahassa, where bamboo 'brass' instruments can still be found. One might also expect wooden trumpets to be particularly widespread, but they appear predominantly in Africa, Europe, and Australia. Often long, they range from straight cylindrical tubes, like the Scandinavian *lur* or the Australian *didjeridu*, to conical tubes with an upturned bell, like the European alphorn. Some are hollowed branches; others involve cutting the branch or tree trunk in half lengthwise before hollowing it and rejoining both halves with whatever comes to hand: tar and osier (*lur*), putty and linen yarn (Lithuanian *daudytė*), animal hide (Ugandan *arupepe*), and bark or gut (alphorn).

The distribution patterns of both conch horns and metal trumpets are historically illuminating. Shells used for blowing include the *triton* (trumpet shell), *cassis* (helmet shell), and *strombus* (true conch) among many other species. The helical interior functions as tubing and a mouthhole is created either by breaking off the point of the shell (end-blown conch) or by boring a mouthhole in the body (side-blown conch). As might be expected from an instrument known since neolithic times, conch horns are found almost everywhere, including inland areas such as Tibet and Central Europe, where they support the existence of early trade routes. Particularly common throughout Oceania, conch horns were formerly associated with religious, ceremonial, military, and signalling functions. Nowadays, however, they are often blown to announce mundane public events. For example, ensembles of up to nine *kele'a* are played at Tongan football matches to sustain general excitement. As sacred ritual instruments, end-blown conch horns have retained their status better in South and East Asia. *Śankh* are blown by Brahmans in Hindu temples throughout South Asia. Known as *dung* in Tibet, *faluo* in China, and *horagai* in Japan, the conch horn travelled through Asia with the spread of Buddhism, the species varying according to local availability and custom. The *horagai* was first mentioned in historical records during the Heian period (794–1185) but might have reached Japan much earlier. Still used by Shugendo Buddhist sects, it is the only traditional lip-vibrated instrument found in Japan.

There were several types of ancient metal trumpets: the Egyptian *ṣnb*, Israelite *ḥatzotzerah*, Celtic *carnyx*, Greek *salpinx*, and the Etrusco-Roman *cornu*, *lituus*, *tuba*, and *buccina*. Long metal trumpets employed by Saracen armies made a great impact on European soldiers during the Crusades. It is possible that these trumpets ultimately derived from the Roman *tuba*. The distribution of long, straight metal trumpets in the non-Western world suggests a strong connection with the world of Islam. In Africa, for example, end-blown metal trumpets are found only in Islamic areas such as Nigeria, Chad, and Central Cameroon. Known as *kakaki* (among the Hausa) or *gashi* (in Chad), these trumpets are narrow cylindrical tubes sometimes more than 2 metres long, with flared metal bells. At the other end of the Islamic world, the silver *nafiri* is one of only two trumpets found in Malaysia. Slightly less than 1 metre long, a single *nafiri* is present in each of the royal *nobat* ensembles maintained by the local sultans. As in Africa, these ensembles play for royal ceremonial occasions and on Islamic holidays. However, not all non-Western metal trumpets are long, straight, or associated with Islam. South Asia has a great variety of metal trumpets of different shapes and sizes, ranging from the S-shaped *narsīgā* of southern Bihar and the double U-shaped Rajasthani *bānkiā* to the long, conical, telescopic Tibetan *dung-chen*.

3. Use and function. One of the most widespread and important functions of trumpets is the marking of power and status. In many parts of the world, trumpets and drums have been part of the regalia associated with kingship. This association continues to the present day: the British monarch, for example, is still heralded on state occasions by military trumpeters. Sometimes such instruments are more than symbolic regalia. In northern Nigeria, for example, the right to kingship itself was vested in the royal trumpets and kettledrums (*kakaki* and *tambari*); a coup d'etat could be effected simply by capturing them. The association between long metal *kakaki* trumpets and Islamic rulers in West Africa is clear, but using trumpets to generate power and mark status is neither limited to metal instruments nor to the Islamic world. Throughout Oceania, conch trumpets were markers of chiefly status, rank, and power. In Rarotonga, for example, the local term for conch was applied to chiefs, rulers, and priests.

Power and status can also be marked in other contexts. There is often, for example, an association between trumpets and gender difference. Sachs and others have attributed it all to sex, specifically to the homology between instrument shape and the shape of sexual organs and to a correlation between aggressive (male) sounds and gentle (female) sounds. This argument confuses sex (a biological distinction) with gender (a culturally constructed distinction). Though it is true that in many parts of the world, trumpets are loud instruments reserved for outdoor use, the separation between male-dominated public and female-dominated private domains is equally widespread. It could be argued that trumpets are played by men because they are played outside, rather than that trumpets are played outside because they are played by men. This applies equally to the traditional associations with regalia, signalling, and ritual, all of which mediate with the outside world in one form or another and thus fall into the public domain controlled, in most cultures, by men.

Trumpets are used to communicate in many ways, for example: European herdsmen use alphorns to call each other across the mountains; Latvian youths play goathorn *āžrags* on summer evenings to announce their intention to marry; Bugandan hunters from Uganda sound their *eng'ombe* (side-blown animal horns) to ensure a successful hunt; and fisherman from Aoba, Vanuatu, blow their conch trumpets, *tapáe*, to summon assistance for bringing in their nets. Not all communication is so pastoral: from the Roman legion to the US Cavalry, trumpets have been an essential part of military life. Communication can also exceed the boundaries of the everyday world: the BaMbuti people of the Democratic Republic of the Congo sound the *molimo* trumpet to wake up the spirit of the forest; Japanese Shugendo Buddhists imitate a lion's roar on the *horagai* to drive out evil spirits; and Fijian islanders use their *davui* conch trumpets to invoke the presence of a god. The sound of trumpets can bridge the gap between temporal and spiritual worlds. In each case, a short loud sound, series of sounds, or rhythmic pattern functions as a signal, a means of carrying a message or an instruction from one person or persons to others often a great distance.

4. The Western trumpet. A member of the family of brass instruments, in its modern form the Western trumpet is a folded tube opening at the end into a bell, with a separate mouthpiece and (usually) three valves. Trumpet playing normally involves overblowing to obtain various members of the harmonic series. Ex.1 shows the harmonic series for a trumpet in 8′ C (i.e. with approximately 8′, or 2.44 metres, of tubing; Roman numerals denote the beginning of each octave, Arabic the individual members). Certain partials, indicated in black, are distinctly sharp or flat (as shown by the direction of the arrows above them) in relation to their equivalents in the equal-tempered scale. For example, the 11th partial is intermediate between *f″* and *f♯″* and the 13th partial intermediate between *g♯″* and *a″*. In performance, pitch can be adjusted slightly by lip technique.

The older 'natural trumpet' is able to produce only the notes of the harmonic series. In the modern valve trumpet the three valves add, in effect, extra lengths of tubing, thus enabling the pitch of 'open' notes to be lowered by a whole tone, a semitone or a minor 3rd respectively. Used in various combinations the valves can lower the pitch by as much as a diminished 5th, making available a chromatic scale from a diminished 5th below the second partial up to the tenth partial or higher. Trumpet parts are traditionally notated in the key of C; the actual pitch sounded depends on the length of the instrument. Natural trumpets were commonly built to pitches between 6′ F and 9′ B♭. In modern valve trumpets the tubing need be only half as long: 'trumpet in C' generally means 4′ C, and *c′* is the second partial, not the fourth.

(i) Sizes and types. The B♭ trumpet common in orchestras and bands nowadays has a tube length of 130 cm and three piston valves. It consists of a tapered mouthpipe (Fr. *branche*; Ger. *Mundrohr*; Ital. *canna d'imboccatura*) 18 to 33 cm long, into which the mouthpiece is inserted; a middle section of cylindrical tubing, including the tuning-slide (Fr. *coulisse d'accord*; Ger. *Stimmzug*; Ital. *pompa d'intonazione*) and the valves together with their associated tubing; and a conical bell

section (Fr. *pavillon*; Ger. *Schallstück, -becher, -trichter,* or *Stürze*; Ital. *campana* or *padiglione*) ending in a flare (Fr. *évasement*; Ger. *Ausladung*; Ital. *sviluppo della campana*) about 12.5 cm in diameter. The cylindrical part of the bore can be between 10.9 mm and 11.9 mm in diameter, depending on the maker and country of origin. Although the bore was traditionally about one-third conical and two-thirds cylindrical, modern manufacturers of piston-valve trumpets have increased the length of the conical section to improve intonation; in some modern trumpets the cylindrical tubing constitutes only about 20% of the total length.

The trumpet in 4′ C, pitched a whole tone above the B♭ instrument, is also common in orchestral work. Indeed, modern trumpeters, because of the variety of musical styles in which they are required to play and the perfection demanded of them in performances, need at least three or four instruments, including ones pitched in B♭ and in C for regular work, in D/E♭, and in high B♭/A (piccolo trumpet; Ger. *Hoch-B/A-Trompete*; Fr. *petite trompette en si-bémol/la aiguë, trompette piccolo*; Ital. *trombino*) for high parts and in Baroque music. The 'quick change' rotary valve which changes the pitch from B♭ to A, favoured by some orchestras at the beginning of the 20th century, is no longer in general use. A low E♭ trumpet is still used in military bands on the Continent, especially in Germany and Italy. It is the band counterpart of the old orchestral valve trumpet in 6′ F.

The orchestral bass trumpet was designed to Wagner's specifications for the *Ring*. Wagner first visualized a huge trumpet pitched an octave below the ordinary 6′ F valve trumpet of his day, with the same length of tubing as a horn or tuba. He later suggested (to the Berlin maker C.W. Moritz) the construction of a four-valve trumpet in 8′ C with crooks for B♭ and A. The resulting instrument has a tube length no greater than that of the 6′ F trumpet played with its longest crooks, but it has a more mellow tone because of its wide bore and large mouthpiece. It is usually played by a trombonist. Wagner demanded of it a large compass, from G♭ to g♭″, and gave it solo passages in every part of its range. Since Wagner, other composers—including Richard Strauss and Stravinsky—have been attracted to write for the bass trumpet.

After World War II piston-valve trumpets spread from France, England, and the USA to most European orchestras, although rotary-valve trumpets—traditionally used in Germany and eastern Europe—remained in use in a few, such as the Berlin PO, the Leipzig Gewandhaus, Dresden Staatskapelle, and the Vienna PO. In the 1980s many orchestras—including some in which they had never been employed—began to use rotary-valve trumpets for the German Classical and Romantic repertory. An instrument of this type has a mouthpipe only about 13 cm long; the valve section is usually inserted between mouthpipe and tuning-slide; the bell is some 13 to 14 cm in diameter.

(ii) History to 1500. Most trumpets of antiquity were short, straight instruments of wood, bronze, or silver,

Ex.1.

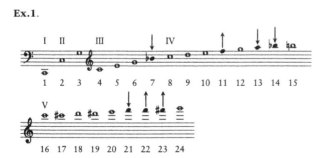

used for both military and ceremonial purposes. The most ancient type—called *šnb* in hieroglyphic inscriptions—is that depicted in Egyptian art of Dynasty 18, accompanying marching soldiers. One scene in Amarna style (late Dynasty 18, from *c*1348 bce) shows it might also be used to accompany the dance. One of Tutankhamun's trumpets (in *ET.C.em*) is made of silver and is 58.2 cm long; the other is of bronze and 50.5 cm long; their bores expand from 1.7 cm at the narrow end to 8.2 cm at the bell. They have no detachable mouthpieces; the lips were applied directly to the narrow end. Their military purpose is confirmed by the divine names inscribed on the instruments; the gods are those of Egyptian army divisions. Herodotus likened the sound of the ancient trumpet to the braying of an ass.

The Assyrians used a similar trumpet, as can be seen on a relief from the time of Sennacherib (reigned 704–681 bce) showing the moving of a colossal bull statue, where two trumpeters stand on the statue, one playing, the other resting (Egyptian trumpeters were also often shown in pairs). The same instrument (*ḥatzotzerah*) was known to the Hebrews. *Numbers* x.2 contains the divine command to Moses, 'Make thee two trumpets of silver, of a whole piece shalt thou make them: that thou mayest use them for the calling of the assembly, and for the journeying of the camps' (Authorized Version). Flavius Josephus (*Antiquities*, iii, §291) described the instrument as a little less than a cubit (about 45 cm) long. Such trumpets were part of the priestly insignia of the Temple from the earliest times; they are represented on the Arch of Titus; and mention of them persists in the Dead Sea Scrolls. They were used as signalling instruments also, in war, in peace, and in royal processions; in the Temple three trumpet blasts accompanied the morning sacrifice, and at the end of a chant section indicated the moment when worshippers should prostrate themselves.

Other early trumpet-like instruments include the Greek (straight, with variable *salpinx* bell-shapes) and the Roman *lituus* (in 'J' shape), *tuba* (long and straight), *buccina* (an animal horn), and *cornu* (in 'G' shape); the Romans inherited two of their brass instruments, the lituus and cornu, from the Etruscans. The Seleucids of the Middle East followed Macedonian practice by using the trumpet in their battle music, as did the Huns when fighting the Chinese Han Empire in the 3rd and 2nd centuries bce. There is a late echo of the Temple trumpet at Dura Europus (now Qal'at as Sāliḥīyah, Syria) where David is shown with a lyre and trumpeters in a synagogue wall-painting dated after the Roman conquest of 165 ce. It is interesting that in a 6th-century Sassanid military orchestra (rock relief; Tāq-e Bostān, nr Kermānshāh) the trumpeters are represented in pairs using an instrument similar to the Roman *tuba*.

According to Sachs, the trumpet disappeared from Europe after the fall of Rome and was not reintroduced until the time of the crusades, when instruments were taken from the Saracens as war booty. Sachs attributed the long form and the shape of the bell to Arabian influence: a late 11th-century fresco in the church of

S Angelo in Formis, near Capua, depicts four angels blowing long, conical, slightly curved trumpets, and is often cited as the first illustration of the imported form. Medieval illustrations of trumpeting angels, for example in the Trier Apocalypse manuscript (D-TRs 31, f.3*v*), have been shown to be part of an older pictorial: the artists were following models derived from antiquity, rather than representing instruments in use in their time. Smithers's attempt (B1989) to show the 'unbroken history of manufacture and use' of metal trumpets in the West has been refuted by Meucci (B1991).

The Church Fathers, writing in Greek and Latin, used the terms 'salpinx' and 'tuba' respectively. In Western art before the crusades (in many depictions of the Last Judgment, for example), animal horns are generally shown. Many Arabic words at various times indicated a straight trumpet. The generic term 'būq', occurring after 800 and describing instruments of both the trumpet and the horn type, might have been derived from the Latin 'buccina'. The *būq al-nafīr* was a large metal trumpet used in the military bands of the Abbasid period (750–1258) and later; in the 14th century it was as long as a man. The term *nafīr* connotates war. From the 11th century, as an instrument designation, it meant any long straight trumpet. Other Arabic words for trumpets in various shapes were *qarnā* and *ṣūr* (named in the Qur'an as the one to be used on Judgment day, probably the predecessor of the *nafīr*). The term 'buisine' was associated with various instrument forms, and was not always applied to a long, cylindrical instrument. By the 14th century, or perhaps as early as 1180, the *buisine* was sometimes made from an animal's horn; in 1240 it was smaller than a *trompe*. It is not certain when the French form of the word began to mean a long metal trumpet as well as the animal-horn type, nor whether the *buisine* more closely resembled the *būq* or the *nafīr*. Another instrument used in the West as a result of contact with the East was the *cor sarrazinois*, a long metal trumpet. The term 'trumba' occurred in Old High German and 'trumbono' in 8th-century Italian sources. The diminutive form 'trombetta' is found for the first time in Dante's *Inferno* (xxi.47), its German derivation 'Trum(m)et' in 1343. In England 'trompette' or 'trumbetta' seem to have meant a straight trumpet.

During the Middle Ages trumpeters played in the low register. Johannes de Grocheo wrote (*De musica*, *c*1300) that only the first four partials of the harmonic series were used, a fact corroborated by the earliest surviving trumpet music. Medieval trumpeters puffed out their cheeks when blowing and produced a tone that was described as airy and trembling, not unlike the vibrato produced by a boy soprano. Until about 1300 trumpeters and many other musicians were vagrants, but during the 14th and 15th centuries their social position gradually stabilized as they found employment as city musicians or, in the case of trumpeters, tower watchmen. Two kinds of ensemble using trumpets came to be differentiated: the shawm-trumpet ensemble (or *alta musica*; the trumpet was later replaced by a trombone) and the trumpet-kettledrum ensemble (the kettledrums appeared toward 1500). (Later, in Germany, these two groups developed respectively into the Stadtpfeifer and the courtly trumpet corps.) The shawm-trumpet ensemble first used the trumpet to play a drone bass. The members of the trumpet-kettledrum ensemble performed in a genre named after the Roman *classicum*, an improvised mingling of various sounds, which by dint of sheer resonance was effective in encouraging troops and frightening the enemy. This type of ensemble became an élite corps of musicians, partly because of its military role in giving signals and performing courier duties. The 14th-century 'Billingsgate trumpet', reputedly the oldest surviving medieval trumpet, was excavated in London in 1984; however, the four sections of a straight trumpet, including a bell and a section with integral mouthpiece, might not have belonged to a single instrument.

About 1400 instrument makers learned to bend the trumpet's tubing: first to an S-shape, soon afterwards with this S-shape folded back on itself to form a loop—a more compact arrangement that has since remained standard. The earliest illustration of an S-shaped trumpet is a wooden relief in the choir stalls of Worcester Cathedral; once dated 1397, it is now thought to have been carved about 1379 (for a modern reproduction see Galpin, 4/1965, pl.49). An S-shaped trumpet made in 1442 by Marcian Guitbert of Limoges was recently discovered, perfectly preserved, in a well in southern France. A very short-lived form, the U-shaped trumpet, is depicted in a Parisian manuscript, the Hours of Charles the Noble (*c*1404, Cleveland Museum of Art). The earliest illustration of the looped form is from the *Très Riches Heures* of Jean, Duke of Berry (*c*1411/13–16). At about the same time the slide trumpet was developed with a mouthpipe that telescoped inside the first length of tubing to enable the player to alter the instrument's length while playing. Tower watchmen adopted the slide trumpet to play chorales; it was also used in church music (but the natural trumpet continued to be used in the trumpet-kettledrum ensemble).

(iii) 1500–1820. Renaissance sovereigns saw in their trumpet ensembles a symbol of their own importance—Matthias Corvinus had 24 trumpeters at his court; in 1482 there were 18 at the Sforza court. They staged tournaments, which the courtly trumpet-kettledrum corps accompanied at close range. In 1548 (not 1528, an error deriving from Altenburg, 1795) the Emperor Charles V issued a decree putting trumpeters under the direct jurisdiction of the sovereign. From that time on the social distinction between trumpeters and other musicians was progressively widened.

During the 16th century the trumpet's compass was extended upwards as far as the 13th partial. Within the trumpet-kettledrum ensemble certain players became responsible for specific registers. Toward the end of the century a five-part ensemble consisted of players capable of playing the following notes (on trumpets in 8′ C): *basso, c; vulgano* or *vorgano, g; alto e basso* or *alter Bass, g–c′–e′; sonata, quinta,* or (later) *principale, c′–e′–g′–c″–(d″–e″)*; and *clareta, soprano,* or *clarino,* from *c″*

(the eighth partial) upwards. Cesare Bendinelli in his method of 1614 (the contents of which appear to derive from the 1580s) gave specific directions for improvising the upper parts in a five-part trumpet ensemble. This music has a distinctive style, which may go back to the Middle Ages: over a drone of tonic and dominant the upper three parts weave their counterpoint. During the same period the trumpet's form became more standardized. The body was usually made of brass, its tubing (with a bore of about 9.5–11.2 mm) rolled from brass sheet about 0.5 mm thick; heavy, ornate ceremonial trumpets were sometimes made of silver. The bell was rolled from brass sheet into a narrow cone, brazed and hammered out on an anvil to a thickness of only about 0.35 mm. The natural trumpet thus comprised two sections of tubing or 'yards', two bends or 'bows', and a bell section. The yards and bows were not soldered but telescoped into each other, and were insulated by a non-permanent material such as beeswax; the joins were covered by an ornamental ferrule or 'garnish'. Circling the middle of the bell section was a round 'boss' or 'ball' (the ball did not cover another joint in the tubing; the bell section was in one piece up to the ferrule). The bell end was strengthened by an embossed rim or 'garland', usually inscribed with the maker's name, mark, town, and sometimes the date. On German trumpets the mouthpipe yard and the bell section were separated from each other by a wooden block, with heavy woollen cord wound around block and tubing; on English trumpets the mouthpipe yard was girdled by an oversized 'ball'. Trumpets were also made in other forms, such as the coiled 'Italian trumpet', which might be identical with the 'Jäger Trommet' illustrated by Praetorius (1620).

In the 16th century Nuremberg began to emerge as the great centre of brass instrument making and remained so throughout the Baroque period; members of the Neuschel and Schnitzer families were the earliest Nuremberg brass instrument makers. There are, however, few extant 16th-century instruments. Two city trumpets made in 1578 by Jacob Steiger of Basle survive (in *CH.B.bm*).

Extant Baroque trumpet mouthpieces differ from modern ones in several ways (fig.1). Their rims were flatter and wider, and there was a sharp edge between cup and throat. The throat, or bore, had a larger diameter, 4 to 6 mm. The shank was often longer and had a larger outside diameter. The sharp edge between cup and throat not only lent brilliance to the tone and enhanced the precision of the instrument's response, but in combination with the wide bore it also made it easier for trumpeters to 'lip' the out-of-tune partials into tune, or even to produce usable notes between the partials, a technique that is difficult if not impossible on a mouthpiece with a V-shaped cup, such as that of a horn. (Playing in tune was perhaps the most important prerequisite for the acceptance of the trumpet into ensembles of strings in the early 17th century.) As with the modern mouthpiece, a shallow cup facilitated playing in the high or Clarino register; a deeper, wider one was more suitable for low or Principale playing.

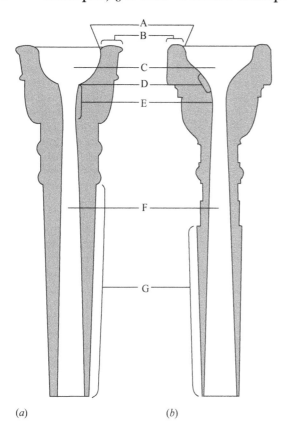

(a)   (b)

Fig.1: *Baroque (left) and modern trumpet mouthpieces: A – inner edge of rim, or 'bite', B – rim facing, C – cup, D – sharp edge (a) or shoulder (b), E – throat or bore, F – backbore, G – shank.*

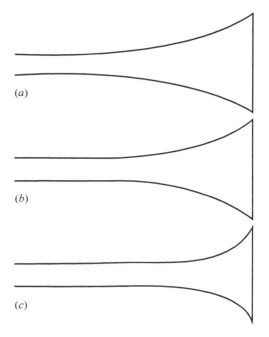

Fig.2: *Three trumpet bells showing the gradual narrowing of the bell throat and flare from the late Renaissance to the late Baroque: (a) Anton Schnitzer, 1581; (b) Hans Hainlein, 1658; (c) Friedrich Ehe, c1700.*

Throughout the 17th and early 18th centuries the form of the trumpet remained the same, although it is possible to distinguish between early, middle, and late Baroque bell flares, as the bell throat became progressively narrower (fig.2). The best-known Nuremberg instrument-making families were Schnitzer, Neuschel, Hainlein, Kodisch, Ehe, and especially Haas. The leading English makers of the time were William Bull, John Harris, and, later, William Shaw. In Germany and England the standard pitch was D or E♭, and the instrument was crooked down to play in lower keys. Independently of one another, both Mersenne (1636–7) and Altenburg (1795) gave the tube length as 224 cm (seven *pieds*, or four *Ellen*), which would yield a pitch slightly lower than modern D. Fine tuning was effected by inserting tuning bits (short prepared lengths of tubing) between the mouthpiece and the instrument or crook. A number of composers, including J.S. Bach, J.L. Bach, Telemann, and Endler also wrote for the shorter F trumpet, called variously *clarino piccolo*, *tromba piccola*, or *kurze Trompete*.

In 1623 an Imperial Society of Trumpeters and Kettledrummers was formed in the Holy Roman Empire by virtue of an Imperial Privilege granted by Ferdinand II. The society (not a guild, a term applicable to craftsmen on a local level) had a twofold function: to regulate

instruction and thus limit the number of trumpeters, and to ensure the trumpet's exclusiveness by restricting where it could be played and by whom. The Elector of Saxony was named its patron and arbiter of its disputes, and its articles were subsequently confirmed by every Holy Roman Emperor up to Joseph II (1767). Saxon mandates 'against the misuse of the trumpet' were issued in 1650, 1661, 1711, 1736, and 1804; revisions of the Imperial Privilege appeared in 1653 and 1747. Nuremberg brass instrument makers formed an association of their own in 1635 which was closely supervised by the city council. Although the organization of trumpeters into a society of more than just local proportions was unique to the Holy Roman Empire, the trumpet enjoyed a similar status in other European countries.

The medieval tournament gave way to the more stylized carousel or equestrian ballet, in which costumed participants formed intricate figures. Since the music of the court trumpet corps was usually improvised, few examples survive. During the 17th century, however, the trumpet was accepted into 'art music', as shown by compositions from that time. Schütz's *Buccinate in neomenia tuba* of 1629 (*Symphoniae sacrae*, vol.1, no.19) was probably the first piece to include a c″ (the 16th partial) for trumpet.

The 'chamber' or 'concert trumpeter' increasingly distinguished himself from the members of the trumpet corps, and performed sonatas, concertos, and church music with the court or municipal orchestras. During the century two styles of trumpet playing developed. Altenburg (1795) referred to them (pp.14 and 23) as *Feldstück-* or *Prinzipalblasen*, and *Clarinblasen*, comparing them directly to techniques used by the ancient Hebrews and known as *teruah* and *tekia*: Luther translated these as *schmettern* and *schlecht blasen* respectively, and the King James Bible as 'blowing an alarm' and 'blowing'. The former style was deemed appropriate for military signals and for the 'outdoor' music of the trumpet corps; the latter, softer style was associated with solo playing in the clarino register. In 1619 Praetorius advised that the trumpet group be separated from the other musicians when called on to play in church, so as not to drown them out. Altenburg wrote that a 'concert trumpeter is [often] spared the weekly playing at table, because through the blaring he would spoil the delicate and subtle embouchure [needed] for clarino [playing]'. 18th-century theorists praised players who were able to manage their instrument as softly as a flute.

The most important centre of Baroque trumpet playing was Vienna, followed by Dresden, Leipzig, Weissenfels, Kremsier (now Kroměříž), Bologna, London, and to a lesser extent Paris and Lisbon. Vienna's elaborate court protocol prescribed the use of trumpets in groups of four, two high (*clarini*) and two low (*trombe*). The Bologna composers Petronio Franceschini, Domenico Gabrielli, and Giuseppe Torelli wrote trumpet parts whose compass often extended to the 16th partial. One or two trumpets were frequently used in Venetian opera toward the end of the century. There was already an important tradition of trumpet playing in Leipzig when Bach arrived there: his predecessors as Kantors of the Thomaskirche had thought well of the instrument, and J.C. Pezel had written and played some difficult trumpet parts. Bach composed much of his most splendid trumpet music for Gottfried Reiche, senior Stadtpfeifer until his death in 1734.

In London, Purcell relied on the trumpeters Matthias, William, and especially John Shore, as Handel later relied on Valentine Snow. French trumpet music retained the heroic *Affekt* perhaps more consistently than did that of any other country; the preludes to *Te Deum* settings by Lully and Charpentier are among the most stirring and best-known examples. Lisbon's trumpet corps ('charamela real') consisted of 24 trumpeters and four kettledrum players, many of them German. Probably the greatest Baroque trumpeter was Johann Heinisch, active at the Viennese court from 1727 to 1750. He was said to have extended the playing range of the trumpet to include high notes that other trumpeters had never envisaged. Trumpet parts in the operas written for the Viennese court by Caldara, Fux, and Georg von Reutter the younger for Heinisch and his colleagues ascend consistently as high as the 20th and sometimes the 24th partial.

The period between about 1720 and 1780 saw both the zenith and the decline of the Baroque trumpet. The technique of playing in the clarino register was developed to the fullest in Vienna and other centres including Salzburg and Fulda. Concertos in which the trumpet is asked to play in the fourth and fifth octaves of its harmonic series were written by Michael Haydn, Reutter, F.X. Richter, and Joseph Riepel. In the slow movement of Reutter's *Servizio di tavola* no.1 (1757) a single trumpeter performs a songlike solo ascending to *f″*. Some of the latest concertos for the Baroque trumpet were written by Leopold Mozart (1762) and J.M. Sperger (1778–9). By then, however, the trumpet concerto as a genre had become old-fashioned. In addition, the accelerating decline of courts, hastened by the French Revolution, deprived the Imperial Society of Trumpeters and Kettledrummers of its socioeconomic foundation. The society was finally dissolved in Prussia in 1810 by the same Friedrich Wilhelm III to whom the Berlin trumpeters had 'most respectfully' dedicated a suite for three trumpets and kettledrums in 1801; Saxony abolished the society in 1831.

In the Classical style of Haydn, Mozart, and Beethoven the trumpet was used mainly as a tutti instrument, although an occasional fanfare at the end of an *allegro* movement called attention to the trumpeters' surviving court function. However, it is wrong to maintain, as has been done, that trumpeters of the Classical period became less skillful: instead, new skills were required. Beethoven, for example, made great demands on endurance. Moreover, the technique of playing in the clarino register was not lost overnight.

In the late 18th and early 19th centuries several attempts were made (before the invention of the valve trumpet) to enable the instrument to play a complete chromatic scale. One early device was the keyed trumpet, for which Haydn and Hummel wrote their concertos. The stop trumpet (Ger. *Stopftrompete*) was usually made with two double bends in its tubing; thus the instrument was short enough for the player to insert his hand in the bell to lower the pitch of the harmonic partials by a semitone or a whole tone. Hand stopping was first used in horn playing (by A.J. Hampel, *c*1760), and was first applied to the trumpet about 1777, by Michael Wöggel of Karlsruhe. Karl Bagans, a German trumpeter of the early 19th century, showed that he knew of keyed trumpets but wrote that a stop trumpet could perform chromatic music even more satisfactorily. J.D. Buhl was the leading French performer on the stop trumpet, the French version of which was built in G and called the *trompette d'harmonie*—as opposed to the military trumpet in E♭ called the *trompette d'ordonnance* on which hand stopping was not used. In Germany the stop trumpet was usually made in G, with crooks to put the instrument into lower pitches. Some early stop trumpets were built in Nuremberg by Johann Leonhard Ehe (iii), but makers elsewhere, such as Michael Saurle in Munich, soon became more important and Nuremberg lost its pre-eminence in brass-instrument making. The *Inventionstrompete* was a stop trumpet with a tuning-slide in U-form, either in the middle of the instrument or in one of the bends. It too was derived from the horn; Hampel's first *Inventionshorn* was built in 1753/4 by J.G. Werner of Dresden. Wöggel's stop trumpet was itself a kind of *Inventionstrompete*; it was bent into a curved shape, like the instrument later known in France as the *trompette demilune* (introduced by Courtois Frères *c*1820). Improved *Inventionstrompeten* were built in the 1790s by A.F. Krause of Berlin.

In England, a new type of slide trumpet was invented about 1798, and was subsequently used throughout the 19th century.

The superiority of the valve system over other methods of making trumpets (and horns) chromatic became clear during the 19th century. The advantage of valves over keys was homogeneity of tone (though perhaps not with the first valved instruments); the advantage over the slide was facility. A valve horn was introduced in Berlin by Heinrich Stölzel in 1814. In 1818 a joint patent was taken out in Berlin by Stölzel and Friedrich Blühmel for both a tubular valve (then called *Röhrenschiebeventil*, now *Schubventil*) and a square piston valve, also known as a box valve (Ger. *Kastenventil*); the latter was applied to the trumpet in 1820.

The two types of valve in use today are the rotary valve and the piston valve. J.F. Riedl of Vienna, working with the horn player Josef Kail, was assigned a five-year patent (later renewed another five years) for a rotary valve in 1835 (not 1832, as previously thought). The piston valve (Ger. *Pumpventil*) was patented by François Périnet of Paris in 1838 as an improvement on the tubular valve which had been Stölzel's invention. Another type of valve sometimes still used (on horns), the double-tube 'Vienna' valve (Ger. *Wiener Ventil*), had been developed in 1823 by Kail and Riedl as an improvement on an earlier double-tube valve produced by Christian Friedrich Sattler of Leipzig by 1819; this type of valve had been developed from Stölzel's original (double-tube) valve of 1814. Leopold Uhlmann of Vienna added cork buffers in 1830, also introducing the clock-spring return action (*Trommeldruckwerk*), one of two in use nowadays on instruments with rotary valves (the other is the spiral spring action (*Spiralfederdruckwerk*), the origin of which is uncertain).

(iv) Since 1820. The first champion of the valve trumpet was Kail, who in June 1826 became professor of trumpet and trombone (both with valves) at the Prague Conservatory. From 1827 he wrote or commissioned the earliest known works for solo valve trumpet (in low D, E♭, and F) with piano or orchestral accompaniment. The valve trumpet was introduced into France in 1826, when Spontini, music director for the King of Prussia, sent a valve trumpet in F and a valve trombone made by Haltenhof to Buhl and Dauverné. The latter recognized the possibilities of the new instrument and immediately published several instruction books. The German prototype had had three tubular 'Stölzel' valves, a type that was improved on—but not invented, as is sometimes claimed—in 1827 by J.C. Labbaye. Halary later made more successful improvements, and on Dauverné's urging produced the first French valve trumpet, with only two valves, in 1828. Even well into the 19th century after valve trumpets had become relatively securely established, trumpeters played on either the valve or the stop trumpet, depending on the music to be performed. The first works in France to use valve trumpets were Chelard's *Macbeth* (1827), Berlioz's overtures *Les francs-juges* (1826) and *Waverley* (1827–8), Rossini's *Guillaume Tell* (1829) and Meyerbeer's *Robert le diable*

(1831). Meyerbeer used both valve and natural trumpets, as did Wagner (*Rienzi*, 1842; *Lohengrin*, 1850). In Germany and England, valve trumpets were made in 6′ F, rarely G, and were crooked down to C and sometimes B♭; French valve trumpets were first made in G, later in F. Trumpets with (tubular) valves had arrived in England in 1831 via Russia, where Prussian instruments had been copied as early as 1825.

A disadvantage of the three-valve system is that the instrument becomes progressively sharper when the valves are used in combination. On modern trumpets the third and often the first valve are usually provided with movable slides (actuated by finger rings or triggers) which may be lengthened by the player as needed to compensate for this acoustical deficiency. 'Compensating systems', by which additional lengths of tubing are automatically brought into play when the valves are used in combination, were developed in Paris as early as 1858; the most successful system, developed by D.J. Blaikley of Boosey & Co., London, in 1874, is still used on low brass instruments. Trumpets and cornets have also been constructed with similar types of compensating systems: J.-B. Arban experimented with them between 1883 and 1888 (after 1885 with the engineer L. Bouvet).

Wagner, Mahler, and Richard Strauss notated their trumpet parts as much as possible in C, indicating the desired transposition above, thus leaving to the performer the question of which instrument to use. The trumpet's pitch could thus change every few bars, especially with Wagner's music, though in no case did trumpeters change crooks as frequently as notated, nor did composers expect them to. The increasing technical difficulty of parts written for the long F trumpet, however, influenced trumpeters to change to a shorter instrument, the 4½′ B♭ or the 4′ C trumpet.

The introduction of the B♭ and C trumpets was also due to the influence of the B♭ cornet, which was invented in 1831 when Halary built a B♭ post horn with valves. The cornet's lowest crook, G, was the highest crook of the French valve trumpet. Because its tubing was shorter and more conical than that of the F or G trumpet, the B♭ cornet was considerably more agile than the trumpet; accordingly French composers came to orchestrate for a pair of cornets and a pair of trumpets. Arban's saxhorn and cornet method (1864) was used as a trumpet method and has continued to influence trumpet playing up to now. In the USA and especially in France toward the end of the 19th century and at the beginning of the 20th, the cornet even threatened to oust the trumpet from the orchestra. The cornet also introduced a different notation, according to which *c″* was no longer the eighth partial but the fourth. The consequent greater distance between adjacent partials (in any part of the register) reduced the chance of 'cracking', or hitting another note besides the one desired. Ex.2 shows the 'open' notes on the modern C trumpet (on the B♭ trumpet and cornet they sound a tone lower).

The transition from the long F to the shorter B♭ trumpet began in Germany, where A. Kühnert of Dresden was one of the first to recognize the possibilities of the

Ex.2.

shorter instrument, about 1850 to 1860. Xavier Teste, first trumpeter at the Paris Opéra, introduced the C (actually D/C) trumpet in France in 1874. By about 1890 the transition was complete. In England the F trumpet was reinstated at the Royal College of Music in 1910 and taught there for a few years, at the insistence of Walter Morrow, but the new generation of players returned to the B♭ instrument.

About 1850, especially in France, England, and the USA, brass-instrument making began to convert to modern industrial methods of manufacture. Some of the most important 19th-century manufacturers, and bitter competitors for the international market, were: Moritz (Berlin), Pelitti (Milan), Sax (Brussels and Paris), Besson (Paris), Červený (Königgrätz; now Hradec Králové), Boosey (London), Hawkes (London), Conn (Elkhart, IN), and Couesnon (Paris). An ideal situation existed before World War II in Neukirchen (now Markneukirchen) and Graslitz (now Kraslice), where specialized makers of bells, valve sections, and other parts lived close together and sold their products to an assembler, whose name appeared on the finished product.

During the early 20th century small-bore instruments were popular in countries in which piston valve trumpets were used. The Conn 22B, widely used in American symphony orchestras, had a bore of 11.12 mm. The Thibouville-Lamy C trumpet, played in France before and just after World War I, had a bore of 11.2 mm, whereas that of the contemporary French Besson B♭ trumpet, the prototype of modern American trumpets, was 11.61 mm. In the 1930s in the USA, after World War II in England and after about 1960 in France, larger-bore trumpets were introduced in symphony orchestras to balance the larger volume of tone produced by the horn and trombone sections, which had already adopted large-bore instruments. Typical bore measurements of B♭ trumpets in use today are: Vincent Bach medium large, 11.66 mm; Bach large, 11.74 mm; Schilke, 11.1 to 11.89 mm; and Yamaha, 10.5 to 11.76 mm. The most popular rotary-valve trumpets throughout most of the 20th century were the smaller-bore model (10.9 mm) used in Vienna and Dresden and made by Heckel, later Windisch, now Meyer, all of Dresden, and the larger-bore model (11.2 mm) used in Berlin and made by Josef Monke of Cologne. At the end of the 20th century a host of new names—Adaci, Baumann, Egger, Ganter, Kröger, Kürner, Lechner, Meyer, Peter, Scherzer, Syhre, Thein, and Yamaha—were vying for the favour of players. American and German trumpets differ in other aspects of construction, which account for the characteristic difference in their sound and response. Besides their generally larger bore, American trumpets have more conical tubing than German ones; the bell is smaller; the mouthpiece cup medium large

as compared with the German very large; and the beginning of the mouthpipe small (9.5 mm) as compared with the German (10 mm).

Although mouthpieces were also standardized at the beginning of the 20th century, they vary widely in width and form of rim, shape and depth of cup, and width of throat, so that the selection of a proper mouthpiece is still an individual matter. Some mouthpieces have a 'double cup', the shoulder between cup and throat being constructed to include a smaller second cup between it and the throat proper. A short cylindrical section in the throat increases the sureness of attack but tends to make the upper register out of tune (fig.2).

Trumpet parts in modern orchestral works frequently reach the d''' first introduced by Mahler and Strauss. Some jazz musicians frequently play up to $b\flat''''$ and even higher, but playing such notes with the required force would tend to deaden the 'classical' trumpeter's sensitivity in the middle and lower registers, where it is all-important. Ideal articulation today demands that every note receive exactly the same attack. Trumpeters have departed considerably from the unequal articulation that was the ideal of the Baroque period and from the manifold subtleties of attack described in most 19th-century methods. Double tonguing (*tu-ku tu*) is done for quick duplets, triple tonguing (*tu-tu-ku tu*, formerly *tu-ku-tu tu*—first applied to the cornet by Arban—and sometimes as in double tonguing *tu-ku-tu ku*) for quick triplets. Because the large-bore instruments in use today require more air, correct breathing and diaphragm support are central in modern instruction. A number of special effects once reserved almost exclusively for jazz are now used in chamber and symphonic music: for example, flutter-tonguing, performed by trilling the dental *R* (although this was used as early as Strauss's *Don Quixote*, 1897); vibrato of varying amplitude and speed, produced by the chin, the diaphragm, or the motion of the right hand; glissandos (accomplished by depressing the valves only halfway); rips, similar to glissandos but with a rapid random action of the valves; singing and playing simultaneously, which results in various tones and beats being produced, best workable in the low register; producing an 'airy' tone, by tightening the lips more than usual and blowing with force so that part of the lip tissue does not vibrate; and even playing multiple notes, by tightening or relaxing the lips unduly and blowing between the partials.

Louis Armstrong (1901–71) was the most influential of early jazz trumpeters. He was the first to use the higher register to $e\flat'''$, and also set standards in jazz phrasing and 'inflection'—the varied attacks, timbres, and vibratos common to jazz trumpeting. Other jazz trumpeters, such as Bubber Miley and Cootie Williams, excelled in growl and plunger-mute effects; trumpeters of the swing period, such as Henry 'Red' Allen and Roy Eldridge, explored high-register smears and rips. Virtuoso demands, already at a high level, were increased still further by the bop musicians Dizzy Gillespie and Clifford Brown, who cultivated special techniques such as half-valving; Miles Davis explored the more subdued timbres of the instrument. Avant-garde jazz trumpeting is represented by Don Cherry, who played a miniature instrument called the 'pocket trumpet', and Woody Shaw. The 'big band' style of orchestral jazz has produced a number of excellent high-note specialists, including Cat Anderson, Maynard Ferguson, Bill Chase, and, toward the end of the 20th century, the flamboyant and versatile James Morrison and Arturo Sandoval. The teaching of jazz at academic institutions has encouraged high-note trumpet methods (by Carlton MacBeth, Roger Spaulding, Claude Gordon, and James Stamp) which are studied by trumpeters of all persuasions, and has furthermore produced a number of jazz players with classical training such as Allan Vizzuti and Wynton Marsalis. The jazz influence on orchestral music can also be seen in the use of new kinds of mute—cup mute, Harmon or 'wa-wa' mute, 'solotone' mute, felt hat and plunger mute—in addition to the traditional straight mute made of wood or metal.

After the introduction of the B♭ valve trumpet in the mid-19th century, even higher instruments were produced. The D trumpet, only half as long as the Baroque D trumpet, seems to have been used in works of Bach and Handel by 1861 in Brussels, and in Germany from about 1885; it appeared in England in a straight form in 1892 and was subsequently folded back on itself like a B♭ trumpet. Several 20th-century composers made use of the D trumpet (the instrument they intended had a narrower bore and a more penetrating tone than the kind generally made nowadays). Such orchestral parts are increasingly played on the piccolo trumpet in B♭ or A. The first piccolo trumpet in G was made by F. Besson for a performance by Teste of Bach's *Magnificat* in 1885. Besson subsequently constructed high trumpets in F/E♭ and E♭/D. The piccolo B♭ was originally developed by Sax (as 'petit Sax-horn suraigu en ut ou en si♭') in 1849 for the première of Berlioz's *Te Deum*, but was subsequently forgotten until 1905 or 1906, when Alexander of Mainz built one which A. Goeyens of Brussels used for performance of Bach's second Brandenburg Concerto, a work he had first performed in 1902 on a small F trumpet. (T. Charlier had been the first to perform this work in the proper high octave on a high G trumpet, in 1898.) The first modern player to adopt the piccolo B♭ for D trumpet parts was Adolf Scherbaum, for whom Leistner of Hamburg constructed one with three different bells in 1951. Scherbaum & Göttner, Schilke, Yamaha, Adaci, and J. Monke have even made piccolo C trumpets, and Schilke has had an order for a piccolo D trumpet. A hindrance to making such tiny trumpets—besides the obvious acoustical difficulties—is the extreme shortness of the second valve slide, which is already of compromise length on the piccolo C trumpet and cannot be pulled out.

Although England was slow to adopt the B♭ or C trumpet, by the 1970s a number of English players were among the most progressive in using an E♭ trumpet in place of the B♭ or C. Unfortunately this involved the loss of a certain fullness of tone, as at the beginning of that century when the B♭ trumpet—called the 'trumpetina' in England—replaced the long F trumpet.

A revival of the natural trumpet of the Baroque period took place in the 20th century. In 1931 Alexander of Mainz built three low-pitch D trumpets ($a' = 415$) after an original by J.J. Schmied (Pfaffendorf, 1767) for the Hoesch Collection (now dispersed); these were tested in concerts of the Kammermusikkreis Scheck-Wenzinger, but with no particular success. Another design built by Alexander, in 8′ pitch with two double bends and two valves, was presented by Werner Menke in 1934. In 1960 Otto Steinkopf, working with the instrument maker H. Finke, devised a trumpet with two vent holes and a transposing hole which not only correct the intonation of the 11th and 13th partials but also improve accuracy by artificially increasing the distance between the partials in the fourth (and fifth) octave. For example, when the hole covered by the ring finger of the right hand is opened, only the 8th, 10th, 12th, 14th, and 16th partials can be sounded, the intervening odd-numbered ones being cancelled out. Walter Holy, first trumpeter of the Cappella Coloniensis, used this instrument with great success in works of Bach and others. The Steinkopf-Finke trumpet was built in coiled form like the instrument held by Gottfried Reiche in the famous portrait by E.G. Haussmann (probably painted in about 1727). Meinl & Lauber (now E. Meinl) and Rainer Egger, working from 1967 with E.H. Tarr, produced trumpets both with and without the three holes after Hans Hainlein (1632), J.L. Ehe (ii) (c1700), J.L. Ehe (iii) (1746), and W.W. Haas; Michael Laird later collaborated with various London makers on a model with four holes. Trumpets with vent holes should not be termed 'natural' (Tarr proposes the neutral term 'Baroque trumpet'). A class for both natural and vented trumpets was set up at the Schola Cantorum Basiliensis (SCB) in 1973 and the instrument subsequently began to be taught in many institutions, notably in Cologne, Karlsruhe, Göteborg, London, Trossingen, and Lyons. J.-F. Madeuf now teaches the natural instrument, thus without vent holes, in Lyons and Basel (SCB).

In 1916 Merri Franquin, professor of trumpet at the Paris Conservatoire, developed a five-valve C trumpet with Jérome Thibouville-Lamy. The fourth valve raised the pitch by a whole tone; the fifth lowered it by a major or minor third, depending on the slide setting. Owing to the complexity of its operation, this instrument never enjoyed wide use. A four-valve trumpet inspired by Franquin was more successful and was played by Roger Voisin during his career as first trumpeter of the Boston SO. The advantages of a whole-tone ascending valve in obtaining correct intonation were also recognized by Armando Ghitalla, Voisin's successor; he encouraged the maker Tottle (Boston) to rebuild Vincent Bach trumpets with a rotary whole-tone ascending valve placed in the middle of the tuning-slide. Renold Schilke's innovations include the tuning-bell, by which the tuning-slide is placed as far toward the bell end of the trumpet as possible, thus reducing internal turbulence and improving the response.

For discussion of trumpet repertory and players, and associated bibliography, *see* GMO.

BIBLIOGRAPHY

A: GENERAL

E.M. von Hornbostel and C. Sachs: 'Systematik der Musikinstrumente', *Zeitschrift für Ethnologie*, vol.46 (1914/R), 553–90

C. Sachs: *The History of Musical Instruments* (New York, 1940/R)

A. Baines: *Brass Instruments: their History and Development* (London, 1980/R1993)

K.A. Gourlay: 'Long Trumpets of Northern Nigeria in History and Today', *AfM*, vol.6/2 (1982), 48–72

R. Meucci: 'Roman Military Instruments and the *Lituus*', *GSJ*, vol.42 (1989), 85–97

D.L. Smithers: 'A New Look at the Historical, Linguistic and Taxonomic Bases for the Evolution of Lip–Blown instruments from Classical Antiquity until the End of the Middle Ages', *HBSJ*, vol.1 (1989), 3–64

R. Boonzajer: 'The Minahassa Bamboo Brass Bands', *Brass Bulletin* (1992), no.77, 38–47

Hajime Fukui: 'The *Hora* (Conch Trumpet) of Japan', *GSJ*, vol.47 (1994), 47–62

C.-G. Alexandrescu: *Blasmusiker und Standartenträger im römischen Heer* (Cluj-Napoca, 2010)

B: THE WESTERN TRUMPET

C. Bendinelli: *Tutta l'arte della trombetta* (MS, 1614; Eng. trans., 1975; facs. ed. with commentary by E.H. Tarr, 2011)

M. Praetorius: *Syntagma musicum*, vol.1 (Wittenberg and Wolfenbüttel, 1614–5, 2/1615/R); vol.2 (Wolfenbüttel, 1618, 2/1619/R; Eng. trans., 1986, 2/1991); vol.3 (Wolfenbüttel, 1618, 2/1619/R)

M. Mersenne: *Harmonie universelle* (Paris, 1636–7/R; Eng. trans. *The Books on Instruments*, 1957)

G. Fantini: *Modo per imparare a sonare di tromba* (Frankfurt, 1638/R); facs. ed. with commentary by E.H. Tarr (Vuarmarens, 2011); Eng. trans., 1975

J.E. Altenburg: *Versuch einer Anleitung zur heroisch-musikalischen Trumpeter- und Pauker-Kunst* (Halle, 1795/R; Eng. trans., 1974)

'Über die neuerlichen Verbesserungen der Trompete und der ihr ähnlichen Blasinstrumente', *AMZ*, vol.17 (1815), 633–8

F.-J. Fétis: 'Cors à pistons', *ReM*, vol.2 (1828), 153–64

K. Bagans: 'On the Trumpet, as at Present Employed in the Orchestra', *American Musical Journal*, vol.1 (1834–5), 252–5

G. Weber: 'Ueber Ventilhorn und Ventiltrompete mit drei Ventilen', *Caecilia* [Mainz], vol.17 (1835), 73–105

H. Eichborn: *Die Trompete in alter und neuer Zeit* (Leipzig, 1881/R)

H. Pietzsch: *Die Trompete als Orchester-Instrument und ihre Behandlung in den verschiedenen Epochen der Musik* (Heilbronn, 1901, 2/1906/R, Ger. and Eng. texts)

V.C. Mahillon: *Instruments à vent*, vol.3: *La trompette* (Brussels, 1907)

F. Jahn: 'Die Nürnberger Trompeten– und Posaunenmacher im 16. Jahrhundert', *AMw*, vol.7 (1925), 23–52

M. Franquin: 'La trompette et le cornet', *EMDC*, vol.2/iii (1927), 1596–637

H. Bouasse: *Instruments à vent* (Paris, 1929/R)

W. Menke: *Die Geschichte der Bach- und Handel-Trompete* (Leipzig, 1934; Eng. trans., 1934/R)

W.F.H. Blandford: 'The "Bach Trumpet"', *MMR*, vol.65 (1935), 49–52, 73–7, 97–101

W. Wörthmüller: 'Die Nürnberger Trompeten– und Posaunenmacher des 17. und 18. Jahrhunderts', *Mitteilungen des Vereins für Geschichte der Stadt Nürnberg*, vol.45 (1954), 208–325; vol.46 (1955), 372–480

Brass Quarterly (1957–64)

H. Bahnert, T. Herzberg and H. Schramm: *Metallblasinstrumente* (Leipzig, 1958, 2/1986)

E. Halfpenny: 'William Shaw's "Harmonic Trumpet"', *GSJ*, vol.13 (1960), 7–13

H. Kirchmeyer: 'Die Rekonstruktion der "Bachtrompete"', *NZM*, vol.122/4 (1961), 137–45

M. Krivin: *A Century of Wind-Instrument Manufacturing in the United States: 1860–1960* (diss., U. of Iowa, 1961)

E. Halfpenny: 'William Bull and the English Baroque Trumpet', *GSJ*, vol.15 (1962), 18–24

F. Lesure: 'Pierre Trichet's *Traité des instruments de musique*: Supplement', *GSJ*, vol.15 (1962), 70–81; vol.16 (1963), 73–84

E. Halfpenny: 'Two Oxford Trumpets', *GSJ*, vol.16 (1963), 49–62

F. Körner: *Studien zur Trompete des 20. Jahrhunderts* (diss., U. of Graz, 1963)

J.M. Barbour: *Trumpets, Horns and Music* (East Lansing, MI, 1964)

Brass World (1965–74)

G.D. Bridges: *Pioneers in Brass* (Detroit, MI, 1965, rev. 2/1968, 3/1972/R)

H. Heyde: *Trompete und Trompeteblasen im europäischen Mittelalter* (diss., U. of Leipzig, 1965)

D. Smithers: 'The Trumpets of J.W. Haas: a Survey of Four Generations of Nuremberg Brass Instrument Makers', *GSJ*, vol.18 (1965), 23–41

J. Wheeler: 'Further Notes on the Classic Trumpet', *GSJ*, vol.18 (1965), 14–22

P. Bate: *The Trumpet and Trombone* (London, 1966, 2/1972/R)

Brass and Woodwind Quarterly (BWQ) (1966–9)

M. Byrne: 'The Goldsmith-Trumpet-Makers of the British Isles', *GSJ*, vol.19 (1966), 71–83

E. Halfpenny: 'Early British Trumpet Mouthpieces', *GSJ*, vol.20 (1967), 76–88

R.E. Eliason: *Brass Instrument Key and Valve Mechanisms Made in America before 1875, with Special Reference to the D.S. Pillsbury Collection in Greenfield Village, Dearborn, Michigan* (diss., U. of Missouri, 1969)

E. Halfpenny: 'Four Seventeenth–Century British Trumpets', *GSJ*, vol.22 (1969), 51–7

Brass Bulletin: International Brass Chronicle (1971–2003)

Sounding Brass (1971–82)

E. Halfpenny: 'Notes on Two Later British Trumpets', *GSJ*, vol.24 (1971), 79–83

D.L. Smithers: 'The Hapsburg Imperial *Trompeter* and *Heerpaucker* Privileges of 1653', *GSJ*, vol.24 (1971), 84–95

K. Pechstein: 'Die Merkzeichentafel der Nürnberger Trompeten– und Posaunenmacher von 1640', *Mitteilung des Vereins für Geschichte der Stadt Nürnberg*, vol.59 (1972), 198–202

E.H. Tarr: 'The Baroque Trumpet, the High Trumpet and the So–Called Bach Trumpet', *Brass Bulletin* (1972), no.2, 30–4, 40–2; (1972), no.3, 44–8, 54–7

K. Wogram: *Ein Beitrag zur Ermittlung der Stimmung von Blechblasinstrumenten* (diss., Technical Institute of Braunschweig, 1972)

D. Altenburg: *Untersuchungen zur Geschichte der Trompete im Zeitalter der Clarinblaskunst 1500–1800* (Regensburg, 1973)

D.L. Smithers: *The Music and History of the Baroque Trumpet before 1721* (London, 1973, 2/1988)

R. Dahlqvist: *The Keyed Trumpet and its Greatest Virtuoso, Anton Weidinger* (Nashville, TN, 1975)

H. Heyde: *Katalog der Blasinstrumente des Musikinstrumentenmuseums der Karl-Marx-Universität Leipzig* (Leipzig, 1975)

Journal of the International Trumpet Guild (1976–)

A. Baines: *Brass Instruments: their History and Development* (London, 1976/R)

P. Righini: 'Dalle trombe egizie per l' "Aida" alle trombe di Tut-Ankh-Amon', *NRMI*, vol.11 (1977), 591–605

D.L. Smithers: 'The Baroque Trumpet after 1721: some Preliminary Observations', *EMc*, vol.5/2 (1977), 177–83; vol.6/39 (1978), 356–61

E.H. Tarr: *Die Trompete* (Berne, 1977, 3/1994, Eng. trans. 2008)

H. Heyde: 'Zur Fruhgeschichte der Ventile und Ventilinstrumente in Deutschland (1814–1833)', *Brass Bulletin* (1978), no.24, 9–33; (1979), no.25, 41–50; (1979), no.26, 69–82; (1979), no.27, 51–9 [with Eng. and Fr. texts]

J. Höfler: 'Der "trompette de ménestrels" und sein Instrument', *TVNM*, vol.29 (1979), 92–132

R. Dahlqvist: 'Some Notes on the Early Valve', *GSJ*, vol.33 (1980), 111–24

M. Haine: *Adolphe Sax (1814–1894): sa vie, son oeuvre, et ses instruments de musique* (Brussels, 1980)

H. Heyde: 'Trompeten, Posaunen, Tuben', *Katalog: Musikinstrumenten-Museum der Karl-Marx-Universität Leipzig*, vol.3 (Leipzig, 1980)

E.H. Tarr: 'Die Musik und die Instrumente der Charamela real in Lissabon', *Forum musicologicum: Basler Studien zur Interpretation der alten Musik*, vol.2 (1980), 181–229

P. Downey: *The Trumpet and its Role in Music of the Renaissance and Early Baroque* (diss., Queen's U. of Belfast, 1983)

P. Downey: 'The Renaissance Slide Trumpet: Fact or Fiction?', *EMc*, vol.12/1 (1984), 26–33

T. MacCracken: 'Die Verwendung der Blechblasinstrumente bei J.S. Bach unter besonderer Berücksichtigung der Tromba da tirarsi', *BJb*, vol.70 (1984), 59–89

C. Ahrens: *Eine Erfindung und ihre Folgen: Blechblasinstrumente mit Ventilen* (Kassel, 1986); Eng. trans. by S. Plank: *Valved Brass: the History of an Invention* (Hillsdale, NY, 2008)

D.L. Smithers, K. Wogram and J.M. Bowsher: 'Playing the Baroque Trumpet', *Scientific American*, vol.254/4 (1986), 108–15

Second Conference of the ICTM Study Group on Music Archaeology: Stockholm 1984, ed. C.S. Lund, vol.2: The Bronze Lurs (Stockholm, 1987)

H. Heyde: *Das Ventilblasinstrument: seine Entwicklung im deutschsprachingen Raum von den Anfängen bis zur Gegenwart* (Leipzig, 1987)

R. Dahlqvist: *Bidrag till trumpeten och trumpetspelets historia: från 1500-talet till mitten av 1800-talet, med särskild hänsyn till perioden 1740–1830* (diss., U. of Göteborg, 1988) [with Eng. summary]

G. Lawson and G. Egan: 'Medieval Trumpet from the City of London', *GSJ*, vol.41 (1988), 63–6

J. Sehnal: 'Die Trompete vom Barock bis zur Klassik', Evropski glasbeni klasicizem in njegov odmev na Slovenskem/Der europäische Musikklassizismus und sein Widerhall in Slowenien: Ljubljana 1988, 53–62 [with Ger. summary]

J. Sehnal: 'Trubači a hra na přirozenou trompetu na moravě v 17. a 18. století, 1. čóst' ('Naturtrompete und Trompeter in Mähren im 17. und 18. Jahrhundert, 1. Teil'), *Acta musei moraviae*, vol.73 (1988), 175–203

J. Webb: 'The Billingsgate Trumpet', *GSJ*, vol.41 (1988), 59–62

Historic Brass Society Journal (HBSJ) (1989–)

F. Anzenberger: *Ein Überblick über die Trompeten- und Kornettschulen in Frankreich, England, Italien, Deutschland und Österreich von ca. 1800 bis ca. 1880* (diss., U. of Vienna, 1989)

K. Polk: 'The Trombone, the Slide Trumpet and the Ensemble Tradition of the Early Renaissance', *EMc*, vol.17/3 (1989), 389–97

D. Lasocki: 'A Bibliography of Writings about Historic Brass Instruments', *HBSJ* (1990–) [annual series]

B. Čížek: 'Josef Kail (1795–1871), Forgotten Brass Instrument Innovator', *Brass Bulletin* (1991), no.73, 64–75; (1991), no.74, 24–9

G. Lawson: 'Medieval Trumpet from the City of London, II', *GSJ*, vol.44 (1991), 150–6

R. Meucci: 'On the Early History of the Trumpet in Italy', *Basler Jb für historische Musikpraxis*, vol.15 (1991), 9–34

R.L. Barclay: *The Art of the Trumpet-Maker: the Materials, Tools, and Techniques of the Seventeenth and Eighteenth Centuries in Nuremberg* (Oxford, 1992)

R. Dahlqvist: 'Pitches of German, French, and English Trumpets in the 17th and 18th Centuries', *HBSJ*, vol.5 (1993), 29–41

E.H. Tarr: 'The Romantic Trumpet', *HBSJ*, vol.5 (1993), 213–61; vol.6 (1994), 110–215

R. Dahlqvist and B. Eklund: 'The Bach Renaissance and the Trumpet', *Euro-ITG Newsletter* (1995), no.1, 12–17

R. Duffin: 'Backward Bells and Barrel–Bells: some Notes on the Early History of Loud Instruments', *HBSJ*, vol.9 (1997), 112–29

T. Herbert and J. Wallace, eds.: *The Cambridge Companion to Brass Instruments* (Cambridge, 1997/R)

G. Doderer: 'Nach Lissabon mit Pauken und Trompeten! Die Verpflichtung eines deutschen Trompeterkorps an den Hof Johanns V. (1723),' *Musica instrumentalis*, vol.3 (2001), 79–103

C. Steele-Perkins: *Trumpet* (London, 2001)

G. Cassone: *La tromba* (Varese, 2002)

G. Dumoulin: 'Cornets in the Brussels Musical Instrument Museum: A Survey and a Checklist of an Outstanding Collection,' *HBSJ*, vol.14 (2002), 425–46

W.R. Kälin: *Die Blasinstrumente in der Schweiz* (Zürich, 2002)

R. Callmar: *Die chromatisierte Trompete: Die Entwicklung der Naturtrompete bis zur Einführung der Ventiltrompete 1750–1850* (diss., Schola Cantorum Basiliensis, 2003)

F. Keim: *Das grosse Buch der Trompete* (Mainz, 2005)

G. Dumoulin: 'The Cornet and Other Brass Instruments in French Patents of the First Half of the Nineteenth Century,' *GSJ*, vol.59 (2006), 77–100

K. Gabbard: *Hotter than That: the Trumpet, Jazz, and American Culture* (New York, 2008)

L.E. Laubhold: *Magie der Macht: Eine quellenkritische Studie zu Johann Ernst Altenburgs Versuch einer Anleitung zur heroisch-musikalischen Trompeter- und Pauker-Kunst (Halle 1795)* (Würzburg, 2009)

MARGARET SARKISSIAN/R (1–3); EDWARD H. TARR (4)

T'rưng [tơ-rưng]. Xylophone of the Central Highlands of Vietnam. The seven to 20 bamboo tubes hang obliquely from two strings on a bamboo frame and are cut in specific ways to tune them, either with the tube partly cut away to the correct length, leaving a long tongue to fit the frame, or with slots of the appropriate length cut into the side of the tube. The t'rưng is played by two performers, each striking the tubes with two wooden round-headed beaters, one playing an ostinato drone with two notes a 4th apart, the other playing the melodic line. The Jörai people's version has 11 tubes.

TRÂN VAN KHÊ/NGUYEN THUYET PHONG

Trường cùng. Slit drum of Vietnam.

Trüstedt, (Wolf-)**Dieter** (*b* Berlin, Germany, 3 Aug 1939). German physicist and experimental instrument builder. He and Ulrike Trüstedt (*b* Altusried, Allgäu, Germany, 24 Feb 1943) formed a duo, performing on electronic instruments of their own design that Dieter has constructed in Munich since 1970. The music is composed by Ulrike, whose scores *Touching* (1978), *Winterfelder* (1980), and *Windharfen* (1981) contain descriptions and illustrations of the instruments.

In *Bewegungs-Hologramm* (1974), movements within a defined space affect a specially devised synthesizer by producing changes in an ultrasonic field. The Lambdoma (1976–7) is a square board of 144 touch-plates for changing the frequency of a specially constructed small monophonic synthesizer; the plates (about a third of which are duplications) produce different transposition ratios, which control the signal from the oscillator. Between 1975 and 2012 the Trüstedts developed a series of instruments called Chin, partly based on the *qin*, a Chinese zither. A typical example of this group (which varies considerably in dimensions) has a narrow, solid cedar body about 150 cm long, divided into sections by two bridges: the outer sections, which are a half and a third of the length of the central one, are called respectively the 'octave' and 'fifth' sections. There are no frets. The five strings (tuned to partials four to eight of the harmonic series) can be rubbed (with fingers or glass rods), struck (with fingers or beaters), plucked (with fingers or a plectrum), bowed (with a violin bow), or blown on by performers or the wind; even the smallest vibrations are picked up by the highly sensitive electromagnetic pickups, which are situated at one end of the central section of the body. A smaller five-string version has also been constructed. Chin instruments have been featured in *Touching* and *Winterfelder* (in which the strings are used to resonate synthesizer sounds); *Windharfen* is scored for two small seven-string Chins, on which the two performers blow. Since 2009, Trüstedt has used a Chin to produce sounds that are altered by a computer.

Trüstedt's first experiment with natural wind and strings involved kites, microphones, and a tape recorder. A wooden board at the end of the nylon kite string amplified the string's vibrations. Between 1974 and 2010 Trüstedt produced a number of large steel-strung, amplified aeolian harp installations. For example, a large 'Windharfe' installed at the University of Ulm in 1991 utilizes an English telephone booth as a listening room with headphones; its sounds have been streamed live over the Internet to computers and mobile phones since March 2010. In these aeolian harps, strings of different thicknesses are tuned to the same pitch or at an octave, each string creating a different overtone series.

At the request of the writer and music producer Joachim-Ernst Berendt, Trüstedt created recordings using sounds generated by the rotation of the Earth and the orbital frequencies of the planets in the solar system, resulting in the CD *Planet Tunes*, released in 2001.

HUGH DAVIES/ANNE BEETEM ACKER

Trutru. Conch horn of Lifu and Lai, Loyalty Islands. See S.H. Ray: 'The People and Language of Lifu, Loyalty Islands', *Journal of the Anthropological Institute of Great Britain and Ireland*, vol.47 (1917), 239–322, 273.

Trutruka. Trumpet of the Mapuche (Araucanian) people of south-central Chile and southwestern Argentina. In the early 18th century the instrument was known as *thouthouca* or *trompette*; it might date back to the early 17th century. It is made from *küla* (*quila* or *colígüe*, mountain bamboo, *Chusquea culeou* or *Chusquea quila*) 3 to 4 metres long and 5 to 6 cm in diameter, with an ox-horn bell attached by vegetable fibres at the distal end. A tube with equal distance between the internal septums is preferred. The *küla* is split in half lengthwise and the septums and loose pulp are removed without damaging the slick inner surface. After drying in the sun the halves are placed together and covered with horse intestine to prevent air leakage. A diagonal cut at the proximal end serves as a mouthpiece. Metal instruments, made from gas- or water-pipes, are known among the Mapuche of Lanalhue, Chile.

The *tuntaman* (*trutrukatufe*, performer) holds the instrument horizontally with help from one or two assistants at the distal end, or rests it on a pole with the horn pointing upwards; he can produce 12 to 13 overtones. The sound of the trutruka is considered magical and facilitates communication between the people and the supernatural world. It is played only by males as a rhythm instrument in the *nguillatún* (fertility rite) and in supplication rituals for rain, food, weather control, and funeral ceremonies. It may also be played for secular entertainment in town squares. Playing requires some exertion and physical strength; *trutruka* pieces are usually short. Pairs of *tuntamanes* play heterophonic duets.

BIBLIOGRAPHY

C. Isamitt: 'Un instrumento araucano, la trutruka', *Boletín latino-americano de música*, vol.1 (1935), 43–6

M. Dannemann: 'The Musical Traditions of the Indigenous Peoples of Chile', *The Word of Music*, vol.19/3–4 (1977), 104–13

JOHN M. SCHECHTER/J. RICHARD HAEFER

Trylodeon. Improved melodeon patented in England (no.2,066, 27 Aug 1860) by Richard Archibald Brooman as agent for Joseph Poole Pirsson. The player controls the registration by finger pressure on the keys. According to the patent claim, each key controls several reeds, producing progressive degrees of loudness. Each reed has its own pallet valve, so arranged that when the key is fully depressed all of its reeds will sound, if pressed less deeply only two will sound, and if depressed slightly only one will sound. If the reeds are tuned slightly out of unison, a vibrato will occur when two or more sound together. Pirsson was an American civil engineer possibly related to the New York piano builders Alexander T. and James Pirsson.

LAURENCE LIBIN

Tsabouna. Greek bagpipe played in the Aegean islands. The bag is made of goatskin, rarely of sheepskin, and the instrument has a double chanter but no separate drone. The chanter normally comprises two cane pipes set in a wooden stock, but occasionally it has twin bores in a single piece of wood, or more rarely a single tube of cane in a wooden stock. The chanter often ends with an upturned bell, or sometimes with an added bell of horn. The reeds are idioglot single reeds, upcut or downcut. The number of fingerholes varies, commonly five in each pipe but sometimes five in one and one, less often two, in the other. The mouthpipe is a tube of wood, cane, or birdbone. The tsabouna is played solo or accompanied by the island drum, the *toubi*. In some islands, notably Karpathos, it is played with the string instruments *lyra* (short-necked fiddle) and/or *laouto* (long-necked lute). See F. Anoyanakis: *Greek Popular Musical Instruments* (Athens, 1979, 2/1991), 168–84.

JEREMY MONTAGU

Tsakara. Percussion plaque of the Gitonga people of the Inhambane region, Mozambique. It is a length of re-used corrugated iron slung from two poles and struck with metal beaters. This is used in dance music, with drums and other loud percussion instruments.

Tsambi. Lamellaphone of the Mayombe region of the Democratic Republic of the Congo. Three types have been reported: a flat-board type with 10 metal tongues; a raft-body type with 11 (apparently) wooden or bamboo tongues; and a box-resonated type with 10 metal tongues. See J.-S. Laurenty: *Les sanza du Congo* (Tervuren, 1962).

FERDINAND J. DE HEN

Tsele. Vessel rattle of the Venda and North Sotho peoples of South Africa. Resembling the Tsonga *ndjele* and the Chopi *njele*, it was formerly made of a calabash containing stones, nowadays usually of a perforated condensed-milk tin pierced by a stick for a handle.

Tsenatsil [sanasel, sinasil]. Sistrum of the Ethiopian Christian Orthodox liturgy. The squared-off U-shaped frame of brass, bronze, silver, or gold is attached at the base to a wooden or metal handle. Two or three metal bars or wires cross between the upright arms of the frame. Each bar carries several thin metal sliding discs or sometimes rings. An open filigree pattern of dots, squares, and other geometrical designs decorates the arms. A tinkling sound is produced when the instrument is shaken. Each part of the tsenatsil has religious meaning and symbolism. Most importantly, the handle represents God, the side arms represent the Old and New Testaments, three discs on the upper cross bar the Trinity, and two discs on the lower bar Jesus as Son of God and of Man. The tsenasil is used exclusively in liturgical chants, dances, and Masses together with the double-headed conical drum *kabaro*. Each priest or deacon holds a tsenatsil in one hand and a prayer staff (*mequamia*) in the other. Apart from the sonorous beats of the *kabaro*, the sistra are rhythmically shaken in unison following given musical rules and the text structure. See M. Powne: *Ethiopian Music, an Introduction: a Survey of Ecclesiastical and Secular Ethiopian Music and Instruments* (London, 1968/R1980).

TIMKEHET TEFFERA

Tshigubu. European-type bass drum of the Venda people of southern Africa, named after the Zulu *isigubhu*.

Tshihoho [mfuhlulu]. Short side-blown horn of the Venda people of South Africa, made from horn, pumpkin stalk, or wood. It is used by boys for signalling. Its alternative name, *mfuhlulu*, means 'ululation'. See P.R. Kirby: *The Musical Instruments of the Native Races of South Africa* (London, 1934, 2/1965/R), 79–80 and pl.29b.

Tshikasa [kikasa]. Drum of the Bena Kalundwe, Luba, and Sanga peoples of the Democratic Republic of the Congo. It has a cylindrical, footed body 1.2 to 1.5 metres long, with a single head nailed on. Among the Luba it is beaten for the enthroning of a chief, or in times of war. See O. Boone: *Les tambours du Congo belge et du Ruanda-Urundi* (Tervuren, 1951), 57 only.

FERDINAND J. DE HEN

Tshikona. Stopped flute ensemble of the Venda of South Africa. The single-note end-blown pipes (*nanga*, pl. *dzinanga*) are made of bamboo, closed by the natural node, the embouchure cut at a right angle. They are blown with the player's tongue extended and hollowed to direct the wind stream. A full set (*mutavha*) consists of 18 to 28 named flutes covering a minimum heptatonic range of two octaves and a 4th at a common shared Venda pitch. Some sets cover up to four octaves. The naming varies, but always contains *phala*, the principal note. A set of 24 flutes made by tshikona teacher Tshoteli Netshivari in 2004 was named, from the lowest note upwards: *tshiaravi, nzhingi, thakula, phala, kholomo, dangwe, veve*, then one more octave with the same names plus four more flutes up to high *phala*, and several duplicates. The players, who may number 60 locally or up to as many as 200 at national events, dance anti-clockwise in a circle around a set of drums: two *ngoma* (large, bowl-shaped, closed drums, struck with sticks) and one or more *murumba* (conical, open, hand-struck drums). The leader-instructor stands inside the circle and indicates the order of events. The flute players were traditionally men and the drummers women, but roles have relaxed in modern times. An all-women group exists, as do university and school groups with children as young as six years. There is only one tshikona tune, but a repertory of many intricate and challenging dance steps; more are continually added. The music can be described as two continuously descending scales a 4th or 5th apart, but the aural impression is complex and serves as a template for much else in Venda music. The tshikona dance is considered the property of hereditary chiefs; its role is thus primarily political and as a marker of Venda identity. It is performed in the course of initiation schools (the ritual process of initiating young people into adulthood) and other public and national events such as openings and installations.

BIBLIOGRAPHY

P.R. Kirby: *The Musical Instruments of the Native Races of South Africa* (London, 1934, 2/1965/R)

J. Blacking: *Venda Children's Songs: a Study in Ethnomusicological Analysis* (Pretoria, 1967/R)

ANDREW TRACEY

Tshilembe. Whistle of the Luluwa people in the Kasayi region, Democratic Republic of the Congo. The wooden barrel-shaped body is about 7.5 cm long. See J.-S. Laurenty: *Systématique des aérophones de l'Afrique centrale* (Tervuren, 1974), 97 only.

FERDINAND J. DE HEN

Tshingufu [tshinguvu, txinguvo] (pl. *inguvo*). Large trapezoidal slit drum of the Lunda and Tshokwe peoples of Angola and the Democratic Republic of the Congo. The Tshokwe slit drum is beaten on both sides with two sticks by the leading drummer of a group of musicians. It may be played solo but usually appears with three or four cup-shaped *ngoma* drums and one or two *mukupiela* drums for festive dances, war songs, wedding songs, and dance songs of the hunters' group. The tshingufu gives the basic beat and provides numerous rhythmic variations. In the Lunda/Lóvua district of Angola it is made from a hollowed tree trunk, and a wire hook on one side of the slit supports two rattling metal rings; it is suspended by thongs from two forked wooden posts and played with two rubber-tipped beaters, either to accompany dancing (with other drums) or to transmit messages. The interval between the two tones is a 5th, and the higher tone is called *mwana* ('child') and the lower *makwend* ('woman').

BIBLIOGRAPHY

G. Knosp: *Enquête sur la vie musicale au Congo belge 1934–1935* (Tervuren, 1968)

B. Schmidt-Wrenger: *Muziek van de Tshokwe uit Zaïre* (Tervuren, 1975)

M.L. Bastin: 'Musical Instruments, Songs and Dances of the Chokwe', *AfM*, vol.7/2 (1992), 23–44

Tshintengula. Whistle of the Kete people of the Democratic Republic of the Congo. The conical wooden body is about 18 cm long. See J.-S. Laurenty: *Systématique des aérophones de l'Afrique centrale* (Tervuren, 1974), 137 only.

Tshiondo. War drum of the Kanyoka people of the Democratic Republic of the Congo. Before the 1920s it was played in the process of manufacturing a chief's drum. *Tshiondo* also denotes a slit drum. See O. Boone: *Les tambours du Congo belge et du Ruanda-Urundi* (Tervuren, 1951), 53 only.

FERDINAND J. DE HEN

Tshipotoliyo (pl. *zwipotoliyo*). Vessel flute of the Venda people of southern Africa. It is made from the spherical shell of the *muthuzwu* wild custard apple (*Oncoba spinosa*) or the *muramba* bush orange (*Strychnos spinosa*). It has two fingerholes and a slightly larger mouth hole. The instruments are made by boys and played in duet, the two flutes being of unequal size. The Tsonga *shiwaya,* the Chopi *chigowilo* (an instrument for young girls), and the Ndau *gorwe* are similar. See J. Blacking: 'Problems of Pitch, Pattern and Harmony in the Ocarina Music of the Venda', *AfM*, vol.2/2 (1959), 15–23.

ANDREW TRACEY

Tshipwidi. Vessel flute of the Luluwa people in the southwestern Democratic Republic of the Congo. It is made from a seed pod about 5 cm long. It supposedly has four fingerholes and is decorated with spots of colour. See J.-S. Laurenty: *Systématique des aérophones de l'Afrique centrale* (Tervuren, 1974), 222 only.

Tshisaji [tshisaandj, tshisaanji, tshisaandji, tshisanji, tshisanshi, tshisazi tsha mudidi]. Term for several types of lamellaphone in western and southern regions of the Democratic Republic of the Congo and neighbouring countries; for many other variants *see* Kisaanj. The variant terms probably reflect minor differences in the use of prefixes and the lack of standard orthography. Tshisaji has been reported as a lamellaphone of the Lunda, with three rows of metal tongues tuned in octaves; it is played to praise the chief, for entertainment, and to accompany narrative songs and dances of circumcised boys and hunters. Tshisaji has also been given as a generic term for the lamellaphone of the Tshokwe; it has metal tongues and is used both solo and to accompany singing. Probably the type most widely used by the Tshokwe is the *tshisaji kakolondondo* with eight to 11 metal tongues mounted on a rectangular wooden board; during performance, it is placed on top of a gourd resonator, the upper quarter of which has been cut away. The instrument has been recorded played by a blacksmith to accompany a song from the secret *mungonge* rites. The *tshisaji mutshapata* has an open box resonator on which are usually fitted 17 tongues. Towards the back of the box is a soundhole to which a membrane (mirliton) is affixed, to add a buzzing sound. Wide metal rings hanging freely on an iron frame by

the lower opening of the box rattle continuously during performance.

Among the other terms, *tshisaandj, tshisaanji,* and *tshisandji* have been used for a board lamellaphone of the Luluwa, a raft lamellaphone of the Luluwa Luntu and Suku, and a box-resonated lamellaphone of the Mvula; *tshisanji* for a lamellaphone of the Luntu, either box-resonated with metal tongues or mounted on a raft-type base with wooden tongues; *tshisanshi* for a lamellaphone of the Luba of the Dibaya region of the DRC; and *tshisazi tsha mudidi* for an instrument of the Binji of the Kasayi region with wooden tongues mounted on a raft-type base.

BIBLIOGRAPHY
F.J. de Hen: *Beitrag zur Kenntnis der Musikinstrumente aus Belgisch Kongo und Ruanda-Urundi* (Tervuren, 1960)
J.-S. Laurenty: *Les sanza du Congo* (Tervuren, 1962), 191, 195
G. Knosp: *Enquête sur la vie musicale au Congo belge 1934–1935* (Tervuren, 1968)
B. Schmidt-Wrenger: *Muziek van de Tshokwe uit Zaïre* (Tervuren, 1975)
J. Gansemans and B.Schmidt-Wrenger: *Zentralafrika* (Leipzig, 1986), 148 only
M.L. Bastin: 'Musical Instruments, Songs and Dances of the Chokwe', *AfM*, vol.7/2 (1992), 23–44

K.A. GOURLAY, PETER COOKE

Tshishiba. Set of two carved wooden whistles of the Kasayi region of the Democratic Republic of the Congo. One, about 15 cm long (called *tshishiba*), is a vessel type with one fingerhole, the other, about 10 cm long (*kashiba*) is Y-shaped and has two fingerholes. Both instruments are decorated with burnt lines. See J.-S. Laurenty: *Systématique des aérophones de l'Afrique centrale* (Tervuren, 1974), 103 only.

FERDINAND J. DE HEN

Tshitiringo. Transverse flute of the Venda of South Africa. It is made from reed; both ends are stopped. There are three fingerholes near the distal end, and sometimes a single hole midway. It is played by boys while herding cattle. The Tsonga *shitloti*; Pedi *naka;* Lovedu *setodiko;* Shona *muranzi, nyere,* and *chinyunjé*; Swazi *umntshingozi*; and Tsonga *msengele* are nearly similar. See P.R. Kirby: *The Musical Instruments of the Native Races of South Africa* (London, 1934, 2/1965/R), 122, pl.43.

ANDREW TRACEY

Tshotsha. Rattles worn for dancing by Tshokwe women in the Democratic Republic of the Congo. They are made from husks of fruit strung together and wound around the ankle.

Tsibïzga. Obsolete end-blown flute of the Kalmyk people of Central Asia, probably related to the Kazakh *sibizgi* and the Tatar-Bashkir *kurai.*

Tsii' edo'ałi [tsii' edo'a'tl] (Apache: 'wood singing') [Apache fiddle]. Single- or two-string 'fiddle', technically a bowed tube zither, of the White Mountain and San Carlos Apache peoples of Arizona. Its origin is unknown. A 30- to 40-cm length of a dried flower stem of the agave plant (*Agave angustifolia*) about 5 to 7 cm in diameter

Tsii' edo'ałi, Apache, 1990s. (Aurelia W. Hartenberger, EdD)

is cut in half and the pith removed except for a 3-cm section left at each end to stop the tube and strengthen it. The two halves are glued back together with pine pitch and wrapped at intervals with sinew or baling wire. A lump of pinyon pine pitch might be melted onto one end to provide rosin for the bow. One string (seldom two) is attached at the proximal end and runs over two low bridges to a long tuning peg inserted laterally through the tube. One or two small soundholes, often triangular, are cut near each end. Old museum specimens are usually shorter than modern instruments, but the maker Chelsey Goseyun Wilson claims that earlier examples were made not only from the stem but also from the heart of the agave and were up to 55 cm long and 15 to 20 cm in diameter at the proximal end.

The bow is made from a bent twig of walnut or sumac, somewhat flattened on the concave side. It is strung with horse hair. The fiddle is held with the proximal end to the player's chest below the breast; the string is fingered by the left hand and bowed with the right. It is played for personal entertainment and often called by the humourous onomatopoetic name *kízh kízh díhí* ('buzz buzz sound'); its sound has been described as thin and weak, faint and dry, and like a wild cat. Early museum specimens are undecorated, but late-19th-century examples have geometric designs incised, and post-1920 examples are often colourfully painted.

BIBLIOGRAPHY
D.P. McAllester: 'An Apache Fiddle', *EthM*, vol.1/8 (1956), 1–5
G. Laczko: *Apache Music and Musical Instruments* (Mesa, AZ, 1981)
C.G. Wilson: *When the Earth was Like New: Western Apache Songs & Stories* (Danbury, CT, 1994) [incl. CD]

J. RICHARD HAEFER/R

Tsimbi. Lamellaphone of the Loango region of the western Democratic Republic of the Congo. It has six or seven metal tongues and a resonator made of a hollowed piece of wood. It is open on the end nearer the player and beak-shaped at the opposite, closed end. The Sundi call it *kongo di longo* and the Suku *kisaanj*. See J.-S. Laurenty: *Les sanza du Congo* (Tervuren, 1962), 194 only.

FERDINAND J. DE HEN

Tsinda [ntshinda]. Drum of the Mbole, Kutu, and Saka peoples of the Democratic Republic of the Congo. The single head is nailed to the footed body, which is decorated with geometrical incisions. It resembles the Nkundo *bondundu*. See O. Boone: *Les tambours du Congo belge et du Ruanda-Urundi* (Tervuren, 1951), 22, 62.

FERDINAND J. DE HEN

Tsindeche. Metal leg bells of the Wanga people of Northern Nyanza district, Kenya.

Tsindza [shinji]. Portable xylophone of Nigeria. The term *tsindza* is used by the Bura people, *shinji* by the adjoining Tera people. The instrument consists of seven wooden bars strung together within a circular frame, each bar being placed above a cow-horn resonator, the tip of which has been replaced by a spider's web mirliton. An unusual feature is that the player has a forked stick in each hand so that he can strike two adjacent keys at the same time or, by turning the stick, one only. The instrument is played either solo or in sets of up to three, usually with drums, to accompany dancing. Similar xylophones are found among the Bachama and Lala (Ga'anda) peoples; the Lala, however, leave the tips of the resonating horns in place and always use their instruments in a battery of seven rested on the ground. See J.G. Davies: *The Biu Book* (Zaria, 1954–6).

K.A. GOURLAY

Tsinidi'ni' [tsindi'ni', cin diṅi']. Bullroarer of the Diné (Navajo) people of the southwestern USA. It is a spatulate flat blade of wood about 20 cm long by 3 to 4 cm wide and 75 mm thick, made from lightning-struck ponderosa pine or oak, with the growing tip of the wood forming the point of the instrument. A hole is bored in the opposite end and a length of mountain sheep hide, a buckskin thong, or a cord 150 to 180 cm long is attached. It is swung by the cord to produce the sound. The wood can be painted a solid colour or with designs; it can also be decorated with three small pieces of turquoise or white shell attached with pitch on one side to create eyes and a mouth. The bullroarer is used to represent thunder, the voice of the Flint People, or supernatural noises in curing ceremonies such as Shootingway, Windway, and Red Antway. It is also used in the ceremonies of the Native American Church.

Similar instruments are found in other southwestern cultures including the Tohono O'odham (*we:wegidakuḍ*), the Mohave (*ual ual*), Apache (*tzi-ditindi*), and Hopi (*tovokimpi*). The Western Apache *gaan* dancers carry a *tzi-ditindi* that consists of two rectangular pieces of wood about 15 to 20 cm long attached by a long cord. One piece serves as a handle while the other is decorated in geometric patterns symbolic of wind and lightening. It is used in curing ceremonies. The O'odham instrument was used in the old *we:igita* or harvest ceremony to simulate the sound of thunder. It consists of one or two wooden blades similar in size to the Apache's, though several museum examples have one blade attached to a 50- to 75-cm stick by a long cord. They were generally undecorated. The Hopi instrument always has only one blade attached to a 60- to 70-cm cord (length measured from the heart to the tip of the fingers of the performer). The distal end of the blade may be carved in a cloud design, and lightning, wind, and corn may be painted on it. The instruments symbolize thunder and wind in *katsina* ceremonies. See C. Kluckhohn and others: *Navaho Material Culture* (Cambridge, MA, 1971).

DAVID P. MCALLESTER/CHARLOTTE
J. FRISBIE, J. RICHARD HAEFER

Tsintsima. Open goblet drum of the Zamfara Hausa people of Nigeria. It has two snares and tuning paste on the head. The head is lapped on a ring and tensioned by parallel cords to rows of horizontal cords, with a single horizontal bracing cord that draws pairs of the vertical cords together for tuning. The instrument, hung from the player's left shoulder and beaten with both hands, is used for praise singing in front of hunters' compounds and at festivities. Previously in wartime it was used by infantry. See K. Krieger: 'Musikinstrumente der Hausa', *Baessler-Archiv* [new ser.], vol.16 (1968), 373–430.

Ts'its'ǫ́ǫ́s ['atsázooł cisǫ́•s]. Whistle used to represent bird calls in ceremonies of the Diné (Navajo) people of the southwestern USA. It is made from a reed stalk or the femur of an eagle and is about 15 cm long. A notch is cut into the upper side of the tube about 3 cm from the top. The tube is blocked at the notch with pitch and a rolled section of corn husk is placed over the opening to direct the air into the lower section. Some sources say the distal end is closed with pitch, but more often the whistle is played with the distal end underwater so that bird-like trills are produced. In the Shootingway ceremony, songs of the last four days are accompanied by the whistle with a beaver- or otter-skin collar attached to it, together with a basket drum (*ts'aa' náhideesh ghał*). The whistle is also used in Lightningway, Mountainway, and Nightway ceremonies and those of the Native American Church.

The *'atsázooł* is a whistle made from the femur of a jackrabbit that has been killed by an eagle. Its sound is believed to invoke the power of thunder as a supernatural being and it is used only in the Beadway and Eagleway ceremonies.

Bee'ídílzóółí is another term for ceremonial whistles. An obsolete end-blown flute formerly used in Enemyway ceremonies and to accompany corn grinding had two names, *ts'sǫǫs* and *ńdilnih*. A child's toy called *t'iis bitąą' bee'ídílzóółí* made by Diné boys consists of a folded cottonwood leaf which is held against the teeth and made to vibrate with the breath. See C. Kluckhohn and others: *Navaho Material Culture* (Cambridge, MA, 1971).

DAVID P. MCALLESTER/CHARLOTTE
J. FRISBIE, J. RICHARD HAEFER

Tsntsgha. Small cymbal of Armenia. While instruments other than the organ are uncommon in the Armenian Apostolic Church, two tsntsgha are sometimes used during the singing of certain *sharagan* (hymns), such as 'Glory to God on High'. Alternatively, a single tsntsgha may be struck with a felted mallet. Some bronze specimens found at Karmir Blur, Yerevan, date from the 7th century bce. They are similar to small modern cymbals.

JONATHAN MCCOLLUM

Tsuchibue. Ancient Japanese clay vessel flute, similar to the *xun* of China and the *hun* of Korea. The numerous examples known from prehistoric Japan are the only unmistakable musical instruments documented in Japan before the *wagon* of the 1st or 2nd century. The earlier of two types is rather flat, often shaped like a turtle or fish, usually with a hole on either surface (one of which is presumed to be a mouth-hole). This might be related to a Chinese type shaped like a 'flattened round fish' found at the neolithic site Huo Shao Guo in 1976. However, some doubt remains as to whether the Japanese specimens are instruments at all. 20 or more have been found, almost all from north Japan and probably dating from the 1st millennium bce. By the Yayoi period (*c*250 bce–*c*250 ce), the second type had appeared, closely resembling the egg-shaped *xun* of Shang and later periods. Several have been found in west Japan, all with four fingerholes on one side and two for the thumbs on the opposite side, and averaging about 7 cm in height. Unlike Chinese examples, however, the mouth-hole is at the broader end of the 'egg'. Several objects from this date might be stone flutes, but no conclusion is yet possible.

BIBLIOGRAPHY
K.-W. Tong: 'Shang Musical Instruments', *AsM*, vol.15/1 (1983), 17–182, 153
D.W. Hughes: 'Music Archaeology of Japan: Data and Interpretation', *The Archaeology of Early Music Cultures*, eds. E. Hickmann and D.W. Hughes (Bonn, 1988)

DAVID W. HUGHES

Tsudi. Pipe of the Chopi people of southern Mozambique. It is made of reed, stopped at the bottom by the natural node or with black beeswax, and is end-blown to sound one note. Unlike other southern African single-note pipes the tsudi is blown with lips alone, without extended tongue. Eight to 16 or more are tuned to a heptatonic scale and played in ensemble. On moonlit nights, boys and young men get away from adult supervision, accompanying themselves with the regular beat of hand rattles and the sound of ankle rattles on one leg only. The leader blows a small metal whistle. On his signal all perform pre-rehearsed, irregular circle-dance steps, while blowing their pipes. The dance is now rare. See H. Tracey: *Catalogue of the Sound of Africa Series* (Roodepoort, 1973), vol.2, 467 only.

ANDREW TRACEY

Tsugaru shamisen [Tsugaru jamisen]. Type of Japanese long lute. The term *Tsugaru shamisen* refers to the region in which the instrument developed, the type of instrument itself, and the music played on it. As a distinct type of *shamisen*, it has several unique features, including a particularly thick neck (*futozao*: 'thick neck'); a very forceful plucking style using a thick spatula-shape plectrum that frequently strikes the dog-skin soundtable in a loud percussive way; a large and heavy sound box; a metal screw (*azumazawari*) on the neck that is adjusted to touch the lowest string in order to produce a vibrating sound; a left-hand style that includes numerous left-hand hammer-on and pull-off techniques on the strings, continually altering the position of plucking; and a popularity in modern culture that has seen the instrument disseminated all over Japan with much new music written for it in solo and crossover styles.

The Tsugaru region is to the west of Aomori prefecture, to the far northwest of Japan's main island of Honshū. This area was historically quite remote and many of its music genres developed with less influence on them than some other styles of Japanese music. The region has many cultural traits that distinguish it from other parts of Japan, such as its own dialect, lacquerware, and performing arts. Tsugaru shamisen has its roots in the late 19th century with the seminal *shamisen* player Nitabō (1857–1928). There were many influences on the music, and some early players were also wandering beggars. Other notable players include Takahashi Chikuzan (1910–98), one of the last of the itinerant blind tsugaru-shamisen performers. The instrument is used in a range of genres, including as accompaniment to folk songs, solo pieces, ensemble, and crossover music. In each style, the sounds of the instrument are dominated by its virtuosic and percussive style of playing. It is also Japan's only true solo *shamisen* tradition, in which a player's long improvisation must avoid repetitiousness.

The modern style of performance developed rapidly after World War II, and especially from the 1960s. There are more than 50,000 players in Japan nowadays, about 20 schools of performance, and many competitions. In the cities of Hirosaki and Aomori in Aomori prefecture, there are several 'live houses' that promote the instrument's music. Younger players often perform in the live houses and some have developed national and international careers.

BIBLIOGRAPHY

N. Suda, K. Daijô, and A. Rausch: *The Birth of Tsugaru Shamisen Music: the Origin and Development of a Japanese Folk Performing Art* (Aomori, 1998)

H. Johnson: *The Shamisen: Tradition and Diversity* (Leiden, 2010)

DAVID W. HUGHES/HENRY JOHNSON

Tsuhni muyake. Duct whistle of the Comanche people of Oklahoma. It is called by other names among many Plains and neighbouring Indian peoples, e.g. the Ute *gusau-ōka*, and the Choctaw *o'skula*. The whistle is made from an eagle, turkey, or goose wing bone about 10 to 18 cm long. Marrow and fat are removed and the proximal end opened for blowing. A V- or U-shaped mouth is cut on the side of the bone about a quarter of the length from the proximal end. A plug made of pitch is inserted in the bone to form a duct directing the air toward the lip of the mouth. The bone may be decorated with incised designs or covered with bead- or quill-work; white eagle feathers are usually attached near the proximal end. A leather thong is attached to the bone so the whistle can be worn around the neck of the player. Bone whistles are used for signalling and in Native American Church ceremonies and are required for the Sun Dance. In some cultures they were and may still be part of a medicine bundle.

J. RICHARD HAEFER

Tsuji, Hiroshi (*b* Aichi-ken, Japan, 10 Dec 1933; *d* Shirakawa, Japan, 22 Dec 2005). Japanese organ builder and organist. He graduated in 1958 from the Geijutsu Daigaku (music school) in Tokyo, where he had become interested in the workings of the school's organ. He served an apprenticeship with the Schlicker Organ Co. of Buffalo, New York, from 1960 to 1963, and with Flentrop Orgelbouw, Zaandam, Netherlands, from 1963 to 1964. Returning to Japan, he opened his own workshop in a Tokyo suburb, and later moved to a larger shop in Shirakawa, Kurokawa. He was the first Japanese craftsman to have undertaken the building of pipe organs in the 20th century. In 1971 he began a study of the historic organs of Europe, and later built several organs based on north European and Italian models, all of which have mechanical action and classical voicing. In 1984 he restored an 18th-century organ in Pistoia, Italy, and in the 1990s also restored the Renaissance organ in the Cathedral of Salamanca, Spain; thereafter some Spanish elements appeared in some of his larger organs. Tsuji built 81 organs between 1964 and 2005, including several practice and continuo organs, and all are characterized by impeccable workmanship, refined sound, and classical case design. Important instruments include those in Tokai University (1975); St Paul's Church, Tokyo (1976); Nagoya Gakuin University (1984); Seinan Gakuin University (1987); Aoyama Gakuin, Shibuya (1994); and the Protestant Church, Kobe (2001). His largest organ (three manuals, 45 stops) was built in 1994/9 for Salamanca Hall in Gifu.

BIBLIOGRAPHY

B. Owen: 'The Organ in Japan', *The Diapason*, vol.68 (Aug 1977), 1ff

P. Planyavsky: 'Hiroshi Tsuji and his Organs', *Reibai to ongaku* [Music and Worship] (Autumn 1981)

BARBARA OWEN/R

Tsula ya noko. Multiple whistle of the Pedi (Northern Sotho) people of southern Africa. It is made from about eight to 12 porcupine quills. The points of the quills are embedded in wax or affixed together; the open ends fan out and are blown across to produce random pitches. They are not tuned. They were formerly used by herbalists to prevent the spread of epidemics. See P.R. Kirby: *The Musical Instruments of the Native Races of South Africa* (London, 1934, 2/1965/R1968), 101–2 and pls.34a (2), 35b.

Tsuridaiko. Large barrel drum, with the heads tacked to the body, of the Japanese gagaku (court music) (*tsuri*: 'suspended'; *daiko/taiko*: generic term for drums). It is about 55 cm in diameter and 15 to 20 cm deep, and is suspended in a stand similar to, but smaller and less ornate than, the *dadaiko* stand. While the *dadaiko* is used in most dance pieces, the much smaller *tsuridaiko* accompanies instrumental pieces and a few small-scale dances. Its elaborately painted front head is struck with two padded sticks. The drum is also referred to as *gaku-daiko* or simply *taiko*, and the term *tsuridaiko* taken literally is occasionally applied to other drums which are suspended from a rope or in a frame. See F. Piggott: *The Music and Musical Instruments of Japan* (London, 1893, 2/1909/R), 160 only.

DAVID W. HUGHES

Tsutsubini. Bamboo stamping tube of the Banoni people, Papua New Guinea. It is about 2 metres long, with one end closed by a node and the other open. The closed end is stamped on a *tatatsuwe* board (about 6 metres long) to accompany women's *dare* songs. The *makau taposa* is a similar instrument, but with the open end split so that it rattles. Both types are stamped directly on the ground for *tsigul* dances, introduced from Buka Island in the 1930s. See R.N. Stella: *Forms and Styles of Traditional Banoni Music* (Boroko, 1990), 39–40.

REGIS STELLA

Tsuur [tsoor]. End-blown flute of western Mongolia. It is made of larch, with three fingerholes. It is used by the Altai-Urianghai people, and playing includes growling into the instrument to produce a low drone. Various traditional melodies (*tatlaga*) are played, often imitating natural sounds such as water, animal cries, and birdsong. The Urianghai called the tsuur 'the father of music' and its prominent place in music-making is reflected in the tradition of beginning a feast with the melody 'In Praise of the Altai' played on the tsuur.

A 17th-century description of the Kalmyk people by Johannes Milan mentions a long flute which makes a deep noisy sound, and the technique of playing the *tsuur* was described by P.S. Pallas (*Sammlungen historischer Nachrichten über die mongolischen Völkerschaften*, vol.1, Frankfurt and Leipzig, 1776/R). A three-hole pipe, *hujia*, in use in Mongolian music during the Manchu dynasty, was believed to possess the magical property of bringing lambs' bones back to life. The classical Mongolian word *čugur* has been used since the 14th century in literary texts. In the epic *Jangar* the tsuur is described as being played together with the *yatuga* or *yatga* (zither) and as having a voice like a swan.

BIBLIOGRAPHY

A.V. Florovskij: 'Ein tschechischer Jesuit unter den Asowschen Kalmücken', *Archiv orientälni*, vol.12 (1941), 162–88

W. Eberhard: 'Lokalkulturen im alten China', vol.1: 'Die Lokalkulturen des Nordens und Westens', *T'oung pao*, vol.37 (1942), suppl.

ANDREA NIXON

Tsuzumi. Generic term for the Japanese hourglass drum with heads laced to the body. In its narrowest sense it refers particularly to the *kotsuzumi*.

Tsuzumi is the only term for drum encountered in Japan's earliest written sources, which purported to chronicle the indigenous culture before the apogee of Chinese and Korean influence. What sort of drum this term referred to is not clear. The only distinct examples of Japanese drums, before the known imports of about the 8th century, are those depicted in two clay tomb figurines (*haniwa*) from a single tomb dating from the 6th or 7th century. Both drums have two heads and are hung diagonally across the chest by straps across the right shoulder. One is barrel-shaped and played with a stick in the right hand and apparently the bare left hand. (A similar technique is used today for the Korean hourglass drum *changgo*.) The other drum, somewhat damaged, is thinner, perhaps slightly narrow-waisted; the hands are positioned as in the other figurine although the stick is missing, if indeed one was ever present.

That *tsuzumi* need not have referred only to hourglass drums can be gathered from occasional extant exceptions such as the pellet drum *furitsuzumi*, the barrel drum *chijin* (the Okinawan pronunciation of *tsuzumi*), and the dancer's prop in the *nō* play *Aya no tsuzumi*. The word *tsuzumi* itself might not be indigenous, since there is no likely native etymology. One scholar has related it, not implausibly, to the Vedic Indian drum name *dundubhi*, and a surviving folk drum of north India is called *tudum*. (*Tsuzumi* would have been pronounced *tudumi* about the 6th century.) It is agreed that the hourglass drum spread from India via China and Korea to Japan.

The oldest extant drums in Japan are kept in the 8th-century Shōsōin imperial repository. There are the bodies of 22 almost identical drums, known as *kuretsuzumi*, about 41 cm long and 14 cm in diameter. Supposedly imported from Korea in the 7th century for use in the lively dancing known as *gigaku*, they are smoothly concave in profile rather than hourglass-shaped; pictorial evidence suggests they would have been hung at the waist and played on both heads with bare hands. The only other Shōsōin drum is a ceramic imitation of a drum body, perhaps a *ni-no-tsuzumi*, showing the subsequently more typical hourglass shape.

Fortunately the Shōsōin also contains the badly damaged remains of one laced drumhead, which confirms the existence in Japan by this time of the technique of first lapping the skins to iron rings and then lacing the resulting stretched heads to each other around the body. The diameter of the head in such cases is approximately twice that of the body.

The earliest representatives of this hourglass drum family seem to have been the graduated series (in ascending order of size) *ikko* (or *ichi-no-tsuzumi*), *ni-no-tsuzumi*, *san-no-tsuzumi*, and *shi-no-tsuzumi* ('number one, two, three, and four *tsuzumi*'). They were used in *gagaku* (court music) and apparently were once played with the bare left hand and a stick in the right hand (as is the current practice with the Korean *changgo*), but the left hand was eventually demoted to simply holding the drum steady. The *ikko* and *san-no-tsuzumi* are still in use in the court orchestra. The *ikko* is about 36 cm long with a head diameter of 24 cm. It is placed horizontally in front of the player, who strikes only the right head. It has long been replaced by the *kakko* in all but a couple of special contexts such as the court orchestra. The *san-no-tsuzumi* is used in the *komagaku* genre of *gagaku*, in which it is limited to three short, simple rhythmic patterns. The diameter of the head is about 42 cm and the body length 45 cm. The drum lies horizontally in front of the player, who steadies it with his left hand while striking only the right head with a thin stick. The only other members of this class are the *kotsuzumi* and *ōtsuzumi*, but the date of their emergence cannot be fixed.

BIBLIOGRAPHY

R. Emmert and Y. Minegishi, eds.: *Musical Voices of Asia* (Tokyo, 1980)

'Tsuzumi', *Ongaku daijiten* [Encyclopedia of Music] (Tokyo, 1981)

A. Tamba: *The Musical Structure of Nō* (Tokyo, 1981)

W.P. Malm: *Traditional Japanese Music and Musical Instruments* (Tokyo, 2000, [incl. CD]

DAVID W. HUGHES/R

Ttimba. Large drum of the Ganda people of Uganda. It has a single head nailed on, and an exaggerated barrel shape with a narrow open end that flares outward at the base. It is suspended from the neck of the player and beaten by both hands. It is the most venerated drum of the Buganda royal court, and was possibly once used by mediums and priests at python centres such as Buddo, where the coronation rites are customarily performed. Ttimba translates as 'python' and a unique feature is the relief carving of a serpent extending around the widest part of the drum. See M. Trowell and K.P. Wachsmann: *Tribal Crafts of Uganda* (London, 1953), 167 and pl.85.

K.A. GOURLAY/PETER COOKE

Ttunttun [thun thun, tuntun]. (1) Basque term for the tabor (*danbolin*).

(2) Basque term for the *tambourin de Beárn*.

Ṭūaṭa. Trumpet of Iraq, known also by the generic name *būq*; it is probably of Zoroastrian origin. It measures up to 120 cm long, and is made from one or more lengths of soldered metal, of which the last forms a bell. The player points the instrument upwards at an angle, one hand framing the mouthpiece and the other supporting the instrument in the middle. These trumpets are an essential part of the ceremony of the ninth day of Muharram, commemorating the martyrdom of Husayn, son of 'Alī (626–680). Several rows of *ṭūaṭa* form the *firqa būqqīa* ('trumpet ensemble'), painted in bright colours; they produce absurd sounds symbolizing the army of Husayn's enemies. See S. Qassim Hassan: *Les instruments de musique en Irak et leur rôle dans la société traditionelle* (Paris, 1980).

SCHEHERAZADE QASSIM HASSAN

Tuba (i). Wide-bore valved brass instrument. It is used as a bass or contrabass member of the band or orchestral brass section. The term is applied to instruments of various sizes and shapes with a wide, conical bore, three to six (rarely seven) valves, and an open (no valves operated) tube length of at least 8′, giving a pedal (fundamental) note of *C* or below. Several members of the tuba family are commonly called by other names, for example the euphonium, bombardon, sousaphone, and

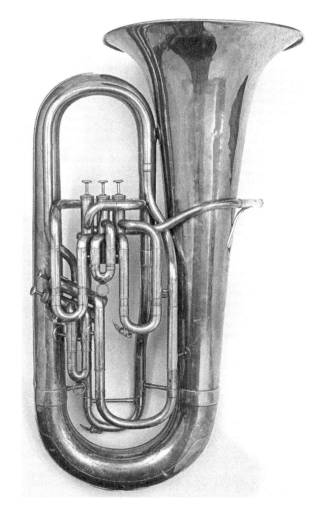

Tuba in 12′ F, five-valve, Barlow model. Besson & Co, London, c1931. (Edinburgh University Collection of Historic Musical Instruments (5848))

helicon. The lower members of the saxhorn group may be included in the tuba family. The Wagner tuba has characteristics of both horn and tuba. The tuba, basically a valved bugle, is a comparative newcomer to the brass section (the first instrument so named, a five-valve *Bass-Tuba*, was introduced in Germany in 1835). Unlike the trumpet and horn, it has no direct ancestors among the valveless brasses; the ophicleide—a keyed brass instrument made in contralto, bass, and contrabass sizes—is probably its closest predecessor. Other bass lip-reed instruments superseded by the tuba are the russian bassoon, bass-horn, and serpent.

Tuba parts are usually notated at sounding pitch, but in British brass bands and French bands the tubas are treated as transposing instruments.

1. Structure. 2. History.

1. Structure. The tuba's wide conical bore (in early instruments interrupted only by the more cylindrical valve system), wide bell, and deep cup-shaped mouthpiece give the instrument a rich, smooth tone and facilitate the sounding of the lowest notes of its harmonic series, including the fundamentals. In timbre the instrument is more akin to the horn than to the trumpet or trombone, but because of its massiveness of tone it is associated with the 'heavy' brass.

Usually the tubing is coiled in an elliptical shape with the bell pointing upright. The helicon and sousaphone, however, are made in circular form: these instruments wrap around the player and rest usually on the left shoulder with the bell reaching up above the head, making the instrument easier to carry while marching. Some upright tubas have been made with the bell pointing forwards; this forward-facing or 're-cording' bell was devised during the 1920s, when the tuba was often substituted for the double bass in recording studios, as techniques were insufficiently developed to record string tone properly. Instruments with this kind of bell have proved serviceable in the band but unsuitable for orchestral use because of the resulting tone quality; hence modern tubas sometimes provide for the attachment of either an upright or a recording bell. Tubas have been built with a left-facing bell (i.e. with the bell to the left of the mouthpiece, as seen by the player); or with a right-facing bell, depending somewhat on whether the instrument has piston or rotary valves. Piston top-valves require a right-facing bell, but piston side-valves (an American development) allow a left-facing bell. The use of rotary valves invariably results in a left-facing bell, allowing the player to use the left hand to adjust the valve slides during performance when necessary. Piston valves are unsuitable if the bore (at the valve) is larger than 19 mm, and rotary valves are faster but less rugged.

Usually there are four valves arranged to lower the instrument's pitch by 1, ½, 1½, and 2½ tones respectively. Used in various combinations the four valves enable the player to produce a complete chromatic octave between the 2nd harmonic and the fundamental. But intonation difficulties encountered when using valves in combination are magnified because of the tuba's large size. The cumulative pitch inaccuracy by the time B' is reached is at least a semitone, causing the note to sound as C unless adjusted in some way. Many players 'lip' the notes down; others, especially in Britain and many parts of the Commonwealth, use a valve system with a mechanism (such as that designed by D.J. Blaikley in 1874) that automatically compensates for intonation errors. A fifth valve, which usually lowers the pitch by a major 3rd, is often added, and sometimes a sixth valve as well; each provides fingering alternatives to improve intonation.

Playing the tuba demands an enormous amount of breath, especially on the larger instruments, but does not require high breath pressure. The lips are normally loose and cushionlike; only in the high register need they be compressed or tense. In the hands of an accomplished performer the tuba can be an agile instrument, but the breath supply must constantly be renewed and, on the larger instruments, the lowest notes must be attacked with deliberation.

Tubas in use in the early 21st century included the tenor tuba in B♭ (Fr. *tuba basse, saxhorn basse*; Ger. *Baryton*; It. *flicorno baritoro, eufonio*), a bass instrument covering much the same range as the cello; bass tubas in F and E♭ (Fr. *tuba contrebasse*; Ger. *Basstuba*; It. *flicorno basso-grave*), contrabass instruments fulfilling a similar function to the double bass; and contrabass tubas in C and B♭ (or, as makers and players would term them, 'CC' and 'BB♭' respectively; the latter is often shown as 'B♭').

The tenor tuba in 9′ B♭ (with an open pedal (fundamental) of $B♭'$) is often designated 'euphonium' when used in bands, especially in Britain, and 'tenor tuba' when used orchestrally. In British practice the euphonium is often played with vibrato; the tenor tuba is not. The instrument has the same tube length as the B♭ baritone (an instrument of the saxhorn type), but its bore is wider. Pedal notes from $B♭'$ down to E' and beyond are available; the upper range extends to $b♭'$ or even higher.

The original German *Bass-Tuba* of 1835 was built in 12′ F and instruments of this pitch were still in common use in orchestras in much of continental Europe in the early 21st century. The band equivalent of the F tuba is the 14′ E♭ instrument (in Britain formerly sometimes called 'bombardon'), which is generally used in combination with the contrabass in 18′ B♭. Until about the 1960s a tuba in 12′ F was commonly used in British orchestras. It was replaced by an instrument in E♭ ('EE♭') with a full bore and four valves, which remained the most common orchestral tuba in Britain in the early 21st century.

The contrabass tuba in 16′ C (with an open fundamental of C') became the standard orchestral type in the USA in the 1940s. In the early 21st century it was being increasingly used in Britain as an alternative to the 'EE♭' instrument, and in continental Europe as an alternative to the F instrument. The 18′ tuba in B♭ ('double B♭' or 'BB♭'), with either three or four valves, is primarily a band instrument; in the USA it occurs regularly in sousaphone form. The so-called CC instrument, though a whole tone higher than the BB♭, usually has as wide a bore, giving it a distinctive and satisfying timbre, while its being pitched in C facilitates fingering in the sharp keys frequently found in orchestral works.

Very large sub-bass and 'subcontrabass' tubas have occasionally been made, but have for the most part proved impractical. In 1851 Adolphe Sax built a *saxhorn-bourdon* in E♭ and four years later an even lower one in BB♭. An even larger instrument, Gustave Besson's *Trombotonar*, also in BB♭, was 3 metres tall. Other giant tubas have been built, but it is not certain which of them has the dubious distinction of being the largest tuba in the world, as one instrument might have a greater length of tubing while another might have a larger bell or a greater volume of tubing.

The unique French six-valve tuba in 8′ C was developed as an all-purpose orchestral tuba, following on the widespread use of the C ophicleide, a French invention. The six valves enabled it to cover a four-octave range and play Wagner contrabass parts as well as ophicleide parts. French composers, having this instrument in mind, have tended to write passages for tuba in a higher range than is usually asked of other tubas. For example, the 'Bydlo' solo in Ravel's orchestration of Musorgsky's *Pictures at an Exhibition*, with a compass of $F\sharp'$ to $g\sharp'$, is well suited to the C tuba but can pose difficulties to players using BB♭ or F instruments.

2. History. During the 1820s several makers, including Stölzel, might have produced valved brass instruments pitched as low as 12′ F. The effectiveness of most of these would have been doubtful since the generally available valves could not be used with the wide bore required in low bugle-horns. In 1827 Stölzel devised a new type of valve, the *Röhrenventil* (later called *Berliner-Pumpe*), a short piston valve of large diameter, which was suited to use on wide bore instruments. The first practical application of the new valve to a low instrument was a *Bass-Tuba* in F introduced by the Prussian bandmaster Wilhelm Wieprecht and the instrument maker J.G. Moritz in 1835 (patented 12 Sept 1835). It was equipped with a variant of Stölzel's valve developed by Wieprecht and Moritz, called the *Stecherbüchsen-Ventil*. The design of the *Bass-Tuba* might have been suggested by the suitability of this kind of valve to an instrument of relatively wide bore through the valves; or else the valve itself might have been the outcome of work carried on perhaps first by Stölzel, later by Wieprecht and Moritz, in developing valved low brass instruments. Wieprecht and Moritz's prototype bass tuba, of which there is a specimen dating from 1838–40 in the Musikinstrumenten-Museum, Berlin, differed in appearance from the modern tuba but displayed some of its important characteristics: it was pitched in F (subsequently the standard pitch of orchestral tubas); it had five valves arranged to lower the pitch of the instrument by 1, ½, 1½, ¾, and 2½ tones respectively; and it could be played down to the fundamental or pedal notes. The instrument was made

from brass with German silver fittings, as are most Continental tubas to this day.

Other makers adopted Wieprecht and Moritz's designs and began producing tubas in various sizes and shapes. The influence of these designs is seen, for example, in the large valved brass instruments ('trombacellos') built by Graves & Co. of Winchester, New Hampshire in the 1840s. Within a few years makers in German-speaking countries began using rotary valves (introduced in practical form in 1835 by J.F. Riedl of Vienna) instead of *Berliner-Pumpen*. The first contrabass tubas in (so-called) CC and BB♭ were built in 1845 by the Bohemian maker V.F. Červený. In France during the 1840s and 50s Adolphe Sax developed the family of saxhorns (ranging in size from sopranino to contrabass), the lower members of which closely resemble modern tubas.

The tuba was soon adopted by bands and orchestras in the German states, but was more slowly accepted in other countries, especially Britain and France, where the ophicleide was firmly established. In France the keyed ophicleide was not superseded at the Paris Opéra until 1874; and although a 'Sax bass' was present at the first known English brass band contest (Burton Constable, 1845), symphony orchestras in England did not introduce tubas until 1863–87 and even then continued to use the ophicleide until the last years of the century. (When he joined the Hallé Orchestra in 1894 Harry Barlow was expected to play both ophicleide and tuba, although it is likely that he played only tuba following Hallé's death in 1895.) It was, in fact, a Frenchman, Berlioz, who was the first major composer to include tubas in his works. He found in the instrument an answer to problems caused by his customary use of large numbers of higher wind instruments. Previously having used several ophicleides to achieve the proper balance, he now substituted tuba for ophicleide in almost all his scores, with the advice that it be doubled at the octave because of its relative weakness in the lower register. Possibly because of this early usage the tuba came to be regarded as a type of ophicleide in France; for many years the F tuba was known as 'ophicléide monstre', while the term 'ophicléide' could mean either *ophicléide à pistons* (i.e. tuba) or the keyed ophicleide. (19th-century German references to *Ophikleide* should be taken to mean *Ventilophikleide*, a tuba in ophicleide form, rather than *Klappenophicleide*, the keyed ophicleide.)

The Faust overture, often cited as Wagner's first work using the tuba, was composed in 1840 but not performed until 1855, after considerable revision including adjustments to the orchestration. Wagner first scored for bass tuba in *Der fliegende Holländer*, first performed in 1843, and specified use of the contrabass tuba in *Das Rheingold* (composed 1853–4). Later in the century Mahler, keenly aware of the distinctive characteristics of each orchestral instrument, often scored solo passages for tuba. Composers of the Second Viennese School, influenced no doubt by Mahler, treated the tuba equally with other individual instrumental voices. An additional tone-colour was provided by the mute, first requested by Richard Strauss in *Don Quixote* (1896–7).

In eastern Europe the tuba was primarily influenced by the distinctive instrument built by Červený, who until the establishment of the Russian maker Šediva (Schediwa) in the early 1880s was apparently the sole supplier to Russia. Červený's *Kaisertuba* appeared in the early 1880s: made in several pitches, with a very large bore, this design was later copied by many other manufacturers. As professor at the St Petersburg Conservatory, Rimsky-Korsakov, who had become well acquainted with the tuba's potentialities while he was inspector of naval bands, influenced Borodin and others in their treatment of the instrument. Early 21st-century Russian orchestras used the largest and deepest tubas, but there is evidence in Tchaikovsky's and Borodin's works that the three-valve E♭ tuba might have been in common use during the 19th century. The great ballet scores of Stravinsky, since they were composed for performances by the Ballets Russes in Paris, tend towards the French practice of writing for the high tessitura, and do not share the deep massive style of Prokofiev and Shostakovich that is typical of 20th-century Russian composers.

In Britain during the late 19th century, orchestral tuba players had often been trained on the ophicleide or euphonium. The F tuba became standard in symphony orchestras, no doubt because players felt more comfortable with it than with a deeper instrument. The E♭ tuba was also found in orchestras, especially amateur ones. Particularly in lighter music, English composers also wrote for the tenor B♭ tuba or euphonium.

During the early part of the 20th century American orchestras, drawing on band practice, often adopted tubas in E♭ or BB♭. German musicians who played in the newly formed American orchestras made the F tuba popular, and American manufacturers such as King began producing German-style tubas. Later in the century the contrabass in CC was adopted in the USA.

At the start of the 21st century German and American bands used contrabass tubas in BB♭ and sometimes C; the E♭ bass instrument was found in school bands. British brass bands included two instruments in E♭ and two in BB♭ (reading in transposed treble clef); military bands employed one of each (reading at concert pitch in the bass clef). French and Italian bands also included E♭ and BB♭ tubas, notated in France in transposed bass clef, and in Italy in concert pitch bass clef.

Although the tuba repertory has been created over a shorter period than that of other orchestral instruments, tuba players are asked to play in a wide variety of styles, partly because of the divergence of opinion among composers of different countries as to exactly what instrument is meant by 'tuba'. Since orchestral parts for the instrument are written at concert pitch in the bass clef, the player can choose which tuba will best fit a given part. The lowest note in the 20th-century symphonic repertory is the *A″* in Max Trapp's Fourth Symphony (1928); *g♯′* or *a♭′* appears regularly in 19th-century French works.

The period since 1945 has been a time of rediscovery of the tuba; jazz musicians, the avant garde, and composers of popular music have demonstrated the instrument's unique character, showing that it can be more subtle and agile than formerly supposed and can produce a wide variety of timbres. Although such avant-garde composers as Melvyn Poore and Krysztof Knittel have on paper extended the compass as far as five octaves, *A″* and *a♭′* may be regarded as the extremes of the range normally required.

The International Tuba and Euphonium Association (ITEA), founded as the Tubists Universal Brotherhood Association in 1968 (renamed in 2000), has actively promoted the instrument and its repertory. At the end of the 20th century it had about 2500 members worldwide.

BIBLIOGRAPHY
G. Kastner: *Manuel général de musique militaire* (Paris, 1848/R)
C. Pierre: *La facture instrumentale à l'Exposition Universelle de 1889* (Paris, 1890)
J. Brousse: 'Tuba', *EMDC*, vol.3/3 (1927), 1674–80
A. Carse: *Musical Wind Instruments* (London, 1939/R)
H. Kunitz: 'Tuba', *Die Instrumentation*, vol.9 (Leipzig,1968)
The Instrumentalist, vol.27/7 (1973) [special tuba issue]
C. Bevan: *The Tuba Family* (London, 1978, rev. and enlarged 2/2000)
H. Heyde: *Das Ventilblasinstrument: seine Entwicklung im deutschsprachigen Raum von der Anfängen bis zur Gegenwart* (Leipzig, 1987)
C.J. Bevan: 'Brass Band Contests: Art or Sport?', *Bands: the Brass Band Movement in the Nineteenth and Twentieth Centuries*, ed. T. Herbert (Milton Keynes, 1991), 102–19
H. Heyde: 'The Early Berlin Valve and an Unsigned Tuba at the Shrine to Music Museum', *JAMIS*, vol.20 (1994), 54–64
R.W. Morris and D. Perantoni, eds.: *Guide to the Tuba Repertoire: The New Tuba Source Book* (Bloomington, IN, 1996, rev. 2/2006/R2007)
E. Mitroulia and A. Myers: 'Adolphe Sax: Visionary or Plagiarist?', *HBSJ*, vol.20 (2008), 93–141

CLIFFORD BEVAN

Tuba (ii). Trumpet-like instrument, the most important of the Roman brass. It consisted of a straight cylinder of bronze or brass or, less frequently, iron or ivory, about 1.2 to 1.5 metres long, and flared at the end. Usually it had a detachable mouthpiece of horn or ivory. Modern reproductions produce about six tones of the overtone series. Several classical references to the instrument as 'terribilis' or 'rauca' suggest that its tone must have been more strident than that of the modern trumpet. Similar instruments existed in ancient Greece, Israel, and Egypt, but the Roman version was directly derived from the Etruscans. Several authors, both Greek and Roman, attributed the invention of the overall type to the Etruscans; although this is obviously untrue, it serves to illustrate the prominence of the Etruscans in the area of brass instruments.

In Etruscan pictorial representations the tuba appears with other brass instruments such as the *cornu* and *lituus* as an instrument of solemn processions for funerals, civic religious ceremonies, and military triumphs. The tuba was used by the Romans for these and other purposes: there survives a rich collection of iconographic and literary evidence.

Although the tuba was not used as frequently in cult music as the *tibia* or the lyre it had a prominent and even number of these instruments was employed; the *legio* III Augusta listed 39 *tubicines* and 36 *cornicines*.

The tuba was also played in the arena: only the *hydraulis* is mentioned more frequently in this connection.

BIBLIOGRAPHY

D. Charlton: 'New Sounds for Old: Tam–Tam, Tuba Curva, Buccin', *Soundings*, vol.3 (1973), 39–47

J. Ziolkowski: 'The Roman Bucina: a Distinct Musical Instrument?', *HBSJ*, vol.14 (2002), 31–58

C.-G. Alexandrescu: *Blasmusiker und Standartenträger im römischen Heer: Untersuchungen zur Benennung, Funktion und Ikonographie* (diss., U. of Cologne, 2010)

JAMES W. MCKINNON

Tuba curva. Crude wind instrument, created during the French Revolution and first heard publicly during the ceremony of Voltaire's reburial on 11 July 1791. No undoubtedly authentic specimen survives. The instrument, probably of brass, had a mouthpiece but was otherwise in one piece without fingerholes and curved into a 'G' shape. Examination of the music written for the tuba curva shows that it was somewhat over 2.5 metres long and made in three sizes to yield a limited harmonic series on the fundamentals *B♭'*, *C*, and *D*. Its sound was described at the time as resembling that of six serpents.

The tuba curva (and its companion instrument, the *buccin*) was created according to a design that satisfied composers' requirements and the aesthetic principles of Revolutionary iconography. Composers needed a new instrument that would provide increased support for the bass in outdoor music. The great majority of tuba curva and buccin scoring is found in choruses or instrumental pieces performed at various festivals of the Revolution. Both instruments assisted in louder episodes in the same limited manner as the natural trumpet; indeed on their first appearance they were described in the score as 'trompe antique' ('antique horns').

In accordance with the neoclassical design of the costumes and emblems of certain festivals, the shape of the tuba curva was taken from antiquity. The model was probably the curved trumpet (cornu) depicted on Trajan's Column, Rome (see P.S. Bartoli: *Colonna Traiana*, 1700, pls.7 and 8). A decorated variant appears in J.-B. de La Borde's *Essai sur la musique* (1780, vol.1, 233). Gossec was the first composer to write for the instrument and Méhul the last, in *Joseph* (1807). Two instruments identified as 'Trompette courbée: tuba curva' by La Borde (1780) have a curved form like the Roman model, but end in a loop with a dragon's head like the 19th-century buccin. The two types were already being confused by Choron in 1813 (*Traité général*).

'Tuba curva' in Chouquet's catalogue of the Paris Conservatoire museum (1884, no.592) was the name given to a 3.4-metre replica of a bronze Pompeian trumpet from the 1st century ce. A supplement to the catalogue (L. Pillaut, 1899) reports Pierre's discovery in 1893 of a U-shaped *tuba curva*.

For bibliography *see* Buccin (i).

DAVID CHARLTON/R

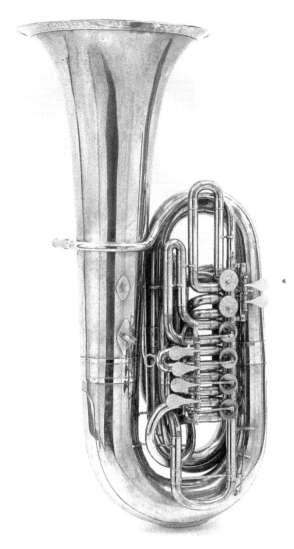

Tuba in 16′ C, six-valve. Alexander, Mainz, c1990.
(Edinburgh University Collection of Historic Musical Instruments(4283))

privileged position there. Its players, the *tubicines sacrorum populi romani*, came to enjoy the rank of priest in imperial times. Each year on 23 March and 23 May a ceremony called the *tubilustrium* took place in which the trumpets used on cult, state, and military occasions were blessed.

Above all the Roman tuba functioned as a military instrument: it accompanied marching, sounded the attack and the retreat, and joined the *cornu* in the heat of battle where its function was both to inspire the Romans and to strike fear into the enemy. Distinctions between the tasks of the various military instruments, namely, tuba, *cornu*, *lituus*, and *buccina*, are seldom clear, but Vegetius's differentiation between the two most important—tuba and *cornu*—seems plausible. In his *Epitoma rei militaris* he claimed that the *cornu* relayed commands to the standard bearers while the louder tuba announced them to the army at large. A surprising

Tuba-Dupré. Wooden soprano ophicleide, with six keys. It was invented by Pierre Paul Ghislain Joseph Dupré (*b* Tournai, Belgium, 28 Sept 1790; *d* Tournai, 12 Oct 1862), who showed it in the 1825 Haarlem Exhibition along with woodwinds and a serpent, all of his making. It was pitched in B♭, an octave above the bass ophicleide in B♭, and must be considered primarily as a military instrument. It has two tubes of maple, bored out and linked at the bow. There is a brass crook which is uncrossed (unlike those of the larger ophicleides) and clamped to the bell. The inscription on the bell reads 'Dupré à Tournay'. The lowest key stands open on the back of the bell and lowers the instrument's pitch by a semitone. The second and third keys are mounted on the front, away from the player, and are pinned into a large saddle, as is the sixth key. The fourth and fifth are mounted on single spherical pillars. The instrument is 73 cm tall from bow to bell, and the crook is 32 cm long. The diameter of the bore expands from 1.1 cm to 11.5 cm at the bell. Six specimens (some of them incomplete) are in the Musée des instruments de musique, Brussels.

According to Plenckers, Dupré built his instrument as an experiment to show that the tone of the ophicleide could be improved by making it of wood. It has been suggested that the tuba-Dupré was popular in Belgium, but there is little documentary evidence to support this.

BIBLIOGRAPHY

Catalogus der voorbrengeelen van nederlandsche volks en konst-vlijt toegelaten ter tweede algemeene tentonstelling geopend binnen Haarlem, July 1825 (Haarlem, 1825)

L.J. Plenckers: *Hoorn-en trompetachtige blaasinstrumenten*, ed. C.C.J von Gleich, vol. 1 (Amsterdam, 1970) [catalogue of the Gemeentemuseum, The Hague]

STEPHEN J. WESTON/R

Tubaphone. Percussion idiophone like a glockenspiel but with triple-plated bell-metal tubes instead of steel bars, giving it a softer sound. The tubes are arranged in keyboard fashion and mounted on a frame. It is typically played with mallets designed for xylophone or glockenspiel. The tubaphone evolved from an earlier instrument called a Pipelaphone, patented in 1888 by John C. Deagan and Joseph Carroll of St Louis and made by the J.C. Deagan Co. of Chicago; it was patented as the tubaphone by Deagan on 6 August 1889 and produced in three configurations: 2-octave $f'-f'''$; 2.5-octave $g'-c''''$; and 3-octave $c'-c''''$. Before 1917 each model was available in low pitch ($a' = 435$) and high pitch ($a' = 454$); beginning in 1917 all Deagan instruments were tuned to $a' = 440$. Each model was available mounted on a frame or on a frame and a floor rack. Before World War I the instrument became popular in British military band music, and Khachaturian included it in his ballet suite *Gayane* (1942, rev. 1957). Imitations of the Deagan instrument are also called tubuphone, tube bells, tubuscampanophone, etc. A Turkish 'tube-phone' (in *US.IN.pas*) has two octaves of brass tubes suspended by thin string from within a wooden frame. The tubes swing when struck, creating a vibrato effect.

Tubaphone is also the name of a model of banjo produced in Boston by Vega from 1909. Its square-sectioned, perforated metal tubular 'tone ring', placed between the wooden rim and the head, is credited with providing a distinctive tone.

RICK MATTINGLY

Tubbs. English family of bowmakers. The family can be traced in London back to the mid-1600s, but the immediate forebear of the bowmakers was the weaver William Tubbs of Bethnal Green, three of whose sons, William (*b* Bethnal Green, London, England, 30 Oct 1770; *d* after 1824), Henry (*b* Bethnal Green, London, England, 27 April 1785; *d* after 1824), and Thomas (*b* Stepney, London, England, Dec 1790; *d* Lambeth, London, England, 29 March 1863), took to bowmaking after 1800, most likely in the workshop of the elder Edward Dodd. The work of the brothers spanned the era of the modernization of the bow, but only Thomas made any quantity of branded works, and so it has not been possible to identify the individual hands in a workshop in which the quality of work was variable.

Tubaphone, Britain, c1925. (Edinburgh University Collection of Historic Musical Instruments (1642))

Thomas is considered the most important maker of the first generation of the family. He became active on his own account in Soho during the early 1820s, ultimately settling in Lambeth where he remained until his death. While many of his bows were marked with his own name, many others were made for the trade, including such noted shops as those of George Corsby, William Davis, and Louis Panormo, much of whose production probably came from Thomas's workshop. His brand-mark was 'T-TUBBS', usually found on the obverse of the handle immediately adjacent to the adjuster. Thomas might have introduced to English bowmaking such features as metal headplates and underplates, the 'Parisian' eye, and tortoiseshell as a material for frogs, while at the same time he preserved such classic English features as the short length, angled frogs, and oval cross-section of the stick. While early bows often have open ivory or ebony frogs and plain tips, later works have the full mounts associated with modern work.

Thomas's son William Tubbs (*b* Southwark, London, England, 20 Nov 1814; *d* Soho, London, England, 28 April 1878) was a highly important bowmaker. He was probably a pupil of his father and of the brothers James and Edward Dodd (ii); he took over the latter's business upon his death, in 1851. From the 1840s onward he was assisted in bowmaking by his sons William, Edward, Thomas, Charles Edward, John, Henry, and above all James. His bows were often made for dealers, although a significant quantity were either branded with his stamp 'W. TUBBS' or sold unbranded. A number of earlier French and English sticks, some better than others, have been seen with gold and tortoiseshell mounts made by William Tubbs, which suggests that someone might have profited from having silver-mounted bows refitted with gold. He also might have begun the practice of replacing the fittings on older English bows, on which the open frog remained characteristic long after the practice had been abandoned on the Continent, with modern mounts. There is a very decided evolution in the style of bows by William Tubbs, the earliest work resembling that of his father and teachers, the middle period showing a more modern approach akin to the similar transformation occurring in France, and finally a smaller, more delicate model quite similar to French and German work from the later 19th century.

William's son James Tubbs (*b* Lambeth, London, England, 25 March 1835; *d* Soho, London, England, 19 April 1921) was by far the most important bowmaker in the family and perhaps in England. While early accounts describe him as being born in Soho, he was in fact born in Lambeth and was baptized in the Church of St Mary Lambeth. He moved to Soho with his father about 1850 and remained there until his death. He was probably a pupil of his father. About 1858 he appears to have been engaged by W.E. Hill as a bowmaker. The bows of this period are frequently outstanding, cleanly made, and with a clear and unmistakably personal style. These bows are frequently shorter, usually mounted in ebony and silver, although chased gold mounts are occasionally seen, and are branded 'W.E. HILL' on each side of the handle and on the frog.

Tubbs's employment by Hill lasted until 1862, when Hill received a gold medal for Tubbs's bows at the International Exhibition of that year, but Tubbs might have continued to make bows for Hill, and might have performed repairs for the firm into the 1870s. Nevertheless, a substantial argument with Hill ensued, occasionally becoming public at such events as the sale of the Woolhouse Estate. Tubbs would later brand his own name over the Hill mark when he came across one of his early bows, and for many years Hills would not sell a Tubbs bow in their shop. The early years were probably not easy, for with some handsome exceptions the wood is not of the best quality. The bows were branded 'J. TUBBS'. Gradually he defined the style that distinguished the rest of his work: the head broad but delicate, with narrow chamfer (in the style of certain Tourte bows), the button of plain silver, the face also of silver, the frog rectangular and with a plain pearl eye (later the heel was rounded and the eye dispensed with). After his father's death, when his brothers entered bowmaking on their own accounts, he changed his brand to 'JAS TUBBS'. His best bows were mounted with gold and ebony, and sometimes the gold was engraved. An octagonal stick is very rare in a Tubbs, as are bows mounted with gold and tortoiseshell or ivory. The bows are distinctive not only visually but also to the player. They have a unique way of gripping the strings, and some claim that if one is accustomed to a Tubbs it is difficult to play with anything else. The Duke of Edinburgh conferred on Tubbs a royal appointment about 1874, and after 1871 Tubbs began offering his annual bow prize to students at the Guildhall School of Music and the Royal Academy of Music.

Well before the turn of the century James Tubbs was helped by his son Alfred (*b* Soho, London, England, 3 June 1862; *d* Soho, London, England, 3 Nov 1909), whose style was in most particulars almost identical with that of James. James's own craftsmanship, however, grew heavier and coarser with age, without affecting his bows' quality. After Alfred's death he began his series of 'Birthday' bows, a special bow with engraved mounts made on each birthday; these bows are now collectors' pieces. He always seems to have worked very quickly. In all he is said to have made, with his son's help, 5000 bows for violin, viola, and cello. Occasionally examples are rather weak, but few makes of bow are preferable to the stronger ones by this remarkable man.

Edward Tubbs (*b* St Pancras, London, England, 28 July 1842; *d* New York, NY, 12 June 1921) was the younger brother of James Tubbs. After working for his father for many years, he opened his own workshop in London in 1868. In 1878, after his father's death, he emigrated to New York in pursuit of a woman whom he would eventually marry. He established a shop in New York City, working primarily as a dealer but also making occasional bows. As such, he became one of the first professionally trained bowmakers to work in the USA. His early bows were stamped 'E. TUBBS', the brand 'E. TUBBS NEW YORK' being adopted after his move. Another brother, Charles Edward (*b* Soho, London, England, 4 Sept 1850; *d* St Pancras, London, England, 3 Feb 1908), opened a shop in 1878 to make and sell bows in competition with his brother James, whose workshop was just doors away on Wardour Street; he used the brand 'C.E. TUBBS'. Another brother, Henry (*b* Soho, London, England, 20 Feb 1854; *d* Soho, Dec 1881) assisted his father in his last years, but his work is today completely unknown. Lastly, another brother, John (*b* Soho, London, England, 23 Feb 1859; *d* New York, NY, 13 Jan 1922), worked for his father and then for the trade after 1878. In 1888 he emigrated to New York, engaging primarily in dealing.

BIBLIOGRAPHY

W.C. Retford: *Bows and Bow Makers* (London, 1964/*R*)

J. Milnes and others, eds.: *The British Violin* (Oxford, 2000)

P.J. Kass: 'English Bow Makers of the Dodd and Tubbs Families', *The Conservation, Restoration and Repair of Stringed Instruments and their Bows*, vol.1, ed. T. Wilder (Montreal, 2010)

CHARLES BEARE/PHILIP J. KASS

Tube (i). Wooden clappers of the Bozo people of Mali. They consist of elaborately carved, diamond-shaped plaques with cylindrical handles, and are played only by women. They are supposed to be related to the plaque clappers of ancient Egypt. See B. Schiffer: *Die Oase Siwa und ihre Musik* (Berlin, 1936).

Tube (ii) [electronic tube, vacuum tube, thermionic valve, valve]. Device for converting alternating current to direct current. Thomas Edison discovered the underlying elements for this effect in 1880 during his light bulb experiments, and the British scientist John Ambrose Fleming first demonstrated a practical device, the 'Fleming diode', in 1904. It is essentially an incandescent light bulb with an extra electrode inside. The filament (the 'cathode') is heated white-hot, boiling electrons off its surface into the vacuum. The extra electrode (the 'anode' or 'plate') then becomes more positively charged than the hot filament and a direct current flows through the vacuum from the filament to the electrode. In 1907, the inventor Lee de Forest patented a similar bulb, but with an additional electrode, a bent wire between the plate and filament called the 'grid', which proved capable of modulating the current between the filament to the plate, thus making the first electronic amplifier, named the 'Audion'. This technique is the basis for all modern vacuum tubes. Design modifications to the cathode, grid, and anode create different amplification capabilities.

Vacuum tubes were an essential component in the development of all electronic technology. Typically made of thin glass, the tubes are fragile, generate considerable heat, and take time to warm up to proper operating temperature. While mostly replaced by solid-state transistor and integrated circuitry by the 1970s, tubes are better for high-power radio frequency (RF) applications, and are considered superior for guitar amplifiers. High-end tube-based guitar amplifiers produce distinctive audio characteristics, including distortion, considered highly desirable by professional electric guitar and bass players. Professional recording studios also value the distinctive characteristics of the older styles of tube-based equipment, and many audiophiles prefer the sound produced by such equipment.

BIBLIOGRAPHY

E. Barbour: 'The Cool Sound of Tubes—Vacuum Tube Musical Applications', *IEEE Spectrum*, vol.35/8 (Aug 1998), 24–5

M. Jones: *Valve Amplifiers* (Oxford, 1995, 4/2012)

ANNE BEETEM ACKER

Tube fiddle. A subcategory of spike fiddle, with tube-shaped resonator, usually made of wood or animal horn. The soundtable is often of snake or lizard skin. Examples include the Chinese *erhu*, the Ganda *endingidi*, and the Central African *taratibu*.

Tube zither. Chordophone, defined by Hornbostel and Sachs as having a body in the form of a tube (with a vaulted or convex surface) which serves as resonator as well as string bearer. In the case of a 'whole-tube zither' the tube is complete; in a 'half-tube zither' the body is cut lengthways. In its simplest form it is idiochord, in which each string is cut from the body of the tube (typically of bamboo) and raised and held taut above the body by bridges. Such instruments are popular in Southeast Asia (e.g. the *keranting* of Malaysia or the *keteng-keteng* of Sumatra), parts of Africa, and Madagascar (the *valiha*). In heterochord tube zithers a string is attached and supported by a pair of bridges. The Chinese *qin* and Japanese *koto* are typical half-tube zithers; sometimes they are called 'long zithers'. The strings of a tube zither may be plucked, struck, or bowed. In the case of the so-called Aeolian zither, the instrument is made to sound by the wind: in Malaysia they are suspended from trees and in Guyana they are stuck into the ground.

There exists a class of instruments, usually termed stick or bar zithers, from South and Southeast Asia, which overlaps the boundaries of the Hornbostel–Sachs classification. Those from South Asia are normally made of naturally hollow bamboo, which falls within the Hornbostel–Sachs definition of stick zithers as 'round sticks which happen to be hollow'; they may also be made from wood hollowed to resemble bamboo, in which case they are strictly tube zithers. Those from Southeast Asia, which are historically related to the South Asian examples and played in a similar manner, may be made from solid wood, in which case they are classified as stick zithers. The India *vīṇā*, for example, was classified by Sachs as a stick zither, and in this he has been followed by most later writers; Marcel-Dubois, however, has suggested that since the *vīṇā* is usually hollow it might better be classified as a tube zither.

Tubular bells [chimes, orchestral chimes] (Fr. *cloches*; Ger. *Glocken, Röhrenglocken*; It. *campane, campanelle*). Set of tuned metal tubes used for bell effects in the orchestra and theatre, real bells being cumbersome, difficult to play with rhythmic precision, and often confused in sound due to the prominence of upper partials. Tubular bells consist of a series of brass or steel tubes ranging in diameter from about 3 to 7 cm; the greater the diameter, the longer the bell tube and the lower the pitch. The compass of a standard set of tubular bells is c' to f'' or g''. Two-octave sets ($f-f''$ or g'') are used in continental Europe, and Kolberg Percussion has produced a three-octave set ($c-c'''$). The tubes hang in a frame mounted in two rows, keyboard-fashion. They are struck at the top edge, which is capped or reinforced with an inner metal disc or pin. For general purposes a rawhide or plastic mallet is employed, one side usually covered with leather or felt for a contrast in tone. The bells are damped by a manual or pedal mechanism. To play large instruments with some tubes 3 metres or more in length, the player stands on a platform; a music stand is incorporated above the instrument.

Tubular bells were introduced by John Hampton of Coventry in 1886, for the peal of four bells in Sullivan's *The Golden Legend*. In 1890 the *codophone*, a set of 15 tubular bells operated by a keyboard, was used in a performance at the Paris Opéra. Gustave Lyon constructed another instrument of this type in 1908. The part for tubular bells is usually written in the treble clef at sounding pitch; earlier composers frequently wrote in the bass clef but probably their instruments did not sound at the pitch written. Outstanding writing for tubular bells can be found in John Ireland's *These Things Shall Be* (1936–7), Britten's chamber opera *The Turn of The Screw* (1954), Messiaen's *Turangalîla-symphonie* (1946–8) and *Chronochromie* (1960), and Boulez's *Pli selon pli* (1959–62).

Tubular bells sound unlike church bells, and are frequently a poor imitation of them. In orchestral situations where the composer obviously had real bells in mind (e.g. Berlioz's *Symphonie fantastique* and Ravel's orchestration of Mussorgsky's *Pictures at an Exhibition*) these are much more effective and their use can be feasible when only one or two pitches are required. For the use of various types of bell in orchestral music, *see* Bell (i). Tubular bells are often incorporated as a stop in church organs, where they can be played from the organ keyboard.

JAMES BLADES/JAMES HOLLAND/R

Tubulon [tubulong]. Popular name for a homemade metallophone comprising a graduated set of slender metal tubes, commonly tuned to a microtonal or other unconventional scale. Tubulons have been made from steel electrical conduit, copper plumbing pipe, and other readily available, relatively inexpensive metal tubing, sometimes recycled. The tubes are cut preferably with a pipe cutter (not a saw) to predetermined lengths and either supported at their nodes or suspended, and struck with beaters. Depending on the octave division (nine to more than 50 pitches per octave have been reported), the tubulon might encompass one or more octaves.

Tudduglag [lelega, gigiugiu]. Xylophone of the Mentawai Islands, Indonesia. Its three or four smooth wooden bars rest on two sticks placed on the ground under their nodal points. Four sticks are pushed into the ground beside the nodes of the highest and lowest bars to hold all in place, with leaves placed between the bars to hold them apart and allow them to vibrate. The bars are beaten by one or two players of either sex, holding two wooden rods each. There is no standard size, but the bars in a set from Sipora measure 61, 53, and 49 cm long. In Pagai the instrument is called a *lelega*. It is played to pass the time in the fields, and to practise for the large *tudukkat* drums. In Siberut the *gigiugiu* is played by boys and men for recreation. See M.H. Rahz: *Musik Mentawai: Kajian Seni Pertunjukan* (Bandung, 1998).

MARGARET J. KARTOMI/ANDREW C. MCGRAW

Tudimba. Lamellaphone of the Luluwa in the Kasayi region, Democratic Republic of the Congo. The Salampasu call it *dudjimba*. It is also designated by the generic name *tshisaandj*. It has 11 wooden tongues and a wooden raft-type body, the middle segment of which is shorter than the outer ones.

BIBLIOGRAPHY

F.J. de Hen: *Beitrag zur Kenntnis der Musikinstrumente aus Belgisch Kongo und Ruanda-Urundi* (Tervuren, 1960), 77ff, 86, 92

J.-S. Laurenty: *Les sanza du Congo* (Tervuren, 1962), 191 only

FERDINAND J. DE HEN

Tudor, David (Eugene) (*b* Philadelphia, PA, 20 Jan 1926; *d* Tomkins Cove, New York, 13 Aug 1996). American pianist, organist, composer, and instrument maker. He studied the organ and theory with H. William Hawke, the piano with Josef Martin and Irma Wolpe (later Rademacher), and composition and analysis with Stefan Wolpe. In 1938 he became Hawke's assistant at St Mark's, Philadelphia, and in 1943 he was appointed organist at Trinity Church, Swarthmore, Pennsylvania, where he also served as organist at Swarthmore College from 1944 to 1948. He taught at Black Mountain College (1951–3), the Darmstadt summer courses (1956, 1958, 1959, 1961), SUNY-Buffalo (1965–6), the University of California at Davis (1967), Mills College (1967–8), and the National Institute of Design in Ahmedabad, India (1969).

Tudor's role as a champion of new music was established as early as 1950, when he gave the American première of Boulez's Second Piano Sonata. From 1960, initially in collaboration with John Cage, he pioneered developments in live electronic music, designing his own sources of sound production, transforming conventional sound-transmitters into sound-generators, programming feedback as a component of the composition, and mixing both input and output matrices. He performed frequently for the Merce Cunningham Dance Company and in 1969–77 he worked with Lowell Cross and Carson Jeffries in creating concert performances and sound environments using four-colour lasers and electronic sounds. In 1966 he developed the 'instrumental loudspeaker' (first used in *Bandoneon!*), in which electronic or other sounds are passed through a container from a loudspeaker at one end to a microphone at the other, and then to a conventional sound system. The concept of the 'instrumental loudspeaker' was used in the four members of a series of concert works and environmental sound sculptures called

'Rainforest', the most important of which is Rainforest IV (1973). The first presentation of Rainforest IV led to the founding, in 1973, of the group Composers Inside Electronics, which, in addition to Tudor, included John Driscoll, Philip Edelstein, Ralph Jones, Martin Kalve, and Bill Viola, younger composers who specialized in live electronic performance, designing special electronic circuits, and constructing sound sculptures and environments.

Tudor also collaborated in visual installations by Jacqueline Matisse Monnier. Some took the form of electro-acoustic environments, in which sounds were either activated by audience-spectator movements or themselves activated lighting, projections, or sculptures. In the Neural Synthesis series (1992–4) a neural-network chip is used to process both analogue and digital signals which in turn, Tudor wrote, 'are gated by the performer, increasing the complexity and unpredictability of the sonic results'. This double goal had been at the centre of Tudor's reformulation of the capacities of musical performance since he began to explore them, at the piano, 40 years earlier.

WRITINGS

'From Piano to Electronics', *Music and Musicians*, vol.20/12 (1971–2), 24–6

BIBLIOGRAPHY

J.D. Fulleman: 'Composers Inside Electronics', *MusikTexte* (1986), no.15, 11–17 [interview]

F. Hilberg: *David Tudors Konzept des 'Elektronifizierten Klaviers' und seine Interpretation von John Cages 'Variations II' (1961)* (Saarbrücken, 1996)

J. Holzaepfel: *David Tudor and the Performance of American Experimental Music, 1950–1959* (diss., City U. of New York, 1994)

Twentieth-century Music, vol.3/11 (1996) [incl. articles *in memoriam* by M.Cunningham, D. Behrman, G. Mumma, P. Oliveros, R. Jones]

HUGH DAVIES, JOHN HOLZAEPFEL

Tudukkat [tuddukan, tuddukat]. Slit drum ensemble of three, sometimes four, instruments of different sizes and pitches, used in the Mentawai Islands, Indonesia. They are used for signalling as well as for musical purposes. The drums are housed in a small covered structure raised approximately 3 metres above ground level and are audible up to 5 kilometres away. Each drum consists of a long piece of palm or other tree trunk, the ends of which are narrowed so that the middle third is ovoid, with a long slit about the width of two fingers. The drums rest horizontally on sticks on the wooden floorboards, and the player beats the middle upper edge of the slit. The largest drum, called *ina* ('mother'), can be about 300 cm long, with a middle diameter of about 30 cm. The other two are called *toga siboito* ('small child') and *toga sikatelu* ('third child', about 150 cm long). Some have carved decorations. There is no standard tuning but a set in central Siberut plays approximately $g\sharp'$, b', and $d\sharp''$, while another plays f', $a\flat'$, and $d\sharp$. The drums are beaten with a thick-headed hammer (*tetete, igra*) about 60 cm long, or one or two wooden rods (*dedega, leleikat*). The *tetete* is used when signalling and for musical purposes, with complex or syncopated improvisatory rhythms, while the *dedega*

is normally used only for musical purposes, providing a regular rhythmic pulse. The music does not accompany dancing or singing but lends lustre to ceremonies. Separate repertories exist for the drums depending on how many are being played. In signalling three drums are used, and each drum phrase (*bag-bag*) has a semantic meaning that describes, for example, the meal to be prepared for the ceremony, or relates that a person has died.

A xylophone in Sipora, also called *tudukkat* or *tuddukan*, performs the same repertory and functions. It has three large wooden bars resting on top of two boat-shaped, wooden resonators. The largest bar, about 100 cm long, sits on one resonator, and the two smaller bars, tune a 5th and an octave higher, share the other resonator. The bars are tuned by thinning their undersides.

BIBLIOGRAPHY

R. Schefold: 'Schlitztrommeln und Trommelsprache in Mentawai', *Zeitschrift für Ethnologie*, vol.98/1 (1973), 36–73

M.H. Rahz: *Musik Mentawai: Kajian Seni Pertunjukan* (Bandung, 1998)

MARGARET J. KARTOMI/ANDREW C. MCGRAW

Tudum. Folk drum of north India. The name, presumably onomatopoeic, has been applied to an earthenware or wooden kettledrum, typically measuring about 30 cm in depth and 40 cm in diameter.

Tuerlinckx. Flemish family of instrument makers. Jean Arnold Antoine Tuerlinckx (*b* Aerschot, Southern Netherlands [later Belgium], 22 Nov 1753; *d* Mechelen, Belgium, 19 Dec 1827) was the son of a clockmaker and amateur harpsichordist. He began to make instruments at the age of 18, by copying a new French clarinet. In 1782 he married Catherine Meikens and moved to Mechelen (Malines) where he established himself as a maker of woodwinds (and also of arrows), and soon began to receive important orders from the Netherlands. Following his brief imprisonment in May 1799 during the French revolutionary period, his business expanded and he gained clients in England, France, and Germany. In 1808 his first wife died, and he married Marie Catherine Clavers in the following year. At the peak of his career, about 1810, he employed 40 workmen in two workshops, one for brasses and the other for woodwinds. He frequently equipped entire military and civil wind bands (*sociétés d'harmonie*) with complete sets of instruments and also dealt in pianos, harps, and printed music. During the 1820s his business declined owing to growing competition from cheaper instruments made by large foreign firms as well as from local manufacturers. A portrait of him by Charles-Pierre Verhulst survives in the Stadsmuseum Hof van Busleyden at Mechelen.

After the death of Jean Arnold Antoine, the business was continued by his eldest son, Corneille Jean Joseph Tuerlinckx (*b* Mechelen, 31 May 1783; *d* Mechelen, 29 Dec 1855), who worked in his father's shop from the age of nine, at the same time learning to play various instruments and studying composition. He helped to found and direct several wind-band societies in Mechelen, for which he composed a great deal of music (in

1828 he was highly placed in a composition contest in Antwerp). In 1835, after the death of his wife, Maria Dochez, whom he had married in 1815, he seems to have largely stopped composing, and about 1840 he probably closed his instrument business owing to decline in trade. The contents of his manufactory, including some 300 unfinished flutes, 200 unfinished clarinets, and many other completed instruments, were sold in 1856.

Since both father and son marked their work 'Tuerlinckx/Malines' or 'Tuerlinckx à Malines', it is almost impossible to distinguish between their instruments. Neither seems to have been a real innovator, though both kept pace with the times. The foreign armies that marched through the Southern Netherlands in the late 18th and early 19th centuries provided them with many opportunities for studying and copying new foreign types of instruments; and, as a result, they produced many new instruments such as the 13-keyed clarinet, the bass clarinet, the contrabassoon, the bugle horn, the russian bassoon, and the ophicleide. They manufactured an astonishing variety of instruments including: fifes, piccolos, and flutes of many sizes; clarinets in C, Bb, and A, *clarinettes d'amour*, and alto and bass clarinets; oboes, small bassoons of various sizes, bassoons, and contrabassoons; natural trumpets, *trompettes d'invention*, and slide trumpets; field bugles and keyed bugles, *clairons*, and ophicleides; *cors de chasse*, natural horns, and *cors d'invention*; serpents and russian bassoons; trombones and *buccins*; harps; a variety of percussion instruments; and possibly even pianos, although it is likely that some at least were made for Tuerlinckx by contractors. The firm's order book for wind instruments sold from 1782 to 1818 and numerous Tuerlinckx instruments are in the Musée des Instruments de Musique, Brussels.

BIBLIOGRAPHY

Catalogue des produits de l'industrie nationale admis à la troisième exposition générale à Bruxelles, au mois de juillet 1830, no.709 (Brussels, 1830)

R. van Aerde: 'Les Tuerlinckx: luthiers à Malines', *Bulletin du Cercle archéologique, littéraire et artistique de Malines*, vol.24 (1914), 13–210; also pubd separately (Malines, 1914)

E. Closson: *La facture des instruments de musique en Belgique* (Brussels, 1935), 71–2

W. Waterhouse: *The New Langwill Index: a Dictionary of Musical Wind-Instrument Makers and Inventors* (London, 1993)

A.R. Rice: *From the Clarinet D'Amour to the Contra Bass: a History of Large Size Clarinets, 1740–1860* (Oxford, 2009)

G.J.J. van Melckebeke: *Notice biographique sur C.-J.-J. Tuerlinckx* (Mechelen, n.d./R2010)

JANE M. BOWERS/R

Tugi [Stucki], **Hans** [Johannes; Hans von Basel] (*b* Basle, *c*1460; *d* Basle, summer 1519). Swiss organ builder. He was the son of a Basle gunsmith and matriculated at Basle University, 1476–7. By about 1500 he was one of the most important organ builders in Switzerland and southwest Germany. He appears to have worked in Mantua Cathedral in 1503. He built new organs in Basle (1487, 1496–9, and before 1510), Mainz (before 1496, perhaps 1490), Brugg (1493 and the following years), Zürich Grossmünster (1505–7), Colmar (before 1513), and Biel (1517–19). He also rebuilt and repaired organs in Basle (1482), Konstanz Cathedral (1489–90; he might also have built a small organ there in 1490–91), Zürich Grossmünster (1511–13), Mainz Cathedral (1514), Berne Minster (1517–19), and Colmar (1513, 1518).

Tugi should not be confused with the German organist Johannes Gross (*b* Nuremberg, Germany, *c*1480; *d* Basle, 1536), who, like Tugi, was known as Hans von Basel; he was organist of Konstanz Cathedral in 1505–6 and of Basle Cathedral in 1507. He was invited to test Tugi's organ in the Zürich Grossmünster in 1507.

BIBLIOGRAPHY

F. Jakob: *Der Orgelbau im Kanton Zürich* (Berne, 1969–71)

J.F. van Os: 'Tugy: reconstructie in de Predigerkirche te Basel', *Het orgel*, vol.83 (1987), 95–103

MANFRED SCHULER

Tuhung. Conical drum of the Kayan and Kenyah peoples of Sarawak, Malaysia. It is about 3.6 metres tall. The single goatskin head is 90 cm in diameter and the opening at the other end 45 cm.

Tu hutta. Antelope-horn whistle of the Fali people of Cameroon.

Tui. Largest slit drum on Pororan Island, Buka, Solomon Islands. It is 2.4 metres long and 1.2 metres high. The other slit drums are the *halan* (150 by 60 cm) and the *king* (90 by 30 cm). The tui is used by itself for signalling and in association with the *king* to accompany dances (*guma*).

The tui is also the largest instrument in the slit-drum ensemble of the Siuai people, southwest Bougainville, Solomon Islands. There the slit drums are kept in the men's clubhouses, each one containing a set of (usually) nine, ranging from 4.5 by 1.5 metres to 1 metre by 30 cm. They are played during the various stages of 'big man' feast-giving ceremonies. See D.L. Oliver: *A Solomon Islands Society: Kinship and Leadership Among the Siuai of Bougainville* (Cambridge, MA, 1955), 379 only.

MERVYN MCLEAN

Tüidük [kargy-tüidük]. Open end-blown flute of the Turkmen people of Central Asia. It is usually made of bamboo with pyrographic decoration, though sometimes of wood. It normally has five burned-in fingerholes, the upper three close together and the two lower more separate, and a high thumbhole.

Ṭuila [ṭuhila, ṭohilā]. Single-string fretless stick zither of central India. The string, of twisted cotton, gut, or silken hemp, is held by a bamboo rod about 2.5 cm thick and approximately the length of the player's arm. It is secured directly to the proximal end of the rod by wrapped cord but attached several centimetres away from the bottom to the curved end of a piece of wood affixed at right angles to the rod. A small oblong hollowed gourd is tied to the underside of the rod near its upper end. The player holds the ṭuila diagonally across his body. He supports it at its lower end with his right thumb as he plucks the string with the second finger of his right hand; his left thumb rests under the neck of the gourd and he stops the string with three fingers of his left hand to produce the instrument's lowest tetrachord. The upper tetrachord is played as harmonics at the 12th, using the same hand position, but the string is lightly touched with the right index finger. The player alternates monophonic playing with polyphony produced by playing each fundamental and its harmonic simultaneously. The open end of the gourd rests against the player's chest and is shaken and pulled to alter the instrument's tone. Mundari ṭuila players use a scale roughly equivalent to the Western 'church Dorian'.

The ṭuila is found particularly in the Mayurbhanj district of Orissa and among the Muṇḍā people of southern Bihar; it is normally played by men. Each player generally makes his own instrument and plays it to accompany group marriage songs or his own singing. The ṭuila repertory includes songs for communal dancing, but the instrument itself is not played with drumming or dancing; in Mundari song texts it is often paired with the kendrā (plucked chordophone). Although the instrument is now rare it still holds a position of respect and symbolic importance in tribal villages.

Elsewhere in Orissa the name ṭuila is applied to drone spike lutes of the South Asian éktār type.

BIBLIOGRAPHY
J. Hoffmann and A. van Emelen: Encyclopedia mundarica (Patna, 1938–50)
K.S. Kothari: Indian Folk Musical Instruments (New Delhi, 1968)
O. Prasad: Munda: Music and Dance (thesis, Ranchi U., 1971)
B.C. Deva: Musical Instruments of India: their History and Development (Calcutta, 1978, rev. 2/1987/R2000)

CAROL M. BABIRACKI

Tu'itu'i [tu'i]. Large pātē (slit drum) of Samoa. Some have a handle by which they can be carried in one hand while being struck by a beater held in the other or by a second person; larger ones are stood on end for beating. The term tu'itu'i in Samoa also formerly referred to lengths of bamboo wrapped in a floor mat and struck with beaters, but this instrument is now called fala. It has a noticeably louder sound than the fala of mats without the bamboo. See R. Moyle: 'Samoan Musical Instruments', EthM, vol.18 (1974), 57–74, esp. 58, 64.

T'ŭkchong. Bronze bell, suspended in a wooden frame, of Korea (t'ŭk: 'special'; chong: 'bell'). It is a survival of one historical type of the Chinese tezhong. In the Korean version the highly decorated frame is about 72 cm tall and 56 cm wide, mounted on two stands of wooden lions, much as in the case of the set of bells p'yŏnjong. The bell itself is about 52 cm tall and 31 cm in diameter at the rim; near the rim there is a raised circle which is struck with a mallet of animal horn, giving the pitch c.

The t'ŭkchong has been made in Korea since the 15th century, but it is considered a purely Chinese instrument and is used only in the ritual music (aak) played in the tungga ('terrace ensemble') at the twice-yearly Sacrifice to Confucius in Seoul. Two strokes on the bell form part of the signal for the ensemble to begin playing; the instrument has no other musical function.

BIBLIOGRAPHY
Sŏng Hyŏn, ed.: Akhak kwebŏm [Guide to the Study of Music] (Seoul, 1493/R), 6.1a,b
Chang Sa-hun: Han'guk akki taegwan [Korean Musical Instruments] (Seoul, 1969), 110ff

ROBERT C. PROVINE

Tuki. General term for the obsolete large upright slit drum of Fila Island, Efate, Vanuatu. See K. Huffman: 'Slitdrums … ', Nabanga (1978), no.74, p.16 only.

Tukku. Gourd vessel rattle of the Kilba (Huba) people of Nigeria. It contains loose baobab seed. Three rattles of different sizes are strung together by a cord and attached to the player's wrists. The medium-sized rattle is held in the left hand, the other two in the right. Ownership is vested in the Mulea (hyena) clan and the rattle is used for the hyena dance during death celebrations.

T'ŭkkyŏng. Lithophone, suspended in a wooden frame, of Korea (t'ŭk: 'special'; kyŏng: 'chime'). It is a survival of one historical type of the Chinese teqing. In the Korean version the highly decorated frame is about 72 cm tall and 56 cm wide, mounted on two stands each consisting of a white wooden goose on a rectangular wooden platform, much as in the case of the p'yŏn'gyŏng lithophone. The chime itself is roughly L-shaped, about 53 cm along one portion and 50 cm along the other, both portions being about 17 cm wide and about 3 cm thick. The chime is struck on the side near one end with a mallet of animal horn, giving the pitch c'.

The t'ŭkkyŏng has been made in Korea since the 15th century from calcite quarried at Namyang in central Korea, but it is considered a purely Chinese instrument and is used only in the ritual music (aak) played in the tŭngga ('terrace ensemble') at the twice-yearly Sacrifice to Confucius in Seoul. Two strokes on the t'ŭkkyŏng form part of the signal for the ensemble to finish playing; the instrument has no other musical function.

BIBLIOGRAPHY
Sŏng Hyŏn, ed.: Akhak kwebŏm [Guide to the Study of Music] (Seoul, 1493/R), 6.2a–3a
Chang Sa-hun: Han'guk akki taegwan [Korean Musical Instruments] (Seoul, 1969), 118f

ROBERT C. PROVINE

Tulak [tula]. Term for various flutes of Central Asia. The tulak is a duct flute of the mountain Tajik people of Tajikistan. The instrument is called nai or tula by the mountain Tajiks of Afghanistan. The tula is also a wooden flute of the Tajiks of Badakhshan; it tapers towards the lower end and is marked by incised bands.

Tulali. End-blown flute of the Philippines. It is made of bagakay, a small variety of bamboo. Its three finger-holes and one thumbhole accommodate a pentatonic scale; the holes are spaced by the width of two of the maker's fingers. The blowing end is encircled by a piece of banana leaf. The tulali is played by men and women as a courting instrument. The Panay Bukidnon people reportedly believe that playing the tulali invites spirits with mystical powers (*tamawo*) to respond by also playing the flute. See C. Dioquino: 'Philippine Bamboo Instruments', *Humanities Diliman*, vol.5/1–2 (Jan/Dec 2008), 101–13.

Tulila. Clarinet of the Mandailing people of northern Sumatra, Indonesia, and various neighbouring groups. It has a quiet tone and was traditionally used by young men in courtship. Preferably it consists of two pieces, the smaller *anak ni tulila* ('child tulila') and the larger *induk ni tulila* ('mother tulila'), each made from a separate bamboo tube open at both ends. The *anak ni tulila* is provided with a single idioglot reed, carved from the bamboo just below the upper end of the tube and reinforced by string at the hinge; the string might also act as a tuning bridle and quieten the sound by reducing the reed's movement. The lower end of the *anak ni tulila* is inserted into the *induk ni tulila*, which has four fingerholes spaced nearly equally from the ends of the tube and from each other. The two tubes are loosely linked with string. The player puts the entire reed into his mouth and stops the tube's open upper end with his tongue. A second, less preferable type of tulila has the reed and fingerholes all on the same tube. The single-piece instruments are about 15 to 18 cm long and two-piece ones about 23 to 25 cm. The diameter of both types typically ranges from 5 to 7 mm.

Played alone, the *anak ni tulila* may be used to imitate bird calls or other sounds of nature. The complete instrument, in either its one- or two-piece form, is strongly associated with the human voice and language; its repertory consists largely of melodies based on well-known local poetry. Since the late 20th century, *tulila* playing and traditional courtship have become rare. See E. Nasution: *Tulila: Musik Bujukan Mandailing* ['Tulila: Mandailing Music of Courtship'] (Penang, 2007).

GINI GORLINSKI

Tullum. Side-blown horn of the Kilba (Huba) people of Nigeria. It is made from the horn of a bush-cow and was originally used by hunters for signalling. It is blown during communal farming and at the *tiwi* dance ceremony to summon performers and when the dance is at its height.

Tulnic. Romanian alphorn from Țara Moților, an ethnographic region in the western Carpathians in Transylvania. It is always straight and conical, made of fir and bound intermittently along its length with osier rings. The tulnic is played almost exclusively by girls and women, sounding mainly the fourth to ninth overtones.

Tülök [kanásztülök]. End-blown bovine horn of Hungary, used chiefly by shepherds for signalling. It is often decorated with incised patterns.

Tulou, Jean-Louis (*b* Paris, France, 11 Sept 1786; *d* Nantes, France, 23 July 1865). French flutist, composer, and flute manufacturer. The son of a bassoonist on the staff of the Paris Conservatoire, he entered that institution at the age of ten. A pupil of Jean-Georges Wunderlich (1755–1819), he won a first prize for flute in 1801. He became first flute at the Théâtre italien in 1805. He replaced Wunderlich in 1813 at the Paris Opéra and was judged by many to be the finest flutist in France. For political reasons he did not receive the chair at the Paris Conservatoire in 1816, but was appointed to this chair in 1829, and held it until his retirement in 1859. From 1831 to 1859 he was an official supplier of flutes to the Conservatoire. During his professorship he was bitterly opposed to the Boehm flute and in 1839 defeated Victor Coche's efforts to institute a class in the Boehm flute.

Tulou began to deal in flutes and established a successful flute factory in 1828. In that year Jacques Nonon (*b* Metz, France, 1802; *d* 1877) submitted a flute for his inspection, and in 1831 the two formed a partnership, with Nonon as foreman. In 1839 the workforce was reported as six in-house and four outside. They produced elegant flutes in the older French style and 12-keyed 'improved' flutes (the 'Système Tulou') with a small key to help the intonation of the $f\sharp''$ and $f\sharp'''$. Their collaboration ended in 1853, both continuing independently. Nonon obtained patents in 1854 for an improved flute and an improved oboe; he exhibited an oboe in Paris in 1855. Besides flutes, surviving instruments with the Tulou mark include a four-key piccolo and an oboe. Tulou left a very large number of excellent compositions and a good *Méthode pour la flute progressive et raisonné* (Paris, 1835/1851/*R*1973). See M. Tellier: *Jean Louis Tulou, flutiste, professeur, facteur 1786–1865* (thesis, Conservatoire de Paris, 1981).

PHILIP BATE/RENÉ PIERRE

Tulum. Bagpipe of Turkey and Azerbaijan. The bag is made of goat- or sheepskin and the cane double chanter is inserted into a trough-like wooden stock; there is no separate drone pipe. Both pipes of the chanter have five parallel fingerholes. Some instruments have a wooden chanter with two parallel bores. The idioglot single reeds are down-cut. In Turkish instruments, two or three of the upper holes in one of the pipes are sometimes sealed with beeswax, and the chanter often has an integral rectangular upturned wooden bell or attached cow-horn bell, or occasionally no bell at all. The mouthpipe has no non-return valve; the player stops the pipe with his tongue. The tulum is the main instrument of the semi-migrant stock-raising population of northeastern Anatolia, but in Azerbaijan it is now rare except in Nakhichevan, where it is used to accompany songs and dances. See L. Picken: *Folk Musical Instruments of Turkey* (London, 1975), 528–49.

R. CONWAY MORRIS, JOHANNA SPECTOR/R

Tulumbas [tulumbaz]. Military kettledrum of Russia and Ukraine. It was beaten by a thong with a bulging end, called a *boshchaga*.

Tumank [tsayantur]. Mouth bow of the Shuar (Jívaro) people of the Ecuadorian Oriente region, made from *guadúa* cane-bamboo. It is plucked with the finger-nails; the player's mouth serves as a resonator. It is used in courting to accompany love songs at sunset. The *paruntsi* is a similar instrument made from a bent cherry-wood sapling with a string of gut or *pita* or *cabuya* fibre. It is played by the Quechua people of Imbabura Province, northern highland Ecuador.

BIBLIOGRAPHY
S.L. Moreno: *Historia de la Música en el Ecuador* (Quito, 1972)
C.A. Coba Andrade: 'Instrumentos musicales ecuatorianos', *Sarance* (Oct 1979), no.7, pp.70–95

JOHN M. SCHECHTER/J. RICHARD HAEFER

Tumao. Single-headed cylindrical drum of the Saramaka Maroon people of Suriname. It is made from a hollow log up to 2 metres long and 15 to 20 cm in diameter. The skin head is attached by a loop of cords wrapped around the edge of the head and laced to a second loop of multiple strands of fibre about 15 cm below the top. The head is tuned by pounding wedges between the fibre loop and the body. Initially four wedges about 40 cm long are put in place. Fine tuning is accomplished by using a series of shorter wedges placed between the larger wedges and the body. Tension can also be adjusted by heating the head. The tumao is played with one hand only, the performer squatting near the drum, which is placed at an angle to the ground.

The tumao, dedicated to the Apuku spirits, plays intermediate rhythm patterns with the *apinti* and *agida* drums. The drums are played only by males; young boys learn by helping to tune the instruments. See M.J. Herskovits and F.S. Herskovits: *Suriname Folk-Lore* (New York, 1936).

J. RICHARD HAEFER

Tumbā [tumbī]. North Indian term literally meaning 'gourd'. It is used in the Hindi-speaking area both for a variable tension chordophone ('plucked drum') with a gourd body and for the double clarinet with a gourd wind cap.

Tumbadora [tumba, conga]. Single-headed drum of Cuba, historically associated with conga and rumba. Use of the term *tumbadoras* to denote a set of three drums dates from the 1950s; previously, these drums were known simply as *tambor* or *tumba* (from the verb *tumbar*, Sp. for 'beating a drum'), hence *tumbadora*. The names given to the individual drums in a set vary geographically, but generally stem from their function: the highest-pitched drum, which carries the improvisational role, is known as *quinto*, *requinto*, or *repicador*; the drum in the middle register, which plays a stabilizing role in the rhythmic locution of patterns and strokes (*toque*), is called *tres-dos*, *tres golpes*, or *un golpe*; and the lowest-pitched drum, which starts the *toque* and maintains a stable pattern, is called *llamador*, *salidor*, *fondo*, *tumbador*, or *conga*. The tumbadoras in the ensemble that accompanies conga (a genre of collective dancing typical of carnival celebrations) are called *congas*. The international music industry that has commercialized tumbadoras abroad also uses the term *conga* for the instrument.

The most common type of tumbadora has a somewhat barrel-shaped body, with the greatest diameter above the mid-point of the length and tapering to an open base of considerably smaller diameter than the head. Sizes range from about 67 to 77 cm tall, with a head diameter of about 20 to 40 cm. The size of the instruments does not always correlate with registers, which depend largely on tuning. This is possible because the low, middle, and high registers of tumbadoras remain within a rather narrow and low timbric spectrum. Heads are traditionally made of bovine or mule skin, but nowadays synthetic heads are not uncommon. Ordinarily the head is fastened by a hoop and stretched by metal tension keys, or less commonly is nailed to the body or stretched by turnbuckles. Handcrafted tumbadoras are built from approximately 25 wooden staves, preferably of pine, although cedar, palm, aguacate, majagua, and oak also are used. The glued staves can be reinforced by metal bands around the body's widest circumference and close to the head and base. Factory-made drums often have a fibreglass body.

Tumbadoras are struck by the hands, using five basic strokes: (1) striking with four fingers near the rim produces a clear tone with distinct pitch; (2) the same stroke produces a muffled tone when the fingers remain in contact with the head; (3) striking the head near the centre with the palm produces a deep, muted tone; (4) sharply slapping the head with quick repetition produces a popping sound; (5) touching the fingers or the heel of the palm lightly to the head produces a gentle tone.

When played by a seated musician, for example in rumba and certain religious ceremonies, the drum is held between the legs and slightly inclined forward to release sound from the open bottom. When incorporated into popular music ensembles, the drum stands upright in a metal tripod with the drummer standing behind it. For parading congas, the instrument hangs from a strap around the drummer's shoulder. When only two tumbadoras are used in *son* ensembles, these are called *macho* (high, male) and *hembra* (low, female). In the congas of eastern Cuba, tumbadoras reinforce the role of *bocúes*. The medium-size *tumbadora* used in the parading Charangas de Bejucal is called *mambisa*.

Tumbadoras present a synthesis of features appropriated from drums of different African origins. Moreover, Cubans subverted the African principle of assigning the oratorical role to the lowest-pitched drum by switching the improvisational function to the tumbadora in the highest register. Dizzy Gillespie has been credited with launching the international popularity of the tumbadora when, in 1947, he engaged the Cuban Chano Pozo to play a 'conga drum' in his jazz band. Leading 20th-century Cuban makers of tumbadoras included the Vergara brothers and Juan Bencomo Pedroso, Gilberto Castillo, and Trinidad Torregosa.

BIBLIOGRAPHY
C.M. Sáenz Coopat and A.V. Casanova Oliva: *Instrumentos de la música folclórico-popular de Cuba*, vol.2 (Havana, 1997), 376–88

C.M. Sáenz Coopat: 'Cuba under Tumbadora', *Diccionario de la música española e hispanoamericana*, vol.10: ed. E. Casares Rodicio, with Victoria Eli Rodríguez and Benjamín Yéepez Chamorro (Madrid 2002), 506–7.

MALENA KUSS

Tumbaknārī. Large goblet drum of Kashmir. It is similar and related to the *tombak* of Iran and the *zirbaghali* of Afghanistan; like the latter, it is usually made of pottery. It is held horizontally on the seated player's lap and left thigh and played with both hands. It is usually played in folk music and to accompany wedding songs such as *chhakkari* and *rove*, when it is used with the *rabāb* (lute), the *sarān* (fiddle), and the *nut* (percussion vessel). See B.C. Deva: *Musical Instruments of India* (Calcutta, 1978).

ALASTAIR DICK

Tumbal. Large kettledrum, part of the insignia of office of the Shehu of Borno in northeastern Nigeria. It is suspended between two Y-shaped sticks and beaten with leather thongs.

Tumbal sardi. Legendary drum of the Fulani people of Adamawa, Nigeria. Originally one of the war drums of Ukba brought from Mecca to Melle, it became the symbol of authority, handed on secretly to the ruler's chosen successor. According to the legend the first drum disappeared when a new ruler, Bondi Lamale, was unable to retrieve the drum from its hiding place, and so a wooden replica was made, also known as *tumbal sardi*. See P.F. Lacroix: *Poésie Peule de l'Adamawa* (Paris, 1965).

Tumboi. Drum chime of the Mbwela and Nkhangala peoples of Angola.

Tumbol [tembol, tumbel]. Drum of Chad.

(1) Large paired conical drum of the Kanembu people of northern Chad. It has a wooden ovoid body and two cowhide heads, laced in an 'X' pattern with single holes for the fastening ties. It is about 55 cm tall with a large diameter of 45 cm and a small diameter of 20 to 40 cm. To increase the tension large wooden pegs are inserted into the lacing holes of the larger head and at the crossing of the X. One of the pair is 'male', the other 'female'. 'Tumbol' is the generic name but the players refer to the female drum as 'tumboli'; its upper head is scraped thinner than the male's. The drums differ in other details. The male has an even number of pegs and the female always has one more, usually eight for the male and nine for the female. Around its middle the female drum has a *kayata* band, the same name as the string of pearls that the young Kanembu women wear around their waists.

The tumbol drums belong only to a person in some position of authority and only caste musicians play them. According to tradition there was once just one drum, and nowadays, for transmitting signals, the male drum alone is struck. For music the drums are used in pairs, hung vertically from posts. Each drum is struck on the larger head by a player with two straight sticks. When necessary a bunch of burning herbs is passed over the heads to heat them and increase the tension.

(2) Large double-headed cylindrical drum of the Tuburi people of southwestern Chad. It has parallel lacing, tightened by horizontal bands. There are no pegs. It is slung from the left shoulder and beaten by the hands.

(3) Double-headed drum of the Tundjer people of central Chad. It is paired with a bigger drum, the *nugara*, and resembles the *kwelli* of northern Chad, which is paired with the *nangara*.

MONIQUE BRANDILY

Tumbullac. Small kettledrum of Albania. The almost hemispherical body is made of wood, clay, or metal in different sizes. It is played by hand as a part of diverse instrumental ensembles in many regions in Albania. Other known designations are *tallamas* in Tiranë, *tollambas* in Berat, *tullumbac* ('balloon') in Dibër, *dumalek* in Zerqan, *tumlek* in Gramsh, and *tumelek* in Drenicë. A variant of the *tumbullac* is the *kadumi* in Central Albania or *kudumi* in Kosovo, where it is beaten with a belt.

ARDIAN AHMEDAJA

Tumdak' [tumdā]. Double-headed drum of the Santal people of Bihar, West Bengal, and Orissa, East India. The body is made of clay. The right head (about 20 cm in diameter) is smaller than the left (about 29 cm), and the centre of the conical body is very gently waisted (inverted bi-conical), though this is concealed by the leather lacings, densely laced in a 'V' pattern, giving a long, truncated conical appearance. Both heads (of cow- or goat-skin) are double, the upper skin (*moudha*) pasted to the lower (*cakki*) and cut away to leave an outer ring. On the right head the upper skin is about 37 mm wide; the lower has a paste (*kharen*) of powdered limestone, gram-flour, half-boiled rice, and soot, dried for three to four days and rubbed smooth with a stone. The paste on the left head (whose upper ring is about 45 mm wide) is thicker, has no soot and is not smoothed. Both heads are beaten by the hands. The *tumdak'* is played, together with the *tāmāk* or *deger* (kettledrum), in community dancing and singing, in the annual hunt and in the outcasting ceremony (*bitlaha*). Both drums are worshipped by the *nayke* priests at the winter solstice. The tumdak' is also called *mādal*, and is played by neighbouring tribes.

BIBLIOGRAPHY
W.G. Archer: *The Hill of Flutes: Life, Love, and Poetry in Tribal India: a Portrait of the Santals* (Pittsburgh, PA, 1974)
B.C. Deva: 'The Santals and their Musical Instruments', *Jb für musikalische Volks- und Völkerkunde*, vol.8 (Cologne, 1977), 36–46

ALASTAIR DICK

Tümïr. Double-headed wooden drum of the Mari people of the Volga-Ural region of Russia. The body is about 60 cm in diameter and 60 to 70 cm deep. The heads are lapped on flesh hoops with wooden counterhoops, and laced together with rope. Tension is adjusted by inserting a short wooden stick in each 'V' of rope and twisting it. There are usually two snares. The drum is used to accompany the *shüvir* (bagpipe) at weddings, and is similar to the Chuvash *parappan*.

Tumpung. Duct flute (whistle) of the Manobo people of the southern Philippines.

Tumtum. General term for musical instruments of the Palau Islands of Micronesia.

Tun [c'unc'un, tunkul, tum, tyum]. Slit drum of Mesoamerica, particularly the Yucatan peninsula, El Salvador, and Guatemala, similar to the Mexican *teponaztli*. Its origins are pre-Hispanic, and it is still predominantly played by Mayan musicians. Usually made of hollowed *hormigo* wood (*Platymiscium dimorphandrum*), it features an H-shaped cut on its upper side that forms two vibrating tongues producing different pitches often a 4th apart. They are struck with mallets, usually rubber-headed. When played, the tun is laid horizontally on the ground, on a stool, or on the musician's lap. It may be played solo, in pairs of different sizes, or in ensembles with trumpets, flutes, fiddles, or guitars.

Guatemalan Mayans also apply the term *tun* to a double-headed cylindrical drum of European origin beaten with two rubber-headed drumsticks. In colonial dictionaries of Mayan languages *tun* can be found to denote trumpets. A similar instrument called *k'utin* or *cutín* is reported among the Ch'orti' Indians of Guatemala, where it is believed to be an instrument *del Señor* ('of God') and is said to recreate the din of thunder. See A. Arrivillaga Cortés: *Exposición no. 6 de Instrumentos Musicales de la Tradición Popular de Guatemala* (Guatemala City, 1982).

ANDRÉS AMADO, MATTHIAS STÖCKLI

Ṭunbūr (pl. *ṭanābīr*). Arabian lyre of the Islamic period; the term is also widely used for a long-necked lute. The term, of Pahlavi origin, is included in the celebrated inventory of the page of the Sassanid king Xhusraw Parviz (590–628), where it appears in a list of musical instruments that includes the *barbaṭ* and the *kinnor*. In the Turkish-Iranian-Indian area, the instrument might be included in the family of long-necked lutes. Although the Arabs readily use the word in this sense, it has also for them denoted a lyre, and this fact has given rise to serious misunderstandings. It is first recorded in Arabic in a line by the poet al-A'shā (*d* 625), who curiously uses the term in its plural form, 'ṭanābīr': 'And the pleasant voices of the *ṭanābīr* [sound] along with a *ṣanj* (harp), deftly touched'. The use of the plural here might recall a similar usage, that of *kinnārāt* for Arabian lyres or *kinārātu* for the lyres of Mari. The inclusion of the *ṣanj* in the second half of the line makes the comparison all the more valid. For this poet, strongly influenced by the civilization of Iran, *ṭanābīr* can refer as much to lyres as to long-necked lutes.

The unexplained transfer of the term 'ṭunbūr' from the lute to the lyre is among the most difficult musicological problems posed by the rise of Islam. The etymology has caused commentators enormous trouble and led lexicographers into aberrations (see Farmer). At the same time, the idea of the ṭunbūr as a lyre can be clarified only by considering the juxtaposition of *mi'zaf* (the official Arabic name for the lyre) and *mizmār* (a wind instrument) as a whole—a tradition of great antiquity: 'Jubal, the father of them that play upon the *kinnor* (string instrument) and the *'ugab* (wind instrument)' (*Genesis* iv.21). This association did not escape certain later writers: 'The *nāy* flute which responds to the lute' (Mas'ūdī: *Murūj al-dhahab*, Paris, 1874, viii.90); 'The Iraqi *mizmār*, which is played with string instruments' (Ibn Ḥajar al-Haythamī: *Kaff al-ra 'ā'*, Cairo, 1937, i.12). To understand that ṭunbūr means a lyre, it is necessary to investigate both the terms *mizmār* and *mi'zaf*, and the substitution of the latter term with 'ṭunbūr'. Some writings interchange from *mi'zaf* to ṭunbūr (as in the canonical and non-canonical *ḥadīth* respectively). In addition, ṭunbūr is used officially, as is *mi'zaf*, as a sign of the coming of the end of the world: 'when the last hour comes and Ibn Maryam (the son of Mary) comes down to you … for he shall break the idols, the cross and the ṭunbūr'. From this it becomes easier to conclude that ṭunbūr should be understood as a lyre.

Although in most cases the term 'ṭunbūr' means a lute, some later authors of the 13th century (e.g. Mutarrazī) connected it, correctly, with the Yemenite *mi'zaf*. It is in the dialectal mutation 'ṭumbūra', and more especially 'ṭanbūra', that the lyre has survived to this day in the area of the Red Sea.

BIBLIOGRAPHY
H.G. Farmer: 'Ṭunbūr', The Encyclopaedia of Islam (Leiden, 1928–38, 3/2007)
A.J. Wensinck and J.P. Mensing: 'Azafa', 'Ṭunbūr', Concordances et indices de la tradition musulmane (Leiden, 1933–69)
J. Robson, ed.: *Tracts on Listening to Music, being Dhamm al-malāhī, by Ibn abī 'l-Dunyā* (London, 1938)
M. Husayn, ed.: *Dīwān al-A'shā* [Poetical Works of al-A'shā] (Cairo, 1950/R)
M. Boyce: 'The Parthian Gosan and Iranian Minstrel Tradition', *Journal of the Royal Asiatic Society* (1957), 10–45, esp. 27
C. Poché: 'David et l'ambiguité' du *mizmār*', The World of Music (Berlin, 1983), vol.2, 58ff

CHRISTIAN POCHÉ

Tunda. Transverse flute of the Ecuadorian highlands. It takes its name from the cane from which it is made. Length, diameter, and number of fingerholes vary. The Quechua people of Imbabura and Pichincha Provinces play these instruments at festivities for St John and SS Peter and Paul in June. See J. Idrovo Urigüen: *Instrumentos musicales prehispánicos del Ecuador* (Cuenca, 1987).

JOHN M. SCHECHTER/R

Tung bok [tunbak]. Lute of the Lepchas people of Sikkim, North India. The body and long unfretted neck are made from one piece of *hopta* wood about 46 cm long. The small resonating bowl, 12 cm in diameter, has a goatskin belly. The strings are plucked with a tiny leather plectrum, which is attached to the end of the instrument with string. The bowl is usually round but some are pear-shaped, and very close in structure to the West Bengal *dotara*, while others have inverted 'U' shapes. The latter are somewhat larger, about 58 cm long overall with the bowl 25 cm long tapering from 15.7 cm wide at the base to 4.2 cm where it joins the neck. The tung bok ordinarily has four tuning pegs, although only three are strung; the fourth is provided for visual symmetry. Decoration is minimal and usually on the back of the bowl. Often striated designs are used, derived from feather or leaf patterns. The strings are tuned in ascending 4ths with the first and third strings tuned microtonally sharp. Many performers make their own tung bok while others commission them from Bengali *dotara* makers, who make them larger still, about 80 cm long overall with a bowl diameter of 29 cm.

ELAINE DOBSON

Tungda. Kettledrum of the Lepcha people of Sikkim, North India, or possibly only a generic term for drum in Sikkim.

Tungtung. (1) Bamboo stamping tube of the Isneg people of the northern Philippines; the Tausug people of the southern Philippines call it *tuntung* and it is known by the Sama (or Samal) peoples as *tuntungan*. Stamping tubes were used by women mediums calling the spirits to visit the human world and cure the sick. Nowadays they are played for recreation, stamping the closed end on flat pieces of rock and covering the open upper end with one hand to a varying extent to change the pitch.

(2) Resonating board of the Yakan people of the southern Philippines. A board about 25 cm wide and 2.5 metres long is suspended from a frame and almost touches the ground. Two large wide-bodied jars, one smaller than the other, are suspended upside down with their narrow mouths almost touching the board in order to catch its resonance. One player beats a fast ostinato on one end of the board while another plays an irregular, improvised beat on the other end and makes dancing steps. An instrument with a similar musical function is a log drum called *edel* by the Kalagan Manobo and *odol* by the Tiboli people of Mindanao.

JOSÉ MACEDA

Tuni. Transverse flute of the Fula people of Sierra Leone. It is made of cane and has three fingerholes. The term may also refer to an idioglot transverse clarinet of the Fula.

Tuning. Adjustment, generally made before playing, of the pitches, intervals, or the overall pitch level of an instrument. Inflections of pitch that form an inherent part of the performance itself are usually thought of as a matter of intonation rather than tuning. The term is also commonly used to refer to the note or (more often) the set of notes or intervals to which a particular instrument is tuned. The tunings, in this sense, of individual instruments are discussed in the articles on the instruments concerned. A third use of the term is in the sense

of the 'tuning system' employed, referring to a model of the scale corresponding to some mathematical division of the octave. For the history of such models in performance practice, *see* Temperaments, Well-tempered clavier, Meantone, Just intonation, and Pythagorean intonation.

Wind instruments in an ensemble are tuned to make their general pitch level uniform by adjusting the length of tubing in each instrument. Tuning slides are shifted in brass instruments, the top joint in a flute, the staple of the reed in an oboe, etc. The extent to which bass reed instruments can be tuned is slight, as each millimetre of difference amounts to a smaller portion of the total tube length than on a treble instrument. On the other hand, the palpable lengthening or shortening of any woodwind instrument will complicate the player's task during performance by tending to put the instrument slightly out of tune with itself: to sound a precise octave above the new basic pitch, for instance, the player must compensate for the fact that the effective tube length provided by the normal fingering is no longer precisely half the overall length. The techniques used for this compensation are likely to affect timbre, volume, or articulation. Hence the intonation and voicing of a good woodwind instrument are displayed best when it is at the pitch level intended by the maker; this is especially true of the oboe, the instrument which provides the *a'* to which the orchestra tunes (this pitch being used because the violas and cellos as well as the violins have a string tuned to A, and this is the cello's highest and hence clearest string). That pitch level itself, however, varies somewhat with temperature, gradually rising as the instrument is warmed by the player's breath.

On string instruments the tuner adjusts the tension and sometimes the sounding length of the string. Gross alterations of tension are avoided because of the danger of breakage and because a pronounced change in the stress borne by the instrument will more or less subtly alter its shape and hence in turn the sounding length, tension, and pitch of any previously tuned strings. (At least two tunings are thus required to raise or lower the pitch level of a piano, the first being unlikely to leave the instrument very well in tune.)

Most keyboard instruments have so many strings or pipes that some of them are far more suitable to begin tuning with than others. The octave around middle C on the keyboard, perhaps *f*–*f'*, is traditional nowadays on the organ (using pipes of the 4′ Principal rank) and on the piano (using the middle of the three strings for each note, the other two being damped by a strip of felt which the tuner inserts). One note, for example *a* or *c'*, is set to a pitch standard from a tuning fork or the like, and then the rest of the octave is tuned through a network of consonant intervals extending from this starting point. Often a chain of 5ths and 4ths is used (for instance A–D–G–C, etc.), but many tuners use 3rds and major 6ths at least as much. Once the initial octave has been set, the tuning is extended to the other octaves and, finally, to the other sets of strings or pipes.

In judging intervals a tuner listens, consciously or subliminally, for beats among the overtones of the two

Table 1

	grand piano	large upright	small upright
d''''			
	1208	1209	1212
d'''			
	1206	1206	1207
d''			
	1202	1204	1206
middle d'			
	1202	1204	1206
d			
	1204	1205	1209
D			
	1209	1211	1216
D'			

notes involved. Hence differences in timbre crucially affect the procedure. It would be difficult to set precisely tempered intervals by a stopped-flute rank on the organ, for example, because its timbre is weak in the odd-numbered members of the harmonic overtone series. In piano timbre a mild degree of inharmonicity obliges the tuner to make all the octaves slightly larger than the theoretical norm of 1200 cents (which would be an octave with a frequency ratio of exactly 2:1). While the proper amount varies with the particular instrument, a general indication is given in Table 1 (based on suggestions made by the Tuners Supply Co. of Boston, Massachusetts). Some of the 'stretch' in the extreme bass and treble, however, is for the sake of a certain melodic bite gained by making the octaves larger than harmonic justness would dictate. In this respect different tuners and musicians have different tastes, but markedly stretched octaves are at best a mixed blessing in chamber music, where a more sober intonation will allow the non-keyboard instruments to blend more resonantly.

On instruments with extremely inharmonic timbre, the criteria for good tuning are quite different. Each Indonesian gamelan, for example, is likely to have its own shading of the *pelog* or *slendro* scale, and these shadings differ far more than the various temperaments of the Western tradition. Yet within each gamelan the unisons and octaves are tuned precisely to achieve certain qualities of beating and, according to Hood (*Selected Reports in Ethnomusicology* (Los Angeles, 1966)), definite patterns of stretching or compressing the octaves for certain notes of the *pelog* or *slendro* scale.

For bibliography *see* Temperaments and Violin intonation.

MARK LINDLEY

Tuning fork (Fr. *diapason*; Ger. *Stimmgabel*; It. *corista*). Metal device (occasionally with resonator) for establishing pitch. It was invented in 1711 by John Shore, Handel's famous trumpeter. Its musical advantages are that its pitch is hardly affected by changes of temperature, that for all practical purposes it retains its pitch permanently, that it is of convenient size, and that its pitch can be adjusted by careful filing. To sharpen it, the tips of the prongs are filed, and to flatten it the prongs are filed inside just above the yoke that joins them (a job better left to an instrument maker). When a fork is struck and held in the air its sound is faint and, for a short time, at least one high partial tone is clearly heard; but if the stem is pressed down on a table, or other hard surface of some size, the fork's note becomes much louder, while the high partial tone fades out at once. The vibrations of the two prongs, away from and towards one another, cause the stem to move up and down, and it is this that sets the surface in sympathetic vibration as a soundboard: the soundboard rapidly drains away the energy of vibration of the fork to produce its own motion, hence the fading of the fundamental note of the fork and the almost instantaneous fading of the high partial tone. This high partial tone of the tuning fork is an interesting and extreme example of the 'inharmonicity' of a mechanical system that can vibrate in a number of different 'modes' and is allowed to vibrate freely. It is not easy to determine the pitch of the first upper partial by ear alone; but in the average fork it is about two octaves and a major 6th above the fundamental, which is the note used for tuning. It is thus incorrect to speak of the 'harmonics' of a tuning fork, for the vibrations of its several tones are inharmonic.

Originally invented for musical purposes, the tuning fork was found to have properties that made it invaluable as a scientific instrument, and as a reference standard of frequency (rate of vibration). For use in the acoustics laboratory a tuning fork was often fitted with a resonance box. In shape this was rather like a large matchbox with one end removed; it had a knob on the top with a hole in it into which the fork could be fitted. Sometimes a cylindrical resonator was used instead. The resonance box, or resonator, has its own note, just as a glass jar has (as one discovers by blowing across the mouth of a test tube), and this note was made slightly different from the note of the fork's fundamental. If the notes were made exactly the same, the resonance box would respond so much that it would drain away the energy of the fork too rapidly and the sound of the fork would fade too soon. The resonance box, not being tuned to the fork, actually alters its frequency, though the alteration is extremely slight. Since the resonator radiates the fundamental tone much more efficiently than the inharmonic high partial tones, a tuning fork and its resonance box produce a practically pure tone, and were often used for that purpose before the availability of electronic signal generators.

Three well-known names are especially associated with the scientific use of the tuning fork in the 19th century for musical objectives. Johann Heinrich Scheibler was the first to devise, in his tuning-fork tonometer, a method of determining with accuracy the absolute frequency of a given musical note and of comparing the frequencies of two notes. Lissajous devised a still more accurate method of comparing the frequencies of two tuning forks which give a mistuned unison, or a mistuned consonance. He viewed, through what is called a Lissajous vibration microscope, the pattern made by the motion of a spot of light reflected in turn on a highly polished area on one prong of each of the two forks which were set to vibrate in planes at right angles to each other. The gradual shifting of this pattern gave him an accurate measure of the difference of frequency. Rudolph Koenig was able to determine absolute frequency by means of his clock-fork, which he used to show that Lissajous' standard fork, intended to record 'diapason normal', really had a frequency of 435.4[5] Hz at 15° C. (The brackets around the 5 is because Lissajous' standard fork, now in Paris (*F.P.cm*), was attached to a resonance box which Koenig, quite rightly, was unwilling to disturb. As a consequence its vibration faded too rapidly to allow him time to ascertain the second decimal place.) Koenig's clock-fork was a beautiful piece of apparatus for maintaining a fork in continuous vibration by mechanical means in order to measure its frequency with great accuracy.

Modern methods use electrical means to keep a fork in continuous vibration for such a purpose. Other electrical means are used to compare a fork's frequency with that of a musical sound. Both devices were used in the chromatic stroboscope (Stroboconn), invented shortly before World War II by physicists in the laboratories of C.G. Conn Ltd, the American musical instrument makers. In this instrument the frequency of a fork whose vibrations are maintained electrically is adjusted by turning a knob that moves a weight along each prong. The vibration of the fork controls the speeds of rotation of patterned discs, there being one disc for each chromatic note in an octave. These discs are illuminated by a gaseous discharge lamp that flashes at the frequency of a sound falling on a microphone. After turning the knob to the right or left, until the pattern on one of the rotating discs appears to stand still, the observer is able to read at once from a graduated scale the deviation of the frequency of the sound from that of the nearest note of the chromatic musical scale at standard pitch (a' = 440 Hz). The material of the fork is a nickel-chromium-steel alloy that makes the fork's frequency practically independent of the temperature.

Since the 1970s crystal-controlled frequency generators and meters, in which the oscillation of an electric circuit is controlled and stabilized by the resonant mechanical vibration of a small slab of crystalline quartz, have replaced equipment based on tuning forks for scientific purposes, and compact electronic tuning meters are used by many musicians. These modern achievements may prompt one to appreciate more fully those of the music physicists of the 19th century who, with none of the electronic resources of the modern acoustics laboratory at their disposal, managed to obtain remarkably precise results.

BIBLIOGRAPHY

G. Stradner: 'Stellt Michael Pacher 1486 eine Stimmgabel dar?', *'Musik muss man machen': eine Festgabe für Josef Mertin*, eds. J. Mertin and M. Nagy (Vienna, 1994), 127–41

K. Winkler: 'Stimmung und Stimmgeräte', *Das Orchester*, vol.43/11 (1995), 24–8

L.S. LLOYD/MURRAY CAMPBELL

Tuning-fork instruments. Instruments, mostly with keyboards, that incorporate tuning forks as the sound source; their descendant the celesta rapidly became a more common alternative. The forks are set in vibration over a resonance chamber or individual resonators and sound a practically pure, and therefore monotonous, tone. One advantage over strings is tuning stability. The first instrument of this type was Charles Clagget's 'Aiuton, or Ever-tuned organ' (1788), in which the forks were bowed by a rotating metal cone. In later instruments, such as the Hilleno patented in the USA by U.C. Hill in 1847, 1858, and 1860 and in the UK in 1873, the forks are usually struck by rebounding hammers like those in a piano. To recreate vowel sounds for acoustic research, Hermann von Helmholtz controlled eight tuning forks (1856, subsequently 12 forks), tuned to the overtone series of a single note, with an oscillating electromagnetic circuit to produce sustained sounds, using an additional fork to stabilize the circuit.

In 1865 Victor Mustel of Paris introduced the Typophone, which was registered in Great Britain in 1866; Vincent d'Indy included it in *Le chant de la cloche* (1885) and Henri Duparc in *L'invitation au voyage* (*c*1870, later revised for orchestra). In 1872 John Milward extended one of the prongs to produce an octave. After 20 years' work Thomas Machell of Glasgow perfected his 'Dulcitone' in 1880; it was used in five works by Percy Grainger, including *The Warriors* (1913–16). Other instruments included the 'Adiaphon' of W. Fischer & E.W. Fritzsch of Leipzig (1882) and the 'Euphonium' of G.A.I. Appunn of Hanau, a five-octave instrument without resonators (1885).

From 1885, in his Elektrophonisches Klavier, Richard Eisenmann used a system of electromagnets and tuning-fork oscillators to excite and sustain vibrations in piano strings. Helmholtz's use of tuning forks as a stable vibrating source for controlling an electrical circuit was extended in the Rangertone organ (1931); the forks maintained electromagnetic tone-wheels at a constant speed, and the tuning of individual notes could be adjusted by changing single forks. The RCA Electronic Music Synthesizer (two models: 1951–2, 1957) included a set of 12 electronically-driven tuning forks as the primary source of sound. Amplified tuning forks are featured in the Kamerton pianino (1950s) from the former USSR and in several compositions of the 1980s and 90s, including works by Denis Smalley (1985–9), Richard Lerman (1976), and Warren Burt (several works for a specially built four-octave set of aluminium tuning forks tuned in 19-note just intonation, with an extended bass range).

H.G. FARMER/HUGH DAVIES/R

Tuning slide (Fr. *coulisse d'accord*; Ger. *Stimmzug*). On wind instruments the tuning slide is a part of the tube that can be pulled out or pushed in to adjust slightly the sounding length and basic pitch of an instrument. On brass instruments the tuning slide is a detachable U-shaped tube of cylindrical bore; it was apparently invented by J.G. Haltenhoff of Hanau in the late 18th century. On woodwind instruments tuning slides consist of tenon-and-socket joints that can be pulled out or pushed in, a more satisfactory way of adjusting the pitch than by using *corps de rechange* (interchangeable middle pieces of varying lengths). The telescopic tuning slide began to appear on flutes towards the middle of the 18th century; Quantz claimed it as his own invention. About 1830, cylindrical tuning slides (*pompes d'accorde*), often adjustable via a rack-and-pinion mechanism, began to appear on some bassoons made in France, Germany, and Austria. However, these slides (five spread across three joints on a bassoon by Savary *jeune*) introduced perturbations into otherwise conical bores. Simple tuning slides were sometimes found on the top joints of Viennese oboes during this era.

On organ pipes, a tuning slide is a movable metal tube surrounding and extending slightly above the top of a cylindrical metal flue pipe; it can be raised or lowered to adjust the length and pitch of the pipe.

HOWARD MAYER BROWN/JAMES B. KOPP

Tuning wire. In organs, reed pipes are tuned to the pitch of a convenient diapason rank (usually a 4′ Principal) by means of a stiff wire of brass or other copper-based alloy that passes through the lead block into which the shallot and tongue are wedged. The angled lower end of the wire presses the tongue against the shallot; the wire is raised (to increase the vibrating length of the tongue and flatten the pitch of the pipe) by tapping the edge of a steel reed knife upwards against the overhang of a filed-out portion of the wire above the block, or the underside of a right-angled bend in it, and lowered (to sharpen the pitch) by tapping the wire downwards. Since the tone as well as the pitch of a reed pipe depends largely on the tongue, tuning exclusively by means of a wire (without also tuning the resonator) can change the tonal regulation of the pipe.

MARTIN RENSHAW/R

Tunkul. Slit drum of the pre-Contact Maya people, known to the Aztec as *teponaztli*; the term is also used for the modern *tun*. The tunkul of the ancient Maya was used as an accompanying instrument for the *zonó* dance. In Yucatán it was commonly laid on the ground rather than on a trestle, as in Aztec usage. Colonial writers mentioned the *teponaztli* (i.e. tunkul) as the indispensable Mayan festival as well as sacred instrument. In 1813 José Granado y Baeza justified its continuing use in religious ceremonies with the claim that *Isaiah* xviii.1 referred to the Yucatán tunkul.

In highland Guatemala the common *tunkul* (also called *c'unc'un* or *tun*) is a horizontal percussion tube with two vibrating tongues, struck with a plain or rubber-tipped mallet or antler, producing two pitches approximately a 4th apart. Two instruments of different sizes are sometimes played together. A confusion in the literature arises from the use in Quichean languages of the word *tun* or *tum* to refer both to the slit drum and to the trumpet.

LINDA L. O'BRIEN-ROTHE/R

Tunshinkidi. Double-headed drum of the Yeke, Luba, and Lomotwa peoples in the Shaba region of the Democratic Republic of the Congo. The body is made of a palm tree log, with both ends hollowed but left solid in the centre. The heads are nailed on. Frequently it is decorated with white and red geometrical patterns. It is suspended from the neck of the player and used to accompany songs of praise to the chief. See O. Boone: *Les tambours du Congo belge et du Ruanda-Urundi* (Tervuren, 1951), 57–8.

FERDINAND J. DE HEN

Túntui [túnduy]. Large wooden slit drum of the Shuár (Jívaro) people of Ecuador (the provinces of Zamora Chínchipe, Morona Santiago, and Napo) and Peru (notably the Peruvian Aguaruna, south of the Marañón River). It is taboo for women and serves to send signals of war, death, or some event. Its penetrating sound can be heard over a radius of 5 km. See C.A. Coba Andrade: 'Instrumentos musicales ecuatorianos', *Sarance* (Oct 1979), no.7, pp.70–95.

JOHN M. SCHECHTER

Tuṇṭuṇe. Drone chordophone or plucked drum, of Maharashtra, western India. The metal string is fastened at the underside of a goatskin membrane pasted over the open bottom of a cylindrical wooden resonator. As in the *coṇak* the string passes through a hole in the membrane and up through the resonator to the upper end of a stick that is nailed vertically to the side of the cylinder; unlike the *coṇak,* however, the string is attached at this upper end to a tuning peg by means of which it is tuned to the tonic of the music performed. The tuṇṭuṇe is held under the left arm and plucked with a small plectrum, giving both a monotone drone and a rhythmic accompaniment to bardic or devotional songs and in folk drama.

The *noone guddalavani burra* of Andhra, south India, is similar save that the resonator tapers and is often of metal. It also accompanies vocal music and, as its name indicates, it is used by soothsayers.

BIBLIOGRAPHY
S. Krishnaswami: *Musical Instruments of India* (New Delhi, 1965, rev. 3/1977), 42
K.S. Kothari: *Indian Folk Musical Instruments* (New Delhi, 1968)
B.C. Deva: *Musical Instruments of India: their History and Development* (Calcutta, 1978), 150

JONATHAN KATZ

Tunumukhu [tamva]. Kettledrum of the Newar musician caste in Kathmandu Valley, Nepal. It accompanies the *mvālī* shawm and *jhyāli* cymbals on ritual occasions such as visits to temples. The clay body is 13 cm deep with a goatskin head 21 cm in diameter secured by 'V' lacing. The drum is tied to the waist of the player by thongs and the two drumsticks hang from the thongs in a cloth bag when not in use. The body of the drum may be decoratively painted.

GERT-MATTHIAS WEGNER, SIMONNE BAILEY

Tuohitorvi [tanotorvi]. Common name for Finnish pastoral horns, sometimes also for clarinet-type instruments.

Tuohitorvi, possibly by Teppo Repo, Finland, c1975. (Edinburgh University Collection of Historic Musical Instruments (3184))

The horns are usually of curved conical form with an integral mouthpiece and without fingerholes, and are made of split, hollowed wood wrapped with birch or other tree bark (commonly alder) to hold the pieces together. The bottle-shaped *pullotorvi* is widely used, especially in Karelia, as is the similar *turu*, about 40 cm long, primarily a pastoral and signalling instrument in Karelia.

A modern version of the tuohitorvi also exists, with five fingerholes and a thumbhole, perhaps a creation by the Finnish former army musician and instrument maker Teppo Repo (who also created a split-wood, bark-covered recorder simulacrum). It is played similarly to the *bockhorn*, using hand stopping to fill the gaps in the range between the fundamental and the first fingerhole pitch. The instrument is popular enough to be used to illustrate tourist brochures and souvenirs.

See R. Parks: 'The Tuohitorvi: *Cornett Survival or Re-Creation?*', *GSJ*, vol.48 (March 1995), 188–93.

JEREMY MONTAGU

Tu-ôl. Transverse flute of the Orang Asli (aborigines) of Peninsular Malaysia. It has one fingerhole at the proximal end, made by piercing the node. By stopping this hole or leaving it open two notes, usually a 4th apart, can be produced. Skeat (1906) claimed that it could produce three notes, and that it was played by holding the palm of the right hand over the open end, and the thumb of the left hand over the small hole in the other end. Flutes of this type listed by Blacking, all from the Senoi, vary in length from about 9.5 to 15 cm, and in diameter from about 1.5 to 3.5 cm.

BIBLIOGRAPHY

W.W. Skeat and C.O. Blagden: *Pagan Races of the Malay Peninsula* (London, 1906)

J.A.R. Blacking: 'Musical Instruments of the Malayan Aborigines', *Federation Museums Journal*, new ser., vol.1–vol.2 (1954–5), 35–52

JACK PERCIVAL BAKER DOBBS

Turali [turahi, tuahi]. Nose flute of Sabah, Malaysia. The Rungus Dusun people of north Sabah use a relatively short instrument from 30 to 38 cm long, while in the Kadazan Dusun communities it can be from 38 cm to 1 metre long. It is made from a piece of *sumbiling* bamboo that is open at one end. At the opposite end, closed by a natural node, a small blowing hole is cut into the node. The tube has three equidistant fingerholes and a thumbhole. It is played by placing the blowing hole directly under one nostril while plugging the other nostril to intensify the airstream. In the district of Tambunan some turali are modified to be blown by the mouth: a blowing hole is cut in the side of the proximal end of the tube and a narrow, circular piece of bamboo is added to cover this hole partially to form a sort of mouthpiece. Because of its soft, sombre tone the *turali* is played by women to mourn the dead and express grief, to imitate melodies of songs or chants, or to wake the family in the morning. It is now also used for personal entertainment.

BIBLIOGRAPHY

E.M. Frame: 'The Musical Instruments of Sabah, Malaysia', *EM*, vol.26 (1982), 247–74

J. Pugh-Kitingan: *Selected Papers on Music in Sabah* (Kota Kinabalu, Sabah, 2004), 31–3

PATRICIA MATUSKY

Turam. Kettledrum of Madhya Pradesh (Bastar district), central India. Its hemispherical wooden or pottery body is about 30 cm in diameter, and the drum is played resting on the ground, the laced head being struck with two sticks. It is used with other instruments by some of the Maria people to accompany dancing or singing. See W. Grigson: *The Maria Gonds of Bastar* (London, 1938, 2/1949).

GENEVIÈVE DOURNON

Ture angwa. Side-blown horn of the Madi people of Uganda. It is an animal horn with a plain oval mouth-hole in the concave side. The tip might be cut off to form a fingerhole. It is used by men and boys in their dances, and is similar to the Acholi *obute*.

Turkish crescent [jingling Johnny, Chinese pavilion] (Fr. *chapeau chinois, pavillon chinois*; Ger. *Schellenbaum*). Percussion stick in the form of an ornamental standard, generally having at the top a conical pavilion or an ornament shaped like a Chinese hat, surmounted by the Muslim crescent—hence its several names. Bells and jingles and usually two horsetail plumes of different colours are suspended from the various ornaments. The plumes are occasionally red-tipped (emblematic of the battlefield). The instrument is held vertically and shaken with an up and down or twisting movement.

The Turkish crescent might have derived from the *tugh*, the symbol of rank of the Ottoman military élite. It developed in Europe in the mid-18th century when jingles were added as decoration, perhaps in imitation of another Turkish instrument, the *cewhan*, a small crescent-shaped stick-rattle with bells, which was not associated with military music. It became an important instrument in the janissary band and was adopted by British Army bands in the late 18th century. From the middle of the 19th century it was discarded by the British, but survives on the Continent in the German lyre-shaped form, *Schellenbaum*.

The Turkish crescent was primarily an instrument of the military band. Hector Berlioz (in his *Grand traité d'instrumentation*, 1843) wrote that the shaking of its 'sonorous locks' added brilliance to marching music. It is included (as *pavillon chinois*) in his *Symphonie funèbre et triomphale*. His 'dream' ensemble of 467 instrumentalists included four *pavillons chinois* among the 53 percussion instruments. See B. Chenley: 'Jingling Johnny: a Note on the Pavillon Chinois', *Berlioz Society Bulletin* (1961), no.36, pp.4–5.

JAMES BLADES/R

Turkish drum. Name by which the bass drum was known in Europe until the beginning of the 19th century. Longer than its diameter, it was played in 'Turkish' fashion, with a heavy, solid wooden beater in one hand and a light switch in the other, as frequently indicated in the music of Haydn, Mozart, Beethoven, and others by notes with stems up or down, the beater on strong beats and the switch on intervening beats.

JEREMY MONTAGU

Turlure [turlurette] (Fr.). (1) Early term for a small bagpipe.

(2) Duct flute of northern France, or by extension any instrument used by itinerant musicians.

(3) *Turlutaine* is a type of bird organ that imitates curlews.

Turner, Daniel (*b* Vancouver, BC, 27 Jan 1952). Canadian luthier, known for making flamenco guitars. He became interested in guitar making while studying flamenco music in Spain in the 1970s; he learned the rudiments of the craft in Andalusia and Majorca and initially copied

traditional *negra* (dark-coloured wood, e.g. Brazilian rosewood) and *blanca* (light-coloured wood, e.g. Spanish cypress) models. In developing his own designs he has emphasized visual aspects through the use of more exotic woods such as quilted bubinga, Port Orford cedar, koa, snakewood, Tasmanian tigerwood, and ziricote. These materials required modifications of the normal forming and bracing of the soundtable. Turner has a limited output of customized, handmade flamenco guitars in various models, mostly produced to order, but in 2012 he was establishing a production company in Brazil to manufacture his 'Sóla'-model nylon-strung electro-acoustic guitar.

Turntablism. Performance technique in which sound recordings are manipulated, typically through the use of two phonographs (gramophones) and an audio mixer. Although the use of phonographs as musical instruments dates to the early decades of the 20th century, turntablism as commonly understood has its roots in hip-hop. Starting in the mid 1970s hip-hop DJs (disc jockeys) in New York developed techniques to transform the sound of commercially recorded vinyl discs, notably by looping (repeating short musical passages, often drum solos) and scratching (pushing a record back and forth underneath the stylus). These techniques, developed by Grandmaster Flash (Joseph Sadler), GrandWizzard Theodore (Theodore Livingston), and others, allowed DJs to transform pre-recorded discs into wholly new music.

The terms 'turntablism' and 'turntablist' came into wide use in the mid 1990s, popularized by the California-based DJ Babu (Chris Oroc) of the DJ group (or crew) The Beat Junkies. 'Turntablist' came to signify a DJ who scratched and mixed records in virtuosic performances, either as a soloist or with a crew. Two developments aided the flourishing of turntablism in the 1990s: advancements in mixer technology that allowed DJs a finer control over the sound, and the growing prominence of DJ competitions known as battles.

Since the 1990s, turntablism has come to be incorporated into an array of musical genres and styles, notably rock and jazz, and the practice has expanded beyond traditional analogue turntables and mixers. In the first decade of the 2000s, the use of digital vinyl emulation systems, which connect turntables to laptop computers and allow the manipulation of digital files, became increasingly common.

BIBLIOGRAPHY

K.F. Hansen: *The Acoustics and Performance of DJ Scratching: Analysis and Modeling* (diss., U. of Stockholm, 2010)

S. Webber: *Turntable Technique: The Art of the DJ* (Boston, 2000, 2/2009)

M. Katz: *Groove Music: The Art and Culture of the Hip-Hop DJ* (New York, 2012)

S. Smith: *Hip-Hop Turntablism, Creativity and Collaboration* (Surrey, 2013)

MARK KATZ

Turoń. Clappers of Poland. The turoń is usually made to imitate the head of a sheep or goat, with a moving lower jaw. Many clappers of this kind (for example a *bocian*: 'stork') are used during Christmas and Easter by folk carol singers.

ZBIGNIEW J. PRZEREMBSKI

Turu (i). Side-blown horn of the Kpelle people of Liberia, made from wood, ivory, or animal horn. It is played in ensembles of four to six, using hocket technique, and also as a voice disguiser to produce animal and bird imitations. Ensembles usually accompany song and dance, with the instrumentalists pausing to sing. *Turu* trumpets are also used separately for signalling.

The name *turu* has also been applied to a drum of Nigeria.

Turu (ii). Signal trumpet of Karelia. It is made of wood wrapped in birch or other tree bark, about 40 cm long, and has no fingerholes. It is primarily a pastoral instrument. The similar Finnish *pullotorvi*, widely used especially in Karelia, is bottle-shaped. See K. Vertkov, G. Blagodatov and E. Yazovitskaya, eds.: *Atlas muzïkal'nïkh instrumentov narodov SSSR* (Moscow, 1963, 2/1975 with 4 discs), 84.

Turú [mburé-mburé, uatupú]. Onomatopoeic generic word for trumpets among the Guaraní people of Paraguay. Compound names such as *turú guazú* ('large trumpet') are descriptive of size or construction material. *Turú* are usually made of *takuara* cane (*Guadua angustifolia*), though also of wood, animal bone (including in earlier times human bone), or cow horn. *Turú* are normally used for sending signals, including formerly battle signals. *Uatupú* refers specifically to a type of trumpet used to attract fish. Despite its name, the *mimby tarará* ('shaking' or 'shivering flute') is not a flute, but a trumpet. See J.M. Boettner: *Música y músicos del Paraguay* (Asunción, n.d.).

TIMOTHY D. WATKINS

Ṭūs (sing.: *ṭāsa*, *ṭāsī*). Small brass cymbals, played in pairs, of the Arabian Gulf region (Bahrain, Abu Dhabi). Used during dances and by *fijiri* pearl divers, their function is to control the rhythmic pattern, particularly in polyrhythmic systems. They are usually accompanied by several drums and water jars (*jahla*, struck on the side or lip), and sometimes accompany other instruments. See P.R. Olsen: *Music in Bahrain* (Bahrain, 2002).

Tüsak. Finger cymbals of the Uzbek people of Afghanistan.

Tutek. Duct flute of Azerbaijan. It is made of lathe-turned wood (usually apricot, mulberry, or walnut) or reed, 24 to 35 cm long. The body can be cylindrical or conical (wider at the upper end), and the exterior can be smooth or ornamented with ring-like projections. The beak-shaped mouthpiece has a movable metal ring to regulate the register: if the ring is lowered to adjust the wind stream and the fingerholes are partly covered, lower pitches can be produced. The tutek has seven fingerholes and one thumbhole, producing a diatonic scale with a range of an octave. Experienced musicians add

chromatic notes by partly covering the fingerholes. The tutek is played by herdsmen while grazing cattle; lyrical melodies, folksongs, and dances are usually played in the upper register. It is also used in ensembles.

JOHANNA SPECTOR/R

Tuttivox. Polyphonic electronic organ developed by Harald Bode and manufactured by Jörgensen Electronic in Düsseldorf between 1953 and the late 1950s. Similar to the Clavioline, it was a portable one-manual instrument with a range of three octaves, which by means of an octave transposition switch could be set within a total compass of five octaves. The sound was generated by 12 oscillators and 12 sets of valve (vacuum tube)-based octave dividers. A second manual, or an octave of pedals, or both could be added. The Tuttivox was used mainly by small dance bands that transported all their instruments in one car; the organ and amp each has a wooden carry/storage case and the organ has a collapsible stand. During the same period Jörgensen also manufactured the Basilika (a two-manual, five-octave church organ with full pedalboard, based on the Tuttivox), Bode's concert model of the Clavioline, and the hybrid Combichord, which consisted of a combined Tuttivox and Clavioline played from a single three-octave keyboard with 38 stop-tabs contained in a console like that of a piano attachment.

HUGH DAVIES/R

Tutu (i). (1) [cucu], Double-headed barrel drum of Nias, Indonesia. It is made of palmwood with deerskin or goatskin heads and ranges from 15 to 36.5 cm long and 15 to 21.5 cm in diameter. Tension is applied to the heads via rattan lacing between the two rattan counterhoops. The tutu is played with bare hands by village shamans to prevent spirits from stealing the soul of a dying person. It is now rare and, along with the *fodrahi* drum, remains one of the few indigenous instruments not incorporated into the modern Christian church service. See J. Kunst: *Music in Nias* (Leiden, 1939), 32.

(2) Small drum of the Marquesas Islands. See R. Linton: *The Material Culture of the Marquesas Islands* (Honolulu, 1923), 403.

MARGARET J. KARTOMI/ANDREW C. MCGRAW

Tutu [cucu] **(ii).** Onomatopoeic term for conch horns in all languages of New Caledonia. In the Paicî language, however, the conch is called *tuu* and this name also refers to the call of the pigeon *déa tuu* (*Ducula goliath*). When heard from a distance, the sound of the pigeon and that of the conch can hardly be distinguished. Conches blown for signalling are reported in early ethnographic notes for New Caledonia; the shells are also decorative objects with powerful symbolism, for example as a metaphor for the conception of life. On the Grande Terre (main island) only the conch *Triton tritonis* is used; it is end-blown, and sometimes the pitch is varied by inserting the fist in the shell. The tutu was used to signal shipping movements and to call meetings, commonly nowadays for prayers or church services. It is also blown to announce a death. Formerly it was sounded also at important moments in yam cultivation, for example, at the beginning of a new harvest or at the ending of an old harvest, but this is no longer done. See M. Leenhardt: *Gens de la Grande Terre, Nouvelle-Calédonie* (Nouméa, 1937, rev. and enlarged 1986).

RAYMOND AMMANN

Tutumetšo. Long conical single-headed drum of the Lovedu and Kwebo (Northern Sotho) peoples of South Africa, resembling the Venda *murumba*. The name refers to its function as the lead drum of a group.

ANDREW TRACEY

Tutut. Reedpipe of the Chuvash people of the Volga-Ural region of Russia. It is presumably made of an expanding spiral of birch bark with a single beating reed of goose quill in the narrower end. It is 45 to 50 cm long, has no fingerholes and is mostly played by shepherds.

Tutz, Rudolf (*b* Innsbruck, Austria, 13 Aug 1940). Austrian wind instrument maker. His great-grandfather Anton Tutz (1842–1919) founded a wind-instrument making firm in Innsbruck in 1875. Anton was succeeded by his son Rudolf I (1880–1952) and grandson Rudolf II (1909–1963). Rudolf III was trained as a woodwind maker in his father's workshop from 1954, and studied at the applied arts schools for metal workers and sculptors in Innsbruck. After an internship at Richard Müller's firm in Bremen (1957–58), he passed his examination for the master craftsman's certificate in woodwind making in 1961. After the death of his father, he took over the family business. In the 1960s he produced a Viennese concert trumpet in collaboration with Josef Hell of the Vienna Philharmonic.

Tutz's important role in the early music movement began in 1963, when he responded to a request from Otto Ulf, founder of the Innsbrucker Festwoche, to produce trumpets in the Baroque style. In 1972 Tutz made the first reconstruction of a basset clarinet for the German clarinettist Hans Deinzer and the ensemble Collegium Aureum. In 1982 the Collegium Aureum made the first recording of Haydn's *Creation* to use copies of historic instruments, with flutes, oboes, and clarinets made by Tutz. In the 1980s Tutz collaborated with the Baroque flutist Barthold Kuijken and the oboist Walter Lehmaier of the Vienna Philharmonic to produce instruments. Since 1998 he has designed modern clarinets in the Austrian style for the firm Uebel (Markneukirchen). His son Rudolf Tutz IV became director of the business in 2003.

Rudolf III was honoured with the Jakob-Steiner-Preis of Tirol (2004), with the title 'Professor' by the Austrian president Heinz Fischer (2008), and with the Kulturehrenzeichen of the city of Innsbruck (2011). See Stadtarchiv/Stadtmuseum Innsbruck, ed.: *Rudolf Tutz—Der Klangmeister* (Innsbruck, 2010).

HEIKE FRICKE

Tuzu abe. Friction sticks of the Lugbara people of Uganda. They are rubbed against a sounding board (*oguru*) during the *nyabmi tuzu* dance. The board is sprinkled with crushed charcoal and fitted and sealed into a trench dug in the ground, about 10 cm deep and 40 by 150 cm along the sides, acting as a resonator. Three girls kneel close to one end of the board, each with a stick held almost at right angles to the board, and rub the stick against the board in slow, measured motion. The length of the stroke is determined by the length of the note, while pressure and attack affect its pitch. For the dance other girls sit around the players, singing and swaying to the rhythm of the sticks. See M. Trowell and K.P. Wachsmann: *Tribal Crafts of Uganda* (London, 1953), 329.

Twenesin. Signalling drum of the Asante people of Ghana. With the expansion of the Akan empire in the precolonial period the drum diffused to other groups in the south including the Krobo and the Guan. See V. Arlt: *Christianity, Imperialism and Culture: the Expansion of the Two Krobo States in Ghana, c. 1830 to 1930* (diss., U. of Basel, 2005), 222.

GAVIN WEBB

Two foot. Term used in reference to organ stops, and by extension also to other instruments, to indicate that they are pitched two octaves above the eight foot or 'normal' pitch now based on $c' = 256$ Hz. A 'two-foot organ' is one whose biggest open Principal pipe is or would be 2′ (60 cm) long at C, irrespective of any larger stopped pipes; nor does the terminology imply that the compass extends to C, since it could apply to a stop or department of any compass. The *Brustwerk* department of the ideal *Werkprinzip* organ was a two-foot Positive organ incorporated in the main organ case.

PETER WILLIAMS

Txalaparta. Basque term for a percussion bar. It is a wooden beam 1 to 2 metres long, about 20 cm wide and of variable thickness. One or two beams are placed on sacks of maize leaves, supported on two large baskets, and beaten by two players, one interpolating his beats with the fixed rhythm of the other. The players hold a thick wooden stick vertically in each hand, beating down on the beam with the end of the stick. In the 1990s some players started to tune the beams and use the txalaparta as a kind of bass marimba, playing melodies and bass lines accompanying other instruments. See H. Leaf: 'An Introduction to the Basque Txalaparta', *GSJ*, vol.60 (2007), 215–19.

SABIN BIKANDI BELANDIA

Txissanje (pl. *issanje*). Lamellaphone of the Tshokwe people of the Lóvua/Lunda district, Angola. It has eight iron tongues, all but the first with folded tin vibrating rings, on a wooden body about 18.5 cm long and 9 to 10 cm wide. Twisted fibres passing through holes in the body bind it to a calabash resonator. A small stick is inserted between the body and the calabash to tighten the fibres. See Museo do Dundo: *Folclore musical de Angola*, vol.1 (1961), 30–1 and figs.57–9.

Txistu. Basque term for the pipe. The *txistu* is a three-holed, cylindrical duct flute about 42 or 43 cm long, played with one hand, leaving the other hand free to beat the tabor (*danbolin*) which hangs from the arm that holds the flute. In the past, the size of the *txistu* varied depending on the maker or the materials available. Iztueta (1824) commented that older pipes and tabors were much larger. Normal use of the word *txistu* to denote the three-holed flute and *txistulari* for its player appears to date from the 20th century; previously, various terms were used.

A typical txistu band, standardized since the late 19th century, consists of two *txistu*, one *silbote* and a side drum. The *silbote*, a bass duct flute also known as *txistu aundi,* is about 63.5 cm long, in two sections, and sounds a 5th lower than the txistu. The *silbote* player uses both hands to manipulate his instrument and is thus excused from taboring.

Early Basque three-holed flutes were made from cane or bird bones, but txistu configured like the one today were first made from cherry, walnut, or for the best quality, boxwood. Later, dark-coloured tropical woods were introduced; these now define the appearance of the instrument, also in iconography. Many instruments made from other materials were painted black to make them look 'authentic'. Metal bands reinforce and decorate the tube. Metal mouthpieces and lips, which stabilize tone production, might date back to the 15th century. A metal ring at the foot of the pipe, for the player's ring finger, allows the little finger to be used to partly stop the end of the pipe and so obtain chromatic notes; the txistu is unique in this respect. In the second half of the 20th century more durable synthetic materials such as ebonite and injection-moulded plastic were introduced. Gancedos, leading makers of all types of three-hole pipes in Amurrio (Alaba), employ both wood and ABS plastic which, apart from having excellent acoustic qualities, can be turned on a lathe.

Music for the txistu sounds an octave plus a 4th higher than notated; e.g., written *c'* sounds *f'''*. Overblowing is normal, as the lowest fundamentals are weak. Beginning in 1980 txistus tuned in F♯ were promoted by the professor of txistu at the Conservatory of Donostia. Since then, tuning at high pitch has been considered more appropriate for traditional music, for playing in the street, and especially for accompanying dance, whilst tuning in F is considered more appropriate for classical and chamber music.

The related *txirula* [*txirola, chirola, chirula, xirula*] is a tabor pipe of the Pyrenees, especially the French Basque side; it is shorter (32 cm) than the *txistu* and shriller, sounding an octave higher than the *silbote*, and is played with the *atabal, ttun-ttun* or *tambourin* de Béarn, often for dancing and carnival plays. Revival of the *txirula* in the mid-20th century centred on Soule and was led by Jean-Mixel Bedaxagar and Mixel Etxekopar. The Basque country is the main area in Europe where the pipe and tabor ensemble survives and the only area where towns maintain a municipal pipe and tabor band.

BIBLIOGRAPHY
J.I. Iztueta: *Gipuzkoako dantza gogoangarrien kondaira edo historia* (San Sebastián, 1824/1990)
J.L. Ansorena Miranda: *Txistua eta Txistulariak. El Txistu y los Txistularis* (San Sebastián, 1996)
Txistulari (journal of Euskal Herriko Txistularien Elkartea (Basque pipe and tabor players association))

SABIN BIKANDI BELANDIA

Txiuolouolo (pl. *iuolouolo*). Small spherical metal pellet bell of European make used by the Tshokwe people of the Lóvua/Lunda district, Angola. Mounted on strips of antelope skin, the bells are attached to the legs of dancers or may be shaken by hand to accompany singing.

Ṭyāmko. Kettledrum of Nepal. The bowl, of various shapes, is made of brass, copper, iron, pottery, or wood, typically with a diameter of 14 to 23 cm and depth of 17 to 23 cm. The skin head is lapped to a hoop that is held to the body with V lacing. It is suspended at waist level from a neck strap and played with two sticks. The drum is not tuned to a definite pitch. It is used by the *damāi* tailor-musicians as part of the *Pañcai bājā* ensemble. See C. Tingey: *Auspicious Music in a Changing Society: The Damāi Musicians of Nepal* (London, 1994).

MIREILLE HELFFER/GERT-MATTHIAS WEGNER,
SIMONNE BAILEY

Tyepondo-pinge. Footed drum of the Senufo people of the Ivory Coast. It has a barrel-shaped body and a single pegged head. These footed drums are normally reserved for male use, but can be played by Senufo women who belong to the Fodonon group.

KONIN AKA

Tymbalon (Fr.). Provençal frame drum with jingles. The term has also been applied to a small folk kettledrum (normally played in pairs).

Tympanocorde. String instrument in the shape of a large banjo and presumably with a membrane soundtable (like a drum head), played with a bow; patented by Bernard in Paris in 1861, it was designed to replace the cello. It is not known whether any were produced or survive.

Tympanon. (1) Frame drum of ancient Greece.
(2) (Fr.) Dulcimer.

Tympanum [tymbal] (Lat., from Gk. *tympanon*). Ancient hand drum. Approximately 30 cm in diameter, it had a rim of metal or wood covered on both sides by skin heads. It is usually shown held in the left hand being struck by the fingertips of the right. Small circles sometimes seen on depictions of the frame are not thought likely to indicate the presence of jingles.

Normally it was associated with the orgiastic cults of Dionysus and Cybele where it appeared almost invariably with the aulos. The absence of any reference to it in Homer or the archaic lyric poets, and its sudden appearance in the art and literature of the 5th century bce, have prompted the suggestion that it came to Greece from Asia Minor in that century with the cult of Cybele and spread thence to the cult of Dionysus; nevertheless, it might only have become more prominent then, since the almost universal appearance of hand drums and pipes in orgiastic cults might speak for its usage in the Dionysian cult of pre-classical Greece.

The use of the instrument certainly increased as the Asiatic cults became more popular. Livy describes its ecstatic function in the cult of Dionysus at Rome, and the introduction of the worship of Cybele to Rome in 204 bce furthered its employment. The many Roman literary references and pictorial representations usually refer to this cult usage. The popularity of the mime from late republican times also extended its use. Interludes of dance and song sometimes supplemented the acting of the *mimi*; among the instruments featured were *tympana*.

BIBLIOGRAPHY

E.R. Dodds: *The Greeks and the Irrational* (Berkeley, 1951)

G. Fleischhauer: *Etrurien und Rom*, Musikgeschichte in Bildern, vol.2/5 (Leipzig, 1964)

T.J. Mathiesen: *Apollo's Lyre: Greek Music and Music Theory in Antiquity and the Middle Ages* (Lincoln, NE, 1999), 173–6

JAMES W. MCKINNON, ROBERT ANDERSON/R

Typotone. One-note pitch pipe patented 17 Jan 1829 by Pierre Pinsonnat, inspector of gold and silver hallmarks in Amiens, France. It is a small rectangular plate of mother-of-pearl or silver pierced with a bevelled-edged rectangular slot, over which is riveted a metal free reed. Grooves cut in the long edges of the plate enable it to be held vertically between the teeth, broadside to the wind flow, while the reed is blown by the player's breath, freeing the hands for tuning an instrument. It was approved for use by the Paris Conservatoire. A mother-of-pearl example (29.7 by 16.6 mm; *US.V.n*), preserved with its original leather case, has a reed of hallmarked gold sounding $a' = 441$ Hz. The *Typotone* was improved by Louis Julien Jaulin under the name *Harmonica-Jaulin*. See M.D. Banks: 'From the Four Winds … A Rare Triple Æolina and a Typotone Both Added to the Alan G. Bates Collection', *National Music Museum Newsletter*, vol.30/3 (Aug 2003), 4–5, repr. in *The Trumpet Call*, vol.5/3 (Sept 2003), 4–5.

LAURENCE LIBIN

Tzamara. Greek end-blown flute of the *floyera* family. It is played mainly by shepherds in the northwest of the mainland. Made from wood or metal, it has seven fingerholes, sometimes an additional thumbhole, and one to four tuning vents depending on its length, which varies from 60 to 85 cm. An alternative name in Thrace, where it is usually made in three joints, is *kavali*.

Tzouras [bouzoukaki]. Greek long-necked lute. The tzouras (*tzoura*: 'small') has a very small carved mulberry-wood or carvel-built, drop-shaped bowl resonator, and a fretted neck equal or nearly equal in length to that of a *bouzouki*. It has three double courses of metal strings tuned in 4ths and 5ths (nowadays sometimes four double courses, tuned by means of machine tuners) that pass over a low bridge to a tailpiece. It is played solo or with a *bouzouki* or *baglamas* (long-necked lutes).

The name *tzoura(s)* also refers to a small *klarino*, and *tzouras* (*tzourlas, souravli*) is a Peloponnesian name for the *floyera* end-blown flute. The *tzamara* (up to 85 cm long) is a longer *floyera* with seven fingerholes, a thumbhole, and three vent holes; the seated player rests its distal end on the ground or on his shoe.

U

U [*kuretakeu* (*kuretake*: type of bamboo); *ōshō* ('large *shō*'); *u no fue* ('*u* type of flute')]. Obsolete Japanese mouth organ. It is a large type of *shō* with a lower range and longer mouthpiece, once used in *gagaku* (court music), specifically in the *tōgaku* repertory from Tang-dynasty China. It might be related to the ancient Chinese *yú* and might have become obsolete during the Heian period (794–1185). The three oldest known surviving examples or fragments are preserved in the Shōsōin repository in Nara. The u had 17 free-reed bamboo pipes of different lengths, each with a fingerhole, inserted into a small lacquered wooden windchest (overall height up to about 92 cm). The pipes were positioned in two similar rows with the tallest pipes in the middle, one row facing the player and the other on the opposite side. The player held the windchest in both hands and inhaled or exhaled while covering the fingerholes to couple the vibrating reeds to their pipes. While the u is no longer used in traditional *gagaku*, some versions of the instrument have been reconstructed and are used in new music. See Shōsōin Jimusho, ed.: *Shōsōin no gakki* [Musical instruments of the Shōsōin] (Tokyo, 1967).

HENRY JOHNSON

Uakti. Brazilian ensemble notable for its use of novel acoustic instruments. The quintet, founded in 1978–9 by the composer, cellist, and instrument maker Marco Antônio Guimarães (*b* 10 Oct 1948), was named for a mythical being of the Tukano people, whose perforated body sounded as wind blew over it, and from whose grave grew palm trees from which flutes were made. Among Uakti's many unconventional instruments, mostly made by Guimarães, are so-called pans, graduated lengths of PVC tubing recalling the tubes of a panpipe but struck by hand or with mallets; marimbas with bars of construction lumber or glass, both types mounted above movable soundboxes; bowed string instruments including the Iarra, a kind of cello with two sets of strings that can be fingered simultaneously, the Chori Smetano, said by its creator, Guimarães's teacher

Walter Smetak, to be able to evoke opposite feelings simultaneously, and the Torre, a PVC tube with strings stretched along it—the tube is turned on its axis by a handle while another person bows it, creating chords that vary with the speed of the turning and the number of strings bowed; and drums such as the Trilobyte, comprising 10 PVC tubes in a frame, with drum heads over the top openings, played melodically by two drummers. Uakti also employs conventional and traditional instruments of several cultures. The group's success, for example in collaboration with Philip Glass, has led to imitation by other musicians seeking new sounds from familiar materials.

LAURENCE LIBIN

Ubah. Medium-sized open conical drum of the Igede people of Nigeria. The drummer sits astride the drum and beats it with his hands; the heel of his foot is often used to vary the tension of the membrane.

Ubete. Pot drum of the Idoma people of Nigeria. It is usually about 1 metre tall and 30 to 40 cm wide with a constricted neck and an everted mouth, across which its head is affixed by rolling it around a lapping ring. The ring is secured by parallel cords to another ring part way down the neck. Large wedges between this ring and the neck are hammered down to tune the head. The spheroidal drum stands upright on the ground on a fibre ring. It is played with sticks for men's dance societies. See R. Blench: 'Idoma Musical Instruments' *African Music*, vol.6/4 (1987), 42–52.

Ubo. Lamellaphone of the Igbo people of Nigeria.

(1) Generic term for any lamellaphone. It encompasses the *ubo agana*, the *ubo agbugba*, and the *ubo oba*, all with either a wooden box resonator or a hemispherical gourd resonator, and the *opanda* with a box resonator.

(2) Six- to nine-tongue lamellaphone, known also as *ubo aka*, *ikpa*, and *akpata*. Traditionally the tongues were of fibre or bamboo, mounted on a flat board with

large resonating holes; it was fitted into a half-calabash. Metal tongues are now more common and three or four instruments are often played together, using only a few tongues on each, for private entertainment, during courtship, or to accompany story-telling. *Ubo aka* now also denotes a lamellaphone with four metal tongues and a rectangular wooden box resonator used on the same occasions as above.

BIBLIOGRAPHY

A.N.G. Okosa: 'Ibo Musical Instruments', *Nigeria Magazine*, no.75 (1962), 4–14

W.W.C. Echezona: 'Ibo Music', *Nigeria Magazine*, no.85 (1965), 45–52

K.A. GOURLAY

Ubo akwara [ubo agala]. Eight-string pluriarc of the Igbo people of Nigeria. It consists of bows of flexible cane bound into a triangular wooden trough resonator. To the upper end of each bow are tied palm-fibre strings which go over a bridge to fasten to a tailpiece. The ubo akwara is plucked with the thumbs and tuned by winding or unwinding the string around the bearer until the correct tension is obtained.

Ubuxhaka [ubuxaka]. Concussion idiophone of the Zulu people of southern Africa. A small bundle of sticks is held and shaken by girls while dancing.

Uchif. Leaf oboe of the Micronesian island of Yap, made of rolled coconut leaf.

Uchiwadaiko. Frame drum of Japan. The name refers to the shape of the instrument: *uchiwa* (fan); *daiko/taiko* (drum). It has a circular wooden or metal frame about 21 to 60 cm in diameter with a handle about the same length as the diameter, and resembles a traditional Japanese flat fan. The single head, of cow or horse hide, can be struck on either side, using a wooden beater. Other names for different forms of frame drums with long handle, and sometimes two heads, include *edaiko*, *etsukedaiko*, and *etsukidaiko*. In some modern settings, the uchiwadaiko is played in sets of different sizes and pitches, and often with other types of Japanese and Western percussion instruments. The handle is held in one hand and the beater in the other. The player might sit or stand while playing, or even walk while chanting. In the Nichiren Buddhist sect, the drummers normally chant the *daimoku* prayer while playing the instrument, which provides metric accompaniment. In this context, the instrument, called *daimokudaiko*, sometimes has the prayer *namu myōhō rengekyō* ('Praise to Lotus Sutra') inscribed on one side of the head. The frame drum is also used in some folk performances and off-stage *kabuki* music (where it often accompanies Buddhist scenes), and to accompany children's dances. Some makers have produced uchiwadaiko of up to 120 cm in diameter, which have a slightly different form and are without a handle. They are normally suspended from four equidistant points in a large wooden frame, and struck with a beater up to 55 cm long and 4 cm wide.

BIBLIOGRAPHY

E. Kikkawa, ed.: *Zusetsu nihon no gakki* [Japanese musical instruments, illustrated] (Tokyo, 1992)

W.P. Malm: *Traditional Japanese Music and Musical Instruments* (Tokyo, 2000)

HENRY JOHNSON

ʿŪd (*oud*; pl.: *ʿīdān*). Short-necked plucked lute of the Arab world, the direct ancestor of the European lute, whose name derives from *al-ʿūd* ('the lute'). Known both from documentation and through oral tradition, it is considered the king, sultan, or emir of musical instruments, 'the most perfect of those invented by the philosophers' (Ikhwān al-Ṣafāʾ: *Rasāʾil* [Letters] (1957), i). It is the principal instrument of the Arab world, Somalia, and Djibouti, and is of secondary importance in Turkey (*ut*, a spelling used in the past but now superseded by *ud*), Iran, Armenia, and Azerbaijan (*ud*). It plays a lesser role in Greece (*outi*), where it has given rise to a long-necked model (*laouto*); the latter is used in rustic and folk contexts, while the ʿūd retains pre-eminently educated and urban associations. In Tanzania, among the Nyamwezi and Swazi/Nguja people, it is known as *udi*; in recent decades it has also appeared in Mauritania and Tajikistan.

For discussion of ʿūd repertory see *GMO*.

1. The term ʿūd. 2. Early history. 3. Description. 4. Models of the ʿūd. 5. Performance and aesthetics. 6. Makers.

1. THE TERM ʿŪD. Literally, *ʿūd* means 'twig', 'flexible rod', or 'aromatic stick', and by inference 'piece of wood'. In Ibn Khaldūn (14th century), *ʿūd* denoted the plectrum of the lute called *barbaṭ*. The etymology of the word has occasioned numerous commentaries, among them the thesis put forth by Farmer that the Arabs adopted the term to differentiate the instrument, with its wooden soundtable, from the similar Persian *barbaṭ*, whose belly is covered with skin. But this can no longer be defended. The choice of the term *ʿūd* depends on a discursive form of Arab thought which required some other word to define the *barbaṭ* before the ʿūd (the same applies to all the instruments of the emergent Islamic world): in this system of ideas, one term refers back to another or is glossed by yet another, leading to a multiplicity of terms. As the *ṣanj* is described as a *wanj*, the *būq* as a *qarn*, the *duff* as a *ṭār*, the ʿūd becomes a synonym of the *barbaṭ*. The skin–wood difference was not taken into account. This play of reference is clearly stated by the 10th-century Andalusian writer Ibn ʿAbd al-Rabbīḥ: 'the ʿūd is the *barbaṭ*'. Other writers such as Ibn Sīnā and Ibn Khaldūn, included the ʿūd under the heading of 'barbaṭ' when speaking of its characteristics. In the 10th century commentaries on pre-Islamic poetry by al-Anbārī (*d* 916) give the ʿūd two semantic meanings: *barbaṭ* and *mizhar; mizhar* was to become a poetic substitute for the ʿūd. Earlier, it could equally denote the lyre, suggesting a process of transference from lyre to lute, the lute gradually acquiring the attributes of previous string instruments and becoming a sublimation of them. This transference is noticeable in the earliest Arabic versions of the Bible, where *kinnor* (lyre) is translated as *ʿūd* (lute).

2. EARLY HISTORY. The transfer of terms for lyre and lute appears more subtly in the myth of the invention of the 'ūd which has been handed down in two variants from the 9th and 10th centuries, the first being Iraqi and the second Iranian. These say that the 'ūd was invented by Lamak, a direct descendant of Cain; on the death of Lamak's son, he hung his remains in a tree, and the desiccated skeleton suggested the form of the 'ūd (a contradiction between archaeological research and mythological tradition; the former assumes a process of evolution from lyre to lute, confirmed by organology). The myth attributes the invention of the *mi'zaf* (lyre) to Lamak's daughter. There is a Chinese legend that the *pipa* lute was created through the division or modification of earlier instruments of the zither type, *zheng* and *zhu*; such a relationship, of lyre to lute or zither to lute, did exist in the Far East. The comparison suggests a common origin for the 'ūd and the *pipa*.

Just as the 'ūd becomes the quintessence of earlier chordophones, it also constitutes their functional synthesis. In the 9th century Māwardī, the jurist of Baghdad, extolled its use in treating illness, a principle allowed and defended in Arab Spain by the 11th-century theologian Ibn Ḥazm. The symbolism lived on until the 19th century: 'the 'ūd invigorates the body. It places the temperament in equilibrium. It is a remedy … It calms and revives hearts' (Muḥammad Shihāb al-Dīn, *Safīnat al-mulk*, Cairo, 1892). There is also evidence that it was played on the battlefield. In any case it was predominantly in secular usage that the 'ūd made its mark, as the only kind of accompaniment to a form of responsorial song known as *ṣawt*, according to written tradition (the *Kitāb al-Aghānī* of al-Iṣfāhānī) and oral tradition (Tunisia and the Arabian Gulf).

The emergence of the 'ūd on the stage of history is an equally complex matter. Two authors of the end of the 14th century (Abū al-Fidā, or Abulfedae, and Abū al-Walīd ibn Shiḥnāh) place it in the reign of the Sassanid King Shapūr I (241–72). Ibn Shiḥnāh added that the development of the 'ūd was linked to the spread of Manicheism, and its invention to Manes himself, a plausible theory because the disciples of Manes encouraged musical accompaniments to their religious offices. Reaching China, their apostolate left traces of relations between West and East, seen in a short-necked lute similar to the 'ūd. But the movement's centre was in southern Iraq, whence the 'ūd was to spread towards the Arabian peninsula in the 7th century. However, the texts mentioning the introduction to Mecca of the short-necked lute as the 'ūd were all written in the 9th and 10th centuries. The 'ūd spread to the West by way of Andalusia.

3. DESCRIPTION. The 'ūd consists of a large soundbox connected to a short neck, features that give it its patent of nobility and distinguish it from the long-necked lute family (*ṭanbūr, saz, baǧlama, setār*, etc.). The body has evolved considerably from the original pear shape (which is perpetuated in our own time by the *qanbūs*, taking on a swelling, rounded form). A spherical shape may even have been envisaged: al-Kindī (9th century)

described the body of the lute as a ball divided in two, but a century later the Ikhwān al-Ṣafā' encyclopaedia (see Shiloah, 1978) suggested harmonious proportions: 'The length must be one and a half times the width; the depth, half the width; the neck, one quarter of the length' (p.203). If the neck measured only 20 cm (its approximate length today), the total length would be 80 cm, with or without the pegbox, making it much the same size as very large contemporary models. Another tradition required the length of the vibrating string from nut to bridge, now about 60 cm, to be equal to the body length, which would leave only 15 cm for the length of the neck (Mīkhā'īl Allāhwayrdī: *Falsafat al-mūsīqā al-sharqiyya* [The philosophy of oriental music], Damascus, 1948).

The body is made from lightweight wood. It consists of a series of 16 to 21 ribs, mentioned as early as the 10th century by the name of *alwāḥ* ('boards') and now called *ḍulū'* ('sides'). In the 19th century the body was called *qaṣ'a* ('receptacle', 'bowl'), and by the classical authors *jism* ('body'). It consists of a strongly rounded back (*ẓahr*) and a flat front surface (*baṭn*: 'belly'; *ṣadr*: 'chest'; or *waǰh*: 'face') made of lightweight wood, which must 'reverberate if it is struck' (Ikhwān al-Ṣafā'). This, the soundboard, is pierced by one quite large soundhole, or (earlier) two small ones; sometimes there are three round or oval soundholes (a design inspired by the lotus flower in Morocco). The holes may be plain or richly ornamented. They are called *shamsiyya* ('little sun'), *qamarāt* ('moons'), or *'uyūn* ('eyes'). The bridge, on the lower part of the belly, is known in classical writings as *musht* ('comb'), and as *faras* ('horse') or *marbaṭ* ('fastening place') today. It bears the strings and stands about 10 cm from the lower edge, which is called *ka'b* ('heel'). (In a recent innovation by Munīr Bashīr, of Iraq, the 11th, low string is not on the traditional bridge but on the lower edge of the soundbox.) The *raqma* ('membrane'), a piece of fish-skin or leather, or occasionally of shell, between the bridge and the soundhole, protects the belly from the strokes of the plectrum. This section may take all kinds of extravagant shapes; a Tunisian example is in the form of a parallelogram. The *raqma* tends to be absent from the modern Iraqi 'ūd.

The neck, joined to the body, is described as *'unq* ('neck') in classical writings, and the *raqba* ('neck') or *zand* ('wrist') today. It extends the upper part of the instrument by some 20 cm and is inserted into the soundbox up to the soundhole. This length, which has been much discussed, is important in the instrument's construction, determining the number and location of the intervals and thus affecting the modes. In early 19th-century Egypt, Villoteau gave the measurement as 22.4 cm; a century later, also in Egypt, Kāmil al-Khulā'ī gave it as 19.5 cm. In modern Egypt, the length of the neck may vary between 18 and 20.5 cm. It is standardized as 20 cm in Syria, but a length of 24.5 cm may be found on Moroccan models, the *'ūd 'arbī* (Arab 'ūd). If the *'ūd 'arbī* is the descendant of an archaic model of Andalusian provenance, the upper part of the instrument may have become shorter. The neck rarely has frets (*dasātīn*), but some are found on the Tunisian lute of Khumayyis Tarnān (1894–1964). Both sides of the neck are inlaid with marquetry to facilitate the learning of the instrument, so providing visual references for the placing of the hand. There is a nut of ivory or bone, called *anf* ('nose') or *'ataba* ('threshold'), at the upper end of the neck before it bends sharply back to become the pegbox. The tuning-pegs are screwed to the pegbox; they are called *mafātīḥ* ('keys') or more commonly *malāwī* ('folds', 'whorls'). The vibrating length of the strings ranges from 60 to 67 cm, according to the model, but lengths as small as 52 cm have been noted.

The quality of material used in the making of the 'ūd is extremely varied; the more the diversity, the better it sounds. This explains the elaborate attention paid to decorative inlay work and the assembling of an impressive number of pieces of wood. The Baghdad lute maker Ḥannā Ḥajjī al-'Awwād (1862–1942) used 18,325 pieces to make a single 'ūd.

Classical lexicographers regarded the wood of the *wa's*, which cannot be identified, as best for the material of the 'ūd. All kinds of wood have been used, some chosen for their aromatic quality (like sandalwood). Some texts recommend the use of a single type; woods mentioned include walnut, larch, beech, maple, cypress, pistachio, oak, mahogany, cedar, and pine for the belly, and ebony for the fingerboard. There is a growing tendency to add inlay work to the 'ūd, whose weight may exceed 800 grams in Arabian lutes but is less in Turkish ones (which are 6 to 8 cm smaller than their Arabian counterparts, and more like the Maghribi 'ūd of the *'arbī* type).

4. MODELS OF THE 'ŪD.

(i) Two-string 'ūd. The thesis of its existence envisages the archaic 'ūd as a counterpart of the *ṭanbūr*, having two strings like that instrument. The argument rests on the names of the strings, two of which are Iranian terms (*bamm* and *zīr*), and two others of Arab origin (*mathna* and *mathlath*). There is no circumstantial documentary evidence to support this hypothesis.

(ii) Four-course 'ūd. The Arabian *'ūd qadīm* (ancient lute), in particular, invited cosmological speculation, linking the strings with the humours, the temperature, the elements, the seasons, the cardinal points, the zodiac, and the stars. The strings may be tuned bass to treble or treble to bass. Bass to treble tuning is represented by al-Kindī (9th century), who advocated tuning the lowest course (*bamm* or first string) to the lowest singable pitch. Placing the ring finger on a mathematically determined length of this string, one moves on to deduce the pitch of the third open course (*mathna*), then that of the second (*mathlath*), and finally the fourth (*zīr*). (This system is also applied to the five-course 'ūd and is still used as a tuning method, following the sequence 1–4–2–3–5 or 1–4–2–5–3.) Adherents of the opposite school (Ikhwān al-Ṣafā') tune from treble to bass. The intention, inherited in part by the Turkish 'ūd, entails pulling hard on the *zīr* (high) string, so that as it approaches breaking-point it gives a clear sound. One then moves on to determine the pitch of the second course (*mathna*), the third (*mathlath*), and finally the fourth (*bamm*). These two schools did not remain entirely separate. But whichever procedure is used, both end up with tuning by successive 4ths, each course being tuned a 4th above the lower course preceding it. Musicologists, Eastern as well as Western, who try to interpret the pitch of these notes in European terms end up with different results.

Although the four-course 'ūd survives in Morocco, as the *'ūd 'arbī*, the tuning does not conform to the pitches inferred from classical treatises: a conflict between oral and written traditions. The Moroccan method seems to be the product of a previous system, the *'ūd ramāl*, which also comprised a sequence of 4ths: *ramāl*, *ḥsīn*, *māya*, *rāghūl*. This 'ūd, like its Tunisian counterpart, may be variously tuned: a feature of these tunings is that they juxtapose the traditional 4ths with the octave and sometimes the 5th and 6th (*D–d–G–c*). The strings of the *'ūd 'arbī* are named *dhīl*, *ramāl*, *māya*, *ḥsīn*; this terminology by no means refers to a fixed pitch standard such as academic and standardized tuition methods call for.

At the time of al-Kindī, two of the courses were made of gut and two of silk. In the 10th century silk became predominant and some texts give the composition of the twisted threads: *bamm* = 64 threads, *mathlath* = 48, *mathna* = 36, *zīr* = 27. The figures for the lower courses of the 'ūd correspond with those of two upper strings of the Chinese *qin*, a fact that has led to speculation about the relationship between Arab and Chinese civilizations by way of the Silk Route.

Another characteristic of the four-course 'ūd is that it is bichordal, having double courses. 13th-century iconography shows that it was already usual to pair the strings at that time, probably to increase sonority but also to allow the development of a more virtuoso type of performance.

(iii) Five-course 'ūd. The addition in Andalusia of a fifth course has been attributed to Ziryāb (8th–9th century), although in theoretical writings it appeared in Iraq with al-Kindī. (The addition of this extra course has a parallel in China.) With Ziryāb the fifth course, known as *awsaṭ* ('intermediary'), a term perpetuated in the 'ūd of Sana'a called *qanbūs*, is placed between the second (*mathna*) and third (*mathlath*) courses. With al-Kindī and his successors, it was to reach the end of the instrument and become the string called *ḥadd* ('high') or the second *zīr*. (According to oral tradition, to obtain an octave on the long-necked lute *baglama* a low string should be placed in the middle; this is done when the neck has few frets.) As the ancient 'ūd did not have a two-octave compass, the appearance of the fifth string corresponded to the demands of a new system. The four-course 'ūd had no need to run right through the octave. Its repertory was performed on a tetrachord or pentachord, transposable an octave higher. With the five-course model, the heptatonic system imposed complete series of octaves. The new lute was called *'ūd kāmil* ('perfect 'ūd').

The five-course 'ūd is the most common and most popular model among performers. It has also been called the '*ūd miṣrī* (Egyptian) because of the finely constructed instruments produced by the lute makers of Egypt, who export them as far as Zanzibar. The people of North Africa have added the dialectal name of *m'sharqī* or *mashriqī* ('of the east'). The method of tuning it, extremely flexible in the 19th century, is now becoming stabilized. These modifications are due partly to the breakup of the Ottoman Empire, which caused a rupture between Turkish and Arab cultures, and partly to the proliferation of teaching methods endeavouring to impose a single type of tuning, running from low to high: *yakā* = G; *'ushayrān* = A; *dūkā* = d; *nawā* = g; *kardān* = c'. However, there are variants reintroducing tuning by 4ths. Thus what is described as 'Aleppo tuning' consists of: *qarār būsalīk* = E; *'ushayrān* = A; *dūkā* = d; *nawā* = g; *kardān* = c'. This latter structure is used in Turkey and Iraq. To answer the practical requirements of present-day notation, a treble clef followed by the figure 8 is used. This procedure has been much criticized by those in favour of using the bass clef. The tuning of the Turkish lute faithfully reflects the Arab type but in reverse, reading in descending order: *gerdâniye* = g'; *nevâ* = d'; *dügâh* = a; *aşîrân* = e; *kaba dügâh* = d (this last, more mobile pitch may equally settle upon G). This outdated tuning represents the 'old school' (*eski akort*), and has now been replaced by an ascending tuning—the 'new school' (*yeni akort*): A–B–e–a–d'–g'. Though it is now considered incorrect in the Syro-Egyptian area, and representative of the old Ottoman school, a tuning method in ascending order survives in Iraq. It consists of: *yakā* = d; *'ushayrān* = e; *dūkā* = a; *nawā* = d'; *kardān* = g'. The compass of the bichordal five-course 'ūd is just over two octaves; in Turkey, it is three octaves with the addition of a low course. Arabian instruments can achieve this by the addition of a sixth course.

(iv) Six-course 'ūd. Two kinds of six-course 'ūd exist: one has six pairs of strings, the other five pairs with an additional low string. The first was found by Jules Rouanet in North Africa towards the end of the 19th century; tuned inclusively, it has since disappeared except in Libya, where it is still made but with different tuning. A similar instrument, found in Syria, is tuned C–E–A–d–g–c'. The instrument with five double strings and a single low one, however, is becoming increasingly usual from Istanbul to Baghdad. It has become common to place the additional string after the highest (or chanterelle). Its pitch is at the choice of the player; no rule is laid down. The presence of the extra string endows the instrument with a wider range and increased ease of playing, allowing the performer to run effortlessly through three octaves. The sixth course is also coming to be used as an intermittent drone, a new phenomenon.

(v) Seven-course 'ūd. Seven-course models, based on a complex system of tuning, were found in Egypt and Lebanon in the 19th century but have not been seen since 1900. There is one exception: the Tunisian, Fawzī Ṣāyib, was a 20th-century master of the seven-course instrument in the six pairs and one low arrangement. A feature of this 'ūd (as described by Villoteau, 1809) was that it reversed the arrangement of strings, placing first the high and then the low strings on the neck from left to right. According to Mīkhā'īl Mushāqa (1800–88), only four of the seven courses were played, the lowest course (*jahārkā*) and the two highest (*būsalīk* and *niḥuft*) being unused in performance.

5. PERFORMANCE AND AESTHETICS. The strings of the modern 'ūd are twisted, or spirally reinforced. They are plucked with a plectrum (*rīsha*: 'quill') made of an eagle's feather and held between thumb and index finger; a shell or plastic plectrum may be used instead. The technique calls for suppleness of the wrist as the plectrum strikes the strings in a simple fall, or combines risings and fallings. Certain teachers, such as Tawfīq al-Ṣabbāgh, claim that a technique similar to the mandolin tremolo was once used. This may have disappeared, but another technique spread rapidly: the *başm* ('imprint'), which was invented by the Egyptian Aḥmad al-Laythī (1816–1913). It consists of substituting for the plectrum touches of the fingers of the left hand, plucking the strings, and introduces light and shade into the execution. Munīr Bashīr (Iraq) extended the technique by using the right hand too; he made it one of the canons of present-day aesthetics of the 'ūd.

There are two schools or conceptions of performance. The first, or 'Ottoman', takes as its principle the ornamentation of the sound, produced by delicate glissandos of the fingers and slight vibratos. The touch of the plectrum on the string sets off a vibration which, in turn, gives rise to an effect of resonance, volume, and controlled intensity. The plectrum does not interfere with the resulting sound. This produces an intimate style of playing, making the interiorized 'ūd a path to meditation. This approach was first promoted in Istanbul by Ali Rifat Çağatay (1867–1935) and Nevres Bey (1873–1937), then by Refik Tal'at Alpman (1894–1947) and Cinuçen Tanrikorur (*b* 1938). It spread to Aleppo (Nash'at Bey, *d c*1930, and 'Abd al-Raḥmān Jabaqjī, *b* 1931), then was developed in Baghdad by Salmān Shukur (*b* 1921), Jamīl Bashīr (1921–77), and Munīr Bashīr (1930–1997).

The second aesthetic approach is Egyptian. The volume is amplified by firm strokes of the plectrum, which makes the strings resonate. This calls for virtuosity in performance, which is conceived of as an exteriorizing factor. The finest proponents of this school have been Ṣafar 'Alī (1884–1962), Muḥammad al-Qaṣabjī (1898–1966), and Farīd Al-Aṭrash (1915–74), who, despite his melodramatic style, breathed a new vitality into the instrument. A synthesis of these two styles is taking place in Somalia, where the manner of performance combines extensive glissandos with the sonorous impact of the plectrum; outstanding proponents of this style include Abdullahi Qarshe and 'Umar Dhule.

With the appearance of new problems of theory, such as the 19th-century division of the octave into 24 quarter-tones, the 'ūd entered a new phase. In the past it was not an ideal instrument for theoretical research, unlike the *ṭanbūr*: 'The 'ūd allows of theoretical demonstrations, but in an imperfect manner' (see Al-Farābī in d'Erlanger, 1930–59, i). However, as the *ṭanbūr* fell into disuse among Arabs during the 19th century, the 'ūd was substituted for theoretical reference. The present-day tendency towards a standardized teaching method based on a Western approach tries first to resolve the problems created by the use of microintervals not provided for in Western treatises, and second to produce teaching manuals adapted to the instrument's evolution. The earliest such course to be published, in 1903, was by the Egyptian Muḥammad Dhākir Bey (1836–1906): *Tuḥfat al-mawʿūd bi taʿlīm al-ʿūd* ('The promise of the treasure, or the teaching of the 'ūd'). Since then, various manuals have tried to 'democratize' the instrument, placing it within everyone's reach and putting forward teaching rules that claim to be universal. They offer instruction in solfeggio and Western theory and give exercises on occidental or oriental modes. They all use Western notation, with modifications of key signature, and place before the student a large repertory, mostly of the 19th and 20th centuries. Notable among proponents of this method of teaching was Muhiddin Targan (1892–1967). This trend has been opposed, in the name of the elementary aesthetic rules of traditional Arab music (i.e. creative liberty and the development of the modal sense). But certain masters of the 'ūd owe something to these newer manuals. Two are outstanding for their instructional value, those by Fuʾād Maḥfūẓ of Damascus (1960) and Mutlu Torun of Istanbul (1993). The manual by ʿAbd al-Raḥmān Jabaqjī of Aleppo (1982) was the first accompanied by audio and video-cassettes. In any event, it is still too early to analyse the consequences of written, standardized tuition in an instrument whose technique has been passed down individually and orally from master to pupil for more than a thousand years.

6. MAKERS. In the past little attention was paid to the field of string instrument making and instrument makers pursued their profession out of the public eye. A greater awareness of their work dates from the second half of the 19th century, in Istanbul, when makers' names became known for the first time. One of them was Manol (1845–1915), an instrument maker of Greek origin from Istanbul, renowned for the exceptional quality of his instruments, which are highly prized in Turkey. The Syrian Naḥḥāt dynasty, originally from Greece, settled in Damascus at the end of the 19th century, and signed their instruments with the name of Ikhwān Naḥḥāt (the Naḥḥāt brothers). The first generation was active in the 1920s and consisted of four brothers, Hannā, Anṭūn, Rūfān, and ʿAbduh Naḥḥāt; the second generation comprised Hannā's two sons Tawfīq and Jurjī, and the dynasty came to an end with Tawfīq's

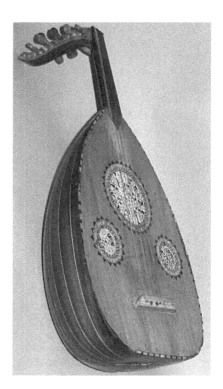

'Ūd, Middle East. (Aurelia W. Hartenberger, EdD)

death in 1946. The Naḥḥāt family, who worked on a small scale as craftsmen, not on the industrial scale usual today, transformed the 'ūd by giving it its pear shape ('*ūd ijjāṣ*, or in dialect '*ūd njāṣ*), and produced extraordinary instruments through their research into the sonority of wood. Specimens of the 'ūd signed by the Naḥḥāt brothers are sought after both by the greatest players, for the exceptional sonority which has been the reason for their success, and by antiquarians and collectors; these models of the 'ūd are the equivalent to the perfection of Stradivarius violins in the Western world.

BIBLIOGRAPHY
A: General. B: Myth of the Invention of the 'Ūd. C: Interchange with China: barbāṭ and 'ud. D: Theory and philosophy. E: Two-string. F: Four-course. G: Five-course. H: Six-course. I: Seven-course. J: Methods.

A: GENERAL
R. d'Erlanger: *La musique arabe* (Paris, 1930–59), vol.1, 165–215; vol.2, 234ff; vol.3, 430ff; vol.4, 420ff

H.G. Farmer: *Studies in Oriental Musical Instruments*, i (London, 1931/R), ii (Glasgow, 1939/R)

V. Sözer: *Müzik ve müzisyenler ansiklopedisi* (Istanbul, 1964)

H. Usbeck: 'Türklerde musik aletler', *Musiki mecmuasi* , no.259 (1970), 27–30

A. al-Ḥifnī: *'Ilm āl–ālāt al–mūsīqīyya* [Understanding musical instruments] (Cairo, 1971), 73ff

Ṣ.A. Rashīd: *Al-ālāt al-mūsiqīyya fī al-ʿuṣūr al-Islāmiyya* [Musical instruments of Islam] (Baghdad, 1975), 36–125

Y. Öztuna: *Türk musikisi ansiklopedisi* (Istanbul, 1976)

H.H. Touma: *La musique arabe* (Paris, 1977)

H. Turnbull: 'The Genesis of Carvel–Built Lutes', *Musica asiatica*, vol.1 (1977), 75–84

Ṣ.M. Ḥamīdī: *Tārīkh ālat al-'ūd wa ṣināʿatuhu* [History and structure of the '*ūd*] (Cairo, 1978)

A. Shiloah: *The Epistle on Music of the Ikhwān al-Ṣafā* (Tel–Aviv, 1978)

J.C. Chabrier: 'Evolution du luth '*ūd* et périodisation des structures musicales arabo–islamiques', *Proceedings of the Ninth Congress of* the Union Européenne des Arabisants et Islamisants, ed. R. Peters (Leiden, 1981), 31–47

L. Ibsen al Faruqi: An Annotated Glossary of Arabic Musical Terms (Westport, CT, 1981)

A.I. Muḥammad: Ṣinā'a ālat al-'ūd fī Baghdād [Manufacture of the 'ūd instrument in Baghdad] (Baghdad, 1986)

R. Mazuela Coll: 'El laud, sultan de los instrumentos musicales', Boletín de la Asociacion Española de Orientalistas, vol.23 (1987), 135–51

[F. Zghonda:] Les instruments de musique en Tunisie (Tunis, 1992)

N. Allao and A.M. Bianquis: 'Luth, luthistes et luthiers', Damas miroir brisé d'un orient arabe, ed. A.M. Bianquis (Paris, 1993), 219–25

J.C. Chabrier: 'Analyse modale du mode/maqam 'Iraquien' lami tel qu'il est joué en la/A par J. Bachir et son luth-'ud: audition et analyse comparative', Ethnomusicologia II [Siena], vol.14 (1993), 111–7

E. Neubauer: 'Der Bau der Laute und ihre Besaitung nach arabischen, persischen und türkischen Quellen des 9. bis. 15. Jahrhunderts', Zeitschrift für Geschichte der arabisch-islamischen Wissenschaften, vol.8 (1993), 279–378

A. Say: The Music Makers in Turkey (Ankara, c1995)

B: MYTH OF THE INVENTION OF THE 'ŪD

Mas'ūdī: Les prairies d'or (Paris, 1874), vol.8, 88ff

H.G. Farmer: 'Ibn Khurdadhbih on Musical Instruments', Journal of the Royal Asiatic Society, no.3 (1928), 509

J. Robson: 'The Kitāb al-malāhī of Abū Ṭālib al-Mufaḍḍal ibn Salāma', Journal of the Royal Asiatic Society, no.2 (1938), 231

T. Grame: 'The Symbolism of the 'ūd', AsM, vol.3 (1972), 25–34

M. Brandily: Instruments de musique et musiciens instrumentistes chez les Teda du Tibesti (Tervuren, 1974), 85ff

A. Shiloah: 'The 'ūd and the Origin of Music', Memoria D.H. Banath dedicata: studia orientalia, ed. J. Blau et al. (Jerusalem, 1979), 395–407

C. Poché: 'David et l'ambiguité du mizmār', World of Music, vol.25/2 (1983), 58–73

C: INTERCHANGE WITH CHINA: BARBĀṬ AND 'ŪD

K. Kessler: Mani (Berlin, 1889), 212, 369ff

A. Grünwedel: Altbuddistische Kultastätten in Chinesisch: Turkistan (Berlin, 1912)

H.G. Farmer: 'Reciprocal Influences in Music 'twixt the Far and Middle East', Journal of the Royal Asiatic Society, vol.66/2 (1934), 327

S. Kishibe: 'The Origin of the p'i-p'a', Transactions of the Asiatic Society of Japan, vol.19 (1940), 261–98

L. Picken: 'The Origin of the Short Lute', GSJ, vol.8 (1955), 32–42

H.C. Puech: 'Musique et hymnologie manichéennes', Encyclopédie des musiques sacrées, ed. Jacques Porte (Paris, 1968), vol.1, 354–86

D: THEORY AND PHILOSOPHY

H.G. Farmer: The Influence of Music from Arabic Sources (London, 1926)

A. Chottin: 'Le luth et les harmonies de la nature', ReM (1940), no.197, 197–203

M. al-'Aqīlī: Al-samā' 'ind al-'Arab [Music among the Arabs] (Damascus, 1966–79), vol.4, 17ff

E.R. Perkuhn: Die Theorien zum arabischen Einfluss auf die europäische Musik des Mittelalters (Walldorf-Hessen, 1976), 77ff

E: TWO-STRING

J.P.N. Land: 'Recherches sur l'histoire de la gamme arabe', Bulletin du sixième congrès international des orientalistes: Leiden 1883 (Leiden, 1884), vol.2, 37–99

H.G. Farmer: Historical Facts for the Arabian Musical Influence (London, 1930/R), 240ff

M. Barkechli: 'La musique iranienne', Histoire de la musique, ed. Roland-Manuel, vol.1 (Paris, 1960), 453–525, esp. 466

F: FOUR-COURSE

H.G. Farmer: 'An Old Moorish Lute Tutor', Journal of the Royal Asiatic Society, vol.64/2 (1931), 349–66; (1932), 99–109, 379–89, 897–904; pubd separately (Glasgow, 1933)

A. Chottin: Tableau de la musique marocaine (Paris, 1938)

H.G. Farmer: 'The Song Captions in the Kitāb al-aghānī al-kabīr', Transactions of the Glasgow University Oriental Society, vol.15 (1953–4), 1–9

H.G. Farmer: The Science of Music in the Mafātīḥ al-'ulūm (Glasgow, 1959)

S. al-Mahdi: La musique arabe (Paris, 1972)

Y. Shawqī: Risāla ibn al-Munajjim fī al-mūsīqā [The epistle of Ibn al-Munajjim on music] (Cairo, 1976)

S. al-Sharqī: Aḍwā' 'alā al-mūsīqā al-maghribiyya [Aspects of Moroccan music] (Mohammadia, 1977)

M. Guettat: La musique classique du Maghreb (Paris, 1980)

G: FIVE-COURSE

R.G. Kiesewetter: Die Musik der Araber (Leipzig, 1842/R1968)

K. al-Khulā'ī: Kitāb al-mūsīqā al-sharqī [Book of oriental music] (Cairo, 1904), 48ff

A. al-Dik: Qānūn aṭwāli al-awtār wa raṭbīqihi 'ala al'ūd [Application to the 'ūd of the rule of string division] (Cairo, 1926)

R. Lachmann: Musik des Orients (Breslau, 1929)

A. Berner: Studien zur arabischen Musik (Leipzig, 1937)

A. Alvarez Bulos: Handbook of Arabic Music (Beirut, 1971)

H: SIX-COURSE

J. Rouanet: 'Les liens de la musique Maghrebine avec le passé', EMDC, I/v (1922), 2914–37, esp. 2927

I: SEVEN-COURSE

G.A. Villoteau: 'Description historique, technique et littéraire des instrumens de musique des orientaux', Description de l'Egypte: Etat moderne, i, ed. E.F. Jomard (Paris, 1809), 846–1016; pubd separately (Paris, 1812)

E.W. Lane: Manners and Customs of the Modern Egyptians (London, 1836)

H. Horeau: Panorama d'Egypte et de Nubie (Paris, 1841)

E. Smith: 'A Treatise on Arab Music, Chiefly from a Work by Mikhâil Meshâkah of Damascus', Journal of the American Oriental Society, vol.1/3 (1847), 173–217

F.J. Fétis: Histoire générale de la musique, vol.2 (Paris, 1869), 107ff

J: METHODS

M. Dhākir Bey: Tuḥfat al-maw'ūd bi ta'līm al-'ūd [The promise of treasure, or the teaching of the 'ūd] (Cairo, 1903)

A. Salāhi: Hocasiz ûd öğrenme usulü [The basis of the 'ūd without a teacher] (Istanbul, 1910)

F. Kopuz: Nazarî ve amelî üd dersleri [Theory and practice of the 'ūd] (Istanbul, 1920)

A. Salâhi: Ilâveli ûd muallimi [Adjunct to the study of the 'ūd] (Istanbul, 1924)

Ş. 'Alī and 'A. 'Arafa: Kitāb dirāsat al-'ūd [Book of 'ūd studies] (Cairo, 1945, 8/1995)

T. al-Ṣabbāgh: Al-dalīl al-mūsīqī al-'āmm [Complete guide to music] (Aleppo, 1950)

S. Erten: Ud metodu (Istanbul, 1956)

G. Faraḥ: Al-'ūd (Beirut, 1956/R1986 as Tamārīn mūsīqiyya li-ālat al-'ūd) ['Ūd exercises]

F. Maḥfūẓ: Ta'līm al-'Ūd ['Ūd method] (Damascus, 1960)

J. Bashīr: Al-'ūd wa tarīqat tadrīsihi [The 'ūd and how to study it] (Baghdad, 1961/R)

S. al-Ḥilū: Dirāsat al-'ūd wa ta'līm al-nūta [Study of the 'ūd and rudiments] (Beirut, 1962)

Z. Yūsuf: Tamrīn lil ḍarb 'alā al-'ūd ['Ūd exercises] (Baghdad, 1962)

L. Fathallāh and M. Kāmil: Al-manhaj al-hadīth fī dirāsat al-'ūd [The modern way to study the 'ūd] (Cairo, 1974)

A.S. Shawqī: Al-ṭarīqa al-ḥadītha fī ta'līm al-'ūd [Modern method of 'ūd instruction] (Casablanca, c1975)

K. Şençalar: Ud öğrenme metodu [Method of 'ūd instruction] (Istanbul, 1976/R)

D. Fakhūry: Ta'līm al-'ūd dūna mu'allim ['Ūd method without a teacher] (Beirut, c1978)

'Abd al-Raḥmān al-Jabaqjī: Ta'līm al-'ūd ['Ūd method] (Aleppo, 1982)

M. Khalifé: Ta'līm al-'ūd ['Ūd instruction] (Beirut, 1983)

'Abd al-Hamīd Mash'al: Dirāsat al-'ūd bi-al-tarīqa al-'ilmiyya [Study of the 'ūd in a scientific way] (al-Jazair, c1985)

O. Akdogu: Ud metodu ['Ūd method] (Izmir, 1987/R)

D. al-Ubira [Cairo Opera House]: Mudāwanāt li-ālat al-'ūd [Notations for the 'ūd] (Cairo, 1993) [staff notation]

I. Labīb and A. Jamīl: al-Tadrībāt al-asāsiyya li-ālat al-'ūd [Fundamental exercises for the 'ūd] (Cairo, 1993) [staff notation]

M. Torun: Ud metodu ['Ūd method] (Istanbul, 1993)

B. Turan: Ud metodu ['Ūd method] (Izmir, 1993)

C. Rouhana: al-'Ūd (manhaj hadīth) [The 'ūd (modern method)] (Beirut, 1995)

CHRISTIAN POCHÉ/R

Uḍäkki. Small hourglass drum of Sri Lanka. It is carved from a single piece of hardwood, such as *jak*, and is usually between 18 and 22 cm long, with a circumference of approximately 30 cm at the head and 18 cm at the waist, where there is usually a narrow boss. Formerly the drum was often lacquered in characteristic Sinhalese fashion, with thin stripes of red, gold, and black, but it is now more often stained in these colours. The two heads, of thin hare or iguana skin, overlap the body of the drum by about 2.4 cm and are stretched over cane hoops. Both hoops and skin are then pierced six times around the circumference and held taut by a single length of hemp (or, more often nowadays, nylon cord) braced diagonally the length of the drum. A circlet of plaited twine (or padded cloth) is passed around the waist of the drum, over the braces. The lower head has a snare of thread or string which gives the instrument a barely audible metallic sound when played. The drum is held in the right hand, which also grips the circlet of plaited twine, using it to tighten or loosen the braces and thus alter the pitch. The left hand plays the upper head only.

The instrument is mentioned in Sinhalese literature from the 16th century onwards and is clearly related, both in name and construction, to the *uḍukku* of Tamil Nadu, although its use is somewhat different. It used to be a favourite domestic instrument of the Sinhalese upper classes, particularly during the 18th century, and although it has died out as a domestic instrument it survives in several other contexts.

The uḍäkki dance is one of the four major dances of the Kandyan tradition. A solo performer sings and dances to the accompaniment of his uḍäkki, playing rhythms which are mirrored in his dance movements. The songs and drumming patterns are traditional but the performance has lost whatever ritual significance it might have had and is now given solely for entertainment. Troupes of uḍäkki players are a prominent feature of the Kandy *Äsalaperahära* (an annual procession), when privileged dancers and drummers escort the Buddha relic through the streets of the town on 11 consecutive nights.

The uḍäkki retains its ritual role in the *Kavkāra maḍuv*, which still plays and sings every Wednesday morning in the Temple of the Tooth, Kandy. A.M. Hocart (1931) described the ensemble as including two uḍäkki players with silver instruments, but a single player with a lacquered or painted instrument is now more usual.

The instrument is sometimes used to accompany rehearsals and dance lessons in Kandyan dance schools, being more portable than the *gāṭa-berē*; it is also one of the instruments used to accompany the rarely performed folk drama of the hill country—*sokari*. It was until recently found in the low-country ritual of *yakunnāṭīma* (demon dancing), where it was involved in healing rituals.

BIBLIOGRAPHY

A.M. Hocart: *The Temple of the Tooth at Kandy* (London, 1931), 17

M.D. Raghavan: *Sinhala Natum: Dances of the Sinhalese* (Colombo, 1967), 173ff

W.B. Makulloluwa: *Dances of Sri Lanka* (Colombo, n.d.), 17

NATALIE M. WEBBER

Udjanga. Lamellaphone of the Ngbaka people in the Ubangi region, Democratic Republic of the Congo. It has seven or eight wooden tongues, the front ends of which are obliquely cut. The rectangular soundbox can be made of one piece of wood or assembled from separate pieces. See J.-S. Laurenty: *Les sanza du Congo* (Tervuren, 1962), 11, 14, 192.

Udongwe. Duct vessel whistle of the Mpondo (Xhosa) people of southern Africa. It is made by inserting a short piece of thick grass into a hollow sphere of soft clay. When the clay dries and hardens a horizontal slit is cut in the grass to act as a lip.

Uebel. German family of woodwind instrument makers, active since the late 19th century in the Vogtland. The Erlbach branch (including the workshop of Gustav Reinhold Uebel, founded in 1910, continued until 1985 by VEB B&S) mainly made Boehm flutes. The branches in Wohlhausen and Markneukirchen obtained prominence primarily in connection with the clarinet maker Oskar Oehler in Berlin. Friedrich Gustav Uebel (*b* Gopplasgrün, 14 Nov 1855; *d* Wohlhausen, 4 June 1915) established his company in Wohlhausen in 1878. He learned woodwind making in Erlbach and worked as a journeyman with H.F. Meyer in Hanover and C. Kruspe in Erfurt. At first he supplied Markneukirchen dealers, but later he offered a wide range of woodwinds under his own name. As early as 1888 he was connected to Oehler, taking over the keywork and producing semi-finished clarinets. Oehler's invention of the forked *f''* mechanism (in 1900/1905) and later improvements were made in conjunction with the successive proprietors of F.G. Uebel. From 1915 to 1936 that company was continued by Uebel's sons Gustav Max (*b* Wohlhausen, 17 March 1881; *d* Wohlhausen, 27 April 1936) and Friedrich Arthur (*b* Wohlhausen, 6 Aug 1888; *d* Markneukirchen, 31 Aug 1963). When Gustav Max died the company split into two, which reunited by steps, beginning in 1963.

Gustav Max Uebel's son Gerhard Rudolf (*b* Wohlhausen, 7 Nov 1915; *d* Ruhpolding, 26 Nov 1991) founded his own company in Wohlhausen. After World War II, he introduced industrial methods and standardization in clarinet manufacturing and owned numerous patents including for a *b'-c♯''* trill mechanism (*Einpunktverbindung*) and forked *f''* cross-mechanism.

By 1911 Friedrich Arthur Uebel had worked directly with Oehler in Berlin. In 1936, when Oehler died, he founded his own workshop in Markneukirchen, with the trademark FAU. He retained many of Oehler's professional customers, and his workshop became the most important in Germany for clarinets in the second third of the 20th century. His further developments of the Oehler clarinet related to the mechanics of the forked *f''* (design registered (DRGM) 1940), the 'new Oehler mechanism' (DRGM 1940/41), and the *e-f* mechanism (previously built as a vent key in the bell for *e*), introduced about 1955.

After Friedrich Arthur Uebel's death, clarinet production was taken over by his nephew G. Rudolf Uebel, and merged with his own company. This was nationalized in 1972 and in 1984 affiliated to VEB B&S, under whom Uebel clarinets were increasingly relegated to batch production. After German reunification, FAU clarinets continued to be produced under the umbrella of the Vogtländischen Musikinstrumentenfabrik (VMI) or the JA Musik GmbH, sometimes in cooperation with the Hans Kreul company in Tübingen. In 2005, the Uebel brand was sold to Arnold Stölzel in Wiesbaden.

BIBLIOGRAPHY

W. Waterhouse: *The New Langwill Index: a Dictionary of Musical Wind-Instrument Makers and Inventors* (London, 1993)

E. Weller: 'Erste Adresse des deutschen Klarinettenbaus', *Rohrblatt*, vol.8/4 (1993), 142–46; vol.9 (1994), 52–60

T. Reil and E. Weller: *Der Klarinettenbauer Oskar Oehler: Meisterleistungen deutscher Instrumentenbaukunst*, vol.1 (Markneukirchen, 2008)

ENRICO WELLER

Uele. Afro-Cuban musical bow. It is made from a short, flexible stick of wood and has a small gourd resonator attached near the lower end of the bow. It is played by striking the vegetal fibre string with a stick, or by the friction of another bow. It can be held between the chin and shoulder and bowed like a violin. The uele is rare and is used only during certain secret and funeral rites of the Congo people, possibly to represent the voices of the dead. See F. Ortiz: *Los instrumentos de la música afrocubana* (Havana, 1952–5), vol.5, 23–4.

JOHN M. SCHECHTER/R

Ueno salamuri. Open, end-blown flute of Georgia. It is also known as *stviri* (Kartli, Kakheti, Tusheti, Pshavi, Meskheti, and Achara). It is made from elder, apricot, or mulberry wood, rarely from the wing-bone of a vulture or the barrel of a sporting gun, and is 38 to 44 cm long. It has five or six fingerholes producing a diatonic scale (e', $f\sharp'$, g', a', b', c'', d''). The instrument can be played solo or to the accompaniment of a *doli* (double-headed drum) or *daira* (frame drum). Its repertory includes herdsmen's signals and tunes, also simple songs and dance-tunes. It is played only by men. See M. Shilakadze: *Kartuli khalkhuri sakravebi da sakravieri musika* [Georgian Folk Instruments and Instrumental Music] (Tbilisi, 1970), 70–3.

NINO RAZMADZE

Ufie [uhie]. Slit drum of the Igbo people of Nigeria. It has two rectangular openings linked by a narrow slit and is made from *cam* wood. It is played in pairs, propped up diagonally by two sticks, by seated players each using two beaters. Use of the ufie is a royal prerogative. It is beaten to wake the ruler at dawn, to announce when his meals are ready, and to send him to bed at night. Its timbre differs from that of other Igbo slit drums, and its sound patterns are immediately recognizable to his subjects. It is sometimes replaced by a vertical footed drum with a single skin. Another slit drum made from *cam* wood is the *ufie-amadi*.

Uganda drum. Term commonly used to describe one of the most widespread types of drum in Uganda and adjoining parts of east Africa. It has two heads, of which only one is beaten, the second being stretched over the base of the drum to hold the lacing. The Uganda drum is generally cylindro-conical, with parallel straight sides for the upper part, the remainder taking the form of a truncated cone. The relative proportions of these two parts vary according to locality. In Buganda the cylindrical section is often longer than the lower section; in Soga this is sometimes reversed.

In the north drums might have an unbroken, curving outline rather than be strictly cylindro-conical. Lacing also varies: for tall drums it may be Y-shaped (two vertical thongs are looped together and knotted into horizontal lacing before continuing together to the base of the drum) as with the *art* of the Lugbara. With shorter drums the lacing is W-shaped (the thongs are threaded alternately through upper and lower skins, often completely covering the wooden body, and the horizontal lacing is absent). On some drums, for example the Toro *nyimba*, a more complex form of lacing combines an intricate X-pattern with a W-pattern and a further X-pattern, each 'layer' being separated by plaited horizontal rings. Tuning is effected by adjusting the lacing, though tuning wedges are sometimes used.

When associated with royalty, drums often appeared in pairs, the Banyoro *nyalebe* and *kajumba* being, for example, one pair. The Banyankore royal *engoma*, however, were formerly beaten daily as solo instruments (*ngoma* and its variants often denote royal drums). Most Uganda drums are beaten with straight sticks, which vary in size and thickness according to the size of the drum; the Lugbara and Kakwa peoples, however, use their hands, as do the Ganda on the larger drums for specific genres such as the popular *baakisimba* and the *embaga* wedding dance. The Amba sometimes squat on their drums to enable the player to move the heel of one foot against the head and thus vary the pitch. Drums are frequently played in tuned sets, for example the Kakwa *leriyo*, which uses four

Uganda drum. (Aurelia W. Hartenberger, EdD)

drums, the Gwere *mansa* set of seven Uganda drums and one single-headed drum, the Gwere *namaddu* set of seven tuned drums (which about 1965 was gradually replacing the Gwere *entaala* (xylophone)), and the better-known Ganda *entenga*, a pentatonic drum chime comprising 12 drums. See M. Trowell and K.P. Wachsmann: *Tribal Crafts of Uganda* (London, 1953).

K.A. GOURLAY/PETER COOKE

Ugbom [ugege, ugele]. Clapperless bell of Nigeria. The ugbom and *ugele* are instruments of the Igbo people, the *ugege* of the Igala. The *ugbom eze* is a double clapperless forged iron bell of the Igbo.

Ugene [ogene, oja ufele]. Clay-bodied globular vessel flute of the Igbo people of Nigeria. It has a single fingerhole opposite the blowhole.

Ugubhu [ugubo, ugubu, ugumbu, inkohlisa]. Unbraced gourd-resonated musical bow of the Zulu people of southern Africa. It is similar in construction and performance practice to the Ngoni *gubo*, Swazi *ugubhu*, Sotho *thomo*, Tswana *segwana*, and the Xhosa *uhadi*. It is a large bow, about 1.5 metres long, with the resonator attached near the lower end, and a single undivided string, made from twisted cow-tail hair, which is struck with a piece of thatching grass.

DAVID K. RYCROFT

Ugwala [gwale, unkwindi]. Unbraced mouth bow of the Zulu and Venda peoples of southern Africa. Among the neighbouring Xhosa it is known as *ugwali* or *igwali*. It apparently derives from the *gora* of the Khoikhoi, and is sounded by blowing and sucking air over a piece of quill that connects one end of the string to the stave. It was played by males but is no longer found among the Zulu. See P.R. Kirby: *The Musical Instruments of the Native Races of South Africa* (London, 1934, 2/1965), 183–4, pl.50*c*.

DAVID K. RYCROFT/R

Uhadi [hade]. Unbraced gourd-resonated musical bow of the Xhosa people of southern Africa. It is similar in construction and performance practice to the Zulu *ugubhu*, but in the uhadi the two fundamentals, obtained by stopping the string with a finger of the hand that holds the bow, are a whole tone apart, rather than a semitone. The term uhadi is also used by the Xhosa to refer to certain Western instruments, for example, the reed organ.

DAVID K. RYCROFT

Uhlmann. Austrian family of wind instrument makers and musicians. The firm was founded by Johann Tobias Uhlmann (*b* Kronach, Upper Franconia, 8 June 1776; *d* Vienna, 12 May 1838), who was granted a licence to trade in Vienna in 1810; he took the oath of citizenship in 1817. In addition to his instrument-making activities he was an oboist at the Theater an

der Wien. In 1833 his sons Leopold and Jakob entered the firm, which already had become one of the most important in the Austrian lands, producing wind instruments of all kinds and exporting them to the rest of Europe as well as to Egypt, Persia, and Brazil. Uhlmann & Söhne's 1836 woodwind price list illustrates a curved basset horn like those made by Koch in Vienna; none of this type by Uhlmann is known to exist. Surviving instruments bearing the marks 'I.T. UHLMANN' or 'J:T:Uhlmann' include a flute, a walking-stick flute, clarinets, straight and angled basset horns, an oboe, an angled cor anglais, bassoons, and contrabassoons.

Jakob Uhlmann (*bap* 19 Dec 1803; *d* 18 Nov 1850) received his licence to trade in 1830 and was also an oboist in the Hofmusikkapelle from 1843. He died of typhoid. His son Jakob jr (*b* 1837; *d* 10 Sept 1871) is recorded at the same address during the following years. The fact that Jakob jr was likewise an oboist has caused some confusion. The younger Jakob played in the orchestra of the court opera, and from 1866 taught at the conservatory of the Gesellschaft der Musikfreunde. He died of pulmonary tuberculosis.

Leopold Tobias Uhlmann (*b* 22 Feb 1806; *d* 8 March 1878) learned his father's trade and applied for his 'freedom' in 1825. In 1830 he received a patent in connection with improvements to the double-piston or Vienna valve, developed by Joseph Riedl and Josef Kail. The new valve was quieter, more airtight and produced less friction. Although Uhlmann used this valve in horns, trumpets, and trombones, it was to prove useful only for the horn; with minor alterations it is used nowadays in the so-called Vienna horn in F. He also invented a water key for the trombone in 1830. Uhlmann also made improvements to the ophicleide, providing it too with Vienna valves. In 1843 he applied for patents for four other improvements: a mouthpiece in which the volume of the cup changes according to lip pressure; a new process for making the flare; an improved rotary valve; and auxiliary keys to improve intonation. Uhlmann was appointed wind instrument maker to the Austro-Hungarian court in 1874. His advertisements proudly mention the firm's exports to Russia and America, and the nine medals won at trade and international exhibitions. After Leopold Uhlmann's death his son of the same name continued the family business. In 1900 the Erste Productivgenossenschaft der Musikinstrumentenmacher (workers' cooperative; founded 1892) took over the stock of the workshop. Surviving instruments bearing the mark 'L. Uhlmann' or 'Leopold Uhlmann' include a bassoon, a trumpet, and a bass valve trombone. A unique double-reed contrabass instrument in brass, pitched in F' with eleven closed-standing keys, is in the Conservatorio di Musica, Parma.

Joseph Uhlmann (*b* 31 Dec 1807; *d* 1 March 1859) also joined his father's business and appears in the Vienna registers as an independent maker of wind instruments from 1846, when he acquired citizenship, until his death. He exhibited a 23-key bass clarinet in the 1854 Munich Exhibition.

BIBLIOGRAPHY
H. Heyde: *Das Ventilblasinstrument* (Leipzig, 1987)

W. Waterhouse: *The New Langwill Index: a Dictionary of Musical Wind-Instrument Makers and Inventors* (London, 1993)

R. Hopfner: *Wiener Musikinstrumentenmacher, 1766–1900* (Tutzing, 1999)

T. Kiefer: 'Tiefstimmige Doppelrohrblattinstrumente von der Harmoniemusik bis in das Blasorchester des 19. Jahrhunderts', in W. Meighörner, ed., *Wissenschaftlicher Jahrbuch der Tirolischer Landesmuseum 2010* (Innsbruck, 2010), 47–99

RUDOLF HOPFNER/R

Uindja. Rattle of the Nzakara people of the Central African Republic and the Democratic Republic of the Congo. It is made of dried fruit shells strung together, and is worn on the arms and legs of dancers.

FERDINAND J. DE HEN

Ujara. Leg rattles of the Igbo people of Nigeria.

Ukari [evkari]. Side-blown horn of the Dakakari people of northern Nigeria. It is made from oryx or roan antelope horn and is used by hunters for signalling and by young men for praising the chief and during wrestling.

Ūkas. Whizzer of Lithuania. It is made from bone, a wooden splinter, a button, or a metal cogwheel; a cord is threaded through two holes in the object and the ends tied together. The player holds the ends of the cord and spins the disc rapidly to wind up the cord. The cord is then stretched and released in turn and thus whirls the buzzing disc. The intensity, pitch, and timbre of the ūkas depend on the material and size of the disc and on the speed with which it is whirled. The ūkas is a toy made and used by children and shepherds.

ARVYDAS KARAŠKA

Ukase. Rattle of the Edo-speaking peoples of Nigeria.

Ukaya. Small circular brass gong of the Digo people of Kenya. It is placed flat on the ground and beaten with two strikers made from plaited grass as part of a tuned drum ensemble.

Uke. Single-headed conical closed drum of the Genya people of the Democratic Republic of the Congo.

'Ukēkē. Mouth bow of Hawaii. It is reputed to be the only indigenous Hawaiian string instrument. It usually has two, or sometimes three strings, traditionally of plant fibre (later of horsehair or gut), stretched over a flexible wooden stave 3 to 4 cm wide and 40 to 60 cm long; the strings are attached in notches or holes at one end and wound around a fishtail-like carving at the other. The upper surface of the stave is flat and the under surface slightly convex. The wood (typically *kauila* or *ulei*) is held at one end between the lips and the strings are plucked with the fingers or a plectrum made of the midrib of a leaf; the player might chant while sounding the instrument. Most specimens have small bridges inserted to keep the strings from touching the stick. Three-string instruments are tuned to tonic, 3rd, and 4th, or tonic, 2nd, and 4th. Most two-string instruments have strings a 3rd or 4th apart. The 'ukēkē is said to have been played by lovers, who communicated by means of its tones. Once considered obsolete, it is now being revived. The term 'ukēkē has also been used in Hawaii to denote the European jew's harp. See H.H. Roberts: *Ancient Hawaiian Music* (Honolulu, 1926/*R*1967), 18.

MERVYN MCLEAN/R

Ukelin. Trade name of a fretless zither popular in the USA from the mid-1920s through the mid-1960s. It is roughly rectangular, about 70 cm long and 19 cm wide, with one end somewhat wider and shaped like the outline of a ukulele body. That end rests on the player's lap and the opposite end rests on a tabletop or chair in front of the player (it can also be held across the lap, or in other positions). The 32 longitudinal wire strings form melody and chord groups, the left hand strumming or plucking four chords, each sounded by four strings, and the right hand using a short violin-type bow to sound the 16 diatonic melody strings, strung at a higher level diagonally in two groups of eight and eight and terminating at the distal end.

The instrument was intended for use by persons with no musical training, using numerical notation, and was

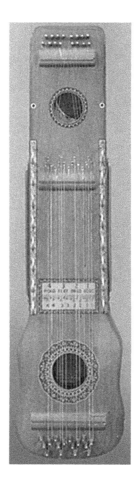

Ukelin, bowed zither, International Music Corp. (© Gregg Miner)

sold inexpensively by travelling salesmen and by mail order. The ukelin's origin is not entirely clear. Supposedly it can be traced to Henry Charles Marx (1875–1946 or 1947), a native of Kansas, who was trained as a woodworker and played the violin. He moved repeatedly around the USA and finally settled in New Troy, Michigan, where in 1927 he opened a small manufactory, the Marxochime Colony, to produce and distribute zithers of various models, assisted by his son, Charles (*d* 1972). Reportedly, their 'violin-uke' was copied by the International Music Company, a subsidiary of Oscar Schmidt International of Jersey City, New Jersey, and sold as the 'ukelin'. According to another account, the instrument was invented in 1923 and patented in 1926 by Paul F. Richter, who assigned the patent to the Phonoharp Co., which merged in 1926 with Oscar Schmidt. Two similar instruments were patented about the same time. In any case, Oscar Schmidt ended production of ukelins in 1964 in reaction to unethical behaviour by some salesmen, and the Marxochime factory ceased operation with the death of Charles Marx.

Ukhombe. Double duct flute of the Xhosa people of southern Africa. It resembles the modern Zulu *uveve*, made of unequal lengths of bamboo.

Ukom. Drum chime of the Igbo people of Nigeria.

Ukpe. Side-blown open-ended trumpet of the Idoma people of Nigeria. It is made from one or more long, narrow gourds fitted together. The instrument gives two notes by covering and uncovering the narrow open end with the thumb, and is played in hocket in groups of four, or sometimes eight.

Ukubu [umunahi, umuduri]. Gourd-resonated musical bow of the Rundi people of Burundi and Rwanda. The string is braced off-centre to the gourd so that the shorter segment of the string sounds about an octave higher than the longer segment. The brace loop holds the gourd to the bow stick. The ukubu is used to accompany singing. See J.-S. Laurenty: *L'Organologie du Zaïre*, vol.4 (Tervuren, 1997), 24.

FERDINAND J. DE HEN

Ukúk [oguk]. Side-blown conch horn of Kosrae, eastern Caroline Islands, Micronesia. See E. Sarfert: 'Kusae', *Ergebnisse der Südsee-Expedition 1908–1910*, vol.2B, bd.4 (Hamburg, 1920), 487.

Ukulele [ukelele] (from Hawaiian: 'leaping flea'). Small guitar-like instrument. It is a hybrid of the virtually identical *machête da braça* and the slightly larger, five-string *rajão* brought to the Hawaiian (then the Sandwich) Islands by immigrants from Madeira. It is differentiated from Madeiran models by utilizing native woods and having gut strings rather than wire, slightly different size and shape, and altered tuning. (The *'ūkēkē*, a mouth bow, is the only string instrument native to Hawaii.) Three Portuguese instrument makers arrived in 1879: Manuel Nunes (1843–1922), who opened the

first shop about 1880, and his associates Augusto Dias (1842–1915) and José do Espirito Santo (1850–1905), who opened their own shops in 1884 and 1886 respectively. The instrument rose swiftly to popularity among the native population: in 1886 ukuleles were used to accompany hula dancers at King Kalakaua's jubilee celebration, and the *Hawaiian Annual* of the same year reported that 'of late they have taken to the banjo and that hideous small Portuguese instrument now called the "taro-patch fiddle"'. The 'taro-patch fiddle' is a large ukulele which appears to be derived from the *machête da rajão*.

Although a US tour by the Hawaiian Glee Club in 1901 included ukulele accompaniments, and a Los Angeles publisher, R.W. Hefflefinger, was advertising 'a self-instructor for the ukulele or Hawaiian guitar and taro-patch' by 1914, the ukulele first truly came to national prominence during the Panama-Pacific Exposition of 1915 in San Francisco. According to the official history of the exposition published in 1917, 'people were about ready for a new fad in popular music at the time of the Exposition and the sweet voices of the Hawaiians raised in those haunting minor melodies you heard at the Hawaiian Building . . . were enough to start a musical vogue'.

In the Hawaiian music fad that swept across the United States, lasting into the 1930s, the ukulele was at the forefront. Its low cost, small size, and light weight, combined with a simple tuning and undemanding technique, were all factors in the ready acceptance of the ukulele for the accompaniment of popular song. Tin Pan Alley songwriters published dozens of novelty songs that mentioned the ukulele in the titles or lyrics. A flood of instruction books, mostly published outside Hawaii, appeared in response to heightened interest. American guitar manufacturers, including Martin, Gibson, and Weissenborn, offered variously sized models; later entrants to the market included Lyon & Healy, Regal, and Harmony, all of Chicago. In 2000 the Kamaka Ukulele Co., founded in 1916, remained the sole mass production operation in Hawaii; independent instrument makers also cater to serious performers.

Numerous entertainers have been associated with the ukulele as virtuoso performers; many have written instructional books as well. Hawaiian players include Ernest Kaai (1881–1962), active from the 1910s to the 30s; Jesse Kalima (1920–80), active from the 1940s to the 60s; and Herb Ohta [Ohta-San] (*b* 1934), who has released several dozen recordings since 1964. In mainland America exponents include Cliff Edwards ['Ukulele Ike'] (1895–1972); Roy Smeck (1900–94); May Singhi Breen (*d* 1970); Arthur Godfrey (1903–83), whose television show in the 1950s sparked a revival of interest; and 'Tiny Tim' (Herbert Khaury; 1925–96). The fashion for the ukulele also spread to Europe, where it was adopted by stars of British music hall; one of the most successful entertainers of the 1930s and 40s, George Formby (1904–61), featured the banjulele: a hybrid instrument combining a banjo body with a ukulele fingerboard, stringing and tuning. In the 1990s a new generation of virtuosos brought renewed attention to the ukulele in Hawaii, foremost among them Troy Fernandez and Israel Kamakawiwo'ole (1959–97).

There are four sizes of ukulele: soprano or standard (46–53 cm long, with 12 to 17 frets), 'concert' (c60 cm; up to 19 frets), tenor (c70 cm, 18 to 22 frets) and baritone (c80 cm, up to 22 frets). Instruments with four strings predominate. The tuning is re-entrant and spans a major 6th, although absolute pitch is not regarded as important: the basic tuning of g'–c'–e'–a' can be raised or lowered to enable the player to accompany in a key that is comfortable for the singer's voice and avoids awkward chord patterns. The different sizes are used to provide variety of timbre and register; traditionally they are made of kou or koa wood. On the tenor and baritone resonance is often enhanced by doubling (or even tripling) the courses, and tuning the doubled strings an octave apart. All four sizes are played predominantly with a strummed chordal style, although the soprano ukulele has also become a virtuoso melody instrument, starting with the work of Jesse Kalima in the late 1950s.

BIBLIOGRAPHY

H.H. Roberts: *Ancient Hawaiian Music* (Honolulu, 1926/R)

J.H. Felix, L. Nunes, and P.F. Senecal: *The 'Ukulele: a Portuguese Gift to Hawaii* (Honolulu, 1980)

A. Tsumera: *Extraordinary Ukuleles: the Tsumura Collection from Japan*, Honolulu Academy of Arts, 8 Sept– 3 Oct 1993 (Honolulu, 1993) [exhibition catalogue]

J. Beloff: *The Ukulele: a Visual History* (San Francisco, 1997)

J. King and J. Tranquada: 'The Singular Case of Manuel Nunes and the Invention of the Bouncing Flea', *GSJ*, vol.60 (April 2007), 85–95

JAY SCOTT ODELL/AMY K. STILLMAN/R

Ulbura [ilpirra]. Aboriginal Australian megaphone. It was first described in 1896, as a short wooden trumpet used by the Aranda people of central Australia; the latest description dates from 1908, and the instrument has now, almost certainly, long disappeared. It was about 60 cm long and 5 cm across. It was probably megaphonic (as opposed to aerophonic) in use, though megaphonic use can lead to lip vibration (as with similar instruments in Papua New Guinea). It was almost certainly used with magical intent in ritual contexts.

TREVOR A. JONES

'Ūlili. Hawaiian spinning rattle, played for instance by a hula dancer while dancing or chanting, or by children as a toy. It consists of three *la'amia* gourds mounted axially on a stick, two of them large and spherical flanking a smaller, somewhat oblong gourd that serves as a grip. The outer gourds, which often contain rattling seeds, spin and whizz when a cord wound around the stick is pulled quickly through a hole in the middle gourd. When released, the cord winds again around the stick in the manner of a yo-yo. Similar instruments elsewhere include the Turkish *nar firildaği*, which employs dried pomegranates, and a Jamaican example that uses a seed on the bottom of the stick as a flyweight.

LAURENCE LIBIN

'Ulī'ulī. Hawaiian vessel rattle. It is made from a single small gourd receptacle containing seeds, fitted with a fibre handle surmounted by an artistically designed flat circular disc fringed with feathers. In 1779 Captain James Cook and his men witnessed the *hula 'ulī'ulī* (gourd-rattle dance) at Kealakekua, Hawaii. The male *'ōlapa* ('dancer') wore *kūpe'e niho'īlio* ('dog-teeth anklets'; the dogs' teeth are strung in multiple rows on a net backing). Dancers now use two 'ulī'ulī the gourd having been replaced by the calabash (introduced from tropical America) or a hard coconut shell; the disc is now of dyed feathers, and occasionally ceramic facsimiles of the anklets are worn by male dancers.

ZANETA HO 'OŪLU CAMBRA

Ulla. Obsolete gongs of Korea (*ul*: 'cloud'; *la*: 'gongs'), the Korean name for Chinese *yunluo*. The set of ten thin disc-shaped metal gongs were mounted in a portable wooden frame in three rows of three with a single gong centred on top. The gongs were tuned ab–bb–c'–db'–eb'–f'–g'–ab'–bb'–c''. The instrument was carried in the left hand by a handle-pole protruding from the bottom of the frame and struck with a mallet held in the right hand.

The instrument is considered Chinese. It appears in a painting of the 18th century showing a provincial governor's procession and in a book of court banquet ceremonies of the early 19th century. From all indications the ulla was used only during the late Chosŏn period (18th and 19th centuries) and limited to processional music and some *tangak* ('Chinese music'). The only extant examples, now in Korea, were brought from Beijing in 1937. See Chang Sa-hun: *Han'guk akki taegwan* [Korean musical instruments] (Seoul, 1969), 114–5.

ROBERT C. PROVINE

Ullmann, (Reinhold) Oskar (*b* Adorf, Germany, 13 May 1875; *d* Leipzig, Germany, 16 June 1938). German brass instrument maker. Son and pupil of the instrument maker Gustav Erhard Ullmann, he claimed in 1903 to be the successor to the firm of J.C.G. Penzel in Leipzig. (It is not clear whether he was joint successor with Robert Schopper on Christoph Hermann Robert Penzel's

'Ulī'ulī, paired vessel rattles, Hawai'i. (Aurelia W. Hartenberger, EdD)

death, in 1880, or whether he gained control after Schopper set up his own business in 1888.) Besides making instruments Oskar assembled valves, bells, and other parts from Markneukirchen suppliers and from the factory of his brother Arno Ullmann in Adorf. His customers were mainly military and youth bands. He is particularly noted for the manufacture of valved brass instruments with special applications. His trumpet in D with three rotary valves was designed for performances of Bach, while another trumpet in B♭ was intended for Verdi's *Aida* (both instruments in *D.LE.u*). Similar to the latter are two E♭ fanfare trumpets (*D.HA.b*). Oskar Ullmann's son succeeded him in 1937 and the factory was destroyed in an air raid in 1943.

BIBLIOGRAPHY

H. Heyde: *Trompeten Posaunen Tuben* (Leipzig, 1980)

G. Dullat: *Verzeichnis der Holz- und Metallblasinstrumentmacher auf deutschsprachigem Gebiet* (Tutzing, 2010), 480ff

NIALL O'LOUGHLIN/R

Ululation [megolokwane, kaklaku, yuyu, ololuge, ologymus, italta, kulavai, ulu-uli, uruli]. Vocal technique of high-pitched sustained wailing or howling with a trilling aspect involving rapid movement of the tongue and uvula. Ululation is practised usually by women in many Arab, African, and Asian cultures. It is associated with celebrations such as weddings, and with grieving. It is used in worship in Eritrean and Ethiopian Orthodox churches. Ululation is also part of audience participation in music of the Shona in Zimbabwe. Western singers such as Joan La Barbera have incorporated ululation into their extended vocal techniques. See J.E. Jacobs: '"Unintelligibles" in Vocal Performance at Middle Eastern Marriage Celebrations', *Text & Talk*, vol.28/4 (2007), 483–505.

SALLY SANFORD

Uluru. Trumpet of the Madi people of Uganda. It is a straight bamboo tube, approximately 22 cm long, to which is attached one or more almost spherical calabashes increasing successively in size, by means of one or two small gourd joints sealed with a sewn leather ring or clay. In one specimen the single calabash is 30 cm long and the joining gourd 7 cm. The calabash has only a small opening, 5 to 7 cm in diameter and surrounded by a ring of cowrie shells, and thus does not serve as a bell but rather as a separate sound vessel. The uluru is played at important dances, and each clan allegedly owns an instrument. See M. Trowell and K.P. Wachsmann: *Tribal Crafts of Uganda* (London, 1953), 348–9.

Umakhweyana [imvingo, inkohlisa, isiqwemqwe, mana, uqwabe, unkoka, unkokha, umakweyana]. Braced gourd-resonated musical bow of the Zulu people of southern Africa. It is similar in construction and performing practice to the Tsonga *xitende* (or *nkoka*), Northern Sotho (or Pedi) *sekgapa*, Tswana *segwana*, Chopi *tshitendole* (or *chitende*), Swazi *makhweyane*, Venda *dende*, Ila and Tonga *kalumbu*, Humbi

mbulu-mbumba, and the Cuban *burumbumba*. The umakhweyana was reputedly borrowed by the Zulu from the Tsonga people of Mozambique early in the 19th century, largely displacing the Zulu *ugubhu* (as also the Swazi *ligubhu*), but it was not adopted by the Xhosa or Southern Sotho. This instrument differs from the unbraced *ugubhu* in that the gourd resonator is slightly smaller and mounted near the centre of the stave instead of at the bottom.

DAVID K. RYCROFT

Umampembe [mampembe]. Whizzer of the Zulu people of southern Africa. It is a toothed disc of wood or gourd segment, pierced with two holes through which a string is looped. The string is wound up between the two hands and the disc is spun by pulling the hands apart to untwist the string. It is used as a children's toy. The Xhosa call it *uvuru*. See P.R. Kirby: *The Musical Instruments of the Native Races of South Africa* (London, 1934, 2/1965), 72.

Umbubu. Bullroarer of the southern Orokaiva people, Northern Province, Papua New Guinea. It is made from a thin slat of palmwood with a hole drilled through one end, and is swung on a string attached to a long stick handle. It is used during initiation ceremonies, with secret flutes, to represent the voice of spirits of the dead. See F.E. Williams: *Orokaiva Society* (London, 1930), 89.

Umbungu. End-blown bamboo trumpet used by a Zulu religious sect in Natal, South Africa.

Umkiki. Single-string fiddle of the Baggara people of western Sudan. The slightly curved neck passes through the hemispherical gourd body. The horsehair string extends from a peg at the top of the neck to a sisal retaining string that crosses a flat bridge and is tied to the projecting end of the spike. The goatskin soundtable has a circular soundhole offset to one side. It is used to accompany *gardagi* songs. The instrument was introduced by immigrant Arabs and is a type of *rabāb*.

Umkwenda. Bamboo scraper of the Nyanja/Chewa people of the Dedza district, Malawi.

Umntjingozi [livenge, umtshingosi]. End-blown harmonic flute of the Swazi people of southern Africa. It resembles the Zulu *umtshingo*. It is made from a slightly conical tube of reed about 75 cm long with an oblique embouchure and the internodes pushed out with a stick, or a stem of the cabbage tree. Opening and closing the distal end with a finger allows production of the overtones of an open or stopped pipe.

The name also applies to a transverse flute with two or sometimes three fingerholes that is open-ended but otherwise resembles the Venda *tshitiringo*. See P.R. Kirby: *The Musical Instruments of the Native Races of South Africa* (London, 1934, 2/1965), 112–3, 126–7.

Umkiki, Western Sudan, c1970. (Edinburgh University Collection of Historic Musical Instruments (2063))

Umpindo [dilele]. Transverse flute of the Luba people in the Shaba region of the Democratic Republic of the Congo. (DRC) The two terms might formerly have referred to different instruments, the *dilele* possibly end-blown, but are now interchangeable. The umpindo is a bamboo tube about 20 cm long and 1 to 1.5 cm in diameter, with a rectangular embouchure 4 cm from the closed end, three fingerholes, and two thumbholes opposite the first and third fingerholes. Traditionally used to encourage warriors or during hunting, the flute is now played mainly for entertainment at feasts to the accompaniment of the *madimba* xylophone and the *ditumba* drum. A few other transverse flutes (but with only three fingerholes) have been reported from the Luluwa and Tetela peoples of the DRC. See J. Gansemans: *Les instruments de musique Luba* (Tervuren, 1980).

K.A. GOURLAY/FERDINAND J. DE HEN

Umqangala. Musical bow originally of the Nguni peoples (Zulu, Swazi, Xhosa, Ndebele) of South Africa. It was spread widely around southeastern Africa in the course of the *Imfecane* diaspora caused by the Zulu leader Shaka in the early 19th century. The stave is usually made of a straight reed, about 60 cm long, with an unbraced plant fibre, sinew, twisted hair, wire, or nylon string, plucked with a finger or plectrum. Similar bows are known by other names, for example *lugube* (Venda), *lekope* (North and South Sotho), *lengope* (Tswana), *chidangari*, *kadimbwa* (Shona of Zimbabwe, Sena of Mozambique), *inkinge* (Xhosa), *gabus* (Korana), *mqangala* (Tsonga), *nkangala*, and *mtangala* (Ngoni). Sometimes a rattle plate with pieces of snail shell attached is added. In the Nguni tradition it is largely played by men, among the Sotho and Venda by women and girls. When played, the string faces outwards and one end of the stave rests in the right corner of the player's mouth, without touching the teeth. This simple instrument is capable of playing any music of southern Africa. Like the jew's harp it uses mouth-resonated harmonics, and by fingering the far end of the string with the left hand, different fundamentals are obtained. See P.R. Kirby: *The Musical Instruments of the Native Races of South Africa* (London, 1934, 2/1965), 220ff, pl.62.

DAVID K. RYCROFT/ANDREW TRACEY

Umreñiduruture. Vessel flute and rattle of the Xavante people of Mata Grosso, Brazil. It is a rather rare instrument, made of a gourd containing the hooves of a pig as rattles, and pierced by two holes; when blown it can emit three pitches, the fundamental and roughly a minor 3rd and perfect 5th above, used melodically. Other aerophones of the Xavante include the *upawã*, a transverse flute without fingerholes, capable of sounding three pitches by varying the blowing pressure or by stopping and opening the open distal end of the bamboo tube, and the *tsidupo*, a double flute made of two bamboo tubes, played in pairs in interlocking fashion. See M. Kuss, ed.: *Music in Latin America and the Caribbean: an Encyclopedic History*, vol.1 (Austin, TX, 2004).

Umrhubhe [umrube, umqunge]. Unbraced friction mouth bow of the Xhosa people of southern Africa. It was formerly played by men but now is used mainly by women of the Mpondo clan. The Zulu *umhubhe* is similar but is nowadays rarely found. In its simplest form the instrument consists of a curved stick about 65 cm long, with a wire or fibre string stretched between the ends. A more elaborate type, now rarely found, has a composite string-bearer comprising a piece of stout reed with a curved stick inserted in one end. Both types are sounded by rubbing the string with a thin reed or stalk, used like a violin bow. One end of the stave rests against the player's slightly parted lips. The other end is held by the left hand, and the string may be stopped with finger or thumb to yield a second fundamental, a whole tone higher than that from the open string. Mouth-resonated harmonics are used melodically. The *utiyane* and the *ipiano* of the Swazi were similar but are now obsolete.

BIBLIOGRAPHY

P.R. Kirby: *The Musical Instruments of the Native Races of South Africa* (London, 1934, 2/1965), 239–40, pl.68.

D.K. Rycroft: 'Friction Chordophones in South–Eastern Africa', *GSJ*, vol.19 (1966), 84–100.

DAVID K. RYCROFT

Umtshingo [ivenge]. Long end-blown harmonic flute of the Zulu and Bomvana (Xhosa) people of southern Africa. It has been likened to the ancient Egyptian flute. Cognate instruments are the Swazi *umntjingozi* (*umtshingosi* or *livenge*), the Mpondo (Xhosa) *umtshingi* (or *ivenge*), the Sotho *lekolilo*, and the Bomvana (Xhosa) *ngcongolo*. It is made of the *ngcongolo* river reed, has no fingerholes, is open at both ends, and the mouthpiece is cut obliquely. The instrument is held obliquely and is sounded by shaping the tongue to serve as an air channel. By overblowing and by alternately stopping and unstopping the end with a finger, the 2nd to 6th harmonic partials (on the open pipe) and 5th, 7th, 9th, and 11th partials (on the closed pipe) are produced, thus corresponding to partials 4 to 12 from an open pipe twice as long. *See* P.R. Kirby: *The Musical Instruments of the Native Races of South Africa* (London, 1934, 2/1965), 111, ill.40, 41.

DAVID K. RYCROFT

Umudende. Clapper bell of the Baganda people of Uganda. It is made from a narrow rectangular strip of iron, folded into the shape of an inverted U, with the clapper suspended inside it.

Umuduri [umuduli, umunahi]. Musical bow of the Hutu people of Rwanda and Burundi. It is a bent wooden stick holding a metal string stretched between the ends. A third of the way along its length the string is braced by a metal ring that brings it slightly closer to the stick; at this point on the stick a hemispherical calabash resonator is attached. The player holds the instrument vertically in his left hand with the open part of the calabash against his chest. His right hand holds two sticks arranged in a V; one stick is used to strike the string, while the other, which has a round vegetable husk containing seeds threaded on to it, strikes the calabash resonator, thus causing the husk to rattle. Variations in pitch and timbre are produced by stopping the string with the index finger of the left hand, and by movement to and fro of the resonator against the chest. The umuduri accompanies the player's singing of songs commenting on everyday events. *See* J.-S. Laurenty: *L'Organologie du Zaïre*, vol.4 (Tervuren, 1997), 24.

K.A. GOURLAY

Umwilenge [umwironke, umwirongi, mwironge]. Notched flute played by Hutu and other herdsmen of Rwanda and Burundi. It is made from a dried, hollow stalk. It has two fingerholes and can be up to 70 cm long. The men play it for pleasure while herding cattle or at night to pass the time. It may also be played for dance.

BIBLIOGRAPHY

F.J. de Hen: *Beitrag zur Kenntnis der Musikinstrumente aus Belgisch Kongo und Ruanda-Urundi* (Tervuren, 1960)

G. Knosp: *Enquête sur la vie musicale au Congo belge 1934–1935* (Tervuren, 1968)

J.-S. Laurenty: *Systématique des aérophones de l'Afrique centrale* (Tervuren, 1974), 281, 283

K.A. GOURLAY

Una corda (Ger. *Verschiebung*). Name often used for the left or 'soft' pedal on the piano, or, in piano music, a direction to play with this pedal depressed. In a modern grand piano this pedal shifts the action sideways so that the hammers strike only two of the three strings provided for each note in the treble and only one of the two strings provided for each note in the bass, while continuing to strike the single strings of the extreme bass. In some triple-strung pianos of the late 18th and early 19th centuries, the una corda pedal caused the action to be shifted so far that the hammers struck only one string throughout the entire range of the instrument, giving the pianist a choice between 'tre corde' (when the pedal was not depressed), 'due corde' (partly depressed), and 'una corda' (depressed completely). In some instruments a stop could be set to limit the shifting of the action to the 'due corde' position, but several composers, notably Beethoven, wrote explicitly for both 'due corde' and 'una corda'. The phrase 'tre corde' (tutte le corde) (It.: 'three strings') in piano music is usually a direction to release the una corda pedal.

The effect produced by depressing the una corda pedal on a grand piano is not merely one of reduced loudness, but also of a change in timbre, so that the sound is not only softer but less brilliant than that from all three strings. This change is due in part to the una corda position causing the string to be struck by a less compressed portion of the hammer covering. (On an upright piano the corresponding pedal merely moves the hammers closer to the strings, so as to shorten their stroke, and the resulting reduction in loudness is not accompanied by any change in timbre.)

The una corda, operated by hand, was introduced in the earliest extant pianos, by Bartolomeo Cristofori, possibly as an aid to tuning. It has been a feature of most grand pianos since the late 18th century, becoming standard on English instruments rather earlier than on German or Austrian ones. *See* D. Rowland: *A History of Pianoforte Pedalling* (Cambridge, 1993).

EDWIN M. RIPIN/DAVID ROWLAND/R

Una-Fon. Small electronic organ manufactured for several years during the 1930s by J.C. Deagan of Chicago. Designed for open-air performance (for use at skating rinks, and for functions such as political meetings and auctions) it could produce the volume and timbre of brass instruments. Two versions were available, respectively with 33 and 49 notes (one oscillator per note), and the instrument could be powered by a large storage battery for outdoor presentations. A Una-Fon was included by Percy Grainger in a rescoring of his *Marching Song of Democracy* (1901–17).

HUGH DAVIES

Undaji [kimpungili, mpungi]. Voice modifier of the Democratic Republic of the Congo (DRC). It is made of reed or a hollow stem of the papaya tree. One end is covered with a thin skin or spider silk mirliton that alters the vocal timbre when the user sings into the other, open end. Although uncommon, it is used throughout the DRC and called by various names including *kimpungili* (Luba) and *mpungi* (Sanga); *undaji* is its Chokwe name. See J.-S. Laurenty: *Systématique des aérophones de l'Afrique centrale* (Tervuren, 1974), 34.

FERDINAND J. DE HEN

Une. Mouth bow of the Igbo people of Nigeria. The player taps the string a stick held in one hand, producing various overtones by changing his mouth shape, and obtains a second fundamental by stopping the string close to one end with a second stick held in the other hand. Now very rare, the une was formerly used for entertainment and to give instructions during wrestling matches and in a children's game.

Ŭng. Obsolete Korean percussion idiophone consisting of a wooden box and a hammer. It was considered of Chinese origin. As described in the treatise *Akhak kwebŏm* (1493), the box was 121.8 cm tall and 18.4 cm square. A long wooden hammer protruded from a hole at the top end of the box and was thumped against the bottom. The ŭng was used only as part of the *mumu* ('military dance') ensemble in ritual music (*aak*). Together with the *a, sang* (drums), and *tok* (idiophone) it was played after the regular sounding of the large drum *chin'go*, that is after every four-note phrase of the very slow melody. See Sŏng Hyŏn, ed.: *Akhak kwebŏm* [Guide to the Study of Music] (Seoul, 1493/R), 6.26a, b.

ROBERT C. PROVINE

Ŭnggo [ŭngbi]. Obsolete long barrel drum of Korea (*ŭng*: 'responding'; *go*: 'drum'). The alternative name *ŭngbi* is given in some historical sources such as the treatise *Akhak kwebŏm* (1493). Its construction was very similar to that of the *sakko*, with which it was always paired, except that the ŭnggo was somewhat smaller (head diameter about 40 cm; length of body about 65 cm). The ŭnggo was included in a large gift of musical instruments sent to Korea in 1116 by the Song Chinese emperor, and Korean examples were constructed in the 15th century. The last was destroyed during the Korean War (1950–53) and extant instruments are reconstructions.

According to the *Akhak kwebŏm*, the ŭnggo was used in the *hŏn'ga* (courtyard ensemble) at court banquets and similar events. It was played only at the end of pieces of music, as part of the closing signal, and was always paired with the *sakko*, which had a corresponding role in starting signals. The ŭnggo has not been in use since the 19th century.

BIBLIOGRAPHY

Chang Sa-hun: *Han'guk akki taegwan* [Korean musical instruments] (Seoul, 1969), 138–9

Sŏng Hyŏn, ed.: *Akhak kwebŏm* [Guide to the Study of Music] (Seoul, 1493/R, 6.7a, *b*

ROBERT C. PROVINE

Unglerth, Simon (*b* c1778; *d* Ljubljana, Slovenia, 14 Nov 1854). Woodwind instrument maker in Ljubljana, Slovenia. He obtained his civic licence on 30 Jan 1801 and is also documented as a turner (*Drechmeister*). As was typical for contemporary instrument makers in Austrian-influenced Slovenia, his woodwinds resemble Viennese counterparts. Extant examples include an eight-key basset horn (in *US.NY.mma*); a czakan (in *DK.K.m*), and an Eb clarinet, a transverse flute in C, and two parts of a flageolet (in *Sl.P.pm*). In 1844 Unglerth received a bronze medal at an industrial exposition in Ljubljana. He is one of few known woodwind makers active in Slovenia from the late 18th century to the mid-19th; others include Matias Poje (*fl* Maribor, c1845) and Michael Pöhm (*b* 1759; *d* Ptuj, 1821). See D. Koter: *Glasbilarstvo na Slovenskem* (Maribor, 2001).

DARJA KOTER

Unguni. Brass gong of the Mairasi people of West Papua, Indonesia. It is about 35 cm in diameter and 11 cm deep. The related *mamonggo* is of the same diameter but 5 to 7 cm deep. Both gongs are suspended from a wall or the player's shoulder by rattan or rope and are struck with a wooden mallet on the central boss. They are played with the *evia* drum and singing during festivals. The gongs are said to be from Seram Islands, obtained by trade with fishermen. Gongs are also reported in other scattered parts of western New Guinea, particularly areas in contact with Maluku. See N. Peckham: 'Day and Night Songs in Mairasi Festival Music', *Irian*, vol.9/1 (1981), 55–65, esp. 58.

DON NILES

Union [uilleann] **pipe.** Type of bellows-blown bagpipe known in Ireland from the 18th century and nowadays widely played. It is also called the *uilleann* (Gaelic: 'elbow') pipe or 'Irish organ'.

Univox. (1) Monophonic, three-octave piano attachment developed by Leslie James Hills and manufactured by Jennings Musical Industries of Dartford, Kent, from about 1952. The sound is generated by a single oscillator. The range of the touch-sensitive keyboard can be set within a total compass of five octaves by means of octave transposition switches, which also permit octave doubling and trebling. Volume is controlled by a knee-lever. From the 1950s until the mid-1970s Jennings also manufactured a range of frequency-divider electronic organs. See A. Douglas: *The Electronic Musical Instrument Manual: a Guide to Theory and Design* (London, 1949, 6/1978).

(2) A range of tube amplifiers, electric guitars, and keyboards produced initially by the Unicord company in Westbury, New York, from the 1960s. About 1971 synthesizers and effects boxes, produced by Korg, were added to the Univox line. Early Univox keyboards were manufactured in Italy by Crucianelli. Manufacture of

Univox guitars was moved to the Matsumoko guitar factory in Japan in 1975 and a new line called Westbury was introduced in 1978. Many Univox products were copies of other manufacturers' and the brand did not have a reputation for quality or innovation, although their effects pedals were well regarded. Both the Super Fuzz pedal used by Pete Townshend and the Univibe made famous by Jimi Hendrix are now collector's items. Univox also distributed Korg and Marshall products in the USA. The line ended when Unicord was purchased by Korg in 1985. *See* M. Wright: *Guitar Stories Vol.2: The Histories of Cool Guitars* (Bismarck, ND, 2000).

HUGH DAVIES/R

Unra. Set of bronze gongs used in Japanese *minshingaku* music, equivalent to the Chinese *yunluo*. For generic discussion of Japanese metallophones, *see also* KANE.

Unverdorben [Unferdorfer], **Marx** [Marc, Max] (*fl* ?mid-16th century). German lute maker, active mainly in Venice and briefly in Bologna. He was a cousin of Luca and Sigismondo (i) Maler and married Angela, the daughter of Giovanni Gisoli (also known as Batilori), with whom Luca Maler made a contract in 1527. In 1530 Maler's son Sigismondo (ii) was apprenticed to Unverdorben for a year, and Unverdorben is mentioned as a beneficiary in Luca Maler's first will, also dated 1530. Shortly afterwards he appears to have moved to Venice, although legacies to the daughters of 'Marco Oserdoni, lute maker of Venice' in Maler's second and last will of 1552 suggest that the family connection was maintained. The Raymund Fugger inventory of 1566 includes 'Eine grosse alte Lauten von Max Unverdorben'. At least nine of his instruments survive, though none is in original condition. These include a fine multi-rib yew instrument (in *GB.L.fb*), labelled 'Marx Unverdorben in Venetia 158 … ', which was rebuilt as a 13-course Baroque lute by Buchstetter of Regensburg in 1747. The Victoria and Albert Museum, London, has a very striking lute back composed of a complex and unsupported marquetry of different woods. The Museu de la Mùsica, Barcelona, has a seven-course lute with a 13-rib back of quilted

maple. The Lobkowicz collection in Nelahozeves Castle near Prague has one instrument converted in the 18th century. A lute with ivory bowl at Harvard University was converted to a 13-course lute by Heinrich Kramer of Vienna in 1706. Another instrument, remade as a theorbo, is in the Museo di Strumenti Musicali, Rome. The stylistic disparity and the date of the Fenton House lute suggest that the surviving instruments represent at least two generations of Unverdorbens.

BIBLIOGRAPHY
M.W. Prynne: 'A Note on Marx Unverdorben', *LSJ*, vol.1 (1959), 58 only
C. Challen: 'The Unverdorben Lute at Fenton House: Conservation in Practice', *EMc*, vol.7/2 (1979), 166–73
S. Toffolo: *Antichi strumenti veneziani: 1500–1800, quattro secoli di liuteria e cembalaria* (Venice, 1987)
S. Pasqual: 'Laux Maler (*c*1485–1552)', *Bollettino della società italiana del liuto*, no.22 (1997), 3–11; no. 13 (1997), 4–13; Eng. trans. in *Lute News*, no.51 (1999), 5–15

LYNDA SAYCE/R

Upanga [upang]. Indian term denoting various reedpipes. The *upang* (*owpunk*) is described in the late 16th century as a tube with a hole in the centre in which is placed a reed (the precise type is not clear). The instrument was played in the aristocratic house orchestra *akhārā*. The *şruti upanga* of central-south India is a drone bagpipe. *See* Abu'l FazI: *Ā'īn-i-akbarī* (*c*1590), trans. H. Blochmann in *The Imperial Musicians* (Calcutta, 1873, 2/1927); trans. H. S. Jarrett, rev. J. Sarkar in *Sangīt*, Bibliotheca Indica, vol.270 (Calcutta, 1948).

ALASTAIR DICK

Upe. Side-blown gourd trumpet of the Ondó Yorùbá people of Nigeria. It is sacred to Ògún, the deity of iron and war.

Upright [vertical] **piano** (Fr. *piano droit*; Ger. *Piano*; It. *pianoforte*). Piano with strings stretched in a vertical plane, rather than horizontally as in grand and square pianos. The earliest reliably dated upright (1739), by Domenico del Mela (1683?–after 1772) of Gagliano, is in the Museo del Conservatorio di L. Cherubini, Florence; possibly modelled after Bartolomeo Cristofori's *cimbalo in piedi, o sia ritto* ('standing, or upright harpsichord'), it is effectively a grand piano set on end, with compass *C/E-c′′′*, an oddly asymmetric case resting on a separate stand, and exposed strings and soundboard. Del Mela might have been associated with Bartolomeo Cristofori, one of whose wills bequeathed tools and furnishings to a del Mela family.

Upright pianos developed in Germany in the mid-18th century. C.E. Friederici of Gera supposedly introduced the 'pyramid piano' (Ger. *Pyramidenflügel*), with strings running diagonally in a symmetrically tapering case. Of three such instruments ascribed to Friederici, two are dated 1745. An anonymous Germanic upright (in *US.NAZ.m*) might be the earliest extant piano built in America.

In 1795 William Stodart of London patented an upright with a tall rectangular case fronted by silk-panelled

Univox, Crumar, c1960. (Photo by Don Kennedy. Courtesy of National Music Centre, Calgary, Canada)

doors; the compartment holds bookshelves at its upper right-hand side. These instruments, placed on legs, stand about 2.5 metres tall. As in earlier uprights, their keys pass under the wrest plank and soundboard, the hammers striking the strings from behind. German and Austrian builders including Jakob Bleyer (1778–1812), Franz Martin Seuffert (1773–1847), Matthäus Andreas (André) Stein (1776–1842), and Joseph Wachtl (*fl* 1803–32) began making 'giraffe' pianos soon after 1800. These instruments are named for their graceful shape, with the right side following the concave curve of the string band and terminating at the top left side with a kind of scroll. Following Biedermeier fashion, giraffe pianos often have multiple pedals for special effects, including janissary and bassoon stops; many also employ drop-action ('hanging') versions of the Viennese action.

Often imposing as furniture, uprights normally stand against a wall and present the player's back to the room, and hence are best suited to domestic music-making. In the early 19th century, experiments with small uprights began. In 1800 Mathias Müller of Vienna made his 'Ditanaclasis', standing about 154 cm tall, and in the same year John Isaac Hawkins of Philadelphia patented his 'portable grand pianoforte', reaching only about 140 cm. These were the earliest instruments with strings rising from the floor. Later forms include Robert Wornum's 'cottage' or 'harmonic' piano (introduced in 1813) and 'piccolo piano' (1826), the latter only 98 cm tall, and the *piano droit* of Johannes Roller and Nicolas Blanchet (Paris, 1827). In 1828 Jean Henri Pape of Paris invented his 'pianino' or 'piano-console', which introduced cross-stringing; French makers excelled in short uprights of this sort. Earlier, Thomas Loud (i) had proposed oblique stringing, like that in Friederici's pyramids, for small uprights; he was granted a British patent in 1802. All of these forms were intended for small spaces, particularly urban apartments. Some more impressive types are the neo-classical 'lyre piano' (Ger. *Lyraflügel*) of *c*1820–40, characteristic of Johann Christian Schleip (*d c*1877, Berlin), which has a lyre-shaped upper case, and the 'harp piano' (especially by Kuhn & Ridgeway, Baltimore, *c*1860), which has sound boxes rather than a normal soundboard, and strings exposed above the keyboard. The Euphonicon, an iron-framed harp-piano patented by Dr John Steward of Wolverhampton in 1841 and manufactured by Frederick Beale & Co., is decorated on all sides and intended to be freestanding.

As compasses were extended, uprights required longer bass strings. In Britain, 'cabinet pianos', with cases extending to the floor and tuning pins at the top, and utilizing tape-check actions developed by Wornum, supplanted earlier uprights, while on the Continent, uprights began to assume shapes more familiar today. Steinway & Sons' full-size uprights incorporate many of the firm's innovations: cross-stringing on a single-piece iron frame, metal action frame (which helps to avoid warping of the action parts), sostenuto pedal, duplex scale, and single bridge. That form dominated the piano market until the Great Depression. Since the 1930s,

modifications have consisted mainly of standardizing smaller sizes and improving actions and scalings. 'Studio' uprights, suitable for teaching and rehearsal studios, classrooms, and similar venues, stand about 115 to 135 cm tall, 'console' pianos about 100 to 115 cm, and 'spinet' pianos 90 to 100 cm. These sizes can accommodate only small soundboards and relatively short bass strings of inferior tone. The shortcomings of the upright have not been resolved, though Darrell Fandrich of Seattle, Washington, has completely redesigned the action, which has never been satisfactory. In 1987 David Klavins of Bonn introduced a modernistic, straight-strung upright more than 3.5 metres tall; its keyboard is near the top of the instrument, and the pianist sits on a platform more than 2 metres above the floor. In the 21st century production of uprights moved mainly to Asia, with cheap models being mass-produced in China and widely exported.

EDWIN M. GOOD/LAURENCE LIBIN

Upwut [wupwut]. Idiophone of the central Caroline Islands of Micronesia. It is made by tying together both ends of two long, young coconut fronds. Holding the resulting knots in each hand, a soft percussive snapping sound is produced by first pushing the knots towards each other and then quickly pulling them apart so that the fronds strike each other. Formerly sounded with chants and practices associated with indigenous spiritual beliefs, the upwut nowadays has connotations of magic and is associated largely with traditional navigation. Islanders sometimes use it to add a soft rhythmic accompaniment to presentations of traditional standing and sitting dances.

BRIAN DIETTRICH

Uranikon. Type of harp-piano or sostenente piano. It was played in Vienna, Regensburg, and Munich in 1806 by the composer, writer, and actor Franz Ignaz von Holbein, who said it had been invented by a group of craftsmen and connoisseurs in Vienna, of whom he was one. The instrument was named by a Prof. Sibicke. Contemporary descriptions of the Uranikon conflict in detail, but apparently it had the form of two conjoined 'antique' harps with their lower halves enclosed in a pedestal that presumably contained the action, operated by a five-octave keyboard. It produced a soft, sweet tone like that of an aeolian harp, sustained without bowing but rather by means of the motion of the keys, thus avoiding the nervous upset associated with the glass armonica. Its crescendos were 'inimitable'. *See* G.C. Busch and J.B. Trommsdorff: *Almanach der neuesten Fortschritte in Wissenschaften, Kuensten, Manufakturen und Handwerken*, vol.12 (1808), 441–2.

LAURENCE LIBIN

Urquhart, Thomas (*fl* London, England, *c*1650–80). English or Scottish violin maker. He was probably a pupil of Jacob Rayman, and was more or less a contemporary of Edward Pamphilon. Urquhart was the most accomplished craftsman of the three. An early, small-sized violin bearing a label with the date 166– (last digit illegible) is of extraordinary delicacy, with a golden varnish of the highest quality. Later instruments are slightly more robust, but excellently finished, and often have a fine red varnish of almost Italian character. Ribs are set into a groove in the back. These instruments are capable of very fine tone, and can often be distinguished from provincial Italian work of the period only by the intriguingly worked scroll, which is incised at the chin and marked with small prickings around the volute. Unfortunately many of the scrolls and labels were removed by unscrupulous dealers and replaced with more Italianate substitutes. It is likely that some of his work was relabelled and sold in his own lifetime by John Shaw, an eminent instrument dealer and music publisher of the period, who was appointed 'instrument maker to his Majesty' in 1687.

Apart from the record of a Thomas Urquhart buried at St Giles-in-the-Fields, London, in 1698, no information about Urquhart's life has yet been unearthed. The family name of Urquhart certainly derives from Inverness, and has led some writers to conclude that he was Scottish.

BIBLIOGRAPHY
W.M. Morris: *British Violin Makers* (London, 1904, 2/1920)
British Violin Making Association: *The British violin: historical aspects of violin and bow making in the British Isles* (Oxford, 1999)
CHARLES BEARE, JOHN DILWORTH/R

Uruá. Paired flutes of the Tupi (Kamayura) people of the Highland Xingu area of Mato Grosso and southern border area of Lake Ipawa, Brazil. The long, one-note cane pipes, with external ducts and no fingerholes, are tied side by side. Two pairs are used for ritual purposes, requiring two players in hocket. The larger instrument of a pair can be up to 2.2 metres long. The uruá are considered teaching and dancing instruments, and also provide the fundamental music of the *Kwarup* ancestral ritual. Young men learn on the smaller *awiraré* panpipes, which are also played in hocket. Sets of uruá and *awiraré* have the same interval relation between the pipes: a semitone between the 1st and 2nd, a minor 3rd between the 2nd and 3rd, and a whole tone between the 3rd and 4th. *See* R.J.M. Bastos: *A musicológica Kamayurá: para uma antropologia da comunicação no alto Xingu* (Florianópolis, 1999).

ALICE LUMI SATOMI

Urumari. Double-headed cylindrical drum of Karnataka state, South India. It has two vellum heads stretched on hoops, which are slightly larger than the drum faces, and laced by ropes. The instrument is struck or rubbed on one side by a curved stick to produce a rumbling sound. It is used in processions and on ceremonial occasions. *See* K.S. Kothari: *Indian Folk Musical Instruments* (New Delhi, 1968).

Urumba. Bass drum of the Tumbuka/Henga people of the Karonga district, Malawi. It is double-headed, with the heads laced on, and is played with two beaters.

Urumi, Southern India. (Virtual Instrument Museum, <http://www.wesleyan.edu/music/vim/>)

Urumi. Double-headed hourglass drum of Tamil Nadu, South India. It is suspended on a neck-strap and struck with a stick on one head and rubbed with a curved stick on the other.

Urusa. Panpipe of the Omagua people of the Peruvian tropical forest region. Other Peruvian panpipes associated with specific tribal peoples are the Ashaninka/Campa *jonkari*, Aymara *siku*, Quechua *antara*, and Witoto and Ocaina four-tube *oribe*.

Ushpulak. Zoomorphic whistle of Afghanistan.

Usindi. Drum of southern Africa.

(1) Small single-headed closed drum of the Sena/Tonga people of the Mtoko district, Zimbabwe. It rests on a three-legged pedestal and is played with sticks, being used with a flute ensemble and other drums.

(2) Single-headed open-ended conical drum of the Nyanja/Manganja people of southern Malawi. Four of these are used in a set of nine tuned *likhuba* drums. *See* H. Tracey: *Catalogue of the Sound of Africa Series* (Roodeport, 1973), vol.2, 175, 187.

DAVID K. RYCROFT

Uskulushi. End-blown duct flute of the Choctaw people of Mississippi, USA. Made by medicine men from a local river cane, the flutes are about 30 cm long and 2.5 cm in diameter, with two fingerholes near the distal end. An opening in the tube about one quarter of the length below the proximal end is partially filled with pine pitch to direct the airflow against the lower lip of the opening. Some flutes are decorated with a medicine man's personal mark or other symbols, such as a snake design, burnt onto the flute's upper side; the proximal end is often wrapped with leather. It is played by medicine men before and during stickball games to conjure for their teams. Formerly, Chickasaw medicine men played similar instruments and the Delaware used them at the start of communal dance songs to encourage the dancers. Each tribe has its own word for cane flutes. *See* F. Densmore: *Choctaw Music* (Washington, DC, 1943).

VICTORIA LINDSAY LEVINE

Ut. Term for the *'ūd* in Turkey, Albania, and Macedonia. For the Albanian instrument, *see* LLAUTË.

Uta. Side-blown gourd horn, with a large calabash bell, of the Ibibio people of southern Nigeria. Four instruments are played in hocket with a large drum and wooden percussion block to form an uta ensemble.

Utete. (1) Mouth bow of the Marquesas Islands. The stick, from 1 to 1.3 metres long, holds a single string of plaited sinnet. In some instruments the string is held taut by the spring of the bow; in others small stones or pieces of wood are used as bridges. One end of the instrument is held in the teeth while the other, supported by the left hand, extends to the side. The string is either tapped rapidly with a coconut leaf midrib or plucked with the fingers of the right hand. It is primarily a women's instrument.

(2) Idioglot jew's harp of Futuna, Samoa, Tonga, and Uvea, made from a strip of coconut leaf 15 to 25 cm long. It is used as a children's toy. In Uvea and Futuna the midrib is torn free for about half the length of the strip and left projecting between 2 to 5 cm at one end. This end is twanged with the finger while the other is held in the mouth. In Samoa and Tonga the midrib is a separate portion lying in front of the leaf or inserted into it and held in place with the left hand.

BIBLIOGRAPHY

R. Linton: *The Material Culture of the Marquesas Islands* (Honolulu, 1923), 408

E.G. Burrows: *Ethnology of Futuna* (Honolulu, 1936), 210

E.G. Burrows: *Ethnology of Uvea* (Honolulu, 1937), 145

R. Moyle: 'Samoan Musical Instruments', *EM*, vol.18/1 (1974), 57–74, esp. 65

R. Moyle: 'Tongan Musical Instruments', *GSJ*, vol.30 (1977), 86–111, esp. 96–7

MERVYN MCLEAN

Utley, Joe Roy (*b* Carter, OK, 22 Oct 1935; *d* Spartanburg, SC, 15 Jan 2001). American collector of brass instruments. A renowned cardiac surgeon, he was also active as a trumpeter. He bought his first trumpet in the early 1950s from Richard E. McFarland in Elk City, Oklahoma, for whose music company he repaired instruments. Initially collecting for his own use, he purchased his first historically significant instrument, a Prussian cornet with three Berlin valves, in 1957.

In the 1980s his interest in historic valve designs and fingering systems led him to the systematic collecting of brass instruments of the soprano range with an emphasis on 19th-century cornet and 20th-century trumpet models. In the 1990s he added historic trumpets of the Nuremberg and English schools to his collection, housed in Spartanburg, South Carolina, and researched the use and distribution of brass instruments with reversed valve order, in which the semitone is positioned at the first valve. With his wife, Joella, also a medical doctor, Utley also collected exemplary work of important 19th- and 20th-century American trumpet makers, and commissioned from David Monette a highly decorated flumpet (trumpet-flugelhorn) that Monette first created for the jazz trumpeter Art Farmer. The Utleys also collected brass instruments during travels to Asia, India, the South Pacific, and elsewhere. In 1999 the Utleys donated his encyclopaedic collection of more than 600 high brass instruments to the National Music Museum in Vermillion, South Dakota, and established there the Utley Institute for Brass Studies.

BIBLIOGRAPHY

R. Utley with S.K. Klaus: 'The "Catholic" Fingering, First Valve Semitone: Reversed Valve Order in Brass Instruments and Related Valve Constructions', *Historic Brass Society Journal*, vol.15 (2003), 73–161

S.K. Klaus: 'The Joe R. and Joella F. Utley Collection of High Brass Instruments: A Trumpeter's Dream Come True', *International Trumpet Guild Journal*, vol.34/4 (June 2010), 38–45

SABINE K. KLAUS

Utur. End-blown flute of the Kambarawa and Lopawa peoples of the Yauri Emirate in Sokoto Province of Nigeria. It is made of bamboo or reed and has four fingerholes. When played, a short piece of horn is held by a thong over the distal end as a bell. *See* P.G. Harris: 'Notes on Drums and Musical Instruments seen in Sokoto Province, Nigeria', *Journal of the Royal Anthropological Institute*, vol.62 (1932), 105–25, esp. 121.

Uyara [aka ogene]. Double wooden clapper bell of the Igbo people of Nigeria. It is shaped like a flattened hourglass with a clapper in each end. It is used in the making of announcements.

V

Vábničky. Hunting lures (decoy calls) of Slovakia. Formerly they were made by the hunters themselves but in recent decades hunters have replaced traditional lures with mass-produced ones, except for deer calls made from horn. The oldest known Slovak example dates from the 14th century. Vábničky produce or modify sound by various means; some are flutes or whistles, others are ribbon reeds, and so on. Many are used to extend the hunter's mouth cavity and so have very thin walls in the part near the player's mouth so as to increase its resonance. Most survive nowadays as toys imitating bird songs and other natural sounds.

IVAN MAČAK

Vaksin [vaccine, banbou, boom pipe, bamboo bass]. One-note trumpet of Haiti and Jamaica. It is a bamboo tube more than 1 m long and 5 to 7 cm in diameter, open at one end with a mouth-hole cut into a node at the other, and wrapped with recycled bicycle inner-tube rubber. The player blows in energetic puffs, producing a low-pitched note; players also tap the bamboo with sticks in order to add an additional layer of percussion. Normally in a *rara* band several vaksin of different pitches sound in alternation to produce an ostinato hocketing pattern. They exploit approximate minor 3rd intervals (creating tritones and arpeggiated diminished chords, but without a harmonic intent), with two of the vaksin often tuned approximately a semitone apart. One of the vaksin pitches generally serves as the tonal centre of *rara* songs. The *rara* ensemble also includes tin trumpets called *konè* (from cornet). *Konè* players may reinforce the vaksin ostinato, play improvised patterns, or hum the melody of the song while blowing to create a mysterious, kazoo-like complement to the song.

GAGE AVERILL/R

Valdímbula. Afro-Cuban lamellaphone. It was invented in the style of the *marímbula* by the Cuban composer and performer Gilberto Valdés (1905–72) for performing Afro-Cuban music. It had four rows of metal tongues plucked by the thumbs. A close collaborator with Fernando Ortiz in folk music research, Valdés later served as president of the Association of Composers of Cuba and directed the National Institute of the Tourism Industry. In that connection, during the 1960s he promoted the development and use of Afro-Cuban instruments. His valdímbula was used in some commercial recordings, but eventually he destroyed it. See F. Ortiz: *Los instrumentos de la música afrocubana* (Havana, 1952–5), vol.5, 117.

JOHN M. SCHECHTER/R

Valdrighi, Luigi Francesco (*b* Modena, Italy, 30 July 1827; *d* Modena, 20 April 1899), Italian count, instrument collector, and music historian. Born into the Modenese aristocracy, he was a well-known expert on local history, music, and organology. He served as secretary at the Estense library in Modena from 1867 to 1891. Most of his instrument collection was donated to the Museo Civico di Storia e Arte Medievale e Moderna. Valdrighi produced the first and largest biographical survey of instrument makers and collectors, *Nomocheliurgografia antica e moderna* (Modena, 1884–94). His *Musurgiana* (Modena, 1879–96, R/Bologna, 1970) comprises 14 essays dealing with Modenese musicians and some organological issues. The latter includes pioneering studies on a 16th-century instrument called 'pianoforte' (probably a harpsichord with a stop for *piano* and *forte* effects), on the 'scrandola' (ratchet), the 'salterio' (Italian plucked psaltery), a consort of crumhorns later acquired by the Musée des Instruments de Musique, Brussels, the 'phagotus' (phagotum; a 16th-century bagpipe), and 19th-century violin innovations made in particular by E.R. Mollenhauer of New York. See M. Lucchi: 'Contributi alla conoscenza di Luigi Francesco Valdrighi', *Antichi strumenti musicali. Catalogo del fondo musicale del Museo Civico di Storia e Arte Medievale e Moderna di Modena* (Modena, 1982), 25–45.

RENATO MEUCCI

Valenzano, Giovanni Maria (*b* Asti, Italy, *c*1750; *d* Rome, Italy, after 1830). Italian violin maker. He appears to have been one of the most widely travelled violin makers of his time and is recorded as having resided and worked in Asti, Trieste, Naples, Padua, Valenza, Nice, Montpellier, Marseilles, and Barcelona. In 1825 he settled in Rome and his work from this final period is generally regarded as his best. His instruments basically follow an Amati model; the later ones are less arched and also have less elongated corners and somewhat wider edges. The scrolls are roundly symmetrical and show wider bevelled turns than normal. The brownish-red varnish over a yellow ground is quite Neapolitan in texture but rather more colourful. See R. Vannes: *Essai d'un dictionnaire universel des luthiers* (Paris, 1932, 2/1951/*R*1972 as *Dictionnaire universel des luthiers* and *R*1981 incl. suppl. 1959).

JAAK LIIVOJA-LORIUS

Valiha. Plucked tube zither of Madagascar. The valiha is one of the oldest Malagasy instruments, originating in Southeast Asia, and it has become the symbol of cultural unity in the island. There are three types, each with local distinguishing features. The vernacular name has been retained in some regions: for example, *volo* among the Tsimihety and *valiha-volo* in remote parts of Imerina. Dialect variants include the Sihanaka name *valeha*, and *baliha*, used in some coastal areas. The Bara name *manibola* denotes a small instrument and *betorky* the larger type. The Sakalava name *marovany* and some of the other local names mentioned are also used to denote a box zither.

The best-known valiha is the one most like the Southeast Asian tube zither. It is usually made from a thick internode of bamboo, which serves as a direct resonator, with open sections of unequal length at each end; the end sections amplify the sound. Traditionally the strings were raised from the outer layer of the internode and reinforced at each end with raffia or sisal binding to prevent them from breaking away. Modern instruments reuse steel strings from various sources, for example guitar strings, unravelled bicycle brake cables, and so on, which are bound on with wire or oxhide, and can have bone or wooden tuning pegs. (The change from bamboo to metal strings was gradual: an instrument at a Paris exhibition in 1900 had 19 bamboo strings and four metal ones, and such a mixture is still seen nowadays.) There are usually 14 strings (of which one or more might be sympathetic), supported by small rectangular bridges made from pieces of gourd. The instrument is held projecting forward from the body, and the strings are plucked with the fingers and thumb of both hands. The bridges are movable, so that the tuning can be adjusted. Normally the bridges at one end are all close to the ends of the strings, while those at the other are each at a different point around the tube so as to produce the required pitches. Soundholes are cut in the side of the internode; they vary in shape according to the maker. The surface of the bamboo is often decorated with pyrographic patterns, sometimes also with cloth and carved pieces of bone nailed to the surface. Nowadays some instruments are made from PVC tubing.

The instrument most common in southern Madagascar is usually made of wood, with an independent amplifier. Two pieces of wood are bound together with wire; animal gut, often from goats, was traditionally used. The instrument has 10 strings and the bridges are triangular. The body rests on the amplifier, which was formerly a wooden box, but nowadays an oilcan is often used.

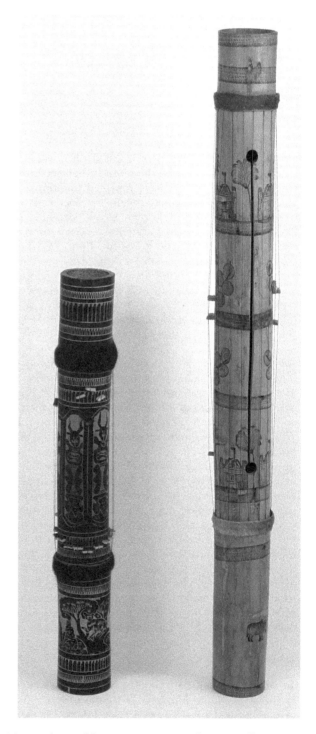

Two modern valihas, wire strung, Madagascar. (© Gregg Miner)

In northern Madagascar instruments are made from hollowed halves of a raffia stem held together by wooden pegs and a raffia tie at each end. The main function of the tie, however, is to hold the strings firmly. As in the original bamboo valiha, the strings (usually 19) are raised from the outer layer of the stem. The movable bridges are rectangular and are made of raffia.

The valiha was originally played only at sacred rituals, but it is now also a secular instrument. In the highland region of the Merina it was played during rites invoking ancestors (the *vazimba*, the first inhabitants of the area) and seeking their goodwill, but it is nowadays little more than a curiosity for tourists. Among the Bara it was played in ceremonies of possession (*bilo*, *sabo*, or *sandratse*), but has become mainly a secular instrument. In the north of Madagascar among the Tsimihety, a musical genre called *osika*, played on the valiha, was included in magic–religious ceremonies, but the instrument has been practically supplanted by the accordion, which was introduced during the 19th century.

Early researchers implied that the valiha was formerly restricted to the aristocracy, especially in Imerina, and played only by men. Oral tradition confirms its use by the aristocracy (which would not preclude its use for rituals), but it seems that women did play the instrument and nowadays it is not unusual to find a woman player in the most important role at a ceremony of Sakalava or Bara rituals.

MICHEL DOMENICHINI-RAMIARAMANANA/R

Valimba [varimba, ulimba]. Xylophone particularly of the Manganja and Sena peoples, and also of the Podzo, Cuabo, Yao, Barwe, and other peoples in the lower Zambezi region of central Mozambique and southern Malawi. Other names for the xylophone include *madudu*, *bachi*, *mambira*, *marimba*, and *ngambi*. The valimba is a heptatonic instrument and the term includes the free-bar type (rough slats or logs laid across two long bundles of grass, sometimes with a shallow trench beneath for added resonance) and the trough-resonated type (all the bars sharing a common resonator box) as well as those having individual gourd resonators with mirlitons (i.e. with openings, usually rectangular, covered with spider egg sac or cigarette paper). The bars are normally made of *mukwa* (kiat, *Pterocarpus angolensis*), the all-purpose musical wood of southern Africa. The frame is often constructed so that the far side of the bars tilt up towards the players who sit with the low notes to their left. While the valimba is generally played singly, the instrument always has more than one player, usually three. The players sit either together on one side or place themselves on opposite sides, and beat the centres of the bars with soft-tipped sticks. Sometimes a fourth player beats only one bass note and/or a special 'rattle bar' fitted with metal jingles or made with one bar loosely tied on top of another. Adjacent players often share one or more bars while playing, resulting in characteristically reduplicated patterns. The compass of the instrument varies from about ten notes in the simpler types to four octaves in the gourd-resonated types. The parts interlock

rhythmically at very high speed; much of the music is related to that of the Zambezi regional lamellaphone traditions and has a strong harmonic framework. The valimba is normally played at night for young people's dances, and is accompanied by singing, rattles, and sometimes a drum.

BIBLIOGRAPHY
A.E. Dziko and M. Strumpf: 'A survey of musical instruments', *Baraza, a Journal of the Arts in Malawi*, no.2 (June, 1984), 36–44
M. Dias: *Instrumentos musicais de Moçambique* (Lisbon, 1986)
A. Tracey: 'Kambazithe Makolekole and his *valimba* group: a glimpse of the technique of the Sena xylophone', *African Music*, vol.7/1 (1991), 82–104

ANDREW TRACEY

Valve (i). Mechanical device for altering the basic tube length of a brass instrument by a predetermined and fixed amount while it is being played.

1. Function and description. 2. History. 3. Compensating and key-changing valves.

1. FUNCTION AND DESCRIPTION. It is a useful, if not strictly accurate, convention to call the lowest vibration frequency theoretically possible in a given air column (mainly governed by its length) the 'fundamental', and its overtones 'harmonics' (the fundamental and the harmonics being referred to collectively as 'partials'), even if they do not quite form a mathematically true harmonic series (for a stricter definition of these terms *see* SOUND, §5(ii)). Ex.1 shows, up to the 16th partial, the notes theoretically obtainable from an 8′ tube, and the portions of the series used for musical purposes on three types of simple or unmechanized brass instrument. Partials 7, 11, 13, and 14 are out of tune with the equal-tempered scale. (For a discussion of the resonance properties of air columns, see ACOUSTICS, §III. Although some skilled players can extend the upper range by eight or more harmonics, such a sequence clearly has little potential in music based on the chromatic scale. If, however, the air column is lengthened by an appropriate amount, a new fundamental and its attendant series of harmonics will be introduced. The valve accomplishes this by, in effect, introducing extra lengths of tubing. Three valves—to lower the fundamental of the primary tube by a semitone, a whole tone and three semitones respectively—when used singly and in combination make available seven different fundamentals. Ex.2 shows how the player can command a chromatic scale with a selection of harmonics from the seven corresponding series. The sounds

Ex.1.

Ex.2.

under 1 are fundamentals. Partials 7, 11, 13, and 14 have been omitted as they are out of tune with the equal-tempered scale and are not used by valved instruments; 15 is seldom used in practice, though the note is a good one. The lines with arrows show the fingering. The void notes between partials 5 and 16 are used only occasionally, for convenience in fingering, since the equivalent sounds can usually be better tuned with standard fingering.

In most brass instruments of fairly narrow bore (trumpets, cornets, etc.) the fundamental is not usually playable and the useful scale begins on the 2nd partial, an octave above. In wide-bore instruments (e.g. tubas) the fundamental is a valuable note; three valves, however, are not sufficient to connect it chromatically with its octave. A fourth valve, bringing in additional tubing to lower the pitch of the instrument five semitones, fills the gap when combined with the basic three valves in different ways and thus renders the instrument fully chromatic from the fundamental upwards. An inherent defect in any additive valve system, however, is that a supplementary tube designed to lower the pitch of an instrument by a given amount will be too short to do this if the main tube has already been lengthened by another supplement. Thus notes requiring the use of two or more valves together tend to be sharp—as much as a semitone in some instances where all three essential valves are combined. On small instruments the player can usually 'pull' or 'lip' the defective notes into tune, but on the larger ones this is hardly possible; consequently, on a tuba, a fifth or even sixth valve may be added to improve intonation. The extra valves are arranged differently by different makers, or according to the ideas of particular players; in six-valve instruments the commonest arrangement is for the fourth and sixth valves to supply a perfect 4th and perfect 5th

respectively. The fifth valve is then tuned to an approximate semitone which can be used to fill in deficiencies elsewhere.

The 'ascending third valve' was until recently favoured by many orchestral and solo horn players, especially in France. In this system the third valve, instead of adding a supplementary section, cuts out a section of the main tube, thus raising the pitch of the instrument. An 'independent' valve system introduced by Sax of Paris in 1852 comprised six valves, each of which added its own complete length of supplementary tubing to lower the fundamental by a semitone more than the preceding length. Thus, using the open note and then each valve in turn, the player could command seven different harmonic series. As applied to the trombone this system had some success, but the weight of the necessary tubing and the generally unfamiliar fingering led to its ultimate disappearance.

Three types of valve are in use today—the piston valve (Fr. *piston*; Ger. *Pump(en)ventil*, *Périnet-Ventil*; It. *pistone*), the rotary valve (Fr. *cylindre rotatif*; Ger. *Drehventil*, *Zylinderventil*; It. *cilindro rotativo*), and the double piston or Vienna valve (Fr. *piston double*; Ger. *Wiener Ventil*; Ital. *pistone viennese*, *pistone sistema viennese*). The first two are used by most brass players and appear to be equally favoured. The Vienna valve is employed nowadays only on horns, and only in the area around Vienna.

The piston valve consists of a cylindrical outer casing of brass and the piston or 'pump'. The latter is a cylinder of thin sheet metal ground into the casing with abrasives so as to be as airtight as possible while able to move freely. It is held at rest in the 'up' position by a spring, either above or below it (the latter is cheaper), according to the maker's preference. Frequently it is made of, or plated with, some metal of low friction when opposed to brass. The casing is perforated to correspond with the main tubing of the instrument and has elbows leading to the supplementary tubing or 'valve slide', which is telescopic and can be pushed in or out for tuning purposes or withdrawn entirely to drain off the moisture that condenses during playing. The structure and interconnection of a normal cluster of three valve cases is shown in fig.1. The wall of the piston is also perforated and is fitted with three transverse tubes so placed that when the piston is in the up position one of these provides a direct passage through the valve, and when it is down the others divert the windway through the supplementary tubing, thus adding its length to the main tubing of the instrument (see fig.2).

The rotary valve also has an outer casing perforated to accommodate the main and supplementary tubing, but the perforations are all in the same plane, placed at four points equidistant from each other. Two tangential passages are arranged so that when the inner part, or rotor, is at rest there is a clear passage through the valve. A quarter-turn of the rotor diverts the windway through the valve slide, which is essentially similar to that of a piston valve (see fig.3). (The rotor can be turned from solid metal or built up from sheet.)

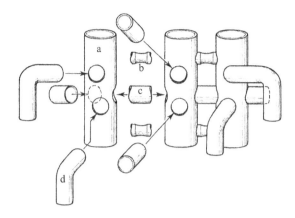

Fig.1: *Structure and interconnection of a normal cluster of three piston valve cases, shown in a partly 'exploded' sketch: a – valve case, b – supporting strut, c – connecting tubing, d – elbow leading to valve slide.*

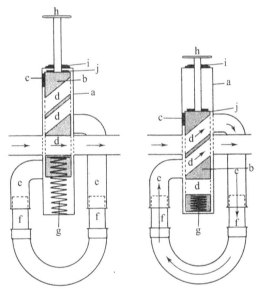

Fig.2: *Piston valve (schematic view) in up position (left) and down position (right): a – outer casing, b – piston, c – guide, d – elbows serving as channels for the airstream, e – additional tubing, or valve slide, f – slide, g – spiral spring, h – finger button, i, j – cork buffer and cork (or felt) washer (both for noise prevention); arrows show direction of air from mouthpiece towards bell.*

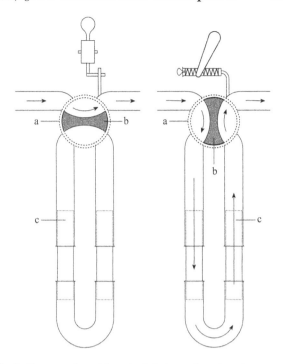

Fig.3: *Rotary valve with articulated crank action, in normal position (left), and with American string action, depressed (right): a – outer casing, b – rotor, c – valve slide; arrows show direction of air from mouthpiece to bell.*

Complications arise, however, in converting a downward finger pressure into rotational movement. Thus various return mechanisms have been devised. The earliest non-tubular valves (Ger. *Federstecher*; first developed in Leipzig in 1821) were activated by a rod around which a spring was wound, both of these elements being enclosed in a short casing otherwise much resembling that of the modern piston valve. Josef Kail's Vienna valves of 1823 were activated by touchpieces attached to long flat springs, a system which was subsequently employed by C.A. Müller of Mainz (first working

for Schott and then on his own). In his patent of 1830 Leopold Uhlmann displayed a type of clock spring in a separate casing anchored to a fixed axle (placed at some convenient point on the instrument) and to the inside of its own casing. To the outside of this is attached the touchpiece, which remains up while at rest. The touchpiece is linked to the rotor by a crank and a connecting rod, so that pushing down on it causes the rod to rotate as far as two buffered 'stops' will allow, at the same time winding up the spring a little. With the release of pressure the spring reverses the movement (see fig.4). When well made this mechanism proves entirely satisfactory, but it is somewhat prone to wear and inadvertent damage.

A mechanism (Ger. *Spiralfederdruckwerk*) developed in the 1840s eliminated the clock spring and casing. Here the touchpiece is kept at rest by a simple spiral spring wound around its axle. A further development was the 'American string action' (Ger. *Schnurmechanik*), patented in 1848 by Thomas D. Paine of Woonsocket, Rhode Island, and also taken up in 1855 by Wenzel Schamal in Prague, on Kail's suggestion. This system also employs a spiral spring at the axle of the touchpiece, from which a connecting rod passes close to the associated valve casing (thereby eliminating the articulated crank), carrying near its end a loop of fine cord anchored to it at two points (at a distance from each other about equal to the valve's diameter). The cord passes round a pulley on the rotor spindle to which it is also fastened (see fig.5). This arrangement gives an efficient and silent

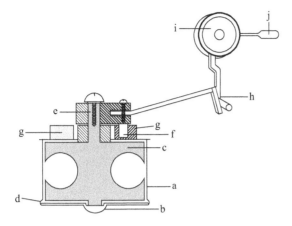

Fig.4: *Section of rotary valve with articulated crank action: a – outer casing, b – valve cap, c – rotor, d – inner cover plate (to support rotor), e – rotor spindle, f – reciprocating driver pivot, g – cork buffers, h – articulated crank, i – spring box containing coiled clock spring (outside ratchet sometimes provided to facilitate alteration of spring tension), j – touch-piece or finger-plate.*

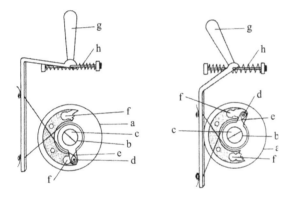

Fig.5: *Return mechanism of a rotary valve with American string action, in normal position (left) and depressed (right): a – valve casing, b – rotor spindle, c – screw to hold rotor in place, d – screw to hold the string in place, e – reciprocating driver pivot, f – cork buffer, g – touchpiece, h – spiral spring.*

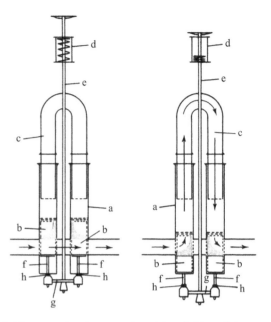

Fig.6: *Vienna valve, in normal position (left) and depressed (right): a – outer casing forming part of the windway, b – pistons, c – valve slide, d – spring box and spiral spring, e – push rod, f – plunger, g – connecting piece, h – cork buffes.*

It is not difficult to explain why the Vienna or double piston valve (see fig.6), once so popular in central Europe, has passed almost completely out of use. Its chief advantage lies in its right-angled windways, producing a gentler tone than is currently in vogue.

2. HISTORY. The first recorded idea for altering the sounding length of a brass instrument other than by means of detachable crooks must, it seems, be credited to Ferdinand Kölbel (*fl* 1735–69), a Bohemian musician active in St Petersburg. He first demonstrated his chromatic horn, Amor-Schall, in 1766. A surviving drawing (see Porfir'yeva and Stepanov, 1998) reveals that his was a kind of omnitonic horn with six push-buttons activating a return mechanism allowing the instrument's tonality to be changed instantaneously. Kölbel's invention bore no fruit. Nor did that of Charles Clagget, an Irishman, who in 1788 obtained an English patent for his 'Cromatic Trumpet and French Horn'. This invention consisted of twinned instruments a semitone apart, with a kind of rotary valve operated by a lever at the mouthpiece end activating first one, then the other instrument. In July 1814 Heinrich Stölzel, a horn player in the court orchestra of Pless, brought to Berlin a horn equipped with two tubular valves (for lowering the pitch of the instrument by a whole tone and a semitone respectively), which he claimed as his invention. This was taken up and exploited by the firm of Griesling & Schlott. Stölzel's idea was to make it unnecessary for a horn player to carry a full set of crooks for all keys. His device permitted the transposition of an F horn into E, E♭, or D without extra crooks.

rotary motion, its only disadvantage being the possible breaking of the cord. String action was also part of the US patent granted in 1866 to Isaac Fiske of Worcester, Massachusetts, for a cornet with three rotary valves activated by vertical rods passing through a casing containing the spring—an arrangement that, except for the string action, very closely resembled one for which Joseph Higham had already obtained a British patent in 1857.

A completely different return mechanism involved long cumbersome levers mounted on leaf springs. It was developed in Bavaria from about 1828 to 1840 and can also be found on instruments by Hirsbrunner (Sumiswald) and certain Saxon makers. Trumpets with two valves of this type, usually with the half step fingered '1' and the whole step '2', can be found on steel engravings of itinerant or peasant musicians into the late 1880s.

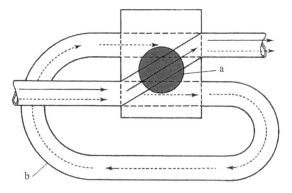

Fig.7: *'Box' valve (piston valve of square section), patented by Stölzel and Blühmel, seen from above (arrows with continuous tails show direction of airstream when valve is in normal position, arrows with broken tails show airstream when valve is depressed): a – finger-button, b – additional tubing (no tuning-slide).*

In the meantime Friedrich Blühmel, a works band musician, had contested Stölzel's primacy with the 'box' valve (Ger. *Kastenventil*; see fig.7), which he demonstrated in 1816 on a trumpet and a horn, each with two valves. He then showed a three-valved trombone in February 1818. Instruments with box valves survive (in *D.B.im*, *D.N.gnm*, and *B.B.mim*). After considerable litigation, the two men finally joined forces. Together they secured a ten-year Prussian patent for both kinds of valve on 12 April 1818, Stölzel furthermore buying out Blühmel's rights for 400 thalers. It is important to note that it was not the specific type of valve, but rather the general principle as applied to brass instruments, which the patent office considered protectable. Later patent applications were often refused for this reason.

Stölzel's tubular valve (or 'Stölzel valve'; Ger. *Schubventil*, Fr. *piston Stoelzel*; Ital. *pistone (sistema) Stoelzel*), in which the lower part of its casing also serves as a windway (see fig.8), is the most common type found on instruments made before 1850, the surviving

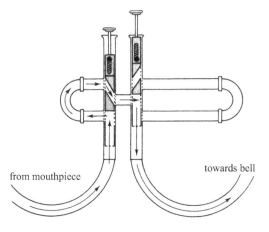

from mouthpiece   towards bell

Fig.8: *Stölzel valves, depressed (left) and in normal position (right).*

instruments often having two such valves. The first were made for Stölzel by Griesling & Schlott of Berlin (c1816–18). Their design was copied very soon by J.F. Anderst (St Petersburg, 1825), Labbaye and Halary (Paris, 1827), Pace and Köhler (London, after 1830), and even James Keat for Samuel Graves (Winchester, New Hampshire, c1837). In London, chromatic Russian brass instruments (a gift to the Second Life Guards band from Tsar Nicholas I, who had purchased such instruments from Griesling & Schlott in 1824) were heard as early as 6 May 1831, and a 'Russian Valve or Stop Trumpet' is illustrated on p.38 of the elder Harper's *Instructions for the Trumpet* of 1835. Despite the somewhat constricted cross-tubes of the piston and the sharp angles involved, valves of this type were still in use on inexpensive French cornets as late as 1916, no doubt because they were relatively easy to make.

When their patent expired in 1828, Blühmel and Stölzel applied for a new one, this time for a rotary valve (which they called Drehbüchsenventil), which both of them had worked on even before their first patent was granted; Blühmel had had a trumpet fitted out with an early kind of rotary valve by 1819. The authorities refused their application, however, for the reason mentioned above. A horn built by an unknown maker between 1828 and 1831, with two of Blühmel's rotary valves, survives (in *D.MK.mim*; for illustration see Heyde, 1987, p.129). It remained for Kail and J.F. Riedl to make the most of this kind of valve (see below).

The next valve to claim attention was a 'transverse spring slide' (British patent no.5013 of 1824) devised by John Shaw of Glossop, Derbyshire, a farmer and part-time brass worker. Its application required that a large part of the main tube of the instrument take the form of a long narrow U, much like the slide of the trombone. Both limbs of the tube passed through twin pairs of piston cases set perpendicular to the plane of the U, and these were bridged by two pistons connected at the top by a cross-tube. When depressed, the paired pistons either short-circuited a section of the main tube or cut in an extra length (see fig.9). No surviving examples are known, and it seems likely that the complexity of the arrangement kept it from being generally adopted.

The twin piston cases of the transverse spring slide anticipated to some extent the Vienna valve, which is still in limited use. A forerunner, with long rods to activate the valves, was built in 1820 by Christian Friedrich Sattler of Leipzig. The first usable double-piston valve was developed by the horn player Josef Kail and the maker Joseph Felix Riedl, who were granted a ten-year privilege on 1 Nov 1823 in Vienna for a two-valved trumpet. This form was eagerly imitated in southern Germany, Saxony, and Mainz but had the disadvantage of allowing condensed water to squirt out, for which reason they were nicknamed Spritzerventile. The addition of a third valve is attested by an illustration in Andreas Nemetz's *Allgemeine Trompeten-Schule* (Vienna, 1828). Leopold Uhlmann made an improvement in 1830 by adding cork buffers which eliminated the squirting; he was not the inventor of this kind of valve, as is sometimes claimed. A far-reaching aspect of Uhlmann's

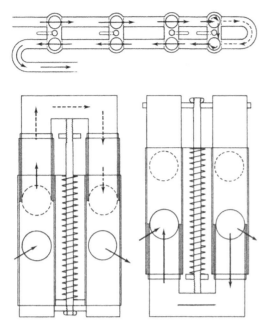

Fig.9: *Transverse spring slide devised by John Shaw: general layout, as applied to the trumpet (top), used as an ascending valve (left), and as a descending valve (right); arrows show direction of air from mouthpiece towards bell.*

privilege, however, was its barrel or clock-spring action (Ger. *Trommeldruckwerk*) described in §1 above.

There were several variants of double-piston valves which strictly speaking are not 'Vienna' valves. The most common were the 'Mainz valves' made by C.A. Müller, the touch pieces of which are activated by elegant leaf springs. Several generations of these valves were known as Altmainzer Maschine (1830–40), alte Neumainzer Maschine, and Neumainzer Maschine (from *c*1833). Another is the so-called Hanoverian model of the 1840s, also called *système belge*, which is held with the valve slides pointing up, the valves being activated by a squat piston-type return mechanism mounted parallel to and at the lower part of the slides. Finally, there were the double-piston valves patented in England on 3 April 1849 by Richard Garrett. His 'registered double piston cornopean' is held with the valve slides pointing down; they are activated by simple touchpieces mounted directly at the top of the moving parts. One example of each of these three systems survives (in *D.BDSA.t*).

Not long after, another important type of valve was designed in Prussia, the Berlin valve (Ger. pl. *Berliner Pumpen*). Formerly attributed to Wilhelm Wieprecht, an important figure in German military music, it is now believed to have been developed in 1827 by Stölzel, and independently by Wieprecht in 1833. Both their patent applications were refused, again for the reason given above. According to Heyde, the inlet and outlet of Stölzel's valve slides are on the same side of the casing, whereas Wieprecht's are on opposite sides so that the valve slide (which often is fixed and does not slide at all) forms a loop passing around or under the casing.

Through Wieprecht's influence, instruments with Berliner Pumpen made by Moritz soon became standard in all Prussian military bands. When the young Belgian Adolphe Sax established himself in Paris in 1842 he immediately (and without acknowledgment) began to make the Prussian type of valve, calling them cylinders, and through the Distin family the Sax version became well known in England (1844–53).

A rotary-action valve ('Rad-Maschine') with Trommeldruckwerk, designed by Kail and Riedl, was given a privilege on 11 Sept 1835. Except for changes in its driving mechanism, this has hardly been improved on since. A trumpet with a form of rotary valve had been produced in the USA by Nathan Adams of Boston, some time before 1825. Another trumpet, with two primitive (and leaky) rotary valves operated by levers, was built about this time by the Swiss makers Schupbach & Guichard in Yverdon. Adams also built a 'permutation trumpet' in 1825 in which paired internal vanes diverted the main windway into and out of the supplementary slides. Other American workers—Thomas D. Paine (US patent no. 5919, 11 Nov 1848), and J. Lathrop Allen, about 1850—produced practical rotary valves, examples of which survive. Paine's rotor contained three passages; thus the air either went straight ahead through the middle one, or was diverted to one side passage and returned via the other. The small-diameter rotor adopted by Allen, however, necessitated some distortion of the windways. A French invention termed 'valvules', which operated on the same principle as Adam's permutation trumpet, was patented in 1834 by the horn player J.E. Meifred and the mechanic Deshays, but proved too costly to pursue.

For some reason the very efficient rotary valve did not become popular in France or England. A few rotary-type instruments were made by A. Courtois, Gautrot, and Sax in Paris, by Distin in London, and by Higham in Manchester. It was only after World War II, with the wide-bore German orchestral horn superseding the old French model, that the rotary valve became familiar in Great Britain. The German type of horn and trumpet had been introduced about a century earlier into the USA, but rotary-valved trumpets were supplanted by those with piston valves after about 1870.

In 1838 John Shaw took out a patent for what he called 'patent swivel valves for brass instruments', and J.A. Köhler acquired the right to manufacture instruments with such valves for a ten-year period. A year or two later Köhler brought out an improved version called the New Patent Lever valve. This was very similar to the *plaques tournantes* or *disques mobiles* which the Parisian maker Halary (ii) had developed (but not patented) in 1835, possibly after designs by John Shaw. Köhler sold a number of instruments with disc valves to the British Army, and no fewer than 18 to the band of the Crystal Palace at its opening in 1854. This type of valve, however (Ger. *Scheibenventil*), with one disc rotating against another fixed one containing the valve slides (see fig.10), generated too much friction to work rapidly enough, and it never gained acceptance.

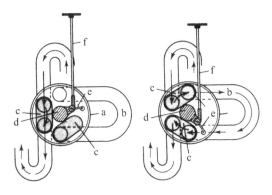

Fig.10: *Patent lever valve, in normal position (left) and depressed (right): a – back plate (fixed) showing attachment of main windways, b – valve slide, c – bows fixed to revolving cover plate, d – spring box, e – 'finger' connected with the revolving outer part of the spring box, and engaged in a ring fixed on the cover plate, thus driving the cover plate around when valve is depressed, f – push-rod and touchpiece.*

In 1838 François Périnet of Paris redesigned and patented (French patent no.9606, 27 Oct 1838) the tubular valve to its present form, now called the piston valve (Fr. *piston*; Ger. *Périnet-Ventil, Pumpventil*; Ital. *pistone, pistone (sistema) Périnet*). He eliminated the sharp angles which had been a feature of the tubular valve, whose windways pass through the bottom of the valve casings. Sax and other French makers soon adopted Périnet's valve (although they continued to make brass instruments with tubular valves and with cylinders as well). Piston-valved trumpets became standard not only in France, but also in England and, after about 1870, in the United States. In the 1930s, such trumpets became known in Germany and Russia as 'jazz trumpets'; after World War II they saw nearly universal use except in a few Germanic tradition-conscious orchestras such as the Berlin and Vienna POs. (After 1965, following the lead of Adolph Herseth of the Chicago SO, rotary-valved trumpets began to be reintroduced in many orchestras for certain works of the symphonic repertory.)

After Périnet's invention and apart from the compensating devices mentioned below, little now remained for instrument makers to do beyond improving the layouts of rotary and piston valves and their cross-passages, to keep them free of constriction and to improve response. New alloys were introduced, notably Monel metal for piston valves, to reduce friction. Engelbert Schmid in Kirchheim (1980) has made improvements to rotary valves (and horn design). Stephen E. Shire's trombone thumb valve (US patent no.7112735, 2006) is a modified rotary valve that, with its straight passage and two side passages, seems to resemble Paine's valve of 1848 mentioned above. The same seems to be true of Christian Lindberg's US patent 5,965,833 (1994), with a straight and a 'Y' windway, respectively. One new type, the Thayer axial valve, invented in 1976 by Orla Ed Thayer (*b* 1 April 1920; *d* 7 June 2009) of Waldport, Oregon,

should be mentioned (with four US patents between 1978 and 1984). A cross between the box valve and the rotary valve, it has been used with great success on trombones; only its size precludes its use on higher-pitched brasses. Noteworthy among newer related designs is the 'free-flow' valve of René Hagmann in Geneva (with Courtois, 1996).

3. COMPENSATING AND KEY-CHANGING VALVES. Modified piston or rotary valves have been employed for two additional functions: to compensate for the increasing sharpness in pitch when two and three valves are used; and to make a brass instrument playable in two or even three different keys by adding supplementary lengths of tubing. The ancestor of both these systems is generally considered to be Besson's register of 1856: a long fourth valve placed horizontally, through which all the supplementary valve slides passed. A still earlier system, however, with a horizontal piston and barrel which closes or extends the tuning slide, was registered by J.B. Ziegler on 7 May 1847.

The first true double horn in Bb/F, its rotary valves possessing two-storey windways, was built from 1896 and registered on 13 Nov 1897 by Fritz Kruspe of Erfurt after an idea by the horn player F.A. Gumpert. Countless models have been derived from it, including the triple horn in F/Bb/F alto (or even Bb soprano), developed from 1958 by Paxman of London after the ideas of the horn player Richard Merewether.

'Compensating' brass instruments, however, do not require in principle an additional valve for intonation correction, for their valves have additional windways automatically throwing into play extra loops of tubing when used in combination. The most successful compensating system was that of D.J. Blaikley of Boosey & Co. (1874, patented in 1878). On trumpets and cornets such a system invariably results in a stuffy response, but on euphoniums and tubas, with their wider and more conical bore, Blaikley's system is efficient and has been widely accepted. A slight disadvantage is that the additional windways have no slides and are thus difficult to clean.

Numerous later inventions were too complicated to have lasting success. J.-B. Arban (1825–89), a professor at the Paris Conservatoire who was almost obsessively concerned with intonation, invented several cornets with compensating systems (his first developed with Sax and demonstrated in 1848). The first compensating 'Cornet Arban' (1883; earlier cornets with a noncompensating system, made by Courtois for Arban, were also so called), manufactured by Auguste Mille, had a lever to lengthen the third valve slide, and a *barillet* (a quick-change rotary valve) that lowered the pitch from C to A (with integrated levers that lengthened the first and second slides accordingly). The second (1884) had an extremely complex compensating system on the first and third valve: no less than ten different tubes emanated from the first valve (one example survives in *F.P.kampmann*). The 'nouveau Cornet Arban' of 1887, produced with L. Bouvet, was a double instrument in C and A: a fourth valve activated by the index finger of the left hand made the key change, and there were two slides per valve. It required an elaborate chart for its 21 fingerings. Even though Arban simplified this system over the following year, after his death the Conservatoire returned to the simple three-valved cornet.

Undeterred, Martin Lessen, who in 1983 had presented a Benge-built four-valve C trumpet after Arban's system, obtained a US patent in 1991 for a compensating C trumpet with only three valves, following the Blaikley system and built by Zigmund Kanstul. The third valve slide passes through valves one and two; a true innovation is that the corrective additional lengths of tubing are contained within the first and second pistons. The advantage of Lessen's instrument is that traditional fingerings can be retained. Time will tell if it is free-blowing enough.

BIBLIOGRAPHY

R. Morley-Pegge: *The French Horn* (London, 1960/R)

M. Vogel: *Die Intonation der Blechbläser* (Düsseldorf, 1961)

P. Bate: *The Trumpet and Trombone* (London, 1966, 2/1972/R)

R.E. Eliason: 'Early American Valves for Brass Instruments', *GSJ*, vol.23 (1970), 86–96

R.E. Eliason: 'Brasses with both Keys and Valves', *JAMIS*, vol.2 (1976), 69–85

J.-P. Mathez: *Joseph Jean-Baptiste Laurent Arban 1825–1889* (Moudon, 1977)

W. Cardoso: *Ascending Trumpets (Trumpets with Ascending Valves)* (Buenos Aires, 1978)

R.E. Eliason: *Early American Brass Makers* (Nashville, 1979, rev. 1981)

R. Dahlqvist: 'Some Notes on the Early Valve', *GSJ*, vol. 32, 1980, 111–24

M. Haine: *Adolphe Sax (1814–1894): sa vie, son oeuvre et ses instruments de musique* (Brussels, 1980)

J. Webb: 'Designs for Brass in the Public Record Office', *GSJ*, vol.38 (1985), 48–54

C. Ahrens: *Eine Erfindung und ihre Folgen: Blechblasinstrumente mit Ventilen* (Kassel, 1986), Eng. transl. by S. Plank: *Valved Brass: The History of an Invention* (Hillsdale, NY, 2008)

G. Dullat: *Blasinstrumente und deutsche Patentschriften 1877–1970: Metallblasinstrumente 2* (Nauheim, 1986)

B. Kampmann: 'Catalogue de la collection d'instruments de musique à vent', *Larigot*, various special numbers (Paris, 1986–2005)

H. Heyde: *Das Ventilblasinstrument* (Leipzig, 1987)

G. Dullat: *Metallblasinstrumentenbau: Entwicklungsstufen und Technologie* (Frankfurt, 1989)

E. Tarr: 'The Romantic Trumpet', *HBSJ*, vol.5 (1993), 213–61

H. Heyde: *Musikinstrumentenbau in Preussen* (Tutzing, 1994)

M. Lessen and A.E. Smith: 'A New Compensating Valve System', *Journal of the International Trumpet Guild*, vol.19/4 (1995), 47–56

A. Myers: 'Design, Technology and Manufacture since 1800', *The Cambridge Companion to Brass Instruments*, ed. T. Herbert and J. Wallace (Cambridge, 1997), 115–30

A.L. Porfir'yeva and A.A. Stepanov: 'Kyol'bel' (Koelbel), Ferdinand', *Musical St Petersburg: Musical-Encyclopedic Dictionary*, ed. A.L. Porfir'yeva (St Petersburg, 1998)

G. Cassone: *La tromba* (Varese, 2002)

G. Dumoulin: 'Cornets in the Brussels Musical Instrument Museum: A Survey and a Checklist of an Outstanding Collection', *HBSJ*, vol.14 (2002), 425–46

N. Eldredge: 'A Brief History of Piston–Valved Cornets', *HBSJ*, vol. 14 (2002), 337–90

R. Callmar: *Die chromatisierte Trompete: Die Entwicklung der Naturtrompete bis zur Einführung der Ventiltrompete 1750–1850* (diploma paper, Schola Cantorum Basiliensis, 2003)

E. Tarr: *East Meets West* (Hillsdale, NY, 2003)

J.R. Utley and S. Klaus: 'The "Catholic" Fingering—First Valve Semitone: Reversed Valve Order in Brass Instruments and Related Valve Constructions', *HBSJ*, vol.15 (2003), 73–161

G. Dumoulin: 'The Cornet and Other Brass Instruments in French Patents of the First Half of the Nineteenth Century', *GSJ*, vol.59 (2006), 77–100

E. Mitroulia, G. Dumoulin and N. Eldredge: 'On the Early History of the Périnet Valve', *GSJ*, vol.61 (2008), 217–29

PHILIP BATE /EDWARD H. TARR

Valve (ii). Term found in some early patent specifications where key (as on a woodwind instrument) is implied. It also occurs occasionally in this sense in early music dictionaries. The term is also used in organ building as an alternative to pallet.

Vamp-horn [vamping-horn]. Type of speaking-trumpet or megaphone invented in 1670 by Samuel Morland and used in English churches into the early 19th century to concentrate and project (albeit with some degree of unavoidable distortion) an individual voice, usually that of the parish clerk or the leader of the choir. It was used musically to give out the first line of a psalm or hymn, to lead congregational singing, or to supply vocally a missing line of harmony. Vamp-horns were originally designed for non-musical uses such as summoning labourers to and from the fields or making announcements to the village community. The device, varying in length from about 90 cm to nearly 2.5 metres, was constructed in a conical shape from thin sheet-iron, with a bore of about 5 cm flaring (in the case of the widest noted example, from Braybrooke, Northamptonshire) to a bell measuring 64 cm; at least one was originally provided with a wooden 'mouthpiece'. The first documented vamp-horn, at Walgrave, Northamptonshire, is noted as being audible at a distance of a mile. Another, from Harrington, Northamptonshire, was built in telescopic sections for ease of transportation. Eight surviving examples are known in England: two each in Northamptonshire and Lincolnshire, and one each in Buckinghamshire, Kent, Nottinghamshire, and Sussex. Their use in churches might have originated in Northamptonshire, where the earliest documentation is found. Although vamp-horns have often been regarded as 'amplifiers', they incorporate no means of supplementing the actual energy supplied by the user.

BIBLIOGRAPHY

S. Morland: *Tuba Stentoro-Phonica, an Instrument of Excellent Use, as well at Sea, as at Land; invented, and variously experimented in the year 1670* (London, 1671)

K.H. Macdermott: *The Old Church Gallery Minstrels* (London, 1948), pp. 33–5 [incl. illustration]

A.C. Cox: 'Vamping Horns', *Journal of the Northampton Museums and Art Gallery* (1968), no.3, pp.19–23

S.J. Weston: 'The Vamping Horn in Northamptonshire', *Harborough Historian* (1989), no.8, pp.5–8

PHILIP BATE/NICHOLAS TEMPERLEY,
STEPHEN J. WESTON

Vaṃśa [bãsurī, veṇu]. Classical Indian term, meaning 'bamboo', 'flute' in Sanskrit. It is the root of common names found in the modern north Indian languages— bãs, bãsī, bãsurī, bãsrī, bãslī, bãsulī—sometimes, but not always, denoting a transverse flute. The

Sanskrit synonym *veṇu,* also used since classical times, is more often adopted in modern south India. The transverse flute is treated here. For ductless end-blown flutes of South Asia *see* NAŘ; for panpipes *see* KUḶAL; for duct flutes *see* PĀVA; and for vessel flutes *see* BORRINDO.

1. Early and classical periods. 2. Medieval period. 3. Post-medieval period and folk traditions. 4. Modern classical transverse flutes.

1. EARLY AND CLASSICAL PERIODS. The term *vaṃśa* does not occur in the oldest literature, the *Ṛgveda* (later 2nd millennium BCE), in which *nāḍī* (Vedic *nāḷī:* 'pipe') is used to refer to the flute of Yama, King of the Dead. Another Vedic term, *vāṇā,* has been interpreted by some, to denote a flute; the contexts in which it occurs, however, suggest a meaning of no more than 'sound', 'speech', or, possibly, 'music'. In later Vedic literature of the 1st millennium BCE the common term for flute is *tūṇava,* of unknown derivation. Here, and into classical times, the flute, together with the *vīṇā* (harp) and *dundubhi* (drum), is frequently recorded.

In the classical period of Sanskrit literature (roughly, the 1st millennium CE) *vaṃśa* and *veṇu* are the terms most used, and classical Indian sculpture and painting (from the 3rd century BCE) show that they referred above all to the transverse flute, played in chamber music and in the drama of court and temple. The *Nāṭyaśāstra* (early centuries CE), attributed to Bharata, places the vaṃśa in the melody section of the classical theatre orchestra, together with strings and singers, and it prescribes the use of bamboo in its making (though decorated depictions in classical sculpture suggest also carved wooden flutes). The major whole tones, minor whole tones, and semitones of the old Indian parent-scales are here correlated with fully open (*vyaktamukta*), shaken (*kampita*), and half-open (*ardhamukta*) fingerings, respectively, and the problem of good intonation in flutes is noticed, with an instruction to follow the strings and singers. The treatise *Nāradīya śikṣā* (of disputed date) correlates the scale of the flute (*veṇu*) with that of the sacred chant *Sāmaveda,* suggesting a Dorian mode for the parent-scale *ṣaḍjagrāma.* In the classical period, also, the flute is established as the emblem of the god Krishna, though in literature the name *muralī* is more common for this instrument. In this period in the south, the Dravidian *kuḷal* of old Tamil literature was an equally important instrument.

2. MEDIEVAL PERIOD. By the Middle Ages the flute, and its music and theory, had been greatly developed, and texts such as the *Saṅgītaratnākara* describe the vaṃśa made in many sizes and with different tunings and materials (including acacia wood, sandalwood, ivory, iron, bronze, silver, and gold, as well as bamboo). This account, partly based on that of earlier writers, gives 15 (or 17) principal models of the vaṃśa, each with its keynote tuned successively to each of the seven degrees of the lower and middle octaves and the upper tonic (much as nowadays, when classical Indian

flutists bring a bag of different-sized flutes to a performance, suited to the range and tuning of different ragas). The four smallest, however, are said to be uncommon in being too shrill. The description of the structure of the vaṃśa is not completely explicit: it is said to be completely uniform and hollow to the thickness of the little finger (i.e. cylindrical). Measurements are given in *aṅgula* ('finger', 'inch'), which the author defines as the length of the top thumb-joint, and which is usually taken as three-quarters of an imperial inch, or about 2 cm (this obviously varies according to the maker, who is often the player and thus makes a flute convenient to his own dimensions). The simple mouth-hole (*phūtkārarandhra* or *mukharandhra*) is two to four 'inches' from the head, in the wall of the flute. The distance from here to the nearest (highest) fingerhole (*tārarandhra*) is the crucial one, and it is in terms of this, not of overall length, that the flutes are enumerated 'one-inch', 'two-inch' etc. up to 12-inch and then 14, 16, 18. There are seven fingerholes, and then, two 'inches' below the lowest hole, a vent ('wind exit hole'). This suggests the lower end of the flute was closed by a node, rather than open as on the modern classical flute of India. The different vaṃśa are named in terms of Hindu number cryptography (e.g. *muni:* 'sage', 'star of the Plough', for the seven-inch). For further details, including discussion of technique, e.g. *ṭīpā* (edge-tone and overblowing), as well as of flute-ragas, see Grosset, 1921.

3. POST-MEDIEVAL PERIOD AND FOLK TRADITIONS. With the spread of Turko-Afghan Muslim rule over the greater part of the Indian subcontinent from the end of the 12th century, the eclipse of the transverse flute as a court and art-music instrument is remarkable. When a flutist is mentioned at a Muslim court, it is often a player of the *nāy* (the Persian oblique flute), and Willard (1834) noted that professional players of the 'bansulee' are few. This is the more remarkable considering that it was during this period that the Krishna cult grew most significantly, and countless homes and temples had their idols of *madanamohana* ('the charmer', 'the seducer') holding a transverse flute. In the modern folk instrument repertory, too, the transverse flute is not common, except in the east—Bengal, Orissa, Assam, and the northeastern areas—where it is frequent and much-loved. This region, especially Assam, is held to produce the best-quality bamboo. Elsewhere, the terms *bā̃s, bā̃sī, bā̃surī* and *bainsirī* are frequent but usually denote folk end-blown flutes, with or without ducts.

4. MODERN CLASSICAL TRANSVERSE FLUTES. During the last century or so, the transverse flute has been redeveloped as an important instrument of northern and southern classical musics. In the south this is credited to Sarabha Sastri (1872–1904). Here, the *veṇu* (Tamil *pullāṅkuḷal* or *pillanagrovi*) is a short bamboo tube, little more than about 30 cm long, but comparatively wide. It is closed by a node at one end, and has eight fingerholes. In its range (about two and a half octaves), use of

ornamentation (*gamaka*), and repertory it follows the voice, the model for all Karnataka instruments. In the same period the *veṇu* replaced the oboe *mukhavīṇā* in the accompaniment of the classical Tamil dance *Bharata nāṭyam*.

The northern or Hindustani concert flute (*bãsrī; bãsurī*) has been developed especially by Bengalis, above all the late Pannalal Ghosh. Here, especially for heavy ragas, a very long flute (at least twice the length of the southern one) is often played, though flutists play a selection of sizes suitable to different pieces. It is closed by a node at the top end, and usually has seven fingerholes, the lowest on the side to accommodate the little finger. Again the model is vocal music, especially the Hindustani 'heavy' form *khayāl* and the lighter *ṭhumrī*, though some mix Hindustani instrumental techniques such as *joř* and *jhālā*.

BIBLIOGRAPHY

N.A. Willard: *A Treatise on the Music of Hindustan* [1834], repr. in Tagore: *Hindu Music from Various Authors* (Calcutta, 1875, 2/1882/R1965)

J. Grosset: 'Inde', *Encyclopédie de la musique et dictionnaire du Conservatoire*, A. Lavignac and L. de La Laurencie, eds., vol.1/pt.1 (1921), 257–376

P. Sambamoorthy: *The Flute* (Madras, 1927, rev. 3/1967)

C. Marcel-Dubois: *Les instruments de musique de l'Inde ancienne* (Paris, 1941)

Śārṅgadeva: *Saṅgītaratnākara* (13th century), ed. S. Subrahmanya Sastri, vol.3 (Madras, 1951)

Bharata: *Nāṭyaśāstra* (early centuries CE), ed. M. Ghosh, vol.2 (Calcutta, 1950; Eng. trans., 1967); ed. M. Ramakrishna Kavi and J.S.Pade, vol.4 (Baroda, 1964)

Nārada: *Nāradīyā śikṣa* (early centuries CE), ed. Sudhakāra Śukla (Datiya, 1964)

K.S. Kothari: *Indian Folk Musical Instruments* (New Delhi, 1968)

B.C. Deva: *Musical Instruments of India* (Calcutta, 1978)

B.C. Wade: *Music in India: the Classical Traditions* (Englewood Cliffs, NJ, 1979)

ALASTAIR DICK

Vāṇá. Ancient Indian, Vedic Sanskrit, term, usually translated as instrumental music of harps or flutes. Sachs (1940) identified it as a flute, perhaps following the Sanskritist Zimmer and relying on a connection with storm gods and thus with wind. A passage in the *Ṛgveda* (i,85,10) refers to blowing the *vāṇá*, but others imply the translation 'voice' or (metaphorically) 'song'. In later Vedic texts *vāṇá* is also referred to as *śatatantu vāṇá*, interpreted as 'hundred-string harp', but is probably only a poetic expression for 'hundredfold speech'. Native ritual etymologists have interpreted this as *śatatantrī vīṇā* ('hundred-string harp', i.e. a harp using ten ten-ply strings).

BIBLIOGRAPHY

A.A. Macdonell and A.B. Keith: *A Vedic Index of Names and Subjects* (London, 1912)

C. Sachs: *The History of Musical Instruments* (New York, 1940)

ALASTAIR DICK

Van Casteel, Henri-Joseph [Henrique] (*bap.* Tournai, Southern Netherlands, 19 Nov 1722; *d* Brussels, Southern Netherlands, 7 June 1790). Flemish harpsichord and piano maker, active in Portugal. He married Catherine-Joseph Pierre in Lisbon on 3 July 1757. A beautiful

grand piano dated 1763 survives (*P.L. mm*), the second oldest extant Portuguese grand. It is constructed like a Portuguese harpsichord but its action is modelled on Cristofori's and the soundboard ribbing recalls the Flemish harpsichord tradition. This might indicate that Van Casteel learned his craft in the Low Countries, perhaps in Tournai beside the harpsichord maker Albert Delin, though this is speculation. Because in 1760 the Lisbon harpsichord maker Manuel Antunes received an exclusive privilege to make and sell pianos for ten years, Van Casteel's 1763 piano might have caused legal problems, resulting in his move to Brussels in 1769. There between 1770 and 1777 Van Casteel published advertisements in the *Gazette des Pays-Bas* for his 'harpsichord with feathers', 'harpsichord with hammers', and 'piano in the English style'. A square piano from 1784 survives (in *A.W.t*). A pyramidal piano formerly attributed to Van Casteel is a forgery (in *B.B.mim*).

BIBLIOGRAPHY

G. Doderer and J.H. van der Meer: *Cordofones de tecla portugueses do século XVIII: clavicórduios, cravos, pianofortes e espinetas* (Lisbon, 2005)

P. Vandervellen: *La facture du piano dans les provinces belges des origines à 1851* (diss., U. libre de Bruxelles—U. of Paris IV/La Sorbonne, 2007)

PASCALE VANDERVELLEN

Van Dam. Dutch family of organ builders. Lammert [Lambertus] van Dam (i) (1744–1820) first trained as an organ builder in Gouda from 1764, presumably with Hendrik Hermanus Hess. As early as 1768 he worked for Albertus Anthoni Hinsz. In 1777 he set up a workshop in Leeuwarden, the capital of Friesland. The house he bought there in 1779 remained in the family as a workshop until 1917. He completed his first organ in Oldeboorn in 1779. This move to Friesland proved to be fortuitous, not only for the firm, but also for the province, in which organs had been scarce, and which gained about 125 organs from the four generations of Van Dam builders. Lambertus (i)'s enlargement of the Hinsz organ of Wassenaar, near The Hague, with a *Rugwerk* helped the firm to receive regular work in the western provinces as well.

Although Lammert did not make many large organs (his largest was Voorburg, 1806; dismantled in 1877), the quality of his work, which initially was in the Hinsz tradition, was highly praised. His later organs, beginning with those in Voorburg and Garnwerd (1809), show a more individual style. His sons Luitjen Jacob (i) (*b* Langweer, 1783; *d* Leeuwarden, 1846) and Jacob (i) (*b* Bergum, 1787; *d* Leeuwarden, 1839) became his partners about 1812 (under the name of L. van Dam & Zonen). Their organ for 's-Gravenzande in 1818 set the style of the second generation of Van Dam builders. From then on the cases were built in the then dominant Biedermeier style, and the tone became milder, with *Bovenwerk* divisions replacing the traditional *Rugwerk* (the last *Rugwerk* was built in 1832). Several organs were also given independent Pedals and the new-style magazine bellows, following in the tradition of the German organ school. When Luitjen Jacob (i) died the firm passed to his oldest son Lammert (ii) (1823–1904), who was joined by his two brothers, Pieter (i) (1824–89) and Jacob (ii) (1828–1907).

The third generation produced 150 new organs over a period of 58 years. Lammert (ii) kept pace with changing tastes and demands and from 1860 onwards the Empire style of façade was replaced with a kind of Regency style, while neo-Gothic façades were also introduced. Internally, from 1852, the windchests of the Great of larger organs were arranged chromatically, while free reeds, string stops, and swell boxes were introduced. Yet the approach to construction, pipe scaling, and voicing remained much the same as that of the 18th century. The largest organ of this generation is the extant three-manual, 40-stop organ of Enschede.

When Lammert (ii) died the firm was continued by his sons Pieter (ii) (1856–1927), Luitjen Jacob (ii) (1850–1915), and Haije (1853–1927). Although at first the organs were still of high quality (even during and after World War I), the rising costs of materials and labour and increasing competition led the company to buy prefabricated organ parts and pipes from mass manufacturers, causing the firm to turn to pneumatic action. This development, along with the conversion of the business to a limited liability company in 1917, estranged the firm from its age-old tradition of excellence. Pieter retired as director in 1926 and in the same year, due to increasing competition from the successful Leeuwarden firm of Bakker & Timmenga, sold the firm to the organ builder A.S.J. Dekker.

BIBLIOGRAPHY

F. Talstra: *Langs Nederlandse orgels: Groningen, Friesland, Drenthe* (Baarn, 1979)

J. Jongepier, ed: *Achter het Friese orgelfront: tentoonstelling orgelbouw in Friesland 1776–1926* (Leeuwarden, 1981)

J. Jongepier: *Orgelbouwers in Friesland* (Leeuwarden, 1992)

ADRI DE GROOT

Vanden Gheyn [Van den Ghein, etc.]. Flemish family of bellfounders, carillon builders, and carillonneurs. Willem Van den Ghein (*d* 1533) from Goorle, near Tilburg, was the ancestor of ten founders who were to produce bells and carillons in Mechelen until 1697. His son Peter (i) (*d* 1561) was one of the first to make carillons. The bells and original barrel of the one he made for the town hall at Zierikzee (Netherlands) in 1554 were moved to the Zuidhavenpoort (at Zierikzee) in the early 1960s, and is the oldest known carillon still chiming. Although built as an automatic instrument, it was also played manually (although possibly not at first). His grandson Peter (ii) (1553–1618) cast a carillon for Monnickendam (Netherlands), which is now the oldest manually played carillon in the world. In 1638 Peter (iii) (1607–59), nephew of Peter (ii), cast the 6-tonne 'Salvator' bell, which still exists, for Ste Gudule, Brussels, with his nephew Peter De Klerck.

After brief periods in St Truiden and Tienen the family settled in Leuven in 1727. Peter (iv) (*b* 1698), a monk, built a number of fine carillons, of which the instruments in Veere (Netherlands) and Steenokkerzeel (Belgium) are extant. His nephew and successor Andreas Jozef (1727–93) is regarded as the most gifted bellfounder to have emerged from the southern Low Countries. Of his 23 carillons, parts of nine have survived at St Truiden; Hasselt; St Lambert, Liège; Huy town hall; Notre Dame, Huy; Turnhout; Schoonhoven; the Nijkerk and Gertrudiskerk, Leuven. His carillon bells are accurately tuned and have a clear sonority; in the treble bells he achieved an even higher proficiency than the Hemony brothers.

Andreas Jozef's son Andreas Lodewijk was the last bellfounder to bear the Vanden Gheyn name. His business was continued by his grandsons André-Louis (1814–88) and Séverin (1819–85) Van Aerschodt, who separated in 1851. Séverin's son Félix (1870–1943) closed the foundry just before World War II. Another dynasty with family ties to the Vanden Gheyns, the Sergeys family, continued to cast bells in Leuven until 1980 when the Belgian bellfounding tradition reached its end.

Matthias Vanden Gheyn (*b* Tienen, 7 April 1721; *d* Leuven, 22 June 1785), brother of Andreas Jozef, was a bellfounder, carillonneur, organist, and composer. He was organist of the Pieterskerk, Leuven, from 1741 and the town's municipal carillonneur from 1745. Widely regarded as the most gifted carillonneur of his time, he was also an expert restorer of organs and carillons. He published two collections of harpsichord pieces and one set of sonatas for harpsichord and violin. A number of other works by Matthias, variously for harpsichord, organ, and carillon, were discovered in manuscript about 1861 by Xavier van Elewyck and copied by him (*B-bc* ms.6255). The eleven virtuoso preludes for carillon in this collection are the earliest surviving genuine compositions for the instrument, and have formed part of the standard carillon repertory since the beginning of the 20th century. Their strict structure and toccata-like character have earned Vanden Gheyn the nickname 'Bach of the Carillon'. The rediscovery of Matthias's autograph of these preludes in 1995 (now *B-LVu* Van Elewyckfonds P-195) led to substantial improvements to Van Elewyck's transcription. Another carillon manuscript, the *Leuvens Beiaardhandschrift* (1755–60; now shelved with the preludes autograph), was probably supervised by Vanden Gheyn. It contains 151 pieces, with dance music, marches, music for formal occasions, and two dazzling variation works: *Les folies d'Espagne* and *Cecilia*.

BIBLIOGRAPHY

X. Van Elewyck: *Matthias Van den Gheyn, le plus grand organiste et carillonneur belge du XVIIIe siècle* (Paris, 1862/*R*)

G. van Doorslaer: 'Les van den Ghein, fondeurs de cloches, canons, sonnettes et mortiers à Malines', *Annales de l'Académie royale d'archéologie de Belgique*, vol.62 (1910), 463–666

R. Barnes: 'Matthias Van den Gheyn', *Bulletin of the Guild of Carillonneurs in North America*, vol.10 (1957), 11–20

P.F. Vernimmen: 'De klokkengieters Vanden Gheyn en Van Aerschodt', *Stad met klank: vier eeuwen klokken en klokkengieters te Leuven*, ed. G. Huybens and others, Leuven Centrale Bibliotheek, 16 June—3 Sept 1990 (Leuven, 1990), 43–61 [exhibition catalogue]

M. and K. van Bets: *De Mechelse klokkengieters (14de–18de eeuw)* (Mechelen, 1998)

LUC ROMBOUTS

Van den Heuvel. Dutch firm of organ builders. Jan Leendert van den Heuvel (*b* 5 Nov 1946) learned organ building with the Flentrop firm. At the age of 20 he set up his own business in his father's painting workshop in Dordrecht. His first organ (1967; one manual, ten stops) was well received and led to a contract for a three-manual, 32-stop instrument for the Singelkerk, Ridderkerk, completed in 1972. This was followed by a new organ for the Lambertuskerk, Strijen (1975; two manuals, 33 stops). In 1975 van den Heuvel was joined by his brother Peter Aart van den Heuvel (*b* 13 Feb 1958); the firm became known as J.L. van den Heuvel-Orgelbouw B.V. in 1979.

The Van den Heuvels' love of French Romantic organs and their music inspired a study tour of Cavaillé-Coll instruments with Michelle Leclerc and Daniel Roth. Much of the knowledge gained from this tour was applied to the construction of the four-manual, 80-stop organ behind an old case for the Nieuwe Kerk, Katwijk-aan-Zee, in 1983. This instrument was received with mixed reactions, some suggesting that quantity had been given preference over musical quality and coherence. However, several prominent French organists, especially Daniel Roth, praised it, and the firm was honoured with a contract to build a unique organ with five manuals, 101 stops (five at 32′, including one on the *Grand orgue*), 147 ranks, 8000 pipes, and 33 windchests in the old case at St Eustache, Paris. This, the largest organ in France (completed in 1989), has a second, electric remote-control console equipped with MIDI. Jean-Louis Coignet and Jean Guillou acted as consultants.

Although the Van den Heuvel firm suffered setbacks at home due to controversies over the quality of their work, it has thrived mainly on foreign contracts, and has built organs for the Martinikerk, Sneek (1986; based on Cavaillé-Coll's model no.8), Victoria Hall, Geneva (1992), the Royal Academy of Music, London (1993), Rotterdam (1996; originally ordered by the Concordian Theological Seminary, Tai-pei, and a sister organ was installed in the Royal College of Music, Stockholm, in 1995), St Franziskus Kirche, Munich (1997), and Katarina Kyrka, Stockholm (2000; three manuals, 62 stops). Also noteworthy are a Van den Heuvel organ in the Holy Apostles Church, New York (1994; three manuals, 32 stops; formerly in Texas), and both a small positive and a large French Romantic instrument in the DR-BYEN (Danish radio and television) concert hall in Copenhagen (2006; four manuals, 91 stops). See J. Jongepier: 'Groot, maar niet groots: over het Van den Heuvel-orgel te Katwijk', *De Mixtuur* (1983), no.44, pp.554–65.

ADRI DE GROOT/R

van der Linden, Paul (*b* Eindhoven, Netherlands, 11 Sept 1957). Dutch oboist and maker of early oboes. He studied recorder and Baroque oboe performance at the Royal Conservatory in The Hague, where his primary teachers were Ricardo Kanji (recorder) and Ku Ebbinge (oboe). Beginning in 1981, courses in instrument building were offered at the Conservatory, which by then had its own workshop, primarily for repairs. After a year of mentoring under the visiting oboe maker Bruce Haynes and recorder maker Frederick Morgan, van der Linden turned to instrument making and opened his own workshop. The first years were devoted mainly to recorders; in the early 2000s he turned exclusively to producing Baroque oboes, which he plays professionally. At his present workshop in Oss, he makes Baroque oboes after Jacob Denner and J.M. Anciuti, Classical oboes after Grundmann & Floth, oboes d'amore after I.C. Eichentopf and I.G. Baur, and oboes da caccia after H. Weigel. The oboes da caccia are covered with leather and fitted with a brass bell in the manner of the more familiar Eichentopf oboe da caccia. In recent years van der Linden has cooperated with the historical oboe maker Piet Dhont, whom he credits for new insights and inspiration.

CHRISTOPHER BRODERSEN/R

Van der Meer, John Henry (*b* The Hague, Netherlands, 9 Feb 1920; *d* Fürth, Germany, 1 Feb 2008). Dutch organologist, musicologist and museum curator. The son of a Dutch father and an English-born mother, van der Meer grew up bilingual and became fluent in at least seven European languages. He received piano lessons from the age of six. From 1938 to 1946 he studied jurisprudence and musicology at the University of Utrecht. His studies were interrupted when he was arrested on his birthday in 1943 together with other men in consequence of the assassination of a Dutch member of the Nazi Schutzstaffel (SS). After detention in the concentration camp of Herzogenbusch (Kamp Vught) he was deported for forced labour in an aircraft engine factory in Strasbourg and a cement plant in Heidelberg until April 1945. In April 1946 he received his doctorate in law, but thereafter taught aural training and other subjects first at the Utrecht higher conservatory, then at the Royal Conservatory of The Hague. In 1954 he became head of the musical instrument collection, library, and drawings and prints collection of the Haags Gemeentemuseum. Two years later, he received his second doctorate, in musicology, also from the university of Utrecht, with the dissertation *Johann Joseph Fux als Opernkomponist*.

On 1 Jan 1963 he was appointed first curator of the newly created department of musical instruments of the Germanisches Nationalmuseum, a position claimed by Ulrich Rück, who had sold his family's collection to the museum the year before. Van der Meer designed the museum's instrument exhibition which, after acquisition of the Neupert collection in 1969, opened in a new building in the same year. In 1979 he published the first modern catalogue of the museum's instrument collection and founded an ongoing collaboration with the editor Florian Noetzel. Van der Meer published more than 170 articles, books, and catalogues, and was a voluminous correspondent and generous mentor. He was among the founders of ICOM-CIMCIM (the International Committee of Musical Instrument Museums and Collections) in 1965 and served as its secretary until 1968. Van der Meer retired in December 1983 and continued his research until shortly before his death. He was honoured with two *Festschriften*, in 1987 and 2001, the Curt Sachs Award of the American Musical Instrument Society in 1986, and the Germanisches Nationalmuseum's Theodor-Heuss-Medal in 2000.

WRITINGS
(*selective list*)
Johann Joseph Fux als Opernkomponist (Bilthoven, 1961)
Verzeichnis der Europäischen Musikinstrumente im Germanischen Nationalmuseum Nürnberg, vol.1: Hörner und Trompeten. Membranophone. Idiophone. (Wilhelmshaven, 1979)
with L. Cervelli and M. Lucchi: *Antichi strumenti musicali. Catalogo del fondo musicale del Museo Civico di Storia e Arte Medievale e Moderna di Modena* (Modena,1982)
with R. Weber: *Catalogo degli strumenti musicali dell'Accademia Filarmonica di Verona* (Verona, 1982)
Musikinstrumente von der Antike bis zur Gegenwart (Munich 1983)
with L.F. Tagliavini: *Clavicembali e spinette dal XVI al XIX secolo. Collezione L. F. Tagliavini*) (Bologna, 1986)
Strumenti musicali europei del Museo Civico Mediavale di Bologna (Bologna, 1993)
with G. Doderer: *Cordofones de tecla portugueses do séc XVIII: clavicórdios, cravos, pianofortes e espinetas* (Lisbon, 2005)
ed.: *Alla ricerca dei suoni perduti/In Search of Lost Sounds* (Briosco, 2006) [catalogue of the Giulini collection]

BIBLIOGRAPHY
F. Hellwig, ed: *Studia Organologica. Festschrift für John Henry van der Meer zu seinem fünfundsechzigsten Geburtstag* (Tutzing, 1987), 535–6 (biography), 537–42 (bibliography to 1983)
F.P. Bär, ed: *Musica instrumentalis. Zeitschrift für Organologie*, vol.3, John Henry van der Meer zum 80. Geburtstag (Nürnberg, 2001), 10–11 (bibliography 1984–2000)

FRANK P. BÄR

van der Poel, Peter Vincent (*b* The Hague, Netherlands, 28 May 1956). Dutch maker of recorders and other early woodwinds. He studied mechanics from 1975 to 1977 at the Delft University of Technology and modern oboe from 1979 to 1981 at the Royal Conservatorium in The Hague, also attending a recorder-making class taught there by Fred Morgan and Ricardo Kanji. He worked as a maker of Renaissance and Baroque recorders and early oboes in The Hague from 1982, in Nieuwegein from 1986, and in Bunnik from 1993, also producing early clarinets, chalumeaux, and bassoons. He exhibited regularly at music festivals in Stockstadt, Germany, and The Hague, and his instruments have been chosen by many prominent performers. His apprentices and assistants included Bodil Diesen (recorders), David Coomber (recorders, *c*1982), Boas Berney (transverse flutes, 1993–9), and Oscar Arguelles (clarinets, *c*2001–10).

JAMES B. KOPP

Van Dinter, Louis Hubert (*b* Weert, Netherlands, 20 Feb 1851; *d* Mishawaka, IN, 9 March 1932). American organ builder, of Dutch birth. The son of organ builder Mathieu H. Van Dinter (1822–1902) and Elizabeth Vermeulen, daughter of an organ builder, he apprenticed at an early age and in 1870 emigrated to the USA with his father and brothers Alphonsus, Franciscus, and Peter Johannes. They began building organs in Detroit in 1875, relocating to a larger factory in Mishawaka, Indiana in 1886, and are said to have built between 150 and 180 organs,

mostly for Roman Catholic churches, in the growing cities and towns of the Midwest. These included instruments for St Hedwig's Church, South Bend, Indiana (1878), St Mary's Church, Detroit (1884), Saints Peter and Paul, Huntington, Indiana (1894), and his family's church, St Joseph's in Mishawaka (1893). After Louis's death his son John Joseph (1889–1954) assumed direction of the company, but on a reduced scale dictated by the decline in business during the Depression, eventually selling the factory and working largely in tuning and maintenance until 1944. See M. Friesen: 'The Van Dinter Organbuilders', *The Tracker*, vol.33/3 (1989), 13–23.

BARBARA OWEN

Vandumbu. Speaking tubes of the Vambwela and Vankhangala peoples of southeast Angola. These are secret instruments used to commemorate dead chiefs. The sounds that are produced, supposed to represent the voices of the chiefs, are the esoteric knowledge of the initiated. The vandumbu are wooden tubes up to 4 metres long with a circular embouchure, cut from tall trees and hollowed, with a mouth often shaped like that of a crocodile or other river animal. The body of each tube is completely wrapped with plant fibre. Throughout the year, these instruments are kept under water by the members of the secret society in a shallow place of the river marshlands. During the ceremony, members bring them up to the village in the darkness and produce fearful sounds. Three vandumbu usually form part of the procession. In front of them walk the players of three smaller lip-vibrated aerophones, about 1.5 metres long and quite narrow in bore, called *nyavikali*. Harmonics up to the 8th or even the 10th partial are blown on some of them. They have a separate mouthpiece similar in size and shape to that of early European trombones.

GERHARD KUBIK/JEREMY MONTAGU

Vangelisti, Pier Lorenzo (*fl* Florence, Italy, *c*1740–85). Italian violin maker. He followed the Stainer model then current in Florence. While many sources consider Vangelisti a follower of Gabbrielli, surviving instruments reveal a far closer affinity to the work of the Carcassi family, particularly in their fine edging, narrow model, and closely placed f-holes. The scrolls, with longish tails and rounded eyes, also suggest the Carcassis. Vangelisti used a small written or printed label on which his name is occasionally spelled 'Evangelisti'. See R. Vannes: *Essai d'un dictionnaire universel des luthiers* (Paris, 1932, 2/1951/R1972 as *Dictionnaire universel des luthiers* and R1981 incl. suppl. 1959).

JAAK LIIVOJA-LORIUS/PHILIP J. KASS

Vanniyayar [vanniyayay] ('tooth-tambourine'). Idioglot jew's harp of the Koryak and Chukchi peoples of Siberia. A narrow rectangular piece of wood or bone has a triangular tongue cut in it. It is played, by pulling a cord through a hole in one end, mainly by women often imitating natural sounds such as animal cries, or wind and rain, or as a courting instrument.

Van Oeckelen, Petrus (*b* Breda, Netherlands, 15 Aug 1795; *d* Harenermolen, Netherlands, 1878). Dutch organ builder, carillon maker, musician, and instrument inventor. His father, Cornelis (*b* 1762; *d* 29 Aug 1837), was a clockmaker and inventor of musical instruments who worked on carillons and started an organ-building business in 1805. Petrus completed his father's last instrument. His brothers were also musicians and gifted craftsmen: Johannes Matthias (1787–1860) was a carillonneur and clockmaker in Breda; and Cornelis Jacobus (1798–1865) was a piano maker and the inventor of several mechanical musical instruments. In Paris in 1861, Cornelis patented the Triolodéon, an improved melodeon in which each note was independently capable of dynamic variation.

In 1810 Petrus left his job as municipal carillonneur in Breda and moved to Groningen, where he learned organ building from H.H. Freytag (*d* 11 April 1811) and his apprentice J.W. Timpe. His first organ was built for the Dutch Reform church of Assen (1814, now in Havelte), re-using older parts. His reputation as a repairer and restorer grew, and he adapted the large organs of Groningen's Martinikerk, Der Aa-kerk, and Zwolle's Grote Kerk in accordance with contemporary musical tastes and practices. Petrus also designed the magnificent case for the 1829 Timpe organ in the Nieuwe Kerk, Groningen, patterned after the famous Müller organ of the Bavokerk, Haarlem.

In 1837 Petrus took over the organ-building firms of his father and Timpe, both recently deceased, and settled in Harenermolen. In 1841 he built one of his first new organs, at the Koepelkerk, Smilde. He secured orders for new instruments through the contacts cultivated by the organist Samuel Trip, who often played the inaugural recitals. Petrus also continued to work on carillons (in 1857 he automated the carillon of the church in Middelstum). He is credited with having invented the free-reed 'Clavier oboe' played from a keyboard; this and a 'Clavier contrabasso' as well as a costumed automaton clarinettist 'somewhat larger than life' were featured in a concert at Dodworth's Hall in New York in 1861 but there credited to Charles van Oeckelen, a pianist and organist who also performed on the 'Alexandre organ' at the Lyceum.

After the death of Petrus his sons Cornelis (Cornelius) Aldegundis (1829–1905) and Antonius (1839–1918) continued their father's work although they produced few organs after 1905. From 1918 the business was run by his chief apprentice Harmannus Thijs (1862–1943); he was succeeded by lesser figures after 1933.

Petrus was an innovator: the first builder to introduce magazine bellows into northern Europe, applied to both new and rebuilt organs; he also made extensive use of metal parts in the action, especially the stop action. He was the first organ builder in the Netherlands to develop a certain degree of mass production: parts were absolutely uniform and made according to standardized procedures, and even the cases could be identical or nearly identical twins, such as those at Usquert and Saaxumhuizen. The churches of Westeremden and Leermens received identical organs in

neo-Gothic cases. With these production methods Petrus was able to build up to three organs per year. Both in quality and quantity, Van Oeckelen's work belongs to the greatest of the 19th century. The sound of his organs can be characterized as stately, heavy, full of gravity, and very well suited to the musical practice of his time. For much of the 20th century Petrus's vigorous rebuilding and replacement of old organs was lamented; however, the quality of that work (especially of his newly built organs) has gained recognition since the 1980s.

BIBLIOGRAPHY

F. Talstra: *Het Groninger Orgelbezit van de Reformatie tot de Romantiek*, Stichting Oude Groninger Kerken, vol.22 (Groningen, 1979)

F. Talstra: *Langs Nederlandse Orgels: Groningen, Friesland, Drenthe* (Baarn, 1979)

J. Holthuis: *Petrus van Oeckelen, Orgelmaker te Harenermolen bij Groningen: Voortzetter of vernieuwer der Groninger orgelmakerstraditie?*, Publicatie Stichting Groninger Orgelland, (Groningen, 1985)

V.B. Lawrence: *Strong on Music: The New York Music Scene in the Days of George Templeton Strong*, vol.3: *Repercussions, 1857–1862* (Chicago, 1999), 453

ADRI DE GROOT/R

Van Peteghem. Belgian family of organ builders. The earliest member of the family to build organs was Pieter Van Peteghem (*b* Wetteren, South Netherlands, 24 Jan 1708; *d* Ghent, South Netherlands, 4 June 1787), who was apprenticed to Guillaume David. Pieter is said to have introduced French features in his specifications. His work was aided from 1767 by his sons Lambertus Benoit (*b* Ghent, 5 March 1742; *d* Ghent, 5 Sept 1807) and Egidius Franciscus (*b* Ghent, 27 March 1737; *d* 5 March 1779), who from the late 1770s worked largely independently of their father and expanded the business geographically. The brothers in turn were succeeded by Lambertus's sons Pieter Karl (1792–1863) and Lambertus Corneille (*b* 1779). Pieter's son Maximilian (1822–70) joined the firm in the 1840s and, adopting a Romantic style, worked until the mid-1860s. Van Peteghem organs survive in many Belgian churches, including those at Denderwindeke, Etikhove, Rozebeke, and Meerle. Particularly noteworthy is their relatively intact Rococo organ in St Martinus Church, Haringe (1778; three manuals, 29 stops, renovated 1993–4). See G. Moortgat: *Oude orgels in Vlaanderen*, vol.1 (Brussels, 1964).

BARBARA OWEN/R

Van Vulpen. Dutch firm of organ builders. It was founded in Utrecht in 1940 by brothers Rijk van Vulpen (i) (*b* Utrecht, 11 April 1921; *d* 15 Nov 1997) and Adrianus (Jos) van Vulpen (*b* Utrecht, 5 July 1922). They had already built their first organ in their father's plumbing workshop from old parts. On 10 March 1952 the third brother, Evert van Vulpen (*b* Utrecht, 2 Jan 1929) joined the firm as a salaried worker, and Rijk van Vulpen (ii) (*b* 3 Aug 1955), son of Adrianus, joined likewise on 1 May 1974. In 1983 Rijk (i) retired, leaving Adrianus as sole proprietor. On 27 March 1997 Rijk (ii) took over the firm and changed the name to Gebr. van Vulpen BV. In 1999 Henk Bouwman (*b* 1 Sept 1938) and Rijk (ii) led the firm. The firm started to blossom in 1950, when they bought the building that has since housed the organ building workshop. All parts and pipes are constructed in-house.

As self-taught builders of mechanical-action church, studio, and house organs, the brothers' initial orientation was inspired by the neo-Baroque organ revival movement, and especially that of Danish builders. They were introduced to this by Lambert Erné, organist of the large three-manual 1957 Marcussen organ of the Nicolaikerk in Utrecht. Their most famous example and landmark instrument is the 1961 two-manual choir organ for St Eusebius in Arnhem, which has a modern yet classically inspired flat façade and a horizontal Trumpet stop. Other significant organs of that period are in Bremen Cathedral (1966) and the Elisabethkirche in Recklinghausen (1973).

After the restoration of the 1756 Matthijs van Deventer organ in the Hermvormde Kerk, Nijkerk (1975–87) and the 1696 Duyschot organ at Hendrik-Ido-Ambacht (1982), and also owing to a changing tide of opinion in the Netherlands, the firm's approach to the building of new organs changed dramatically to one more fully based on Dutch styles from before the 20th century. This is exemplified by lower mixtures, wider pipe scales, more lead in the pipe metal, and an overall warmer sound. The firm employs both historically inspired and modern case designs.

Other notable restorations are: the 1733 Hinsz organ of the Petruskerk, Leens (1967); the 1786 Bätz organ, Petruskerk, Woerden (1971); the 60-stop, three-manual 1830 organ of Utrecht Cathedral, containing much 16th-century pipework (1985); the 1686/1720/1860 organ of the Nicolaaskerk, Vollenhove (1977); and the 1738 Hinsz organ of the Broederkerk, Kampen (1993; new Pedal and *Rugwerk* added).

The most significant organs built since the 1970s were for the Stephankirche, Andernach (1983); the Maranathakerk, Woerden (1983); the Buurkerk, Utrecht (1984); the Rehobothkerk, Utrecht (1984); the Hervormde Kerk 'de Ark', Ede (1986); the Gereformeerde Kerk Vrijgemaakt, Zuidhorn (1989); the Hervormde Kerk, Arnemuiden (1990); the Hervormde Kerk, Renkum (1994); and the large three-manual organ in North-Germanic/Dutch tradition for the Hervormde Kerk of Ouddorp (1994). More recently the firm has built organs for the Hervormde Kerk, Meerkerk (2001; two manuals, 13 stops); St Martinuskerk, Stein (Limburg) (2007; two manuals, 18 stops); and the Hervormde Gemeente, Gouda (2009; two manuals, 30 stops), each tuned to a different temperament.

The firm, which in 2010 had 14 workers, has contributed to the production of somewhat standardized, small and large chamber organs, and has delivered new organs to Germany, Norway, Austria, and the Czech Republic. See G. Verloop, ed.: *Small Organs in Holland: a Description of Some Modern Instruments* (Schagen, 1978).

ADRI DE GROOT/R

Vara bungas ('copper drum'). Kettledrum of Latvia. It is a hemispherical brass or copper kettle, placed on a tripod, with a diameter of about 60 cm and height 30 to 50 cm. A skin head is attached by a metal hoop that is held and tightened by seven or eight screws. The earliest written evidence is from the 13th century, but it is frequently mentioned in documents of the 17th and 18th centuries, when it was used in military units, often together with trumpets. Several Latvian folksong texts mention 'copper drums on the back', apparently a poetic reflection of the medieval military tradition, when paired kettledrums were strapped on the back of one soldier, while another soldier followed and drummed with two sticks. A 16th-century Livonian chronicle mentions a kettledrum in a church tower in Riga, as a signalling instrument. Kettledrums have been also used inside churches, possibly to synchronize congregational singing. See V. Muktupāvels: *Latviešu mūzikas instrumentu sistemātika* [Systematics of Latvian Musical Instruments] (diss., U. of Latvia, 1999).

VALDIS MUKTUPĀVELS

Vargāns [vargas, zobu spēles]. Heteroglot jew's harp of Latvia. The earliest archaeological evidence is from the end of the 13th century, while most historical examples are from the 14th century to the 17th. The frame is made of iron or bronze, 5 to 8 cm long and 2 to 5 cm wide. The tongue is made of forged iron. Most of these instruments are found in the vicinity of medieval castles or towns. The playing tradition extended throughout the 19th century and sporadically into the second half of the 20th century, when a revival began. The known repertoire is dance music—mostly polkas. See V. Muktupāvels: 'Musical Instruments in the Baltic Region: Historiography and Traditions', *The World of Music*, vol.44/3 (2002), 21–54.

VALDIS MUKTUPĀVELS

Variable tension chordophone [plucked drum]. Type of plucked, single-string chordophone principally of South Asia. The resonating body is a vessel such as a gourd, wood or metal cylinder, or clay pot with base excised, one opening covered with skin. A gut or metal string extends perpendicularly or nearly so from the middle of the skin (where it is typically secured by a button, washer, or wooden strip behind the skin) to the middle of a wooden stick or a small pot, either of which is held by the player's hand, or to a flexible neck attached to the side of the resonator, or to a yoke attached to both sides of it. Pitch is altered by varying the string tension either directly by the player's hand or arm, or indirectly by flexing the neck or yoke. Sachs termed this type of instrument a 'plucked drum' (Ger. *Zupftrommel)* although he knew that the string is 'the primary vibrator'. Others have shown that these chordophones are 'frequency-doublers' because, owing to the string's vibration in a plane perpendicular to that of the membrane, the fundamental is an octave higher than if the string

Variable tension chordophone. Plucked drum, gopiyantra. The two arms are pressed together by the fingers while the string is plucked, thus changing the length and tension of the string, and so varying the pitch in a continuous glissando. (Jeremy Montagu Collection, Oxford)

were parallel to the membrane. Instruments in which tension is varied by deflection of the string by the player's finger or by stopping, for example the Indian sitar, *surbahār or vīṇā*, or the koto, steel-string guitar, etc., cannot be categorized as variable tension chordophones.

The *gopīyantra* of Bengal and Orissa in east India and Bangladesh (and the similar *ṭokāri* of neighbouring Assam) has a yoke made from a split-bamboo fork whose upper node is left whole and whose separated lower ends are nailed or bound to the sides of the body. The string, usually a steel wire, is attached at the top to a tuning peg inserted laterally through the upper node. The string is sometimes plucked with the index finger of the right hand while it is holding the instrument, or plucked with the right hand while the left holds the body of the instrument. When the sides of the fork are squeezed and released the pitch rises and falls. The *gopīyantra* is played by Baul and Sadhu religious mendicant singers to accompany their singing or dancing. The name, meaning 'the instrument of [Krishna's loving companions] the milkmaids', appears to be literary; in the countryside it is usually called *ektārā* ('monochord') or *khamak*.

The body of the *ānandalaharī* is a wooden cylinder open at both ends and somewhat barrel-shaped or conical, tapering inward toward the top. The lower opening is covered by a complete skin and the upper opening by a skin with its centre cut away; both skins

are laced to plaited leather hoops and braced by cord V-lacings, each having a metal tuning-ring, giving an inverted Y-shape. (Older models had only a lower skin, glued on.) A gut string is looped through two holes to a protective button (or piece of bamboo, etc.) in the centre of the lower skin, and passes up through the body as a double string to a handle formed from a small brass pot, itself covered with skin at the proximal opening and attached in the same way. The body is tucked into the player's left armpit and the string tensioned by the left hand gripping the pot; the right hand plucks the string with a small plectrum of bone, plastic, or other material. The pitch of the string can be greatly and instantly varied to produce a dramatic accompaniment for song or dance; the instrument can play both rhythmic and melodic music, with swooping portamento leaps within about an octave. The *ānandalaharī* is used especially by Baul religious mendicant singers.

This type of instrument has several sub-types, widespread in the Indian subcontinent, with wood, metal, clay, or gourd resonators. These include the *jhamalikā (jamidikā)*, a beggar's instrument of Maharashtra and the Deccan, and the *jamuku* of Andhra, which accompanies ballad singing, particularly in the Godavari area, but with these the body is a brass tube, roughly 22.5 cm in diameter and 25 cm long, covered at the lower end by a skin, from the centre of which a gut string passes up to a wooden handle.

The instrument is held under the left arm and the string, plucked by the right hand, is tensioned by the left hand pulling the stick. The *dudhukī* (*dhudhkī*) of Orissa differs in having a barrel-shaped wooden body. It is played by male and female snake charmers to accompany their songs. The body of the *bagilu* of Gujarat resembles a wooden frame drum and its string is of iron wire. The *bhapang* of Rajasthan has a gourd body, 16 cm to 18 cm high, with the two ends excised and a goatskin nailed over the larger opening. The thick gut string, fastened to the centre of the skin, is plucked with a small plectrum. Among the Jogi communities of Alwar and Bharatpur in west Rajasthan the *bhapang* accompanies epic-religious ballads and devotional songs. The *premtāl* of Uttar Pradesh, is also called *tumbā* ('gourd') and has a gourd body. Other variable tension chordophones include the *pulluvān kuḍam* and *apang*.

BIBLIOGRAPHY

S.M. Tagore: *Yantra-koś* (Calcutta, 1875/R1977)

C. Sachs: *Die Musikinstrumente Indiens und Indonesiens* (Berlin and Leipzig, 1914, 2/1923)

S. Ray: *Music of Eastern India* (Calcutta, 1973)

B.C. Deva: *Musical Instruments of India* (Calcutta, 1978)

C.J. Adkins and others: 'Frequency–doubling Chordophones', *Musica asiatica*, vol.3 (1981), 1–9

L.E.R. Picken: 'The "Plucked Drums": *Gopīyantra* and *Ānanda laharī*', *Musica asiatica*, vol.3 (1981), 29–33

ALASTAIR DICK/JEREMY MONTAGU

Variable tension drum. Term occasionally applied to an hourglass drum whose pitch is changed by pressing the head tension cords toward the waist of the drum.

Variacord. Electric piano developed by Dr Pollak-Rudin and Ernst Werndl in Vienna and completed by 1937. It resembled a baby grand in size but was semicircular and had no soundboard. Its strings were activated and their vibrations picked up by electromagnets, of which there were several to each string, positioned at different points along its length; the player could switch between them to obtain different timbres. A special mechanism produced mandolin-like repetitions of the sound. See P. Donhauser: 'Von Forschergeist und Alt–Wiener Werkmannsarbeit', *Blätter für Technikgeschichte*, vol.71 (2009), 151–74.

HUGH DAVIES/PETER DONHAUSER

Variophon (i). Photoelectric composition machine, four models of which were developed in Leningrad between 1930 and 1949 by Evgeny Aleksandrovich Sholpo, inspired by experiments in graphic sound which he made with Arseny Avraamov at the end of 1929 and later on his own.

In May 1930, while working at Alexander Shorin's Central Laboratory of Wire Communication in Leningrad, Sholpo applied for a patent on a 'method and device for the production of a periodic sound track on film', later named the *Variophon*. Supplementary applications claimed improvements, and he obtained copyright on 31 August 1931. In October 1930 he applied for a patent on a method of additive synthesis of graphic soundtracks: 'a mechanism for the transformation and addition of harmonious fluctuations with different amplitudes'.

A shaped vane, or 'acoustical drafter', rotating between a length of film and a beam of light, shaped the optical recording, producing different pitches related to the ratio of speed of rotation of a disk and the speed at which the film moved. The first version of the Variophon was built with assistance from the composer Georgy Rimsky-Korsakov in 1931 at Lenfilm Studios. It was capable of producing artificial soundtracks and allowed easier access to different timbres by means of paper disks with images of appropriate shapes, rotating in a light beam synchronously with a moving filmstrip. Although the first version was made with wooden parts affixed by wires and tuned with ropes, it already incorporated one of the most crucial devices—a mechanism for the precise and continuous changing of the speed of rotation of the optical disk; i.e. a means of controlling pitch with the possibility of synthesizing continuous glissandos as well as any microtonal scale. The composer had full freedom to work with polyrhythmic combinations and almost unlimited tempos.

An improved second model was constructed that by 1936 allowed flexible and exact control over pitch, dynamics, and timbre, with a deep vibrato option. This model could produce soundtracks with up to 12 parallel voices using multiple exposures. Even compared with the more advanced third and fourth versions, it produced the most impressive quality and complexity of sound. Unfortunately it was destroyed by a shell in January 1944, shortly before the end of the siege of Leningrad.

Sholpo did not regard timbre as being very important until he was joined in the late 1930s by the acoustician Boris Yankovsky, who had worked with Avraamov in Moscow before undertaking his own researches, which included an exploration of timbre. In 1939 Sholpo began developing the third version of the *Variophon*, which was almost finished by 1941 but remained nonfunctional until 1946 due to critical mistakes in its construction. In the fourth and last model, constructed at the Sound Recording Institute in Moscow from about 1949 under Sholpo's supervision, magnetic tape was substituted for film as the storage medium; but this version was never finished. When the laboratory was closed in 1950 the instruments were declared non-functional and were discarded.

A similar approach to graphic sound, partly influenced by Sholpo's work, was pursued in the ANS graphic sound synthesizer developed in Moscow during the 1930s–50s by Evgeny Murzin.

BIBLIOGRAPHY

V. Solev: 'Synthetichesky Zvuk', *Kino* (Jul 31, 1935), 4

G. Anfilov: *Fizika i muzika* (Moscow, 1960, 2/1964); Eng. trans, as *Physics and Music* (Moscow, 1962).

A. Smirnov: *Sound in Z: Experiments in Sound and Electronic Music in Early 20th-century Russia* (London, 2013)

HUGH DAVIES/ANDREI SMIRNOV

Variophon (ii). Electronic wind synthesizer with breath controller, invented in the mid-1970s in the acoustics department of the Musicological Institute at the University of Cologne by Jobst Peter Fricke, Wolfgang Voigt, and Jürgen Schmitz (*b* Brühl, Germany, 12 April 1952). A prototype called the Martinetta was produced by Ernest Martin KG. The Variophon was developed by Schmitz in collaboration with Helmut Reuter in 1978, and manufactured from 1979 by Realton, a firm founded by Reuter in Euskirchen. It consists of a recorder-like tube mouthpiece, a 38-note keyboard and a separate control panel. To keep the circuitry secret, the circuit boards are encapsulated in epoxy resin. The mouthpiece and keyboard are differently combined in the various models; they can be attached to form a wind instrument held vertically, in which the narrow keyboard takes the place of conventional fingerholes and keys; or the two elements can be separate, in which case the monophonic keyboard console resembles a small electronic organ or piano accordion. The control panel includes four sockets (six on the professional model) into which a selection of plug-in cards can be inserted; on each of these are stored digitally the sounds of one of the principal orchestral woodwind and brass instruments, and there are also saxophone and panpipe modules. Any combination of modules can be used simultaneously, producing unison sounds; the professional model offers, in addition, the alternative of two lines moving in parallel, each line consisting of three voices of different timbre. The fundamental tuning of the instrument can be fixed, by means of an automatic transposition switch, in C, B♭ or E♭ (also F in the professional model). All traditional mouth articulations are effective and their impact can be adjusted electronically to suit individual modules. Glissando is also possible. Schmitz specialized as a performer on the Variophon. The original analogue algorithms were later transferred to a new digital platform in order to improve the sound production process. See M. Oehler and C. Reuter: 'Dynamic Excitation Impulse Modification as a Foundation of a Synthesis and Analysis System for Wind Instrument Sounds', *Mathematics and Computation in Music. First International Conference, MCM 2007* (Berlin, Heidelberg, New York, 2009), 189–97.

HUGH DAVIES/R

Varnish. Transparent coating applied to the surface of an object to enhance its appearance and provide protection. Typical historical varnishes are made from natural organic substances (resins, oils, dyes, etc.) and, in lesser amount, inorganic additives (driers, fillers, pigments, etc.). Varnishes can be classified by basic composition (e.g. oil varnish, spirit varnish) or function (ground varnish, colour varnish, protective varnish). With the term varnish, luthiers often mean the entire coating system, from the ground to the top layer. Opaque lacquers or coatings imitating East Asian lacquers are not addressed in this entry, which focuses on historical European string instrument varnishes.

Most wooden instruments are partially or totally covered with transparent coatings. Research has primarily been focused on varnishes for bowed and plucked instruments, while transparent finishes on keyboard and woodwind instruments have received little consideration. Formerly, it was assumed that varnishes on musical instruments must have had a special, even secret composition exerting a supposed acoustic influence on the instrument body. This assumption is unsubstantiated. On the contrary, the sources attest that the composition and function of coatings on lutes, guitars, violins, viols, etc. were not fundamentally different from varnishes and glazes on paintings or furniture. This does not mean that varnishes do not affect the sound of instruments, but providing shine, visual depth, colour, and protection of the wood seem to have been the most important roles of the varnish. Until the 18th century, the soundboards of instruments with a glued bridge (e.g. lutes, guitars, harpsichords) were kept unvarnished. It is even possible that until the 18th century instrument makers considered varnishes to have a deleterious acoustic effect, especially upon plucked instruments with gut strings.

Historical sources confirm that plucked and bowed instrument varnishes were (in most cases) made and applied by their makers. Since the Renaissance, two main types of varnish have been used: clear or red. Letters from the Venetian lute maker Moise Tieffenbrucker describe a singular invention of a new type of crimson red and green varnish (1580). This is the only indication that there were apparently also green varnishes. Red varnishes appear to have been held in high esteem. Correlations appear between the use of intensively red-tinted varnishes and wealthy instrument-making centres such as Venice, Cremona, Nuremburg, and Salzburg (particularly during times of economic prosperity), possibly because expensive dyestuffs were required to obtain an intense red colouration. In less exclusive production centres such as Milan, Naples, Mirecourt, Neukirchen, and Mittenwald, almost clear or goldish varnishes were normal. On contemporary paintings, string instruments are almost invariably depicted as either white or pale gold. It can therefore be assumed that red varnishes were much less common than colourless ones. As they age, natural resins and oils become increasingly dark and brittle, and colourant fades. Thus, the historical typology of colourless and red varnishes on old instruments is less apprehensible nowadays.

At least since the Renaissance, musicians and collectors have often preferred old plucked and bowed instruments over new ones. Natural appearances of aging, such as darkening and craquelure or wear and patina were appreciated because they indirectly contribute to the 'authenticity' and sense of value of the instrument. As early as the 17th century, lute and violin varnishes were (unlike varnishes on furniture and paintings) regarded as an integral part of the original instruments, hence worthy of preservation. As a result, most old violins retain at least part of their original varnish. Despite aging and frequent polishing of the original varnishes, the large number of extant violins of the 17th and 18th centuries allows recognition of distinctive varnishes from each lutherie centre. From the 19th century at the latest, varnishes on fine stringed instruments were regarded as a type of 'abstract paint layer' and, like easel paintings, were given a transparent final varnish or final polish to enhance and protect them.

'Classical' Italian varnishes, Cremonese in particular, became legendary and are still revered. They are characterized by an exceptionally luminous and profound golden or red colour on a particularly reflective golden ground, which enhances the wood structure. The ground layer is vital to the outstanding appearance of Italian instruments. There has been endless, often misleading speculation about the methods and materials used by the 17th and 18th century schools of Italian violin makers, of whom Antonio Stradivari is the most celebrated. In recent years multidisciplinary scientific investigations on a large group of instruments have obtained significant new findings. A two-layer system has been generally established: a ground layer that fills the upper wood cells, and the actual varnish. Italian instruments, from 16th-century lutes to Stradivari violins, reveal an oil-resin-based ground. Instruments from north of the Alps generally show a glue-based ground. Mineral particles have been largely ruled out as main constituents of the ground layer. The main specificity of the Italian varnish system might reside in the oily nature of the ground.

The actual varnish consists, before the mid-18th century, fundamentally of mixtures of drying oil and resins of the pine family. From a chemical perspective, the main differences among historical instrument varnishes (except the ground layer) reside in the colouring system. While Italian Renaissance lute makers and early luthiers from the north of the Alps coloured their red varnishes with soluble colourants or highly heated resins, Cremonese and Venetians luthiers of the 17th and 18th centuries used very fine crimson lake pigments. To achieve the vibrant optical effect of his famous red varnishes Stradivari mixed crimson lakes with finely ground red iron oxide or cinnabar particles. However, even with modern analytical methods, the exact composition of historical varnishes remains somewhat uncertain, although they were not specially formulated for instruments.

BIBLIOGRAPHY

E. Mailand: *Découverte des anciens vernis italiens employés pour les instruments à cordes et à archets* (Paris, 1859)

C. Reade: *A Lost Art Revived: Cremona Violins and Varnish* (Gloucester, 1873) [orig. pubd in *Pall Mall Gazette*]

G. Fry: *The Varnishes of the Italian Violin-Makers of the Sixteenth, Seventeenth and Eighteenth Centuries and their Influence on Tone* (London, 1904)

G.L. Baese: *Classic Italian Violin Varnish* (Fort Collins, CO, 1985)

S. Pollens: 'Historic Lute and Violin Varnishes', *Journal of the Violin Society of America*, vol.8/2 (1987), 31–40

E. Fontana, F. Hellwig, K. Martius: *Historische Lacke und Beizen auf Musikinstrumenten in deutschsprachigen Quellen bis 1900* (Nuremberg, 1999)

B.H. Tai: 'Stradivari's Varnish: A Review of Scientific Findings, Part I', *Journal of the Violin Society of America: VSA papers*, vol.21/1 (2007), 119–44

J.P. Echard, B. Lavédrine: 'Review on the Characterisation of Ancient Stringed Musical Instruments Varnishes and Implementation of an Analytical Strategy', *Journal of Cultural Heritage*, vol.9/4 (2008b), 420–9

B.H. Tai: 'Stradivari's Varnish: A Review of Scientific Findings, Part II', *Journal of the Violin Society of America: VSA papers*, vol.22/1 (2009), 60–90

J.P. Echard, B. Soulier: 'Stradivari's Varnish: a chemical analysis', *The Strad*, vol.121/1440 (April 2010), 48–51

T. Wilder, ed: *The Conservation, Restoration, and Repair of Stringed Instruments and Their Bows* (Montreal and London, 2010), vol. 1, 567–706

B. Soulier: 'Resonanzen vergessener Oberflächen: Lautenfirnisse der Renaissance Teil 1', *Zeitschrift für Kunsttechnologie und Konservierung*, vol.25/2 (2011), 324–38

BALTHAZAR SOULIER

Varpelis (pl. *varpeliai*; diminutive of *varpas*). Small clapper bell of Lithuania. It can be pear-shaped, conical, or cylindrical, and is usually made of metal, although bells of clay are also known. Archaeological finds confirm that from the 11th century such metal bells were attached to horse harnesses, sometimes with jingles. Into the 20th century metal varpeliai were hung on the necks of grazing farm animals. After both World Wars bells were often made from empty artillery shells. The varpelis was used in various rituals at Christmas and during Lent, at weddings, funerals, and so on. Until the mid-20th century potters used a clay bell in market places to attract customers. Small *varpeliai* were hung on roadside shrines (*stogastulpiai* or *koplytstulpiai*); known as *vejo varpeliai* ('wind-bells'), they were sounded by the wind, producing a quiet ringing. Likewise, suspended bars of wood rattled against one another in the wind.

ARVYDAS KARAŠKA/R

Vas Dias, Harry (*b* Amsterdam, Netherlands, 3 Jan 1924). American maker of historical oboes, of Dutch birth. His early education was in London. In 1940 vas Dias emigrated with his family to New York City. After serving with the Dutch East Indies air force during World War II, he returned to New York and studied oboe at Adelphi College with Lois Wann and with Harold Gomberg of the New York Philharmonic and the Juilliard School. He gained orchestral experience with the National Orchestral Association and took posts with numerous orchestras; while playing with the Birmingham Symphony (Alabama) in 1970–73, he first came into contact with the Baroque oboe through a visit from the ensemble Concentus Musicus of Vienna. He then studied with Paul Hailperin and Michel Piguet at the Baroque Performance Institute, Oberlin, Ohio. Hailperin, an American who had been working with Concentus and making oboes in Europe, encouraged vas Dias to develop his own designs after historical models.

In 1974 vas Dias stopped performing professionally in order to concentrate on oboe making. His first instruments were based on oboes by Jacob Denner and Thomas Stanesby Sr in New York collections. Vas Dias relocated to Decatur, Georgia, and by 2012 had made more than 450 oboes and oboes d'amore after some dozen 17th- and 18th-century designs. He makes instruments one at a time in his home workshop, taking about two weeks for each. He receives high praise for the finish of his oboes and his understanding of the acoustic properties of different woods. Notable performers who play his oboes include Marc Schachman (Aulos Ensemble) and John Abberger (American Bach Soloists and Tafelmusik). Vas Dias was one of the first to register the importance of Baroque oboe reed design, and published articles for the guidance of players. Craftsmen trained by him include Daniel Betsill and Dan Noonan.

BIBLIOGRAPHY

N. Post: 'Harry vas Dias: Baroque Oboe Maker', *The Double Reed*, vol.3/3 (1980)

H. Vas Dias: 'Making Reeds for the Baroque Oboe', *Journal of the International Double Reed Society*, vol.9 (1986); reprinted from 'Rohrbau für Barockoboen', *Tibia*, vol.2/80 (1980), 107–13

GEOFFREY BURGESS/R

Vatelot, Etienne (*b* Provins, France, 13 Nov 1925). French violin maker and restorer. He came from a long line of luthiers; his great-great-grandfather was a guitar maker. In 1942 he began training with his father, Marcel Vatelot, one of France's foremost luthiers, who opened his workshop in Paris in 1909. From there Etienne went in 1946 to learn to make new instruments under Amédée Dieudonné in Mirecourt, then in Massy Palaiseau with Victor Quenoil. He spent a few months in New York in 1949 before rejoining his father. In 1959 Marcel Vatelot handed over the business to his son, staying on as a consultant and making his almost daily contribution at the shop until his death, in September 1970. In the meantime Etienne Vatelot's skill, knowledge, and reputation continued to grow; he was president of the French Violin Makers' Society from 1966 to 1969, and was appointed to the Légion d'Honneur in 1972. Many other honours followed. In 1975 he founded the Vatelot Foundation to support disadvantaged apprentices. His opinion as an expert on old instruments has been widely sought and highly regarded, and he has also been especially noted for his expertise in tonal adjustments. He published the definitive work on French bows, *Les archets français* (Paris, 1976), whose detailed photographs (in colour) make it an invaluable study. In 1998 Vatelot turned over the operation of his shop to Jean-Jacques Rampal, the son of the flutist Jean-Pierre Rampal, who was a close friend. An international violin-making competition was named for Vatelot in 1991.

CHARLES BEARE/R

Vater, Christian (*b* Hanover, Germany, bap. 11 Oct 1679; *d* Hanover, Germany, 25 Jan 1756). German organ and harpsichord builder. He learned organ building from his father, Martin Vater. He is known to have worked for Arp Schnitger as journeyman in 1697 and 1700, and then set up on his own about 1702. He became organist to the court of the Elector of Hanover (later King George I of England) in 1708–9, and court organ builder in 1714. By 1716–17 he had to his credit 33 new or renovated organs. Most of his work was done in the electorate of Hanover, the bishopric of Osnabrück, and

the county of Oldenburg, but he also worked for the landgraves of Kassel and Darmstadt, and in Amsterdam he built a new organ for the Oude Kerk (1724–6) and rebuilt an instrument in the Westerkerk (1726). Like his brother Anton (1689–after 1759) in Paris, Christian Vater was in demand as a builder of harpsichords and clavichords. His son Johannes succeeded him as organ builder to the court of Hanover.

Organs by Vater survive at Bockhorn, Oldenburg (1722); Wiefelstede, Oldenburg (from 1729); St Nikolai, Gifhorn (1748); and Hohenrode, near Bad Hersfeld (built for Gestorf, 1749). Surviving cases are to be found at Wathlingen (1707), Melle, near Osnabrück (from 1722), Riessen (1738), Zeven (1750), and elsewhere. Vater's Amsterdam organ, which was substantially altered and enlarged as early as 1738 by Johann Caspar Müller—probably a brother or cousin of Christian Müller—now contains only a few ranks of pipes by Vater. He built slider chests, having no appreciation for the spring chest. His instruments, with their well-balanced specifications, are typical of the late Baroque organ in northern Germany.

A single-manual harpsichord by Christian Vater is in the Germanisches Nationalmuseum, Nuremberg. It has two 8′ registers, a short-octave compass of G'/B'-e''', and a double bentside. Although its rose is inscribed 'MARTINVS VATER/ORGEL VND INSTRVM MACHER M.F. HANNOVER', it is signed 'Christian Vater/Hannover 1738/in December/Nr 193' under the soundboard. Replicas of this instrument have been made by Alberto Cozani, Matthias Griewisch, Bruce Kennedy, Andrea Restelli, and other modern builders. It was also the basis for certain harpsichord kits manufactured by Zuckermann Harpsichord International.

Anton Vater settled in Paris in 1715; several harpsichords dating from the 1730s have been ascribed to him.

BIBLIOGRAPHY

R. Skupnik: *Der hannoversche Orgelbauer Christian Vater, 1679–1756* (Kassel, 1976)

D.H. Boalch: *Makers of the Harpsichord and Clavichord 1440–1840* (Oxford, 3/1995)

HANS KLOTZ/R

Vaucanson, Jacques de (*b* Grenoble, France, 24 Feb 1709; *d* Paris, France, 21 Nov 1782). French inventor of musical automata. As a child he showed a talent for making clocks. After receiving a Jesuit education, he joined the order of Minims. He then studied anatomy under the surgeon Claude-Nicolas Le Cat and was encouraged by another surgeon, François Quesnay, in the building of automata to demonstrate the physiology of living creatures. Seeking to study human breathing, Vaucanson began in 1733 to build his automated flute player (*fluteur automate*). He completed the life-size figure, outwardly modelled on a marble statue by Charles Antoine Coysevox in the Tuileries gardens, in 1738. An array of nine crank-driven bellows powered a variable blowing mechanism, allowing the automaton to play a transverse flute with expressive articulations and dynamics. A separate system of cords, chains, axles, and pulleys, driven by a pegged cylinder and levers, moved the android's leather-covered fingers to stop the toneholes. The two mechanisms were powered by a weight.

Observers reported that the automaton played 11 (or 12 or 14) tunes 'like a master'. In a dissertation presented to the Royal Academy of Sciences, Vaucanson characterized the flute player as an acoustical experiment testing the influence on pitch of blowing pressure, shape of the oral aperture, and the flute's sounding length. The academy acknowledged his achievement and allowed him to add the particle 'de' to his name.

Later in 1738, Vaucanson created two more automata: an eating, digesting, and defecating duck; and the *joueur de tambourin*, an android dressed as a Provençal shepherd, which played 20 tunes on the 'flageolet provençal' and 'tambour de Marseille' (pipe and tabor). Vaucanson noted that the tabor pipe was dependent on finely differentiated blowing pressures to produce its overblown registers, and that finely coordinated and rapid 'tonguing' was required. After exhibiting the three automata in Paris, Vaucanson exhibited them on a tour through France and Italy. In 1743 he sold them to an entrepreneur from Lyon, who continued the exhibition tours throughout Europe during the 1740s. The three automata have not survived, but they are described in Vaucanson's pamphlet (1738). Vaucanson later turned his attention to the automation of weaving; his automated loom of 1747, now at the Musée des arts et metiers, Paris, was an important precursor of the Jacquard loom.

BIBLIOGRAPHY
J. Vaucanson: *Le mécanisme du fluteur automate* (Paris, 1738/R Paris, 1985; R and Eng. trans., Buren, 1979)
A. Doyon and L. Liaigre: *Jacques Vaucanson, mécanicien de genie* (Paris, 1967)
J. Riskin: 'The Defecating Duck, or, The Ambiguous Origins of Artifical Life', *Critical Inquiry*, vol.29/4 (2003), 599–633

JAMES B. KOPP

Vaudry. French family of harpsichord makers. While they apparently flourished in Paris for at least two generations, only Jean-Antoine Vaudry (*b* c1680; *d* 1750) has been confirmed as a harpsichord maker. He lived in the rue St Jacques, but otherwise nothing is known of him. A document of 1718 names a Vaudry as 'maître seul faiseur d'instruments de musique du Roi', indicating that he made instruments for the French court. The only extant Vaudry instrument, a double-manual harpsichord (at *GB.L.v*), has the inscription 'Vaudry a Paris 1681' on the underside of the soundboard and was likely made by an older relative of Jean-Antoine. This instrument was supposedly owned by the Duchesse du Maine, who reportedly had the underside of the lid decorated to match the room where she kept it in the Château Savigny-les-Beaunes after 1718. Rebuilt several times and at some point fitted with an organ beneath its case, the instrument was restored in the mid-1970s by Derek Adlam. The crude painting on the lid underside contrasts with the chinoiserie decoration on the case sides, based

on engravings by Jacques Stella and finely executed in gold, silver, and bronze on a black background. The harpsichord has fairly thin case walls of walnut, 8′ + 8′ + 4′ disposition, G′/B′-c‴ compass (extended in the 18th century but restored to 50 notes), a shove coupler, two hand stops, and a short scaling indicating it was tuned to *a*′ = 392 Hz. Its distinctive complex soundboard ribbing has 11 light ribs distributed about the board and crossing under the 8′ and 4′ bridges. Replicas have been made by Nikolaus Damm, Owen Daly, Kevin Fryer, Andrew Garlick, and others. See D.H. Boalch: *Makers of the Harpsichord and Clavichord 1440–1840* (Oxford, 3/1995).

ANNE BEETEM ACKER

Vega. American firm of instrument makers. It was established in Boston in 1889 by Carl and Julius Nelson, John Palm, and John Swenson. Initially the firm produced guitars and mandolins as well as a few zithers and bandurrias. In 1898 it was consolidated with the Standard Band Instrument Co., formerly owned by Thompson and Odell, also of Boston; this resulted in the addition of brass instruments (excluding french and bass horns) to Vega's production. The firm of A.C. Fairbanks, noted for its high-quality banjos, was acquired in 1903 or 1904. By the 1930s Vega had produced more than 96,000 banjos, 40,000 guitars, 40,000 mandolins, and 30,000 trumpets, gaining a high reputation for its banjos, particularly up to 1937 and for the Whyte Laydie, Tubaphone, and Vox models. In 1970 Vega was bought by C.F. Martin, which in 1971 moved production to its plant in Nazareth, Pennsylvania, and also sold some imported instruments under the Vega brand. In 1979 Martin sold Vega to the Galaxy Trading Corp., an Asian conglomerate with offices in Santa Fe Springs, California, and production moved to Korea. 'Vega' banjos, bearing little resemblance to the classic Vega instruments, were also made in Japan. In 1989 the Deering Banjo Company of Spring Valley, California, purchased the Vega name from Galaxy and resumed domestic production of Vega banjos as a high-end line. In 1998 Martin included a Deering-made Vega banjo in its so-called Kingston Trio set, which included two guitars.

JAMES BOLLMAN/ARIAN SHEETS/R

Veit [Veith], **Huns** [Hanß] (*b* c1600/10; bur. Naumburg, Germany, 20 Dec 1661). German brass instrument maker and tower musician, presumably a son of Rudolf (Rudloff) Veith, a tower musician from Wanßleben, who became a Naumburg citizen in 1601. A trombone signed by Rudolf was at the Musikinstrumenten-Museum, Berlin, in 1922; parts of its slide survive there. Two of Huns's trumpets survive, dated 1646 and 1651 (*D.B.im*). The latter, pitched in modern E♭, is the only known pre-19th-century slide trumpet (*tromba da tirarsi*). It is of the Renaissance type, its bell has an early Baroque flare, and its slide—which was lost during World War II but had been measured—was nearly 56 cm long. It might be one of the 'two brand-new slide trumpets' listed in an inventory of 1658 from St Wenzel, Naumburg, whence it came to the Musikinstrumenten-Museum in 1890. Huns's son Johann Christoph Veith (*b* Naumburg, 27 April 1629; *d* Naumburg, 21 Dec 1690) was his successor; he was both a wirepuller and trumpet-maker.

BIBLIOGRAPHY

K. Restle: 'Die Naumburger Blasinstrumente im Berliner Musikinstrumenten–Museum', *Saale-Unstrut-Jahrbuch*, vol.3 (1998), 61–72

G. Dullat: *Verzeichnis der Holz- und Metallblasinstrumentmacher auf deutschsprachigem Gebiet* (Tutzing, 2010)

EDWARD H. TARR

Vejiga (Sp.: 'bladder'). Inflated animal bladder used as a percussion instrument in Panama and Puerto Rico. The bladder, usually that of a pig or cow, about 20 to 30 cm in diameter, is struck with a stick to provide rhythmic accompaniment to the music and movements of the 'little devil' street dancers. It may be worn as part of a dancer's costume. In the *gran diablos* ('big devils') ceremony the sound of the instrument symbolically mimics the fight between good and evil.

In Loiza, Puerto Rico, at the *Fiestas de Santiago Apostol* ('St James festival'), a popular street character is called the *Vejigante*, named for the vejiga made from an inflated cow's bladder that he carries. He represents the Moors in the battle between good and evil. While the primary purpose of the bladder is as a rhythmic instrument, the character will sometimes chase children and hit them with it to knock off evil spirits.

J. RICHARD HAEFER

Velviool. Dutch name for an imitation of a violin, with leather body, made by a San in southern Africa about 1880. The *tamboer* is a similar Dutch-named imitation but made of wood and goatskin by a Griqua (Khoikhoi), also in the 19th century. See P.R. Kirby: *The Musical Instruments of the Native Races of South Africa* (London, 1934, 2/1965), 246 and pl.71*a*.

Vena [venava, rāvaṇa vīṇā]. Long-necked spike fiddle of Sri Lanka, now obsolete. The form *vena* is Sinhalese; *venava* and *rāvaṇa vīṇā* are Sanskrit. The instrument had two strings, a coconut-shell body, and a wooden neck, and the bow sometimes had jingles attached to one end. The fiddle is depicted in many temple paintings and woodcarvings, but was very probably an importation from India, as its name suggests. It was particularly associated with the court of King Vīra Parākrama Narendrasiṃha, who reigned in the early 18th century and whose three Indian wives probably brought musicians with them from their native Kerala.

NATALIE M. WEBBER

Vent. (1) (Fr.) Wind, as in *instruments à vent*, wind instruments.

(2) Unstopped side hole of a wind instrument; it determines the effective sounding length of the air column. The highest tone hole open when a given pitch is fingered is called the 'primary vent' for that pitch. A 'register vent' (also called 'register hole' or 'octave vent')

is used to cause the pitch to jump to a higher octave (in a conical tube) or 12th (in a cylindrical tube). Shawms and some other woodwinds sometimes have uncloseable vents drilled near the bell to enhance timbre and pitch stability.

(3) Ventil (Ger.; It. *ventile*) means a valve. A *Ventilhorn* is a valve horn. In a pipe organ, a ventil turns on or off the wind supply to a windchest, allowing a combination of stops on that chest to be drawn in advance and sounded or silenced as a unit, by means of a pedal (hence 'combination pedal') or hand lever controlling the ventil.

Ventapane, Lorenzo (*fl c*1800–*c*1843). Italian violin maker. His instruments date from soon after 1800 until after 1830. It seems certain that he was a pupil of one of the Gaglianos, possibly of Giovanni, or of his son, Nicola Gagliano (ii), whose work his own very much resembles. In the varnish and in many details Ventapane's instruments are nearly identical to those made by the Gaglianos, usually being distinguished by a certain flatness towards the edges, where a Gagliano would often be rather full in model. His peg placement, use of paper in purfling, and rather vertical soundholes look typically Neapolitan. Like the later members of the Gagliano family, Ventapane was variable in the quality of his work. Visually some of his instruments are dull, even crude, though others are attractive and carefully made; all, when well adjusted, have that Neapolitan character of tone which makes Ventapane an important name among players. He is one of the best-known Neapolitan violin makers outside the Gagliano family.

Less significant makers named Vincenzo Ventapane (*fl* 1750–1800) and Pasquale Ventapane (*fl* 1860; said to be Lorenzo's brother) also worked in Naples.

CHARLES BEARE/R

Ventura, Angelo Benedetto (*b c*1781; *d* 1856). Italian instrument inventor, composer, and teacher. He worked in London from at least 1813. He taught Princess Augusta Charlotte from that year until her death in 1817. This opportunity, and an early partnership with Edward Light, enabled him to create and market several hybrid harp-lute-guitars, for which he gave lessons and published simple song arrangements and 16- or 32-bar compositions. His most important invention was the Harp Ventura, patented in 1828, a 17- to 19-string harp-lute, measuring about 83 x 33 x 13 cm, and tuned to an open C chord with descending diatonics. This was perhaps the most flexible harp-lute for song accompaniments with awkward modulations, or in unusual keys. Its seven pushstops (later levers) raised the open strings by a semitone, using forks similar to Erard's single-action harp *fourchettes* of the 1780s.

Ventura's other inventions were the single-finger-board 12-string Imperial *Otavino*; the 13- or 14-string Imperial Harp-Lute (first announced in 1813); the Imperial Lyre with 12 strings; and the Ventura Guitar, with a tone-altering mechanism incorporated into the six-string neck and a long, floating seventh string with chromatic sharping levers, patented in 1828. At the 1851 Great Exhibition in London, Ventura displayed five instruments, four of them new: the New British Ventura, a shield-shaped guitar-type instrument with nine single strings; the New English Cetra, 'an improvement on the old Spanish guitar', with six strings and much altered body shape; the Venturina, a small four-string guitar; and the Lyre Ventura, a small instrument with 12 strings arranged in six double courses and played with a plectrum (also perhaps known as a mandolin-lute). Of his previous inventions, only the Harp Ventura was represented.

All of Ventura's instruments appear to have been intended mainly for such elegant ladies as those to whom his compositions are liberally dedicated.

BIBLIOGRAPHY

R.B. Armstrong: *Musical Instruments*, pt.2 (Edinburgh, 1908)

S. Bonner: *Angelo Benedetto Ventura* (Harlow, 1971)

STEPHEN BONNER/GREGG MINER

Verdalonga, José (*b* Guadalajara, Spain; *fl* late 18th century and early 19th). Spanish organ builder. Little is known of his activity, but he must have been of considerable importance, judging by the organs that he either built or repaired. In 1796–7 he constructed an organ for Toledo Cathedral, with enclosed and unenclosed reeds from 32′ to 2′ and two small pedalboards; he also built instruments for the cathedral of S Isidro in Madrid and Soria Cathedral. At the beginning of the 19th century he rebuilt and modified the two organs in the choir at El Escorial, and restored the 'Emperor's' organ in Toledo Cathedral. His work as an organ builder was carried on by his son and pupil, Valentín (who worked with him in Toledo), and his son-in-law Leandro Garcimartín, reputedly the last great organ builder of his period in central Spain. Valentine Verdalonga's large organ for Seville Cathedral (1825) was destroyed in an earthquake in 1888. See A. Justo Estebaranz: 'Valentín Verdalonga y sus órganos en Sevilla y Cádiz a comienzos del siglo XIX', *Laboratorio de Arte*, no.18 (2005), 455–64.

JOSÉ LÓPEZ-CALO/R

Vermeij, Koen (*b* Haarlem, Netherlands, 24 Feb 1942). Dutch clavichord builder and researcher active in Aerdenhout. He was educated at the choristers' school of St Bavo Cathedral in Haarlem and at the Amsterdam Conservatory, where he studied music education and the recorder (1962–69). He built his first clavichord as a hobby in 1960 and assembled three from kits. He began building clavichords from technical drawings in 1976 while teaching school music at the Sweelinck Conservatory in Amsterdam (1970–95) and directing a chamber choir that he founded in 1972. Between 1978 and 2011 (the first four years working with Jan Oudshoorn, then alone) Vermeij produced 56 clavichords, three of them after the 1763 Hass (*GB.E.u*) but mainly after designs of Christian Gottlob Hubert. In 1985 he began research on all extant Hubert instruments, resulting in *The Hubert Clavichord Data Book*, and in 1999 he restored the 1772

Hubert clavichord (University of Freiburg, on loan to *D.BKZ.st*). His studies led to a series of important publications on Hubert's clavichords, which give detailed insight to Hubert's construction methods and contributed to the popularity of his designs among modern copyists and performers; these publications also set a high standard for documentation. Vermeij was a co-founder of the Nederlands Clavichord Genootschap (1987) and editor of its journal, *Het Clavichord* (1988–96) and initiated and edited the succeeding journal *Clavichord International* (1997–2003). He has also performed on the clavichord and taught both amateur and professional instrument builders, including Sander Ruys. Since 2002 Vermeij has studied watchmaking and focused on restoring old timepieces.

WRITINGS

Tuning & Maintenance of the Clavichord (Amsterdam, 1992)

'A Contribution to Dating Hubert Clavichords', *De Clavichordio I, Proceedings of the International Clavichord Symposium 1993*, ed. B. Brauchli and others (Turin, 1994), 171–8

'Eighteenth–century Lovers of the Clavichord, Which Makers did They Prefer?', *De Clavichordio II, Proceedings of the International Clavichord Symposium 1995*, ed. B. Brauchli and others (Turin, 1996), 105–14

with L. Bemmann: 'Vom Anonymus zum Hubert Heidelbergiensis/or a New–Found Hubert Clavichord', *Clavichord International* vol.2/2 (Nov 1998), 56–9

'In Praise of the Five–octave Fretted Clavichord', *De Clavichordio III, Proceedings of the International Clavichord Symposium 1997*, ed. B. Brauchli and others (Turin, 1998), 47–51

The Hubert Clavichord Data Book (Bennebroek, 2000)

'Keylever Tail Width as a Tool for Assigning Keyboard Instruments', *GSJ*, vol.56 (2003), 175–80 (on Hubert's keyboard proportions)

Korte geschiedenis van het clavichord (Aerdenhout, 2007, English trans. 2012)

'Christian Gottlob Hubert's Workshop and the Tafelklavier', *De Clavichordio IX, Proceedings of the International Clavichord Symposium 2009*, ed. B. Brauchli and others (Magnano, 2010), 131–49

LAURENCE LIBIN

Vermeulen flute. Slide-operated flute developed from 1965 by Greta Vermeulen, Dutch flutist, and computer specialist at the Institute of Sonology at the University of Utrecht. It was designed particularly for use in contemporary music. The instrument, which is held vertically, has two concentric cylindrical tubes, the inner one of brass, the outer one of stainless steel; these operate on the principle of the slide trombone, and there are no keys or fingerholes. The ebonite top joint is T-shaped and includes the mouthpiece, which is based on that of the transverse flute but has no lip-plate. The range is *c′* to *a‴* (rather narrower than that of the normal flute), with a much softer fundamental range of a major 6th upwards from *c′*.

Several models of the Vermeulen flute have been built: the first (transverse with three concentric tubes) was constructed by A. Hessing of Deventer in 1965; the second (vertical with two tubes) in 1972 at the Technical University in Delft; and the third by P. van Swol of Van Doorn in De Bilt in 1973. An instrument with a narrower bore, built in 1979, proved unsatisfactory. Additions include a built-in microphone, and a mute (1975) in the form of a cap for the lower end, which converts the instrument into a closed pipe and adds a 4th to the range above and below the normal compass; only odd-numbered harmonics are possible with the mute. Several compositions for the Vermeulen flute have been written by Dutch composers.

BIBLIOGRAPHY

G. Vermeulen: 'Report on the Vermeulen Flute', *Sonorum speculum* no.56 (1974), 22–35 [parallel Eng. and Ger. text]

G. Vermeulen: 'Pitch Problems of a Performer', *Interface*, vol.14/1–2 (1985), 109–24

HUGH DAVIES

Verschueren. Dutch firm of organ builders. Leonard (Léon) Hubert Verschueren (1866–1957) trained as a cabinetmaker with the firm of Maarschalkerweerd in Utrecht (1886–90) before founding a pipe-making workshop in his native village of Heythuysen, Limburg, on 5 May 1891. Within a few years he was supplying more than 30 organ builders at home and abroad with pipes and parts. In 1896 he built his first entirely new organ, a one-manual mechanical-action instrument for the Hervormde Noordkerk, Schagen (later removed to Oudesluis). After 1904 Léon developed the business with South German organ builder Max Bittner (*d* 1955), making all parts in-house (a rarity at the time). Tonally their instruments blended South Dutch, Walloon, Rhineland, and, through Bittner, South German styles. Actions were pneumatic (a well-preserved example from 1929 is in the Petruskerk, Gulpen).

Verschueren was very struck by the Klais organ in the abbey of Rolduc, which was built in accordance with the principles of the *Orgelbewegung*. In response he changed his design for the new instrument at St Dyonisius, Schinnen, adopting electropneumatic cone chests and a neo-Baroque specification. His *magnum opus*, for the Catharinakerk, Eindhoven (1936, restored 1990; main and altar organ, 71 stops), remains the most important organ of this type in the Netherlands. He maintained this style of building into the 1950s.

In the mid-1930s the firm was joined by Léon's sons Léon Gerard Joseph (1903–86) who later became its director, George Emile (1909–85) who ran the Tongeren (Belgium) branch from 1937 (which became independent in 1951 and closed in 1998), and Frans Joseph Jacques (1914–86), who after training with the Kuhn firm in Männedorf headed the pipeshop and voicing department. In 1946, another son, Antoine Henri Joseph (1911–72) joined as administrator. During the post-war period the firm's production of new organs reached its height. Instruments, some still employing electric action, were exported to the USA and Japan. *Rugwerk* divisions were introduced in 1948, and the firm's first tracker-action organ was made in 1953. From 1948 to 1969, Henri Grados, who had trained with Cavaillé-Coll-Convers, worked part-time on reed voicing and taught younger voicers.

About 1970 Willem Talsma and Hans van der Harst led the firm into the historically informed organ building movement. Under Leonard (Léon) Francis Maria Verschueren (*b* 1947), son of Frans Joseph Jacques and managing director from 1977, the firm set about rethinking its methods, using fine instruments of the past as exemplars. Among the most important instruments is the organ built at the Lambertuskerk, Wouw (1984), which is rooted in the 17th- and 18th-century Hollandic tradition. From the mid-1980s Verschueren continued to build new instruments along historically informed lines, as well as restoring and reconstructing old organs with great success. On its centenary in 1991 Queen Beatrix bestowed upon the firm the title *Hofleverancier* (purveyor to the court). During the late 1990s the firm was chosen to restore the large three-manual Hagerbeer organ in the Pieterskerk, Leiden, to its 1643 condition, a project of international importance and the largest historical organ tuned in meantone in the Netherlands. At the close of the 20th century the firm boasted 28 employees, shipping pipes to the USA and organs to locations across Europe and North America. In 2004, Leonard Francis was knighted by Queen Beatrix in recognition of his work. By 2011 the firm's opus list (including restorations) had exceeded 1,100 instruments.

BIBLIOGRAPHY

J. Jongepier: 'De restauratie van het orgel in de St.–Cathrien te Eindhoven', *Het Orgel*, vol.88 (1992), 20–6

P. van Dijk: 'Continuiteit en ontwikkeling: recent werk van Verschueren Orgelbouw', *Het orgel*, vol.91 (1995), 133–41

P. van Dijk: 'Hundert Jahre Verschueren Orgelbouw betrachtet aus niederländischer Perspektive', *ISO News*, vol.9 (1995), 25–36

ADRI DE GROOT/R

Vessel flute. Aerophone in which the body of the pipe is globular or vessel-shaped rather than tubular. The best-known example is the ocarina. Vessel flutes date back to remote antiquity. Most vessel flutes have fingerholes; where they do, the action of opening them raises the pitch irrespective of the order in which the holes are opened; the change in pitch is related solely to the sizes of the apertures. Where there is only one fingerhole the instrument is referred to as a vessel whistle.

An early type of vessel flute is the *xun* of the Han Chinese, which was made of baked clay and usually had five fingerholes (or more in later examples). In ancient Egypt vessel flutes made from a gourd or a hollowed coconut were regarded as possessing magic powers. Pre-Columbian vessel flutes have been found in Guatemala; they are regarded as sacred and powerful and might have been used during shamanic curing. In Peru during the 14th century and early 15th, the Chancay of the central coast produced vessel flutes. Chroniclers report that the Chibcha Indians played such instruments at the time of first European contact. Vessel flutes are played by the Iawa and Bora peoples in the Peruvian tropical forest region, where they are made of beeswax or clay; they are also used in Colombia, sometimes in the *chirimía* ensemble, in Panama (where they are played by Guaymi Indians), and Costa Rica. In Africa, vessel flutes are mainly made from gourds and fruit shells; the same is true of Oceania. In North America, gourd vessel flutes of American Indians are found in certain east coast regions. In Europe, where the modern ocarina was invented about 1860 in Italy, older clay vessel flutes have long been popular

Vessel flute. Russian folk ocarina in the shape of a cow, with the duct in the tail and two fingerholes on each side of the body. (Jeremy Montagu Collection, Oxford)

as folk instruments; in Romania, for example, ovoid or carrot-shaped instruments with ten fingerholes as well as zoomorphic instruments with fewer are made. Small vessel flutes with several fingerholes, sometimes suspended from a cord around the neck, are widely popular craft items.

Another type of vessel flute is the whistling pot.

Vessel rattle. Term used in the Hornbostel–Sachs classification for an indirectly struck idiophone in which internal or external objects strike either against each other, the vessel's walls, or usually both. The vessel can be natural or artificial, and the pellets natural inclusions such as dried seeds (as in a gourd), or inserted objects. Those vessels with rattling objects affixed to an external net slipped over the surface are also classified as vessel rattles.

Veuze. Bagpipe of southeastern Brittany and the northern Vendée, especially around Nantes, the Guérande peninsula, and Basse-Vilaine, France. Said to be the oldest Breton bagpipe, it is documented from the 16th century. It consists of a long double-reed chanter (*levriad*) with six fingerholes, one thumbhole and a pair of unstopped holes near the base, a single-reed shoulder drone or drones (*bourdon*) usually in three segments, a short blowpipe (*sutell*), and a bag (*poche*). The chanter is usually pitched in C or D, occasionally in A, B♭, or G. Distinct from the *biniou*, and still in use until about 1940, the *veuze* was later revived.

CLAUDIE MARCEL-DUBOIS/R

Vevlira [hjulgiga, lyra, lira, lirepilk]. Swedish hurdy-gurdy. It is shaped like an oblong box, the sides of the lower part rounded and slightly narrowing at the upper end. The back is flat, the top flat or slightly arched, with a one-piece frame. Extant examples have 12 to 19 keys and two drone strings. Only a few are known and the instrument is sparsely documented in historical sources. According to folklore records, it was still to be found on the island of Gotland during the 19th century. Like other old folk instruments, it is now enjoying a revival among younger musicians in Sweden. See B. Kjellström: 'Om folkliga instrument', *Folkmusikboken*, vol.1, ed. J. Ling, M. Ramsten, and G. Ternhag (Stockholm, 1980), 158–211.

BIRGIT KJELLSTRÖM

Viaule. Guitar of Sri Lanka with 13 strings and a narrow body, now obsolete. Its name and construction point to its Portuguese origins, and it was used exclusively by the artisans of Ceylonese-Portuguese extraction to accompany popular dancing and song. See C.M. Fernando: 'The Music of Ceylon', *Journal of the Royal Asiatic Society, Ceylon Branch*, vol.13/45 (1894), 183–189, esp. 183.

NATALIE M. WEBBER

Vibraphone [vibraharp]. Tuned metallophone of the bar percussion family, similar in appearance to the xylophone. Developed in the USA in the early 20th century, it is often used in jazz ensembles, has become integral in percussion ensembles, and is occasionally required in orchestral and chamber music. Commonly known as the 'vibes', it produces sounds through vibrations of metal bars amplified by a special type of tube resonator, or electronically, producing a pulsating tone. The bars (an alloy), which are arranged keyboard-fashion, are suspended on cords at their nodal points. They are (in contrast to the raised mounting of the bars of the normal orchestral xylophone) level-mounted to facilitate the use of three or more mallets. Yarn-wound rubber mallets are normally used. The usual range of the vibraphone is three octaves (*f–f‴*). The instrument has a clean, bell-like tone of long duration, and is equipped with a sustain/damper pedal operated by the player. The instrument's outstanding feature is its unique vibrato. In the tube-resonated model this is obtained by the repeated opening and closing of the upper (open) ends of the resonators by means of revolving vanes (flat metal discs). The vanes are attached to a spindle that is driven by an electrical motor mechanism. The repeated breaking up of the sound causes it to emerge in a series of pulsations, the speed of which is governed by adjusting the revolution rate of the spindle. When no vibrato is desired the vanes are set to rest in a vertical position, leaving the resonators fully open.

The desire for the extraordinary in early 20th-century vaudeville shows was probably responsible for the introduction of the vibraphone to the percussion section as a novelty sound. In 1916, Hermann Winterhoff of the Leedy Manufacturing Company applied a mechanical vibrato to a 'steel marimba' in which a human-voice-like effect was produced by lowering and raising the tubular resonating chambers by means of a motor-driven apparatus. In 1921 a development of the original principle was applied, whereby the vibrato was obtained by opening and closing the upper (open) ends of the resonators by means of revolving discs. By the mid-1920s the vibraphone was an integral part of the jazz dance orchestra. In 1927, J.C. Deagan & Co. made improvements to the Leedy instrument, making the bars of aluminium instead of steel, refining their tuning to make a smoother sound, and introducing a pedal-controlled damper to control the sustain. The Deagan design became the template for later instruments; prominent vibraphone manufacturers in the early 21st century include Adams, Deagan, Musser, Premier, Ross, and Yamaha. These instruments all include vibrato control knobs. Experiments with electronic amplification resulted in such instruments as the Deagan ElectraVibe, released in the early 1970s, where no tube resonators are used, each bar being individually fitted with a pickup transducer.

Some years elapsed before the vibraphone was frequently employed in classical compositions, Darius Milhaud being one of the first to score for the vibraphone in *L'annonce faite à Marie* in 1933. There are challenging vibraphone parts in Pierre Boulez's *Le marteau sans maître* (rev. 1957), Gunther Schuller's *Seven Studies on a Theme of Paul Klee* (1959), Milhaud's *Concerto for Marimba and Vibraphone* (transcribed in 1947 from his *Suite for Piano and Orchestra*), and Toru Takemitsu's *Raintree* (1981); Steve Reich has used vibraphones and other mallet instruments in a number of works, including *Mallet Quartet* (2009); percussionist Bob Becker has also featured the instrument in compositions for keyboard percussion ensemble. The vibraphone has been most commonly used as a featured instrument in jazz by such virtuoso performers as Red Norvo, Lionel Hampton, Bobby Hutcherson, Milt Jackson, Gary Burton, David Friedman, Dave Samuels, Joe Locke, and Stefon Harris. The instrument is frequently used with its vanes stationary (with the motor off) and is played with a deft four-mallet technique (two mallets in each hand) that includes hand, finger, and mallet dampening.

BIBLIOGRAPHY

J. Blades: *Percussion Instruments and their History* (London, 1970, 3/1984)

A. Clark: *Jazz Styles and Analysis: Vibes* (Chicago, 1980)

R. Cook: *The Complete History of the Leedy Drum Company* (Anaheim, 1993)

JAMES BLADES/THOMAS BRETT/R

Vibra-slap. Rattle consisting of a trapezoidal, open-ended wooden box enclosing a frame of loosely held metal slugs or pins, to which is attached a roughly U-shaped, flexible metal rod handle bearing a wooden ball at the other end. The player holds the bent rod in the middle and strikes the ball with the palm of the other hand; the vibrations of the rod activate the rattling pins to produce a sound that quickly dies away. The vibra-slap

was invented by the American musician and engineer Martin Cohen in an effort to imitate the sound of the jawbone rattle. The vibra-slap has been widely used by Latin American bands and in film scores and pop music since the 1970s. It is manufactured by Latin Percussion, the company Cohen founded in his garage in 1964 (owned since 2002 by the Kaman Music Corporation). In 2006 Cohen was honoured by the Percussion Arts Society for creating the world's largest percussion instrument company and for his innovations.

HUGH DAVIES/R

Vibrato (It., from Lat. *vibrare*: 'to shake'). Regular fluctuation of pitch or intensity (or both), either more or less pronounced and more or less rapid; it can be regarded as both an ornament and a technique of tone production. This article is concerned only with Western art music, though vibrato is important in the musics of many different cultures. The Italian term 'tremolo' is also occasionally used for vocal vibrato. Terminology used in music was not standardized until the 20th century; earlier terms, primarily applied to vocal vibrato, include: *flattement, flatté, balancement, balancé, plainte, langueur, verre cassé; tremolo, tremolo sforzato, ardire, trilletto; Bebung, Schwebung*; and sweetening, depending on the effect wanted or technique used. Terminological uncertainties arise because vibrato can be regarded as a complex of 'quivering' ornaments which might be modified in performance depending on the desired expression or the emotion to be aroused. Neither intensity nor tempo, therefore, can be clearly determined, and many Baroque or Classical kinds of vibrato are only distantly related to our present concept. 'Wobble' (exaggerated, slow or irregular vibration of the singing voice) is a technical fault, and not to be regarded as vibrato.

Vibrato as a device can be found throughout Western music with descriptions dating from early medieval sources to the present day, but the techniques have varied. Historical descriptions are often vague and do not make clear how the vibrato was actually produced, but it seems always to have been accepted as an ornament until the first quarter of the 20th century, when its continuous use gradually became the norm.

1. Techniques. 2. Measured vibrato. 3. History.

1. TECHNIQUES. On string instruments vibrato is produced by moving the finger on the string backwards and forwards, aided by the wrist and sometimes by the forearm. On fretted string instruments such as viols 'two-finger' vibrato (also known as the close shake or *langueur*) was used, the first finger being placed firmly on the string and the second making a trilling movement near to it, thus creating an undulation of about an eighth- to a quarter-tone. Only with the little finger was a 'normal' vibrato comparable to modern practice allowed as a substitute for the usual technique (sources in England and France agree on the subject). German violin sources of the late 17th century and the 18th also

describe a vibrato produced without the usual rocking movements of the finger; here too, a slight beating of the string in a trill-like movement without altogether leaving it is described (Petri suggests combining this technique with the inward and outward movement of the finger, thus actually describing the changes in finger pressure explained by Tartini and Leopold Mozart in their tutors). Two-finger vibrato on the violin (the 'Gypsy trill') is not mentioned explicitly. One unclear passage in Mersenne could point to it, but more likely a beat (mordent) is meant; Tartini refers to it in passing. Rocking of the fingers has always been the usual technique for producing vibrato on string instruments of the violin family. The amount of wrist or arm movement differs according to different schools of violin playing.

On plucked instruments the same device (known variously in history as tremolo, *tremolo sforzato, verre cassé, soupir, mordant*) is found. The lower strings of the lute, however, demand a stronger movement: here the string is pulled back and forth (indicated by the same symbol as the mordent; on higher strings the vibrato is indicated by <).

On wind instruments during the 17th and 18th centuries vibrato was normally produced by a trill-like movement (usually made with stiff fingers) over a hole some distance from the ones covered, thus producing a very slight fluctuation in pitch. Breath vibrato is described early in the 16th century but seems to have been abandoned because of its bad effect on breathing technique. The *flattement* (sweetening, *Bebung* or *Klopfen*) was in use throughout the 17th and 18th centuries and at the beginning of the 19th. There was some experimenting in the second half of the 18th century, resulting, for example, in Lusse's rolling of the flute to produce a vibrato by slight changes of the embouchure. When all these forms as well as the written-out measured vibrato (see below) became obsolete, there seems to have been a period with little or no vibrato on wind instruments; only in the 20th century did 'breath' (diaphragm) vibrato become generally accepted as the norm, even if it is still not universally used on all wind instruments (e.g. clarinets, horns, Viennese oboes).

Vocal vibrato is regarded as standard if the voice is well supported; during the 16th to 18th centuries it was supposed to be small and was considered virtually non-existent. It is impossible to establish whether 'vibrato-free production' (described at least until the end of the 19th century) denotes a sound entirely without vibrato in the modern sense; statements that the singing voice differs from the speaking voice in that it contains an almost inaudible vibrato rather suggest that it does not. Some Baroque treatises mention a vocal sound wholly without vibrato as an ornament, which would support the hypothesis that a well-trained Baroque voice normally used minimal vibrato. The same sources mention not only ornamental non-vibrato but also ornamental vibrato. The technique of the latter is described somewhat vaguely, as 'breath vibrato'. Changes in singing technique later suggest that sound production changed in the latter half of the 19th century; vibrato would thus have had a higher priority before that time.

2. MEASURED VIBRATO. Measured vibrato, now all but obsolete, was much used throughout the 17th and 18th centuries and in part of the 19th, mostly in orchestral music to underline passages (see below). On string instruments it is rendered by controlled pressure changes of the bow (indicated by a wavy line, and about M.M.60 or 120; a well-known example is found in the scene with the Cold Genius in Purcell's *King Arthur*). The choice of quavers or semiquavers serves to suggest the tempo. On wind instruments a measured breath vibrato is indicated with the same device. Singers also use it; here too, the beats should be strictly in time. This kind of vibrato is often said to be an imitation of the tremulant stop of the organ. Such indications as staccato (or, eventually, such counter-indications as andante) show that repeated quavers or semiquavers in slow movements were generally considered to point to the use of measured vibrato, although the actual performance may sometimes have been less a vibrato than something akin to a portato (as suggested by Roger North); from the mid-18th century on, German writers distinguish between 'Tremolo' and 'Tragen der Töne'.

In ensemble music of the 17th and 18th centuries, measured vibrato is often the only kind accepted, as the specific technique, which relies mostly on carefully gauged fluctuations in intensity, helps the players to stay together and reduces the risk of intonation problems.

Although normal vibrato is also to some extent measured, and most measured vibrato involves fluctuations of pitch, both kinds were mainly connected with only one of their characteristics. As a rule, measured vibrato has strong emotional connotations; its use survives well into the 19th century, most clearly in opera, but also in the symphony. Unlike an ornamental 'normal' vibrato, it produces some degree of continuity.

3. HISTORY. In Western music vibrato has been documented since the Middle Ages. It may have been in use as an ornament even in early Christian music, but here documentary confirmation is lacking. During the 16th century it became fashionable as a mannerist ornament, and towards the end of the century there seems to have been at least one (polyphonic) singing school that would eventually accept it as some sort of a continuous device. It was then associated with bravura and ornamentational skill (hence the term *ardire*, sometimes used for bravura vibrato) and was used as the basis of trilling ornaments. This more or less continuous vibrato was rejected by practitioners of solo singing and the new style in Italy, and slowly also elsewhere (in Germany the injunction to sing with a tremulous voice, found in singing tutors for boys, became obsolete during the first half of the 17th century, although some tutors, following tradition, advocated its use until the latter years of the century). As

a result of this change of style, vibrato is described as an (occasional) ornament, thus conveying a meaning in accord with Baroque conceptions of passions or with a character as portrayed in a given piece of music. Even in singing tutors of the time it was not mentioned as a substantial element in sound production; there is a clear distinction between the small 'natural' vibrato of the well-placed voice, which is considered the same as a non-vibrated instrumental sound, and the audible ornamental vibrato. The association with well-defined passions lacks meaning if vibrato is used continuously as a means of musical tone production (see Seashore). According to 17th- and 18th-century sources, vibrato was associated with fear, cold, death, sleep, and mourning, and was generally perceived as a 'feminine' ornament (hence denoting also sweetness or loveliness, as reflected in many of the names given to it); its use in this way was eventually superseded by the more modern idea of using vibrato to embellish the tone.

During the Baroque vibrato was used sparingly, for emphasis on long, accentuated notes in pieces with an affect or character to which it was suited. Being regarded as an ornament, in principle it was used on single notes like any other. It was usually denoted by wavy lines; in tablatures a cross (×) has the same meaning. Most of the signs used appear either in tutors or in French amateur music where unspecified ornaments are often indicated by a cross (+). Less common ornaments such as vibrato or glissando were in theory used only by soloists. In the second half of the 18th century there was a tendency towards more vibrato; in some circles it may even have been used continuously.

By the mid-18th century vibrato was gradually identified with some of its more positive connections, especially the sweetness of sound quality ('lieblich'). With many performers it seems to have been in nearly constant use – at least on all longer notes. Such theorists as Leopold Mozart, Simon Löhlein, and Tromlitz warn against overuse. In Classical orchestral works there are many written-out forms of vibrato or similar effects; as a rule these are measured (bow) vibrato, thus allowing small groups to be in time and in tune despite its use. Vibrato at that time also spread among amateur musicians; finger vibrato on woodwind instruments as described for amateurs was already known, because relatively little technical knowledge was needed to produce it (English and French sources of the late 17th and early 18th centuries). The early 19th century saw, again, a much more restricted use of the device.

The extensive use of vibrato and measured vibrato in the last decades of the 18th century brought a reaction at the beginning of the 19th; a tendency developed towards a stricter use of prescribed measured vibrato in the symphonic repertory of the first half of the 19th century, and tutors warn against overuse of the normal vibrato, still described as an ornament and not as part of basic sound production. This becomes clear in the fact that during the first three decades of the 19th century wind tutors still describe finger vibrato as the standard technique. Nor do singing tutors mention vibrato as a part of normal tone, and even at the beginning of the 20th century Leopold Auer expressed reservations about the spread of continuous vibrato, which he in no way advocated. In opera abundant use is made of the measured vibrato for dramatic effect until the very end of the 19th century, suggesting that members of Italian opera orchestras were not expected to use left-hand or normal breath vibrato.

In the 20th century absence of vibrato, except for some wind instruments, came to be regarded as a special effect to be employed for character delineation. Only when continuous vibrato began to establish itself did treatises or 'tutors' on vibrato in singing and playing begin to appear; there are none devoted solely to the subject until the 20th century. It would seem that the use of metal strings to replace gut strings in the orchestra went hand in hand with an increasing demand for continuous left-hand string vibrato; before this, left-hand vibrato was still reserved for particular effect, as for example in Schreker's *Der ferne Klang* (1912). Not until the 20th century was 'incorrect' vibrato first seen as a problem; earlier, it had simply been considered as resulting from generally poor technique (especially where singers and wind players were concerned). Continuous vibrato is a 20th-century phenomenon, indicating in itself that the older ornament has lost its expressive power. Regular vibrato has thus become a normal element of sound production, hence an important component of singing and playing technique.

Measured vibrato is as a rule written out by the composer, although use ad libitum may exist. It is used mainly to convey fear and awe, but also supplication and mercy. In late 17th-century German sonatas a tremolo movement is often inserted as a slow movement; this use is also documented by Roger North for the Italian style in general. In his church cantatas, Bach made ample use of measured vibrato, usually with a particular purpose, although there are indications that he and his contemporaries also used it to indicate ensemble vibrato. Especially in small ensembles this use of bow vibrato helps to avoid fluctuations in pitch and speed. Measured vibrato was still used freely by Italian opera composers of the 19th century to denote feminine mourning passions. As a technical exercise it was still taught to string players at the beginning of the 20th century; symphonies of the latter half of the 19th century still have passages with measured vibrato, suggesting that not only in opera orchestras was continuous vibrato (left-hand vibrato for strings) not established before the introduction during the 20th century of metal strings. These paved the way for changes in violin technique and sound perception, one of which was the increasing use of continuous vibrato, not only for solo use. After a period of virtually universal use, playing with little or no vibrato has become increasingly popular through the revival of early music and early singing and playing techniques.

BIBLIOGRAPHY

C.E. Seashore, ed: *The Vibrato* (IA City, IA, 1932)

C.E. Seashore, ed: *Psychology of the Vibrato in Voice and Instrument* (IA City, IA, 1936)

C. Brown: 'Bowing Styles, Vibrato and Portamento in Nineteenth–Century Violin Playing', *JRMA*, vol.113 (1988), 97–128

E. Fiebig: 'Ein tüchtiger Musiker und angesehener Bürger: Johann Christoph Pezel, Stadtpfeifer in Bautzen von 1681 bis 1694', *Das Orchester*, vol.43, no.5 (1995), 10–16

F.E. Kirby: 'The Germanic Symphony of the Nineteenth Century: Genre, Form, Instrumentation, Expression', *JMR*, vol.14 (1995), 193–221

D. Manning: 'Woodwind Vibrato from the Eighteenth Century to the Present', *Performance Practice Review*, vol.8 (1995), 67–72

G. MOENS-HAENEN/R

Vicentino, Nicola (*b* Vicenza, Italy, early 1510; *d* Milan, Italy, *c*1576). Italian theorist and instrument inventor. Little is known of his early years, but he probably came under the influence of the humanist Giangiorgio Trissino in Vicenza. At some time during this period he was ordained to the priesthood, but his interest seems to have been chiefly in the theoretical examination of the diatonic, chromatic, and enharmonic genera, and their practical application. It is not known when Vicentino arrived in Ferrara, where he was probably employed by Cardinal Ippolito II d'Este. Although he lacked an official connection with the ducal court, Vicentino gave music instruction to several members of Duke Ercole II's family. By 1561 Vicentino had completed not only the *archicembalo* discussed in the fifth book of *L'antica musica* but had also built an *archiorgano* constructed along similar lines and capable of reproducing the sounds of all three genera (described in a publication dated 25 Oct 1561).

Ercole Bottrigari in *Il Desiderio* (1594) stated that Vicentino died during the plague of 1575–6; his pastoral activities would certainly have exposed him to infection, and his post was vacant by 1577. His *archicembalo* passed into the ownership of Prospero Visconti.

Vicentino's fame rests on the treatise *L'antica musica ridotta alla moderna prattica*. The work as a whole is divided into two main parts. The first, a single book 'della theorica musicale', is based chiefly on Boethius but with an emphasis on those elements that support Vicentino's own ideas. The other part contains five books 'della prattica musicale', the first of which concentrates chiefly on a discussion of various intervals in their melodic functions, extended to encompass the possibilities of the three genera. The second concentrates on vertical function of intervals in contrapuntal practice. The third deals chiefly with the eight diatonic modes and their extension into chromatic and enharmonic forms. The bulk of the fourth applies all of these concepts to composition. The fifth submits the principles and theories of the previous books to the definitive test of performance on his *archicembalo*, which was so constructed that any type of microtonal composition could be played on it. Vicentino's instrument is provided with two keyboards, each containing three ranks or orders of keys. The diagram (fig.1) shows the disposition of the orders and the notation used by Vicentino for each sound. The names of the notes make clear the progression from one order to the next, the denomination of each note in the succeeding orders being derived from the name of the note in the first. Thus, in moving from *A la mi re primo* (A, in the first order) to the second order, the notation is given as G♯, but the note is called *A la mi re secondo*. In other words, Vicentino preferred to think of the location of his notes with reference to the keyboard rather

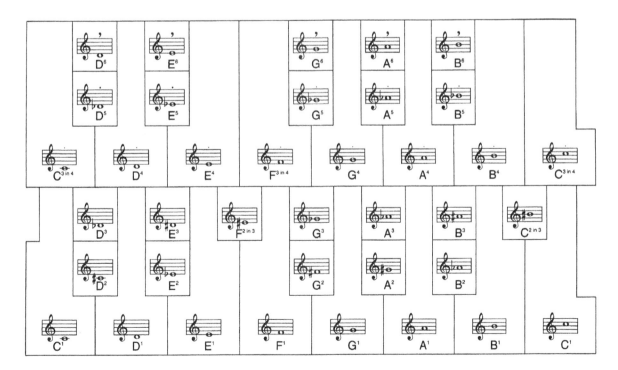

Fig.1: *Diagram showing the disposition of the orders and the notation used by Vicentino for his archicembalo.*

than to the staff. The first order is made up entirely of white keys that correspond to those found in most keyboard instruments. The second order contains the black keys most frequently used in the 16th century: F♯, G♯, B♭, C♯ and E♭. The keys of the second order are split and raised to provide for the third order, which is then completed by the insertion of shortened black keys between the semitones E–F and B–C. This order contains the less commonly used semitones: G♭, A♭, A♯, B♯, D♭, D♯, E♯.

The second frame begins with the fourth order, which contains the same white keys as the first order, but pitched a *diesis* higher. This interval, equal to half a minor semitone or a fifth of a tone, is represented notationally by a dot over the note. The notes of the fifth order are G♭, A♭, B♭, D♭ and E♭, all a *diesis* higher than the corresponding notes in the second and third orders. The sixth order resembles the first diatonic order by using plain notes, but is a comma (equal to half a *diesis*) higher in sound than the first order. The notes are G, A, B, D and E, with the symbol of a comma over each note.

Vicentino's novel and visionary concepts remain a witness to the battle of those musicians of 16th-century Italy who sought a new and contemporary art. From their innovations emerged the free chromatic style of the *seconda pratica* of the 17th century and the stabilization of tuning into the equal temperament of more modern times. For discussion of Vicentino's musical work and full bibliography see *GMO*.

WRITINGS

Descrizione dell'arciorgano (Venice, 1561; trans. in Kaufmann, *JMT*, vol.5, 1961)

L'antica musica ridotta alla moderna prattica (Rome, 1555/R1959, 2/1557; Eng. trans., 1996)

BIBLIOGRAPHY

H.W. Kaufmann: 'Vicentino's Arciorgano: an Annotated Translation', *JMT*, vol.5 (1961), 32–53

H.W. Kaufmann: 'More on the Tuning of the *Archicembalo*', *JAMS*, vol.23/1 (1970), 84–94

P. Niedermüller: 'La musica cromatica ridotta alla pratica vicentiniana: Genus, Kontrapunkt und musikalische Temperatur bei Nicola Vicentino', *Neues musikwissenschaftliches Jb*, vol.6 (1997), 59–90

D. Daolmi: *Don Nicola Vicentino arcimusico in Milano* (Lucca, 1999)

HENRY W. KAUFMANN/ROBERT L. KENDRICK/R

Vierling, Oskar (*b* Straubing, Lower Bavaria, Germany, 24 Jan 1904; *d* 1986). German physicist, electroacoustic engineer, and instrument inventor. After earning an engineering degree from Ohm-Polytechnikum in Nuremberg and then working at a telegraph firm in Berlin, in 1928 he began working on the development of electronic instruments at the Heinrich-Hertz Institut für Schwingungsforschung at the Technische Hochschule in Berlin, where he completed his doctorate in physics in 1937. In 1938, Vierling began lecturing in physics and electroacoustics in Hanover, becoming a professor in 1944. Beginning in 1941 he conducted weapons, encryption, and communications research. After World War II he designed surveillance devices at a laboratory he created in Ebermannstadt, near Nuremberg, where in 1949 he established his firm as Oskar Vierling

GmbH. From 1949 to 1955 he was also a professor of physics at the Fakultäten Theologie und Philosophie of the Universität Bamberg. He held more than 200 patents.

Vierling helped Jörg Mager construct the Sphärophon in 1925 and assisted in the design of the Neo-Bechstein-Flügel in 1928–30. In 1931 he built an electrically amplified violin, the Elektro-Geige, and a similar cello; the string vibrations are sensed by electromagnetic pickups, amplified, and sent to a loudspeaker, and the amplifier can be used to alter the timbre. In 1932 Vierling began to develop the Elektrochord electroacoustic piano, manufactured by the August Förster piano firm from 1934. Along with Winston E. Kock (developer of the Baldwin organ) and his student Fritz Sennheiser, he created the Kdf-Grosston-orgel for the 1936 Olympic games. The Grosston-orgel was an oscillator-based organ with a reverberation device that simulated the acoustics of a large church, but was heard through the stadium loudspeakers. In 1937 Vierling constructed a set of electroacoustic bar chimes, and in 1938–9 he assisted Harald Bode in developing the Melodium and a two-manual version of the Warbo Formant-Orgel.

The term 'Vierling organ' is applied to three models of an Electronic organ developed by Vierling and manufactured by his company between 1950 and 1961; it was then licensed to Ludwig Eisenschmid & Sohn in Munich who produced it until 1976. The instruments were designed for use in churches; one of the larger two-manual organs was installed in the new Festspielhaus in Salzburg in 1960. In the mid-1950s the company took over the remaining stock of the bankrupt manufacturers of the AWB organ, which was thereafter sometimes called the Vierling organ. From 1961, the Vierling firm devoted itself exclusively to the production of electroacoustic measuring and testing devices and data-processing equipment. In 1982, an Elektrochord completed in 1938 was restored for display at the Deutsches Museum, Munich.

WRITINGS
(*selective list*)

'Elektrische Musik', *Elektrotechnische Zeitschrift*, vol.33 (1932), 155–9

'Das elektrische Musikinstrument', *Zeitschrift des Vereins Deutscher Ingenieure*, vol.76 (1932), 625–30, 741–5

Das elektroakustische Klavier (diss., Technische Hochschule, Berlin, 1936)

'Der Formantbegriff', *Annalen der Physik*, vol.418 (1936), 219–32

Eine neue elektrische Orgel, (Berlin, 1938)

BIBLIOGRAPHY

W. Voigt: 'Oskar Vierling, ein Wegbereiter der Elektroakustik für den Musikinstrumentenbau', *Das Musikinstrument*, vol.37/1–2 (1988), 214–21

HUGH DAVIES/ANNE BEETEM ACKER

Vigneron, Joseph Arthur (*b* Mirecourt, France, 30 July 1851; *d* Paris, France, 13 June 1905). French bowmaker. He served his apprenticeship in Mirecourt with Claude Charles Husson, then worked for Jean Jacques Martin until about 1880. From 1880 to 1888 he worked in Paris for Gand & Bernardel Frères, and then Gand & Bernardel.

In 1888 he opened his own shop. Vigneron developed a strongly individual style that remained constant throughout his career. His best bows rank with the finest of his day, showing elegant craftsmanship and superb quality pernambuco. The sticks are usually round but with a pronounced widening at the lower edges, giving a distinctive triangular cross-section, and the heads have broad chamfers, especially at the throat. His bows are branded 'A.VIGNERON À PARIS'.

On J.A. Vigneron's death, his shop was taken over by his son André Vigneron (*b* Mirecourt, France, 19 Sept 1881; *d c*1924). Andrè came to Paris with his father and apprenticed under him, then worked closely with him from 1900 to 1905. His early work is much like his father's, but later he developed his own style, with a tall, narrow and somewhat elongated head, a narrower chamfer, and smaller collar to the button. He used his father's brand and later 'ANDRE VIGNERON À PARIS', and for some work the brand 'VIGNERON—PARIS'.

BIBLIOGRAPHY

E. Vatelot: *Les archets français* (Nancy, 1976)

B. Millant and J.F. Raffin: *L'Archet* (Paris, 2000)

JAAK LIIVOJA-LORIUS/PHILIP J. KASS

Vihuela (Sp.). Plucked chordophone on which the strings, made of gut, were generally arranged in six or seven courses, each probably paired in unison. Closely related to the lute, it flourished mainly in Spain and in areas under Spanish influence in the 15th and 16th centuries. Under the name *viola* (or *viola da mano*) it was also known in Italy and Portugal. At various times the word was applied to string instruments of the viol family, distinguished according to the method of playing them: *vihuela de pendola* (or *peñola*: 'with a quill') in medieval sources; *vihuela de arco* ('with a bow') from the 15th to the 18th centuries; *vihuela de mano* ('with the hand', i.e. with the fingers) in several 16th-century sources from Aragon and Naples. By the 16th century, however, the unqualified term 'vihuela' usually referred to the finger-plucked instrument.

1. Structure and history. 2. Technique.

1. STRUCTURE AND HISTORY. The structure and early history of the vihuela are very closely linked with those of the guitar and viol. The vihuela was probably developed in the 15th century as a plucked alternative to the *viola de arco*. Outside the Spanish sphere of influence, vihuelas were designated with guitar-related terms during the 16th century. The vihuela in the Musée Jacquemart-André of the Institut de France, Paris, is the earliest known example in Europe that has been fully examined and measured. It is a large instrument, dating from the early 16th century, with a body 58.4 cm long. The inward curve at the waist is small and the body is shallow in relation to its surface area. The neck is long and narrow and the head is flat and set back at a slight angle. Multiple roses set into the soundboard and the construction of the body and neck of more than 200 small pieces of contrasting woods add to the distinctive appearance of the instrument, suggesting it might have been an apprentice's examination piece. Its size suggests that it was tuned at a fairly low pitch. Two other vihuelas are known to survive. One (in *F.P.cm*), with body 43.3 cm long and string length of 64.5 cm, has a back made of deeply fluted double-curved ribs, a feature it shares with a 1581 five-course guitar by Belchior Diaz (in *GB.L.cm*), perhaps used by other luthiers from the last years of the 16th century. The other instrument, which probably dates from the 17th century, belonged to St Mariana de Jesús (1618–45) who, according to witnesses, used to accompany herself singing praises of Christ the Bridegroom; it shows characteristics akin to a Baroque guitar with a deep body about 55 cm long and pronounced curves at the waist.

Nassarre, writing in 1724, gave a set of proportions to which a vihuela should be constructed, though his interest was mainly antiquarian. His proportions would give a body of greater depth than those of the three extant instruments. The many pictorial representations of vihuelas from the 16th century show a great variety of basic shapes, ranging from a narrow outline in relation to its length, to a broader and rounder shape; there is usually a single elaborately carved rose, and in some instances surface decorations are set into the soundboard.

Bermudo (1555) gave diagrams of vihuelas tuned at *Gama ut*, C *fa ut*, D *fa ut*, A *re*, D *sol re*, B *mi*, and E *la mi*; but these, he made clear, were only to facilitate the transposition of compositions in staff notation into tablature for the vihuela. Nevertheless he described instruments of different sizes, and it is clear that several different pitches were known since a number of duos in Valderrabano's *Silva de Sirenas* (1547) demand tunings a minor 3rd, a 4th, and a 5th apart. Milán, by the consistent placing of modal finals on certain frets, implied a variety of nominal tunings for his instrument, including E, G, F$\sharp$, and A; but in practice he suggested that the pitch should be taken from the first (highest) course, which should be tuned as high as possible without breaking. Among other writers, opinion was divided as to whether the first or fourth course was the better one from which to begin.

The intervals of tuning for which almost all surviving music was written are identical with those of the lute, that is (from the sixth—i.e. lowest—course upwards): 4th–4th–major 3rd–4th–4th. Bermudo, however, gave several other schemes. For a certain 'small new vihuela' he named the notes as *G–B–d–g–b–d'*. For vihuelas of seven courses he gave three tunings. The first of these, 5th–4th–5th–4th–5th–4th, provides a range of 22 notes on the open strings. The second, *G'–C–F–G–c–f–g*, he described as new and perfect (he also gave an accompaniment in this tuning for the *romance Mira Nero de Tarpeya*). His third tuning, 5th–4th–major 3rd–5th–4th–minor 3rd, imitated that of a guitar on the lower four strings and a bandurria on the upper three; a clever musician could, he said, divide music suitable for this type of vihuela between those two instruments. Music given by Fuenllana in his *Orphenica Lyra* (1554) for a vihuela of five courses requires the same intervals of tuning as the six-course instrument with the top course removed.

The usual number of gut frets on the neck of the vihuela was ten, and considerable attention was given to devising methods of placing these to obtain an exact intonation. Bermudo, who favoured a Pythagorean temperament, expressed great concern about the difference in pitch of certain notes according to whether they have to serve as *mi* or *fa* (the lower or higher note of a semitone) in the mode of a particular composition. Suggestions for overcoming this difficulty include the use of a double fret composed of two thicknesses, either of which could be selected at will, or the actual moving of the fret to suit the mode. The latter method was advocated by Milán (1536), who prefaced a fantasia and a *romance* with this instruction: 'raise the fourth fret a little [towards the nut] so that the note of the said fret will be strong *[mi]* and not feeble *[fa]*'; and by Valderrábano, who said: 'lower the fourth fret a little towards the rose', which meant tuning it to a *fa* fret. Seeking the note on another course and fret was also mentioned by Bermudo.

Literary references indicate that the word 'vihuela' was used in Spain from the 13th century onwards. It appears in the *Libro de Apolonio* (*c*1250), the *Poema de Alfonso Onceno* by Alfonso XI of Castile *(d c*1340), and the famous *Libro de buen amor* of the 14th-century poet Juan Ruiz, who distinguished between the *vihuela de arco* and the *vihuela de peñola*. Tinctoris described the vihuela in the 15th century as an instrument invented by the Spaniards and called by them and the Italians *viola* (or *viola sine arculo*). It was, he said, smaller than the lute and flat-backed, and in most cases had incurved sides. During the last years of that century the guitar and the vihuela appear to have evolved side by side, the guitar with its four courses being a popular instrument, largely used for accompanying songs and dances, while the vihuela was favoured by virtuoso players, although evidence indicates its use among the lower classes as well. Some virtuosos were employed in households of the nobility, but the finest achieved great fame as royal musicians at the Spanish court, where music was highly esteemed. The children of Ferdinand and Isabella, the Catholic monarchs who reigned at the turn of the century, were trained in music, especially the young prince Juan who possessed, among other chamber instruments, vihuelas and viols which it is said he could play. Although abundant evidence indicates the use of the vihuela in royal and noble establishments at this period, the first printed music appeared years later, in Milán's book of 1536.

During the reign of Emperor Charles V the vihuela reached the height of its development as an instrument of the musical élite. The emperor employed mostly Flemish musicians in his chapel; he entrusted the secular music activities to native players, however, and in private music-making the vihuela had a prominent role. It continued to be held in high regard at the court of Philip II, where in 1566 the celebrated blind composer

and player Miguel de Fuenllana was listed as *musico de camara* to Isabel de Valois, the king's third wife. Towards the end of the century its position seems to have been undermined by the increasing popularity of the guitar, and a few years later Sebastián Covarrubias Orozco wrote (in his *Tesoro de la lengua castellana o española,* Madrid, 1611) that:

> This instrument [the vihuela] has been held in great esteem until our own times, and there have been excellent players, but since the invention of the guitars there are very few who apply themselves to the study of the vihuela. This is a great loss, because every kind of written music can be played on it, and now the guitar is nothing but a cow-bell, so easy to play, especially when strummed, that there is not a stable-boy who is not a musician of the guitar.

Apart from the composer–players whose names have survived through their books, a few other famous players are mentioned in publications of the time. Bermudo named not only Narváez but also Luis Guzman, Martin de Jaen and Hernando de Jaen ('citizens of Granada'), and Lopez ('musician to the Duke of Arcos'). Francisco Pacheco in his *Libro de descripción de verdarderos retratos* (1599) included a portrait of the blind player Pedro de Madrid with a seven-course vihuela and commented, 'Seville is honoured by such a son', and also one of Manuel Rodriguez, 'player of the harp and viguela'. Vicente Espinel in his *Relaciones de la vida del escudero Marcos de Obregón* (Madrid, 1618), described how he heard Lucas de Matos play on a seven-course instrument together with Bernardo Clavijo on the keyboard and the latter's daughter on the harp, adding that their music is 'the best I have heard on my life'.

The apparent preference for the vihuela over the lute in Spain has been explained by a theory that the lute was repudiated because of its Moorish origin. This theory, however, overlooks the fact that many aspects of Islamic culture remained firmly established in Spain long after the final expulsion in 1492, and still remain so. Among musical instruments, the rebec continued in use into the 16th century; and many Moorish themes frequently appear in the words of 16th-century songs. Moreover, a growing body of evidence suggests that the lute was more commonly used than has been generally supposed.

Tinctoris stated that an instrument identical with the vihuela was played in Italy, and indeed pictures and a few musical sources and literary references confirm its presence there in the 16th century. Francesco Canova da Milano is known to have performed on the vihuela as well as on the lute, and the title of his book of 1536, *Intavolatura di viola o vero lauto*, indicates that the pieces it contains were intended for either of these instruments. Other Italian players of the vihuela, including the composer Giulio Severino, are mentioned by Scipione Cerreto in his *Della prattica musica vocale et strumentale* (Naples, 1601). Some documentary and pictorial evidence of the use of the *viola* in Portugal can be traced, and the names of a few famous players, such as Peixoto da Peña, Domingos Madeira, and Alexandre de Aguiar, are known.

The vihuela, along with other European instruments, was taken to Latin America during colonization. A soldier named Ortiz, who was a great player of the vi-huela, accompanied Cortés in the conquest of Mexico; according to the chronicler Bernal Díaz de Castillo, the natives learned very soon how to make instruments, including 'very good vihuelas'. A letter of about 1583 from the Jesuit priest Fernão Cardim refers to the early establishment of schools of singing and playing in Christianized villages; the *viola* was among the instruments taught. Furthermore, the archives of Buenos Aires contain many references to the sale of strings for the *biguela* and strings for frets between 1597 and 1736. *Biguelas* are also mentioned in wills and other documents.

Santa Mariana de Jesús' instrument, now kept as a relic in the church of the Compañía de Jesús in Quito, Ecuador, has six double courses. Four instruments (in *MEX.M.ma* and *MEX.M.mb*) have been claimed to be descendants of the vihuela, constructed by native craftsmen; together with other members of the plucked-string family, such as the *cuatro* in Venezuela, they strongly suggest a common ancestry in the 16th-century vihuela and guitar.

2. TECHNIQUE. Though there is little written evidence about the technique of the left hand in vihuela playing, this can hardly have differed in any significant way from that used on the lute. There is a brief mention by Venegas de Henestrosa, and Fuenllana explained how a finger of the left hand may divide a course in two by stopping only one string, thus obtaining an additional voice in the counterpoint; this technique was also employed by the Italian lutenist Vincenzo Capirola about 1517.

Right-hand technique was dealt with in some detail, especially for the playing of rapid passages known as *redobles*. Three methods are given. *Dedillo* (marked *dedi* in some sources) consists of a rapid movement inwards and outwards with the index finger; it was considered unsatisfactory by Fuenllana since the string is touched by the flesh of the finger on the inward stroke but by the nail on the outward. *Dos dedos* (marked *dosde* in some sources) consists of the alternating movement of the thumb and the first finger, as used in the rest of Europe at this time. According to Venegas de Henestrosa, *dos dedos* had two variants: *figueta castellana* ('Castilian'), with the thumb held outside the fingers, and *figueta estranjera* ('foreign'), with the thumb held inside the fingers, as in 16th-century lute technique. The third method involves alternating the index and second fingers; Fuenllana and Venegas de Henestrosa praised this as being the most perfect way of playing, and Fuenllana added, 'as I have said to you, to strike with a stroke without the intrusion of the nail or any other kind of invention has great excellence, because only in the finger, as a living thing, the spirit lies'.

For discussion of vihuela repertory *see GMO*.

BIBLIOGRAPHY

J.M. Ward: *The Vihuela de mano and its Music, 1536–76* (diss., New York U., 1953)

D. Gill: 'A Vihuela in Ecuador', *LSJ*, vol.20 (1978), 53–5

J. Griffiths: 'At Court and at Home with the Vihuela de Mano', *JLSA*, vol.22 (1989), 1–27

E. Bermudez: 'La vihuela de la iglesia de la compañía de Jesús de Quito', *Revista Musical Chilena*, vol.47/179 (1993), 69–77

C. Bordas: 'La construcción de vihuelas y guitarras en Madrid en los siglos XVI y XVII', *La guitarra en la historia*, vol.6 (1995), 47–67

J. Griffiths: 'Extremities: the Vihuela in Development and Decline', *Luths et luthistes en Occident París*, 1999, 51–61

A. Corona-Alcalde: *The Players and Performance Practice of the Vihuela and its Related Instruments, the Lute and the Guitar, from c1450 to c1650 as Revealed by a Study of Musical, Theoretical and Archival Sources* (diss., U. of London, 1999)

J. Romanillos and M. Harris Winspear: *The Vihuela de Mano and the Spanish Guitar: A Dictionary of the Makers of Plucked and Bowed Musical Instruments of Spain (1200–2002), String Makers, Shops, Dealers and Factories* (Guijosa, 2002)

A. Corona-Alcalde: 'L'organographie de la vihuela', *Aux origines de la guitare: la vihuela de mano*, ed. J. Dugot (París, 2004) 16–28

J. Dugot: 'Un chef–d'oeuvre du XVIe siécle: la vihuela du Musée Jacquemart-André', *Aux origines de la guitare: la vihuela de mano* (París, 2004), 50–61

F. Gétreau: 'L'iconographie de la vihuela', *Aux origines de la guitare: la vihuela de mano*, ed. J. Dugot (París, 2004), 41–9

H. Minamino: 'The Spanish Plucked *Viola* in Renaissance Italy', *EMc*, vol.32/2 (2004), 177–92

J. Martínez González: 'Arqueología de la vihuela de mano, savia nueva por madera vieja', *Nassarre*, vol.21 (2005), 265–77

M. Morais: 'A Viola de Mão em Portugal', *Nassarre*, vol.22 (2006), 393–462

C. González and others, eds.: *Estudios sobre la vihuela* (Madrid, 2007) [incl. A. Corona-Alcalde: 'La vihuela en la Nueva España', 67–84; C. González: 'La vihuela E.0748 del Musée de la Musique en Paris', 97–111; J. Romanillos: 'La construcción de la vihuela de mano y de la guitarra española en las ordenanzas y en los inventarios de taller de violeros y guitarristas españoles', 113–25; C. Bordas: 'De violero a guitarrero: la actividad del gremio de violeros de Madrid (ca. 1577–ca. 1808)', 127–40]

DIANA POULTON/ANTONIO CORONA-ALCALDE

Vihuela mexicana. Five-stringed small guitar of Mexico. Commonly known as the vihuela, it is played in the *mariachi* ensemble as a harmony and rhythm instrument, and should not be confused with the Spanish *vihuela de mano*. It has a loud, crisp, rapid-decay sound. The soundbox is typically 39 cm long with a 29 cm maximum width, a 28 cm neck with four to six movable nylon frets, and 50 cm string length. The maximum depth of the sides is 10.5 cm plus an additional 6 cm depth to the apex of the vaulted, angled back. Wooden pegs inserted from the rear of the pegboard are traditional but nowadays most vihuelas have mechanical tuners. The tuning is *a-d'-g'-b-e'* but sometimes the lowest three strings are tuned an octave higher. The soundhole (*boca*) is surrounded by *nácar* (mother of pearl) and wood inlay in a starburst pattern, and the purfling has intricate *limoncillo* wood inlay. The woods used to build vihuelas are the same as those for *guitarrones*.

The vihuela is strummed between the *boca* and the neck, and is supported using a normal guitar strap in the *boca*, allowing the vihuelista freedom to play the intricate *monicos* (strums) of *sones* and *huapangos*. The Morales family of Guadalajara and Sevillano family of Tijuana are the premier builders of vihuelas nowadays. See R. Baltazar Arteaga: *Manual Teórico-Practico para Vihuela* (Obregón, n.d.).

J. RICHARD HAEFER

Vijole [skripka, smuigas, spēles]. Fiddle or violin of Latvia. The earliest written evidence is from the first half of the

17th century. The earliest museum examples are from the end of the 19th century, but most collected violins are from the first half of the 20th century, and they show little variation in form and construction: length is 57 to 62 cm, width 20 to 22 cm, with four strings. Some eyewitnesses wrote in the 18th century that Latvian peasants made their violins skilfully with just a knife. Replacing the vanishing piping tradition in the 18th century, vijole became the most popular dance music instrument and was played either solo or in various ensembles: the core of such ensembles was a violin with a chord zither in western, central, and northern Latvia, with a hammer dulcimer in south-eastern Latvia, or with a button accordion in all Latvia, plus frame drum, triangle, double bass, mandolin, or other instruments. Solo violin playing was more characteristic in Vidzeme in central and northern Latvia, with the solo violinist named *spēlmanis*; here one can see a certain similarity with the Swedish *spelman* tradition.

BIBLIOGRAPHY

Ī. Priedīte: *Ko spēlēja sendienās* [What They Played in the Olden Days] (Riga, 1983)

V. Muktupāvels: 'Musical Instruments in the Baltic Region: Historiography and Traditions', *The World of Music*, vol.44/3 (2002), 21–54

VALDIS MUKTUPĀVELS

Vilepill. Duct flute of Estonia, typically made of pine; also known as *pajupill* ('willow pipe') or *haavapill* ('aspen pipe'). It could have a variable number of fingerholes, or, as a harmonic flute played by stopping the open end, none at all. It was usually played outdoors while grazing cattle or while on watch at night by the camp fire. Nowadays *vilepill* can be used generically to denote flutes of various types. In Setomaa *valipill* reportedly denoted two flutes blown simultaneously.

Villādivādyam. Composite instrument of Tamil Nadu and Kerala, south India, combining an implosive aerophone, idiophone, and chordophone. The instrument consists of four elements: a bow (*vil, villa*) about 240 cm long, of wood or metal; several bronze bells hung along the bow; two sticks with jingling rings; and a large terracotta pitcher. The instrument is played by two singers. One singer holds the middle of the bow, string upwards, against the neck of the pot, with his left arm slipped between the string and the wood of the bow;

he beats the mouth of the pot with a rigid fan held in his right hand, and the side with a small coin in his left. The main singer beats the string with the sticks. It is played in an ensemble, which includes the drums *uḍukkai* and *ghaṭa*, two *jālra* (cymbals), and a pair of *kaṭṭa* (wooden clappers), to accompany songs called 'bow-songs' (Tamil *villupattu*, Malayalam *villadichanpatte*), a form of popular entertainment performed generally at temple festivals.

BIBLIOGRAPHY

P. Sambamoorthy: 'Catalogue of Musical Instruments Exhibited in the Government Museum, Madras', *Bulletin of the Madras Government Museum*, vol.2/3 (1931)

P. Sambamoorthy: *A Dictionary of South Indian Music and Musicians* (Madras, 1952–71), vol.2, 274, pl.33

PRIBISLAV PITOËFF

Villu [vil, villukottu, onaviṭṭu]. Struck musical bow (*villu*: 'bow') of Kerala, south India. The bow itself is a spathe of palm leaf, about 82 cm long, and the string a strip of thin bamboo, affixed into slots at either end of the bow by terminal knobs. It has been classified wrongly as an idiophone because of its wood-like string, but this would have no tension or pitch unless stretched. It is held vertically on the right upper chest and shoulder by the left hand, with the string facing forward; the string is beaten with a light bamboo stick held in the right hand. The villu provides a purely rhythmic accompaniment in *villinmel* and *thayambaka* and in the harvest festival songs (*onapaṭṭu*), with which it is closely associated. Alternative names are *onavillu* ('harvest festival bow') and *villukoṭṭu* ('bow percussion').

BIBLIOGRAPHY

P. Sambamoorthy: *Catalogue of Musical Instruments Exhibited in the Government Museum, Madras* (Madras, 3/1962)

K.S. Kothari: *Indian Folk Musical Instruments* (New Delhi, 1968)

ALASTAIR DICK

Vin. Sassanian horizontal angular harp; also a plucked chordophone of medieval Armenia.

Vīṇā [veena]. The principal indigenous term for chordophones in India and other countries of South Asia. The name (and its later derivatives: Tamil *vīṇai*; New Indo-Aryan *bīṇā, bīṇ*, etc.) has been used for almost three millennia to denote the main type of the age: the

Vīṇā, South India, early 20th century. This "Thanjavore Veena" has a total of seven strings: Four main strings and three Talam strings, with seven wooden tuning keys, and 24 brass frets. The bridge is made of rosewood and inlaid with brass. (Aurelia W. Hartenberger, EdD)

musical bow (§§1 and 5 below); the early harps (§2); the short lute (§3); the medieval stick or tube zithers (§4; for discussion of classification *see* TUBE ZITHER); bowed chordophones (§5); and various descendants of the above in the contexts of both folk (§6) and high art (§§7–9) traditions, including the modern south Indian vīṇā, a lute (§8). In technical literature the instruments described as *vīṇā* often bear a distinguishing epithet.

The Hindu stick zithers, depicted since the 6th century but probably older, have been considered the classic vīṇā or *bīṇ* instruments for a millennium and a half. The term is also found, mainly in folk contexts, denoting various aerophones (for example the *bīṇ, nāgbīṇ,* and *bīṇ jogī* in north India and the *mukhavīṇā* in the south); this may reflect an ancient use of bamboo for both string and wind instruments. The name has been brought back into use in modern writings either to re-name existing instruments of non-Indian name and origin or, with more propriety, to name new variations or inventions (§10).

1. Early history. 2. Harps. 3. Lutes. 4. Medieval stick zithers. 5. Bowed chordophones. 6. Folk stick zithers. 7. The Hindustani *bīṇ.* 8. *Sarasvatī vīṇā.* 9. Fretless *vīṇā.* 10. 19th-century ephemera.

1. EARLY HISTORY. The name *vīṇā* is first documented in the *Yajurveda* (*c*1000 BCE). It is not found in the earlier *Ṛgveda,* nor in the *Atharvaveda,* but another term in those texts, *vāṇā,* has been interpreted by some scholars and later Indian ritual etymologists, probably wrongly, as a chordophone. A possible chordophone, however, referred to in these earliest written sources is the *gārgara* or *karkarī,* which might have been a musical bow resonated on a skin-covered pot or gourd (a bowed *gargarah* is mentioned in the *Sāmaveda* as accompanying a hymn to Indra). Some ideograms of the pre-Aryan Indus culture (3rd–2nd millennia BCE) might show a curved stick with three or four strings, more safely interpreted as polychord bows (which could have evolved into the later harps or bow harps) than as harps proper. From the *Ṛgveda* on, there are frequent references to the 'song' of the archer's bow which, though not always to be taken literally, do show the importance of this weapon as a probable progenitor of chordophones. The *pināka* or *pinākī vīṇā* of post-Vedic Sanskrit texts was doubtless this; the medieval Sanskrit *pinākī* and later northern *pināk* is a bowed bow, while the southern *vil* or *villu* are struck bows.

An analogy between the vīṇā and the human body, a correspondence expressing the deep impregnation of ancient Indian thought upon musical thinking, is given in the *Aitareya Āraṇyaka* (*c*500 BCE). Vocal sounds were assimilated to a human vīṇā and the different parts of the musical instrument were correlated with the head, the tongue, the fingers, the stomach, and the skin of the body. The *Nāradīyaśikṣā* (early Christian era), a phonetic handbook to ensure the correct performance of *Sāmvedic* chant, mentions two kinds of vīṇā, the *gātra* ('bodily') *vīṇā* and the *dāravi* ('wooden') *vīṇā.* The *gātra vīṇā* is called *śarīra vīṇā* by Bharata in the *Nāṭyaśāstra.* The *Kāṭhaka* recension

of the *Yajurveda* contrasts the vīṇā, said to be associated with animals (*paśu*), with the *kāṇḍavīṇā,* associated with plants (*oṣadhi*). The meaning of the latter (*kāṇḍa*: 'internode of cane') makes it likely to have been a tube or a stick zither, possibly idiochord; it is not known if it had an extra resonator, though the term *alābuvīṇā* ('bottle-gourd vīṇā') occurs in later texts (the *Śrautasūtras*). The later stick zithers, though not appearing in high-art iconography until about the second half of the 5th century CE, probably go back to these early forms. At the same time, it is clear that *vīṇā,* unqualified, at this period denoted the harps or bow harps, whose animal components are referred to. Sachs suggested (1914) that the name *vīṇā,* which is possibly non-Aryan in form, derived from an ancient Egyptian harp name *bint,* but the north Indian vernacular form *bīṇ* is very much later, and ancient India's contacts were rather with Mesopotamia, where arched harps were also found. On stronger grounds, the name might derive from a pre-Aryan root meaning 'bamboo' (possibly Dravidian, as in the Tamil *veṟam*: 'cane'), giving also *veṇu* ('bamboo', 'flute'), and *veṇa* ('caneworker'). In this case the name would have originated with early tube or stick zithers.

2. HARPS. Arched harps are assumed to have reached South Asia from the ancient Middle East. The transmission is undocumented, but evidence from the Indus civilization (*c*3000–1750 BCE) suggests the harp's early presence in the subcontinent at a period of trade contact with Mesopotamia. Various types of vīṇā—not all necessarily harps—are mentioned in the Vedic canon (1st millennium BCE) as instruments of ritual, and in classical literature (*c*500 BCE onwards) as instruments of court entertainment music. The latter role is confirmed for the harp by the earliest (mainly Buddhist) art from the 2nd century BCE until about the 6th century CE, in which kings, nobles, minor deities, and courtesans are depicted playing the harp, either solo or to accompany song and dance. The harp continues to appear sporadically in iconography to the end of the 1st millennium, but seems then to have died out in South Asia, with the possible exceptions of the *waji* of Nuristan and the *bīṇ bājā* of Madhya Pradesh.

The South Asian harps varied in size, construction and playing technique. Apart from angular harps known in Gandhāra (northwest India), all were horizontal arched (or bow) harps: the curved wooden neck, terminating bluntly or with an inward-curling scroll, merged at the lower end with a wooden boat-shaped resonator, the soundtable of which was of skin pierced with soundholes. The gut or vegetable-fibre strings typically numbered seven (*citrā vīṇā*); instruments of nine (*vipañcī vīṇā*), ten, and, by the 7th century CE, 14 strings (the Tamil *yāḻ*) are also attested. The strings appear to have been attached to the arch by means of tuning-cords. The internal construction of the instrument is unclear, no specimens having survived. The 'bow-harp' type, in which the resonator is attached beneath one end of the arch, and in which the strings are attached to the arch at both ends in the manner of a polychord musical bow, can occasionally be identified in iconography, and is represented today by the *waji* and the *bīṇ bājā*. This type is distinct from harps elsewhere in Asia, most of which have a separate string-bar (e.g. the Burmese *saùng-gauk*), and perhaps derives from indigenous musical bows (see §1) under the influence of harps from West Asia.

In iconography to about the 4th century CE the harp is shown beneath the player's left arm (supported, if the player stands, by a sling). The right hand plucks the proximal (inner) surface of the string-plane, either with the fingers or with a large plectrum (*koṇa*). The left hand damps and/or plucks from the distal (outer) side. Later, however, the instrument is held beneath the right arm; the right-hand fingers pluck on the distal side while the left hand appears to raise the pitch of individual strings by pressing, with the crooked left thumb, near the point of attachment to the arch. This later method of playing, shown in reverse (as though the player were left-handed) when the player faces the viewer's left, resembles the technique of the Burmese harp.

Certain features of Indian music theory appear to reflect the importance of the harp at the time of its earliest formulation. Thus the theoretical 'consonance' (*saṃvāda*) of perfect 4ths and 5ths might reflect the attested simultaneous plucking of two strings. Early texts explicitly describe the tuning and scale system in terms of the seven-string *vīṇā*, and their use of modes with differing dominants and finals perhaps indicates an instrument on which no one pitch is inherently fundamental to the others (as it is on monochords).

3. LUTES. In South Asia, short-necked lutes first appear in the Graeco-Buddhist art of the 1st century CE to the 3rd of Gandhāra, the extreme northwestern province of ancient India which borders on Central Asia; it is thought that they spread thence to the Indian subcontinent. They appear in Buddhist art from the 2nd century CE to the 6th, and thereafter sporadically in Hindu art to the end of the millennium. They generally occur in the same contexts as harps.

In Gandhāran art a wide variety of types is found. The resonator is ovoid or barbed, with or without soundholes. The strings, generally three or four, are attached to a straight, lute-type bridge, or pass over a flat rectangular bridge, similar to that later characteristic of various Indian instruments. The short, slender, unfretted neck often terminates in a rather bulky pegbox with laterally inserted pegs. The player normally stands, but the instrument is held in various positions and is plucked with fingers or plectrum. In peninsular Indian art larger, generally five-string, uniformly pear-shaped lutes appear, resembling the Chinese *pipa* in outline. They have a curved string-bar, no soundholes, a long, slender, perhaps backwards-curving pegbox, and in some cases frets; the plectrum appears not always to have been used. The player sits or stands, and usually holds the lute horizontally, at waist height.

Of various unidentified instrument names in Sanskrit literature, *kacchapī* ('tortoise') *vīṇā* is thought to denote a lute type.

4. MEDIEVAL STICK ZITHERS. In the second half of the 1st millennium CE various types of single-string stick zither with gourd resonators supplanted the harp- and lute-*vīṇā* as instruments of court music and assumed an important role in religious iconography. Though not iconographically attested before about 475, they might have been indigenous folk instruments before their adoption into art music (see §1 above). The type survives in the modern north Indian *bīṇ*, and in various folk instruments including the *ṭuila, kullutan rājan, jantar, king,* and *kinnarī vīṇā*. The Arab geographer Ibn Khurdadbih (*c*820–912) reported that 'The Indians have the *kankala* which has but one string stretched across a gourd. And it serves them in place of the lute or harp'. The name *kingra* appears in other Arab writings as well as in the poetic work of Amir Khusrau (1253–1325), who also mentions the *alawan*, another type of stick zither. In addition to innumerable representations in late Buddhist and (especially) medieval Hindu art, there are very detailed descriptions by the 13th-century musicologist Śārṅgadeva (*Saṅgītaratnākara*, chap. 6), who distinguishes three principal types: *ālāpinī, ekatantrī* ('one-string'), and *kinnarī vīṇā*. These types can be identified in iconography of the late 5th century to the 13th, where they are associated particularly with the deities Shiva (as patron of the arts) and Sarasvatī (goddess of learning). Thus this class of *vīṇā* became the symbol of the arts.

All the stick zithers comprised a bamboo or wooden tube, along which a single string (of gut, sinew, silk, cotton, or metal) was stretched. At the lower end the string passed over a rectangular bridge with a convex upper surface, which caused a buzzing effect when the string vibrated; at the other end the string was attached to the body either directly, tied to a rope wrapped around it (as on the ancient harps), or (on the metal-stringed *kinnarī vīṇā*) with the aid of a tuning peg. Additional resonators could be attached. The flat curved bridge and hooked tailpiece of early Indian stick zithers show striking similarities with those of an ancient Egyptian round-necked lute dating from the 18th dynasty and preserved in the Cairo Museum. Although no other evidence supports any assumption, it is possible that indigenous monochord stick zithers developed during a period of trade between the ancient Middle East and South Asia.

On the *ālāpinī*, a hemispherical cup made from half a hollowed dried gourd was fastened behind the upper end of the tube; the opening of this cup was pressed against the player's chest to form a closed resonance chamber. A similar gourd on the *ekatantrī* and *kinnarī vīṇā* was held higher, resting on the player's shoulder; on the latter a second and even third gourd could be attached lower down the instrument. Drawings of a single-gourd and two-gourd *vīṇā* of the *ekatantrī* type, respectively called *ballakī* (*vallakī*) and *bipanchī* (*vipancī*), figure among other Indian instruments in the *Ghunyat 'ul munyā* (1374–75), the earliest known Persian work on Indian music. Śārṅgadeva's description of playing technique on the *ālāpinī* (*Saṅgītaratnākara*, chap.6) is the earliest evidence for a technique still adopted for certain single-string stick zithers of South and Southeast Asia. These include the *ṭuila* of eastern India, the *phīn nam tao* of Thailand, and the *sāṭīev* of Kampuchea, all of which are characteristically played partly or wholly in harmonics (compare also the single-string box zither *đàn bầu* of Vietnam). The instrument is held by the left hand in such a way that the gourd is pressed against the player's chest by the left thumb; the left-hand fingers are able to stop the string in 'first position' only. The middle finger of the right hand plucks the string, while the extended forefinger of the same hand lightly touches it at selected harmonic nodes; a complete scale in harmonics can be obtained over one or more octaves. By varying the stopping positions of the left-hand fingers, a variety of scales and temperaments is possible, only the harmonics of the open string being of fixed pitch. Ornamental pitch inflection is achieved by moving the stopping finger after the string has been plucked.

It may be noted, first, that in order to produce an ascending scale of harmonics, the right hand touches the string at points successively nearer the distal end. The true nature of harmonics, as depending on equal division of the string, is thus disguised, and was not apparent to early Indian theorists: Śārṅgadeva is unable to explain how the first and fifth degrees are both produced from the open string. Secondly, and most remarkable for a monochord, the texture can be polyphonic, for both the fundamental and a harmonic can be simultaneously audible. This effect is attested both for the *ṭuila* and for the *sāṭīev*.

The fretless *ekatantrī* is described in the *Saṅgītaratnākara* as the most respected vīṇā. Its large and long tube allowed a holding position giving greater freedom of movement for the left hand, which is shown stopping the string with a wooden slider (*kamrikā*) along its full length. Thus a wide range was available without recourse to harmonics, and the instrument's compass and expressiveness, akin to vocal abilities because of the sliding technique, were highly appreciated. The right hand plucked with both first and second fingers, as on the modern *bīṇ*. A similar technique was used on the *kinnarī vīṇā*, where, however, a variable number of high, fixed frets (from 12 to 14 in Śārṅgadeva's account) assisted left-hand fingering; the slider was not used on this instrument.

Śārṅgadeva also mentions, but does not describe, a *nakula* of two strings, a *tritantrikā* of three strings, and a *mattakokilā* of 21 strings (this last possibly a board zither).

5. BOWED CHORDOPHONES. These are mentioned in or described by medieval Sanskrit texts. The *Saṅgītaratnākara* (early 13th century) gives a detailed description of the bow and of two instruments played with it. The *pināki* ('bow') vīṇā was a musical bow, with a staff 41 Hindu 'inches' (about 80 cm) long, 2.25 Hindu inches (4 cm) thick in the centre, and tapering to 1.25 Hindu inches (2.25 cm) at the upper end and 1 (2 cm) at the lower. Two small terracotta *kheṭoka* (probably the 'inverted cups', perhaps resonators, of the later *Ā'īn-i-akbarī*) are affixed to each end at the back, and the string is threaded and tied through holes near each end. The lower end of the bow was placed on a gourd resonator held on the ground by the feet, and the upper end leant against the shoulder. The string was stopped by the stem of a small gourd held in the player's left hand.

The playing bow (*cāpa, dhanu*, both, like *pināka*, meaning 'bow') is described in a precise account perhaps unequalled in medieval times. It was 21 Hindu inches (about 40 cm) long, but reduced (by curvature) to a hair length of 'two fists' (not a standard measurement, but perhaps about 30 cm), and 3 Hindu inches (about 5.75 cm) thick, except for the last third of an inch (about 7 mm) at each end, which was 0.75 Hindu inches (about 1.5 cm) thick. To these whittled-down ends would be attached the hair ('of horse's tail'), with resin (*rāla*) from the *sāl* tree (*Shorea robusta, Vatica robusta*) applied before playing. The bowing action is not described by Śārṅgadeva. The account of the *pināk*, also called *surbatāna* (*sur-bitāna* in Jarrett's translation), given by Abu'l Faẓl three-and-a-half centuries later adds that the main string was of gut, and that it was played like the *ghichak*, or Central Asian spike fiddle. In the late 18th century, the bowed *pināki* had become rare but was yet recorded and drawn by a Flemish painter settled in Calcutta, François Baltazard Solvyns (1760–1824), who remarked: 'The *Pennauck* is now as seldom heard in India as in the other provinces of Asia'. It is reported for the Ho of Bihar in the 19th century, but might have become obsolete. Pre-medieval references to the *pināki* cannot be taken as proof of bowing, as the term refers to the main bow; though a plucked musical bow seems rare in the subcontinent, beaten forms are still found.

Another bowed instrument is described by Śārṅgadeva under his own pen-name, the *niḥsaṅkā vīṇā* ('Niḥśaṅka's vīṇā'), though he does not claim to have invented it. The description of the instrument, though not clear, indicates a string four hands long tied at its upper end to a piece of wood and at its lower end to another piece (measuring one-and-a-half hands), whose last two 'inches' are whittled to a spike one 'inch' thick. A gourd is attached near the bottom. The top of the instrument is held to the left base of the chest, and the bottom held flat on the ground in the crook of the left knee by the right leg. It is played with a bow like the *pināki*, but a thimble of dried leather (*peśī*), stiffened with an inside rod (*koṇa*), or the rod alone, can be used to stop the string. The *niḥsaṅkā vīṇā* can produce ragas in three registers. The instrument might be interpreted as a spike fiddle, but the use of the terms *kāṣṭha* and *dāru* ('wood', 'log') for the neck suggests something heavier. The *sārān* of Kashmir (Śārṅgadeva's family homeland) is held in similar fashion by the legs (but reversed). The manner of stopping the strings of these two vīṇā is probably the origin of the analogous method on the modern *sāraṅgī* type, and possibly the author took a documented medieval name, *sāraṅga*, and made a play on his own.

6. FOLK STICK ZITHERS. Many of the aspects of the medieval stick zithers described above (§4) survive in

folk instruments throughout the subcontinent, though the name *vīṇā/bīṇ* is rare. The *ālāpinī* type appears to survive in India only in the Orissan *ṭuila*. Whether the sliding fret rod technique of the *ekatantrikā* has descended to the modern concert instruments (see §9 below) through maintained folk traditions is not clear. However, the instrument that has contributed most to the concert vīṇā (see §§7–8 below), and which is most widespread in various shapes and sizes, is the *kinnarī vīṇā*. This was the most developed medieval type, which had raised fixed frets and a high (pinnate) nut and tuning peg; it was finger-plucked and played primarily by division of a single string, though often had one or more drone or punctuating strings. Of this type are the small stick zithers of the eastern tribal peoples, such as the *kullutan rājan* and the *jantarungrai* of the Saora, the *memerājan* of the Savaras, and the *deka* (or *doka*) of the Kondhs; others include the large *kinnarī vīṇā* of Karnataka and the *jantar* of Rajasthan, the smaller *jantar* of Madhya Pradesh (now bowed), the *ghangri* of Maharastra and Gujarat, and the *king* of Panjab and Jammu. The several types of vīṇā listed by Abu'l Faẓl in the 16th century (see §7 below) might also have been folk instruments to some extent.

7. THE HINDUSTANI *BĪṆ*. The vīṇā, often found in the north Indian vernacular form *bīṇ*, is mentioned in Muslim court records during the Sultanate period: the king of Kashmir Zain-ul Abidin (reigned 1423–1474), a great music lover 'ordered the decoration of musical instruments like the Rubab and Bin (Vina) in gold' and the Afghan sultan Sikandar Lodi (reigned 1489–1517) had 'four boy slaves skilled in *chang, qānūn, bīṇ*, and *tunbur*'. It is also recorded in the early Mughal period as three-stringed, together with the two-string *kinnarī vīṇā, ādhaṭi*, and *kingṙa*, and the fretless *sirbīṇ* and *amṛtī*. However, with its five or six metal strings, the *yantra* was played alongside the *bīṇ* in the *akhāṙā* chamber orchestra and might have been the most important vīṇā of this time. Mughal and Deccani paintings from the 16th century show that these had evolved from the medieval *kinnarī vīṇā* type into what is substantially their modern form, though rather smaller. In the three centuries of Mughal rule the *bīṇ* and the *rabāb* were the chief instruments of court music. The descendants of Akbar's (reigned 1556–1605) chief musician Tansen, the Seniyā, formed a dynasty whose musical authority matched that of the Mughal emperors in polity; they were organized in two main branches as the *rabābiyā* and the *bīṇkār* (players of the *rabāb* and *bīṇ*), descended from Tansen's son Vilas Khan and from his daughter Sarasvati respectively, the terms applying even to singers.

The body of the *bīṇ* is a long, hollow, wooden 'stick' (*daṇḍdi* etc.), or tube, sometimes carved outside with nodes to resemble bamboo and capped at both ends with brass tubing, to which two large bottle-gourds (*tumbā; ālābu, lāu*) are attached some way below the ends near each end of the fret area. It is described in the 16th century as a 'yard' long with 16 frets, and early Mughal painting shows a high nut to which one

of the three strings (the melodic one) rises sharply over the frets from a string-guider binding, the two others being stretched laterally along the tube on either side of the frets. This nut, peculiar to the *kinnarī vīṇā*, disappeared during the 18th century. By the end of the century, the *bīṇ* had a length of about 109.5 cm with 19 frets and seven strings (four melodic and three side strings), and in the 19th century a length of about 122 cm long with 24 frets and seven strings (this being now standard although since the 1960s the *bīṇ* can have one additional side string). In the following description of the instrument's structure, measurements for a rare 17th-century court *bīṇ* (kept in *F.P.cm*) and a more recent 19th-century one (in *IRL.D.nm*) are indicated in parentheses. The strings were of metal (brass and steel). The gourds were almost whole (about 23–26.5 cm high, 34–37 cm wide, and 5–7 mm thick), and were attached by plaited leather thongs passing up from an interior supporting wooden disc through an intermediate wooden bobbin and holes in the stick; a round hole (about 13–12 cm wide) was excised in their base. Modern *bīṇ* can have their gourds attached by a heavy brass screw-tube. Both frets (about 2 to 4 cm high) and nut (about 2.5 cm) are thin (4 to 5 mm) upright brass-capped wooden plates; they are straight on top but carved below in an arch that fits on the neck and is held by a traditional cement of wax and soot (frets are also sometimes tied on the tube as on a *sitār*). The peg area has a typical bilateral arrangement of five main pegs (two on one side and three on the other), and a clockwise disposition of strings 1 to 5 from above the nut on the right side (player's view) to the same position on the left; strings 1 to 4 pass over the nut from right to left (i.e. with the main string nearest to the player's right hand, an arrangement similar to that of the southern vīṇā, but differing from the Rajasthani *jantar* and the West-Asia-derived lutes *rabāb, sitār*, and *sarod*). String 5 runs down the left side of the neck, and strings 6, 7 and sometimes 8 pass from pegs below the nut down the right. A complex bridge-piece is fitted into the lower opening of the tube, often carved as the front of a peacock, with deep, curving bone or ivory surfaces on its back and wings for the three sets of strings tied around projecting pin string holders below each section (for the curvature, *see* SITĀR and TAMBŪRĀ).

Fowke (1788) gives the 18th-century Seniyā *bīṇ* tuning as (from player's right to left) *a′–d–A–e–c♯–A*: the first two strings, of steel, are the tonic drones (*cikārī*), to the right of the stick; of the others (of brass), the third and fourth are the melody strings (tuned a 4th apart and giving on 19 frets two octaves and a tone, chromatic almost throughout), while the fifth to seventh (the last to the left of the stick) form a drone triad similar to that given for the 19th-century *rabāb*.

By the early 19th century steel was used for the first melody string, and in that century a tuning with four melody strings, *d–A–E–A′*, became standard, giving a range of three and a half octaves on the 23 or 24 frets. This, with the two *cikārī* on the right and the drone string on the left (usually tuned to the middle tonic), provided a model for the developing Hindustani lutes (*sitār, sūrbahār*) in the 19th century, and remains the modern tuning. The thickness of the strings increased in the course of time along with the size of the *bīṇ*. Today, the steel melody string (*nayaki*) has a diameter of 0.40 mm or 0.45 mm and the thicker one (*karaj*), made of brass or bronze wire, can reach 1.20 mm. Accordingly, the resulting string tension varies from 23 to 56 kg.

The main strings of the *bīṇ* are played (as in §8, below) with downward strokes of two metallic plectrums (*mizrāb*) placed on the right index and middle fingers (tied-on fish-scale plectra are mentioned), and the side-strings with upward strokes of the little fingers (on the left side the thumb or the little finger is also used occasionally to sound the drone string on the left side of the tube). The instrument is held across the body, with the left gourd on the shoulder and the right on the hip, the player formerly kneeling or standing (a position appropriate to a court servant). Sideways pulling of the strings for large-scale portamento (*mīṇḍ*) originated on the vīṇā class, and hence also, perhaps, the important element of raga repertory, *ālāp* (a free-tempo improvised development of the mode making considerable use of portamento, and much elaborated since the 19th century also by the *sitār* and *sūrbahār*). Some of the elements of instrumental *jor* and *jhālā* also owe their existence to the *bīṇ*, which was the first instrument to have the punctuating side-strings now known as *cikārī* (two side strings were already present on the early Mughal *bīṇ* and they may have been inspired from the doubled-back open string of the medieval and folk *kinnari vīṇā*). The *bīṇ* is also played in metric compositions with the drum *pakhāvaj* but here the typically Hindu subordination of instrumental to vocal style has resulted in an absence of distinctively instrumental compositional styles.

In the 1960s a modified and larger *bīṇ* was conceived by Zia Mohiuddin Dagar (1929–90) in association with the well-known Calcutta instrument maker Murari Adhikari (1928?–2006), owner of the famous workshop Kanai Lal & Sons. To facilitate the handling and control of this heavier *bīṇ*, Dagar adopted a seated cross-legged playing position, similar to that of the *sarasvatī vīṇā* (*see* §8). The diameter of the teak wood tube is larger and its walls are thicker than those of a traditional *bīṇ*. The gourd resonators are also larger, as are the wooden frets (attached to the tube with waxed flax ligatures instead of the usual cement), which are edged with thick rounded nickel-silver bars. Finally, an additional *cikārī* string was added to the right side strings, tuned in unison with the lower one of the two others. This *bīṇ* is plucked by the nails of the first and middle fingers. The pad of the ring finger is also used, mainly to soften the sound of the steel string and to render deep mellow sounds on the heavier bronze strings. Although the string gauges and tension are heavier and the pitch is higher than on a regular *bīṇ*, deflection of the strings can encompass a 5th.

The *bīṇ* is sometimes known as the *rudra vīṇā* (the vīṇā of the ascetic god Shiva, the great *yogi*), and it has strong Tantric-Yogic associated symbolisms. Since it has no soundtable, the forward projection of the sound is weak, but it vibrates powerfully into the body of the player. According to oral tradition, the *rudra vīṇā* was created by Lord Shiva, the stick with its nodes is regarded as the *merudaṇḍa* (both the human spine and the cosmic axis) and the gourds as the breasts either of Shiva's wife Parvati or of Sarasvatī, goddess of arts and learning. The length of the fret area is traditionally given as nine fists—i.e. the distance from the navel to the top of the skull (seat of the three octaves: navel, throat, and head).

8. *Sarasvatī vīṇā.* This is a large, long-necked, plucked lute, the principal chordophone (nowadays together with the Western violin) of south Indian classical music. It is played mainly by members of the *brāhman* caste in the four southern states of India (Tamil Nadu, Andhra Pradesh, Kerala, and Karnataka), and is usually employed only in the art-music tradition. Famous schools of technique/style evolved in the courts of the rajahs and continued to flourish under British rule. In modern times, technique, style, and repertory are increasingly influenced by Hindustani music from the northern states. Resistance to these influences has been strongest in the Mysore school of vīṇā playing.

The name refers to the icon of the Hindu goddess Sarasvatī playing the vīṇā (Sarasvatī is shown playing *ālāpinī* and *ekatantrī vīṇā* in 12th-century Jain palm-leaf manuscripts). She is displayed holding a *sarasvatī vīṇā* in most *brāhman* houses and places of education in south India. Sarasvatī is the goddess of *vidyā*—that supreme understanding of the nature of life which, in Hindu thought, permits the release of the individual from the cycle of reincarnation. The meaning given to the icon is that the pursuit of music leads to this understanding.

(i) Structure. The *sarasvatī vīṇā* is a long-necked lute, a later development than the stick zithers described above and which are often found in southern medieval sculpture. Tamil tradition ascribes changes in the vīṇā to the reign of Raghunatha Nayaka of Tanjore (1614–32). In terms of historical organology, the instrument's origins are hybrid. The main body derives from the long-necked barbed *rabāb*, much cultivated at the pre-Mughal Deccan Muslim courts. It also recalls the folk drone lute *tambūrī* of Karnataka and Andra Pradesh. As on the *rabāb* and the *tambūrī*, the neck and shell are sometimes in one piece; hence also the flange where they meet, a vestige of the barb, and the open, bent-back animal-motif pegbox. The wooden soundtable, the bridge (combining vīṇā and lute principles as on the *sitār*), and the stylized shoulder-and-ribs pattern on the shell, similar to the southern *tambūra*, derive from the long-necked lutes, originally carvel-built. A final layer of features— the embedded chromatic frets, the mock-gourd upper resonator, the stringing and tuning, and the playing technique—originate in the stick zither tradition. This

vīṇā is thus a unique blend of South Asian types, perhaps about three centuries old.

Of the modern instrument, two types are recognized: the Tanjore and the Mysore. The latter is made of blackwood and the former of lighter jackwood. Other differences lie mainly in the decoration of the instruments (the Tanjore vīṇā is much more elaborately carved and brightly painted) and in the position of the soundholes on the table.

The body has three main parts. The shell (*kayi, kuḍam*) is hemispherical and hollowed from a single piece of wood, often with mock 'shoulder-and-ribs' carving on the back. The heavy hollow neck (*daṇḍi*) has straight sides rounded at the back and tapering lightly towards the top; a second resonator (*burra*), of gourd, metal, or papier-maché, is screwed into a small metal cup affixed to the back of the neck below the nut. The pegbox is bent back, and open at the front, with a bilateral peg arrangement (two on the right, two on the left); it terminates in a dragon (*yāli*) head design (sometimes there is also an opening compartment for accessories). These three parts are often separate, but for tone quality the *ekadaṇḍi vīṇā*, with shell and neck of one piece, and above all the *ekāṇḍa* or *ekavada vīṇā*, with all three parts solid, are specially prized. A projecting ledge (*gvantu*; made formerly of deer horn or ivory but nowadays often of plastic) around the sides and back of the neck and shell joint is found on some types. The shell is covered by a round, thin, slightly bent wooden soundtable (*yeddapalaka*), which has two decorated soundholes about 5 cm in diameter in the upper quadrants. The bridge (*gurram* or *kudirai:* 'horse') is in the centre of the soundtable; it is similar to that of the *sitār*, with a wooden, bench-shaped trestle about 6.5 cm wide and 3 cm deep, but covered with a metal plate. The four main strings pass over the top, and the three *tāla*, or side strings, over a buttress-like metal arc that extends from the right side of the bridge down to the soundtable.

The neck is covered by a thin board (*daṇḍipalaka*). Along each side is a raised ledge (*maruvapalaka*) to which is applied a cement of wax and lamp-black which holds the frets (*metlu*) in place (small metal pins are also mentioned for this purpose.) The frets are straight brass bars, rounded on top and about 5 mm thick; there are 24, giving two full chromatic octaves on the first of the four main strings. The strings (two of steel, two of brass) are fitted in right-to-left descending order (see §7 above). The three side strings (of steel) pass from their pegs in the side of the neck, below the nut and over three small ivory knobs.

All seven strings are secured below the bridge to thick wires (*langar*) with fine-tuning devices in the form of sliding metal rings attached to an inferior string holder, a unique development on Indian lutes.

(ii) Technique. The player sits cross-legged on a mat; the secondary resonator attached below the neck of the instrument rests on the left knee and the main resonator rests on the mat, touching the right knee. The instrument is played tilted forwards. The left arm encircles the neck to fret the melody strings, the fret positions

giving a 12-note scale roughly equivalent to Western equal temperament. The left forearm, moving up and down the smooth surface of the neck, also supports and balances the vīṇā (it is considered sacrilegious to play the vīṇā left-handed).

The melody strings are struck (downwards only) with the nails of the middle and forefingers of the right hand and muted with the fingertips. The melody string nearest the *tāla* strings is called *sāraṇī* and is tuned to the system-tonic (*shaḍja*). The next string (*pañcama*) is tuned a 4th below, and the next (*mandra*) an octave below the *sāraṇī*; the fourth string (*anumandra*) is tuned an octave below the *pañcama*. The *sāraṇī* is played for most of the time, with occasional descents to the *pañcama* and very occasional descents to the *mandra*.

The melody strings are stopped with the forefinger and middle finger of the left hand. The player develops a groove from the corner of the nail across the tip of each finger within which the string slides, the method of playing being up and down single strings. The low string tension permits pitch movements of up to four semitones by deflection of the string downwards and along the fret. The player deflects, or 'pulls', the *sāraṇī* under the *pañcama* (and the *pañcama* under the *mandra*), while simultaneously muting the *pañcama* etc. with the underside of the tips of both fingers.

The large frets and absence of a fingerboard permit the player to sound notes without using the right hand by gliding up to a fret from a pitch below and/or by deflecting the string behind a fret. Both types of melodic movement are called *gamaka*. *Gamaka* executed by deflecting the string are conceived as continuous movements between the 12 pitches of the scale plus seven other '*gamaka*' pitches (located roughly midway between tonic and minor 2nd; major 2nd and minor 3rd; major 3rd and perfect 4th; augmented 4th and perfect 5th; perfect 5th and minor 6th; major 6th and minor 7th; and major 7th and supertonic). Different, and complex, configurations of such melismatic movements characterize different ragas.

In the Mysore tradition, facility in executing *gamaka* is highly regarded; in deflected *gamaka* the timing is often deliberately complex and asymmetrical. The Mysore vīṇā masters teach the skill of alternating struck notes, which mark rhythmic accents, and *gamaka*, which through their relative dynamics and complex timing mask—or conceal—rhythmic accents.

The three *tāla* (metre) strings are tuned to the system tonic, the octave above and the perfect 5th between. They are struck (upwards only) with the nail of the little finger of the right hand.

9. FRETLESS *VĪṆĀ*. The *vicitrā vīṇā* and *goṭṭuvādyam* are respectively the unfretted tube zither and lute of north and south Indian classical musics. They are played, Hawaiian-guitar style, by a smooth sliding-block in the left hand and plucking by the right. Both appear to be modern instruments dating from the 19th century; there might be a historical relationship with the medieval *ekatantrikā*, which is played similarly (see §4 above),

or with the 16th-century *sirbīn*. By the end of the 18th century, F.B. Solvyns depicted a fretless *vīṇā* with two gourds, one melody string and three side strings, called *kuplyan* and played by a Brahmin he heard in Calcutta. This *vīṇā*, fretted with a rod in the left hand, was probably one of the last survivors of the medieval *ekatantrī*. The *goṭṭuvādyam* ('block instrument') is structurally a *sarasvatī vīṇā* without frets, but, uniquely for a southern classical instrument, it has from seven to 13 sympathetic strings, which run from their pegs (set in the distal side of the neck) through and along the fingerboard under the main strings. The instrument rests on the floor before the player, with the resonator to his right. The sliding-block is of hardwood. The first melody course, nearest to the player, is a bichord tuned to an octave. The instrument is plucked by the fingers, and its repertory is principally the classical vocal raga compositions of Karnataka music. The *goṭṭuvādyam* is also called the *mahānātaka vīṇā*, suggesting an origin in dramatic music.

The northern *vicitrā* ('colourful') *vīṇā* is structurally a hybrid of the *bīn sitār* type: it has a wide neck (about 10 cm) which is flat on top and rounded in section beneath (about 3 cm deep), and pegs for the sympathetic strings set in the proximal side (the playing position is as for the *goṭṭuvādyam*). The neck terminates on the right in an integrated, wood-covered resonator, which in some cases is smaller and pear-shaped, in others larger and similar to that of the *sitār*. The instrument rests on two large bottle-gourds which are screwed into the back of the neck. The main strings are tuned in descending 4ths and 5ths (see §7); the slider (*baṭṭa*) is a glass egg.

In recent decades, a modified version of the Western acoustic cutaway guitar, played on the lap in the Hawaiian style, entered the Hindustani classical tradition. The 'Hindustani slide guitar', as it is generally called, has six to eight main metal strings, 12 to 14 sympathetic strings (*tarab*) and two side strings (*cikārī*) as on the *bīn* and the *sitār*. Two plectra, on the thumb and the forefinger of right hand, play the strings while a smooth metal or wooden rod held in the left hand stops the strings.

10. 19TH-CENTURY EPHEMERA. Among the early modern Indian writers on music and collectors of instruments the name of Raja Sir Saurindro Mohun Tagore of Calcutta (1840–1914) is pre-eminent. In addition to much writing in Bengali and English, he collected and commissioned many Indian instruments for presentation to museums in London, Paris, Brussels, and New York. His otherwise excellent work is, however, somewhat marred by an attempt to give Sanskritized *vīṇā* names to instruments that did not in practice bear them: thus *rudra vīṇā* (see §7) for the long-necked *rabāb; śāradīya vīṇā* ('autumnal lute') for the *sarod* (even though he admits in the same sentence that the name means 'to sing' in Persian); and *kacchapī vīṇā* and *tritantrī vīṇā* for the flat-backed *kachvā sitār* and small amateur *sitār* respectively (admitting that both in practice are termed *sitār*). While the term *vīṇā*, in the long sweep of Hindu

culture, has at times been used to denote any string instrument, this usage often implied an indigenous origin for the group which was neither useful nor justified, and which misled some Western museum curators and writers on organology.

Further, some objects of Tagore's collecting were of his own creation and had an ephemeral existence: examples were the 'vīṇā' with a *sitār* neck terminating in a violin body, the *kāca vīṇā* (a glass *sitār*), the *bharata vīṇā* (a *kachvā sitār* with skin soundtable), the *vipancī vīṇā* (see §2) with a waisted gourd resonator, the *prasāriṇī vīṇā* (a *sitār* with two necks) or the *śruti vīṇā* (a *sitār* with frets which could be arranged to give the ancient Indian 22-microtone scale). The *rañjanī vīṇā*, however, was of the hybrid *bīn sitār* type, which had some vogue in the 19th century.

BIBLIOGRAPHY

F. Fowke: 'On the Vina or Indian Lyre', *Asiatick Researches*, vol.1 (1788), 295; [repr. in Tagore: *Hindu Music* (1875)]

F.B. Solvyns: *Les Hindoûs, ou Description de leurs mœurs, coutumes et cérémonies*, vol.2 (Paris, 1810)

S.M. Tagore: *Hindu Music from Various Authors* (Calcutta, 1875, 2/1882/R1965)

C.R. Day: *The Music and Musical Instruments of Southern India and the Deccan* (Delhi, 1891/R1974)

L. Schroeder, ed.: *Yajurveda* (Leipzig, 1900)

C. Sachs: *Die Musikinstrumente Indiens und Indonesiens* (Berlin and Leipzig, 1914, 2/1923)

A.K. Coomaraswamy: 'The Parts of a Vīṇā', *Journal of the American Oriental Society*, vol.50 (1930), 244–253; vol.51 (1931), 47–50 vol.57 (1937), 101–103

Rāmāmātya: *Swaramelakalānidhi* (c1550); ed. M. S. Ramaswami Aiyar (Annamalai, 1932)

C. Marcel-Dubois: *Les instruments de musique de l'Inde ancienne* (Paris, 1941)

C. Sachs: *The History of Musical Instruments* (New York, 1941)

Abu'l Fażl: *Ā'īn-i-akbarī* (c1590); trans. F. Gladwin (1783); trans. H.S. Jarrett, rev. J. Sarkar in *Saṅgīt*, Bibliotheca Indica, vol.270 (Calcutta, 1948), 260ff

A. Halim: *Muslim Contribution to The Development of North Indian Music* (Bombay, 1948–9)

L.E.R. Picken: 'The Origins of the Short Lute', *GSJ*, vol.8 (1955), 32–42

Bharata: *Nāṭyaśastra* (4th–5th centuries); ed. M. Ghosh, ii (Calcutta, 1956; Eng. trans., 1961); ed. M. Ramakrishna Kavi and J. S. Pade, vol.4 (Baroda, 1964)

Śārṅgadeva: *Saṅgītaratnākara* (13th century); ed. S. Subrahmanya Sastri, vol.3 (Madras, 1951)

Parameśvara: *Vīṇaa lakṣaṇia*, ed. J. S. Pade, Gaekwad's Oriental Series, no.131 (Baroda, 1959)

V. Shankar: 'The Process of Vīṇā Fretting', *Journal of the Music Academy Madras*, vol.30 (1959), 125–9

J. Becker: 'The Migration of the Arched Harp from India to Burma', *GSJ*, vol.20 (1967), 17–23

J. Kunst: *Hindu-Javanese Musical Instruments* (The Hague, 2/1968)

E.W. te Nijenhuis: *Dattilam: a Compendium of Ancient Indian Music* (Leiden, 1970)

G.H. and N. Tarlekar: *Musical Instruments in Indian Sculpture* (Pune, 1972)

F.J. de Hen: 'A Case of Gesunkenes Kulturgut: the Toila', *GSJ*, vol.29 (1976), 84–90

B.C. Deva: *Musical Instruments of India: their History and Development* (Calcutta, 1978)

R.V. Ayyangar: *Gamaka and Vādanabheda: a Study of Somanātha's Rāga Vibodha in a Historical and Practical Context* (diss., U. of Pennsylvania, 1980)

W. Kaufmann: *Altindien*, Musikgeschichte in Bildern, vol.2/8 (Leipzig, 1982)

R. Knight: 'The Harp in India Today', *Ethnomusicology*, vol.29/1 (1985), 9–28

D. Bhattacharya: *Musical Instruments of Tribal India* (New Delhi, 1999)

S. Sarmadee, ed.: *Ghunyatu'l munya. The Earliest Persian Work on Indian Classical Music* (New Delhi, 2003)

P. Bruguière: 'An Historical Account of the Fretted Vina and its Precursors', *Hindustani Music, Thirteenth to Twentieth Centuries*, ed. J. Bor and others (New Delhi, 2010)

ALASTAIR DICK (1, 5–8 (I), 9–10); GORDON GEEKIE (8 (II–III)); RICHARD WIDDESS (2–4)/PHILIPPE BRUGUIÈRE

Vinaccia. Italian family of violin and mandolin makers, active in Naples from the mid-18th century to the 1930s. Gennaro Vinaccia (i) (*c*1710–*c*1788) seems to have been the oldest member of this extensive family; he and his sons Antonio (*c*1734–before 1796), Giovanni (*c*1730–after 1795), Vincenzo (*c*1740–*c*1802), and Nicola (*c*1745–*c*1780) produced numerous plucked and bowed string instruments. Later generations directed most of their attention to mandolins and guitars, only occasionally producing instruments of the violin family.

Antonio's three sons, Domenico, Gaetano (i) (*c*1764–after 1847), and Mariano (*c*1760–*c*1808), were accomplished mandolin makers; Gaetano also made violins. The label of one mandolin made by Mariano reads '*Marianus Vinaccia fu. Antonii/fecit anno 1796 in via Costantii no. 18/Neapoli*', establishing his relationship to Antonio and setting Antonio's death before 1796. However, one instrument with a label of Antonio is dated 1802, suggesting the existence of a second Antonio.

The Vinaccias are considered to have developed the so-called Neapolitan mandolin model in the mid-18th century. The first extant mandolin-type instrument by Gennaro is a tenor mandola made in 1744; it is the oldest example featuring the characteristics that came to define the Neapolitan style. 18th-century Vinaccia mandolins are of very high quality and are eagerly sought by collectors.

By the end of the 18th century, the Vinaccia family were regarded as among the most important Italian makers of mandolins and guitars, along with the Filano and Fabricatore families. Their workshops were located in the same area of Naples and their instruments share characteristics that came to define the 19th-century Neapolitan school of guitar and mandolin making. Most of their extant instruments are ornate and sophisticated.

Like instruments by the Fabricatore family, those by the two first generations of Vinaccias are characterized by elaborate decoration, which includes profuse use of mother-of-pearl inlays on a red or black shellac paste background; richly engraved mother-of-pearl plaques; extensive use of tortoiseshell over gold leaf which in some examples covers most of the instrument except the soundtable; exquisitely carved clasp; and use of ivory for bindings, inlays, and decorative buttons on the peghead.

The violins of Gennaro, Antonio, and Vincenzo follow the Gagliano school; the instruments by Vincenzo more closely resemblance the Guarneri model. Their varnish is typically Neapolitan in texture and ranges in colour from golden yellow-brown to red-brown.

Pasquale Vinaccia (*b* 20 June 1806; *d c*1885), son of Gaetano, followed the innovative trend of his family; he developed mechanical tuners for mandolins and led in the transition from brass to steel strings. One of the most renowned makers of his time, he made a mandolin and a guitar for Queen Margaret of Savoy. His labels, reading '*Pasquale Vinaccia e Figli/Fabbricanti di strumenti armonici/di S.M. la regina d'Italia/Rua Catalana 53 …* ', indicate collaboration with his sons, Achille (*c*1836–?*c*1927), Gennaro (ii) (*c*1832–?*c*1933), and Federico (*c*1839–after 1884). Evidence of a fourth son of Pasquale named Antonio is found in a label of an undated mandolin: *Antonio Vinaccia/fu Pasquale/Fabbricante di strumenti Armonici/Napoli*. Nothing further is known about him.

Achille and Gennaro later founded Fratelli Vinaccia, a manufactory (employing 25 or more workers and apprentices) dedicated almost exclusively to the large-scale production of mandolins, although a few guitars are extant. Their labels claim awards from expositions in Chicago (1893) and London (1898) and mention their work for the Queen. The apparent longevity of Achille and Gennaro is suggested by dates on their instruments' labels; however, it is possible that other family members inherited control of the company after their deaths and retained the brand name. The label of a mandolin by Fratelli Vinaccia made in 1900 includes the name of Carlo Munier (*c*1859–*c*1911), the virtuoso mandolin player and innovative developer and teacher of mandolin technique, who was the great-nephew of Pasquale Vinaccia.

Gennaro's son Gaetano (ii) (*c*1855–after 1927) was also an accomplished mandolin maker. The labels of his late instruments show the same address as some of the Fratelli Vinaccia instruments. Other apparent members of the Vinaccia family active as luthiers include another Gaetano, who died before 1898, and his son Giuseppe, who was active late in the 19th century. Their specific relationship to the family is unclear.

A number of apprentices from the Vinaccia workshops, including among others A. Salvino, Gennaro Rubino, Stridente, Pasquale Ancara and Pasquale D'Isanto, Fratelli de Angelis, Michele Maratea, Michele Varano, Pasquale Esposito, Gaetano Esposito, and Giuseppe Seraphino, eventually opened their own shops, which spread the Vinaccia style and reaffirmed the characteristics of the Neapolitan mandolin.

BIBLIOGRAPHY

J. Tyler and P. Sparks: *The Early Mandolin* (Oxford, 1989)

G. Antonioni: *Dizionario dei costruttori di strumenti a pizzico in Italia dal XV al XX secolo* (Cremona, 1996)

G. Accornero: *Rosa Sonora: esposizione di chitarre XVII—XX secolo* (Savigliano, 2003)

P. Sparks: *The Classical Mandolin* (Oxford, 2005)

JONATHAN SANTA MARIA BOUQUET

Vincentius [Vincenti]. (*fl* 1515). Italian instrument maker from Livigmeno (possibly Livignano, Tuscany). His harpsichord constructed in 1515–16 (*I.S.ac*) is the oldest known to survive (one made in 1521 by Hieronymus Bononiensis formerly held this distinction). An inscription on the Vincentius harpsichord indicates that it was made for Pope Leo X in 1516, and a signature on the underside of the soundboard reveals that it was started on 18 Sept 1515. Although the harpsichord was made in a style consistent with other early harpsichords, and probably with a single register, its compass cannot be definitely established. It might have been *C/E–f′′′*, although *FGA–g′′′a′′′* is also possible.

Another harpsichord maker called Vincentius (*fl* 1610–12), of Prato, also made harpsichords (now at *D.LE.u*, at *US.PP.vc*, and at *D.N.gnm*).

BIBLIOGRAPHY

D. Wraight: 'Vincentius and the Earliest Harpsichords', *EMc*, vol.14 (1986), 534–8

D. Wraight: *The Stringing of Italian Keyboard Instruments c1500–c1650* (diss., Queen's U. of Belfast, 1997), vol.2, 311–14

DENZIL WRAIGHT

Viol [viola da gamba, gamba] (Fr. *viole*; Ger. *Gambe*; It. *viola, viola da gamba*). Type of bowed string instrument with frets. It is usually played held downwards on the lap or between the legs (hence the name 'viola da gamba', literally 'leg viol'). It appeared in Europe towards the end of the 15th century and subsequently became one of the most popular of all Renaissance and Baroque instruments and was much used in ensemble music. As a solo instrument it continued to flourish until the middle of the 18th century. In 18th- and 19th-century American and British usage the term bass viol was applied to a four-string instrument of the violin family. For discussion of the viol's repertoire, and associated bibliography, *see GMO*.

1. Structure. 2. 15th-century origins. 3. Continental Europe *c*1500 to *c*1600. 4. England. 5. Italy from *c*1580. 6. France from *c*1600. 7. Germany and the Low Countries from *c*1600. 8. The modern revival.

1. STRUCTURE. During its history the viol was made in many different sizes: *pardessus* (high treble), treble, small tenor, tenor, bass, and violone (contrabass). Only the treble, tenor, and bass viols, however, were regular members of the viol consort. The *pardessus de viole* did not emerge until the late 17th century, and the violone—despite its appearance in the 16th century—was rarely used in viol consorts. The alto viol was rarely mentioned by theorists and there is some doubt as to how often it was used, or if it existed as a distinct size. Instruments called 'lyra' and 'division' viols were relatively small basses used in the performance of solo music in England.

According to Mace's guidelines (A1676) a consort or 'chest' of viols should be 'all truly and proportionably suited' in shape, wood, and colour, but especially in size. The string length from nut to bridge on the treble viol, for instance, should ideally be exactly half that on the bass viol, the treble being tuned an octave higher than the bass. Application of this principle to the tenor viol is aided by the downward *a gamba* playing position; if it were applied to the tenor member of the modern string quartet, the result would be a viola too large for comfort.

The shape of the viol was extremely variable during much of its early history. Some 16th-century instruments show the influence of the guitar family or the violin family. A few have a festooned outline in the manner of an orpharion or bandora. By the 1540s a distinctive shape had evolved in Venice, which is characterized by steeply down-sloping shoulders and a narrow upper body. A significant number of examples by Francesco Linarol and Antonio and Battista Ciciliano (if authentic) have been preserved (in *A.W.km* and *B.B.mim*), and the shape is also recorded in paintings by Titian, for example *Venus and Cupid with a Lute player, c*1565. The most characteristic form of viol, however, with its deep ribs, sloping shoulders, and middle bouts appeared early in the 16th century and became fairly standard during the 17th and 18th centuries. The viol is very lightly constructed, both the belly and the back being made of very fine wood. The belly is gently arched, whereas the back is flat, except at the top, where it slopes in towards the neck. A few crossbars are usually fixed to the back to reinforce it. The ribs of the viol are usually quite deep (often reinforced with linings of parchment or linen), and since neither the belly nor the back projects beyond them there are no overhanging 'edges'. The neck of the Renaissance viol and early 17th-century English viol was thick and rounded. In the course of the 17th century the neck became flatter, and on the later French instruments, it was sometimes very thin, resembling that of a lute. Jean Rousseau (A1687) described how the late French makers gave the viol its 'final perfection' by setting the neck at a greater angle, and also by reducing the overall thickness of the wood. Frets, made from pieces of stretched gut, are tied around the neck in a special fret knot. Normally, double frets are used. There are usually seven frets placed at intervals of a semitone, but, according to Simpson (A1659), an eighth might be added at the octave. All frets can be finely adjusted to improve the tuning. Simpson said that the strings should lie close to the fingerboard 'for ease and convenience of Stopping'.

Most viols have six strings, but the solo bass viol played on the Continent during the Baroque era often had seven and the *pardessus* five. The standard tuning of the six-string viol was a sequence of 4th, 4th, major 3rd, 4th, 4th. Thus the three principal types of viol in a consort are tuned as follows: *d–g–c′–e′–a′–d′′* (treble); *G–c–f–a–d′–g′* (tenor); and *D–G–c–e–a–d′* (bass). Players of the alto viol sometimes prefer a tuning in which the position of the major 3rd is altered: *c–f–a–d′–g′–c′′*. English (and possibly some Continental) bass viol players occasionally tuned their lowest string down to *C*. French Baroque bass viols often had a seventh string (*A′*), an innovation attributed to Jean Rousseau in 1687 to Sainte-Colombe. This string, like the *D* and *G* strings, would be overspun with silver or another metal, all three preferably having the 'same covering', according to Jean-Baptiste Forqueray (who experimented also with half-covering on the *c* string). The 18th-century French *pardessus* was usually tuned *g–c′–e′–a′–d′′–g′′*; from the 1730s the five-string *pardessus* was tuned *g–d′–a′–d′′–g′′*.

Like other fretted instruments such as the lute, the viol could have been tuned and played in equal temperament. Some 16th-century theorists such as Ganassi advocated a form of meantone temperament. This would have meant tuning the central 3rd purer and enlarging slightly the four 4ths between remaining open strings. The frets would then have been adjusted to achieve at least some of the unequal tones and semitones that this temperament requires. The fact that any single fret determines the intonation for all six strings, however, must have imposed severe limitations on its use. Modern experiments suggest that meantone intonation on the viol is best reserved for pieces with a very limited range of key.

All viols, whether supported on the calves (like the tenor and bass) or on the knees, are played in an upright, almost vertical, position. The bow is held in an underhand grip, the palm facing upwards. Simpson (A1659) wrote:

> Hold the Bow betwixt the ends of your Thumb and two foremost fingers, near to the Nut. The Thumb and first finger fastned on the Stalk; and the second fingers end turned in shorter, against the Hairs thereof; by which you may poize and keep up the point of the Bow.

The wrist should be relaxed, since quick notes 'must be express'd by moving some Joint nearer the hand; which is generally agreed upon to be the Wrist'. Heavy accents are not idiomatic to the viol because the essence of both the up- ('forward-' or 'push-') and the down-bow ('back-bow' or 'pull-bow') is a movement across the string and not a movement downwards with the weight of the arm above the bow, as it is in violin bowing. Light accents, however, can be obtained by means of a small increase in pressure at the beginning of a stroke. This small pushing accent is more easily and naturally achieved with an up-bow. Thus viol bowing is the exact reverse of violin bowing and, as Simpson wrote, 'When you see an even Number of Quavers or Semiquavers, as 2, 4, 6, 8. You must begin with your Bow forward' (i.e. with an up-bow).

The early viol bow is characteristically convex (like an unstretched archer's bow) rather than concave like a violin bow. A concave design is found in some 18th-century French bows: this gives the advantage of a more sensitive response to nuance. The player governs tension by pressure with the middle finger directly on the hair; pressure on the stick itself would merely cause the hair to bend towards the arc of the stick. According to Danoville (A1687) a viol bow 'must be of Chinese wood, and should not be too heavy, because it makes the [bowing] hand clumsy, nor too light, because then it cannot play chords [easily] enough; but a weight proportioned to the hand, which is why I leave that to the choice of the one who plays the Viol'. Rousseau, however, wrote: 'But it seems to me that one finds many other sorts of woods used to make Bows, which are no less good than Chinese wood'. Chinese wood is almost certainly snakewood, but Trichet pointed out that brazilwood (of which pernambuco is a superior variety) was also known in France, and other wood was certainly known in England.

Because of the lightness of its body construction and the relatively low tension of its strings, the viol is extremely resonant and readily responds to the lightest stroke of the bow. Its tone is quiet but has a reedy, rather nasal quality which is quite distinctive and makes it an ideal instrument for playing polyphony, in which clarity of texture is of the greatest importance. On the other hand the viol is less successful in music to be danced to, partly because its sound is rather restrained, but also because it cannot accent heavily enough.

The viol's capacity for resonance is enhanced by the way the left hand takes advantage of the frets. The finger presses the string down hard directly behind the fret and thereby produces an effect akin to that of an open string. A vital technique for achieving resonance—as well as for facility in fast passagework—is the use of 'holds', whereby each finger, once placed behind a fret, remains there even after the note has been played, until it has to be moved to another position. This technique enables the instrument, in Simpson's words, 'to continue the Sound of a Note when the Bow hath left it'. For this, as for multiple stops, the fact that the placing of the frets guarantees stability of intonation enables the left hand to assume a greater variety of postures than would be possible on an unfretted instrument such as a violin or cello.

During the 16th and 17th centuries there were many highly skilled viol makers, particularly English craftsmen such as John Rose, Henry Jaye, and Richard Meares. Outstanding makers of the late 17th and 18th centuries included Barak Norman in England, Michel Colichon, Nicolas Bertrand, and Guillaume Barbet in France, Jacob Stainer in the Tyrol, and Joachim Tielke's workshop in Hamburg. Makers of the *pardessus* included Jean-Baptiste Dehay ('Saloman') and Louis Guersan.

2. 15TH-CENTURY ORIGINS. The characteristic playing position of the viol seems to have been known in Europe as early as the 11th century, when waisted fiddles were played like viols, resting on the lap or between the knees with the bow held above the palm. A 12th-century miniature depicts an unusually large instrument of this type, which is sometimes referred to as the medieval viol. Rebecs were also played in this way, as is shown in the famous 13th-century *Cantigas de Santa María*. By the early 14th century, however, this method of playing bowed instruments had almost completely disappeared from Europe. But in Aragon rebecs were played *a gamba* throughout the 14th and 15th centuries, as shown for example in a mid-15th-century Aragonese miniature of King David (*GB-Lbl* Add.28962, f.82) and in a painting of St Anthony Abbot by the Almudévar Master (Juan de la Abadía; in *GB-Cfm*). The Aragonese rebec thus provides a link between the general disappearance of the *a gamba* playing posture at the end of the 13th century and its re-emergence two centuries later with the Renaissance viol.

Viols appear in late 15th-century paintings from the Aragonese province of Valencia. A painting of the Virgin and Child, by a follower of Valentín Montolíu, comes from the Maestrazgo, a mountainous region to the north of the Valencian district of Castellón de la Plana. It is one of the earliest known representations of the Renaissance viol, dating from about 1475. By 1500 the viol was regularly depicted in angelic consorts by Valencian, Majorcan, and Sardinian painters. In the Cagliari Museo Nazionale is a fine full-length picture of an angel viol player, painted about 1500 by the Sardinian Master of Castelsardo. This shows a fairly typical early Spanish viol with an extremely long narrow neck, frets, lateral pegs, central rose, very thin ribs, and tenor-sized body with the characteristic viol shape, waisted but with marked corners. Like most other Valencian viols of this period it does not have a raised fingerboard, and instead of an arched bridge the strings pass over a low uncurved bar attached to the belly. In other paintings the strings are actually fixed to the bar as on a plucked instrument. The Castelsardo Master's viol with its long neck, thin ribs, and generally slim outline appears to have been a tall instrument, quite distinct from the shorter, deeper-bodied viol that became standard in Italy during the 16th century. Later Valencian viols of the type pictured by the St Lazarus Master do, in fact, have shorter necks and wider, deeper waists, but still retain the thin ribs. On the belly of this particular instrument is a pattern of ornaments characteristic of the *vihuela de mano*. Iconographic evidence suggests that the viol was the result of applying the traditional Aragonese technique of rebec playing to a new bowed instrument whose size and body construction were essentially those of the plucked *vihuela de mano*. For such instruments, the term *vihuela de arco* seems appropriate.

The viol quickly spread across the Mediterranean through the Balearic Islands and Sardinia to Italy. Its advance was probably assisted by the Borgia family from Valencia, from whose ranks came two popes, Calixtus III and Alexander VI. It was during the pontificate of Alexander VI (1492–1503) that viols began to appear in Rome and in cities to the north, such as Urbino and Ferrara, that were dominated by the Borgias. Some of the earliest representations of viols in Italian art are by painters working in those areas: Costa in Ferrara, Francia in Bologna, and Raphael (as well as Timoteo Viti) in Urbino and Rome.

The court of Isabella d'Este at Mantua seems to have been particularly receptive to new Spanish instruments of all kinds, which included the *vihuela de mano* and possibly a Spanish form of lute, as well as the viol. In the last decade of the 15th century Lorenzo de Pavia, Isabella's agent, was frequently involved in the purchase or repair of a range of instruments made 'in the Spanish manner': the 'viola spagnola', the 'viola a la spagnola', the 'liutto a la spagnola', and the plain 'spagnola'. It is probable that one of the earliest viol consorts ever made was the one provided for Isabella by Lorenzo from a workshop in Brescia.

In 1493 the chronicler Bernardo Prospero reported that some Spanish musicians had come from Rome to Mantua playing viols 'as tall as I am' ('viole grande quasi come me'). These Spanish players had probably come from Valencia to Rome with Rodrigo Borgia (Alexander VI). Their 'viole grande' may have been long-necked Spanish viols. Tall, slim viols with long necks appear

also in Italian paintings of this period, notably in Lorenzo Costa's *Virgin and Child Enthroned with Saints*, on an altarpiece dated 1497 (in S Giovanni in Monte, Bologna), and Timoteo Viti's painting of the same subject (Pinacoteca di Brera, Milan). In other early 16th-century Italian paintings the viol appears as a more fully developed instrument. Raphael in his *Allegory of St Cecilia* (*c*1513–16; Pinacoteca Nazionale, Bologna) depicted a tenor viol with a carved lion's head scroll and nearly all the characteristics of a typical 17th-century instrument: deep ribs, sloping shoulders, flat back bending in at the upper end towards the neck, two c-holes, frets, six pegs, and a slightly arched belly. This picture illustrates the most important single change that the viol underwent in Italy: the older flat-bridged Valencian type gave way to the instrument with an arched bridge and a fingerboard. In effect, Italian makers enabled the viol, which had hitherto probably had a melodic and a drone-playing capability only, to develop into an instrument fully equipped to play an individual line in a polyphonic ensemble. As a direct result of this fundamental change of identity, there was now the need to make viols of different sizes. At first, only two sizes, tenor and bass, were required. Ensemble music for which these sets of large viols were well suited included textless polyphony, and frottolas which could be performed by solo voice and instruments.

Although there is no iconographic evidence of any viol-like instrument in 15th-century German art, numerous references to groups of 'Geigen' players in archival sources suggest that a tradition of string consort playing began to take root north of the Alps, and that German instrumentalists employed in the Italian courts played a significant role in the early development of the viol as an ensemble instrument. However, the term 'Geige' itself was a generic one, which could with equal reason be taken to refer to other bowed or plucked instruments or to mixed ensembles. The first iconographic evidence that the viol had entered the domains of Maximilian I comes in the early years of the 16th century.

A bass viol is pictured in Grünewald's famous Isenheim altarpiece (1512/13–15), although the bowing technique of the player is obviously unrealistic. Martin Agricola in his *Musica instrumentalis deudsch* (A1529) hinted at the southern origins of viols by describing them as 'grosse welschen Geygen' ('large Italian fiddles'). The curious woodcuts of 'grosse Geygen' printed by Agricola, like some Valencian depictions of viols, show instruments without fingerboard, bridge, or tailpiece; the strings pass over a rose and are attached to a bar on the belly. Woodfield noted that the large majority of extant depictions of this instrument come from Basle—Agricola's woodcut, for example, derives directly from that in Virdung's *Musica getutscht* (Basle, 1511). He suggested that the origins of its characteristic shape may lie in the flamboyant lira da braccio outlines of the kind depicted by Cima da Conegliano, woodcuts of which were readily available in Basle.

Early German theorists point to the closeness of the relationship between the viol and lute. Judenkünig, for example, equated the viol with the lute. Both instruments are pictured together on the titlepage woodcut of his 1523 treatise, and in the introduction he stated that his instructions were for both. Yet the viol is scarcely mentioned in the text and all the musical examples are for lute, so it is not clear how the viol player was expected to use the treatise. Some early Renaissance writers classified bowed and plucked instruments together. Tinctoris (*De inventione et usu musicae, c*1487) wrote of two types of 'viola', 'sine arculo' ('without a bow') and 'cum arculo' ('with a bow'), as though they were members of the same family.

3. CONTINENTAL EUROPE *c*1500 TO *c*1600. The terminology of the viol family during the 16th century was varied and at times extremely confusing. The generic word 'viola' (viol) included two quite different instruments, the viola 'da braccio' (i.e. 'arm' viol) and the viola 'da gamba' (i.e. 'leg' viol). Few writers before the middle of the century, however, used either modifying phrase. While some Italian and Spanish writers used the phrase viola 'da arco' or vihuela 'de arco' (i.e. bowed viol) in order to distinguish the viol from plucked instruments, the clarifying phrase 'de arco' was often omitted. Further confusion was caused by the widespread use of the word 'viola' to refer to the lira da braccio. Some theorists, therefore, referred to the 'fretted' viol, the *lira* being unfretted. The title-page of Ganassi's viol tutor (A1542) is unusually specific in its reference to the 'violone d'arco da tasti' ('bowed fretted viol'). The terminology of viol consorts was at times equally inconsistent. Italian writers, for example, often described consorts in terms of the bass instrument, the violone. Thus, references to 'violoni' or 'violoni da gamba' do not necessarily imply a consort consisting entirely of bass viols. The term 'violoni', however, can easily be confused with 'violini' or 'violons', meaning violins. In fact, isolated references to viols in literary works, inventories and account books are often ambiguous.

Despite the confusing terminology, there is ample evidence that the viol was popular at many 16th-century courts. Baldassare Castiglione wrote enthusiastically of the viol consort ('quattro viole da arco') in his *Il libro del cortegiano* (Venice, 1528; Eng. trans. by T. Hoby, 1561), a vivid description of life in an early 16th-century court: 'The musicke with a sette of violes doth no lesse delite a man: for it is verrie sweet and artificiall'. Theorists too commented on the upper-class status of the viol. Jambe de Fer (A1556), for example, wrote that the viol was played by 'gentlemen, merchants and other men of virtue' as a pastime, whereas the violin was usually considered a 'professional' instrument of the lower classes, often played in the streets to accompany dances or to lead wedding processions. Shakespeare attests to the viol's noble status; and Moll in Dekker and Middleton's *The Roaring Girl* (1611) is deeply indignant when her porter refers to her viol as a 'fiddle', although another character suggests that the viol is considered by many as 'an unmannerly instrument for a woman'.

It would be wrong, however, to suggest that the viol was played only by amateurs for their private enjoyment. Many courts employed professional viol players—sometimes complete consorts—to perform in the musical *intermedi* given at royal weddings or other special occasions. In 1502, at the wedding of Alfonso d'Este and Lucrezia Borgia at Ferrara, one of the *intermedi* included music played by six viols. Throughout the century, the viol consort remained an essential part of the Renaissance *intermedio* 'orchestra'. It was most frequently used with other consorts of instruments, such as flutes or trombones, and sometimes in even larger ensembles. Some of the viol players hired for these special occasions were doubtless skilled professionals able to perform elaborate ornamentation. The names of several celebrated violists have survived; Ganassi mentioned two in his treatise—Giuliano Tibertino and Lodovico Lasagnino. The popularity of the viol with amateur players resulted in the publication of several viol tutors. Many general treatises on music, too, included sections devoted to viol playing or viol music.

Ganassi was the first writer to describe in detail the standard method of holding the viol—firmly between the knees, but with the knees not impeding the bow stroke. His method is illustrated on the titlepage woodcut of *Regola rubertina*. Yet iconographic evidence shows that viols were often played in positions other than those recommended in textbooks. Two of the famous viol players pictured by Paolo Veronese in his *Marriage at Cana* (1562–3) in the Louvre are holding their viols in an almost horizontal position. This posture was condemned by Ganassi. Bass viol players are sometimes pictured standing, with their viols either resting on the ground or supported on a small stool (as described by Jambe de Fer), or even held against the body with no visible means of support at all. This last method, illustrated by the woodcut in Judenkünig (A1523) and in several illustrations of processions, looks highly improbable since the player has to support the weight of the instrument while playing it. Jambe de Fer, however, described a device used by players of the bass *viola da braccio* to help take the weight of their instrument. This consisted of a small hook worn by the player which could be attached to an iron ring fixed to the back of his instrument—an arrangement which may on occasion have been adopted by bass viol players. But despite these and other unusual playing positions, the standard posture as described by Ganassi remained almost unchanged and was firmly advocated by later 17th-century English theorists.

In the second volume of his viol tutor (A1543) Ganassi described fingering techniques in some detail. He gave five different fingerings for a scale (shown in ex.1). It is clear from his fourth and fifth alternatives that he intended the viol player to make full use of high positions. Indeed, his ricercares for solo viol contain some quite extended high passages, up to a 9th above the open top string. Alternative fingerings avoid unnecessary string crossing (ex.2). The ricercares for solo viol and the madrigal arrangement for voice and viol contain many chords, some of which are facilitated by Ganassi's use of the *barré* (one finger laid flat across two or more strings).

Ex.1.

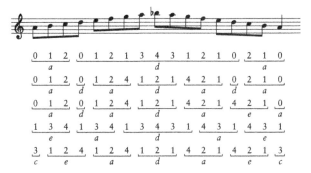

Ex.2.

The characteristic 'underhand' viol bowing was described by Ganassi. He started with the basic techniques, such as the grip with the thumb and middle finger holding the bow and the index finger applying the required amount of pressure; the different types of bow stroke; the use of arm in sustaining long notes, and the wrist in playing fast passagework; and the need to keep the bowing arm firm but flexible. The correct use of up- and down-bows is explained at great length. Moreover, some of the musical examples have bowing marks, a dot beneath a note or letter indicating a down-bow, and the absence of a dot an up-bow. There are no slur marks as such, but there are occasionally two consecutive up- or down-bows, both articulated. Ortiz's *Trattado* suggests that groups of two or three fast notes ('semiminimas') should be played in one bow. But the quick passagework in Ganassi's ricercares for solo viol is fully bowed out, usually with up-bows on the strong beats.

Ganassi's most interesting comments concern the style of good viol playing and the variety of tone which a good viol can produce. In the section on bowing, for example, he wrote that the best place to bow is at a distance of four fingers' width from the bridge. But he also described the rougher sound of the strings near the bridge and their more restrained sound near the fingerboard. The viol player, it would seem, was completely at liberty to use these different sound qualities if he so desired. Ganassi also referred to a 'tremar' (shaking) of the bowing arm and the left hand, possibly an indication of tremolando and vibrato. These and similar passages all serve to emphasize Ganassi's view that viol playing should be above all else expressive, and that the best way to play expressively is to imitate the human voice. To illustrate this, one of his most important points, he compared the viol player to the orator, who expresses his meaning to his listeners by gestures of the hand and changes in the tone of his voice. In the same way, he wrote, the good viol player should aim at variety and be sensitive to the music that is being

played; and should not, for example, bow with vigour in 'sad and afflicted' music.

The earliest printed source of viol tunings is Agricola's *Musica instrumentalis deudsch* (A1529), which gives the following tunings: *f–a–d′–g′–c″* (*discantus*); *c–f–a–d′–g′* (*altus, tenor*); *G–c–f–a–d′–g′* (*bassus*). These tunings are clearly based on a single sequence of intervals for the whole consort, and consequently the position of the third varies within the consort. Most later theorists gave tunings in which all viols have the same sequence of intervals.

Ganassi devoted a large section of his tutor to explaining four 'regole' (rules) for consort tuning. The first three are given in Table 1. The fourth rule, which according to Ganassi was used by most players, is rather different. Entitled 'Modo de sonar una quarta piu alta' ('how to play a 4th higher'), it consists of a tuning for five-string viols (Table 2). It seems that the purpose of this tuning was to enable the performer to play in a higher position on a viol tuned to a lower pitch. The tenor viol, for example, is tuned just like the bass viol of the first three tunings without its lowest string: [*D*–]*G–c–e–a–d′*. The note *g′*, therefore, which in the first tuning is the open top string, has to be played on the fifth fret above the top string. In other words, the fourth rule involves a change of position, not pitch. Gerle gave an identical tuning for viols with five strings. Unlike Ganassi, however, he implied that a sixth string could be added, a 4th below the other five. A six-string bass, therefore, would presumably be tuned [*A′*–]*D–G–B–e–a*, although Gerle did not actually give the low notes in any of his charts.

Theorists of the late 16th and early 17th centuries gave one of two tunings. Cerreto and Mersenne gave the normal 'd tuning' as in Ganassi's first and second rules. Zacconi, Banchieri, Cerone, and Praetorius gave a '*G* tuning', a 5th lower. Banchieri, for example, gave the tunings in Table 3. The problem of these two quite

Table 1

	Soprano	Tenor	Bass
Rule 1	*d–g–c′–e′–a′–d″*	*G–c–f–a–d′–g′*	*D–G–c–e–a–d′*
Rule 2	*d–g–c′–e′–a′–d″*	*A–d–g–b–e′–a′*	*D–G–c–e–a–d′*
Rule 3	*c–f–b♭–d′–g′–c″*	*G–c–f–a–d′–g′*	*D–G–c–e–a–d′*

Table 2

Soprano	Tenor	Bass
d–g–b–e′–a′	*G–c–e–a–d′*	*D–G–b–e–a*

Table 3

violone in contrabasso (violone)	*D′–G′–C–E–A–d*
violone da gamba (bass)	*G′–C–F–A–d–g*
viola mezana da gamba (tenor, alto)	*D–G–c–e–a–d′*
quarta viola in soprano (treble)	*G–c–f–a–d′–g′*

different tunings is partly one of confusing terminology. The 'tenor' viol of the low-pitched consort was the exact equivalent of the 'bass' viol of the high-pitched consort. Thus the name given to a viol depended more on its relative position in the consort than on its absolute size or pitch. Very little music appears to have been composed for the low *G*-tuned consort; almost all 16th- and 17th-century viol music is for the higher *d*-tuned instruments. It has therefore been suggested that the low-pitched viols were used in concerted music, doubling other instruments and voices. The origins of the low *G*-tuned viol consort remain something of a mystery. The relationship between the low-pitched viols of the late 16th century and the earlier five-string viols described by Gerle and by Ganassi in his fourth rule may be significant (Table 4).

An interesting regional variant in viol tunings was given by Jambe de Fer, who contrasted the tunings of Italy and France. His 'Italian' tuning follows the standard sequence of intervals (4th–4th–3rd–4th–4th). In France, however, it was apparently the custom to play on five-string viols tuned to a sequence of 4ths without the 3rd. This 'French' tuning is confirmed by Mareschall's *Porta musices* (Table 5).

The first printed source of solo viol music is Ganassi's *Regola rubertina*, which includes several ricercares for viol and one madrigal arrangement for viol and voice. The ricercares are short 'improvisations' consisting of running scales, cadential flourishes, and some double stopping. In the arrangement of the madrigal *Io vorei dio d'amor* the viol accompanies the voice with a series of chords. This most interesting piece was probably intended as an imitation of the chordal style of playing associated with the *lira da braccio*. *Regola rubertina* also includes three exercises for practising various intervals. Some similar exercises are given in Mareschall's *Porta musices*; like Ganassi's they are intended to help the student practise difficult intervals and awkward leaps. The art of playing divisions (i.e. improvising ornaments) was an essential part of the musical education of all 16th-century musicians, and Ortiz devoted the whole of his treatise on viol playing to this subject. His musical examples include ornamented cadential patterns for viol consort, freely ornamented versions of

vocal pieces for solo viol and keyboard, and 'improvisations' over well-known bass patterns like the folia and the romanesca. Ortiz's arrangements of Sandrin's chanson *Doulce memoire* and Arcadelt's madrigal *O felici occhi miei* are among the most beautiful 16th-century pieces for solo viol. The ornamentation is restrained but by no means confined to standard cadential patterns. Towards the end of the century a small bass viol, the viola bastarda, was developed specifically to perform divisions.

4. ENGLAND. The viol was introduced into England sometime early in the reign of Henry VIII, perhaps by members of the van Wilder family. In 1526 two viol players, Hans Hossenet and Hans Highorne, entered regular employment at a monthly salary of 33s. 4d. In contrast with Italy and Germany, where its impact was immediate, there is little evidence to suggest that the viol spread rapidly into English society, and not until the 1530s is there any significant evidence of ownership of viols outside the royal court. In 1540 the appointment of Henry VIII's 'newe vialles', who comprised a complete consort of string players from Venice, Milan, and Cremona, provided a strong impetus to the growth of the viol's popularity in England. Despite their official Italian identities, Henry's viol players were in fact Jews from northern Italian sephardic communities. The rapidly increasing popularity of the viol at the Tudor court is reflected in the inventory of Henry VIII's great collection of instruments (*GB-Lbl* Harl.1419), compiled at the end of his reign in 1547. It includes an item 'xix Vialles great and small with iii cases of woodde covered with blacke leather to the same'. A few years later, English viol players were employed: in 1549 Thomas Kentt was 'admitted to the Vialles in place of great Hans deceased', and from 1554 Thomas Browne appeared regularly in the lists of players.

The introduction of the viol into the curriculum of London choir schools during the reign of Henry VIII marked a new era of growth in England. By the mid-century selected choirboys at the Chapel Royal, St Paul's Cathedral, and Westminster Abbey were receiving regular tuition. In 1582 Sebastian Westcote, the Master of the Children at St Paul's, bequeathed to the Almonry his 'cheste of vyalyns and vialles' for the use of the pupils. For a while in the 1560s the children viol players of St Paul's occupied an especially prominent place in the ceremonial and theatrical activities undertaken by their school. At the Goldsmiths' Annual Feast on 17 June 1560, for example, company members were regaled with musical entertainment during their meal: 'And all the dynner tyme the syngyng chyldren of Paules played upon their vialles & songe verye pleasaunt songes to the delectacion & rejoysynge of the whole companie'. Incidental music and song accompaniments were also provided for plays. The interlude 'Wyt and Science' (*c*1545) by John Redford, organist of St Paul's, calls for a viol consort on stage: 'Heere cumth in fowre wyth violes and syng'. The long-term influence of the choirboy viol players was considerable. Generations of trained

Table 4

Gerle	[A']–D–G–B–e–a
Ganassi	D–G–B–e–a
Praetorius	A'–D–G–B–e–a
	(or G'–C–F–A–d–g)

Table 5

Jambe de Fer		Mareschall	
dessus	e–a–d'–g'–c"	discant	f♯–b–e'–a'–d"
taille	B–e–a–d'–g'	tenor	B–e–a–d'–g'
bas	E–A–d–g–c'	bass	E–A–d–g–c'

musicians entered the wider musical community in young adulthood with their viol playing skills. Furthermore, musical genres which had some early association with the choir schools (the *In Nomine*, the consort song, and the consort anthem) retained a prominent place in the English repertory for the instrument.

The extent to which viol playing was taken up by amateur players in 16th-century England has been the subject of some controversy. However, there was a steady increase in the ownership of sets of viols in large Elizabethan households. In 1537, to take an early example, the accounts of the Earl of Rutland show that 53s. 4d. was paid for 'four viols bought at London'. Neither this, nor the activities of the choirboy consorts, however, prove the existence of a strong tradition of amateur playing; not until the beginning of the 17th century did the viol consort achieve widespread currency. Even then, pictorial evidence of its popularity remains surprisingly scarce. The painting of Sir Henry Unton from shortly after 1596 (in the National Portrait Gallery, London) is exceptional. It depicts a domestic consort of five viol players seated round a table. A typical 17th-century 'chest' of viols as described by North included two trebles, two tenors, and two basses.

With the instruments of the younger John Rose (*d* 1611), the English viol found its classic outline (although not all surviving Rose instruments are to this pattern). His father, also named John (*fl* 1552–61), was well established as a viol maker by the mid-16th century and successfully exported his instruments to Italy. John Stow rated the son's gifts 'as a maker of Bandoras, the Voyall de Gamboes and other instruments' as 'far exceeding' those of his father (*Annales*, 1631). John Rose's viols in the elegant classical shape share the same basic features of the Venetian instruments of Ventura Linarol (*b* 1539/40): both are lightly built with sloping shoulders, deep ribs, and a flat back with the bend and slope towards the neck, and the table and back meeting the ribs flush at right angles. A distinctive feature of English viol design, perhaps developed by Rose himself, was the use of five pieces of wood for the belly. A further characteristic of some of Rose's surviving instruments, which was used by the later English makers, is extravagant decoration using geometrical designs in purfling and cross-hatching etched out with a hot needle. The viols of Henry Jaye (*fl* c1610–67) of Southwark were the most prized in the mid-17th century. Two other makers of particular importance were Richard Meares and Barak Norman; the latter's surviving bass viols are generally of the smaller division size, which seems to have been preferred in the late 17th century and early 18th.

Instruction books on viol playing appeared during the 17th century. Robinson's *The Schoole of Musicke* (A1603) and Playford's *A Breefe Introduction* (A1654) were intended primarily for consort players. For viol players wishing to learn the solo techniques of the lyra and division viols there were Playford's *Musick's Recreation on the Lyra Viol* (A1652), Simpson's remarkably comprehensive *The Division-Violist* (A1659), and Hely's *The Compleat Violist* (A1699). The

Table 6

slur ⌒	thump ⌒	hold ✓

existence of a flourishing school of solo viol playing led to some refinements of technique including the slur, the 'thump' or pizzicato (on the lyra viol), and the hold (see §1 above and Table 6). Hume even made use of the *col legno*, instructing the player to 'Drum this with the back of your bow'. On the more basic matters of posture, bowing, and fingering, 17th-century writers mainly followed their 16th-century predecessors. The importance of a correct or 'decent' posture, however, was given particular emphasis. Simpson, for example, criticized the playing of fast notes with the whole arm, on the grounds that 'it will cause the whole body to shake, which (by all means) must be avoyded; as also any other indecent Gesture'. There was also controversy about how best to use the elbow joint in bowing. Some, like Simpson, preferred it rigid; others, like Mace, 'Something Plying or Yielding to an Agile Bending'.

Consorts of viols continued to be popular in England longer than on the Continent. As North observed, 'the use of chests of violls, which supplyed all instrumental consorts, kept back the English from falling soon into the modes of forrein countrys, where the violin and not the treble viol was in use'. In fact it was the bass viol that lasted the longest, for despite North's comments, the 'extraordinary jolly' violin had begun to rival the treble viol quite early in the 17th century. The popularity of the violin was finally established during the Restoration period. Charles II detested the contrapuntal fancies of viol consorts, preferring instead the 'brisk and arie' sound of violins. Yet the bass viol lingered on as an amateur instrument, particularly for playing basso continuo lines, because of its subtle tone and ease in executing fast passages. Samuel Pepys enjoyed evenings devoted to 'the vyall and singing'; the practice of singing to an improvised chordal accompaniment on the bass viol (as an alternative to the lute or theorbo) persisted throughout the 17th century.

The earliest source of English consort music is Henry VIII's songbook (GB-Lbl Add.31922; ed. in *MB*, vol.18, 1962, 2/1969), which dates from the early 16th century. The short, textless 'consorts' contained in that manuscript were probably not composed with any particular instrument in mind. The most significant development in late 16th-century consort music was undoubtedly the growth of idiomatic writing for the viol. On the Continent ricercares, fantasias, and canzonas were still being described as 'da sonar' ('to be played'). But in England instrumentation was often specified in more detail. Thus English composers were able to distinguish between the comparatively restricted range of the voice and the wider compass of the viol. Tomkins, for example, commenting on a series of fantasias by Ferrabosco (*GB-Lbl* Add.29996), wrote 'made only for the vyolls and organ which is the Reason that he takes such liberty of compass which he would have Restrayned; if it had bin made for voyces only'. Playing above the frets, therefore, became quite common as the viol's upper register was increasingly exploited. The solo viol repertory was also influential in the development of idiomatic consort music.

The development of idiomatic writing is perhaps best seen in the 'broken' consorts of the early 17th century in which bowed, plucked, keyboard, and wind instruments were combined. During the 17th century many different instrumentations were tried, including both consort viols and solo lyra and division viols, as for example in the consorts for treble, bass, and lyra viols by Ferrabosco and Hume, the consorts for violin, division viol, theorbo, and harp by William Lawes, the duets for keyboard and bass viol published in *Parthenia In-Violata* (RISM *c*1614), and the fantasia-suites for one or two violins, bass viol, and organ by Ferrabosco and Coprario.

There can be little doubt that viols were often used in the performance of vocal music. Directions such as 'Apt for Viols and Voyces' or 'to be played on Musicall Instruments' are frequently found on the titlepages of late 16th- and early 17th-century publications. The English consort song, which dates from the mid-16th century, was written specifically for viols and solo voice or voices.

By the mid-17th century newer forms such as the suite or 'sett', a flexible combination of fantasias and dances, were becoming increasingly popular. There were also some important changes in instrumentation. The 'whole' consort of three to six viols was often replaced by the 'broken' consort of violins, bass viols, and organ. The organ, in fact, became a regular member of the viol consort. Parts for the organ varied from simple score reductions of the viol parts (as in the magnificent set of five-part fantasias by Jenkins) to completely independent parts, sometimes with quite extended solo sections (as in Jenkins's airs for two trebles, two basses, and organ). Locke and other Restoration composers wrote much music for the new instrumentation of one or two trebles (viols or violins), bass viol, and organ.

The bass viol remained popular with amateur musicians well into the 18th century and even into the 19th, as both a solo and an accompanying instrument, and the arrival in England during the 1758–9 season of Carl Friedrich Abel, the instrument's last famous virtuoso, stimulated a short-lived but significant revival of interest. Abel's playing, according to Burney 'was in every way complete and perfect' and his compositions 'easy and elegantly simple'. After his death in 1787 Burney remarked that Abel's 'favourite instrument was not in general use and will probably die with him'.

Gainsborough, an enthusiastic amateur, and a friend of Abel, wrote to a friend on 4 June 1772: 'I'm sick of Portraits and wish very much to take my Viol da Gamba and walk off to some sweet Village when I can paint Landskips and enjoy the fag End of Life in quietness and ease'. Another artist who studied 'viol di gamba' in his youth (*c*1766) was Thomas Jones. One of the aristocratic enthusiasts for the viol at this period was Lady

Spencer. The Althorpe accounts in 1773 and 1774 (*GB-Lbl* Althorpe F 184) contain references to the purchase of two complete sets of viol strings, to the 'Puting a Viol da Gamba in order', and to the supply of a 'Bow for the Viola da Gamba'. Mrs Howe wrote to Lady Spencer on 29 Dec 1779 (*GB-Lbl* Althorpe F 45) that she was looking forward to 'hearing one of y r new pieces of musick upon y r Viol de gambo'. The only 18th-century public performance with piano and viola da gamba so far recorded took place at Coopers' Hall in King Street, Bristol, on 17 Jan 1771. The programme included: 'a song by Miss Marshall, accompanied by the Piano Forte and Viol de Gambo' and 'a favourite Lesson on the Harpsichord by Miss Marshall, accompanied by the Viol de Gambo'. The last work with a part for 'Viola di Gamba' to be published in England was perhaps no.7 of William Jackson's *Twelve Songs*, op.16 (*c*1790).

5. ITALY FROM *c*1580. Virtuosity on the bass viol first reached spectacular heights with the Italian school of viola bastarda playing, the seeds of which are found in the madrigal improvisations of Ortiz (1553). The fully fledged *bastarda* style flourished from about 1580 to 1630; the first published compositions were by Girolamo Dalla Casa (*Il vero modo di diminuir*, 1584) and the last by Vincenzo Bonizzi (*Alcune opere di diverse auttori a diverse voci, passaggiate principalmente per la viola bastarda*, 1626). In addition to its solo role, the viol continued to be used in ensembles. Pietro de' Bardi, in a letter to G.B. Doni (1634), recalled Vincenzo Galilei's *stile rappresentativo* setting of Dante's lament of Count Ugolino (performed with the Florentine Camerata in 1582) as being 'intelligibly sung by a good tenor and precisely accompanied by a consort of viols'. Monteverdi's scoring of *Orfeo* (1607) includes three *bassi da gamba*. In this work, as in the *intermedi* of the previous century, the contrasting instrumental timbres have an important symbolic significance: the viol family was associated with the gods, the supernatural and the nobility, and the bass members were thus suitable for depicting the underworld (with trombones). Monteverdi later specified a *contrabasso da Gamba* in his *Combattimento di Tancredi et Clorinda* of 1624 (published 1638).

As the 17th century progressed the viols were gradually ousted by the violin family: already by the time of Monteverdi's *Orfeo* the treble had fallen to the brilliant and fashionable violin (though it continued to be used in Germany until the middle of the century and in England and France for even longer). By the second quarter of the century Italian string continuo parts increasingly demanded the new cello. Writing from Rome in 1639, the French virtuoso André Maugars lamented

as for the viol, there is no one in Italy now who excels at it; and indeed it is very little played in Rome, at which I was greatly astonished, since formerly they had Horatio [Bassani] of Parma, who did marvellous things with it and left to posterity some very fine pieces.

Nevertheless the viol family did not die out. There is evidence that consorts of viols still persisted in cultural isolation, for example, in Sicily and in convents, and the bass viol is specified in two Venetian operas of the 1670s, Petronio Franceschini's *Arsinoe* (1676) and Carlo Pallavicino's *Nerone* (1679). Ten patterns survive by Stradivari for a 'Viola da Gamba of the French Form' from 1701, and a number of fine Italian six- and seven-string instruments from the first two decades of the 18th century also exist. And despite its unpopularity at the time of Maugars' visit, it appears to have been particularly in Rome that an interest in the viol was rekindled in the early 18th century, notably by the patrons Benedetto Pamphili and F.M. Ruspoli. Pamphili employed a viol player named 'Monsieur Sciarli' and Ruspoli retained Bartolomeo Cimapane to play at his Sunday afternoon *conversazione*; and in 1708 the celebrated German virtuoso E.C. Hesse visited Italy, performing in Rome, Naples, and Venice.

The most significant compositions with bass viol are Handel's cantata *Tra le fiamme* (1707) and his sumptuous *Oratorio per la Resurrezione* (1708), composed for Pamphili and Ruspoli respectively. In the opening sonata of *La Resurrezione* the bass viol makes an arresting entrance as a member of the concertino group paired with the solo violin (played in the first performance by Corelli). Handel assigned to the viol melodic lines (commonly as the second part in a trio texture), Italianate arpeggiated figurations and figured bass; the choice of the viol for a Resurrection oratorio is in keeping with the German association of the viol representing the solace of the Resurrection.

6. FRANCE FROM *c*1600. There was a strong late Renaissance tradition of viol playing in France, encouraged by the Académie de Poésie et de Musique which, under the direction of Jacques Mauduit, included viol consorts in its concerts. At first, as in Italy, viols were used to accompany voices, but soon purely instrumental genres became popular. The fantasias by Du Caurroy and Le Jeune and later Métru, Roberday, Du Mont, and Louis Couperin are evidence of this. These fantasias do not, however, exploit the resources of the viol as distinctively as their English counterparts. Indeed, many were played by viol consort, organ, or other instruments according to the choice of the performers. Idiomatic English consort music was also known in France, and Mersenne chose a fantasia by Alfonso Ferrabosco (ii) as an illustration of viol music in his *Harmonie universelle* (1636–7). The viol was not only used in consort; Trichet recommended it as 'highly suitable for all musical ensembles'. Herouard recalled a group comprising 'a lutenist, a harpsichordist and violist named Pradel, an excellent player if ever there was' playing for Louis XIII in 1609.

Mersenne considered the viol to be the instrument that most perfectly imitated the human voice. He described the standard French viol as having six strings (tuned in 4ths with a 3rd in the middle) and his illustration of the modern viol portrays the classical English model. Jean Rousseau (A1687) credited Sainte-Colombe with introducing silver-covered strings, adding

the seventh, low A string, and developing a left-hand position in which the thumb fell behind the second finger instead of the first, as was common practice on the theorbo. This gave the left hand greater flexibility, and Rousseau especially commended Sainte-Colombe for his ability to imitate all the vocal graces. Sainte-Colombe's new hand position was the one that survived into the 18th century but for a while it caused deep division between the old-fashioned players led by De Machy, who remained faithful to the theorbo hand position, and the progressives of Sainte-Colombe's school.

From about 1675 to 1760 the French virtuoso bass viol school led the rest of Europe in viol playing. The viol was often played in private concerts in the salons of the nobility, and professional players began to arrange recitals themselves; according to Titon du Tillet, Sainte-Colombe was known for 'concerts *chez lui*, where two of his daughters played, one on the treble viol and the other on the bass, thus forming a *concert* for three viols with their father, which was a great pleasure to listen to'.

Both Louis XIV and Louis XV employed a viol player among their *Musiciens ordinaires de la chambre du roy*, and a demand for teachers arose as the instrument came to be considered a fashionable one for the nobility themselves to play. Amateur players at court included the Regent, the Duke of Orleans, and Louis XV's daughter Princess Henriette Anne. Continuo playing constituted an important role for the viol in chamber music, and it was as a continuo instrument that it appeared in the *petit choeur* of the Académie Royale de Musique from the time of Lully until at least 1726, when Quantz heard Roland Marais and Jean-Baptiste Forqueray perform. But only rarely, as for example in the *air* 'Beaux lieux' added to the second version (1708) of Destouches' opera *Issé*, was the viol given an obbligato part.

Four important sources of information on viol playing were printed between 1685 and 1687: collections of *pièces de viole* (prefaced by long *avertissements*) by De Machy and Marais, and treatises by Danoville and Jean Rousseau containing comprehensive instruction on playing technique, the instrument and bow, tuning, and ornamentation. 18th-century information is found in *avertissements* (particularly to the later collections by Marais), in Hubert Le Blanc's *Défense de la basse de viole* (A1740) and in a series of letters from Jean-Baptiste Forqueray to Friedrich Wilhelm of Prussia which discuss the construction and stringing of the instrument as well as its playing technique. In the late 17th century, taste dictated playing in the 1st or half-position whenever possible, but by the 18th century viol players began using the upper positions on the three top strings to avoid changing position unnecessarily. From 1717 Marais frequently used positions from the seventh fret upwards, known as the *petit manche*. Jean-Baptiste Forqueray developed this technique still further when, inspired by the mid-18th-century virtuoso violinists such as Leclair, he aimed to achieve a smooth and unified line by extensive use of the *petit manche*, on both high and low strings. This produced new and unusual tone colours and enabled him to obtain an exotic new range of chords (not only in the *petit manche* but also combined with open strings). The *pièces de viole* were often, when composed by a viol player, carefully marked with fingering, bowing, and ornament signs. Viol ornaments included the rare semitone glissando (called by Marais the *coulé de doigt*) and a form of vibrato in which a finger is placed on the string, touching the one on the fret, beating lightly on the string 'with an even shaking movement'. This kind of vibrato, which Marais indicated by a horizontal wavy line, was often preferred to a one-finger vibrato (used on the modern cello and indicated by Marais with a vertical wavy line), except of course when the note itself was played by the little finger. Vibrato is regularly marked only in *tombeaux, plaintes*, and suchlike pieces; the *coulé de doigt* was regarded as suitable for 'languishing melodies' (see Table 7), generally on the second finger and ascending, though according to Rousseau it could be used descending as well.

Jean-Baptiste Forqueray drew special attention to the bowing hand: 'it should express all the passions … [the middle] finger presses on the hair to make more or less sound, and by pressing and relaxing imperceptibly this makes the expression both soft and loud'. By 1725 a variety of different bow strokes had been developed, including enormous slurs of 24 notes and more, portato bowing on both single notes and chords, and the tremolo. Le Blanc described the rich yet airy and resonant sound that the great French viol players made:

> Père Marais and Forcroi le Père … strove to make a sonorous sound, like the Great Bell of St Germain, which they achieved by playing on air just as they recommended, that is to say that having bowed a stroke they allowed time for the string to vibrate.

He went on, however, to distinguish between the 'old' style of Marais which resembled 'so much the plucking of the lute and guitar' and the 'new' mid-18th-century technique characterized by the imperceptible bow change 'which reproduces and multiplies the expression like the Sun's rays'.

The French style of virtuoso writing for the viol is characterized by an extensive use of chords, which are particularly idiomatic to the viol because of its frets. De Machy likened writing for the viol without chords to playing the harpsichord or organ with only one hand.

The French bass viol was a large, lightly built instrument, which generally had seven strings though some survive with six. Le Blanc described its tone as like 'the voice of an Ambassador, delicate and even

Table 7

∿	two-finger vibrato
⌇	one-finger vibrato
ɔ	trill
×	mordent
t	tiré (down-bow)
∕	coulé de doigt
1, 2, 3, 4	1st, 2nd, 3rd, 4th finger
4̈	4th finger on 3rd string

a little nasal, always being highly proper'. The internal workmanship was extremely delicate: the linings were of linen or parchment and occasionally a series of little cubes of wood was used between the table and ribs to increase the adhesive area. Michel Collichon (*fl* 1666–93) was highly regarded as a maker in the latter half of the 17th century. Nicolas Bertrand and Guillaume Barbey were the most celebrated of the next generation, their finest viols being valued at around 100 livres. Both Marin Marais and Antoine Forqueray possessed instruments by Barbey; nonetheless the outstanding viol in the inventory taken at Marais' death was 'une viole Anglaise fait par Robert Grille en mil six cens seize' valued at 600 livres. Jean-Baptiste Forqueray believed Barbey to be 'the best maker we have had for the shape, thickness, quality and dimensions' and explained that his father had two of Barbey's viols 'l'une pour les pièces, l'autre pour l'accompagement'. He also wrote on the importance of setting up the viol correctly so as to obtain a free sound and promote ease of playing, and the necessity of the strings being in true proportion to one another. He advocated that the lowest four strings be covered with the same covering (the C string half covered) and warned that too much rosin on the bow would make it liable to squeak and dull the tone. By the 1740s the 'pardessus de viole' was valued more highly than the bass; André Castagnery's bass viols were priced at six livres whereas his pardessus were estimated at between 10 and 12 livres in the inventory taken at his death in 1747. The finest pardessus of Jean-Baptiste Salomon (1713–48) and Louis Guersan were the most expensive instruments of their genre at up to 38 livres; some of Guersan's pardessus and quintons were still valued at between 30 and 36 livres in 1770.

Between the late 17th century and mid-18th the bass viol was gradually superseded throughout Europe by the cello as the string continuo instrument. In the early Baroque period, the bass member of the violin family had been less refined in tone than an 18th-century cello, so the viol was preferred for its beautiful sound and ease in playing fast passages. But as the cello and its stringing were improved, and instrument making in general was developed, the cello was favoured because it was better suited to supporting the louder 18th-century ensemble. It overtook the viol first in Italy, where fine cellos were made from the middle of the 17th century, and later in France as well as in England and Germany as the Italian innovations in cello making and playing spread to the rest of Europe. Le Blanc and Jean-Baptiste Forqueray fought a fierce rear-guard action on behalf of the bass viol, but though Forqueray's talents were highly respected, Ancelet remarked in his *Observations sur la musique, les musiciens et les instrumens* (Amsterdam, 1757) that 'the Violoncello, which is without doubt one of the most beautiful instruments … is generally used everywhere … Only the Basse de Viole declared war on the Violoncello, which won the victory'.

In France, unlike the rest of Europe, treble viols remained popular long after the demise of the viol consort. Rousseau emphasized the vocal character of the instrument and the need to adopt 'la delicatesse du Chant' and 'to imitate all a beautiful Voice might do with all the charms of the Art'. He proceeded by stressing that 'one must not abandon the spirit of the instrument, which does not wish to be treated like a violin, with which it is correct to animate, in place of which it is correct for the *Dessus de Viole* to flatter'. By about 1700 the *dessus* had become popular among noble ladies; it was believed to be more appropriate for women to play a small viol on their lap rather than a violin on their shoulder.

As the vogue for the new Italian violin sonata grew, the six-stringed *pardessus de viole* was developed on which the low *d* of the treble viol was exchanged for a high *g''*, enabling players to reach top *d'''*, necessary for playing violin music, in 1st position. By the time Michel Corrette published his *Méthode pour apprendre facilement à jouer du pardessus de viole a 5 et à 6 cordes* (A1748) a new variant, the quinton, had been 'invented', strung with the bottom three strings like the lowest three on the violin and the top two in the manner of the pardessus: *g–d'–a'–d''–g''*. Corette described this 'new instrument' as having the refined 'flute-like treble of the *pardessus de viole* and the sonorous bass of the violin' adding that 'it sounds much better than the ordinary *Pardessus*'; he recommended it unreservedly for 'violin sonatas and concertos'. Corette, Ancelet, and Brijon praised the playing of Mlle Levi, who rendered 'her instrument equal to a violin by the beauty of her playing'. By the 1760s a third type of pardessus, with four strings tuned like a violin, had emerged. The celebrated violinist L'abbé *le fils* mentioned it on the title page of his *Principes* (1761): 'Those people who play the four-string *Pardessus* can use these *Principes*, they only have to remember to give the opposite significance to the bowing signs'. And Brijon remarked in his *Méthode nouvelle et facile pour apprendre à jouer du par-dessus de viole* (A1766) that 'in Paris lots of people play the *pardessus* with four strings'. Interestingly Brijon, who was a violinist, suggested using an overhand bowing on the pardessus. The pardessus' popularity outlived that of the bass viol; as late as 1783 the *Almanach musical* advertised 'trois Maistres du pardessus de viole'.

7. GERMANY AND THE LOW COUNTRIES FROM *c*1600. During the late 16th century and the first half of the 17th a number of English musicians took up employment in Germany, Denmark, Austria, the Low Countries, and Spain. Among them were six virtuoso violists: William Brade, Thomas Simpson, Walter Rowe, Daniel Norcombe, Henry Butler, and William Young. They had a major effect on the development of Continental viol playing, Rousseau declaring that it was the 'English who were the first to compose and play chordal pieces on the viol, and who exported their knowledge to other Kingdoms'. The German predilection for consorts of low instruments is clearly evident in the many sacred works scored for multiple bass viols, both alongside other instruments and as a consort of their own. Ensembles consisting of three viols with two violins superimposed were common, as was a consort of four viols. Often the inner parts of 17th-century cantatas are simply marked 'viola' and it is uncertain whether they were intended for violas *da gamba* or *da braccia*; in the middle of the century it seems that whichever instrument was more readily available took the part, but later the violas *da braccia* increasingly ousted the violas *da gamba*. Idiomatic bass viol parts appear in eight of Buxtehude's cantatas; his *Jubilate Domino* for alto, viol, and continuo demands a range of three and a half octaves (*D* to *a''*) and begins with a 'sonata' for viol and continuo; both *Laudate pueri* and *Ad cor: vulnerasti cor meum* are scored for five bass viols.

In central and southern Germany the viol continued to be used in sacred compositions until the 1680s, after it had fallen from favour in the north. Viols were not, however, the exclusive preserve of Protestant music. Roman Catholic Austria maintained a tradition of viol playing, despite the prevailing taste for Italian music, from the time of John Price (i) and William Young until the 1730s. Here as in north Germany viols were associated with the affect of *lamento*, and were used in the uniquely Viennese Passiontide genre, the *sepolcro*. A.M. Bononcini, Antonio Draghi, and G.B. Pederzuoli all wrote for the viol as did Emperor Leopold I.

With the universal acceptance of the Italian four-part string quartet as the core of the 18th-century orchestra, the viol lost its position in the instrumental ensemble of Protestant church music. However, 18th-century composers occasionally chose to employ its unusual timbre for special effect, particularly in Passions and funeral compositions. Telemann used two in his funeral cantata *Du aber, Daniel, gehe hin* and C.P.E. Bach also employed two in his *St Mark Passion*. The outstanding composer of 18th-century sacred music for viol was J.S. Bach, who scored for it in three sacred cantatas (BWV76, 106, and 152), the *Trauer Ode* (BWV198), and three Passions. His most famous arias with obbligato viol are 'Es ist vollbracht' in the *St John Passion* and 'Komm süsses Kreuz' in the *St Matthew Passion*; the latter is preceded by an arpeggiated recitative and features a virtuoso chordal obbligato (originally conceived for lute)—Bach's only truly idiomatic writing for the viol in the French virtuoso style. In these arias Bach, following the 17th-century tradition, used the viol to symbolize the lament for and the kingship of the person of Christ.

The German-Netherlandish virtuoso viol school had its roots in the English division style, as exemplified by Nicolaus a Kempis's divisions on Philips's *Pavana dolorosa* (Antwerp, 1642), but towards the end of the 17th century it came under the influence of the latest virtuoso techniques of the thriving Italian-inspired Austro-German violin school. The marriage of ideas was facilitated by the fact that many 17th-century German string players, such as Schop, Nicolaus Bleyer, and Biber, played both the violin and the viol.

There were three distinct German schools of viol making, emanating from Austria and south Germany,

Saxony and central Germany, and north Germany and the Baltic. Of the Tyrolean school, viols survive by Busch, Hiltz, and Kögel from the first half of the 17th century, some of which use a festoon outline. The most celebrated maker was Jacob Stainer, who modelled his viols on those of William Young. He generally built a traditional flat back and shoulders, although the influence of the Italian violin is equally apparent in his characteristically strongly contoured, carved table and, latterly, his use of f-holes. Hawkins praised Stainer's instruments for their 'full and piercing tone'. In the Saxon area of central Germany, Hoffman was a leading maker, working in Leipzig. Viols of the north German and Baltic tradition demonstrate a strong influence from English makers and used bent fronts in two, three, four, five, or seven pieces until about 1710. Joachim Tielke was Germany's most renowned viol maker, securing commissions for his highly prized instruments from the nobility and royalty. About 50 viols from his prolific workshop survive; all of them are basses. As a gifted and creative craftsman, Tielke developed the Anglo-German model he inherited. In about 1683 he largely forsook the traditional flat back and began to carve a solid gently arched back without bent shoulders; his workshop's viols from that date thus became heavier than their English and French counterparts, and also favoured a thicker two-piece front. Until 1685 he maintained the north German tradition of carving rosettes in the belly of his viols but after that date they only occur on his most extravagantly ornamented instruments. By 1696 he had settled for a neck of 30.5 cm although three sizes of bass viol are found. Tielke is particularly renowned for his consummate powers of decoration. All his extant viols have carved heads (most commonly women's or lions' heads). Vine leaves and blossoms are his favoured form of motif; they appear in relief on the sides and back of the pegbox and in white (ivory) and black (ebony) inlay on the fingerboard and tailpiece. Tielke also worked with tortoiseshell and, in his most elaborate designs, silver and gold.

At the same time as the bass viol was losing popularity in France, it enjoyed a final flowering at the court of Frederick the Great in Berlin, where there had been a strong tradition of viol playing since the time of Brade and Rowe. The court viol player Ludwig Christian Hesse (1716–72), described by Hiller as 'incontestably the greatest viol player in our time in Europe', inspired sonatas, trios, and concertos in the remarkably virtuosic 'Berlin' style from composers such as J.G. Graun, C.P.E. Bach, Christoph Schaffrath, and J.G. Janitsch. Interest in the viol in Berlin finally faded when Friedrich Wilhelm switched his allegiance to the cello in the early 1770s.

Further south, viol playing lingered on. Burney reported that Elector Maximilian Joseph III of Bavaria played the viol until his death in 1777 adding that 'next to Abel, [he] was the best performer on the viol da gamba I have ever heard'. The Austrian baryton virtuoso Andreas Lidl also played the viol; Burney commended his playing for its 'exquisite taste and expression'.

Dictionary articles around the turn of the century affirm the viol's demise; Gerber declared that 'if you wanted a viola da gamba, you would have to dig up a stringless, worm-eaten example from some court music room' (*Neues historisch-biographisches Lexikon der Tonkünstler*).

8. THE MODERN REVIVAL. Not long after the viol finally died out in Austria and Bohemia, the French, notably Fétis, considered it ripe for revival and included it in a series of 'concerts historiques' in the 1832–3 season. A reviewer in the *Neue Zeitschrift für Musik* pointed out that Fétis's viol was tuned like a cello, but added that it sounded a little more 'tender'. In 1859 the viol featured prominently in Julius Rietz's opera *Georg Neumark und die Gamba*. Rietz, a cellist, conductor, and musicologist, was a close friend of Mendelssohn and deeply involved in the revival of 18th-century music. For the performances of the opera the court library loaned an instrument by Tielke, which was played by the virtuoso cellist Bernhard Cossmann.

From the mid-1870s the pursuit of resurrecting the viol was taken up predominantly by cellists curious about the ancestry of their instrument (the viol was then considered to be the precursor of the cello). The distinguished cellists Auguste Tolbecque and Paul de Wit acquired bass viols and stimulated interest by playing them in public. At first they played Tartini, Boccherini, and Mendelssohn but they soon focussed their attention on the riches of the bass viol literature. Tolbeque performed one of Rameau's *Pièces de claveçin en concerts* in April 1880 with Saint-Saëns and the flutist Paul Taffanel; the reviewer in *Le ménestrel* observed that the performance would have been improved had Saint-Saëns played a harpsichord instead of the piano. In 1889 the *Musical Times* reported that a Société des Instruments Anciens had been formed in Brussels by Louis van Waefelghem, Louis Diémer, Jules Delsart (bass viol), and Laurent Grillet 'for the study and practice of instruments once in general favour but now almost unknown to our concert rooms, such as the clavicembalo, the viola da gamba, the viol d'amore … members of this body have already given historical concerts with much success'. This society disbanded within a decade, but was followed in 1901 by the Société des Instruments Anciens Casadesus, formed by Henri Casadesus with encouragement from Saint-Saëns, in which Henri's sister-in-law Lucette played the viol.

Most performers on the bass viol in the late 19th century and first half of the 20th played the viol like a cello, with an endpin, a cello-like thin and rounded neck and fingerboard, a cello bow, and no frets. In addition the viol was fitted with a thick, cello-like bass bar and soundpost, and heavily reinforced with thick linings to support its unnatural set-up. Arnold Dolmetsch was intuitively aware that the viol was being misunderstood, despite his initial scanty knowledge of the instrument and its music. In the 1890s, after considerable research into music and instruments of the 16th to 18th centuries, he began to give concerts on original instruments including viols. *The Times* reported in 1892 how 'Mr Dolmetsch brought forth several interesting concerted works for the viols—among them a beautiful "Dovehouse Pavan" by Alfonso Ferrabosco ... Miss Dolmetsch displayed her remarkable skill on a viola da gamba in a long chaconne by Marin Marais, a composer whose revival is entirely due to Mr Dolmetsch'. These concerts won the recognition of the Bloomsbury circle, and Bernard Shaw speculated prophetically:

> If we went back to old viols ... I suppose we should have to begin to make them again; and I wonder what would be the result of that ... if our fiddle-makers were to attempt to revive them, they would probably aim at the sort of 'power' of tone produced by those violins which ingenious street-players make out of empty Australian mutton tins and odd legs of stools.

In 1938, the year before Dolmetsch's death, Percy Scholes wrote that the viol was played by 'a small (but growing) body of devoted students'. Many of these were in fact pupils of Dolmetsch, but Paul Grümmer's *Viola da Gamba-Schule* (Leipzig, 1928) shows that a parallel revival was taking place in Germany, pioneered by the scholar Max Seiffert and the instrument maker Peter Harlan. Grümmer encouraged his pupil, the young Swiss cellist August Wenzinger, to nurture his interest in the bass viol, and in 1933 Wenzinger was one of the founders of the Schola Cantorum Basiliensis (the first institution for the research, performance, and teaching of early music), where he taught the viol. Viol playing was uncommon in America until after World War II. However, in 1929 the American Society of Ancient Musicians was founded in Philadelphia by Ben and Flora Stad, who were inspired by the playing of Casadesus with whom they had both studied in Paris in the early 1920s. The viol made slow but sure progress in the 1950s. It was not without provocation that Vaughan Williams wrote to Michael Kennedy on 9 May 1957:

> With regard to that aria in the Matthew P. about bearing the Cross. I was told that at the first performance under Mendelssohn this was the hit of the evening—apparently they used to encore things they liked at those early performances. I have an idea that I will put it in my next performance. But it will have to be rearranged for three cellos. I will not have a viola da gamba inside the building.

The viol's post-war renaissance is marked by three distinctive styles of playing: English, German, and Netherlandish. The English school stems from Dolmetsch and has been closely associated with the performance of English consort music. The German school' of playing was originally centred on the work of Wenzinger in Basle. Although his style was derived from the same primary sources as the English school, his manner of playing might be seen as its antithesis. His performance was characterized by an intense, rhythmically animated manner, driving forward to the cadence in long sustained melodic lines. Wenzinger's influence on American playing is particularly significant; as early as 1953 he spent a term lecturing and teaching at Harvard and in the 1970s he made frequent visits to the Oberlin summer school. The Netherlands school of viol playing is the youngest of the three and had its origins in the playing of the Belgian Wieland Kuijken. Jordi Savall has recorded much of the solo viol repertory and has been a highly influential teacher at Basle.

The American John Hsu was a player of distinction who developed an intensely subtle bowing technique which moulded the melodic line into a series of gestures, which he expounded in his *Handbook of French Baroque Viol Technique* (E1981). Alison Crum's *Play the Viol* (B1989) primarily addresses the amateur market. In 1998 Paolo Biordi and Vittorio Ghielmi published a more advanced and comprehensive tutor entitled *Methodo completo e progressivo per viola da gamba*. Since World War II interest in the viol has been fostered in England by the Viola da Gamba Society (founded in 1948) and in the USA by the Viola da Gamba Society of America (1963), both of which publish scholarly journals. German-speaking countries are served by the Viola da Gamba Mitteilungen of Switzerland. By the late 1970s interest in viol playing had spread throughout the English-speaking world, Europe, and Japan. Universities and music colleges purchased consorts of viols; adults took up the instrument as amateurs; and children were introduced to it without first having developed a modern violin or cello technique. In 1991 Marais became a household name in France after the success of the film *Tous les Matins du Monde*, loosely based on the lives of Sainte-Colombe and his pupil.

In the late 20th century many excellent instruments were built based on classical models, by makers such as Jane Julier, Dietrich Kessler, and David Rubio in Britain, François Bodart in Belgium, Pierre Jacquier and Guy de Ra in France, Tilman Muthesius and Ossenbrunner in Germany, and Paul Reichlin in Switzerland. Fine copies of Baroque bows were made by Boumann (Netherlands), Landwehr (Germany), Fausto Cangelosi (Italy), Patigny (Belgium), Hans Reiners (Germany), and Luis Emilio Rodriguez (Netherlands). The viol's unusual sound inspired works from many 20th-century composers, including George Benjamin (*Upon Silence*, 1990), Tan Dun (*A Sinking Love*, 1995), Barry Guy (*Buzz*, 1994), Thea Musgrave (*Wild Winter*, 1993) and Peter Sculthorpe (*Djlile*, 1995).

The late 20th century brought experiments with electrification of the viol by makers such as François Danger of Petit Couronne, France; Eric Jensen of Seattle, Washington; and Jonathan Wilson of Sylmar, California. Their designs range from Danger's electrified acoustic and solid-body electric Altra-Gamba models, which feature an asymmetric, ergonomic body, to Eric Jensen's solid-body brace-mounted design, developed since 1983. In the early 21st century, Jan Goorissen of Ruby Instruments, Arnhem, Netherlands, developed the Ruby Gamba, a seven-string electric viol with 22 tied nylon (adjustable) frets giving a compass of more than six octaves; the Ruby Spine model is designed especially for plucking, either with fingers or a plectrum. Jonathan Wilson's eccentric-shaped GuitarViol, available in acoustic or electric solid-body type, is basically a bowed guitar with a tall bridge like a viol's.

BIBLIOGRAPHY

A: 16TH- TO 18TH-CENTURY STUDIES. B: GENERAL. C: ENGLAND. D: ITALY. E: FRANCE. F: GERMANY.

A: 16TH- TO 18TH-CENTURY STUDIES

S. Virdung: Musica getutscht (Basle, 1511/R)

H. Judenkünig: *Utilis et compendiaria introductio* (Vienna, c1515–19)

H. Judenkünig: *Ain schone kunstliche Underweisung* (Vienna, 1523); ed. H. Mönkemeyer as *Die Tablatur*, vol.10 (Hofheim am Taunus, 1970)

M. Agricola: *Musica instrumentalis deudsch* (Wittenberg, 1529/R, enlarged 5/1545; Eng. trans., ed. W. Hettrick, 1994)

H. Gerle: *Musica teusch* (Nuremberg, 1532, enlarged 3/1546/R as *Musica und Tablatur*)

G.M. Lanfranco: Scintille di musica (Brescia, 1533/R); Eng. trans. in B. Lee: *Giovanni Maria Lanfranco's 'Scintille di musica' and its Relation to 16th-Century Music Theory* (diss., Cornell U., 1961)

S. di Ganassi dal Fontego: *Regola rubertina* (Venice, 1542/R); ed. W. Eggers (Kassel, 1974); Eng. trans. in *JVdGSA*, vol.18 (1981), 13–66

S. di Ganassi dal Fontego: *Lettione seconda* (Venice, 1543/R); ed. W. Eggers (Kassel, 1974)

D. Ortiz: *Trattado de glosas* (Rome, 1553); ed. M. Schneider (Berlin, 1913, 3/1961)

P. Jambe de Fer: *Epitome musical* (Lyons, 1556); repr. in F. Lesure: *AnnM*, bk.6 (1958–63), 341–86

V. Galilei: *Dialogo della musica antica et della moderna* (Florence, 1581/R)

G. Dalla Casa: *Il vero modo di diminuir* (Venice, 1584/R)

S. Mareschall: *Porta musices* (Basle, 1589)

R. Rognoni: *Passaggi per potersi essercitare* (Venice, 1592) [lost, MS copy by F. Chrysander, US-SFsc]

L. Zacconi: *Prattica di musica* (Venice, 1592/R, 2/1596)

S. Cerreto: *Della prattica musica vocale et strumentale* (Naples, 1601/R)

T. Robinson: *The Schoole of Musicke* (London, 1603); ed. D. Lumsden (Paris, 1973)

A. Banchieri: *Conclusioni nel suono dell'organo*, op.20 (Bologna, 1609/R, 2/1626 as *Armoniche conclusioni nel suono dell'organo*; Eng. trans., 1982)

P. Cerone: *El melopeo y maestro* (Naples, 1613/R)

M. Praetorius: *Syntagma musicum*, vol.1 (Wittenberg and Wolfenbüttel, 1614–5, 2/1615/R); vol.2 (Wolfenbüttel, 1618, 2/1619/R; Eng. trans., 1986, 2/1991); vol.3 (Wolfenbüttel, 1618, 2/1619/R)

F. Rognoni: *Selva de varii passaggi* (Milan, 1620/R)

M. Mersenne: *Harmonie universelle* (Paris, 1636–7/R; Eng. trans. of the books on instruments, 1957)

J. Playford: *Musick's Recreation on the Lyra Viol* (London, 1652, 4/1682/R)

J. Playford: *A Breefe Introduction to the Skill of Musick* (London, 1654) [many later edns]

C. Simpson: *The Division-violist* (London, 1659, 2/1667/R as *Chelys: minuritionum artificio exornata/The Division-Viol*, 3/1712)

T. Mace: *Musick's Monument* (London, 1676/R)

De Machy: 'Avertissement' to *Pièces de violle* (Paris, 1685/R)

M. Marais: 'Avertissement'to *Pièces à une et à deux violes* (Paris, 1686/R)

Danoville: *L'art de toucher le dessus et basse de viole* (Paris, 1687/R)

J. Rousseau: *Traité de la viole* (Paris, 1687/R)

B. Hely: *The Compleat Violist* (London, 1699)

E. Loulié: *Méthode pour apprendre à jouer la violle* (MS, F-Pn, c1700) [transcr. in Cohen (1966)]

E. Titon du Tillet: *Le Parnasse françois* (Paris, 1732/R)

H. Le Blanc: *Défense de la basse de viole contre les entreprises du violon et les prétentions du violoncel* (Amsterdam, 1740/R)

M. Corrette: *Méthode pour apprendre facilement à jouer du pardessus de viole à 5 et à 6 cordes* (Paris, 1748; Eng. trans., 1990)

C.R. Brijon: *Méthode nouvelle et facile pour apprendre à jouer du pardessus de viole* (Lyons, 1766)

J.A. Hiller, ed.: *Wöchentliche Nachrichten*, vol.11 (1766)

B: GENERAL

E. van der Straeten: *The History of the Violoncello, the Viol da Gamba, their Precursors and Collateral Instruments* (London, 1914/R)

T. Dart: 'The Fretted Instruments, III: the Viols', *Musical Instruments Through the Ages*, ed. A. Baines (Harmondsworth, 1961, 2/1966/R), 184

N. Dolmetsch: *The Viola da Gamba: its Origin and History, its Technique and Musical Resources* (London, 1962, 2/1968)

W. Bachmann: *Die Anfänge des Streichinstrumenspiels* (Leipzig, 1964, 2/1966; Eng. trans., 1969)

C. Dolmetsch: 'The Pardessus de Viol or Chanterelle', *The Strad*, vol. 76 (1965), 99–103; repr. in *JVdGSA*, vol.3 (1966), 56–9

M. Cyr: 'The Viol in Baroque Paintings and Drawings', *JVdGSA*, vol.11 (1974), 5–16

G.J. Kinney: 'Fray Juan Bermudo's Methods of Measuring Frets', *JVdGSA*, vol.11 (1974), 90–101

D. Abbot and E. Segerman: 'Gut Strings', *EMc*, vol.4 (1976), 430–7 *EMc*, vol.6/1, vol.6/4 (1978) [special viol issues]

R.D. Leppert: 'Viols in Seventeenth–Century Flemish Paintings: the Iconography of Music Indoors and Out', *JVdGSA*, vol.15 (1978), 5–40

T. Pratt: 'The Playing Technique of the *dessus* and pardessus de viole', *Chelys*, vol.8 (1978–9), 51–8

P. Tourin: *Viol List: a Comprehensive Catalogue of Historical Viole da Gamba in Public and Private Collections* (Duxbury, MA, 1979)

H.M. Brown: 'Notes (and Transposing Notes) on the Viol in the Early Sixteenth Century', *Music in Medieval and Early Modern Europe*, ed. I. Fenlon (Cambridge, 1981), 61–78

M. Lindley: *Lutes, Viols and Temperaments* (Cambridge, 1984)

J. Rutledge: 'Towards a History of the Viol in the 19th Century', *EMc*, vol.12 (1984), 328–36

I. Woodfield: *The Early History of the Viol* (Cambridge, 1984)

K. Coates: *Geometry, Proportion and the Art of Lutherie: a Study of the Use and Aesthetic Significance of Geometry and Numerical Proportion in the Design of European Bowed and Plucked String Instruments in the Sixteenth, Seventeenth and Eighteenth Centuries* (Oxford, 1985, 3/1991)

A.H. König: *Die Viola da Gamba* (Frankfurt, 1985)

K. Moens: 'Authenticiteitsproblemen bij oude strijkinstrumenten', *Musica antiqua*, vol.3/4 (1986), 80–7, 105–11

S. Bonta: 'Catline Strings Revisited', *JAMIS*, vol.14 (1988), 38–60

J.R. Catch: 'James Talbot's Viols', *Chelys*, vol.17 (1988), 33–9

T. Crawford: 'Constantijn Huygens and the "Engelsche Viool"', *Chelys*, vol.18 (1989), 41–60

A. Crum: *Play the Viol* (Oxford, 1989, 2/1992)

C.H. Ågren: 'The Use of Higher Positions on the Treble Viol', *Chelys*, vol.19 (1990), 44–54

A. Viles: '*New Grove* Index for Viol Players', *JVdGSA*, vol.27 (1990), 55–75

T Stronks: 'A Viola da Gamba Bibliography', *A Viola da Gamba Miscellany: Utrecht 1991*, ed. J. Boer and G. van Oorschot (Utrecht, 1994), 141–162

I. Woodfield: 'The Basel *gross Geigen*: an Early German Viol?', ibid., 1–14

A. Crum with S. Jackson: *Play the Viol: The Complete Guide to Playing the Treble, Tenor and Bass Viol* (Oxford, 1992)

P. Holman: '"An Addicon of Wyer Stringes Beside the Ordenary Stringes": the Origin of the Baryton', *Companion to Contemporary Musical Thought*, ed. J. Paynter and others (London, 1992), 1098–115

A. Ashbee: 'The Society's Indexes: a Way Forward', *Chelys*, vol.23 (1994), 73–9

A. Otterstedt: *Die Gambe: Kulturgeschichte und praktischer Ratgeber* (Kassel, 1994)

M. Smith: 'The Cello Bow Held the Viol–Way: once Common, but now almost Forgotten', *Chelys*, vol.24 (1995), 47–61

E. Segerman: 'Viol–Bodied Fiddles', *GSJ*, vol.49 (1996), 204–6

J. Bryan: 'In Search of the Earliest Viols: Interpreting the Evidence from a Painting by Lorenzo Costa', *The Viola da Gamba Society of Great Britain Newsletter*, no.131 (2005)

J.B. Rutledge: *Megaviol: a Bibliography of the Viols* (<http://www.unc.edu/~jbr/MEGAVIOL.DOS>)

C: ENGLAND

E.H. Meyer: English Chamber Music (London, 1946/R, rev. 3/1982 with D. Poulton as Early English Chamber Music)

J. Wilson, ed.: *Roger North on Music* (London, 1959)

J.T. Johnson: 'Violin versus Viol in English Fantasia–Suites', *JVdGSA*, vol.15 (1978), 88–101

P. Olds: 'The Decline of the Viol in Seventeenth–Century England: some Observations', *JVdGSA*, vol.17 (1980), 60–9

D. and J. Baker: 'The Browning', *Chelys*, vol.10/4 (1981), 4–10

I. Harwood: 'A Case of Double Standards? Instrumental Pitch in England c1600', *EMc*, vol.9 (1981), 470–81

I. Graham-Jones: 'Some Random Thoughts on Pitch in English Viol Consort Music in the Seventeenth–Century', *Chelys*, vol.11 (1982), 20–3

D. Kessler: 'Viol Construction in 17th–Century England: an Alternative Way of Making Fronts', *EMc*, vol.10 (1982), 340–5; vol.11 (1983), 145–6

C. Monson: *Voices and Viols in England, 1600–1650* (Ann Arbor, 1982)

J.R. Catch: 'Praetorius and English Viol Pitches', *Chelys*, vol.15 (1986), 26–32

M. Remnant: *English Bowed Instruments from Anglo-Saxon to Tudor Times* (Oxford, 1986)

E. Segerman: 'On Praetorius and English Viol Pitches', *Chelys*, vol.17 (1988), 24–7

A. Otterstedt: *Die englische Lyra-Viol: Instrument und Technik* (Kassel, 1989)

I. Payne: 'The Provision of Teaching on Viols at Some English Cathedral Churches, c1594–c1645', *Chelys*, vol.19 (1990), 3–15

P. Holman: *Four and Twenty Fiddlers: the Violin at the English Court 1540–1690* (Oxford, 1993, 2/1995)

P. Holman: *Life After Death: The Viola da Gamba in Britain from Purcell to Dolmetsch*, (Woodbridge, 2010)

D: ITALY

P. Allsop: 'The Role of the Stringed Bass as a Continuo Instrument in Italian Seventeenth–Century Instrumental Music', *Chelys*, vol.8 (1978–9), 31–7

M. Edwards: 'Venetian Viols of the 16th Century', *GSJ*, vol.33 (1980), 74–91

W.F. Prizer: 'Isabella d'Este and Lorenzo da Pavia, Master Instrument-Maker', *EMH*, vol.2 (1982), 87–127

M.D. Banks: 'North Italian Viols at the Shrine to Music Museum', *JVdGSA*, vol.21 (1984), 7–27

H.M. Brown and K.M. Spencer: 'How Alfonso della Viola Tuned his Viols and How he Transposed', *EMc*, vol.14 (1986), 520–33

P. Ferrari: 'La liuteria veneziana del Cinquecento e la viola da gamba di Antonio Ciciliano del Museo Civico di Bologna', *Flauto dolce*, vol.17–18 (1987–8), 49–53

H.M. Brown: 'The Trecento Fiddle and its Bridges', *EMc*, vol.17 (1989), 307–29

G.M. Ongaro: 'New Documents on a Sixteenth–Century Venetian Viol Maker', *JVdGSA*, vol.27 (1990), 22–8

E: FRANCE

F. Lesure: 'La facture instrumentale à Paris au seizième siècle', *GSJ*, vol.7 (1954), 11–52

F. Lesure: 'Le traité des instruments de musique de Pierre Trichet', *AnnM*, vol.3 (1955), 283–387; iv (1956), 175–248; also pubd separately (Neuilly-sur-Seine, 1957; Eng. trans., 1973)

F. Lesure: 'Un querelle sur le jeu de viole en 1688: Jean Rousseau contre Demachy', *RdM*, vols.45–6 (1960), 181–99

Y. Gérard: 'Notes sur la fabrication de la viole de gambe et la manière d'en jouer, d'après une correspondance inédite de J.B. Forqueray au Prince Frédéric-Guillaume de Prusse', *RMFC*, vol.2 (1961–2), 165–71

A. Cohen: 'An Eighteenth–Century Treatise on the Viol by Etienne Loulié', *JVdGSA*, vol.3 (1966), 17–23

S. Milliot: *Documents inédits sur les luthiers parisiens du XVIIIe siècle* (Paris, 1970)

M. Benoit: *Musiques de cour: chapelle, chambre, écurie, 1661–733* (Paris, 1971)

H. Bol: *La basse de viole du temps de Marin Marais et d'Antoine Forqueray* (Bilthoven, 1973)

G.J. Kinney: 'Writings on the Viol by DuBuisson, DeMachy, Roland Marais, and Etienne Loulié', *JVdGSA*, vol.13 (1976), 17–55

J. Hsu: *A Handbook of French Baroque Viol Technique* (New York, 1981)

L. Robinson: *The Forquerays and the French Viol Tradition* (diss., U. of Cambridge, 1981)

M. Sicard: 'The French Viol School Before 1650', *JVdGSA*, vol.18 (1981), 76–93

F: GERMANY

J.A. Sadie: 'Handel: in Pursuit of the Viol', *Chelys*, vol.14 (1985), 3–24

K. Polk: *German Instrumental Music of the Late Middle Ages* (Cambridge, 1992)

M. O'Loghlin: 'Ludwig Christian Hesse and the Berlin Virtuoso Style', *JVdGSA*, vol.35 (1998), 35–73

F. and B. Hellwig: *Joachim Tielke: Kunstvolle Musikinstrumente des Barock* (Munich, 2011)

IAN WOODFIELD/R (1–3); IAN WOODFIELD (WITH LUCY ROBINSON)/R (4); LUCY ROBINSON/R (5–8)

Viola (i) (Fr. *alto*; Ger. *Bratsche*). The term 'viola' now refers to the alto (or, more properly, to the alto-tenor) member of the violin family (for earlier meanings, see §2 below). The viola came into being in northern Italy at about the same time (not later than 1535) as the other members of the violin family.

1. The modern instrument. 2. Earlier meanings of the term 'viola'. 3. Violas as 'instruments of the middle'. 4. Viola construction in the 19th and 20th centuries. 5. Usage.

1. THE MODERN INSTRUMENT. The viola, in general, has the darker, warmer, richer tone qualities of the alto voice as opposed to the lighter, more brilliant soprano of the violin. The strings are tuned to *c–g–d'–a'*, a 5th below the violin. Its highest string (*a'*) may produce something of a contrast in timbre to the other strings: on some violas more piercing and nasal. The lowest string (*c*) of a fine viola is capable of a clear, beautiful, resonant, and powerful tone eagerly sought by both makers and players. Viola tone, however, can be less assertive, more mellow, even subdued at times. To produce optimum strength of tone and, especially, beauty and depth on its lower strings, the ideal size for a viola would make it too long for the player's arm.

Viola size has never been standardized as to length of body, depth of ribs or width of bouts. To replicate the acoustical results of the violin (whose length is standardized at an average of 35.5 cm), the viola would require a body half as long again as the violin's (approximately 53 cm). Full-sized violas can range in body length from 38 to more than 48 cm. However, while the smallest viola can rarely produce a truly powerful and resonant C-string sound, the largest are virtually impossible for most players to handle. Differing sizes of violas are best explained by a maker's intention to produce an instrument basically alto or tenor in tone quality although the differing lengths of players' arms and the demands of the repertory are certainly pertinent factors. For practical reasons the most utilized violas probably have body lengths in the 41 to 43 cm range.

Just as the length of the viola varies from instrument to instrument, so, naturally, does the sounding length of the strings (i.e. the open string measured from inside the nut to the inside of the top of the bridge). On the modern violin this length is standardized at about 33 cm. On a typical modern viola with a fairly substantial body length (for example, 42.5 cm, as on the 'Tertis' viola; see §4 below), the corresponding open-string length is about 38.5 cm. An extant specimen of a large viola of the late 16th century (made by Gasparo da Salò; in *GB.O.ua*) has a 44.5 cm body, but the open-string length is only 36.2 cm because the instrument still has its original short neck.

The strings of the viola were originally gut, but a wound C string must have been used in the 18th century and probably also a wound G string in the 19th. In modern practice, wound strings (i.e. with metal wound over gut, synthetic, or metal cores) are often used for all four strings to aid their capacity to 'speak', to improve their evenness of tone and response from string to string, to stabilize intonation and to reduce breakage. The fingering and bowing techniques of the viola are similar in principle to the violin's, and many technical studies (e.g. Kreutzer, Ševčík) are simply transposed down a 5th for the viola. Differences in technique are related to the viola's larger size. For one thing, its weight and size suggest that it be held with its scroll slightly lower than is common on the violin. Viola fingering, while similar to that of the violin, utilizes more half-position playing and demands greater left-hand expansion. The vibrato is generally somewhat wider and less intense on the viola than on the violin. While viola bowing is in principle similar to that of the violin, the viola player uses somewhat greater energy on the viola's thicker strings to make them 'speak' properly, while the bow itself is generally heavier and slightly shorter.

2. EARLIER MEANINGS OF THE TERM 'VIOLA'. By 1535 the alto-tenor violin (the modern viola) was established as one of the three principal members of the violin family, but it was not called 'viola' because at that time the term had a variety of meanings both general and specific. About 1500 'viola', in the most general sense, might mean any bowed string instrument. From this general sense, the Italian term *viola* (Fr. *vielle*; Ger. *Fidel*) was modified in various ways to describe a specific family or a specific instrument. Examples from the 16th and 17th centuries are the *viola da braccio* ('arm viola'; a member of the violin family), *soprano di viola da braccio* (violin), *viola da gamba* ('leg viola'; a member of the viol family), and *basso di viola da gamba* (bass viol). Later instances are the *viola d'amore* and *viola pomposa*.

When used before approximately 1550, 'viola' might also have the specific meaning of a Renaissance fiddle or a *lira da braccio* (but not generally a rebec). Frequent statements to the contrary notwithstanding, the unqualified term 'viola', used alone, rarely if ever means violin. However, the converse is sometimes true: in Venetian usage around 1600, 'violino' might mean viola (alto violin) as well as violin proper (for example in Zacconi, *Prattica di musica*, 1592; G. Gabrieli, *Sonata pian e forte*, 1597).

In the 17th and 18th centuries 'viola' is often used with adjectives to denote different registers (but not change of tuning, which, whatever register was involved, moved invariably upwards in 5ths from *c*). In Albinoni's *Sinfonie e concerti a cinque* op.2 (1700), for example, two of the partbooks are labelled 'Alto Viola' and 'Tenor Viola' for what are respectively viola I and viola II parts, one playing in the alto register and the other in the tenor; Handel's op.3 no.1 concerto has one part marked 'Alto Viola' and another 'Tenor' in the Walsh edition of 1734. Similarly, in the five-part French ensembles described by Mersenne (1636–7) the three 'parts of the middle' are all violas (all with the customary *c* tuning), but of differing sizes and playing in different registers. Hence the 24 Violons du Roi included *haute-contre or haute-contre taille* (contralto or contral-to-tenor: viola I), *taille* (tenor: viola II), and *quinte* or *cinquiesme* (fifth: viola III).

By the 18th century 'viola' (alto violin) was equated with *viola da brazzo* (braz.), from *viola da braccio* (see above); hence *Bratsche*, the modern German term for viola (alto violin). Brossard's *Dictionaire* (Paris, 1703) ties the two sets of meanings together, equating *braz. I* with *haute-contre* (alto viola or viola I), *braz. II* with *taille* (tenor viola or viola II) and *braz. III* with viola III. Brossard also mentioned 'viola IV', but said it was not used in France. The term 'violetta', used in the 16th century to mean 'violin' or even 'viol' in certain contexts, often refers in the 18th century to the viola (alto violin). Adjectives can also alter the meaning: *violetta marina*, for instance, is a species of viola d'amore.

3. VIOLAS AS 'INSTRUMENTS OF THE MIDDLE'. Historically, the viola was 'the instrument of the middle', being used for both the alto and tenor registers: in the 16th and 17th centuries, a four-part ensemble might use two violas; and a five-part ensemble, three violas (see references to Mersenne, §2). This distribution accounts for the relatively large number of violas produced in these two centuries by makers of the time, including such famous ones as the various members of the Amati family in Cremona and, in Brescia, Gasparo da Salò and Maggini. The distribution of parts explains also why the sizes of violas varied from very large models, needed to play in the deep tenor register, to small models for playing in the higher alto register.

Some of the tenor violas are so large as to be barely playable on the arm. The huge Andrea Amati tenor viola of 1574 (now in *GB.O.ua*) has a body length of 47 cm. That of the Stradivari 'Medici' tenor viola of 1690 (now in Florence) is 48 cm. With regard to such very large violas, the late viola virtuoso William Primrose once remarked: 'The viola is difficult enough without having to indulge in a wrestling match with it'. Few of these large tenors still exist. Besides expected attrition over the years, a number were later altered and shortened to make them easier to manage for viola players of a later period.

This was one reason why few violas were made in the first part of the 18th century; instruments were already in plentiful supply in varying sizes from the past, and, in addition, the large tenors were cut down to the prevailing requirements of a smaller model that became favoured after 1700. Also, violas were in less demand for musical reasons. The typical ensemble texture of the early 18th century was four parts, the usual orchestral distribution becoming two violin parts, one viola part, and one cello-bass part, as opposed to as many as three viola parts in certain five-part ensembles in the 17th century. Moreover, two of the prevailing forms of chamber music, the solo violin sonata and the trio sonata, rarely used a viola part at all. (For usage of the viola in concertos of the early 18th century, see §5 below.) It is therefore not surprising that, although 600 or so Stradivari violins, violas, and cellos survive, Beare cites only ten Stradivari violas in existence, and some of them were made in the 17th century.

4. VIOLA CONSTRUCTION IN THE 19TH AND 20TH CENTURIES. With the perfecting of the modern (Tourte) bow around 1785, a new era in string playing began. Around 1800, the viola, like the violin, went through various alterations to increase string tension and carrying power and to facilitate technique, especially left-hand fingering and shifting. Such changes involved a lengthened and angled-back neck and fingerboard, a longer and heavier bass-bar, somewhat heavier strings (the lowest being wound; see §1), and a somewhat higher bridge. New violas made in the 19th and 20th centuries conformed to these specifications, and earlier instruments were altered as needed to fit the new conditions. The new-model (Tourte) bow was ideally suited to drawing out the increased power and fuller tone inherent in the new-model viola.

Some 19th-century makers were possessed with the notion of improving the viola acoustically by lengthening or enlarging the body. In the middle of the century, Vuillaume experimented making a viola with extremely wide bouts and Charles Henri of Paris built a viola with the entire left side larger than the right. In 1876 Hermann Ritter introduced a *viola alta* (built by K.A. Hörlein); Wagner was interested enough to use this instrument in the orchestra at Bayreuth. However, while Ritter's viola, which was about 48 cm in body length, was acoustically desirable, it was effective only in proportion to the length of the player's arms.

Beginning in 1937 the English viola virtuoso Lionel Tertis (1876–1975), after long experience and experiment, began collaborating with the violin maker Arthur Richardson to create a model viola intended to combine fullness, depth, and beauty of tone in a full-size viola still manageable by the player. This 'Tertis' model, first heard in concert in 1939, has since been produced by a number of craftsmen around the world, and is illustrated and described in Tertis's autobiography (1953).

Other novel approaches to viola construction, inspired by musical and acoustic considerations, have continued to the present time. In the 1960s, Carleen Hutchins, after earlier research by Frederick Saunders, designed and built a whole new violin family of eight instruments, acoustically scaled to the violin as the ideal. Of the eight instruments of this new family (including two pitched above the present violin and one below the present double bass), four are new and three are re-scaled instruments. Among the latter is the 'viola', re-scaled to a body length of more than 53 cm, and played like a cello, using an endpin, although some viola players have chosen to play this instrument in the traditional way. In the 1990s, David Rivinus developed his ergonomic Pellegrina viola with expanded upper left and lower right bouts, tilted fingerboard, and off-centre neck. This viola, with a standard body-length measurement of 40 cm but an acoustic length of 50.8 cm, attracted considerable attention and favour particularly from orchestral viola players.

By the late 20th century electric and MIDI violas, including five- and six-string 'violins' (c–g–d'–a'–e'' and F–c–g–d'–a'–e'', respectively) were being produced in a variety of shapes and sizes by an increasing number of makers. Although an acoustic viola can be amplified with a microphone pick-up attached near the bridge or the f-hole, a dedicated electric viola will use built-in piezo or magnetic pickups located in or under the bridge. Some of these built-in pickups (the best known are made by Barbera Transducer Systems and Zeta Music Systems), with appropriate pre-amplification systems, produce a remarkably beautiful tone quality scarcely distinguishable from a fine acoustic viola sound.

5. USAGE. The best viola makers have often successfully minimized the inherent acoustical difficulties discussed above and a fine viola, played by a true artist, is therefore capable of a beauty and variety of tone and effects of virtuosity that are thrilling and moving in the alto-tenor register. However, the viola has always suffered as a solo instrument by comparison with the greater brilliance of the violin and the strength and depth of the cello. Both violin and cello can compete more successfully with the orchestra in concertos, and this explains why, over the years, composers have written innumerable violin concertos, a fair number for cello and until recently comparatively few for viola. Before 1740 the viola was seldom treated as a soloist in any context, generally being banished to the decent obscurity of the accompaniment, realizing the harmony of the middle parts. At the low point of its fortunes the instrument was described by J.J. Quantz (*Versuch*, 1752):

> The viola is commonly regarded as of little importance in the musical establishment. The reason may well be that it is often played by persons who are either still beginners in the ensemble or have no particular gifts with which to distinguish themselves on the violin, or that the instrument yields all too few advantages to its players, so that able people are not easily persuaded to take it up. I maintain, however, that if the entire accompaniment is to be without defect, the violist must be just as able as the second violinist.

After about 1740 the viola began to enjoy a new lease of life. It was treated increasingly as a solo instrument in concertos, and during the lifetime of Haydn, Mozart, and Beethoven a good many changes took place in the treatment of the viola in chamber music. The changes came about partly because a basic concept of late 18th-century chamber music was that a single player played each part (thus setting chamber music apart from the orchestra where each string part, at least, was played by several players). In this context a violist of any attainment would become increasingly impatient simply playing the harmonic filler 'parts of the middle' while the first violin was playing the main melodies. Composers of early quartets made the inner parts of string quartets more interesting by giving them thematic motifs or even, from time to time, main melodies, obbligato parts, or virtuoso figuration. This factor in turn animated the solo player to greater mastery of the instrument's technique.

A greater equality of part-writing and a notable advance of viola technique can be observed in the mature chamber music, especially string quartets, of Mozart and Beethoven. Unusual at this time is the exploiting of the colour possibilities of the higher register of the C string in the fugal last movement of Beethoven's op.59 no.3, where the viola player is required to play on the C string in the 5th position.

Mozart, in his concerto for violin and viola (Sinfonia concertante κ364/320d, 1779), treated the violin and viola as equal partners. He thus made technical demands of the viola quite unprecedented at that time, requiring the player to reach the 7th position. He also scored the concerto so that the natural brilliance of the violin is somewhat muted, while the natural reticence of the viola is somewhat brightened and amplified. This was done by using the key of E♭ for the concerto and by writing a scordatura part for the viola. The key of E♭ is not a brilliant one for the violin (none of the open strings serves to reinforce the principal notes of this key). The same is normally true of the open strings of the viola, but Mozart followed the practice of writing the part in D, with the strings tuned up a semitone. This 'transposition scordatura' means that the viola player fingers the music as if it were in the key of D, but it sounds in E♭. This particular retuning increases the tension on the strings making the viola a bit more brilliant and slightly louder; three of the four viola strings—now tuned to what is enharmonically d♭, a♭, e♭' and b♭'—reinforce the tonic, subdominant and dominant notes of the main key of E♭; and finally, it is easier for the viola player to play in D than in E♭. The technique of tuning the viola up a semitone or whole tone was used in several late 18th- and early 19th-century pieces.

Several viola methods, somewhat analogous to those for violin and cello, were published at the end of the 18th century and the beginning of the 19th. Early in the 19th century an outstanding method by A.B. Bruni (c1820) and viola studies by Bartolomeo Campagnoli and J.-J.-B. Martinn were published. In the 20th century the viola began to share in the technical advances of the violin (most viola players having begun their training as violinists). The trend towards virtuosity became much more pronounced when, for instance, players were obliged to cultivate the highest positions on the lower three strings. Also in the 20th century the viola was increasingly called upon, especially the viola soloist in chamber music, to perform special effects such as col legno bowings (e.g. Schoenberg), rebounding pizzicatos (Bartók), glissandos, harmonics, and so on. Developments in fingering were similar to those for the violin and are enshrined in the methods of Dolejši

(1939) and Primrose (1960) as well as in the 20th-century repertory.

Berlioz had already shown (1834) how magical a *sul ponticello* could sound in an arpeggio passage for solo viola against muted orchestral strings (in 'Marche des pèlerins' from his *Harold en Italie*). Such demands by composers meant that an efficient technique was slowly being acquired by viola players in all types of instrumental music. In much 20th-century chamber music, the technical demands on the viola are often as great as on the other parts. Treated mainly as a tenor in early times, the viola had also been used occasionally as an alto or even, for special effect, as a bass. The cultivation of tone-colour of different registers after 1800 led composers to use the viola as any voice-part of the ensemble for momentary effect. To increase power and sonority, special violas such as Hermann Ritter's *viola alta* were introduced into the orchestra.

For full discussion of viola repertory, and associated bibliography, see *GMO*.

BIBLIOGRAPHY

A: GENERAL. B: REPRESENTATIVE METHODS.C: PERIODICALS.

A: GENERAL

H. Berlioz: *Grand traité d'instrumentation et d'orchestration modernes* (Paris, 1843, 2/1855/R; Eng. trans., 1856, rev. 2/1882/R by J. Bennett)

H. Ritter: *Die Geschichte der Viola alta* (Leipzig, 1876/R)

H. Ritter: *Die fünfsaitige Alt-Geige* (Bamberg, 1898)

E. van der Straeten: 'The Viola', *The Strad*, vols.23–26 (1912–6) [series of articles]

W. Altmann: 'Zur Geschichte der Bratsche und der Bratschisten', *AMz*, vol.56 (1929), 971–2

W. Altmann, ed.: *Die Bratsche: Mitteilungsblatt des Bratschisten-Bundes* (Leipzig, 1929–30)

L. Tertis: *Beauty of Tone in String Playing* (London, 1938; repr. in *My Viola and I* (London, 1974))

H. Besseler: *Zum Problem der Tenorgeige* (Heidelberg, 1949)

G. Pasqualini: 'Referendum internazionale sulla viola moderna', *Santa Cecilia*, vol.8 (1959), 81–3

H. Kunitz: *Violine/Bratsche* (Leipzig, 1960)

G. Pasqualini: 'Risultati sul referendum', *Santa Cecilia*, vol.9 (1960), 73–4

C.M. Hutchins: 'The Physics of Violins', *Scientific American*, vol.207/5 (1962), 78–84, 87–93

D.D. Boyden: 'The Tenor Violin: Myth, Mystery, or Misnomer', *Festschrift Otto Erich Deutsch*, ed. W. Gerstenberg, J. LaRue and W. Rehm (Kassel, 1963), 273–9

D.D. Boyden: *The History of Violin Playing from its Origins to 1761* (London, 1965/R)

S.M. Nelson: *The Violin and Viola* (New York, 1972)

M. Rosenblum: 'The Viola Research Society', *American String Teacher*, vol.23/2 (1973), 29–30

A. Arcidiacono: *La viola: gli strumenti musicali* (Ancona, 1973)

L.C. Witten: 'Apollo, Orpheus, and David', *JAMIS*, vol.1 (1975), 5–55

Y. Menuhin and W. Primrose: *Violin and Viola* (London, 1976, 2/1978)

F. Zeyringer: *The Problem of Viola Size* (New York, 1979)

M.W. Riley: *The History of the Viola*, vol.1 (Ypsilanti, MI, 1980; 2/1993) [incl. full bibliography]

M.W. Riley: 'The Early Development of the Viola by Luthiers of the Brescian and Cremonese Schools', *Journal of the Violin Society of America*, vol.5/1 (1980), 120–52

D. Gill: 'Vihuelas, Violas and the Spanish Guitar', *EMc*, vol.9 (1981), 455–62

M. Robinson: *The Violin and Viola* (London, 1983)

S. Ponjatovskij: *Istorija al'tovogo iskusstva* [The history of the viola] (Moscow, 1984)

C.A. Johnson: *Viola Source Materials: an Annotated Bibliography* (diss., Florida State U., 1988)

A.M. Woodward: 'Observations about the Status, Instruments, and Solo Repertoire of Violists in the Classic Period', *Journal of the Violin Society of America*, vol.9/2 (1988), 81–104

F. Zeyringer: *Die Viola da braccio* (Munich, 1988)

M.W. Riley: *The History of the Viola*, vol.2 (Ann Arbor, MI, 1991)

D. Pounds: *The American Viola Society: a History and Reference* (n.p., 1992, 2/1995)

M. Fox: 'Crazy but Correct Viola', *New York Times* (4 Aug 1997)

C. Alvergnat: *L'Alto depuis son origine* (Lyon, 1999)

F. Lainé: *L'alto—Mnémosis Instruments* (Bressuire, France, 2010)

B: REPRESENTATIVE METHODS

M. Corrette: *Méthodes pour apprendre à jouer de la contre-basse à 3, à 4, et à 5 cordes, de la quinte ou alto et de la viole d'Orphée* (Paris, 1773/R)

Complete Instructions for the Tenor Containing such Rules and Examples as are necessary for Learners with a Selection of Favorite Song-Tunes, Minuets, Marches, etc. (London, n.d. [between 1782 and 1798])

M. Woldemar: *Méthode d'alto contenant les premiers élémens de la musique* (Paris, c1800)

?F. Cupis: *Méthode d'alto précédé d'un abrégé des principes de musique de différents airs nouveaux dont plusieurs avec variations et terminé par un long caprice ou étude* (?Paris, ?1803)

M.J. Gebauer: *Méthode d'alto contenant les principes de musique avec les gammes accompagnées dans tous les tons suives de petites pièces en duo tirées des plus célèbres auteurs tels que Haydn, Mozart, Boccherini &c* (Paris, c1805)

A.B. Bruni: *Méthode pour l'alto viola contenant les principes de cet instrument suivis de 25 études* (Paris, c1820)

J.-J.-B. Martinn: *Nouvelle méthode d'alto contenant des gammes et exercises dans tous les tons, douze leçons en duos et trois sonates faciles* (Paris, n.d. [between 1826 and 1830])

R. Dolejší: *Modern Viola Technique* (Chicago, 1939/R)

W. Primrose: *Technique is Memory: a Method for Violin and Viola Players Based on Finger Patterns* (London, 1960)

H. Barrett: *The Viola: Complete Guide for Teachers and Students* (Birmingham, AL, 1978, 2/1996)

S.L. Kruse: *The Viola School of Technique: Etudes and Methods Written between 1780 and 1860* (diss., Ball State U., 1985)

C: PERIODICALS

The Strad (1890/91–)

Hindemith-Jb (1971–)

Newsletter of the American Viola Research Society (1973–8)

Journal of the Violin Society of America (1975–)

British Viola Research Society Newsletter (1976–83)

Newsletter of the American Viola Society (1978–85)

The Viola: Yearbook of the International Viola Research Society (Kassel, 1979–)

British Viola Society Newsletter (1983–)

Journal of the American Viola Society (1985–)

Strings (1986–)

DAVID D. BOYDEN/ANN M. WOODWARD/R

Viola (ii). Portuguese term for string instruments with a waisted body like that of the guitar. Construction of violas was governed by regulations published in 1572 in Lisbon. Nowadays, the term mostly denotes plucked folk instruments with more or less pronounced incurved sides, a neck topped by a pegbox or pegboard, and a flat soundboard and back. Strings are mostly of steel or brass, *bordões* (bourdons) being thicker strings of nylon, gut, or wire overspun with brass or copper. Violas may accompany one or more voices, or be played solo, or integrated into instrumental ensembles. When used for vocal accompaniment, tuning is adjusted to suit a singer's range.

Portuguese convention, contrary to custom elsewhere, is to call *guitarra* those instruments having the strings attached to a tailpiece and without incurved side (like the Portuguese guitar), whereas *viola* refers to waisted instruments whose strings are attached to a string-holder glued to the soundboard. However, appellations are intermixed, and thus the name 'guitarra' may be given to the classical guitar (also named *guitarra clássica* or *guitarra espanhola*, with the variant *guitarrinho*) and to electric guitars (*guitarra eléctrica*). The term *violão* may be applied to the classical guitar, which has a larger body than the traditional viola, hence the augmentative suffix '-ão'. Other types include *viola acústica* (as opposed to *viola eléctrica*), *viola francesa*, *viola dedilhada* (to distinguish it from the bowed viola, called *viola d'arco*), *viola de cravelhas* or *viola de fado* (with six thicker strings), and *viola de jazz* (six strings, with f-holes on the soundboard). The *violão baixo* (bass guitar) has four thick strings; it can be played upright, often supported on an endpin. An even larger model is called the *violão contrabaixo*. The *violão-harpa* has at times six fretted strings plus five unfretted bourdons.

Types of the Portuguese viola include:

(1) *Viola amarantina*, one of the two distinctive violas of Minho (the northwest region of Portugal), modern models being easily recognisable by the two symmetrical heart-shaped soundholes pointing outwards, situated about three-quarters up from the bottom, above the waist. It has five double courses of metal strings secured to a convex string-holder glued at the centre of the lower bout, below a thin straight bridge. It is smoothly figure-8-shaped. The soundboard and back are flat and almost parallel, and the fingerboard ends close to the soundholes. Most versions have ten complete frets and seven gradually shorter frets at the treble side. Traditionally, the ten tuning pegs are placed in two parallel rows, five on each side of the long, flat peghead, which has a hole in the centre. The name *amarantina* links this viola to the city of Amarante, northeast of Porto. It is frequently played for dances, accompanying the *rabeca chuleira* and other folk instruments.

(2) *Viola beiroa*, chiefly used in the eastern area north of the river Tejo. It has 12 strings and pronounced side curves. The circular soundhole is the same distance above the waist as the bridge is below it. Uniquely among violas, it has an extra pegbox on the bass side of the neck just above the heel, where two strings are attached, known as '*requintas*' or '*cantadeiras*', nowadays tuned as a treble double bourdon; they cross a small nut on the upper bout, offset from the centre-line of the instrument. All the strings are attached to a string-holder, with seven pins for five double courses plus the two bourdons, glued below the main bridge. The soundboard extends slightly onto the flat neck, which carries ten frets. The tuning pegs are perpendicular to the flat rectangular headstock and the additional smaller pegbox. The body shape of the *viola beiroa* resembles only that of the *viola campaniça*. Historical examples are rare and the traditional performance techniques are now obsolete. The instrument's last known uses were in the first half of the 20th century at the *dança dos*

homens, a special dance from Lousa, a small village north of Castelo Branco, and at ceremonies or feasts in that part of the Beira region. The *requinta* size of the *viola beiroa* is a smaller version, tuned higher than the normal one.

(3) *Viola braguesa*, from Braga, the district capital of Minho, which gave its name to the most popular instrument of northwest Portugal. It is played solo or in ensemble. The waist of the body is more pronounced than that of the *viola amarantina*, and it has a longer neck which ends in a heel and is level with the soundboard. It has ten frets and the ten tuning pegs are perpendicular to the long, flat, carved headstock. The five courses of metal strings may be tuned according to the *moda velha* ('early fashion') or the *mouraria velha* ('old Moorish-quarter fashion'). Dividing the body roughly in five parts, there are: at the first fifth from the tail, the end of the bottom inlay decoration; at the second, a straight thin bridge preceded by an arched string-holder; at the third the waist; and at the fourth and fifth the tops of the three soundholes. There are three main types of soundholes; the most common is called *raia*, a semi-circular shape, with two smaller teardrop shapes above an internal bar. Circular or oval soundholes were used in the past.

The similar *viola toeira* from central Portugal also has ten frets and a level fingerboard. The strings form two triple courses plus three double courses. The headstock is flat and usually carved. There can be profuse ornamentation inlaid on the lower part of the soundtable and around the oval soundhole, placed horizontally above waist.

Smaller *braguesas*, referred to as *requinta* (the common Portuguese name for higher-tuned instruments) and, even smaller, *requintinha*, currently being made with a differently shaped headstock and a circular soundhole, are usually played by children or to reinforce the melody in ensembles.

(4) *Viola campaniça*, whose name denotes its rural origin, coming from the Alentejo, south of the river Tejo. It has a narrow waist like the *viola beiroa*'s, but lacks the extra strings and has the bridge placed roughly at the centre of the lower part of the body. Currently this type is built with 12 pegs in the rectangular headstock and six pins on the string-holder, but players use only five or four courses, and it is said that they sometimes use the upper peg holes to hold spare tuning pegs, the extra pegs having possibly originated in the former use of double and triple courses. There are ten frets on the neck, with two or three shorter frets on the soundboard on the treble side. The purfling around the circular soundhole, which is placed above the waist, often represents a compass rose. Although very popular in the past, especially played in feasts and balls, it is now rarely used.

(5) *Viola da terra*, whose name is mainly given to folk instruments from the Portuguese archipelago, the Azores, and which are also called *violas de arame*, a name applied to all violas with wire (*arame*) strings. These are distinguished as '*violas de arame do continente*' (Iberian Portugal) and '*violas de arame das ilhas*'

(instruments from the Portuguese archipelago), or to specific violas from Madeira and Azores. There are five sizes: *meia-viola* (half *viola*, also called *requinta* or *machete*, although not necessarily the *cavaquinho* type so-called in Brazil), *viola de três-quartos* (three-quarters *viola*), *viola boieira* (basically four-fifths), *viola inteira* (full *viola*), and *viola-violão* (larger *viola*).

The *viola de arame madeirense* or *da Madeira* frequently has nine strings, attached to the bridge or to a string-holder below it. These are arranged as three double courses, one single (which can also be doubled), and a last treble course, tuned by pegs in a flat rectangular headstock. The fingerboard, usually with 14 frets, extends over the soundtable as far as the soundhole or surrounding inlay, whose lower radius is level with the waist or above it. It commonly accompanies popular music.

In the Azores there is one type of *viola de arame* from the island of S. Miguel, the *viola micaelense*, and two from the island of Terceira, the *violas terceirense*. The *micaelense* has decorative inlays on the lower body and at the body edges, and heart-shaped soundholes (similar to those of the *viola amarantina*), which are united by an inlayed filament. These, together with an elegant waisted outline and the presence of a mirror ('for the player's beauty') at the centre of the flat rectangular headstock, give this viola a distinctive appearance. It has two triple courses, with two brass or steel strings plus a bourdon at the treble end, and three double courses of steel and brass, attached to a string-holder glued to the soundboard, with two silhouettes of birds carved on the sides (deriving from the early belief that the archipelago was named for the bird '*açor*'). A short straight bridge is placed about two-thirds of the body length above the tail. There are usually 12 frets up to the heel and a further number along the extended fingerboard, which reaches almost the top of the soundholes. This instrument is said to be present in every household, traditionally kept over the couple's bed for protection.

The *viola terceirense* is common on the island of Terceira, also in the Azores. During the centuries following the colonisation of the island in the 15th century, this instrument was highly appreciated as an item for trade or the acquisition of property, being listed also in the fiancée's dowry. This viola has three triple courses followed by three double courses, a fourth triple course being added on the 18-string type. The strings are attached to a string-holder glued at the centre of the lower body, with a thin straight bridge slightly above it. Like the *viola micaelense*, it might have a mirror along the central part of the flat headstock, and might be highly decorated on the soundboard. The fingerboard extends to the inlay surrounding the circular soundhole, with ten frets to the heel and about seven over the table.

In Brazil, *viola de arame* denotes the metal-stringed folk violas of Portuguese origin, including the *viola caipira*, or variants such as *viola de pinho, sertaneja, nordestina, cabocla, cantadeira, de dez cordas, chorosa, de queluz, serena, brasileira*, etc.

BIBLIOGRAPHY

J.L. Almeida: *Cordofones portugueses* (Porto, 2000)

E.V. Oliveira: *Instrumentos musicais populares portugueses* (Lisboa, 2000)

P.L. Bastos: *Discovering the fascinating craft of historical musical instruments in Portugal* (Castelo Branco, 2014)

PATRÍCIA LOPES BASTOS

Viola alta. Large viola introduced in 1876 by the German violist Hermann Ritter (*b* Wismar, Mecklenburg, Germany, 16 Sept 1849; *d* Würzburg, Germany, 25 Jan 1926). He studied music at the Hochschule in Berlin and art and history at Heidelberg University. The history of musical instruments attracted him, and profiting by some practical hints in A. Bagatella's *Regole per la costruzione di violini* (Padua, 1786), he devoted some time to constructing a large viola. This new instrument, built in Würzburg by K.A. Hörlein (1829–1902), was an exact enlargement of a violin based on the same acoustical properties (the normal viola being a compromise). Tuned like the viola, it had a large body (*c*48 cm long) intended to improve resonance and tonal brilliance, in contrast to the characteristically veiled and slightly nasal quality of smaller violas. Ritter toured extensively, writing and arranging a great deal of music for his instrument. In 1879 he was appointed professor of the viola and history of music at the music school in Würzburg. The viola alta was exhibited in 1876; Wagner was interested and asked Ritter to cooperate at the Bayreuth Festival. By 1889 five of Ritter's pupils were in the Bayreuth orchestra playing the viola alta. In 1898 a fifth string (*e″*) was added. In 1905 Ritter founded the Ritter Quartet, which used kindred instruments. His book, *Die Geschichte der Viola alta und die Grundsätze ihres Baues* (Leipzig, 1876, 2/1877/*R*1969, 3/1885), traces the history of the instrument, which subsequently lost favour, possibly because of its unwieldy size; it is no longer played.

BIBLIOGRAPHY

G. Adema: *Hermann Ritter und seine Viola alta* (Würzburg, 1881, 2/1890)

H. Ritter: *Die fünfsaitige Alt-Geige* (Bamberg, 1898)

WATSON FORBES/R

Viola bastarda. Style of virtuoso solo bass viol playing favoured in Italy from about 1580 to about 1630, which condensed a polyphonic composition (madrigal, chanson, or motet) to a single line, whilst retaining the original range, and with the addition of elaborate diminutions, embellishments, and new counterpoint. The term viola bastarda does not denote an instrument but has been misinterpreted to mean one. All viola bastarda music is written for the standard viol tuning, of 4ths with a 3rd in the middle. It most commonly uses the lowest string tuned to *D* (like the modern bass viol) but sometimes the lowest string is a *G* (using the range of a modern tenor) or an *A*; some players also used a tuning based on *A′* or *G′*.

Regarding the instrument's size, Francesco Rognoni, whose compositions use the D tuning, stated: 'The viola bastarda … is an instrument which is neither a tenor nor a bass viol, but which is between the two in size'.

However, the term in 16th-century descriptions seems to refer to the instrument's function rather than to its size; in addition, the wide pitch range of the lowest note for surviving works indicates that viols of different sizes were used as appropriate or as available.

References to the viola bastarda by Praetorius and Adam Jarzębski are misleading. Praetorius, in his *Syntagma musicum*, vol.2 (1618, 2/1619), gave a variety of tunings that would appear to be more appropriate to the lyra viol than the viola bastarda. Jarzębski used the title 'viola bastarda' for the bass viol part in his trio and quartet sonatas, which are of a modest range and only occasionally ornamented with divisions. Jarzębski's misnomer might have arisen because he worked at the court of Sigismund III of Poland, where Francesco Rognoni had also been employed.

BIBLIOGRAPHY

Veronika Gutmann: 'Viola bastarda: Instrument oder Diminutionspraxis', *Archiv für Musikwissenschaft*, vol.35/3 (1978), 178–209

S. Saunders: 'Giovanni Valentini's "In te Domine speravi" and the Demise of the Viola Bastarda', *JVdGSA*, vol.28 (1991), 1–20

LUCY ROBINSON/R

Viola da braccio (It.). 16th- and 17th-century term for a member of the violin family. 'Da braccio' ('on the arm'), as opposed to 'da gamba' ('on the leg'), was one of the ways the generic word *viola* was qualified in 16th-century Italian to distinguish the violin from the viol. At this stage it was usually applied to the complete family: in the printed score of Monteverdi's *L'Orfeo* (1609) five-part passages evidently intended for two violins, two violas, and bass are collectively labelled 'Viole da braccio'. Later in the century it became customary to restrict the term to the alto, tenor, and bass parts of string consort music while the soprano parts were given the more precise label 'violino'. The first setting of 'Beatus vir' in Monteverdi's *Selva morale e spirituale* (Venice, 1641) calls for '6. voci concertato con due violini & 3 viole da brazzo ouero 3 Tronboni', while a sonata by Clemens Thieme (1631–68) composed about 1660 (*S-Uu*) is said to be for two 'Violini', two 'Trombetti', and four 'viole di Braccio'—the last being parts in alto, tenor, and bass ranges. By then it was becoming more common to restrict 'viola da braccio' (or sometimes just 'braccio') to viola parts. *Bratsche*, the most common German word for viola, preserves a form of this usage in modern terminology.

PETER HOLMAN

Viola da gamba. Italian term for the viol (literally, 'leg viol'). During the 16th century bowed string instruments were sometimes classified according to the way in which they were held during performance, the viol being designated 'leg viol' and the violin 'arm viol' (*viola da braccio*). From the mid-17th century the bass instrument of the viol family was most regularly used, and 'viola da gamba' gradually assumed its modern specific meaning of bass viol. By the time of the final phase of the viol's popularity in England, from the 1770s into the early 19th century, corrupt forms of the original Italian term, occasionally found since the early 17th century, had become the norm, for example 'Viol de Gambo'; 'viol-de-gamba'; 'Viol di Gamba'; 'Viol da gamba'; 'Viol di Gambo'. The abbreviated form 'gamba' is nowadays frequently used.

IAN WOODFIELD

Viola d'amore (Fr. *viole d'amour*; Ger. *Liebesgeige*). Kind of viola popular during the late 17th century and the 18th; also a stop on the Romantic organ that imitates its timbre. Although its shape and size vary considerably, normally the viola d'amore is about the size of a viola but has physical characteristics of a viol: flat back, wide ribs flush with the top and back, sloping shoulders, and a carved head (typically a blindfolded cupid) surmounting the pegbox. The soundholes commonly resemble a 'flaming sword' and a rosette is usually present. The instrument is held under the chin like an ordinary viola. Its tone, not so brilliant or powerful as that of the viola, is singularly sweet and resonant. Usually it has six or seven bowed strings, which cross the top of the bridge, and six or more sympathetic strings, which run through holes in the bridge and under the unfretted fingerboard to the long pegbox. Other combinations of strings exist. Its wide range encompasses those of both violin and viola.

1. History. 2. Uses.

1. HISTORY. The 'flaming-sword' soundholes (an Islamic symbol) and sympathetic strings suggest a Middle Eastern influence. The earliest known mentions of the instrument appear in a letter of the Hamburg musician Johann Ritter ('Viole de l'amour', 9 Nov 1649) and in John Evelyn's diary (20 Nov 1679):

> I dind at the Master of the Mints with my wife, invited to heare Musique which was most exquisitely performed by 4 of the most renouned Masters, *DuPrue* a *French-man* on the Lute: Signor *Batholomeo* Ital: on the Harpsichord: & Nicolao on the Violin: but above all for its swetenesse & novelty the *Viol d'Amore* of 5 wyre-strings, plaied on with a bow, being but an ordinary Violin, play'd on *Lyra* way by a *German*, than which I never heard a sweeter Instrument or more surprising ....

Extant instruments and early writings show two main types of viola d'amore: first, a smallish, shallow-ribbed, viol-shaped type and a higher-ribbed model, both with metal bowed strings and no sympathetic strings, known since the 17th century and likely used by Bach, Telemann, and Graupner; and second, a larger type prevalent during the 18th century, of viola body-length but viol-shaped and equipped with gut bowed strings and wire sympathetic strings. Some late 17th-century examples have sympathetic strings, but the earliest known reference to these is in Joseph Majer's *Museum musicum* (1732). Other 17th- and 18th-century writers who described the instrument include Speer (*Grund-richtiger ... Unterricht*, 1687, rev., enlarged 1697), Brossard (*Dictionaire de musique*, 1703), Mattheson (*Das neu-eröffnete Orchestre*, 1713), Walther (*Musicalisches Lexicon*, 1732), Eisel (1738) and Rousseau (*Dictionnaire*, 1768). Mattheson extolled its 'tender and languishing effect' and regretted that 'its use should not be greater'. Leopold Mozart (*Versuch*, 1756) wrote that the viola d'amore was 'a special kind of violin that sounds lovely in the stillness of the night' and emphasized that it permitted many different tunings. Albrechtsberger (1790) called it a 'pleasant chamber instrument'.

The abundance of extant 17th- and 18th-century violas d'amore shows that the instrument was in great demand, particularly in Austria, Germany, Bohemia, and Italy. Inventories of instruments and manuscripts of religious music with viola d'amore obbligato in Austrian and Swiss monasteries indicate the popularity of violas d'amore in 18th-century monastic life. Notable makers, many of them Bohemian, include J.A. and Mathias Albani, Johann Paul Alletsee, Lorenzo and Tomaso Carcassi, J.U. Eberle, Tomaso Eberle, four members of the Gagliano family, Matteo Gofriller, Giovanni Grancino, G.B. Guadagnini, J.G. Hellmer, T.A. Hulinzky, members of the Klotz family, C.F. Landolfi, Pietro Mantegazza, Vincenzo Ruggieri, Jacob Stainer, J.P. Schorn, Lorenzo Storioni, David Tecchler, P.A. Testore, and Joachim Tielke. Plans for a viola d'amore from the Stradivari workshop exist (1716) but no corresponding instrument is known. Two cornerless Stradivari violas d'amore from 1727 and 1728 have been altered into other types of instruments.

For most of the 18th century the viola d'amore was tuned in the key of the composition it was to play. Mattheson and Walther wrote that the instrument was tuned in either C minor or C major: $g–c'–e\flat'(e')–g'–c''$. In addition to the C (minor or major) tuning Eisel offered another: $F–B\flat–d–g–c'–g'–b'$. Compositions from the first half of the 18th century employ many scordatura tunings. Majer listed 16 for the viola d'amore in 1732. By the end of the century, however, the standard tuning was in D major: $A–d–a–d'–f\sharp'–a'–d''$. The sympathetic strings were tuned in unison with the bowed strings. 18th-century music for the viola d'amore was sometimes notated to sound as written (as in the music of J.S. Bach and Graupner), but more often notated in scordatura, whereby the composer would write $g–d'–a'–e''$ for the four highest open strings, which were tuned to $d'–f\sharp'–a'–d''$ in the D major tuning (or other pitches in different tunings). Fingered notes were indicated accordingly. Notes written in the bass clef (when it was used for the three lowest strings) sounded an octave higher. Ex.1 illustrates typical viola

Ex.1: Schmidt: Sinfonia for viola d'amore, violin, and basso.

d'amore notation. Attilio Ariosti in his 'lessons' for viola d'amore and continuo used a unique notation system, placing the alto clef in its usual position and the soprano clef on different ledger lines to indicate hand position rather than actual pitch.

2. USES. Among the earliest known works with obbligato viola d'amore are J.C. Pezel's cantata *Des Abends, Morgens und Mittags* (MS, 1690, *D-F* MsMus.449) and Wilderer's *Il giorno di salute* (1697). Ariosti, Giovanni Bononcini, Fux, Keiser, Mattheson, Alessandro Scarlatti, Stölzel, and Telemann also included it in orchestras for cantatas, operas, Passions, and similar works. Biber's Partita no.7 for two violas d'amore and continuo from the *Harmonia artificiosa-ariosa* (1696) is an early use in instrumental chamber music.

J.S. Bach used the viola d'amore to great effect in his cantatas *Schwingt freudig euch empor* BWV36c, *Tritt auf die Glaubensbahn* BWV152, and *Der zufriedengestellte Äolus* BWV205, and the first setting of the *St John Passion* (1724). Other outstanding works include Telemann's concerto for flute, oboe d'amore, and viola d'amore with strings and harpsichord. During the second half of the 18th century and early 19th the viola d'amore appeared frequently in solo and chamber compositions by Albrechtsberger, F. Benda, J. Eybler, A. Girànek, Haydn, Heinichen, Hoffmeister, Locatelli, Pepusch, Pez, Pezold, Quantz, F.W. Rust, Carl Stamitz (a virtuoso on the instrument), and J.C. Toeschi. Baroque composers, primarily interested in the special timbre of the instrument, tended to ignore its multiple-stop and chordal possibilities. Late 18th-century composers, however, made abundant use of double and multiple stops as well as arpeggios, harmonics, and left-hand pizzicato.

The popularity of the viola d'amore declined during the 19th century despite its effective use in Meyerbeer's *Les Huguenots* (1836) and Ferenc Erkel's *Bánk bán* (1861), but revived in the 20th century owing to rising interest in old instruments generally and a growing taste for exotic sounds. Outstanding players such as Louis van Waefelghem, Walter Voigtländer, Carl Wunderle, and Carli Zoeller, and the efforts of the performer-composers Paul Hindemith and Henri Casadesus, enhanced its appeal. In his *Technique de la Viole d'amour suivie de 24 Préludes* Casadesus advocated a chromatic tuning for the sympathetic strings to capture pitches and overtones other than those of the open bowed strings. Both Casadesus and van Waefelghem led early-music groups that gave the viola d'amore wide exposure. Hindemith's *Kammermusik* no.6 for viola d'amore and chamber orchestra (1927) and *Kleine Sonate* for viola d'amore and piano (1923) and Frank Martin's *Sonata da chiesa* for viola d'amore and organ (1938) were the first major 20th-century compositions for viola d'amore. Numerous other 20th-century composers included the instrument in operas and chamber music. The Viola d'Amore Society of America was created in 1977. Its activities focus on frequent international congresses, yearly newsletters, fostering editions of old and new music, and encouraging luthiers.

For full discussion of viola d'amore repertory and associated bibliography see *GMO*.

BIBLIOGRAPHY

J.P. Eisel: 'Von der Viole d'Amour', *Musicus autodidaktos* (Erfurt, 1738/*R*), 31–6

L.T. Milandre: *Méthode facile pour la viole d'amour* (Paris, 1777/*R*)

F.A. Weber: 'Abhandlung von der Viole d'Amour oder Liebesgeige', *Musikalische Real-Zeitung* (5, 12, 19 Aug; 9, 16, 23 Sept 1789)

F. Wiese: *Theoretischer Unterricht für die Viole d'Amour* (Darmstadt, c1850)

J. Král: *Anleitung zum Spiele der Viole d'Amour* (Hamburg, c1880)

C. Zoeller: *New Method for the Viole d'amour* (London, 1885)

E. de Bricqueville: *La viole d'amour* (Paris, 1908)

W. Voigtländer: *Der moderne Viola d'amore-Spieler: systematisch geordnetes Übungsmaterial zur Erlernung des Viola d'amore-Spiels für Violinspieler* (New York, 1914)

P. Shirley: *The Study of the Viola d'amore* (New York, 1920)

D. Fryklund: 'Bidrag till kännedomen om viola d'amore', *STMf*, vol.3 (1921), 1–36

E. Lesser: 'Zur Skordatura der Streichinstrumente mit besonderer Berücksichtigung der Viola d'amore', *AcM*, vol.4 (1932), 123–7, 148–60

K. Stumpf: *Neue Schule für Viola d'amore* (Vienna, 1957/*R*)

K. Stumpf: 'Die Viola d'amore in der neuen Musik', *Musikerziehung*, vol.21 (1968), 175–7, 228–31

J.H. van der Meer: 'Zur Frühgeschichte der Viola d'Amore', *IMSCR XI: Copenhagen 1972*, 547–55

M. Vogel: 'Was hatte die "Liebesgeige" mit der Liebe zu tun?', *Musicae scientiae collectanea: Festschrift Karl Gustav Fellerer zum siebzigsten Geburtstag*, ed. H. Hüschen (Cologne, 1973), 609–15

P. Hindemith: 'Über die Viola d'amore', *Hindemith-Jb*, vol.4 (1974–5), 158–65

H. Danks: *The Viola d'amore* (Halesowen, 1976, 2/1979)

M. Rosenblum: *Contributions to the History and Literature of the Viola d'amore: A Translation and Expansion of Werner Eginhard Köhler's 'Beiträge zur Geschichte und Literatur der Viola d'amore'* (diss. New York U., 1976)

K. Stumpf: 'Die Viola d'amore: Tradition oder Weterentwicklung', *Musikerziehung*, vol.34 (1980), 70–6

A. Martin: 'Die Viola d'amore im 20. Jahrhundert', *Das Orchester*, vol.32 (1984), 952–4

E. Küllmer: *Mitschwingende Saiten: Musikinstrumente mit Resonanzsaiten* (Bonn, 1986)

W. Schrammek: 'Die Viola d'amore zur Zeit Johann Sebastian Bachs', *Bach Studien*, vol.9 (1986), 56–66

H. Boatwright: 'A Memoire: Paul Hindemith and the Viola d'amore', *Newsletter of the Viola d'amore Society of America*, vol.16/2 (1992), 13–6

M. Rônez: 'Aperçus sur la viole d'amore en Allemagne du Sud vers 1700', *Amour et sympathie: Limoges 1992*, 223–71

J.-P. Vasseur: '1800–1990: Viole d'amour, tradition ininterrompue', *Amour et sympathieLimoges*, 1992, 173–218

M. and D. Jappe: *Viola d'amore Bibliographie* (Winterthur, 1997)

M. Rosenblum: 'Cupid's Strings', *The Strad*, vol.110 (1999), 176–81; continued as 'Bridging the Gap', 276–80

V. Montanucci: 'Italian Musicians and the Viola d'amore in the First Half of the 18th Century', *Newsletter of the Viola d'amore Society of America*, vol.27/2 (2003), 7–12

H. Berck: *Die Viola d'amore—Geschichte, Bau, künstlerische gestaltung, Repertoire, Methodik, Literatur* (Neu-Isenberg, 2008)

A. Dipper: 'Andrew Dipper and his Copy of a Stradivarius Viola d'amore', *Newsletter of the Viola d'amore Society of America*, vol.33/2 (2009), 7–15

B.T. Sroczynski; *Viola d'amore* (Warsaw, 2010)

MYRON ROSENBLUM

Viola da spalla [violoncello da spalla] (It.). 18th-century name given to a smaller variant of a cello, with four to six strings. It is played at shoulder height with the instrument held sideways across the player's chest by a strap over the shoulder (It. *spalla*) and rested on the lap, or it can be played while standing. The instrument was possibly an outcome of experiments with metal-wound gut strings, aimed at producing a good tone from relatively short strings.

Zaccaria Tevo (1706) mentions the viola da spalla as an instrument that plays bass parts in an ensemble. Musicians from the Veneto, such as Tevo, frequently referred to the bass member of the violin family as a *viola*, and his viola da spalla is probably an equivalent of the *violoncello da spalla* mentioned by Bartolomeo Bismantova, who gives its tuning as *D* (or *C*)–*G*–*d*–*a*. Johann Mattheson followed Tevo's usage, but added considerable detail—including the playing position and the use of a strap to keep the instrument in place—in his account of the viola da spalla, which he described along with the violoncello and *bassa viola* as a small bass violin. J.F.B.C. Majer, *Museum musicum* (1732), added that the viola da spalla, taken now as an equivalent of the cello, can also be held between the legs. Jacob Adlung, *Anleitung zu der musikalischen Gelahrtheit* (1758), simply equated the viola da spalla with the cello.

Iconographic evidence—formerly taken as bizarre or incompetent renditions of violins or violas—confirms the use of a shoulder-held cello during the period reported by these writers. An illustration in the cello music of Giuseppe Torelli's *Concertino per camera* op.4 (1688), for example, shows a standing figure with just such an instrument. Significantly, the engraver of this publication, Carlo Buffagnotti, was himself a cellist who held the rank of *suonatore* in the Accademia Filarmonica of Bologna.

In the late 20th century the viola da spalla was revived for Baroque music performance, notably by the luthier Dmitry Badiarov in The Hague and the performer Sigiswald Kuijken. The nearly up-and-down bow stroke is comfortable, and high positions on the fingerboard are easily reached.

BIBLIOGRAPHY

G. Barnett: 'The Violoncello da Spalla: Shouldering the Cello in the Baroque Era', *JAMIS*, vol.24 (1998), 82–107

B. Wissick: 'The Cello Music of Antonio Bononcini: Violone, Violoncello da Spalla, and the Cello "Schools" of Bologna and Rome', *Journal of Seventeenth-Century Music*, vol.12/1 (2006)

D. Badiarov: 'The Violoncello, Viola da Spalla and Viola Pomposa in Theory and Practice', *GSJ*, vol.60 (2007), 121–45

D. Badiarov: 'Errata, and More on the Violoncello da Spalla of the Italians', *GSJ*, vol.61 (2008), 324–5

M. Vanscheeuwijck: 'Recent Re-Evaluations of the Baroque Cello and What They Might Mean for Performing the Music of J.S. Bach', *Early Music*, vol.38/2 (2010), 181–92

GREGORY BARNETT/R

Viola di fagotto (It.; Ger. *Fagottgeige*). Bowed string instrument of south German/Austrian origin, in use from about 1670 to 1782. It is supposed to have had the range and tuning of a cello but to have been held on the arm like a viola. It was probably the bass equivalent of the treble *Schalmei Geige*, and most likely was also the *viola piffero* encountered in instrumental pieces by J.H. Schmelzer. Its gut strings were wound with silver or copper wire that presumably struck the fingerboard when bowed, thereby producing a buzzing sound recalling a bassoon's. Leopold Mozart wrote that some people inaccurately called the instrument *Handbassel* (apparently the same as *viola da spalla*). See M. Spielmann: '"Violino Pifferato" und "Viola di Fagotto"', *Die Viola: Jb der Internationalen Viola-Gesellschaft*, vol.7 (1985), 50–6 [with Eng. summary, 96].

HOWARD MAYER BROWN/STEPHEN BONTA/R

Violalin. Five-string viola introduced by Friedrich Hillmer of Leipzig (later Berlin) before 1800. The young violinist and singer Friederike Klinsing studied with Hillmer and in 1815 performed together with him, using the violalin. It was still being played in public by his son Joseph in 1840. Like the *viola pomposa*, Woldemar's *violon-alto* and Ritter's *viola alta*, the instrument was an attempt at the combination of violin and viola.

Hillmer in 1799 also reportedly invented the 'Polychord', a ten-string instrument smaller than a contrabass, which it resembled, with a fingerboard and neck that could be lengthened or shortened to change the pitch of the instrument; however, this description might be garbled. See C. Sachs: *Real-Lexikon der Musikinstrumente* (Berlin, 1913, R/1964), 412.

LAURENCE LIBIN

Violaline. Type of mandolin with violin- or viola d'amore-shaped body. Said to have been invented and patented in Paris about 1900 by Georges Contal (*b* Mirecourt, 19 April 1874) and made in a range of sizes, the violaline has four pairs of fretted strings like a mandolin's, but supposedly a quieter sound. Violalines bearing the label and patent mark of Jérôme Thibouville-Lamy appear to date from about 1910 to about 1920 (*F.MIR.ml* has an example). Mandolin-violin hybrids such as this were widespread from the late 19th century. See W. Lütgendorff: *Die Geigen- und Lautenmacher vom Mittelalter bis zur Gegenwart* (Frankfurt/Main, 1904), 112.

LAURENCE LIBIN

Viola napoletana [viola spagnola, viola a la spagnola]. Term found in 16th-century Italian sources, normally denoting the plucked vihuela because of its association with Spain.

Viola pomposa (It.). Five-string viola, tuned either *c*–*g*–*d'*–*a'*–*e''*, that is like a regular viola with an additional *e''* string, or possibly *d*–*g*–*d'*–*g'*–*c''* as Galpin suggested. It was in use from about 1725 to about 1770 and was played on the arm. Some writers (e.g. H.C. Koch and J.G. Graun) also called it *violino pomposo*. The only surviving music for the instrument comprises two duets for flute and viola pomposa or violin by G.P. Telemann (from *Der getreue Music-Meister*), a double concerto by J.G. Graun, two *sonate da camera* by J.G. Janitsch, and a solo sonata with continuo by C.J. Lidarti. The invention of the instrument was erroneously ascribed to J.S. Bach by several late 18th-century writers, apparently because they confused the viola pomposa with the violoncello piccolo, which Johann Christian Hoffmann of Leipzig made for Bach and for which Bach occasionally wrote. Late in the 20th century the viola pomposa was revived in various forms (e.g. the asymmetric Peligrini Pomposa by David Rivinus, Portland, OR) and music is again being composed for it.

BIBLIOGRAPHY

U. Drüner: 'Violoncello piccolo und Viola pomposa bei Johann Sebastian Bach: zu Fragen von Identität und Spielweise dieser Instrumente', *BJb 1987*, 85–112 [summaries in Eng., Fr.]

D. Badiarov: 'The Violoncello, Viola da Spalla and Viola Pomposa in Theory and Practice', *GSJ*, vol.60 (2007), 121–45

HOWARD MAYER BROWN/R

Violetta (It.). Word used at various times to mean viol, violin, viola, or cello. G.M. Lanfranco (*Scintille di musica*, Brescia, 1533) wrote about 'violette da arco senza tasti' (small bowed violas without frets), which might be rebecs but are more likely violins. Tuned in 5ths with the higher members of the family having only three strings, they are the equivalent of the *kleine Geigen* described by Martin Agricola (1529) and other 16th-century German writers. This usage also appears in other 16th- and 17th-century sources, for example in Pietro Cerone's *El melopeo y maestro* (Naples, 1613). Zacconi (*Prattica di musica*, 1592) called the treble viol a *violetta piccola*, a term Praetorius (*Syntagma musicum*, 2/1619) used both for treble viol and for violin. Sebastiano Cherici, observing the Venetian usage of his time (wherein the term 'viola' was used for the larger size of the bass violin, 'violetta' for the smaller), applied the term 'violetta' to the small bass violin or cello in his *Inni Sacri* (1672). The compass of Cherici's part for the instrument was *D–e'*. Banchieri (*L'organo suonario*, Venice, 2/1611) discusses a *basso violetta da brazzo*, which is tuned in 5ths, one octave below the violin.

In the 17th and 18th centuries *violetta* commonly meant 'viola'. On the other hand, J.G. Walther, in his *Musicalisches Lexicon* (1732), defined it as a bowed string instrument that played a middle part, either a viola or a small viola da gamba ('eine Geige zur Mittel-Partie, sie werde gleich auf Braccien, oder kleinen Viole di Gamben gemacht'). Telemann might have been observing this practice when he called for the 'violetta' as an alternative to the 'violin' in several orchestral parts for two of his violin concertos (*Musikalische Werke*, xxiii, no.6 in F and no.8 in G). Given the range of the parts, either viola or bass viola da gamba would serve as suitable substitutes.

The English violet is a kind of viola d'amore.

The term *violetta* can also denote an organ stop.

BIBLIOGRAPHY

S. Bonta: 'From Violone to Violoncello: a Question of Strings', *JAMIS*, vol.3 (1977), 64–99

S. Bonta: 'Terminology for the Bass Violin', *JAMIS*, vol.4 (1978), 5–42

J. Catch: 'No, not Anyone's Violetta', *Chelys*, vol.23 (1994), 90–91

HOWARD MAYER BROWN/STEPHEN BONTA

Violetta marina (It.). Obsolete bowed chordophone with sympathetic strings. Structurally it probably resembled the viola d'amore. It was developed by Pietro Castrucci (*b* Rome, 1679; *d* Dublin, 29 Feb 1752), leader of Handel's opera orchestra in London for more than 22 years. Two obbligato parts inscribed 'violette marine per gli Signori Castrucci' occur in the hero's sleep aria in Handel's *Orlando* (1733), and a part for one instrument is included in *Sosarme* (1732); the 'violetta' in *Ezio* (1732) and *Deborah* (1733) might refer to the same instrument. A brief passage by Burney (*History*, ii, 1782, 698) is the chief source of information about the violetta marina, though it is possible that it was identical with the English violet.

STEPHEN BONTA

Violetta piccola (It.). According to Lodovico Zacconi's *Prattica di musica* (Venice, 1592), book 4, chap.56, a descant viol. Praetorius, in *Syntagma musicum*, ii (2/1619), used the term to mean either descant viol or violin. An instrument identified as a violetta piccola (in *GB.L.v*) has four strings like a violin, and steeply sloping upper bouts like a viol's.

Violin (Fr. *violon*; Ger. *Violine, Geige*; It. *violino*; Sp. *violín*). Soprano member of the family of string instruments that includes the viola and cello (the contrabass is also usually considered to be a member of the violin family though in some of its features—all explicable in terms of the practicalities of playing such a large instrument—the influence of the viol family is apparent: it is tuned in 4ths rather than 5ths, historically had a variable number of strings and normally has sloping shoulders and a flat back that is angled so that the upper section slopes inward towards the neck).

I. The instrument and its technique. 1. Introduction. 2. Structure. 3. History to 1600. 4. History and use, 1600–1820. 5. Since 1820. II. Extra-European and folk usage. 1. Europe. 2. Middle East and South Asia. 3. Southeast Asia.

I. The instrument and its technique.

1. INTRODUCTION. The violin is highly developed acoustically and has extraordinary musical versatility. In beauty and emotional appeal its tone can rival that of its model, the human voice, but at the same time the violin is capable of particular agility and brilliant figuration, making possible the expression of moods and effects that may range from the lyric and tender to the brilliant and dramatic. Scarcely another instrument can produce so many nuances of expression and intensity. The violin can play all the chromatic semitones or even microtones over a four-octave range, and, to a limited extent, the playing of chords is within its powers. In short, the violin represents one of the greatest triumphs of instrument making. From its earliest development in Italy the violin was adopted in all kinds of music and by all strata of society, and has since been disseminated to many cultures across the globe (see §II below).

The most important defining factor of the Western orchestra, ever since it emerged during the 17th century, has been the body of 'strings' (i.e. violin-family instruments) playing together with (usually) more than one player to a part. The violin (and violin family), however, had originated well before the 17th century—the three-string violin was certainly in existence in the 1520s and perhaps even earlier—and by the early 17th century the reputation and universal use of the violins were such that Praetorius declared (*Syntagma musicum*, vol.2, 2/1619): 'since everyone knows about the violin family, it is unnecessary to indicate or write anything further about it'.

The present article concerns the structure and functions of the Western violin; for discussion of its repertory see *GMO*.

2. STRUCTURE.

(i) Components of the modern violin. The violin is constructed of some 70 parts, which require masterly skill to cut and assemble. Acoustically it is one of the most complex of instruments (see §2(ii) below). The body is a hollow box (fig.1) about 35.5 cm long, consisting of an

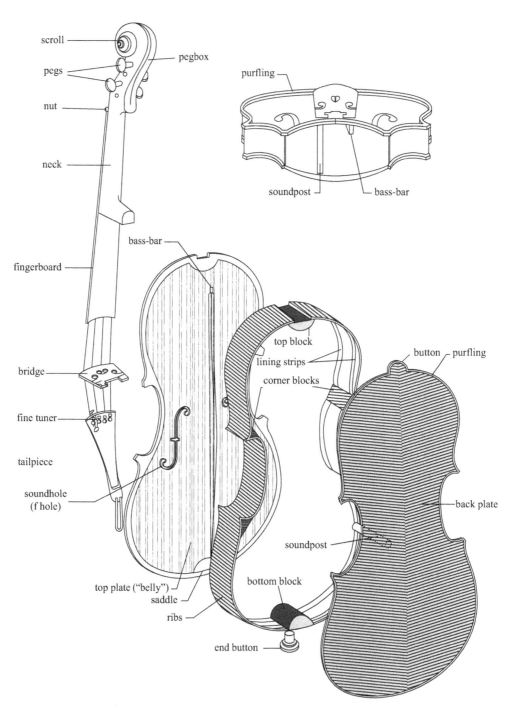

Fig.1: *Component parts of the modern violin.*

arched top plate ('belly') and arched back plate, joined by sides ('ribs') of slightly varying heights (a typical Stradivari measurement is 2.8 cm at the top end of the instrument and 3.2 cm at the bottom). The edges of the belly and back are not flush with the ribs as is usual in a viol, but project beyond, overhanging the ribs slightly. The belly is made of softwood, generally European spruce, and the back and sides are fashioned of hardwood, usually maple. The neck, pegbox, and scroll are also customarily of maple. The fingerboard runs along the neck and extends over the belly towards the bridge; it is now normally made of ebony. It is unfretted, a feature that distinguishes the violins from the viols.

Both top and back can be made of one piece of wood, or (much more usually) of two pieces joined. The wood may be cut either radially 'on the quarter' (fig.2*a* and *b*) or in layers ('on the slab'). One-piece backs (either quarter- or slab-cut; see fig.2*c* and *d*) are not uncommon but one-piece slab-cut tops are rare because for acoustical reasons they seldom give satisfactory results. Radial cutting is generally favoured, especially for tops, because the properties of the various radial sections are about the same from one piece to another. Fig. 3 shows how a radial section is split from the top and the resulting two sections then glued base to base. In this way, the resulting piece of wood will have the same properties relative to the join in the middle. The appearance of the wood surface depends on which of the two methods of cutting is used. The 'waves' in the veined wood

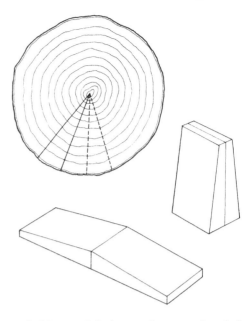

Fig.3: *Radial Section Split (cut on the quarter) and glued base to base.*

are generally called 'curls', and in the one-piece back shown in fig.2*c* these are seen to run continuously upwards from left to right. In two-piece backs the curls (if there are any) would not be continuous because they would be interrupted by the join in the middle (as in the 'Messiah' Stradivari violin). The pattern of curls is referred to as 'figure'. Highly figured wood looks very beautiful, but it is not necessarily acoustically better than plainer maple (which has often been used by the great makers).

Figure is distinct from 'grain', the latter being the arrangement of the fibres of the wood which are distributed in alternating strata of impacted resin (summer growth when the sap is rising) and paler wood (winter carbohydrate growth). In a cross-section of a tree trunk the grain is seen as annular rings, but in radial sections used for violin backs and bellies they appear as parallel lines running longitudinally. The grain is generally more prominent in the spruce of the belly than in the back where the eye tends to be distracted by the figure in the maple. The distance between the parallel grain lines varies, sometimes being narrow ('close' grain), sometimes wider ('open' grain); for violins the ideal range is between 1 and 2 mm. In a typical belly the spacing of the grain lines widens symmetrically from the centre join. Grain is important acoustically since the resin lines conduct sound while the carbohydrate growth acts as a damper; the balance of these two features, especially in the belly, determines the suitability of the wood.

The four strings of the violin are anchored in the upper end of the tailpiece, strung over a carefully fitted bridge of maple, then carried over and above the fingerboard to the ebony (or ivory) nut and secured by the pegs of ebony (or rosewood) in the pegbox (fig.1). The latter is crowned by an ornamental scroll. At the lower end of the violin, the tailpiece is secured by the tailgut

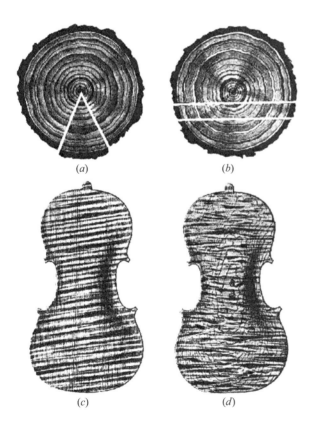

(a)   *(b)*

(c)   *(d)*

Fig.2: *Wood cut (a) on the quarter, and (b) on the slab, with the resulting appearance of one-piece violin backs (c, d) made from each.*

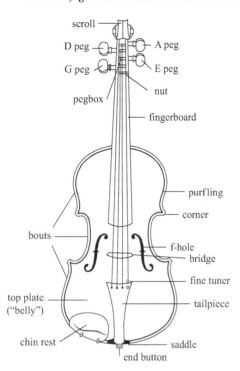

Fig.4: *Features of the modern violin.*

(traditionally a heavy piece of gut but now sometimes wire or nylon) that runs over the ebony saddle (figs.1 and 4) and is looped over, and secured by, the end button ('end pin'). The tension of the strings is regulated by turning the pegs to bring the four strings to their proper pitches: *g, d', a'* and *e''*. In modern violins the steel E string (and sometimes the others also) is generally fine-tuned by means of a mechanical adjuster attached to the tailpiece (figs.1 and 4).

The strings were originally all gut. From the 1660s, however, the lowest (G) string was commonly wound with silver wire to give a better response. Nowadays violinists generally use wound strings for the D and A strings as well and also use a steel E string, the latter being far more durable. Other kinds of stringing were developed in the 20th century; strings with a steel core (overwound with, usually, silver) or a core of synthetic material (e.g. nylon). Both types are widely used, though neither has displaced the gut-core string as the preferred choice of most professional players.

Inside the violin, the top-, bottom-, and corner-blocks and the side linings (see fig.1) strengthen and stabilize the structure. The soundpost and bass-bar give additional support for the interior of the instrument. The soundpost, ordinarily of spruce, stands vertically between back and belly and is located below the right foot of the bridge—not directly under the bridge's foot but on a line with it, slightly towards the tailpiece. The position of the soundpost is critical in producing the best sound. The bridge too must be fitted exactly to the contours of the belly and is positioned in line with the notches of the f-holes. The bass-bar, also normally of spruce, is

glued to the undersurface of the belly, running under the left foot of the bridge. Like the soundpost, the bass-bar helps support the top and also serves an acoustical purpose (see §2(ii) below). The chin rest, if present, is made of wood (usually ebony) or vulcanite. Many players also attach a shoulder rest to the underside of the instrument. These devices, the first invented by Spohr about 1820 (though much improved since) and the second a 20th-century development, make it possible for players to support their instruments without assistance from the left hand.

The beautiful design and shape of the violin are not merely ornamental but are functional to a considerable degree. The vaulting of the back and the belly is essential for strength and for acoustical reasons, the whole body being designed to furnish the best amplification of sound. The narrow waist—that is, the 'middle bouts'—permits ease of bowing on the highest and lowest strings. The scroll is decorative, although the instrument may be hung up by it. The line of purfling that runs just inside the outer edge of back and belly not only emphasizes the beauty of the outline but also minimizes cracks and prevents any damage to the overhanging edges from going further into the body. Some acoustical experts think that purfling might be a factor in the tone. The soundholes (f-holes) and the bridge are basically acoustical in function (see §2(ii) below), though their actual forms are influenced by decorative considerations. In any case, early bridges vary in design somewhat from modern bridges.

Finally, the varnish, so beautiful in the finest violins, is functional as well as decorative, being indispensable as a preservative. Varnish cannot improve the tone, but if it is too hard, too soft or badly applied it can prevent the best tone qualities inherent in the instrument from being realized.

The composition of the Cremona varnish, which contributes so much to the visual beauty of a Stradivari and other Cremonese violins, remains something of a mystery, although there could not have been anything very mysterious about it in its time. Jacob Stainer in the Austrian Tyrol, for example, knew all about it, and the Venetian makers used an equally fine varnish. However, easier and quicker methods of varnishing were later applied, and by 1750 or 1760 the old process had nearly disappeared, G.B. Guadagnini being one of the last (*c*1780) to use Cremona varnish. Nevertheless, excellent varnishes are again being used nowadays.

Distinctive structural characteristics of the violin from *c*1600 to *c*1785 ('Baroque violin') are described in §4(ii) below.

(ii) Sound production and acoustics. Any violin has a certain potential of volume, whose realization depends partly on 'accessories'—the type of strings and their tension, the type of bridge, the quality of the bow, even the type of chin and shoulder rests—and partly on the skill of the player. Fingering, vibrato, bow speed and pressure, and the relative placing of the bow between the bridge and the end of the fingerboard all have a direct bearing on dynamic and tonal characteristics.

When the bow sets the string or strings in motion, the vibrations are transmitted to the belly and the back via the bridge and the soundpost. The soundpost renders the right foot of the bridge (the nearest to the E string) effectively immobile, leaving the left one relatively free to transmit vibrations to the bass-bar and belly (which functions as the soundtable of the instrument) and thence, through the sides to the back (whose primary function, however, is as a reflector). The total area of the soundbox then further amplifies the vibrations and transmits them eventually to the ear of the listener. The soundholes operate as a secondary and complementary acoustical system, adding considerably to the resonance.

The quality and character of the tone depend on the vibrating string and how well its fundamental pitch frequency and upper partials are received and transmitted by the wood of the violin's body. The string vibrates (for any given pitch) not only as a whole—that is, as stopped between nut and bridge by the player's finger—but also in various parts of its length so as to produce the other harmonics of the fundamental, thus giving richness and complexity to the timbre. Some individual tones are the result of the complex interaction of as many as 20 upper partials in addition to the fundamental.

The role of the violin body is to amplify and project the string vibrations to the outer air. What makes a particular violin good is the degree to which it transmits the string vibrations of the fundamental and its harmonics with equal response over the whole register of the instrument. The tone of the violin, then, depends initially on the capacity of the many resonance frequencies of the wood to respond to the string vibrations. Many makers, when adjusting the final thicknesses of the back and belly of a new violin, tap the plates (or fix them in a clamp and bow their edges) to tune them. The notes produced are known as 'tap tones'. (The natural resonance of the interior air space—the so-called 'air tone'—has a frequency normally in the area of the D string in superior violins.)

Many experiments have been made, especially in the last 70 years, to determine which factors affect the timbre of a single note or of all the notes of a particular violin, thus distinguishing one violin from another. Modern acoustics, using electronic equipment, has shown that some previously accepted theories, including the 'formant' theory, will have to be modified or even discarded. There are still major questions regarding the acoustics of the violin (not to mention related areas in the physiology of hearing) that are not yet completely or satisfactorily answered—for example, what makes a violin a 'good' one, and whether old violins are better than modern ones (the best available answer to the second question is 'Not necessarily').

Since its origins, the violin has undergone a considerable evolution of detail to meet the changing requirements of successive generations of performers and composers. The first century and a half of the 'true' violin culminated in the magnificent 'classical' model of Antonio Stradivari shortly after 1700. But this was not the end of the instrument's evolution; in the early years of the 19th century it was altered in a number

of respects to attain greater power and a more mellow tonal quality (see §5 below). It was in this era, too, that the Tourte bow gained universal acceptance.

Nowadays the violin is a more powerful instrument, supporting greater tensions and pressures thanks largely to the move away from gut strings described above. These changes in the violin (and bow) were occasioned by (and made possible) new styles of music and new techniques of playing. Whether we regard these changes as improvements is an entirely subjective matter. Many musicians now take the view that a particular repertory will be served best by performing it with instruments set up and played in the way the composers of the time expected. It is in response to this approach that so many violinists have now acquired 'Baroque', 'Classical', or even 'Renaissance' violins (while some, too, perform Romantic literature on violins strung as they would have been in the 19th century).

For an account of attempts to make mechanically self-playing violins, *see* VIOLIN PLAYER, AUTOMATIC.

3. HISTORY TO 1600.

(i) Antecedents and origins. As with many instruments, the violin has traditionally been defined mainly by its shape. However, it came into being at a period of rapid change and adventurous experimentation in instrument making, and the 'classic' outline only became standard in Italy about 1550; in northern Europe non-standard variants were still in use well after 1600. For this reason studies of the early violin need to take into account the way it was played and how it was used as well as its appearance, and need to be informed by a wide understanding of the development of instruments and instrumental music in the late Middle Ages.

15th-century pictures show two main types of bowed instrument: the alto-range medieval fiddle, usually with five or more strings (one of which could be a bourdon running off the fingerboard), and the small pear-shaped rebec, with two or three strings. Both are routinely depicted with a flat bridge or no bridge at all, which means that they must have been used essentially to play monophonic music in chords—the way folk survivals such as the Greek *lira* and the Norwegian Hardanger fiddle are still played today. To play single-line polyphonic music on them would have required arched bridges of the modern type, and there is no convincing evidence of these before the second half of the 15th century, when polyphony played on pairs of soft, or *bas*, instruments became fashionable. Johannes Tinctoris (*De inventione et usu musice*, *c*1481–3) described a bowed *viola* with strings 'stretched in a protuberant manner so that the bow … can touch any one string the player wills, leaving the others untouched' and reported a recent performance in Bruges of polyphonic songs played on fiddles by the brothers Jean and Charles Fernandes.

The instruments played by the Fernandes brothers probably had three strings tuned in 5ths—the most usual tuning by that time, according to Tinctoris—and must have been similar to the earliest alto/tenor members of the violin family. However, there is no indication that they, or any other bowed instrument, had been developed in more than one size as early as the 1480s. The idea of creating instruments in sets or consorts of several sizes to make them suitable for polyphonic music was first developed in the 14th century with the *bombarde*, a tenor-range shawm, and was subsequently applied to the flute, the recorder, and the *douçaine*, all apparently made in sets in the 15th century. This 'consort principle', as we might call it, does not seem to have been applied to bowed instruments until the 1490s, when the earliest viol consorts were apparently developed on the orders of Isabella d'Este, wife of Francesco Gonzaga of Mantua, from a large, single-size, guitar-like drone instrument recently imported into Italy from Catalonia. Isabella ordered three viols of two sizes from an unnamed maker in Brescia in March 1495, and a letter dated 19 March 1499 reveals that her brother Alfonso was in Venice and wanted to order five 'viole da archo' made 'in all the possible sizes [modi] in the world', which suggests that the third size, the soprano, had been developed by then.

The consort principle was apparently applied about a decade later to the fiddle, producing the violin family. Circumstantial evidence suggests that it happened in Ferrara, Isabella d'Este's home town. A three-string violin-like instrument and a large four-string viola-like instrument are depicted in Ferrarese wall paintings executed between about 1505 and 1510, and two Ferrarese court documents suggest the existence of a violin consort by 1511. References to 'Una viola, zoè un basso' and 'Una viola, zoè un tenore' in an inventory of that year can be identified as violins by a process of elimination: 'Viole da gamba', 'lauti', and 'violoni alla napolitana' (vihuelas) are also listed. On 20 Dec 1511 'maestro Sebastian da Verona' was paid to look for timber for making 'violette' for the Ferrara court, and for repairing its 'viole e violoni'. In 16th-century Italian, violins were usually distinguished from the larger-bodied viols by the addition of the descriptive phrases 'da braccio' and 'da gamba' to the generic term *viola*, or by qualifying it with the diminutives *violette* and *violini* and the augmentative *violoni*. It should be emphasized that these terms applied to violins and viols as a class, irrespective of the size of particular instruments. *Violino* did not specifically mean a soprano violin, nor *violone* a contrabass viol, until much later.

The viol and violin families seem to have been developed as part of a humanist cultural agenda that preferred 'noble' strings to 'ignoble' winds. Isabella d'Este commissioned a cycle of allegorical paintings for her *studiolo* in which string instruments are consistently associated with virtue, spiritual love, and harmony, while wind instruments are associated with vice, sensual love, and strife. Isabella also followed the traditions of female patronage of music in preferring soft string instruments to loud winds, with their indecorous warlike and phallic associations. The two families should therefore be seen as complementary, and were usually played as alternatives by professional musicians in the 16th century, though the viol was also played by amateurs. The viol, soft, sonorous but rather lacking in attack, was suitable for serious contrapuntal music and for accompanying the voice, while the sprightly violin was quickly recognized as the ideal vehicle for the new composed polyphonic dance music that developed soon after 1500.

The Ferrarese wall paintings show instruments that conform surprisingly closely to the later standard shape of the violin, with four corners. However, the earliest Brescian violins might have had only two corners, connecting a broad lower half to a narrower upper half. The shape can be seen in several early pictures of viols, as well as a vihuela and a *lira da braccio* depicted in an intarsia panel made between 1506 and 1508 for the door of one of Isabella d'Este's cabinets at Mantua. We know nothing of the earliest violin makers apart from Sebastian of Verona (assuming he was the person who made the Ferrarese violin consort), although G.M. Lanfranco (*Scintille di musica*, 1533/R) mentioned the Brescians Giovanni Giacobo dalla Corna and Zanetto da Montichiaro as makers of 'Liuti, Violoni, Lyre & simili'. Zanetto's son Peregrino [Pellegrino] Micheli, Girolamo di Virchi, Gasparo da Salò [Bertolotti], and G.P. Maggini continued to make stringed instruments in Brescia, though a rival tradition was established in Venice by Francesco Linarol and his son Ventura. With Andrea Amati and his sons Antonio and Girolamo [Hieronymus] (i), the centre of Italian violin making moved to Cremona.

(ii) Sizes and tunings. According to the first detailed description of the violin family, in Lanfranco's *Scintille di musica*, there were four sizes of 'Violette da Arco senza tasti' (also called 'Violetta da Braccio, & da Arco'), 'Soprano', 'Contraalto', 'Tenore', and 'Basso', with three tunings; the alto and tenor were tuned in unison. In other words, the consort consisted of a single violin, two violas of different sizes, and a bass violin. This disposition, confirmed by later treatises, was the standard one for 16th-century violin consorts, though a third viola was added when five-part dance music became common after 1550. Scorings with two violin parts were gradually adopted in most countries during the 17th century, though the French court orchestra, the 'Vingt-quatre violons', retained the old layout until after 1700. The earliest violin consorts probably consisted entirely of three-string instruments. Sylvestro di Ganassi dal Fontego (*Lettione seconda*, 1543/R) gave the sizes pitched a 5th apart, as in wind consorts of the period: the bass was tuned *F–c–g*, the violas *c–g–d'*, and the violin *g–d'–a'*.

This simple and logical arrangement was soon complicated by the addition of a fourth string. Lanfranco's system of specifying the intervals between the strings rather than absolute pitches implies the use of a three-string violin and viola tuned as in Ganassi, but with a four-string bass tuned *B♭'–F–c–g*. This tuning, with the fourth string at the bottom extending the range downwards, is the one given by the majority of 16th- and 17th-century sources; given the limitations imposed by the plain gut strings of the time, it must have been used on large instruments with long string lengths, such as the two in an illustration of the banquet for the marriage in 1568 of Duke Wilhelm to Renée of Lorraine. *C–G–d–a* and *F–c–g–d'* were specified by Praetorius (*Syntagma musicum*, vol.2, 1618, 2/1619/R), while Adriano Banchieri (*Conclusioni nel suono dell'organo*, 1609/R) specified *G–d–a–e'*. *F–c–g–d'* and *G–d–a–e'* were evidently arrived at by adding the fourth string at the top rather than the bottom, and were probably used on instruments made small enough to be played standing or walking along, supported, in the words of Philibert Jambe de Fer (*Epitome musical*, 1556), 'with a little hook in an iron ring, or other thing, which is attached to the back of the said instrument quite conveniently, so it does not hamper the player'.

Jambe de Fer was the first writer to record four-string violins and violas, with the fourth string placed at the top as in the modern tunings. It extended their ranges in 1st position to *c'''* and *f''* respectively, their normal top notes in ensemble music throughout the 16th and 17th centuries. However, Lodovico Zacconi (*Prattica di musica*, 1592/R), copied by Daniel Hitzler (*Extract aus der Neuen Musica oder Singkunst*, 1623), gave *F–c–g–d'* as an alternative for the viola, adding the fourth string at the bottom, and this has given rise to the modern notion of the 'tenor violin'. Large violas tuned in this way might have existed about 1600, but they are not required by the inner parts of 16th- and 17th-century violin consort music, which never go below *c*, the lowest note on the ordinary viola.

(iii) Dissemination. (1) Italy. Little is known about how the violin consort spread outside the Este-Gonzaga circle, for there are few reliable references to it prior to the second quarter of the 16th century, by which time it was widely distributed both sides of the Alps. Northern Italy, repeatedly invaded and fought over by French and imperial armies at the time, was not a promising environment for the creation and survival of documents, and, according to Jambe de Fer, 'few persons are found who make use of it [the violin] other than those who, by their labour on it, make their living'; it was not played by the literate classes, who might have discussed it in correspondence or literature. We also have no means of knowing whether some of the many unqualified references to *viole*—such as the 'quattro suonatori di liuto, viole e altri strumenti' who appeared in a Bolognese triumphal car in 1512, or the *viole* heard in a play during the Roman carnival of 1519—were to violins rather than viols.

The French language is less ambiguous in this respect, since the terms *viole* and *violon* seem to have been used consistently to distinguish between the viol and violin from the beginning. It is not surprising, therefore, that the largest body of unambiguous early references to the violin is in the French-language accounts of the dukes of Savoy, who ruled Savoy and Piedmont from Turin. There was a payment to a group of 'vyollons' from Vercelli as early as 1523, and dozens of professional groups across northern Italy were evidently using violins by the 1540s and '50s, often in small towns such as Abbiategrasso, Desenzano, Rovereto, and

Peschiera. A large town such as Milan might support several groups: one day in December 1544 four violinists entertained the Duke of Savoy during the day, and four others in the evening. In general, the Savoy accounts give the impression that by then the violin consort was the most popular choice of professional groups—wind instruments are rarely mentioned—and was being used by quite humble classes of musician.

The violin spread with remarkable rapidity during the first half of the 16th century, in part because it was often cultivated by independent, mobile family groups, who recruited their own personnel, composed or arranged their own music, often made their own instruments, and were prepared to travel great distances to work for the right patron. The largest courts employed enough musicians to allow groups to specialize in particular instruments, though most groups had to be versatile: the six-man Brescian group that Vincenzo Parabosco recommended to the Farnese court in January 1546 played *viole da brazo* as well as seven types of wind instrument. The normal practice of the time was to use the various instrumental families as alternatives on a musical menu rather than ingredients in a single dish, choosing them according to circumstances: violins were suitable for dancing, viols for serious contrapuntal music and for accompanying the voice, loud wind instruments for playing outdoors, and so on. However, mixed ensembles became more and more common in the second half of the 16th century: Parabosco particularly recommended 'the combinations of these instruments, one type with another, and combined in various ways with vocal music' because it was 'something unusual and so new'.

(2) France and England. A Parisian woodcut dating from 1516 shows that consorts of bowed instruments were known in France in the second decade of the century, however unlikely the situation (the players are Plato, Aristotle, Galen, and Hippocrates) and fanciful the details. A six-man group described variously as 'viollons, haulxboys et sacquebuteurs' and 'violons de la bande françoise' was already established at the French court by 1529. The musicians all have French names, so they might have come into contact with the violin while accompanying the French court on its forays south of the Alps. But several groups of Italian violinists served in Paris during the 1530s and 40s, and about 1555 a violin consort led by Balthasar de Beaujoyeux is said to have arrived there from the Milan area.

It is not clear when an orchestral violin band was established at the French court, for a number of received 'facts' seem to be no more than hearsay. For example, the idea that Andrea Amati made a complete set of 38 instruments for Charles IX (reigned 1560–74) seems only to go back to a statement in Jean-Benjamin de La Borde's *Essai sur la musique ancienne et moderne* (1780/R), and Moens (B1998) has recently challenged the authenticity of the surviving instruments decorated with devices relating to Charles IX (see §V below). In any case, they include small- as well as large-pattern violins, which were probably made for different pitch standards and are unlikely to have been played together in a single band. However, legal agreements between members of the Paris musicians' guild, the Confrérie de St Julien-des-Ménétriers, show that groups of orchestral size were formed in the middle of the 16th century—there are instances of nine players in 1547, eight in 1551, and 11 in 1552—and violins are always given as one of the options, usually as an alternative to cornetts, when particular instruments begin to be mentioned in the 1580s.

The violin was apparently brought to England by a group of six Jewish string players from Milan, Brescia, and Venice who arrived at Henry VIII's court in the spring in 1540; the institution they founded served successive monarchs up to the beginning of the Civil War in 1642, and during the Restoration it formed the basis of the 24 Violins. Surviving documents suggest that violins began to appear in English aristocratic households in the 1560s, and began to be taken up by town waits, theatre groups and the more humble classes of musician about 1600. Most violins played in 16th-century England were probably imported or made by the instrumentalists themselves. Members of the Lupo family, who served in the court violin consort between 1540 and 1642, are known to have made instruments, though the earliest English violin maker so far identified is the Cambridge University wait Benet Pryme: an inventory drawn up at his death in 1557 includes 'vii vyalles & vyolans' valued at £3, as well as 'a nest of unp[er]fyte vyall[e]s' and 'unp[er]fytt regall[e]s & oth[e]r lu[m]ber'—evidently the contents of a workshop.

(3) Germany and Poland. The same pattern was repeated in German-speaking areas of Europe. The violin consort at Munich was founded by four members of the 'Bisutzi' family in the 1550s, and was enlarged about 1568, probably for Duke Wilhelm's marriage with Renée of Lorraine. The five newcomers, who included three members of the Morari family, might have been part of Renée's entourage; the court at Nancy acquired a set of violins as early as 1534. Italian violinists (including three members of the Ardesi family from Cremona) were at the Viennese court by the 1560s, at Weimar in 1569, at Innsbruck in the 1570s and 80s, and at Hechingen in the Black Forest from 1581. Italian instruments mentioned in inventories include a set of Brescian 'geig' at Augsburg (1566), 'Ein Italinisch Stimwerckh von Geigen, darinn ein discant, drey tenor und ein Bass' at Baden-Baden (1582), and 'Funf venedische geugen' at Hechingen (1609).

The use of the term 'Geige' presents another thorny terminological problem. About 1400 it seems to have been used in opposition to *Vedel* to distinguish the rebec from the medieval fiddle, just as it was used about 1600 in opposition to *Phyolen* or *Violen* to distinguish violins from viols. Early 16th-century German writers such as Sebastian Virdung (1511), Hans Gerle (1532), and Martin Agricola (1529, 5/1545) used the term *Geigen* for both instruments, qualifying it with *grossen* and *kleinen* as in Italian terminology of the period. These treatises illustrate *kleinen Geigen* with instruments shaped like rebecs, so it is not clear when the term began to be used for the violin. In 1545 Agricola

described a third type, the 'Polischen Geigen'; there are no illustrations but the instrument was apparently played without frets, using fingernails to stop the strings. It had three strings; there was also a four-string bass version. Several violin makers, including Mateusz Dobrucki, Bartłomiej Kiejcher, and Marcin Groblicz the elder, are known to have been active in 16th-century Poland, and some apparently 16th-century Polish violins survive, often with non-classic shapes, though not enough research has been done into them (or contemporary German instrument making for that matter) for us to be sure at present what relationship they had with Italian violin-making traditions.

By 1600 the violin consort must have been one of the most familiar sounds in the courts and towns of northern Europe. But in the northern Italian courts, its cradle, it seems to have been in decline. Regular violin consorts do not seem to have been employed at the Mantuan and Ferrarese courts in the late 16th century—Mantua hired *violini* from Parma and Casalmaggiore in 1588, presumably because it had no group of its own—and in 1608 the Florentine court recruited 12 violinists from France. Vincenzo Giustiniani wrote in about 1629 that consorts made up of a single type of instrument, 'with the uniformity of sound and of the consonances, became tiresome rather quickly and were an incentive to sleep rather than to pass the time on a hot afternoon'. He associated shawms and 'bands of violins' with unfashionable milieus such as 'festivals in small towns and country districts, and also in the great cities at the festivals of the common people'. As discussed below, the fashion in advanced musical circles in Italy was for mixed ensembles, in which the violin was often used without the other members of its family. The lead in the development of violin consorts passed to northern Europe, and it was more than half a century before Italy recovered it.

(iv) Usage. (1) Consort dance music. It cannot have been an accident that the violin consort developed at a time of profound change in courtly dance and dance music. Soon after 1500 the pavan and its related saltarello or galliard replaced the old basse danse. The new dance music was composed rather than improvised, and was usually written in simple block chords in four, five, or six parts with the tune in the soprano rather than the tenor. As an increasingly popular vehicle for courtly dancing, violins must be regarded as a principal option for consort dance music, though the repertory continued to be written in a neutral style, with limited ranges so that it could be played on as many different types of instruments as possible. Composers only began to specify particular instruments when they began to write in idioms that favoured one rather than another, and that did not happen until after 1600. The odd exception, such as the five-part dances printed in Beaujoyeux's *Balet comique de la Royne* (Paris, 1582/*R*; ed. in MSD, vol.25, 1971), proves the rule: the accompanying text mentions that they were played on violins in the original performance, though there is nothing intrinsically violinistic about them.

(2) New roles. The violin family was particularly associated with dance music throughout the 16th century, though it acquired a new role and a new repertory when it began to be used in churches. There are references to Brescian *violini* playing in church as early as 1530 and 1538, and the Venetian Scuola Grande di S Rocco employed 'sonadori di lironi' (probably violins rather than viols, for viols could not be played on the move) in 'masses and processions' from at least 1550. The four-part ensemble canzonas of the 1570s and 80s were doubtless played mostly by conventional monochrome consorts, though the development of polychoral music in the 1590s inevitably involved the creation of ensembles mixing cornetts and trombones with violins—which usually involved detaching particular sizes of violin from the rest of the consort.

Violins were also used in secular mixed ensembles. In the 1589 *intermedi* a five-part sinfonia by Luca Marenzio was played by 'dua Arpe, due Lire, un Basso di viola, due Leuti, un Violino, una Viola bastarda, & un Chitarrone', while a chorus by Cristofano Malvezzi was accompanied by 'quattro leuti, quattro viole, due bassi, quattro tromboni, due cornetti, una cetera, un salterio, una mandola, l'arciviolata lira, un violino'. A third type of mixed ensemble involving the violin was the sets of *passaggi* or variations on the soprano parts of vocal music, intended to be accompanied by a keyboard reduction of the original vocal lines. This virtuoso repertory, the ancestor of the early Baroque violin sonata, was doubtless partially conceived for the agile, expressive violin, though Dalla Casa only specified 'fiato, & corda, & di voce humana' while Bassano used the standard formula 'con ogni sorte di stromenti' for the solo part.

Histories of instrumentation have traditionally focused on Italian ad hoc ensembles, though the English mixed or broken consort was arguably more significant, since it was the first to have a scoring that was sufficiently standardized to attract a sizeable repertory that exploited its peculiar characteristics. It was developed in the 1560s and 70s, possibly at Hengrave Hall near Bury St Edmunds, and consisted of violin or treble viol, flute or recorder, bass viol, lute, cittern, and bandora. The treble viol is mentioned in some of the early descriptions of the group, and is called for in the collections of mixed consort music published by Thomas Morley (1599, 2/1611) and Philip Rosseter (1609), though all the surviving pictures show a violin, and one of the manuscripts of mixed consort music (at *GB-Cu*) has pages headed 'Treble violan' and 'The treble violan parte'. Furthermore, there is some evidence that the word 'viol' in Elizabethan English could mean a violin.

(v) Authenticity and surviving instruments. The study of the early violin relies on written and iconographical sources, as well as on surviving instruments. Dozens of instruments from the violin family preserved in museums and private collections are attributed to 16th-century makers such as Zanetto di Montichiaro, his son Peregrino, and Gasparo da Salò, all from Brescia, the Venetian Ventura Linarol, the Cremonese Andrea Amati, Dorigo Spilmann from Padua, and Gaspar

Tieffenbrucker from Bologna and Lyons, as well as to anonymous makers. Attributions to Tieffenbrucker and a number of obscure builders are no longer taken seriously, but other instruments are still used as trustworthy evidence material. Current knowledge on the early violin is based on instruments attributed to about six Italian builders, on some anonymous examples, and on a few, mainly Italian, iconographical representations. Surviving instruments of primitive (or 'rustic') form are given dates mainly in the first half of the 16th century, while instruments resembling modern violins are said to be from the second half of the century.

These widely accepted views on the early violin need to be questioned. Thorough critical examination of the instruments at stake has cast doubt on their authenticity: signatures on instruments attributed to a single maker usually differ greatly and are often poorly forged; several instruments said to be from the same maker might show substantial differences of design or construction; some components of an instrument have been shown to have different origins or to have been heavily adapted or restored, whether or not with fraudulent intent. The signature, shape and construction of many of these instruments are thus unreliable and therefore useless as evidence material for the study of the 16th-century violin. Proven historical facts uphold this conclusion. For example, while it is true that a Paris account dating from 1572 mentions a 'violin façon de Cremone', it is almost certain that the long-held belief that Andrea Amati made an extensive range of instruments for King Charles IX of France is false: close investigation of preserved instruments bearing the arms of Charles IX uncovers too many inconsistencies for them to be from a single maker. We therefore have no clear picture of the violins made by the early famous masters. *Lire da braccio* and viols attributed to 16th-century makers have the same problems of authenticity and therefore are also unreliable as reference material.

However, a small number of little-known instruments from the 16th century or the early 17th have been preserved practically in their original form: considered together with iconographical sources and folk instruments with archaic forms from later periods, these can shed new light on the construction and shape of a representative part of late 16th-century violin making. Perhaps the most remarkable of the surviving instruments are a group of five instruments attributed to members of the Klemm family from Randeck, near Freiberg in Saxony, and now in Freiberg Cathedral (where they are held by a group of angel musicians in the roof of one of the chapels). The group is a rare example of a complete violin consort, consisting of a small three-string descant violin (or violino piccolo), a treble violin, a tenor violin, and two bass violins, all with four strings. These instruments share characteristics that are at variance to those of the violins attributed to famous 16th-century makers, but that often recur in regional varieties of fiddle that persisted in later periods (and in some cases are still played), including the 17th-century *Allemannische* violin (then common in the Black Forest and German-speaking districts of Switzerland and

France), the Norwegian Hardanger fiddle, the Swedish *nyckelharpa*, the Sorbian *Klarfidel* (Cz. *skřpsky*) of the Jihlava district of the Czech Republic, the Polish *mazanki*, and 18th- and early 19th-century violins from North and South America. These shared characteristics include the following: a strongly curved belly and back; long and pointed bevelled corners to the ribs; an entirely or partly flat pegbox back; a deeply cut scroll clearly separated from the pegbox; painted decorations on the belly and back; lobe and brace forms on the tailpiece and fingerboard; the belly carved with a thickening in the inside (instead of separate bass-bar); the neck fitted directly into the body rather than into a top-block; the absence of a bottom-block; and the ribs anchored into grooves cut into the back and belly.

4. HISTORY AND USE, 1600–1820.

(i) The instrument. (1) Violin makers. At the dawn of the 17th century, the violin was beginning to develop a role as an expressive and virtuoso solo instrument. New idiomatic repertory appeared at a rate which suggests an almost feverish excitement in its possibilities. Already two towns, Brescia and Cremona, had emerged as pre-eminent in the manufacture of the instrument. Brescia had been known for its string instruments since early in the 16th century; its reputation as a centre for violin making was established principally by two makers, Gasparo da Salò and Gio Paolo Maggini. Cremona's fame was due at first to Andrea Amati and his descendants. In the early 17th century his sons Antonio and Girolamo (i) were making superb instruments, working together as 'the brothers Amati'. The violins made by Girolamo's son Nicolò are generally considered the pinnacle of the Amatis' achievement. Although the family's traditions were carried into the next generation by Girolamo (ii), Nicolò's mantle passed to more illustrious makers outside the family, most notably Antonio Stradivari but also Andrea Guarneri. Guarneri in turn founded a dynasty, the most distinguished member being his grandson Giuseppe Guarneri ('del Gesù'). The latter has for the past two centuries been regarded the greatest maker after Stradivari. His contemporary Carlo Bergonzi was followed into the trade by a son and grandsons. Numerous references in writings of the period point to the prestige of acquiring a Cremona violin. English court records from 1637 onwards distinguish between the purchase of Cremona and other, by implication more ordinary, violins. In the early 18th century Roger North observed that so many fine instruments had been imported 'that some say England hath dispeopled Itally of viollins'.

Distinguished violin makers in other parts of Italy in the late 17th century and the 18th included Matteo Goffriller, Sanctus Seraphin, and Domenico Montagnana in Venice, David Tecchler and Michael Platner (*fl* 1720–50) in Rome, the Gagliano family in Naples, Giovanni Grancino and the Testore family in Milan, Camillo Camilli and Thomas Balestrieri in Mantua, Giovanni Tononi in Bologna, and his son Carlo in Bologna and Venice.

One non-Italian maker was of cardinal importance in the 17th century: Jacob Stainer, who worked in Absam in the Tyrol. His characteristically high-arched violins are easily distinguished from Cremonese models and were greatly prized (and imitated) in the 17th and 18th centuries. Two other centres were the source of a large number of well-made, though not especially sought-after, violins. Mittenwald in Germany became identified with violin making in the 17th and 18th centuries through the work of Mathias Klotz and his descendants, and to this day it has sustained a reputation as a centre for violin making (and for the teaching of the craft). Mirecourt in France had similar associations in the 17th and 18th centuries, though many makers who learned their skills there moved on to Paris. (The last and most famous of these was Jean-Baptiste Vuillaume, who left in 1818.) By the early 19th century Paris had in fact taken over as the violin-making capital of the world; Nicolas Lupot, especially, was thought to have absorbed the principles of Stradivari better than the makers still working in Cremona. Fine instruments were produced by his friend and business associate François-Louis Pique and by his apprentice Charles-François Gand. (Paris was also identified with bows of the most advanced design and superb craftsmanship thanks to the work of the Tourte family.)

Preferences in the late 18th century do not match up with the modern view that Stradivari represents the doyen of violin makers. The 1785 edition of the *Encyclopédie Méthodique* names Jacob Stainer as the maker of 'greatest reputation' followed by the Amatis (and principally Andrea and the brothers Amati rather than Nicolò). 'Among the skilled makers of more recent date', Stradivari is singled out as having made 'a very large number of good violins; the merit of his instruments consists in their masculine, powerful, and melodious tone'. This hierarchy was endorsed in the later 18th century by the violin makers Antonio Bagatella (1786) and Giovanni Antonio Marchi (1786) and, in a less clear-cut way, the theorist Francesco Galeazzi (1791). The change in fashion is thought to have started in France, thanks to G.B. Viotti's persuasive playing in the 1780s on Stradivari and Guarneri instruments. Michel Woldemar expressed a preference for Stradivari and Guarneri over Amati and Stainer because of their more vigorous sound but also because he considered the less pronounced arching more convenient for holding the violin when playing virtuoso music. A history of violin making written by the Abbé Sibire (1757–1827), *La Chélonomie, ou Le parfait luthier* (Paris, 1806), culminates in a paean to Stradivari:

> I prostrate myself in front of the patriarch of violin makers. ... If in his century a competition had been staged in which all the great violin makers had been judged by their best works, the five Amatis would have obtained honourable mention, Stainer would have been runner-up, but without hesitation and unanimously, Stradivari would have been awarded the prize. ... The first six are simply admirable, each one in a particular aspect of the art, while the last is perfection itself.

That reputation remains intact: 'Stradivari' has become a byword for perfection and value.

(2) Characteristics of 'Baroque' and 'Classical' violins. Violins of the Baroque period are distinct in a number of basic features from their modern counterparts. The neck projects straight out from the body so that its upper edge continues the line of the belly's rim. The neck is affixed by nails (or occasionally screws) through the top-block rather than mortised into it as in modern instruments. The fingerboard is wedge-shaped and shorter than the modern fingerboard. Bridges were cut to a more open pattern and were very slightly lower. The bass-bar was shorter and lighter and the soundpost thinner. Violins (and violas) lacked chin rests. The tone of these instruments is brighter, clearer, less loud and less 'mellow' than that of their modern counterparts.

Such a summary, necessarily peppered with inexact comparative adjectives, may be useful enough; but getting beyond it is no easy matter. Throughout the period all these instruments underwent change, which took place unevenly in different parts of Europe. To acknowledge this is to recognize the term 'Baroque violin' as merely a serviceable generalization. Instruments that have never been altered are scarce and might be of dubious value as models: their survival intact may be attributable to their lack of appeal to discriminating players. Contradictions and approximations in other sorts of evidence create difficulties. The James Talbot manuscript of *c*1695 (*GB-Och* Music MS 1187) gives measurements for a whole range of wind and string instruments but its laconic notes are sometimes tantalizingly inconclusive. Another late 17th-century manuscript, the violin method attributed to Sébastien de Brossard (*F-Pn* Rés.Vm), contains a few apparently detailed measurements, but these are surprising. The bridge, for example, seems thinner rather than thicker than modern bridges: 'about a *demie-ligne*' (1,125 mm) for the base, and the top should be 'thin, but not too much so or it will cut the strings'.

The term 'Classical violin' is another convenient generalization. The key features of violins that were used in the second half of the 18th century and the early years of the 19th were the size of the soundpost and bass-bar and the length of the neck and fingerboard. (Chin rests and shoulder rests still did not exist.) Not surprisingly, these dimensions on Classical instruments lie mostly somewhere between 17th-century and modern averages. This is not to say that the Classical violin should be regarded as a 'transitional' instrument, at least not without acknowledging that the violin has always been and continues to be in a state of transition.

Hardly any extant soundposts can be positively identified as late-18th-century, but the manuscript treatise on violin making completed by the Bolognese violin maker G.A. Marchi in 1786 suggests that some makers must have been inserting soundposts as large as the modern standard (6.5 mm), with a diameter 'such that it can only just pass through the f-holes'. More substantial bass-bars were used as the century progressed—but the picture is far from simple. Surviving examples show great variation within an overall trend towards increase in mass. Compared with Baroque period models,

original necks from the later 18th century seeming tend to be longer and are slightly tilted back. Fingerboards show considerable variation in length (and besides, some late-18th-century players were using instruments built long before). Mozart owned an early-18th-century Mittenwald violin that still has its original fingerboard (long enough to play up to *d′′′*). An unaltered 1783 violin by Antonio Gragnani (*US.W.si*) allows for a range of a 12th above the open string, that is, up to *b′′′*. Marchi noted that it was better to copy longer fingerboards 'because some players today are so good that they can exploit the whole length'. Galeazzi advised that fingerboards should be long enough to produce the note two octaves above the open string.

Throughout the 19th and 20th centuries, the most sought-after violins were those made in the previous two centuries, especially Cremonese instruments. But virtually all of these have been altered to bring them into line with later ideas about tonal quality and strength in a violin. Quite a lot of updating must have taken place as an incidental by-product of repairs and more drastic alterations. Many over-confident makers and repairers took it into their heads to adjust the thicknesses of backs and bellies on instruments that came into their workshops. By Marchi's own account, he made comparatively few new instruments since he was kept very busy repairing and 'improving the quality and strength of tone' of old instruments. (He mentions in particular reducing cellos to smaller forms.)

Antonio Bagatella, in his *Regole per la costruzione de' violini* (Padua, 1786), said that he got his break as a violin maker because Tartini sent many violins to him for adjustment. He described altering a great many old violins to give them either a 'voce humana' (suitable for solos) or a 'voce argentina' (for orchestral playing). The essay gives dimensions for the neck (virtually modern length) and bass-bar (puzzlingly small), and describes in detail how the soundpost should be fitted; but it never even hints that those found in older instruments would need altering. Bagatella described a gadget he had invented for ensuring that the neck is correctly aligned, and from this it is clear that he was still using the traditional way of affixing the neck to the body with nails through the top-block.

The Hills, in their pioneering study of Stradivari (B1902), quoted from the journal of Dom Vicenzo Ascensio who described alterations he made to the quintet of Stradivari instruments at the Spanish court in the 1783. In the interests of what he called 'improving the tone' Ascensio almost certainly modernized the dimensions of neck and bass-bar (though claiming to be following Stradivari's principles). But this was all mixed up with more barbaric acts; Ascensio, too, 'corrected' thicknesses, as shown by his description of repairs to the violoncello:

> I pieced the centre, replaced the bar by one adjusted to mathematical proportions based on that of Stradivari. I corrected the thicknesses, pieced the four corner-blocks, took the back off and inserted a piece in the centre, as it was too thin. I had to replace the neck, which I did in the most careful manner. I then adjusted the instrument, the tone of which was rendered excellent by all these changes.

Marchi, Bagetella, and Ascensio were among many craftsmen working in the second half of the 18th century who participated (at least piecemeal) in what we now see as something of a revolution: the adaptation of old instruments to modern requirements. The nonchalance with which they write about what would now be considered fundamental transformations in an instrument suggests that much of the modernization must have been carried out with no other aim than to apply current best practice in the craft. It was only from the early 19th century onwards that the practice of replacing bass-bars and resetting necks was explicitly acknowledged. In 1806 the Abbé Sibire wrote at some length on the subject in *La Chélonomie*. He described these structural changes as a response to changes in musical expression:

> I shall confine myself hereafter to a daily occurrence .... It is a kind of restoration (loosely called) which is purely accessory and yet at the same time crucial. This is a process which does not imply the slightest deterioration and yet which virtually every old violin, no matter how well preserved it is in other ways, could not avoid: REBARRING. The revolution which music has experienced needs to be replicated in instrument making; when the first has set the style, the other must follow. ... Formerly it was the fashion to have necks well elevated, bridges and fingerboards extremely low, fine strings, and a moderate tone. Then the bass bar, that necessary evil in the instrument, could be short and thin because it was sufficient for it to have enough strength to sustain the weight of five to six pounds which the strings exerted on it. But since then music, in becoming perfect, has placed a demand on violin making. The tilting back of the neck, the raising of the bridge, of the fingerboard, and the amplification in sound, necessitate increasing by a full third the resistant force. Repairers have only one choice: strengthening the old bar, or replacing it with a new one.

Vincenzo Lancetti (*Notizie biografiche*, Milan, 1823) suggested that the process of replacing necks was in full swing by the end of the 18th century and implied that this started in Paris: 'About 1800 the Brothers Mantegazza were restorers of instruments who were often entrusted by French and Italian artists to lengthen the necks of their violins, after the Paris fashion, an example which was followed by amateurs and professionals all over North Italy'.

Violin strings in the 17th and 18th centuries were usually gut, although metal stringing was known and liked for a short time at the beginning of the Baroque period. In his *Syntagma musicum*, vol.2 (2/1619) Praetorius expressed the opinion that 'when brass and steel strings are used on these instruments they produce a softer and lovelier tone than other strings'. There were various types of gut string. Exactly what 17th-century musicians understood by such terms as 'minikins', 'gansars', 'catlines', 'Lyons', and 'Pistoy basses' is not absolutely clear, but the vehemence with which these were variously recommended or condemned indicates that the distinctions were important. The invention in the late 20th century of strings made of roped gut to which the term 'catline' has been appropriated is not based on secure historical evidence, although they can sound good.

By the early 18th century gut strings wound with silver were being used on various instruments. These appear to have been invented in Bologna in the mid-17th century. They must have reached England by 1664 since John Playford (i) advertised them then as a 'late invention ... which sound much better and lowder than common Gut Strings, either under the Bow or Finger'. Because they allowed for an increase in mass without an increase in diameter (and consequent loss of flexibility), covered strings could produce good-sounding bass notes from a shorter vibrating length than pure gut strings of the same pitch. For the violin this meant a more resonant and refined-sounding G string. There is, however, evidence that in parts of Europe (notably Italy and Germany) violinists continued using pure gut G strings until well into the 18th century. French sources mention strings that are half covered ('demi-filée', i.e. wound with a single open spiral of metal thread). The manuscript treatise attributed to Brossard recommends them for the D string. Such strings are extremely resonant and mediate well between the covered G string and a pure gut A.

For discussion of bows of the period *see* BOW.

(ii) Technique and performance practice. (1) Treatises. Roger North wrote of techniques 'which may be knowne but not described'. Some subtleties are indescribable, and some, particularly in the 17th century, might have been kept as mysteries of the trade. For all that, the most obvious sources of information on technique and performance practice are treatises. A great deal of fascinating information is contained in two great encyclopaedic works, Praetorius's *Syntagma musicum* and Mersenne's *Harmonie universelle* (1636–7). With these outstanding exceptions, however, most 17th-century treatises were written by generalists and directed at amateur players, and confine themselves to rudimentary matters. This tradition of what Boyden (1965), picking up on the title of a 1695 publication, called 'self-instructors' continued throughout the first half of the 18th century.

Many tutors addressed to amateurs do little more than sketch the topography of the fingerboard and provide a few simple tunes. Speer (1697) concluded his instructions for the violin with the frustrating comment: 'a true teacher will be sure to show his student what remains: how to hold the violin properly, how to place it on the breast, how to manage the bow, and how to play trills, mordents, slides and tremolos combined with other ornaments'. Where these writers did venture into technical matters their advice may be suspect. Some, like Prinner (1677) and Berlin (1744), are manifestly non-specialist since they were probably not string players and set out (like Speer) to give instruction in a whole range of musical instruments. Such volumes are, however, not entirely without interest. John Lenton's *The Gentleman's Diversion, or the Violin Explained* (London, 1693), for example, manages—despite its quite explicit targeting of hobbyists—to give us some tantalizing glimpses of the practices of advanced players in turn-of-the-century England. Even such a publication as Robert Bremner's *Compleat Tutor for the Violin* (London, after 1761) helps in an oblique way to fill out the picture. Addressed to beginners, its eight pages of instruction contain almost nothing useful about violin technique. But it includes a charming frontispiece of a violinist with portraits behind him of Corelli and Handel (an indicator of taste), a revealing one-page dictionary of musical terms, and a fascinating advertisement for musical accessories (e.g. 'mutes or sardines') sold by Bremner.

The picture changed markedly in the mid-18th century with an explosion of treatises written by real violinists for those aspiring to be real violinists: Geminiani's *The Art of Playing on the Violin* (London, 1751), Leopold Mozart's *Violinschule* (Augsburg, 1756), Herrando's *Arte y puntual explicación del modo de tocar el violín* (Paris, 1756), and L'abbé *le fils*'s *Principes du violon* (Paris, 1761). Two other manuals should really be included in this group: Quantz's *Versuch einer Anweisung die Flöte traversiere zu spielen* (Berlin, 1752), since it contains a great deal which is specifically relevant to violin playing, and Tartini's *Traité des agréments*, published posthumously in 1771 but circulating in manuscript for some years before that. Of the many later 18th-century manuals, probably the most significant are G.S. Löhlein's *Anweisung zum Violinspielen* (1774), the French publications of C.R. Brijon (1763), T.-J. Tarade (*c*1774) and Antoine Bailleux (1798), and the first volume (on violin playing) of Francesco Galeazzi's *Elementi teorico-pratici di musica* (1791).

All of these treatises must be approached with a sense of context and hence of the limits of their applicability. Quite apart from broad differences in stylistic orientation, performers obviously had diverse ideas, then as now, on matters of technique and interpretation.

Geminiani, the pupil of Corelli, is often regarded as an exponent of an Italian violin tradition, but by 1751 he had become fascinated with French music. The hybrid character of his style led John Potter to observe in 1762, 'his taste is peculiar to himself', and even his great admirer, Sir John Hawkins, doubted 'whether the talents of Geminiani were of such a kind as qualified him to give a direction to the national taste' (1776). Hence he should be regarded as a rather idiosyncratic guide to Baroque practice. It is difficult even to establish a context for some volumes. Giuseppe Tartini's precepts were published in the *Traité des agréments de la musique* (Paris, 1771) shortly after his death, but it is generally assumed that at least some of it must have been written before 1756 since Leopold Mozart referred in his *Violinschule* (1756) to Tartini's remarks on the augmented-2nd trill, and virtually plagiarized Tartini's notes on vibrato. It is not known when exactly this work was compiled or how much of it was written by pupils; neither is it clear how to reconcile, for example, Tartini's advice (in the letter to Signora Maddalena Lombardini) to 'make yourself a perfect mistress in every part of the bow' with his puzzling injunction (in the 'Rules for Bowing') never to play near the point or heel. As sources of information on performance practice, treatises must take their place alongside other invaluable (but often also equivocal) forms of evidence such as paintings, observers' accounts of performances, records of payment for instruments and musical services—and, most importantly, the music itself.

(2) Holding the violin. Where exactly on the upper body the violin rested was not completely standardized until late in the 18th century. In the early Baroque era, violinists might hold their instruments almost as low as their waists (as some traditional fiddlers still do). When Nicola Matteis arrived in England in the 1670s, observers were struck by the way he held the violin against 'his short ribs'. Many players preferred to support the violin against their chests just beneath the collar-bone. John Playford (i) (1654), addressing amateurs, advocated this breast position, but so too did Geminiani writing nearly a century later with much more accomplished players in mind. Even in the later 17th century some chose to rest the violin on the collar-bone with the option of using their chins to steady the instrument, particularly when shifting. Lenton (C1693) advocated resting the instrument on the collar-bone but without chin pressure:

> I would have none get the habit of holding an Instrument under the Chin, so I would have them avoid placing it as low as the Girdle, which is a mongrel sort of way us'd by some in imitation of the *Italian*. … The best way of commanding the Instrument will be to place it something higher than your Breast your fingers round and firm in stopping.

Obviously, none of these positions can be regarded as standard. G.B. Rangoni's essay on Nardini, Lolli, and Pugnani published in 1790 argues that:

> Just as each person is differently built, it follows that the position of the instrument shouldn't be the same for all; and that making anyone hold the violin in a way contrary to their natural bearing (which is always related to the constitution of their limbs) would introduce obstacles in a student's progress and prevent the development of their talent.

As early as 1677, however, Prinner asserted that the violin should be held 'so firmly with your chin that there is no reason to hold it with the left hand—otherwise it would be impossible to play quick passages which go high and then low or to play in tune'. Corrette (C1738) and Berlin (C1744) both regarded chin support as essential when shifting (advice repeated by Bailleux in 1779). In 1756 Leopold Mozart offered violinists a choice between a chest-high hold (elegant, he thought, but inconvenient for shifting) and an under-the-chin method (comfortable and efficient). In the same year, Herrando stated simply that 'The tailpiece must come under the chin, being held by it there, turning the head slightly to the right'.

Various other methods in the second half of the 18th century describe the violin as being held on the collar-bone without specifying whether or not to stabilize it with the chin. In 1761 L'abbé *le fils* proposed that the chin should be on the G string side of the instrument, but this practice was apparently still not completely accepted by the end of the 18th century. In 1796 Francesco Galeazzi attacked the idea of playing with the chin on the E string side, and his vehemently defensive tone makes it clear that this must still have been an issue; he claimed that it looked ridiculous, necessitated unwieldy movements with the bow and numbed the left ear because of the proximity of the instrument. The Paris Conservatoire *Méthode* of 1803 states quite unequivocally that 'the violin is placed on the collar-bone, held by the chin on the left-hand side of the tailpiece, and inclined a little to the right'. By the late 18th century chin pressure on one side or the other must have been standard; but this meant something quite different from modern practice. Bartolomeo Campagnoli's treatise of 1824 stresses that the pressure exerted by the chin on the tailpiece must be light and that the head should be held as upright as possible. The inventor of the chin rest, Louis Spohr, listed among its advantages the fact that it makes it easier to hold the head upright. He claimed in his *Violinschule* (1832) that in the ten years since he had invented it, the chin rest had found favour with many violinists; but the *Méthode de violon* (1858) by the great Belgian violinist Charles-Auguste de Bériot fails to acknowledge its existence.

With the exception of Herrando, all of these writers identified shifting as the principal reason for applying pressure with the chin. Yet it is obvious that many skilled violinists who held the instrument beneath the collar-bone (and probably others who held it on the collar-bone but without chin support) were capable of playing virtuoso repertory requiring an advanced shifting technique. Even Prinner, the earliest and most vehement advocate of chin-on playing, conceded (1677): 'I have known virtuosos of repute who irrespective of this put the violin only against the chest, thinking it looks nice and decorative'.

Pictorial evidence from the 17th and 18th centuries seems to reflect what must have been a genuine diversity in ways of holding the violin. A number of paintings, in fact, depict several violinists, each holding his instrument differently, playing in a single ensemble. For all that, the vast majority of violinists depicted in the art of the period use holds in which the chin could not be used to stabilize the instrument. Geminiani's instructions for shifting are predicated on such a hold and we can only assume that many virtuosos had mastered such a technique (as, in fact, a good number of period instrument players did in the later 20th century).

It might be that chin stabilization was disdained by 17th-century virtuosos but adopted by amateurs as a stratagem that got them around the most perplexing technical problem: that of shifting. In the course of the 18th century the situation reversed itself; by about 1800 professional players were unanimous in resting the chin (however lightly) on the tailpiece, while chin-off methods (especially ways of holding the violin lower than the collar-bone) were the preserve of tavern and traditional fiddlers. (There is a parallel with the adoption of the end-pin on the cello, recognized as a possibility by the early 18th century but spurned by advanced players for almost two centuries thereafter.)

For discussion of bowing technique and other aspects of performing style on the violin in this period *see* Bow; Col legno; Pizzicato; Scordatura, §1; Vibrato.

5. Since 1820.

(i) The instrument. (1) The violin. Most violins made before about 1800 have been modified to yield greater tonal power and brilliance. The flat-model Stradivari

flourished as concert instruments, while the highly arched, smaller-toned Stainers and Amatis lost their former popularity. The main body of the violin remained unaltered despite further attempts at 'acoustical improvement', ranging from the construction of instruments from metals, glass, leather, plastics, and ceramics to experiments with various shapes, notably Félix Savart's trapezoidal violin with straight sides and straight slits for soundholes (1817) and François Chanot's guitar-shaped model with small crescent soundholes (also of 1817).

During the 1960s and 70s, Carleen Hutchins and her associates developed a 'concert violin', with a longer, revamped body and larger f-holes, and a string octet, compromising mathematical, acoustical, and violin-making principles to produce instruments in different frequency ranges that possess the dynamic power and timbre of the violin family. These instruments range from the contrabass violin (body length 130 cm, tuned E'–A'–D–G) to the small treble (or 'sopranino') violin (tuned an octave above the normal violin).

Experiments with building electric instruments based on the violin family, often with solid bodies and amplified usually by means of one or more sets of electromagnetic pickups or contact microphones, have continued since the 1920s. The kit-like Raad violin was developed in the late 1970s to dispense with the earlier primitive arrangement of surface pickups and to cultivate a more sophisticated sound. By allowing the instrument's signal to be amplified, modified or altered through changes in frequency response, rapid changes in amplitude, harmonic alteration (of overtones), echo and reverberation effects, and distortion, it has served a wide range of classical and popular musical styles.

(2) Makers. The burgeoning concert activity and educational opportunities of the early 19th century increased demand for instruments, especially for cheaper 'factory fiddles', mass-produced in France at Mirecourt and in Germany at Mittenwald and Markneukirchen. Mirecourt is still a centre for specialist craftsmen, having a violin-making school and a small factory that produces high-quality instruments at reasonable prices by implementing some mechanized processes. Similar schools have been established in recent years in Britain (especially in London and Newark-on-Trent), the USA, Italy (Cremona), Switzerland (Brienz), Poland (Poznań), and many other countries.

Although there were some significant 19th-century Italian makers such as G.F. Pressenda (1777–1854), Giuseppe Rocca (1807–65), and Gaetano Chiocchi (1814–81), the leadership in violin making passed to the French, notably Nicolas Lupot (1758–1824), F.-L. Pique (1757–1822), and Lupot's pupils C.-F. Gand (1787–1845) and S.-P. Bernardel (1802–70). Most influential was Jean-Baptiste Vuillaume (1798–1875), who worked for François Chanot and Simon Lété in Paris before establishing his own business in 1827. In 1855 he purchased Luigi Tarisio's collection of fine Italian violins. His talented workforce copied these instruments, including the 'Messiah' Stradivari, producing many high-quality violins. Most of these bear Vuillaume's label and brand, serial number, and the date of manufacture. Among skilled craftsmen who worked for Vuillaume were Paul Joseph Bailly (1844–1907), Honoré Derazey (1794–1883), and Hippolyte Silvestre (1808–79).

J.F. and J.B. Cuypers, the sons of J.T. Cuypers (1724–1808), continued their father's work in The Hague, but to a lesser standard. Central to the British violin market was the firm of W.E. Hill & Sons, formally established in 1835, as well as the family businesses of J.T. Hart, the younger Georges Chanot, Edward Withers, and John Beare. Several skilled foreign luthiers also lived and worked in Britain, among them the younger B.S. Fendt (1800–52), George Craske (1795–1888), and J.F. Lott (1776–1853).

Leading 20th-century makers included C.G. Becker (1887–1975), Sergio Peresson (1913–91), Dario D'Attili (1922–2004), David Burgess (*b* 1953), Luiz Bellini (*b* 1935), and Samuel Zygmuntowicz (*b* 1956) in the USA; Annibale Fagnola (1866–1939), Giuseppe Fiorini (1861–1934), Cesare Candi (1869–1947), Fernando Sacconi (1895–1973), Vittorio Bellarosa (1907–79), Francesco Bissolotti, and Giovanni Battista Morassi (*b* 1969) in Italy; Joachim Schade and Eugen Sprenger (1882–1953) in Germany; Pierre Gaggini (1903–2006), Etienne Vatelot (*b* 1925), and Frédéric Becker in France; the Portuguese Antonio Capela (*b* 1932); and the Czechs Přemysl Špidlen, Vilém Kužel, and Tomáš and Vladimír Pilař, as well as several fine Japanese craftsmen. In the postwar resurgence of violin making in Britain the work of William Luff (1904–93), Thomas Earle Hesketh (1866–1945), Geroge Wulme-Hudson (1862–1952), Arthur Richardson (1882–1965), Maurice Bouette (1922–92), Wilfred Saunders (*b* 1927), Clifford Hoing (1903–89), Lawrence Cocker (1912–82), Roger Hargrave (*b* 1948), and Gimpel Solomon (*b* 1934) was outstanding. The early music revival encouraged craftsmen such as Ronald Prentice (*b* 1932), Derick Sanderson (*b* 1932), Colin Irving (*b* 1945), Rowland Ross, David Rubio (*b* 1934), and numerous followers to make reproduction instruments to Baroque dimensions.

(3) Strings and accessories. A report by François-Joseph Gossec presented to the Institut national, later published in *Procès-verbaux de l'Académie des beaux-arts*, vol.1 (1937), 156–61, puts forward some of the perceived disadvantages of gut stringing: the need to keep them moist; their tendency to unravel; their sensitivity to variation in atmospheric temperature; and the common incidence of knots. Yet despite the increased preference for overspun D strings and these well-publicized disadvantages of gut stringing, H. Welcker von Gontershausen strongly advocated all-gut stringing (*Neu eröffnetes Magazin musikalischer Tonwerkzeuge*, Frankfurt, 1855). However, the combination of plain gut E and A, high-twist gut D and a G with copper, silver-plated copper or silver round wire close-wound on a gut core was the norm throughout the 19th century. The gut E was gradually replaced by a more durable and responsive steel variety, with the metal adjuster for greater facility in fine tuning, championed by the violinists Willy Burmester (1869–1933) and Anton Witek.

Only a few performers, most notably Fritz Kreisler, persevered with a gut E string as late as 1950. Flesch (*c*1923) documents the use of an overspun A string, while the high-twist D was replaced by gut with aluminium winding. By the mid-20th century, flat-ribbon and flat-ground round windings (with interleaved plastic) were applied to roped steel and plastic as well as gut, for A, D and G strings; the development of more flexible woven core led to the introduction of metal strings, which have the advantages of longer wear, easier tuning with adjusters (usually on specially designed tailpieces), minimal stretching, and precise moderation of thicknesses for true 5ths. However, their perceived tonal inferiority and the additional pressures they place on the instrument have encouraged a preference for metal-wound strings with a gut or nylon core. Early-music specialists employ gut strings almost exclusively; this revival of interest is prompting research into, and attempts at reconstructing, the manufacturing techniques of the late Renaissance period and the Baroque.

Mutes of various types and weight have been employed. The three-pronged clamp model (sometimes two- or five-pronged) made from wood, metal, ivory, or, latterly, Bakelite remained virtually unchallenged until the mid-19th century, when Vuillaume, J.F.V. Bellon, and others attempted (with little success) to introduce models that could be applied more quickly and conveniently. In the 20th century, designs for mutes that are stored between the bridge and the tailpiece, notably the 'Tourte', 'Heifetz', and 'Roth-Sihon' models, gained preference.

The chin rest has become a standard accessory, ensuring the stability of the instrument and increased left-hand mobility. Invented by Spohr about 1820, it was originally of ebony and placed directly over the tailpiece, not to the left side as later became customary. The chin rest only gradually achieved general approbation but has come to be adopted by most modern violinists. It is normally made from wood (usually ebony or rosewood) or vulcanite, and is available in numerous forms and sizes.

Pierre Baillot (1834) was the first to recommend 'a thick handkerchief or a kind of cushion' for the correct and comfortable support of the instrument. The production of shoulder rests has been a growth industry since the 1950s, designs ranging from wooden models made in various sizes, to pads affixed to metal frames that grip the instrument with feet covered with rubber protectors, and to inflatable cushions. Late 20th-century pedagogical trends largely discouraged their use, due to their perceived adverse effect on tone quality and their causing unwanted body tensions for many violinists.

(4) The bow. Apart from some minor 19th-century additions and unsuccessful attempts to improve the bow, Tourte's standardized design has remained unsurpassed. The most significant of his French successors worked in Paris or Mirecourt, notably Jacques Lafleur (1757–1833) and his son Joseph René (1812–74), Jacob Eury (1765–1848), Etienne Pajeot (1791–1849), Nicolas Maire (1800–78), Jean Dominique Adam (1795–1865)

and his son Grand-Adam (1823–69), and François Lupot (1775–1838); their bows are generally more heavily wooded and slightly shorter than Tourte's. Lupot adopted a narrower outline for the head and probably added (c1820–30) the metal underslide to prevent wear on the nut caused by friction with the stick.

Vuillaume trained and hired countless bowmakers (among them Dominique Peccatte, Joseph Fonclause, Pierre Simon, J.P.M. Persoit, and F.N. Voirin) in his workshops and disseminated the best qualities of Tourte's work, publishing in 1856 a theory that the taper of Tourte's sticks generally corresponded to a logarithmic curve. Among Vuillaume's inventions were: a tubular steel bow, which was championed by C.-A. de Bériot and Alexandre Artôt, but generally lacked the resiliency of its wooden counterpart, was deficient in balance, and kinked, dented, or bent easily; and the 'self-hairing' bow with fixed frog. His other experiments achieved more lasting approbation, notably the round-edged frog or curved ferrule combined with the stepped bottom plate for a good spread of hair at the heel, the indentation of the channel and track of the frog, and the combination of rear and upper heel plates into one right-angled metal part.

Peccatte (1810–74), Joseph Henry (1823–70), Simon (1808–81), and Voirin (1833–85) also challenged the supremacy of Tourte's legacy, striving for a lighter, more elegant product. Particularly characteristic were the slimmer and less square profile of the head and the different camber, the progression of which was moved closer to the head for additional strength in the stick. The balance was redressed by a reduction in the diameter of the lower end of the stick, with the frog appropriately in proportion.

Outstanding among Voirin's successors were Louis and Claude Thomassin and Eugène Sartory. The Thomassins were trained by Charles Bazin (1847–1915), himself an imitator of Voirin. Louis later worked for Voirin and succeeded to his business (1885), while Claude worked for Gand & Bernardel, Caressa, and Caressa & Français in Paris, before opening his own workshop there (1901). Sartory's predominantly round sticks are indebted to Voirin and A.J. Lamy but are characterized by their smaller heads and greater strength and weight. Among other leading makers of the fortified Voirin model were J.A. Vigneron, Victor and Jules Fétique, and E.A. Ouchard (1900–69).

French bowmaking declined during the two World Wars, but the products of André Chardon (1867–1963), Louis Gillet (1891–1970), Jacques Audinot (b 1922), Jean-Paul Lauxerrois (b 1928), Jean-Jacques Millant (1928–98), B.G.L. Millant (b 1929), and André Richaume (1905–66), most of whom returned to the style and hatchet head of Peccatte and Tourte, are well respected. The Mirecourt bowmaking tradition was revived with the establishment of a school (1971–81) under the direction of Bernard Ouchard (1925–79) and, later, Roger-François Lotte (b 1922). Among its distinguished 'graduates' are Stéphane Tomachot, Jean Grunberger, Pascal Lauxerrois, Benoît Rolland, Christophe Schaeffer, Martin Devillers, Sylvie Masson, and Jean-Yves

Matter. Along with Didier Claudel, Masson and Matter are among France's principal makers of reproduction pre-Tourte bows.

Bowmaking in 19th-century Britain was founded on the work of the Dodd and Tubbs families, who favoured functional durability over artistic craftsmanship. John Dodd (1752–1839) experimented with various weights, shapes of head, lengths and forms of stick, and mountings on the nut, his somewhat crude product approximating to the Cramer type, which, together with the bows of his father Edward Dodd (1705–1810), most likely served as his model. Many of his bows are slightly shorter and lighter than Tourte's, and his early examples lack a metal ferrule. William Tubbs (1814–78) and his son James (1835–1921) retained the robust qualities of the Dodds but softened the angularity of the earlier English style. William was the first significant maker to use silver or gold (as opposed to ivory or ebony) facings for the head.

Samuel Allen (1848–c1905) was the chief inspiration behind the 'Hill bow'. Preserving the robust English tradition, this model was developed by makers in the workshops of W.E. Hill, notably W.C. Retford (1875–1970), William Napier (1848–1932), Sydney Yeoman (1876–1948), Charles Leggatt (1880–1917), and Frank Napier (1884–1969). Among other talented trainees in Hill's workshops were Arthur Barnes (1888–1945), Edgar Bishop (1904–43), Albert Leeson (1903–46), W.R. Retford (1899–1960), Berkeley Dyer (1855–1936), A.R. Bultitude (1908–90), Malcolm Taylor (b 1933), and William Watson (b 1930). Garner Wilson (b 1930), Brian Alvey (b 1949), Michael Taylor (b 1949), John Stagg (b 1954), and John Clutterbuck (b 1949) have become leading British makers, while history reserves a niche for Lawrence Cocker's cane bows. Matthew Coltman (b 1955) and Brian Tunnicliffe (b 1934) are among the prominent British makers of reproduction pre-Tourte bows.

Germany became known during the 19th century for the mass-production of bows made from a cheaper and harder substitute for pernambuco wood, sometimes called 'Braziletta'. There were few specialist bowmakers of international repute, but the work of Nikolaus Kittel (1839–70), Ludwig Bausch (1805–71), and the Knopf, Nürnberger, Pfretzschner, and Weidhaas families, is well respected. Siegfried Finkel (b 1927) continued the Weidhaas tradition in Switzerland and his son Johannes (b 1947) worked in London and the USA. The roll of distinguished recent American bowmakers includes John Bolander Jr, William Salchow (b 1926), José da Cunha (b 1955), John Lee (b 1953), and Charles Epsey (b 1946). Christophe Landon (b 1959) is renowned for his reproduction pre-Tourte bows, as are the Netherlanders Luis-Emilio Rodriguez and Gerhard Landwehr.

20th-century inventions included the highly arched Vega (or 'Bach') bow. Promoted in the 1950s by Emil Telmányi and Albert Schweitzer to address the misconception that Bach's polyphonic violin music should be sustained precisely as written, it enabled all four strings to be sounded individually or in combination, its hair tension being controlled by a mechanical lever operated by the thumb. It had no precedent in the Baroque and made little impression. With supplies of pernambuco dwindling, bows of fibreglass, metal, graphite fibre, and other materials have been introduced, but without ousting the conventional pernambuco from its favoured position.

Traditionally, bowhair comes from the tails of white horses, but some players use black horsehair or synthetic substitutes such as nylon, arguably to coarser tonal effect. Bronisław Huberman (1882–1947) made experiments with fine-gauge wire which also yielded mixed tonal results.

(ii) Technique. (1) Historical outline. Giovanni Battista Viotti, the 'father of modern violin playing', was trained in the classical Italian tradition by Pugnani and first went to Paris in 1782. There he taught or inspired the founders of the French violin school (Baillot, Rode, and Kreutzer), who exerted an immense influence on violin playing in the 19th century. Viotti's cantabile was based on Tartini's maxim 'per ben suonare, bisogna ben cantare'. He was also one of the first to appreciate the specific beauties of the lowest (G) string, including its high positions; and his concertos unite the singing style, the brilliance of passage-work, and such specialized bowings as the 'Viotti' stroke. In addition, Viotti persuaded the Parisians of the beauty of the Stradivari violins; and he might have assisted Tourte in creating the modern bow.

The Italian school reached its final flowering in Nicolò Paganini, who aroused audiences to hysterical enthusiasm by the technical perfection and verve of his playing and by the intense projection of his hypnotic personality. His music uses practically all known technical devices in a grand, virtuoso, and frequently novel manner, including glissandos, harmonics of all types, pizzicatos of both right and left hand, octave trills, the solo on the G string alone (a speciality of his), multiple stops, extensions and contractions of the hand, and the scordatura. Staccato, ricochet, and mixed bowings of all sorts were also among his stock in trade.

Paganini and Pierre Baillot set the technical standard of the early 19th century. A school of violin playing similar to the Paris school was founded in Brussels in 1843 by Charles-Auguste de Bériot, who, like the Parisians, was heavily indebted to Viotti. Among Bériot's illustrious successors were Hubert Léonard, Henry Vieuxtemps, Henryk Wieniawski, and Eugène Ysaÿe; the latter's bowing facility, energetic personality and golden tone became legendary.

The Germans were generally more conservative in technique and more serious in musical attitude than the French, whose virtues included great technical facility, elegance, and imagination. Spohr was astonished by the accuracy of intonation of Paganini and Ole Bull but was unimpressed with such virtuoso devices as their elaborate harmonics, intense vibrato, bounding bow, and the air played solely on the G string. Spohr's pupil Ferdinand David made an important contribution to the violin pedagogy in his *Hohe Schule des Violinspiels* (1867–72).

Among David's pupils was Joseph Joachim, whose editions of such works as the Mendelssohn and Beethoven violin concertos reveal much about the technique of the 19th century and the implied ideas of expression (including the deliberate portamento slide in shifting).

Sharp distinctions in schools of instruction became less clear in the course of the 19th century. There was a strong tendency to mix the teachings of various schools, to amalgamate their styles and, under outstanding teachers, to select the best from all methods. The old Italian training was grafted on to the newer precepts in France and Belgium, and the results, in turn, to various teachings in Vienna, Prague, Leipzig, and Budapest. Leopold Auer upheld the Franco-Belgian tradition at the St Petersburg Conservatory, while in Prague, Kiev, and Vienna Otakar Ševčík revolutionized and systematized basic technique, especially of the left hand, by a system of numberless exercises based on the semitone system (rather than the diatonic system, as previously). Among the most distinguished teachers to appear in the course of the 20th century were Carl Flesch, Max Rostal, Lucien Capet, Pyotr Stolyarsky, Louis Persinger, and Ivan Galamian.

(2) Sources of information and pedagogical literature. Baillot's *L'art du violon* (Paris, 1834), perhaps the most influential violin treatise of the 19th century, easily surpasses in detail Baillot, Rode, and Kreutzer's *Méthode de violon* (Paris, 1803), previously adopted by the Paris Conservatoire. Baillot's influence was perpetuated by his pupils François-Antoine Habeneck (*Méthode*, Paris, c1835, incorporating extracts from Viotti's unfinished treatise), Delphin Alard (*Ecole du violon*, Paris, 1844), and Charles Dancla (*Méthode élémentaire*, Paris, 1855). The celebrated études of Rode, Kreutzer, and Gaviniés helped to consolidate the teachings of the French violin school. The principal contributions of the Belgian school are Bériot's *Méthode de violon* (Paris, 1858) and Léonard's *Méthode* (Paris, 1877).

Karl Guhr's *Über Paganinis Kunst die Violine zu spielen* (Mainz, 1831) focuses on specific aspects of Paganini's performing style, while Spohr's *Violinschule* (Vienna, 1832) and David's *Violinschule* (Leipzig, 1863) are more comprehensive. The important three-volume *Violinschule* (Berlin, 1902–5) of Joachim appears to have been written largely by Joachim's pupil Andreas Moser.

Flesch attributed the development of technique and pedagogy in the late 19th century principally to Dont, Schradieck, Sauret, and Ševčík, although the works of Kayser and Courvoisier are also noteworthy. Flesch's *Kunst des Violin-Spiels* (Berlin, 1923–8) is a synthesis of the techniques and artistic priorities of the principal schools of violin teaching in the 19th and early 20th centuries. His *Urstudien* (1911) also contributed to the systematic development of left-hand technique, and his *Hohe Schule des Fingersatzes auf der Geige* (first published in Italian, Milan, 1960) significantly loosened traditional concepts of fingering.

Other notable 20th-century pedagogical literature includes Capet's *Technique supérieure de l'archet* (Paris, 1916), Auer's *Violin Playing as I Teach it* (New

York, 1921), Demetrius Dounis's *Künstlertechnik* (Vienna, 1921), Elma and Erich Doflein's *Geigenschulwerk* (Mainz, 1931), Galamian's *Principles of Violin Playing and Teaching* (Englewood Cliffs, New Jersey, 1962), and various works by Menuhin and Bronstein. Kato Havas and Paul Rolland focused on developing relaxation, control, and coordination. The 'Suzuki method' revolutionized violin teaching in some areas, allowing pupils to develop artistic potential simultaneously with technical skills. However, most 20th-century sources were based on traditional methods; few account for the extended harmonic language, diversity of styles, and the resultant technical and rhythmic demands of much contemporary music. Exceptions include Galamian and Neumann's *Contemporary Violin Technique* (New York, 1966) and Zukofsky's *All-Interval Scale Book* (New York, 1977), which are essentially modern approaches to scales and arpeggios, and study books by Hindemith, Adia Ghertzovici, and Elizabeth Green.

(3) Posture and manner of holding the violin. Not until the early 19th century was there general agreement on the optimum posture and manner of holding the violin. A 'noble' and relaxed position was recommended, with head upright, feet normally in line but slightly apart, and body weight distributed slightly towards the left side. The seated position preserved the erect trunk but required the right leg to be turned inward slightly to avoid 'fouling' the bow. 20th-century attitudes were generally more flexible, emphasizing comfort and ease while prohibiting exaggerated body movement; but Flesch (1923) stressed the importance of feet placement, recommending a 'rectangular' leg position in which the feet are close together; an 'acutangular' position in which the feet are separated, with either right or left foot advanced and the body weight on the rear foot; and his favoured 'spread-leg' position.

Although Spohr's chin rest was originally positioned directly over the tailpiece, a chin-braced grip on the left of the tailpiece gained universal approval by the mid-19th century, affording firm support for the instrument and allowing it to be held horizontally at shoulder height and directly in front of the player at almost 90 degrees. Optimum freedom of left-hand movement and bow management was thus achieved; some violinists employed a pad to increase security and comfort and avoid raising the left shoulder. The right arm adopted a position closer to the player's side than formerly, requiring the violin to be inclined more to the right for optimum bowing facility on the lowest string. Baillot (1834) prescribed an angle of 45 degrees, Spohr (1832) 25 to 30 degrees. Flesch, Suzuki, and most 20th-century teachers recommended that the violin be held parallel to the floor.

(4) Fingering and shifting. The 'Geminiani grip' (ex.1) remained the most common guide to correct elbow, hand, wrist, and finger placement (in 1st position) until well into the 20th century. The hand and fingers generally formed a curve to enable the top joints of the fingers to stop the strings from the same height. With the chin-braced violin hold, shifting proved less precarious, the left hand was able to move more as a unit than

before, and a closer relationship developed between shifting and phrasing. Baillot (1834) acknowledged this interrelationship, demonstrating Kreutzer's frequent shifts for brilliance of effect and Rode's more uniform tonal objectives, incorporating *ports de voix*. Baillot's discussion of *ports de voix* and expressive fingering provides clues to the mechanics of shifting. Anticipatory notes (unsounded) indicate the method of shifting, the stopped finger sliding forwards (or backwards) in order to be substituted by another finger. Spohr (1832) endorsed this, especially for rapid shifts involving leaps from a low to a high position in slurred bowing without glissando (ex.2), and illustrated a fast shift in which the highest note is a harmonic (ex.3). A sliding effect is clearly intended in another Spohr example (ex.4), and Habeneck (c1835) and Baillot (1834) allowed the tasteful introduction of portamento, especially in slow movements and in sustained melodies when a passage ascends or descends by step. Bériot (1858) used signs to indicate three types of *port de voix: vif, doux*, and *traîné*.

Exploitation of portamento as an 'emotional connection of two tones' (commonly in slurred bowing and with upward shifts) to articulate melodic shape and emphasize structurally important notes became so prevalent in the late 19th century that succeeding generations reacted strongly against the false accents it created, its slow execution and its use for convenience in shifting rather than expressive purpose. Flesch (1923) distinguished three portamento types: a straightforward one-finger slide; the 'B-portamento', in which the beginning finger slides to an intermediary note; and the 'L-portamento', in which the last finger slides from an intermediary note (ex.5). The first two types were commonly employed in the early 20th century, but the L-portamento was rarely used until the 1930s. Broadly speaking, the execution of portamento became faster, less frequent, and less prominent as the century progressed.

In shifting, the odd-numbered positions began to be emphasized, and an increased use of semitone shifts

Ex.1: The 'Geminiani grip'.

Ex.2: Adagio from Spohr, Violin Concerto no.10 in A op.62, 2nd movement.

Ex.3: From Rode, Violin Concerto no.7, 2nd movement, quoted in Spohr, *Violinschule*, p.209.

Ex.4: Allegro from Spohr, *Violinschule*, no.45 (6th position), bar 58.

Ex.5: (a) One-finger slide; (b) 'B-portamento'; (c) 'L-portamento'.

Ex.6: (a) From Baillot, *L'art du violon* (Paris, 1834); (b) From Geminiani, *The art of playing on the violin* (London, 1751).

facilitated achievement of the prevalent legato ideal. The higher positions were exploited more frequently for expressive reasons, particularly of sonority and uniformity of timbre. The fingered-octave technique, first discussed by Baillot (1834), gradually gained favour for its greater clarity and accuracy, and less frequent displacements of the hand. Geminiani's fingering for chromatic scales, largely ignored by his contemporaries and successors, achieved more positive recognition in the 20th century when re-introduced by Flesch (1923), due to its greater evenness, articulation, and clarity. However, the diversity of systems used in 20th-century methods and studies confirms that fingering is a matter for individual decision rather than textbook regulation.

Many 19th-century violinists opted for a more advanced thumb position to achieve greater mobility and facility in extensions, sometimes avoiding formal shifts between positions. Some of Paganini's fingerings, for example, anticipate the flexible left-hand usage of modern violin technique, in which contractions, extensions and 'creeping fingerings' liberate the hand from its customary position-sense and the traditional diatonic framework. In 20th-century music this was demanded by increased chromaticism, whole-tone, microtone, and other scale patterns, and non-consonant double and multiple stopping. The increased use of glissandos (by, for example, Xenakis: *Pithoprakta*, 1956; *Syrmos*, 1959; and *Aroura*, 1971) and Feldman's experiments with intonation systems are also significant (e.g. Violin Concerto, 1979; *For John Cage*, 1982; *Piano, Violin, Viola, Cello*, 1987). The general application to violin fingering of Cage's concept of a 'gamut'

of sounds, in which a specific string is assigned for a specific pitch (e.g. *Six Melodies for Violin and Keyboard*, 1950), revealed new possibilities of structural and timbral organization.

(5) Vibrato. Up to the early 20th century vibrato was employed sparingly as an expressive ornament linked with the inflections of the bow. It served to articulate melodic shape and assist in cantabile playing and was employed particularly on sustained or final notes in a phrase, at a speed and intensity appropriate to the music's dynamic, tempo, and character.

Spohr (1832) described four kinds of vibrato: fast, for sharply accentuated notes; slow, for sustained notes in impassioned melodies; accelerating, for crescendos; and decelerating, for decrescendos. Like Baillot (1834), he emphasized that deviation from the note should be scarcely perceptible. Baillot expanded the vibrato concept to include three types of 'undulated sounds': left-hand vibrato; a wavering effect caused by variation of pressure on the bowstick; and a combination of the two. He recommended that notes should be begun and terminated without vibrato to achieve accuracy of intonation and provided examples of Viotti's vibrato usage, some of which link the device with the 'swell' effect.

Joachim (1902–5) and Auer (1921), among others, recommended selective use of vibrato; Ysaÿe's vibrato, though more perceptible, was restricted to long notes. Flesch (1923) attributed the reintroduction of continuous vibrato (previously practised in the second half of the 18th century) to Kreisler, though it should probably be accredited to Lambert Massart, Kreisler's teacher. By the late 1920s vibrato was considered more a constituent of a pleasing tone than an embellishment. Most theorists advocated a combination of finger, hand, and arm movements for optimum vibrato production, but Rolland also included the shoulder.

Several 20th-century composers prescribed extreme applications of vibrato, even reversing traditional usages by demanding intense, fast vibrato in soft passages, or a slow, wobbly vibrato in loud passages; others employed the ornamental vibrato-glissando in which the finger slides up and down the string, creating a siren-like sound (e.g. Penderecki, String Quartet no.1). By contrast, the *senza vibrato* indication has been used increasingly for contrast or special effect.

(6) Special effects. Universal acceptance of harmonics was slow to materialize, but interest was eventually aroused by virtuosos such as Jakob Scheller and Paganini. Paganini introduced the technique of artificial harmonics in double stopping, and, by using harmonics, extended the range of the G string to at least three octaves. Chromatic slides, single trills, trills in double stopping, double trills, all in harmonics, and some pseudo-harmonic effects were incorporated into his vocabulary.

The use of the index finger for pizzicato was customary in the 19th century, but the right-hand thumb was occasionally employed, the instrument sometimes being held guitar-fashion for sonorous arpeggiation of chords or for soft passages. Berlioz (1843) recommended the second finger for most pizzicatos but suggested using the thumb and first three fingers in appropriate rapid passages. Left-hand pizzicato was employed by Paganini and later composers such as Bartók and Penderecki, sometimes in combination with right-hand pizzicato or simultaneously with bowed notes (e.g. Bartók's *Contrasts*). Paganini's Introduction and Variations on Paisiello's 'Nel cor più non mi sento', for example, employs left-hand pizzicato in accompanying, melodic and decorative roles, and the 15th variation of his *Carnaval de Venise* involves pizzicato for both left and right hands. Sculthorpe also employs left-hand pizzicato extensively (e.g. in *Requiem*).

Pizzicato techniques demanded by composers in the 20th century included the prescription of various pizzicato locations (e.g. mid-point of the string, at or behind the bridge, or either side of the stopping finger) or specific plucking agents (e.g. with the nail or the fleshy pad of the finger), requiring strings to be stopped with the fingernail for pizzicato, perpendicular strumming and oblique strumming of chords, or specifying pizzicato with alternating fingers (e.g. Crumb, *Four Nocturnes*). A 'scooping' technique was developed to obtain mellow, resonant pizzicatos in single and double stopping. Other effects involved 'flicking' the string with the nail, pizzicato glissando using the finger or peg (Crumb), pizzicato tremolo (Bartók), 'snap' pizzicatos (introduced by Biber but popularized by Bartók), pizzicato natural harmonics (Crumb), and pizzicato with vibrato in varying degrees.

Scordatura gradually lost popularity during the 19th century, although it never became obsolete; Mazas, Spohr, Paganini, Bériot, Prume, Winter, Baillot, Bartók, Mahler, Scelsi, and Ligeti are among those who have employed it. Ligeti's *Ramifications* (1968–9) for 12 solo strings, which requires half the ensemble to be tuned a quarter-tone higher than normal pitch, reflects 20th-century interest in microtones, initiated by Julián Carrillo's experimental 'sonido 13' system (of equal-tempered quarter-tones) of the 1890s. Among others who experimented with microtonal effects for expressive purposes or as an integral compositional device were Ives (*Quarter-tone Chorale* op.36), Bartók (Sonata, 1944), Hába, Vishnegradsky, Penderecki, Cage, Boulez, Husa, Szymanowski, Takemitsu, and Crumb.

Sculthorpe and other 20th- and 21st-century composers have prescribed unconventional violin sounds, including tapping on various parts of the instrument or on the strings with the fingers or with a wood, metal, glass, or plastic beater. Others have exploited sounds extraneous to the violin, using percussion, sounds such as floor stamping or finger snapping, or vocal sounds in combination with violin playing. Pre-recorded tape has further expanded the range of texture and effect, notably in Reich's *Violin Phase*.

II. Extra-European and folk usage.

1. EUROPE. From Praetorius's time the violin rapidly penetrated throughout Europe finding favour among all strata of society wherever there was already a native tradition of bowed string playing (rebecs, fiddles, viols, bowed zithers, etc.); this was probably because of its greater dynamic range and more flexible tone. Nevertheless, use of indigenous predecessors of the violin persisted for centuries making it hard to be precise about the chronology of the diffusion of the violin. Alexandru (1983) remarked on three aspects of the transfer to the violin: firstly, wherever this happened there was a tendency to apply to the violin a playing technique learned from earlier indigenous instruments; secondly, despite its perfection of form, there were often modifications to the structure of the violin (e.g. adding sympathetic strings in the case of the Norwegian Hardanger fiddle); thirdly, different tunings were adopted to facilitate the execution of the characteristic repertory of each region.

(i) Scandinavia and western Europe. In this region cheap instruments were readily imported because they proved ideal for dance music, but numerous native variants also appeared. The violin often retained the name of the older instrument, for instance, in the British Isles the term 'fiddle' or variants of it is still used synonymously for the violin, though often a difference in the status of the music or the performer is implied in use of one term or the other: fiddlers play indigenous airs and dance music, violinists play a 'classical' European repertory. In these regions the instrument was often used solo, the playing style making much use of the open strings as variable drones to enrich the musical texture and help with rhythmic accentuation. Until the middle of the 20th century, most musicians rarely played outside the 1st position; they used the left hand to hold the fiddle along the arm and against the chest rather than under the chin.

Less is known about traditions of fiddling in England than elsewhere in the British Isles. This is probably because there were few, if any, English publishers over the centuries who were interested in fiddle music specifically, compared with those in Scotland and Ireland. But fiddlers' tune books have been discovered from several areas of England, especially the north, which suggest that the fiddle was popular in the countryside, even if the pipe and tabor and, from the 19th century onwards, free-reed instruments such as the concertina were more frequently favoured by musicians attached to morris and sword dance groups. By contrast, the popularity of the fiddle in both Scotland and Ireland is attested by large collections of the repertory, both printed and manuscript, and the proximity of the two traditions by a considerable overlap in the repertory. By the late 18th century a semi-classical influence was discernible in the repertories of fiddler-composers such as William Marshall and Simon Fraser, but found its chief exponent in the flamboyant person of James Scott Skinner (1843–1927). His influence has been considerable in Scotland, causing many humbler fiddlers to try to emulate his style and technique.

Since the mid-19th century in Scotland, Ireland, and Scandinavia the custom of concerted playing has developed along with fiddlers' societies. The building of community halls and specialized dancing venues led to the single dance fiddler being joined by other players, notably of the accordion, piano, and drums. One outcome of the folk revivals in all these countries has been the growth of importance of the 'session': usually taking place in public houses, small informal groups of instrumentalists, often including a fiddler, meeting together to play for their own enjoyment (and not usually for dancing).

In Wales, the fiddle (*ffidil*) superseded the bowed lyre (*crwth*) during the 18th century as the principal bowed folk instrument and was eventually to challenge the harp as the main accompanying instrument for popular dance (although both instruments frequently performed together in that capacity). From the 18th century onwards, however, dance was vigorously condemned by puritanical nonconformist religion; whereas during the 19th century the harp was retained as a symbol of nationality and granted a respectable place within the eisteddfod, the *ffidil* was doomed to be associated almost solely with taverns and wild celebrations. By the end of the century it was almost extinct, and played only by Roma families until around World War I. More lately it has been revived by Welsh folk-dance and song groups.

In Portugal the violin has kept the older name *viola*; indigenous bowed instruments are distinguished by the name *rebecca* (from 'rebec'). The Portuguese played a major role in the dispersal of the violin throughout the world; they took it with them to their trading posts and colonies in the East, e.g. Goa, India, and the port of Melaka in Malaysia, as well as along the coast of Angola in Africa.

(ii) Eastern and southeastern Europe. As the violin displaced indigenous instruments, it became a favoured instrument of Roma musicians. Sarosi reported (1978) that as early as 1683, 'nearly every nobleman has a Gypsy who is a fiddler or locksmith'. Two violins, a string bass, and a plucked instrument make a typical dance ensemble in central Europe, Romania, and the Balkans.

The violin is the most popular folk instrument in Poland. The *skrzypce* is made by villagers themselves out of a single piece of wood, apart from the soundboard, and has three or four strings. The *skrzypce podwiązane* or *skrzypce przewiązane* is an ordinary violin with a match or small stick placed under the strings and then bound, so that it can be played as in the 1st position but in a higher register; in the 19th century this instrument began to replace the *mazanki*, a small fiddle with three strings that was played along with the bagpipe (*dudy*). The *skrzypce* is played chiefly as the melody instrument in folk bands. In Slovakia the *oktávka* (octave-violin) and the *shlopcoky* (scuttle-shaped violin) are used as well as the standard violin. Instruments are played solo, in combinations such as bagpipe and violin, or in diverse ensembles of bowed string instruments.

In Romania the *vioară* (violin) is known under several different local names. Players, particularly in Oltenia and Muntenia, use a wide range of scordatura

to facilitate the playing of certain tunes, to obtain unusual sounds and to imitate other instruments, such as the bagpipes. The *contră* of Transylvania has only three strings (tuned *g–d'–a*), which are stretched over a notched bridge and bowed simultaneously to obtain chords. The violin in southwest Moldova usually has seven sympathetic strings, probably a relic of the Turkish *kemençe*, with sympathetic strings. The Stroh violin, called *vioră cu goarnă* ('bugle violin') or *higheghe* in Bihor, became widespread between the two World Wars (it was invented in London for use in gramophone recording studios at the turn of the 20th century). *Lăutari* (professional folk musicians) make the instrument themselves, replacing the soundbox with a metal bell and resting the strings on a small mica sheet.

The *smuikas* of Lithuania is also often made by the musicians themselves and accordingly is found in a great variety of sizes and forms, of varying quality. The back and sides are made of maple, apple, or ash, the belly of fir or pine and the bridge and tuning-pegs of oak, hornbeam, beech, or ash. The instrument may have three, four, or more strings, usually tuned in 5ths, but in bands the tuning is adapted to suit the concertina and the clarinet. The player sometimes places a small piece of wood on the soundboard to muffle the timbre; experienced musicians adorn dance melodies with melismata and double or triple stopping. Similar traditions of violin playing are also found in neighbouring countries such as Estonia, where the instrument is known as the *viiul*, and Belarus, Moldova, and Ukraine, where the *skripka* has its own folk technique. The instrument is usually tuned in 5ths, but higher and lower tunings are used depending on the genre of music. Players use mainly the bottom two strings, more rarely the third. Fiddle playing has been an established profession in many Belarusian towns since the 17th century and the instrument maintains a strong role in rural musical life.

2. MIDDLE EAST AND SOUTH ASIA. The violin has been adopted in a wide range of indigenous art music, from North Africa to South India, and each culture has adapted the holding position to meet its own requirements. In many cases the first introduction of the instrument to these countries was in European-influenced, popular music contexts, such as café music of the Middle East. The violin has shown its flexibility and power as an accompanying instrument, especially where a voice sets the model in timbre and phrasing, as well as for solo playing. In Morocco, one or more violins take a leading part in the vocal-instrumental *nawbā* suites played by traditional orchestras. In North Africa and Turkey it is usually called *keman* (from the generic term *kemençe* or *kamānche*, the latter used for spike fiddles) and is often played in an upright position, resting on the seated player's thigh. In Iran, the violin is the only Western instrument to be admitted without reservation into traditional music because it is possible to play the whole of the *kamānche* repertory on it when technique and articulation are suitably adapted. Its great success at the beginning of the 20th century threatened the existence

of the *kamānche*, and it has now quite eclipsed the traditional instrument.

In India, where it was introduced in the 17th century, the violin became prominent in the classical music of the South from about 1800 after B. Dīkṣitar and his pupil Vadivelu adopted it for accompanying vocalists at the court of Travancore. It is usually played with the scroll resting on the right foot of the player, who sits cross-legged; the other end is wedged against his left shoulder. The player's left hand is thus free for the complex *gamaka* of Karnatak music. The strings are tuned to tonic and 5th of the lower and middle octaves at a pitch nearer that of the Western viola pitch. At this pitch level it gives, in the view of Bandyophadaya, 'a deep and melodious sound perfectly suited to male musicians'. When accompanying a singer, the violinist's role is to 'shadow' the soloist, echoing each phrase in a virtually continuous canon. During the last two decades of the 20th century, virtuosos such as L.K. Subramaniam elevated the violin to the status of solo instrument. This has been accompanied by changes in technique, the earlier two-finger left-hand technique, derived from that for the *vīṇā*, developed into one involving all four. In northern India, Pakistan, and Bangladesh, where the classical vocal styles *dhrupad* and *khayāl* are more long-breathed and relaxed, the violin is much less common in vocal accompaniment; here it is in competition with the deeper-toned, indigenous *sārangī* fiddle. However, violins form an essential section in each of the modern *filmi* orchestras of the South Asian broadcasting and television industries. Alternative north Indian names are *behālā*, *bela* (Hindi), and *behālā* (Bengali), which probably derive from the Portuguese *viola*; in Goa, where the Portuguese ruled for over four centuries, the violin is called 'rebec'.

The violin was brought to Sri Lanka by Parsi theatrical troupes from Bombay during the 19th century. The *ravikiñña* is now used by the Tamils for playing Karnatak music and, less often, for *rukada* (string-puppet plays).

3. SOUTHEAST ASIA. The violin was introduced into Southeast Asia by the Portuguese during the 17th century, and became known as the *biola* from the Portuguese name. European instruments were played in European fashion in colonial houses by slaves of varied origin. In Batavia (Jakarta) in 1689, a bride who had 59 slaves referred in a letter to 'a slave orchestra which played the harp, viol and bassoon at meal-times' (Boxer, 1965, p.240). Ensembles combining Malay instruments and styles with European ones entered the Malay courts of the Riaulinggu archipelago, East Sumatra, and the Malay peninsula. The Osinger people of East Java use the *biola* in their *gandrung* ensemble. It is played in several other ensembles, including the *orkes Dul Muluk* (theatre ensemble) of parts of South Sumatra, the *orkes gambus* of northern Java, Sumatra, and Malaysia, and the *orkes Lampung* of Lampung, Sumatra. *Biolas* are usually made locally by hand and are generally tuned like the European viola.

Biyolin is the term used for the violin by many groups in the Philippines. The instrument is used to play European-type songs in serenades or for entertainment in town feasts. String players for city symphony orchestras are sometimes recruited from the provinces where musical traditions date back to training by Spanish friars in the 17th century. More recently, the *biyolin* has been introduced into the music of some indigenous northern groups.

BIBLIOGRAPHY

A: CATALOGUES, BIBLIOGRAPHIES, GENERAL HISTORIES. B: MAKERS, ASPECTS OF VIOLIN MAKING. C: TREATISES, METHODS. D: COMMENTARIES ON TECHNIQUE. E: TO 1600. F: AFTER 1600.

A: CATALOGUES, BIBLIOGRAPHIES, GENERAL HISTORIES

F. Regli: *Storia del violino in Piemonte* (Turin, 1863)

W. Sandys and S.A. Forster: *The History of the Violin* (London, 1864)

J.W. von Wasielewski: *Die Violine und ihre Meister* (Leipzig, 1869, rev. 8/1927/R by W. von Wasielewski)

G. Hart: *The Violin and its Music* (London, 1881/R)

E. Heron-Allen: *De fidiculis bibliographia: being an Attempt towards a Bibliography of the Violin and all Other Instruments played with a Bow in Ancient and Modern Times* (London, 1890–4/R)

A. Moser: *Geschichte des Violinspiels* (Berlin, 1923, rev. 2/1966–7 by H.J. Nösselt)

A. Bachmann: *An Encyclopedia of the Violin*, ed. A.E. Wier (New York and London, 1925/R)

M. Pincherle: *Feuillets d'histoire du violon* (Paris, 1927)

E. van der Straeten: *The History of the Violin* (London, 1933/R)

F. Farga: *Geigen und Geiger* (Zürich, 1940, rev. 7/1983 by K.F. Mages, W. Wendel and U. Dühlberg; Eng. trans., 1950, rev. 2/1969)

S. Babitz: *The Violin: Views and Reviews* (Urbana, IL, 1955, 3/1980)

E. Leipp: *Le violon: histoire, esthétique, facture et acoustique* (Paris, 1965; Eng. trans., 1969)

B.G. Seagrave and J. Berman: *The A.S.T.A. Dictionary of Bowing Terms for String Instruments* (Urbana, IL, 1968)

W. Kolneder: *Das Buch der Violine: Bau, Geschichte, Spiel, Pädagogik, Komposition* (Zürich, 1972, 3/1984; Eng. trans., 1998)

E. Melkus: *Die Violine: eine Einführung in die Geschichte der Violine und des Violinspiels* (Berne, 1973/R, enlarged 2/1977, 4/1979)

V. Schwarz: *Violinspiel und Violinmusik: Graz 1972* (Vienna, 1975)

D. Gill, ed.: *The Book of the Violin* (Oxford and New York, 1984)

R. Stowell, ed.: *The Cambridge Companion to the Violin* (Cambridge, 1992)

R. Dawes, ed.: *The Violin Book* (London, 1999)

J. Milnes, ed.: *Musical Instruments in the Ashmolean Museum* (Berkhamstead, 2011)

B: MAKERS, ASPECTS OF VIOLIN MAKING

A. Bagatella: *Regole per la costruzione de' violini, viole, violoncelli e violoni* (Padua, 1786/R; Eng. trans., 1995)

G.A. Marchi: *Il manoscritto liutario di G.A. Marchi* (Bologna, 1786); ed. and Eng. trans. as *The Manuscript on Violin Making/Il manoscritto liutario*, ed. R. Regazzi (Bologna, 1986)

E. Heron-Allen: *Violin-Making, as it was and is* (London, 1884, 2/1885/R)

G. Fry: *The Varnishes of the Italian Violin-Makers* (London, 1904)

W.M. Morris: *British Violin-Makers, Classical and Modern* (London, 1904, 2/1920 as *British Violin-Makers*)

O. Möckel: *Die Kunst des Geigenbaues* (Leipzig, 1930, 6/1984)

F. Hamma: *Meisterwerke italienischer Geigenbaukunst* (Stuttgart, 1931, rev. 2/1964 by W. Hamma as *Meister italienischer Geigenbaukunst*, with Eng. trans., rev. 4/1976)

C. Bonetti: *La genealogia degli Amati liutai e il primato della scuola liutistica cremonese* (Cremona, 1938; Eng. trans., 1989, as *A Genealogy of the Amati Family of Violin Makers, 1500–1740*)

J.H. Fairfield: *Known Violin Makers* (New York, 1942, 7/2006)

E.N. Doring: *How Many Strads? Our Heritage from the Master* (Chicago, 1945, 2/1999)

J. Michelman: *Violin Varnish: a Plausible Re-Creation of the Varnish Used by the Italian Violin Makers between the Years 1550 and 1750* (Cincinnati, 1946)

J.W. Reiss: *Polskie skrzypce i polscy skrzypkowie* [Polish violins and violinists] (Warsaw, 1946)

F. Hamma: *Meister deutscher Geigenbaukunst* (Stuttgart, 1948, 2/1961; Eng. trans., 1961 as *German Violin Makers*)

K. Jalovec: *Italští houslaři/Italian Violin Makers* (Prague, 1952; edn in Eng. only, 1957, 2/1964)

R. and M. Millant: *Manuel pratique de lutherie* (Paris, 1952/R)

Z. Szulc: *Słownik lutników polskich* [Dictionary of Polish violin-makers] (Poznań, 1953)

C.M. Hutchins: 'The Physics of Violins', *Scientific American*, vol.207/5 (1962), 78–84, 87–93

S. Milliot: *Documents inédits sur les luthiers parisiens du XVIIIe siècle* (Paris, 1970)

A. Gauge: '"La lutherie" at Mirecourt', *Journal of the Violin Society of America*, vol.3/3 (1977), 68–79

Verband Schweitzerische Geigenbaumeister: *Alte Meistergeigen: Beschreibungen, Expertisen* (Frankfurt am Main, 8 vols., 1977–82)

M. Brinser: *Dictionary of Twentieth Century Italian Violin Makers* (Irvington, NJ, 1978)

C. Taylor: 'The New Violin Family and its Scientific Background', *Soundings*, vol.7 (1978), 101–16

F. Prochart: *Der Wiener Geigenbau im 19. und 20. Jahrhundert* (Tutzing, 1979)

F. Mele: '19th- and 20th-Century Violin Makers', *The Strad*, vol.90/1074 (1979–80), 912–5

R.B. Nevin: 'Violin Varnish', *The Strad*, vol.90/1074 (1979–80), 446–8

P.L. Shirtcliff: 'The Violin–Making Schools of Europe', *The Strad*, vol.90/1074 (1979–80), 442–5

H. Heyde and P. Liersch: 'Studien zum sächischen Musikinstrumentenbau des 16./17. Jahrhunderts', *Jb Peters*, vol.2 (1980), 230–59

C. Vettori: *Linee classiche della liuteria italiana/The Classic Lines of Italian Violin Making* (Pisa, 1980)

G. Tumminello: *Arte, artigianato, società: dall' albero al violino, lavoro e creatività* (Cremona, 1981)

W. Prizer: 'Isabella d'Este and Lorenzo da Pavia, "Master Instrument Maker"', *EMH*, vol.2 (1982), 87–127

J.S. and W.R. Robinson: *The Guarneri Mold and Modern Violin Making* (Oklahoma City, OK, 1982)

I. Vigdorchik: *The Acoustical Systems of Violins of Stradivarius and other Cremona Makers* (Westbury, NY, 1982)

A. Cohen: 'A Cache of 18th Century Strings', *GSJ*, vol.36 (1983), 37–48

A. Lolov: 'Bent Plates in Violin Construction', *GSJ*, vol.37 (1984), 10–15

D. Rubio: 'The Anatomy of the Violin', *The Book of the Violin*, ed. D. Gill (Oxford and New York, 1984), 17–47

E.J. Ward: *The Strad Facsimile: an Illustrated Guide to Violin Making* (Kaneoho, HI, 1984)

K. Coates: *Geometry, Proportion, and the Art of Lutherie* (Oxford, 1985)

R. Doerr: *Violin Maker's Handbook* (Battle Creek, MI, 1985)

K.D. Marshall: 'Modal Analysis of a Violin', *JASA*, vol.77/2 (1985), 695–709

P.L. Polato: 'Liutai veneziani nei secoli XVI, XVII e XVIII: ricerca documentaria nell'Archivio di Stato di Venezia', *Flauto dolce*, no.12 (1985), 6–15

W.S. Gorrill and N. Pickering: 'Strings: Facts and Fallacies', *Journal of the Violin Society of America*, vol.8/1 (1986), 27–40

W. Hamma: *Geigenbauer der deutschen Schule des 17. bis 19. Jahrhunderts/Violin-Makers of the German School from the 17th to the 19th Century* (Tutzing, 1986)

R. Hargrave: 'Safety Pins', *The Strad*, vol.97/1154 (1986–7), 116–8

R. Hargrave: 'Tried and Tested', *The Strad*, vol.97/1155 (1986–7), 194–9

R. Hargrave: 'Keeping Fit', The Strad, vol.97/1156 (1986–7), 257–8

A. Dipper and D. Woodrow, ed. and trans.: *Ignazio Alessandro Cozio di Salabue: Observations on the Construction of Stringed Instruments and their Adjustment, 1804, 1805, 1809, 1810, 1816* (Taynton, 1987)

K. Moens: 'Der frühe Geigenbau in Süddeutschland', *Studia organologica: Festschrift für John Henry van der Meer*, ed. F. Hellwig (Tutzing, 1987), 349–88

S. Bonta: 'Catline Strings Revisited', *JAMIS*, vol.14 (1988), 38–60

D. Draley: 'The Transition of the Amati Workshop into the Hands of Stradivari, 1660-1684', *Journal of the Violin Society of America*, vol.9/3 (1988), 71–97

H.M. Brown: 'The Trecento Fiddle and its Bridges', *EMc*, vol.17/3 (1989), 309–29

O. Adelmann: *Die alemannische Schule: archaischer Geigenbau des 17. Jahrhunderts im südlichen Schwarzwald und in der Schweiz* (Berlin, 1990)

F. Dassenno and U. Ravasio: *Gasparo da Salò e la liuteria bresciana tra Rinascimento e Barocco* (Brescia and Cremona, 1990)

T. Drescher: *Die Geigen- und Lautenmacher vom Mittelalter bis zur Gegenwart* (Tutzing, 1990)

P. Kass: 'The stati d'anime of S. Faustino in Cremona: Tracing the Amati Family, 1641 to 1686', *Journal of the Violin Society of America*, vol.12/1 (1992), 3–85

D. Rosengard: 'Cremona after Stradivari: the Bergonzi and Storioni Families', *Journal of the Violin Society of America*, vol.12/1 (1992), 91–162

Liuteria e musica strumentale a Brescia tra Cinque e Seicento: Salò 1990, ed. M. Bizzarini (Brescia, 1992)

C. Beare and B. Carlson: *Antonio Stradivari: the Cremona Exhibition of 1987* (London, 1993)

D.G. Plowright: *Dictionary of British Violin and Bow Makers* (Exmouth, 1994)

B.W. Harvey: *The Violin Family and its Makers in the British Isles* (Oxford, 1995)

J. Jaskulski, J. Podbielski and R.J. Wieczorek: *Polakowi tylko boga a skrypic: dzieje lutnictwa na ziemiach polskich di II wojny światowej* [To a Pole, the almighty and a violin: history of the violin-making art in Poland until the Second World War] (Poznań, 1996)

J. Beament: *The Violin Explained: Components, Mechanism, and Sound* (Oxford, 1997)

K. Moens: 'Vuillaume et les premiers luthiers/Vuillaume and the First Violin Makers', *Violons, Vuillaume, 1798–1875: un maître luthier français du XIXe siècle/Violins, Vuillaume, 1798–1875: a Great French Violin Maker of the 19th Century, Musée de la Musique, 23 Oct 1998–31 Jan 1999* (Paris, 1998), 130–8, 160–2 [exhibition catalogue]

R. Hoepfner, ed.: *Meisterwerk der Geigenbaukunst* (Vienna, 2002)

T. Wilder, ed.: *The Conservation, Restoration, and Repair of Stringed Instruments and Their Bows* (Montreal and London, 3 vols., 2010)

C: TREATISES, METHODS

S. Virdung: *Musica getutscht* (Basle, 1511/R)

M. Praetorius: *Syntagma musicum*, vol.1 (Wittenberg and Wolfenbüttel, 1614–5, 2/1615/R); vol.2 (Wolfenbüttel, 1618, 2/1619/R; Eng. trans., 1986, 2/1991); vol.3 (Wolfenbüttel, 1618, 2/1619/R)

M. Agricola: *Musica instrumentalis deudsch* (Wittenberg, 1529/R, enlarged 5/1545; Eng. trans., ed. W. Hettrick, 1994)

H. Gerle: *Musica teusch* (Nuremberg, 1532/R, rev. 3/1546/R as *Musica und Tabulatur*)

G.M. Lanfranco: *Scintille di musica* (Brescia, 1533/R); Eng. trans. in B. Lee: *Giovanni Maria Lanfranco's 'Scintille di musica' and its Relation to 16th-Century Music Theory* (diss., Cornell U., 1961)

S. di Ganassi dal Fontego: *Regola rubertina* (Venice, 1542/R); ed. W. Eggers (Kassel, 1974); Eng. trans. in *JVdGSA*, vol.18 (1981), 13–66

S. di Ganassi dal Fontego: *Lettione seconda* (Venice, 1543/R); ed. W. Eggers (Kassel, 1974)

P. Jambe de Fer: *Epitome musical* (Lyons, 1556); repr. in F. Lesure: 'L'epitome musical de Philibert Jambe de Fer', *AnnM*, vol.6 (1958–63), 341–86

R. Rognoni: *Passaggi per potersi essarcitare* (Venice, 1592)

L. Zacconi: *Prattica di musica* (Venice, 1592/R)

F. Rognoni: *Selva di varii passaggi* (Milan, 1620/R)

G. Zanetti: *Il scolaro* (Milan, 1645)

J.J. Prinner: *Musicalischer Schlissl* (MS, 1677, *US-Wc*)

J. Lenton: *The Gentleman's Diversion, or the Violin Explained* (London, 1693, 2/1702 as *The Useful Instructor on the Violin*)

Nolens volens, or You Shall Learn to Play on the Violin Whether You Will or Not (London, 1695)

The Self-Instructer on the Violin (London, 1695, 2/1700 as *The First, Second and Third Books of the Self-Instructor on the Violin*)

D. Merck: *Compendium musicae instrumentalis chelicae, das ist: kurtza Begriff, welcher Gestalten die Instrumental-Music auf der Violin, Pratschen, Viola da Gamba, und Bass gründlich und leicht zu erlernen seye* (Augsburg, 1695)

G. Muffat: *Florilegium secundum* (Passau, 1698; ed. in *DTÖ*, vol.4, Jg.2/ii, 1895/R)

M. Corrette: *L'école d'Orphée, méthode pour apprendre facilement à jouer du violon dans le goût françois et italien avec des principes de musique et beaucoup de leçons* (Paris, 1738/*R*, enlarged 2/1779)

J.-J.C. de Mondonville: *Introduction to Les sons harmoniques*, op.4 (Paris and Lille, 1738)

H. Le Blanc: *Défense de la basse de viole contre les entreprises du violon et les prétentions du violoncel* (Amsterdam, 1740/*R*)

J.D. Berlin: *Musikalske elementer* (Trondheim, 1744); ed. B. Korsten (Bergen, 1977)

R. Crome: *The Fiddle New Model'd, or a Useful Introduction for the Violin* (London, c1750)

F. Geminiani: *The Art of Playing on the Violin* (London, 1751/*R*1952 with introduction by D.D. Boyden)

L. Mozart: *Versuch einer gründlichen Violinschule* (Augsburg, 1756/*R*, 3/1787/*R*; Eng. trans., 1948, as *A Treatise on the Fundamental Principles of Violin Playing*, 2/1951/*R*)

G. Tartini: *L'arte del arco* (Paris, 1758); repr. in J.B. Cartier: *L'art du violon* (Paris, 1798, enlarged 3/c1803/*R*)

The Compleat Tutor for the Violin: Containing the Best and Easiest Instructions for Learners to Obtain a Proficiency on that Instrument (London, after 1761)

L'abbé le fils [J.-B. Saint-Sévin] *Principes du violon* (Paris, 1761/*R*, 2/1772)

C.R. Brijon: *Reflexions sur la musique et la vraie manière de l'exécuter sur le violon* (Paris, 1763/*R*)

G. Tartini: *Lettera [dated 1760] del defonto Signor Giuseppe Tartini alla Signora Maddalena Lombardini: inserviente ad una importante lezione per i suonatori di violone* (Venice, 1770; Eng. trans., 1771, 2/1779/*R*) [It., Eng., Fr. and Ger. edns repr. in G. Tartini: *Traité des agréments de la musique*, ed. E.R. Jacobi (Celle, 1961)]

G. Löhlein: *Anweisung zum Violinspielen* (Leipzig and Züllichau, 1774, enlarged 3/1797 by J.F. Reichardt)

T.-J. Tarade: *Traité du violon* (Paris, c1774/*R*)

M. Corrette: *L'art de se perfectionner dans le violon … suite de L'école d'Orphée* (Paris, 1782/*R*)

A. Lolli: *L'école du violon en quatuor* (Berlin and Amsterdam, c1784)

I. Schweigl: *Verbesserte Grundlehre der Violin* (Vienna, 1786, 2/1795 as *Grundlehre der Violin*)

F. Galeazzi: *Elementi teorico-pratici di musica con un saggio sopra l'arte di suonare il violino analizzata, ed a dimostrabili principi ridotta*, vol.1 (Rome, 1791, enlarged 2/1817, Eng. trans., ed. A. Franscarelli (diss., U. of Rochester, 1968); vol.2 (Rome, 1796), Eng. trans. of pt 4, section 2, ed. G.W. Harwood (MA thesis, Brigham Young U., 1980)

J.A. Hiller: *Anweisung zum Violinspielen für Schulen und zum Selbstunterrichte* (Leipzig, 1792)

M. Woldemar: *Méthode pour le violon* (Paris, 1795-8)

A. Bailleux: *Méthode raisonée pour apprendre à jouer du violon* (Paris, 1798/*R*)

J.-B. Cartier: *L'art du violon* (Paris, 1798, enlarged 3/c1803/*R*) [incl. G. Tartini: *L'arte del arco*]

M. Woldemar: *Grande méthode ou étude élémentaire pour le violon* (Paris, 1798-9, 2/1802-3)

G.G. Cambini: *Nouvelle méthode théorique et pratique pour le violon* (Paris, c1800/*R*)

P. Baillot, P. Rode, and R. Kreutzer: *Méthode de violon* (Paris, 1803/*R*)

B. Campagnoli: *Nouvelle méthode de la mécanique progressive du jeu de violon … op.21* (Leipzig, 1824; It. trans., n.d.; Eng. trans., 1856)

K. Guhr: *Über Paganinis Kunst die Violine zu spielen* (Mainz, 1829; Eng. trans., rev., 1915; new Eng. trans., 1982, ed. J. Gold)

L. Spohr: *Violinschule* (Vienna, 1832; Eng. trans., 1843)

P. Baillot: *L'art du violon: nouvelle méthode* (Paris, 1834)

G. Dubourg: *The Violin* (London, 1836, rev. 5/1887 by J. Bishop)

J.-D. Alard: *Ecole du violon: méthode complète et progressive* (Paris, 1844)

H. Wieniawski: *L'école moderne* op.10 (Leipzig, 1854)

C.-A. de Bériot: *Méthode de violon* op.102 (Paris, 1858)

F. David: *Violinschule* (Leipzig, 1863)

F. David: *Die hohe Schule des Violinspiels* (Leipzig, 1867-72, 2/1903)

O. Ševčík: *Schule der Violin-Technik* op.1 (Prague, 1881)

O. Ševčík: *Schule der Bogentechnik* op.2 (Leipzig, 1895)

J. Joachim and A. Moser: *Violinschule* (Berlin, 1902-5; Eng. trans., c1907; trilingual edn, 1959, rev. M. Jacobsen)

O. Ševčík: *Violinschule für Anfänger* op.6 (Cologne, 1901)

C. Flesch: *Urstudien für Violine* (Berlin and Leipzig, 1911)

L. Capet: *La technique supérieure de l'archet* (Paris, 1916)

D.C. Dounis: *Die Künstlertechnik des Violinspiels/The Artist's Technique of Violin Playing* op.12 (New York, Leipzig, and Vienna, 1921)

A. Jarosy: *Die Grundlagen des violinistichen Fingersatzes* (Berlin, 1921; Fr. orig., Paris, 1924, as *Nouvelle théorie du doigté*; Eng. trans., 1933, as *A New Theory of Fingering*)

C. Flesch: *Die Kunst des Violin-Spiels*, vol.1 (Berlin, 1923, 2/1929; Eng. trans., 1924, 2/1939; new Eng. trans., 2000); vol.2 (Berlin, 1928; Eng. trans., 1930)

L. Auer: *Graded Course of Violin Playing* (New York, 1926)

E. and E. Doflein: *Geigenschulwerk* (Mainz, 1931, 2/1951; Eng. trans., 1957)

I.M. Yampol'sky: *Osnovï skripichnoy applikaturï* [The principles of violin fingering] (Moscow, 1933, enlarged 3/1955; Eng. trans., 1967)

S. Babitz: *Principles of Extensions in Violin Fingering* (Philadelphia, 1947; enlarged 2/1974 as *Violin Fingering*)

C. Flesch: *Alta scuola di diteggiatura violinistica* (Milan, 1960; Eng. trans., rev., 1966/*R*, as *Violin Fingering: its Theory and Practice*; Ger. orig., ed. K. Rebling, Frankfurt, 1995, as *Die hohe Schule des Fingersatzes auf der Geige*)

W. Primrose: Technique is Memory: a Method for Violin and Viola Players Based on Finger Patterns (Oxford, 1960)

I. Galamian: *Principles of Violin Playing and Teaching* (Englewood Cliffs, NJ, 1962, 2/1985)

I. Galamian and F. Neumann: *Contemporary Violin Technique* (New York, 1966)

Y. Menuhin: *Violin: six lessons with Yehudi Menuhin* (London, 1971/*R*)

R. Gerle: *The Art of Practising the Violin: with Useful Hints for All String Players* (London, 1983)

D: COMMENTARIES ON TECHNIQUE

A. Pougin: *Viotti et l'école moderne de violon* (Paris, 1888)

M. Pincherle: 'La technique du violon chez les premiers sonatistes français (1695-1723)', *BSIM*, vol.7 (1911), no.8, 1-32; no.9, 19-35; no.10, 10-23

G. Beckmann: *Das Violinspiel in Deutschland vor 1700* (Leipzig, 1918, music suppl. 1921)

A. Moser: 'Die Violin–Skordatur', *AMw*, vol.1 (1918-9), 573-89

E. Lesser: 'Zur Scordatura der Streichinstrumente', *AcM*, vol.4/3 (1932), 123-7, 148-60

T. Russell: 'The Violin "Scordatura"', *MQ*, vol.24/1 (1938), 84-96

P.G. Gelrud: *A Critical Study of the French Violin School (1782–882)* (diss., Cornell U., 1941)

I.M. Yampol'sky: *Russkoye skripichnoye iskusstvo: ocherki i materialï* [Russian violin playing: essays and materials] (Moscow, 1951)

M.W. Riley: *The Teaching of Bowed Instruments from 1511 to 1756* (diss. U. of Michigan, 1954)

A. Wirsta: *Ecoles de violon au XVIIIème siècle d'après les ouvrages didactiques* (diss., U. of Paris, 1955)

S. Babitz: 'Differences between 18th–Century and Modern Violin Bowing', *The Score*, no.19 (1957), 34-55; rev., pubd separately (Los Angeles, 1970, enlarged, 2/1975)

B. Seagrave: *The French Style of Violin Bowing and Phrasing from Lully to Jacques Aubert (1650–730)* (diss., Stanford U., 1958)

D.D. Boyden: *A History of Violin Playing from its Origins to 1761* (London, 1965)

G.J. Kinney: 'Viols and Violins in the Epitome Musical (Lyon, 1556) of Philibert Jambe de Fer', *JVdGSA*, vol.4 (1967), 14-20

E. Winternitz: *Gaudenzio Ferrari: his School and the Early History of the Violin* (Milan, 1967)

F. Neumann: *Violin Left Hand Technique: a Survey of Related Literature* (Urbana, IL, 1969)

A. Silbiger: 'The First Viol Tutor: Hans Gerle's Musica Teusch', *JVdGSA*, vol.6 (1969), 34-48

A. Wirsta: *L'enseignement du violon au XIXème siècle* (diss., U. of Paris, 1971, addenda, 1974)

R. Donington: *String Playing in Baroque Music* (London, 1977)

R. Stowell: 'Violin Bowing in Transition', *EMc*, vol.12/3 (1984), 316-27

P. Walls: 'Violin Fingering in the 18th Century', *EMc*, vol.12/3 (1984), 300–15

S. Monosoff: 'Violin Fingering', *EMc*, vol.13/1 (1985), 76–9

R. Stowell: *Violin Technique and Performance Practice in the Late Eighteenth and Early Nineteenth Centuries* (Cambridge, 1985)

G. Moens-Haenen: *Das Vibrato in der Musik des Barok: ein Handbuch zur Aufführungspraxis für Vokalisten und Instrumentalisten* (Graz, 1988)

P. Walls: 'The Influence of the Italian Violin School in 17th–Century England', *EMc*, vol.18/4 (1990), 575–87

P. Allsop: 'Violinistic Virtuosity in the Seventeenth Century: Italian Supremacy or Austro–German Hegemony?', *Il saggiatore musicale*, vol.3/2 (1996), 233–58

E: TO 1600

F. Lesure: 'La communauté des joueurs d'instruments au XVIe siècle', *Revue historique de droit français et étranger*, 4th ser., no.31 (1953), 79–109

D.D. Boyden: 'The Tenor Violin: Myth, Mystery or Misnomer?', *Festschrift Otto Erich Deutsch*, ed. W. Gerstenberg, J. LaRue, and W. Rehm (Kassel, 1963), 273–9

B. Geiser: *Studien zur Frühgeschichte der Violine* (Berne, 1974)

K. Moens: 'Problems of Authenticity of Sixteenth Century Stringed Instruments', *CIMCIM Newletter*, vol.14 (1989), 41–9

K. Polk: 'Vedel und Geige—Fiddle and Viol: German String Traditions in the Fifteenth Century', *JAMS*, vol.42/3 (1989), 504–46

L. Libin: 'Early Violins: Problems and Issues', *EMc*, vol.19/1 (1991), 5–6

K. Moens: 'La "nascita" del violino nei Paesi Bassi del sud: alla ricerca di un lougo dove collocare l'inizio della storia del violino', *Monteverdi: imperatore della musica*, ed. M. Tiella (Rovereto, 1993), 84–131

R. Baroncini: 'Contributo alla storia del violino nel sedicesimo secolo: i "sonadori di violini" della Scuola Grande di San Rocco a Venezia', *Rececare*, vol.6/1 (1994), 61–190

K. Moens: 'De eerste violisten in Antwerpen, 1554–1560', *Musica antiqua*, vol.11/1 (1994), 170–3

K. Moens: 'De vroege viool in Brussel', *Musica antiqua*, vol.11/2 (1994), 53–9

K. Moens: 'De viool in Antwerpen op het einde van 16de eeuw', *Musica antiqua*, vol.12/1 (1995), 16–20

K. Moens: 'Geiger in der Münchner Hopfkapelle zur Zeit Lassos und ihre Bedeutung für die Frühgeschichte der Violine', *Yearbook of the Alamire Foundation*, (1995), 383–413

K. Moens: 'Renaissancegamba's in het Brussels Instrumentenmuseum', *Bulletin van de Koninklijke Musea voor Kunst en Geschiedenis*, vol.66 (1995), 161–237

K. Moens: 'Violes ou violons?', *Musique—images—instruments*, no.2 (1996), 18–38

P. Holman: *Dowland: Lachrimae (1604)* (Cambridge, 1999)

F: AFTER 1600

D.D. Boyden: 'Monteverdi's Violini Piccoli alla Francese and Viole da Brazzo', *AnnM*, vol.6 (1958–63), 387–402

E. Dann: 'The Second Revolution in the History of the Violin: a Twentieth–Century Phenomenon', *Journal of the Violin Society of America*, vol.4/1 (1977–8), 48–56; repr. in *College Music Symposium*, vol.17/2 (1977), 64–71

S. Bonta: 'Terminology for the Bass Violin in Seventeenth–Century Italy', *JAMIS*, vol.4 (1978), 5–42

D. Cox: 'The Baroque Violin', *Journal of the Violin Society of America*, vol.8/1 (1986), 57–70

C. Bordas: 'Les relations entre Paris et Madrid dans le domaine des instruments à cordes (1800–1850)', *Musique—images—instruments*, no.1 (1995), 84–97

DAVID D. BOYDEN/PETER WALLS/R (I, 1–2, 4);

PETER HOLMAN/R (I, 3, I–IV); KAREL MOENS (I, 3, V);

ROBIN STOWELL/R (I, 5); PETER COOKE, ALASTAIR DICK

AND OTHERS (II)

Violin intonation. Term for pitch inflection practised mainly by players of unfretted, bowed string instruments, The two types of intonation considered here are the just and meantone complex used from the Renaissance into the 19th century, and the 'Pythagorean-functional',

starting in the second half of the 18th century but widespread only in the 20th century.

1. Just and meantone intonations. 2. Pythagorean and 'expressive-functional' intonation.

1. JUST AND MEANTONE INTONATIONS.

(i) Just (i.e., syntonic). The main feature of this intonation is the purity of 5ths, 3rds, and their inversions. In 1754 Tartini stated that the untempered syntonic diatonic scale was precisely what he himself used on the violin. He and his pupils checked the perfect intonation of the above intervals by means of the 'third sound', i.e. by the beat-tone produced by each of the above intervals; Leopold Mozart's *Violinschule* (1756) recommends the same test. Just intonation in violin performance poses three practical problems:

Problem 1. In order to obtain both pure 3rds and 6ths and a non-shifting reference pitch, one 5th in each four must be narrowed by a syntonic comma (= 21.5 cents), an alteration making that 5th dissonant. In the diatonic scale the narrowed 5th, usually D–A or A–E, clashes with the pure-5ths tuning generally adopted for the open strings. So performers avoided playing on open strings not only to preserve uniformity of timbre, but also to preserve the purity of 3rds and 6ths: see e.g. Johann Philipp Kirnberger (1786–7).

Problem 2. The alterations introduced in the 5ths create whole tones of two different sizes: minor (*t*) and major (*T* = *t* + 1 comma). The scale of C begins with the succession *T-t*; complications arise if one tries to transpose the same melody into all keys while maintaining the same relative size of intervals: at each instant the violinist must choose between two notes that differ by just a comma (i.e. by about 2 millimetres in the central part of the fingerboard). Francesco Galeazzi (1791) states that the best performers apply syntonic tuning in the strictest fashion, shifting the major and minor tones according to the key; he also gives a chart showing such shifts for each key then in use. Only the most skilled virtuosos, however, were capable of such 'commatic' adjustments; ordinary violinists always put their fingers in the same positions in whatever key they were playing, thus altering the character of the composition when transposed. Alexander Malcolm (1721), Hubert Le Blanc (1740), and Charles Delezenne (1827) provide evidence on this matter.

Problem 3. Theorists of various periods never agreed on a single type of just intonation, i.e. on the relative position of the major and minor tones. The physicist Jacques-Alexandre Charles, who observed virtuosos such as Giambattista Viotti and Pierre Baillot, in 1802 describes the syntonic scale they used when playing alone: in their C major scale, unlike the syntonic scale of ancient theorists, they made the step G to A a major tone and A to B a minor tone.

David Boyden observed (1951) that 'while just intonation as a complete harmonic system of fixed notes … may be relegated to the limbo of some musical fourth dimension, its flexible application by violinists to melody and to certain harmonic intervals can hardly be denied as a historical fact'. This observation finds support in Robert Bremner's *Some thoughts on the performance of concert music* (1777), in the section 'Concerning pure intonation'.

(ii) Meantone. Meantone intonation is obtained by distributing the above-mentioned alteration of one 5th equally among the four 5ths, each of which is therefore narrowed by a quarter comma. In this way the three previous difficulties disappear, because (1) excessively tempered 5ths no longer exist, (2) the major and minor tones unite around a mean value, and therefore (3) no distinction arises among various types of syntonic scale. Given that the 'quarter comma' (or allied temperaments) was the standard tuning of harpsichords and especially organs well into the 18th century, it automatically eliminated pitch disagreement between instruments with fixed and free intonation.

Most fingering charts confirm this kind of intonation, prescribing sharps tuned lower than the enharmonically equivalent flats, and not taking into account the comma: see e.g. Robert Crome (*c*1740–50), Francesco Geminiani (1751), [Du Perron] (1769), Georg Simon Löhlein (1774). Favouring this enharmonic differentiation was the type of fingering prescribed by Leopold Mozart (1756), widespread through the 18th century and still used in the first decades of the 19th: a given note and its chromatic accidentals (e.g. D–D♯, D–D♭) were realized with the same finger, which naturally led one to play the sharp lower than the enharmonically equivalent flat. The Florentine *maestro di cappella* Giovanfrancesco Becattelli (1726) testifies to the performance of such enharmonic distinctions by violinists.

So, leaving aside the matter of whether their syntonic system was 'flexible' or 'rigid', pure or tempered (i.e. meantone)—subtleties that, even if attested by the sources, could be questioned by the sceptical—we can at least conclude that in those centuries performers on unfretted bowed instruments employed a 'just-meantone' kind of intonation, because beside the above-mentioned enharmonic differentiation, their major 3rds were close to the 'just' ratio (5:4).

Turning to the tuning of open 5ths, only a few authors advise narrowing them, and this practice is mentioned only in periods and regions in which keyboard instruments were still tuned to more or less 'regular' meantone temperaments. Jean-Philippe Rameau (1737) points out that, on the violin, the three pure 5ths G–D–A–E would form a major 6th sharp by a comma: the violinist Jean-Pierre Guignon (Giovanni Pietro Ghignone) assured him that 'skilled masters' were narrowing them slightly 'to sweeten the hardness of the 6th in question'. As late as 1834, the Florentine composer Luigi Picchianti states that to correct the defect of the 6th 'it is indispensable that the three fifths should be slightly flat, and this is how violin players make them in practice, and most without knowing why'.

(iii) Enharmonic intonation and ornamentation. Supposing that a violinist, playing in 'just-meantone', was presented with a harmonic succession of the type B–D♯ followed by C–E♭, the rise from D♯ to E♭ would have to distinguish the so-called 'enharmonic diesis', equal to about a fifth of a tone. Such a passage can be found, for example, in the *Sonata terza* by Marco Uccellini (1660) and in the *Sinfonia XI* by Alessandro Stradella (*c*1670–80). In France, on the contrary, keyboards with split keys were scarce and violinists were not accustomed to such passages. In the earthquake scene of *Les Indes galantes* (1735) Rameau's players failed to produce the quarter-tone A♯–B♭, so he had to reduce the piece 'to common music', as he himself complained.

Jean-Jacques Rousseau (1768) condemned the type of enharmonic succession employed by Rameau, praising instead the 'enharmonic of the Italians', exemplified by the first recitative of Pergolesi's cantata *Orfeo*. This style, characterized by rapid modulations to distant keys, can be identified with the style called 'metabolic' (i.e. 'modulating') by G.B. Doni and Kircher, and 'enharmonic' by Domenico Mazzocchi (1638), though it does not respect the true melodic pattern of the Greek enharmonic genus. The reason for this identification lies in the fact that the extreme 'metabolic' notes, sharped or flatted, belong to the higher rows of keyboards known as 'chromatic' or 'enharmonic'. For instruments of the violin family this style can be found in Giovanni Valentini's *Sonata a 5* (first half of the 17th century), Georg Muffat's *Sonata violino solo* (Praga 1677, whose *continuo* requires a *cembalo cromatico*), Attilio Ariosti's *Il Coriolano* (1723, scene 'Spirate, o iniqui marmi'), and *Fuga—Diatonico Enarmonico Cromatico* from Nicola Porpora's violin sonata (1754).

While scantly used as harmonic intervals, the quarter-tones were for the most part played as ornamental notes. Giovanni Andrea Angelini Bontempi (1695) provides an example of this practice (which he calls 'spesso enharmonico') as it was taught to the *cantori* in Roman schools, embellishments already prescribed for vocal compositions by Emilio de Cavalieri (1599–1600), Ottavio Durante (1608), and Domenico Mazzocchi (1638). The same kind of ornamentation was used by violinists. Michel Woldemar (1798) transcribes a performance in Paris by Nicola Mestrino: most of the melodic notes are reached through an 'echelle enharmonique', i.e. by a slide. This kind of embellishment is already mentioned in 1618 by Fabio Colonna, who calls it 'strisciate di voce', and by the Venetian Giordano Riccati (1736), who states that such 'grace notes of charm [...] using the slide' were 'done all the time by violinists and singers'. Such shifting was favoured by the type of fingering then used for chromatic notes, illustrated by L. Mozart (§1.i). The fashion then extended to all strings of Vienna's orchestras, until it was given a definite name: the *maniera smorfiosa* (i.e. the 'mincing style') of the Italians. Still in Vienna, Antonio Salieri (1811) condemns it as 'an abuse of sliding the finger up and down the string [... changing] a harmonious body into a collection of whining children and miaowing cats'. This *maniera smorfiosa* was later used by Paganini and by some virtuoso cellists. Such excessive use of portamento can be heard in late 19th- and early

20th-century recordings and persisted in British orchestras in the 1920s.

2. PYTHAGOREAN AND 'EXPRESSIVE-FUNCTIONAL' INTONATION. By the mid-18th century, modern tonality had begun to impose itself on intonation: for example, the pull of the tonic on the leading tone and of the sixth degree on the minor 7th ensured that these two diatonic semitones, from being 'large' (as in the syntonic-meantone system), were reduced to 'small'. In the division of the tone the sharp (say, C♯) therefore became sharper than the enharmonically equivalent flat (say, D♭). This narrowing of the diatonic semitones obviously affected the major 3rd, which from being pure (ratio 5:4) was widened by a syntonic comma and became Pythagorean (ratio 81:64). Abbé Pierre-Joseph Roussier (1770) first reported this change of intonation, referring to 'Monsieur Duport for the cello in Paris and Monsieur Vachon for the violin'. Roussier was followed by Anton Bemetzrieder (1776), who furthermore noticed that the intonation of the virtuosos, though clearly of the Pythagorean type, had a strong 'expressive' or 'functional' component, the size of the semitones being dependent on nuances desired by the performer, according to the harmonic and melodic context. In 1791 Galeazzi also realized, with surprise, that for violinists the leading semitone was small instead of large (in contrast to what was prescribed by the just intonation that he upheld). Shortly after Galeazzi's treatise, Bartolomeo Campagnoli published his violin method, the first to prescribe a Pythagorean type of intonation explicitly; only in certain cases does he allow the sharps and flats to be united by what he calls 'temperament' (temperamento).

The natural tendency to lower the pitch of the flats was probably one of the factors that during the 18th century favoured attempts to admit into practice the seventh harmonic, i.e. the prime number 7. The first violinist to declare that he made use of it was Tartini (who employed it in the form of a minor 7th, ratio 7:4), followed by Michele Stratico. Compared to the just-intonation 7th, the new 'septimal' interval had the size of an enharmonic quarter-tone, as noted by Jean-Adam Serre (1753) and Tartini himself (1754). Still in this period, the composer Francesco Bianchi tells us that violinists also utilised the septimal ratio (14:9) to confer more expression on the Neapolitan 6th.

All this evidence notwithstanding, throughout the 19th century tests by the physicists Delezenne, Helmholtz, Georges Guéroult, and John A. Zahm provided results still favouring just intonation; Zahm, referring to such violinists as Reményi, Joachim, Popper, Wilhelmj, and Ole Bull, remarked that in their performances, unaccompanied by equal-tempered instruments, 'one can always hear distinctly the Tartini, or beat-tones, that add such richness and volume to violin music'. On the contrary, the physicists Alfred Cornu and Ernest Mercadier arrived in 1869 at the conclusion that Pythagorean intonation was preferred melodically and just intonation harmonically. Only in the early 20th century did the neo-Pythagorean tendency begin to be widely reported, both in solo and in string-quartet performances. String players in large orchestras had instead to compromise with the fixed intonation of wind instruments, the number of which had been constantly increasing since the late 18th century: equal temperament satisfied this requirement, together with the addition of vibrato.

Actual practice in the 19th century must have been considerably conditioned by emotional-psychological factors. For example, Bernhard Romberg, in his method for the cello (1840), asserts that the leading tones in minor keys were pitched higher than those in major keys. In 1862, the physicist Alexandre-Pierre Prevost gave a skilled violinist a tune in C major, asking him to transpose it to F♯ major and then to G♭ major: in the last key the performer introduced 'several modifications that gave the piece a certain sweetness, which to my [Prevost's] ears seemed to bring it closer to a minor mode'. This is indirectly explained by a deeply rooted conviction among musicians, already recorded about 1774 in the *Traité du violon* by Théodore-Jean Tarade: 'Many people believe that the flats always give minor keys and the sharps major keys: this is an error'.

BIBLIOGRAPHY
(only modern sources, in which previous sources are examined)
D.D. Boyden: 'Prelleur, Geminiani, and Just Intonation', *JAMS*, vol.4/3 (1951), 202–19
J. M. Barbour: 'Violin Intonation in the 18th Century', *JAMS*, vol.5/3 (1952), 224–34
J.H. Chesnut: 'Mozart's Teaching of Intonation', *JAMS*, vol.30/2 (1977), 254–71
R. Stowell: *Violin Technique and Performance Practice in the Eighteenth and Early Nineteenth Centuries* (Cambridge, 1985)
P. Barbieri: 'L'intonazione violinistica da Corelli al Romanticismo', *Studi musicali*, vol.19/2 (1990), 319–84
P. Barbieri: 'Violin Intonation: a Historical Survey', *Early Music*, vol.19/1 (1991), 69–88
B. Haynes: 'Beyond Temperament: non–Keyboard Intonation in the 17th and 18th Centuries', *Early Music*, vol.19/3 (1991), 357–81
M. Vogel: *Die Naturseptime: Ihre Geschichte und ihre Anwendung* (Bonn, 1991)
R. Philip: 'Traditional habits of performance in early–twentieth–century recordings of Beethoven', *Performing Beethoven*, ed. R. Stowell (Cambridge, 1994), 195–204
J. Fyk: *Melodic Intonation, Psychoacoustics, and the Violin* (Zielona Góra, 1995)
R. Jackson: 'From PPR to PPO: New Directions, New Challenges', *Performance Practice Review*, vol.10/2 (1997), 137–51
C. Brown: *Classical and Romantic Performing Practice 1750–1900* (Oxford, 1999)
M. Hewitt: *The Tonal Phoenix: a Study of Tonal Progression through the Prime Numbers Three, Five and Seven* (Bonn, 2000)
S. Standage: 'Historical Awareness in Quartet Performance', *The Cambridge Companion to the String Quartet*, ed. R. Stowell (Cambridge, 2003), 127–48
D. Waterman: 'Playing Quartets: a View from the Inside', *The Cambridge Companion to the String Quartet*, ed. R. Stowell (Cambridge, 2003), 97–126
P. Barbieri: *Enharmonic Instruments and Music 1470–1900* (Latina, 2008), 107–77
C. Di Veroli: *Unequal Temperaments: Theory, HIstory and Practice* (e-book: Bray, Ireland, 2008), 295–307

PATRIZIO BARBIERI

Violino grande (It.: 'large violin'). Bowed string instrument that expands the sonority and range of the violin. It was constructed by the chemist, engineer, and luthier Hans Olof Hansson (*b* 1919; *d* 16 June 2003) of

Sollentuna, Sweden, in 1963–6 for the Polish-Swedish violinist Bronisław Eichenholz. Early experiments directed to similar ends were carried out by Hansson's former teacher Otto Sand, who constructed the unsuccessful 'E-viola' (an ordinary viola fitted with a fifth string) in 1961. The violino grande unites elements of the violin and viol families, and is similar in size to a viola but shaped like a viol; its five strings, tuned in 5ths from *c* and played with a normal viola bow, give it the combined range of the violin and viola. A gently arched bridge facilitates multiple stopping. In making the instrument Hansson utilized the results of many years' research into the purported 'secrets' of old Italian varnish, concentrating in particular on the wood primer used before varnish was applied. Music for the violino grande has been composed by Krzysztof Penderecki and by several Swedish composers. Hansson's papers are in the library of the Catgut Acoustical Society at the Stanford University Center for Computer Research in Music and Acoustics.

BIBLIOGRAPHY

H.O. Hansson: 'Constructional Principles for Bow Instruments Applied to Violino Grande, the Five–Stringed New Member of the Violin Family', *J. Acoust. Soc. Am.*, vol.46/1A (July 1969), 120 only

O. Nordwall: 'The *violino grande*', *PNM*, vol.7/2 (1969), 111–4

HUGH DAVIES/R

Violino piccolo (It.). Small violin on which high violin parts were played from the late 16th century to the 18th. Its function is comparable to that of a piccolo flute; however, the size of the now rarely heard instrument continues to be debated. The violino piccolo was variously pitched up to a 5th higher than the full-size violin (hence sometimes called in German Terzgeige, Quartgeige, etc.) to accommodate high parts, which could then be played principally in the 1st position. Although violin virtuosos played in the 6th or 7th position by the end of the 17th century, the average violinist normally did not exceed the 3rd or 4th position. The violino piccolo was therefore specified when composers wished to extend the range of the violin upwards. As shifting became a standard part of violin technique in the 18th century, the violino piccolo, as it was originally conceived, became obsolete until its revival for 'early music' in the 20th century.

Violini piccoli existed as early as the late 16th century; several *claine discant* violins are listed in an inventory, dated 1596, of the collection in Schloss Ambras, near Innsbruck. Praetorius (*Syntagma Musicum* 2/1619) noted that the instrument was common in his day. His treatise demonstrates that the *Klein Discant Geig* was significantly smaller than a full-size violin, having a body length of roughly 27 cm. It had four strings, was tuned in 5ths, and was pitched a 4th higher than the full-size violin.

The dimensions of Praetorius's *Klein Discant Geig* closely match those of a basically unaltered violino piccolo (body length of 26.6 cm) from the workshop of the brothers Antonio and Girolamo Amati (1613, Cremona; in *US.V.n*). A number of violins with body lengths of 23 to 27 cm survive by makers such as Pietro Antonio Cati

(1741), Giuseppe Guarneri, Klemm, and both Antonio and Omobono Stradivari. They are similar in length to a modern ¼-size violin, but built for an adult hand rather than for teaching children; they have distinctly thicker necks, slightly wider fingerboards, and somewhat larger pegboxes than children's instruments.

The earliest music specifically calling for the violino piccolo is Monteverdi's opera *Orfeo* (1607). J.S. Bach specified the violino piccolo in three compositions: Cantatas nos.96 and 140, and the First Brandenburg Concerto. Many present-day violinists choose to perform these parts on so-called ⅞-size violins, rather than on smaller instruments. Numerous examples of ⅞-size violins with body lengths of about 34 cm (only 1 or 2 cm less than the size of standard violins), survive from the 17th and 18th centuries, but no persuasive arguments have been offered to clarify the use for which they were originally intended. Clearly, they are neither the *Klein Discant Geig* described by Praetorius nor could they represent the violino piccolo described by Leopold Mozart in his *Violinschule* (1756). All the bowed string instruments known to Mozart are described in the introduction to his tutor. He notes that the violino piccolo is smaller than the ordinary violin and is capable of being tuned to a much higher pitch. Most significant is his remark that violini piccoli were no longer needed to play the high violin parts since by then violinists were accustomed to shifting into higher positions. Therefore, Mozart notes, the small violins were used instead to train young boys. These remarks suggest that the violino piccolo in the mid-18th century was significantly smaller than a ⅞-size violin and was more likely the size of the 1613 Brothers Amati instrument.

Concertos, sonatas, orchestral suites, and cantatas featuring the violino piccolo were composed as late as the third quarter of the 18th century. Composers whose works call for it include Dittersdorf, Doles, Erlebach, Förster, Fux, Harrer, Janitsch, Krause, Pfeiffer, and Rosetti.

BIBLIOGRAPHY

A. Moser: 'Der Violino Piccolo', *ZMw*, vol.1 (1918–19), 377–80

J. Schlosser: *Die Sammlung alter Musikinstrumente* (Vienna, 1920/*R*)

N. Bessaraboff: *Ancient European Musical Instruments* (Cambridge, MA, 1941), 301, 353–6

D.D. Boyden: 'Monteverdi's *violini piccoli all francese* and *viole da brazzo*', *AnnM*, vol.6 (1958–63), 387–402

L. Sirch: 'Violini piccoli all francese e canto alla francese nell' *Orfeo* (1607) e negli *Scherzi musicali* (1607) di Monteverdi', *NRMI*, vol.15 (1981), 50–65

P. Liersch: 'Bericht über die für die Bachgedenkstätte gearbeitete Kopie des Violino piccolo Cati 1741', *Cöthener Bach-Hefte*, vol.3 (Köthen, 1985), 57–64

M.D. Banks: 'The Violino Piccolo and Other Small Violins', *EMc*, vol.8 (1990), 588–96

MARGARET DOWNIE BANKS

Violin player, automatic. Mechanical instrument incorporating at least one violin that is bowed and fingered automatically. Normally this is placed in the case of an upright expression piano or reproducing piano, and the playing mechanism of both piano and violin is operated by a musical programme in the form of a pneumatic paper-roll system.

The principle of the 'endless bow', often in the form of a rosined wheel, is an ancient one, and characteristic of such instruments as the hurdy-gurdy. Designs for keyboard instruments applying this principle go back to Leonardo da Vinci. Makers of fairground organs and orchestrions such as Gavioli, Mortier, and J.D. Philipps sought to imitate a string tone using specially voiced, narrow-scaled organ pipes. During the 18th and 19th centuries, however, attempts were made to construct an automatic violin player. The first practical and reliable instruments were made by Hupfeld in Leipzig, beginning about 1900. After two unsuccessful prototypes, they produced the Phonoliszt Violina in 1907 (put on the market in 1908). This spectacular instrument uses as a base a Hupfeld Phonoliszt expression piano—later a reproducing piano was used—having three violins each with one string played by a pneumatic fingering system. The violins are set vertically, with the necks lowermost, in a cupola set into the case of the piano. A circular rotating bow, strung with horsehair, encompasses the violins and is driven at variable speeds between seven and 32 r.p.m. by a pneumatic motor. When a note is to be sounded, the violin with the appropriate string is pushed outwards so that the string makes contact with the rotating bow. At the same time a small pneumatic motor presses a mechanical 'finger' onto the string to stop it at the required pitch. A wide range of expressive possibilities is available through varying the speed of the bowing wheel or its pressure on the string, the provision of a bridge mute, and a vibrato effect caused by an eccentric rotating wheel attached to the tailpiece of the violin. Duet or trio passages can be played by the violins sounding together, and the violins are accompanied by the reproducing piano; the effect is extremely convincing.

Another model was designed for use in public places such as restaurants and bars, having two music rolls that could be played interchangeably, and therefore non-stop, when accompanying silent films. A later version had six violins.

A Swedish engineer, Henry K. Sandell, employed by the Mills Novelty Company in Chicago, took the Swedish *nyckelharpa*, or keyed fiddle, as his model, and in 1905 produced the Automatic Virtuoso—an electrically operated violin with a perforated paper roll. The instrument created a sensation on a tour of Britain in 1908. On 13 March the *Birmingham Gazette* reported: 'Everything that a fine violinist could do, the machine did, and did perfectly. It executed trills and shakes, picked the strings, or played sliding notes just as the composition demanded, and throughout there was no sound or sign of mechanical origin save only the slight buzzing of the motor'. The company then placed this device in a cabinet with a symmetrically strung 44-note piano, and called it the Violano-Virtuoso. In this coin-operated machine the violin is placed horizontally; for each of the four strings there is a separate small celluloid disc 'bow' and pitch is controlled by four rows of electromagnetic 'fingers'. The electromagnetic action also included variable-speed bowing and variable vibrato.

The firm tried to capitalize on the popularity of the Violano-Virtuoso with the Viol-Cello (which had an additional side-cabinet containing a cello, forming a piano trio), the Viol-Xylophone (which replaced the piano with a metal-bar xylophone), the String Quartette (with three violins and a cello), and the Melody Violin (a two-manual keyboard from which 'any number of violins from one to a hundred' could be played with an electric mechanism), but none of these achieved the same success.

Other makers of automatic violin players included Hegeler & Ehrlers of Oldenburg (the Geigenpiano, 1906–8), E. Dienst of Leipzig (Sebstspielende Geige, 1910–12), Popper of Leipzig (Violinovo, 1930–31), and J.D. Philipps & Söhne of Frankfurt. The last experimented with a violin in one of its Paganini orchestrions (c1910–14) but opted in the end for violin-toned organ pipes in its Paganini Violin Piano (piano-orchestrion). None of these had the success of the Hupfeld instrument.

BIBLIOGRAPHY

L. Hupfeld: *Dea-Violina* (Leipzig, 1909)

H.N. Roehl: *Player Piano Treasury* (Vestal, NY, 1961, 2/1973)

Q.D. Bowers: *Put Another Nickel in: a History of Coin-Operated Pianos and Orchestrions* (Vestal, NY, 1966)

Q.D. Bowers: *Encyclopedia of Automatic Musical Instruments* (Vestal, NY, 1972)

A.W.J.G. Ord-Hume: 'The Violano–Virtuoso and its Swedish Origins', *Music & Automata*, vol.1 (1983–4), 134–42

J. Brauers: *Von der Äolsharfe zum Digitalspieler: 2000 Jahre mechanische Musik, 100 Jahre Schallplatte* (Munich, 1984)

M. Kitner and A. Reblitz: *The Mills Violano-Virtuoso: the Famous Self-Playing Violin and Piano* (Vestal, NY, 1984)

H. Jüttemann: *Mechanische Musikinstrumente: Einführung in Technik und Geschichte* (Frankfurt, 1987)

ARTHUR W.J.G. ORD-HUME

Violin Society of America. Society founded in 1973 to promote the art and science of making, repairing, and preserving bowed string instruments and their bows. Membership is open to all who share an interest in the violin, viola, cello, bass, and related instruments, and their bows, reflecting a diverse range of interests, including craftsmanship, acoustics, innovation, the history of instruments and performers, technique, performance practice, repertory, and other matters pertaining to instruments of the violin family. In 2011 the society, headquartered in Maitland, Florida, had more than 1400 members, with 29% from outside the USA.

The group holds an annual convention, offering lectures, demonstrations of violin and bow making, exhibits, and performances, and is well known for its biannual international competition for new instruments and bows. It publishes the refereed *Journal of the Violin Society of America* and *VSA Papers*, as well as a newsletter, and maintains a website. Jointly with Oberlin College, the VSA has sponsored summer workshops (since 1986) and holds an extensive collection of violin-related books (collected by founding member Herbert Goodkind).

In 2004, the Catgut Acoustical Society (CAS), which had been founded in 1963, joined the VSA as an independent Forum. The founder of CAS, Carleen Hutchins, and other CAS leaders have worked to increase and diffuse the knowledge of musical acoustics and instruments, and to promote the application of scientific principles to the construction of instruments in the violin family. Hutchins published the *CAS Journal* for some 30 years; after 2004, this was replaced by *VSA Papers*.

CAROLYN BRYANT/R

Violon-alto. Viola with five strings tuned *c–g–d'–a'–e''* supposedly designed or proposed by Michel Woldemar (*bap.* Orléans, 21 Sept 1750; *d* Clermont-Ferrand, 19 Dec 1815) in the late 18th century. Woldemar was a violinist, composer, and teacher; he is not known to have made instruments. The violon-alto, for which he composed a concerto, might have been a development of the quinton.

Violone (It.: 'large viol'). In modern terminology, the double bass viol, the direct ancestor of the double bass. Historically, the term has embraced a variety of meanings: it was originally used, from the 1530s onwards, to denote any size of viol. Francesco Prandi, in his treatise of 1606, applied the term to a low-pitched viola da gamba. In numerous Italian publications dating from 1609 to the 1730s the term refers to the early, larger size of the bass violin that existed before the invention of wire-wound strings in the mid-17th century (after which time it was reduced in size and became known as the violoncello). In some parts of Italy after 1660 (and subsequently in other countries) the term denoted the double bass. The complexity of usage has led to continuing controversy as to the exact meaning of the term.

1. Italy. 2. Germany, Austria and other countries.

1. ITALY. In 16th-century Italy 'violone' was a generic term for the viol family (see Ganassi, *Regola rubertina*, 1542, and Ortiz, *Trattado de glosas*, 1553); it distinguished the viol family from the violins, which in some early sources are called 'violette'. By about 1600 'violone' had come to stand for a large bass viol. Banchieri (*Conclusioni nel suono dell'organo*, 1609, 2/1626) referred to the 'violone da gamba', tuned *G'–C–F–A–d–g* (a 5th below the normal six-string bass viol), and to a larger instrument, 'violone del contra-basso', tuned *D'–G'–C–E–A–d*. It is not clear when the term 'violone' first became associated with the bass violin. The bass part of Caterina Assandra's motet *O Salutaris hodie* (*Motetti* op.2, Milan, 1609), which employs the typical Baroque trio scoring for strings, calls for a 'violone'; this was probably the early, larger form of the bass violin, as opposed to Banchieri's violone da gamba. The first known instance of the term 'violone' being specifically associated with the violin family is found in Giovanni Ghizzolo's motet *Quem terra pontus* (*Seconda raccolta de' sacri canti*, Venice, 1624) which is scored for 'due canti o tenori con due violini et chitarrone o violone da brazzo'. The confusion in terminology persisted into the early 18th century; the *Vocabulario degli Accademici della Crusca* (Florence, 4/1729) defined violone as 'a large viol, which is also called "bass viol" and, when of smaller size, "violoncello"'. Corelli's use of the term 'violone' should be interpreted as signifying a bass violin or 'violoncello'.

2. GERMANY, AUSTRIA AND OTHER COUNTRIES. Praetorius, who cited Italian sources (including Agazzari) in *Syntagma musicum*, pt.2 (2/1619), illustrated in *Theatrum instrumentorum* (1620) a five-string 'Gross Contra-Bas-Geig' (pl.V) and a six-string 'Violon, Gross Viol-de Gamba Basz' (pl.VI), both fretted and tuned in 4ths; the length of the latter has been estimated at 114 cm, the former instrument at 80 cm. He also referred to the 'Bas-Geig de bracio', later known as 'violoncello'. To avoid confusion he emphasized the distinction between 'Violonistam' (bass player) and 'Violinistam' (violin player). Schütz (*Musicalische Exequien*, 1636) referred to the violone, or Gross Bassgeige, as 'the most convenient, agreeable and best instrument to go with the concertato voice with the accompaniment of a quiet organ'. Several German authorities of the late 17th century and early 18th give tunings that correspond with the Italian. The earliest known instructions for the instrument are by Johann Jacob Prinner (*Musicalischer Schlissl*, 1677, MS in *US-Wc*), with the tuning *F'–A'–D–F♯–B*. Georg Falck (*Getreu und gründliche Anleitung*, 1688), Daniel Speer (*Grundrichtiger … Unterricht*, 2/1697), J.F.B.C. Majer (*Museum musicum*, 1732), and J.G. Walther (*Musicalisches Lexicon*, 1732) all give the tuning *G'–C–F–A–d–g* (Walther has *E* rather than *F* for the third string). J.P. Eisel (*Musicus autodidactus*, 1738) gave *G'–C–E–A–d–g* for the 'Basse Violon' and, for a larger violone, a tuning a 4th lower; he also mentioned a four-string 'violone grosso' tuned in 5ths *C'–G'–D–A*. Janovka (*Clavis ad musicam*, 2/1715) cited the tuning *G–A–d–g* for the violone and an octave below that for the violone grosso. The lower tuning (with *E'* as an alternative for the bottom string) corresponds with that given in 1694 by Bartolomeo Bismantova in his instructions for violone and violoncello (*I-REm* Regg.E.41). Among the composers who apparently distinguished between the violone and the violone grosso are Schütz and Bach. Georg Muffat (preface to *Florilegium secundum*, 1698) stated that the instrument called 'contrabasso' in Italy went under the name 'violone' in Germany; he distinguished between this and the 'Welsches Violoncino' or 'Bassetl' (the later cello). Walther considered the old violone preferable to the harsher bass violin (cello); but Quantz (*Versuch einer Anweisung die Flöte traversiere zu spielen*, 1752) wrote of the so-called 'German violone' with five or six strings which 'has justly been abandoned'. By Leopold Mozart's time (1756) the double bass, 'commonly known as violone', usually had four or five strings but sometimes only three. Koch (*Musikalisches Lexikon*, 1802) referred to 'violone' as meaning double bass. Writing in England, both Pepusch (*Rules, or a Short and Compleat Method for attaining to Play a Thorough Bass*, c1730) and Prelleur (*The Modern Musick-Master*, 1731) unambiguously identified the violone as the double bass, as did Brossard (*Dictionaire de musique*, 1703) in France, where the term 'violone' was not usual by this date.

BIBLIOGRAPHY

S. Bonta: 'From Violone to Violoncello: a Question of Strings', *JAMIS*, vol.3 (1977), 64–99

S. Bonta: 'Terminology for the Bass Violin in Seventeenth-Century Italy', *JAMIS*, vol.4 (1978), 5–42

P. Brun: *Histoire des contrebasses à cordes*, (Paris, 1982; Eng. trans., 1989)

S. La Via: 'Violone e violoncello a Roma al tempo di Corelli: terminologia, modelli organologici, techniche esecutive', *Studi corelliani IV: Fusignano* 1986, 65–91

S. Bonta: 'Catline Strings Revisited', *JAMIS*, vol.14 (1988), 38–60

A. Planyavsky: *Der Barockkontrabass Violone* (Vienna, 1989; Eng. trans., 1998)

M. Urquhart: 'The 17th Century Violone', *Journal of the International Society of Bassists*, vol.21/3 (1997), 18–21

S. Bonta: 'Five Essential Errors in Planyavsky's Baroque Double Bass Violone', *Journal of 17th Century Music*, vol.6/2 (2000)

THARALD BORGIR/STEPHEN BONTA (1);

ALFRED PLANYAVSKY/R (2)

Vipwali. Long, goblet-shaped, single-headed drums of the Mbwela-Nkhangala people of eastern Angola. They are called *jingoma* among the Lwena-Luvale peoples. The latter often group six of these drums together as a chime and play them together with a two-note, gourd-resonated xylophone, *jinjimba*.

GERHARD KUBIK/R

Virchi [Virchinus, Virchis], **Girolamo di** [de] (*b* Brescia, *c*1523; *d* after 1574). Italian cittern maker. The best known member of a family of instrument makers and musicians, he was the friend and possibly the teacher of the violin maker Gasparo da Salò, for whose son, Francesco, he stood as godfather in 1565. Documents from 1559 to 1569 record his activity: in 1568, for example, he paid a salary to two carvers, which would account for the high quality of decorations on his extant instruments. A document of 1563–1564 cites him as 'magister citharum'. A cittern by Virchi was in the Musikinstrumenten-Museum, Berlin (lost in World War II), and another one of particularly fine construction is in the Kunsthistorisches Museum, Vienna. Two more citterns may be ascribed to him on account of their rich carving and decoration: one (formerly attributed to Stradivari) is in the Musée de la Musique, Paris, and the other is in the Ashmolean Museum, Oxford.

His brother Benedetto (*b* c1520; *d* after 1568) was also a cittern maker, whose son Bernardino (*b* c1565; *d* after 1624) was an organ builder who studied with, and worked for the Antegnatis. Girolamo's son Paolo Virchi (1551–2 May 1610), court musician at Ferrara and Mantua, published a cittern tablature (1574). See U. Ravasio: 'Il fenomeno cetera in area bresciana', *Liuteria e musica strumentale a Brescia tra Cinque e Seicento: Salò 1990*, vol.1 (1992), 123–56.

UGO RAVASIO

Virdung [Grop], **Sebastian** (*b* ?Amberg, *c*1465; *d* after 1511). German theorist and composer. His father, Wernczlein (or Wenntzlaw) Vierdung, adopted the name Grop in 1469; he earned citizenship in Amberg (1475), then in Nuremberg (1486). Sebastian matriculated at Heidelberg University in 1483. By 1486 he was studying law while employed as an alto singer in the chapel of Count Philip, Elector Palatine, at Heidelberg. No record tells of Virdung's gaining a degree; by 1489, however, he had become a priest, as befitted the holder of an ecclesiastical benefice awarded him that year by the elector. Despite an accusation of slander against him in 1490 Virdung maintained his reputation, receiving a second benefice in 1500 at Stalburg Castle; at this time he bore the title of chaplain. From about 1505 Virdung was employed at the Württemberg chapel of Duke Ulrich in Stuttgart. By January 1507 he had formally left his posts at Stuttgart and Stalburg and been appointed succentor at Konstanz Cathedral, where his duties included teaching the choirboys and seeing to their physical welfare. A year later, in Jan 1508, he was dismissed for being 'erratic and negligent with the boys'.

In 1510, at the Diet of Augsburg, Virdung was soliciting support to complete and publish a comprehensive treatise in German, *Ein deutsche Musica*. Unable to find funding, he produced a greatly truncated version, covering only the section on musical instruments, which he published at Basle in late summer 1511. This work, entitled *Musica getutscht*, is the earliest printed treatise in the West to deal exclusively with musical instruments and aspects of their performance and pedagogy. It is also one of the earliest works on music in a vernacular tongue. Virdung hoped that dedicating this smaller treatise to Wilhelm Honstein, Bishop of Strasbourg, who had shown interest in the larger work, would elicit subvention for its completion. However, his magnum opus was never published, and the manuscript does not survive.

Musica getutscht contains much material appearing in print for the first time, including illustrations of musical instruments in current use arranged by organological categories, German keyboard tablature, German lute tablature, recorder fingering charts, and instructions with diagrams on aspects of performance. The author presents his material as a dialogue between himself (Sebastian) and his more erudite friend, Andreas Silvanus—most likely the latinized name of Andreas Waldner, a colleague of Virdung's at Heidelberg. Sebastian acts as the more knowledgeable of the two regarding contemporary musical instruments and performing practice, while Andreas takes the role of the initiate.

Virdung's treatise provides insights into music history, both in his era and earlier. It is here, for example, that the invention of German lute tablature is attributed to Conrad Paumann (*d* 1473). On the issue of whether black keys be considered *musica ficta* or notes from the Greek chromatic genus, Virdung, citing Boethius, sides with the latter view. He expresses his conviction by lambasting Arnolt Schlick for having espoused the former view in his treatise *Spiegel der Orgelmacher und Organisten*, published earlier in 1511. To this attack, which included cruel allusion to his blindness, Schlick retorted angrily several months later (Nov 1511) in the introduction of his subsequent publication *Tabulaturen etlicher Lobgesang und Lidlein uff die Orgeln und Lauten* (1512), in which he castigates Virdung for his pretentious 'knowledge' of Greek language and theory and for the numerous errors in the musical examples of *Musica getutscht*. Most of these errors result from Virdung's pedagogically inspired decision to transcribe the notes exactly, as demonstrations of instrumental notation, rather than to generate playable pieces.

Hints as to Virdung's date of death come from a treatise originally commissioned as a Latin translation of *Musica getutscht* but which, despite the presence of the original woodcuts, took on an identity quite its own: Othmar Luscinius's *Musurgia seu praxis musicae*, written about 1517 but published in 1536 and 1542. In his dedication (1536) Luscinius writes that 'unmistakable signs' in *Musica getutscht* (i.e. frequent references to the larger work) make clear that 'Sebastian was prematurely taken away from the living' before publication of his magnum opus could be realized. Virdung's death, then, took place after Schlick's harsh words (printed in 1512) and before the writing of *Musurgia* (c1517).

The popularity of both Virdung's subject matter and his illustrations inspired a second edition of *Musica getutscht* sometime between 1511 and 1521, and four derivative works in as many languages between about 1517 and 1529. In addition to the Latin *Musurgia*, these are Martin Agricola's *Musica instrumentalis deudsch*, in German (Wittenberg, 1529/R, enlarged 5/1545); the anonymous *Dit is een seer schoon boecxken*, in Flemish (Antwerp, c1528; exemplars from 1554 and 1568 survive); and the anonymous translation into French of this last work, *Livre plaisant et tres utile* (Antwerp, 1529).

Virdung follows a bipartite plan in *Musica getutscht*, first providing an illustrated instrumentarium and then offering elementary instructions for three representative instruments in preferred order of study: clavichord, lute, and recorder. He also expounds the basic principles of intabulation. He places instruments in three traditional categories—strings, winds, and percussion—and bases his subgroups on the instrumental notation appropriate to each. String instruments have four subdivisions: (1) those with keyboards, for which keyboard tablature is used in teaching and playing: clavichord, virginal, harpsichord (*clavicimbalum*), clavicytherium, hurdy-gurdy and presumably *harpfentive* (named but not pictured); (2) those with frets, for which (whether bowed or plucked) lute tablature is used: lutes, *quintern* (a small lute-like instrument) and viols (*gross geigen*); (3) those with multiple open strings and no keyboards or frets (tablatures are not discussed): harps, psaltery and hammered dulcimer; and (4) those with one to three strings and no frets, for which tablatures are not practical (thus rendering them 'unprofitable instruments'): rebecs (*clein geigen*) and tromba marina.

Wind instruments come in three subgroups: (1) those that can be blown by a person and have fingerholes, for which a tablature resembling fingering charts can be used (Virdung's wind tablature is unique): shawm, tenor shawm (*bombardt*), tabor pipe (*schwegel*), fife (*zwerchpfeiff*), recorders, *russpfeif* (four-hole fipple flute), curved horn (with four holes), gemshorn, cornetts, bladder pipe, crumhorns, and bagpipe; (2) those that can be blown by a person but do not have fingerholes (listed but not discussed): trombones and trumpets (military trumpet [*felttrummet*], *clareta* [high trumpet], and tower trumpet [*thurner horn*]); and (3) those that cannot be blown by a person and are sounded by bellows, for which keyboard tablature is used: organs (large organ, positive, regal, portative).

Virdung defines percussion instruments as those 'made of metal or other resonant substances'. Since he accepts only instruments capable of carrying melody, the sole representatives in this category are hammers and anvil, chime bells, and tuned clapper bells. He dismisses drums (military kettledrums [*grossen herpaucken*], side drums, and small drums) as 'devilish', for they cause 'a smothering and a drowning of all sweet melodies'. He also rejects the following: (1) 'foolish instruments': jew's harp, non-pitched bells, hunting horn, 'field horn' (*acher horn* = coiled horn), clappers, and 'beater on the pot' (*britschen uff dem hafen*); (2) 'tomfoolery' (*göckel spill*, literally 'juggler play'): whistles, birdcalls, leaves or keys into which one blows, and xylophone (*hültzig gelechter*, literally 'wooden laughter'); and (3) all instruments not represented by extant examples that could be played and heard—obsolete instruments known only from pictures or descriptions. (Virdung does bow to the prevailing reverence for antiquity, however, by including the fictitious 'instruments of Jerome', which he recognizes as allegorical.)

Most of the pictures in *Musica getutscht* cannot be taken with modern expectations of technical accuracy; their presence, as in other books at the time, offered enhancement of the text through pleasing suggestion of an object. They do, however, give insights into the relative importance of certain features. The clavichord keyboard, for example, was drawn accurately (but it appears in mirror image in the print). The flat bridge on the viol shows that instrument's relationship to the vihuela. The depiction of the recorder family conveys information about consort performance: these instruments came in three sizes a 5th apart—discant, alto/tenor, and bass—not four, as has been assumed. Three sizes sufficed for playing four-part music at the time, the normal disposition being one each of bass and discant and two of alto/tenor. Shawms are shown in two sizes and crumhorns in four, although the fingering charts for crumhorns in three sizes published by Agricola several decades later (1529–45) suggest pictorial misrepresentation in this instance.

As a practice piece for intabulation, Virdung provides his own sacred lied, a four-part setting of a rhymed translation into German of three Marian responsories: *O haylige, onbeflecte, zart iunckfrawschafft marie*. His keyboard and lute intabulations of this song in *Musica getutscht* are, by his own admission, literal transcriptions from staff notation to tablature intended only to demonstrate the principles involved; he pledges to provide idiomatic (and playable) versions in the larger work. For discussion of Virdung's compositions, see *GMO*.

WRITINGS

Musica getutscht (Basle, 1511/R1882) with index by R. Eitner, *PÄMw*, vol.11; R1970 with commentary by K.W. Niemöller, DM, 1st ser.: Druckschriften Faksimiles, vol.31

BIBLIOGRAPHY

H.H. Lenneberg: 'The Critic Criticized: Sebastian Virdung and his Controversy with Arnold Schlick', *JAMS*, vol.10 (1957), 1–6

F. Krautwurst: 'Bemerkungen zu Sebastian Virdungs Musica getutscht (1511)', *Festschrift Bruno Stäblein*, ed. M. Ruhnke (Kassel, 1967), 143–56

G. Stradner: 'Bemerkungen zu den besaiteten Tasteninstrumenten in Sebastian Virdungs "Musica getutscht … "', *Der klangliche Aspekt beim Restaurieren von Saitenklavieren: Graz 1971*, 79–86

E.M. Ripin: 'A Reevaluation of Virdung's *Musica getutscht*', *JAMS*, vol.29 (1976), 189–223

G. Stradner: 'Neue Erkenntnisse zu Sebastian Virdung's "Musica getutscht" (Basle, 1511)', *Mf*, vol.29 (1976), 169ff

C. Meyer: *Sebastian Virdung: Musica getutscht: les instruments et la pratique en Allemagne au début du XVIe siècle* (Paris, 1980) [incl. transcrs. of 5 songs, 131–45]

M. Staehelin: 'Bemerkungen zum geistigen Umkreis und zu den Quellen des Sebastian Virdung', *Ars musica, musica scientia: Festschrift Heinrich Hüschen*, ed. D. Altenburg (Cologne, 1980), 425–34

G. Stradner: *Spielpraxis und Instrumentarium um 1500 dargestellt an Sebastian Virdung's 'Musica getutscht' (Basle 1511)* (Vienna, 1983)

B. Bullard: *Musica getutscht: a Treatise on Musical Instruments (1511) by Sebastian Virdung* (Cambridge, 1993)

BETH BULLARD

Virgil practice clavier. Toneless keyboard developed by the American Almon Kincaid Virgil (*b* Erie, PA, 13 Aug 1839 or 1842; *d* St Petersburg, FL, 15 Oct 1921) in support of his physiologically based piano teaching system, published as *The Virgil Clavier Method* (1889–96). The method emphasized correct technical development during early stages of study, with particular emphasis on legato playing and key release. In 1878 in Peoria, IL, Virgil and his wife, Antha Minerva (née Patchen; 1852–1939), opened a music school, which continued until 1883; the Virgils then moved to New York and later opened schools in Chicago (from late 1896 or 1897 to 1900), London and Berlin (1895–6), Boston (1899), and St Petersburg, Florida (1917–21). Dissatisfied with his pupils' tendencies to acquire poor habits at the keyboard, as early as 1872 Virgil began to develop a practice clavier with adjustable touch-weight, on which the only sound produced was a click on the down- or up-stroke (or both). In theory, everything would be learned and practised at the toneless keyboard so that, on transfer to a piano, fail-safe results were virtually guaranteed.

In 1883 or 1884 Virgil first marketed his practice keyboard, the Techniphone. This used a barely adjustable click-sound mechanism, which generated a snapping effect (for both up- and down-clicks) through the flexing of spring steel tabs. No surviving example is known. In 1890 the company began production of the 'Perfected Practice Clavier', an improved direct-striker action model, which had a click feature with on and off levers at each end of the keyboard, and a 56.5- to 565-gram touch-weight adjustment lever over the keyboard; the device had folding legs and was declared portable, although the full 7⅓-octave model weighed between 41

and 45 kg. By 1896, some 3600 instruments had been manufactured.

After separating in 1900, the Virgils ran competing Clavier Method schools in New York. As well as publishing her own version of the method (1902–5), Antha established a clavier factory in Bergenfield, NJ, and brought out an improved model designed by her second husband, Amos Cole Bergman (1865–1948). The 'Tekniklavier' (or 'Tek') incorporated an improved, more adjustable action. Like the A.K. Virgil instruments, it was offered in a choice of wood finishes and the 7⅓- and 5⅓-octave models were equipped with folding legs. Both factories also made truly portable four- and two-octave suitcase models. Practice keyboards continue to be used wherever a low noise level is desirable, although electronic keyboards have supplanted mechanical types.

BIBLIOGRAPHY

H. Brower: *Piano Mastery* (New York, 1915–17)

D.A. Nahm: *The Virgil Clavier and Keyboard Pedagogy Method* (diss., Catholic U. of America, 1983) [extract (biography) in *Piano Quarterly*, vol.33 (1985), 48ff]

D.A. Nahm and R.E. Sheldon: 'The Virgil Practice Clavier', *Encyclopedia of Keyboard Instruments*, vol.1: *The Piano*, ed. R. Palmieri (New York, 1994)

ROBERT E. SHELDON, DOROTHEA A. NAHM/R

Virginal [virginals] (Fr. *virginale*, *épinette*; Ger. *Virginal, Instrument*; It. *arpicordo*, *spinetta*, *spinettina*). Smaller type of harpsichord, usually with only one set of strings and jacks and with only one keyboard (except for the double virginal; see below).

1. Nomenclature and construction. 2. Italy. 3. Flanders. 4. England and other northern European countries.

1. NOMENCLATURE AND CONSTRUCTION. The precise application of the term 'virginal' is much debated, in part because of its use in England to denote all quilled keyboard instruments well into the 17th century. Although some writers still reserve the term for rectangular instruments, present usage generally applies it to instruments whose strings run at right angles to the keys, rather than parallel with them as in a harpsichord or at an oblique angle as in a spinet. A distinction based on the supposed uniqueness of a virginal's having two bridges resting on free soundboard is no longer tenable, since this is also the case with some harpsichords in which the wrest plank is hollowed out under the nut (wrestplank bridge), and some virginals have one bridge deadened by a massive plank underneath the soundboard. However, 'spinet' is often applied to polygonal Italian virginals (in English and in German) because of the similarity to the Italian word 'spinetta'. The late 16th-century Italian name for the rectangular virginal was 'spinetta', while the most common word for polygonal instruments was 'arpicordo'. During the 17th century, however, 'spinetta' came to be accepted in Italy as a generic term for any plucked keyboard instrument smaller than a harpsichord. The term 'clavicordio' was used in the 16th century to mean any kind of plucked keyboard instrument, but also specifically

for the polygonal virginal. The word 'virginale' did not appear in this sense in Italian usage until the 20th-century revival of early music. (For further discussion of terminology, *see* SPINET; for Flemish usage, see §3 below.)

The derivation of the term 'virginal' remains in dispute, the association with the Latin *virga* ('rod') being unproved and that with Elizabeth I ('the virgin queen') being without foundation. The term probably derives in some way, however, from the instrument's association with female performers—possibly this results from a confusion between 'timbrel' (a frame drum played by women since biblical times) and the 'cymbel' in such terms as 'cembalo' and 'clavicymbel'—or from its tone, which some theorists likened to a young girl's voice (*vox virginalis*). The term 'pair of virginals', to be found in early literature derived from organ terminology, denotes a single instrument.

In contrast to those of a spinet, the long bass strings of a virginal are at the front, making it possible to build the instrument in a wide variety of shapes, from squat rectangles to more or less graceful polygons, depending on whether the keyboard is inset or projecting. The rectangular form would appear to have been the earliest. It is cited in the manuscript treatise of Paulus Paulirinus of Prague (c1460), who described the virginal as 'an instrument having the shape of a clavichord and metal strings making the sound of a harpsichord'. This form was also the one known to Virdung, who showed a small rectangular instrument with a projecting keyboard having a range of just over three octaves (*FG–g″*, lacking *F♯*) in his *Musica getutscht* (1511). Non-rectangular instruments appear in early 16th-century Italian representations, notably intarsias in the Vatican and in Genoa Cathedral, as well as Giorgione's well-known *Concert* in the Pitti Palace, Florence, all dating shortly after 1510. An earlier example is the intarsia from about 1506 in Isabella d'Este's *grotta* in the Palazzo Ducale, Mantua, which probably represents an instrument made for her in 1496 by Lorenzo da Pavia and is the earliest example of a *C/E–c‴* compass in a virginal. Like the intarsia in the Vatican, this instrument has some curved case sides and suggests that virginals might have been made in a variety of shapes before the straight-sided, pentagonal design became established.

The bridges of Italian virginals are invariably parallel-sided with a moulding on the top edge, but northern European instruments usually have a triangular section. The right-hand bridge of any virginal usually has a pronounced curve in the treble; this was always bent in Italian virginals but could be sawn in other traditions. Instruments at quart, quint, and octave pitch sometimes have the right bridge (at least partly) made of straight sections. In the northern European traditions the left-hand bridge is virtually straight, but most Italian virginals have a curve at the bass end.

In a typical virginal the jacks are placed along a line running from the front of the instrument at the left to the back of the instrument at the right. The key levers are, correspondingly, quite short in the bass and quite long in the treble, giving the keyboard of the virginal a characteristic touch, and, in some cases, making it difficult to play notes in the extreme bass easily and quickly. The jacks (one for each key) are arranged in pairs and pluck in opposite directions, so that the pairs of jacks are separated by closely spaced pairs of strings. In Italian instruments, each jack passes through a slot in the soundboard and in the solid ('box') register or jackslide (about 4 cm by 3 cm) glued to the underside. In northern European virginals each pair of jacks is usually served by a single slot in the soundboard, together with another slot below in a thin guide above the keys. Leather on the soundboard and lower guide provides a quiet bearing surface for the jacks.

Although virginals were made in many shapes, the internal bracing is similar for the different types. A brace extends from the front to the back of the case at each side of the keyboard; this can be supplemented by corner blocks. A liner around the inside of the case supports the soundboard and carries the hitchpins; the wrest pins (tuning pins) are held by a larger piece of hardwood. In rectangular instruments a separate diagonal hitchpin rail and wrest plank are provided. The back corners of rectangular Italian virginals were sometimes cut off, as shown by the 1593 virginal by Giovanni Celestini (in *GB.L.cm*). A few employ the false inner-outer construction in which a thick softwood case is fitted with cypress veneer and half-mouldings to make it appear as if a cypress instrument were in an outer case. The oldest known such instruments are by Joseph Salodiensis (c1570) and Celestini (1587). By far the most common Italian construction method used thin (3 to 5 mm) cypress case sides with mouldings on the top and bottom edges, as in Italian harpsichords. Many of these thin-cased virginals were kept in a painted outer case.

The case joints of Italian virginals are mitred, as might be expected considering the thinness of their wood; accordingly, it is noteworthy that the corners of the 1548 Karest virginal are dovetailed, even though the wood is scarcely thicker. Otherwise, the structure of the instrument is hardly different from that of an Italian example, except for the replacement of the solid Italian jack register by a complete counter-soundboard mortised for the jacks and serving as a lower guide (this feature is also found in a number of German and English instruments, and dovetailing of the case joints in German harpsichords and clavichords persisted into the 18th century).

Later Flemish virginals have thick cases, like those of Flemish harpsichords, and are assembled before the bottom is put on rather than being built from the bottom up. As with the Italian instruments, however, the two principal braces run from the front of the instrument to the back at the ends of the keyboard. The decoration of these instruments normally corresponds to that of the Flemish harpsichords, either plain paint or marbling outside and block-printed papers inside, except for the inside of the lid, which might have a painted landscape on it. A few examples are painted with arabesques instead of being papered, but this must have been relatively uncommon. The inclusion of a Latin motto on the inside of the lid, the jackrail, or around the inside of the case above the soundboard was quite common, and this is also seen in German instruments. The case-side covering the keywell (the 'fallboard') was usually hinged to the case along its underside. The decorated inside face, sometimes with a motto, was thus displayed when the fallboard was opened.

2. ITALY. Numerous Italian 16th-century virginals have survived. Some are elaborately decorated, for example the 1577 Rossi instrument (in *GB.L.v*) inset with precious and semi-precious stones. More typical was a plain cypress case with fine mouldings, but sometimes the casework was set with intarsia work in contrasting coloured woods, as in the 1523 Francesci de Portalupis virginal (in *F.P.cm*). All of these virginals have a rose in the soundboard, usually made of three or four layers of wood veneer, pierced in intricate gothic or geometric designs. Sometimes carved brackets were set on either side of the keyboard. Ivory was sometimes used for the natural-key covers, but boxwood was most commonly used, with ebony-topped sharps. Most instruments by Venetian makers had projecting keyboards, and virginals from the Milan–Brescia area had partly recessed keyboards, but exceptions to these traditions are found in both regions. There is no overwhelming acoustical advantage in one system or the other. Almost all 16th-century virginals have a compass of *C/E–f‴*, and later 17th-century examples only *C/E–c‴*. Early 16th-century instruments were made with a compass of *FGA–f‴*, but in the few instruments that survive the keyboard has since been modified. Some 17th-century virginals (for example by Francesco Poggi and Stefano Bolcioni) had split keys for *d♯/e♭* and *g♯/a♭*. Flemish and Italian virginals usually ended on a *C/E* short octave. A well-known instrument, 'Queen Elizabeth's Virginal' (in *GB.L.v*), is Italian, probably by Giovanni Baffo. Its original keyboard had a compass of *C/E–f‴*, but a *C–c‴d‴* (that is, no *c♯‴*) keyboard was later installed, presumably in order to alleviate the difficulty of the non-chromatic bass. In turn, this keyboard was later modified to the present compass of *G′/B′–c‴*. English virginals tend to have a wide compass (see §4 below).

Modifications, which have obscured the history of the Italian harpsichord, were not undertaken often for the virginals. It was relatively difficult to replace keyboards with those from other instruments because the pairwise jackslide tends only to match the keyboard for which it was made. Nevertheless, some virginals had their scale changed and keyboard altered to keep them abreast of changing musical requirements.

Considerable discussion has been devoted to the question of the pitch of Italian virginals (*see* HARPSICHORD for a detailed discussion): it has been argued that the long scales (usually corresponding to *C/E–f‴* compasses) were intended for low pitches. Most 16th-century Italian virginals have scales between 30.5 cm and 35 cm at *c″* (with only a few being shorter). These instruments were, however, designed to be strung in iron wire, which requires a longer scale than brass wire, and

means that this long scale came to a normal pitch (that is, for 35 cm about a tone below *a′* = 440).

Although most Italian virginals were designed for iron wire, some were quite clearly intended for brass wire at the same pitch (by reason of their scaling; for further details, *see* HARPSICHORD), such as the 1693 instrument by Cristofori (in *D.LE.u*). Several rectangular instruments by the 17th-century maker Honofrio Guarracino are examples of the latter. They have the tuning pins on the left-hand side and only one bridge on free soundboard, with the result that the sound is much brighter than that of most virginals and closely resembles that of a bentside spinet. These virginals by Guarracino appear to have been the continuation of a Neapolitan tradition: a similar instrument was made by Alessandro Fabri in 1598. Because instruments of this design are unknown further north of the Italian peninsula, this design might have been influenced by Spanish virginals. Virtually nothing is known of the latter, but Naples was under Spanish administration at that time, so the introduction of Spanish instruments would have been possible. The use of brass wires on virginals in the 16th century is believed to have been uncommon, but Isabella's intarsia virginal was probably so strung; the pitch would have been about a 4th above normal 8′ pitch (*a′* = *c*415–440).

Italian makers (unlike Flemish makers; see §3, below) all adopted similar scalings and plucking points, thereby giving a fairly uniform character to their instruments. The sound of an Italian virginal is usually louder than that of an Italian harpsichord, since the virginal has two bridges on free soundboard. However, as with all keyboard instruments with a plucking action, it is possible to vary the volume considerably by voicing the plectra.

A few virginals were made with two sets of 8′ strings although this was not common. Four such instruments are known: two by Donatus Undeus (1623, *B.B.mim*; 1633, *ZA.C.u*), one by Celestini (1594, *D.H.km*), and an unsigned instrument attributed variously to Undeus and to Celestini (but probably by the latter; in *GB.L.fb*). Another rectangular virginal, made by Celestini in 1610 (*B.B.mim*), does not have the usual pairwise arrangement of jacks: instead each string is separated from the next string by one jack. On the nameboard this instrument is described as an 'arcispineta'. Other Italian makers whose instruments gained a high reputation at the time included Domenico da Pesaro, Vito Trasuntino, and Alessandro Trasuntino (no instruments by the latter two makers survive).

3. FLANDERS. Although the tonal resources of the virginal (which has a single set of strings and is seldom equipped with any means of changing timbre) are more limited than the harpsichord's, it nonetheless occupies a crucial position both in musical life and in the development of quilled instruments in general in the 16th and 17th centuries. Harpsichords certainly existed throughout this period north and south of the Alps, but they are more rarely represented in paintings, drawings, and so on than are virginals, and it must be concluded that they were much less common than

the smaller, simpler, and cheaper instruments. In addition, the sound of the virginal is excellently suited to most of the keyboard literature of the period. That the virginal occupied a central position in Flemish instrument building is well illustrated by the fact that in the rules for the admission of keyboard instrument makers to the Antwerp Guild of St Luke (drafted in 1557) the piece of work to be submitted by a candidate was specifically designated as 'a rectangular or polygonal virginal' ('een viercante of gehoecte clavisymbale'), and no mention of harpsichords is made at all. Furthermore, the Ruckers family made many more virginals than harpsichords.

The earliest surviving Flemish virginal, like those depicted in Flemish paintings from before 1565, is thin-cased and polygonal. These instruments thus bear a superficial resemblance to their Italian counterparts, the most obvious difference being that their keyboards are entirely recessed rather than wholly or partly projecting; however, some Italian virginals of false inner-outer design have completely recessed keyboards. In appearance, the Flemish polygonal instrument seems somewhat heavier than does one of the graceful Italian design. Possibly the Flemish polygonal design was transmitted to the Low Countries by way of Germany. It is known that some of the earliest 15th-century makers working in the Low Countries came from Cologne: of the earliest string keyboard instrument maker in Flanders, Hans van Cuelen (Hans from Cologne; *fl* 1509–57), little is known, but Joes Karest (builder in 1548 of the oldest surviving Flemish virginal) headed the instrument makers' petition to the Guild of St Luke in 1557 as they sought to be admitted as instrument makers and not grouped with the painters. A German harpsichord of 1537 made by Hans Müller in Leipzig shows striking resemblances to thin-cased Italian harpsichords. However, the answer as to where these harpsichord or virginal designs originated probably lies in the 15th century, and about this period so little is known in detail that answers can be no more than speculative. As is often the case with inventions, similar designs might have been developed simultaneously in different parts of Europe.

As noted above, however, the guild regulations make it clear that rectangular as well as polygonal instruments were being made in Antwerp in the 1550s, and presumably these instruments were also thin-cased. Although no example from this period survives, the earliest Flemish depiction of a rectangular virginal (an engraving by Cornelis Cort printed in 1565, based on a painting by Frans Floris from ten years earlier, now lost) shows an instrument without a lid, suggesting that it was thin-cased and intended to be kept in a stout outer case like an Italian instrument. Yet by the end of the 1560s, it would seem, a thick-cased rectangular instrument very much like those now considered typically Flemish had come into being, since a painting by Michiel Coxcie purchased by Philip II of Spain in 1569 clearly shows an instrument of this kind, which seems immediately to have superseded the thin-cased types in the Low Countries.

At the end of the 16th century, three types of virginal were being made in Flanders: one with the keyboard centred in one of the longer sides, one with it placed off-centre to the left (called 'spinett' by Claas Douwes), and one with it placed off-centre to the right ('muselar'). The centre-keyboard design in normal-pitch virginals is known only from one instrument, that made for the Duke of Cleves, and it is impossible to say whether this was an isolated example or a design that was later forgotten. Octave (4′) instruments retain their central placement of the keyboard, although this is virtually obligatory because of their small size. The difference in the placement of the keyboard is important since it determines the placement of the jacks in relation to the two bridges. With the keyboard placed to the left, the jacks run in a line close to the left-hand bridge; therefore the point at which the jacks pluck the strings is close to the mid-point in the treble and well away towards the left end in the bass. This is also true with virginals with centrally placed keyboards, although the displacement of the plucking point from the centre of the strings in the bass is reduced. Because of this varying plucking point, the timbre of these virginals gradually changes from flute-like in the treble to reedy in the bass, being similar in this respect to the timbre of a harpsichord. Muselars, with their keyboard at the right, have their strings plucked at a point near the centre for virtually their entire range, producing a powerful, flute-like tone that varies little from treble to bass. Both spinetten and muselars were made in a variety of sizes, the smaller ones presumably tuned to higher pitches and the smallest ones clearly tuned an octave above the largest ones. Among the surviving instruments, muselars are more numerous in the full-size examples, spinetten in the smaller sizes.

The earliest surviving example of a muselar is in the double virginal by Hans Ruckers (*d*1598) and is dated 1581 (*US.NY.mma*): it is entirely possible that Ruckers invented the muselar design, even though the other characteristics now associated with Ruckers's work are to be found in virginals made by the preceding generation of makers, notably Hans Bos (*fl* at least 1543–72) and Marten van der Biest (*fl* at least 1557–84). Muselars always have both their bridges resting on free soundboard, in contrast to the spinetten and the polygonal instruments, which often appear to have had the bridge at the left deadened by a plank underneath the soundboard. Ruckers's practice in this regard was not consistent; the smaller spinetten all seem to have the left-hand bridge deadened, but some of the full-size examples have both bridges resting on free soundboard. Muselars have the further distinction of being the only virginals normally provided with any means of changing timbre. A substantial number of the surviving examples have an *arpichordum* stop, which can be engaged to produce a buzzing sound in the tenor and bass to contrast with the clear, flute-like sound of the alto and treble.

The culmination of the Flemish virginal makers' art was the double virginal called 'mother and child' by Joos Verschuere-Reynvaan (*Muzijkaal kunst-woordenboek*,

2/1795), a usage apparently sanctioned by the makers, since the original Ruckers numbers on surviving examples include an 'M' and a 'k' for *moeder* and *kind* on the large and small instruments respectively. These instruments consisted of a virginal of normal size (the 'mother') with a compartment next to its off-centre keyboard in which a removable octave instrument (the 'child') was housed. The octave instrument was designed to be coupled directly to the larger one. An oblique slot was cut in the bottom of the octave instrument, and if the jackrail of the 'mother' was removed and the 'child' was put on top of it in place of the jackrail, the larger instrument's jacks reached through the slot to touch the underside of the octave instrument's key levers. Thus when a key of the 'mother' instrument was depressed its jack pushed upwards on the back end of the corresponding key of the 'child', causing the octave instrument to sound at the same time as the larger one. In addition, the octave instrument could be played separately, either when in place on top of the larger instrument or entirely removed from it. Instruments of this kind appear to have been imitated in Germany and Austria, and an Innsbruck inventory made in 1665 mentions a virginal in which two smaller ones were contained, 'all three of which could be placed on one another and sounded together'.

4. ENGLAND AND OTHER NORTHERN EUROPEAN COUNTRIES. Unlike some Italian and Flemish examples, the surviving English virginals are all rectangular. Their cases are typically of oak, and the lids were always originally vaulted. The decoration is also standardized: the outsides of the cases are plain, ornamented only by ironwork strap hinges and locks, but the insides are given stylized and colourful embellishment including paintings on the lid and fallboard, generally of landscapes with figures, painted decorations on the soundboard, and gilt embossed papers contrasting with finely cut mouldings, normally of cedarwood, sometimes painted. The natural keys are usually boxwood, with dark sharps, occasionally inlaid, although instruments survive with snakewood or ebony naturals and solid ivory sharps. The compass of early virginals is often from *C* to *c'''*, later instruments usually having a very wide *G'/B'–f'''* compass, although three instruments from the mid-1660s have compasses extending down chromatically to *G'* or below. The short scalings, often based on a *c'''* string length of 6 inches (15.24 cm), suggests that many instruments were strung in iron at a high pitch standard, probably one or two semitones above *a'* = 440. Other instruments were built to pitches one or two semitones below this high pitch, and there is one instrument, the orphan of a mother-and-child virginal made by Thomas White (*c*1600–60; private collection, the only such instrument known to have been made in England), which was designed to play a 5th above the standard high pitch.

The virginal in England probably developed in the early part of the 16th century, influenced by early instruments from Flanders and the Spanish Netherlands. There are many references to virginals in this period,

including several in the inventory taken at the death of Henry VIII in 1547. Although a number of these were probably made on the Continent, about 20 virginal makers are known to have worked in Britain in the 16th century. The typical layout and decorative scheme found in the surviving instruments were most likely established by the last quarter of the century.

The instruments date from 1638 to 1684, although two undated examples are probably earlier. The White family appear to be the most prolific of the early makers, judging from surviving examples. Five of Thomas White's instruments are extant, including an unusual instrument with double stringing from *G'/B'* to *A* (privately owned), then single strung to *f'''*. His son James has left two instruments (1656, *GB.L.ml*; 1661, Bunratty Castle, Ireland). Later virginal makers of note include Stephen Keene (*c*1640–1719) and John Player (*c*1634–*c*1706), who both went on to make spinets, Adam Leuersidge (*fl* 1650–70), and the Exeter makers John Loosemore (1613–81) and Charles Rewallin (*fl* 1657–97). Loosemore, Rewallin, and James White were also involved in making or repairing organs.

Praetorius (*Syntagma musicum*, ii, 2/1619/*R*), who also mentioned placing virginals on top of one another, depicted a rectangular instrument differing in several respects from the developed Flemish design, rather resembling pre-Ruckers examples in having a central keyboard and a jackrail supported at the left by an arm extending from the bass end of the key well. The instrument shown by Praetorius also has a larger range than the regular Flemish virginal compass of four octaves with a bass short octave (*C/E–c'''*), its keyboard extending to *d'''*, with divided accidentals in the lowest octave to provide the *F♯* and *G♯* not ordinarily available with the *C/E* short octave. Also, the E♭ keys are divided in the remaining octaves to sound D♯, thereby extending the range of available keys to include E major and E minor. As with virtually all northern European virginals, a tool box is set in the space to the left of the keyboard.

Although polygonal virginals of this region were, like their Italian counterparts, normally housed in outer cases, this does not seem always to have been true of the rectangular instruments. Praetorius did not show a lid for the instrument he illustrated (presumably to save space), although the presence of a hinged front board to cover the keys strongly suggests that the instrument had one; it would be of great interest to know whether such a lid would have been vaulted like those shown in French illustrations of the 1580s, on the title page of *Parthenia* (London, 1612–13), and found on all surviving English virginals, which range in date from 1641 to 1679. Despite the fact that the English instruments seem to be patterned on Flemish spinetten, the vaulted lid, the method of supporting the left end of the jackrail, and the shorter scaling of English virginals suggest that they actually derive from the same non-Flemish tradition represented by Praetorius's illustration and the surviving 17th-century harpsichords and virginals from Germany and France—a tradition also represented by the polygonal Flemish virginals from the mid-16th century.

Outside Italy the making of rectangular virginals seems to have come to an end by the close of the 17th century, these instruments having been replaced by bentside spinets. Since only one bridge of a spinet is on free soundboard, the sound of a spinet resembles that of a harpsichord, and it might be for this reason that taste changed in favour of the spinet and against the virginal. The spinet is typically somewhat smaller than a rectangular virginal, but the scalings employed in both instruments are similar. Polygonal virginals and spinets usually have less soundboard area in the low tenor and bass than do rectangular virginals; this can impart a clearer, reedier character to the sound. Some virginals resembling square pianos but with a plucking mechanism were made in the early 19th century in Italy. The last dated of these (1839, *D.LE.u*) is by Alessandro Riva of Bergamo.

The importance of the virginal has been exaggerated by some, who, unaware that the term was used for all plucked keyboard instruments in England, assume that the music of Byrd, Bull, Gibbons, Tomkins, and others was intended specifically for these single-strung instruments. However, as is made clear by the title-page illustration of *Parthenia In-violata or Mayden-Musicke for the Virginalls and Bass-Viol* (*c*1624–5), which shows a harpsichord rather than the rectangular instrument of the earlier version of *Parthenia*, the music of the 'virginalist composers' was not intended to be restricted to the virginal. Other writers have relegated the instrument to a status rather lower than that of the modern upright piano. The proper assessment of the virginal lies between these extremes. Despite the limitations imposed by a single register, virginals are useful and remarkably versatile instruments with special qualities of their own, on which virtually the entire literature of their period can be played with considerable success.

For a discussion of the instrument's repertory, and further bibliography, see *GMO*.

BIBLIOGRAPHY

G. Zarlino: *Le istitutioni harmoniche* (Venice, 1558/*R*, 3/1573/*R*); Eng. trans. of pt 2, 1968, as *The Art of Counterpoint*)
A. Banchieri: *L'organo suonarino* (Venice, 2/1611/*R*)
C. Douwes: *Grondig ondersoek van de toonen der musijk* (Franeker, 1699/*R*)
R. Russell: *The Harpsichord and Clavichord* (London, 1959, rev. 2/1973 by H. Schott)
F. Hubbard: *Three Centuries of Harpsichord Making* (Cambridge, MA, 1965, 2/1967/*R*)
M.M. Velimirović: 'The Pre-English Use of the Term "Virginal"', *Essays in Musicology in Honor of Dragan Plamenac*, ed. G. Reese and R.J. Snow (Pittsburgh, 1969), 341–52
G. Leonhardt: 'In Praise of Flemish Virginals of the Seventeenth Century', *Keyboard Instruments: Studies in Keyboard Organology*, ed. E.M. Ripin (Edinburgh, 1971, 2/1977), 42–46
E.M. Ripin: 'On Joes Karest's Virginal and the Origins of the Flemish Tradition', *Keyboard Instruments: Studies in Keyboard Organology*, ed. E.M. Ripin (Edinburgh, 1971, 2/1977), 65–73
J.H. van der Meer: 'Beiträge zum Cembalobau der Familie Ruckers', *Jb des Staatlichen Instituts für Musikforschung Preussischer Kulturbesitz* (1971), 100–53
N. Meeùs: 'La facture de virginales à Anvers au 16e siècle', *Brussels Museum of Musical Instruments Bulletin*, vol.4 (1974), 55–64
J.H. van der Meer: 'Studien zum Cembalobau in Italien', *Festschrift Ernst Emsheimer*, ed. G. Hillestrom (Stockholm, 1974), 131–48, 275–9

N. Meeùs: 'Epinettes et "muselars": une analyse théorique', *La facture de clavecin du XVe au XVIIIe siècle: Leuven* 1976, 67–78
J. Koster: 'The Mother and Child Virginal and its Place in the Keyboard Instrument Culture of the Sixteenth and Seventeenth Centuries', *Ruckers klavecimbels en copieën: Antwerp* 1977, 78–96
S. Howell: 'Paulus Paulirinus of Prague on Musical Instruments', *JAMIS*, vols.5–6 (1979–80), 9–36
G. Nitz: *Die Klanglichkeit in der englischen Virginalmusik des 16. Jahrhunderts* (Munich, 1979)
N. Meeùs: 'The Nomenclature of Plucked Keyboard Instruments', *FoM-RHI Quarterly*, no.25 (1981), 18–20
J. Barnes: *Making a Spinet by Traditional Methods* (Welwyn, Herts., 1985) [with reference to instruments by S. Keene]
L.F. Tagliavini and J.H. van der Meer, eds.: *Clavicembali e spinette dal XVI al XIX secolo* (Bologna, 1986)
A.E. Beurmann and A. Pilipczuk: 'A Rarity in the Art of Harpsichord Building: the 1594 Venetian Virginal by Celestini', *Das Musikinstrument*, vol.40/10 (1991), 66–68
L. Stella: 'La spinetta di Domenico da Pesaro delle collezione "Luigi Ciceri"', *Societât Filologjche Furlane*, vol.46/2–3 (1994), 25–35
D.H. Boalch: *Makers of the Harpsichord and Clavichord, 1440–1840* (Oxford, 3/1995)
G.G. O'Brien: 'Two Virginals by Gian Francesco Antegnati', *Gli Antegnati: Studi e documenti su una stirpe di organari bresciani del Rinascimento*, ed. O. Mischiati (Bologna, 1995), 50–62
D. Wraight: *The Stringing of Italian Keyboard Instruments, c1500–c1650* (diss., Queen's U. of Belfast, 1997)
D. Wraight: 'Principles and Practice in Stringing Italian Keyboard Instruments', *Early Keyboard Journal*, vol.18 (2000), 175–238
G. O'Brien: *Ruckers: a Harpsichord and Virginal Building Tradition* (Cambridge, UK, 2008)

EDWIN M. RIPIN/DENZIL WRAIGHT/R (1–2);
EDWIN M. RIPIN/DENZIL WRAIGHT (3–4)

Virtual instrument [software synthesizer]. Term for computer software designed to simulate or duplicate the functionality of other instruments. A software synthesizer is any computer program capable of sound synthesis using stock computing hardware. Virtual instruments can be software synthesizers, or a collection of sound samples of an instrument that is being emulated. One reason for using software emulations is to duplicate the look, sound, and feel of an older instrument, particularly if the user has no access to the original. Hard-to-find equipment, such as the Moog Minimoog and ARP 2600 analogue synthesizers, is nowadays synthesized as software.

The most common virtual instruments are designed to work within music sequencer software, although many can function as stand-alone programs. Virtual instruments are played by means of a connected MIDI controller (keyboard, drum pads, etc.) and heard through the computer's audio output. Popular sequencing software such as Logic, Pro Tools, and Cubase all support virtual instruments. Different 'plug-in' formats for software synthesizer and audio effect programs are used to integrate virtual instruments into the host sequencer software. In 2010 the four most common formats were RTAS (Pro Tools), VST (Steinberg), AU (Apple), and DirectX (Windows). Most sequencer programs support one or more of these formats. AU and DirectX are proprietary to Apple and Windows, respectively. The most widely supported format is VST (Virtual Studio Technology), created in 1996 by Steinberg Media Technologies GmbH (since 2005 a subsidiary of Yamaha). The VST standard was made available to third-party developers, leading to a large variety of VST instruments and effects. Hundreds of VST programs are freely available on the Internet, although their quality varies. The desire to use virtual instruments on stage has led to innovations such as the Muse Research Receptor, a dedicated hardware device that functions as a host for virtual instruments and effects. This host eliminates the need to rely on a computer, and streamlines the interface for easier use.

BIBLIOGRAPHY

M. Collins: *A Professional Guide to Audio Plug-ins and Virtual Instruments* (Waltham, MA, 2003), 1–9

J.O. Smith: *Physical Audio Signal Processing: for Virtual Musical Instruments and Digital Audio Effects*, vol.3 (Menlo Park CA, 2006), 1–6

J. Aiken: *Software Synthesizers: The Definitive Guide to Virtual Instruments* (Montclair, NJ, 2003), 1–24

BRANDON SMITH

Vis-à-vis Flügel. Term for a combination of two wing-shaped string keyboard instruments built so that they share a common bentside and that the keyboards are 'facing' (Fr. *vis-à-vis*) each other. Pairs of harpsichords combined in this way were known at the end of the 17th century. Johann Andreas Stein made vis-à-vis instruments consisting of a harpsichord and a piano. From the late 19th century until about 1930 Pleyel constructed as many as 50 rectangular vis-à-vis pianos; their size (2.5 metres long) and weight (nearly 600 kg) as well as their complicated structure, including a single massive iron plate, unitary soundboard, and a coupling mechanism, made them impractical for most purposes, but a restored example has been used since 1996s by the Egri-Pertis piano duo.

Visser, Pieter A. (*b* Amsterdam, Netherlands, 3 Nov 1940). American organ builder, of Dutch birth. He studied drafting and mechanical engineering in the Netherlands, apprenticed with the Verscheuren firm in 1954 while also studying drafting and mechanical engineering at night, and later studied organ building in Ludwigsburg, Germany, earning his Master certificate in 1959 and emigrating to the USA in December of the same year. In Los Angeles he worked briefly as a voicer for Holzinger Organs before going to the Wicks firm in Illinois in 1961, employed there as an installer and finisher until 1966, when he left organ building to work as an airline pilot and flight engineer, meanwhile consulting with various American organ builders. In 1973 he returned to organ building, first with the Berkshire Organ Co., then in partnership with Texas native Jan Rowland in Houston, Texas, under the Visser-Rowland name. Visser next relocated to Magnolia, Texas, as Visser Associates, later moving to Tomball, Texas. The firm's organs (by 2013 more than 130 had been completed and many more rebuilt or restored) are largely mechanical-action instruments housed in modern casework, and range in size from small house organs to concert-hall instruments. Among their most notable organs are those in Bates Recital Hall, University of Texas, Austin (1983), First Presbyterian Church, Stamford, Connecticut (1991), and Woodale Church, Eden Prairie, Minnesota (2008; 114 ranks, with five-manual tracker console and four-manual electric action console).

BIBLIOGRAPHY

P. Visser: 'The Organbuilder's Art', *The American Organist* (March 1983), 38ff

'An Organ for All Times', *Texas Monthly*, vol.12, no. 1 (1984), 82ff

BARBARA OWEN/R

Vitruvius Pollio (*fl* 1st century BCE). Roman architect. His reputation is based primarily on the treatise *De architectura*, comprising ten books and dedicated to Emperor Augustus. In the introductory section (i.1.8–9) he asserts that music is essential to the education of the architect, along with drawing, geometry, history, philosophy, medicine, law, and astronomy. A musical education enables one to perform accurately such diverse tasks as tightening the cords on projectile military engines, designing acoustical enhancements for theatres, and building water organs and other instruments. These remarks anticipate three passages in *De architectura* that explicitly address musical subjects.

In his discussion of theatre construction (v.3–9), Vitruvius comments on the importance of acoustical considerations in site selection as well as in the design of the structure itself. The site should neither produce an echo nor deaden the voice, and the ascending rows of seats must not obstruct the sound waves. A brief summary of Aritoxenian harmonic theory provides the background for a discussion of vases designed to resonate to various musical notes. According to Vitruvius, such vases served as acoustical enhancements in many theatres in Greece and Italy, though apparently not in Rome.

In a discussion of the architect's concern with climate (vi.1.5–7) Vitruvius draws an analogy between geographical latitude and a musical scale. Understanding that Rome would have been Vitruvius's point of reference, the reader is to imagine a circular plane figure defined by the horizon. Perpendicular to this is a triangle whose three defining points are due north, due south and the celestial north pole. This triangle represents the outline of a string instrument called the *sambukē*, though with the strings stretching vertically. The shorter strings, to the south, explain the supposed higher-pitched voices of peoples from the tropical regions, while the longer strings correspond to the deeper voices of northern peoples.

The last book of *De architectura* is devoted to the construction of various machines; it includes a detailed description (x.8) of the parts and operation of the water organ.

DENISE DAVIDSON GREAVES

Vivo. (1) Bamboo nose flute of Tahiti and the Austral Islands. In Tahiti it is about 25 to 30 cm long. Tuning and number of tone holes are not standardized but three or four fingerholes and a thumbhole are normal. Modern instruments are undecorated, although old ones were decorated with burn marks and wrapped with braided sinnet. Formerly used to accompany singing and dancing, this *vivo* is played nowadays primarily in musical presentations and competitions. The name *vivo* has also denoted end-blown bamboo flutes such as one with three fingerholes of Hiva Oa (Marquesas), also known as *ki* and on Ua Pou as *puhakahau*. See R. Linton: *The Material Culture of the Marquesas Islands* (Honolulu, 1923), 408.

(2) End-blown bamboo whistle of Mangareva (French Polynesia) and Mangaia (Cook Islands), probably post-contact. See P. Buck: *Ethnology of Mangareva* (Honolulu, 1938), 399.

(3) Flute (type unknown) of Rarotonga (Cook Islands) and the Tuamotu Islands (French Polynesia). See E. Tregear: 'A Paumotuan Dictionary', *Journal of the Polynesian Society*, vols.2–4 (1893–5), 160; S. Savage: *A Dictionary of the Maori Language of Rarotonga* (Wellington, 1962), 460.

(4) Jew's harp of Pukapuka (Cook Islands), made from coconut leaf and used as a toy by children. See E. and P. Beaglehole: *Ethnology of Pukapuka* (Honolulu, 1938), 212.

MERVYN MCLEAN/JANE FREEMAN MOULIN/R

Viyanzi. End-blown single-note flute of the Zaramo people of Tanzania. Thirteen are used in a stopped flute ensemble.

Vizugo. Wooden bell of the Shambala people of Tanzania.

(1) An hourglass-shaped double bell with three clappers at each end.

(2) A trough-shaped rectangular bell with numerous clappers suspended from a cord.

Vlier (Flemish) [krabber, pinet]. Belgian zither. It is a variant of the *hommel*, consisting essentially of a rectangular fretbox, or sometimes only a fretboard, bearing six to 11 wire strings in two groups, melody and drone. The number of strings varies according to region. The type called *pinet* has a larger soundbox added below the fretbox. Further sub-types can be distinguished according to shape. The instrument is placed on a table and strummed with a plectrum while being fretted with a wooden rod. The frets, usually of metal but sometime only indicated by deeply burned spaces, are mainly diatonic (the first frets can lie more than a tone apart, depending on the region), enabling melodies to be played in Dorian, Mixolydian, and Aeolian modes. See F.J. de Hen: 'Folk Instruments of Belgium, Part 1', *GSJ*, vol.25 (1972), 87–132.

FERDINAND J. DE HEN

Voboam. French family of guitar makers, active in Paris from 1630 to 1730. René Voboam (*c*1606–71) was known as a master instrument maker from 1631 onwards. Jacques Prévost was apprenticed to him in 1638, and Dimanche Drouin the following year; at that time he was working at rue St-Honoré. A guitar bearing his name, dated 1641, is preserved in the Ashmolean Museum, Oxford. Three more guitars, made with tortoiseshell and mother-of-pearl, may be attributed to him. One marked 'Voboam 1668' was in the former collection of Maurice Le Roux, Paris; the other two are preserved

in the Musée Masséna, Nice, and the RCM, London. By the end of his career he was working at rue Traversière.

(Nicolas) Alexandre (*b c*1633; *d* after 1691), son of René, signed his first guitars in 1652. Lütgendorff also listed a theorbo, dated 1661. In 1671 Alexandre married Anne Bourdet, the sister of the harpsichord maker Jacques Bourdet the elder. He worked at rue des Arcis, where he stayed until 1692 (the date of his last signed instrument). Between 1673 and 1679 he signed his instruments 'Alexandre Voboam Le Jeune'. 11 guitars are known; three others are attributed. Jean (*b c*1633; *d* after 1691), also son of René, worked first as a musician. He is first mentioned as a master instrument maker in 1680. Seven guitars bearing his signature, dated between 1676 and 1692, are preserved.

Jean-Baptiste (also known as 'Jean'; *b* 1671; *d* after 1731) worked 'préau de la foire Saint-Germain'. He was a prominent member of the guild of instrument makers, and signed the inventories taken after the deaths of Nicolas Bertrand (1725) and Pierre Véron (1731). Seven guitars and two viols, signed and dated between 1697 and 1730, are known. His son Jean-Baptiste began an apprenticeship with Jean-Claude Goujon in 1740, but the contract was broken the following year.

Voboam guitars are characteristic of the 17th century. They have five double courses and a flat back, and are built with narrow proportions and parallel bracing from one side to the other of the rose. A plaque on the front of the head bears the signature and date. Very often the binding of the soundboard, fingerboard, head and rose is made of a diagonal pattern of ivory and ebony. The rose is deep and made of several layers of paper stamped out. The bridge is flanked with ebony flowers or moustaches. Though the Voboams built standard instruments (with backs made of strips of cedar, walnut, or exotic wood, inlays of ebony and ivory, and sides often made of ebony) they also made more luxurious instruments incorporating tortoiseshell and mother-of-pearl. The designs of the guitars' heads and their inlay patterns are characteristic to the individual family members. Three instruments are still preserved with their original cases, stamped with coats of arms. Many paintings and engravings from the 17th century, and later works of art by Jean-Antoine Watteau, Jean-Marc Nattier, Jacques-André Portail, and Louis de Carmontelle, attest the fame of Voboam guitars among amateurs.

BIBLIOGRAPHY

W.L. von Lütgendorff: *Die Geigen- und Lauten-macher vom Mittelalter bis zur Gegenwart* (Tutzing, 1904–90)

F. Gétreau: 'René, Alexandre et Jean Voboam: des facteurs pour "La Guitarre Royalle"', *Instrumentistes et luthiers parisiens: XVIIe–XIXe siècles* (Paris, 1988), 50–73

H. Charnassé and S. Milliot: 'Les Voboam: précisions sur la filiation des célèbres facteurs de guitare', *Recherches sur la musique française classique*, no.27 (1991–2), 219–23

F. Gétreau: 'La dynastie des Voboam: nouvelles propositions pour le catalogue de leur oeuvre', *Musique—Images—Instruments*, no.2 (1996), 185–94

F. Gétreau: 'Recent Research about the Voboam Family and Their Guitars', *JAMIS*, vol.31 (2005), 5–66

FLORENCE GÉTREAU

Vocalion. Type of reed organ. The instrument was developed by the inventor James Buchanan Baillie Hamilton [John Baillie-Hamilton] (*b* Scotland, 20 Jan 1837; *d* London, after 1926), originally in an attempt to combine the sounds of free reeds and attached or sympathetic strings. Hamilton's ideas might have emerged from a 13 Nov 1872 patent by John Farmer, who later shared several patents with Hamilton. A vocalion with triple-tongue reeds was demonstrated in Harrow on 23 Jan 1875 and described at the Royal Institution of Great Britain on 21 May 1875. A modified instrument in which wires were attached to heavy reed tongues was demonstrated before the Royal Musical Association in 1883 and patented in 1884, but the wires were deleted from the three-manual vocalion built at William Hill's organ factory and shown at the International Inventions Exhibition of 1885 in London. In the same year Hamilton, who appears to have worked briefly with the Canadian organ builder S.R. Warren, exhibited the vocalion in the USA; he began to manufacture such instruments in Worcester, Massachusetts, in 1886. Shortly thereafter production was turned over to the New York Church Organ Co., and in 1890 to the piano makers Mason & Risch, who continued manufacture in Worcester. In 1901 the firm was called the Vocalion Organ Co. In 1903 this firm was absorbed by the Aeolian Co., which continued to make vocalions until about 1910. Aeolian had already begun in the 1890s to use vocalion reeds for their 'Orchestrelle' player organs. The firm also produced self-playing organettes under the names 'Syreno' and 'Tonsyreno'.

Ranging in size from foot-operated single-manual models to models with two (or occasionally three) manuals and pedal, the vocalion is basically a reed organ on the pressure system, but with unusually wide reeds connected to chambers called 'qualifying tubes', which permit note-by-note regulation. It is therefore somewhat bulkier than the average reed organ, but produces a smoother, more powerful, and more varied sound. This characteristic made the vocalion, often decorated with a façade of dummy organ pipes, popular for use in small churches in the late 19th century and early 20th. A vocalion built in 1898 by Mason & Risch and restored in 2003, with 24 sets of reeds played from three manuals and pedal, is in the Waldesian Church, Pisa, Italy.

BIBLIOGRAPHY

J.H. Richards: 'The Vocalion', *Reed Organ Society Bulletin* (Feb 1985), 3–7

K.B. Williams: 'The Vocalion and its Manufacturers—Some History', *Reed Organ Society Bulletin*, vol.8/4 (Nov 1989), 25–8

K.B. Williams: 'Morris S. Wright and his Contributions to the Vocalion', *Reed Organ Society Bulletin*, vol.8/4 (Nov 1989), 29–31

BARBARA OWEN/R

Vocal vibrato [jitter]. In Western singing, a pitch fluctuation, or frequency modulation (FM), employed as a technique to ornament a note or colour the overall timbre of a voice. It is produced by subtle movements in the cricothryroid muscle, which is involved in raising pitch. Vibrato is regarded by some voice scientists and musicians as a way expression is encoded into the acoustic signals. Classical voice training has been shown to enhance a singer's ability to conform to aesthetically pleasing standards of vibrato use. Nowadays, a controlled, cultivated vocal vibrato has a sinusoidal wave pattern with a rate between 5.5 to 7 undulations per second and a pitch extent of about 50 to 150 cents, i.e., from a quarter-tone to three-quarters of a tone. For performing popular music, pre-Romantic music, folk music, and choral music, the acceptable range of modulation is often smaller. Where singers distinguish between major and minor semitones, and in vocal works requiring fine pitch distinctions and microtones, the extent of FM is normally no more than 50 cents and often less. These parameters vary widely in non-Western singing.

Singers of early music, choral music and various styles of popular music often employ amplitude modulation (AM) vibrato, or intensity vibrato, known also as 'shimmer' and 'tremolo'. The mechanisms involved in producing AM are less clearly understood and can involve subtle variations in sub-glottal pressure as well as an acoustic interaction between the harmonics produced by the larynx and the resonance of the vocal tract. While FM vibrato predominates in string instruments and AM predominates in wind instruments, singers often use FM and AM vibratos at the same time. The slower the vibrato rate, the greater a listener's perception of pitch fluctuation. A singer's control over vibrato is partly a function of laryngeal position.

FM is inherent in certain vocal styles and not in others. For example, little to no vibrato is a characteristic of 'belting'. However, many belters mix in vibrato occasionally, sometimes on consonants as well as vowels.

BIBLIOGRAPHY

C. Seashore: *The psychology of the vibrato in voice and instrument* (IA City, 1936)

J. Sundberg: 'Acoustic and psychoacoustic aspects of vocal vibrato', in P. Dejonckere, M. Hirano, and J. Sundberg, eds., *Vibrato* (San Diego, 1995), 35–62

C. Dromey, L. Reese, and J.A. Hopkin: 'Laryngeal–Level Amplitude Modulation in Vibrato', *Journal of Voice*, vol.23 (2009), 156–63

SALLY SANFORD

Vocoder. Electronic device for analysing and resynthesizing sounds. The original Vocoder ('voice coder') was developed by Homer Dudley in 1936 at the Bell Telephone Laboratories in Murray Hill, New Jersey, for telephonic applications; it has also proved a valuable tool in speech research and has found applications in electroacoustic music. Speech, music, or other sound is analysed by a set of filters, each covering a different band of frequencies, that subdivide the entire audio spectrum; the fundamental frequency of the input is used as the 'programme' in a modulation process to control the frequency of an audio oscillator (which supplies 'buzz') and a noise generator ('hiss'). The resulting signal is then passed through a second set of filters, each of which is 'tuned' by the amount of electrical information received by their counterparts in the first set, recreating the original signal electronically. A telephone line can intervene between the analysis and synthesis sections.

About 1960 a vocoder was incorporated into the Siemens Synthesizer, which probably offered the first opportunity for musicians to use the device. Since about 1970 several manufacturers, including Bode Sound, Moog, Korg, Roland, EMS, Sennheiser, Synton, Eventide, and Doepfer, have produced vocoders (some of which are controlled from a keyboard) primarily for use in electronic music studios or in live performances of rock music; the 'harmonizer' is a similar device. Such vocoders permit the timbre and articulation of one sound source (usually a voice) to control another. Simpler devices for producing 'talking (or singing) instruments', particularly in films, include the Sonovox (c1938) and, from the early 1970s, various 'voice boxes' ('voice tubes') used in rock music, which impart vocal qualities with the larynx and mouth respectively. The 'phase vocoder' (1966) is a software program developed at Bell, which has found a role in computer music since the late 1970s, primarily for time compression or expansion.

In 1937 Dudley and others developed the speech synthesis section of the Vocoder to produce the Voder ('voice operation demonstrator'), a successor to the keyboard-controlled speaking machines devised from the end of the 18th century onwards. The filters are controlled by two independent five-note keyboards. The right thumb also operates a 'quiet' key for fricative consonants and three central 'stops' for plosive ones, and there is a pitch-control pedal for inflection; a left-hand wrist-bar switches between 'buzz' and 'hiss' (also combinable) to give voiced and unvoiced qualities. In 1948 researchers at Bell developed the Visible Speech machine, using graphic sound in the form of speech 'notation' to control the coder section of a Vocoder.

BIBLIOGRAPHY

H. Dudley: 'Synthesizing Speech', *Bell Laboratories Record*, vol.15 (1936), 98–102

H. Dudley, R.R. Riesz, and S.S.A. Watkins: 'A Synthetic Speaker', *Journal of the Franklin Institute*, vol.227/6 (1939), 739–64; repr. in Speech Synthesis, ed. J.L. Flanagan and L.R. Rabiner (1973)

H. Dudley: 'The Vocoder Remakes Speech', *Proceedings of the Institute of Radio Engineers*, vol.28 (1940), 1–47

J.L. Flanagan and L.R. Rabiner, eds.: *Speech Synthesis* (Stroudsburg, PA, 1973)

T. Rhea: 'Harald Bode's Frequency Shifters and Vocoders', *Contemporary Keyboard*, vol.6/2 (1980), 86 only

C. Roads and others: *The Computer Music Tutorial* (Cambridge, MA, and London, 1996), 148, 444–6, 549, 566–77, 1094–9

D. Tompkins: *How to Wreck a Nice Beach: the Vocoder from World War II to Hip-Hop* (New York and Chicago, 2010)

HUGH DAVIES

Vogler, Georg Joseph [Abbé Vogler] (*b* Würzburg, Germany, 15 June 1749; *d* Darmstadt, Germany, 6 May 1814). German theorist, teacher, keyboard player, organ designer, and composer. His theory of harmony influenced 19th-century approaches to music analysis. His music is noteworthy for chromatic harmony, colouristic orchestration, and melodic borrowings from folk tradition and exotic cultures. His radical concept of organ design aroused widespread interest and controversy; his writings on the reform of sacred music foreshadowed the Cecilian movement.

The son of a Würzburg instrument maker, Vogler attended a Jesuit Gymnasium before enrolling in humanistic studies at Würzburg University in 1763. Subsequently he studied common and canon law, first at Würzburg, then at Bamberg. In 1770 he obtained a post as almoner at the Mannheim court of Carl Theodor, the Elector Palatine. Politically resourceful, he soon attained prominence in the court's musical life, secured the elector's favour, and was granted the financial means to pursue musical study in Italy (from 1773). There he studied briefly with Padre Martini in Bologna and spent a longer period in Padua, where he studied theology and became a disciple of the theorist Francesco Antonio Vallotti. In Rome, he was granted membership in the Accademia dell'Arcadia, and Pope Pius VI named him papal protonotary, chamberlain, and Knight of the Golden Spur.

Vogler returned to the Mannheim court in November 1775 and in this new phase of his career, he acquired the titles of spiritual counsellor and second Kapellmeister. He founded a music school, the Mannheimer Tonschule, and began publishing didactic writings. Following the removal of the electoral court to Munich in 1778, Vogler remained temporarily at Mannheim. In 1780 he travelled to Paris to win approbation for his theory of harmony from the Académie Royale des Sciences, and during the next three years he had works performed both in Paris and at Versailles. He then went to London (1783), where the Royal Society approved his theoretical system. Summoned to Munich to succeed Andrea Bernasconi as first Kapellmeister in 1784, he remained there only until 1786, when he entered the service of Gustavus III, King of Sweden, as music director and teacher of the crown prince. At Stockholm he resumed his pedagogical work but was also permitted to continue his travels, and in 1792, following the assassination of his royal patron, he set off on a journey that took him to Gibraltar, Cádiz (where he was mistaken for a spy and arrested), Tangier, and further into the Mediterranean in search of ancient, orally transmitted traditions of modal singing.

In 1793 Vogler returned to Stockholm, where he retained an official post under Gustavus Adolphus IV until 1799. His subsequent wanderings as a performer, organ designer, and teacher included sojourns in Copenhagen (1799–1800), Berlin (1800–01), Prague (1801–2), and Vienna (1802/3–5). After spending two years in Munich, he received a court appointment at Darmstadt in August 1807. There, Vogler continued to compose and undertake ambitious projects, including a 'monument to the science of organ building', the Triorganon: a huge organ to be equipped with 13 manuals distributed among three separate consoles, which remained unfinished in Munich at the time of his death.

In his theoretical handbooks, treatises and essays Vogler aimed to apply harmonic principles in terms understandable to amateurs as well as professionals. To make tangible his theoretical calculations, he devised an eight-string *Tonmaass* (or octochord), a latter-day monochord whose fixed bridges furnished string divisions in nine to 16 parts. As a theorist of acoustics and organ design, he proposed a simplification system whose principles—including economy of materials, reliability of wind pressure, and acoustical enhancements—were embodied in his Orchestrion, a compact, transportable organ. Initially completed at Rotterdam in 1790, but later modified, it used free reeds and exploited the principle of difference tones to eliminate the large and costly pipes otherwise needed to produce low notes. Though deplored by conservative organists, the simplification system was implemented in the renovation of more than 30 church organs, including instruments in Berlin, Munich, Prague, and Salzburg.

Vogler's work was seldom free from controversy. He was chided for his eccentricities, and detractors denounced him as a charlatan. He nevertheless enjoyed the admiration of patrons and pupils throughout his career, and in retrospect he stands out as an innovative musical thinker and practitioner. His accomplishments not only added a colourful voice to European musical life of the late 18th century and early 19th, but also exerted far-reaching influence on his successors.

For fuller discussion of his theoretical writings and musical compositions, and extensive bibliography, see *GMO*.

WRITINGS
(*selective list*)
Tonwissenschaft und Tonsezkunst (Mannheim, 1776/R)
Stimmbildungskunst (Mannheim, 1776)
Entwurf eines neuen Wörterbuchs für die Tonschule (Frankfurt, 1780)
Data zur Akustik (Leipzig, 1801); also pubd in *AMZ*, vol.3 (1800–1), 517–25, 533–40, 549–54, 565–71
Ueber die harmonische Akustik (Tonlehre) und über ihren Einfluss auf alle musikalische Bildungs-Anstalten (Munich, 1806)
Gründliche Anleitung zum Clavierstimmen, für die, welche gutes Gehör haben, nebst einer neuen Anzeige, jedes Saiteninstrument vortheilhaft und richtig zu beziehen (Stuttgart, 1807)
Harmonisch-akustische Bemerkungen über den Theater-Bau (MS, c1807, D-DSsa, D 4, Nr. 695)
'Abt Voglers Vertheidigung seines Simplifications–Systems für den Orgelbau', *Neue fränkische Chronik*, vol.3/50 (1808), 775–80
Über die Oxydazion der schwingenden Metallkörper (MS, 1809, D-DSsa, D 4, Nr. 695)
Vergleich der Kempeln'schen Sprach-Maschine mit dem, der Menschenstimme täuschend nachahmenden, singbaren Orgel-Register, von dieser Ähnlichkeit 'Vox humana' genannt (MS, 1810, D-DSsa, D 4, Nr. 695), also pubd as 'Ueber Sprach– und Gesang–Automaten, ein akustischer Versuch', *Sammlung einiger im Frankfurter Museo vorgetragenen Arbeiten*, vol.1 (Frankfurt, 1810), 118–30

BIBLIOGRAPHY
E. Rupp: *Abbé Vogler als Mensch, Musiker und Orgelbautheoretiker unter besonderer Berücksichtigung des sog. 'Simplificationssystems'* (Ludwigsburg, 1922)
H. Spies: *Abbé Vogler und die von ihm 1805 simplifizierte Orgel von St. Peter in Salzburg* (Mainz, 1932, 2/1940)
H. Schweiger: 'Abbé Voglers Simplifikationssystem und seine akustischen Studien', *KJb*, vol.29 (1934), 72–123
H. Schweiger: *Abbé G.J. Voglers Orgellehre* (Vienna, 1938)
D.J. Britton: *Abbé Georg Joseph Vogler: his Life and his Theories on Organ Design* (diss., Eastman School of Music, 1973)

MARGARET GRAVE/R

Voice. The quintessential human instrument, capable of unsurpassed tonal and melodic expressivity and nuance. Vocal sounds reflect individual anatomical differences as well as cultural, stylistic, and technique influences. The vocal mechanism is made up primarily of cartilaginous and other soft tissues. Vocal production involves coordination of complex physiologic processes, engaging the lungs and respiratory muscles (wind source), the vocal folds (vibrator/oscillator; also called vocal cords), the pharynx, mouth, nasal and head cavities (resonator), as well as the tongue, lips, teeth, and palate (articulator). The lips also radiate sound outward. The great capacity for variation in each of these areas, and for variation in more than one area at the same time, leads to a strong association of the voice with individual identity.

1. Phonation and vocal mechanism. 2. Acoustical analysis of the voice.

1. PHONATION AND VOCAL MECHANISM. Phonation refers to the production of sound waves in the larynx (voice box). Phonation takes place during exhalation as the respiratory system supplies air through the vibrating vocal folds, which interrupt and break the air stream into smaller units or puffs of air. The resulting sounds are filtered through a resonator system and then transmitted outside the mouth. Singing, speaking, humming, and other vocal sounds usually involve practised regulation of air pressure and breath-stream mechanics, and balanced control of the inspiratory (chiefly the diaphragm) and expiratory muscles (chiefly the abdominal and intercostal muscles). This muscular antagonism requires some degree of experience or training to develop. Various methods are used in breathing for singing (often termed 'breath support' in Western vocal pedagogy) and different breath strategies will affect the vocal timbre and intensity. Singing tends to require greater lung capacity than normal speech, because musical phrases tend to be of longer duration than spoken phrases. Singing also often entails much higher air pressure than speech, sometimes reaching 40 to 50 cm (water gauge) at the top of the soprano range compared to a range of 4 to 9 cm for normal speech. The airflow is controlled by opening and closing the glottis, the space between the vocal folds. With sufficient subglottal air pressure, if the vocal folds are close enough, the Bernoulli effect will assist in their adduction.

The fundamental frequency of vocal fold oscillation determines the pitch of the voiced sound. This frequency is a function of the length and tautness of the vocal folds and the subglottal air pressure. Length and stiffness are regulated by the intrinsic muscles of the larynx. The cricothyroid muscle contracts to raise pitch, and the thryoarytenoid muscle contracts to lower and thicken the vocal folds, lowering the pitch. The thyroarytenoid muscle also contracts during the singing of high notes in a natural register, in order to widen the area of vocal fold contact to increase loudness and overtones. The thyroarytenoid is passive in the male falsetto and the female whistle registers. Firm adduction of the vocal folds is correlated with high intensity vocalization and higher air pressure. The vocal fold is made up of materials that let it simultaneously adjust tension and elongation. Most of the material is muscle tissue.

Inside each vocal fold is a ligament that can stretch and elongate, and inside the ligament are muscles that can contract. Covering the outside of the vocal fold is a soft, pliable mucous membrane that oscillates and sustains vibration.

The vocal folds are relatively small (about 1/5 the size of an oboe reed) given the amount of sound they can produce. Measurement of the vocal fold lengths will vary slightly depending on the methodology used. Voice scientists distinguish between the membranous, vibrating length (Lm or MVFL) of the vocal folds, and the cartilagenous length (Lc), which does not vibrate. Total vocal fold length is the sum of the membranous and cartilagenous lengths. At rest, an adult woman's vocal folds will average about 16 mm in total length, with a range between 12.5 and 17.5 mm; an adult male's will average approximately 23 mm, ranging 17 to 25 mm.

Vocal fold oscillation is influenced by the length and shape of the vocal tract, comprising the entire space above the glottis extending to the nostrils. The average length of the adult vocal tract is 17.5 cm. The vocal tract is capable of many adjustments that modify sound; it serves as a filter for the sounds generated by the vocal folds. It functions like a tube resonator, though it is a much smaller tube than those of most wind instruments. Because the phonatory tube is closed at the lower end, its resonating frequencies include only odd-numbered partials. The singer can vary the length of the phonatory tube by a few centimetres only, either by lowering the larynx or by pursing the lips, but even this small change will create significant differences in tone colour. The vocal tract can boost certain harmonics simultaneously, storing energy from one part of the vibration cycle to add back at another point to increase amplitude, augmenting the adduction and abduction of the vocal folds. This 'formant tuning' varies in different styles of singing to make optimal use of inertive reactance (a slow response to an applied pressure). Different singing styles employ different 'set-ups' or shapes of the vocal tract. In Western classical singing, the 'singer's formant' is obtained with a relatively narrow opening just above the vocal folds (the laryngeal vestibule) and a wide pharynx.

Voice phonation also involves mechanisms for pitch, loudness, and stress, which assist the listener in decoding meaning and expressive intent. The suprasegmental function of the voice is highly complex, with many continuously adjusting laryngeal elements including vocal fold length and tension, vocal tract length, and rate and amount of airflow. Expiratory flow must be sufficient to create plosive, aspirate, and fricative noises for words to be intelligible.

The ultimate locus of control of the voice is the brain. The neuromotor systems utilized in phonation evolved for different purposes, such as swallowing, breathing, and maintaining the airway. Certain aspects of involuntary processes can influence the voluntary ones, and very delicate neuromuscular coordination and regulation are required in order to sing well. Within the brain, the cerebral cortex is the primary music

processing area. Neuroscientists are only beginning to study singers in detail, chiefly focusing on Western opera singers. Experienced opera singers have been shown to have more activity in the primary motor cortex, the dorsolateral prefrontal cortex, and the inferior parietal cortex, than untrained singers. Singers of words simultaneously activate music and speech centres in the brain. If a person's speech centre becomes damaged, the singing centre can compensate. Within the cerebral cortex, Broca's area, Wernickes' area, and Brodmann's area are involved in vocal processing. Fine-tuned proprioceptive processing and sensory relay also involve the basal ganglia and cerebellum. In addition, the periaqueductal gray matter in the midbrain is involved in coordinating respiratory, laryngeal, and oral movements in singing as well as in speech. The neuromuscular firing can be intricate and very rapid; a soprano's vocal folds open and close 1,046.5 times per second at 'high C' (c'''). Many peripheral cranial nerves are also involved in voice production, controlling the movements of the jaw, mouth, lips, tongue, palate, pharynx, and vocal tract.

2. ACOUSTICAL ANALYSIS OF THE VOICE. In the laboratory, voice sounds are analysed according to fundamental frequency (perceived as pitch); frequency perturbation or jitter (perceived as pitch fluctuation or vibrato); frequency range or maximum phonational range measured in semitones from the highest to lowest notes produced (usually greater than the singing range used in performance); intensity or amplitude in dB of the vocal signal (perceived as loudness); and intensity perturbation or shimmer (perceived as intensity vibrato). Pulmonary function is also measured, with flow volume measured in litres per second. The airflow rate is the flow volume divided by the maximum phonation time. Subglottal pressure is difficult to measure noninvasively. The contact of the vocal folds is measured with electroglottography (EGG), which can indicate how the vocal folds close and for what duration. Spectrographic studies can also indicate the positioning and formant tuning of the vocal tract, and help to distinguish differences in timbre as well as differences in vowel sounds.

Singers and listeners tend to describe the voice in more subjective terms such as bright/dark, small/big, forward/back, light/heavy or lyric/dramatic, clear/breathy, clean/raspy, speech like/ringing, nasal (twangy)/non-nasal, free/forced/, vibrant or with vibrato/straight, and in tune/out of tune. Intelligibility of diction and intensity of emotional expression are other criteria for describing vocal quality. For more extended discussion and bibliography, see *GMO*.

BIBLIOGRAPHY

J. Sundberg: *The Science of the Singing Voice* (DeKalb, IL, 1987)
I. Titze: *Principles of Voice Production* (Englewood Cliffs, NJ, 1994/R)
J. Potter (ed.): *The Cambridge Companion to Singing* (Cambridge, 2000)
S. McCoy: *Your Voice: An Inside View* (Princeton, NJ, 2004)
M. Benninger and T. Murray (eds.): *The Singer's Voice* (San Diego, CA, 2008)
D. Miller: *Resonance in Singing* (Princeton, NJ, 2008)

J. Kreiman and D. Sidtis: *Foundations of Voice Studies: An Interdisciplinary Approach to Voice Production and Perception* (Malden, MA, 2011)

SALLY SANFORD

Voice classification. System used chiefly in Western opera and choral music to determine the voice part or role(s) to which a singer is assigned. The system involves a set of generally accepted, but not internationally standardized criteria, some more subjective than others, based primarily on range and secondarily on actual (rather than potential) output power ('weight'), agility, tessitura, and/or timbre. With the advent of television and DVD, extra-vocal considerations, such as physical attributes and acting ability, have become secondary criteria.

Since the 19th century, six main categories of Western voice types have been recognized. Female voices are classified by range (high, middle, low) as soprano, mezzo soprano, or contralto (though some women can also sing in the tenor range); male voices as tenor, baritone, and bass. Children who have not reached puberty are often designated as trebles and sometimes further classified by gender (e.g. boy soprano). Mezzo soprano has historically been regarded as a sub-category of soprano, connoting a soprano voice with a short upper range or connoting a timbral difference, but mezzo soprano tends now to be considered a legitimate category of its own, though the lines between the two are often blurred. (Mezzo soprano has also been considered a sub-category of contralto.) In the 20th century, a seventh voice type was revived in Western voice classification: the countertenor, which has the highest range of the male voices. In the 17th and 18th centuries, castrato voices were also classified as soprano or alto.

Despite advances in voice science, voices are even now rarely classified by physiology and technique. The only area where this is currently done is with the countertenor, which is often classified by whether or not falsetto is employed. The falsettist is further categorized by range: male alto or sopranist.

Both tessitura (the area of the range in which the voice is judged to have its best quality and greatest ease in production for prolonged periods) and the locus of registration events (*passaggio* or 'break') are gaining importance as co-determinants in voice classification for Western-trained singers. Usually the optimal tessitura is determined by the part of the range that presents no difficulties with shifts in register or *passaggio*.

Sometimes repertoire serves as a means of classification, encompassing the vocal characteristics and techniques deemed stylistically appropriate to it: jazz, blues, soul, gospel, pop, country, folk, rock, cross-over, Broadway, or contemporary commercial music (CCM). Within Western classical music, the second half of the 20th century saw the rise of the 'early music' singer and the 'contemporary music' singer, both of whom use techniques outside the mainstream.

In Western choral music, voice classification is chiefly by range (from high to low) in a four-category model: soprano, alto, tenor, and bass. Within these broader categories, soprano is often further subdivided by range into soprano I and soprano II; alto may be divided by gender into countertenor and female alto or contralto and also divided by range into alto I and alto II; tenor may similarly be divided by range; and bass may also be divided by range into baritone and bass or bass I and bass II. Choral score order follows this classification.

In Western classical music, and especially in opera, the size or weight of the voice is an important aspect of classification that also usually includes characteristics of agility and timbre. Voices that are perceived as 'light' or 'lighter' are termed 'lyric' and are considered to be agile and bright. 'Heavy' voices are designated 'dramatic' and regarded as less agile and more powerful, with a rich, dark timbre. The Italian term *spinto* or *lirico spinto* is used for a lyric voice that has sufficient power and heft for dramatic climaxes.

Timbral characteristics depend on the particular frequencies that are emphasized through resonance decisions by the singer, but these characteristics also result from the physiological size and shape of the vocal tract. Normative associations hold that higher voices with shorter vocal fold length will have a smaller vocal tract with a resulting bright(er) timbre and that lower voices with longer vocal fold length will have a longer vocal tract with a resulting dark(er) timbre. Rarer voices depart from the norm in the relationship of the size of the vocal folds and the size of the vocal tract, e.g. the dramatic soprano, which has a shorter vocal fold length and a longer vocal tract, and the lyric contralto, which has a longer focal fold length and a shorter vocal tract. Further investigation is needed to determine if additional physiological differences in the vocal folds themselves contribute to timbral differences.

Agility is another important secondary classification criterion. It is possible that differences in agility between voice types are due to physiological differences in intrinsic laryngeal musculature. Voices with great agility and facility in fast passagework are classified with the term 'coloratura'.

The German Fach ('profession') system is the most widely used method of voice classification in Western opera. It was developed in the early 20th century to enable European opera houses to simplify casting by grouping roles according to their vocal demands and assigning them to specific voice types. The system grew out of the diversity of repertoire being performed and the need to use the same singer in multiple roles. It led to an expansion of voice categories. The system offered some contractual protection for singers, who could know that they would not be asked to sing a role unsuited to their voice. The system has been criticized because once assigned to a particular Fach a singer could be 'pigeon-holed' and find it difficult to gain other roles that are considered to require a different Fach.

The Fach system was not developed scientifically, but much of its terminology has been carried over into modern voice classification. It was codified in the mid-20th century by Rudolph Kloiber, whose first criterion was whether a role was 'serious' or 'comic'. Kloiber's

Table 1 German Fächer, based on Kloiber

Serious			
Lyrischer Sopran	Lyric Soprano	*c'–c'''*	A light voice with beautiful melodiousness (*Schmelz*); rich (*edle*) lines
Jugendlich-dramatischer Sopran	Young Dramatic Soprano	*c'–c'''*	A lyric soprano voice with greater volume that can shape dramatic high points
Dramatischer Koloratursopran	Dramatic Coloratura Soprano	*c'–f'''*	A flexible voice with extended high range; dramatic penetrating power
Dramatischer Sopran	Dramatic Soprano	*g–c'''*	With great volume, a metallic voice; great penetrating power
Dramatischer Mezzosopran	Dramatic Mezzo Soprano	*g–b''* or *c'''*	A lithe, metallic 'in-between Fach' voice with dark colour, which often with increasing maturity later develops into a high dramatic Fach. Good high range
Dramatischer Alt	Dramatic Alto	*g–b''*	A flexible, metallic voice with mature high and low range; dramatic penetrating power
Tiefer Alt (Kontra-Alt)	Contralto	*f–a''*	Full, thick voice with greater depth
Lyrischer Tenor	Lyric Tenor	*c–d''*	Light, flexible and melodious voice and extended high range
Jugendliche Heldentenor	Young Heroic Tenor	*c–c''*	Metallic voice that can be lyric in places as well as dramatic in high points; rich tenoral shading
Heldentenor	Heroic Tenor	*c–c''*	Weighty instrument with great volume in the middle and lower range, often with a baritonal shading
Lyrischer Bariton	Lyric Baritone	*B–a♯'*	Light, flexible voice with beautiful lines and extended high range
Kavalierbariton	Cavalier Baritone	*A–g'*	A metallic voice that can be lyric in places as well as dramatic in high points; manly, rich baritonal shading
Heldenbariton/Hoher Bass	Heroic Baritone	*G–f♯'*	Weighty, projecting instrument that has a soaring high range and is well equipped with a good, uniform, strong middle and bottom
Seriöser Bass (Tiefer Bass)	Basso Profondo	*C–f'*	Thick voice with darker shading, great low range
Comic			
Lyrischer Koloratursopran	Lyric Coloratura Soprano	*c'–f'''*	Very flexible, light voice with extended high range
Spielsopran (Soubrette)	Soubrette	*c'–c'''*	Tender, flexible voice, delicate appearance
Charaktersopran	Character Soprano	*b–c'''*	An 'in-between' Fach that is equipped with great ability in characterization
Spielalt (Lyrischer Mezzosopran)	Lyric Mezzo Soprano	*g–b''*	A flexible instrument with great ability in characterization
Spieltenor	Tenor buffo	*c–b'*	A slender voice with great ability in characterization
Charaktertenor	Character Tenor	*A–b'*	An 'in-between' Fach equipped with great ability in characterization
Spielbariton	Baritone buffo	*B–a♯'*	A slender, flexible voice with great ability in characterization
Charakterbariton	Character Baritone	*A–g'*	Powerful voice able to modulate; fine ability in characterization
Spielbass (Bassbuffo)	Comic Bass/Bass buffo	*E–f'*	Slender, flexible voice with ability in characterization
Charakterbass (Bassbariton)	Bass Baritone	*E–f'*	Large voice with fine ability in characterization
Schwerer Spielbass (Schwerer Bassbuffo)	Heavy Bass buffo	*D–f'*	Voluminous voice with great compass

voice types with their ranges and descriptions (translated) appear in Table 1. Additional categories have subsequently been added to Kloiber's, such as the light lyric mezzo soprano and the full lyric mezzo soprano.

BIBLIOGRAPHY

R. Kloiber, W. Konold, and R. Maschka: *Handbuch der Oper* (Kassel, various editions, 1973–2002)

R. Boldrey: *Guide to Operatic Roles and Arias* (Dallas, 1994)

S. Cotton: *Voice Classification and Fach: Recent, Historical and Conflicting Systems of Voice Categorization* (diss., U. of North Carolina at Greensboro, 2007)

SALLY SANFORD

Voice flute. Recorder with lowest note *d'*, a 3rd below the treble recorder. The name is seen in a manuscript compiled by James Talbot *c*1690–1700 (*GB-Och* Music MS 1187), who named the London maker Peter Bressan

Voice flute in D, Baroque fingering, Joseph Bradbury, England, probably early 18th century. (Edinburgh University Collection of Historic Musical Instruments (2491))

(1685–1731) as his authority, and most surviving voice flutes are by Bressan. Sharing the Baroque transverse flute's range (at least through the first two octaves), the voice flute probably served mostly as a substitute for it. A quintet attributed to Jacques Loeillet, however, includes two transverse flutes and two *flûtes de voix* with continuo.

Voice modifier. Acoustic device that alters the sound of the human voice, typically by amplification, distortion, or changing its apparent location. The only such implements appearing in the Hornbostel-Sachs classification are those with a vibrating membrane (e.g. kazoo, *undaji*, comb-and-paper, and eunuch flute); however, many voice modifiers lack a membrane. Voice modifiers affect vocal sounds; they are distinguished from timbre modifiers that affect the sounds of instruments other

than the voice. (Electronic modification is not considered here, neither is the use of the voice to modify the sound of an instrument.) The use of voice modifiers in heightened speech forms can shift the listener's focus from speech to music.

Voice modifiers may be grouped into four categories according to the manner in which the voice interacts with the device: deflected (for example, frame drums, vessels, or coconut shells); focused without obstruction (tubes, megaphones); focused through vibrating or filtering material (masks, kazoos, mirlitons, the singer's hands); or altered by pressing or striking the throat (*boğaz çalma* of the Anatolian Yörük). These categories sometimes overlap, as in the *tereri* of the Nekgini people in Papua New Guinea: an unobstructed bamboo tube, partly split lengthwise, adds the sounds of the vibrating instrument to the modified voice.

Voice modifiers are used for sacred or ritual purposes predominantly in tropical regions, most notably in Africa (Cameroon, Côte d'Ivoire, Democratic Republic of the Congo, Gabon, Malawi, Mozambique, Nigeria, Republic of the Congo, Rwanda), Amazonia, Papua New Guinea, and Vanuatu. The Australian *ulbura* might also be used to modify the voice. The Dan of Côte d'Ivoire have elaborate masks that affect the voice in different ways, through both instruments and costumes; their *gee kpa* 'doffed masks', however, consist only of sound, without a mask or instrument other than the voice, thus challenging standard notions of 'mask' and 'modifier'.

Outside of the tropics, people use voice modifiers for sacred or secular purposes. Examples include the *kal'ni* from the Siberian island of Sakhalin, the use of masks in Japanese Nō performance, Canadian Inuit singing into a pot, the Indian *nyāstaranga*, possibly the Māori *pūtōrino*, and novel uses by avant-garde composers and improvisers who work in European-influenced genres.

Because many types of voice modifiers involve a tube held to the mouth, they have often been described erroneously as flutes or trumpets. They have also been called 'voice masks', 'voice distorters', 'voice disguisers', 'speaking tubes', or 'resonating tubes'. It is likely that ethnomusicologists will identify more cultures that use voice modifiers, as documentation increases and confusion regarding terminology lessens.

Papua New Guinea provides a good example of a region having a variety of traditions involving the ritual use of voice modifiers. While voice modifiers might be considered a step between the voice alone and its replacement by an instrument, for most traditions in Papua New Guinea, they are believed to transform human voices into spirit voices. Voice modifiers are particularly varied and important in male ritual activities, where tube and vessel forms can be distinguished. Tubular modifiers are typically made of bamboo, although gourds and branches are used in some areas. The walls of the tube are usually solid, although sometimes they are split in order to vibrate. Solid-wall tubes range from 30 cm long to more than 4 metres. The distal ends of the shorter tubes are always open, while those of the longer tubes can be open or placed in leaves or into a vessel, frequently a drum without a skin: the resultant sound has thus been modified twice. Vessel-form modifiers are less common, but conches and coconut shells are used. Leaves are also reported as an alternative to coconut shells in one area. Different forms are associated with certain parts of the country; no society uses all of them.

Although reported in scattered parts of the southern Papua New Guinea mainland, voice modifiers are primarily associated with ritual activities in the northern part and in regions of New Britain and New Ireland. According to the tradition involved, they might be used singly, in pairs, or in larger ensembles. On the mainland around Madang and the Rai Coast, gourd voice modifiers are used simultaneously with bamboo ones with split sides, other non-esoteric instruments (drums, slit drums, rattles), and singing to create the voice of the spirits called *tambaran* in Tok Pisin (pidgin). The method of producing spirit voices is only revealed to initiated males. While women dance to their performances, the darkness of night hides the way such sounds are produced.

Local Papua New Guinean terms for voice modifiers include *mai* (bamboo type used by the Iamtul of East Sepik Province), *kanggut* (gourd type used by the Ngaing of Madang Province), *kaapu naing* ('mother of the spirits'; gourd type used by the Nekgini of Madang Province), and *mavela* (small coconut shell containing orchid leaves, used by the Uniapa of West New Britain Province).

BIBLIOGRAPHY

D. Balfour: 'Ritual and Secular Uses of Vibrating Membranes as Voice–Disguisers', *Journal of the Royal Anthropological Institute of Great Britain and Ireland*, vol.78 (1948), 45–69

C. Sachs: *The Wellsprings of Music*, ed. Jaap Kunst (New York, 1965), 84–5

B. Hauser-Schäublin: 'The Mai Masks of the Iatmul', *Oral History*, vol.11/2 (1983), 1–53

D. Niles: 'Altérateurs de voix de Papouasie–Nouvelle–Guinée: Ou comment la confusion des donnés appauvrit l'organologie', *Cahiers de musiques traditionnelles*, vol.2 (1989), 75–99

A. Norborg: *A Handbook of Musical and Other Sound-Producing Instruments from Equatorial Guinea and Gabon* (Stockholm, 1989)

L. Fernandez: *Brésil: Enauené-Naué et Nhambiquara du Mato Grosso.* CD with booklet (Lausanne, 1995)

R. Reigle: 'Sacred Music of Serieng Village, Papua New Guinea', diss. with 2 CDs (University of California at Los Angeles, 2001)

ROBERT REIGLE, DON NILES

Voicing. The means by which the timbre, attack, loudness, etc., of the pipes or strings of keyboard instruments and some non-keyboard wind instruments are given their desired quality and uniformity.

1. Organ pipes. 2. Wind instruments. 3. String instruments.

1. ORGAN PIPES. Without 'voicing', it is unlikely that a newly made organ pipe, however accurately formed, would speak at all (save possibly with a rough and irregular sound). A voicer has therefore to make a number of fine manipulations and adjustments to each pipe. In flue pipes, a basic adjustment concerns the amount of wind that is allowed to issue from the flue or windway. This can be controlled either by increasing or de-

creasing the size of the toe-hole (a method common since the mid-18th century) or by leaving the toe-hole open and widening or narrowing the flue itself. Both methods are still used, often in combination.

Also of importance is the 'cut-up' of the mouth (the height of the mouth in relation to its width). A high cut-up yields a smoother, more fundamental tone, while a lower one encourages harmonic development but at a loss of fundamental. Thus flutes are usually cut up on the high side, while strings or quintadenas are on the low side, principals or diapasons being somewhere in between. Wind pressure is a factor in determining the best cut-up, because the cut-ups must be correspondingly higher or lower for a similar sound to be produced from identical pipes on higher or lower wind pressures; the exception to this would be a pipe with an extremely narrow toe-hole, usually in a string-toned stop. It is essential that the plane of the upper lip is parallel to that of the lower lip. If the languid is too low or the upper lip pulled out too far, the pipe is said to be 'quick' and in extreme cases will overblow; if the languid is too low or the upper lip pressed in too much, the pipe will be 'slow' and in extreme cases will cease speaking. Flutes are generally voiced on the quick side, strings on the slow side, and principals just barely quick enough to overblow or flutter when forced beyond their normal wind pressure. In wooden pipes the block (corresponding to the languid) is immovable, and the adjustments made by the voicer will consist in modifying the height of the upper lip, the position of the cap, the angle and width of the flue, and sometimes the angle of the upper lip.

Some fine adjustments that affect the tone of flue pipes include arching or 'skiving' of the upper lip, changes to the height and bevel of the languid face, and 'nicking' of the languid edge. Until the end of the 18th century it was customary to blunt or 'counterface' the languid edge, which tended to discourage the 'sizzle' in the sound of an unnicked or lightly nicked pipe. This practice was in many instances continued into the 19th century and was revived by some 20th-century builders. A knife-edged languid requires shallow, widely spaced nicking to achieve the same purpose; a small amount is usually necessary to fine regulation, and does not adversely affect articulation or 'chiff'. Deep, close nicking, however, particularly when done on the lower lip as well as languid, destroys both chiff and harmonic development; this was extensively practised in the early 20th century and is still necessary for modern string-toned pipes. Many larger flue pipes have projections ('ears') at the sides of their mouths that help to focus the sound and sometimes need adjustment by the voicer. 'Beards' below the ears or 'rollers' between them were developed in the 19th century to stabilize the speech of narrow-scaled pipes and are also adjusted by the voicer.

In reed pipes the thickness and curvature of the reed tongue are the major factors determined by the voicer. The tongues are usually of 'half-hard' brass (although some tone-colours require soft brass or harder phosphor bronze) and are cut to size by the voicer. Both the width of the tongue and the opening in the shallot affect tone somewhat, but the most critical operation in reed voicing is the curving of the tongue, done with a burnisher on a wood or metal block. Too little curvature will produce weakness or silence; too much will make the attack slow. Pipes of the trumpet type usually speak best when the tongue has a slight extra curvature at its tip. Until the late 19th century it was common to file reed tongues slightly thinner at the end, to improve attack at low wind pressures. High pressures used in the early 20th century necessitated thicker tongues, often weighted (by an amount adjusted by the voicer) at their tip in the lowest two or three octaves. Such tongues produced a smoother, more fundamental tone. The loudness of reed pipes is regulated not on the toe, which is usually fully open, but by adjusting the length of the resonator in conjunction with the vibrating length of the reed tongue. Very fine adjustments are sometimes made to the length by which the shallot projects from the block.

Organ pipes are usually pre-voiced in the builder's workshop by means of a small organ called a 'voicing jack'. This device has interchangeable racks to accommodate pipes of various sizes, so that the pipes are within easy reach of the keyboard, with the voicer's tool shelf above. Racked at the back of the voicing jack is a permanent set of pipes to which the set being voiced can be tuned, since the loudness or softness of the voiced pipe will affect its tuning length. Voiced pipes are placed in the organ while it is set up in the workshop, and further adjustments are made. Final voicing, called 'finishing', can take several months for large instruments and is done after the organ is installed.

2. WIND INSTRUMENTS. As in the case of organ flue pipes, the voicing of recorders concerns the proportions of the windway (flue) and its alignment in relation to the labium. In the finest Baroque instruments, and modern copies of them, the windway is slightly curved and the player's breath is concentrated on the labium through a fairly narrow channel, giving an intense and slightly reedy quality to the tone. In some mass-produced instruments the voicing is more 'open', giving less resistance to the player's breath; the resulting sound is relatively bland and lacking in overtones.

The term 're-voicing' is used for adjustments to the block or to the 'roof' (i.e. the upper surface) of the windway.

3. STRING INSTRUMENTS. The voicing of harpsichords and other quilled instruments involves reducing the length, width and particularly the thickness of the quill or plastic or leather plectra so as to arrive at an even touch of the desired lightness and a tone of uniform loudness without any notes having a different timbre from that of their neighbours. Thinning the plectrum reduces the loudness of the tone and lightens the touch; narrowing the plectrum tends to brighten the tone. The voicing and regulation procedure also involves adjusting the point in time at which the plectrum plucks the string as the key is depressed. Usually this is accomplished by adjusting the length of the portion of the jack below the plectrum, in such a way that the plucking order in an instrument with two or more registers is 'staggered'.

The voicing of pianos involves altering the hardness of the sub-surface felt of the hammers by pricking them with needles of appropriate size once the hammer has been properly shaped with sandpaper or a file. Additional work with a heated iron or chemical treatment can also be done to produce a brighter timbre and to achieve a better balance between the densities of the felt on the outside and the inside of the hammer. But the part of the hammer's surface that actually strikes the string is almost never pricked or ironed. The voicing of early pianos (or reproductions) with leather-covered hammers involves similar operations. Also, since the leather is usually glued only to the front and back of the hammer head, the tone can be made duller by inserting a needle under a layer of leather to stretch it.

BIBLIOGRAPHY

G.A. Audsley: *The Art of Organ-Building*, vol.2 (New York, 1905/*R*), 592ff, 623ff

W.B. White: *Modern Piano Tuning and Allied Arts* (New York, 1917, rev. and enlarged 5/1946 as *Piano Tuning and Allied Arts*), 190ff

W. Ellerhorst: *Handbuch der Orgelkunde* (Einsiedeln, 1936/*R*), pp. 273ff, 315ff

N.A. Bonavia-Hunt and H.W. Homer: *The Organ Reed* (New York, 1950)

J. Mertin: 'Thoughts on Determining Cut Up in Flue Pipes', *ISO Information*, no.9 (1973), 633–9

L.G. Monette and C. Stevens: *Organ Tonal Finishing and Fine Tuning* (Baton Rouge, LA, 1981)

E.L. Kottick: *The Harpsichord Owner's Guide* (Chapel Hill, NC, 1987), 90ff

L.G. Monette: *The Art of Voicing* (Kalamazoo, MI, 1992)

P. Pelto: 'Four Voicing Techniques: Analysing the Perception of Sound', *Organ Yearbook*, vol.25 (1995), 101–22

BARBARA OWEN (1); EDGAR HUNT/FRIEDRICH VON HUENE (2); EDWIN M. RIPIN/JOHN KOSTER (3)

Voigt. German family of musical instrument makers in Markneukirchen (to which the following refers, including birth and death data). Lutherie dominated the family's craft in the 18th century, beginning with Adam Voigt (*b* c1674; *d* 19 Feb 1737), who in 1699 became a member of the Neukirchen violin makers' guild. By 1850, 23 Voigts were counted as guild masters, their high-arched violins epitomizing the old Vogtland style. The most important masters were Johann Georg Voigt (four masters with the same name about 1800), Johann Friedrich Voigt, called 'Fritz' (*b* 17 Dec 1778; *d* 4 Sept 1840), and Johann Christian Voigt II (*b* 15 April 1766; *d* 13 Feb 1846). The last also made guitars, and in the 19th century several other Voigts also turned to guitar making, and later to bow and zither making. In the 20th century, Arnold Voigt (*b* 13 May 1864; *d* 26 Sept 1952) and Werner Voigt (*b* 25 Feb 1911; *d* 9 May 1982) adopted the modern Italianate style of violin making.

From the end of the 18th century, members of the family were also active as brass instrument makers. The brothers Johann Friedrich (*b* 25 Aug 1756; *d* 7 Nov 1826) and Johann Georg Voigt (*b* 28 Nov 1759; *d* 19 Dec 1843), who apprenticed with Johann Georg Eschenbach, were founding members of the wind instrument makers' society in 1797. Two grandchildren of Johann Georg Voigt advanced the division of labour in Vogtland brass instrument manufacture: Theodor Voigt (*b* 13 Aug 1830; *d* 13 March 1902) founded a valve business in 1850, later continued by Reinhard Voigt, while Moritz Voigt (*b* 26 June 1836; *d* 8 Sept 1926) founded a bell-making business in 1878, later continued by William Voigt. Both companies operated over three generations to the middle of the 20th century, and other workshops in the region nowadays continue a similar specialization.

The workshops of Helmut Voigt and Jürgen Voigt remain active as brass instrument producers, especially of trombones. The luthiers of the family are now based in Bavaria; Jochen Voigt works as a violin maker in Garching near Munich, and Claus Voigt as a guitar maker in Edling.

BIBLIOGRAPHY
W. Waterhouse: *The New Langwill Index: a Dictionary of Musical Wind-Instrument Makers and Inventors* (London, 1993)
B. Zoebisch: *Vogtländischer Geigenbau, vol.1: Biographien und Erklärungen bis 1850* (Horb am Neckar, 2000)
E. Weller: *Der Blasinstrumentenbau im Vogtland von den Anfängen bis zum Beginn des 20. Jahrhunderts: Untersuchungen und Dokumentationen zur Geschichte eines Gewerbezweiges der Musikinstrumentenindustrie* (Horb am Neckar, 2004)

ENRICO WELLER

Voirin, François Nicolas (*b* Mirecourt, France, 19 Dec 1833; *d* Paris, France, 4 June 1885). French bowmaker. After serving his apprenticeship in Mirecourt he worked from 1855 to 1870 for J.-B. Vuillaume in Paris. After briefly returning to Mirecourt he established his own business at 3 rue du Bouloi, Paris, where he worked until his sudden death. He was a prolific maker and his bows were of superb quality; he is generally regarded as the most important bowmaker of the second half of the 19th century.

Voirin's bows show a radical departure from the predominant Tourte model of the first half of the century. The dimensions of the stick and head are thinner and smaller, and to retain strength he used only the finest pernambuco possible. He also began the camber directly behind the head; this feature was taken up not only by his pupils Thomassin and Lamy but also Eugène Sartory, Victor and Jules Fétique, and E.A. Ouchard among others; he also influenced German makers. Voirin's early bows, i.e. those made in the Vuillaume workshop and carrying the Vuillaume brand, are somewhat stouter than his later ones. After 1870 his work exhibits a rare elegance of line; the frogs are either regular or sometimes rounded in Vuillaume's style and the buttons are normally two-banded. In more recent times players have often dismissed Voirin's bows as being too light; this is most often true of the cello and viola bows with the former ranging in weight from 70 to 75 grams. The violin bows, however, fall largely within the normal range (i.e. 58 to 60 grams) and continue to be in demand.

After his death, Voirin's widow continued the business for some years, branding his pupils' work with her husband's brandmark, 'F.N. VOIRIN À PARIS'. Most of these bows appear to lack the strength of the originals.

BIBLIOGRAPHY
J. Roda: *Bows of the Musical Instruments of the Violin Family* (Chicago, IL, 1959)
W.C. Retford: *Bows and Bowmakers* (London, 1964)
E. Vatelot: *Les archets français* (Paris, 1976)

CHARLES BEARE/JAAK LIIVOJA-LORIUS

Voit. German firm of organ builders in Karlsruhe-Durlach. The firm was founded in 1764 by Johann Heinrich Stein (1735–67) of Heidelsheim, and continued by his cousin Georg Markus Stein (1738–94), organ and piano builder to the court of Baden-Durlach; after the latter's death it passed by his daughter's marriage to Johann Volkmar Voit (1772–1806) of Schweinfurt, scion of a Franconian family who had built organs since the mid-17th century; he succeeded Stein as court organ builder. His brother Carl Friedrich Voit was also an instrument maker. In 1807 Johann Ludwig Wilhelm Bürgy (1761–1838) of Niederflorstadt married Volkmar Voit's widow and ran the workshop until 1835. He was succeeded by his stepson Louis Voit (1802–83) who ran the firm until 1870. It was then taken over by the latter's sons Heinrich (*b* Durlach, 18 March 1834; *d* Durlach, Oct 1914) and Carl (1847–87). After Carl's death, Heinrich's sons Emil (1864–1924) and Siegfried (1870–1938) were taken into the firm as partners, and it became known as H. Voit & Söhne. They experimented with electrification and introduced a movable electric console in 1903. One of few organs in Bulgaria is theirs in the Catholic church of St Paul in Rousse, Bulgaria (1908; one manual and pedal, 13 stops). Heinrich Voit Jr (1871–1926) and Julius Voit (1883–1955) later joined the firm. In 1930 Siegfried Voit retired from the business, and the workshops were taken over by their former manager Karl Hess (1879–1943), who renovated the Voit organ in St. Bonifatius Church, Karlsruhe (1908/49; three manuals, 44 stops). After World War II, under the direction of Hess's widow, Annie (1900–81), the much diminished firm continued in business until about 1959. Hans Voit (1904–94), son of Heinrich Jr, founded a separate firm in Stendal in 1930.

Voit & Söhne was the leading firm in its field in the former Grand Duchy of Baden, at times employing about 50 staff, and by 1930 it had built more than 1500 organs. The firm also provided parts to other makers. It acquired fame beyond the immediate locality through a series of organs built for concert halls: the Treviris Hall, Trier (1900); the Festhalle, Koblenz (1902); the Rosengarten, Mannheim (1903); the Stadthalle, Heidelberg (1903); the National Hungarian Royal Academy of Music, Budapest (1907); the hôtel particulier du Comte de la Revélière, Paris (1912); the Smetana Hall, Prague (1912); and the Stadthalle, Krefeld (1917).

BIBLIOGRAPHY
H. Fischer: *100 Jahre Bund deutscher Orgelbaumeister, 1891–1991* (Lauffen, 1991)
E. Wagner and others: *Die Voit-Orgel in der Stadthalle Heidelberg* (Heidelberg, 1993)

H. Fischer and T. Wohnhaas, eds.: *Lexikon süddeutscher Orgelbauer* (Wilhelmshaven, 1994)

M. Zepp: '" … ein Meisterwerk der bekannten Orgelfabrik H. Voit & Söhne in Durlach …" Die Geschichte der Voit–Orgel im Kurhaus Baden–Baden', *Ioculator Dei. Festschrift für Andreas Schröder zum 60. Geburtstag*, ed. M.G. Kaufmann (Freiburg, 1999)

M.G. Kaufmann: 'Die Heinrich Voit & Söhne–Orgel … in der katolischen Pfarrkirche St. Cyriacus Karlsruhe–Bulach', *Organista et homo doctus: Festschrift Rudolf Walter zum 90. Geburtstag*, eds. R. Walter and A. Reichling (Sankt Augustin, 2008), 129–42

HERMANN FISCHER/R

Voix mixte (Fr.: 'mixed voice'). Vocal technique involving the blending of the chest and head registers in the middle range, especially in male singers. Manuel García (*Traité complet de l'art du chant*, Paris 1840–47/*R*) was the first to define the term, although the practice is described much earlier. Tosi (*Opinioni de' cantore antichi e moderni*, Bologna, 1723; Eng. trans., 1742, 2/1743 as *Observations on the Florid Song*) urged the male singer 'to leave no Means untried' to unite the two registers, 'for if they do not perfectly unite, the Voice will be of divers Registers, and must consequently lose its Beauty'. Although García defines this term as a mixture of the two basic registral mechanisms, he also considers the term 'improper' as the actual mixing of mechanisms is physiologically impossible. He argues that the effect was created by the use of a *mezzo voce* (half voice) in the chest register.

ELLEN T. HARRIS

Voix sombrée (Fr.: 'darkened voice'). Technique of voice production. It was made famous by the singing of Gilbert Duprez during the 1830s. He is said to have carried the chest register up to *c″*. Duprez (*L'art du chant, Paris*, 1845) called this technique *voix sombre* or *voix couverte* (covered voice). 'Covering' involves the darkening of the vowels, for example, from 'ah' to 'uh', resulting in a physiological change in mechanism first described by the physicians H. Diday and J.-E. Pétrequin in their 'Mémoire sur une nouvelle espèce de voix chantée' (*Gazette médicale de Paris*, vol.8, 1840) as a lowering of the larynx. Covered tone is used as an expedient to admit more of the head tone into the area of the break between the head and chest voice, allowing these to be better united. When used in the highest register, as by Duprez, the technique produces a sound of great volume and intensity but can be vocally damaging. The voix sombrée became highly controversial as a voice type and was vigorously attacked by Etienne Jean Baptiste (called Stéphan de la Madelaine) in his *Oeuvres complétes sur le chant* (Paris, 1875). Duprez himself is reported to have tired easily because of his use of the voix sombrée, and had a short career.

Manuel García (*Traité complet de l'art du chant*, Paris 1840–47/*R*) does not discuss voix sombrée as a voice type; rather, he distinguishes between *timbre clair* and *timbre sombre* as distinct vocal qualities in both head and chest voice and discusses these in terms of offering 'the student a throng of resources which permit him appropriately to vary the expression of the voice'. He equated the use of *timbre sombre* in the chest voice with *voix mixte*.

OWEN JANDER/ELLEN T. HARRIS

Volckland, Franciscus [Franz] (*b* Berlstedt, nr Weimar, Germany, 5 June 1696; *d* Erfurt, Germany, 23 Dec 1779). German organ builder. He trained with J.G. Schröter in Erfurt, possibly after some initial experience with the Berlstedt organ builder Johann Conrad Vockerodt, and in 1716 became an assistant to the organ builder Lortzing in Ohrdruf. In 1718 he settled in Erfurt, where he first worked as a brewer and fruit seller; in 1720 he unsuccessfully sought a privilege as an organ builder. There followed a legal dispute, lasting several years, with Schröter, who felt himself threatened by Volckland's competition. By 1721, however, he was building organs, and he married in 1722. At the time of his death he was well-to-do and held in high repute as an organ builder.

Volckland's productivity was highest between 1725 and 1750. His organ specifications are dominated by an abundance of 8′ foundation stops, mixtures (including the Tierce), and copious wooden pipework as well as Zimbelsterns and Glockenspiels. In addition to these typical 18th-century Thuringian features, he also made frequent use of the 4′ Hohlflöte in the Pedal division. The majority of Volckland's organs are of medium size; he did not build large or three-manual instruments. A number of his organs still survive in the area of Erfurt, including Mühlberg (1729), the Cruciskirche, Erfurt (1732–7), Bindersleben (1743), Elxleben, near Arnstadt (1750), and Tröchtelborn (1758–61).

BIBLIOGRAPHY

J. Adlung: *Musica mechanica organoedi*, ed. J.L. Albrecht (Berlin, 1768/*R*); ed. C. Mahrenholz (Kassel, 1931)

F. Friedrich: 'Franciskus Volkland: Organ Builder', *Early Keyboard Studies*, vol.7/3 (1993), 6–8

H. Brück: 'Franz Volckland (1696–1779). Ein Erfurter Orgelbauer der Bachzeit', *Thüringer Orgeljournal* (Arnstadt, 1999)

FELIX FRIEDRICH/R

Voller. English family of violin makers. The brothers William (*b* Marylebone, London, 10 May 1854; *d* Streatham, London, 19 Dec 1933), Alfred (*b* Marylebone, 22 April 1856; *d* Salcombe, Devon, 22 March 1918), and Charles (*b* Marylebone, 24 Nov 1865; *d* Paignton, Devon, 9 Jan 1949) were self-taught but achieved a high standard as copyists. Each learned a stringed instrument in childhood (William, viola; Alfred, cello; Charles, violin). William first set up as a music teacher, but through contacts with Frederick Chanot (1857–1911) and George Hart II (1860–1939), began in the 1880s and 90s to copy classical Italian instruments with his brothers' assistance. Violins copied include the 'Red Cross Knight' (1691) and 'Circle' (1701) by Stradivari and the 'D'Egville (1735) and 'Leduc' (1743) by Guarneri 'del Gesù', as well as work by other Italian makers including Guadagnini, Landolphi, and Nicolò Gagliano. Characteristics of the Vollers' output include the use of ebony for the purfling blacks, sourcing of old wood, inclusion of genuine parts from Italian classical instruments, and accurate imitation of varnish wear patterns.

Their labels usually either declare a model—for example 'EXACT COPY OF 'THE LEDUC'/GUARNERI DATE 1745/HART & SON'—or are reproduction labels of Italian makers; these might have been inserted by others. Some of the latter instruments ended being sold as genuine Italian work, and the Vollers were the makers of a celebrated fake, the 'Balfour' Strad—the subject of notorious legal proceedings, though the Vollers were not personally implicated in the fraud. Later in their careers the brothers did private restoration work for prominent players including Lionel Tertis and August Wilhelmj, and had commercial dealings with Wurlitzer of New York and Hamma of Stuttgart. Despite the fine quality of their work the Vollers kept a low profile in the violin trade, working from home and styling themselves 'musician' or 'music teacher' on official documents. See J. Dilworth, A. Fairfax, and J. Milnes: *The Voller Brothers* (Oxford, 2006).

JOHN MILNES

Voltage control (Fr. *commande par tension;* Ger. *Spannungssteuerung*). In electronic music, a means by which the functions of certain electronic devices can be controlled by the application of external voltages. A change in the voltage applied results in a proportional change in the behaviour of the signal-producing or processing device that is being controlled. Theoretically any function of such a device that can be controlled manually (e.g. by turning a knob) can be made to respond to applied voltages if suitable circuitry is designed. In practice the most usual applications are to be found in the voltage-controlled oscillator (VCO) and the voltage-controlled amplifier (VCA), in which respectively frequency and amplitude can be controlled by an external voltage. The range of voltages used in musical applications of voltage control is normally quite small: in the case of the voltage-controlled oscillator it is typical to find a ratio of one volt per octave (and therefore one-twelfth of a volt per semitone).

One of the first pioneers of electronic music to appreciate the importance of the principle of voltage control was the Canadian inventor Hugh Le Caine. His 'electronic sackbut', completed in 1948, incorporated a voltage-controlled oscillator. In 1955 he designed a multichannel tape recorder whose speed could be varied by control voltages operated from a three-octave keyboard or a ribbon controller. In the USA Harald Bode made limited applications of voltage control in a modular 'signal processor' or sound synthesizer constructed in 1959–60, which in turn influenced Robert A. Moog when he began experimenting in 1964 with what was to become, at the end of that year, the first commercially manufactured analogue synthesizer. In the early 1960s Donald Buchla constructed independently several voltage-controlled modules, from which the Buchla synthesizer was developed in 1966.

The principle of voltage control is central to the operation of analogue synthesizers, many of whose component devices are voltage-controllable. Thus a device can be used to control one or more others, which in turn can control further devices, and so on. To take a simple example, a low-frequency oscillator (that is, one producing frequencies below the audible spectrum) can be used as the source of a varying voltage to control another oscillator that operates within the audio spectrum; the frequency of the latter oscillator tracks the waveshape of the former, producing an audible variation in pitch. This kind of automated frequency control led to the development of the sequencer, a device designed to deliver sequences of control voltages.

One reason why voltage control became such an important technique is because any piece of equipment capable of delivering a voltage that varies within an appropriate range can be used as the controller of voltage-controlled devices. This has led to a proliferation of control equipment employing many different principles of interaction between the user and the electronic circuitry.

Keyboards and ribbon controllers were available with the first analogue synthesizers. A synthesizer keyboard is generally of conventional design; to each key is assigned a voltage from a pre-set range of voltages divided into equal fractional steps. Often the range of voltages itself can be increased or decreased by the user, so that any desired interval steps (including microtones) can be delivered from the keyboard to a voltage-controlled oscillator. Some keyboards can deliver a second control voltage by means of a circuit that tracks the speed of the key as it is depressed. Typically this is sent to a voltage-controlled amplifier, so that a faster stroke gives a louder sound. However, the decision as to what is controlled by what is normally the choice of the user: the second control voltage could as easily control a second oscillator or a voltage-controlled filter. In other keyboards, further sources of control voltages are pressure on the key bed and lateral movement of the key.

The glide strip or ribbon controller consists of a contact strip (usually of metal) placed above a strip of electrically resistive material. A single contact, made by pressing the finger down on the ribbon, causes a certain voltage to be sent to the receiving device, and the signal continues until the contact is broken by lifting the finger. By sliding the finger along the strip, continuous transitions between control voltages can be effected, resulting in glissandos if the output is sent to a voltage-controlled oscillator.

By the 1980s the number of control devices available had increased. The joystick, capable of movement in two (sometimes three) dimensions, can simultaneously control two voltage outputs, one for each axis of its motion. Touch-plates, which deliver voltages proportional to the degree of capacitance between the performer and the plate, and photoelectric cells, the action of which is dependent upon the amount of light falling on them, have been used in a variety of ways.

Other electronic devices are designed to convert external signals, such as those created by a musical instrument, into a form in which they can be used as control voltages. The envelope follower gives voltages derived from the amplitude of a varying audio signal; a frequency-to-voltage converter tracks the fundamental pitch of any input and supplies a voltage proportional to its frequency. A random voltage source, externally triggered, delivers unpredictable voltages by sampling and holding levels read from a source of white or pink noise. More unusual sources of control voltages have been tapped, for example, the earth's magnetic field (by Charles Dodge), and the alpha waves of the brain (by David Rosenboom and others) gathered by means of electrodes attached to the scalp.

The American composer Morton Subotnick developed a system of control voltages derived from tape tracks on which amplitude-modulated oscillator tones were pre-recorded (normally three to each track). During performance or recording, the voltage-control information is extracted by band-pass filters and envelope followers and relayed to the appropriate sound modules. In this way, several control voltages can be applied concurrently. This system, called 'ghost electronics' by the composer because only the effects, and not the sounds, of the pre-recorded tracks are heard, has been used both for tape compositions (for instance the *Butterfly* series) and live electronic pieces. The sound processors are called 'ghost boxes'. Since 1982 the voltage-control information has been stored in a digital memory and then applied through digital-to-analogue converters, thus eliminating the need for tape recorders.

Voltage control has provided composers and performers with many means of controlling their electroacoustic sound material. Now that digital technology permits even greater precision of control, a wider diversity of controller interfaces has been developed for composition and performance. The work of Moog's Big Briar company concentrated entirely on this area, which is also featured in some digital synthesizers, such as the SSSP in Toronto.

BIBLIOGRAPHY

H. Bode: 'A New Tool for the Exploration of Unknown Electronic Music Instrument Performances', *Journal of the Audio Engineering Society*, vol.9/4 (1961), 264–6

H. Le Caine: 'A Tape Recorder for Use in Electronic Music Studios and Related Equipment', *JMT*, vol.7/1 (1963), 83–97

R.A. Moog: 'Voltage–controlled Electronic Music Modules', *Journal of the Audio Engineering Society*, vol.13/3 (1965), 200–6

D. Johnson: 'A Voltage–Controlled Sequencer', *Electronic Music Reports*, no.4 (1971), 119

A. Strange: *Electronic Music: Systems, Techniques and Controls* (Dubuque, IA, 1972, 2/1983)

W.G. Landrieu and L. Goethals: 'Electronic Programming of Electro–Acoustical Music', *Interface*, vol.2/1 (1973), 71–99

J. Chadabe: 'The Voltage–Controlled Synthesizer', *The Development and Practice of Electronic Music*, ed. J. H. Appleton and R. C. Perera (Englewood Cliffs, NJ, 1975), 138–88

F.L. McCarty: 'Electronic Music Systems: Structure, Control, Product', *PNM*, vol.13/2 (1975), 98–125

C.A.G.M. Tempelaars: *Sound Signal Processing* (Utrecht, 1977)

N. Collins and J. d'Escriván, eds.: *The Cambridge Companion to Electronic Music* (Cambridge, 2007)

RICHARD ORTON

Votey, Edwin Scott (*b* Ovid, NY, 1856; *d* Summit, NJ, 21 Jan 1931). American organ builder and inventor. In 1873, when his family moved to West Brattleboro, Vermont, he entered the Estey Organ Co. as an office boy, four years later becoming a traveling salesman for that firm throughout western New York State. In 1883 the Detroit music dealer C.J. Whitney purchased the Detroit Organ Company (a maker of reed organs), renamed it the Whitney Organ Company, and hired Votey as technical director and William R. Farrand (1854–1930), son of a local drugstore owner, as administrator. After Whitney retired, in 1887, the name of the firm was changed to the Farrand & Votey Organ Company. Farrand & Votey acquired the assets the Granville Wood Co. in 1890, and in 1892 or 93 the noted Roosevelt Organ Works in New York. In the latter year the firm built its largest organ, for the World's Columbian Exposition in Chicago. Other notable organs built under the Farrand & Votey name included those for Aeolian Hall, New York (1893) and St Ignatius Church, San Francisco (1896). In 1897 this partnership dissolved, with Votey taking over the organ operation as the Votey Organ Co., which was purchased by the Aeolian Company and reorganized under the Aeolian-Votey name. The firm built a new factory in Garwood, New Jersey, where manufacture began in 1900. In 1895 in Detroit Votey had invented a roll-operated automatic piano-playing device, the Pianola, which by 1898 was already being manufactured by the Aeolian firm.

In 1901 Votey left to go to Boston as a partner in the long-established George Hutchings firm, which reorganized in that year as Hutchings-Votey. When that firm's factory was destroyed by fire in 1904, he returned to the Aeolian firm as secretary and treasurer, and in 1917 became vice-president and general manager. From 1910 Votey lived in Summit, New Jersey, where he was active in civic affairs and was a director of a local bank. From his earliest years in the organ trade Votey was noted for his inventiveness, and between 1886 and 1929 was granted 21 patents for improvements in reed and pipe organ mechanisms, including some related to the self-playing devices for which Aeolian would eventually be known. During World War I, at the former Wright Brothers airfield at Dayton, Ohio, Votey helped develop Charles Kettering's automatically controlled (drone) bomber, for which Aeolian contracted to produce the pneumatic mechanisms.

BIBLIOGRAPHY

'Edwin S. Votey', *The American Organist*, vol.14/3 (1931), 152ff

J.J. Hammann: 'History of the Farrand & Votey Organ Company', *The Tracker*, vol.32/2 (1988), 18ff

R. Smith: *The Aeolian Pipe Organ and its Music* (Richmond, VA, 1998)

BARBARA OWEN/R

Vowles, William Gibbons (*b* Bristol, England, 1826; *d* Churchill, Somerset, England, 25 Feb 1912). English organ builder. He was trained by Joseph Munday, whose business was founded by John Smith in 1814. In 1856 Vowles founded the Bristol firm of W.G. Vowles Ltd. His early work included the rebuilding of the organs of Bristol Cathedral (1861) and St Mary Redcliffe (1867). In 1860 the firm moved from Castle Street to extensive premises in St James's Square and developed factory production methods. After his retirement in 1908 the firm became a limited company, whose catalogue of that year offered a range of 17 standard specifications from one to three manuals and gave details of 510 instruments supplied to locations principally in Bristol, Gloucestershire, Somerset, and South Wales. Some organs were exported to South Africa, India, and the West Indies. On 29 March 1924 the factory was destroyed by fire; the firm suffered further damage during World War II and was eventually absorbed by J.W. Walker & Sons in 1959. See 'Messrs. Vowles' Organ Works', *Work in Bristol: a Series of Sketches of the Chief Manufactories of the City* (Bristol, 1883), 162–77.

CHRISTOPHER KENT

Vredeman [Vredman, Vreedman], **Michael** (*b* Mechlin, Southern Netherlands, *c*1562; *d* Utrecht, Netherlands, 19 Jan 1629). Netherlands maker of viols and citterns. He was the son of the carilloneur and composer Sebastian Vredeman. He settled in Utrecht where he acquired citizenship in 1583. He published a book describing one of his inventions, *Der violen cyther met vijfsnaren en nieuwe sorte mélodieuse inventie, twe naturen hebbende, vier parthijen spelende* (Arnheim, 1612). He also published a music collection called *Der Cyteren lusthoff*.

BIBLIOGRAPHY

G. van Doorslaer: 'De toonkunstenaars der familie Vredeman', *Bulletin de l'Académie royale d'archéologie de Belgique* (Antwerp, 1920), 29–43

R. Visscher: 'Vredeman', *Nieuw Nederlandsch biografisch woordenboek*, ed. P.C. Molhuysen and P J. Blok, vol.7 (Leiden, 1927)

HOWARD MAYER BROWN

Vuhudendung. Mouth bow of Pentecost, Vanuatu. The stick is about 50 cm long, slightly curved, flat, and thin. The string, made from a creeper, passes from a hole near one end to a stud or spur formed on the other. It is held by the teeth and the single string is struck with a double stick. See O.T. Mason: 'Geographical Distribution of the Musical Bow', *American Anthropologist*, vol.10/11 (1897), 377–80.

Vuillaume, Jean-Baptiste (*b* Mirecourt, France, 7 Oct 1798; *d* Paris, France, 19 March 1875). French violin maker and dealer. His activities in the middle of the 19th century dominated the trade and contributed importantly to the making of new instruments and bows. Vuillaume was born of an old but undistinguished violin-making family in Mirecourt. In 1818, having trained with his father, he went to Paris to work for François Chanot, moving to the workshop of Lété in 1821. There he progressed, and in 1823 began to sign his own instruments, giving each one a serial number. In 1828, after he had made about 100 new instruments, the connection with Lété was dissolved, and Vuillaume established his own workshops at 46 rue Croix des Petits-Champs. He remained there until 1858, when he moved to a large and elegant house in the rue Demours at Les Ternes.

Vuillaume's first instruments were heavily varnished a deep, dark red all over, but were otherwise excellently made, rather in the style of Lupot or Pique. By 1827 he

must have seen enough fine old Italian violins to realize that a large part of their attraction was the picturesque wear of the varnish, and that, as Charles Reade put it, 'violins are heard by the eye'. Vuillaume quickly became the pioneer of imitation, and as soon as his violins were visually acceptable they sold speedily and trade began to flourish. Assistants were engaged and production increased, and the imitations became more and more accurate and impressive. Vuillaume had an excellent eye for old instruments, in which he dealt from early on, and his increasing expertise and understanding of the old Cremonese makers contributed largely to the success, tonal as well as visual, of his own violins. His was soon the leading Paris violin shop, and by 1850 the first shop in Europe conducting business in every country.

In his dealings in old instruments, Vuillaume had the opportunity of handling many of the world's finest. His greatest day came early in 1855, after the death of the Italian dealer and recluse Luigi Tarisio. Hastening south, Vuillaume was able to purchase the entire stock, including fine examples of all the best Italian makes. The greatest single prize was the 'Messiah' Stradivari, made in 1716 but in unused condition, a violin of which Tarisio had often spoken in Paris, though the dealers there doubted its existence. As was his habit with the more spectacular instruments that he was able to acquire, Vuillaume made a number of very good copies of the 'Messiah'. Modelled after Guarneri 'del Gesù', Nicolò Amati, and Maggini as well as Stradivari, Vuillaume's copies have seldom if ever been mistaken for the originals. They have a distinctive appearance, and, since there are so many, they are easily recognized. After the first few years of experiment, Vuillaume developed firm ideas about how worn varnish should look. He did not, however, make any but the most half-hearted attempt to reproduce knocks and scratches and other normal signs of centuries of use. His instruments are copies, therefore, rather than fakes. All but a very few bear Vuillaume's own label, and a minute brand on the interior of back and table, the serial number, and the date of manufacture. More than 2000 of the best quality were produced, each closely supervised and varnished by Vuillaume himself. In addition there were the 'Sainte Cécile' instruments, a less expensive line, made for Vuillaume but without his direct participation.

Vuillaume's achievement in supervising the manufacture of bows was no less worthy, and many of the best French makers were his workmen and pupils. These included (dates indicate approximate duration of employment): Persoit (1825–38), Dominique Peccatte (1826–35), Joseph Fonclause (1830–40), Nicolas Maline (*c*1840–50), Jean Grandadam (1842–53), Joseph Henry (*c*1847–50), Pierre Simon (*c*1847–50), François Peccatte (1852–53), François Nicolas Voirin (1855–70), Jean Joseph Martin (1858–63), Nicolas Maire (1860), Charles Peccatte (1866–70), Justin Poirson (1870), Charles Claude Husson (1870–74), and Prosper Colas (1873–74). He also employed non-French bow makers, including Thomas Jacobsen (1830–35), Ludwig Bausch (1840), Emst Liebich (ii) (1850), J.C. Nürnberger (1860), and H.R. Pfretzschner (1870).

Vuillaume's innovations with bows did not survive beyond the end of the century. The hollow steel bow was inadequate, but the 'self-rehairing bow' was at least a good idea. The hair, purchased in prepared hanks, could be inserted by the player in the time it takes to change a string, and was tightened or loosened by a simple mechanism inside the frog. The frog itself was affixed to the stick, and the balance of the bow thus remained constant when the hair stretched with use. He also designed a round-edged frog mounted to the butt by means of a recessed track, which he encouraged his bow makers to use; other details of craft, however, make it possible to identify the actual maker of many Vuillaume bows. The bows are stamped, often rather faintly, either 'VUILLAUME À PARIS' or 'J.B. VUILLAUME'.

Many of Vuillaume's later instruments were left fully varnished: his reputation made, it was no longer necessary to simulate age. His influence was felt among makers all over France, but perhaps especially in Mirecourt, where magnificent craftsmanship continued well past the turn of the century. His instruments were and are successful largely because of his admiration and understanding of the Cremonese masters. (For details of his three-string octobass (1851), see DOUBLE BASS.)

Several brothers of Jean-Baptiste were also violin makers. Nicolas Vuillaume (b Mirecourt, 21 May 1800; d Mirecourt, 14 April 1872) worked for him in Paris from 1832 to 1842 but returned to Mirecourt to establish a successful business as a dealer and manufacturer. He was the maker of the Ste Cécile and Stentor violins. Nicolas-François Vuillaume (b Mirecourt, 13 May 1802; d Brussels, Belgium, 16 Jan 1876), another brother and pupil of Jean-Baptiste, worked for him from August 1824 until 1828, then went to Brussels where he remained until his death. He too was primarily a copier, and if he did not quite have the talent of his brother, his instruments are nevertheless very good and much sought after. A nephew, Sébastien Vuillaume (b Mirecourt, 18 June 1835; d Paris, 17 Nov 1875), was also a violin maker of some note.

BIBLIOGRAPHY

C. Reade: *Cremona: Violins and Varnish* (Gloucester, 1873/R) [orig. pubd in *Pall Mall Gazette* (Aug 1872)]
E. Doring: *Jean Baptiste Vuillaume of Paris* (Chicago, 1961)
R. Millant: *J.B. Vuillaume: sa vie et son oeuvre* (London, 1972)
E. Vatelot: *Les archets français* (Nancy, 1976)
B. Millant and J.F. Raffin: *L'Archet* (Paris, 2000)
S. Milliot: *Histoire de la lutherie parisienne du XVIIIe siècle à 1960*, vol.3: *Jean-Baptiste Vuillaume et sa famille: Nicolas, Nicolas-François et Sebastien Vuillaume* (Spa, 2006)
CHARLES BEARE, JAAK LIIVOJA-LORIUS/PHILIP J. KASS

Vul mi myel. Drum of the Alur people of the eastern Democratic Republic of the Congo. It is small, double-headed, and used for dances. See O. Boone: *Les tambours du Congo belge et du Ruanda-Urundi* (Tervuren, 1951), 72.

Vuvă. Single-headed frame drum of Romania; a type of *daire*. It is of medium size without jingles, but has one or more little bells attached inside the frame. It is played in north Oltenia and Muntenia at weddings and other entertainments by a *vuvar*. The playing technique consists of rubbing the membrane with the thumb (sometimes sprinkled with rosin), which produces an intermittent raw sound ('vuvuit'), which has given the instrument its onomatopoeic name.

TIBERIU ALEXANDRU

Vuvuzela. Plastic trumpet of South Africa, now widely mass-produced. Most are brightly coloured, about 62 to 65 cm long with integral mouthpiece, and sound near $b\flat$. First developed commercially in South Africa about 2000, the vuvuzela caught on worldwide when South Africa hosted the FIFA (Fédération Internationale de Football Association) Confederations Cup in 2009 and the World Cup in 2010. Millions were sold worldwide and it became the 'sound of the World Cup', adored in South Africa but also abhorred because its dangerously loud sound (up to 113 dB at 2 metres from the bell) obscured players' communication on the field and took the place of the hitherto well-known choral singing of South African crowds. FIFA considered banning the instrument but yielded because of its popularity in South Africa. An attempt was made to develop a pentatonic 'vuvuzela orchestra' on the lines of the traditional one-note pipe ensembles of South Africa, but this effort succumbed to commercial interests. Later a kudu-horn-shaped vuvuzela was manufactured, whose improved shape was not, however, mirrored in its sound. The horn has been banned from many venues.

Despite various assertions, the vuvuzela does not descend from traditional African horns, except to the extent that South Africans use side-blown animal horns for signalling and as noise-makers. The Church of Shembe in KwaZulu-Natal tried unsuccessfully to claim ownership of the vuvuzela on the grounds that they developed a longer, wooden, end-blown trumpet during the 20th century. Others have also tried to claim its invention, but similar one-note horns of sheet metal have long been popular at sporting events and for signalling.

The word *vuvuzela* was invented along with the instrument, based on the onomatopoeic syllable common in southern African languages—*vu, fu, fe*, and so on—for the sound of blowing, plus the applicative verb ending *-zela* as used in Zulu and Xhosa.

ANDREW TRACEY

Wachtl, Joseph (*fl* Vienna, Austria, *c*1800–35). Austrian piano maker. Along with Franz Martin Seuffert (1773–1847) and Jacob Bleyer (1778–1812), with both of whom he partnered early in his career, Wachtl was supposedly a pupil of Anton Walter. He obtained Viennese citizenship and received his masters qualification in 1805. An inscription on a pyramid piano (*D. LE.u*) identifies him as 'bürgerl. Orgel- und Instrumentmacher', but it is not known whether he completed any organs. He is remembered particularly for making fancy upright pianos of pyramid and giraffe forms, typically with five-and-one-half- to six-octave compass and three to five pedals. Wachtl married Bleyer's half-sister about 1811, and Bleyer bequeathed his estate to Wachtl. About the time of Bleyer's death, Seuffert obtained his master's qualification and left the partnership, supposedly over a disagreement concerning the 'invention' of their upright pianos. Wachtl evidently continued work on his own at least until 1832, when his firm was reportedly liquidated, although directories record the name until 1835.

Wada (i) [wuasa, huala]. Vessel rattle of the Mapuche (Araucanian) people of south-central Chile and southwestern Argentina. It is made from an undecorated gourd (*Lagenaria vulgaris* or *Lagenaria siceraria*) about 14 cm in diameter with dried seeds or pebbles inside, and pierced at the bottom by a 20-cm wooden handle. It is used only by the *machi* (shaman, usually female) or her assistants (*yegül*) to accompany sacred prayers and fertility rites.

Wada (ii). Name of a sacred single headed drum of the Venda people of South Africa. The drum was presumably made in the 19th century and reportedly kept in a cave in the village of Domboni, ancestral home of the Nefolovhodwe family, who were its guardians. Wada is associated with ancestor spirits. At least until the 1920s it was occasionally used in *tshikona* (reed pipe) dance performances. Various myths relate futile attempts by white people to remove it from its home

in the 1930s, after the Domboni residents were forcibly dispossessed of their ancestral land. Since the late 1930s Wada has been deposited in a hollow baobab tree in the Muswodi district; it is suspended from a pole within the large trunk and not allowed to touch the ground. It is described as being of a more squared shape than rounded, of an ochre colour, and devoid of carvings. The head is of oxhide, although some people believe it is of human skin. A single small wooden beater lies near it. At least into the 1990s Wada remained a revered symbol of cultural and regional identity and resistance to land appropriation. Other sacred drums include the legendary Ngoma-lungundu, revered as a supernatural creature by the ruling Singo clan. Civundika was a sacred drum of the Rozvi people of Zimbabwe. See J. Kruger: 'Wada: a Sacred Venda Drum', *South African Journal of Musicology*, vol.16 (1996), 48–57.

Waga. Ankle rattles of the Birom people of Nigeria. They are made from small containers of *Borassus* palm leaves inside which are placed small stones, shot, or grain. The containers are affixed to a cord which is wound four times around the ankle.

Wägg. Panpipe of Nissan, Green Islands, Papua New Guinea.

Wagner. German family of brass instrument makers. Gustav Adolf Wagner (*b* Cunewalde, Germany, 22 March 1865; *d* Dresden, Germany, 20 Jan 1941) was the son of the piano tuner and maker Karl Friedrich Wilhelm Wagner. From 1879 to 1883 he apprenticed with the firm of Friederich Albin Heckel in Dresden and then worked with Gebrüder Alexander in Mainz, F. Schmidt in Cologne, and Altrichter in Frankfurt an der Oder. In 1889 he returned to Heckel. In 1904 he took over the firm of Moritz Eschenbach, renaming it Gustav A. Wagner and concentrating on trumpet manufacture. He had made a 'Bach' trumpet in D in 1900, but mostly made standard orchestral trumpets in B♭ with three rotary valves, after the Heckel model. He also made some other brasses such as tenor valve trombones.

Some of the valves in Wagner models were made by the firm of Martin Peter of Markneukirchen. Gustav Adolf's two sons, Richard G. Wagner (*b* Dresden, 18 Nov 1891; *d* Dresden, 12 June 1965) and Kurt Wagner (*b* Dresden, 26 Feb 1898), learned their trade in the family business, continuing their father's work in Dresden. From 1934 instruments bore the name Richard G. Wagner. In 1939 illness forced Gustav's withdrawal from the business. The factory was bombed in 1944. After World War II, Richard reestablished the business on a limited basis in Dresden. Kurt, who had concentrated on instrument manufacture and repairs, took over the firm on his brother's death, continuing it as a repair shop until 1980; no new instruments were made. In 1987 Norbert Walsch acquired Wagner's tools for use in his newly founded workshop. See H. Heyde: *Musikinstrumenten-Museum der Karl-Marx-Universität Leipzig, Katalog, vol.3: Trompeten Posaunen Tuben* (Leipzig, 1980).

NIALL O'LOUGHLIN/R

Wagner, Joachim (*b* Karow, nr Genthin, 13 April 1690; *d* Salzwedel, Altmark, 23 May 1749). German organ builder. He was probably taught by Matthias Hartmann of Magdeburg (a pupil of Arp Schnitger), and he worked for two years with Gottfried Silbermann in Freiberg, together with Zacharias Hildebrandt (from Silesia). In 1719 Wagner built his first organ (Marienkirche, Berlin). He then set up his business in Berlin and immediately became the leading Prussian organ builder. In the following 30 years he built nearly 50 organs, including several in Berlin (his largest being in the Garnisonkirche), Potsdam (Erste und Zweite Garnisonkirche), Brandenburg (Cathedral; extant), St Katharinen (Gotthardkirche), Magdeburg (Heiliggeistkirche), Wusterhausen (St Peter und Paul; extant), Angermünde (extant), and Trondheim Cathedral, Norway (extant). Wagner's highly individual style derives from his synthesis of north German and Silesian styles with that of Silbermann, combined with his own new ideas and inventions.

Wagner's specifications are based on that of the Silbermann organ in Freiberg Cathedral (1710–14); Wagner adapted this model according to the size of his organs and added new features. The specification of the Pedal organ is the same in his medium organs as in his large ones; therefore a coupler to pedal is not necessary. The Mixture in the *Hauptwerk* is a Scharff (Ger.: 'sharp', i.e. five ranks including a Tierce). If there is a Principal 16′ in the Pedal, there will also be a tapered Gembshorn 8′ in place of an Octava 8′. Usually there is a Quinta 6′ in the Pedal. All Wagner organs have a compass of *CD–c‴* in the manuals, and *CD–c′* or *d′* in the Pedal. Wagner's style was copied by his pupils Peter Migendt, Ernst Marx, and Gottlieb Scholtze (who completed Wagner's last organ at St Marien, Salzwedel, in 1751).

BIBLIOGRAPHY

J.F. Walther: *Die in der königlichen Garnisonkirche zu Berlin befindliche neue Orgel* (Berlin, 1727)

H.H. Steves: 'Der Orgelbauer Joachim Wagner', *AMf*, vol.4 (1939), 321–58; vol.5 (1940), 17–38

W. Bergelt: *Die Mark Brandenburg: eine wiederentdeckte Orgellandschaft* (Berlin, 1989)

W. Bergelt, D. Kollmannsperger and G. Raabs: *Joachim Wagner, Orgelmacher (1690–1749)* (Regensburg, 2012)

DIETRICH KOLLMANNSPERGER

Wagner, Johann Gottlob [Jean Théophile] (*b* Medingen, Lower Saxony, 4 June 1741; *d* Dresden, Saxony, 21 July 1789). German maker of keyboard instruments. His brother Christian Salomon (*b* Medingen, 1754; *d* Dresden, between 1812 and 1816) joined him in partnership in 1773. Together they introduced the *Clavecin roïal*, a square piano providing a remarkable variety of timbres and dynamic capabilities. It employs bare wooden hammers in a simplified version of Cristofori's action, omitting the check and the intermediate lever. Gottlob announced the new instrument in 1774; his report, reprinted by Forkel (1779), describes four pedals (knee-levers in extant examples) for making timbre changes (*Veränderungen*): (1) a so-called harp stop, lowering a fringe of cloth to mingle with the strings, giving a pizzicato effect; (2) engaging underdampers, normally disengaged; (3) a moderator, inserting soft leather tabs between the hammers and the strings; (4), a swell, lifting a cover, normally resting above the soundboard, to give a sudden *forte* or a crescendo. With none of these in use the instrument sounded like a harpsichord with dynamic capability. The underdampers could be engaged to control unwanted resonance. Engaging the underdampers alone gave a harp sound, while the moderator plus the harp stop imitated a lute. The moderator alone imitated the pantalon, while the moderator and underdampers together gave the sound of the pianoforte.

At least ten examples of the *Clavecin roïal* (some restored) survive, dating from 1783 to 1797, the latest two by Christian Salomon, and the last bearing the production number 805. Gerber relates that after Johann's death Christian made a three-manual harpsichord (1796), worked on a method of quilling harpsichords to make quill replacement unnecessary, and built a harpsichord that produced dynamic effects by lifting the lid, and made the sounds of the flute and the bassoon without using pipes.

BIBLIOGRAPHY

J.N. Forkel, ed.: *Musikalisch-kritische Bibliothek*, vol.3 (Gotha, 1779, repr. Hildesheim, 1964), 322–8

E.L. Gerber: *Neues Historisch-Biographisches Lexikon der Tonkünstler*, vol.4 (Leipzig, 1813/14, repr. Graz, 1966), 494

M.R. Latcham: 'The *Clavecin roïal* of Johann Gottlob Wagner in its eighteenth-century context', *Geschichte und Bauweise des Tafelklaviers*, ed. B.E. Hans Schmuhl and M. Lustig (Augsburg and Michaelstein, 2006), 127–84

MARGARET CRANMER/MICHAEL LATCHAM

Wagner, Johann Michael (*b* Schmiedefeld, 1727; *d* Schmiedefeld, 1801). German organ builder. With his brother Johann Christoph Wagner (*b* Schmiedefeld, *c*1725; *d* after 1770), Johann Michael (i) was the most prominent member of a family of organ builders resident over several generations in Schmiedefeld, Thuringia. In 1764 the brothers produced a claviorgan; evidently they also made harpsichords and clavichords. The family history is not completely clear. Other members active as organ builders in the same workshop were Johannes Wagner (1733–1804), Johann Michael (ii) (1760–99) and Johann Friedrich (the two sons of Johann Michael (i)), Johann Michael (iii) (1798–1876), and Johann Gottlob (1771–1800; not to be confused with the earlier piano maker of the same name in Dresden). At various times members of the family worked with other organ builders: Johann Michael (i) was with Hofmann in Gotha from 1741 to 1747, and from 1747 to 1751 he worked with Johann Caspar Beck (1703–74) of Herrenbreitungen on the rebuilding of the organ in the Stadtkirche, Laubach, Hessen. He also collaborated with Johann Caspar Holland on the organ of the Kreuzkirche, Dresden (1789), one of the greatest of the Wagner instruments. He served as court organ builder to the principality of Bernburg, although his application in 1755 for the same position in Altenburg, to succeed T.H.G. Trost, was unsuccessful.

The Wagner workshop in Schmiedefeld supplied organs as far away as Saxony and the Netherlands. The specifications of the Wagners' instruments display typical characteristics of central German organs of the 18th century: full Principal chorus, mutation stops, and relatively copious reeds, but also various flute stops. Mixtures contain the Terz. The Wagners made their cases in the Rococo style. One innovation of the Wagner brothers—the division of wind in the main wind trunk—became especially influential. Other organs by the Wagners (it is often not possible to ascribe instruments to particular family members) include those at Döschnitz (1750–1), St Marien, Suhl (1757–62), Vachdorf (1770), Schmiedefeld (1770), the Groote Kerk, Arnheim (1770; three manuals), and Gersfeld (1784–7). Johann Andreas Heinemann was a partner in the Wagner workshop before setting up on his own in Laubach.

BIBLIOGRAPHY

U. Dähnert: *Historische Orgeln in Sachsen* (Leipzig, 1980)

H. Fischer and T. Wohnhaas: *Lexikon süddeutscher Orgelbauer* (Wilhelmshaven, 1994)

H. Haupt: *Orgeln in Ost- und Südthüringen* (Bad Homburg, 1995)

FELIX FRIEDRICH/R

Wagner tuba. Brass instrument devised by Wagner for use in the *Ring* to provide a more solemn sound than that available from the horn. In form, *Tuben* (the common plural) follow the familiar Teutonic low-brass oval, with four rotary valves operated by the left hand, the fourth usually lowering by a perfect 4th. The compass of the tenor tuba in B♭ is E♭–f″; of the bass tuba in F, B♭–a′. The conical bore progresses gradually from a horn mouthpiece to a bell some 25 cm diameter. Wagner scored for a quartet of two tenors, played when required by the fifth and seventh horn players, and two basses, played by the sixth and eighth.

Wagner was possibly inspired by instruments he saw during an 1853 visit to Sax's Paris workshop. Schröder's Deutsches Horn has also been cited as a possible inspiration, but the Cornon, invented by Cerveny in 1844, has more similarities with the Wagner tuba and was present in Austrian military bands, which Wagner heard in Venice while working on the *Ring*.

The Tuben were not available for the Munich premieres of *Das Rheingold* in 1869 and *Die Walküre* in 1870, so the parts were played by military musicians on their normal instruments. The initial set of Tuben, made by Johann George Ottensteiner of Munich and first heard in a concert performance of *Götterdämmerung* in Vienna on 1 March 1875, established a reputation for problematic intonation (caused primarily by the long bell throat and consequent free-blowing characteristics) that has lasted to this day. Two years later Carl Moritz of Berlin provided another set, sometimes considered the first true Wagner Tuben but still presenting intonation problems. Those made by Gebr. Alexander in 1890 (first heard at Bayreuth) came to be considered the definitive design. Other European makers, notably Paxman of London, have also manufactured Tuben.

For the Lamoureux Concerts in Paris in 1888 Fontaine-Besson's cornophones were used, following earlier Parisian experiments using saxotrombas with 'pavillon reversible': a bell that could be swivelled to either a raised position (for loud passages) or floor level (for a subdued and mysterious sound). In London, where there had been unsatisfactory performances of *Ring* excerpts conducted by Richter in 1877, Henry Wood commissioned a set of instruments from Mahillon of Brussels. In saxhorn form, with four in-line Périnet (piston) valves operated by the right hand and normally a trombone mouthpiece, intonation was as secure as on any other valved bugle-horn. They might have been used in the Grand Wagner–Mottl concert at Queen's Hall in April 1894 and were certainly heard at the 1908 Norwich Festival. The instruments' ability to sound solemn, dignified, and heroic as stipulated by Wagner was shown when they were rediscovered in the early 1990s and successfully used in performances by the New Queen's Hall Orchestra. These were essentially Wagner tubas (and described as such at the time), their workaday saxhorn appearance contrasting strongly with the aesthetic qualities of true Tuben.

In the opera house, the Tuben are normally placed alongside the contrabass tuba and horns, with the trumpets (including bass trumpet) and trombones (including contrabass trombone) on the opposite side of the pit. In Wagner's scores, the Tuben are logically positioned above the contrabass tuba, but later composers have sometimes positioned them with the horns (above the trumpets). Wagner's vacillations over which transpositions to use for the instruments have led to significant problems for players and conductors, and there are passages over which there is still disagreement. Later composers have thus had to make decisions without the benefit of established practice. Wagner used five different transpositions.

Bruckner was next to utilize Tuben (in the 7th, 8th, and 9th symphonies), followed by Stravinsky (*Le Sacre du printemps* and *The Firebird*), Schoenberg (*Gurrelieder*), Strauss (*Elektra, Die Frau ohne Schatten,*

Alpensinfonie), and numerous minor Teutonic composers. They have also attracted the avant-garde (Lutyens, Henze), pop arrangers (Gene Page for the Motown Sound), and, from about 1964, film and television composers: it was claimed in 2002 that one out of every four American film scores stipulated Tuben.

The first double Wagner tuba, after the fashion of the double horn, was made in 1908 by Kruspe, and full double Tuben are now available, but it has been claimed that these lack the required contrast in timbre between the F and B♭ instruments. At Edinburgh University, acoustical investigations into influences on response, timbre, and intonation in the Wagner tuba and related instruments did not show particular problems with intonation, although later instruments performed better; the double Wagner tuba unexpectedly showed the greatest variation in brassy timbre between the two sides of the instrument. These scientific conclusions thus fail to confirm two of the characteristics commonly perceived by players: poor tuning and the double instrument's lack of differentiation between the F and B♭ sides. It may be fair to conclude that these perceptions result from the musicians' relative lack of familiarity with what is primarily a doubling instrument.

BIBLIOGRAPHY

R. Gregory: *The Horn: a Comprehensive Guide to the Modern Instrument and its Music* (London, 1961)

J. Webb: 'Mahillon's Wagner Tubas', *GSJ*, vol.49 (1996), 207–12

C. Bevan: *The Tuba Family* (Winchester, 2000)

W. Melton: *The Wagner Tuba: a History* (Aachen, 2008)

L. Norman, A. Myers, and M. Campbell: 'Wagner Tubas and Related Instruments: an Acoustical Comparison', *GSJ*, vol.63 (2010), 143–58

CLIFFORD BEVAN

Wagon [yamato-goto]. Six-string long zither of Japan. Its name (*wa/yamato:* 'Japan'; *gon/goto:* 'zither') reflects its accepted status as Japan's only indigenous stringed instrument. Before the importation of the *koto* from China about the 7th century, the word *koto* designated this instrument, which has changed little since the 8th century. Made of paulownia wood, it resembles the *koto* in general shape but narrows gradually from the player's left to right (from about 24 to 15 cm); its length ranges from 188 to 197 cm and its thickness from 4 to 8 cm. The strings converge towards the right, rather than remaining parallel as on the *koto*. Like the *koto*, the wagon has a movable tuning bridge for each string, is slightly convex laterally and is generally made of a hollowed upper part closed by a flat bottom. The *koto*-type bridges are made from the unpeeled forks of maple twigs, although nowadays actual *koto* bridges are sometimes used. Setting it apart from all other Asian long zithers is the row of six projecting 'teeth' at the left end, which serve as attachment points for the strings. These teeth may be squared off or petal-shaped. Each string is tied to a thick cord which is in turn attached to one of the teeth – a feature seen already on 8th-century models and presumably derived from Korea (as the *kayagûm* has the same feature).

The tuning is non-consecutive (re-entrant): one typical tuning is *d'–a–d–b–g–e* from the string nearest the player. Two main playing techniques are combined, both unlike any traditional *koto* technique. In one, all six strings are strummed with an oval plectrum in the right hand, and the left hand then damps all but one string. In the other, the left-hand fingers also pluck strings. A string is never pressed to the left of the tuning bridge to raise its pitch.

The Shōsōin, Japan's 8th-century imperial treasure-house preserves eight wagon, basically like the modern instrument in all essentials. Several had feet, as on the *koto*, indicating that they were placed on the floor as is usual today; this contrasts with evidence from 5th- to 6th-century *haniwa* funerary sculptures and 8th-century poetic references, which indicate that the instrument was placed on the lap. At least 15 archaeological specimens, mostly fragmentary, are known from sites dated between the 1st and 7th centuries; near both ends of that timespan there are examples from Kyushu and the Tokyo area, the two likely extremities of the contemporary distribution of Japanese-speaking people. When surviving, the projecting teeth are rectangular and have no string-hole, suggesting that the strings were tied around the teeth. The three earliest examples have six teeth and the two latest five, refuting the commonly held view that the five-string form developed into the six-string form. The earlier examples are all flat boards, although some had a resonating box attached along part or all of their length, from about 41 cm to 150 cm. All narrow towards the playing end. Some of the movable bridges have survived. The degree of craftsmanship varies tremendously, pointing to the use of the wagon at various levels of the social hierarchy. The longest example is the most elaborate and one of the earliest: found in Fukuoka, Kyushu, it is thought to date from the 1st or 2nd century. On its underside are neatly chiselled grooves to receive a box resonator, which does not survive but would have been about two-thirds the length of the instrument. Obviously of specialist manufacture, this instrument suggests, in the absence of earlier specimens within Japan, that it was at least influenced by a foreign model. (A roughly trapeziform instrument, possibly a type of zither, was found at the Nōso site, Mie Prefecture, which might date from the 2nd century BCE.)

Nearly 20 *haniwa* (small-scale, low-fired clay figures decorating tombs) from the late 5th to the 7th century depict wagon. The fact that all but one of these figures are from east Japan (the Kantō area) is due to the distribution of *haniwa* styles, not to the absence of wagon in west Japan, as archaeological evidence shows. In all clear cases but one the performer is a male and the wagon rests across his thighs. It often slants down to his left somewhat and/or tilts away from his body, recalling the playing positions of early Chinese zithers and of the Korean zithers *kayagûm* and *kōmun'go*. Difficulty in modelling the strings is presumably responsible for what seem to be three- and four-string versions. Often the player is using the left hand as well as or instead of the right, and in one case he holds a large oval plectrum in the right hand—a giant version of the modern plectrum. There is one well-modelled specimen of a wagon without a player: five clearly etched strings connect to the five teeth, apparently being tied around them. These strings run over a common lower bridge and are gathered into a small circular hole about a quarter of the way in from the right end. What might be the two sides of a resonator run along the underside, but the expected bottom panel is absent (if indeed any was intended). The resonator sides end just past the string-hole, resulting in a seemingly unnecessary extension of the top to the right beyond the bridge and resonator—a feature shared with some excavated examples and one specimen (in *J.NR.s*), but not with modern wagon. Also, the *haniwa* instrument has concave sides when seen from above; this feature occurs in one excavated example and the majority of *haniwa* ones, but again not in modem wagon.

Comparison with other East Asian long zithers fails to find a single likely parent for the wagon. Quite possibly the wagon was an indigenous invention, albeit inspired by earlier long zithers.

BIBLIOGRAPHY

W. Malm: *Japanese Music and Musical Instruments* (Tokyo, 2000) [incl. CD], 43–5

K Hayashi and others: *Shōsōin no gakki* [Musical instruments in the Shōsōin treasury] (Tokyo, 1967) [with Eng. summary]

E. Harich-Schneider: *A History of Japanese Music* (London, 1973)

E. Kikkawa: 'Genshi jidai no koto o kangaeni' [Thoughts on prehistoric koto], *Kikan hōgaku*, vol.18 (1979), 124ff

D. Hughes: 'Music Archaeology of Japan: Data and Interpretation', *The Archaeology of Early Music Cultures*, ed. E. Hickmann and D. Hughes (Bonn, 1988), 55–87

M. Mizuno: 'Kinkafu izen no koto' [*Koto* before the *Kinknfu*], *The Archaeology of Early Music Cultures*, ed. E. Hickmann and D.Hughes (Bonn, 1988), 128–41

DAVID W. HUGHES/R

Wahl, Jacob Valentin (*b* Landskrona, Sweden, 3 March 1801; *d* Landskrona, 26 Nov 1887). Swedish manufacturer of wind instruments in Landskrona. Wahl made instruments from 1818 and studied instrument manufacture in northern Germany from 1824 to 1826. From 1827 on, he was supplying Swedish regimental bands and musicians with flutes, clarinets, bassoons, keyed bugles, trumpets, and trombones. He employed up to 10 workers in the 1840s, including Olof Ahlberg and Lars Ohlsson. Wahl's early competitors included Johan Hägerström in Stockholm (a brass maker who received a privilege from the The Royal Swedish Academy of Music in 1818) and P.A. Carlsson (1779–1843; woodwinds and brasswinds) in Karlskrona. During the 19th century, woodwinds were usually imported to Sweden, or manufactured by Swedish woodworkers such as A.G. Swensson (1802–78) in Linköping.

From 1840, Wahl pioneered Swedish making of valved brasses, which were similar to Prussian models, with a narrow conical bell and wide bore, most often with 'Swedish fingering' (the third valve lowers the harmonic series by two tones, not 1½). Until the 1860s, his firm dominated brass instrument manufacture in Sweden. Wahl was succeeded by Hans Jacob Hasselgren (*d* ?Landskrona, 1905). In turn, Johan Fredrik Friberg and Nils Petter Johansson (*d* ?Landskrona, 1911) ran the business from 1905 until about 1910. Some of the firm's tools, patterns, business records, and a few surviving instruments are in the Landskrona Museum, Sweden.

BIBLIOGRAPHY

H. Nilsson: 'Instrumentmakare I.V. Wahl och hans verkstad', *Kulturens årsbok* 1942 (Lund, 1942), 77–111

A.-M. Nilsson: 'Brass Instruments in Small Swedish Wind Ensembles During the Late 19th Century', *Historic Brass Society Journal*, vol.13 (2001), 176–209

ANN-MARIE NILSSON

Waisvisz, Michel (*b* Leiden, Netherlands, 8 July 1949; *d* 18 June 2008). Dutch composer, inventor of instruments, and performer. He was self-taught. He became acquainted with electronics at the age of 16, when his father built a theremin. In the late 1960s he worked at the electronic music studio at the Royal Conservatory in The Hague. His music-theatre works, including *Avonden over jazz* (1975, with Maarten van Regteren Altena), *Mathilde bestelt een componeerapparaat* (1978, with Moniek Toebosch), *De slungels* (1981), and *Memories of the Waiscrack* (1982), often feature his instruments, which have also been frequently exhibited since 1974. From 1981 he was director of the Studio voor Elektronische Muziek in the Netherlands.

De Slungels was the first theatrical piece to be performed entirely by robots. Using these theatrical robots, Waisvisz studied both the relationship between man and machine and ways of improving the operation of electronic systems. An important step in this respect was the development of *De Handen* (hands), a sensitive instrument with which material stored in the computer can be played in real time. Variants on this same principle are *De MIDI-Conductor* (1985) and *Het Web* (1990), the latter a complex of wire sensors connected to a computer music system and manipulated by a single finger movement. Waisvisz also appeared with 'LiSa', a software instrument that is a live sampling system, controlled by *De Handen*. 'Operation LiSa' involves audience collaboration; sounds sampled from the audience are immediately turned into music.

Waisvisz's first instrument was a tape recorder playback head mounted on a stand, past which lengths of pre-recorded magnetic tape are moved backwards and forwards manually. From 1969 he developed the *Kraakdoos* (cracklebox), which is based on the instability of electronic circuits, usually considered undesirable. Waisvisz constructed a number of electronic instruments based on this principle, in which the performer connects parts of a specially designed oscillator circuit by means of body resistance. This tactile approach offers a great range of precise control and more complex sound structures than are possible with one comparable conventional oscillator. The idea underlying these interactive instruments or 'gestural controllers' is that, just as with acoustic instruments, the physical action of making music must be visible to the public. In view of the great importance he attached to interaction with the public and to a refined and dynamic quality of sound, on principle he never published any work on CD.

While he was developing the Kraakdoos Waisvisz also modified a Putney synthesizer – by adding a special set of controls resembling a keyboard – so that it could be played in a similar way: he performed on this until his own crackle synthesizer was completed in 1974. In 1975 Waisvisz developed a light-screen based on the technique of graphic sound.

Waisvisz applied the cracklebox principle not only to concert instruments but also to his music theatre performances: *De electriciteit* (1974) includes an electrified fencing match in which sparks and loud crackles are produced and cause changes on a television monitor; in the children's piece *Violen Paultje* (1977, with Toebosch and Maurice Horsthuis) an 'American violin' in the shape of a machine gun has a single string as well as crackle touch-plates to make appropriate noises. Other constructions include a large fly with aluminium foil wings, which contains a buzzing electrical circuit that is switched on and off as required, and the Aanraker (1978), a small musical stage on which the bare feet of the two performers make connections between large touch-plates (contact between the performers also affects the sounds). Waisvisz also devised a number of theatrical 'props' based on the cracklebox, such as a group of dynamo-powered units mounted on a bicycle, and crackle systems controlled by a modified cuckoo clock, by pressure pads concealed under mats, and by wired cutlery and crockery. Waisvisz elaborated this theatrical side in appearances with diverse musicians and artists.

BIBLIOGRAPHY

M. Waisvisz: *De Kraakdozentenioonstelling* (Amsterdam, 1975) [exhibition catalogue]; section trans. as 'The Cracklebox Project', *Musics*, no.7 (1976), 7

F. Lagerwerff: 'Michel Waisvisz en het cultuuronderzoek van deze tijd', *Jazz nu* (1979), 193ff

HUGH DAVIES, JACQUELINE OSKAMP/R

Wait [wayt, wayte] (from Old Fr. *gaite*, a watchman; Arabic *ghayṭa*, a shawm).

(1) Watchman at the gate of a town or castle, or a household watchman, who commonly used a horn or shawm to signal the approach of people requiring admittance, but the watchman was not a musician.

(2) By extension, a civic minstrel permanently employed by a town, equivalent to the German *Stadtpfeifer* and the civic pipers of Italy and elsewhere. At first they formed the standard loud band of two or three shawms and a slide trumpet (later, a sackbut); it was probably their use of the shawm that led to the name 'waits' being attached to them. At the time of their institution at Beverley (1405) and Norwich (1408) the term 'wait' was still applied to any player of the wayte-pipe (3).

(3) An instrument of the shawm family; sometimes called 'wayte-pipe', it probably derived its name from the household wait (1) who played it. The seal of Edward III's *vigilator* John Harding clearly shows crossed shawms, but their size is not ascertainable. The wait is almost certainly the treble shawm, perhaps to be identified with the 'small pipes' of the *Black Book of the Exchequer*.

BIBLIOGRAPHY

L.G. Langwill: 'The Waits: a Short Historical Study', *HMYB*, vol.7 (1952), 170–83

G.R. Rastall: *Secular Musicians in Late Medieval England* (diss., U. of Manchester, 1968)

R. Rastall: Review of D. George, ed.: *Lancashire*, Records of Early English Drama (Toronto, 1991), *ML*, vol.74 (1993), 417–21

RICHARD RASTALL/R

Waji [wuj]. Chordophone of Nuristan (formerly Kafiristan), eastern Afghanistan. It is played by people of Dardic heritage and language but there is no record of its being used by the Dards on the Pakistan side of the border. It consists of a string holder (a relatively thick, bow-shaped piece of wood) and a boat-shaped wooden resonator, pointed at both ends but flat-bottomed and waisted, which is covered with a skin laced by thick thongs. The skin might be pierced with several soundholes. The string holder passes through two holes in the centre of the skin and projects upwards on either side; it appears to be supported by the skin alone, but in some cases is braced by double cords that pass around the ends of the resonator and the bow and are wound tight by wooden pins tucked into the holes. There are two main shapes, sizes, and tunings. On the smaller model, roughly one-third of the almost semicircular bow projects upwards to the front of the instrument and two-thirds to the rear. There are four strings that pass through holes near the lower front end of the bow (here somewhat flattened) and are held by knotting; at the other end they pass over small knobs to thick tuning loops or cords hung with long tassels and wound around the bow. One four-string model has been said to be tuned to a Phrygian tetrachord: $e'-f'-g'-a'$. On the larger size, which has five strings, the arch of the bow is more gradual and the lower front end rests more flatly on the skin.

The waji is held diagonally across the left side of the body and is cradled on the outside by the left arm. The right hand strums the strings with a small wooden plectrum, while the left fingers deaden the unwanted strings in different homophonic patterns. The waji is probably a direct descendant of the ancient Indian bow harp; it is possible that the name itself derives from the Sanskrit *vādya* through Prakrit *vajja* ('instrument'). The *waji* is played as a solo instrument and to accompany song. See T. Alvad: 'The Kafir Harp', *Man*, vol.54 (1954), 151–4.

ALASTAIR DICK

Waka-pinkillo. Duct flute of Bolivia. It is made of cane about 45 to 50 cm long and 2.5 cm in diameter, with two fingerholes and one thumbhole, and a square opening at the duct. Overblowing produces multiple harmonics. It is held by and played in the left hand and may be used together with a *caja* or *wankara* (*huncara*), a small double-headed drum suspended from the little finger of the left hand and struck with a stick in the right hand. It is used to accompany the *waka-waka* (or *waka-thokhori*) dance, which simulates a bullfight, and other agricultural dances performed at Carnival. It was perhaps brought to Bolivia by the Spaniards.

The *waka-waka* is a similar duct flute of Irpa Chico, 30 km south of La Paz, Bolivia. It is also used to accompany agricultural dances, all apparently of post-Contact origin.

J. RICHARD HAEFER

Walch. German family of woodwind makers. About 50 makers of this name are documented between 1610 and 1873, and instruments by at least seven of them are known. Their output included recorders, French flageolets, double recorders, transverse flutes, tabor pipes, walking-stick flutes, *deutsche Schalmeis*, oboes, and clarinets, as well as toy instruments and other turned wooden objects. The known instrument makers were born in Berchtesgaden and died there or in nearby Bischofswiesen. The attribution of marks to individual family members is often doubtful, and only that of Paul Walch is documented with certainty.

Instruments of the Walch family made during the 17th and 18th centuries largely conform to German and Austrian traditions. Older instrument types such as the tabor pipe and *deutsche Schalmei* were made longer in Berchtesgaden than elsewhere. In the 19th century the focus shifted towards making instruments for folk music. Original models were developed, including the *berchtesgardener Fleitel*, a narrow-bore variant of the Baroque recorder, which survived into the 19th century as a folk instrument. In all types of recorder and flute made by the family, a great variety of sizes and tunings is notable.

(1) Augustin Walch (i) (*b* c1610; *d* 4 April 1678), son of Bartholomäus Walch (*b* 1644), was documented in 1652 as 'woodwind instrument maker at Aschahlehen, married, five children, one servant'. Most instruments with the mark 'A: WALCH' are attributed to him. According to the style of construction, however, they may be attributable to Augustin Walch (ii) (*b* 28 Feb 1668) or his brother Andreas (*b* 20 Nov 1672).

(2) Georg Walch (*b* 31 Oct 1690; *d* 1769), brother of Augustin (ii) and Andreas, lived at the inn *Zum Siegel auf der Stanggass*. He acquired master's rights as a woodwind maker in 1716. Most instruments marked 'G: WALCH' are attributable to him, except a double recorder dated 1662 and other instruments older in style. Among the surviving instruments marked G: WALCH are recorders, tabor pipes, transverse flutes, clarinets, and an oboe. He is thought to be the earliest maker of a clarinet d'amour or alto clarinet.

(3) Lorenz Walch (*b* 10 Aug 1735; *d* 19 April 1809), son of (2) Georg Walch. He learned the craft in his father's workshop and became a master flute and recorder maker. Instruments with the mark 'L: WALCH' are attributed to him. His surviving instruments include recorders, double recorders, transverse flutes, tabor pipes, and *deutsche Schalmeis*.

(4) Johann Georg Walch (*b* 1 Dec 1764), oldest son of (3) Lorenz Walch. Instruments marked 'IG. WALCH' are attributable to him or to an earlier Johann Georg Walch (*b* c1688). Because of their early style of construction, recorders and a tenor oboe are attributed to the earlier Johann Georg.

(5) Andreas Walch (*b* 9 Nov 1777), son of (3) Lorenz Walch and brother of (6) Lorenz Walch. At his marriage to Gertrud Aschauer (14 Feb 1803), he was named as a master flute (and recorder) maker and prospective owner of the *Siglerlehens* (perhaps his grandfather's property, with similar name, mentioned above). The mark 'ANDRÉ WALCH/BERCHTESGADEN' on transverse flutes and clarinets is probably his.

(6) Lorenz Walch (*b* 6 June 1786; *d* 24 Feb 1862), son of (3) Lorenz Walch and brother of (5) Andreas Walch. From 1808 he was owner of the *Rosspointlehen in der Stanggass*. At his wedding in 1809 he was described as a master flute (and recorder) maker. He and his ten children worked in a shop associated with the following marks: 'LORENZ WALCH' with a rosette or cloverleaf, and 'LORENZ WALCH/BERCHTESGADEN', with a cloverleaf or five-petal flower. These marks are found on recorders, flageolets, a double recorder, tabor pipes, a cane flute, and clarinets.

(7) Johann Paul Walch (*b* 18 Sept 1810; *d* 16 Sept 1873), son of (6) Lorenz Walch. He took over his father's property, the *Rosspointlehen*. He was probably the last instrument maker of the family. Three marks are seen on his known instruments: 'PAUL WALCH' with a star; 'PAUL WALCH/BERCHTESGADEN' with a rosette; and 'PAUL WALCH/BERCHTESGADEN' with a crown and star, the last probably used after 1849. Surviving instruments include recorders, flageolets, tabor pipes, piccolos, walking-stick flutes, and clarinets.

(8) Lorenz Walch (*b* 25 Nov 1811; *d* 18 Feb 1881), son of (6) Lorenz Walch and brother of (7) Johann Paul Walch. Zimmermann attributed instruments marked 'LORENZ WALCH/BERCHTESGADEN' to him, but the style of surviving instruments led Bruckner to attribute them to (6) Lorenz Walch.

BIBLIOGRAPHY

J. Zimmermann: 'Die Pfeifenmacherfamilie Walch in Berchtesgaden: Ein Beitrag zur Geschichte der Holzblasinstrumente', *Zeitschrift für Instrumentenbau*, vol.57 (1937), 175–7, 200–2
H. Bruckner: 'Die Pfeifenmacherei in Berchtesgaden', *Tibia*, vol.4 (1979), 289–96
G. Dullat: *Verzeichnis der Holz- und Metallblasinstrumentenmacher auf deutschsprachigem Gebiet von 1500 bis Mitte des 20. Jahrhunderts* (Tutzing, 2010), 489–91

PETER THALHEIMER

Walcker. German family of organ builders. The firm was founded in 1780 in Cannstadt by Johann Eberhard Walcker (1756–1843). His son Eberhard Friedrich Walcker (*b* Cannstadt, 3 July 1794; *d* Ludwigsburg, 2 Oct 1872) moved the business to Ludwigsburg (Württemberg) in 1820. Eberhard's op.1, a small one-manual organ (1821), is preserved in the Ludwigsburg castle chapel. In 1833 he completed a large new organ for the Paulskirche in Frankfurt am Main, representing a new tonal concept with a large variety of flue stops of varied timbre and volume, extended with free reeds and several expressive devices, and two pedalboards (a design he would use in several large organs). The success of this organ brought him important commissions even abroad, such as those for St Peter's Lutheran Church, St Petersburg (1840), and St Olai's, Tallin (1842). He introduced the cone chest (*Kegellade*) in 1840 and used this system exclusively from 1842 onwards. In 1842 he formed a partnership with Heinrich Spaich (*b* 21 June 1810; *d* 1908), his associate since 1834, creating the firm E.F. Walcker & Spaich. Large instruments of this period were built for the Stiftskirche in Stuttgart (1845), Zagreb Cathedral (1855), Ulm Minster (1856; 100 stops), the Music Hall, Boston (1863), and St Etienne, Mulhouse, Alsace (1866; highly esteemed by Albert Schweitzer).

Walcker's two eldest sons, Heinrich (*b* Ludwigsburg, 10 Oct 1828; *d* Kirchheim unter Teck, 24 Nov 1903) and Fritz (*b* Ludwigsburg, 17 Sept 1829; *d* Ludwigsburg, 6 Dec 1895), became associates in 1857 (when the company was renamed E.F. Walcker & Cie.), followed by Karl (*b* Ludwigsburg, 16 March 1845; *d* Stuttgart, 19 May 1908) in 1872, and in 1887, when Spaich's partnership ended, by Paul (*b* Ludwigsburg, 31 May 1846; *d* Frankfurt an der Oder, 6 June 1928) and Eberhard (*b* Ludwigsburg, 8 April 1850; *d* Ludwigsburg, 17 Dec 1926). After Eberhard Friedrich's death, the firm was run by his sons, and organs were built for the Saalbau, Frankfurt (1872), the Votivkirche in Vienna (1878), Riga Cathedral (1884), the Petrikirche, Hamburg (1884), the Neues Gewandhaus, Leipzig (1884), and the Stephansdom, Vienna (1886). The firm began using tubular-pneumatic action in 1889 and electropneumatic in 1899. In 1916 the firm of Wilhelm Sauer in Frankfurt an der Oder (managed since 1910 by Paul Walcker) became the property of the Walcker family but was continued under Sauer's name; his most notable organ, made in 1913 for the Jahrhunderthalle, Breslau (now Wrocław), is now in Wrocław Cathedral.

Oscar Walcker (*b* Ludwigsburg, 1 Jan 1869; *d* Ludwigsburg, 4 Sept 1948), a grandson of Eberhard Friedrich, while interested in architectonic and tonal aspects of the organ, also successfully represented the firm's business interests. The almost 2000 organs built under his direction, when the number of employees increased to more than 200, include those at Reinoldikirche, Dortmund (1909), Michaeliskirche, Hamburg (1912), the musicology institute of the University of Freiburg im Breisgau (the 'Praetorius' organ, 1921, with Willibald Gurlitt), City Hall, Stockholm (1925), the Exposición Internacional Barcelona (1929), and the Kongresshalle, Nuremberg (1936). In 1916 Oscar succeeded Paul as manager of Wilhelm Sauer, but daily oversight was given to Karl Ruther (*b* Überlingen, 7 Nov 1867; *d* Ludwigsburg, 24 Nov 1956). Oscar Walcker took an eager interest in the Alsatian *Orgelbewegung*, which advocated mixtures and mutations on all keyboards, but he

retained an interest in Swell divisions. He was made an honorary DPhil for his work on the 'Praetorius' organ, which turned his interest towards the German *Orgelbewegung*. During the 1930s Walcker built a few tracker organs and developed, in cooperation with Hans Henny Jahnn, a two-manual tracker chamber organ with slider chests (a 'series' instrument).

In 1948 Oscar's grandson Werner Walcker-Mayer (*b* Ludwigsburg, 1 Feb 1923; *d* Saarbrücken, 13 Nov 2000) began running the firm. Under his management output grew to about 3200 organs, among them those for Ulm Minster; Zagreb Concert Hall; the Mozarteum, Salzburg; the concert hall for the Gesellschaft der Musikfreunde, Vienna; the Stiftskirche, Stuttgart; the Liszt Academy of Music, Budapest; the Bogotá concert hall; Trinitatiskirche, Berlin; Göttweig Abbey; Zagreb Cathedral; Methodist Temple, Evansville, Kentucky; First Baptist Church, Toccoa, Georgia; the Chopin Academy of Music, Warsaw; and St Peter's Catholic Church, Sinzig (1972; specially designed for the performance of avant-garde music). Walcker-Mayer also reconstructed the antique Roman Aquincum (Hungary) organ's pipes and published his findings as *Die römische Orgel von Aquincum* (Stuttgart, 1970; Eng. trans., 1972).

In 1965 Walcker-Mayer founded the Walcker-Stiftung für Orgelwissenschaftliche Forschung, which still exists and which organizes symposia and publishes books. He received the honorary doctorate from the Albert-Ludwigs University, Freiburg im Breisgau, in 1980. The firm moved from Ludwigsburg to smaller premises at Murrhardt-Hausen in 1974 and again in 1985 to Kleinblittersdorf, Saarland. Large projects were carried out in collaboration with a sister company (independent from 1986) founded in 1957 and from 1961 onwards based in Guntramsdorf, near Vienna. In 1999 the Walcker firm in Germany went bankrupt; by then almost 6000 instruments had been built. Of Werner Walcker-Mayer's four sons who previously worked in the company, Gerhard (*b* Ludwigsburg, 3 July 1950) started his own business in 1988 in Saarbrücken and Michael (*b* Ludwigsburg, 5 May 1957) continued the Guntramsdorf shop as his own company from 2000. In 2011 Gerhard was joined in his business by his son Alexander under the new name E.F. Walcker Orgelbau GmbH, thus connecting his firm to the Walcker company heritage broken by the bankruptcy of 1999.

From 1945 onwards, the Wilhelm Sauer Orgelbau was led by Anton Spallek, in 1966 succeeded by his son Gerhard. The company was nationalized in 1972 by the German Democratic Republic, but was returned to the Walcker firm in 1990, and a new workshop was built in Müllrose. From 2000, after the bankruptcy of the German Walcker company, the Sauer company was continued under the direction of Peter Fräßdorf (*b* Frankurt an der Oder, 29 Sept 1944).

BIBLIOGRAPHY

O. Walcker: *Erinnerungen eines Orgelbaumeisters* (Kassel, 1948)

J. Fischer: *Das Orgelbauergeschlecht Walcker in Ludwigsburg* (Kassel, 1966)

H.H. Eggebrecht, ed.: *Orgelwissenschaft und Orgelpraxis: Festschrift zum zweihundertjährigen Bestehen des Hauses Walcker*

(Murrhardt-Hausen, 1980) [incl. H. Fischer and T. Wohnhaas, 'Eberhard Friedrich Walcker (1794–1872)', pp.160–97]

F. Moosmann and R. Schäfer: *Eberhard Friedrich Walcker (1794–1872)* (Kleinblittersdorf, 1994)

H. Fischer: 'Die Orgeln der Paulskirche', *Von der Barfüßerkirche zur Paulskirche: Beiträge zur Frankfurter Stadt- und Kirchengeschichte*, ed. R.Fischer (Frankfurt/Main, 2000), 401–21

H.J. Busch: 'Das "leuchtende Dreigestirn": Die Werkstätten Ladegast, Sauer und Walcker und der deutsche Orgelbau des 19. Jahrhunderts', *Die Düdelinger Kirche und ihre Stahlhut-Orgel, mit Beiträgen über Kirchenkunst, Orgelbau und Orgelmusik sowie einer Monografie über die Orgelbauer Georg und Eduard Stahlhut* (Dudelange, 2002), 165–84

Organ, Journal für die Orgel (2003, no.2): special issue devoted to E.F. Walcker, with a report on the international Walcker symposium held in Schramberg, 26–8 Sept 2002

HANS KLOTZ/THEODOR WOHNHAAS/PAUL PEETERS

Waldhorn (Ger.). Hunting horn. Wagner (*Tannhäuser*) and Brahms (Trio, op.40) used the term Waldhorn to specify a valveless horn. Waldhorn also sometimes denotes a folk oboe made of conically wrapped bark secured with a stick or thorns piercing the wider end. As an organ stop from the mid-19th century the Waldhorn was usually a reed of 8′ or 16′ pitch, but the name was also applied, earlier and later, to certain powerful flute ranks, and at 4′ or 2′ pitch it is sometimes synonymous with *Waldflöte*.

LAURENCE LIBIN

Waldorf Electronics GmbH [Waldorf Music GmbH]. German manufacturer of synthesizers and other electronic musical instruments, founded in Waldorf (near Bonn) in 1988 by Wolfgang Düren, who was previously the German distributor for the audio synthesizer firm PPG (Palm Products GmbH). Waldorf Electronics was declared insolvent in February 2004, but was reformed as Waldorf Music GmbH in 2006.

Waldorf technology was based on the PPG Wavecomputer developed from 1980 by Wolfgang Palm. Their Microwave Synthesizer was released in 1988, followed in 1992 by the Wave and in 1995 by the Pulse, a monophonic analogue synthesizer. The popular Q, a digital signal processor-driven vir+tual analogue synthesizer, was released in 1999. The PPG Wave 2.V, a virtual reconstruction of the earlier Wave 2.3 synthesizer, was released in 2000. The 2002 RackAttack is Waldorf's percussion synthesizer. The business's revival in 2006 brought the Zarenbourg electric piano, which is based on a sampled Steinway Model B grand and distinctively has wooden keys. In 2007 the relatively small Blofeld synthesizer was introduced at a lower price point; a keyboard and samples were added in 2008. Waldorf produced the entirely software-based virtual synthesizer Largo, for both Macintosh and Windows PC platforms, in 2009. Partnering with Rolf Wöhrmann of TempoRubatos, Waldorf released a wavetable synthesizer for the iPad in 2012. Waldorf technology has been incorporated into products by Digidesign Inc. (USA), Terratec (Germany), TC Works Soft- und Hardware (Germany), and Steinberg Media Technologies AG (Germany).

Waldteufel (Ger.: 'forest devil'). Whirled friction drum, used as a toy. It is a small container like a tiny drum or tin can with one end open, and a cord passed through one or two closely spaced holes in a membrane covering the opposite end. The cord is looped around a handle by which the can is whirled, producing a growling sound as vibration caused by friction of the cord against the rosined handle is transmitted to the membrane. These noisemakers are usually made by the player and have also been produced commercially, for example in Markneukirchen in the late 19th century.

Walet-hkok [walet-chaùng]. Clapper of Myanmar. It is made from a piece of bamboo approximately 90 to 120 cm long, split in half and narrowed down most of its length, leaving a short split section full-width at the top, and another short section whole at the bottom to hold the two halves together and act as a hinge. The player grips the narrowed lengths, one half in each hand, and strikes the top sections together. The walet-hkok marks the beat in the *hsaìng-waìng* ensemble and in smaller ensembles such as the *ò-zi* (goblet drum) and *dò-bat* (double-headed drum) groups.

JOHN OKELL

Walker. English firm of organ builders. Joseph William Walker (*b* London, 17 Jan 1803; *d* London, 1 Feb 1870) was reputedly 'parlour apprentice' to George Pike England in London; he worked with W.A.A. Nicholls (England's successor) and then set up business as a pipe maker. He built his first organ in 1827 and established his own business in 1828, first in Soho, then on Tottenham Court Road, London. Joseph Walker's instruments are notable for their full-toned diapasons and bright upperwork; most had one or two manuals but he built larger organs for the Exeter Hall (1839), Highfield Chapel, Huddersfield (1854), and the International Exhibition of 1862. Under his youngest son and successor, John James Walker (*b* 21 Aug 1846; *d* 19 Sept 1922), the firm secured a series of prestigious contracts including Holy Trinity, Sloane Square, London (1891), St Margaret's, Westminster (1898), and York Minster (1903). All these instruments were characterized by a restrained opulence in which fully developed flue choruses coexisted with strings, orchestral reeds, and bright flutes.

The firm played a significant part in the reform of English organ building after 1945. Influenced by collaborations with Ralph Downes at Buckfast Abbey, Devon (1952), and Brompton Oratory (1954), the typical Walker organ of the period had a neo-classical tonal scheme and electropneumatic action. Examples include the Italian Church, Hatton Garden, London (1959), Corpus Christi, Osmondthorpe (1962), Ampleforth Abbey (1963), Liverpool Metropolitan Cathedral (1967), and Blackburn Cathedral (1969).

The Walker family retained control until the death of the founder's grandson Reginald Walker, MBE. In 1975 J.W. Walker & Sons Ltd, reconstituted under management of Robert Pennells, a previous employee, moved its premises from Ruislip, Middlesex, to Brandon, Suffolk; since then it has increasingly concentrated on building new mechanical-action instruments (Albert Hall, Bolton, 1985; St Martin-in-the-Fields, London,

1990; St Chad's Cathedral, Birmingham, 1993). Pennells was joined in the business by his son, Andrew Pennells (*d* 1999), who had been apprenticed to Klais Orgelbau in Bonn. After Robert Pennells retired, Sebastian Meakin, a former Walker apprentice also trained in Germany, took over direction of the firm, which has added premises in Devises, Wiltshire. Overseas installations include more than 90 in the USA since 1984, and Adelaide Town Hall (four manuals, 61 stops).

Surviving organs from the earlier phase of the firm's history include those at St Mary's, Bermondsey (1853), Romsey Abbey (1857 and 1888), St Cross Hospital, Winchester (1863 and 1907), St Mary's, Portsea (1891), Bristol Cathedral (1907), and the Church of the Sacred Heart, Wimbledon (1912 and 1935).

BIBLIOGRAPHY
C. Clutton and A. Niland: *The British Organ* (London, 1963/*R*, 2/1982)
R. Downes: *Baroque Tricks* (Oxford, 1983)
N.J. Thistlethwaite: *The Making of the Victorian Organ* (Cambridge, 1990)

NICHOLAS THISTLETHWAITE/R

Walking-stick instrument (Fr. *canne à musique*; Ger. *Spazierstockinstrument*). Walking sticks (canes) that incorporate whistles, rattles, and other simple musical instruments are plentiful, often unsigned, and difficult to date. Because of their convenient shapes, flutes and other woodwinds are especially numerous as walking-stick instruments. The death inventory of Henry VIII lists 'ten fluttes … caulled pilgrim staves'. A cane recorder by Richard Haka (*c*1646–1705) is at the Gemeentemuseum in The Hague. As with weapons, parasols, and other devices melded with canes, novelty was valued in all such instruments; the woodwind maker George Brown advertised 'German cane flutes, for the accommodation of those gentlemen that wou'd recreate themselves abroad' (*Dublin Courant*, 16 Jan 1747). Combination flute/oboe walking sticks by members of the Scherer family (*fl* Butzbach, 1711–78) are in the Metropolitan Museum of Art, New York, and the Hessisches Landesmuseum, Darmstadt. Ulrich Amman (1766–1842) was renowned for making cane flutes, often decoratively carved; a cane clarinet (*F.P.cm*) and a combination cane flute/clarinet (*D.N.gnm*) by him survive. A walking-stick trumpet signed by C[ornelius] Steinmetz (Dresden, 1723–80), is reportedly preserved.

Romantic connotations of nature and music were often conjoined in walking-stick instruments. The protagonist in Ludwig Uhland's poem 'Das Schifflein' (1810) 'unscrews the cap of his walking stick and joins the tones of the flute with the din of the horn'. Dozens of makers, including Doke, Merklein, Schölnast, and J.T. Uhlmann, produced walking-stick flutes, recorders, flageolets, harmonicas, and ocarinas during the 19th century. Clarinets survive by Felchin, Pourcelle, and Sauerhering, and a basset horn by Strobach of Carlsbad. A bagless chanter and drone by P. Hutcheson survives; the player blows into both through a central stock. Most surviving walking-stick trumpets are bent double and valveless, although some late models have small valves and associated coiled tubes.

Walking-stick clarinet in B♭, 8-key Continental, c1850. (Edinburgh University Collection of Historic Musical Instruments (142))

Adelung's *Grammatisch-kritisches Wörterbuch der Hochdeutschen Mundart* (Leipzig, 1801) defined *Stockgeige* (*Stockfidel*) as a small, narrow violin in the shape of a stick or staff. Usually the violin forms the body of the stick; a removable cover protects the strings and bridge, and the handle often serves as a chin rest that can be unscrewed so that the small bow can be stored inside the body. An example by Moritz Wilhelm Glaesel survives (in *US.B.mfa*). In a rarer version from 18th-century France, the violin is removed from the hollow cane for playing. Walking-stick violins were offered by Markneukirchen makers into the 1920s, about the time that walking sticks in general passed from fashion. In 18th-century Hungary the *csákányfokos* combined an iron hatchet with a duct flute; the later *csakan* or *Stockflöte*, also popular in Austria, was a flageolet in the shape of a walking stick. Musical accessories found in canes include music stands, conductor's batons, kazoos, tuning hammers, tuning forks, and sirens.

BIBLIOGRAPHY
H. Moeck: 'Spazierstockinstrumente: Czakane, Englische und Wiener Flageolette', *Festschrift to Ernst Emsheimer on the Occasion of his 70th Birthday*, ed. G. Hilleström, Studia instrumentorum musicae popularis, vol.3 (Stockholm, 1974), 149–280
C. Dike: *Cane Curiosa: From Gun to Gadget* (Paris and Geneva, 1983), 123–43
M. Betz: *Der Csakan und seine Musik: Wiener Musikleben im frühen 19. Jahrhundert dargestellt am Beispiel einer Spazierstockblockflöte* (Tutzing, 1992)

TONY BINGHAM, JAMES B. KOPP

Walpen. Swiss family of organ builders. They were active over three generations in the Valais and central Switzerland, in frequent collaboration, initially, with the Carlen family. Johannes Martin Walpen (*b* Reckingen, Switzerland, 1723; *d* Reckingen, 1782 or 1787) was a son of the master tanner Andreas Walpen (1698–1739) and of Cäcilia (née Carlen; 1699–1779), a sister of Matthäus Carlen, the founder of the Carlen family business. He worked exclusively in the Valais, frequently in collaboration with Carlen. He had three sons: Joseph Ignatius Walpen (1761–1836) was also an organ builder in Reckingen; Johannes Sylvester Walpen (*b* Reckingen, 1767; *d* Lucerne, 1837) married Katharina Carlen (*b* 1766), daughter of the organ builder Felix Carlen, and moved in 1802 to Lucerne, where he lived until his death; Wendelin Walpen (*b* Reckingen, 1774) settled eventually as an organ builder in Sierre. The families that remained in the Valais died out or gave up organ building as a profession, but the Lucerne branch flourished. Sylvester Walpen (1802–57), son of Johannes Sylvester, enjoyed a high reputation in central Switzerland. His brother Georg Walpen (1810–51) was active only as an assistant.

The Walpens built very traditional, purely mechanical slider-chest organs, and even in the 19th century followed 18th-century principles of construction throughout. A stylistic peculiarity of the cases is the curving cornices over the side panels of the front. There is no systematic study of the life and work of the Walpen family, and the attribution of certain organs—and even their precise differentiation from the Carlen ones—is difficult and often a matter of dispute.

Organs built or rebuilt by the Walpens include those by Johannes Martin at Reckingen (1746), Naters (1761), and Münster (1776–81); by Johannes Sylvester at Meiringen (1789), Frutigen (1809), Beatenberg (1812), and at St Martin, Chur (1816); by Sylvester at Ringgenberg (1827), Grindelwald (1838), Luthern (1839), Walchwil (1845), Habkern (1846), Frauenthal (1851), Risch (1854), Unterseen (1854), Ufhausen, and in St Leodegar und Mauritius, Lucerne (choir organ); and by Wendelin at Raron (1837–8) and Saint Martin, near Sion (1840).

BIBLIOGRAPHY
R. Bruhin: 'Die Orgeln des Oberwallis', *Vallesia*, vol.15 (1960), 179–230
R. Bruhin, ed.: 'Das Traktat von 1752 des Johannes Walpen aus Reckingen über den Bau von Orgeln und Instrumenten', *Vallesia*, vol.26 (1971), 187–226
R. Bruhin: 'Die Orgelbauer Walpen aus Reckingen (Goms)', *Blätter aus der Walliser Geschichte*, vol.18 (1982), 83–98

FRIEDRICH JAKOB

Walter, (Gabriel) **Anton** (*b* Neuhausen an der Fildern, nr Stuttgart, 5 Feb 1752; *d* Vienna, 11 April 1826). Austrian piano maker of German birth. He was the most famous Viennese piano maker of his time. He was in Vienna by 1780, when he married the widow Schöffstoss. In 1790 he was granted the title 'Imperial Royal Chamber Organ Builder and Instrument Maker'. About 1800 his stepson Joseph Schöffstoss joined the firm, by then employing up to 20 workmen. Of the instruments produced, dating from about 1780 to 1825, approximately 3% survives, comprising about 20 pianos built before 1800 and an equal number after that date. The former are usually inscribed 'Anton Walter in Wien' to which is added 'u(nd) Sohn' in the latter. Several museums and private collections preserve playable instruments by Walter.

If Johann Andreas Stein invented the German action (with hammers mounted in wooden pivot forks on the keys, combined with a hammer escapement mechanism with upright hoppers), Walter was probably the first to develop it. He thus configured the Viennese action (with brass pivot forks and forward-leaning hoppers), adding a back-check to catch the returning hammers, thereby preventing the unwanted rebound that could occur with the new configuration. The oldest pianos (*c*1785) by Walter that survive in original condition have this Viennese action, which became standard in Walter's pianos after about 1790, and in Viennese pianos generally. Contemporary sources, including one of Beethoven's letters, attest to the mechanical and musical qualities of Walter's pianos.

The firm was highly regarded in musical and aristocratic circles throughout the Hapsburg empire until about 1810, after which his instruments were overshadowed, first by those of Nannette Streicher and then by those of Conrad Graf. Walter's current fame rests on Mozart's having acquired a Walter piano about 1782. This instrument was radically altered by Walter about 1800. As with his other early pianos, it is not known when its present action was installed, or when the knee levers (for the dampers) replaced the original hand stop. For these reasons Mozart's piano should not be relied upon as evidence when discussing the performance of his music.

BIBLIOGRAPHY
M.R. Latcham: 'Mozart and the Pianos of Gabriel Anton Walter', *EMc*, vol.25 (1997), 382–400
S. Berdux and S.Wittmayer: 'Biographische Notizen zu Anton Walter', *Mitteilungen der internationalen Stiftung Mozarteum*, vol.48 (2000), 13–106
M.R. Latcham: 'Johann Andreas Stein and Anton Walter. A comparison of two piano makers', *Early Keyboard Journal*, vol.24 (2006), 39–68
R. Steblin: 'Anton Walter's Difficult Early Years in Vienna: New Documents, 1772–9', *JAMIS*, vol.33 (2007), 42–83

MICHAEL LATCHAM/R

Walter Piano Co. [Charles R. Walter Piano Company] American firm of piano makers, founded by Charles R. Walter (*b* Watseka, IL, 8 May 1927). The son of a baker, Walter graduated from the University of Illinois in engineering physics (1947) and in 1964 joined the C.G. Conn Company, where he became head of the piano division. Conn at that time produced Janssen upright pianos; when these were discontinued, in 1969, Walter took over their production in Elkhart, Indiana. He and his wife began to produce well-regarded console pianos under his own brand—Charles R. Walter—in 1975, making two models, about 109 cm and 114 cm tall. They remain the foundation of the company's output and are characterized by very strong back posts, either a Renner or a Chinese-made 'Walter' action (the latter in the less expensive models), and longer keys than in most consoles for more grand-like touch and control. The soundboard and bridge design allows the bass strings to be the same length as on a typical 173-cm grand. In 1991, the company introduced fine grand pianos of 170 cm and 190.5 cm lengths, designed by Delwin Fandrich. Each grand soundboard rib is individually crowned according to its position on the board as well as being mortised into the inner rim. The grands have Renner actions and feature adjustable hitchpins allowing precise adjustment of bearing on the bridge. Like the consoles, the grands are available in a variety of furniture styles. All pianos feature solid brass hardware, including the pedals.

The company is a family organization run by Charles Walter and his wife, with several next-generation members and spouses on the staff. Every piano is checked out and signed by a family member before shipping.

EDWIN M. GOOD/R

Wamsley [Walmsley, Warmsley], **Peter** (*fl* London, *c*1725–45). English maker of violins, violas, and cellos. Although the foremost English maker of his time, following Daniel Parker and Nathaniel Cross, his reputation suffered with the publication of Sandys and Forster's *The History of the Violin*, in which his instruments were criticized for having had the wood worked too thin. The repetition of this allegation has tended to obscure his considerable merits as a maker.

Wamsley was evidently a pupil of Cross, and inherited from him a respect for the work of Stainer and for a pleasing pale golden varnish of rather brittle consistency. Later he developed a much softer dark brown oil varnish, quite satisfactory from the tonal viewpoint and similar in all but colour to that used by the Forsters in the second half of the century. In his woodwork he was one of the makers who exaggerated Stainer's archings by hollowing out too much towards the edge, but in thus leaving his edges thin in wood he was doing no worse than near-contemporaries such as Rombouts in the Netherlands, most of the Florentines and dozens of fine German and Austrian makers. In the relatively few instances where his instruments have not been treated harshly by the passage of time, they are both handsome in appearance and of fine quality tonally. His numerous cellos are the forerunners of an English

school of making which is often regarded by players as second only to the best of the Italians. He made quite a number of violins, and also a few violas of good size.

Wamsley's shop, at the sign of the Harp and Hautboy in Piccadilly, was taken over by his pupil, Thomas Smith. Another pupil was Joseph Hill, perhaps the most successful London maker of his time, and the first of the Hill dynasty of violin makers and experts.

BIBLIOGRAPHY
W. Sandys and S.A. Forster: *The History of the Violin* (London, 1864)
W.M. Morris: *British Violin Makers* (London, 1904, 2/1920)

CHARLES BEARE/JOHN DILWORTH

Waniguchi. Bell of Japan. The name refers to the instrument's form: *wani* (crocodile); *guchi/kuchi* (mouth); it is also called *kinko* ('metal drum') and *uchinarashi* ('struck sound'). It is a circular, vertically suspended vessel made of bronze, copper, or iron, shaped like two gongs joined together, with a narrow bulging opening (the mouth) along the lower half of the circumference, with two circular, or near circular, projections, one at each end of the mouth. While made in various sizes, it is typically about 20 to 30 cm in diameter and several centimetres deep. It is suspended within a wooden frame by cord from two metal rings joined to the upper part of the rim. It is struck on the outside by a thick rope beater that hangs in front of and central to the playing side, which is usually decorated with symbolic markings consisting of a central striking point, concentric lines, and other symbols. The player swings the rope so that a padded part of it strikes the central point. Alternatively, it is occasionally struck by a padded beater held in the player's hand. The oldest known waniguchi is dated 1001, and it is first mentioned in the *Meitokuki* (*c*1394), which chronicles the Meitoku war (1391–94). At Shintō shrines and Buddhist temples, visitors can strike the waniguchi to call a deity. A version of the waniguchi is used in offstage kabuki music to represent the instrument's normal religious context.

BIBLIOGRAPHY
J. Okazaki, ed: *Butsugu daijiten* [Dictionary of Buddhism] (Tokyo, 1982)
E. Kikkawa, ed.: *Zusetsu nihon no gakki* [Japanese musical instruments, illustrated] (Tokyo, 1992)

HENRY JOHNSON

Waning [laba wai, wani, laba]. Drum of Flores, Indonesia. It has a cylindrical wooden body, often closed at the bottom, and one goatskin head affixed by leather straps attached to a counterhoop. The head is tuned by moving wooden pegs placed between the straps and the body of the drum. Two are used in the *gong waning* ensemble in the central Sikka region: the larger *waning inan*, about 35 cm in diameter and 60 cm long, played with a bare hand and a stick in the other hand, and the smaller *waning anak*, about 25 cm in diameter, played with two sticks. The drums lie on the ground, the musicians sitting upon them. The ensemble includes up to five medium-sized, shallow bossed gongs (*gong* or *go*) ranging from 35 to 20 cm in diameter and named, from low to high pitch: *inan, depun, beit, udon,* and *anak.* Single gongs are held in the left hand and struck with a rubber-padded mallet held in the right, performing rapid interlocking patterns; the gong is damped against the chest. These patterns are semi-improvised, the higher gongs being allowed more freedom. One or two larger suspended gongs may be added to play slower ostinatos. A bamboo time keeper (*saur*) is laid upon the ground and struck in rapid alternation with two unpadded wooden sticks to signal the beginnings of passages, while the waning cues their ends. In the Sikka region the *gong waning* ensemble accompanies social dances, often performed by women twirling scarves. Singers may spontaneously join the ensemble. Kunst suggests that a xylophone (*do'u da*) of five bars hung vertically upon two strings is added to a similar gong and drum ensemble in the Manggarai region.

BIBLIOGRAPHY

J. Kunst: *Music in Flores* (Leiden, 1942)

P. Bos: *Biographies of Florenese Musical Instruments and Their Collectors* (Amsterdam, 1995)

P. Yampolsky: disc notes, *Music of Indonesia 8; Vocal and Instrumental Music from East and Central Flores,* Smithsonian Folkways SFW CD 40424 (1995)

ANDREW C. MCGRAW

Waning anak. Idiochord tube zither of the Sikka area of Flores, Indonesia. Its seven strings are raised from the cortex of an old stout bamboo tube about 50 cm long. Each string is raised by a bridge at both ends. It is played together with a *letor* (xylophone).

MARGARET J. KARTOMI

Wanj. Arab harp of the 7th to 10th centuries. The name was taken into Arabic from the Pahlavi (*wann*) through two lines of al-A'shā (d 625): 'Chinese *mushtaq, wann* and *barbat* to which a *ṣanj* answers if it starts to hum', and 'the *ṣanj* has sounded ['*azafa*] to which the call of the *wann* replied' (variants on a proclamation by the page of King Xhusraw Parviz, 590–628, on musical instruments). Usage has maintained the literary association of the two terms, which explains the transfer of the suffix modifying *wann* to *wanj.* The wanj is likened to the *ṣanj* as it is a harp; this juxtaposition of similar or related instruments seems to be characteristic of Near Eastern thought. The historian Ṭabarī (d 923), discoursing on instruments, attributed them to Tūbīn (or Tūbāl), son of Lamak, 'who was the first to play the wanj and the *ṣanj*'. This reversed order appears in early Arab translations of *Daniel* where the orchestra of Nebuchadnezzar includes 'wanj and *ṣanj*'; subsequent versions give '*rabāb* and *sanṭīr*'. The substitution of *wanj* by *rabāb* accentuates the semantic erosion of the term. Syriac lexicography shows an identity of wanj, *jank* (*chang*), *ṣanj*, and ten-string harp (Payne-Smith: *Thesaurus syriacus,* 1876–1901, 'Qiṭoro'). Late references to the wanj come from the end of the 9th century ('the music of the people of Khurasān and their neighbours was with the *muwannaj* and upon it were seven strings. And its rhythm was like the rhythm of the *ṣanj*: H.G. Farmer, 'Ibn Khurdadhbih on Musical

Instruments', *Journal of the Royal Asiatic Society*, 1928, 511) and in the 10th century (al-Khwārizmī: 'as for the *ṣanj* which is a stringed instrument ... it is the *wanj*'; Farmer, *Science of Music in the Mafātīḥ al-'Ulūm*, London, 1959, 3). According to Jāhiz (*Kitāb al-Tāj*, Paris, 1954, 53), players of the wanj were hierarchically at the bottom of the social scale, in the third category, among the jokers and buffoons, along with those of the *ma'azif*.

Arab lexicographers have broadened the context and blurred the instrument's identity as a harp, for example Ibn Manẓūr (14th century): 'The wanj is the *mi'zaf*, the *mizhar*, the '*ūd*, it is a kind of *ṣanj*' (Lisān al-'Arab, 'wanj'). Although recorded by later Arab lexicographers, the term has been abandoned in favour of *jank*, because *ṣanj* (initially meaning a harp) was transformed into percussion. In the 18th century it was introduced into Western musical lexicography: J.B. de La Borde (*Essai sur la musique*, Paris, 1780) identified *wann* with psaltery and *wenedge* with lute. Probably the instrument never existed in Arab culture except as a substitute for *ṣanj*. But the term should be noted for its place in Iranian culture: the historical line shifted from Khorasān to Nuristan (Afghanistan) where, in the late 19th century, it was noted in field research as a four-string bow harp: *wuj* or *waj*, or *wanz, waji,* or *vaj,* corruptions of *wann* and wanj.

BIBLIOGRAPHY

G.S. Robertson: *The Kafirs of the Hindu-Kush* (London, 1896)

H.G. Farmer: 'The Instruments of Music on the Taq–i Bustan Bas Reliefs', *Journal of the Royal Asiatic Society* (1938), 397–412 [repr. in *Studies in Oriental Musical Instruments*, 1978]

J. Robson: 'The Kitāb al-malāhi of Abū Ṭālib al-Mufaddal ibn Salama', *Journal of the Royal Asiatic Society* (1938), 231–49, esp. 244

M. Ḥusayn: *Dīwān al-A'shā* [Complete poetic works of al-A'shā] (Cairo, 1950)

H.G. Farmer: 'The Music of Islam', NOHM, vol.1 (1957/R1975), 421–78

H. 'Alī Mahfūz. *Qāmūs al-mūsīqā al-'Arabiyya* [Dictionary of Arab music] (Baghdad, 1975)

J. Jenkins and P. Rovsing Olsen: *Music and Musical Instruments in the World of Islam* (London, 1976)

P. de Tarrazi: *Syria's Golden Age* (repr., Aleppo, 1979), 67 only

CHRISTIAN POCHÉ

Wankara [wankarita]. Two-headed log drum of the Bolivian Alti Plano. It is about 50 cm in diameter and about 15 cm deep; the heads, of goat or sheep hide, are laced together in a V pattern. It has a snare (*chariera*) across the bottom head made from animal intestines to which cactus spines can be attached to amplify the resonance. It is played with a drumstick (*baqueta, wajta*) about 30 cm long tipped with a 7-cm hide ball. The drum accompanies Quechua ensembles of *pinkillos* (duct flutes), *sikuris* (panpipes), *lakitas* (panpipes), or *paceños* (end-blown notched flutes). The drums are played in groups of seven in the *sikuri* ensembles.

The similar *pfutu-wankara* is a higher-pitched, double-headed log drum about 60 cm deep and 45 cm in diameter. The drum stick is similar to that of the *wankara* but with a smaller leather ball. Indians and mestizos use these drums in the dance of the *tundiquis* from La Paz, to imitate rhythmic patterns brought by black slaves to Bolivia.

The *wankarita*, also called *retuela*, is about 30 cm in diameter and 60 cm deep. The two heads are laced together in a V pattern with a secondary cord around the middle of the drum. It is played with two sticks about 30 cm long, the top 10 cm wrapped in leather. It is used in *kena*, *chokela*, and *pinkullu* ensembles. See M.P. Baumann: 'Music of the Indios in Bolivia's Andean Highlands', *The World of Music*, vol.25/2 (1982), 80–98.

J. RICHARD HAEFER

Wa:pk kuikuḍ End-blown flute of the Tohono O'odham (Papago) Indians of southern Arizona and northern Sonora, Mexico. It consists of two internode sections of *wa:pk* ('river cane', *Phragmites communis*) and about 4 cm of each adjoining section for a total length of 48 to 55 cm and 2.5 to 4 cm diameter. The two end nodes are perforated, but the centre node is left intact and is bridged by a rectangular hole cut in the side of the instrument and covered with a piece of cloth or leather. Three fingerholes are cut in the lower portion of the flute. The index finger of the left hand is placed over the cloth or leather to help direct the air over the internal partition, thus creating a flue for the passage of air, and allowing for minor adjustments in the airstream. The fingerholes are controlled by the right hand.

One does not 'play' the flute but rather 'sings' it. Although the cane flute may have been used as a courting instrument and in the *wi:gita* (harvest) ceremony, it is more often played for self-entertainment. O'odham flutes are decorated in geometric patterns burnt into the exterior surface of the cane. The Akimel O'odham (Pima Indians) historically had a similar instrument.

The Yuman flute, *wĭlwĭl'tĕlhuku'p*, named after a small bird, the *wĭlwĭl*, has three to five fingerholes and is longer (70 cm) than the *wa:p kuikud*. Traditionally the Yuman flutes were played by two or three young men to attract the attention of a young lady. The Apache *sul* has three to five fingerholes. It is normally of cane ('giant reed', *Arundo donax*), but substitute materials such as metal pipe or gun barrels were used in the late 19th century. Although played as a courting instrument, it is also used for self-entertainment. The traditional Diné (Navaho) *ńdilnih* was made of cane or a mature sunflower stalk 25 to 60 cm long and 3 cm diameter, with four to six fingerholes. The pith was removed and the holes burnt with a hot iron rod. The flute was reportedly a toy, used by young girls while grinding corn, or used as a courting flute by young men. The modern Diné instrument is derived from that of the Ute and is similar to the Plains-style *siyotanka*; made from cedar, redwood, or other hard wood, 45 to 55 cm long and 3 to 4 cm in diameter, with six fingerholes and a carved animal-shape wind-stop.

BIBLIOGRAPHY
F. Russell: *The Pima Indians: Twenty-sixth Annual Report of the Bureau of American Ethnology* (Washington, DC, 1905)
C. Kluckhohn and others: *Navaho Material Culture* (Cambridge, MA, 1971)
J.R. Haefer: *Musical Thought in Papago Culture* (diss., U. of Illinois, Urbana, 1981)

MARY RIEMER-WELLER/J. RICHARD HAEFER

Warbo Formant-Orgel. Electronic keyboard instrument (not an organ) developed in Hamburg in 1937 by Harald Bode with the German violinist Christian Wamke; the title 'Warbo' was derived from their names. The console, which resembled a small upright piano, had a 44-note keyboard that was only partially polyphonic—a maximum of four notes could sound simultaneously. This was the first application of the technique of 'assignment', now common in certain types of synthesizer, in which only a selection of the keys depressed at any time (in this case the four highest) are connected to the oscillators that produce the sound. A choice of two complementary timbres, produced by means of formant filters, was available, and they could be assigned to any pairing of the four voices; two volume pedals enabled the performer to balance the two channels. Variable envelope control permitted a choice of attacks that included percussive qualities. Some 50 knobs and switches controlled these functions. About 1939 Bode, assisted by Oskar Vierling, developed a version of the instrument with a second manual and a 30-note pedalboard, both of which were monophonic.

BIBLIOGRAPHY
H. Bode: 'Bekannte und neue Klänge durch elektrische Musikinstrumente', *Funktechnische Monatshefte* (1940), no.5, 72 only
T. Rhea: 'Harald Bode's Four-Voice Assignment Keyboard (1937)', *Contemporary Keyboard*, vol.5/12 (1979), 89 only

HUGH DAVIES

Ward, Cornelius (*b* ?Liverpool, *c*1796; *d* London, 1 Feb 1872). English maker of woodwind and percussion instruments. He is reputed to have been a music seller in Liverpool from about 1805 to 1811, but references in the city directories are possibly to another Ward family, active in the instrument-making firm (R.J.) Ward & Sons (Liverpool, *fl* 1848–1931). He has also been confused with a different Cornelius Ward (1814–1903), who was an organist and composer.

By 1815 Ward was a foreman with the flute-making firm of Monzani & Hill, and in 1818 he was reportedly making flutes for Drouet at 20 Conduit Street. From 1836 to 1859 he had his own instrument-making business at 36 Great Titchfield Street, and during that period he made his greatest contribution to instrument development. In 1859 he was at 87 Portland Road and after 1860 he moved to 172 Great Portland Street, where his business was last recorded in 1870. While working for Monzani & Hill in 1830 Ward was commissioned by Chevalier Anne-Toussaint Florent Rebsomen, who had lost his left arm in battle, to make a flute that could be played with the right hand only. Ward's flute, a professionally made version of an earlier instrument made by Rebsomen himself, is a masterpiece of ingenuity.

Ward was supposedly making flutes as early as 1819; his models are documented with certainty from 1831. About 1831 Ward claimed to have made a flute under the direction of Captain J.C.G. Gordon, who had also had a flute made in Theobald Boehm's workshop. A later controversy, in which it was claimed that Boehm had plagiarized Gordon's invention, appears to have been stoked by Ward, who stated that 'Gordon is entitled to most credit in the affair'. The controversy was ended in favour of Boehm.

In 1842 Ward was producing a version of Boehm's 1832 flute system. Also in 1842 Ward patented his own system, with a fully vented mechanism, with open G♯ and open D♯ keys, and with foot-joint keys operated by wires attached to keys for the left thumb. Despite his exquisite craftsmanship, the flute was not a commercial success. Ward's 'Terminator' was a cam-operated device to move the stopper in the flute's headjoint to compensate for the extension of the tuning slide.

In 1837 Ward concentrated on the tuning of timpani, patenting a system of cable tensioning operated by a single handle and linked to a pitch indicator. At the same time he patented devices for tensioning heads of side and bass drums, replacing rope with screw tensioning. In 1853 he patented the Cymbal Drum for combined bass drum and cymbal effects.

Ward introduced the needle spring, a significant development in woodwind instrument manufacture, to England in 1842 (it first appeared in Paris, c1837). Examples of Ward's clarinets are known, and, under the guidance of Giuseppe Tamplini (1817–88), principal bassoonist at Her Majesty's Theatre from 1847, Ward was the first to apply Boehm's system to the bassoon. These bassoons, with 23 covered holes, were first exhibited at the Great Exhibition of 1851, the year of their French patent. Tamplini's influence led him to obtain a British patent in 1853. Tamplini exhibited two of these bassoons at the International Inventions Exhibition of 1885.

BIBLIOGRAPHY

G. Tamplini: *Brevi cenni sul sistema Bohem [sic] e della sua applicazione al fagotto* (Bologna, 1888)

R.S. Rockstro: *A Treatise on … the Flute* (London, 1890, rev. 2/1928)

J. Blades: *Percussion Instruments and their History* (London, 1970, rev. 3/1984)

C. Ward: 'The Flute Explained' (1844), *Readings in the History of the Flute*, ed. R. Bigio (London, 2006)

J. Lancaster and P. Spohr: 'The Extraordinary Chevalier Rebsomen', *Pan: the Journal of the British Flute Society*, vol.27/1 (2008), 25–41

GRAHAM MELVILLE-MASON/ROBERT BIGIO

Warren. Canadian family of organ builders and organists, of American origin. Samuel Russell Warren (i) (*b* Tiverton, RI, 29 March 1809; *d* Providence, RI, 30 July 1882) trained as an organ builder with Thomas Appleton of Boston, with whom he worked sporadically during the early 1830s. In 1836 he emigrated to Montreal, where a year later (after a short-lived partnership with George W. Mead) he formed his own firm to build pipe organs and harmoniums, eventually selling pianos, seraphines (reed organs), accordions, and flutes as well. His brother, Thomas D. Warren (1815–63), was also an organ builder, working with Appleton from 1836, briefly becoming a full partner under the name Appleton & Warren (1847–50) before joining his brother in Montreal.

Samuel became the outstanding figure in 19th-century Canadian organ building. He was the first in Canada to use Harmonic Flutes, free reeds, and orchestral stops, and he was the first to adopt the Barker lever (c1851) and hydraulic bellows (1860–61; at the Wesleyan Chapel, Montreal). His patents include one for a piano and several for improvements to the organ. He built more than 350 organs all over Canada and the USA, although only a handful are extant unaltered. These can be found in Chambly, Quebec; Frelighsburg, Quebec; Clarenceville, Quebec; and Dorchester, New Brunswick. A four-stop melodeon dating from about 1865 is at the Sharon Temple Museum, Sharon, near Toronto.

His youngest son, Charles Sumner Warren (*b* Montreal, 30 Nov 1842; *d* Rochester, NY, 5 July 1933), became his partner in 1876 under the name S.R. Warren & Son. Another son, Samuel Prowse Warren (*b* Montreal, 18 Feb 1841; *d* New York, 7 Oct 1915), was a noted organist, a teacher in New York, and a co-founder of the American Guild of Organists.

Charles moved the firm to Toronto in 1878. Extant organs from this period include those at St Michael's Cathedral, Toronto (1886), and Deschambault, Quebec (1892). In 1896 he sold the business to Dennis W. Karn but continued to work for him; in 1898 the firm moved to Woodstock, Ontario. Charles's sons, Frank Russell Warren (1867–1953), Samuel Russell Warren (ii) (1892–1965), and Mansfield Warren (dates unknown), also worked in organ building until the late 1940s; they founded a separate company, the Warren Church Organ Co., in 1907, also in Woodstock, and built the Chautauqua organ the same year.

BIBLIOGRAPHY

S.R. Warren: *Réponse au sujet de la construction, de l'examen des rapports et des certificats concernant la réception de l'orgue de l'église paroissiale de Montréal …* (Montreal, 1864)

P. Jennings: 'Samuel P. Warren', *Music* [Chicago], vol.17/Nov–April (1899–1900)

'In Memory of S.P. Warren', *The Diapason*, vol.7/2 (1 Jan 1916)

H. Kallmann, G. Potvin, and K. Winters, eds.: *Encyclopedia of Music in Canada* (Toronto, 2/1992)

K.J. Raudsepp: 'The Warrens', *The Tracker*, vol.43/1 (1999), 9–26

KARL J. RAUDSEPP/R

Warren, Kenneth. American firm of violin dealers and repairers. It was founded in Chicago in 1926 by Kenneth James Warren (*b* Erie, PA, 24 Sept 1899; *d* Chicago, IL, 2 June 1985). He studied with the violinist Leon Samatini at the Chicago Musical College and began a career as a professional player, before becoming head of the violin department of the Chicago branch of the Rudolf Wurlitzer Co. In 1948 his son Kenneth Nelson Warren (*b* Chicago, IL, 8 April 1929; *d* Floral City, FL, 16 March 1990), who trained with the violin maker John Hornsteiner, joined him in his business, which became Kenneth Warren & Son; in 1968 Kenneth N. Warren's son James Anthony Warren (*b* Chicago, IL, 15 May 1953) also entered the business, three generations thus being active in the firm. It became one of the most important and respected dealers and appraisers for old violins in the USA, and its repair department was outstanding. Among the master craftsmen who have worked for the department were John Hornsteiner, Zenon Petesh, and Tchu Ho Lee. The firm also made violins; in 1975 it established the Kenneth Warren & Son School of Violinmaking, which was sold in 1982 to become the Chicago School of Violinmaking. In that year the firm moved from its original offices on Jackson Street to South Dearborn Street, and it moved again in 2013 to North Wells Street.

PHILIP J. KASS

Wasamba. Sistrum of the Maninka people of Guinea and the Manding peoples of Mali. It is an L-shaped frame strung with calabash discs. The rattle is used by circumcised boys for dance rhythms.

Washboard. Scraped idiophone in the form of a domestic washboard or scrubbing board: a corrugated panel, usually of wood, metal, or molded glass, against which wet clothes are rubbed to loosen dirt. Its use as a rhythm instrument supposedly originated among African Americans in the 19th century, but it is also used in Europe, for example in Lithuania where it is called *skalbimo lenta*. It is played by scraping a nail, fork, or thimbles over the corrugations to produce a loud, staccato rhythm. Cowbells, woodblocks, and improvised metallophones are often attached to add tonal variety. Some washboard players place two boards back to back and sit astride them while playing with both hands. Washboard bands were instrumental groups in which a single washboard player supported the rhythm. Early washboard bands included string instruments and were frequently augmented by other improvised instruments such as a washtub bass (probably derived from the African ground bow), comb-and-paper, or kazoo, as well as a harmonica. They were closely related to children's 'spasm bands' of New Orleans. Typical performances by folk washboard bands are *Diamond Ring* (1930) by Walter Taylor and the Washboard Trio, and Chasey Collins's *Atlanta Town* (1935). Washboards were frequently used to accompany blues vocalists, and at least one singer, Washboard Sam (Robert Brown), played a washboard while singing, as on his *Rack'em Back* (1938) or *Levee Camp Blues* (1941).

Almost alone among folk instruments the washboard sometimes appeared in jazz bands, examples being Floyd Casey's crisp and forceful rhythms on numerous Clarence Williams recordings, including *Beer Garden Blues* (1933), and Jimmy Bertrand's driving

Washboard, Besson & Co, c1935. (Edinburgh University Collection of Historic Musical Instruments (2129))

accompaniments to Louis Armstrong and Erskine Tate's large 'Vendome Orchestra' on *Stomp Off, Let's Go* (1926). In the early 1930s the related groups of The Washboard Rhythm Kings and Washboard Serenades recorded extensively, often with two trumpets and three reed instruments. In the 1950s the washboard was the favoured rhythm instrument of 'skiffle bands', but its novelty soon declined and the instrument returned to the folk idiom of blues. *Zydeco* (music of Afro-French Creoles of rural southwest Louisiana and Texas) bands frequently used washboards after World War II. A later development was the wearing of a corrugated metal vest, played with thimbles. Cleveland Chenier was the most notable exponent of this technique, as on *Zydeco et pas sale* (1965) by his brother, accordionist Clifton Chenier.

BIBLIOGRAPHY

P. Oliver: 'Jug and Washboard Bands', *Jazz on Record*, ed. A. McCarthy (London, 1968)

C. Seemann: 'Washtub Bass', *Sing Out!*, vol.22/4 (1973), 14–15

J. Broven: *South to Louisiana: the Music of the Cajun Bayous* (Baton Rouge, 1983)

B. Rust: 'Clarence Williams Jug and Washboard Band', Philips 13653 A-JL [disc notes]

PAUL OLIVER/R

Washburn, George. Trademark of the Lyon & Healy Co. of Chicago, a musical merchandise business founded in 1864 by George Washburn Lyon and Patrick J. Healy. 'George Washburn' was applied to their own manufacture of high-quality guitars from 1883, mandolins and zithers from 1885, banjos from 1892, and ukuleles from 1915. About 1928 the trade name 'George Washburn' and the musical merchandise activities other than piano and harp manufacture were acquired by the Tonk Bros. Co., which continued to sell instruments under the name into the 1930s. The Tonk Bros. Co. was acquired by C.G. Conn Ltd in 1947.

In 1973, the trade name and production inventory was purchased by Beckman Musical Instruments, the American distributor for the Japanese electronics firm Roland. It was again sold in 1977 to the Chicago firm Fretted Industries, Inc., which in 1978 announced the production in Japan of instruments bearing the Washburn name. After Rudy Schlacher bought out co-owner Rick Johnstone's share of Fretted Industries in 1987, the firm became known as Washburn International, marketing a wide range of guitars, other string instruments, and sound equipment under the Washburn, Oscar Schmidt, Soundtech, and Randall trade names. At the end of the 20th century most of the production was based in Korea, with some instruments at the top end of the range manufactured in the USA. In 2003, Washburn International purchased U.S. Music Corp. and adopted the acquired company's name.

BIBLIOGRAPHY

J. Teagle: *The Washburn: Over One Hundred Years of Fine Stringed Instruments* (New York, 1996)

H. Pleijsier: *Washburn Prewar Instrument Styles* (Anaheim Hills, CA, 2008)

JAY SCOTT ODELL/ARIAN SHEETS

Washint. End-blown flute of Ethiopia. It is made, usually by the player, of a kind of bamboo (*schembeko*) in various lengths and pitches, and has four to six equidistant fingerholes, with any unused ones covered with adhesive paper. It is held obliquely, blown against the straight rim, and played traditionally by male shepherds in the Amhara and Tigray regions, often to improvise luxuriant ornamentations on folk melodies. It is also used for war songs and entertainment songs. The use, tuning and repertory of the washint were modified during the 1960s when it was brought to Addis Abeba and entered the orchestra of the National Theatre. To be able to play the four traditional pentatonic anhemitonic scales (*tizita*) of northern and central Ethiopia, a washint player needs four flutes with different, unequidistant fingerhole arrangements. He might have seven sizes of each flute (one for each key from A to G) in order to match the range of singers. Nowadays the washint is also played in urban ensembles with singers, lyre (*krar*), one-string fiddle (*masenqo*), and *kabaro* drums; the string instruments tune to the pitch of the washint.

BIBLIOGRAPHY
Musical Instruments of Ethiopia. Catalogue of the Collection of the Ethiopian Museum of the Institute of Ethiopian Studies (Addis Abeba, 1999)
C. Lacombe: *De la tradition au folklore: une représentation de la diversité musicale éthiopienne dans les 'traditional restaurants' d'Addis-Abeba, Ethiopie*, thesis, St Etienne University, France (2009)
CLAIRE LACOMBE

Washtub bass. Improvised chordophone consisting of an inverted metal washtub (which acts as a resonator), with a string attached at one end to the tub's bottom and at the other end to a long upright stick such as a broom handle; different pitches are obtained by moving the stick to vary the tension on the plucked string. It was played in the 1920s and 30s in Afro-American blues and jug bands. The similar tea-chest bass, using a large wooden box as the resonator, was used by British skiffle groups in the 1950s and 60s. Both types have counterparts among the South Asian variable tension chordophone group. The related *tura* of the Marquesas Islands is made of a large can or plastic container with a long stick and a string of fishing line. It is used to accompany informal singing at parties.

LAURENCE LIBIN, JEREMY MONTAGU

Wasp. Small analogue–digital hybrid synthesizer designed by Chris Huggett with rock musician Adrian Wagner and manufactured between 1978 and 1981 by their firm, Electronic Dream Plant (EDP), in Combe, near Oxford. The Wasp was also briefly available in kit form. This synthesizer has a two-octave, solid, monophonic 'keyboard' with pitch-bend and portamento controls; the diatonic keys, knobs, and lettering are yellow on a black background, to match the instrument's name. For a real keyboard, it substitutes flat copper plates under a printed vinyl sticker. The conductive plates sense skin capacitance to trigger the associated pitches. The Wasp contains two oscillators, a white-noise generator, a filter, and an envelope shaper, and offers various voltage-controlled features, as well as a small built-in loud speaker and sockets for connecting to other EDP products. The circuitry incorporates a digital pitch-coding system which facilitates links with other devices, including microcomputers. In its shiny black plastic case and with batteries in place, the Wasp weighs only 1.8 kg (a deluxe version with wooden case and conventional keyboard is heavier but still easily portable). Although relatively inexpensive, small, and rather fragile, the Wasp was powerful and versatile for its time and developed an enduring following. EDP developed a still smaller model, the Gnat, with one oscillator and pulse width modulation, and the Caterpillar, a three-octave keyboard controller with four-voice polyphony. Other EDP creations included the Keytar, a guitar controller based on the Wasp, which was never produced, and a microcomputer-based 252-step sequencer called the Spider.

In 1981 Adrian Wagner left the company to form Wasp Synthesizers Ltd, which produced a small number of slightly modified Wasps and Gnats. The rather rapid demise of the EDP in 1982 after an initial success in opening up a new market was at least partly the result of competition from several Japanese companies with mass-production facilities. Huggett went on to found the Oxford Synthesizer Company, where he created the more sophisticated OSCar synthesizer, with Paul Wiffen and Anthony Harris-Griffin. The OSCar has a three-octave keyboard and dual oscillators and is an early example of a programmable synthesizer with an arpeggiator and a step sequencer. Huggett worked next on the S1000 sampler for Akai and then joined Novation where he designed synthesizers and controllers including the SuperNova.

BIBLIOGRAPHY
'Industry Profile: Electronic Dream Plant Limited', *Electronics and Music Maker* (May 1981), 70
C. Carter: 'EDP Wasp', *Sound on Sound* (Feb 1995) (<http://www.soundonsound.com/sos/1995_articles/feb95/edpwasp.html>)
HUGH DAVIES/ANNE BEETEM ACKER

Water drum. Percussion instrument that exploits the special sound-conducting qualities of water.

(1) A single-headed drum of the North American Indians and the Chaco and Guaycurú Indians of Argentina and Paraguay, having as a distinctive feature a

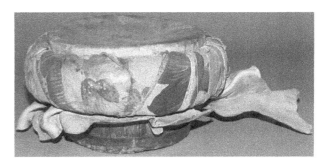

Iroquois water drum, c1800s. (Aurelia W. Hartenberger, EdD)

hollow body containing water. The volume of water is adjusted for tuning purposes and the head is dampened before use, usually by inverting the drum. The body can be of wood or an earthenware or iron pot or kettle. Wooden drums can have a bung hole in the side so that the quantity of water can be changed without removing the head, and ceremonial materials such as ash or pollen can be inserted. A padded wooden stick is generally used as a beater, but the Iroquois use an unpadded stick for their small *ka'nohko'wah* drum, and the Chaco of Paraguay sometimes use a gourd or the hand.

Water drums have been found in eastern North America among the Chickasaw, Creek (*tamamápka*), Delaware, Cherokee, Iroquois (*ohgiwe ka'nohko'wah*), Seminole, Shawnee (now in Oklahoma, but formerly in the northeast), and Yuchi (*dīdanê*). Elsewhere in North America the water drum has a scattered distribution: it is found in the western Great Lakes region among the Ojibwa (*miti'gwakik*), on the Plains among the Omaha (*ne'xegaku*) and, more recently, in ceremonies of the Native American Church (peyote drum); and in the southwest among the Apache (*ísal dàdestl'ooní*) and the Navajo (*ásaa'yilghaalí*).

(2) Percussion instruments without membranes, used as drums in Africa, New Guinea, Latin America, and occasionally elsewhere, and known by a great variety of names including 'water gourd'. One type, used mostly by women over a wide area of the West African savanna lands, is made by floating a hemispherical section of a gourd upside-down in water within a larger vessel (half-gourd or pail, for example). The smaller gourd is beaten with a spoon or a small stick. The resultant sound, which is used rhythmically in ensemble with other percussion instruments, usually as an accompaniment to song and ritual, funeral and rejoicing dances, combines the concussive click of two hard objects with a soft low-pitched booming tone. The *assakhalebo* of Niger, Mexican *jícara de agua*, Cuban *jícara de joba*, Yaqui *bakubai*, *djidounou* of the Malinke, Dioula, and Bambara peoples of Ivory Coast, and the *tembol* of Chad belong to this category.

In New Guinea the instruments have a hollow wooden body shaped like an hourglass drum, but with open ends. They are played like a stamping tube and one end is pounded against the surface of water during male initiation ceremonies in the Chambri Lakes.

MARY RIEMER-WELLER (1), PETER COOKE/R (2)

Waterhouse, William (Robert) (*b* London, England, 18 Feb 1931; *d* Florence, Italy, 5 Nov 2007). English bassoonist, instrument collector, and organologist. He studied at the RCM under Archie Camden and began his career in the Philharmonia Orchestra. He played with the Royal Opera House Orchestra, 1953–5, and as first bassoonist in the Italian-Swiss Radio Orchestra in Lugano, 1955–8. He became first bassoonist of the LSO in 1958, the Melos Ensemble in 1959, and from 1964 to 1982 was first bassoonist of the BBC SO. Waterhouse's collection of more than 60 bassoons was exhibited at the 1983 Edinburgh Festival; his catalogue of the collection traces the historical development of the instrument.

Waterhouse drew on evidence from surviving woodwind and brass instruments, archival data, and global correspondents in his major expansion of the pioneering work of Lyndsay G. Langwill (*The New Langwill Index*, 1993). The combined Langwill–Waterhouse research archives is now at the Edinburgh University Collection of Historic Musical Instruments. Waterhouse contributed articles on the bassoon, related instruments, and the flageolet to the 1980 and 2001 editions of *Grove*. He published numerous articles, reviews, obituaries, and translations in the *Galpin Society Journal*, *Tibia*, *Early Music*, and other periodicals. While serving as honorary curator of the musical instrument collections of RNCM (where he was appointed professor of bassoon in 1966), he compiled an online catalogue, later published in an illustrated edition.

WRITINGS
(*selective list*)

The Proud Bassoon [exhibition catalogue] (Edinburgh, 1983)
The New Langwill Index: a Dictionary of Musical Wind-Instrument Makers and Inventors (London, 1993)
Bassoon, Yehudi Menuhin Music Guides (London, 2003)
Royal Northern College of Music: Catalogue of the Collection of Historic Musical Instruments, ed. Anna Wright (Manchester, 2010)

LYNDESAY G. LANGWILL/JAMES B. KOPP

Water key [spit valve] (Fr. *clef d'eau*; Ger. *Wasserklappe*; It. *chiave d'acqua*). Small sprung, pivoted lever on brass instruments (though seldom on horns), with an attached pad covering the end of a short 'chimney' projecting from the bore, used to release condensate trapped inside the tubing. Liquid is released when the player opens the hole by depressing the touchpiece of the key while blowing silently into the instrument. Some instruments have more than one water key. Though the origin of the water key is uncertain, there was one on the hibernicon, a contrabass horn patented in 1823 by J.R. Cotter of Co. Cork. A water key also features in the Stuckens 1826 French patent specification of an omnitonic horn. Leopold Uhlmann patented a water key for a valve trombone in Vienna on 12 July 1830. Jean-Louis Halary patented the 'Siphon' water key for the trombone in Paris in 1845. In the late 20th century Renold Schilke replaced the flat cork pad with a rubber plug inserted into the chimney. A successful invention has been the Amado water key, a sprung piston device designed by Ray Amado and adopted for trumpets by the Getzen Co. with the aim of reducing air turbulence and smoothing the bore by eliminating the 'chimney'. Another recent device, the Saturn water key promoted by Denis Wedgwood, uses a stainless steel ball held in place by a helical spring.

Other methods of releasing trapped moisture include removing and shaking out tuning slides (still normal on horns), and on woodwinds, drying the bore by passing through it a feather or a soft absorbent swab attached to a string.

BIBLIOGRAPHY
R. Morley-Pegge: *The French Horn* (London, 1960, 2/1973)
R. Dahlqvist: 'Some Notes on the Early Valve', *GSJ*, vol.33 (1980), 111–24

H. Weiner: 'Friedheim's Reservoire: a Failed Precursor to the Trombone Water Key', *HBSJ*, vol.17 (2005), 81–4

DAVID K. RYCROFT, REINE DAHLQVIST, EDWARD H. TARR/R

Water organ [hydraulic organ] (Fr. *orgue hydraulique*; Ger. *Wasserorgel*; It. *organo idraulico*; Lat. *organum hydraulicum*). Kind of automatic organ without bellows. Its pipes are sounded by air compressed directly by water impelled by natural forces (e.g. by a waterfall). Water organs play without human intervention once they are set in action. Ancient and modern writers have frequently confused them with the Greco-Roman hydraulis, a pneumatic organ in which air was supplied by hand-operated air pumps and water was used to steady the wind-pressure. Unlike the steam organ, which employs 'wet' air, no water coursed through the musical pipes of the water organ. Apart from the method of blowing, the water organ is similar to the barrel organ, having a pinned cylinder carrying the musical programme, a windchest, and pipework.

Water organs were described by Ctesibius (3rd century BCE), Philo of Byzantium (3rd century BCE), and Hero of Alexandria (*c*62 CE). Like water clocks (*clepsydra*) of Plato's time, they were not mere playthings but might have held particular significance in Greek natural philosophy, which used models and simulacra of this type. In antiquity hydraulically blown pipes imitated birdsong and produced the awe-inspiring sound emitted by Memnon's statue at Thebes. For the latter, solar heat was used to syphon water from one closed tank into another, thereby producing compressed air for sounding the pipes.

Arab and Byzantine engineers developed, among other devices, an automatic water organ (described by the Banū Mūsā in their 9th-century treatise; see Farmer, 1931), and a 'musical tree' at the palace of Khalif al-Muqtadir (ruled 908–32). By the end of the 13th century hydraulic automata had reached Western Europe. During the Renaissance water organs again acquired magical and metaphysical connotations among followers of the hermetic and esoteric sciences. Organs were placed in gardens, grottoes, and conservatories of palaces and mansions to delight onlookers with music and with displays of automata—dancing figurines, wing-flapping birds and hammering cyclopes—all programmed by the pinned cylinder. Other types of water organ were hidden and simulated musical instruments apparently being played by statues in mythological scenes such as Orpheus playing the viol and the contest between Apollo and Marsyas.

The most famous 16th-century water organ was at the Villa d'Este in Tivoli. Built about 1566–9 by Lucha Clericho (perhaps Luc le Clerc; completed by Claude Venard), it was fed by a waterfall and described by Mario Cartaro in 1575 as playing 'madrigals and many other things'. G.M. Zappi (1576) wrote: 'When somebody gives the order to play, at first one hears trumpets which play awhile and then there is a harmony …. Countless gentlemen could not believe that this organ played by itself … but they rather thought that there was somebody inside'. The mechanism is illustrated in a 1576 drawing by Claude Venard. In 1611–13 the organ was rebuilt to a new design: besides automatically playing three pieces of music, the new organ was also provided with a keyboard. Destroyed during the 18th century, it was rebuilt in 1999–2003 (by Rodney Briscoe), incorporating the original stone air-chamber. Other Italian gardens with water organs were at Pratolino, near Florence (designed by Bernardo Buontalenti, built by Giovanni Battista Contini, 1568–*c*1583); Isola di Belvedere, Ferrara (before 1599, on a design by the hydraulic engineer Giovanni Battista Aleotti); Palazzo del Quirinale, Rome (built by Luca Biagi in 1598, rebuilt in 1647–8 by Matteo Marione under direction of Athanasius Kircher; restored 1990); Villa Aldobrandini, Frascati (see below); Florence, Palazzo Pitti (1645, built by Vincenzo Sormani); Parma and Colorno (see below); one of the Royal Palaces at Naples (1746); and Villa Doria Pamphilj, Rome (see below). Of these only the one at the Palazzo del Quirinale survives.

The water organ in the Villa Aldobrandini (Belvedere) was made in 1617–19 by Giovanni Guglielmi in a hall frescoed by Domenichino, with the instrument incorporated into a reconstruction of Mount Parnassus: its nine muses held real wind instruments to their mouths, and atop the mountain Apollo played a 30-note psaltery with real brass strings; of the music, only the *Aria dell'organo di Frascati* survives, attributed to Bernardo Pasquini. Other musical devices, a centaur and a cyclop, were housed just outside the hall; the original tune (*Ballo del Ciclope*) for the cyclop device appears in Braga, Portugal, Biblioteca Pùblica, MS 964. The organ was restored in 1759 by Celestino Testa; nowadays only the statues survive. Testa also made (1760) the musical faun of the Villa Doria Pamphilj; a second organ echoed some measures of the tune played by the faun. At the Farnese palace in Parma, in 1619 Simone Ongaro from Innsbruck installed automatic singers and players plus a barrel organ from Nuremberg. In the nearby Farnese palace at Colorno, inside the 'Grotta incantata' the French engineer Jean Bailleul built in 1718–24 an astounding water-operated musical 'Comedy', with many complex scenes in succession (destroyed only a few years later).

In the early 17th century, water organs were built in England; Cornelius Drebbel built one for King James I, and Salomon de Caus built several at Richmond. There was one in Bagnigge Vale, London, the summer home of Nell Gwynn (1650–87), and Henry Winstanley (1644–1703), the designer of the Eddystone Lighthouse, is thought to have built one at his home in Saffron Walden, Essex. At Heidelberg Castle, de Caus laid out gardens famous for beautiful and intricate waterworks, A water organ survives in the gardens at Heilbronn, Württemberg, and parts of one at the Wilhelmshöhe gardens in Kassel. The brothers Francini constructed splendid waterworks and organs at Saint Germain-en-Laye and Versailles.

By the end of the 17th century, however, interest in water organs had waned. As their upkeep was costly they were left to decay and were soon forgotten; by

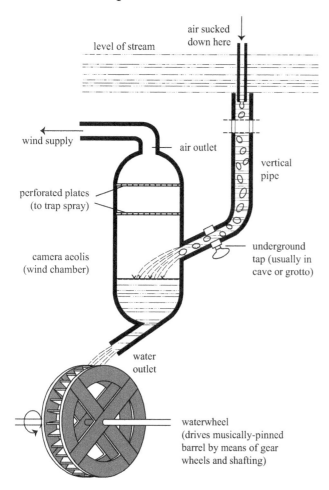

level of stream

air sucked down here

wind supply

air outlet

vertical pipe

perforated plates (to trap spray)

camera aeolis (wind chamber)

underground tap (usually in cave or grotto)

water outlet

waterwheel (drives musically-pinned barrel by means of gear wheels and shafting)

Fig.1: *Diagram showing the blowing system of a water organ.*

1920 not one survived (the so-called water organ at Hellbrunn Castle, Salzburg, is a pneumatic organ driven by hydraulically operated bellows). Their mechanism was subsequently misunderstood until the Dutch engineer Van Dijk pointed out in 1954 that the method of air supply to the water organ was the same as that formerly used in forges and smelting works. The most important factor is the natural ability of water, when drawn by gravity into an outlet, to suck air in with it. In fig.1 air is drawn through a small pipe placed within a larger vertical pipe, which takes water from a stream, pond or stabilizing reservoir. Both water and air arrive together in the *camera aeolis* (wind chamber) which is situated considerably below the head of the water. The longer the vertical pipe the greater the volume of air sucked in. Water and air separate in the chamber and the compressed air is driven into a wind-trunk atop the chamber, to blow the organ pipes. The water leaves the chamber at the same rate as it enters and drives a water wheel, which in turn drives the pinned cylinder and the movements attached. To start the organ, the tap above the entry pipe is turned on and, given a continuous flow of water, the organ plays until the tap is closed. The above-mentioned air pipe could be omitted or could be installed alongside the main vertical water conduit: this latter solution can be seen in a

reconstruction of a water organ by the Jesuit Francesco Lana Terzi (1686), which fills a gap in a similar scheme by Kircher (1650) by adding the missing air supply. A few water organs had simple wind-pressure regulating devices. At the Palazzo del Quirinale, the water flows from a hilltop spring (once abundant, now only sufficient to play the organ for about 30 minutes at a time), through the palace itself into a stabilizing 'room' some 18 metres above the *camera aeolis* in the organ grotto. This drop provides sufficient wind to power the restored six-stop instrument.

Among Renaissance writers on the water organ, Salomon de Caus was particularly informative. His book of 1615 includes a treatise on making water organs, advice on tuning and registration, and engravings showing the instruments, their mechanisms and scenes in which they were used. It also includes an example of suitable music for water organ, the madrigal *Chi farà fed' al cielo* by Alessandro Striggio (i), arranged by Peter Philips.

BIBLIOGRAPHY

S. de Caus: *Les raisons des forces mouvantes* (Frankfurt, 1615, 2/1624) [basis of part of I. de Caus: *Nouvelle invention de lever de l'eau* (London, 1644; Eng. trans., 1659)]

A. Kircher: *Musurgia universalis* (Rome, 1650/R)

F. Lana Terzi: *Magisterium naturae et artis […]*, vol.2 (Brescia, 1686)

H.G. Farmer: *The Organ of the Ancients from Eastern Sources, Hebrew, Syriac and Arabic* (London, 1931)

R. Giorgetti: 'Gli organi idraulici e gli automi musicali della Villa Medicea di Pratolino', *Strumenti e musica*, vol.40 (1988), no.3, pp.41–3; no,pp.49–50

A. Latanza: *Il ripristino dell'organo idraulico del Quirinale* (Rome, 1995)

P. Barbieri: 'Organi automatici e statue "che suonano" delle ville Aldobrandini (Frascati) e Pamphilj (Roma). Monte Parnaso, Ciclope, Centauro e Fauno', *L'organo*, vol.34 (2001), 5–175

P. Barbieri: 'Ancora sulla "Fontana dell'organo" di Tivoli e altri automata sonori degli Este (1576–619)', *L'organo*, vol..37 (2004), 187–221

P. Barbieri: 'Giambattista Della Porta's "singing" hydraulis and other expressive devices for the organ, c1560–860', *JAMIS*, vol.32 (2006), 145–66. Rev. and transl. as 'L'hydraulis dalla voce "gargante" di Giambattista Della Porta e altri accessori "lirici" per l'organo, c1560–860', *Informazione organistica*, vol.19/3 (2007), 211–37

SUSI JEANS/ARTHUR W.J.G. ORD-HUME/PATRIZIO BARBIERI

Waterphone. Instrument invented in 1967 and patented in 1975 (US patent number 3,896,696) by Richard A. Waters and manufactured individually to order by him, formerly under the company name Multi-Media in Sebastopol, California. The Waterphone combines the principles of the nail violin and a water-drum. Various sizes have been produced; the earliest ('Standard') had a resonator 17.8 cm in diameter. In 2011 the 'Mega-Bass' (40.6 cm in diameter) was popular. The Standard model consists of a stainless steel bowl resonator containing water, the dome-shaped top of which opens into a vertical unstopped, cylindrical tube that serves as a handle. Current models ('Whaler', 'Bass', and 'MegaBass') are constructed from flat, stainless steel pans. Around the edge of the resonator are attached 25 to 55 nearly vertical bronze rods, which (depending on the model) are tuned in equal or unequal 12-note or microtonal systems. The rods can be struck with sticks or Superball mallets or rubbed by a bow or the hands. Movement of water in the resonator produces timbre changes and glissandi. The Waterphone has inspired many imitations and further developments. It has been played in a wide variety of musics, including rock, jazz, and compositions of Tan Dun and Sofia Gubaidulina, and has been featured in many film and television soundtracks. It is also an important element in the Gravity Adjusters Expansion Band founded by Waters in 1967. Waterphones have been displayed in museums as works of sonic art. The instrument is very light and can be taken into water; it has been played by Waters and by Jim Nollman while swimming, to communicate with whales and other cetaceans. Waters's business was for sale in 2011.

HUGH DAVIES/LAURENCE LIBIN

Waters, Richard Adolphus (*b* Dubois, PA, 19 Sept 1935). American kinetic sculptor and painter. Since 1966 he has invented and performed on instruments and sound sculptures, the best-known of which is the Waterphone. Other instruments devised by Waters include the Mytar (based on the sitar), Corrugahoms (multi-octave, using two or more corrugated pipes), revolving sound generators (resembling large, pivoted Waterphones, tuned microtonally), water-gong-drums (based on Waterphone-like resonators) and other novel instruments and sound devices. In 1967 Waters and Lee Charlton founded the Gravity Adjusters Expansion Band, which performs improvisations on conventional instruments, synthesizer, Waterphones, and other instruments developed by Waters, and also the 'slide horn' (with a tenor saxophone mouthpiece) devised by Lee Charlton. They produced two albums, 'One' and 'Hole in the Sky'.

HUGH DAVIES/R

Watson, John R(oger) (*b* St Louis, MO, 28 March 1952). American organologist, instrument maker, and conservator. After receiving a BMus degree from Houghton College (1974), he independently studied historical instrument making, producing 32 reproduction keyboard instruments. Since 1988 Watson has worked for the Colonial Williamsburg Foundation, where he holds the position of Conservator of Instruments and Mechanical Arts and (since 2008) Associate Curator of Musical Instruments. He is also a conservator in private practice. His research focuses on historical keyboard instruments and issues of conservation ethics and documentation, and he has written and lectured extensively on balancing the desire to restore old instruments to playable condition with the need to preserve the valuable historical evidence present in the details of their original construction. In addition to his scholarly writings, he has developed software to assist in documenting the conservation of artifacts and served as administrator and chief editor of the *Clinkscale Database of Early Pianos, 1700–1860* (<http://www.earlypianos.org/>), a research database dedicated to the worldwide cataloguing of pianos made before 1860.

WRITINGS

'Historical Musical Instruments: a Claim to Use, an Obligation to Preserve', *JAMIS*, vol.17 (1991), 69–82

D. Blanchfield: 'Theory and Practice in the Conservation of Musical Instruments', *Journal of the Violin Society of America*, vol.16 (1999), 11–24

'Instrument Restoration and the Scholarship Imperative', *Early Keyboard Journal*, vol.19 (2001), 7–31

'Conservation of Six Historic Organs at Colonial Williamsburg', *The Tracker*, vol.46 (2002), 22–34

ed.: *Organ Restoration Reconsidered: Proceedings of a Colloquium* (Warren, MI, 2005)

'The Restorative Conservation of Organs: A Conceptual Roadmap', *The Organ Yearbook*, vol.37 (2008)

Artifacts in Use: the Paradox of Restoration and the Conservation of Organs (Richmond, VA, 2010)

Changing Keys: Keyboard Musical Instruments for America, 1700–1830 (Williamsburg, VA, 2013)

EDMOND T. JOHNSON/R

Watson, William (Bill) **David** (*b* St Pancras, London, 6 Oct 1930). English bow maker. He joined the firm of W.E. Hill & Sons in 1945 as the first apprentice taken on since the workshop's manager Arthur Bultitude (1908–90) had himself been apprenticed, in 1922. After six months in the case-making department, Watson undertook a six-year bow apprenticeship under William Charles Retford (1875–1970), and he counts the Hill makers William Napier (1848–1932), William Grieve Johnston (1860–1944), and Retford himself among his major influences. Except for a two-year break for National Service, he remained with the Hill firm until 1962; his bows made for Hill bear the stamped number '7'. In 1962 he established his own workshop in Hanwell, West London, moving to Denham, Buckinghamshire, in 1963. Watson's bows are cleanly and precisely made, the sticks generally being stronger than most, though without extra weight. Typically they are stamped 'W.D.WATSON.LONDON'. Watson is also well known as a restorer of fine old bows, nowadays in Falmouth, Cornwall. See J. Milnes, ed.: *The British Violin* (Oxford, 2000).

JOHN MILNES, TIM BAKER

Wauqu. Vessel flute of the Chipaya people of the department of Oruro, highland Bolivia. It is made of clay or of a tropical fruit shell in an oval shape about 10 cm long and has a mouth-hole and a smaller tone hole on the side. Approximate pitches $b\flat''$ and g'' have been reported. The instrument is incorporated into the hocket melody performed on a pair of *maizu* panpipes. See M.P. Baumann: 'Music, Dance, and Song of the Chipayas (Bolivia)', *Latin American Music Review*, vol.2 (1981), 171–222.

Wave organ. Electronic organ developed by (Frank) Morse Robb (*b* Belleville, ON, 22 Jan 1902; *d* Belleville, 5 Aug 1992) during 1926–7, patented in 1928, and manufactured by the Robb Wave Organ Co. in Belleville between 1934 and 1938; it was designed specifically for use in churches. The sounds were generated by electromagnetic tone-wheels, one for each note, which produced waveforms derived from oscillograph patterns of those of a pipe organ. An early model had a touch-sensitive keyboard, but this was later abandoned. In 1932 a five-octave, single-manual instrument was constructed, and from 1934 between 16 and 20 two-manual Wave organs (with 32-note pedalboard) were manufactured. The instrument was successfully demonstrated in department stores and at a concert in Toronto (1936), but although it was well received, Robb had to abandon the project in 1938 owing to lack of financial backing; he then turned to inventing mechanical packing devices and designing silver wares. The Wave organ was one of the earliest electronic organs and was an exact contemporary of the Cellulophone and Coupleux-Givelet organ. See J.J. Brown: *Ideas in Exile: a History of Canadian Invention* (Toronto, 1967), 236.

HUGH DAVIES/R

Wa-wa [wah-wah]. Onomatopoeic term derived from the sound created by the regular boost and cut of treble frequencies. It is applied to devices that produce this effect, notably the Harmon mute for the trumpet and trombone, and to an electronic signal processor unit, generally operated by means of a pedal.

Way, David Jacques (*b* Elk Creek, NE, 28 June 1918; *d* Stonington, CT, 4 Feb 1994). American publisher and harpsichord maker. After attending Black Mountain College near Asheville, North Carolina, he took several printing positions in New York, specializing in limited fine-arts editions. In 1965 he built one of Wolfgang Zuckermann's slant-side kit harpsichords, sparking an enthusiasm for that instrument that lasted the rest of his life. In 1969 his publishing firm, October House, published Zuckermann's *The Modern Harpsichord.* Shortly thereafter he purchased Zuckermann's business and closed his printing and publishing endeavors.

Way began his career as a harpsichord builder by continuing the production of the kit instrument. Soon he designed a larger, more complex slant-side kit. In 1971 the harpsichord builder William Hyman became Way's adviser, and after Hyman's death (1974) his apprentice John Bennett moved to Stonington, Connecticut, where Way had moved his business in 1973. There, under Bennett's direction for 11 years, about 20 unfinished orders of Hyman's were eventually completed in Way's workshop under the Hyman name. The demand for kits, at their height mass-produced for Way by a factory in Philadelphia, fell off in the 1980s, and the Stonington shop increasingly turned out custom instruments of numerous designs, as well as limited runs of harpsichord and pipe organ kits. Meanwhile Way had built an international network of dealers, including from 1973 Marc Ducornet in Paris; in 1982 Way went into partnership with Ducornet, who thenceforth designed and made parts for most of their instruments. After Way's death Zuckermann Harpsichords was managed by Ducornet's former apprentice Richard Auber, who eventually purchased the business from Way's widow. In 1999 the arrangement with Ducornet dissolved and Ducornet continued his own work as 'The Paris Workshop', while Zuckermann Harpsichords International continued operations in Stonington. See S.-M. Kosofsky: 'David

Jacques Way, Harpsichord Maker, 1918–94', *Early Music*, vol.22/2 (1994), 363–4.

EDWARD L. KOTTICK/R

Way, George Harrison (*b* San Francisco, CA, 8 Jan 1891; *d* Elkhart, IN, 21 Feb 1969). American drummer and instrument maker. Childhood drum lessons and itinerant positions as drummer with several troupes led to a position as salesman and drummer with George B. Stone & Son Drum Manufacturing Company of Boston in 1910. Way founded Advance Drum Co. in Edmonton, Alberta, Canada, about 1915, selling products built of components from the USA. In 1922 he began working for Leedy Manufacturing Co. of Indianapolis, continuing as sales manager after Leedy became a division of G.C. Conn in 1928. Way left the company in 1942 when exigencies of World War II caused widespread changes in the industry. During his 20-year tenure, Way was responsible for innovations in drum construction, the introduction of new products, and the continued development of the drum set. He was also responsible for new concepts in marketing.

During World War II, Way successively established George H. Way Co. and worked for Slingerland Drum Co. in Chicago. After a failed venture opening the Hollywood Drum Shop, he returned in 1948 to a position with the Leedy division of Conn, and in 1951 he was in charge of a merger of two of Conn's divisions to form Leedy and Ludwig. Conn then dropped their percussion business in 1954, at which point Way established the George Way Drum Company in Elkhart, Indiana. He purchased the Leedy factory building and began the manufacture of several signature lines of drums and accessories. In 1962 Way lost control of the company, which was acquired by Camco. He then worked for Rogers Drum Company for a few months before establishing GHW Drum Company, which continued in operation under the leadership of his widow for only a few years following his death.

BIBLIOGRAPHY

R. Cook: *The Complete History of the Leedy Drum Company* (Fullerton, CA, 1993)

J. Aldridge and M. Kaskell: 'George H. Way Camco–Drum Workshop', *Guide to Vintage Drums*, ed. J. Aldridge (Anaheim, CA, 1994), 40–47

JAMES H. COOK

Waza. End-blown calabash horn of the Berta people of western Ethiopia and southern Sudan. It is used only in ensembles of 10 or 12. Waza are made in different sizes and consist of several conical segments of calabash joined to form the tube. The smallest eight horns require three or four segments, larger ones need up to six. The Berta cultivate special types of calabash plants to make waza. Every one within a set is named according to the sound it produces or to its musical function; such as *wazalu* ('important *waza*; first *waza*'), *adolo bala* ('small leaf'), *shinir bala* ('small donkey'), *agondo* ('wild animal'), and *nely dang* ('gigantic lady'). The names vary according to locale and dialect. Waza are constructed by experienced makers who fix the sizes and pitches of the pipes starting from the shortest tube, *wazalu*. The pipes are 40 to 220 cm long and 4 to 6 cm in diameter at the blowing end. A special glue called *adegela*, or honey wax, is used to join the segments. The larger pipes are additionally supported by several long bamboo strips that run along the outside and are fastened with twine from tree bark or with other vegetable cords. Also, thin bamboo sticks are pushed into the tube crosswise for support. A funnel-shaped gourd segment serves as a mouthpiece. Water is poured into the horn before performance to close any splits. Each waza produces one pitch, and a minimum of five musicians play in hocket to create the required melodic and rhythmic patterns.

A side-blown horn called *angari* accompanies the waza ensemble. It is made of a goat's horn approximately 35 cm long. The oval embouchure is near the tip of the horn, which is decorated with fringes of animal hair, shells, and colourful beads. Another accompanying instrument is the *pale*, a forked branch that is beaten with a thick wooden mallet (occasionally the tip of an animal horn) called *bulu*. Additionally, *asese* gourd rattles join the ensemble.

The smallest five waza (together called *waza bala*, 'group of small waza') are held horizontally by the players, who stand upright while relaxing their shoulders in order to be able to take strong breaths. The ends of the long waza (together called *waza dang*, 'group of large waza') rest on the ground. The *waza bala* players simultaneously play the *bulu-pale* percussion set: each of them holds the waza in the left hand while the *pale*, placed on the right shoulder, is beaten by the *bulu* held in the right hand.

Like other aerophone ensembles, the waza ensemble served formerly as a symbol of status and authority of the traditional Berta courts, and the set was therefore kept in a special place within the royal palace. Nowadays, a chieftain or clan leader is assigned to preserve such sets, to be taken out of his house whenever a musical performance takes place. During performance the musicians usually create a circle that is surrounded by a singing and dancing group of men and women. As with all other Berta aerophone ensembles, the waza are played exclusively by males, while female participants are limited to shaking the *asese* and singing and dancing. Waza performances take place mostly during the harvest season between September and the beginning of November. During the rainy season and the beginning of autumn it is taboo to play the waza because people believe that the noise of the wind would provoke evil spirits who could destroy the crop. Another custom related to waza performance is the slaughtering of an animal such as a sheep or goat before playing the instruments. The blood is sprinkled on the instruments as well as in the house where they are kept. Nowadays the waza ensemble performs for entertainment at ceremonial and ritual events and also at big annual music festivals.

BIBLIOGRAPHY

A. Simon: 'Trumpet and Flute Ensembles of the Berta People in the Sudan', *African Musicology: Current Trends*, vol.1 (A Festschrift presented to J.H.K. Nketia), ed. J. Cogdell Djedje (Los Angeles, 1989), 183–217

A. Simon: 'Zur Musik der Berta: Feldforschungen im Sudan', *50 Jahre Musikwissenschaftliches Institut in Hamburg*, ed. P. Petersen and H. Rösing (Frankfurt am Main, 1999), 151–68

T. Teffera: *Aerophone im Instrumentarium der Völker Ostafrikas* (Berlin, 2009)

TIMKEHET TEFFERA

Weber. American firm of piano makers. Albert Weber (i) (*b* Bavaria, Germany, 8 July 1828; *d* New York, NY, 25 June 1879) a gifted pianist as a child, emigrated to New York in 1845. He apprenticed as a piano maker in the workshop of Charles J. Holden, then worked several years in Van Winkle's piano factory. In 1852 he established his own shop at 103 West Broadway in Manhattan. Following a disastrous 1854 fire, he moved to a larger factory at Broome and Crosby Streets, which the thriving firm quickly outgrew. By 1869, when Weber opened an impressive showroom at 108 Fifth Avenue, the firm had become the sixth largest producer of pianos in the USA, with gross annual sales of $221,444. Weber was succeeded by his son, Albert Weber (ii) (*b* New York, 1858; *d* after 1896), who established a branch in Chicago in 1880; the first Weber Concert Hall was opened there in 1883, and was later replaced by a still larger concert hall.

While not innovative piano makers, the Weber firm produced instruments of high quality, and the Webers themselves were widely respected in the trade. A 21 Dec 1894 *New York Times* article lauded Weber (i) as having been 'a thoroughly skilled manufacturer and an able business man', who 'achieved a high reputation, owing to the marked degree of excellence—musical, artistic, and mechanical—with which he endowed the noble instrument still bearing his name'.

At its height, the firm produced 1500 instruments annually. Albert Weber (i) has been credited with introducing the term 'baby grand' for a small grand piano. Although not in the forefront of concert instruments, Weber pianos were played by such artists as Carreño, Hofmann, and Paderewski, and were widely used in mid- and late-19th-century theatres. They were shown with success at international exhibitions, including those at Philadelphia (1876), London (1887), Paris (1889), and Chicago (1893). In 1903 the firm was purchased by the Aeolian Co., which produced Weber pianos until 1985. In 1987 the piano manufacturer Young Chang acquired the label and continues to produce Weber-brand instruments, redesigned by Delwin Fandrich. The higher-end Albert Weber line, made in South Korea, have better actions, and an unusual asymmetrically tapered soundboard and asymmetrically crowned ribs, both intended for better bass sound, while the less expensive Weber line is made in China.

BIBLIOGRAPHY

D. Spillane: *History of the American Pianoforte* (New York, 1890/R1969)

[Weber and Co.]: *Progress of Time* (New York, 1897)

A. Dolge: *Pianos and their Makers* (Covina, CA, 1911/R1972)

L. Fine: *Acoustic and Digital Piano Buyer* (Jamaica Plain, MA, spring 2013)

NANCY GROCE/R

Weber [Webber], **Ferdinand** (*b* Borstendorf, Saxony, 6 May 1715; *d* Dublin, Ireland, bur. 25 Oct 1784). Irish keyboard instrument maker of German origin. His certificate of apprenticeship states that he learned organ building under Johann Ernst Hähnel of Lower Meissen between 10 Dec 1728 and the same date in 1735. He worked about 1745–8 in London before settling in Dublin about 1749 (residing at 71 Marlborough Street from *c*1750 onwards). He married Rachel Wilcocks in 1755, and after his death she carried on the business with their son Thomas Ferdinand (bap. Dublin, 19 April 1756) at 75 Marlborough Street, until her own death in 1789. The piano maker William Southwell was an apprentice of Weber's; Robert Woffington, who succeeded Weber as the leading organ builder in Dublin until the establishment of William Telford's firm about 1832, might also have been his pupil.

Weber's work is first mentioned in Faulkner's *Dublin Journal* (10–14 Oct 1749), which states that 'Mr. Weber from Dresden has built a very curious organ for the Cathedral Church of Tuam, and the said Weber is repairing the organ of St. Nicholas Church in Galway'. After 1761, when he built the organ for Christ Church in Cork, Weber's activities as the leading Irish maker of keyboard instruments are more fully documented. His accounts for the years 1764–83 record the cost of his instruments, number of clients, and his purchase and sale of porcelain (probably from Meissen). Besides building organs in Dublin for St Catherine's, St Thomas's (1767), and St Werburgh's (1767), he tuned the organs in most of the important Dublin churches, including Christ Church Cathedral, where he held the contract between 1766 and 1784 at a yearly salary of £10, as well as the instrument in Kilkenny Cathedral. The only remaining traces of his pipework, however, are the Great organ Flutes of the rebuilt instrument in St Werburgh's.

Weber was also a skilled maker of stringed keyboard instruments and regularly supplied them (on at least one occasion a piano) to concert venues in Dublin. Five harpsichords, two spinets (one dated 1780), and single examples of a clavicytherium (?1764) and a square piano (1772) survive. The harpsichords, all single-manual instruments, share many similarities with those of Kirkman and Shudi; three have the unusual compass F', $G'–g'''$ (without $F\sharp'$). The clavicytherium (8′, 8′, 8′, $G'–g'''$) has special jacks and an ingenious single-spring mechanism to return the horizontal jacks. Both spinets have the compass $G'–g'''$ and are of the same design, although one was meant for leather plectra rather than quills. The piano (*US.NY.mma*; $G'–f'''$) has a sliding hammer rail and two hammers per note (leather-covered wood and soft pad) for contrasting tones, plus a nag's head swell, and two pedals in addition to hand stops.

BIBLIOGRAPHY

T. de Valera: 'Two Eighteenth-century Musical Instrument Makers', *Dublin Historical Record*, vol.36/4 (1982–3), 122–31

J. Nex and L. Whitehead: 'A Copy of Ferdinand Weber's Account Book', *RMARC*, ed. J. Wainwright, vol.33 (2000), 89–150

L. Libin: 'Ein bemerkenswertes Tafelklavier von Ferdinand Weber', *Musica instrumentalis*, vol.3 (2001), 143–6

J. Nex and L. Whitehead: 'The Stringed Keyboard Instruments of Ferdinand Weber', *Aspects of Harpsichord Making in the British Isles*, Historical Harpsichord No.5, ed. J. Koster (Hillsdale, NY, 2009), 116–53

BRIAN BOYDELL/LANCE WHITEHEAD

Weber, Franz (*b* Oberperfuss, nr. Innsbruck, Austria, 1 July 1825; *d* Oberperfuss, Austria, 16 April 1914). Tyrolean organ builder. His father, Mathias Weber (*b* Oberperfuss, 24 Feb 1777; *d* Oberperfuss, 16 May 1848), was a self-taught piano maker and organ builder whose organs include those at Völs, near Innsbruck (1826), Ladis (contract 1841), and Bichlbach (1844). Franz learned with his father and in 1852 for a short time with Balthasar Pröbstl in Füssen. Among his numerous works are the organs at Fulpmes (1852–3), Bruneck parish church (1855; 32 stops), Pfalzen (1857; enlarged 1868), Stilfes (1860), Zams (1861), Ausservillgraten (1862), Telfes in Stubai (1865), Oberperfuss (1867), Fliess (1869), Flaurling (1875), St Nikolaus, Innsbruck (1882), Kaltenbrunn (1883), and Oberleutasch (1893; known as the 100th organ). He employed several apprentices; his most important assistant was his brother Alois (*b* 31 Aug 1813; *d* 30 Aug 1889), and he was later joined by his son Johann (1860–1947).

Weber was of a conservative disposition; his instruments continued the tradition of the post-Baroque both in specification and tone quality into the late 19th century. He retained use of the slider chest and tracker action all his life. The brilliant *plenum* of his organs is coloured by a high-sounding Cornet. The auxiliary manual, whose windchest he characteristically placed in the lower part of the organ, always has a 2′ stop (even when there are only four stops), to which is often added a mixture or a Cimbel. He developed an independent style in his organ screens whose detailed craftsmanship makes his instruments unmistakable. See A. Reichling: *Orgellandschaft Südtirol* (Bozen [Bolzano], 1982).

ALFRED REICHLING

Weber, (Jakob) **Gottfried** (*b* Freinsheim, Pfalz, 1 March 1779; *d* Bad Kreuznach, 21 Sept 1839). German lawyer, music theorist, and writer on instrument acoustics. He published numerous important writings on harmonic theory and composition, and was himself a competent flutist, cellist, keyboard player, and conductor. Under the influence of the physicist Ernst Florens Friedrich Chladni, Weber in 1812 published an article on improving the horn, and in 1816 he began to outline his systematic theories of the acoustics of wind instruments. He invented a trombone with double slide, produced in 1816 by Johann Heinrich Haltenhof. The music publisher Schott of Mainz opened an instrument factory about 1818, and in 1824 began publication of *Caecilia*, an influential music periodical edited by Weber that included articles on acoustics by Chladni and the physicist Wilhelm Weber (no relation), among others. Various wind instruments 'of new invention' advertised by Schott in 1828 reflected Weber's positivistic spirit, including clarinets designed by Iwan Müller, bassoons designed by Carl Almenräder, and keyed trumpets designed by Carl August Müller.

WRITINGS

(*selective list*)

'Wichtige Verbesserung des Horns', *AmZ*, vol.14 (1812), 759–64

'Versuch einer praktischen Akustik des Blasinstrumenten', *AmZ*, vol.18 (1816), 33–44, 49–60, 65–74, 87–90

'Einige Vorschläge zur Vervollkommnung und Bereicherung der Bass-Instrumenten', *AmZ*, vol.18 (1816), 725–9, 749–53

'Praktische Resultate aus der … Akustik der Blasinstrumente', *AmZ*, vol.19 (1817), 809–14

'Wesentlichen Verbesserungen des Fagottes', *Caecilia*, vol.2/6 (1825), 123–40

'C. Almenräder's weitere Fagott-Verbesserung', *Caecilia*, vol.9/34 (1828), 128–30

'Über Ventilhorn und Ventiltrompete mit drei Ventile', *Caecilia*, vol.17/66 (1835), 73–105

BIBLIOGRAPHY

A. Lemke: *Jacob Gottfried Weber: Leben und Werk* (Mainz, 1968)

B. Höft: 'Gottfried Weber (1779–1839): ein Porträt', *Mitteilungen der Arbeitsgemeinschaft für mittelrheinische Musikgeschichte*, vol.42 (1981), 45–62

HEIKE FRICKE/JAMES B. KOPP

Weber, Rainer (*b* Leipzig, Germany, 3 Feb 1927). German wind instrument maker and restorer. He is noted for his restorations and fine reproductions of early wind instruments including crumhorns, shawms, dulcians, rauschpfeifen, cornetts, recorders, rackets, gemshorns, sorduns, oboes, bassoons, and portatives. He took up the organ as a schoolboy and visited many old organs in north Germany. He became first a mechanic and later a painter and commercial artist. In Berlin he was trained by Gerhard Muchow to restore pictures and wood carvings and also learned to play the recorder, oboe, and bassoon. His taste for music of the 15th to the 17th centuries led to an unsuccessful search for instruments with sounds like those of the old organs he loved. He learned wood-turning at Hamburg and made his first instruments there in 1947, simply to produce the sounds he wanted for amateur music-making.

He was encouraged to start his own workshop in 1950 and in 1960 moved to Bayerbach in Bavaria, by which time he was making historical copies that were ever more faithful to their originals. In latter years his main career was as a leading restorer of historic woodwinds for numerous private collectors and museums, having had through his hands during his long career more than 900 instruments, at least 100 of them recorders. His restoration reports, a volume of which he published, are models of their kind: revealing the use of the most modern techniques, they are nevertheless informed by a deep knowledge of and respect for the techniques employed in former times. His most outstanding achievement was probably to have saved some particularly notable instruments from threatened destruction, including the crumhorns in the Accademia Filarmonica, Verona. Weber published an important corpus of articles concerned with both woodwind history and restoration topics (for a bibliography, see E. Fontana, ed.: *Festschrift Rainer Weber* (Halle, 1999)).

WRITINGS

J.H. van der Meer: 'Some Facts and Guesses Concerning Doppioni', *GSJ*, vol.25 (1972), 22–9

'Tournebout—Pifia—Bladderpipe (Platerspiel)', *GSJ*, vol.30 (1977), 64–9

J.H. van der Meer: *Catalogo degli strumenti musicali dell'Accademia filarmonica di Verona* (Verona, 1982)

'Die Restaurierung von Blasinstrumenten', *Per una carta Europea del restauro: Venice 1985*

Zur Restaurierung von Holzblasinstrumenten aus der Sammlung von Dr Josef Zimmermann in Bonner Beethovenhaus (Celle, 1993)

'Historische Holzblasinstrumente, Originale—Kopien—Nachschöpfungen', *Der 'schöne' Klang: Festschrift des GNM Nürnberg* (Nuremberg, 1996)

'Säulenblockflöten—Columnarflöten—Colonnen?', *Musica instrumentalis*, vol.1 (1998), 94–105

'Early double reeds', *GSJ*, vol.55 (2002), 233–41; 'Addendum', *GSJ*, vol.56 (2003), 280–81

'Einblicke in originale Blockflöten aus dem 16. bis 18. Jahrhundert', *Neues musikwissenschaftliches Jahrbuch*, vol.15 (2007), 21–65

CHRISTOPHER MONK/R

Wegmann. German family of organ builders. Johann [Hans] Conrad Wegmann (*b* Affeltrangen or Affoltern am Albis, Switzerland, bap. 22 June 1699; *d* Frankfurt am Main, Germany, 4 Oct 1738), son of a cabinetmaker, became court organ builder in Darmstadt and married in that same year. His organs at the Barfüsserkirche, Frankfurt (1736) and at Wörsdorf (1737) were both completed by his journeyman and successor, Johann Christian Köhler (*b* Groß-Rosenburg an der Saale, Germany, 31 July 1714; *d* 1761), who married Wegmann's widow in 1739. In 1740 Köhler moved the business to Frankfurt, where it rose to prominence. His 36 extant instruments recall those of Stumm in tone, but their façades are distinctive.

Köhler in turn was succeeded by his stepson Philipp Ernst Wegmann (*b* Darmstadt, Germany, 14 Aug 1734; *d* at sea, 26 July 1778), who received his indentures from his stepfather on 16 May 1756. Philipp Ernst became a citizen of Frankfurt on 20 Aug 1762, and was appointed court and state organ builder to the Prince of Hessen-Darmstadt. His organs included those for the Liebfrauenkirche, Frankfurt (1763; two manuals, 20 stops), Lauterbach (1763; two manuals, 34 stops), Bobenhausen (1766; two manuals, 18 stops), Alter Peterskirche, Frankfurt (1771), St Christoph, Mainz (1773; two manuals, 24 stops), and Gross Eichen (1773; one manual, 11 stops).

After Philipp Ernst's death his children Johann Benedikt Ernst Wegmann (*b* Frankfurt, 19 Feb 1765; *d* Frankfurt, 6 Sept 1828) and Maria Anna Wegmann (*b* Frankfurt, 27 Feb 1764; *d* Frankfurt, 24 Oct 1802) inherited the firm. It was managed by their mother and the foreman, Johann Friedrich Meynecke, while Meynecke was training the young man, who became a citizen of Frankfurt on 21 March 1796. Wegmann organs of this period included those at Gräfenhausen (*c*1780; one manual, 13 stops), Sulzbach (1781; one manual, 19 stops), Nieder-Erlenbach (1781; one manual, 13 stops), Schotten (1782; two manuals, 28 stops), Götzenhain (1784; one manual, 14 stops), St Katharine, Frankfurt (1821; repair), and Johann Benedikt Ernst's last work, at Offenthal (1822).

Maria Anna married Johann Ebert, the organist of St Katharine, Frankfurt, and their two sons joined the firm. Johann Ebert Jr (*b* Frankfurt, 29 Sept 1790; *d* Frankfurt, 1 Jan 1860), initially a carpenter, became a citizen of Frankfurt on 2 Feb 1815 and obtained his licence as an organ builder on 17 March 1842. George Christoph Ebert (*b* Frankfurt, 28 Aug 1797; *d* Frankfurt, 22 March 1871) took the citizen's oath as an organ builder in Frankfurt on 15 June 1835. The brothers maintained the St Katharine organ (1829–33) and undertook a project at Frankfurt-Nied (1833).

The Wegmanns and Köhler belonged to the Middle-Rhine-Main-Franconian school of organ building. They used comprehensive Principal choruses with strong four-rank Mixtures in small instruments, six-rank in large ones. Also characteristic were the bass-treble division of Sesquialteras, in combination with a Cornet, and the use of Gamba, Salicional and Fugara as solo stops. Typically the *Hauptwerk* contained Trumpet and Fagotto reeds, and a Vox humana appeared in the *Positiv*.

BIBLIOGRAPHY

F. Bösken: 'Orgel', §V, 10a: 'Geschichte der Orgel seit 1500, Westdeutschland, Südteil', *MGG*

F. Bösken, H. Fischer, and M. Thömmes: *Quellen und Forschungen zur Orgelgeschichte des Mittelrheins. Bd. 2: Das Gebiet des ehemaligen Regierungsbezirks Wiesbaden*, parts 1 and 2 (Mainz, 1975)

H. Fischer: 'Johann Christian Köhler, Orgelbauer in Frankfurt am Main', *Acta Organologica*, vol.31 (2009), 217–75

FRANZ BÖSKEN/R

Wegscheider, Kristian (*b* Ahrenshoop, Germany, 20 Jan 1954). German organ builder and restorer. After army service and training with a cabinetmaker, he was apprenticed to the Jehmlich firm in Dresden, rising to become head of restorations. For Jehmlich he supervised work on the 1714 Gottfried Silbermann organ in Freiburg cathedral and the 1808 Lütkemüller in Güstrower cathedral. He then briefly joined the restoration staff of the instrument museum of the Karl Marx University (University of Leipzig) before opening his own workshop in Dresden Neustadt in 1989; he obtained his Meisterbrief in 1990. Wegscheider's first independent project was a new organ for Allstedt Castle in Mansfeld, noteworthy for using only traditional materials and for enabling performance in either of two temperaments. Subsequent projects included restoration of a small Silbermann organ (1734) at Bremen cathedral and replication of it for the Silbermann Museum in Frauenstein. Meanwhile Wegscheider's workshop expanded and relocated in 1993 to Rähnitz. A major restoration of Zacharias Hildebrandt's 1722 masterpiece at St Nicholas in Langhennersdorf was completed in 1996. Extensive experience with Silbermann and Hildebrandt organs led to contracts for new instruments based on their concepts, and to collaboration on several projects, including the Noack organ for Christ the King Lutheran Church in Houston, Texas (1995; two manuals, 30 stops, inspired by Hildebrandt). Wegscheider built another Hildebrandt-influenced organ for the Stuttgart Musikhochschule (2006; two manuals, 21 stops). In 2006–7 he collaborated with Jehmlich in restoring the Silbermann organ at the Freiburg Petrikirche (two manuals, 32 stops). By 2009 Wegscheider's workshop had restored numerous organs by Silbermann and builders of his school, and built 30 new instruments on historical principles. See J.H. Kuznik: 'Kristian Wegscheider: Master Restorer and Organbuilder', *The Diapason*, vol.100/5 (2009), 23–5.

LAURENCE LIBIN

Weidhaas. German bow makers. Ewald Weidhaas (1869–1939) was apprenticed to Hermann Pfretzschner. His son and pupil Paul Weidhaas (1894–1962) worked for Bausch and in Paris for Victor Fétique (whose name is sometimes stamped on his own bows), and then established a workshop in Markneukirchen; his daughter married Siegfried Finkel. Their son Johannes S. Finkel (*b* 1947) continues the family tradition in Switzerland.

Weigle. German firm of organ builders. It was founded in Stuttgart in 1845 by Carl Gottlieb Weigle (*b* Ludwigsburg, 19 Nov 1810; *d* 1882), formerly an apprentice to his brother-in-law, Eberhard Friedrich Walcker. Weigle built some 100 organs by 1880, when his son Wilhelm Theodor Friedrich Weigle (*b* Stuttgart, 17 Nov 1850; *d* Stuttgart, 6 Jan 1906) took over the company; he moved it to Echterdingen in 1888. There he patented (1893–4) a type of loud, high-pressure metal pipe (Stentor) with mouth extending across half the pipe's circumference, like a steam whistle; it did not endure. Yet under his direction the firm produced well-regarded pneumatic-action organs and exported instruments overseas. In 1902 the firm escaped bankruptcy. Together with J. & P. Schiedmayer, in 1908 Weigle built for the Protestant church in Eichwalde a hybrid harmonium and nine-stop pipe organ, called Parabrahm from an Indian term meaning 'perfection' and 'completion'; two others were built, in 1916 and 1921, but only the 1908 example (restored 2002) survives in its intended form.

After Wilhelm Theodor's death his sons Friedrich, Karl, Julius, and Gotthold continued the firm; in 1937, Friedrich (1882–1958) became the sole owner, succeeded by his son Fritz Weigle (*b* 1925). The company closed in 1985, but in 1986 Fritz's son Joachim F. Weigle (*b* 1960), who had apprenticed with Gerhard Schmid in Kaufbeusen, founded his own workshop, in St Johann-Upfingen near Reutlingen; he had completed nine instruments by 2008.

In the early 1980s the original Weigle firm had 35 to 45 employees and built organs ranging from positives to large church and concert-hall instruments. Important examples, which incorporate slider chests and tracker action, include those in the collegiate church, Tübingen (1965); Friedrichshafen Castle Church (1970); the Protestant church, Heiligenhafen (1974); the Catholic church, Trennfurt (1976); the Protestant church, Schriesheim (1977); St Martin's, Metzingen (1979); St Magnus's, Bad Schussenried (1979); the Protestant church, Katarini, Greece (1981); St Nikolaus's, Neuerburg (1981); St Martin's, Neuffen (1982); St Stephan's,

Würzburg (1983); St Pius, Oberhausen (1983); and the collegiate church, Mosbach (1983). The largest of these organs have up to 58 stops. See H. Fischer: 'Weigle, Carl Gottlieb', *Biographisch-Bibliographisches Kirchenlexikon*, vol.13 (Herzberg, 1998).

WALTER SUPPER/R

Weinreich, Gabriel (*b* Vilnius, Lithuania, 12 Feb 1928). Physicist and acoustician of Lithuanian birth, naturalized American in 1949. Youngest son of the great Yiddish linguist Max Weinreich, he emigrated to the USA with his family during World War II. He studied physics and atomic physics at Columbia University (BA 1948, MA 1949, PhD 1953). For 25 years he carried out research in semiconductor physics, first at Bell Telephone Laboratories and subsequently at the University of Michigan, where he was appointed to a chair in physics in 1964.

In 1977 he commenced a series of important studies in the physics of musical instruments with a landmark paper describing and analysing the tonal effects of the interaction between multiple strings struck by a single piano hammer. Several investigations into the acoustics of the violin followed, in which he developed innovative experimental methods and theoretical descriptions of the dynamics and radiation field of violins, including the first absolute measurements of violin radiativity, and discovered the violin's 'directional tone colour'. His unique approach, open-minded but always scientifically rigorous, shed much light on these frequently discussed but still controversial topics. He also made significant contributions to the acoustical investigation of woodwind and brass instruments, and to the computer synthesis of musical sounds. He worked on development of a 'digital bow' and electric violins, and on the theory and design of loudspeakers. He retired in 1995, but remained active in research. He was ordained a priest in the Episcopal Church in 1986. Among many honours, in 1991 he was awarded the Médaille Étrangère by the French Acoustical Society, and the Silver Medal in Musical Acoustics in 2008 by the Acoustical Society of America.

WRITINGS

'Coupled Piano Strings', *JASA*, vol.42 (1977), 1474–84

'What Science Knows about Violins—and What it Does not Know (Klopsteg Memorial Lecture)', *American Journal of Physics*, vol.61 (1993), 1067–77

with A. Hirschberg and J. Kergomard, eds.: *Mechanics of Musical Instruments* (New York, 1995)

MURRAY CAMPBELL/R

Weissenborn, Hermann Christof (*b* Hanover, Germany, June 1863; *d* Los Angeles, CA, 30 Jan 1937). American instrument maker of German birth. He is famous for wood-bodied Hawaiian steel guitars he manufactured in Los Angeles between 1915 and 1937. Little is known about his life in Germany. Weissenborn arrived in New York in 1902, then moved in 1910 to Los Angeles, where he worked as a piano repairman. He briefly partnered with one Fritz Pulpaneck to make violins, but an opportunity to build steel guitars shortly arose. Steel-guitar maker Chris J. Knutsen arrived in Los Angeles in 1914 to make instruments for music publisher and teacher Charles S. DeLano, but could not keep up with the demand for DeLano-branded Kona Hawaiian guitars, particularly with the growing Hawaiian music craze and the impending Panama Pacific Exposition. DeLano turned to other string instrument makers in the Los Angeles area, including Weissenborn. His earliest steel guitars are almost indistinguishable from Knutsen's as he learned the craft; however, his craftsmanship was superior. Weissenborn was soon making Hawaiian guitars with his own paper label, experimenting with tone woods such as spruce and maple as well as koa, an acacia sub-species found only in Hawaii. By about 1920 Weissenborn had settled on koa almost exclusively as his wood of choice, and in addition to his own brand was manufacturing steel guitars under private label arrangements for large department stores with brands such as Italian Madonna and Maui.

In 1923 Weissenborn established a factory to increase production. The production models included a burned-in brand rather than a paper label, and were offered in four styles from plain to fancy ornamentation. The factory also turned out Spanish guitars in four styles that paralleled the steel guitars, as well as a limited number of ukuleles, mandolins, pectrum guitars, and perhaps even violins. He also continued to make Kona guitars for DeLano. East Coast distribution was handled by Henry Stadlmaier until 1928 when Tonk Brothers of Chicago took over national distribution. By 1930 the demand for steel guitars was ebbing, and Weissenborn's production declined. Some of the rarest of Weissenborn's steel guitars include ones with solid square necks built during the period from 1916 to 1922, and so-called teardrop models built in the 1930s.

GEORGE T. NOE

Weisshaar, Hans (*b* Wildberg, Germany, 25 Aug 1913; *d* Los Angeles, CA, 24 June 1991). American violin maker and restorer, of German birth. He was born to musical parents, and as a young man studied violin making at the school in Mittenwald, Bavaria. After further experience in Switzerland, the Netherlands, and Germany, he emigrated to the USA in 1936, working as a restorer first with Emil Herrmann in New York, then with Lewis & Son in Chicago, and again with Herrmann until his workshop closed in 1945. During his time with Herrmann he worked under Fernando Sacconi. In 1947 he established his own business in Hollywood, California; it rapidly gained an international reputation from the excellence of his restorations.

Weisshaar was also an important teacher of restoration, and the alumni of his workshop represent many of the most important violin makers, bow makers, and restorers working nowadays. He put many of his ideas into the book *Violin Restoration: a Manual for Violin Makers* (Los Angeles, 1988), which he co-wrote with his assistant Margaret Shipman (*b* Denver, CO, 7 Oct 1946). Shipman had joined the workshop in 1969 and subsequently acquired the shop, continuing its operation after Weisshaar's death. In 2004 she in turn sold the business to Georg Eittinger (*b* Ingolstadt, Germany,

10 Sept 1965), who had previously worked with Weiss-haar, with Peter Benedek in Munich, and with Withers, Morris and Smith, and J. & A. Beare in London before returning to Los Angeles, and who has continued the high standards for which the firm is known.

Weisshaar's son Michael (*b* Chicago, 4 Nov 1942) and daughter-in-law Rena (*b* Berlin, Germany, 8 Feb 1940) also worked in the shop but in 1975 chose to open their own business in Costa Mesa, California. Both studied in Mittenwald, and have specialized in violin making, repairs, and dealing. Since 1999 they were joined by their son Daniel (*b* Los Angeles, 15 Sept 1967), who trained under Bernard Camurat in Paris and Michael Becker in Chicago.

PHILIP J. KASS

Weli-gugu. Small zoomorphic slit drum of the Zande people of the Democratic Republic of the Congo. See J.-S. Laurenty: *Les tambours à fente de l'Afrique centrale* (Tervuren, 1968), 140.

Well-tempered clavier. Term used in particular by J.S. Bach ('Das wohltemperirte Clavier') to signify a tuning system suitable for all 24 keys. The fame of Bach's 48 preludes and fugues, two in each of the 12 major and 12 minor keys (in fact only the first book, 1722, bore the title) led to the mistaken assumption that *wohltemperirt* was a standard technical term in Bach's day to designate a particular tuning; and on the basis of this assumption a difference of opinion arose as to whether it was equal temperament. Bach's choice of title disallows any form of regular meantone temperament (which would have a wolf 5th) and calls for a tuning well adapted to all 24 keys; but equal temperament was not the only such scheme employed at that time. Moreover, while many theorists, including Meckenheuser (1727), Sorge (1748), and Marpurg (1756), referred to equal temperament as a good tuning or even as the best of the good tunings, other influential theorists from Werckmeister in the 1680s to Bach's former pupil Kirnberger in 1776 held that a good temperament 'makes a pleasing variety' (Werckmeister, 1697) or does not 'injure the variegation of the keys' (Kirnberger, 1776–9).

There is no proof that Bach explicitly endorsed the latter view, but there is clear evidence that had he done so he would still have rejected the tunings advocated by his former pupil Kirnberger: they contain a pure major 3rd between C and E, whereas Bach had evidently taught Kirnberger to temper all the major 3rds larger than pure (see Marpurg, 1776, p.213). Thus not even the scheme referred to by scholars as 'Kirnberger III', in which the four 5ths C–G–D–A–E are each tempered by ¼ comma, would have conformed to Bach's practice, and the tuning primarily advocated by Kirnberger is an even more unlikely candidate as it obliges the two 5ths G–D–A to be diminished by the excessive amount of ½ comma each.

A selection of 18th-century temperaments that Bach would more probably have considered 'good' is shown in fig.1, which shows how much the various triadic concords are tempered according to each scheme, and how large the semitones are. Each hexachord

diagram represents a spiral in which F, A, and C♯ are to the right of B♭, D, and F♯; the unit of measure employed is the one most often used by 18th-century German theorists: 1/12 of the Pythagorean comma, or the amount by which each 5th is diminished in equal temperament (approximately 2 cents). To the right of each diagram the semitones are given in cents, and each row covers half the octave: by reading the numbers zig-zag between the two rows, one can see how the semitones vary according to their relation to the circle of 5ths. (In fig.1*b*, for example, the leading notes to C, G, D, and A are 110, 106, 102, and 98 cents beneath them respectively.) Fig.1*c* is a theoretical model; Werckmeister suggested that in practice he might leave C–G–D–A as in ¼-comma meantone temperament (tempered 2¾; units instead of 3). Fig.1*e* is a modern, approximate reconstruction to exemplify a style of tuning, not a specific theoretical model.

Bach would undoubtedly have been grateful to find any of these tunings (except perhaps the last one) on the organ. A hint of his more subtle preferences may be found in the remarks of his one-time pupil Lorenz Mizler (1737), his very well-informed friend G.A. Sorge (1748), and his son-in-law J.C. Altnickol (1753) to the effect that Johann Georg Neidhardt was a better theorist of tuning than Werckmeister. It is doubtful whether Bach had any one secret mathematical formula of his own; he was not so mathematically inclined in matters of theory. Werckmeister, Neidhardt, and Sorge all pointed out that circumstances such as the social ambience, the presence or absence of transposing instruments, the use of Cammerton *versus* Chorton, or the chromaticism of the music could have a bearing upon the exact nuance of temperament to be preferred, and Bach was probably no less exacting; according to his son C.P.E. Bach, no one else could tune a keyboard instrument to his satisfaction. C.P.E. Bach's own tuning advice allows for a few 5ths to be left untempered (implying a slightly unequal temperament), and he endorsed the mathematically vague instructions of Barthold Fritz (1757), which were ostensibly intended to render all keys 'equally pure', but actually tend to favour the diatonic 3rds.

Table 1 shows by what fraction of a comma the 5ths are tuned smaller than pure according to various theoretical well-tempered systems. Several of them distribute ¼ of the Pythagorean comma among the three 5ths C–G–D–A; ⅙ among E♭–B♭–F–C, and ⅓ among A–E–B–F♯–C♯–G♯. As fig.1 shows, the tempering of any 3rd or 6th will vary inversely with the sum of the tempering among the 5ths or 4ths that it comprises in the chain. (If the sum of tempering among them is an entire syntonic comma, 11 units, the 3rd or 6th will be pure; if they are all pure, the 3rd or 6th will be tempered by an entire syntonic comma; etc.) Of Werckmeister's schemes, only the one singled out by Christiaan Huygens, Sorge, and Marpurg in their discussions of Werckmeister is included in Table 1. The systems of Kellner and Barnes are modern proposals for the music of Bach, and share with Werckmeister's scheme a musically unfelicitous mixing of tempered and untempered 5ths among the

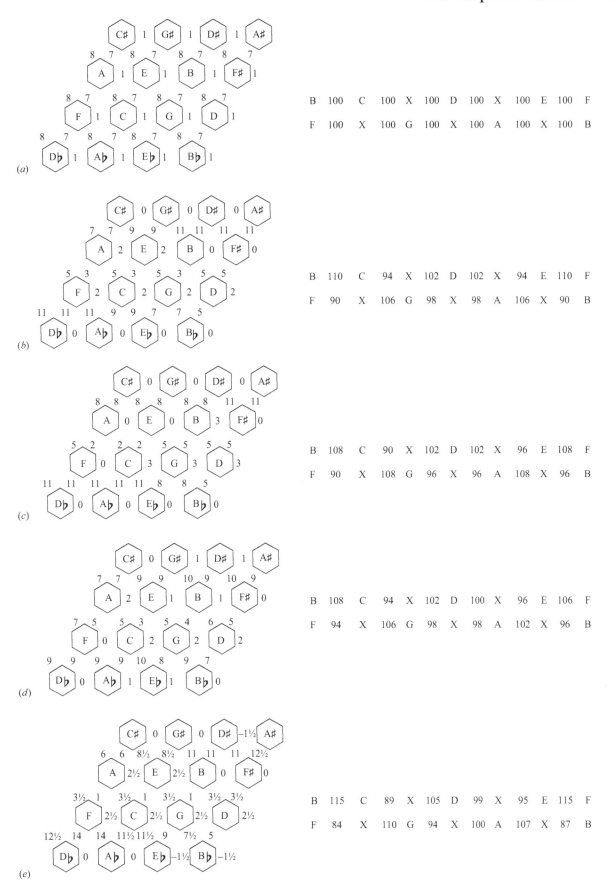

Fig.1: *Some well-tempered keyboard tunings: (a) equal temperament; (b) Vallotti's system; (c) Werckmeister's favoured system for the 'chromatic genus'; (d) one of Neidhardt's most preferred systems; (e) an approximation of French 18th-century 'tempérament ordinaire' without a wolf 5th.*

Table 1 Distribution of the Pythagorean comma in 12 'good' temperaments

																								Pure 5ths
Werckmeister (1681)	A♭	0	E♭	0	B♭	0	F	0	C	1/4	G	1/4	D	1/4	A	0	E	0	B	1/4	F#	0	C#	0	G# 8
Kellner (1977)	A♭	0	E♭	0	B♭	0	F	0	C	1/5	G	1/5	D	1/5	A	1/5	E	0	B	1/5	F#	0	C#	0	G# 7
Young (1800)	A♭	0	E♭	0	B♭	0	F	0	C	1/6	G	1/6	D	1/6	A	1/6	E	1/6	B	1/6	F#	0	C#	0	G# 6
Vallotti (*d* 1780)	A♭	0	E♭	0	B♭	0	F	1/6	C	1/6	G	1/6	D	1/6	A	1/6	E	1/6	B	0	F#	0	C#	0	G# 6
Barnes (1979)	A♭	0	E♭	0	B♭	0	F	1/6	C	1/6	G	1/6	D	1/6	A	1/6	E	0	B	1/6	F#	0	C#	0	G# 6
Lambert (1774)	A♭	0	E♭	0	B♭	0	F	1/7	C	1/7	G	1/7	D	1/7	A	1/7	E	1/7	B	1/7	F#	0	C#	0	G# 5
*Young (1800)	A♭	0	E♭	0	B♭	1/12	F	1/12	C	1/6	G	1/6	D	1/6	A	1/6	E	1/12	B	1/12	F#	0	C#	0	G# 4
Sorge (1744)	A♭	0	E♭	1/12	B♭	1/12	F	0	C	1/6	G	1/6	D	1/6	A	0	E	1/6	B	1/12	F#	1/12	C#	0	G# 4
Neidhardt (1724–32)	A♭	0	E♭	0	B♭	1/12	F	1/12	C	1/6	G	1/6	D	1/6	A	1/12	E	0	B	1/12	F#	1/12	C#	1/12	G# 3
Neidhardt (1724)	A♭	0	E♭	1/12	B♭	1/12	F	0	C	1/6	G	1/6	D	1/6	A	1/12	E	0	B	1/12	F#	1/12	C#	1/12	G# 3
Neidhardt (1724–32)	A♭	0	E♭	1/12	B♭	0	F	0	C	1/6	G	1/6	D	1/6	A	1/6	E	1/12	B	1/12	F#	0	C#	1/12	G# 4
Lehman (2006)	A♭	0	E♭	1/12	B♭	1/12	F	1/6	C	1/6	G	1/6	D	1/6	A	1/6	E	0	B	0	F#	0	C#	1/12	G# 3
*Mercadier (1776)	A♭	0	E♭	0	B♭	0	F	1/12	C	1/6	G	1/6	D	1/6	A	1/6	E	1/16	B	1/16	F#	1/16	C#	1/16	G# 3
equal temperament	A♭	1/12	E♭	1/12	B♭	1/12	F	1/12	C	1/12	G	1/12	D	1/12	A	1/12	E	1/12	B	1/12	F#	1/12	C#	1/12	G# 0

*systems originally formulated in terms of the syntonic comma

diatonic notes. (Werckmeister, 1697, p.32, did this in order to convert from ¼-comma meantone temperament by returning only some of the notes and yet to make C–E larger than pure.) Lambert's 1/7-comma arrangement might be regarded as a kind of synthesis of the four schemes preceding it in Table 1. The remaining systems are more elaborate in that they provide for more than one size of tempered 5th. Of Neidhardt's schemes, those which he recommended for a large or small town have been included, and Bach probably favoured something along these lines. The first volume of *Das wohltemperirte Clavier* was composed before the publication of any of these schemes, however, and may rather have been inspired by a non-mathematical book on the musical significance of unequal temperament published by Johann Mattheson in 1720; Bach visited Hamburg at the end of the same year and probably met Mattheson.

For the 3rds involving a sharp or flat, an averaging of the rigidly mathematical theoretical schemes of 'good' unequal temperament that Bach might have known about would be better suited to the subtle demands of his music than would any one of those schemes on its own. This is because the unit of measurement used by even the most meticulous of the German theorists of the day, 1/12 Pythagorean comma, is not fine enough to represent the nuances as subtly as a good tuner can control them by ear. The theoretical problem could have been overcome by dividing the unit, but none of the theorists did that.

One point which emerges from a comprehensive study of Bach's organ music, however, is that the most heavily tempered major 3rd was the one above C♯/D♭. Bach would, for instance, more readily treat F♯ minor as transposed Phrygian than transposed Dorian, and so would characteristically use F♯–A♯ in a more straightforward way than C♯–E♯ as a vertical sonority. This can be observed in such chorale settings as *Aus tiefer Not* (BWV687), *Erbarm dich* (BWV721), and *Herzlich tut mich* (BWV727). On the other hand, the 'St Anne' Prelude (BWV552) shows that the nuances of tempering on at least some organs available to Bach were subtle enough that he could compose virile, allegro organ music in E♭ major. The climactic (albeit inverted) D♭ triad towards the end of the Passacaglia in C minor (BWV582) occurs at such a stressful moment that some harshness in the intonation is, in this particular context, expressively apt. In a quieter way the tender effect of the relatively low intonation, in a 'good' temperament, of D♭ (and, though to a lesser extent, of A♭) when used as the 7th in a dominant 7th chord is tellingly exploited in such well-known chorale-preludes as *O Mensch bewein'* (BWV622) and *Schmücke dich* (BWV654). To tune really well for Bach, one should think in such terms and test with some characteristic examples of his fine use of the various notes of the chromatic scale.

The modern schemes included in Table 1 are only two of several neo-Baroque keyboard temperaments invented since the mid-1970s. These have often been improved upon after being tried out for a while. For instance, the Frobenius organ at Queen's College, Oxford,

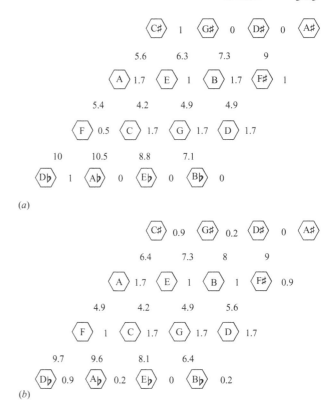

(a)

(b)

Fig.2: *Some neo-Baroque organ temperaments: (a), (b) Queens College, Oxford, in the 1980s and as improved in 1992.*

was tuned in the 1980s to the scheme shown in fig.2*a*. In 1992 the tuning was improved by raising slightly the chromatic notes and F, thereby letting D–F♯ be tempered more than F–A, preventing E♭–G from being tempered distinctly more than B–D♯, and likewise gaining a better balance between the temperings of A♭–C and E–G♯. The result is shown in fig.2*b*.

Bradley Lehman's assertion, first published in 2005, that Bach represented a favoured temperament by means of a pattern of shapes in what seems to be a decorative squiggle across the title page of Bach's 1722 manuscript has sparked vigorous controversy and further attempts to define Bach's tuning methods. For additional discussion of the musical characteristics and historical importance of well-tempered tunings, *see* TEMPERAMENTS. Instructions for tuning some of them have been published by Lindley (1977), Jorgenson (1977: 304, 323), and Blood (1979), and some have been reduced by Barbour to tables showing the distance (in cents) of the 11 notes of the chromatic scale above C.

For bibliography *see* TEMPERAMENTS.

MARK LINDLEY/R

Welte. German family of instrument makers, notable for developing various types of mechanical instrument. The firm, which began by making musical clocks and, from about 1848, barrel-operated orchestrion organs, was founded by Michael Welte (1807–1880) in 1832 at Vörenbach and later moved to Freiburg where it flourished under direction of Edwin Welte (1876–1957) and his brother-in-law Karl Bockisch; a branch opened in New York in 1865. The firm introduced perforated paper rolls instead of pinned barrels for orchestrions as early as 1885, and applied roll-playing mechanisms to player pianos by 1895. In 1904 M. Welte & Söhne introduced the first reproducing player piano under the name of 'Welte-Mignon'; it was developed and marketed in cooperation with Popper & Co. Originally in the form of a separate roll-operated player mechanism ('Vorsetzer') placed in front of the keyboard of a normal piano, it was later built into specially constructed grands and uprights by such prominent makers as Bechstein, Steinway, and Gaveau; in New York Welte-Mignon mechanisms were manufactured under licence to the Auto Pneumatic Action Co. Welte soon adapted this mechanism to player pipe organs of considerable complexity, some to specifications by Max Reger; these were sold under the trade name 'Welte-Philharmonie'. Many prominent musicians, such as Albéniz, Debussy, Grieg, Mahler, Paderewski, and Ravel, recorded for Welte. About 1933 Edwin Welte (1876–1957) designed the Lichtton-Orgel (an electronic organ operated by photocells), also known as the Welte organ. The firm suffered as interest in mechanical pianos and organs declined and it was liquidated shortly after the Freiburg premises were destroyed in 1944.

BIBLIOGRAPHY
Q.D. Bowers: *Encyclopedia of Automatic Musical Instruments* (Vestal, NY, 1972)
H. Weiss-Stauffacher and R. Bruhin: *Mechanische Musikinstrumente und Musikautomaten* (Zürich, 1975; Eng. trans., 1976)
HOWARD SCHOTT/LAURENCE LIBIN

Wembe. Side-blown animal horn of the Chaga/Meru people of the Arusha district, Tanzania.

Wender, Johann Friedrich (*b* Dörna, nr Mühlhausen, Thuringia, bap. 6 Dec 1655; *d* Mühlhausen, 13 June 1729). German organ builder. He rebuilt the organ at Divi-Blasii-Kirche, Mühlhausen, in 1687–91 (to a plan by J.G. Ahle); he built an organ at Seligenstadt Abbey, 1695; one at the Neue Kirche, Arnstadt, 1701–3 (two manuals, 23 stops; tested and played by Bach), and he enlarged the organ at Divi-Blasii, Mühlhausen, in 1708 (three manuals, 37 stops; to a plan by Bach). He also built an organ at the Maria Magdalen-Kirche, Mühlhausen, in 1702 (today preserved in Dörna), and at the Severikirche, Erfurt, in 1714 (the case survives); enlarged one at Merseburg Cathedral in 1714–16 and built one at the Kaufmannskirche, Erfurt, in 1728–9. His work was much in demand; among those who had a high opinion of it were Bach, Kuhnau, and Mattheson (who ranked him with Gottfried Silbermann).

In his Principal choruses Wender aimed at the classical arrangement (8′, 4′, 2⅔′, 2′, Mixtur, Zimbel, on the *Hauptwerk*; 4′, 2′, 1⅓′, Sesquialtera, Zimbel, on the Positive—even his Pedal upperwork normally included a Mixtur). He also included other flute stops of various kinds (16′, 8′, 4′ on the *Hauptwerk*; 8′, 4′, 2′ on the Positive); reeds were restricted to 8′ Trompete on the Great, with 16′ Posaune and 8′ Trompete on the Pedal, where

he often added (in the older style) higher stops, such as 2′ Cornett and 1′ Rohrflöte.

One of Wender's pupils was Johann Christian Dauphin, who later moved to Kleinheubach am Main, and another might have been his son-in-law Johann Nikolaus Becker, who later became court organ builder to the Prince of Kassel. Wender's son, Christian Friedrich Wender (dates unknown), restored the organ at the Marienkirche, Mühlhausen (1735–9). His reputation did not equal his father's.

BIBLIOGRAPHY
G. Stauffer and E. May, eds.: *J.S. Bach as Organist: His Instruments, Music, and Performance Practices* (Bloomington, IN, 1986)
W. Meinhold: 'Der Mühlhäuser Orgelbauer Johann Friedrich Wender und sein Wirken im Bereich des mitteldeutschen barocken Orgelbaues', *Mühlhäuser Beiträge zu Geschichte, Kulturgeschichte, Natur und Umwelt*, vol.10 (1987), 36–41
H. Fischer and T. Wohnhaas, eds.: *Lexikon süddeutscher Orgelbauer* (Wilhelmshaven, 1994)
F. Friedrich: *Orgelbau in Thüringen: Bibliographie* (Kleinblittersdorf, 1994)
HANS KLOTZ/FELIX FRIEDRICH/R

Wenthin, Joachim Friedrich (*b* Otterstedt, nr Bremen, 10 Aug 1746; *d* 27 May 1805). German organ builder, also active in the Netherlands. His largest organ, a two-manual, 40-stop instrument (destroyed in World War II) was completed for the Grosse Kirche St Cosmas und Damian, Emden, in 1779. Other important organs were built at Backemoor (1783), Zweins (1785), Nieuwolda (1787; his best-preserved instrument), Reepsholt (1789), Wolthusen (1790), Westerende (1793), Groothusen (1798), and Weener (1779–82), to which he added a *Brustwerk* and the last freestanding Pedal towers in northern Germany, and rebuilt the case in Rococo style. Wenthin introduced Rococo-style organ cases to East Friesland, along with 'modern' southern stops including the Viola di Gamba, Salicional, the labial Cornet, a wooden Traversflöte, Unda maris, and Vox angelica. He also employed equal temperament. Knock called Joachim Friedrich 'a famous artisan'.

His son Joachim Wenthin (*b* 12 Dec 1778; *d* c1850) continued the workshop after his father's death and followed his style, working on organs in Emden, Uithuizen (1816; now Niehove), and in Westphalia at Lotte (1807), Halverde (1817), and Tecklenburg (1838). He moved to Tecklenburg about 1820 and entered into partnership with W. Meese in 1840. It is thought that he also built chamber organs.

BIBLIOGRAPHY
W. Kaufmann: *Die Orgeln Ostfrieslands: Orgeltopographie* (Zürich, 1968)
F. Talstra: *Langs Nederlandse Orgels: Groningen, Friesland, Drenthe* (Baarn, 1979)
S. Tuinstra: 'Het Schnitger–Wenthinorgel te Weener (Ostfriesland)', *Het orgel*, vol.81 (1985), 293–9
ADRI DE GROOT

Werckmeister, Andreas (*b* Benneckenstein, Thuringia, Germany, 30 Nov 1645; *d* Halberstadt, Germany, 26 Oct 1706). German theorist, organist, organ examiner, and composer. His numerous treatises provide important documentation regarding organs and their tuning and musical thought in Germany in the 17th century. Werckmeister spent his whole life in the relatively confined area of Thuringia on the northeastern slopes of the Harz Mountains. His parents quickly recognized his musical gifts and sent him to an uncle, Christian Werckmeister, organist at Bennungen, near Sangerhausen, to study the organ and begin his general education. In 1660 he enrolled in the Gymnasium at Nordhausen and two years later moved to the Gymnasium at Quedlinburg, where another uncle, Victor Werckmeister, was Kantor. On 24 December 1664 he became organist at Hasselfelde, near Blankenburg, and remained there for ten years. He then served briefly as organist and notary at nearby Elbingerode and in 1675 returned to Quedlinburg, where through his uncle's recommendation he obtained the positions of organist at the collegiate church of St Servatius and at the court of Anna Sophia I, abbess and Countess Palatine; from 1677 he was also organist at St Wiperti. He took up his last post, as organist of St Martini, Halberstadt, in 1696.

Though not educated at a university, Werckmeister was widely read in classical as well as contemporary literature. He frequently referred in his writings to a number of German theorists, including Baryphonus, Calvisius, Gibelius, Kuhnau, Lippius, and Printz, and felt specially indebted to Michael Praetorius, whose unpublished manuscripts were (according to his *Organum Gruningense redivivum*) in his possession. He also knew treatises by Glarean and by such important Italian authors as Artusi, Galilei, and Zarlino. His own writings spread his influence widely in Germany in the 18th century: his treatises were often cited and discussed by such writers as Adlung, Mattheson, and Walther. Walther went to Halberstadt in 1704 especially to visit him, and this led to an instructive correspondence and obviously influenced Walther's treatise *Praecepta der musicalischen Composition* (1708).

Werckmeister was as celebrated an organ examiner as he was an organist. His *Orgel-Probe* provides a vivid picture of the methods he used in testing new or renovated instruments and, together with his report on the organ built in 1596 at the castle at Gröningen, near Halberstadt, has significantly furthered the success of modern efforts to revive interest in the building of organs suitable for the performance of Baroque music. He is well known for his innovations in the tuning of keyboard instruments, though he has been incorrectly credited with the introduction of equal temperament, which he never described accurately. For the perfect 5ths G–D, D–A, A–E, and B–F♯ he used a tuning slightly tempered by a quarter of a comma, while the eight other 5ths remained pure. In his system the 3rds varied from those a quarter of a comma too large to others equalling Pythagorean tuning. His method did, however, enable organists and harpsichordists to move through the 12 keys of the chromatic scale with satisfactory musical results. Although it stopped short of equal temperament, in which all semitone steps are equal, his contribution was the penultimate step in that direction.

For discussion of Werckmeister's theoretical writings and musical compositions, and extensive bibliography, see *GMO*.

WRITINGS
(selective list)

Orgel-Probe, oder Kurtze Beschreibung, wie und welcher Gestalt man die Orgel-Wercke von den Orgelmachern annehmen, probiren, untersuchen und den Kirchen liefern könne und solle (Frankfurt and Leipzig, 1681, 2/1698/R as *Erweiterte und verbesserte Orgel-Probe*, 5/1783; Eng. trans., 1976)

Musicalische Temperatur, oder Deutlicher und warer mathematischer Unterricht, wie man durch Anweisung des Monochordi ein Clavier, sonderlich die Orgel-Wercke, Positive, Regale, Spinetten und dergleichen wol temperirt stimmen könne (Frankfurt and Leipzig, ?1686–7[lost], 2/1691/R)

Hypomnemata musica, oder Musicalisches Memorial, welches bestehet in kurtzer Erinnerung dessen, so bisshero unter guten Freunden discurs-weise, insonderheit von der Composition und Temperatur möchte vorgangen seyn (Quedlinburg, 1697/R)

Cribrum musicum, oder Musicalisches Sieb (Quedlinburg and Leipzig, 1700/R, 2/1783)

Musicalisches Send-Schreiben (Quedlinburg and Aschersleben, 1700) [trans., with commentary, of A. Steffani: *Quanta certezza habbia da suoi principii la musica* (Amsterdam, 1695)]

Organum Gruningense redivivum, oder Kurtze Beschreibung des in der Grüningischen Schlos-Kirchen berühmten Orgel-Wercks (Quedlinburg and Aschersleben, 1705); ed. P. Smets (Mainz, 1932)

BIBLIOGRAPHY

J.M. Götzen: *Der Welt-berühmte Musicus und Organista wurde bey trauriger Leich-Bestellung des Weyland edlen und Kunst-Hocherfahrnen Herr Andreae Werckmeisters* (Halberstadt, 1707/R)

J.G. Walther: *Musicalisches Lexicon, oder Musicalische Bibliothec: Studienausgabe im Neusatz des Textes und der Noten*, ed. Friederike von Ramm (Leipzig, 1732; Kassel, 2001)

D.-R. Moser: *Musikgeschichte der Stadt Quedlinburg von Reformation bis zur Auflösung des Stiftes (1539–1802): Beiträge zu einer Musikgeschichte des Harzraumes* (diss., U. of Göttingen, 1967)

P. Williams: 'J.S. Bach, Orgelsachverständiger unter dem Einfluss Andreas Werckmeisters?' *BJb* 1982, 131–42; *BJb* 1986, 123–5

Bericht über das Werckmeister-Kolloquium aus Anlass des 340 Geburtstages von Andreas Werckmeister am 30 November 1985. (Blankenburg, 1986)

GEORGE J. BUELOW/R

Werkprinzip (Ger.: 'department principle'). Term coined probably during the German organ revival movement (*Orgelbewegung*) of the 1920s to describe the system for building organs in which each division ('department') or *Werk* (i.e. a keyboard with its chest or chests and pipes) has its own separate structure. For convenience the keyboards (manual or pedal) are brought together at one console, but the earliest examples of the Chair organ (Utrecht, *c*1390) might also have had their keyboard separate, behind the organist. Structurally separate but acoustically an entity, an organ could be built up of several discrete divisions depending on requirements. A likely order of size is as follows:

Hw
Hw + dep. pedal
Hw + Bw + dep. pedal
Hw + Rp + dep. pedal
Hw + Rp + independent pedal
Hw + Bw + pedal towers
Hw + Rp + pedal towers
Hw + Bw + Rp + dep. pedal
Hw + Bw + Rp + pedal towers
Hw + Ow + Bw + Rp + pedal towers

(Hw = *Hauptwerk*; dep. pedal = pedal pulldowns; Bw = *Brustwerk*; Rp = *Rückpositiv*; Ow = *Oberwerk*; pedal towers = 1 or 2 chests in tall boxes to right and left).

Usually, each department is built up on a Diapason rank (16′ pedal, 8′ Hw, and so on), hence the wrong explanation of the term as denoting '*Werke* based on a *Prinzipal*'. Almost all organs before about 1700 were built according to one or another of the plans; exceptions were those French, southeast European, Spanish, and English organs in which subsidiary chests were placed within the main case (*cadireta interior*, Echo, solo Cornet). The system's reputed advantages are that separate cases ensure maximum resonance and dispersal, departments can be added (at Lüdingworth, Hw/Bw of 1598, Rp/towers 1682), and such departments have different functions and sounds; non-Werkprinzip organs also allow for this, however, and the strongest reason for building Werkprinzip organs today is that the organ music of 1500–1720 was written for this type.

PETER WILLIAMS

Werner, Johann Georg (*b* Lippersdorf, Saxony, *c*1710; *d* Dresden, *c*1772). German brass instrument maker. He was documented in 1719 as a journeyman, and in 1728 as an instrument maker with citizen's rights in Dresden. Between 1753 and 1755 he devised a new horn in nine tonalities, from B♭ alto to B♭ basso, after Anton Hampel's instructions. Although it was claimed that the invention was later imitated by the Viennese maker Anton Kerner, the latter apparently created a unique set of terminal crooks, possibly with a general tuning slide, while Werner reportedly had adapted slide crooks to three different horn sizes. No such instruments are known to survive. In 1760 Werner was in partnership with his former apprentice Johann Gottfried Leuthold (*b* Dresden, *c*1720; *d* Dresden, 28 Aug 1728), who succeeded him in 1772. Surviving instruments include a hunting horn dated 1740 and a trumpet dated 1733. See W. Waterhouse: *The New Langwill Index: a Dictionary of Musical Wind-Instrument Makers and Inventors* (London, 1993).

RENATO MEUCCI

Wheatstone. English firm of music publishers and instrument makers. Although supposedly established in London about 1750, the earliest identifiable figure in the business was Charles Wheatstone (1768–1823), who came from a Gloucester family and who was active in London from about 1791. The firm was known as Wheatstone & Co. from about 1815 and about 1816 had a branch or agency at Bath. Charles's brother William (*b* Gloucester, 17 Aug 1775; *d* London, 12 July 1854) moved with his family to London in 1806, where he became a flute teacher and manufacturer and music seller on his own account from about 1813, holding patents for improvements to the instrument. He also published a number of books of airs for the flute.

William's sons, the future Sir Charles Wheatstone (*b* Gloucester, 6 Feb 1802; *d* Paris, 19 Oct 1875) and William Dolman (*b* Gloucester, 1804; *d* London, 30 Aug 1862), entered their uncle's business, which they took over following his death, and William senior then

amalgamated his own business with theirs about 1826. From his youth onwards the younger Charles's attention was largely directed towards scientific subjects, including optics, sound vibrations, and electricity. He was famous for his inventions in telegraphy, but he also invented the English concertina and Symphonium (a free-reed mouth organ with button keys), the patents for which were taken out between 1829 and 1844 and held by the Wheatstone firm for many years. In 1822 he invented the Acoucryptophone, a mechanical instrument described as a lyre-shaped chest hanging on a rope from the ceiling; it was wound with a key and imitated the sounds of orchestral instruments. Charles became a Fellow of the Royal Society, and was knighted in 1868.

The Wheatstone firm published a prodigious amount of sheet music, mostly of a popular nature. It also did an extensive trade as makers of and dealers in musical instruments, especially concertinas. The firm's fortunes declined during the 20th century, and the concertina business was acquired by Besson & Co. about 1944, that firm being itself taken over by Boosey & Hawkes in 1948. Small-scale production of Wheatstone concertinas was maintained until the mid-1970s, when the name, machinery, and stock were sold off to Steve Dickinson, who continued to manufacture instruments under the Wheatstone trademark.

BIBLIOGRAPHY

W.G. Adams: 'On the Musical Inventions and Discoveries of the Late Sir Charles Wheatstone, F.R.S', *PMA*, vol.2 (1875–6), 85–91

B. Bowers: *Sir Charles Wheatstone FRS, 1802–1875* (London, 1975)

A.W. Atlas: *The Wheatstone English Concertina in Victorian England* (Oxford, 1996)

FRANK KIDSON/WILLIAM C. SMITH/PETER WARD JONES/R

Whelpdale, Maxwell & Codd. British piano firm. Founded in 1876 by W.M.Y. Maxwell (*d* 1939) and William John Whelpdale (*b* Dec 1852; *d* 1914) as Whelpdale & Maxwell Ltd, the firm was initially created to import Blüthner pianos. With the death of W.J. Whelpdale, his son Arthur (*b* 1882) became an active partner. After a hiatus during World War I, Whelpdale & Maxwell resumed importing Blüthner pianos, but also contracted with Cremona Ltd in 1919 to manufacture pianos under the Welmar brand, a name reportedly created from the partners' names.

Cremona Ltd was founded in 1914 by the piano designer and technician Clarence Edward Lyon (1883–1960), the son and grandson of piano makers. Charles Squire, from another piano-making family, joined as a partner in 1919 and brought the brand name Squire & Longson. Cremona made well-designed, well-built instruments under various names for different retailers. For the Welmar and other Cremona-brand pianos Edward de Gruchy Whomes (1878–1960) devised improved soundboard production methods that included gluing the ribs onto pre-compressed, pre-shrunk soundboards. Alfred Knight (1899–1974) designed new angular, girder-like iron frames in the 1920s for the Cremona instruments; he opened his own factory in 1936. In the 1920s Cremona pioneered the use on pianos of sprayed cellulose lacquer finishes, which contributed to a fire that destroyed the factory in 1929. The factory reopened in 1931, but ensuing financial and production difficulties caused Cremona Ltd to close in 1934.

In 1934 Whelpdale & Maxwell purchased the Cremona designs and equipment, hired many former Cremona employees, and opened a new factory on Clapham Park Road, London. There they produced Welmar uprights and grands that were popularly called 'English Blüthners', because they emulated the Blüthner sound and appearance. During World War II, the firm was allowed to continue making pianos primarily for armed forces entertainment troupes. The Concentration of Industry Act required the factory to be shared with John Broadwood & Sons Ltd, Sir Herbert Marshall & Sons Ltd, and George Rogers & Sons Ltd. The factory also made wooden aircraft parts and wheels for gun carriages. In 1945 the long-time employee (and Arthur Whelpdale's nephew) Jack Codd became a partner, and the business name was changed to Whelpdale, Maxwell & Codd Ltd. That same year they purchased Sir Herbert Marshall & Sons Ltd, thus acquiring the high-end Marshall & Rose brand and an expanded dealer network. The Marshall & Rose pianos thereafter built by Whelpdale were identical to the Welmar pianos except for slight differences in case style.

During the 1960s Whelpdale, Maxwell & Codd partnered with William de Blaise (b Latvia, 1907) to make cases for modern harpsichords which Blaise's staff completed at a rate of up to 60 per year. These heavily constructed harpsichords have a plywood case with open bottom and employ piano-size keys, high-tensile steel strings, leather plectra, and a metal reinforcing plate.

In 1993 Whelpdale, Maxwell & Codd acquired the good will, trademarks, designs, and manufacturing equipment for the upright piano lines of the recently liquidated Bentley Piano Company Ltd, including the Bentley, Grover, Knight, Rogers, Steinberg, Hopkinson, and Zender brands. Their production was moved to the Clapham factory. Each line used different designs and construction methods, creating a range of tonal characteristics. In 2000 Whelpdale purchased the Woodchester Piano Company, which had opened in the old Bentley factory, creating the British Piano Manufacturing Co. as a wholly owned subsidiary. By this time their brands included Welmar, Knight, Marshall & Rose, Hopkinson, Steinberg, Stroud, Bentley, Woodchester, and Lipp, as well as the Knightsbridge piano made for Harrod's department store, and the Eavestaff which was made in China. In addition, they produced Broadwood pianos under licence for John Broadwood & Sons. By 2001 the company was making about 600 uprights a year while still importing Blüthner pianos and Blüthner's lower-priced Haessler line. In 2001 Whelpdale moved all operations to the Woodchester factory in Stroud, but many of the experienced Whelpdale employees chose not to move. This lack of skilled workers and problems of combining two very different lines contributed to the failure by 2003 of the British Piano Manufacturing Co. The brand names from the Woodchester factory were purchased by an import and distribution firm, Intermusic Ltd, of Poole, Dorset, and thereafter the names were applied to Chinese pianos having no resemblance to the pianos made in Clapham.

BIBLIOGRAPHY
L. Fine: *The Piano Book* (Boston, 4/2001)
E. Kottick: *A History of the Harpsichord* (Bloomington, 2003)
A. Laurence: *Five London Piano Makers* (London, 2009)

ANNE BEETEM ACKER

Whio ('to whistle'). End-blown wooden flute of the Māori people of New Zealand (Aotearoa). It is unlikely ever to have been common. It was reportedly made of two split pieces of *mataī* wood (*Podocarpus spicatus*), hollowed and lashed together in the same manner as the *pūtōrino* and *pūkāea*. It is said to have had three fingerholes and a thumbhole. No instrument matching this description is known, but confirmation of its historical existence was provided by Ernest Dieffenbach (1843), who equated it with the *pōrutu*. The term was reportedly applied also to flutes of human bone, known also as *kōauau*. See M. McLean: *Māori Music* (Auckland, 1996), 199–200.

MERVYN MCLEAN

Whip [clappers, slapstick] (Fr. *fouet, claquette*; Ger. *Holzklapper, Peitsche*; It. *frusta*). Concussion idiophone, or clappers, used to imitate the sound of a whip crack. The whip consists of two pieces of hard wood about 10 cm wide and 45 cm long, hinged together at one end and provided with a strap or handle on each leg; the player slaps the two surfaces together. A variant known as a slapstick incorporates a spring and requires only one hand to operate. The effect of several whip cracks in rapid succession is created by a 'double whip': two whips mounted side by side on a board, one operated by each hand.

The sound of a whip has been connected with musical activity for many centuries. An Assyrian bas-relief from Nimrud shows a dancer carrying a whip in his right hand, apparently for use as a timekeeper. A similar custom exists to this day in eastern Europe. Composers to make use of the whip effect range from Adolphe Adam (*Le postillon de Lonjumeau*, 1836) to John Adams (*Nixon in China*, 1987) and Thomas Adès (*Living Toys*, 1998; the whip is played by the principal french hornist). In Britten's *The Burning Fiery Furnace* (1966), a multiple whip of four different sounds or pitches is required. The slapstick was extensively used for comic effect in 20th-century cartoon film scores, music halls, and vaudeville, hence the term 'slapstick comedy'.

An actual whip, or lash, creates a loud crack not from the motion of its tip, but from a loop that travels along the length of the whip, accelerating until it exceeds the speed of sound and creates a sonic boom.

JAMES BLADES/JAMES HOLLAND/R

Whispering. Unvoiced vocalization technique involving a slight adduction of the vocal folds but not enough to create pitch, while still using the articulation of normal speech. Activity in the abductor muscles (the posterior cricoarytenoid) is increased in order to prevent vocal fold vibration. There is a smaller supralaryngeal

Whip effect, James Blades, probably mid-20th century. (Edinburgh University Collection of Historic Musical Instruments (2904))

aperture than in speech, creating constriction in the larynx.

Stage whispering is a louder form of whispering that has been a part of theatrical technique at least since the mid-19th century. Quiet whispering uses about twice the airflow rate of normal speech and loud whispering uses about three times the airflow. The activity in the thryopharyngeous muscles is two times greater in stage whispering than in quiet whispering, with even greater constriction in the supralaryngeal aperture. For many actors and singers, stage whispering, which is intended to be heard by the audience, can also involve some soft phonation.

Other types of unvoiced vocalization without pitch include gasping, panting, and sighing. Gasping involves a strong, sudden intake of breath through the mouth with sufficient adduction of the vocal folds so that the inhalation is audible. In panting, both inhalation and exhalation are audible during rapid, shallow, short breaths. Sighing is an audible exhalation with a slow, gentle release of the breath.

In the 20th century composers such as Ruth Anderson, Luciano Berio, Eric Chasalow, George Crumb, Olli Kortekangas, Gary Kulesha, Bernhard Lewkovitch, Witold Lutosławski, Elizabeth Vercoe, and Ilja Zeljenka began to incorporate unvoiced vocalizations into their music. Electronic amplification enabled singers such as Bing Crosby, Billie Holiday, and Frank Sinatra to make vocal nuances such as a whisper or sigh audible in live performance.

BIBLIOGRAPHY

S. Mabry: *Exploring Twentieth-century Vocal Music: A Practical Guide to the Innovations in Performance and Repertoire* (Oxford, 2002)

K. Tsunoda: 'The Roles of the Posterior Cricoarytenoid and Thropharyngeous Musicles in Whispered Speech', *Folia Phoniatrica et Logopaedica*, vol.46 (1994), 129–51.

SALLY SANFORD

Whistle (Fr. *sifflet*; Ger. *Pfeife*, *Signalpfeife*; It. *fischietto*; Sp. *silbato*). Short, usually high-pitched flute ('edge aerophone'), either without fingerholes or with no more than one (e.g. the cuckoo whistle; therefore, the pennywhistle, which has six fingerholes, is a duct flute, but not a whistle within this definition). Whistles can be of wood, cane, metal, plastic, glass, stone, shell, or any other material capable of containing a column or body of air. The distinction between flutes and whistles is difficult to establish (a small organ flue pipe or a tube of a disjunct panpipe, such as is used in Lithuania and by the Venda people of southern Africa, could be defined in the same way); it is normally considered that flutes are used for music and whistles for signalling, leaving a grey area for those instruments that are used, either by the same or by different peoples, for both purposes (e.g. swanee whistle). Whistles are blown in all the ways used on flutes: via a duct, across the side or the end, or into a notch. Whistles can be multiple (e.g. the police whistle) or single, and either tubular or with a vessel as the body, in the latter case sometimes with a captive pellet to add a roll to the sound, as with the football referee's whistle. They have been known to most cultures from prehistoric times to the present day.

JEREMY MONTAGU

Whistling. In humans, sound made by forcing breath across a small aperture formed by partly closed lips, by the teeth, or by the fingers resting on the tongue; also the technique of making this sound. The breath can be egressive or ingressive, enabling long phrases without using circular breathing. The mouth and vocal tract form the resonance chamber. Frequency changes are determined by subtle movements of the mouth and tongue; loudness is controlled by breath pressure.

The 'pucker' whistle (*sporgendo*) is the most common technique: the lips are tensed, rounded, and protruded, while the tongue tip is typically against the lower front teeth, enabling a very pure, penetrating tone quality. Palatal whistling involves placing the sides of the tongue on the roof of the mouth with the tip of the tongue just above the front teeth while gently blowing air over the tongue. Finger whistling involves usually placing two fingers or the index finger and the thumb together and inserting them in the mouth while pressing the tongue back into the mouth at its tip while keeping the lips taut over the teeth. Some finger whistlers use one finger from each hand. A sub-category of finger whistling is the Japanese *yubibue* technique, invented by Daizo Tamura (1913–2010) in the 1930s; he used one bent finger inserted knuckle-first into the mouth while bending the tongue backwards. Hand whistling involves folding one hand over the other and blowing though parallel thumbs, making the hands into an ocarina.

Most amateur whistlers have a range of about c'''–c''''; professional whistlers can have a three-octave range or greater, but most whistling occurs within the compass of the piccolo. The dynamic range is limited. Articulation, vibrato, and ornaments can be achieved by various means involving the lips, tongue, and vocal tract.

Whistling likely originated as a means of communication. Some languages, such as Siblo Gomero (of the La Gomera Canary Islands), are based on whistling. An early example of notated whistling occurs in an *air de* cour, 'Près de la belle Iris', published in the *Mercure Galant* in Dec 1710. Mozart praised the whistling of the virtuoso violinist Karl Michael von Esser (1737–*c*1795), though he was less enthusiastic about Esser's violin playing. Art whistling reached a zenith in the vaudeville era. Coloratura whistling, drawing on repertory from opera and art-song literature, was developed in Austria by performers such as Hans Tranquillini (*d* 1895), known as Baron Jean, and Joseph Bratfisch (1847–92). Guido Gialdini (1878–*c*1943) (born Kurt Abramowitsch), popular in the 1920s, was another famous coloratura whistler in this tradition. The last Viennese art whistler was the transsexual Rudolph Schmid (1925–2005), who took the name Jeannette Schmid and, under the stage name Baroness Jeannette Lips von Lipstrill, toured internationally and appeared on Broadway.

'Warbling', a whistling style emulative of birds, was the hallmark of the Woodward School, founded in Los Angeles in 1909 by Agnes Woodward (1873–1938). Her student Bing Crosby (1904–77) was a well-known warbler as well as singing actor. Marge Carlson, also a champion warbler, subsequently ran the Woodward school, renaming it the California School of Artistic Whistling.

The golden age for whistling in the USA was during the 1930s and 1940s, when whistlers regularly toured with big bands. Amateur whistling was so prevalent that it was banned in streetcars and in some municipalities. Some attribute the decline in amateur whistling to the invention of the transistor radio, but interest in whistling has been re-kindled since the late 1970s through the establishment of whistling competitions and conventions, the largest of which is the International Whistlers Convention in Louisburg, North Carolina.

BIBLIOGRAPHY

S. Wallon: 'Une "Chanson à siffler" au temps de Louis XIV', *Revue de Musicologie*, vol.54/1 (1968), 102–5

T.A. Wilson and others: 'Experiments on the Fluid Mechanics of Whistling', *JASA*, vol.1B (1971), 366–72

F. Newman: *MouthSounds: How to Whistle, Pop, Boing, and Honk for all Occasions … and then Some* (New York, 2004)

SALLY SANFORD

Whistling pot [whistling bottle, whistling water jar] (Sp. *vaso silbador*). Vessel whistle of pre-Contact American cultures from Peru to Mexico. It is a single- or double-chamber ceramic vessel with a small duct whistle formed in the spout. When it has two chambers, these are connected by a tube; one of the chambers has a zoomorphic or anthropomorphic spout that includes the whistle, and the other has an opening into which water can be poured. Tilting the vessel forces the water into the second chamber, compressing the air within and sounding the whistle. Blowing directly into the opening is also possible. Single-chamber vessels, with both a whistling spout and a fill opening, can also be sounded either by sloshing water within or blowing into the opening. No iconographic evidence supports the historical use of either method of sounding.

Thousands of ancient whistling pots have been found, and new ones are being produced nowadays. In double-chamber exemplars from the Moche (*c*200 BCE to *c*750 CE) and Chimú (*c*900 to *c*1460 CE) cultures, the whistle spout is usually shaped like a bird, a symbol of supernatural flight and power associated with shamans. Lack of contextualizing evidence has led to speculation about the instrument's function; interpretations include a valued gift, a ritual implement capable of inducing trance, and a medium of communication with spirits. Iconography from several ancient cultures that flourished in northern Peru associates whistling pots with Andean funerary art. See D.A. Olsen: *Music of El Dorado: the Ethnomusicology of Ancient South American Cultures* (Gainesville, FL, 2002), 127–33.

MALENA KUSS

White (i). English family of virginal makers, active in London. Of 22 known English virginals, 7 were built by members of the family. Thomas (i) was the father of Thomas (ii), and Gabriel Townsend apprenticed with him, so he was almost certainly a virginal maker. Thomas (ii) (bur. London, 5 Jan 1660) lived in Old Jewry, London. A surviving ottavino (1638, private collection) by him is most likely the child of a mother and child virginal, the only known example of this type made in England. His virginal of 1642 (*GB.L.v*) is the second-oldest known English virginal. It has a Flemish-style soundboard painting and naive paintings inside the lid and on the drop front. Other extant examples of his work are also typical English virginals (1651, *GB.Y.m*; 1653, Duke of Devonshire, Hardwick Hall, England). Thomas (iii) was admitted free of the Joiners' Company in 1669. A typical English virginal at the National History Museum, Cardiff, is probably by this Thomas White, but there has been some speculation about the date, possibly 1684. James, son of Thomas (ii), is recorded from 1656 to 1670. James was admitted free of the Joiners' Company by patrimony, 1 Dec 1656. He is mentioned as a virginal maker in Old Jewry in 1664. Probably he was an organ builder as well, as the will of the organ builder Ralph Dallam (*d* 1672) mentions his partner 'Mr James White Citizen and virginal maker of London'. Two rectangular virginals by James survive (1656, *GB.L.ml*; 1661, Bunratty Castle, Ireland), both of typical English construction with short octaves. The 1656 instrument's case is decorated with gilt embossed paper with the Plantagenet royal arms. See D.H. Boalch: *Makers of the Harpsichord and Clavichord 1440–1840* (Oxford, 3/1995).

ANNE BEETEM ACKER

White (ii). American violin makers. The brothers Ira and Asa White are generally considered the first truly professional American violin makers, and many of the following generation of Boston violin makers studied or worked with them. The claim that their father, John White Jr (1785–1869), was a violin maker was discounted by Ira's son, Daniel. Ira Johnson White (*b* Barre, MA, 9 July 1813; *d* Melrose, MA, 19 Dec 1895) was reportedly self-taught, creating his first violin from scavenged materials. By about 1830 he moved to Boston; his earliest known instrument is dated 1833. He exhibited instruments in Boston four times between 1839 and 1856, garnering awards of various levels. From 1845 to 1849 he was in business with a younger brother, James Henry White (1817–82), who repaired instruments. In 1850 Asa joined Ira in partnership at 52 Court Street and then 86 Tremont Street. They sold a variety of instruments (including imports), music, and accessories. A few guitars and drums from this period bear their label, but no bowed string instruments do. After examining Cremonese instruments in 1843, Ira began to adopt a classic style that commanded a high price for the time. After termination of his partnership with Asa in 1863 he moved to nearby Malden, and then to Melrose, where he lived and worked until his death.

Asa Warren White (*b* Barre, 8 Aug 1826; *d* Boston, 12 Nov 1894) learned violin making from Ira and also worked with a maker named Giradol (or Giraudot). From 1863 to 1869 he operated the Tremont Temple Music Store, was in partnership with Louis Goullaud until 1876, and then relocated to 50 Bromfield Street. In 1879 he briefly moved to Chicago, but by 1881 he returned to Boston, running a shop at 147 Tremont Street until 1888. He finally moved to South Boston, working for a few years at 633 East Broadway before dying in poverty. He participated in Boston exhibitions in 1874 and 1878, receiving gold and silver medals respectively. Besides the violins he made, he imported unvarnished instruments from Germany and regraduated and varnished them for resale. Based on the numbering system on his labels, he may have produced more than 400 instruments, which reportedly included a limited number of violas, cellos, violas da gamba, violas d'amore, and guitars. He was issued patents for a violin chinrest in 1869, a folding music stand in 1872, and a violin bow in 1887. The bow design requires two to three laminations of wood to increase lateral stiffness without adding weight.

BIBLIOGRAPHY
E. Wall: *The John White Family in the Boston Musical Scene, 1829–1935* (Salem, MA, 1978)
J.A. Gould: 'The Early Violin Makers of New England', *Journal of the Violin Society of America*, vol.16/1 (1999), 57–9
D. Kuronen: 'Early Violin Making in New England', *JAMIS*, vol.28 (2002), 5–62

DARCY KURONEN/R

Whitechapel Bell Foundry. Official name since 1968 of a bell foundry located in Whitechapel Road, East London. The origins of the foundry can be traced back to 1420 in the person of master bellfounder Robert Chamberlain. From 1570 its bells have been produced by members of the following families: Mot (16th century); Carter, Bartlett, and Clifton (17th century); Phelps, Lester, Pack, Chapman, and Mears (18th century); Mears, Stainbank, and Lawson (19th century); and Hughes (from 1904). From 1865 to 1968 the foundry was known as Mears & Stainbank. It is best known for making tower bells, both single and in diatonic sets, these mostly for swinging in the manner of English change-ringing, but some rung stationary, as chimes. From the early 19th century or earlier, it has also made handbells. At first these were mostly diatonic sets of 8 to 12 bells used to practise change-ringing; but as handbell music grew more popular in the 20th century it began to produce chromatic sets of 25 to 60 bells. Early in the 20th century the firm made sets of hemispherical bells, but these are no longer produced. Nowadays handbells comprise about one-fifth of its output. The foundry has also produced several carillons and it also manufactures bell frames, headstocks, wheels, clappers, and other accessories. During World War II it made military castings.

The Whitechapel Bell Foundry is widely known for the fine tone and tuning of its handbells. In tuning large bells for change-ringing, its present founders (along with others in England in the first part of the 20th century) replaced the dissonant augmented 7th interval between the lowest two partials with a full octave. Many older ringers complained that changes on such bells did not sound so pleasing, and it was found particularly inappropriate to extend or replace parts of an old set with parts of a new one. Consequently the Whitechapel foundry now usually adheres to a refined form of the old standard when restoring or enlarging peals of bells.

Whitechapel bells have been widely exported; a set was sent to St Petersburg in 1747 and a change-ringing peal was made for Christ Church, Philadelphia, in 1754. The two most famous individual bells by Whitechapel founders are the first Philadelphia Liberty Bell (cast 1752, cracked in the same year) and the second Big Ben of Westminster (cast 1858, still in use). Big Ben weighs 13.5 tonnes and is the largest bell ever cast by this foundry. Whitechapel continues to cast bells for sites throughout the world. In 2004 it finished replacing 58 of the 74 bells of the carillon at the Riverside Church, New York, reputedly the heaviest carillon in the world.

PERCIVAL PRICE/CHARLES BODMAN RAE/R

Whiteley, William (*b* Lebanon-Goshen, CT, 1789 or 1790; *d* Knoxboro, NY, 25 March 1871). American maker of woodwind instruments. Whiteley ran a music store and woodwind-making shop in Utica, New York, from 1810 to 1853. He probably learned the trade from Erastus Wattles (1778–1839) in Lebanon-Goshen before the family moved to New York. In 1816 he published *The Instrumental Preceptor*, one of the earliest American woodwind instruction books, revealing some of the music teaching methods and popular repertory of the day. The remains of his shop, discovered in 1965 by Frederick R. Selch and Victor Fell Yellin, show in some detail the process he used in making flageolets, flutes, and clarinets. More than 50 instruments signed by Whiteley survive. They include a barrel organ and two bassoons, as well as flageolets, fifes, flutes, and clarinets. He made one- to eight-key flutes and five- to ten-key clarinets. He leased a barrel organ to Trinity Episcopal Church in 1811 and was engaged to play it. Clarinets appear to have been his specialty, for the many surviving examples show that he made them in a wide variety of sizes (F, E♭, C, B♭, and B♭/A) in both Continental and English styles. His shop employed no more than one or two workmen, and each instrument is distinctive in design detail. His apprentice from 1832 and long-time associate, James A. Rich, continued the business for a short time after Whiteley retired, making brass instruments as well as woodwinds. Whiteley's significance lies in the volume and variety of clarinets he made, his publication, and the revealing remains of his shop. The Frederick R. Selch Collection of musical instruments and materials, including the remains of Whiteley's shop, is available for study at Oberlin College, Oberlin, Ohio.

BIBLIOGRAPHY
M.M. Bagg: *Pioneers of Utica* (Utica, 1877)
R.E. Eliason and F.R. Selch: 'William Whiteley, Utica, New York, Musical Instrument Maker', *JAMIS*, vol.36 (2010), 5–57

ROBERT E. ELIASON/R

Whithorn [May-horn, peeling-horn]. Rustic oboe constructed seasonally of green willow bark wrapped into a conical shape about 45 cm long or longer and fastened with hawthorn or blackthorn spines. A double reed made of a separate piece of flexible bark is inserted in the narrow end. It was widely used in Europe under different names, mainly by herdsmen for signalling; in England it was used in the Savernake Forest, Wiltshire, during the Whit Monday hunt and by Morris dancers in Headington, Oxfordshire, to announce May morning. It was also used as a child's toy and by itinerant vendors and tradesmen. It produces one loud sound which can be caused to fluctuate in pitch by variation of breath pressure. See H. Balfour: 'A Primitive Musical Instrument (the Whit-Horn)', *Reliquary and Illustrated Archaeologist*, vol.2 (1896), 221–4.

HÉLÈNE LA RUE/R

Whizzer [buzzer, spinning disc]. Free aerophone akin to the bullroarer, both being termed 'whirling aerophone' in the Hornbostel-Sachs classification. It differs from the bullroarer in that it reciprocates, spinning in its own plane, whereas the bullroarer spins on its axis. A whizzer is usually shaped like a disc, less often like a blade, or is a bone such as a pig phalange. It has two central holes through which a cord is threaded and its ends tied together to form a loop. The player holds one end of the loop in each hand, and spins it to form a tight twist; a fast outward pull on the twisted loop causes it to unwind rapidly and then wind up again in the opposite direction. The whizzer makes a humming sound as it spins, the pitch varying with its speed. Whizzers are known as toys but are also often associated with ritual or magic. Examples from around the world are called by various names (often onomatopoeic) such as *fur-fur*, *koororohuu*, *snorra*, *ūkas*, *umampembe*, and *uvuru*.

For example, Latvian names for whizzers include *dūcenis*, *smurkšķis*, *švurksts*, *ūkšķis*, *žūža*, and *žvūrgzdyns*; Latvian examples dating from the 10th century to the 17th are frequently excavated, and modern ones were used at least until the mid-20th century. In Skrapar, southern Albania, children sometimes make the *fugë* whizzer from a large button. In northern Albania the whizzer is known as *vrulë* and *vruletë*; among

Whithorn, Puku people, coastal region, Cameroon. Coiled strip of leaf, pinned with a long thorn, and a double reed of leaf. (Jeremy Montagu Collection, Oxford)

the Albanian Çamë people, living partly in Albania and partly in Greece, it is known as *zvurë*.

A variant form, sometimes called a whirligig, exists also in many countries. A rod or stick pierces through an object such as a large seed (Jamaica), a bamboo tube (Thailand), a walnut or pomegranate (Turkey), and so on, that serves as a handle, with a similar object affixed on top of the stick to act as a flywheel. A string passes through a hole in the handle and is wound around the stick, with usually a toggle on the other end of the string to make it easier to hold. Pulling the string spins the stick within the handle, the flywheel producing enough inertia to make the string wind up again, so making the buzz, which has also an idiophonic component as the stick rubs against the handle. Similarly, the friction of the string loop adds to the sound of the disc type.

The Albanian *bredhkaçe*, for example, is made of a corn stalk put through a pine cone or of a spindle of wood with a nutshell on the top. A larger variety called *vërvudë* in Skrapar is also known as *ujk* ('wolf') because it howls like a wolf. In the Labëri region (southwestern Albania) the *vidhivudë* has a spherical flywheel 7 to 10 cm in diameter. The yo-yo, some types of which are designed to make a sound, might derive from such instruments.

BIBLIOGRAPHY
P.R. Kirby: *The Musical Instruments of the Native Races of South Africa* (London, 1934, 2/1965), pl. 24/B.
L. Picken: *Folk Musical Instruments of Turkey* (London, 1975), 45–52, 343–6
V. Muktupāvels: 'Musical Instruments in the Baltic Region: Historiography and Traditions', *The World of Music*, vol.44/3 (2002), 21–54

JEREMY MONTAGU, ARDIAN AHMEDAJA, VALDIS MUKTUPĀVELS

Whizzing bow. Type of musical bow sounded by swinging it rapidly around, as with a bullroarer. It is found in

West Africa, China, Indonesia, and parts of Latin America, and is classified in the Hornbostel-Sachs system as a free aerophone (whirling). Examples include the Javanese *ower-ower*, also known as the *sara mbele* in the Wolowaru area of Flores, Indonesia, and as *jata* in other areas of Flores. It is a strip of young coconut palm leaf about 15 cm long and 3 cm wide, folded widthwise and lengthwise. The leaf spine is detached and threaded through both ends of the folded leaf, forming a bow between the two ends. A long string is attached at one end of the leaf. The folded leaf sections vibrate as the instrument is swung, but, unlike a bullroarer, it does not rotate as it whirls. In Flores it is a girls' toy. The Balinese *guangan* is made of two narrow slats of bamboo, up to 2 metres long and 5 cm wide, attached to a large kite, which when flown produces a drone not unlike that of the Indian *tambura*.

Wia [yua, hua, wiik, wua]. Wooden notched flute of northern Ghana, particularly of the Builsa and Kasena Nankani peoples. It typically has two or three fingerholes and is played with drums and xylophones, or alone by shepherds and hunters, sometimes for signalling or as a bird call. The wia is also found in south-central Benin, particularly as an accompanying instrument for the Fon music *tchinkoumé*. Fon names for the wia include *kpeté* and *koué*. In the Volta region the Ewe refer to it as *ekpe*. Some modern African compositions employ the wia. A modern commercial version, 12 cm long, has two fingerholes, one on either side, in protrusions covered by thumb and index finger.

GAVIN WEBB/R

Wiard. Modular synthesizer manufacturer owned and operated in Milwaukee, Wisconsin, by Grant Richter (*b* Racine, WI, 1956). Richter, a design engineer at Micronetics International, Inc. from 1990 to 1999, collects vintage synthesizer equipment and was a founding member of the Midwestern Electronic Music Ensemble (MEME). Wiard produces two series of modules (all with a distinctive blue front panel with a Celtic knot design): the custom-order 300 line and the less expensive, less versatile FracRac-compatible 1200 line. Richter describes the Wiard system as a cross between the ARP 2600 and Buchla Music Easel. Production of the 1200 series ended in March 2012, but several module designs have been licensed to other manufacturers. The popular Miniwave, a wavetable audio and control voltage processor, licenced to Blacet Research, makes use of EPROMS (erasable programmable read-only memories) to hold 256 waves that can be tailored to specific functions, either using available wavetables, or by programming the EPROMS with Richter's Wave256 software. The synthesizer module manufacturer Malekko is reissuing early Wiard designs in Eurorack format.

The versatile 300 series modules are built by Grant Richter and provide most classic modular system functions. As of 2012, the eight modules available provided among them four oscillators, two single voltage-control amplifiers (VCA), two stereo VCA/ring modulators, three multimode filters, four envelope/lag processors,

Detail view of a row of Wiard 300 Series modules with Bantam Jacks option. (Cary Grace)

a random voltage source, an eight-stage sequencer, and six four-way multiples. The Sequantizer module can double as a waveshaping oscillator and frequency divider, while the Envelator module can act as a dual low-frequency oscillator, mixer, VCA, chaotic function generator, and voltage-controllable attack, decay, sustain, and release. The Waveform City module can function as a simple analogue oscillator and is one of the few wavetable oscillators that can respond to audio-frequency modulation. The Classic VCO module provides a purely analogue oscillator.

ANNE BEETEM ACKER

Wicks Organ Co. American organ building firm. It was incorporated by 1908 by the brothers Louis J. Wick (1869–1936), Adolph A. Wick (1873–1943), and John F. Wick (1881–1948) in Highland, Illinois. Louis and John were originally watchmakers, and Adolph a cabinetmaker. In 1899 they together had built an organ in Louis's workshop for the local Catholic church, where John was organist. The firm's earliest organs employed mechanical or tubular-pneumatic action, but in 1914 the Wicks developed a direct-electric windchest action which, unlike the electropneumatic actions employed by most other builders of this period, opened the individual pipe valves without pneumatic assistance. Refinements of this system, which facilitated the unification or duplexing of small organs, were patented in 1922 and 1929, and the direct-electric system, although since copied by others, continued to be the hallmark of this firm's work. Many of their early organs were small, some made to stock designs, but organs of the pre-war period also included some of significant size, including those for Temple Beth El, Detroit (1935), and Holy Name Parish, West Roxbury, Massachusetts (1938), the latter voiced by Henry Vincent Willis, who briefly worked for the Wicks firm at that time.

John Henry Wick (1912–40) and Martin M. Wick (1919–2002), sons of John F. Wick, entered the firm during this period, Martin becoming its president in 1948. The firm thrived in the postwar period and their organs were ultimately found throughout the USA. A line of small organs was developed for homes, schools, and small churches, but the firm also produced some significant large organs, including those for Sacred Heart Cathedral, Rochester, New York (1966), First Methodist Church, Peoria, Illinois (1977), and a 92-rank instrument for Morehouse College in Atlanta (1982). John Sperling began a long career as tonal director in 1957, and about 1993 Mark Wick succeeded his father as president, with Barbara Wick as chairman of the board. During this later period a large organ for St Helene's Cathedral in Helena, Montana, was built (2008) and a new version of the small stock design was developed that comprised both pipe and digital voices. By 2010 the Wicks opus list, including rebuilds, exceeded 6400 instruments. In 2011 the firm ceased manufacturing but continued with maintenance work.

BIBLIOGRAPHY

W.H. Barnes: *The Contemporary American Organ* (Glen Rock, NJ, 8/1964)

'Wicks Number One', *The American Organist* (July 1972), 40

M.W. Perin: 'The Wicks Organ Company', *The American Organist*, vol.23/2 (1989), 56–8

K.W. Capelle and M.W. Haberer: 'Martin M. Wick', *The American Organist*, vol.27/3 (1993), 67–8

BARBARA OWEN/R

Widhalm, Leopold (*b* nr Vienna, Austria, 2 Oct 1722; *d* Gostenhof, Nuremberg, Bavaria, 10 June 1776). Austrian luthier, active in Germany. Apparently his style was formed in part by work on old Bolognese lutes. Some consider him the most important 18th-century violin maker in Germany outside Mittenwald. In 1745 he took a job in the Nuremberg shop of Barbara Schelle (*d* 1781), daughter and successor of the luthier Sebastian Schelle (1646–1744). Widhalm and Barbara Schelle married in 1746, instigating a legal dispute with Leonhard Maussiell (1685–1760), who had wanted to take over the business, which grew into the largest of its kind in Nuremberg, producing excellent lutes and violins. Widhalm was a fine craftman who often used handsome material. His primary inspiration was Jacob Stainer, from whose violin model he appears seldom to have departed. Widhalm's best violins have a soft orange or orange-red varnish, others light brown. Occasionally he made dark, almost black violins of small merit. He made very good cellos and violas. Instruments of the same character as his, and with the same label and interior brand 'L.W.', came from the couple's sons Martin Leopold Widhalm (1747–1806) and Gallus Ignatius Widhalm (1752–1822). Their grandson Johann Martin Leopold Widhalm (1799–1855), also participated in the business. See K. Martius and T. Drescher: *Leopold Widhalm und der Nürnberger Lauten- und Geigenbau im 18. Jahrhundert* (Frankfurt am Main, 1996).

CHARLES BEARE/LAURENCE LIBIN

Wieck, Wilhelm (1828–74). German piano maker, active in Dresden. He is sometimes supposed to have been a pupil of Blüthner. A maker of no special distinction, he is remembered chiefly because he was a cousin of the celebrated pianist Clara Wieck (the wife of Robert Schumann). Probably he made mostly square pianos; few of his instruments are extant. A rosewood-encased grand of about 1860, the only Wieck piano in the USA, is in the music department of the University of California at Berkeley. Another grand, of six-and-three-quarter-octaves range, has belonged since the 1970s to the Robert-Schumann-Haus in Zwickau, and another, of 1866, is in the Schumann-Haus in Leipzig.

Clara's father, Johann Gottlob Friedrich Wieck (*b* Pretzsch, Saxony-Anhalt, 18 Aug 1785; *d* Loschwitz, Saxony, 6 Oct 1873), operated a music store that sold and rented pianos, some bearing his name; a square piano signed 'Friedrich Wieck' is on loan to the Grassi Museum, Leipzig.

Wieprecht, Wilhelm (Friedrich) (*b* Aschersleben, Saxony-Anhalt, 10 Aug 1802; *d* Berlin, Germany, 4 Aug 1872). German musician and instrument designer. He was the most important member of a prominent musical family. After receiving instruction in wind instruments from his father, Wieprecht studied in Dresden and Leipzig and in 1824 was appointed a royal chamber musician in Berlin. In 1825 he reorganized a military band, introducing some valved instruments. From 1828 to 1843, while remaining a civilian he accepted various positions of leadership, ranging from the regimental band of the Royal Life Guards to the entire Prussian military musical establishment. At the founding of the German Empire in 1871, Wieprecht's musical organization was introduced in all the other German states.

His interest in wind instruments brought him into contact in 1828 with the firm of Griesling & Schlott, makers of the first practical piston valves. Soon after, he entered into a long-lasting association with J.G. and C.W. Moritz. Wieprecht's name has been associated with the plump-looking Berlin valve (Ger. pl. *Berliner Pumpen*), for which he was refused a Prussian patent in 1833. However, there were actually two types of Berlin valve. Wieprecht's (which he called a 'Stecherbüchsen-Ventil') is distinguished by its valve loops, with inlets and outlets on opposite sides of the valve casing, while a model devised by Stölzel (called by him a 'Röhrenventil'), for which a patent had been refused in 1827, has slides, with inlets and outlets on the same side of the casing. Patented or not, the Berlin valves were so successful that Adolphe Sax fitted many of his instruments with them, calling them 'cylindres' (not to be confused with rotary valves, collectively called *Zylinder-Maschine* in German.) A meeting between Sax and Wieprecht in Koblenz in 1845 was inconclusive.

In 1835, with J.G. Moritz, Wieprecht was granted a Prussian patent for a revolutionary new instrument, the wide-bore chromatic 'Bass-Tuba' with five valves (later expanded to six). His preoccupation with problems of intonation presented by the combination of two or three valves led to his invention in 1838 of the 'piangendo', a device allowing valved brass instruments to play portamento.

Wieprecht's enthusiasm for military music was not confined to brass; in 1839 he devised the Bathyphon, a military-style contrabass clarinet, made by the firm of Skorra. He also invented the '16füssiger Orgelbass' (1845), a bass double-reed woodwind with covered system; it was played by one hand on a one-octave keyboard. This led to C.W. Moritz's development of the 'Claviatur-Contrafagott', patented in 1856.

Wieprecht's letters to various German musical papers (*c*1845) give the most complete near-contemporary account of early valve mechanisms.

BIBLIOGRAPHY

A. Kalkbrenner: *Wilhelm Wieprecht, Direktor: sein Leben und Wirken nebst einem Auszug seiner Schriften* (Berlin, 1882)

H. Heyde: *Das Ventilblasinstrument* (Leipzig, 1987)

H. Heyde: 'The Early Berlin Valve and an Unsigned Tuba at the Shrine to Music Museum', *JAMIS*, vol.20 (1994), 54–64

PHILIP BATE/EDWARD H. TARR

Wier [Weyer]. German crumhorn makers active from the late 15th or early 16th century to the mid-16th century in Memmingen. Their instruments are marked with a single, double, or triple reverse 'f'; this symbol corresponds to an 'I' or 'J' in contemporary script. Judging by the marks and by documented activity over a wide period (1513–65), there appear to have been two or three crumhorn makers of this name: Jörg (i) (*d* ?before 1530), Jörg (ii) (*b c*1485–90; *d* ?1549), and Jörg (iii) (*fl* ?1557–65). References occur to a 'Jörg Weyer' in Memmingen records of 1513, 1518, and the 1520s, sometimes describing him as a town musician; these could concern Jörg (i) or Jörg (ii) or both of them. The listing of voters for the referendum in 1530 on the proposals of the Augsburg Reichstag includes only one Jörg Weyer (he was one of the small minority of voters who rejected the Reformation proposals); it seems therefore that Jörg (i) had died before 1530. References to the name after that date must be to Jörg (ii), as are probably those to an unnamed Memmingen crumhorn maker. In 1549 the records of Nuremberg, which had bought crumhorns from Memmingen in 1539, mention the death of 'the crumhorn maker', believed to be Jörg (ii). However, a great bass crumhorn marked with the double reverse 'f' (*CZ.P.nm*) survives from the Rožmberk (Rosenberg) court band, which was established in 1552; this suggests that crumhorns were still being made with the Wier mark after the death of Jörg (ii). The maker might have been the 'Jörg Weyer' mentioned in the Memmingen records in 1557 and 1565, probably a son of Jörg (ii). No other crumhorn makers are known to have been active in Memmingen or Nuremberg.

Differing marks on surviving Wier instruments are correlated with different designs. The single reverse 'f' mark is found on small, unkeyed crumhorns, mostly of type II. The double reverse 'f' mark is found only on instruments of type III. Two crumhorns of type III, with decorated key covers dated 1522 and 1524 (now in *A.W.km* and *I.R.ms*), carry the name 'Ioerg Wier' and a double mark. The latter instrument is also marked with a triple reverse 'f', the only known occurrence of this form. (The Schnitzer family of wind instrument makers,

active at the same period in Nuremberg and Munich, used a similar system of single and double marks.)

30 Wier crumhorns survived until World War II (more than half of all surviving crumhorns), when two were lost. Most of these were made by Jörg (ii); all sizes, from soprano ('Exilent') to great bass, are represented. The instrument dated 1522, an extended tenor, is the earliest dated crumhorn with extension keys, and the Wiers might have been responsible for developing the classic type III crumhorn. Wier crumhorns were greatly sought after; the courts at Dresden, Ambras (near Innsbruck), Rožmberk, and Trent (the prince-bishop's court) are all known to have owned sets, as did the city of Nuremberg and probably Augsburg. A set in the old cathedral in Salamanca is thought to have been there since the 16th century.

BIBLIOGRAPHY

B.R. Boydell: *The Crumhorn and other Renaissance Windcap Instruments* (Buren, 1982), chap.5

L. Cervelli: *Antichi strumenti in un moderno museo: Museo Nazionale degli Strumenti Musicali, Roma* (Rome, 2/1986, ed. R. Meucci)

J. Hanchet and R. Schlenker: 'Bedeutender Fund in Salamanca, Spanien: Entdeckung und Untersuchung der Pommern und Krummhörner in der mittelalterlichen Kathedrale in November 1983', *Tibia*, vol.11 (1986), 125–30

W. Waterhouse: 'A Hitherto Unrecorded Crumhorn in Belgium', *Galpin Society Newsletter*, vol.16/Oct (2006), 2–3

BARRA R. BOYDELL/R

Wietfelt. German family of woodwind instrument makers, active in Burgdorf (dates below refer to Burgdorf). Hans (*b c*1620; *d* 1687/98) was a fishmonger and brewer before 1687, when he was described as a 'Pfeifenmacher'. His son Harmen (Hermann) (bap. 27 Jan 1669; *d* ?Burgdorf, after 1727) supplied two bassoons and three oboes to the local court in 1715–16. In England, a 1720 inventory listed 'a basson [*sic*] made by H. Wietzfell'. E.L. Gerber (*Historisch-Biogaphisches Lexikon der Tonkünstler*, Leipzig, 1790–92) described Harmen as 'famed far and wide for his excellent oboes and bassoons … his father and his brother Johann follow the same trade but do not nearly approach him in skill'. Harmen had a brother Johann, not otherwise known as a maker, in addition to the maker Johann Erich described below. A bassoon marked 'Harm. Wietfelt/Burgdorf' survives at the Horniman Museum, London.

Philipp Gottlieb (bap. 7 Nov 1706; *d* 12 Dec 1768), a son of Harmen, was described in 1738 as a 'widely famed maker of musical instruments'. He reportedly repaired a flute for Frederick the Great. His son Philipp Gottlieb (*bapt* 14 April 1743; *d* 28 Aug 1793) was described at his death as an instrument maker and brewer. Four marks, each including the words 'G. Wietfelt' or 'Gotlieb [*sic*] Wietfelt', are attributable to either the father or the son. Surviving instruments with these marks include an oboe, a clarinet, and a bassoon.

Friedrich Christian Ludwig (*b* 7 or 28 Dec 1781; *d* 25 Oct 1821), son of the second Phillip Gottlieb, was described upon his death as a 'tradesman, also distiller and instrument maker'. Another son, Andreas Heinrich (*b* 17 May 1771; *d* 26 March 1829), was described in 1796 as a musical instrument maker; he was also a wind player in the military. One of the later Wietfelts was evidently known for his bassoons, so much that 38 bassoons, delivered in 1788 by C.W. Sattler to J.A. Crone, were described as 'Wittfeld [*sic*] models with the D♯ key'.

Other early Wietfelts of unknown relationship were described as instrument makers. A bassoon marked 'Erich/Wietfeld' (at *D.HA.b*) has been attributed to Johann Erich, possibly Harmen's nephew, who married in Burgdorf in 1715. Friedrich Martin (Martinus Friedrich) Wietfelt (*b* 9 Nov 1704; *d* after 1749) was described, when his son married in 1770, as an 'experienced instrument maker'.

BIBLIOGRAPHY

W. Waterhouse: *The New Langwill Index: a Dictionary of Musical Wind-Instrument Makers and Inventors* (London, 1993)

H. Heyde: 'Entrepreneurship in Pre–Industrial Instrument Making', *Musikalische Aufführungspraxis in nationalen Dialogen des 16. Jahrhunderts*, ed. M. Lustig and others (Michaelstein and Augsburg, 2007), 25–63

G. Dullat: *Verzeichnis der Holz- und Metallblasinstrumentenmacher auf deutschsprachigem gebeiet* (Tutzing, 2010), 501–2

JAMES B. KOPP

Wilbrook [Willbrook, Wellbroke], **John** (*fl* London, 1730–39; will proved 22 Dec 1739). Harpsichord and spinet maker. He might be linked to a John Wellbroake baptized in Newton Ferrers, Devon, on 27 Sept 1666, or to the Hanoverian harpsichord maker Hermann Willenbrock, although no direct evidence supports either supposition. His premises from about 1735 were in Rupert Street, St James's, Piccadilly, where the harpsichord maker Heming Lockton also briefly resided. Wilbrook's double-manual harpsichord dated 1730 (Mirrey Collection, *GB.E.u*) resembles typical later 18th-century English instruments, except that its keyboards have ebony naturals and skunk-tail accidentals. The underside of the soundboard is inscribed 'Johannes Wilbrook Londini fecit Tabel's man', indicating that, like Burkat Shudi and Jacob Kirkman, he was an employee and perhaps apprentice of Hermann Tabel. A bentside spinet of his also survives. A 'Clavichord made by Wilbrook' advertised for sale in the *Country Journal or The Craftsman* on 9 June 1733 suggests that he produced a wider variety of keyboard instruments. His daughter, Ilse Maria, married the trumpet and horn maker John Christopher Hoffmaster in St James's, Piccadilly, on 1 March 1741.

BIBLIOGRAPHY

G. O'Brien: 'The Double-manual Harpsichord by Francis Coston, London, *c*.1725', *GSJ*, vol.47 (1994), 2–32

D.H. Boalch: *Makers of the Harpsichord and Clavichord, 1440–1840* (Oxford, 3/1995), 208, 682

LANCE WHITEHEAD

Wilhelm, Karl (*b* Lichtental, Romania, 5 July 1936). Canadian organ builder of German ancestry. He was brought up near Weikersheim, in southern Germany, and was apprenticed between 1952 and 1956 to Aug. Laukhuff in Weikersheim, where he received his diploma. In 1957 he joined W.E. Renkewitz in Tübingen, and later worked for Metzler & Söhne in Diedikon, Switzerland. In 1960 he emigrated to Canada to establish the department of

mechanical-action organs at Casavant Frères. In 1966, when he became a Canadian citizen, he set up his own business at St Hyacinthe, Quebec, delivering his first instrument to Christ Memorial Lutheran Church, Montreal (1966). His opus 5 (two manuals, 19 stops), built the following year for St-Bonaventure, Montreal, stands out as an exceptional example of his early work. His first three-manual organ was built in 1972 for Trinity Church, Southport, Connecticut; this was immediately followed by the magnificent instrument for St Matthias Anglican Church, Westmount, Montreal. The latter organ is arguably one of his best three-manual instruments. In 1974 he moved to Mont-St-Hilaire, Quebec, where by 2004 he had completed 160 organs, including 13 three-manual instruments, the largest being the 50-stop organ at St Andrew's Presbyterian Church in Toronto (1983). Other notable large organs include those at Christ Church Cathedral in Montreal (1980; three manuals, 42 stops), L'Abbaye Saint-Benoit-du-Lac in St-Benoit, Quebec (1999; three manuals, 42 stops), and St John Catholic Church in Fenton, Michigan (2003; three manuals, 44 stops). The last organ he built was for Asbury United Methodist Church in Livermore, California (2004; two manuals 24 stops); since then he has been active as an organ consultant and technician. Wilhelm's organs are found throughout Canada and the USA, and as distant as South Korea.

Wilhelm's organs are exclusively mechanical-action instruments, designed in a range of styles (French, German, Italian, or a mixture). His organs are not replicas but remain faithful to the *Werkprinzip* principle, incorporating suspended actions and flexible winding systems, as well as unequal temperaments. The specifications and voicing of his instruments are patterned after classical traditions. His individual stops are noted for their purity of sound, his well-balanced ensembles for their fullness of tone. His small instruments, including positives and regals, are regarded as highly as his larger organs.

BIBLIOGRAPHY

A. Bouchard: 'Evolution de la facture d'orgue au Canada entre 1960 et 1975', *Organ Yearbook*, vol.9 (1978), 70–82

K.J. Raudsepp: *Organs of Montreal*, vol.1 (Montreal, 1993)

KARL J. RAUDSEPP/R

Wilkinson & Sons. English firm of organ builders. It was founded in Kendal about 1829 by William Wilkinson (1805–70). His uncle Thomas Greenwood was a member of a Halifax weaving family who began building organs about the time of Wilkinson's birth and continued in Yorkshire until about 1860. Wilkinson, too, was initially taught handloom weaving but might have learned about organ building from his uncle. The specification of Wilkinson's first known organ, for Ebenezer Methodist Church, Northowram, near Halifax, has not survived, but another, for the New Connexion Chapel (1834), had one manual and six stops, without pedal. Nothing more is known of Wilkinson's early work, and the story that he collaborated with William Sturgeon, the inventor of the electromagnet, in applying electromagnetic action to an organ, has not been substantiated.

Wilkinson began full-time organ building in 1856 in partnership with his son, Thomas (*c*1835–1917); their first organ was finished the following year. Wilkinson & Son also undertook piano tuning and repairs, and served the local families of William Wordsworth and John Ruskin. Father and son built mainly small organs, excepting one of three manuals for Ulverston Parish Church (1866). Thomas directed the firm after his father's death and embarked on more ambitious projects beginning in 1880, when, against competition from William Hill & Son and other leading London builders, he won a commission for a four-manual, 54-stop organ for the Preston Corn Exchange; completed in 1882, this masterpiece (recently destroyed) established Wilkinson's reputation and led to other substantial commissions, including a three-manual, 37-stop organ for St George's Church in Kendal (1883). About this time Thomas's sons William Greenwood and Croft Wilkinson joined the firm as Wilkinson & Sons.

Work continued on a substantial scale in the northern counties until about 1900, after which the company built and rebuilt organs on a more modest scale. After Thomas's death the firm was directed by his sons and from 1935 by Croft's daughter, Margaret. The business was finally acquired in 1957 by Rushworth & Dreaper of Liverpool.

BIBLIOGRAPHY

G. Sumner: 'Thomas Wilkinson of Kendal and the Organ in Preston Public Hall', *JBIOS*, vol.1 (1977), 26–48

G. Sumner: 'Wilkinson of Kendal and the Organ in St. George's Church, Kendal', *BIOS Reporter*, vol.21/1 (Jan 1997)

MICHAEL SAYER/R

Williams, Peter (Frederic) (*b* Wolverhampton, West Midlands, England, 14 May 1937). English musicologist and organist. He was a scholar at St John's College, Cambridge (BA 1958, MusB 1959), where he studied with Thurston Dart and Raymond Leppard, and where he took the doctorate in 1963 with a dissertation on English organ music and organs 1714–1830; from 1964 he studied the harpsichord with Gustav Leonhardt. In 1962 he went to Edinburgh University as lecturer in music and subsequently became reader (1972), professor (1982), and dean (1984). In 1969 he was appointed director of the Russell Collection of Harpsichords and Clavichords at the university, and from 1992 honorary consultant and honorary professor. He became professor and university organist at Duke University, North Carolina, in 1985, and director of its Center for Performance Practice studies in 1988. He was appointed John Bird professor at the University of Wales, Cardiff, in 1996. He founded the *Organ Yearbook* in 1970 and is its editor, and also general editor of the facsimile series *Biblioteca organologica*. He was chairman of the British Institute of Organ Studies from 1997 to 2007 and has been a vice-president of the Royal College of Organists since 2004.

Williams is a clear and vigorous writer on music, with firm views on organ structure and history acquired during extensive research on European visits; he has also written on interpretation, notably concerning continuo accompaniment. In a manner characteristic of Dart's pupils, his work shows a clear-cut relationship between study of source material, instruments, and practical performance, and his own thoughtful and often original harpsichord interpretations of, for example, Bach and Couperin have been praised. He has edited numerous volumes of keyboard music by Bach, Handel and others, and is general editor of Bach's organ music for the New Oxford J.S. Bach Edition. For full bibliography see *GMO*.

WRITINGS
(*selective list*)

'The Organ in the Church of St John, Wolverhampton', *The Organ*, vol.41 (1961–2), 8–15

English Organ Music and the English Organ under the First Four Georges (diss., U. of Cambridge, 1963)

'The First English Organ Treatise', *The Organ*, vol.44 (1964–5), 17–32

The European Organ, 1450–1850 (London, 1966/R, 2/1968)

'Equal Temperament and the English Organ', *AcM*, vol.40 (1968), 53–65

S. Newman: *The Russell Collection and Other Early Keyboard Instruments in Saint Cecilia's Hall, Edinburgh* (Edinburgh, 1968)

'The Earl of Wemyss' Claviorgan and its Context in Eighteenth-Century England', *Keyboard Instruments: Studies in Keyboard Organology*, ed. E.M. Ripin (Edinburgh, 1971, 2/1977), 75–84

'Some Recent Developments in Early Keyboard Instruments', *ML*, vol.52 (1971), 272–80

A New History of the Organ from the Greeks to the Present Day (London, 1980)

The Organ Music of J.S. Bach (Cambridge, 1980–4/R 2003)

'J.S. Bach's Well-Tempered Clavier: a New Approach', *EMc*, vol.11 (1982), 46–52, 332–9

'The Snares and Delusions of Musical Rhetoric: some Examples from Recent Writings on J.S. Bach', *Alte Musik: Praxis und Reflexion*, ed. P. Reidemeister and V. Gutmann (Winterthur, 1983), 230–40

ed.: *Bach, Handel, Scarlatti: Tercentenary Essays* (Cambridge, 1985) [incl. 'Figurenlehre in the Keyboard Works of Bach, Handel and Scarlatti', 327–46]

'Was Johann Sebastian Bach an Organ Expert or an Acquisitive Reader of Andreas Werckmeister?', *JAMIS*, vol.12 (1986), 38–54

B. Owen: *The Organ* (London, 1988)

'Theophilus and Early Medieval Technology', *Organ Yearbook*, vol.22 (1991), 95–117

The King of Instruments: How Churches Came to Have Organs (London, 1993)

The Organ in Western Culture, 750–1250 (Cambridge, 1993)

'The Idea of Bewegung in the German Organ Reform Movement of the 1920s', *Music and Performance during the Weimar Republic*, ed. B. Gilliam (Cambridge, 1994), 135–53

'Towards a Close Reading of Philipp Emanuel Bach', *Eighteenth-Century Music in Theory and Practice: Essays in Honour of Alfred Mann*, ed. M.A. Parker (Stuyvesant, NY, 1994), 143–58

J.S. Bach: a Life in Music (Cambridge, 2007)

DAVID SCOTT/R

Williams & Sons. Canadian instrument manufacturer and seller, founded in 1855 by Richard Sugden Williams (*b* London, 12 April 1834; *d* Toronto, Feb 1906). Williams arrived in Hamilton, Ontario, in 1838 and in his teens was apprenticed to the melodeon maker William Townsend in Toronto. In 1855 Williams opened a small shop in Toronto selling imported square pianos and instruments that he made, including mandolins, banjos, and, later, melodeons. Over the next 20 years the R.S. Williams Co. expanded to include guitars, violins, brass instruments, pianos, and larger reed organs. Williams acquired an interest in the Canadian Organ & Piano Co.

in Oshawa, Ontario, in 1873 and took control in 1889. The company became R.S. Williams & Son when Richard's son Robert (*b* 1854) joined the company in 1880, and the Canadian Organ & Piano Co. was renamed Williams Piano Co. in 1902.

By the beginning of the 20th century Williams claimed to have the largest instrument factory in Canada, producing upright, grand, and player pianos and some pipe organs in Oshawa. Robert became president of the company after his father's death. By 1920, 250 employees were manufacturing 240 pianos monthly. Brands made or distributed by Williams included Beethoven, Canada, Ennis, Everson, Krydner, New Scale Williams, Plaola (player pianos), Princess, Schubert, and Williams.

When Richard Sugden Williams Jr (1874–1945) entered the company in 1909, it became R.S. Williams & Sons. Williams Jr, considered an expert in violins, employed skilled craftsmen from France, Holland, Italy, and Canada to make violins after Stradivari and others. By 1919 branches were open in Montreal, Calgary, and elsewhere. The company became the Canadian distributor for Edison phonographs and records in 1900 and for Westinghouse and Magnavox radios by 1926. The piano and organ factory in Oshawa closed in 1932, but mandolins, banjos, and guitars continued to be sold in Toronto in the firm's retail outlets. The retail side of the business was sold to B.A. and F.A. Trestrail in 1928 but continued under the name R.S. Williams Co., Ltd in Toronto and later as a warehouse-type operation until it closed in 1951 or 1952.

BIBLIOGRAPHY

W. Kelly: *Downright Upright: a History of the Canadian Piano Industry* (Toronto, 1991), 91–3

H. Kallmann, G. Potvin, and K. Winters, eds.: *The Encyclopedia of Music in Canada*, (Toronto, 2/2002), 1408–9

JESSE MOFFATT

Willis, Henry (*b* London, England, 27 April 1821; *d* London, England, 11 Feb 1901). English organ builder. He was articled to John Gray about 1835 but left before completing his apprenticeship to work with Wardle Evans of Cheltenham, an organ builder and maker of harmoniums. Willis later claimed to have developed a two-manual reed organ with Evans (1841) and to have met Dr Samuel Sebastian Wesley when it was exhibited in London. This meeting was the prelude to an association that was to be of considerable significance in Willis's career.

Meanwhile, Willis returned to London and set up in business as a pipe maker and organ builder (*c*1845). By 1848 he was at 2½ Foundling Terrace, Gray's Inn Road, moving subsequently to 18 Manchester Street (1851–9) and then 119 Albany Street (1859–65), and finally acquiring a remarkable circular building in Camden Town ('The Rotunda Organ Works') previously used as a studio by Robert Burford, a painter of cycloramas. His first major contract was the rebuilding of the organ in Gloucester Cathedral, which he completed in 1847 for £400; he provided a 12-stop, full-compass Swell and described this job as his 'stepping stone to fame'. This was premature, though he rebuilt the organ in Tewkesbury

Abbey in 1848 and about the same time journeyed to France to meet Aristide Cavaillé-Coll and C.S. Barker, inventor of the pneumatic lever.

Much of Willis's eventual success can be attributed to his technical skills. He was one of the great artist-engineers of the 19th century. Not only was his workmanship of the highest order, he satisfied the demands of the rising generation of concert organists for a more musically flexible instrument able to render orchestral scores convincingly. In the church sphere, he met the requirements of architects who wanted to remove central screens and expose vistas. In each case, the exploitation of the pneumatic principle first developed by Barker and Cavaillé-Coll offered a way forward. The long series of Willis patents includes pneumatic thumb pistons for effecting instantaneous changes of registration (1851), improvements in the design of pneumatic levers (1851, 1853), and a crescendo pedal (1857) and blow-tube for operating swell shutters (1861), both activated pneumatically. Other patents describe improvements in pallet design to lighten the touch (1851, 1861, 1862). Later, Willis won favour with architects when he used the new tubular-pneumatic action (which dispensed with the need for a mechanical connection between key and pallet) to achieve the physical division of large organs; the most famous example was St Paul's Cathedral (1872), with others at Durham (1876) and Salisbury (1877). His development of tubular-pneumatic action began in the 1850s and was confirmed by patents issued in 1868 (drawstop action) and 1889 (Vincent Willis's invention of an all-pneumatic mechanism).

Tonally, Willis's early work appears relatively conservative. Although it impressed by its sheer size (70 stops) and the novelty of thumb pistons, Willis's organ for the Great Exhibition (1851), with its duplication of chorus registers and conventional selection of 'fancy' stops, seemed to be pursuing a line of development that Hill had discarded as obsolete 15 years earlier. Yet it impressed Dr Wesley sufficiently for him to acquire part of the Exhibition organ for Winchester Cathedral (1854) and to support the awarding of the contract for the monster organ for St George's Hall Concert Room, Liverpool (100 stops), to Willis. Completed in 1855, the Liverpool organ retained anachronistic features such as G'-compasses, duplication, and unequal temperament (all at Wesley's insistence), but the skilful application of the pneumatic lever turned what might have been a disaster into a qualified triumph, and Willis was later able to repair the organ's shortcomings (1867, 1896). There were more economic schemes from this period that hinted at future trends: at Carlisle Cathedral (1856) 11 of the 35 stops were reeds, and the Swell flue chorus with its Flageolet 2′ and Echo Cornet already presented the appearance of an enclosed accompanimental division rather than a secondary chorus *à la* Hill.

In his instruments of the 1860s further characteristics of Willis's mature style can be detected. Powerful yet brilliant reeds, using closed shallots, weighted tongues, and harmonic resonators in the treble, spoke on wind pressures appreciably higher than the fluework and dominated the choruses; the flue choruses were made up of pipes of relatively small scale, narrow-mouthed, and blown hard. The result was an intense ensemble that blended well and lent itself to a gradual crescendo from *piano* to full organ. Tierce mixtures added to the intensity, and slotting (creating a rectangular slot near the top of a flue pipe as part of the voicing process) encouraged clarity in the bass. The *Pedale* (Willis's favoured terminology) might have a complete flue chorus up to a mixture as well as a weighty 16′ reed (often called Ophicleide). In all of Willis's instruments from the 1860s onwards there would be a variety of refined orchestral and accompanimental voices—Gedacts, Violas, Harmonic Flutes, Claribel Flute, Gemshorn, Corno di bassetto, and perhaps an enclosed undulating register in the modern French manner. This 'middle' period saw some of Willis's finest achievements: two organs for the Alexandra Palace (1868, 1875), the Royal Albert Hall (1871), St Paul's Cathedral (1872), and Salisbury Cathedral (1877).

The later instruments lose none of the refinement and superb finish, but some of the vigour and brilliance of the earlier organs is absent. Wind pressures were increased (at Truro Cathedral, 1887, the lowest was 10 cm); the Pedal reed became a climax stop and the Pedal upperwork disappeared; mixtures and mutations became fewer and less assertive. Willis's last cathedral organ, for Lincoln (1898), had 58 stops, but only one mutation and six ranks of mixture.

The engineering of Willis's organs is always impressive. The Liverpool organ might have been old-fashioned in its tonal design, but the spaciousness of its layout and the finish of its component parts represented a novel standard in English organ building. Willis frequently adopted a horizontal layout for the manual windchests—Great, Choir and Swell, one behind the other—and although he made increasing use of tubular-pneumatic action, and even electropneumatic action in large organs for difficult sites (Canterbury Cathedral, 1885), his preference for most of his career was for tracker action, pneumatically assisted in the larger instruments. Beginning with the big concert organs of the 1860s and 70s his consoles set a new standard in elegance and accessibility, with their solid ivory stop-heads, overhanging keys, and angled jambs. Willis frequently installed the concave and radiating 'Wesley–Willis' pedalboard (said to have been suggested to him by Wesley at the 1851 Exhibition) though it did not find much favour with other builders until after his death in 1901.

Such was Willis's reputation in the closing years of his career that the music journalist F.G. Edwards proposed that he be given the title 'Father' like his distinguished forebears, John Howe and Bernard Smith. For half a century following his death his pre-eminence among Victorian builders was hardly questioned. Today, a more measured judgment acknowledges him as a tonal and mechanical engineer of genius, while reasserting the pivotal role of William Hill in the development of the Victorian organ pre-Willis and paying due regard to Willis's contemporaries (and rivals) Thomas Hill and T.C. Lewis. Willis's success owed everything to

his ability to satisfy the desire of many influential organists for an organ that mirrored the power and colour of the orchestra and had the mechanical equipment to exploit these characteristics to the full. Yet his instruments provoked strong reactions. For every organist who applauded the direction that Willis had taken, there was another who deplored it.

In 1878 Willis had taken his two sons, Vincent (*c*1841–1928) and Henry (ii) (*b c*1851), into partnership. Vincent withdrew in 1894. The financial difficulties in which 'Father' Willis left the firm overshadowed Henry (ii)'s tenure, and he took his own son, Henry (iii) (1889–1966), into partnership in 1910. Henry (iii) rapidly assumed control of the firm, and under his direction it was responsible for two of the most important organs of the first half of the 20th century—Liverpool Cathedral (1912–26) and Westminster Cathedral (1922–32).

Most of 'Father' Willis's larger organs have been destroyed or extensively rebuilt, but among whole or partial survivals can be mentioned Lambourn Parish Church, Berkshire (1858), Reading Town Hall (1864, 1882), St George's, Preston (1865), St George's, Tiverton, Devon (1870), Union Chapel, Islington (1873), St Paul's Cathedral (1872), Salisbury Cathedral (1877), Truro Cathedral (1887), Blenheim Palace, Library (1891), Hereford Cathedral (1893), Oxford Town Hall (1897), and St Bees Priory, Cumbria (1899). Smaller instruments are more numerous, but even they are becoming rarer, and they should be jealously guarded.

BIBLIOGRAPHY

E.J. Hopkins and E.F. Rimbault: *The Organ: its History and Construction* (London, 1855, 3/1887/*R*)

Interview, *MT*, vol.39/663 (1898), 297–303

W.L. Sumner: *Father Henry Willis, Organ Builder, and his Successors* (London, 1957)

C. Clutton and A. Niland: *The British Organ* (London, 1963, 2/1982)

N.J. Thistlethwaite: *The Making of the Victorian Organ* (Cambridge, 1990)

S. Bicknell: *The History of the English Organ* (Cambridge, 1996)

NICHOLAS THISTLETHWAITE

Willson Band Instruments. Swiss brass instrument makers. Willy Kurath Sr (*b* Flums, 4 June 1929) founded the firm in 1950 as a repair workshop for brass and woodwind instruments in Flums, canton St Gallen. From 1943 to 1947 Kurath studied instrument making with his uncle Ernst Giger in Winterthur; from 1947 to 1950 he worked for Pini in Heerbrugg and Reiner in Thun, and subsequently for Getzen in Elkhorn, Wisconsin. In 1955 he built a new workshop in Flums and produced his first self-developed high brass instruments with rotary valves. Research and development of euphonium and tuba designs commenced in the same year. In 1965 a larger workshop was erected at the same location and the firm's name changed from Kurath to 'Willson Band Instruments Switzerland'; the current facilities were built in 1970. Willson produces a full line of brass instruments but has specialized in euphoniums, horns, and tubas. Innovations include 'compact bells' (seamless bells made stress-free in one piece) and, in 1993, the patented 'Rotax' rotary valve system, raising air-passage efficiency to 100%; this system is also sold to other brass makers. Kurath retired in 1991, and direction of the firm passed to his son Willy Kurath Jr (*b* Flums, 1 Feb 1961), who had trained at Willson from 1976 to 1980. See W.R. Kälin, *Die Blasinstrumente in der Schweiz* (Zürich, 2002).

HOWARD WEINER

Wind-cap [reed-cap] **instruments.** Wind instruments on which the reed, usually a double reed, is enclosed within a rigid cap (Ger. *Windkapsel, Mundkapsel*; Fr. *capsule à vent*) normally of wood. The player blows through a hole at one end of the wind cap, causing the reed to vibrate freely; because there is no contact between the lips and the reed the tone cannot be affected by direct lip pressure as it is with an open reed. Overblowing is not usually possible, so the range of most wind-cap instruments is restricted to those notes that can be fingered directly, normally a 9th; in some cases this range is increased by the use of keys, and there is evidence that the range of crumhorns was extended downwards by underblowing (blowing with less than usual wind pressure). The wind cap also protects the reed from damage. On many such instruments, the players sometimes removed the wind-cap to play, as scattered evidence confirms.

Wind-cap instruments are related to the bagpipe and the bladder pipe, in which a reed vibrates freely within a bag or bladder; they differ from them significantly, however, in that the rigid wind cap allows articulation by the interruption of the flow of air through the reed by tonguing, whereas the flexible bag or bladder maintains a reservoir of air under pressure so that the reed vibrates continuously and cannot be affected by tonguing. True wind-cap instruments are first recorded in the late 15th century—the crumhorn in 1488 in Italy, and the wind-cap shawm in 1493 in Germany.

The origins of the wind cap are uncertain: it might have evolved from bagpipes and bladder pipes, probably not by the simple replacement of the flexible bag with a rigid cap, but by the development of the wooden stock of the bagpipe chanter or the protective collar round the reed of a bladder pipe. Certain hornpipes of the later Middle Ages, known as 'mouth pipes', had a piece of horn at the upper end surrounding the reed (usually a single reed); when pressed against the mouth for playing, this horn structure functions, in effect, as a primitive wind cap. Instruments of this type survived into the 18th century in Wales and Scotland, where they were known respectively as pibcorn and stock-and-horn. However, these mouth horns were found primarily in Atlantic Europe, particularly in Britain and Spain, areas not associated with the early occurrence of true wind-cap instruments. Meyer has speculated that the wind cap evolved from the pirouette that supported the player's lips on many early reed instruments.

During the Renaissance a wide variety of wind-cap instruments was developed, of which the crumhorns and wind-cap shawms such as the *Schreyerpfeife* were the main representatives. These instruments fell out of use in art music during the 17th century, by which time changes in musical taste and the requirements of composers had made their small compass and lack of expressive range seem unacceptably restricted. Some wind-cap shawms survived as folk instruments into the 19th century, and the practice chanter of the Highland bagpipes represents a modern survival of the wind-cap principle.

Wind-cap instruments may be grouped in four categories:

(i) Crumhorns and related instruments with cylindrical bore. The crumhorn was the principal wind-cap instrument from the late 15th century to the early 17th; it is associated mainly with Germany, northern Italy, and the Low Countries. Although predominantly cylindrical, the bore flares slightly in the lower, curved section of the body. The cornamusa, a rare form of straight, soft 'crumhorn' with muted bell, was little known outside Italy, though Praetorius (2/1619) described it. There are isolated references in Germany and Bohemia to 'straight crumhorns', which might have resembled the cornamusa. The 'basset: Nicolo' illustrated by Praetorius, a bass instrument like a straight crumhorn, can also be included in this group.

(ii) Wind-cap shawms with conical bore. The shawm with wind cap rather than open reed appears in iconographical sources, especially from Germany in the 16th century and France in the 17th. It is often depicted in the context of popular rather than art music. Praetorius illustrated a small detachable wind cap that fitted over the reed of the normal *discant Schalmey* (treble shawm). The extent to which detachable wind caps were used is not known.

The most extensively documented wind-cap shawm is the *Schreyerpfeife*, an instrument with expanding conical bore. It is recorded in German sources associated with town and court musicians from the 1520s and continued in use until the late 17th century. Considerable confusion has been caused by Praetorius's use of the plural form of the name and its synonym 'Schryari' for a different type of instrument, the shape of whose bore is not clear. His description and illustrations of three instruments, the smallest of which is quite different from the other two, might deal with a rare group of instruments which he happened to have seen; they are not known from any other source.

Mersenne pictured a family of wind-cap instruments that he called the *hautbois de Poitou*, used in the *grande écurie* of the French court in the 17th century. But payroll records from the time suggest that such instruments, when played with wind-caps, were known by the name *musette de poitou*. Another French wind-cap shawm, the *cléron pastoral*, described only by Trichet, appears to have resembled the *Schreyerpfeife* closely.

The German word *Rauschpfeife* was used in the 16th century to refer to wind instruments in general and to shawms (both with and without wind cap) in particular.

(iii) Bagpipe chanters used as wind-cap instruments. Mersenne commented that 'all the bagpipe chanters must be sounded with covered reeds [but] they make a much more graceful and vigorous sound when played in the mouth rather than connected to the bag, because the notes can be articulated with the tongue'. He illustrated three such chanters used separately with wind caps: one has two parallel cylindrical bores and two reeds, one a conical bore, and the third a cylindrical or possibly slightly conical bore. The use of the name 'cornamusa' in Italian and other Romance languages both for bagpipes and for a wind-cap instrument suggests that the latter might have been derived directly from a bagpipe chanter, and that the practice of using chanters independently might have been widespread.

(iv) Miscellaneous wind-cap instruments. The late Renaissance was a period of great advances in instrument building, and there are records of a number of wind-cap instruments that were rare or unique and that might have been no more than isolated experiments. The name 'Kortholt' was used by Praetorius for a wind-cap instrument of this type, in effect a wind-cap *Sordun*.

Two instruments that are probably examples of *doppioni*, as described by Zacconi, survive (in *I.VE.af*). They are 'double' in that each has two conical bores of different pitch. They probably originally had wind caps but were subsequently adapted for use with open reeds on crooks.

The term *dolzaina* (or 'douçaine') remains problematic: it might have been used at times for the crumhorn, but it was also clearly used to refer to instruments without wind caps.

BIBLIOGRAPHY

L. Zacconi: *Prattica di musica* (Venice, 1592/*R*)

M. Praetorius: *Syntagma musicum*, 3 vols.: i: *Syntagmatis musici tomus primus: Musicae artis analecta* (Wittenberg and Wolfenbüttel, 1614–15, 2/1615/*R*); ii: *Syntagmatis musici tomus secundus: De organographia* (Wolfenbüttel, 1618, 2/1619/*R* [with pictorial suppl., *Theatrum instrumentorum*]; Eng. trans., New York, 2/1962/*R*; new Eng. trans., Oxford, 1986, 2/1991); iii: *Syntagmatis musici tomus tertius: Termini musici* (Wolfenbüttel, 1618, 2/1619/*R*)

M. Mersenne: *Harmonie universelle* (Paris, 1636–7/*R*; Eng. trans. of the bk on insts, 1957)

I. Hechler: 'Die Windkapselinstrumente: Geschichte, Speilweise, Besetzungsfragen', *Tibia*, vol.2 (1977), 265–74

B.R. Boydell: *The Crumhorn and Other Renaissance Windcap Instruments* (Buren, 1982)

K.T. Meyer: *The Crumhorn: its History, Design, Repertory, and Technique* (Ann Arbor, 1983)

BARRA R. BOYDELL/R

Windchest [soundboard] (Fr. *sommier*; Ger. *Windlade*; It. *somiere*; Sp. *secreto*). In an organ, the long, broad, but rather shallow wooden structure that collects wind under pressure from the bellows or reservoir and distributes it to the pipes as required. In the classical organ the heart of the windchest is a wooden grid, which is partitioned into as many grooves or note channels as there are notes in the keyboard compass; above this are the table, stop mechanism and upperboard (or 'toe board', on which the pipes stand). Below the grid is an enclosed substructure, the pallet box, which receives the wind from the wind trunk and contains a row of pallets, one for each of the notes on the keyboard. Each pallet is held by a spring to cover the underside of a groove in the grid above, and is connected directly or indirectly to a key. When a key is depressed the pallet opens, and wind is admitted to the corresponding groove and then directed via holes in the table, slider and upperboard to the foot or feet of the appropriate pipe(s), depending on the operation of the stop mechanism.

Many forms of windchest have been devised: before about 1420 all organs had only one sound per chest (i.e. no stop mechanism), but in the course of the next century three important inventions allowed builders to give separate sounds: the multiple chest (where a key would connect to two chests), the spring chest (where a 'stop' had its own row of secondary pallets admitting wind individually to its pipes), and the slider chest. The latter became the most commonly used mechanical action windchest. Many other forms and variations (e.g. ventil or membrane chests), were devised during the 19th century in order to cope with the commercial expansion of organ building and with the increase in organ size and the new types of key action. One variety, the cone chest (*Kegellade*) uses conical valves. The application of electricity to the organ encouraged the invention of even more types (e.g. unit chest, pitman chest), but the principle of the slider chest has proved capable of very flexible application.

James Talbot (MS, *c*1695, *GB-Och* Music 1189) used the term 'soundboard' to mean the whole wind-distributing apparatus, and 'wind-box' for the pallet box. The term 'soundboard' has been more common in Britain, and 'windchest' in the USA. For further discussion *see* ORGAN.

MARTIN RENSHAW/R

Wind chime [aeoliphone]. Term applied to a set of plaques or tubes suspended so that they can be activated by the wind, either through concussion or percussion (the instrument is classified as an idiophone). The sounding elements can be made of metal, glass, bamboo, stone, porcelain, shell, or other resonant material. Often they hang around a central clapper that is attached to and moved by a wind-blown vane. The plaques or tubes might be tuned to a scale or chord and struck individually in random order. When suspended outdoors, a wind chime can be an attractive garden ornament or can be used to startle birds; sometimes the sound is believed to have apotropaic power. A single bell with a wind-blown clapper is widely found in Asia, but the term 'chime' implies a set.

In the orchestra, the player activates the chimes by hand stroker (in which case the appelation 'wind chime' is inaccurate); bamboo chimes create a loud 'thwack' when pushed together sharply between the two hands. Although not a precision instrument, wind chimes were being used increasingly in all types of music at the beginning of the 21st century. Glass wind chimes appear in Birtwistle's *The Mask of Orpheus* (1973–84), Boulez's *Notations I–IV* (1977–80), and Henze's *Voices* (1973); shell wind chimes in Henze's *Compases para preguntas ensimismadas* (1969–70) and *Das Floss der 'Medusa'* (1968, rev. 1990); and glass, shell, and bamboo chimes in Messiaen's *Des canyons aux étoiles* (1970–74).

A similar instrument is the mark tree, a set of 30–40 thin brass tubes, graduated in length from 10 to 30 cm and suspended from a stick. When lightly stroked it produces a shimmering glissando. The mark tree (named after its inventor, Mark Stevens) was, in the early 21st century, widely used in all types of music from pop to orchestral.

JAMES HOLLAND/R

Wind gauge. Device for measuring wind pressure, usually that of organs, at the windchest, in the trunks, and so on. According to German authors (Werckmeister, Adlung, Töpfer) a gauge was first invented by Christian Förner in 1667, but he might only have been publicizing a perfected example. The device had a single column of water which was raised a measurable extent when placed above any air vent (e.g. a pipe-hole in the chest). Töpfer (*Die Orgelbaukunst*, 1833) improved its reliability by giving it a double column. The water-manometer (E.J. Hopkins's 'anemometer') has an S-shaped transparent tube placed on its side; in a bend of this the water rests until moved by the pressurized air admitted at one end of the tube. The pressure of air is measured as the difference between the lower and upper surfaces of water in the bent tube. Thus '2½″ wind' (i.e. about 6 cm) indicates that the surface pushed by the air fell 1¼″, the other surface beyond the bend raised 1¼″ (3 cm).

PETER WILLIAMS

Wind machine [aeoliphone]. Sound-effect device used on the stage and elsewhere to simulate the sound of wind. It commonly consists of either a barrel framework covered with silk or coarse canvas that rubs against the slats of the frame as the barrel is rotated, or an electric fan in which the blades are replaced by lengths of cane. In either device a rise and fall in volume and pitch is gained by a rise and fall in the speed of rotation, and in the case of the barrel by a tightening and loosening of the fabric. An electric wind machine sometimes produces a low-pitched but discernible hum when the machine is turned on but not in use: the unwanted hum might be audible when the orchestra is playing *pianissimo*. Nowadays wind sounds can be synthesized electronically and projected through loudspeakers.

Wind machine, c1920. (Edinburgh University Collection of Historic Musical Instruments (1169))

A wind machine is occasionally requested in orchestral scores, for example Strauss's *Don Quixote* (1896–7), Ravel's *Daphnis et Chloé* (1909–12; as 'eoliphone'), Milhaud's *Les choéphores* (1915), Schoenberg's *Die Jakobsleiter* (1917–22), and Vaughan Williams's *Sinfonia antartica* (1949–52), in which there is an instruction that the instrument be 'out of sight'.

JAMES BLADES/JAMES HOLLAND/R

Wind trunk (Fr. *porte vent*; Ger. *Windkanal*). Large tube, usually wooden or metal, for conveying the wind of an organ from the bellows to the windchest. In medieval organs the one central wind trunk was called *fistula maxima*. Ideally wind trunks should be capacious and avoid sharp bends in order to reduce turbulence in the wind. Devices are often applied to wind trunks to stabilize the wind or produce a tremolo.

Windway. Ambiguous term which, taken literally, may refer to any passage conveying air in a musical instrument. There are, however, two recognized special connotations.

(1) In a wooden flue pipe of an organ the windway is the passage between the opening of the pipe foot and the flue, which is the slot between the face of the block and the inner side of the cap or lower lip (fig.1*a*). The form of the windway determines the size and shape of the air jet that impinges on the upper lip, and through the formation of edge-tones energizes the air column. The throat is that part of the windway hollowed out of the block; its conformation influences the timbre of the pipe. In metal pipes the flue is formed between the edge of the languid and the lower lip derived from the wall of the pipe foot (fig.1*b*).

(2) The windway of a recorder is itself the flue and is a simple passage formed by working a flat on the plug (block) of the instrument and a corresponding groove in the head (fig.1*c*). In certain sophisticated flageolets the windway is sometimes enlarged above the flue proper, forming a receptacle for a piece of sponge to absorb the moisture of the breath.

PHILIP BATE

Winkel, Dietrich Nikolaus [Diederich Nicolas] (*b* Lippstadt, Westphalia, 1776; *d* Amsterdam, Netherlands, 28 Sept 1826). German inventor, mechanic, and builder of automatic organs, active in Amsterdam. About 1814 he invented the familiar metronome based on a double pendulum, an oscillating rod with a weight at each end. J.N. Maelzel (1772–1838) met Winkel in Amsterdam, patented Winkel's idea in London and Paris and commercialized it in 1816 under his own name. Several of Winkel's barrel organs survive; they display a high level of ingenuity and craftsmanship. One is labeled Weckbrodt & Winkel (Amsterdam, *c*1812) but Weckbrodt is otherwise unknown. Despite his skill, Winkel was commercially unsuccessful and died impoverished.

In 1821 Winkel invented the Componium (Ger. *Komponium*), a mechanical instrument of the orchestrion type. It was operated by a weight-driven 'composing

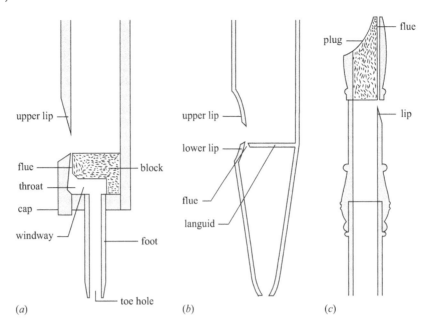

Fig.1: *Diagrams to show the windway in (a) a wooden organ pipe, (b) a metal organ pipe, (c) a recorder.*

machine' that used two pinned wooden cylinders to control the pitch and duration of notes sounded by organ pipes. Pins also activated a triangle and drum. The cylinders shifted sideways automatically in alternation, so that their rows of pins and hooks engaged the pipe valve mechanism in a random sequence of two-measure phrases comprising a single theme. Eight variants of the phrases were pinned onto the cylinders.

The unique surviving Componium measures 270 by 142 by 57 cm without its missing case; the separately pumped bellows occupies the rectangular base below the composing machine, with its cylinders mounted one above the other, and wooden and metal pipe ranks at the top. Winkel displayed it in Amsterdam, London, and Paris, but it was not commercially successful and was seized by creditors. Thereafter it passed to successive owners including the organ builder Aristide Cavaillé-Coll and the collector Auguste Tolbecque, who attempted to repair it. Tolbecque sold it in 1879 to Victor-Charles Mahillon and it is now in the Brussels Musical Instruments Museum, where it was restored by Richard Krcal about 1962–3 and recorded. Nowadays it is no longer playable, but in 1999 the museum produced a computer simulation. Its seven remaining cylinders hold a popular repertory of works by Mozart, Moscheles, Spohr, and others, in addition to the two-measure phrases.

BIBLIOGRAPHY

Nieuw Nederlandsch Biografisch Woordenboek, vol.3 (Leiden, 1914), cols.1437–38

J.H. de Maeyer: 'Het Componium van Diederich Nicolaus Winkel', *Handelingen van het XXVIe Vlaams Filologencongres* (Ghent, 1967), 547–63

P.J. van Tiggelen: *Componium: the Mechanical Musical Improvisor* (Leuven, 1987)

GUY OLDHAM/R

Winkler, Allan (Garret) (*b* Minneapolis, MN, 9 Dec 1948). American harpsichord maker. He grew up in a family of musicians and builders: his grandfather worked for the Holtkamp Organ Company and his father played flute in the Minneapolis SO. He attended Boston and Suffolk universities (in Boston, MA). A friendship with the harpsichord maker Eric Herz led to an apprenticeship in 1971. In 1977 he opened a workshop in Cambridge, then Somerville, then Charlestown, and finally in Medford (all in Massachusetts), where his shop has been located since 2003. His intent has been to produce instruments that reflect the materials and practices of the historical builders, and that are well suited to present-day performers' needs.

A member of the 'Boston School', he counts as one of his mentors William Dowd, who counselled him to develop designs other than those commonly available in the 1970s. He offers three styles of French double-manual harpsichords (after Donzelague, Hemsch, and François-Étienne Blanchet II); a French single; a German double (after Fleischer); two German singles (after Fleischer and Vater); and a German unfretted clavichord (after Schiedmayer). Since 1987 he has been a consulting keyboard technician and restorer for the Museum of Fine Arts, Boston, where he was instrumental in the restoration of its 1736 Hemsch harpsichord, among others. As of 2012 Winkler had produced 52 harpsichords (including virginals and spinets) and five clavichords, for which he made his own open-wound strings.

EDWARD L. KOTTICK/R

Winnen. French family of woodwind instrument makers. Its most important members were Nicolas Winnen (*b* before 1788; *d* c1834) and his son Jean Winnen *cadet* (*b* Paris, 21 Jan 1795; *d* Paris, 12 Nov 1867). Nicolas

Winnen established his business in 1788 in rue de la Monnoye, Paris. The same year he married Anne Victorie Thieriot, daughter of the maker Prudent Thieriot. By 1805 he had moved to rue Froidmanteau, then to rue St Honoré, where he worked until his death. Although he was occasionally listed as 'Winen' as early as 1809, he marked his instruments 'VIENNEN/A PARIS'. Fétis wrote in 1834 that Winnen had invented some years earlier a 'pompe' (tuning slide) with mechanical adjustment for the wing joint of the bassoon. Surviving instruments include a fife, a piccolo, flutes, clarinets, and bassoons.

His son Jean continued the business, working by 1839 at rue St Denis 398. In 1834 and 1839 Jean won medals for a wide-bell bassoon invented with his father in 1832. Designed to provide 'nearly quadruple' the volume of a bassoon (using a stronger reed and new fingerings), this at first descended to *C*. In 1844 Jean took out a patent on a revised version known as the *bassonore*, descending to *B♭'*. One example (in *F.P.cm*) has a broadly flaring wooden bell and several relocated tone holes. In 1845 Jean joined dozens of other French woodwind makers in signing a protest against the adoption of Sax's new instruments by the French war ministry. His instruments are signed 'VIENNEN/CADET/A PARIS' or as 'WINNEN/A PARIS'. Surviving instruments include flutes, oboes, an english horn, clarinets, bassoons, and bassonores. A bassoon (also in *F.P.cm*) has ferrules decorated with engine-turned brass bands and obliquely mounted keys signed [C.H.] FELIX MECANICIEN, listed 1825–30 as a clarinet maker in Paris. The flutes of both Winnens often have a single key and the clarinets five, while the oboes and bassoons are more elaborate, with seven or nine keys. A fragment of an oboe d'amour, made by either Nicolas or Jean, survives (*F.P.cm*). Another son, Nicolas Prudent Winnen (*d* Warsaw, 1848) was described in 1819 as an instrument maker.

BIBLIOGRAPHY
L.A. de Pontécoulant: *Organographie* (Paris, 1861/*R*1973)
C. Pierre: *Les facteurs d'instruments de musique* (Paris, 1893/*R*1971)
W. Waterhouse: *The New Langwill Index: a Dictionary of Musical Wind-Instrument Makers and Inventors* (London, 1993), 432–3
NIALL O'LOUGHLIN/JAMES B. KOPP

Winternitz, Emanuel (*b* Vienna, Austria, 4 Aug 1898; *d* New York, 22 Aug 1983). American organologist and curator of Austrian birth. He gained an LLD at the University of Vienna in 1922 and taught philosophy of law at the University of Hamburg, where he studied aesthetics with Ernst Cassirer. He also studied music privately and took piano lessons with various teachers. Escaping the Nazis in Vienna in 1938, he emigrated with few possessions to the USA, where he was first a lecturer at the Fogg Museum of Harvard University (1938–41) and then lecturer and keeper of the collection of musical instruments at the Metropolitan Museum of Art, New York (1941–9). In 1949 he became curator of musical instruments as the Metropolitan Museum made the collection a separate department of the museum. He held this post until his retirement, in 1973. He also lectured at Columbia University (1947–8) and was a visiting professor at Yale, Rutgers, the City University of New York, and the State University of New York at Binghamton. In the early 1960s he was among the founders of the International Committee for Museums and Collections of Musical Instruments (CIMCIM).

Largely self-taught in organology, Winternitz explored several areas of his field including the history of instruments, instruments as works of art, and music iconography. His *Musical Instruments of the Western World* (1966) is a splendid collection of photographs with descriptive comments and an introductory essay placing the instruments in their social and artistic context. His monograph on Gaudenzio Ferrari shows what contributions iconography can make to historical musicology, in this case to the question of the origins of the violin. He also contributed seminal studies of composers' manuscripts. At the Metropolitan Museum Winternitz organized concerts using some restored instruments from the collection. Assisted by Edwin Ripin he arranged a systematic exhibition of part of the collection in new, permanent galleries, opened in 1971. After retiring from the museum, Winternitz continued for several years to teach organology and iconography at the City University of New York.

WRITINGS
Keyboard Instruments in the Metropolitan Museum of Art (New York, 1961)
Musical Instruments of the Western World (London and New York, 1966; Ger. trans., 1966 as *Die schönsten Musikinstrumente des Abendlandes*)
Musical Instruments and their Symbolism in Western Art (New York, 1967, 2/1979) [incl. list of writings, 235–8]
'The Crosby Brown Collection of Musical Instruments: its Origin and Development', *Metropolitan Museum Journal*, vol.3 (1970), 337–56
Leonardo da Vinci as a Musician (New Haven, 1982)

BIBLIOGRAPHY
J.H. van der Meer: 'Encounters with Emanuel Winternitz', *CIMCIM Newsletter*, no.6 (1978), 3–9
L.H. Kopp: 'Music forgotten and remembered: The life and times of Emanuel Winternitz', *Music in Art: International Journal for Music Iconography*, vol.29/1–2 (Iconography as a source for music history) (2004), 6–13
H.-J. Winkler: 'Fascinated by Early Music: Paul Hindemith and Emanuel Winternitz', *Music in Art: International Journal for Music Iconography*, vol.29/1–2 (Iconography as a source for music history) (2004), 14–19
PAULA MORGAN/R

Wirbel (i) (Ger). The tuning peg of a string instrument. A *Wirbelkasten* is a pegbox. Other compound terms applied to constituent parts of various instruments include *Stimmwirbeln* or *Wirbellöcher* (tuning pegs or pins) and *Wirbelstock* (the wrest plank of a keyboard instrument).

Wirbel (ii) (Ger.). A drumroll. A *Wirbeltrommel* is a tenor drum.

Wirsching, Philipp (*b* Bensheim, Germany, 7 Feb 1858; *d* Milwaukee, WI, 10 Dec 1926). American organ builder of German birth. A graduate of Würzburg University, he also received training in organ building with

Laukhuff and Ladegast in Germany. He emigrated to America in 1886 and established the Wirsching Church Organ Co. at Salem, Ohio, in 1888. Soon afterwards he developed a form of the German cone-chest action. In 1895 he became manager of the Pittsburgh branch of the Farrand & Votey firm, but in 1905 reorganized his own company and built a number of electric-action organs for churches and residences, including a self-playing organ for the Maharaja of Mysore, India, and a large three-manual organ for Queen of All Saints Church, Brooklyn, New York (1913). Until August 1909 his firm also produced small organs, some with self-player units, for the Art Organ Company of New York. In 1918 the Wirsching Organ Co. completed an organ with electropneumatic action for the Singer Theatre in New York. Wirsching espoused an orchestral tonal ideal and promoted his instruments as progressive; for example, he was an early proponent of 32-note pedal-boards and developed a sophisticated tubular pneumatic coupling action that attracted the attention of his supporter George Ashdown Audsley.

BIBLIOGRAPHY

'Philipp Wirsching, Organ Builder', *The Tracker*, vol.24/1 (1979), 6
J.M. Stark: 'The Art Organ Company of New York', *The Tracker*, vol.49/2 (2005), 13–23

BARBARA OWEN/R

Wirth, Franz (*fl* Vienna, Austria, *c*1870–1930). Austrian piano maker. He studied with Ludwig Bösendorfer and worked independently building uprights and grands (especially short grands, with either Viennese or English action) at various locations in Vienna from 1879 to 1929. His factory was expanded in 1885, and by 1900 employed some 50 workers producing as many as 300 pianos annually. The factory produced a total of nearly 13,000 instruments, many of them exported to eastern and southern Europe, including Russia, where the young Tchaikovsky had a Wirth grand purchased in St Petersburg. Wirth received several awards and court appointments. He might have been a descendant of Franz Joseph Wirth (*fl* Augsburg, late 18th century), an organ and piano maker known chiefly from a square piano of 1798 (in *D.M.dm*).

Wistenius, Jonas (*b* Vist outside Linköping, Sweden, 1700; *d* Linköping, 1777). Swedish organ builder who founded the Linköping tradition of organ building. A farmer's son from Vist parish, he trained with Johann Josua Mosengel and Georg Caspari in Königsberg (now Kaliningrad) between 1726 and 1738, as well as with Kurebinske in Belgard and Johann Kloos in Riga. He obtained his charter in 1742, then opened a workshop at Linköping; he worked also as a weaver and merchant. Among his output are at least 70 well-documented instruments (he himself claimed to have built a total of 96) which are mostly one-manual organs with pulldown pedals. Extant examples are those at St Gertrud, Västervik (1744; 20 stops, manual and pedal); Åtvid (1751; reconstructed 1957); Askeryd (1760); Skällvik (1762; original specification restored 1963). Wistenius built in a slightly different style than his contemporaries of the Cahman school, showing the influence of his teachers; this work was continued by his pupils Lars Wahlberg, Anders Wollander, and Pehr Schiörlin. Schiörlin took over Wistenius's workshop and continued it until his death in 1815.

BIBLIOGRAPHY

H. Åstrand, ed.: *Sohlmans musiklexikon* (Stockholm, 1975–9)
E. Erici and A.Unnerbäck: *Orgelinventarium, Bevarade klassiska kyrkorglar I Sverige* (Stockholm, 1988)
N. Fredriksson: 'Eighteenth Century Swedish Organ-building in a Baltic Perspective', in *The Nordic-Baltic Organ Book: History and Culture*, ed. A. Frisk, S. Jullander, and A. McCrea (Göteborg, 2003), 122–34

BENGT KYHLBERG/GÖRAN GRAHN

Wiszniewski [Wiśniewski]. Polish family of organ builders and piano makers, from Danzig (Gdańsk). The dynasty was founded by two sons of a joiner, Johann Jacob Wiszniewski. The elder brother, Jacob Bernhard (*b* Insterburg [Wystruć, now Černiachovsk, Kaliningrad district, Russia], 13 Aug 1799; *d* Danzig, 22 July 1867), was an employee, son-in-law, and maybe pupil of the piano and organ builder Christian Ephraim Arendt in Danzig. From 25 Feb 1820 he ran a workshop in Bromberg (Bydgoszcz), then from 1822 worked abroad, in 1823 in Strasbourg (where he turned pages for Liszt during a concert), and in autumn 1824 for J.B. Streicher in Vienna. From March 1825 he ran a piano and organ workshop in Danzig, where he received his warrant in 1833 and on 6 Nov 1843 was appointed Prussian Royal Court instrument maker. In 1847 he had his own shop in Königsberg (Kaliningrad), where he competed with C.J. Gebauhr. As well as producing pianos in several models including giraffes and grands, Wiszniewski built organs for churches in Berent (Kościerzyna) (1826), Mariensee (Przywidz) (1832), Sobowitz (Sobowidz near Gdańsk) (1835), Neufahrwasser (Nowy Port, now part of Gdańsk) (1840), and in 1835 he repaired the famous organ in Oliva.

In 1833, together with his brother Friedrich Benjamin, he patented an improved English action, with more efficient damping, moveable backchecks, and adjustable hammer rail. In 1836 he incorporated a reed organ in a grand piano, and made pianos with iron tubular braces according to a Viennese pattern. He also patented a wide, hollow rail, placed as a resonator beneath the standard bridge. Under this assembly, in the soundboard, were two or three openings with flaps operated by a pedal, intended to provide *crescendo* and *diminuendo* effects for long tones and chords. A grand piano shown in 1843 at the Berlin and Königberg exhibitions was bought by the king of Prussia, thus gained Wiszniewski the title of Royal Court instrument maker. At that time the company, one of the largest of its type in Prussia, employed 22 workers and exported grands to Liverpool, Ireland, Amsterdam, and America. Further patents followed, and the company's pianos were used in recitals by Sigismund Thalberg, Louis Haupt, Antoni Kątski, and Hans von Bülow. On 25 Feb 1867 Jacob Bernard turned his plant over to his son Felix.

Jacob Bernard's younger brother, Friedrich Benjamin (*b* Gumbinnen [Gąbin, now Gusiev, Kaliningrad district,

Russia], ?1802; *d* Danzig, 25 Jan 1854), worked with him from about 1830, and later independently. His grand with Erard action was awarded a second-class medal at the 1855 Paris Exhibition. After his death his business was run by his brother-in-law and collaborator Otto Arendt, later by Adolf Weise, and from 1868 to 1873 by Friedrich Benjamin's son Philibert Friedrich (*b* Danzig 23 Nov 1836; *d c*1890), who also ran a piano factory and store in Elbing (Elbląg) and simultaneously in Danzig from about 1861.

Eugen Adalbert (*b* Danzig, 28 April 1826; *d* Danzig, 27 May 1888), son and pupil of Jacob Bernhard, visited Berlin and Vienna in May 1846 to perfect his skills. He ran a piano workshop and store in Bromberg from about 1850, and from the end of 1857 in Danzig. In 1855 he presented five grands at a local craft exhibition that gained him general appreciation. He shipped instruments to Russia and had a branch in Frankfurt an der Oder for some time. His pianos were endorsed by Józef Wieniawski, Hans von Bülow, and W. Grahn (a piano teacher and conductor in Bydgoszcz).

Felix Theodor (*b* Danzig, 10 Oct 1829; *d* after 1873), second son and pupil of Jacob Bernhard, was trained in several factories. From Nov 1857 he ran his own workshop in Danzig, and in 1867–9 he also ran his father's business. After a few years he concentrated on selling imported instruments.

BIBLIOGRAPHY

W. Renkewitz and J. Janca: *Geschichte der Orgelbaukunst in Ost- und Westpreussen von 1333 bis 1944*, vol.1 (Würzburg, 1984), 258
H. Heyde: *Musikinstrumentenbau in Preussen* (Tutzing, 1994)
B. Vogel: 'The Story of the Wiszniewski Family, Piano Makers of Gdansk', *Muzyka Fortepianowa*, vol.11 (1998), 43–53

BENJAMIN VOGEL

Witcher, Jay (*b* Chico, CA, 10 Nov 1934). American harp maker. He holds a bachelor's degree in civil engineering from the University of California (1956) and studied control theory at UCLA while working as an aerospace engineer in the 1960s. He learned woodworking as a child from his father and made copies of early keyboard instruments after graduating from college. After leaving the aerospace field in 1969, he researched early harps at the insistence of participants in the early music movement; consequently he revived the making of old Irish brass-wire-strung harps and began his continuing collaboration with the Irish harper Gráinne Yeats, who revived the playing of these instruments. Witcher has been credited with introducing the replication of historical harps to the USA and contributing importantly to the renewal of interest in their repertory. His sources are old harps preserved in museums, iconography, and literary descriptions; he has also created original designs including nylon-strung 'folk' harps and student harps of various sizes, all scaled in accordance with his understanding of the physics of strings. Since 1970 Witcher has produced some 1100 unmechanized harps, including wire-strung Irish types and Renaissance-style double- and triple-strung harps, as well as medieval lyres and fiddles, some strung with gut. His wood

comes from a hardwood dealer in New Brunswick, Canada; he makes his own hardware. In past years has had two formal apprentices but as of 2013 he worked alone at his shop in Houlton, Maine, where he has been located since 1980.

Withers. English family of violin makers, repairers, and dealers. Edward Withers (i) (1808–75) founded his firm in London by purchasing that of R. and W. Davis in 1846. Davis had been associated with the well-known violin maker John Frederick Lott, with whom Withers had clearly studied. Withers's output was considerable and of fine quality; for a time he employed Charles Adolphe Maucotel and Charles Boullangier, émigrés from France. The premises were at 31 Coventry Street.

Edward Withers (ii) (1844–1915) was apprenticed to his father at an early age, also working with Lott. Like his father, he copied the work of Stradivari and Guarneri (mainly the latter), and it is said that he made about 200 instruments in addition to his repair work. In 1878 the business moved to 22 Wardour Street, where it remained; on the death of Edward Withers (ii) it was continued by his three sons, Edward Sidney Munns Withers (1870–1955), Bernard Sidney Withers (1873–1942), and Douglas Sidney Withers (1879–1962), with the emphasis shifting from making new instruments to repairing and selling old ones. In Oct 1969 Bernard's son Edward Stanley Withers (1904–1987) retired and was succeeded by Dietrich M. Kessler; on the latter's retirement in 1987, the firm passed into the hands of Adam Whone (*b* 1956), who moved the offices to 2 Windmill Street. The firm formally closed in 1998.

George Withers (1847–1931), another son of Edward Withers (i), established his own business in St Martin's Lane about 1876 before moving to 22 Leicester Square. There he built up a highly regarded dealing and restoring business, in which he was joined by his sons Guarnerius and Walter George, both good craftsmen trained in Mirecourt. The firm closed in April 1932.

BIBLIOGRAPHY

A. Whone: *Edward Withers Ltd: 230 Years of Violin Craft in Soho* (London, 1996)
J. Milnes, ed.: *The British Violin* (Oxford, 2000)

CHARLES BEARE/PHILIP J. KASS

Witten, Laurence Claiborne (*b* Cincinnati, OH, 3 April 1926; *d* Vero Beach, FL, 18 April 1995). American instrument collector. Born into a wealthy family, Witten earned a music degree from Yale (1951) before opening a rare book and manuscript dealership in New Haven, Connecticut; he later moved to Southport. He and his wife collected pre-Columbian art, antique automobiles, vocal recordings, and rare bowed and plucked string instruments, in which he had become interested during the 1950s. Relying on advice from dealers and his own informed intuition, beginning in the 1960s Witten bought string instruments of high quality, along with accessories and fittings, related books, documents, graphics, and luthiers' tools. His acquisitions, both of individual items and assemblages (notably, the Salabue-Fiorini-De Wit-Herrmann collection of violinmakers' labels), included important 17th- and 18th-century Italian instruments by famous makers that are considered models of their types (although many show old alterations), as well as some interesting earlier examples, formerly owned by the Bisiach family, Emil Herrmann, and Lord Astor among others.

Witten's reputation was tarnished by scandal surrounding a notorious map that he sold, but the instrument collection he formed is esteemed by violin connoisseurs, and his scholarly writings demonstrate his serious intent. A heart attack in 1983 prompted him to offer the collection for sale; it was bought the following year for $3 million by the Shrine to Music Museum at the University of South Dakota (now *US.V.n*) and named the Witten-Rawlins Collection to recognize the generosity of its major donors. Since then, Witten's former holdings, augmented by complementary acquisitions, have been the focus of much study, and some have been lent for temporary exhibitions elsewhere. See A.P. Larson: 'The Witten-Rawlins Collection', *Journal of the Violin Society of America*, vol.12 (1992), 13–21.

LAURENCE LIBIN

Wittenz [Bitenc], **Andreas** [Andrej] (*b* Ljubljana, Slovenia, 1802; *d* Ljubljana, after 1856). Slovenian piano maker. He was taught by an unknown piano maker in Vienna where he obtained his trade licence. His three extant grand pianos (*c*1835, *SI.L.nm*; 1856, *SI.P.pm*; private collection, Slovenia), of Biedermeier style and marked *And. Witenz/in/Laibach*, resemble those of Ignaz Bösendorfer. In 1835 Wittenz's application for a trade licence in Ljubljana was rejected, but local archives document his activity there as a piano maker, repairer, tuner, and seller. In 1841 he received a silver medal at an industrial exposition in Graz and in 1844 another silver medal at an exposition in Ljubljana. See D. Koter: 'Izdelovalci glasbil na Slovenskem 1606–1918', *Muzikološki zbornik/Musicological annual*, vol.39 (2003), 123–52.

DARJA KOTER

Wittmayer. German manufacturer of harpsichords, spinets, and clavichords of modern design (*Serien Instrumente*). The company was founded in Wolfratshausen by the organist Kurt Wittmayer (*b* Hermannstadt, 22 Nov 1917; *d* Bad Tölz, 4 Sept 1997) in 1949 after he moved from Munich, where he had begun building harpsichords in 1947 with Rudolf Schüler as Wittmayer & Schüler while both were students. Although the two builders worked independently after Wittmayer moved to Munich, their instruments have many similarities, particularly their jacks. Recognizing that the sound of his Serien models 'was not ideal' (as he wrote to Wallace Zuckermann), in the late 1960s Wittmayer expanded production to include copies after traditional models. To overcome acoustic deficiencies, some of Wittmayer's early, very heavy modern harpsichords were fitted with electronic amplification and loudspeakers installed in the soundboard; one of these was sold to the Indianapolis Symphony after it had been used by Herbert von Karajan with the Berlin Philharmonic in a concert in New York. Isolde Ahlgrimm, Glenn Gould, and Malcolm Hamilton are among performers who recorded with Wittmayer's modern harpsichords. As of 1969, Wittmayer estimated that his firm was making 400 production models annually. Wittmayer also restored some historical instruments, including Mozart's Anton Walter piano. Wittmayer's daughter Susanne (*b* 1949) remains active as a builder and historian of early keyboard instruments.

BIBLIOGRAPHY

W.J. Zuckermann: 'The Modern Harpsichord: 20th Century Instruments and their Makers', (New York, 1969), 195–8

S. Berdux, ed.: *Festschrift für Kurt Wittmayer* (Munich, 1999)

ANNE BEETEM ACKER, LAURENCE LIBIN

Wobble organ. Monophonic electronic instrument (not an organ) patented as a musical entertainment device by the electrical engineer Larned A. Meacham of New Providence, New Jersey, on 6 March 1951 (no.2,544,466). The frequency of a single oscillator with a pitch range of approximately two and a half octaves was controlled by a 'wobble arm' moved by the player's right hand around a calibrated quadrant dial; vibrato was also produced with the 'wobble arm'. The left-hand controls included a push-button for the articulation of individual notes, which was combined with a volume control. The 'wobble organ' was normally used in a set of four, played by four performers seated around a table; in this case the frequency range of the instruments would usually be set to soprano, alto, tenor, and bass, and each would be given a different timbre by filtering the sawtooth wave produced by the oscillator. Meacham published directions for home assembly of the inexpensive, easy-to-use device. He held other patents in the field of electronic tone generation, amplification and detection, telephonic communication, semiconductors, etc. See L.A. Meacham: 'Tomorrow's Electronic Barbershop Quartet', *Popular Mechanics Magazine*, vol.97/1 (Jan 1952), 237–49, 322–4.

HUGH DAVIES/R

Woeckherl [Wöckerl], **Johannes** [Hans] (*b c*1594; *d* Vienna, Austria, 4 May 1660). Austrian organ builder. He worked on various projects at the collegiate church, Heiligenkreuz, near Vienna, between 1607 and 1650 and built a new organ for St Augustine, Vienna, in 1640. He supplied positives for St Mauritius, Kroměříž (1655), and Olomouc Cathedral (1658), and a new organ for the Church of Our Lady, Wiener Neustadt. His organ in the Franciscan church, Vienna (1641–2; two manuals, 20 stops; restored 2010), follows the style favoured by the Passau organ-building families of Freundt and Putz, as far as can be known from the existing original material; it is said to be the oldest organ in a church in Vienna and is noted also for its richly carved case with painted doors.

BIBLIOGRAPHY

H. Klotz: *Über die Orgelkunst der Gotik, der Renaissance und des Barock* (Kassel, 1934, rev. 2/1975)

O. Eberstaller: *Orgeln und Orgelbauer in Österreich* (Graz and Cologne, 1955)

G. Hradetzky: 'Organ Building in Austria', *ISO-Information*, vol.10 (1973), 691–720

Österreichisches Musiklexicon (Vienna, 2006)

HANS KLOTZ/R

Woffington. Several Irish organists and instrument makers bore this name; they probably belonged to the same family.

(1) Robert Woffington (i) (*d* Dublin, 24 June 1750). Organist in Kilkenny and Dublin. In 1720 he was one of the committee of four experts who testified to the unsatisfactory nature of Thomas Hollister's new organ in St Werburgh's, Dublin.

(2) John Woffington (*fl* 1720–?1758). Organist in Dublin, ?son of (1) Robert Woffington (i). In 1725 he was appointed to St Michan's, where he was also responsible for tuning and repairing the organ. There appear to have been at least six John Woffingtons in Dublin in the 18th century, and it has not been possible to distinguish their careers with certainty.

(3) Robert Woffington (ii) (*d* Dublin, *c*1820). Organist, organ builder, and piano maker. His business, at 9 William Street, is listed in Dublin directories from 1787 until 1835. The firm retained his name after his death, though occasionally it was listed under the names of his sons, Thomas and Abraham. Robert Woffington is said to have been a pupil of Ferdinand Weber, the leading Dublin organ builder of the 18th century, and was a partner of William Gibson at 6 Grafton Street, Dublin (1775–8). A claviorgan (1780) and a boudoir organ by him (*c*1800–10) display a very high standard of workmanship (both are at *IRL.D.nm*). In 1807 he built a large organ for St Andrew's; this was destroyed by fire in 1860. He is mentioned as assistant organist at St Mary's in 1766 and was organist there from 1773 until 1785. Abraham (*d c*1856) worked at the Valuation Office, though he appears to have retained an interest in his father's business, which was carried on by Thomas until 1835.

BRIAN BOYDELL/R

Woissa [woyssa, weyssa]. Notched flute of the Hamar, Benna, and Beshada peoples of southern Ethiopia. It is a bamboo or reed tube 30 to 45 cm long and about 2.5 cm in diameter, with four fingerholes producing five pitches with approximate intervals (treble to bass): major 2nd–major 2nd–minor 3rd–major 2nd. It is played by young, unmarried girls while protecting the sorghum fields. Through the sound of their flutes, the girls are believed to guarantee a successful harvest. The term *woissa* means 'that which causes to stand erect', evoking the ideas that playing the flute causes the sorghum to grow well, and that it keeps the girls alert. In addition it can allude to a man's erection; hence, customarily only young males produce woissa flutes for the women. Although the woissa is a female instrument (especially when used for tasks in the fields), it is occasionally played by men to serenade their sweethearts; a couple will recognize their own melody.

Among the Maale people of southern Ethiopia, the four-holed notched flute is called *shulungo*. It is 37 cm long, 2 to 2.5 cm in diameter, and sounds the approximate intervals: minor 3rd–major 2nd–minor 3rd–major 2nd. Like the woissa, it is played solo primarily by women and young girls while protecting the ripening grain, during breaks in field work, and to calm infants. Young girls also create their own melodies to signal their lovers to meet them, or they might dedicate melodies to their parents or other family members. Occasionally the *shulungo* accompanies group songs along with concussion idiophones and rattles.

The Ari people of southern Ethiopia play a similar notched flute called *shungul*; there, however, it is typically a male instrument. Boys play it while watching the fields, while men use it on various private and social occasions. The repertory comprises only instrumental pieces stemming from traditional work songs (e.g. harvesting) as well as love, epic, and entertainment songs. The flute produces five pitches at the approximate intervals: minor 3rd–major 2nd–major 2nd–major 2nd. The Ari also have a flute called *woissa*, but these are stopped end-blown flutes without fingerholes, played in ensembles of six.

BIBLIOGRAPHY

N. Mohaupt: 'Instruments of the Hamar', *Musical Instruments of Ethiopia* (Addis Ababa, 1999)

T. Teffera: *Aerophone im Instrumentarium der Völker Ostafrikas* (Berlin, 2009)

TIMKEHET TEFFERA

Wokor. Portable slit drum of the island of Vanua Lava, Vanuatu. It is made of bamboo or wood, up to 1 metre long and about 25 to 30 cm in diameter. The slit of the wooden drum has one thinner lip which is struck, and a narrower cylindrical extension at both ends on which the drum can be elevated between two wooden forks or carried by two persons walking while the drummer strikes the instrument. The wokor accompanies several dances and can be part of the *elrediti* dance ensemble that consists also of the *timiatwos* (large membranophone), *wéviriakon* (a bag filled with dry seeds and shaken), and *lalöbur* (a sounding board beaten with wooden sticks). The *timiatwos* and large *wokor ding* (*ding* means 'large') are fixed in position and are forbidden for women to touch, but the portable wokor can be played by women to accompany their dances. In this case the woman who plays the wokor leads the dance.

RAYMOND AMMANN

Wókun kurukur. Percussion staves from the islands of Chuuk, Micronesia. They are carved in lengths of approximately 1.4 metres from *kurukur* (wild orange tree), a hardwood that is resonant when dried. While the staves are often left undecorated, museum specimens collected during the early 20th century exhibit intricately painted designs. Nowadays dried bamboo is often used for the staves. In dance performances called *tukuyá*, men hold a single staff with both hands and strike it rhythmically against those of opposing performers. See F.M. LeBar: *The Material Culture of Truk* (New Haven, CT, 1964), 380–81.

BRIAN DIETTRICH

Wolf, Guntram (Franz Theodore) (*b* Kronach, 25 March 1935; *d* Kronach 4 Feb 2013). German maker of historical and modern woodwinds. Following university studies in archaeology and completion of the teacher's examination, Wolf began a systematic exploration of old woodwinds, studying examples in museum collections. His early efforts were undertaken as an enthusiastic amateur, but by 1992 he had passed the *Meisterprüfung* in woodwind making. His workshop in Kronach dates from that year. Since then, Guntram Wolf Holzblasinstrumente GmbH has grown to offer one of the most extensive ranges of historical and modern woodwinds. Among the several models of dulcian and early bassoon produced are a Baroque bassoon after the HKICW original from the Waterhouse collection, and a low-pitch bassoon after Haka. Classical- and Romantic-era bassoons along with two models of early contrabassoon are also offered, as are several models of shawm, Baroque-, Classical-, and Romantic-era oboes, and a complete line of chalumeaux and clarinets.

Modern instruments include several models of bassoon, in standard maple as well as bird's-eye maple and yew, woods unique to the Wolf brand. Wolf offers a full line of quart, quint, and octave mini-bassoons. Fitted with a simplified fingering system, the mini-bassoons are intended for children; with the full fingering they are geared towards more advanced players. Modern oboes include a French conservatoire model and a Vienna oboe, the latter available either with Viennese or conservatoire keywork. Wolf is one of very few makers currently offering the Vienna oboe.

In recent years, Wolf has branched out into new-instrument design. Together with Benedikt Eppelsheim of Munich, Wolf has developed the contraforte, a radical redesign of the Heckel-system contrabassoon, touted for its stable tuning, simplified fingerings, and above all its ability to be heard in orchestral tuttis. Another innovation is the Lupophone, a new bass oboe designed as a replacement for the Heckelphone. In developing new designs, Wolf has been assisted by his children, Peter (*b* 1968), who also functions as the firm's second-in-command, and Claudia (*b* 1966), who is responsible for the implementation of computer-aided design (CAD). Wolf credits his prior acoustical research and the use of advanced manufacturing technologies such as CAD and computer-numerical-control (CNC) as factors in the success of the new designs.

CHRISTOPHER BRODERSEN

Wolf (i). The name given to two undesirable and unpleasant sound effects that may occur in musical performance, one having to do with temperament and tuning, the other with a structural peculiarity in an instrument that sometimes gives rise to intonation difficulties.

On keyboard instruments with tuning systems that do not provide a note intended for use as A♭, playing G♯ instead, with E♭ in the same chord, produces an unpleasant effect, supposed to resemble the howling of a wolf. In Pythagorean intonation the wolf 5th is smaller than pure by 23½ cents, a quantity known as the Pythagorean comma. But the wolf 5th in any regular meantone temperament (where the 'good' 5ths are tempered two or three times as much as in equal temperament) is considerably larger than pure. The tuner who follows a scheme containing a wolf 5th might choose some other location for it than G♯–E♭. C♯–A♭ was occasionally used in the 15th century and D♯–B♭ in the 17th for meantone temperament; B–F♯ was favoured, or rather disfavoured, by many 15th-century practitioners of Pythagorean intonation. On normal keyboard instruments, just intonation is virtually bound to involve more than one wolf 5th, including one among the diatonic notes, for instance D–A or G–D.

Apart from the context of tuning systems, the term 'wolf' is used to refer to certain individual notes which, owing to the structure of an instrument, are too loud or too soft or difficult to play quite in tune, compared with other notes. This kind of wolf is due to an irregularity in the resonance of the instrument which either enhances or absorbs (damps) one particular note, or to a strong and sharply defined resonance frequency that happens to be slightly sharper or flatter than some note of the scale. The latter situation is often found at the major 6th or perhaps 7th above the open G-string of the cello, and is sometimes rectified by squeezing the body of the instrument with the knees or by attaching a 'wolf mute' to the G-string behind the bridge; in violins of poor craftsmanship a wolf is often found an octave above the open G-string. On the old French (and also English) bassoon, the *a* was characteristically weak and unstable because its hole was particularly small and high up on the butt joint. Another classic example occurred on the old valved french horn in F, where frequently either the *b♭'* or *b'* (notated *f''* or *f♯''*) would be weaker than adjacent semitones, and a strong lip was needed to avoid 'cracking' the note. When a pipe organ is placed in a resonant building, some notes are liable to be emphasized by this resonance, and these are softened during regulation by slightly closing the foot-holes. See W. Güth: 'The Wolf Note in the Cello', *The Strad*, vol.90 (1979) 355–7, 434–5.

GUY OLDHAM, MARK LINDLEY

Wolf (ii). American family of keyboard instrument makers. Thomas Andres Wolf (*b* Escanaba, MI, 17 Sept 1947) and Barbara [née Brown] Wolf (*b* Beloit, WI, 8 Dec 1948) met as teenagers at Interlochen Arts Academy, where Barbara studied piano and Thomas the double bass. He made his first harpsichord at age 16 from a Zuckermann kit. They went on to study at the New England Conservatory in 1966, marrying in 1967. By 1969 both had begun two-year apprenticeships in Boston with Eric Herz, followed by three years with Frank Hubbard. (After the harpsichord maker William Dowd closed his Boston shop in 1988 he spent five years of semi-retirement in the Wolf workshop and made his last harpsichord there.)

In 1974 Thomas began conservation training at the Smithsonian Institution, beginning a long association in which he and Barbara have provided restoration and maintenance for the museum's early keyboard collection. The Wolfs established their own workshop in late 1975 in Washington, DC. Their first piano, made in 1976, was a copy of a Jean-Louis Dulcken instrument (previously attributed to J.A. Stein) that Thomas had restored at the Smithsonian, helping to establish its correct authorship. The Wolfs were among the first Americans to copy early pianos accurately, producing models based on originals by Gottfried Silbermann (1746–9), J.-L. Dulcken (c1788), Anton Walter (c1790), Johann Schantz (c1800), Nannette Streicher (c1815), and, most recently, Bartolomeo Cristofori (1722).

After moving to The Plains, Virginia, in 1992, they undertook a research trip in 1996 to examine the earliest surviving grand pianos. In 2000, with the 1722 Cristofori from Rome on loan to the Smithsonian, they were able to intensively study and document the instrument, resulting in its first modern reproduction. During 2002 Thomas was a James Smithson Fellow at the National Museum of American History, compiling his research on early pianos. He also began building double basses and violones (signed 'Thomas Andres'); in 2009 one of his Prescott-model basses won an international prize for tone. The Wolfs continue to make harpsichords, clavichords, and early pianos, to restore and maintain antique instruments for museums and collectors, and to provide instruments, tuning, and technical services for concerts and recordings. See K. Rivers: 'From Vienna to Virginia', *Piano & Keyboard*, no.171 (Nov/Dec 1994), 42–9.

CAROLYN BRYANT/R

Wolff, Auguste (Désiré Bernard) (*b* Paris, France, 3 May 1821; *d* Paris, 9 Feb 1887). French piano manufacturer. He studied the piano with Pierre-Joseph-Guillaume Zimmermann and composition with Fromental Halévy at the Paris Conservatoire. Between 1842 and 1849 he taught piano at the Conservatoire, then abandoned a musical career and turned to piano manufacturing. In 1853 he became a partner of the piano and harp maker Camille Pleyel. Wolff married Marguerite Thomas, the niece of the composer Ambroise Thomas and daughter of the cellist Charles Thomas. In 1855, after Pleyel's death, Wolff took over the Pleyel company and introduced important innovations to its organization and the construction of its instruments. The company name was changed from 'Ignace Pleyel et Compagnie' to 'Pleyel Wolff et Compagnie' in Jan 1857. Wolff began altering the production process and the types of instruments produced. Soon the firm was constructing nine models of piano (six uprights and three grands). Harp making was suspended in 1855 and production of square pianos ended in 1858. In 1857 Wolff devised his *piano-pédalier* (patent no.36535, 10 May 1858), a two-octave-and-a-4th independent pedal piano that could be adapted to any ordinary grand or upright. From 1863 Wolff developed new piano actions which, while maintaining the light touch and ease of dynamic control of Camille Pleyel's single-escapement mechanism, allowed faster repetition. About 1870 Wolff presented his new cross-strung grand pianos and designed a small, relatively wide baby grand (which Charles Gounod nicknamed *crapaud*, 'toad') that was one of Pleyel's best-selling models for many years. Among Wolff's inventions of this period are the *clavier transpositeur* (patent no.96783, 3 Oct 1872), a moveable keyboard that could be installed above any piano keyboard, allowing transposition into any key, and the *pédale tonale pour pianos* (patent no.107617, 8 June 1876). This consists of a pedal—placed between the damper and una corda pedals—and a one-octave chromatic keyboard (called the tonal keyboard) situated above the piano keyboard. The pianist depresses the keys on the small keyboard corresponding to notes to be sustained, and depresses the centre pedal. A system of rods releases the selected notes from the dampers in all octaves while the other notes are damped normally.

Wolff introduced advanced industrial organization in his factory and social benefits for his workers, including economic support in case of accident or sickness, interest-free loans and favourable pension policies, a school for employees' children and for young apprentices, free recreational activities, a 3000-book library, a choir, and a wind band. Wolff's musical and technical knowledge as well as his innovative industrial decisions made him one of the greatest piano manufacturers and led him to leading roles on the judging panels at international exhibitions. His official honours included being named Chevalier de la Légion d'Honneur in 1862. Like Camille Pleyel, Wolff died without a male heir. He was succeeded by his son-in-law, Gustave-Frantz Lyon, who had married Wolff's daughter, Marie Ernestine Germaine, in 1883.

BIBLIOGRAPHY

M. Haine: 'La manufacture de piano Pleyel dans la seconde moitié du XIXe siècle: un modèle de réalisations sociales', *Revue internationale de musique française*, vol.13 (1984), 75–89

J.-J. Trinques: *Le piano Pleyel d'un millénaire à l'autre* (Paris, 2004)

J. Jude: *Pleyel, 1757–1857. La passion d'un siècle* (Fondettes, 2008)

G.P. Di Stefano: 'Pleyel after Pleyel: the instruments of Auguste Wolff and Gustave Lyon at Universal Exhibitions', *Musique, Images, Instruments*, vol.13 (2011), 69–91

GIOVANNI PAOLO DI STEFANO

Wolff, Hellmuth (Silvio Gustav) (*b* Zürich, Switzerland, 3 Sept 1937; *d* Montreal, QC, 20 Nov 2013). Canadian organ builder of Swiss birth. He was apprenticed to Metzler & Söhne, and received further training with several firms in Europe and the USA, including Rieger in Austria and Charles Fisk in Gloucester, Massachusetts. In 1963 he emigrated to Canada, where he worked as a designer for Casavant Frères in their newly established mechanical-action department. He designed their organs for St Pascal, Kamouraska, Quebec (1963); Our Lady of Sorrows, Toronto (1964); and Marie-Reine-des-Coeurs, Montreal (1965).

After a brief period working as a voicer and designer in Geneva, he returned to Canada in 1966 to work with Karl Wilhelm, before establishing his own business in Laval, Quebec, in 1968. James Louder (*b* 1948) joined the firm as an apprentice in 1974, eventually becoming a partner in 1988. The firm was incorporated under the name Wolff & Associés Ltée in 1981. By 1997 Wolff had built 40 instruments, ranging from a small one-rank practice organ to the organ with four manuals and 50 stops built for Christ Church Cathedral, Indianapolis, Indiana (1989). Other important instruments include those for Cornell University (1972); the Trappist monastery, Oka, Quebec (1973); St John the Evangelist, New York (1974); Eighth Church of Christ, Scientist, New York (1977); Trinity Cathedral, Davenport, Iowa (1979); Travis Park United Methodist Church, San Antonio, Texas (1985); Kalamazoo College, Michigan (1988); and the University of Kansas (1996; a French Romantic organ). Drawing inspiration mainly from French and German classical traditions, Wolff's instruments, however, offer more eclectic and modern designs while exclusively using mechanical actions.

Wolff has on occasion produced instruments that are more distinctly historical, such as Redpath Hall, McGill University, Montreal (built in the French Classical style), and Knox College, University of Toronto. The latter organ (especially the pipework of the main divisions) is closely modelled on the 1725 Swedish Baroque organ built by J.N. Cahman in Leufsta Bruk. These two instruments were the first of their kinds in Canada. In 1993 Wolff constructed a new tracker organ in a historic case (presumably made by the 19th-century American-Canadian builder Samuel Russell Warren) at the Church of the Visitation in Montreal. About half of the stops in this instrument are made from restored Warren pipework. In 1994 Wolff moved the 1959 Rudolf von Beckerath instrument (the first modern tracker organ built for a church in Canada) from the former Queen Mary Road United Church in Montreal to Mountain Side United Church, Westmount. The instrument was meticulously restored and augmented. The firm's most ambitious organs were installed in 2005 in Christ Church Cathedral in Victoria, BC (op.47; four manuals, 61 stops) and in 2008 in Winspear Concert Hall at the University of North Texas, Denton (op.50; three manuals, 60 stops).

WRITINGS
(selective list)
J. Louder: 'Future Trends/Zukünftige Tendenzen', The Tracker Organ Revival in America/Die Orgelbewegung in Amerika, ed. U. Pape (Berlin, 1978), 74–102
'L'orgue de la salle Redpath de l'université McGill', L'orgue à notre époque, ed. D. Mackey (Montreal, 1982), 1–12
'Knox College Chapel, University of Toronto', The Historical Organ in America, ed. L. Edwards (Easthampton, MA, 1992), 47–65
'Inventions in Organbuilding', ISO Journal, vol.31 (June 2009), 65–73
'The Organ in Quebec, an Introduction', ISO Journal, vol.34 (May 2010), 8–16
'History of Wolff & Associés', ISO Journal, vol.34 (May 2010), 17–19
'The Organ Reform in Canada', ISO Journal, vol.37 (April 2011), 44–58

BIBLIOGRAPHY
U. Pape: Organs in America/Orgeln in Amerika (Berlin, 1982), 51–2, 144–6, 185–6
A. Bouchard: 'Wolff & Associés Ltée', Encyclopedia of Music in Canada (Toronto, 2/1992).
K.J. Raudsepp: Organs of Montreal, vol.1 (Montreal, 1993)

KARL J. RAUDSEPP/R

Wŏlgŭm. Obsolete four-string plucked lute of Korea (wŏl: 'moon'; gŭm: string instrument). It is similar to the Chinese ruan, from which it takes its alternative name, wanham (Chin. ruanxian), and identical in written name but different in construction from the Chinese yueqin. According to the treatise Akhak kwebŏm (1493), the wŏlgŭm was 104 cm long with a round soundbox about 37 cm in diameter and a long thin neck with 12 frets; a small 13th fret, positioned under only two strings, was placed on the circular soundtable. The wŏlgŭm was tuned and played similarly to the Korean lute tang-pip'a.

A possibly related instrument appears in tomb paintings of about the 6th century CE, but there is no mention of the wŏlgŭm in the official history of the Koryŏ period (918–1392). According to the Akhak kwebŏm the wŏlgŭm was a Chinese import, but it was nevertheless played only in hyangak ('native music'). The wŏlgŭm fell into disuse during the 19th century. Surviving examples in Korea differ in a few details from the descriptions in the Akhak kwebŏm. Two similar instruments of the 8th century, referred to as genkan, are in the Shōsōin repository in Nara, Japan.

BIBLIOGRAPHY
Sŏng Hyŏn, ed.: Akhak kwebŏm [Guide to the study of music] (Seoul, 1493/R1975), 7.3a, b
Hayashi Kenzo: Dongya yueqi kao [Investigations of East Asian musical instruments] (Beijing, 1962), 244ff.
Chang Sa-hun: Han'guk akki taegwan [Korean musical instruments] (Seoul, 1969), 97–8

ROBERT C. PROVINE

Wonga. Whistle of the Barambo people of the Democratic Republic of the Congo. It is carved out of wood, spindle-shaped, and about 14 cm long. See J.-S. Laurenty: Systématique des aérophones de l'Afrique centrale (Tervuren, 1974), 183.

FERDINAND J. DE HEN

Wonjo. Side-blown animal horn of the Tetela people in the Central Basin, Democratic Republic of the Congo. It is about 60 cm long. See J.-S. Laurenty: Systématique des aérophones de l'Afrique centrale (Tervuren, 1974), 323.

Woodblock (Fr. bloc de bois, tambour de bois; Ger. Holzblock, Holzblocktrommel; It. cassa di legno). Term for a small wooden slit drum, generally signifying the Western orchestral instrument. Woodblocks derive from rectangular wooden slit drums (ban) used as time-beaters by the Han Chinese, hence the occasional specification 'Chinese woodblocks'. However, the two-note cylindrical woodblock, with a slit tube at each end and a solid mid-section, is of Western origin. In ragtime and jazz usage, the woodblock is often referred to as 'clog box' or 'tap box'.

The orchestral woodblock generally is a rectangular block of teak or similar heavy hardwood with one or two slotted longitudinal cavities. It varies from about 15 to 25 cm long, 8 to 15 cm wide, and 7 to 10 cm deep. Its tone is resonant and penetrating. Normally it is affixed to a special holder with two prongs fitting into two holes on the underside of the block, or rests on a felt-covered surface, and is struck on the top or the edge above the slot with wooden drumsticks or beaters such as those used for the orchestral xylophone.

The *muyu* ('wooden fish') woodblocks of China and the similar Japanese *mokugyo* and Korean *mokt'ak* ('wood bell') all have important roles in religious ritual, hence the term 'temple blocks'. The *muyu* entered Western usage by way of early ragtime and 1920s jazz bands. These roughly spherical wooden blocks, carved to resemble a stylized fish with a mouth stretching around half the circumference and a handle opposite the mouth, differ in pitch according to their size (about 7 to 15 cm in diameter), internal volume, and size of the mouth opening. Usually grouped in a graduated set of four or five, they are played with drumsticks or similar beaters, and provide rhythmic structure and 'oriental colour'. In incidental music they have supplied many effects such as the sounds of horses's hooves and a dripping water tap.

Composers frequently confuse the rectangular woodblock and the spherical temple block, failing to distinguish which is required. Those calling for woodblocks in orchestral works include Walton in *Façade* (1921–2: 'block' and 'woodblocks', i.e. temple blocks); Prokofiev in his Fifth (1944) and Sixth (1945–7) Symphonies ('legno') and Copland in *Music for a Great City* (1964: 'woodblocks, high and low'). Cage's *Amores* (1943) requires seven woodblocks, and Gerhard's Symhony no.2 (1957–9) even more. Britten specified two tuned woodblocks in his church parables *The Burning Fiery Furnace* (1966) and *The Prodigal Son* (1968), and Tippett called for a series of five notes (*d′*, *e′*, *f′*, *g′*, *c♯″*) in *The Knot Garden* (1966–9: 'temple blocks').

BIBLIOGRAPHY

J. Blades: *Percussion Instruments and their History* (London, 1970, rev. 3/1984)

N. Del Mar: *Anatomy of the Orchestra* (London, 1981)

JAMES BLADES/JAMES HOLLAND/JEREMY MONTAGU

Woodstock Percussion Inc. [Woodstock Chimes]. American manufacturer of wind chimes, headquartered in Shokan, New York. The company was founded in 1979 by the percussionist Garry Kvistad (*b* Oak Park, IL, 9 Nov 1949). Kvistad studied music at the Interlochen Arts Academy, Oberlin College Conservatory of Music and Northern Illinois University and taught at NIU and the University of Cincinnati College Conservatory of Music. He was a co-founder of the Blackearth Percussion Group, collaborated with composer Lukas Foss, and performed professionally with orchestras in the USA and Europe; in 1980 he began performing with Steve Reich and Musicians and since 2002 he has toured with the percussion ensemble NEXUS. In 1987 he formed the Balinese gamelan Giri Mekar, active in the Hudson Valley of New York State, and in 2011 joined the faculty of Bard College Conservatory of Music. Kvistad made his first metallophone in 1974, using aluminium from discarded lawn chairs, then turned to manufacturing wind chimes of metal, bamboo, and 'capiz' shell, tuned to various scales such as Celtic, Indonesian, Navajo etc. Other Woodstock products include wind bells, suspended gongs, and musical fountains. The company also distributes toy and educational instruments and is known for environmental sensitivity and socially responsible operation.

LAURENCE LIBIN

Woodwind instruments (Fr. *bois*; Ger. *Holz, Holzblasinstrumente*; It. *legni, strumentini di legno*; Sp. *instrumentos de madera*). Term used to describe instruments, in particular Western orchestral instruments, of the flute, recorder, and reed-activated types, whether made of wood or of some other material (e.g. ivory, bone, or metal). For further details, see entries on individual instruments.

Worch, Hugo L. (*b* Potsdam, Germany, 15 Nov 1855; *d* Washington, DC, 14 Nov 1938). American collector of and dealer in keyboard instruments, of German birth. His father, Christian, had a music business in Trenton, New Jersey, from about 1858 to 1861, and in Washington from 1863 to 1868 and again in 1883; Worch and his brother Emil took this over in 1883, and after Emil's death his widow and Hugo continued the business as Hugo Worch & Co. from 1884 until 1895. After 1895 the firm of Hugo Worch sold instruments (including pianos sold under the Worch name but manufactured elsewhere), sheet music, and, as tastes changed, gramophones, recordings, and radios. The firm went out of business in 1960 on the retirement of Hans Hugo Worch, who had bought it from his brother Carl and sister Paulina in 1954.

In the 1880s Worch began collecting keyboard instruments that showed the development of the American piano industry from the 1790s to 1850. Later he added to his collection examples of clavichords, harpsichords, and pianos by such European makers as Shudi, Ruckers, Stein, and Broadwood. From 1921 to 1938 he held the title of honorary custodian of musical instruments at the Smithsonian Institution. Absorbed with the history of the piano, he acquired a collection of some 170 keyboard instruments and more than 2000 photographs showing details of keyboard construction. From 1914 his collection of keyboard instruments, including about 130 pianos, formed the nucleus of the keyboard collection at the Smithsonian National Museum of American History. His library of more than 3000 books relating to keyboard construction and 500 bound volumes of American sheet music was dispersed after World War II.

BIBLIOGRAPHY

Who's Who in the Nation's Capital (Washington, 1922)

C. Larson: 'The Hugo Worch Collection of Keyboard Instruments', *Antiques Journal*, vol.7/11 (1953), 15ff

CYNTHIA ADAMS HOOVER

Wordsworth & Maskell. English firm of organ builders. It was established in Leeds in 1866, and became known as Wordsworth & Co. in 1888 and Wood Wordsworth & Co. in 1920. It later incorporated the businesses of Abbott & Smith (1975), and Andrews & Co. and Thomas E. Hughes of Bradford. Wordsworth & Maskell built more than 160 organs, mainly for the counties of Lancashire (about 60 organs), Lincolnshire (23), and Yorkshire (about 80), including more than 50 in Leeds. Perhaps most prestigious was their four-manual organ for Epping Parish Church (1895). They exported organs to Australia, Canada, India, Newfoundland, Russia, and the West Indies; a typical example, unique in Australia, is at St Luke's Anglican Church (formerly Christ Church) in Enmore (1883; two manuals, 13 stops, restored by Peter D.G. Jewkes, 2009–11). Wordworth & Maskell were employed by Canon Frederick Heathcote Sutton, the Victorian ecclesiologist, to build organs for restored churches; one example of high quality from 1879 survives at Brant Broughton, Lincolnshire. The Snetzler organ in St Margaret's Church, King's Lynn, was rebuilt by Wordsworth in 1895. Wood Wordsworth & Co. worked extensively on the organs in Lincoln Cathedral, Leeds Parish Church (1965), Leeds Town Hall (1972), and Worcester Cathedral (organ removed in 2006) before closing in 1981. Among the firm's apprentices was Brian Peter Wilson (d 2010), who rose to become chief voicer. The firm's papers covering 1866 to 1957 are held by the West Yorkshire Archives Service, Leeds.

MICHAEL SAYER/R

Wornum. English family of music publishers and piano makers. Robert Wornum (i) (b ?Berkshire, 1742; d London, 1815) was established in Glasshouse Street, London (c1772–7), and then at 42 Wigmore Street (c1777–1815). He published many small books of dances and airs for the flute or violin and also made violins and cellos. His son Robert Wornum (ii) (b London, bap. 19 Nov 1780; d London, 29 Sept 1852) went into partnership with George Wilkinson in a piano business in Oxford Street in 1810. A fire destroyed their facilities in October 1812, and the subsequent financial strain caused the partnership to be dissolved in March 1813. Wilkinson then opened his own firm and Robert (ii) moved to the Wigmore Street address, where after his father's death he continued making pianos, moving in 1832 to Store Street, Bedford Square. He played an important role in developing the first successful small upright pianos.

In 1811 Robert (ii) invented a 99-cm-tall bichord upright with diagonal stringing and overdampers called the 'Unique', followed by the vertically strung, 137-cm 'Harmonic' in 1813. The patent shows an action that resembles the Geib square piano action but with the hammer shank vertically above the jack, which acts directly upon a notch in base of the shank. By 1828 he had completed the development of his cottage piano action, which became very popular and was copied by Pape and Pleyel in their 'pianino'. Wornum was not, as was formerly thought, the inventor of the tape-check action for upright pianos, which facilitated rapid repetition – Herman Lichtenthal first patented it in 1832 – but he did patent his own version in 1842 (no.9262), using woven tape (still in use) instead of Lichtenthal's leather

strap. He devised down-striking actions for grands and used a down-striking tape-check action in his 'Albion' squares (1844). He introduced a 'pizzicato' stop operated by a pedal that pushes the dampers against the strings, and he experimented with placing the soundboard above the strings. His son, Alfred Nicholson Wornum (b London, bap. 9 Sept 1814; d London, 1888), also an inventor, succeeded him as head of the firm, which operated as Robert Wornum & Sons from 1861 until it closed in 1900, by then in the hands of Alfred's daughter and her husband.

BIBLIOGRAPHY

R.E.M. Harding: *The Piano-Forte: its History Traced to the Great Exhibition of 1851* (Cambridge, 1933/*R*, 2/1978/*R*)

C. Ehrlich: *The Piano: a History* (London, 1976, 2/1990)

K. Mobbs: 'Stops and other Special Effects on the Early Piano', *EMc*, vol.12/4 (1984), 471–6

PETER WARD JONES/ANNE BEETEM ACKER

Wot. Circular panpipe of Laos and northeastern Thailand. It has stopped bamboo pipes of graduated length affixed with beeswax around a central structural core. Originally known in Kalasin province as a toy used by children, who swing it on a string or throw it to produce musical sounds, it was adopted as an instrument for playing tunes in the 1970s. It has achieved such popularity that it has become the symbol of the city of Roi Et, where large statues of the wot stand throughout the town. See L.E.R. Picken: 'The Sound-producing Instrumentarium of a Village in North-East Thailand', *Musica asiatica*, vol.4 (1984), 213–44.

TERRY E. MILLER

Wotton, Thomas (*fl* Oxford, England, ?1449–89). English organ builder. He or perhaps his father received payment in 1449 for an organ for New College chapel, Oxford. In 1486 he constructed a 'pair of organs' (i.e. an organ) for the chapel of Magdalen College, Oxford, for the sum of £28, and in 1488 repaired it for 40s. In 1487 he entered into an agreement with R. Fitzjames, warden of Merton College, to make a similar instrument, also for £28. The late 17th-century antiquary Anthony

Wot (bamboo bundle panpipe), Nathuland, Indonesia. Nine pipes arranged in scale order in a circle. The player rotates the instrument to select each pipe with the black wax centre towards his mouth. (Jeremy Montagu Collection, Oxford)

Wood wrongly believed that Wotton's first name was William and that he was the father of Lambert Simnel, pretender to the English throne in 1487. An account of this misguided theory is given in S. Jeans: 'Wotton, the Organmaker, of Lambert Simnel Fame: Was he William or Thomas?', *JBIOS*, vol.11 (1987), 50–53.

GUY OLDHAM/STEPHEN BICKNELL/R

Wrest pin [tuning pin] (Fr. *chevilles*; Ger. *Stimmwirbeln, Wirbellöcher*). Metal peg around which one end of the strings of a harp, piano, harpsichord, clavichord, zither, and so on is wound. The wrest pins are turned to increase or decrease the tension of the strings, thereby raising or lowering their pitch and enabling the instrument to be tuned. Modern wrest pins are made of hardened steel (sometimes plated or blued), have accurately formed square or rectangular heads that fit an appropriately shaped tuning key or 'hammer', are lightly threaded from the blunt end to be inserted into the wrest plank or other part into which they are driven, and have a hole through which the end of the string is passed before it is wound around the pin. In earlier instruments, wrest pins were forged from iron (rarely brass) rod and the head flattened by hammering on an anvil; the opposite end was not threaded, but often lightly knurled and slightly tapered. Until the 19th century wrest pins were rarely drilled to accept the end of the string because the softer wire formerly used for strings could be wound directly around the pins without slipping. (An exceptional wrest pin of bone, recently excavated at Merton Priory, London, and presumably of medieval origin, is drilled and has a rectangular head.) Wrest pins in early instruments are generally smaller in diameter than those in modern pianos, since the string tension they had to withstand was much lower—approximately 9 kg for a piano string at the beginning of the 19th century compared with 77 kg in the mid-20th century.

EDWIN M. RIPIN/R

Wrest plank [pin block] (Fr. *sommier*; Ger. *Stimmstock*). The thick piece of hard wood into which the wrest pins (tuning pins) of a piano, harpsichord, clavichord, and so on are driven. In early instruments the wrest plank was made from solid timbre, usually oak, walnut, or beech. In modern pianos it is usually of cross-laminated maple or beech and is supported by the cast-iron frame that bears the strain imposed by the strings. Holes are drilled in the wrest plank for insertion of the wrest pins, often at a slight angle, better to resist the pull of the strings.

EDWIN M. RIPIN/JOHN KOSTER

Wright, Elbridge G. (*b* Ashby, MA, 1 March 1811; *d* Boston, MA, 15 March 1871). American maker of brass instruments. He began his career in Roxbury, Massachusetts, in the late 1830s. In 1841 he moved to Boston, where he continued to make keyed and valved brasses. A 'keyed trumpet' (probably a keyed bugle) made by Wright was exhibited in the 1841 Massachusetts Charitable Mechanic Association fair. A trumpet of his with Vienna twin-piston valves (*US.W.si*) dates

from 1845. Thereafter a wide variety of brass instruments came from his shop, and his excellent E♭ keyed bugles brought him considerable fame. Many of these instruments were made of silver and gold as presentation pieces for famous bandleaders and soloists. The most elaborate of them is a 12-key bugle in E♭ of solid gold made for D.C. Hall in 1850 (*US.DB.hf*).

Wright's string-action rotary-valve saxhorns in circular, over-shoulder, and upright designs set a standard of excellence for the industry during the 1850s and were widely used during the Civil War. Wright was among the first to equip his instruments with Périnet piston valves. His B♭ cornet with these valves was introduced in 1866 and continued to be produced after his death by succeeding makers. He received endorsements from prominent players, among them, in 1868, the distinguished hornist Carl August Hamann.

About 1869, the Boston Musical Instrument Manufactory was formed from a merger of the employees of E.G. Wright and of Graves & Co. Although both Wright and Graves might have helped form the new company, neither of them continued with it. For the last two years of his life Wright worked with D.C. Hall and B.F. Quinby.

BIBLIOGRAPHY

R.E. Eliason: 'Bugles Beyond Compare', *JAMIS*, vol.31 (2005), 67–132

R.E. Eliason: 'D.C. Hall and the Quinby Brothers', *JAMIS*, vol.33 (2007), 84–161

ROBERT E. ELIASON/R

Wright, Thomas (*b* Stockton-on-Tees, co. Durham, England, 18 Sept 1763; *d* Wycliffe Rectory, nr. Barnard Castle, England, 24 Nov 1829). English musician and inventor. He held various posts as organist in northeast England. He is noted as the inventor of a pocket metronome, consisting of a weighted string swinging across a wooden arc marked from zero in tens. Each movement of his *Concerto for the Harpsichord, or Piano Forte, with Accompaniments* (London, *c*1796) bears an indication of speed—thought to be the first metronome marks on a published piece of music: the instruction 'minim = 28' in the concerto's 'Advertisement' indicates that the oscillation of a weighted string measured over the breadth of 28 harpsichord or piano keys (in preference to inches) goes to a minim. Wright seems to have marketed a simple pendulum working in this way, which he considered more practicable than the timekeepers of Loulié, Sauveur, and others. He also invented an organ attachment to a square piano, which plays a set of organ pipes at will without impairing the instrument's use as a piano. His various devices are described in the preface to his concerto. See J.C. Kassler: *The Science of Music in Britain, 1714–1830* (New York, 1979), vol.2, 1083–4.

FRANK KIDSON/R

Wulf, Jan. (*b* Orneta, Poland, 1735; *d* Oliwa, Danzig, Poland, 11 March 1807). Polish organ builder. He was the son of 'Wulf of Orneta' (probably 'Wulf of Malbork', who worked on the organ in Pelplin Cathedral as the assistant of Daniel Nitrowski at various times between 1674 and 1680). In 1758 Wulf went to Danzig; Abbot J. Rybiński of the Cistercian monastery in Oliwa sent him to north Germany and the Netherlands for three years for further training. On his return Wulf built the little organ (of which the case still exists) in the monastery church; on 22 Jan 1763 he entered the order (as Father Michaeł) and began work on the large organ. In 1776 he was ordained and in 1778 stopped work on the instrument, which was completed between 1791 and 1793 by R.F. Dalitz of Danzig. Before its renovation (1934–5), the organ had 83 stops on three manuals and pedal, including 49 foundation stops, 24 mixtures and mutations, and 10 reeds; it sounded three-quarters of a tone above modern concert pitch. The instrument was the largest old organ in Poland and represented a synthesis of southern and northern Polish styles.

BIBLIOGRAPHY

J. Gołos: *Polskie organy i muzyka organowa* (Warsaw, 1972; Eng. trans., 1992, as *The Polish Organ*, vol.1: *The Instrument and its History*)

E. Smulikowska: *Prospekty organowe w dawnej Polsce* (Wrocław, 1989; Eng. trans., rev. 1993, as *The Polish Organ*, vol.2: *Organ-Cases in Poland as Works of Art*)

HANS KLOTZ

Wurlitzer (i). German family of woodwind instrument makers in the Saxon Vogtland. The 23 members, living in Wernitzgrün and Erlbach near Markneukirchen, mainly made clarinets. Direct relationship to Franz Rudolph Wurlitzer in Schöneck, later in Cincinnati, Ohio, is uncertain.

The first woodwind maker in the family was Johann Friedrich Wurlitzer (*b* Erlbach, 29 June 1801; *d* Wernitzgrün, 6 Oct 1878). After apprenticeship, probably with Johann Georg or Christian Friedrich Steiniger in Erlbach, he established himself in the early 1820s as a 'Pfeifenmacher' in Wernitzgrün. His workshop book and representative instruments (at *D.MK.mim*) give insight into the development of clarinet making to the mid-19th century.

With his sons the family separated into the Erlbach and the Wernitzgrün lines (birth and death data below relate to these towns unless otherwise stated). In Wernitzgrün, Friedrich Ferdinand (*b* 15 July 1823; *d* 13 March 1866) and his son Friedrich Albert (*b* 12 Nov 1852; *d* 16 May 1923) continued Johann Friedrich's workshop. The son and successor of Friedrich Albert was Oskar Clemens Wurlitzer (*b* 24 March 1883; *d* 4 Jan 1964), who made good clarinets with German and Oehler key systems. His successors were his sons Clemens Oskar Heinz (*b* 10 Aug 1912; *d* 10 Dec 1977) and Gerd (*b* 18 April 1941). The firm collaborated with Hans Berninger, a clarinettist in the Leipzig Gewandhaus Orchestra, to develop the Berninger-Wurlitzer clarinet. This model, with automatic tuning mechanism (patented 1932) for correcting the pitch of written *e*, was sold mainly through the C.A. Wunderlich dealership in Siebenbrunn. Other workshops in Wernitzgrün were those of Max Wurlitzer (*b* 29 Jan 1881; *d* 29 April 1947) and Paul Wurlitzer (*b* 29 Oct 1892; *d* 25 July 1975).

The founder of the Erlbach branch was Heinrich Eduard Wurlitzer (*b* Wernitzgrün, 29 Aug 1835; *d* Erlbach, 6 June 1920). Two of his sons settled as woodwind instrument makers in Boston, Massachusetts, and Leipzig, respectively: Edward Henry II (*b* 15 Sept 1862; *d* Boston, 1911) and August Bernhard (*b* 30 May 1878; *d* Leipzig, 14 July 1958). Another son, Paul Oskar (*b* 19 July 1868; *d* 13 May 1940), founded his own firm in 1892. He made a wide range of clarinets, flutes, and other woodwind instruments, often in simple versions. Paul Oskar's eldest son was the clarinet maker Fritz (Ulrich) Wurlitzer. Paul Oskar's two younger sons, Arno (*b* 17 April 1890; *d* 11 July 1961) and Kurt Paul (*b* 22 Oct 1899; *d* 12 Jan 1977), specialized in clarinets in the German and Oehler systems; they continued their father's business together until 1951, when they separated. Arno's workshop was continued until 1989 by Gerhard Wurlitzer (*b* 2 June 1922), and the workshop of Kurt Paul until 2005 by his son Dieter (*b* 12 June 1939).

BIBLIOGRAPHY

E. Weller: 'Die Wurlitzers—175 Jahre Holzblasinstrumentenbau in der vogtländischen Familie', *Rohrblatt*, vol.10 (1995), 15–20, 50–55, 107–14

E. Weller: *Der Blasinstrumentenbau im Vogtland von den Anfängen bis zum Beginn des 20. Jh.* (Markneukirchen, 2004)

NICHOLAS SHACKLETON/ENRICO WELLER

Wurlitzer (ii). American firm of instrument makers and dealers, of German origin.

1. History of the company. 2. The Wurlitzer harp. 3. The Wurlitzer electronic organ.

1. HISTORY OF THE COMPANY. Rudolph Wurlitzer (Franz Rudolph Wurlitzer; *b* Schöneck, Saxony, 31 Jan 1831; *d* Cincinnati, OH, 14 Jan 1914) came to the USA in 1853; he settled in Cincinnati and began dealing in musical instruments in addition to working in a local bank. It is likely that he was one of a long line of Saxon instrument makers, beginning with Heinrich Wurlitzer (1595–1656), a lute maker. By 1860 he had a thriving trade and is said to have been a leading supplier of military wind instruments and drums during the Civil War. In 1865 he opened a branch in Chicago and in 1872 joined his brother Anton to form the partnership of Rudolph Wurlitzer & Bro. On 25 March 1890 the firm was incorporated as the Rudolph Wurlitzer Company. Rudolph served as president of the corporation from 1890 to 1912 and as chairman from 1912 to 1914.

Rudolph's eldest son, Howard Eugene (*b* Cincinnati, 5 Sept 1871; *d* New York, NY, 30 Oct 1928), joined the firm in 1889. He guided the general business management, aggressively involving the firm in the increasingly popular automatic instrument trade. Through the purchase of manufacturing operations of the DeKleist Musical Instrument Works in North Tonawanda, New York (1908), and of the Melville Clark Piano Co. in DeKalb, Illinois (1919), Howard established the company as a leading instrument manufacturer and dealer. He served as president from 1912 to 1927 and as chairman from 1927 to 1928.

The artistic development of the firm stemmed from the second son, Rudolph Henry Wurlitzer (*b* Cincinnati, 30 Dec 1873; *d* Cincinnati, 27 May 1948). In 1891 he went to Berlin, where he studied the violin with Emanuel Wirth (of the Joachim Quartet), the history of instruments with Oskar Fleischer, and acoustics with Hermann von Helmholtz. From the violin expert August Riechers he acquired a basic knowledge of violins and violin making. Returning to Cincinnati in 1894 he joined the company as a director, and in addition to serving as treasurer and secretary (1899–1912), vice-president (1912–27), president (1927–32), and chairman (1932–42), he developed the violin department.

The third son, Farny Reginald Wurlitzer (*b* Cincinnati, OH, 7 Dec 1883; *d* North Tonawanda, NY, 6 May 1972), provided technical and manufacturing expertise. After graduating from the Cincinnati Technical School, he went to Germany in 1901 to learn German and to serve apprenticeships with various manufacturers, including six months at Phillips & Söhne, makers of automatic pianos and orchestrions in Bockenheim, near Frankfurt. He returned to Cincinnati in 1904 to join the company, first as a sales representative, and in 1907 as head of the automatic musical instrument department. In 1909 he moved to North Tonawanda to take charge of the Rudolph Wurlitzer Manufacturing Company, formed after the purchase of the manufacturing operations of DeKleist, and in 1910 bought the Hope-Jones Organ Company of Elmira, New York. In 1933, also under Farny in North Tonawanda, the firm began to manufacture coin-operated phonographs. Farny was president of the corporation from 1932 to 1941, chairman from 1942 to 1966, and chairman emeritus from 1966 to 1972. In 1934 R.C. Rolfing joined the company as vice-president and general manager, and at the beginning of his presidency (1941–67) the offices moved from Cincinnati to Chicago; the corporate name was changed in 1957 to the Wurlitzer Company. In the 1980s the president of the company was George B. Howell, the chairman was A. Donald Arsen, and the corporate headquarters were in DeKalb, Illinois. The company split in the 1980s: the keyboard division was acquired in 1988 by Baldwin Pianos, which used the Wurlitzer name for a range of upright and grand pianos. Gibson Guitar Co., which acquired Baldwin in 2001, continued to use the Wurlitzer name for some models as late as 2007; by 2010, Gibson no longer marketed Wurlitzer keyboard instruments.

The Wurlitzer Company had the knack of sensing the demands of the musical public. The emphasis was first on importing and selling: an advertisement of 1865 lists a wide variety of instruments and accessories for sale. The company commissioned drums during the Civil War and had pianos carrying the name of Wurlitzer made from 1880. When automated instruments became popular in the United States in the 1880s, Wurlitzer became leading sellers for the Regina Music Box Company, which in 1896 at the request of the Wurlitzers equipped their 27-inch disc-changer machines with coin slots. In 1899 they marketed the Wurlitzer Tonophone, an electrically powered piano fitted with a coin slot and a cylinder pinned with ten tunes. The success of this coin-operated piano led to the development of other coin-operated machines (among them the Pianino, Mandolin Quartette, and Mandolin Sextette).

When silent films were introduced, Wurlitzer was ready by 1910 for theatre music with the introduction of the Wurlitzer Hope-Jones Unit Orchestra, known as 'the Mighty Wurlitzer' theatre organ, fitted with brass trumpets, tubas, clarinets, oboes, chimes, xylophones, drums, and many other sounds and effects. For smaller theatres Wurlitzer Photoplayers were developed. In the late 1920s Wurlitzer developed coin-operated gramophones: first, in 1934, the P-10 jukebox, with ten selections, then a machine with 24 selections in 1946 (model 1015, 'The Bubbler'), and by 1956 they had produced their Centennial model with 200 selections. When they ceased production of jukeboxes in 1974, nearly 750,000 had been manufactured. In 1985 the Wurlitzer jukebox operation was acquired by the Nelson Group of Companies. It was sold in 2006 to the Gibson Guitar Corp., which manufactures Wurlitzer jukeboxes at a German manufacturing plant.

In 1935 the company introduced a console upright piano, and in 1947, following trends in the musical instrument trade, they began to produce electronic instruments; the most important of these were electronic organs (*see* §3 below), but they also marketed stringless electric pianos based on struck tuned reeds, originally designed by Benjamin F. Miessner (model EP-100, from 1954) and subsequently by Harald Bode (EP-200, from 1968); later they marketed digital electric pianos. About 1960 they introduced the first commercial electronic drum machine, the Side Man.

The violin department became one of the world's leading centres for rare string instruments. Begun by Rudolph Henry Wurlitzer after his training in Germany, by 1918 the violin collection included more than 200 instruments, including several by Stradivari and Guarneri. Jay C. Freeman joined the Wurlitzer branch in New York in 1920 to head the violin department. Under his leadership the firm bought in 1923 the Betts Stradivari of 1704 and in 1929 the important Rodman Wanamaker Collection. Rudolph Henry's son Rembert Wurlitzer joined the department in 1930, and became a violin authority and a strong supporter of 20th-century American violin makers. In 1949 the violin department became independent of the parent company, and was directed by Rembert.

2. THE WURLITZER HARP. For many years Wurlitzer imported from Europe harps made by Erard, Erat, Dodd, Grosjean, and others; the repair of these harps at the Cincinnati store indicated the need for a harp that could better withstand the American climate and the demands of contemporary music. In 1909 the company began harp production at its Chicago factory, under the direction of Emil O. Starke, who had been for 20 years an associate of George B. Durkee at the Lyon & Healy harp factory. Like the Lyon & Healy harp, the new Wurlitzer harp was a far sturdier instrument than its European

prototypes; its special features included body ribs of maple and a patented anchor and shoulder brace which minimized the need for frequent regulation of the harp action.

At the 1915 International Exposition in San Francisco the Wurlitzer harp was awarded a medal of excellence. Soon harpists and important conductors, including Walter Damrosch and Leopold Stokowski, endorsed the instrument. Alberto Salvi, the Italian-born virtuoso who acquired the medal-winning harp, stated that even after seven years of touring, playing 1000 solo concerts, neither travel nor climate changes damaged the harp. By 1924 Wurlitzer was advertising more than eight different styles of harp, from a 43-string instrument of 'Grecian' design to a 'Grand Concert' one of 'Gothic' design. The latter, Style DDX, was 182 cm tall, weighed more than 35 kg and had 47 strings ranging from C′ to g″″. A 46-string version of Style DDX was also introduced.

In tone, craftsmanship, and appearance the Wurlitzer harp competed successfully for many years with the Lyon & Healy harp, and both instruments were generally preferred to their European counterparts because of their durable construction. Owing to economic conditions and changes within the parent company, Wurlitzer ceased harp production in the late 1930s, but harps with the mark 'Starke Model' engraved on the brass plate remain among the finest pedal harps ever made.

3. THE WURLITZER ELECTRONIC ORGAN. The Wurlitzer Company began the manufacture of electronic organs in 1947 at its factory in North Tonawanda, New York. In 1946 Wurlitzer had taken over from the Everett Piano Co. the Orgatron (based on a patent by Miessner), in which the vibrations of reeds operated by suction were converted into voltage variations by means of electrostatic pickups and were made audible through a loudspeaker; a modification of this principle was used in the first Wurlitzer electronic organ, which was marketed in 1947. Between 1959 and the mid-1960s these were phased out and all new models were fully electronic.

Most Wurlitzer electronic organs have two manuals and pedals, and are primarily for home use; an important group are the 'spinet' organs (introduced 1952) in which two manuals (each usually having 44 notes) are staggered, their ranges overlapping by one octave. Most models feature an additional Leslie tremulant loudspeaker. For some years, starting with the Model 4037 in 1971, all Wurlitzer organs, except the smaller spinet models, included the Orbit III Synthesizer (not strictly a synthesizer, though it incorporates some synthesizer features) on a third, principally monophonic, manual with a compass of two octaves. During the early 1970s some models incorporated a cassette tape recorder. Advances in electronic technology from about 1970 made possible several new devices that are included in many home organs: rhythm and 'walking bass' units, arpeggiators, memories, and a choice of chord systems. Digital electronics were introduced in 1980, permitting among other things the storage of different registrations in a

memory. After acquiring Wurlitzer in 1988, Baldwin continued to use the Wurlitzer name for electronic models for a time. Production of Wurlitzer electronic organs ceased before Baldwin was acquired by Gibson Guitar Co. in 2001.

BIBLIOGRAPHY
A. Dolge: *Pianos and their Makers*, vol.1 (Covina, CA, 1911/R), 209ff
The Wurlitzer Harp Catalogue (Chicago, 1924)
J.H. Fairfield: *Known Violin Makers* (New York, 1942, 5/1988)
J.H. Fairfield: *Wurlitzer World of Music: 100 Years of Musical Achievement* (Chicago, 1956)
H.E. Anderson: *Electronic Organ Handbook* (Indianapolis, IN, 1960), 239–50
Q.D. Bowers: *Put Another Nickel in: a History of Coin-operated Pianos and Orchestrions* (New York, 1966), 71ff
N.H. Crowhurst: *Electronic Organs*, vol.3 (Indianapolis, IN, 3/1975), 105–21
T. Rhea: 'B.F. Miessner's "Stringless Piano"', *Contemporary Keyboard*, vol.4/4 (1978), 62 only; repr. in *The Art of Electronic Music*, ed. T. Darter and G. Armbruster (New York, 1984), 21–2
J.W. Landon: *Behold the Mighty Wurlitzer: the History of the Theatre Pipe Organ* (Westport, CT, 1983)
R. Rensch: *Harps and Harpists* (London and Bloomington, IN, 1989)
B. Carson: 'A Parade of Exotic Electric Pianos and Fellow Travellers', *Keyboard*, vol.19/12 (1993), 147–9, 154–6
R. Ederveen: 'A century of Wurlitzer harps: 1909–2009', *The American Harp Journal*, vol.22/1 (2009), 56–61
CYNTHIA ADAMS HOOVER/R (1); ROSLYN RENSCH (2); HUGH DAVIES/R (3)

Wurlitzer, Fritz (Ulrich) (*b* Erlbach, Germany, 21 Dec 1888; *d* Erlbach, 9 April 1984). German clarinet maker. He was born into a family of woodwind instrument makers and worked initially in the shop of his father, Paul Oskar Wurlitzer. He set up an independent workshop about 1930. During the 1930s he collaborated with the clarinettist Ernst Schmidt, adding refinements to both Oehler-system and Boehm-system clarinets. Wurlitzer's Schmidt-Kolbe system (initially involving Louis Kolbe, a maker in Altenburg) is a modification of the Oehler system with more even venting, resulting in an exceptionally full and even tone in the low register. Most of these instruments have a very wide bore (15.2 mm), perhaps the widest ever used in German-style instruments. They were widely played and especially favoured in the Netherlands. The Schmidt Reform Boehm-system utilizes standard Boehm-system fingering but carries several additional vents, resulting in a very even tone closer to the German sound than to the French. Wurlitzer also made fine basset horns, bass clarinets and even a contrabass clarinet; his lower clarinets were still highly prized at the beginning of the 21st century.

Herbert Wurlitzer (*b* Erlbach, 19 Dec 1921; *d* Neustadt an der Aisch, Germany, 8 May 1989), a son of Fritz Wurlitzer, worked with his father until 1959, when he established his own workshop, first located in Bubenreuth, later in Neustadt an der Aisch. Although he made a slightly simplified version of the Reform Boehm-system clarinet, he preferred the standard Oehler system, and most of his instruments follow the latter. His soprano clarinets were almost universally regarded as unrivaled among Oehler-system instruments during the last quarter of the 20th century. His workshop remained active after his death.

BIBLIOGRAPHY
E. Weller: 'Die Wurlitzers', *Rohrblatt: Magazin für Oboe, Klarinette, Fagott und Saxophon*, vol.20 (1995), 15–20, 50–55, 107–14
E. Weller: *Der Blasinstrumentenbau im Vogtland von den Anfängen bis zum Beginn des 20. Jahrhunderts* (Markneukirchen, 2004)

NICHOLAS SHACKLETON

Wurlitzer, Rembert (*b* Cincinnati, OH, 27 March 1904; *d* New York, NY, 21 Oct 1963). American violin dealer and authority on instruments of the violin family. He was the only son of Rudolph Henry Wurlitzer, director of the Wurlitzer Company in Cincinnati. In 1924, after two years at Princeton University, he was sent to Mirecourt to learn violin making under Amédée Dieudonné. The following year he spent six months in London as the guest of Alfred Hill of W.E. Hill & Sons, who introduced him to violin connoisseurship. He returned to Cincinnati and became a vice president of the family business. In 1937 he moved to the firm's violin department in New York, which he established as an independent company under his own direction in 1949. In 1951 he was joined by the Italian restorer Simone Fernando Sacconi (1895–1973).

After Wurlitzer's death the business was continued with considerable success by his widow, Anna Lee Wurlitzer, née Little (*b* 29 July 1912; *d* Dec 2005), to whom Wurlitzer's posthumous US patent (29 April 1969) for a violin bow was assigned. She was aided by Sacconi and his assistant Dario D'Attili (1922–2004), who later as manager upheld the firm's high standard. In 1965 Mrs Wurlitzer purchased the Hottinger Collection, comprising some 30 outstanding Italian violins, including a dozen by Stradivari. The firm closed in autumn 1974.

Wurlitzer's business was unrivalled in the USA and was patronized by leading musicians and collectors. His vast knowledge and photographic memory enabled him to identify many Italian masterpieces. His firm kept careful records of every instrument examined, and their certificates of authenticity are widely accepted as valid.

CHARLES BEARE/R

Wuwu. (1) Bullroarer of the Koko people, Yodda Valley, Northern Province, Papua New Guinea. See A.C. Haddon: 'Migrations of Cultures in British New Guinea', *Journal of the Anthropological Institute of Great Britain and Ireland*, vol.50 (1920), 237–80, esp. 249.

(2) Vessel flute of Blanche Bay, Gazelle Peninsula, New Britain. It was a fruit shell, about the size of a large apricot, into which a mouth-hole and three fingerholes were cut. It was played only by women. *See* O. Finsch: *Ethnologische Etfahrungen und Belegstücke aus der Südsee* (Vienna, 1888–93), 28.

Wuxian. Obsolete five-string lute of the Han Chinese (*wu*: 'five'; *xian*: 'string'). The instrument is also known as *wuxian pipa*. Like the four-string version, it had a pear-shaped shallow resonating chamber, but the wuxian differed in its straight pegbox and in its number of strings. It was plucked either with the fingers or with a large wooden plectrum. As a popular string instrument it enjoyed a wide circulation during the Tang dynasty (618–907 CE) but subsequently fell from favour. The wuxian was introduced both to Japan (where there is a beautifully decorated *gogen biwa*—as the Japanese pronounce the same pictograph—at *J.NR.s*) and to Korea. See Cheung Sai-bung: *Zhongguo yinyue shilun shugao* [Draft examinations into Chinese music history] (Hong Kong, 1974–5), 253–4.

ALAN R. THRASHER

Wyvern organ. Electronic organ, several models of which were manufactured from 1966 by Wyvern Church Organs in Bideford, Devon, continuing as Wyvern Organ Builders Ltd in Fernhurst, near Haslemere. Preceding models from the 1950s were designed by Kenneth Burge (who had been involved in two companies manufacturing electronic organs that bore his name) and some later ones by Tony Koriander. Burge founded the Wyvern firm in 1966 and in 1968 was joined by Arthur Lord, former general manager of the John Compton Organ Co., who served Wyvern as artistic advisor. In 1977 the National Research and Development Corp. (latterly the British Technology Group) invited Wyvern to engineer a digital tone-generation system; in 1978 they produced the prototype of the fully computerized Bradford Computing Organ, designed by Peter Comerford of the University of Bradford.

Since then, the sounds in the Wyvern organs have been generated digitally. A minimum of five very-high-frequency oscillators (one for each of two possible specifications—'English' and a neo-Baroque 'Classical'—on each of two manuals, and one for the pedals) use two stages of frequency division to produce successively the 12 semitones of the highest octave and all the lower octaves. The length of time that different organ pipes take to speak was reproduced by computer-designed graduated frequency attack, and the 'chiff' attack found in some flute stops on pipe organs could be included as an optional feature. A harpsichord unit was also available. More recently, Wyvern adopted a new tone-generator system based on sound-sampling technology; a version allowing note-by-note voicing, adjustment of apparent location of sound sources, and emulation of unsteady wind was adapted for custom-built Wyvern organs, some with four manuals. Some installations combine electronic and pipe components. See P.J. Comerford: 'Bradford Musical Instrument Simulator' *IEE Proceedings*, vol.128/5 (1981), 364–72.

HUGH DAVIES/R

X

Xalam [halam, khalam]. Half-spiked lute of the Wolof people of Senegambia. The strings (one to eight, commonly five), formerly of raffia or bark twine or animal hide or hair, nowadays of nylon, are attached by leather tuning laces to one end of the dowel-like fretless neck, then pass over a fan-shaped bridge and through the soundhole in the cowhide soundtable, and are attached to the exposed end of the neck within the carved, trough-shaped resonator. Related griot plucked lutes with a fan-shaped bridge, varying in size and tuning, include the Fulbe *hoddu*, Moor *tidinit*, Songhay *molo*, Soninke *gambare*, and the Mande *koni* complex (e.g. Maninka *koni*, Xasonke *koni*, Bamana/Bambara *ngoni/nkoni*, and Mandinka *kontingo*).

Four types of Wolof *xalam*s are the *bopp*, *nderr bopp/nderr*, *nderattul*, and *joxé*. They are differentiated primarily by the wall thickness of the resonator. *Xalamkats* (xalam players) usually refer to only two kinds of xalams due to the lack of consistency in the wall thickness: the *bopp*, larger with longer strings, thicker walls, heavier and deeper sound; and the *nderr*, smaller with shorter strings, thinner walls, and a brighter sound. When played in an ensemble, the *bopp* ('bass xalam') serves to accompany, while the *nderr* functions as the leader or soloist. Generally, the *bopp* and *nderr* both have five strings but are tuned differently. The two main tunings (*fodet*) are the *nderr* tuning called *fodeti ardiné* ('leader') and the *bopp* tuning called *fodeti ordinaire* ('follower'). *Nderr fodeti ardiné* involves an octave between strings 1 and 2; the strings are respectively tuned: *f′, f, b♭, g′, a′*. The *bopp* is ordinarily tuned with a 7th between strings 1 and 2: *d′, e, a, f′, g′*.

In playing, the right-hand wrist generally rests on the soundtable. The right-hand index finger plucks strings 2 and 3 upward; the middle finger plucks strings 4 and 5 upward; the thumb plucks string 1 downward. Exceptionally, for projection the index finger strokes downward in very fast passages. An important occasional right-hand technique (from Senegambian *kora* playing) involves tapping the resonator. This tapping serves as an 'answer' to the melody 'question' and adds rhythmic drive. The left-hand index, third, and fourth fingers press strings 2 and 3 against the neck to produce different pitches. The outside strings 1, 4, and 5 are fixed in pitch and serve as melody and drone strings. A special left-hand technique is called *bos* ('touching'). To ornament the melody notes, the fingernails lightly press the plucked strings to create a vibrato. This technique is noted in transcriptions by the presence of a small *b* to the right of the affected note.

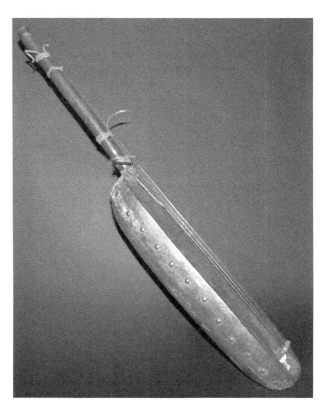

Xalam, plucked lute, Wolof people, West Africa, early 20th century. (Aurelia W. Hartenberger, EdD)

339

Xalamkats are considered *gewels* (equivalent to the Mandinka *jali*) and function as praise-singers, seers/healers, emissaries between chiefs and villages, advisors to leaders, and genealogists.

BIBLIOGRAPHY

M.T. Coolen: 'The Wolof Xalam Tradition of the Senegambia', *Ethnomusicology*, vol.27/3 (1983), 477–98

E. Charry: 'Plucked Lutes in West Africa: an Historical Overview', *GSJ*, vol.49 (1996), 3–37

E. Charry: *Mande Music* (Chicago, 2000)

AURELIA W. HARTENBERGER

Xạmsa'mikạn [xaws mewktses]. Scallop-shell rattle of indigenous peoples of the North American northwest coast. The term literally means 'shellfish rattle' in the Kwakwạkạ'wakw language; *xaws mewktses* means 'new rattle' in Salish. It exists in two forms: (1) A number of scallop shells strung on a long cord, with the concave sides of pairs of shells facing each other; the rattle is shaken by hand; (2) Two pairs of shells tied to cord held in a dancer's fist. The rattles are said to have come to the Kwakwạkạ'wakw from the Coast Salish of Comox and are used in the *xwixwi* dance at times of life transitions, such as marriage, inheritance, and death.

J. RICHARD HAEFER

Xaphoon. Trademark for a single-reed, keyless bamboo aerophone invented about 1973 by Brian Wittman in Maui, Hawaii, and later patented in the USA and Japan. Ordinarily pitched in B♭, C, or D, it employs a tenor saxophone reed with standard metal ligature, and produces a two-octave chromatic scale sounding one octave lower than a recorder of equivalent length, about 32 cm for the C instrument. It overblows at the 12th. Its tone, described as a cross between a saxophone's and clarinet's, and its relatively easy fingering have found favour among some popular musicians as well as amateurs. The name Xaphoon derives from another made-up word, 'bamboozaphone'. In 2000 Wittman introduced a less expensive model called 'Pocket Sax', made of injection-molded plastic by Indiana Plastics in Elkhart, IN. By 2010 some 60,000 Xaphoons and about the same number of Pocket Saxes had been manufactured.

LAURENCE LIBIN

Xeremía. Single or double clarinet of Ibiza in the Balearic Islands. It is made from wood or cane, 3.5 to 6.5 mm in diameter, and is cylindrical, with a cylindrical bore. It usually has four fingerholes and a thumbhole, and is sometimes pentatonic, though some single-pipe versions have as many as six fingerholes plus a high thumbhole. The idioglot downcut single reeds are constructed separately or, more often, formed from the sounding tube itself. The double xeremía, made of cane tubes, is called *reclam de xeremíes*, *xeremía besona*, or *xeremía doble*; it is similar in construction to the Egyptian *zummāra*. A pastoral instrument, the xeremía is now fairly rare. Some examples terminating with a

small bell made from the tip of a horn or a whelk shell might have been made for the tourist trade.

JEREMY MONTAGU

Xiao. Vertical notched flute of the Han Chinese. The name *xiao* (pronounced 'hsiao') is onomatopoeic. Regional names include *dongxiao*, *chiba*, and *yuping xiao*.

The xiao is constructed of bamboo, with an inward-sloping notch at the upper end, five fingerholes plus one thumbhole, and two or more vent holes near the lower end, through which colourful tassels are sometimes attached. Overall lengths vary regionally. For flutes pitched in D (all holes closed), the sounding length, defined by the vent holes, is about 50 to 52 cm, depending upon bore size and configuration. Range is two octaves plus one tone (d'–e'''), though on the southern *dongxiao* several higher pitches can be obtained. Xiao are made in C and E as well. Either the left or right hand may cover the upper three holes, the other hand covering the lower three.

Four types are commonly differentiated:

(1) *Zizhu xiao* ('purple bamboo' xiao), most characteristic of the Jiangnan region of central-eastern China. Longest of the regional variants (about 75 cm or more overall), this type is constructed from a species with long, straight internodal sections and relatively narrow bore (about 1.2 to 1.4 cm). While called 'purple bamboo', the colour is closer to dark brown. It has a U-shaped notch carved through the uppermost node (which otherwise closes off most of the opening). Refined in tone and moderate in volume, this *xiao* is played solo, in duet with *qin* or *zheng* zithers, or in small ensembles such as Jiangnan *sizhu* ('silk-bamboo'). Performance techniques are generally plain, with minimal ornamentation (see *qudi* techniques under D1).

(2) *Dongxiao* ('open xiao'), employed in *nanguan* music of southern Fujian province and Taiwan, where it is also known as *chiba* ('1.8 [Chinese] feet'). The *dongxiao* (55 to 60 cm long overall) is made from 'stone bamboo' (*shizhu*) or other relatively thick species. It has a U- or V-shaped notch at the top node—which unlike the other *xiao* types is completely open—and the lower end is cut at ground level from the bamboo root. In theory, the instrument should have ten nodal outcroppings, though some variants have only nine. Due to its large internal diameter (about 2 cm at the blow-hole), the *dongxiao* is capable of greater volume than the other vertical types, especially suitable within the context of the *nanguan* ensemble. Performance requires more elaborate finger techniques, notably trills and lead-in grace notes.

(3) *Yuping xiao* (Yuping: a region in Guizhou province, south-central China). This flute is made from a species of long, slender, lightly coloured (and often elliptical) bamboo popularly known as 'water bamboo' (*shuizhu*). The *yuping xiao* is about 65 cm long overall, with a very small U-shaped notch penetrating the top node, and decorative images (mountains, waterfalls, etc.) and poems carved or painted on the front. Because

of the instrument's small size (especially its notch), tone production requires a carefully formed embouchure. Its thin but refined and quiet tone make it most suitable for solo performance, though it is often valued as an art object as well.

(4) *Yaxiao* ('refined xiao'), a semi-chromatic adaptation of the *zizhu xiao*, dating from the 1930s, specifically for performance with the *qin* zither. The *yaxiao* differs from the other types in that it is typically pitched in C (rather than D), and has seven fingerholes plus a thumbhole (rather than five plus one), allowing two additional chromatic pitches (eb' and ab') compatible with *qin* temperament.

The history of Chinese vertical flutes is one of constantly changing terminology. Inscriptions on oracle bones (about 12th century BCE) reveal the names of two flutes, *yan* and *guan*, though no archaeological examples of these have been found. The *Zhouli* text and others of the 3rd century BCE mention the names *di* (a name later applied to transverse flutes) and *guan* ('pipe', a name later applied to reed-pipes). Both had fingerholes and presumably notches as well. The *di* of this period must have been a four-holed flute, because during the Han dynasty (206 BCE to 220 CE) the poem *Changdi fu* ('long *di* poem') reports that a thumbhole hole had been added. Other early writings cite another vertical flute, the six-holed *qiangdi*, an instrument of the Qiang minority culture of western China. This instrument was quite long and slender and might have been related to the unnotched vertical flute of Western Asia (see NAY). But the Chinese vertical flute *di* was already documented in late Zhou literature as a standard instrument employed in ritual ensembles. Several centuries later, a note in the *Fengsu Tongyi* (*c*175 CE) explains the *di* flute's cultural significance as an embodiment of the Confucian concept of *di*, a different character meaning 'to wash away evil from the mind' and identify with noble thoughts.

The vertical flute has also been closely associated with Chinese experiments in temperament theory, since the instrument had fewer pitch variables than did stringed instruments or bells. However, the flute's roughly equidistant fingerhole positions—which yielded whole-tone and three-quarter-tone intervals—obviously did not coincide with the new orthodoxy of circle-of-5ths temperament, because numerous attempts were made to correct this discrepancy. Most notable of the early attempts is that of the 3rd-century CE court theorist Xun Xu, who repositioned the fingerholes based upon mathematical calculations, thereby permitting the performance of whole and half steps. Records suggest that the change was not well received by local musicians, who preferred the older tradition. Subsequent attempts (during the 7th century and later) resulted in the construction of sets of 12 flutes (pitched a semitone apart), to correspond with the 12 chromatic pitches of imperial court theory.

During and soon after the Tang dynasty (618–907 CE), the most significant type of vertical flute was known as *chiba guan*, or simply *chiba*. Chen Yang, in his influential treatise *Yueshu* (*c*1100 CE), explained that the *chiba*, at 1.8 (Chinese) feet, was twice the length of the 'yellow bell' pitch (*huangzhong*, foundation pitch of the empire), which was calculated on a closed tube of 0.9 feet. Thus, the *chiba*, an open-tube flute, theoretically sounded the same pitch, achieving correspondence with the universe. The Shōsōin Repository in Japan preserves eight short *chiba* ('shakuhachi' in Japanese) dating from the 8th century. These flutes are constructed of bamboo, jade, and ivory, between 34 and 44 cm long, with outward-cut notches and five fingerholes plus one thumbhole. Due to their size and positioning of fingerholes, some scholars believe the Shōsōin flutes might have been modeled on the calculations of Xun Xu.

After the Tang, the name *chiba* was found less frequently in the literature (perhaps because of changes in measurement systems), and by the Song dynasty (960–1279) the name *dongxiao* became more common. Among local musicians of southern Fujian province, both names are used. The present-day *dongxiao* (*chiba*), which is more than 10 cm longer than the Shōsōin flutes, may well have been in use by the late Song period. Japanese scholars believe that this longer *chiba* was reintroduced into Japan about the mid-15th century. Except for the number of fingerholes and cut of the notch, the present *dongxiao* and the Japanese *shakuhachi* look strikingly similar.

Throughout these periods, other names appeared, such as *shudi* ('vertical *di*') and *changdi* ('long *di*'), primarily identifying long, thin notched flutes. These are regularly depicted in the cave art at Dunhuang (Gansu province) and in scrolls and other paintings. According to the scholar Zhu Xi (1130–1200), the long flute was called xiao or *xiaoguan* ('xiao pipe') by his time (the term *di* increasingly used to identify transverse flutes). No flutes from this period have been found, but a six-hole xiao of porcelain resembling today's *zizhu xiao* and dating from the Ming dynasty (1368–1644) is kept at the Palace Museum in Beijing. Other Ming flutes of porcelain and jade survive in private collections, including two *dongxiao* types from Fujian province. A larger number of 19th-century xiao are preserved in museums throughout China, North America, and Europe, including handsome red-lacquered Confucian ritual flutes decorated with gilded dragon motifs.

Traditional xiao repertory is based upon several conservative sources. From the *qin* zither tradition, *Guanshan Yue* ('Moon over the mountain pass') and *Meihua Sannong* ('Plum blossoms, three variations') are representative; from the Hakka *zheng* tradition, *Chushui Lian* ('Emerging lotus blossoms') is standard; from Jiangnan *sizhu* and Minnan *nanguan* ensemble traditions, *Nishang Qu* ('Rainbow costume melody') and *Meihua Cao* ('Plum blossoms') are respective examples. But an equally large source has emerged from the old *qupai* melodies, such as *Liuyao Jin* which, during the mid-20th century, was transformed into *Fuoshang Dian* ('Buddha ascending to the temple').

BIBLIOGRAPHY

A.C. Moule: 'A List of the Musical and Other Sound-producing Instruments of the Chinese', *Journal of the Royal Asiatic Society, North China Branch*, vol.39 (1908), 1–160; repr. separately (Buren, 1989), 64–7

Hayashi Kenzō and others: *Shōsōin no gakki* [Musical instruments in the Shōsōin] (Tokyo, 1967) [with Eng. summary] i–xxiv, 54ff

Tong Kin-woon: *Shang Musical Instruments* (diss., Wesleyan U., 1983); repr. in *AsM*, vol.15/1 (1983), 166–73

Lu Songling: 'Chiba chutan' [Preliminary study of the *chiba*], *Quanzhou lishi wenhua zhongxin gongzuo tongxun*, no.1 (1985), 9–18

Liu Dongsheng and others, eds.: *Zhongguo yueqi tujian* [Pictorial guide to Chinese musical instruments] (Ji'nan, 1992), 114–15, 119–21

Peng Mumu: 'Di (Chi) he Xiao' [Di (chi) and xiao], *Yueqi*, no.1 (2004), 90–92

H. Goodman and Y.E. Lien: 'A Third Century AD Chinese System of Di-Flute Temperament', *GSJ*, vol.62 (2009), 3–24

ALAN R. THRASHER

Xipro de afilador [silbato de afilador]. Panpipe of Galicia, Spain. It is carved from one thin, flat piece of wood about 11 cm long and 9 cm wide, with 10 drilled holes of graduated depth instead of individual tubes, producing a diatonic scale (tuned if necessary by inserting wax in the holes). The diagonal, closed lower end is usually carved as the profile of a horse's head. It is played by street vendors and craftsmen (*afilidor*, knife sharpener) to advertise their presence.

MAURICIO MOLINA

Xirribita. Term that can refer to a violin, or rabel, of the Basque region; or to a struck box zither, or tambourin de Béarn, of the same region. The term *xirribitari* denotes a performer of either instrument.

Xiurell. Ceramic whistle of Mallorca, Spain. It is made in anthropomorphic or zoomorphic shapes such as horse, demon, bird, or bull and is usually 7 to 15 cm tall. Sometimes one small chamber is filled with water and its sound imitates birdsong. It is sold in street fairs during religious festivities, and accompanies Christmas songs, among other uses. See B. Coll Tomàs and G. Rossello Bordoy: *Ceràmica Popular a les Balears* (Palma, 1997).

MAURICIO MOLINA

Xiyaogu. Hourglass-shaped drum of the Han Chinese, historically known as *zhanggu* ('stick drum'). Several related drum types were introduced from India or Central Asia into the Chinese courts of the Sui and Tang dynasties (6th to early 10th centuries CE), though according to Chen Yang's *Yueshu* ('Treatise on music') of 1104, the *zhanggu* was obtained from Central Asia when Fu Jian (338–85) invaded the state of Kucha. Chen points out that in later times the *zhanggu* was distinguishable by its playing technique: a stick was used to strike the right head, the open hand playing the left. Their common feature is the South Asian tradition of lacing the two drumheads together, rather than tacking them onto the body. Body contour and striking method, however, differ from one historic type to another.

The xiyaogu ('narrow waist drum')—not to be confused with the barrel-shaped *yaogu* ('waist drum') which is merely held at the waist—is a large hourglass-shaped drum (between 60 and 80 cm long), with over-wide heads attached to metal hoops (about 40 cm in diameter) extending beyond the body rims and secured by connective lacing. Historically, the body was constructed from either wood or ceramic. It was played by dancer-musicians, and was suspended from the neck with a strap and struck with a stick in one hand and open palm of the other. The xiyaogu and related drum types are well documented in Dunhuang cave art (Gansu province) from about the 6th century CE onward, in the 10th-century CE Wangjian reliefs (Sichuan province), and in the early 12th-century treatise *Yueshu* and other sources. Following their introduction into Korea and Japan during the Tang-Song period (7th to 13th centuries CE), these drums became less prominent in China, though the xiyaogu is still pictured in the 18th-century treatise *Lülü Zhengyi*. The xiyaogu is especially well preserved by Korean musicians—both in Korea and in northeastern China—where it is known by its earlier name, *zhanggu* (Korean: *changgo*). In Japan, the *san-no-tsuzumi* is another survival in a slightly different form, and the smaller *kotsuzumi* is distantly related. *Xiyaogu*-type drums are still played by the Yao and other minority cultures of South China.

Several related drum types with overwide laced heads were also popular during the Tang-Song period. These include the *maoyuangu*, a smaller hourglass drum with a thicker 'waist', struck by the hands (but shown with sticks in one source); the *dalagu* (a possible transliteration of the Persian *dholak*), a small hand-struck barrel-shaped drum also with overwide heads; and the very important *jiegu* ('jie', a tribal name), with a short cylindrical shell and overwide heads, struck with two sticks. The *jiegu*, a leading percussion instrument in Tang court ensembles, was absorbed into Japanese *gagaku*. These drum types all have clear affinities with South Asian drums, but they have been obsolete in Han China for many centuries. *See* GU for bibliography.

ALAN R. THRASHER

Xizambi [tshizambi, chizambi, zambi, chimazambi]. Scraped unbraced mouth bow (also known as 'friction bow') played by men among the Tsonga and Shangana-Tsonga peoples of Mozambique and South Africa and their neighbours, including the Hlengwe, Karanga and Ndau of Zimbabwe and the Chopi, Tswa and Ndau of Mozambique. Tsonga chiefs once employed a court xizambi player as part of their entourage. The light, curved stave is 36 to 48 cm long and has a series of notches cut along one side. The ribbon-like string is made from a strip of leaf from the *murara* ground palm or the swamp rush *Typha capensis*. One end of the stave is held by the left hand; one or more fingers are used to stop the string. The other end of the stave rests against the cheek and chin so that the string passes between the slightly parted lips without touching them. To sound the instrument, the right hand crosses the body to rub a rattle stick (pierced through two fruit shells containing small stones) rapidly to and fro across the serrations in the front (distal) side of the stave. Mouth-resonated harmonics (partials 9 or more) from the open or stopped string are used melodically, as with the jew's harp.

The *nxoronxoro* of the !Kung Khoisan of Angola, Namibia, and Botswana is similar, often larger and heavier, but it is the left hand that reaches right across the body to hold the far end of the stave while the right hand, holding a plain stick without rattles, rubs the serrations on the back (proximal) side. A second short stick may be used instead of the fingers to stop the string.

BIBLIOGRAPHY
P.R. Kirby: *The Musical Instruments of the Native Races of South Africa* (London, 1934, 2/1965/R1968)
T. Johnston: 'Xizambi Friction–bow Music of the Shangana–Tsonga', *AfM*, vol.4/4 (1970), 81–95
H. Tracey: *Catalogue of the Sound of Africa Series* (Roodeport, 1973)
DAVID K. RYCROFT/ANDREW TRACEY

Xul [ah-xul, xolb, pito, tzijolaj, zicolaj]. End-blown duct flute of the Mayan peoples of Guatemala. It is traditionally made of cane, but nowadays also of PVC pipe or metal. Length and diameter vary widely. It usually has six fingerholes, but three or four are also reported. Its duct is formed by a piece of wax. Sometimes played in pairs, the *xul* is usually played singly together with one or two drums, especially the *tamborón* or *q'ojom*. This ensemble accompanies dance dramas such as the Dance of the Moors and Christians, processions, and activities in religious brotherhoods.

Another xul type is side-blown and made of bamboo, with a hollow ball of beeswax near the blowing end frequently filled with rattlesnake rattles, and with an aperture over which a membrane is stretched as a mirliton.

In the dual Mayan organology all these flutes belong to the *su'* category, together with other wind instruments such as the *chirimía* or the trumpet. No apparent relation has been reported between the xul and the *zul*, a five- or six-hole end-blown flute of Nicaragua. See L.L. O'Brien: 'Marimbas of Guatemala: the African Connection', *The World of Music*, vol.25/2 (1982) 99–104.

MATTHIAS STÖCKLI

Xun. Globular flute of the Han Chinese. The xun (pronounced 'hsün') is an egg-shaped vessel of baked clay, with a blow-hole at its apex and usually three to eight fingerholes distributed in various patterns. Imperial court examples vary between about 8 and 13 cm in height. Because of its globular wind chamber, the xun has a range of only about one octave, without usable overtones, though lower pitches can be obtained by rolling the flute inward, as a transverse flute is rolled inward to flatten a pitch.

The ancient legacy of this Confucian ritual instrument in China is equalled only by the *qing* stone chime. Numerous small proto-xun clay flutes, about 5 to 8 cm in height, irregularly ball-shaped, egg-shaped, and fish-shaped, have been found in Neolithic sites from about 5000 BCE and later. The flutes found in Zhejiang province and Shaanxi province have blow-holes but no fingerholes, suggesting that they were possibly bird-calls. Flutes found in neighbouring Shanxi province have blow-holes and two fingerholes, with a range of about a 4th.

Instruments now identified as xun, found in late Shang sites (c1200 BCE) of Henan province, are roughly the same size, though in the shape of a large egg (standard thereafter), and generally with five fingerholes (three at the front, two at the back). One important decorative characteristic found on some Shang instruments is the *taotie* design (face of a mythical animal on the outer surface). These flutes are believed to have been employed with other instruments in early court rituals.

The significance of the xun within Confucian ideology is cited in the *Shijing* ('Classic of Poetry', c7th century BCE): 'the elder brother plays xun, the younger brother plays *chi* [transverse flute]', with commentary stating that 'our minds, as brothers, must be in harmony', a reminder of the need for social accord within the family. A note in the *Erya* (c3rd century BCE) states that 'a large xun is like a goose egg, with a flattened bottom and six holes; a small one is like a chicken egg'. The reference to 'six holes' might mean five fingerholes (standard in archaeological finds) plus one blow-hole. The Han dynasty text *Fengsu Tongyi* ('Common Meanings in Customs', c175 CE) and other sources give construction details for the flutes of this period. Later sources, such as *Yueshu* (c1100), show that by the 12th century there were several varieties of xun, most slightly larger, with between six and eight fingerholes.

By the Qing dynasty (1644–1911), the xun used in court rituals had acquired a new standardized form and decoration: an egg-shaped globe, 8.5 cm in height, six fingerholes (four in front, two in back), lacquered bright red with gold dragon and cloud motifs.

Apart from its use in Confucian ritual, the xun has enjoyed a minor renaissance in China since the 1980s. Newly constructed nine-hole xun flutes, with additional chromatic capability, are now played in recitals and in contemporary-music ensembles. Related globular flutes include the Korean *hun*, the Vietnamese *huân*, and the Japanese *tsuchibue*.

BIBLIOGRAPHY
Chuang Pen-li: 'A Historical and Comparative Study of Hsün, the Chinese Ocarina', *Bulletin of the Institute of Ethnology, Academia Sinica* (1972), no.33, 177–253 [with Eng. summary]
Cao Zheng: 'Xun he xunde zhizuo gongyi' [The *xun* and art of its construction], *Yueqi*, (1982), no.4, 5–7; no.5, 4–6
Tong Kin-woon: *Shang Musical Instruments* (diss., Wesleyan U., 1983); repr. in *AsM*, vol.15/1 (1983), 152–66
Li Chunyi: *Zhongguo shanggu chutu yueqi zonglun* [Survey of ancient excavated musical instruments from China] (Beijing, 1996), 386–407
ALAN R. THRASHER

Xylophone (from Gk. *xylon*: 'wood'; Fr. *xylophone, claquebois*; Ger. *Xylophon, Holzarmonika*; It. *silofono*). Percussion instrument with one or more tuned bars (often called keys) of bamboo, wood, or synthetic material of graduated length and pitch. For similar instruments made of stone or metal, *see* LITHOPHONE or METALLOPHONE.

1. General. 2. Europe. 3. Africa. 4. Southeast Asia. 5. Pacific. 6. Latin America.

1. GENERAL. Xylophones are widely used in Europe and the Americas, Africa, Southeast Asia (mainland and insular), Melanesia, and the Marquesas Islands in Polynesia. Their prehistoric origins are unknown. Xylophones appear in the traditional music of Hungary, Austria, the Czech Republic, and other Central and Eastern European countries, as well as in modern Western concert and popular music, especially jazz. They take many different forms: for example, a set of bars (or slabs, tubes, etc.) can have one resonator (e.g. a pit or trough in the ground) for the entire instrument, or each bar can have a separate resonator.

Individual bars, each supported at two nodes of vibration, can be loose or temporarily or permanently attached to their support. They can rest on the legs or thighs of a player, on straw bundles or logs, or be suspended from cords. Insulating material such as rubber or plastic knobs, grass bundles, or cloth strips can interpose between bars and support to permit free vibration of the bars.

When the bars are suspended, the cord-and-bar assembly can be attached to the sides of a trough resonator or to vertical posts, or one end of the assembly can hang from a vertical post and the other be tied to the player's leg or waist to form a curved arrangement. When played, the bars can be horizontal, oblique, curved, or vertical in relationship to the ground. The instrument can rest on the ground, be held in playing position by the performer, or hang from a cord slung over the player's shoulders; the player can sit or stand facing the lengths or the widths of the bars. In modern Western orchestral xylophones the bars are arranged chromatically like a piano keyboard; elsewhere the arrangement varies. One, two, or three single beaters, or two pairs of beaters, can be used to strike the middle or near the ends of the bars; the heads of the beaters are usually wrapped with cloth or rubber if the bars are struck at the middle. Several persons can play the same instrument, or the notes of an instrument can be distributed among different players. They can be assigned single melodic lines (for one hand or two), octaves, interlocking pitch patterns, or rhythmic patterns.

Hornbostel and Sachs classified the xylophone as an Idiophone, 'sets of percussion sticks' (Hornbostel–Sachs number 111.212), and divided xylophones into two major types: those with bedded bars and those with suspended bars. Olga Boone, in her 1936 study of xylophones in the Belgian Congo (now Democratic Republic of the Congo, or DRC), delineated two major types: those with loose bars and those with permanently fixed bars (the latter divided into those with or without resonators); she paid particular attention to the ways in which bars and resonators are mounted or attached, tuning patterns, nomenclature, and distribution.

In discussing the xylophone's putative origins in Africa or Asia, she felt that conclusions were premature and that other, nonmusical evidence was needed to support any hypotheses. Later studies by A.M. Jones and P. Kirby favouring an Asian origin of the African xylophone lack full supporting evidence and are generally regarded today as unconvincing.

In India and China, the xylophone with trough resonator and suspended bars is considered a foreign instrument, Burmese in origin. Outside China, the xylophone with trough resonator and bedded bars is associated with Chinese communities. In West Java, for example, the *gambang* xylophone is played by the leader of the ensemble (*gambang leromong*) that accompanies song and dance at Chinese weddings. As a solo instrument, the *gambang* was played by Javanese women of Chinese ancestry to accompany the singing of *pantun* poetry. In Japan, the *mokkin* with 16 or 17 bedded bars is used in the *geza* offstage music for kabuki theatre. A similar xylophone was associated with Japanese societies that performed Chinese music of the Qing dynasty beginning in the 1820s and 1830s.

An instrument that came into J.-P. Rameau's possession was also regarded as Chinese, though Rameau and later authors did not accept its Chinese provenance (see Schaeffner, 1955). In his discussion of Chinese tunings (*Code de musique pratique*, 1760), Rameau stated that it came from the Cape of Good Hope, and there is reason to believe, in the light of contemporary trade routes, that it could have been brought to the Cape from Java or elsewhere in the East Indies. After Rameau's death (1764), Burney referred to such an instrument in the possession of Abbé Arnaud as Chinese (*BurneyH*, i.38; iii.32). A sketch of the instrument appeared in La Borde (*Essai sur la musique ancienne et moderne*, 1780) with the caption 'Instrument Chinois', noting that Rameau improperly called the instrument *orgue de Barbarie*, that it was brought from the Indies and that it belonged at that time to Arnaud. The sketch shows a xylophone with bedded bars resting over a trapezoidal trough; the shape of the instrument resembles that of similarly constructed xylophones in insular Southeast Asia. The shape of the instrument's base, the number of bars and the fanciful beaters provide possible further clues to its origin. The *gambang* xylophone used in the folk theatre *lenong* of Jakarta has bedded bars resting on a trapezoidal base, which is open, as in La Borde's illustration; the *gambang* of the classical *gamelan pelog-salendro* in West Java can also have an open trapezoidal base. La Borde's sketch shows 18 bars, while Burney mentioned a two-octave range or 11 pitches; the *gambang* of West Java commonly has 17 or 18 bars. Other features, for example curved beaters, are related to the trough xylophones of the Philippines and Sabah (Malaysia) or the tube xylophone of West Java.

2. EUROPE.

(i) History. The first published mention of the xylophone in Europe was in 1511, when Schlick (*Spiegel der Orgelmacher und Organisten*) referred to it as *hültze glechter* ('wooden clatter'). Agricola (*Musica instrumentalis deudsch*, 1529) called a series of 25 wooden bars *Strohfiedel* ('straw fiddle'). Praetorius (*Theatrum instrumentorum*, 1620) showed a series of 15 bars about 15 to 53 cm in length, arranged diatonically in a single row, pyramid fashion (like Agricola's example). Mersenne (1636–7) illustrated and described

two instruments (named *claquebois patouilles* and *eschellettes*) of grander scale. One has 17 bars, which are struck on the underside with individual beaters and arranged like a keyboard. In general, however, the European xylophone before modern times was a simple instrument with wooden bars loosely strung together or resting on ropes of straw, giving rise to the name *Strohfiedel*. It was very much an instrument of itinerant musicians until the 19th century, when it rose to prominence as a solo instrument and attracted the notice of Mendelssohn, Chopin, and Liszt, all of whom spoke of the expertise of Michal Guzikow, a Polish virtuoso. Mendelssohn said, 'I must own that the skill of the man beats everything that I could have imagined, for with his wooden sticks resting on straw, his hammers also being of wood, he produces all that is possible with the most perfect instrument'. Guzikow's instrument consisted of 28 wooden bars arranged semitonally in four rows resting on five straw supports.

During the 19th century the European xylophone appeared under various names and guises (*xylosistron*, *tryphon*, etc.). The orchestral instrument had four rows and was similar in many ways to that of Guzikow. The bass notes were nearest the player, with the centre two rows corresponding to the white keys of the piano and the outer rows to the black keys. Ferdinand Kauer's *Sei variazioni* (c1810) contains solo passages for the xylophone, possibly the earliest orchestral use of the instrument. In 1852 it was mentioned in J.G. Kastner's *Les danses des morts*. Better known is Saint-Saëns's use of the instrument to represent rattling bones in his *Danse macabre* (1874), and later (as 'Fossiles') in *Le carnaval des animaux* (1886). The playing technique of the four-row instrument differed from that of the modern xylophone, and apparently sightreading was particularly difficult. The modern xylophone originated about the turn of the 20th century, although the four-row instrument is still played in Eastern Europe. Early 20th-century composers who scored for the xylophone include Mahler (Sixth Symphony, 1903–4); Puccini (*Madama Butterfly,* 1904); Strauss (*Salome,* 1905); Elgar (*Wand of Youth,* Suite no.2, 1908); Debussy (*Ibéria,* 1909); Stravinsky (*The Firebird,* 1909–10); and Delius (*Eventyr,* 1917). In his last work (*Turandot,* completed by Alfano, 1926) Puccini wrote for xylophone and *xylofon basso* (the latter part now usually played on a marimba using fairly hard sticks). An extended and florid part for xylophone occurs in Havergal Brian's 'Gothic' Symphony (1919–27).

Complex writing for the xylophone has revolutionized its use compared with the demands of earlier composers, who, with occasional exceptions such as Stravinsky in *The Wedding* (1923), wrote only short passages. The demands on the modern xylophonist are heavy, especially in Tippett's *The Vision of St Augustine* (1960–5) and many of his subsequent compositions, such as *Concerto for Orchestra* (1962–3) and Third Symphony (1970–72); Messiaen's *Chronochromie* (1960); Boulez's *Le marteau sans maître* (1952–4, rev. 1957); and Henze's Piano Concerto no.2 (1967) and *Ode an der Westwind* (1953). The part in Boulez's *Le marteau sans maître* (1953–5, rev. 1957) was widely regarded as unplayable when first published. Works using the xylophone as a solo instrument include Alan Hovhaness's *Fantasy on Japanese Woodprints* (1965) and Thomas Pitfield's Sonata for xylophone (1967). The keyboard xylophone is now virtually obsolete, but Bartók scored for it (*Tastenxylophon*) in *Bluebeard's Castle* (1911); nowadays the part is usually played on two xylophones.

The xylophone part is written (mostly in the treble clef) an octave lower than its sounding pitch, although Messiaen and Birtwistle mostly notated xylophone parts at sounding pitch. Normally only one staff is used; exceptions include Ravel's *Ma mère l'oye* (1911; 'Laideronette'), where it is given a double staff.

(ii) Construction. The arrangement of the modern Western instrument follows that of a piano keyboard. Deagan of Chicago is thought to have been the first to take the single-row Guatemalan and other Central American instruments as a model for producing the keyboard-derived version, which superseded the older four-row pattern. As with other bar-percussion instruments, the bars are either suspended from cords passing through their nodal points, or they rest at their nodes on a cushion of felt or similar insulation. In general the row of bars corresponding to the black keys of the piano is raised, keyboard fashion. The compass of the orchestral xylophones is generally either four octaves ascending from c', or three and a half octaves ascending from f' or g'. The larger instrument is preferable to avoid octave transposition often necessary on a smaller instrument. The bars are of the finest rosewood (or wood of similar resonance and durability), or of new synthetic materials such as Kelon (a pultrusion silicate) or Klyperon, prepared from synthetic reinforced resins. The pitch of each bar is governed by its length and thickness; thinning the underside of the bar lowers the pitch considerably. In the modern orchestral xylophone each bar is suspended over a tube resonator whose air-column frequency matches the pitch of the bar. The bars give a bright penetrating sound when struck with hard-headed mallets. Softer beaters produce a mellow sound and are especially useful on the lower notes.

3. AFRICA.

(i) Introduction. Oral traditions mention the xylophone in the 13th-century kingdom of Mali; the first written reference, also from Mali, comes from the mid-14th century. Describing two Muslim festivals at the court, Ibn Battūta (*Travels in Asia and Africa, 1325–1354,* trans. H.A.R. Gibb, 1929) mentioned an instrument made of reeds with small calabashes at its lower end. In the second half of the 16th century, dos Santos, a Portuguese missionary living among the Karanga in what is now Mozambique, mentioned the *ambira,* a gourd-resonated instrument. From the mid-17th century onwards, European travellers to the western coast of Africa refer to the instrument, most often with calabash resonators; the most common names for it were *bala, balafo(n),* and *ballard(s)* in West

Africa and *marimba* in the Bantu-speaking areas—the same terms used by writers referring to the instrument in the Caribbean and Central and South America.

Early 20th-century European studies of the African xylophone paid particular attention to organological features of instruments in Berlin and Tervuren museum collections. Olga Boone focussed on construction details and tuning measurements of xylophones of the former Belgian Congo (DRC) according to ethnic origin, the distribution of xylophone types there and in other areas of Africa, and the social context of the instrument. She examined 108 xylophones at the Musée du Congo Belge (now the Musée Royal de l'Afrique Centrale) in Tervuren. Her discussion proceeds from the simpler instruments to the more complex; however, she stated that her order of categories did not necessarily represent stages of evolution. The present discussion is primarily concerned with physical characteristics of the instrument, based on the types distinguished by Boone; additional types are included for those instruments not found in the DRC. There are two main categories: xylophones with loose bars, in which the bars are independent of each other and their support, and those with fixed bars, in which the bars are permanently attached between themselves and to their support.

(ii) Loose bar xylophones. For performance, loose bars are assembled on temporary supports, which can be the player's legs, banana-tree logs, straw bundles, or logs padded with grass. Bars can be completely loose with upright sticks placed between them to prevent their striking each other. Alternatively, holes can be bored in the side of the bar near each end through which a cord is strung and twisted around the dividing upright sticks. Sticks can also be placed vertically between bars at one side of the instrument and through a hole in the middle of each bar at the other side. Bars are normally struck near their ends with wooden sticks.

A xylophone type intermediate between loose and fixed bars is found among the Sena people in central Mozambique and the Lozi in western Zambia where bars strung to each other are temporarily mounted on straw bundles; performers strike the middle of the bars with wooden or rubber-tipped sticks.

(a) Leg xylophones. Bars rest on the seated player's thighs or (as in Madagascar) shins. The instrument is played by young girls or boys as part of initiation activities in Senegal; it is also used as a noisemaker to keep birds and monkeys out of gardens. The instrument's resonance can be enhanced by a hole in the ground, or by a pot or calabash placed underneath it. Two to seven bars are played by one or two players.

Distribution: Senegal, Guinea, Sierra Leone, Ivory Coast, Togo, Benin, southeast Nigeria, Central African Republic, Zambia, Malawi, and Madagascar.

(b) Pit xylophones. A pit can be an integral part of the loose bar xylophone. Four to 13 bars are mounted across grass bundles or banana-tree logs placed at opposite sides of a pit. Among the Yoruba in southwest Nigeria and the Gun in southeast Benin, two such xy-

lophones are played together, one or both instruments over a pit. If the instrument is large, the player sits between two groups of bars with his legs in the pit. This type of xylophone can be used as a practice instrument, as in northwest Ghana, where it is played by children, students of the instrument, and adults without a gourd-resonating xylophone. Among the Luba of the southern DRC, the tuning of the bars for an instrument that will have individual resonators is tested by laying the bars across a pit, or mounting them on banana-tree logs or across a hollow calabash.

Distribution: Guinea, Burkina Faso, Ghana, Benin, Nigeria, Chad, Central African Republic, southeast DRC, northwest Uganda, and southern Malawi.

(c) Log xylophones. Instruments consisting of loose bars resting across banana-tree logs, or a combination of straw bundles (for insulation) and banana-tree logs, appear in many parts of sub-Saharan Africa. They have from six to 22 bars, which are usually larger than those of any other type of African xylophone. It is common for two to as many as six players to interlock different melodic patterns on the same instrument, or two players facing each other can each play one instrument. The bars are usually struck near their ends with one or two plain wooden beaters.

Distribution: Guinea, Liberia, Ivory Coast, Nigeria, Cameroon, Gabon, Central African Republic, Chad, northern DRC, Malawi, Mozambique, Tanzania, Uganda, and southwest Ethiopia.

(iii) Fixed bar xylophones.
(a) Without calabashes. Bars are mounted on runners, or a resonator such as a box or trough, to which insulation material is attached. In northwest DRC, two pairs of beaters are used by one player, and adjacent bars are commonly tuned in octaves. The instrument with runners, found in northwest DRC and among the Yaka in southwest DRC, can have crosspieces at the ends to keep the runners apart. The instrument with bars resting on a trough resonator appears in northwest DRC, southeast Nigeria, and central Mozambique. The box-resonated xylophone is found near the southeast coast of Kenya, on the islands of Zanzibar and Pemba, and in northeast Tanzania.

Among the Igbo of southeast Nigeria, two bars are attached to a grass collar that surrounds the top of an open clay pot.

(b) With one or two calabashes (individual resonators). A bar is suspended from cords strung through holes near its ends and attached to the upper ends of two arcs of wooden sticks glued to the top of the resonator. The player changes the instrument's timbre by closing and opening the mouth of the resonator with the left hand. The instrument can be played in groups of two or more, with each one tuned differently, and is commonly used at hunting ceremonies.

Distribution: southeast DRC, Zambia, and southern Malawi.

Parallel curved poles and two crosspieces form the support frame of an instrument with two calabashes. The ends of the cords that suspend the bars pass over the crosspieces and are tied to the ends of the poles, and the calabashes are suspended on rods placed in holes in each of the poles.

Distribution: among the Tshokwe and Lunda of south-central DRC and the Luvale of eastern Angola.

(c) With multiple calabashes. Instruments differ from area to area in their type of frame construction and the attachment of bars and calabashes. Many xylophones in the DRC and neighbouring areas have in common an arc, or bail, which is attached to the sides of the frame (see types 1–3, 5–6 below). The bail keeps the instrument in the proper playing position in front of the player when it is slung from his shoulders. When the player is seated, he can stabilize the instrument by balancing the bail with his feet. The bars can rest on insulation material or on leather cords, or they can be suspended. Calabashes can be hung from the framework or glued to a frame; they are either suspended directly by rods, or by strings secured to rods fastened across a horizontal frame. The calabashes can be glued to a centre board, which can have holes to accommodate them. While a round or elongated calabash is the most common resonator, bamboo, cattle horn, or wood is also used. Buzzing membranes (mirlitons) are attached to one or more holes in the bottom or side of each resonator; when they are attached to the side, ancillary tubes or round pieces of calabash can be added to protect the membranes. The instrument is played with one to four rubber-tipped beaters, and the bars are struck in the middle; occasionally two players play the same instrument. Several different xylophones can be played in the same ensemble.

Type 1: with resonators suspended from rods (Boone 3a). Two runners are attached to the ends of the bail and insulation is fixed to their top edge; rods pierce the calabashes near their tops and pass through holes in the sides of the runners. Rattan is intertwined around the tops of the calabashes to secure them. The bars are strung together by cords and rest on the insulation. Some modern instruments do not have a bail but have legs inserted between the ends of the runners and the crosspieces at the end of the instrument, so that the player can stand.

Distribution: south-central and southeast DRC, southwest Zambia, and southern Malawi.

Type 2: with suspended bars (Boone 3b). Parallel curved poles constitute the frame for this instrument. The bars are strung on two cords that pass over the crosspieces or ends of the bail and are tied to the ends of the poles and the crosspieces or ends of the bail. The calabashes are strung on cords and are fixed to a rattan cord encircling the poles. On large instruments with a more pronounced curve from the central bars to either end of the instrument (found among the Lunda and Tshokwe of Angola), the suspended calabashes are supported by rods that pass through holes in the poles; the suspended series of bars is held firm by another cord that goes through the cord on the underside of the bars and is attached to the poles. On the xylophone of the Nsenga people in central Zambia, the cord from the underside of the bars to the runners also secures the rods that suspend the calabashes. This instrument is fixed between poles set vertically in the ground, and the bars hang vertically; on the Lunda and Tshokwe instruments, the plane of the bars is oblique to the ground. When two Tshokwe instruments are played together, the second can consist only of bars suspended between vertical poles, with a round pit in the ground below the centre of the instrument.

Distribution: southwest DRC, eastern Angola, and central Zambia.

Type 3: with quadrilateral frame. This combines characteristics of types 1 and 2, and appears to have been modified early in the 20th century. The support now consists of a four-sided frame with parallel ends whose sides taper towards the smallest bars. A bail is attached to the ends of the frame, and insulation material is fixed to the upper edges of its sides. The calabashes are suspended from rods placed in holes in the sides of the frame and hang below their respective bars in order to obtain the best resonance. Thus the arrangement of the resonators is staggered. The bars formerly rested on the insulation material, a cord passing through a hole in the far side of the bar, under another cord attached to the insulation material, back to the surface through the same hole, and under the insulation cord between bars; on the near side, a cord went over the bar and through the insulation material between bars. An additional pair of thicker cords is now added to suspend the bars from the top, passing through the bar attachment cords. In effect, the thin cords become loops for the suspension cords between bars and between the holes. The suspension cord passes under a thin cord strung through two vertical holes on the far side of the bar and is knotted to the thin cord between bars; on the near side, the thick cord passes through the thin cord between bars.

Groups of four or five different sizes of these xylophones are part of the *mendzan* ensemble in Cameroon and Gabon; each instrument has its own name and can overlap in pitch with the instrument next in size. One such ensemble in Cameroon has individual instruments with 11, 11, 10, 4, and 4 bars, while such an ensemble in Gabon consists of instruments with 9, 9, 8, 6, and 2 bars. Reserve bars are added to the larger instruments during construction. Thick beaters of soft wood are used to strike the middle of the bars.

Distribution: south and south-central Cameroon and northern Gabon.

Type 4: with calabashes suspended obliquely. Two horizontal poles extending through holes in side pieces that rest on the ground form the support for this instrument, which is more than 2 metres long. Elongated calabashes, with an oblique cut at one side of their mouths, are suspended from the pole nearest the player and are secured by a thick supporting rope of braided bark to the second pole, so that they are almost parallel to the ground when the instrument is in playing position. The 21 or 22 rectangular bars rest on thongs stretched across the poles and are tuned to a heptatonic scale by thinning the centre of the playing side to leave a raised portion from the nodal point to each end, where designs are carved. The bars are strung together by a thong that passes through a hole in the flat section of the bar at the edge of the raised portion, goes around the support thong, and passes back to the surface through the same hole. The instrument is played by two men using five beaters. The player of the highest-pitched bars begins the performance with an ostinato pattern played in octaves or other intervals, or with a single melodic line distributed between his two hands. The player of the lowest bars interlocks a different melodic pattern with his right hand and adds a rhythmic bass pattern characterized by repeated pitches with two beaters in his left hand. The ends of these beaters cross in his hand so that they spread in an angle of almost 90 degrees, facilitating wide leaps. The Venda instrument, *mbila mtondo*, was formerly an important instrument played at the chief's kraal.

Distribution: northern Transvaal, among the Venda, Kwebo, and Lovedu.

Type 5: with centre board and bridges (or distance pieces) (Boone 3c). The frame of the instrument consists of a flat centre board with calabash resonators inserted into circular holes, and wooden bridges tied across the board between the holes. The ends of the bridges are tied to each other by leather thongs, which extend the length of the instrument and also serve as tension thongs to support the bars, which are strung together by another set of cords. On some instruments insulation is attached to the edges of the centre board. The calabashes are fixed to the centre board by resin applied to the edges of the holes on both sides of the board. In Nigeria, the resonators are long and slender calabashes, cowhorns, or wooden cones in the shape of cowhorns. For the ten-bar instruments of the Azande in the northeast DRC, a pair of beaters in each hand enables the player to strike octaves on adjacent bars. The most common tuning pattern (where numbers indicate the degree of the pentatonic scale) is: 2–2′–3–3′–4–4′–5–5′–1′–1, with the lowest octave pair on the player's right. Among the Chopi of Mozambique, the centre board has two tenons on each end that fit into holes in the legs of the instrument, while the ends of the curved or rectangular bail fit over the tenons. The bars rest on tension thongs and are supported by thin wooden bridges attached by fibre to the centre board between each pair; the tension thongs pass through holes near the ends of the bridges. The bars are strung together by a pair of long leather cords. The cord further from the player passes through a hole in the bar, under the supporting tension thong and back to the surface through the same hole; the near cord goes over each bar and under the tension thong between bars.

Distribution: (with bridge between bars): east-central Nigeria, northern Cameroon, southern Chad, southwest Central African Republic, northeast DRC, and southern Sudan; (with bridge between pair of bars): southern Mozambique and northern Transvaal.

Type 6: with centre board and insulating cushions (Boone 3d). This instrument resembles the preceding one, except that the bars rest on insulating cushions mounted at some distance parallel to and on either side of the centre board, rather than on cords stretched between bridges. The centre board and the insulating cushions, which consist of fibre, bark cloth, or some other material covering wooden branches, are attached to the ends of the curved bail, though on some instruments the insulation is attached to the edges of the centre board. Some instruments have bridges; some have calabashes suspended from a piece of rattan, the ends of which are inserted into the insulating cushions. In some areas, four beaters are used by each player. In northwest DRC, adjacent bars are tuned in octaves, usually in the order: 2–2′–3–3′–4–4′–5–5′–1′–1.

Distribution: northwest DRC, south-central Central African Republic, and southern Chad (with bridges).

Type 7: with centre board set within oval frame. An oval-shaped wooden bar surrounds the entire instrument. The bars are suspended, and the cowhorn resonators are glued and tied to the solid curved base, the back of which is engraved with abstract designs. Six to eight bars are encircled by cords near the ends of each bar, and the ends of the cords are attached to the oval frame; they are oblique to the mouths of the resonators. The seated player supports the instrument between his knees at the middle of the oval frame, and a pair of Y-shaped wooden beaters allows him to strike octaves simultaneously. The bars on a Bura instrument, the *tsindza*, are arranged: 3–4–5–1′–1–2′–2.

Distribution: northeast Nigeria.

Type 8: with open frame. Bars are mounted on an open framework consisting of four vertical and eight horizontal strips of wood lashed together. Round calabash resonators are suspended below each bar by means of suspension rods that extend across and beyond the limits of the upper horizontal frame. In order to accommodate all the resonators within the framework, they are arranged in two zig-zag rows. The suspension rods for the resonators are secured to the frame by leather strips; another long cord or leather strap serving as insulation for the resting bars then passes over the rods, and a third long twisted cord secures the bars together on each side of the instrument. The latter cords are tied to the tops of the vertical posts, and sometimes also to the horizontal crosspieces at each end of the instrument.

The size of the instrument varies. Smaller instruments (in the west and central area of distribution) can rest on the ground, or be slung from the player's shoulders with the instrument perpendicular or parallel to the body. The row of bars curves slightly at the broader end of the instrument, where ogee-shaped horizontal crosspieces also accommodate the larger calabashes within the frame. Larger instruments (in the eastern area of distribution) rest on the ground in performance. The curvature of the row is more pronounced, allowing room for the large resonators and making the entire row easily accessible. The number of bars ranges from 12 to 21. Tuning is predominantly heptatonic, though the instruments of Burkina Faso, Ghana, and Ivory Coast are pentatonic. The player uses a pair of rubber-tipped beaters and can also wear bells around his wrist. The generic term for the instrument is *balo* or *bala*. In the eastern area of distribution, a commonly used term is *gyil*, with prefixes or suffixes to denote specific types, sizes, or contexts of usage. Xylophones are often played singly or in groups with other instruments. To the west, among Manding-speaking peoples, it is often played by professional musicians of the *jali* caste; in Burkina Faso, Ghana, and Ivory Coast, it is an important instrument at funeral ceremonies.

Distribution: Senegal, the Gambia, Guinea, Sierra Leone, Liberia, northeast Ivory Coast, Mali, southwest Burkina Faso, and northwest Ghana.

4. SOUTHEAST ASIA.

(i) Insular. Of the many types of xylophone found in this area, the instrument with bars resting on cloth or rattan strips at the edges of a wooden trough (trough xylophone with bedded bars) is common in classical gamelan ensembles in Java, Madura, Sumatra, and Kalimantan. A Central Javanese double gamelan can have two or three xylophones (one for *salendro* tuning and one or two for *pelog* tuning), but only one is played at a time. In folk gamelan or other ensembles in Java and Bali, for example the Balinese *gamelan joged* and *gambang*, more than one type of xylophone can be played simultaneously.

Xylophones with suspended bars or tubes show the greatest variety. A few examples of a type with bars suspended over individual resonators—often a substitute for another instrument—are found in Bali, but that country's most ancient ensembles (*caruk, gambang,* and *luang*) have a trough-resonated xylophone with suspended bars. A common term for the xylophone in this area is *gambang* (*gabbang, gambangan*), but it can mean a different type of instrument depending on the ensemble in which it is used; in Sabah, Malaysia, and the southern Philippines, *gabbang* always refers to a trough xylophone with bedded bars. The beaters, with rubber on the curved underside, are delicately carved in a bird- or kidney-shapes and resemble the simpler curved beaters used for the *calung renteng* in West Java.

(ii) Mainland. Comparatively few xylophone types are found on the mainland. A two- or four-bar xylophone has been reported in West Malaysia. Suspended tubes or wooden bars in a rope ladder arrangement appear in central Vietnam and northeast Thailand. Among the Jorai, Bahnar, and Rhade people in Vietnam, the *torung* consists of 14 to 20 tubes suspended between two players, one of whom holds an end of the cord; the other end is tied to the second player's leg. In Thailand, the *kaw law* or *bong lang* with 12 wooden bars is played by the Lao people in Kalasin province. The upper end of the instrument is tied to a tree and the lower end to the player's leg. These instruments resemble the *calung renteng* of West Java, though the order of the tubes and bars and the type of beater differ.

In Kelantan, Malaysia, groups of ten players, each with a xylophone with one bar suspended over a coconut resonator (*kertok kelapa*), compete with similar groups; two such instruments may also accompany the harvest dance. The trough-resonated xylophone, *gambang,*

with bedded bars, appears only in the Malaysian court gamelan of Trengganu, where it accompanies the *joget* dance. The xylophone with bars suspended over a trough resonator is important in classical instrumental ensembles in Thailand, Kampuchea, and Laos and is also used for chamber music in Myanmar. The leader of the Thai, Kampuchean, and Laotian *pī phāt* and *mahōrī* ensembles plays the *ranātēk*, an instrument with 21 bars suspended over a curved resonator and resting on a pedestal. In enlarged versions of the same ensembles, a larger xylophone (*ranāt thum*) is added: 17 bars are suspended over a rectangular resonator with sloping sides and a curved upper surface. The instrument, larger in the *pī phāt* than in the *mahōrī* ensemble, rests on short legs, sometimes with casters. The same type of xylophone might have been used in an ensemble that accompanied the *ashek* dance at the 16th- and 17th-century Malay court of Patani, and later at the Kelantan court. Women played an instrument thought to have been a boat-shaped xylophone, and a set of 11 drums, while a man played the *rebab*; the xylophone and set of drums were also used to accompany *pantun* singing. In Kelantan, barrel drums have now replaced cylindrical drums, while a set of seven gongs has replaced the xylophone in the ensemble that accompanies the dance.

In Myanmar, the *pat-talā* with 20 to 25 (usually 24) bars suspended over a curved resonator and resting on a pedestal is played with an end-blown flute (*palwei*), or in chamber music as vocal accompaniment; it is taught by *hsaīng-waīng* musicians as a beginner's instrument. It was also played at the Chinese court during the Qing dynasty (1644–1911); a description (in the *Ta Qing hui tien*, 1899) of the smaller of two Burmese ensembles that played for banquets includes the 22-bar 'pa-ta-la', as well as harp, the *mī-gyaùng* zither, a three-string bowed lute, the *palwei* flute, a drum, and a pair of cymbals.

The xylophone is rare in India. Surviving examples have bars suspended above a curved resonator, resting on a central pedestal. The *kashtha tarang* with 22 bars is used as a solo instrument in certain modern ensembles. Popley (1921), who identified the instrument as Burmese, used the nomenclature *bastran* for a 20- or 21-bar instrument. Another xylophone, *patti-taranga*, has a rectangular resonator resting on short round legs, with ten suspended bars (Schaeffner, 1935). Historical literature refers to neither instrument, and they are not used in folk traditions.

5. PACIFIC. The leg xylophone is common in west Melanesia and is used primarily for courtship; in some areas, women are not allowed to see it. The instrument appears on the Gazelle Peninsula of New Britain, on New Ireland, the Duke of York Islands, and Tami Island, in the Morobe region of eastern Papua New Guinea. Usually two wooden bars (convex on the upper side, flat on the underside) are laid over the player's thighs and struck with two sticks. The player can sit with his legs over a pit or over a mound of earth; alternatively, the bars can rest on banana tree logs or branches. Names for the instrument include *tinbuk, timbuk, timbul, tin-*

but, timboik, tutupele, or *lau lau.* The two-note instrument is used for playing signal patterns. On New Ireland and the Duke of York Islands, the xylophone is played for dancing; only on Tami Island do women play the xylophone, at times when they must be absent from the village.

6. LATIN AMERICA. The xylophone in Latin America, known as the 'marimba', is popular in Mexico, Nicaragua, Costa Rica, El Salvador, Guatemala, Colombia, and Brazil; in Suriname (as *gambang*) it is used in gamelan ensembles by musicians of Javanese descent. In Brazil, however, it has lost its former importance as a solo instrument and now only accompanies such dances as the *congada.* The two types of marimba still in use in Brazil are portable and have six and 11 bars, respectively, struck with wooden sticks.

The marimba is the most popular folk instrument in the Guatemalan Republic and has come to be a symbol of Guatamalan independence. It is believed to be of African origin, introduced during the early colonial period by African slaves. This argument, which is not undisputed, rests mainly on the similarity of the *marimba de tecomates* (the original form of the Guatemalan instrument) to African xylophones, the African derivation of the word 'marimba', and the lack of archaeological evidence for the existence of marimbas in pre-Columbian America.

The earliest account of the marimba in Guatemala appears in the work of Domingo Juarros, a 17th-century historian, who lists it among instruments played by the Amerindians in 1680. During the 18th century it became widely dispersed among the Amerindians, and its presence is noted at public events, both civil and religious. The growing popularity of the marimba among Latinos in the 19th century led to the expansion of the range to five and, later, six and seven octaves, allowing the addition of a fourth player. During the celebration of Guatamalan independence in 1821, the marimba took its place as the national instrument.

The *marimba de tecomates* has bars or percussion plates suspended above a trapezoidal framework by cords that pass through threading pins and the nodal points of each bar. Beneath each bar hangs a tuned calabash resonator, near the base of which a vibrating membrane of pig intestine is affixed to a ring of wax surrounding an aperture. This mirliton produces a characteristic buzzing called *charleo* when the bars are struck. The older form of this marimba, the *marimba de arco,* is portable and is carried by a strap attached to the ends of the frame and passing across the player's shoulders. The bars are kept from touching the player's body by an arched branch (*arco*) affixed to the framework. A later type has four legs and lacks the *arco.* The nearly diatonic range employs 19 to 26 bars. A bar's pitch can be raised during performance by applying a lump of wax, sometimes mixed with bits of lead, to its underside. For this reason such marimbas are called *marimba de ceras* (marimba 'of wax'). The bars are struck with mallets (*baquetas*) made of flexible wooden sticks with strips of raw rubber wrapped

around the heads to form a ball. The tips of the mallets intended for bass bars are soft; those for treble bars are harder and smaller. One to three players hold a mallet in each hand, or two in one hand and one in the other. Other pitches can be produced by striking the extreme ends of the bars with the wooden end of the mallet. The *marimba de tecomates* is now seldom played by Latino musicians, who prefer more Westernized forms of the instrument.

During the last quarter of the 19th century, the *marimba sencilla* was developed, in which *cajones harmonicos,* wooden boxes constructed to resemble gourds, were substituted for gourd resonators. In other particulars, the *marimba sencilla* is identical to the *marimba de tecomates.* During this period, the *marimba de cinchos* (also called *marimba de acero, marimba de hierro*), with metal bars and box resonators, became popular and was played with guitar accompaniment. Types with glass bars and others with bamboo-tube resonators were also developed.

The addition of chromatic bars to the diatonic scale was a late 19th-century development, usually attributed to Sebastian Hurtado in 1894. The name of this type, *marimba doble,* refers to the double row of bars for diatonic and chromatic pitches. Unlike the arrangement of a piano keyboard, in which sharp keys stand to the right of their corresponding naturals, in many Guatemalan instruments the sharps are placed directly behind the naturals.

The *marimba doble* is often played in pairs: the larger, *marimba grande,* has a range of six and a half octaves (about 78 bars) and uses four players; the smaller *marimba cuache* (also called *marimba picolo, marimba requinta,* and *marimba tenor*), ranges over five octaves (about 50 bars) and uses three players. To these two instruments are often added a three-string bass, snare or bass drums, cymbals, accordion, and wind instruments such as saxophones, trumpets, or clarinets. While the folkloric character of contemporary *marimba doble* ensembles is somewhat obscured by the influences of popular Latin American and North American styles, highland village *marimba sencilla* ensembles still maintain traditional style and repertory.

The marimba in Colombia can have as many as 25 bars or as few as 21, though 24 is usual. The bars are made of various palm woods but most frequently of *chontaduro.* Each bar has a resonator of *guadua* bamboo. The bars are placed on the frame in a single row in groups of four, each group being separated from the other by a *pasador* (crosspiece) of *chonta.* The *pasadores* are part of the framework that supports the bars and resonators and also function as points of visual reference for the players. Beginning with the smallest bar and moving downwards, the groups of four bars are known alternately as *tablas duras* and *tablas blandas.* In a group of eight the highest *dura* and the lowest *blanda* form an octave. A series of 24 bars is thus composed of three disjunct octave segments: 8765 4321, 7654 3217, 6543 2176. The seven highest bars are tuned to produce approximate neutral 3rds between bars 8, 6, 4, 2 and bars 7, 5, 3. The remaining bars are tuned in octaves with the bars above them. On the marimba itself the bars are of course arranged in reverse order from that indicated above: the highest octave segment is to the right and the lowest to the left. Each of the two players uses two sticks tipped with small balls of raw rubber; one plays the *bordón* (an ostinato lower part), the other the *requinta* or *tiple* (upper part).

The *marimba-orquesta*, an ensemble incorporating a marimba, is widely popularized in Mexican tourist centres. The instruments are frequently municipal property, and musicians can be exempt from certain other civic responsibilities by virtue of their service in these groups. The ensemble plays music from the *son* repertory and makes constant use of *corrido* accompaniments.

BIBLIOGRAPHY

M. Praetorius: *Syntagma musicum*, vol.2 (Wolfenbüttel, 1618, 2/1619/R1955 and 1980)

M. Mersenne: *Harmonie universelle* (Paris, 1636–7/R1963; Eng. trans., 1957)

E. Modigliani: *Fra i batacchi indipendenti* (Rome, 1892)

R. Shelford: 'An Illustrated Catalogue of the Ethnographical Collection of the Sarawak Museum: Musical Instruments', *Journal of the Royal Asiatic Society,* vol.40 (1904), 3–59

F. Swettenham: *British Malaya: an Account of the Origin and Progress of British Influence in Malaya* (London, 1906/R, rev. 2/1948/R, rev. 3/1955/R)

D.M. Campbell: *Java: Past and Present* (London, 1915)

C. Sachs: *Handbuch der Musikinstrumentenkunde* (Leipzig, 1920, 2/1930/R)

M. Courant: 'Essai historique sur la musique classique des Chine et Corée', *EMDC,* vol.1/1 (1921), 77–241

H.A. Popley: *The Music of India* (New Delhi, 1921, 2/1971)

E.S.C. Handy: 'The Native Culture in the Marquesas', *Bernice P. Bishop Museum Bulletin* (1923), no.9, 3–358

C. Sachs: *Die Musikinstrumente Indiens und Indonesiens* (Berlin, 1915, 2/1923)

C.K. Meek: *The Northern Tribes of Nigeria* (London, 1925/R)

W. Kaudern: *Musical Instruments in Celebes* (Göteborg, 1927)

J.S. Brandts Buys and A. Brandts Buys-Van Zijp: 'De toonkunst bij de Madoereezen', *Djawa,* vol.8 (1928), 61–349

E.M. Loeb: 'Mentawei Religious Cult', *University of California Publications in American Archaeology and Ethnology,* vol.25/2 (1929), 186–247

O. Rutter: *The Pagans of North Borneo* (London, 1929/R)

C. Sachs: *Geist und Werden der Musikinstrumente* (Berlin, 1929/R1975)

J. Kunst: *A Study on Papuan Music* (Weltevreden, 1931/R1967 in *Music in New Guinea*)

C.K. Meek: *Tribal Studies in Northern Nigeria* (London, 1931/R)

S. Nadel: 'Marimba–Musik', *Akademie der Wissenschaft in Wien, Philosophisch-Historische Klasse,* vol.212/3 (1931), 3–63

V.E. Korn: *De Dorpsrepubliek Tnganan Pagringsingan* (Santpoort, 1933)

E.M. von Hornbostel: 'The Ethnology of African Sound-Instruments', *Africa,* vol.6/3 (1933), 277–311

J. Kunst: *De toonkunst van Java* (The Hague, 1934; Eng. trans., rev. 2/1949, enlarged 3/1973)

Nio Joe Lan: 'Chinese Songs and Plays in Batavia', *China Journal,* vol.23/4 (1935), 198–200

A. Schaeffner: 'L'instrument de musique', *Encyclopédie française,* vol.16 (1935)

O. Boone: *Les xylophones du Congo belge* (Tervuren, 1936)

A. Schaeffner: *Origine des instruments de musique* (Paris, 1936/R)

J. Kunst: *Music in Nias* (Leiden, 1939)

G. Jacob: *Orchestral Technique* (London, 2/1940, rev. 3/1982)

S. de Ganay: 'Le xylophone chez les Sara du Moyen Chari', *Journal de la Société des africanistes,* vol.12 (1942), 203–40

J. Kunst: *Music in Flores* (Leiden, 1942)

J. Kunst: *Muziek en dans in de buitengewesten* (Amsterdam, 1946)

B. Costermans: 'Muziekinstrumenten van Watsa–Gombari en omstreken', *Zaire,* vol.5 (1947), 515–42; vol.6 (1947), 629–63

W. Fagg: 'A Yoruba Xylophone of Unusual Type', *Man,* vol.50/11 (1950), 145 only

A. Schaeffner: 'L'Orgue de Barbarie de Rameau', *Mélanges d'histoire et d'esthétique musicales offerts à Paul-Marie Masson* (Paris, 1955/R1980 in *Essais de musicologie et autres fantaisies*)

F.-J. Nicolas: 'Origine et valeur du vocabulaire désignant les xylophones africains', *Zaire,* vol.11/1 (1957), 69–90

H. Fischer: *Schallgeräte in Ozeanien* (Strasbourg and Baden-Baden, 1958/R1974)

A.M. Jones: 'Indonesia and Africa: the Xylophone as a Culture Indicator', *Journal of the Royal Anthropological Institute,* vol.89/2 (1959), 155–168; repr. in *AfM,* vol.2/3 (1960), 36–47

F.J. de Hen: *Beitrag zur Kenntnis der Musikinstrumente aus Belgisch-Kongo und Ruanda-Urundi* (Tervuren, 1960)

L. Bouquiaux: 'Les instruments de musique Birom (Nigeria Septentrional)', *Africa-Tervuren,* vol.8/4 (1962), 105–11

P. Collaer: 'Ozeanien', *Musikgeschichte in Bildern,* vol.1/1 (Leipzig, 1965)

P.R. Kirby: *The Musical Instruments of the Native Races of South Africa* (London, 1934, 2/1965)

D.T. Niane: *Sundiata: an Epic of Old Mali* (London, 1965, rev. 2/2006)

P.R. Kirby: 'The Indonesian Origin of Certain African Musical Instruments', *African Studies,* vol.25/1 (1966), 1–19

C. McPhee: *Music in Bali; a Study in Form and instrumental Organization in Balinese Orchestral Music* (New Haven and London, 1966/R1976)

Folklore Musical de Angola/Angola Folk-Music, vol.2: *Povo Quioco/Chokwe People* (Lisbon, 1967)

L.A. Anderson: 'The African Xylophone', *African Arts,* vol.1/1 (1967), 46–9, 66–9

B. Sárosi: 'Die Volksmusikinstrumente Ungarns', *Handbuch der europäischen Volksmusikinstrumente,* vol.1/1 (Leipzig, 1967)

H.M. Sheppard: 'Joget Gamalan Trengganu', *Journal of the Malaysian Branch of the Royal Asiatic Society,* vol.11 (1967), 149–52

L.A. Anderson: 'A Reassessment of the Distribution, Origin, Tunings and Stylistic Criteria in African Xylophone Traditions', *African Studies Association,* vol.11 (Los Angeles, CA,1968)

L.A. Anderson: *The Miko Modal System of Kiganda Xylophone Music* (diss., UCLA, 1968)

P.R. Kirby: 'Two Curious Resonated Xylophones from Nigeria', *African Studies,* vol.27/3 (1968), 141–4

G. Knosp: *Enquête sur la vie musicale au Congo belge 1934–1935* (Tervuren, 1968)

J. Kunst: *Hindu-Javanese Musical Instruments* (The Hague, rev. and enlarged 2/1968)

F. Bebey: *Musique de l'Afrique* (Paris, 1969; Eng. trans., 1975 as *African Music: a People's Art*)

G. Rouget: 'Sur les xylophones équiheptaphoniques des Malinké', *RdM,* vol.55 (1969), 47–77

H. Tracey: *Chopi Musicians: their Music, Poetry, and Instruments* (London, 1948/R1970)

A.M. Jones: *Africa and Indonesia: the Evidence of the Xylophone and Other Musical and Cultural Factors* (Leiden, 1964/R1971)

J. Maceda: 'Classification and Distribution of Musical Instruments in the Philippines', *The Musics of Asia* (Manila, 1971), 24–37

H. Zemp: *Musique Dan: la musique dans la pensée et la vie sociale d'une société africaine* (Paris, 1971)

E. Richards: *World of Percussion* (Sherman Oaks, CA, 1972)

M. Sheppard: *Taman Inderà: a Royal Pleasure Ground: Malay Decorative Arts and Pastimes* (London, 1972)

R.D. Trimillos: *Tradition and Repertoire in the Cultivated Music of the Tausug of Sulu, Philippines* (diss., UCLA, 1972)

R. Schefold: 'Schlitztrommeln und Trommelsprache in Mentawai (Indonesien)', *Zeitschrift für Ethnologie,* vol.98 (1973), 36–73

D.C. Szanton: 'Art in Sulu: A Survey', *Sulu Studies,* vol.2 (1973), 3–69

K. Gourlay: *A Bibliography of Traditional Music in Papua New Guinea* (Port Moresby, 1974/R1980)

G. Innes: *Sunjata: Three Mandinka Versions* (London, 1974)

L. Kunz: 'Die Volksmusikinstrumente der Tschechoslowakei', *Handbuch der europäischen Volksmusikinstrumente,* vol.1/2 (Leipzig, 1974)

M.T. Osman: 'Traditional Drama and Music of Southeast Asia', *International Conference on Traditional Drama and Music of Southeast Asia: Kuala Lumpur 1969,* ed. T.O. Mohd (Kuala Lumpur, 1974)

Selected Reports in Ethnomusicology, vol.2 (1975) [Southeast Asia issue]

W.P. Malm: 'Chinese Music in Nineteenth–century Japan', *AsM,* vol.6 (1975), 147–72

C.D. Grijns: 'Lenong in the Environs of Jakarta: a Report', *Archipel,* vol.12 (1976), 175–202

E.A. Manuel: 'Toward an Inventory of Philippine Musical Instruments', *Asian Studies,* vol.14 (1976), 1–72

P.-C. Ngumu: *Les Mendzang: des chanteurs de Yaoundé: histoire, organologie, fabrication, système de transcription,* Acta ethnologica et linguistica (1976), no.34

E. Schlager: 'Rituelle Siebenton–Musik auf Bali', *Forum ethnomusicologicum: Basier Studien zur Ethnomusikologie,* vol.1 (1976)

M. McLean: 'An Annotated Bibliography of Oceanic Music and Dance', *Polynesian Society Memoir* (1977), no.41

N. McLeod: 'Musical Instruments and History in Madagascar', *Essays for a Humanist: an Offering to Klaus Wachsmann,* ed. C. Seeger (New York, 1977), 189–215

M. Omibiyi: 'Nigerian Musical Instruments', *Nigeria Magazine* (1977), nos.122–123, 14–35

W. Chen: *Qing shi yue zhi zhi yanjiu* [Studies on the Music Section of the Qing History] (Taipei, 1978)

J. Maceda: 'Report of a Music Workshop in East Kalimantan', *Borneo Research Bulletin,* vol.10/2 (1978), 82–104

P. Collaer, ed: 'Südostasien', *Musikgeschichte in Bildern,* vol.1/3 (Leipzig, 1979)

J. Gansemans: *Les instruments de musique Luba (Shaba, Zaire)* (Tervuren, 1980)

J. Meel: 'Verspreiding en verscheidenheid van de xylofoon in Afrika', *Africa-Tervuren,* vol.26/3 (1980), 79–83

C. Salmon: 'Literature in Malay by the Chinese of Indonesia', *Etudes Insulindiennes-Archipel,* vol.2 (Paris, 1981)

B. Dean: 'Mr Gi's Music Book: an Annotated Translation of Gi Shimei's *Gi-shi Gakufu', Monumenta nipponica,* vol.37/3 (1982), 317–32

E.M. Frame: 'The Musical Instruments of Sabah, Malaysia', *EthM,* vol.26 (1982), 247–74

A.A. Mensah: 'Gyil: the Dagara–Lobi Xylophone', *Journal of African Studies,* vol.9/3 (1982), 139–54

R. Garfias: 'The Marimba of Mexico and Central America', *LAMR,* vol.4/2 (1983), 203–28

L. Kaptain: *Maderas que cantan* (Tuxtla Gutiérrez, 1991)

J.B. Camposeco Mateo: *Te' son, chiab' o k'ojom: la marimba de Guatemala* (Guatemala City, 2/1994)

LOIS ANN ANDERSON (1, 3–4, 5); JAMES BLADES (2); GEORGE LIST, LINDA L. O'BRIEN-ROTHE. (6)

Xylorimba [xylo-marimba, marimba-xylophone]. Name given to a xylophone with extended range, embracing the low pitches of the marimba and the highest-sounding bars of the xylophone. The compass of the xylorimba is up to five octaves: *C* to *c''''*1. As the marimba-xylophone it was a popular instrument in the USA and Britain in the 1920s and 1930s, particularly in vaudeville. The lower notes of the xylorimba sound more like a xylophone than a marimba on account of the bars being thicker and narrower than those of a modern marimba (the bars of the xylophone and the marimba are shaped differently to emphasize different overtones).

The terms have been a source of confusion and are not consistently applied. Many composers have called for 'xylorimba', including Berg (Three Orchestral Pieces, op.6, 1914–15), Boulez (e.g. *Le marteau sans maître,* 1953–5, rev. 1957), and Messiaen, but invariably the parts were written for a four-octave xylophone. Stravinsky's *The Flood* (1961–2) includes a part for 'marimba-xylophone', but a marimba was intended. The parts in Roberto Gerhard's *Hymnody* (1963; with two players at one instrument) were originally labelled 'xylorimba', but this was later changed to 'marimba'. Boulez wrote for two true xylorimbas (each of five octaves) in *Pli selon pli* (1957–62); the parts have sometimes been played on two xylophones and two marimbas.

JAMES BLADES/JAMES HOLLAND/R

Xylosistron. Friction idiophone developed about 1807 by the organ builder Johann Andreas Uthe of Hohlstädt by Sangerhausen, later court organ builder in Dresden. It resembled Chladni's Euphon, consisting of a series of horizontal, tuned wooden bars arranged in two rows like a keyboard. The bars were stroked by the player, who wore rosined gloves. A larger variety, called *Xyloharmonikon,* was introduced by Uthe in 1810 and equipped with a keyboard.

Xyu [xi-u, pí lè]. Wooden oboe, akin to the Chinese *suona,* of the Hmong people of northern Vietnam, Laos, northeastern Thailand, and southern China. It has six fingerholes and a thumbhole and is played for instance at receptions of important guests, funerals, and weddings. See L.Ó Briain: *Hmong Music in Northern Vietnam: Identity, Tradition and Modernity* (diss., U. of Sheffield, 2012).

Y

Yaguradaiko [rōko]. Barrel drum of Japan. The name refers to its former context of performance (*yagura* or *rō*: turret/tower). The drum is especially known for its use in *sumō* (Japanese wrestling), when it announces the event, and from some historical *kabuki* performances, when the drum was positioned atop a high stage. It is about 60 cm long and 27 cm in diameter. The two heads are affixed to the wooden body by one or two rows of broad-headed nails. The drum can be positioned in several ways, including placing it on a tiny stand at a 45-degree angle in front of the player, who kneels perpendicular to the drum, or on a high stand at a similar angle for a standing player. The higher head is struck by two slender wooden sticks. See M. Yamaguchi: 'Sumo in the Popular Culture of Contemporary Japan', *The Worlds of Japanese Popular Culture: Gender, Shifting Boundaries and Global Cultures*, ed. D.P. Martinez (Cambridge, 1998/R).

HENRY JOHNSON

Yagwìn [lagwìn, hkwet-hkwìn]. Cymbals of Myanmar. They are approximately 30 cm in diameter and are struck together. These cymbals are essential in the *hsaìng-waìng* ensemble and in smaller Burmese folk music groups such as those led by the *ozi* and *dò-bat*.

JOHN OKELL

Yak. End-blown bamboo notched flute of Korea. Made of 'yellow bamboo', it has three fingerholes and is required to produce only a single chromatic octave. The player uses two right-hand fingers and one left-hand finger; frequently fingerholes are partly covered to obtain the necessary pitches. When the melody calls for notes in the higher octave they are simply transposed down into the basic compass of the instrument.

The name *yak* refers to an ancient Chinese flute written with the same pictograph, *yue*. Chinese *yue* were given to Korea in 1116 as part of a large bequest of instruments from the Song emperor, but they were apparently intended to function only as dancers' implements.

The treatise *Akhak kwebŏm* (1493) gives the length of the yak as 56.9 cm and describes it both as a dancers' prop and as a musical instrument in its own right, for use in ritual music (*aak*); it also describes the fingering techniques involved.

The yak is now considered a purely Chinese instrument and is played only in the ritual music at the twice-yearly Sacrifice to Confucius in Seoul, producing a rising glissando at the end of each long note of the slow melody. It is used as a dance implement in the same ceremony, being held in the left hands of the 64 dancers during the Civil Dance.

BIBLIOGRAPHY
Sŏng Hyŏn, ed.: *Akhak kwebŏm* [Guide to the study of music] (Seoul, 1493/R1975), 6.13b–14*a*, 28*a*
Chang Sa-hun: *Han'guk akki taegwan* [Korean musical instruments] (Seoul, 1969), 30 only

ROBERT C. PROVINE

Yak-berē [ruhunu-berē]. Double-headed cylindrical drum of Sri Lanka, the low-country equivalent of the *gäta-berē*. The long, heavy body of the drum is usually made from *kitul* palm wood. Its length varies to suit the performer: the maker should measure a length of three times the player's hand-span and three finger-widths for the length, and one hand-span for the diameter. This produces an instrument from about 66 to 71 cm in length and 23 to 25 cm in diameter. The deerskin heads are held in place by hoops of plaited leather or creeper, through which a leather thong about 14 metres long is passed 12 times to brace the hoops. A sling of hemp is attached to the drum and passed around the player's waist, holding the drum at hip level. Unlike the *gäta-berē* it is always held horizontal. It is played with bare hands, with a rotating movement from thumb to little finger, and it produces a rather dead, low-pitched sound, lacking the brilliance of the *gäta-berē*.

The Sinhalese term, in the south of the island, is *ruhunu-berē*. *Yak-berē* is more widely used but strictly speaking applies only when the drum is used in *yakun-näṭīma* (devil dancing); a third name, *devol-berē*, refers to its use in the *devol-maḍu* ceremony, where local deities are supplicated. In the past *yakun-näṭīma* ceremonies were nearly always performed to cure diseases thought to have been caused by a demon (*yaka*): the dancer donned a succession of masks and danced around the afflicted man in an effort to exorcize the demon. The yak-berē played the drum mnemonics for the dancer's movements, slowly at first, but accelerating to a frenzied pace in the hope of inducing a trance in the dancer–exorcizer. The ritual is rarely, if ever, performed nowadays. The yak-berē is also the main instrument used in *kōlam,* a folk drama of the south, also masked but with a strong narrative element.

The drum is also known occasionally *as magul-berē,* since it is used in the south to play the inaugural (*magul*) rhythms that herald any important festival or ritual event.

BIBLIOGRAPHY

W.A. de Silva: 'Articles Used in Sinhalese Ceremonial Dancing', *Journal of the Royal Asiatic Society, Ceylon Branch,* vol.28 (1921), 71–80

O. Pertold: *Ceremonial Dances of the Sinhalese* (Dehiwala, 1930/R1973), 63–108

H. Keuneman: 'Sinhalese Drums', *Ceylon Observer Pictorial* (1960)

C. de S. Kulatillake: *Metre, Melody and Rhythm in Sinhalese Music* (Colombo, 1976)

W.B. Makulloluwa: *Dances of Sri Lanka* (Colombo, [1976]

NATALIE M. WEBBER

Yaktāro. Drone spike lute of Sindh, Pakistan. Its name means literally 'monochord', like the South Asian *ektār,* of which it is the Sindi equivalent, although it generally has two strings. A round-section wooden neck, terminating in a lathe-turned bobbin at each end, passes through two-thirds of a skin-covered gourd. The metal strings pass from two frontal pegs at the upper end over a clay or metal bridge in the middle of the skin soundtable and are affixed to the lower end of the neck. The yaktāro is held over one shoulder and plucked by the forefinger, the player often holding in his other hand the *ḍaṇḍo* (stick rattle) or *capřun* (clappers) to accompany his own singing of *kāfi* or *kalām* Sufi songs; an accompaniment is often also provided by a clay pot (the *dilo* or the *ghaghar*). As well as a drone the yaktāro provides rhythmic backing in various *tār* (metres, equivalent to *tāl*), such as *tintār, kalvāro, dhādhro,* etc. See N.A. Baloch: *Musical Instruments of the Lower Indus Valley of Sind* (Hyderabad, 1966, 2/1975).

ALASTAIR DICK

Yāḷ [yāzh]. Name of the arched harp in old Tamil literature of South India. In the *Cilappatikāram* (?2nd century CE) and other texts it is described as having a resonator (*pattar:* 'wooden trough'); a skin-covered, curved neck (*kōṭu:* 'horn') to which the strings (*narampu:* 'gut') are attached at one end by leather tuning-cords (*tivavu*); and, probably, a string-bar (*tantirikaram*) in the resonator to which the strings are attached at the other end (possibly called *oṛṛuṛupu*). It has been said to have had a tuning-bar (*māṭakam*), an oblong piece of wood lying on the resonator, with holes through which the strings passed, and pins (*āṇi*) to hold them tight. Reference is made to yāḷ with 7, 14, 19, and 21 strings, in different tunings. The harp was covered with a colourful cloth and used to accompany song and in the dance orchestra, where it followed the *kuḷal* (flute). It is mentioned until about the 7th century, when it begins to be replaced, as in the north, by the *vīṇā* (Tamil *vīṇāi*) stick zithers. See S. Ramanathan: *Music in Cilappatikaaram* (diss., Wesleyan U., Middletown, CT, 1974).

ALASTAIR DICK

Ya'lu [yalulu]. Obsolete end-blown flute of the Maidu people of California. Other names for it were Kato *telbul* and Wailaki *telbil.* It was made of a thin tube of elder wood 25 to 45 cm long, open at both ends and pierced by four fingerholes drilled roughly equidistant from one another near the middle (flutes with six or eight holes are mentioned). The blowing end was chamfered to a sharp edge. Except for the musical bow (*mawu* or *mawuwi*), this was the only instrument used by California Indians separately from singing, and the only one capable of producing melodies. It was never used in ceremonial music but was described as being played in courtship or for pleasure. It was sometimes used by young people seeking spiritual power while wandering in solitary places; the players hummed into the instrument.

RICHARD KEELING

Yamadagoto. Zither of Japan. The name denotes a type of *koto* of the Yamada-ryū performance tradition. The instrument resembles the *gakusō, chikusō,* and *ikutagoto,* but some of the component parts have a slightly different shape, and the instrument does not have the lavish decoration that is often found on earlier types of *koto.* Usually it has six or seven strings. The body is about 182 cm long, 25 cm wide at the head (the end to the player's right), 24 cm wide at the tail, and 8 cm tall. It has an oblique dragon's tongue inside the head extremity; a soundhole towards each end of the backboard, with the one under the head having an oval shape; an ivory strip across the nut at the head end; and a rounded tail extremity. This form of *koto* is widely used for the Ikuta-ryū and many other everyday traditions of *koto* performance. The plectra have tightly rolled paper rings that fit over the fingertips, and rounded ivory picks. The player kneels facing the head end on the side by the highest-pitched string. See H. Johnson: *The Koto: a Traditional Instrument in Contemporary Japan* (Amsterdam, 2004).

HENRY JOHNSON

Yamaha. Brand name of musical instruments (and other products) manufactured by Yamaha Kabushiki Kaisha (i.e. Yamaha Corporation), Hamamatsu, Japan. The firm was founded in 1887 by Torakusu Yamaha (*b* Wakayama Prefecture, Japan, April 1851; *d* Hamamatsu, Japan, 8 Aug 1916), a watchmaker who built the first Japanese

Yamaha CP 70 electric grand piano, c1970s–1980s. (Aurelia W. Hartenberger, EdD)

harmonium in that year. In 1888 the firm employed fewer than ten craftsmen; a year later there were 100. In 1897 the company was named Nippon Gakki Seizo KK (Japan Instrument Manufacturing Co.). In 1899 the Japanese Ministry of Education sent Torakusu Yamaha to the USA to learn about building pianos; in 1900 his firm was making uprights, and in 1902 produced its first grand. Expansion was steady through the prosperous period following World War I. The factory base was moved from Tokyo and Yokohama to Hamamatsu in 1922. Yamaha began building pipe organs in 1932. By 1935 they introduced the Magna electronic organ, and in 1942 their first acoustic guitar. During World War II the piano factory made airplane propellers, while other areas of the company made airplane engines for the Mitsubishi Zero.

After World War II the company began collaboration with the Nippon Kangakki (Japan Band Instrument) company, founded as Egawa in 1892 and renamed in 1920, whose brand name is Nikkan. The companies jointly set up an experimental department for wind instruments in 1965 and merged in 1970. In 1953 the company's fourth president, Gen'ichi Kawakami (1912–2002), spent 90 days observing living standards and production methods in Europe and the USA. On his return he introduced technical advances, mass-production methods, and new products and began to emphasize the popularization of music; the firm also branched out into many other consumer product areas.

In 1966 Renold Schilke, an expert in brass instrument design, became a consultant. That same year saw the introduction of Yamaha's first electric guitars and drums. The present factory in Hamamatsu opened in 1970; by the mid-1970s it was reportedly making 30% of the world production of both wind instruments and pianos. In 1973, Yamaha purchased the Everett Piano Co. of South Haven, Michigan, making uprights there

until 1986 when they moved all USA piano manufacturing to their Thomaston, Georgia, factory. The Yamaha brand name was applied to all the firm's products from its centenary in 1987.

The company, which nowadays produces pianos, wind instruments, electronic instruments, concert and marching percussion, guitars, drums, and audio equipment, has developed into a huge complex of diversified interests with 94 subsidiaries and more than 26,000 employees. Factories and partnerships are located in the USA, Germany, Mexico, China, Indonesia, and Taiwan. In 2008, Yamaha purchased the Bösendorfer piano company. Piano models range from console uprights to a well-regarded concert grand. Yamaha produces the D-Deck and Stagea pipe organs primarily for the Japanese market. By the early 21st century, Yamaha was the largest producer of musical instruments in the world. Since 1900, they have produced over six million pianos. Instrument design and manufacture are heavily automated, and quality is consistently very good.

Yamaha has produced many models of electronic instruments, including the Electone organs, electric and electronic pianos (including digital models in the Clavinova series), electric guitars, monophonic and polyphonic synthesizers (from 1975), synthesizer modules, string synthesizers, home keyboards (PortaSound and Portatone ranges), remote keyboard controllers, wind controllers (WX series, developed with Sal Gallina), guitar synthesizers, samplers, sequencers, and electronic percussion systems. A great success was the DX7 synthesizer (1983–86), of which possibly 280,000 were sold. Coinciding with the beginnings of MIDI, Yamaha's DX/TX range of 'algorithmic' Frequency Modulation (FM) synthesizers were based on John Chowning's research at Stanford University (1967–71). In 1984 Yamaha introduced the first specialized music computer (CX-5M), in which FM synthesis was combined with the short-lived MSX computer standard; the company subsequently produced home computer music systems featuring a synthesizer module and licensed software. Sampling and physical modelling techniques licensed from Stanford University were used in their Virtual Acoustic synthesizers from 1994. In 1997, Stanford and Yamaha became partners in a licensing programme to promote development of their respective intellectual properties in computer tone generation and sound synthesis. In 2003 Yamaha introduced Vocaloid software for Windows PCs, which synthesizes the previously recorded voices of singers in English and Japanese. Some of Yamaha's more sophisticated synthesizers have had an optional breath controller. The scale on which the company manufactures electronic instruments enabled it in 1976 to be the first musical instrument manufacturer to develop its own LSI (large-scale integration) chips, each equivalent to millions of transistors and other components.

Yamaha's hybrid acoustic/digital pianos with MIDI include the Disklavier (1986), which contains fibre-optic sensors to register the movement of keys and hammers and solenoids to control their operation; MIDI grand pianos; and the Silent Piano, which has optional digital output to headphones, speakers, mixer, or computer. The Avantgrand digital piano, introduced in 2009, incorporates a complete grand piano action to enable a realistic touch. Its sound, derived from samples of a Yamaha concert grand, is played back from loud speakers positioned in the Avantgrand's small soundboard. Resonators in the soundboard and under the keybed simulate acoustic piano reverberation.

Yamaha maintains its own departments of wood processing (for pianos and guitars), metal processing (for pianos and brass instruments), machine making, electronics, and chemicals. There is a research and development division for keyboard, brass, and woodwind instruments, and special instruments are made for individual players.

The first Yamaha Music School was founded in Tokyo in 1954; by 2010 more than 700,000 students were enrolled in Yamaha Music Schools in more than 40 countries. The Yamaha piano instruction method does for beginners on the piano what the Suzuki method does for the violin. The Yamaha Foundation for Music Education, established in 1966, sponsors concert series and music competitions.

BIBLIOGRAPHY

N.H. Crowhurst: *Electronic Organs* (Indianapolis, 1960, 3/1975), 123–32

J. Chowning and D. Bristow: *FM Theory & Applications by Musicians for Musicians* (Tokyo, 1986)

S. Trask: 'Made in Japan: Eastern Intrigue', *Music Technology*, vol.2/3 (1988), 50–3

M. Vail: *Vintage Synthesizers: Groundbreaking Instruments and Pioneering Designers of Electronic Music Synthesizers* (San Francisco, 1993, 2/2000), 162–7

J. Colbeck: *Keyfax Omnibus Edition* (Emeryville, CA, 1996), 128–41, 180–88

P. Forrest: *The A–Z of Analogue Synthesisers*, vol.2 (Crediton, 1996), 214–39

HUGH DAVIES, EDWIN M. GOOD, EDWARD H. TARR/
ANNE BEETEM ACKER

Yamilango. Drum of the Yeke people in the Shaba region, Democratic Republic of the Congo. It is a very large, double-headed instrument, part of the king's regalia. The heads, of buffalo, antelope, or elk skin, are laced together and beaten with two sticks. The yamilango may be played only by the king and only on official occasions. See O. Boone: *Les tambours du Congo belge et du Ruanda-Urundi* (Tervuren, 1951), 60.

FERDINAND J. DE HEN

Yanagawa shamisen. Type of long-neck Japanese lute. The instrument is named after Yanagawa Kengyō (*d* 1680), a blind male professional musician who influenced much *shamisen* music of his time. The instrument is thought to be very similar to the one used early in the *shamisen*'s existence in Japan, in the latter half of the 16th century. Its distinctive features include its particularly thin neck (*hosozao*, about 2.4 cm wide), a large curve just before the neck enters the soundbox (although some other types of *shamisen* also have this curve in contrast to the *jiuta shamisen*), a very slender ivory plectrum with a narrow spatula-shaped end, and

a small piece of brocade on the top of the soundbox upon which players rest the right arm whilst playing (in contrast to a cover on other *shamisen* that fits over the entire top part of the box). The instrument is used especially in the Yanagawa-ryū *shamisen* performance tradition, which is based in Kyōto, although some similar thin-neck *shamisen* are also used by *geisha* in the same city. Tsuda Michiko (1924–2003) was especially influential in promoting the use of this unique type of *shamisen*. Its music is lyrical in style. Nowadays, the instrument is frequently heard in performances by members of Kyōto Tōdō-kai playing an older style of music known as *kumiuta* (songs with *shamisen* accompaniment), as well as some other traditional types of music for the instrument.

BIBLIOGRAPHY

M. Tsuda: *Kyōto no hibiki: Yanagawa shamisen* [The sounds of Kyōto: Yanagawa Shamisen] (Kyoto, 1998)

H. Johnson: *The Shamisen: Tradition and Diversity* (Leiden, 2010)

HENRY JOHNSON

Yanagisawa. Japanese saxophone manufacturing company, headquartered in Tokyo. It traces its roots to 1894, when its founder, Tokutaro Yanagisawa, began repairing imported instruments used by Japanese military musicians. He established his firm in 1896 (reputedly the first in Japan to manufacture Western woodwinds) and in 1921 opened a factory for trumpets and cornets. Among instrument makers trained by Yanagisawa was the flute maker Koichi Muramatsu. Tokutaro's son Takanobu took over the family business and designed his first prototype saxophone in 1951. Regular production began with a tenor sax in 1954, followed by introduction of alto and baritone models and in 1968, the first Japanese soprano and sopranino saxes. In 1977 a new line of soprano, alto, and tenor models was announced, bringing the full line to 15 models in five ranges. Further models were introduced from the 1980s into the 2000s. The company makes saxophones of phosphor bronze and silver as well as standard brass. Until 1978 the company's saxophones were made as stencil instruments, to which other manufacturers such as Conn, Selmer (USA), and Martin (who provided some of the designs) added their insignia. Thereafter Yanagisawa marketed the instruments under its own brand, which has achieved considerable distinction among professional musicians. Nowadays under direction of Nobushige Yanagisawa, the Yanagisawa Wind Instruments Co., Ltd (incorporated in 1961) is one of Japan's most internationally recognized saxophone manufacturers, alongside the larger and more wide-ranging Yamaha company.

STEPHEN COTTRELL/R

Yanggŭm. Trapeziform hammer dulcimer of Korea (*yang*: 'western'; *gŭm*: 'string instrument'). It is also known as *kurach'ŏlsa kŭm* ('European wire-string instrument'). The yanggŭm is about 71 cm on its longest side, 47 cm on the parallel side, and 28 cm on the two shortest sides; it has 14 quadruple courses of steel wires and two long bridges. Seven courses go over one bridge and under the other, and seven do the opposite. The instrument's range is *eb* to *db''*. The wires are struck with a single slip of bamboo (left of the right bridge, right of the left bridge, and left of the left bridge), and the technique is not very developed. Unlike most other Korean melodic instruments the yanggŭm is incapable of pitch shading or vibrato.

The yanggŭm, basically the same instrument as the Persian *sanṭūr*, was brought to Korea from China in the 18th century, having been brought to China in the 16th century by Christian missionaries. A Korean description and notation book for the instrument, *Kurach'ŏlsa kŭmbo*, survives from the early 19th century. The yanggŭm is now used only in mixed ensembles for aristocratic music such as the suite *Yŏngsan hoesang*. See Chang Sa-hun: *Han'guk akki taegwan* [Korean musical instruments] (Seoul, 1969).

ROBERT C. PROVINE

Yangqin. Hammered dulcimer of the Han Chinese. *Yang* in its original form means 'foreign'; *qin* is generic for string instruments. The *yangqin* is also traditionally known as *hudie qin* ('butterfly *qin*', in reference to its double-wing-shaped body) and *daqin* ('beaten *qin*'). The Japanese *yōkin*, used in *minshingaku* music, is equivalent.

The instrument, made of hardwood (commonly maple, elm, or birch), is trapezoidal. Its parallel widths measure 78 and 118 cm, with the greater width facing the player. The sides measure 51 cm, forming 70-degree angles with the greater width; the resonator is 8 cm deep. Earlier models generally have smaller dimensions with varied contours: some have straight sides and slightly rounded corners, others have rounded sides and fluted widths. The thin soundboard, made of white pine or other softwood, is slightly arched. The baseboard is flat and made of softwood or nowadays plywood. Held against the soundboard by pressure of the strings are several long bridges. Early models have two bridges; recent models have three to five full-length bridges and one or more short bridges. Each bridge has seven to 13 chess-pawn-shaped projections that support the courses of strings.

The yangqin rests on a stand. The strings are struck with two slender bamboo beaters (*qinzhu*) padded with rubber on the round striking end. Tremolos and broken and arpeggiated chords are common in the repertory, as are harmonics, glissandos, striking with the backs of the beaters for a percussive sound, and use of different damping effects.

The strings on older instruments are made of copper (more recently of brass and steel) and organized in two groups (left and right), each tuned diatonically, with double (or more) courses of strings for each pitch position. Strings run from their tuning pins on the right, over a common right nut, across their respective bridge projection, over the left nut, and are fastened to hitch pins on the left side. Strings in the right group pass through spaces located between each bridge projection on the left row and vice versa. The left bridge is positioned on the soundboard so as to divide its strings in a 2:3 relationship (such as 20 cm on the left side, 30 cm on the right). With this particular division, these strings sound two pitches a 5th apart, one on each side of its bridge (e.g. *sol–re, la–mi*, etc., on right and left sides, respectively). Traditional tuning (especially in south China) distinctively requires that *ti* and *fa* be positioned on either side of the same bridge as a perfect 5th, with *ti* roughly 50 cents flat (from equal temperament) and *fa* 50 cents sharp. Placement of the right bridge, however, requires no such precise positioning since only the strings on its left side are utilized (for lower octave pitches). The traditional instrument ranges over little more than two octaves, depending upon its number of bridges.

The yangqin is an adaptation of the Persian *sanṭūr*, which was introduced to coastal areas of Guangdong province in South China late in the Ming dynasty (1368–1644). There is also some evidence of the dulcimer's introduction via an inland route, through regions of Northwest China (Xinjiang) in the early Qing dynasty (mid-18th century). Mentioned frequently in the literature of the 18th to early 20th centuries, the yangqin was readily accepted into the local Cantonese and Chaozhou ensembles, where it remains important. It is also used to accompany narrative singing in Sichuan province, and in northern vocal genres such as *Erren tai*. In the late 20th century, it was gradually accepted into *sizhu* ('silk-and-bamboo') ensembles in the Jiangnan area of central-eastern China.

Within the conservatory music tradition, the yangqin has a sizeable solo repertory, is an important accompaniment instrument, and is valued for its harmonic support in chamber ensembles and orchestras. Since the 1950s, the composition of new works, influenced by Western European art music, sparked development of a yangqin with greater range and resonance that could accommodate Western tonalities. The instrument was enlarged and resonance increased by using three or four strings per course for middle and upper registers. Rows of bridges were added and the number

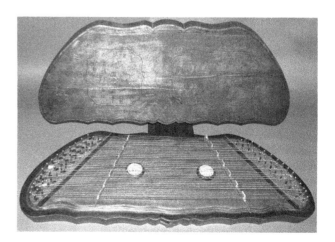

Yangqin, hammered dulcimer, Kuang-tung Province, China. (Aurelia W. Hartenberger, EdD)

of projections on each bridge increased. Makers also experimented with different tuning mechanisms such as movable metal sliders and cylindrical rollers placed underneath the strings.

Although the earliest modernization of the yangqin began in the late 1950s in Beijing, standardization of the two most influential models, commonly called the 401 and 501, took place only in the 1970s. The model 401 (1971) introduced changes that quickly became the norm for all factory-made models: in addition to the original side tuning panels, a raised panel was added for the placement of cylindrical rollers underneath strings; frequently changed pitches used metal sliders (located on the left panel) in addition to rollers placed inside the tracks of the metal sliders; the nuts which were once located at the inner edge of the original outer panels were relocated to a ridge between the raised and lower outer panels. In addition, small tuning platforms, each with one roller, were placed near the top middle section and used for tuning the upper register. Rollers, when moved to the right or left, change pitch by varying the vibratory length of the string.

The precise 2:3 ratio for string lengths pitched a 5th apart is no longer necessary due to the tuning rollers on either side of the bridge. While many pitches in the row are still tuned a 5th apart, others are a tritone or 4th apart. The 401 has a four-octave range G–g'''. Its larger size accommodates four rows of bridges plus a supplementary bridge at the upper left. The right three bridges have nine to ten projections each and the strings are struck only to the left of the bridges. The left bridge has 13 projections and the strings are struck on either side of the bridges.

The 401 makers wanted to create a model that could play Chinese pentatonic melodies with ease, while at the same time allow for Western harmonies and key changes. The result was a largely whole-tone pitch layout that overlaps in range across rows of bridges such that their pitch complement completes the chromatic pitch series. (For example, the far right row is tuned in ascending whole tones from G to c' while the row to its left is tuned from $c\sharp$ to f'. When combined, the two rows cover all chromatic pitches from c to $c\sharp'$.) While this makes it difficult to play adjacent chromatic pitches quickly, it retains a pitch layout that favours the playing of pentatonic melodies.

The still larger 501 (87 to 122 cm wide, 56 cm long, 10 cm deep), developed in 1978, was built upon the modifications of the 401. The 501 has a range of E–c'''' and five rows of bridges plus one supplementary bridge in the lower right corner. The most significant change is the addition of a second left bridge designed for strings to be played on both sides. For the first time, the chromatic pitches are arranged side by side between the two left bridges. The 501 was developed in response to new repertoire featuring greater tonal complexity and technical virtuosity. Recently, instrument makers have experimented with dampers operated by pedals, but these have not yet become standard.

BIBLIOGRAPHY

A.C. Moule: 'A List of the Musical and Other Sound–Producing Instruments of the Chinese', *Journal of the Royal Asiatic Society, North China Branch*, vol.39 (1908), 1–160; repr. separately (Buren, 1989), 118–20

Liu Dongsheng and others, eds.: *Zhongguo yueqi tujian* [Pictorial guide to Chinese instruments] (Ji'nan, 1992), 276–81

Xu Pingxin: 'Zhongwai yangqin de fazhan yu bijiao' [Development and comparison of Chinese and foreign *yangqin*], *Yueqi* (1992), no.1, 7–10; no.2, 11–5; no.3, 1–5; no.4, 8–11

A. Thrasher and G. Wong: 'Yangqin', *Yueqi: Chinese Musical Instruments in Performance* (Vancouver, 2011), 113–28

ALAN R. THRASHER/GLORIA N. WONG

Yareíto. Drum of Oriente Province, Cuba. The body, about 40 cm long and smaller in diameter, consists of 12 staves from the trunk of a *yarey* palm, hence the name of the instrument. The single head is attached with nails, and the drum is open at the lower end. The body is encircled with a small belt of wire, cactus fibre, or iron chain tightened with wedges placed against (not into) the sides. The belt has nothing to do with tensioning the head. The instrument, of African origin, is always struck by the hands in ensembles with the *tumba de monte*, a small snare drum. See F. Ortiz: *Los instrumentos de la música afrocubana* (Havana, 1952–5), vol.4, 179–80.

JOHN M. SCHECHTER/R

Yates, Roger (*b* Solihull, England, 24 Oct 1905; *d* Rutland, England, 1975). English organ builder. He trained in the Willis factory from 1922 to 1928 when he acquired the business (established 1859) of Charles Francis Lloyd in Nottingham, moving to Bodmin in Cornwall in 1935. After service in the Royal Navy he moved to Michaelstowe, Cornwall, where he worked until suffering a stroke in 1972. He was a strong advocate of classical traditions of organ building, and favoured simple instruments with mechanical action and light wind-pressures. His 46-stop organ in All Saints Church, Oakham (1937, rebuild of 1872 Brindley & Foster) had complete choruses on three manuals and Pedal, but when replaced in 1996, it comprised an assortment of miscellaneous pipework. His last completed organ is in Dartington Hall, Devon, and his archives are at the Loosemore Centre for organ and early music studies at Buckfastleigh, Devon. Yates also undertook the sensitive restoration of historic organs and harpsichords, and self-published a short monograph, *Organ Building* (1937). See L. Elvin: *Pipes and Actions: Some OrganBuilders in the Midlands and Beyond* (Lincoln, 1995), 240–55.

MICHAEL SAYER/R

Yatga [yataga, yatuga]. Mongolian half-tube zither with movable bridges. Traditionally, the instrument varies in size and tuning even within one ethnic group, as evidenced by two Chahar Mongol instruments collected by Haslund-Christensen: one (now in *DK.K.m*) measures 114.5 cm long by 21.6 cm wide; a second (in *S.S.e*) measures 153.4 cm long by 22 cm wide. The tuning of the instrument used by Sünit Mongols was pentatonic in the sequence of the Chinese *zhi* mode. Similarly, the ten-string Ordos Mongol zither described by van Oost in *La musique chez les Mongols des Urdus* (1915–16) lacked the *mi* and *ti* of the Western solmization series.

The earliest documentation of the classical Mongolian term *yatuga* (or *yatugan*) occurs in a Mongolian–Chinese dictionary of 1389, where it is paired with the Chinese *zheng*, an instrument described in the *Yüan shih* (1370), a history of the Yüan (Mongol) dynasty, as having 13 strings. It was also used in the Mughal courts of Central Asia. Persian sources use the Mongolian word 'yatugan' for a zither with movable bridges, and a 15th-century poem written in old Uzbek (Chagatay) also mentions the *yatugan*. An 18th-century source refers to a Kalmyk *yattagan* with gut strings. Mongolian sources of the 19th and early 20th centuries describe a *yatga* with 14 strings. During the Qing dynasty (1644–1911), the 12-string yatga was a court instrument, the number of strings symbolizing the 12 ranks within the palace. It was used to entertain the aristocracy and also was played by the aristocracy. The ten-string yatga was played by Living Buddhas and consequently surrounded by ritual. Three recently discovered 18th- and 19th-century song manuscripts for performance in Nomyn Khan monasteries contain notations for the yatga. The ten-string yatga was also used during worship at ritual cairns or *oboo* and during sports, such as horse racing, held on such occasions.

The yatga appears in epics and legends in relation to both court and religious contexts. The Kalmyk heroic epic-cycle *Janggar* tells how a 16-year-old princess played on the seven lower bridges of a yatga that had 82 bridges and 8000 strings. It was used for interludes during recitations of Buryat epics and, as with other Mongolian instruments, was played to animals to persuade a mother to accept her rejected young.

Traditionally, the musician knelt on the ground to perform, laying the narrower end of the yatga on his thigh and supporting the wider end on the ground. Some Mongol groups made strings from a goat's small intestines, after a process of stretching, boiling, and drying. Others used horsehair, as on the Tuvan *chadagan* and Kazakh *zshetïgan*. In Inner Mongolia, horsehair was replaced by silk and, more recently, metal wound around gut or metal. The Inner Mongolian yatga has two rows of bridges. Strings can be plucked by the nails or by various plectra including leather caps (for thumb and finger) to which is attached a small piece of horn.

The yatga was used in ensembles in Urga (now Ulaanbaatar) in 1923. During the early years after the communist revolution of 1924, the yatga fell into disuse, probably because of its traditional aristocratic and religious connections. It was revived as a 'national' instrument of the Mongolian People's Republic during the 1950s, with Korean-style instruments. The 13-string yatga now used to accompany singing and played in instrumental ensembles has a single row of bridges. Seated on a chair rather than on the floor, the player rests the instrument on the knees with it sloping downwards to the floor on his or her left, or plays an instrument supported by legs or a stand. The right-hand

fingernails are used to pluck the open strings. The left-hand fingers apply pressure to the strings which pass over small bridges, each wedged between a string and the soundboard, to produce vibrato, pitch alterations (accidentals), and other embellishments, as well as special plucking effects. The most common type of yatga nowadays has 21 strings; it is about 162 cm long and tuned pentatonically. Higher-pitched instruments are shorter.

BIBLIOGRAPHY

T.S. Vizgo: *Muzikal'niye instrumentï Srednei Azii* [Musical instruments of Central Asia] (Moscow, 1980)

S. Büted and A. Magnaisüren: *Yatgyn Garyn Avlaga* [A handbook for the *yatga*] (Ulaanbaatar, 1987)

L. Erdenechimeg: *The Historical Tradition of the Mongolian Yatga* (Ulaanbaatar, 1995)

L. Erdenechimeg and T. Shagdarsüren: *Chin Süzegt Nomyn Han Hiidiin gür duuny bichig* [*Gür* song notation from Chinsüzegt Nomyn Khan Monastery] (Ulaanbaatar, 1995)

C.A. Pegg: *Mongolian Music, Dance, and Oral Narrative: Performing Diverse Identities* (Seattle, 2001) [incl. CD]

CAROLE PEGG

Yatugalig. Bowed zither of Mongolia, related to the Chinese *laqin*; it is now obsolete. An 8th-century Chinese source describes an instrument, *yazheng*, as a zither bowed with a bamboo stick. The *Yuan shi* (1370), a history of the Yuan (Mongol) dynasty in China, describes a seven-string zither (*qin*) bowed with bamboo, and this is noted in other Mongolian orchestras of that period. In an 18th-century imperial five-language dictionary the Mongolian name yatugalig is linked with the Chinese term *yaqin*. In the Manchu dynasty Mongolian ensembles included a ten-string bowed zither, *yazheng*. A Mongolian musician is reported to have played a bowed zither called a *dzeng* in the early 20th century, and the bard Luvsan (*d* 1943) played on a bowed instrument he called a *chin*. A related instrument is the *ajaeng*, bowed long zither, of Korea.

BIBLIOGRAPHY

L. Picken: 'Early Chinese Friction-Chordophones', *GSJ*, vol.18 (1965), 82–9

R.F. Wolpert: 'Einige Bemerkungen zur Geschichte des Streichinstruments in China', *Central Asiatic Journal*, vol.18/4 (1974), 253

ANDREA NIXON

Yaylı tanbur. Bowed (*yaylı*) version of the Turkish *tanbūr*. The normal *tanbur* was first bowed by the composer Tanburi Cemil Bey in the 1910s, but by the 1930s the much louder *yaylı tanbur* was invented, apparently as a type of *cümbüş*, with that instrument's characteristic skin-head resonator. Its body is usually bowl-shaped, made of glued wooden strips or, less expensively, of spun aluminium. The wooden neck, with geared tuning machines, is 104 to 110 cm long, affording a 120-cm vibrating string length. It normally has 31 tied nylon frets in the lower octave and 24 in the higher octave, though players often move, add, or subtract frets. All but the highest course of its three or four metal bichords (tuned in 5ths, 4ths, and/or octaves according to the melodic mode) are intended to vibrate sympathetically, only the highest bichord being bowed and fingered. The lower bichords often sound octaves, while the playing course is tuned in unison, normally to *d*. Often both strings of the bowed course occupy the same slot in the nut and bridge so that the strings touch one another along their length. The bridge beneath this course is elevated to facilitate bowing. The instrument rests upon the left knee or on the lap and is bowed underhand, usually with a violin or cello bow. The yaylı tanbur is seldom played in classical and folk musics but finds a home in light classical *fasıl* ensembles in urban Turkish restaurants, bars, and cabarets. See E.B. Ederer: *The Cümbüş as Instrument of 'the Other' in Modern Turkey* (Santa Barbara, CA, 2007).

ERIC BERNARD EDERER

Yazheng. Bowed half-tube zither of China (*ya*: 'creak'; *zheng*: 'zither'). The instrument is mentioned in the *Jiu Tangshu* ('Old History of the Tang Dynasty', completed 945 CE) with the comment, 'The yazheng is made to creak with a slip of bamboo, moistened at its tip'. An early illustration of the yazheng appears in Chen Yang's *Yueshu* ('Treatise on Music') of 1104, showing a long zither with a slightly convex soundboard (closely resembling a *zheng*), approximately nine strings, and an L-shaped playing implement. Yazheng was also referred to as *qin* (a different character from the seven-string scholar's zither) from the Song to the Ming dynasties. The 13th-century encyclopedia *Shilinguangji* ('Comprehensive Record of the Forest of Affairs') states that the instrument had seven strings, each with a movable bridge underneath. *Da Qing huidian tu* ('Illustrations for the Compendium of Administrative Laws of Qing', 1899) describes the yazheng as having ten strings played with a straight wooden stick.

The yazheng was first documented at the Tang court, in a visiting ensemble from Nanzhao Kingdom (modern Yunnan). Iconography depicting the yazheng performing court banquet music and accompanying sung poetry suggests the instrument grew in popularity in the central plain from the 12th century onwards. By the 14th century the seven-string yazheng had been exported to Korea, where it is still played, while a source of 1607 states that the instrument was played in Mongolian music.

The yazheng is now found only in regional folk ensembles in Shanxi, Shandong, and Hebei provinces, often under different names, such as *waqin*, *foqin*, and *zhuqin*. A version known as *chengni* is also played by the Zhuang minority in Guangxi. These surviving instruments are shorter, with seven to 14 strings and soundboards ranging from slightly convex to a 180-degree half circle. Supported with the left hand on the bottom of the instrument, the end rests against the performer's shoulder or chest while being bowed with a long horsehair bow.

BIBLIOGRAPHY
L. Picken: 'Early Chinese Friction-Chordophones', *GSJ*, vol.18 (1965), 82–9
Zhongguo yinyueshi tupian [Photographs of Chinese music history] (Beijing, 1988), 57, 149

HAN MEI

Yenjing. Dulcimer of the Uyghur people of Central Asia. It is similar to the Chinese *yangqin*, and since that instrument is thought to have derived from the Persian *santūr*, possibly transmitted via Uyghur areas, the yenjing might have been the origin of the *yangqin*.

JEREMY MONTAGU

Yeye. Cylindrical slit drum of the Konda people of the western Democratic Republic of the Congo. It is made from wood, 30 to 50 cm long and 15 to 20 cm in diameter, and has a square hole at both ends of the slit. The yeye is held in the crook of the left arm and is beaten with one stick; it accompanies dancing. The Konda *ikookole* slit drum used to accompany the *bobongo* dance is similar.

FERDINAND J. DE HEN

Yo. Obsolete clapperless handbell of Korea, considered to be of Chinese origin. According to the treatise *Akhak kwebŏm* (1493) it was 23.7 cm tall and 20.6 cm in diameter at the open end, with a handle 11.9 cm long attached to the closed end. The player held the bell by the handle in his left hand and struck it with a mallet held in the right. It was used in ritual music (*aak*) at sacrificial rites, when the *mumu* ('military dance') was being performed. It was played, together with the *sun* and the two bells called *t'ak*, on the third and fourth beats in every four-beat phrase. The Chinese bell *zhong* is similar. See Sŏng Hyŏn, ed.: *Akhak kwebŏ* [Guide to the study of music] (Seoul, 1493/R1975), 2.4*b* and 6.25*b*.

ROBERT C. PROVINE

Yodelling. Singing or calling using a rapid alternation of vocal registers.

1. Terminology. 2. Definition and technique. 3. Distribution of yodelling in non-Alpine contexts.

1. TERMINOLOGY. The German verb *jodeln* (to yodel) comes from the Middle High German verb *jôlen* (to call or cry and to sing), found in numerous sources since about 1540; *jôlen* remains in Alpine dialects to the present. According to Grimm and Grimm (1877), the verb *jo(h)len* or *jola* is derived from the interjection *jo* and might have gained the additional 'd' for vocal-physiological reasons. The forms *jo(h)ha*, *jodle(n)*, *jodeln*, and *jödele* evolved from so-called *jo* and *ju(c)hui* calls and are closely related to other regional expressions such as *juchzen*, *jutzen*, *ju(u)zä*, and *juizä* in Switzerland; *lud(e)ln*, *dud(e)ln*, *jorlen*, *jaudeln*, and *hegitzen* in Austria; *johla* in the Allgäu region of Germany; and *jola*, *zor(r)en*, *zauren*, *rug(g)us(s)en*, and *länderen* in the Appenzell region of Switzerland. Other languages use translations of the German *jodeln*, as in French, *jodler* (*iouler*) or *chanter à la manière tyrolienne*; in Swedish, *joddla*; in Japanese, *yŏderu*, etc.

2. DEFINITION AND TECHNIQUE. The following features are generally understood under 'yodelling': (1) singing

without words, in which the play of timbres and harmonics is emphasized in the succession of individual, nonsensical vocal-consonant connections (such as 'jo-hol-di-o-u-ri-a'), which are also (2) connected in a creative way with the technique of continuous and rapid change between the natural and falsetto registers. (3) The tones, often performed in large intervallic leaps, are either smoothly connected during the continuous change of register (register break) or are additionally broken up in traditional styles by glottal stops. Well-trained yodellers employ a vocal range of up to three octaves. Through the change of yodelling syllables and of vocal register, a continuous timbral transformation emerges which results from the shifting number of overtones and stress of fundamental tone and overtones. The falsetto register almost always has fewer partials than the chest voice, which usually has a continuous row of (15–20) overtones of relatively strong intensity. However, sonographic and acoustic-phonetic investigations of yodelling sounds reveal inconsistencies that can be traced to a differentiation that should be made between a supported and an unsupported falsetto voice. Of particular significance for the timbral spectrum of individual tones are the relationships between open vowels, such as a, œ, and ɑ and lower pitches in the natural register, as well as between closed vowels, such as i, y, and u and higher pitches in the falsetto register. Most yodelling uses a lowered larynx ('yawning position') and an expanded resonance space.

3. DISTRIBUTION OF YODELLING IN NON-ALPINE CONTEXTS. By the beginning of the 19th century, yodelling had gained popularity and had been introduced to European cities by travelling 'natural' and 'Alpine' singers and by national singing societies and singer families from the Tyrol (Zillertal), Styria, and Carinthia. Travelling entertainers spread the 'yodelling style' in presenting a combination of songs and yodels in popular Viennese theatrical plays. Owing to international cultural contact, the presence of enthusiasts in different cultures and especially the influence of disseminating media, Alpine-like yodelling is now practised outside Europe. In Tokyo the Japanese Jodler-Alpen-Kameraden cultivate this technique. In Seoul the first yodelling club was established in 1969, and the Korean Yodel Association was founded in 1979.

(i) Cowboy yodellers. In the USA and Canada immigrants and their descendents yodel in Bavarian, Austrian, or Swiss fashion. Many traditional cowboy songs end with a yodel refrain. The image of the yodelling cowboy was spread by musical events at rodeos, radio shows (such as Melody Ranch featuring the Oklahoma Yodelling Cowboy, Gene Autry), records, and Hollywood westerns. Among these yodelling cowboys, Jimmie Rodgers (1897–1933), known as 'Mississippi Railroad Man', 'Yodeling Ranger', and the 'Blue Yodeler', developed the fine points of the yodel song: the change of timbre according to register, abrupt glottal stops, and gentle slurring.

(ii) Yodel-like singing. This can be found in Central European Alpine regions and in many mountainous and forest regions of other geographic areas. In the polyphonic songs of the Tosks of Albania, two yodel-like voices are accompanied by a sung drone. In Georgia, vocal polyphony as a harmonic basis to a higher 'yodelling' voice is known as krimanchuli. Related vocal techniques can be found in Ethiopia, Rwanda, the Democratic Republic of the Congo, Angola, Burundi, Gabon, and other African countries. Among the Khoisan and the !Kung of southern Angola, for example, a canon-like technique using one to four yodelling voices produces contrapuntal-like effects during which the relative positions of the voices vary. The Aka yodellers stand out in that they produce four to six or even 13 overtones in the 'high register'. In the 'deep register', on the other hand, the tones display a sound spectrum of homogeneous overtones with greater intensity; however the fundamental tone is hardly existent or only very weak.

Yodel-like melodies and songs also occur in Asia and in the boundary region between Melanesia and Polynesia. In the southern highlands of Papua New Guinea, the Huli have two kinds of yodel-like songs: the solo-istic and alternating falsetto song (u) of the men and the repetitive and yodel-like singing with fixed timbre (iwa) performed during work. On Savo in the Solomon Islands, in reference to the solo voice it is said that one takes the song deep (neo laua) when singing with natural voice and uses a high voice (taga laua) when changing register and singing with falsetto. In addition to three-voice polyphony, the sudden, characteristic register change of two solo voices is supported by a vocal drone.

Falsetto and calls, screams, and ululation that alternate between the normal register and falsetto are important among most native groups of North and South America. Among the Bororo in Brazil, the 'o-ie o-ie i-go' vocalization in hunting songs is characterized by additional elements of a yodel-like larynx technique. Additional comparative research in the future might extend the concept of yodelling in its details. It has already been established that yodel-like singing need not necessarily be tied to large intervals. Sonographic research has shown that two 'different' pitches (one in the natural register and the other in the falsetto register) can have a common fundamental tone and still belong to different registers.

BIBLIOGRAPHY

J. and W. Grimm: 'Jodeln', Deutsches Wörterbuch, vol.4/2 (Leipzig, 1877/R)

W. Senn: '"Jodeln": eine Beitrag zur Entstehung und Verbreitung des Wortes—mundartliche Bezeichnungen', Jb des österreichischen Volksliedwerkes, vol.11 (1962), 150–66

W. Graf: 'Sonographische Untersuchungen', Handbuch des Volksliedes, vol.2, ed. R.W. Brednich, L. Röhrich, and W. Suppan (Munich, 1975), 583–622

M.P. Baumann: Musikfolklore und Musikfolklorismus: eine ethnomusikologische Untersuchung zum Funktionswandel des Jodels (Winterthur, 1976)

H.J. Leuthold: Der Naturjodel in der Schweiz: Entstehung, Charakteristik, Verbreitung (Altdorf, 1981)

C. Luchner-Löscher: Der Jodler: Wesen, Entstehung, Verbreitung und Gestalt (Munich, 1982)

S. Fürniss: *Die Jodeltechnik der Aka-Pygmäen in Zentralafrika: eine akustisch-phonetische Untersuchung* (Berlin, 1992)

F. Födermayr: 'Zur Jodeltechnik von Jimmie Rodgers: Die Blue Yodel', *For Gerhard Kubik: Festschrift*, ed. A. Schmidhofer and D. Schuller (Frankfurt, 1994), 381–404

B. Plantegna: *Yodel-ay-ee-ooo: the Secret History of Yodeling Around the World* (New York, NY, 2004)

E. Fink-Mennel: *Johlar und Juz: Registerwechseinder Gesang im Bregenzerwald: mit Tonbeispielen, 1937–1997* (Graz-Fedlkirch, 2007)

M. Echternach and B. Richter: 'Vocal Perfection in Yodeling: Pitch Stabilities and Transition Times', *Logopedics, Phoniatrics, Vocology*, vol.35 (2010), 6–12

MAX PETER BAUMANN/R

Yokobue. General term for any Japanese transverse flute, but particularly the *shinobue*. The same characters can be read *ōteki*, which nowadays denotes the *ryūteki*, another kind of transverse flute.

Yokota, Munetaka (*b* Tokyo, Japan, 14 March 1952). Japanese organ builder. He is a leading researcher and implementer of 17th- and 18th-century German construction techniques. After taking his degree in economics at Gakushuin University (1974), he apprenticed with the organ builder Hiroshi Tsuji before joining John Brombaugh's workshop in Eugene, Oregon, in 1978. From 1984 to 1990 he was artist-in residence at Chico State University, California, where he built a large, path-breaking organ in the style of Gottfried Silbermann using local materials and only volunteer help. In 1994 he was appointed guest professor at Göteborg University in Sweden, where he was the artistic leader of the ambitious undertaking, completed in 2000, to reconstruct, for Göteborg, Arp Schnitger's 1699 organ for Lübeck Cathedral. Subsequent projects include an organ closely modelled after the 1776 A.G. Casparini organ in Vilnius for the Eastman School of Music in Rochester, New York (inaugurated 2008), and two instruments inspired by another lost Schnitger masterpiece, formerly at Berlin's Charlottenburg Castle Chapel, for the Korean National University of the Arts in Seoul (completed 2006) and for Cornell University in Ithaca, New York (completed 2011). Yokota, whose affiliation with Göteborg continues, is especially noted for his expertise in replicating historical metal pipework.

Yokuë. End-blown secret flute of the Lake Sentani area of northeast Irian Jaya (West New Guinea). It is as long as a hand and has no fingerholes. Forearm-length flutes are called *keru* and arm-length flutes *ivare*. See J. Kunst: *Music in New Guinea* (The Hague, 1967), 130.

Yolum. Heavy ankle bell of the Kabre people of northern Togo. It is worn during the warriors' dance procession.

Yom biBagirmi. Six- or seven-string arched harp of the Birom people of the Jos Plateau of Nigeria, reputed to originate from the Bagirmi people, south of Lake Chad. It has a wooden boat-shaped resonator covered with goatskin. The strings are attached to the neck by tuning pegs and at the other end to a metal plate with holes in it. Formerly restricted to use by men to accompany singing, the harp now appears in instrumental ensembles for general entertainment. See L. Bouquiaux: 'Les instruments de musique Birom (Nigeria Septentrional)', *Africa-Tervuren*, vol.8/4 (1962), 105–11.

Yomkwo [riyom ko]. Idiochord raft zither of the Birom people of Nigeria. It is made from reeds of equal length and thickness. The strings, loosened strips of the surface, pass over two wooden bridges; their ends are bound with thin fibre which can be adjusted for tuning, and the point at which they are plucked is reinforced by bindings of the same fibre, which also adds mass to the strings and thus lowers the pitch. The zither has 11 to 18 strings, arranged in sets of two or three and tuned an octave apart. Some instruments have a small woven container on the back with seeds or small pebbles inside. The yomkwo is usually plucked with the thumbs and it is used for self-accompaniment or, recently, as part of an instrumental ensemble with arched harp, scraper, and gourd rattles.

The *zunzum* of the Kagoro people of Nigeria, with 15 or 18 strings, is constructed and played in the same manner as the *yomkwo*. In the 18-string version two central sets of strings have identical tuning. See L. Bouquiaux: 'Les instruments de musique Birom (Nigeria Septentrional)', *Africa-Tervuren*, vol.8/4 (1962), 105–11.

Yondo. Metal percussion tube of the Teda people of Tibesti, Chad. Traditionally the yondo is played by slapping it against the player's thigh or shin, but it can also be struck against a bottle.

Yonggo. Shallow two-headed barrel drum of Korea (*yong*: 'dragon'; *go*: 'drum'). It has two tacked cowhide heads, roughly 35 to 40 cm in diameter, and a body about 20 to 25 cm deep. The body of the yonggo is often decorated with brightly coloured dragon motifs; there is also an undecorated version of the drum, used in folk music and normally called *puk*.

The history of the yonggo is not well documented, but the drum resembles two instruments (*taego*: 'large drum', now obsolete; and *sogo*: 'small drum') described in the treatise *Akhak kwebōm* (1493). The yonggo is now used in military processional music (*tae-ch'wit'a*) and as an accompaniment for folk narrative singing (*p'ansori*). In military music it is suspended, skin upwards, by a shoulder sash attached to two metal rings on the drum body; the standing player strikes it with two large mallets. In narrative singing the player sits and the drum is placed upright on the floor in front of him; he strikes the left head with his open left palm, and both the right head and wooden body with a slender wooden mallet which is held in his right hand.

BIBLIOGRAPHY

Sŏng Hyŏn, ed.: *Akhak kwebōm* [Guide to the study of music] (Seoul, 1493/R1975), 8.9*b*

Chang Sa-hun: *Han'guk akki taegwan* [Korean musical instruments] (Seoul, 1969), 135 only

ROBERT C. PROVINE

Yoochin. Mongolian board zither. The name might have originated through confusion with the round-bodied lute, *yueqin*, which was also played in Mongolia and called *yoochin*, or *biivlig*. The struck zither was more often known as *yanchin*, or *yanchir*, from the Chinese *yangqin*. Instruments of different sizes and with various numbers of strings have been used in Mongolia; they have had from 12 to 24 bridges, each with two to four metal strings. The yoochin is used in ensembles and has no traditional Mongolian repertory. See A. Chuluundash: *Yoochindoj sur'ya* [Let's learn the *yoochin*] (Ulaanbaatar, 1969).

ANDREA NIXON

Yotsudake. Clappers of Japan. They consist of two pairs of bamboo pieces, one pair held in each hand (*yotsu*: 'four'; *dake*: 'bamboo'). Each piece is about 10 to 12 cm long, 4 to 6 cm wide, and 1 cm thick and slightly curved around the longitudinal axis. The convex faces strike each other. The pieces can be lacquered to give a sharper sound, or often just trimmed with red around the edges. In most of Japan the two pieces are attached to the thumb and middle finger by means of a short cord, but in Okinawan classical dance the pieces are simply held in the crooked hand. The yotsudake were once used by certain itinerant performers, and in the *kabuki* theatre in *geza* (off-stage) music this connection is maintained. See W.P. Malm: *Traditional Japanese Music and Musical Instruments* (Tokyo, 2000) [incl. CD].

DAVID W. HUGHES

Young, John (*b* ?London, England, *c*1672; *d* London, *c*1732). English music printer, publisher, and instrument maker. Young's father was also John, but since he was still alive in 1693, he was evidently not the John Young who was appointed musician-in-ordinary to the king as a viol player on 23 May 1673 and who had died by 1680. Young was apprenticed to the music seller and publisher John Clarke and was established on his own by 1695. His publications included *A Choice Collection of Ayres for the Harpsichord or Spinett* by Blow and others (1700); William Gorton's *A Choice Collection of New Ayres, Compos'd and Contriv'd for Two Bass-Viols* (1701); the fifth and sixth editions of Christopher Simpson's *Compendium* (1714); and other works. Young also had a high reputation as a violin maker, working from premises at the 'Dolphin and Crown' at the west corner of London House Yard in St Paul's Churchyard. His violin-playing sons, John (*b* London, 23 Aug 1694) and Talbot (*b* London, 25 June 1699; *d* London, bur. 24 Feb 1758), both joined the business, which was memorialized in a catch printed in the *Musical Companion* (1726):

You scrapers that want a good fiddle well strung,
You must go to the man that is old while he's young;
But if this same fiddle you fain would play bold,
You must go to his son, who'll be young when he's old.
There's old Young and young Young, both men of renown,
Old sells and young plays the best fiddle in town. . . .

John the younger in turn had a son, yet another John Young (*b* London, 1 March 1718; *d* London, 30

April 1767), who was a violinist and organist. Talbot Young became the best-known violinist of the family. With his father, Maurice Greene, and others, he established a series of weekly music meetings from about 1715. Held initially at the Young's premises, they eventually became known as the Castle Society concerts. About 1741 the Young's business passed into the hands of Peter Thompson (*d c*1759), who had probably had an association with the firm since about 1731. Thompson worked at the sign of the 'Violin and Hautboy'; his business continued under family direction into the 19th century, and many violins bearing the Thompsons' label were probably made for them by others.

PETER WARD JONES/R

Young Chang. South Korean manufacturer of acoustic and digital pianos and other instruments. The company was founded in 1956 by brothers Jai-Young Kim, Jai-Chang Kim, and Jai-Sup Kim. Initially they sold Yamaha pianos in Korea. In 1962 they incorporated as Young Chang Akki Co. Ltd. Beginning in 1964, Yamaha helped the company build a factory and sent partially completed pianos there for completion. By 1971 Young Chang were manufacturing and exporting pianos under their own name; the relationship with Yamaha ended in 1975. Thereafter, Young Chang produced Wurlitzer-brand pianos for Baldwin, Weber pianos for Samsung, and private-label pianos for large retailers and distributors. In 1979 they opened an integrated factory for instrument manufacture in Inchon; a North American distribution subsidiary opened in 1984. That same year they constructed an automated piano warehouse at the Inchon factory. In 1985 Young Chang purchased the Weber brand from the Aeolian Corporation, and in 1990 they bought Kurzweil Musical Systems, producer of electronic pianos, MIDI controllers, and loud speakers. Also in 1990 Young Chang began digital piano sales in Korea and established a research and development facility in Boston. In 1995 the company hired Joseph Pramberger, previously a Steinway engineer and manufacturing executive; he developed two lines of significantly improved pianos that bore the Pramberger name until he died in 2003.

In 1996, when Young Chang opened a huge factory in Tianjin, China, the company was among the world's largest piano manufacturers. In 1999 Young Chang began to manufacture the Boston line of grands and uprights designed by Steinway, and from 2001 to 2005 produced Steinway's Essex line. Samick acquired a 46% controlling interest in 2004, but antitrust rulings quickly forced sale of the interest, and in September 2004, Young Chang filed for bankruptcy. In May 2006 a contract that had given Samick exclusive North American distribution rights for all Young Chang and Kurzweil products was invalidated, returning those rights to Young Chang. While North American sales and distribution were in litigation, the company suffered a large decline. However, in June 2006 Hyundai Development Company purchased an 87% stake in Young Chang, and thereafter Hyundai automotive engineers upgraded

Young Chang's factories in Inchon and Tianjin. In 2009, Delwin D. Fandrich was employed to redesign all the pianos in the product line. Consequently improved quality and the infusion of capital and resources by Hyundai enabled Young Chang to regain prominence in the world piano market. In 2011, the company had subsidiaries in Canada, the USA, and Europe. Other music-related products manufactured by Young Chang include guitars, saxophones, flutes, violins, cellos, electronic organs, synthesizers, and speakers.

ANNE BEETEM ACKER

Yu. Scraper in the form of a carved wooden tiger, used in Chinese imperial rituals. The crouching tiger is about 60 cm long. Its 'backbone' is lined with a row of 27 thin wooden chips inserted into slots, though on some instruments the back itself is serrated for the same effect. A rasping sound is produced when a bamboo whisk, its playing end split lengthwise into strips, is drawn along these serrations. The resultant sound is primarily a function of the split sections of the whisk vibrating against each other. The tiger rests on a hollow box that acts as a resonator.

No specimens have been excavated, but 19th-century examples remain in Confucian shrines and museums. The instrument's ancient history is attested by references in the *c*7th-century BCE *Shijing* ('Classic of Poetry') and many sources of later periods, and it is illustrated in the 18th-century CE *Lülü Zhengyi*. Together with the *zhu* idiophone, the yu maintained a firm position in the imperial court ritual ensemble until the early 20th century, when the ritual itself was abandoned. By the late 20th century, both instruments had been revived within the Confucian ritual. The player draws the whisk three times along the backbone to signal the conclusion of a ritual hymn. The symbolic implication of stroking the back of a tiger, as suggested in early texts, is to tame or subjugate the beast and remain alert to the possibilities of danger. The Korean *ŏ* is a related instrument.

The name *yu* also denotes a historic Chinese mouth organ.

BIBLIOGRAPHY

A.C. Moule: 'A List of the Musical and Other Sound–Producing Instruments of the Chinese', *Journal of the Royal Asiatic Society, North China Branch*, vol.39 (1908), 1–160; repr. separately (Buren, 1989)

Liu Dongsheng and others, eds.: *Zhongguo yueqi tujian* [Pictorial guide to Chinese instruments] (Ji'nan, 1992), 105 only

A. Thrasher: 'The Changing Musical Tradition of the Taipei Confucian Ritual', *CHIME Journal* (2005), nos.16–17, pp.7–33

ALAN R. THRASHER

Yua [wua, hua]. End-blown notched wooden flute or whistle found throughout northern Ghana particularly among the Builsa and Kasena Nankani peoples. It is played with drums and xylophone or alone by shepherds and hunters, sometimes for signalling or as a bird call. A modern commercial version, 12 cm long, has two fingerholes, one on either side in protrusions covered by thumb and index finger.

LAURENCE LIBIN

Yubul [yāvŭl]. Conch horn of the Yap Islands of Micronesia.

Yue. End-blown flute of the Han Chinese, used in court rituals. Pictographs from the late Shang dynasty (*c*12th century BCE) show what appears to be a small panpipe-type instrument, with bamboo pipes in a single raft bound together in the middle with fibre or cord. While disagreement exists as to whether this image represents a panpipe or two or more end-blown flutes bound together, the pictograph was ultimately equated with the character yue commonly interpreted as a panpipe. Yet, the *c*3rd-century BCE *Zhouli* text indicates that the yue is a single end-blown flute with three fingerholes; the name might simply have been transferred to an instrument of this type. The yue retained this end-blown form into the 12th century CE, when it was included in a large imperial gift to Korea. As employed nowadays in government-sponsored Confucian rituals (notably in Taiwan), the yue has become an unplayed ritual flute, a lacquered bamboo tube without notch or fingerholes, carried by young male dancers. See Tong Kin-woon: *Shang Musical Instruments* (diss., Wesleyan U., 1983); repr. in *AsM*, vol.15/1 (1983), 17–182.

ALAN R. THRASHER

Yueqin. Lute of the Han Chinese. Literally 'moon *qin*', the name is often popularly translated as 'moon lute'. The short neck is inserted into a circular resonator 36 cm in diameter and 5 cm deep, with softwood (commonly *wutong*) soundtable and back. Overall length is 60 cm. Four long tuning pegs are inserted laterally into the pegbox, and eight to 12 bamboo frets are glued to the neck and upper part of the soundtable. On traditional lutes, two double courses of silk strings are tuned a 5th apart. The instrument has a two-octave range and is played with a plectrum.

The yueqin is historically related to several Han Chinese lutes, especially the *qinqin*, *shuangqing*, and *ruanxian*. The *qinqin* ('Qin [kingdom] *qin*') has a long fretted neck, often only two or three strings (pitched about one octave lower than the yueqin), and a scalloped or 'plum blossom'-shaped resonator (about 90 cm long overall). The *shuangqing* (literally 'double clear') or *shuangqin*, known since the 18th century, resembles the *qinqin* in size, though it has four strings and an octagonal resonator. These instruments can all be traced back to the ancient *ruanxian*, which was described by different names in the literature of the Han dynasty (206 BCE–220 CE).

The yueqin (essentially a *ruanxian* with short neck) and *qinqin* (a *ruanxian* with small scalloped soundbox) remain in use. The *qinqin* is especially common in Chaozhou and Cantonese traditions of south China, and the yueqin is most frequently employed in Beijing opera ensembles. Yueqin variants are also used in accompaniment of dance songs and other genres of the Yi and other minority peoples of southwest China.

During the instrument reforms of the mid-20th century, the yueqin retained its former size, but its strings were reduced from four to three, and tuned to separate pitches for an extended range. In spite of this change,

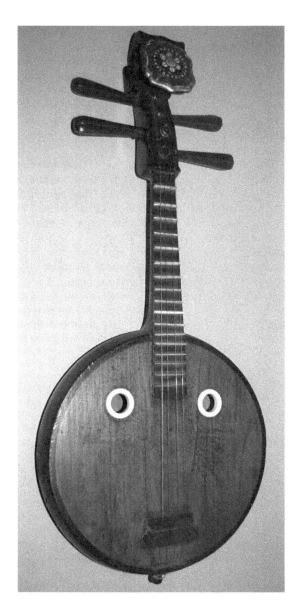

Yueqin, China; ivory rings in sound holes have been replaced with modern bone rings. (Aurelia W. Hartenberger, EdD)

the new *yueqin* has not won wide acceptance into the modern Chinese orchestra. However, the traditional *yueqin*, *qinqin*, and *shuangqing* continue to be used in regional common-practice traditions.

BIBLIOGRAPHY

A.R. Thrasher: *La-Li-Luo Dance-Songs of the Chuxiong Yi, Yunnan Province, China* (Danbury, CT, 1990), 43–51 [incl. CD]

Liu Dongsheng and others, eds.: *Zhongguo yueqi tujian* [Pictorial guide to Chinese instruments] (Ji'nan, 1992), 212–5

A.R. Thrasher and G.N.Wong: *Yueqi: Chinese Musical Instruments in Performance* (Vancouver, 2011), 73–87

ALAN R. THRASHER/GLORIA N. WONG

Yuge. Side-blown wooden horn of the Kakwa people of Uganda. It is a straight conical tube which narrows at the mouthpiece so that the tip terminates with a knob in the shape of a truncated pyramid with six sides. The instrument is about 140 cm long and 25 cm in diameter at the open end; it has a plain mouth-hole and no fingerhole. It is blown to summon people to dancing, and is played at the dance to 'make the drums sound sweet'. In the Democratic Republic of the Congo the yuge is known by the Bongo and Bwende peoples, who play it in sets of three and two respectively. See M. Trowell and K.P. Wachsmann: *Tribal Crafts of Uganda* (London, 1953), 353 only.

Yuk [jug, bas jug]. Lowest-pitched xylophone in the *kolintang* orchestra in Minahasa, North Sulawesi. The longest bar on its single row measures about 90 cm. It is normally played with a pair of padded hammers.

Yuka. Set of three single-headed drums associated with Bantu-affiliated descendants of Kongo peoples in Cuba. The largest drum is called yuka (Bantú: 'beating' or 'striking') or *caja*, the most common name for the instrument of largest dimensions in various ensembles of African provenance. The same applies to *mula* for the medium-sized drum, which initiates the rhythmic locutions of patterns and strokes (*toques*), and *cachimbo* for the smallest drum, which stabilizes the basic rhythmic pattern. The three drums are tuned to low, middle, and high tones, respectively.

Yuka drums are built by the drummers, and, since the tradition is practised only by a handful of families nowadays, a new drum might be built only to replace a deteriorated one. A drum is made from a single cedar or avocado log, which must be dried before being hollowed. Some are painted but the roughness of the wood is preserved. Skin from a cow's belly yields the ideal sound but ram and calf skin are also used. Formerly sharp sticks were used to attach the head, now nailed. In the past a tall unfinished drum might be partly buried upright with the top exposed and surrounded by posts across which ox skin was stretched before being attached. The heads were tuned by heating at a fire. Some drums have metal hoops around the body to prevent splitting, and some have tin sheets nailed to their base to avoid deterioration from contact with the ground.

Each yuka drum is played by a standing musician, with the instrument between his legs. A belt of leather, hemp, or rope attached by rings to the drum near the head can suspend it from the drummer's waist. Typical dimensions for the *caja* range from 135 cm tall with diameters of 29 cm for both the head and base, down to 99 cm tall with a head 24.5 cm in diameter and base 19 cm. The *mula* ranges from 136 tall with 31-cm head and 33-cm base, to 101 cm tall with 23-cm head and 19-cm base. The *cachimbo* ranges from 139 cm tall with 30-cm head and 26-cm base, to 100 cm tall with 22-cm head and 16-cm base.

The *caja*, which carries the improvisational role, is played with a wide variety of hand strokes. The *mula* and *cachimbo*, however, alternate hand strokes with a stick (held in the left hand for the *mula* and right hand for the *cachimbo*) that beats the body of the drum. In addition, the ensemble requires a *guataca* or another iron, such as a *cencerro*, and a pair of sticks beating the body of any of the drums, a practice referred to as 'making *coco* or *guagua*'. In the past, drummers also wore small wrist maracas called *nkembis* as an added timbric layer of shakers.

Yuka drumming can be traced to the second half of the 19th century, and, until the 1940s, was known throughout Cuba. The term *yuka* also refers to the dancing, the *toques*, and the events in which the drums participate. The set was associated with secular festivities and accompanied dancing and singing that recalled historical accounts and events from everyday life. After the societies (*cabildos*) dedicated to specific ethnolinguistic groups such as the Congos began to disappear, yuka drumming moved to the house-temples of popular syncretic religions. In addition, yuka drums joined other ensembles in patron-saint celebrations. Sets were built as recently as 1984 and perhaps later. See M.E. Vinueza González: *Instrumentos de la música folclórico-popular de Cuba*, vol.1 (Havana, 1997), 188–98.

MALENA KUSS

Yumanwusmangge. Ensemble of seven bamboo transverse flutes and one hourglass drum or *kundu*, peculiar to the southernmost Iatmul village of Aibom, Papua New Guinea. The ensemble formerly played in the ceremonial house at a feast in honour of the pottery goddess, Yumanwusmangge, but now plays on occasions of widespread famine or sickness. The flutes are arranged in three pairs playing antiphonally plus one solo player, with the drummer leading the ensemble by adopting a particular pattern from a repertory of at least 12 different rhythms. The flutes are shorter than *wabi kain* flutes (most are less than one metre long) and are without fingerholes. The flutes and drum are known by the names of ancestors and therefore remain secret to the families concerned.

GORDON D. SPEARRITT/R

Yunluo ['cloud gongs']. Set of brass gongs, of the Han Chinese. Yunluo gongs are basin-shaped, with flat faces, narrow rims turned back 90 degrees, and thin flanges extending outward. The gongs are all of the same diameter (about 8 to 9 cm) but of varying thickness, the thicker ones sounding higher pitches, the thinner lower. While numbers have varied regionally, the most common traditional pattern is of ten gongs framed in three vertical rows of three gongs, with a single gong at the top of the middle row. Smaller sets are rare, but sets of 13 or 14 gongs have been documented. The gongs are suspended vertically, each in an individual cubicle, by three cords passing through holes in its flange. They are struck with a thin beater tipped with a small cylindrical head of horn or ivory. Yunluo are pitched in different keys, following regional practice. Ten-gong instruments typically have diatonic ranges of a 10th or 11th, the latter realized by omitting one non-pentatonic pitch. A standard tuning for a set pitched in D, for example, has a diatonic range *a'* to *d'''* (with the high *c♯'''* omitted).

Traditional frames, ornately decorated on their top and bottom horizontal supports, measure about 55 cm tall by 40 cm wide, with a short handle extending from the bottom. When played with a walking ensemble in ritual ceremonies, as in funeral processions, the instrument is held by the handle. When played with a seated ensemble, as in Xi'an *guyue* music, it is supported in a stand resting on a table, where it is often paired with a matching instrument side by side.

The yunluo is mentioned in 14th-century Chinese sources by the name *yun'ao*, though visual evidence indicates it existed earlier. By the 18th century, it had become an essential melodic instrument in Buddhist and Daoist ritual ensembles throughout North China, and in several regional percussion-based ensembles, such as Sunan *chuida*, *shifan luogu*, and Xi'an *guyue*. These traditions are still performed. During the 1950s, the yunluo was redesigned for concert use: the small frames converted into large stands; the number of gongs increased to 24 and more (some sets tuned chromatically); and mallets with either hard or soft tips used for different effects. A Korean adaptation of the yunluo is the *ulla*. See LUO for bibliography.

ALAN R. THRASHER

Yunost' [Junost] (Russ.: 'youth'). Transistor-based analogue electronic organ. It was developed in 1965 in a special laboratory (established in 1964 by Vyacheslav Mescherin, founder of the Moscow Orchestra of Electromusical Instruments) at the military factory for radio-electronic devices in Murom, central Russia. The Yunost' was one of the electronic instruments that made up the V. Mescherin Band, which played dance music on Radio Moscow.

The first version, weighing about 25 kg, had a five-octave keyboard, six-octave pitch range, vibrato capability, four registers (16′, 8′, 4′, 2′), a tone-correction button, and a volume control pedal. It was based on 12 analogue top-octave oscillators with related octave dividers, covering the whole frequency range. These oscillators could be adjusted by means of 12 controls located at the rear of the instrument. Since the oscillators were unstable and always slightly out of tune, and the octave dividers produced only the square waveform, it had an easily recognizable sound. The second version (YUNOST-70), produced in 1970, was very similar to the first but added a glissando feature. The YUNOST-73 had a new design and much wider possibilities. It could produce effects of vibrato, glissando, percussion, sustain with continuous duration control, repeat with continuous control of tempo, and had a small sequencer to record a composition without a microphone. It also had a five-octave keyboard but with a musical range of eight octaves and six registers for octave synthesis. The last version (YUNOST-75), developed in 1975, was a portable version of the previous one with a wider range of effects (frequency vibrato, timbre vibrato, timbre percussion, drum and brushes imitation, and timbre glissando).

HUGH DAVIES/ANDREI SMIRNOV

Yvyra'í [ywyra'í]. Percussion sticks of the Guaraní Indians of interior and coastal Brazil, Argentina, Paraguay, and Bolivia. Also called *popyguá* or *ỹvyporá*, they are made from sticks of *guadjayvi* wood 35 to 40 cm long by 1 cm in diameter, attached to each other by vegetable fibres at one end. They are generally shaken to produce rhythmic beats and a tremolo during the singing of sacred songs. The yvyra'í have their origin in Mbyá Guaraní mythological narratives related to the sticks used by the Creator, Ñamandu Ru Etê. They are used only by males. In some villages, each man has his own instrument, which can be understood as a symbol of power. See F. Müller: 'Etnografia de los Guarani del Alto Paraná', *Steyler Missionswissenschaftliche Institut e.V.* (1989), 1–133 [trans. of 'Beiträge zür Ethnographie der Guarani-Indianer im östlichen Waldgebiet von Paraguay', *Anthropos*, vol.29 (1934), 177ff; vol.30 (1935), 151ff].

KILZA SETTI

Yzaguirre Sanz, Felix de (*d* 1736, Mexico City). Spanish organ builder working in New Spain. He was co-signatory with his brother Tiburcio (Yzaguirre) Sanz (they used their names differently for professional reasons) for the installation of the Jorge de Sesma organ in Mexico City Cathedral from 1692 to 1695. In 1698 Yzaguirre modified the organ by replacing two unspecified registers in the Great with a new Flautado de Madera and Rochela and one in the Chair organ with an Espigueta (Chimney flute); adding a mounted block in order to spread out the pipes on the chest of the Chair organ; constructing new pipes to replace those that did not work; repairing the bellows, wind conduits, windchests, the eight largest Contras, and the Corneta de ecos; and retuning. He charged 1500 pesos for the work. Yzaguirre maintained the cathedral's organs from Feb 1698 until May 1704, when he was fired for wanting too much money for another repair.

From Oct 1699 to May 1700 he repaired the organ at the Royal Convent of Jesús María in Mexico City, and later signed a contract with the Jesuits for an organ in La Profesa in Mexico City, a project that he turned over to his brother so that he could move to Puebla to build a large new organ for the cathedral there. That organ would be Yzaguirre's magnum opus. Although largely modelled on the Sesma organ for Mexico City, it differed by being a true 16′ organ with both Flautado and Bardón at 16′ pitch, Quint 5 ⅓′, and Sobre Címbala on the Great, and an 8′ Chair organ. Like the Sesma organ, this one was very innovative and, when the organist in Puebla proclaimed himself unfamiliar with many of the registers, the organists from Mexico City had to be brought to Puebla to evaluate Yzaguirre's work. Claims and counterclaims about the organ were exchanged with authorities of Puebla Cathedral and went unresolved for many years.

Yzaguirre later returned to work briefly in Mexico City Cathedral and was paid in May 1731 for three repairs to the organs. He had married in Mexico City in 1694. A son, Nicolás de Yzaguirre, became an organ builder and applied for, but was not granted, the post of organ curator at the cathedral after the completion of the Nassarre organs in 1736. Nicolás built an organ for the Convent of Jesús María in Mexico City in 1774. See E.C. Pepe: 'Innovaciones peninsulares introducidas en la Nueva España para construir órganos: Jorge de Sesma en la Catedral de México (1695) y Félix de Yzaguirre en la de Puebla (1710)', *Harmonia mundi: los instrumentos sonoros en Iberoamérica, siglos XVI al XIX*, ed. L. Enríquez (Mexico City, 2009), 261–79.

EDWARD CHARLES PEPE

Z

Zabumba [zambumba, bumbol]. Snare drum of El Salvador and Brazil. It is a double-headed cylindrical drum with a wooden body 20 to 30 cm deep and 40 to 56 cm in diameter. Zabumba is also called *bumbo, bombo, bumba, caixa grande, tambor grande,* or *Zé-Pereira,* preserving some Portuguese names. It is also known as *zambê* in Rio Grande do Norte and *alfaia* or *bombo* in the Pernambucan *maracatu* dance.

Traditionally, zabumba players also make the drums. The goatskin (or other animal skin) heads are attached by a system of hoop and cords. Squeezing or loosening the cords raises or lowers the pitch. The head can also be heated by the sun or fire to stretch and tune it.

The commercial zabumba, called *bumbo zabumba,* used in brass and military bands, has a stainless steel or zinc body, heads made of acrylic or nylon, and rim held in place by butterfly or Allen bolts. It is 15 cm deep and 16 to 22 cm in diameter. It hangs vertically in front of the player's chest from a shoulder strap (*talabarte*), with the lower-pitched head on top. The upper skin is played with one wooden drumstick (or two in the case of brass bands) called *massa* ('mass'), *maceta* or *maçaneta* ('knob'), *resposta* ('answer'), or *baqueta macia* ('soft stick') and is 20 to 45 cm long. The end of the stick is covered with a soft cloth or leather.

The handmade zabumba is used in two musical genres that are emblematic of Northeastern Brazil: the *banda de pífanos* and *baião,* though nowadays these genres may use an industrial zabumba, modified with a wooden body. The precision of the rhythm depends on the *bacalhau,* a thin drumstick about 35 cm long made of tree branches, bamboo, strands of fibre from coconut trees, or synthetic material, striking the higher-pitched head.

The word *zabumba* also refers to the ensemble *terno de zabumba,* which uses two *pífanos* or *pifes* (side-blown flutes), one zabumba, and one *tarol.*

Handmade zabumbas are used in diverse traditional performances such as the *maracatu* or *cambinda,* a dance-courtship-procession that depicts the coronation of kings, and are associated with carnivals of Pernambuco and Paraíba. They also define the steps of the *coco,* a dance with satiric, erotic, or comical texts, and accompany *congadas* or *bailados,* local dances in São Paulo.

BIBLIOGRAPHY

G.C. Peixe: 'Zabumba, orquestra nordestina', *Revista Brasileira de Folclore,* vol.10/26 (1970), 15–38

G. Béhague: *Musiques du Brésil: de la cantoria a la samba-reggae* (Paris, 1999) [incl. CD]

G.M. Dantas: *A performance musical do zabumbeiro Quartinha* (diss., U. Federal da Paraíba, 1999)

ALICE LUMI SATOMI

Zaclitrac [triquelitraque]. Portuguese *matraca,* consisting of a board holding two or three axles with several small wooden hammers on each. These hit the board when it is shaken. Children use it in some festivities, especially in the northern region.

PATRÍCIA LOPES BASTOS

Zamataba. Single-string harp of the Fang people of Gabon. It is played exclusively by women.

Zambomba [sanbomba, simbomba, ximbomba, zambumbia, eltzagor, furro]. Friction drum of Spain and the New World. In Spain, the zambomba accompanies Christmas carols. The membrane of the instrument is pierced with a stick on which the player's hand rubs up and down. The Basque *eltzagor* is made from an earthenware pot covered with a membrane through which the friction stick is inserted. The term *simbomba* is used in Catalonia, and *ximbomba* in both Catalonia and the Balearic Islands, where the instrument accompanies festive songs. In Ecuador the earthenware zambomba is played by mestizos of Pichincha province; a cane serves as the friction stick. The Guatemalan zambomba, of uncertain origin, has a fixed stick. See C.A. Coba Andrade: 'Instrumentos musicales ecuatorianos', *Sarance,* vol.7 (1979), 70–95.

JOHN M. SCHECHTER

Zambuna. Drum of the Hausa people of Nigeria.

(1) Pair of single-headed closed goblet drums of the Katsina Hausa. Both are suspended from the player's left shoulder so that they hang almost horizontally at waist level. He beats them with the fingers of his left hand and a stick in the right hand. The drums are used for the chief of Kurfi village, in whose ownership they are vested; for the performance of praise epithets, which implies that they are differently pitched so as to reproduce word pitch patterns as well as syllabic rhythms, and to accompany singing. See D.W. Ames and A.V. King: *Glossary of Hausa Music and Its Social Contexts* (Evanston, IL, 1971), 39 only.

(2) Name for the *tabshi* kettledrum.

Zamonga. Whistle of the Sango people in the northern Democratic Republic of the Congo. The cylindro-conical wooden tube is typically about 38 cm long and is partly covered with animal skin. See J.-S. Laurenty: *Systématique des aérophones de l'Afrique centrale* (Tervuren, 1974), 180.

FERDINAND J. DE HEN

Zampogna [sampogna]. Italian term for bagpipe. The instrument, characteristic of southern Italy, Sicily, and Malta, is mouthblown; it has two divergent chanters (for separate hands) and two or three drones inserted in the same stock as the chanters. In the Marches, drones might be absent. The bag is traditionally made of goat- or sheepskin turned inside out. The zampogna is mainly played with the *piffaro* and often with the tambourine, but in eastern Sicily and Calabria it is played solo, with another zampogna, or with zampogna and tambourine. The zampogna is reputedly the only bagpipe having all conical pipes with double reeds, sometimes nowadays made from plastic. The pipes and stock are typically made of olive or fruitwood. The chanters are tuned and positioned according to regional tradition, typically with the soprano chanter for the right hand and the bass for the left. Related bagpipes with single reeds include the *surdullina* of Catanzaro and Cosenza, and the *ciaramella* (*ciaramedda*) of Southern Calabria and Messina and Catania in Sicily. The Museo della Zampogna is located in Scapoli, Molise.

Zampoña. Generic Spanish term used by mestizos for Andean panpipes. The zampoña of Gral, Bilbao Province, Potosí Department, on the Bolivian Altiplano, has its pipes ranked in double rows and is played in pairs; one having two ranks with eight pipes in each, and the other two ranks with seven pipes in each. One rank in each linked pair is closed. The tubes of the second rank are open and cut, at an angle, to half the length of the closed tubes; they sound two octaves higher. The open pipes sound indirectly when the closed pipes are blown and amplify the sonority. Zampoñas elsewhere may have the open tubes the same length as the matching closed pipes, producing notes one octave higher. The ensemble that performs *wayñus* (dance songs) at the fiesta of Santiago (July 25) in Gral includes two sizes of panpipes, a pair called *sanja* and another called *liku*. See M.P. Baumann: 'Music of the Indios in Bolivia's Andean Highlands (Survey)', *The World of Music*, vol.25/2 (1982), 80–96.

Zampoña is also the Spanish term for bagpipe.

JOHN M. SCHECHTER/R

Zanetto [Joannetto] **da Montichiaro** (Micheli) [de Michaelis] (*b* Roma de Monteclaro', Italy, 1489–90; *d* Brescia, Italy, 26 April 1560–12 Aug 1561). Italian viol and violin maker. His instruments are supposed to be the earliest extant examples of the Brescian school. G.M. Lanfranco (*Scintille di musica*, Brescia, 1533) praised the work of 'Zanetto Montechiaro'. He is variously recorded in Brescian city records from 1527 as 'Joannettus de li violettis', 'magister a liriibus', 'magister a violonis et violis', and 'di liuti'. He was excused

Zampogna, Calabria, Italy, late 18th or 19th century. (Edinburgh University Collection of Historic Musical Instruments (1707))

from duty in the register of night guards of 1549–50 because he had reached the age of 60. A six-string viol with its apparently original label 'Zanetto in Bressa' (in *B.B.mim*) shows its maker to have been an excellent designer and craftsman. A smaller viol, from Bisiach (in *US.V.n*), also has a Zanetto label. Several other instruments are attributed to him. The authenticity and original forms of all these instruments demand further investigation; nevertheless, Zanetto appears to be very important in the early history of the violin. He is the earliest violin maker about whom sufficient documentation exists to draw a picture, however tentative, of his life and work.

His son, Peregrino [Pellegrino] Micheli (*b* Brescia, Italy, *c*1520; *d* Brescia, Italy, 1606–20 July 1609), was also a fine maker. He is recorded as a maker of 'viole, lire, cittare, lauti et altri instrumenti'. A tenor viola with the label 'Peregrino f[ilius] q[uondam] m[agistro] Zanetto' in Brescia is in the National Music Museum, Vermillion, South Dakota, and a bass viol with a carved scroll and an unusual body shape (in *F.P.cm*) is attributed to him. His three sons, Giovanni (*b c*1562; *d* after 1619), Battista (*b c*1568; *d* before 1615), and Francesco (1579–1615), worked with him.

BIBLIOGRAPHY

F. Dassenno and U. Ravasio: *Gasparo da Salò e la liuteria bresciana tra Rinascimento e Barocco* (Brescia, 1990)

U. Ravasio: 'Vecchio e nuovo nella ricerca documentaria su Gasparo da Salò e la liuteria bresciana', *Liuteria e musica strumentale a Brescia tra Cinque e Seicento: Salò 1990*, ed. M. Bizzarini and R. Cafiero (Brescia, 1992), 25–43

K. Moens: 'Problems of Authenticity in Sixteenth–Century Italian Viols and the Brussels Collection', *The Italian Viola da Gamba: Proceedings of the International Symposium on the Italian Viola da Gamba: Magnano 2000*, ed. S. Orlando (Solignac and Turin, 2002), 97–114

CHARLES BEARE/UGO RAVASIO/R

Zanfona [chanfona, zanfonia, sanfonha, sanfona]. Hurdy-gurdy of Spain, formerly used for example in Pontevedra province, Galicia. Certain types were used to accompany the singing of romances. In Catalonia the instrument is known as *viola de roda* and in parts of Castille as *gaita de pobre*.

MAURICIO MOLINA

Zang. Finger cymbals of central Asia. They are documented from the Sassanid Empire (224–651 CE). The related name *zanj* is used for cymbals in Iraq. In Uzbekistan *zang* denotes a wrist or ankle bracelet with small brass or copper pellet bells, worn by dancing girls. *Zang-i kaftar* ('dove bells') are small metal pellet bells of northern Afghanistan; they are worn on the knuckles of lute players to accentuate rhythmic patterns. *Zangak* is a medieval Armenian name for a bell; the oldest bronze examples excavated in Armenia date from the middle of the 2nd millennium BCE.

Zanj [ṣandj]. Term used for cymbals in Iraq. Zanj are made of brass or bronze, variable in size, and with two small holes in the dome for the holding strap. They are used in the army, church, and for religious processions of all sorts. The name can also be used for finger cymbals, though other names such as *tchumpāra* or *tcharpālāt* are more common for these smaller instruments, which measure only 4 to 5 cm in diameter. See S.Q. Hassan: *Les Instruments de musique en Irak et leur rôle dans la société traditionnelle* (Paris, 1980), 19–21.

JEREMY MONTAGU

Zanoli, Giacomo (*fl c*1737–61). Italian violin maker. He probably studied with his father, Giovanni Battista (Johannes Baptista) Zanoli, and left his hometown of Verona to work in Padua (a cello made there, his earliest known instrument, is dated 1737) and Venice (where he registered for jury duty in 1747, and where a brother was reportedly a bass singer in the choir of San Marco). After his father's death he returned to Verona and took over his workshop, the only one of note in that city. He was by no means an innovatory maker, his violins generally following classical Italian patterns (especially in his Venetian-oriented cellos) but with Germanic influence in their rather square arching, deeply curved waist, upright soundholes of Tyyrolean style, and walnut linings. His long pegboxes and large, tight scrolls are distinctive. While the table wood is invariably excellent, Zanoli often used rather ordinary Italian maple for the backs. Not all his works are of equal merit but his better instruments are varnished an attractive light golden orange-brown or red-brown. See R. Vannes: *Essai d'un dictionnaire universel des luthiers* (Paris, 1932, 2/1951/*R*1972 as *Dictionnaire universel des luthiers* and *R*1981 incl. suppl. 1959).

JAAK LIIVOJA-LORIUS/R

Zapateado. Form of foot percussion. It involves rapid stamping and tapping of the heels and toes (shod in a flamenco shoe) in a rhythmic fashion associated with flamenco. The feet are relaxed and most of the work is done by the lower leg, which initiates the movement with a backswing of the foot by bending the knee almost 90 degrees off the floor before dropping the foot down adjacent to the instep of the standing foot. Digs and stamps allow the dancer forward and lateral movement. Digs are executed with a backswing of the foot landing on ball of the foot slightly behind the standing foot. The stamp (*golpe*) also begins with a backswing, landing with forward movement as the heel strikes the floor. Modern flamenco shoes (*zapatos* for women and *botas* for men) have thick soles, elevated heels, and small tacks on both the toe and heel. Female dancers face the added challenge of executing rapid footwork while wearing a heavy dress with a long train (*bata de cola*) that has to be kicked out of the dancer's path.

SALLY SANFORD

Zapotecano. Marimba of Central America. Popular in both mestizo and indigenous cultures since the 19th century, it is found from southern Mexico south through Nicaragua and is a predecessor of the modern Mexican-Guatemalan marimba. It is distinguished from the modern marimba by its small size (rarely more than three octaves) and the use of gourds as resonators for the bars (*claves*). The bars are made from local hardwoods such as *hormigo* (*Triplaris surinamensis*) or *cocobolo*

(*Dalbergia retusa*). Beeswax is adhered on the underside of the bars to tune them and is also used to secure the pig-intestine membrane (mirliton) that covers a hole near the bottom of each resonator.

J. RICHARD HAEFER

Żaqq. Maltese mouth-blown bagpipe. The bag is traditionally made of calf, goat, or dog skin, with the hair exposed. The blowpipe (*mserka*), made of cane or rubber and without a valve, is tied into a foreleg. The double chanter (*saqqafa*), inserted into the neck, has two downcut idioglot single reeds. The cane pipes, the left one having five fingerholes and the right having one fingerhole, are set into a cane yoke. The bell is usually a decorated ox horn with a serrated rim.

The żaqq is traditionally played at Christmas, Carnival, and *L-Imnarja*, the feast day of St Peter and St Paul, celebrating the end of harvest. The player uses a series of motifs and variations repeated in various combinations. Rhythmic accompaniment is provided by the *tanbur* (tambourine) and in Carnival by the *rabbâba* or *żafżafa* (friction drum).

BIBLIOGRAPHY

J.K. Partridge and F. Jeal: 'The Maltese *żaqq*', *GSJ*, vol.30 (1977), 112–44

A. Borg-Cardona: 'Making the Maltese *żaqq* bag', *Chanter* (Winter 2005), 22–8

SYLVIA MOORE/ANNA BORG-CARDONA

Zarabanda. Among the Maya of Guatemala and Chiapas, Mexico, the word may denote instrument ensembles, musical genres of probable Spanish origin, or particular music events. As a string ensemble it may include one or more three- or four-string *rabels* or violins, some rudely constructed of half a calabash, or of wood with deerskin sides, and played with loose horsehair bows; one or more six-string guitars or five-string *guitarrillos* or *tiples*; the now obsolescent *bandurria*, *bandola*, or *bandolín*; and an *arpa* (diatonic frame harp), often beaten with a padded stick by a musician who alternately beats a snare drum. To this ensemble might be added an *adufe* (frame drum) or an accordion. Among the Q'eqchi', the zarabanda mostly includes a violin, a *guitarrilla*, and a harp whose soundbox is additionally beaten by hand or with a drumstick.

LINDA L. O'BRIEN-ROTHE/ANDRÉS AMADO

Zarb [dombak, tombak]. Goblet drum of Iran, known since the early 19th century. It is used in entertainment music and in some folk traditions (e.g. those of Lorestān), and is the only percussion instrument of Iranian art music. The zarb is made from a single block of walnut or mulberry wood, turned and hollowed with a skin glued to the upper end. It is 40 to 45 cm tall and 20 to 28 cm in diameter. Many examples are extensively decorated with mother-of-pearl segments set into wax or other materials on the body. It was used originally as an accompanying instrument, but its technique was considerably developed by the virtuoso Hossein

Teherāni (1911–76), who extended the range of beating methods and sonorities and exploited its potential as a solo instrument. Iranian gymnasiums (*zurkhāne*: 'house of force') use an earthenware zarb, about 70 cm in diameter, to provide a rhythmic background for exercises. Its powerful tone and beating technique distinguish it from its classical counterpart. The zarb can be likened to the Afghan *zirbaghali*, which however differs in playing technique.

BIBLIOGRAPHY

N. Caron and D. Safvate: *Iran: les traditions musicales* (Paris, 1966)

J. During: *La musique iranienne: tradition et evolution* (Paris, 1984)

JEAN DURING

Zare. Ankle rattle of the Bisa people of Burkina Faso. It is a chain of vessel rattles, made from woven reed leaves containing seeds, which is wound four or five times around the ankle. It is used for dances, such as the popular *diassa* dance.

Zari. Metal ring clappers used by the Ada people in Niger and by the Zamfara Hausa and Kebbi in Nigeria. A circular iron tube, formed into an open ring about 30 cm in diameter, is held in the left hand and struck by a smaller ring about 15 cm in diameter held in the right. The rings are not quite closed and one end of the larger is expanded by forging it into an open bell shape; the smaller is also expanded but only into 'open lips' shape. Among the Ada the zari is used by singers specializing in blacksmithing; the songs provide their own accompaniment which, since each person plays a set rhythm, is polyrhythmic. See K. Krieger: 'Musikinstrumente der Hausa', *Baessler-Archiv*, new ser., vol.16 (1968), 373–430, esp. 375.

Zarlino, Gioseffo [Gioseffe] (*b* Chioggia, Italy, ?31 Jan 1517; *d* Venice, Italy, 4 Feb 1590). Italian theorist and composer. His book *Le istitutioni harmoniche* (1558) is especially important for its discussion of intervals and tuning. Zarlino received his early education among the Franciscans. He is recorded at Chioggia Cathedral as a singer in July 1536 and as an organist in 1539–40. He must have been ordained by 1540, because on 27 April he was elected 'capellano' and *mansionario* of the Scuola di S Francesco, Chioggia. He moved to Venice in 1541 and became a pupil of Willaert. He was appointed *maestro di cappella* of S Marco, Venice, on 5 July 1565 and held this post until his death. Among his pupils were Claudio Merulo, Giovanni Croce, Girolamo Diruta, Vincenzo Galilei, and Giovanni Maria Artusi.

Le istitutioni harmoniche united speculative theory with the practice of composition. The composer must not be content to master his craft; he should know the reason for what he does, and this can be discovered through an alliance of the rational and sensory faculties. The first two parts (they are designated 'books' in the 1573 edition) present the traditional curriculum of *musica theorica* from a fresh viewpoint. In part 1 Zarlino reviews the philosophical, cosmological, and mathematical basis of music. Part 2 sets forth the Greek tonal system and supplants it with a modern theory of consonances and tuning. Zarlino synthesized critically a vast compendium on music, philosophy, theology, mathematics, and classical history and literature.

Having observed, like Ramis de Pareia, Gaffurius, Spataro, and Lodovico Fogliano before him, that 3rds and 6ths were not consonant in the ratios handed down by Pythagorean theory, he sought a system that would permit sweet-sounding imperfect consonances. The Pythagoreans had limited the class of intervals they called consonant to those produced by the first four divisions of a string: the octave, 2:1; 5th, 3:2; 4th, 4:3; octave plus 5th, 3:1; and double octave, 4:1. Zarlino extended the upper limit to the divisions of the string into two, three, four, five, and six equal segments. Thus the number six, 'numero senario', epitomized the formal cause—the 'sonorous number' ('numero sonoro')—that generated consonances out of the 'sounding body' ('corpo sonoro'). The elevation of the determinant of consonance from four to six permitted the admission of several more intervals: the major 3rd, 5:4; the minor 3rd, 6:5; and the major 6th, 5:3. The minor 6th, 8:5, which remained outside this sanctuary, had to be rationalized as the joining of a perfect 4th and a minor 3rd.

Before the newly gained consonances were legitimately practicable, a tuning that yielded them consistently had to be devised. The syntonic diatonic, which Ptolemy had praised (as Zarlino learned from Gaffurius) because its tetrachord was made up entirely of superparticular ratios (descending 9:10, 8:9, 15:16), fitted Zarlino's needs, and it could be adapted to the Western ascending scale (pt 2, 39), from *C* to *c*: 9:8, 10:9, 16:15, 9:8, 10:9, 9:8, 16:15. This scale lacked the symmetry of the two descending disjunct tetrachords of the Greeks, as in *e* to *E*, but for Zarlino it had the overriding virtue of containing, reduced to an octave, the consonances as generated by the first six divisions of the string in the order of the sonorous numbers—octave, 5th, 4th, major 3rd, minor 3rd.

Zarlino acknowledged that the numerical criteria that he established in parts 1 and 2 for the tuning of the consonances did not apply to instrumental music, which employed artificial tunings made necessary by the imperfection of instruments. But in the natural medium of the voice it was possible, he maintained, to realize all the inherent perfection of harmony. His theoretical foundations had a brief life, however. Almost immediately the scientist Giovanni Battista Benedetti (in his *Diversarum speculationum*, 1585) demonstrated mathematically that a choir singing consistently according to the intervals of the syntonic diatonic would deviate progressively further and further from the starting pitch. Galilei in his *Dialogo* of 1581 raised similar objections and also pointed out numerous instances in which Zarlino had misunderstood his ancient sources. Zarlino replied at great length in his *Sopplimenti musicali* (1588), in which he displayed much greater penetration into the ancient authors, particularly Aristoxenus and Ptolemy, who had been published in 1562 in a

Latin translation by Gogava, than in *Le istitutioni harmoniche*; but he failed to refute Galilei's valid criticisms.

For discussion of Zarlino's music, and fuller bibliography, see *GMO*.

WRITINGS
(selective list)
Le istitutioni harmoniche (Venice, 1558/*R*, 3/1573/*R*; Eng. trans. of pt 3, 1968/*R*, as *The Art of Counterpoint*; Eng. trans. of pt 4, 1983, as *On the Modes*)
Dimostrationi harmoniche (Venice, 1571/*R*)
Sopplimenti musicali (Venice, 1588/*R*)

BIBLIOGRAPHY
C.V. Palisca: 'Scientific Empiricism in Musical Thought', *Seventeenth-Century Science and the Arts*, ed. H.H. Rhys and others (Princeton, NJ, 1961), 91–137; repr. with pref. note in *Studies in the History of Italian Music and Music Theory* (Oxford, 1994/*R*2001), 200–35
D.P. Walker: 'Some Aspects of the Musical Theory of Vincenzo Galilei and Galileo Galilei', *PRMA*, vol.100 (1973–4), 33–47; repr. in *Studies in Musical Science in the Late Renaissance* (London, 1978), 14–26
P. Barbieri: *Acustica, accordatura e temperamento nell'Illuminismo veneto* (Rome, 1987)
R. Airoldi: *La teoria del temperamento nell'età di Gioseffo Zarlino* (Cremona, 1989)
M. Lindley: 'Zarlino's 2/7-Comma Meantone Temperament', *Music in Performance and Society: Essays in Honor of Roland Jackson*, ed. M. Cole and J. Koegel (Warren, MI, 1997), 179–94

CLAUDE V. PALISCA/R

Zawzaya. Oblique end-blown rim-flute of Mauritania. It is made from an acacia root and has up to six fingerholes. Shepherds use it to imitate the cries of animals, give signals, and tell stories.

Zech, Jacob (*b* Bad Dürkheim, Germany, 25 July 1832; *d* San Francisco, CA, 13 Sept 1889). American piano maker, of German origin. After the death of his father, Franz Phillip Zech (1789–1849), a piano maker with whom Jacob studied, he went to New York and worked for five years at Nunns & Clark and Steinway. In May 1856 he moved to San Francisco, where he began by repairing pianos, and by March 1857, had built his first instrument. The following September two square pianos of his manufacture were exhibited at the Mechanics Institute Fair. In 1860 he opened a small factory; six years later he moved to a larger one employing two workmen. By 1867 he had built 494 instruments, including concert grands. Successes at other California exhibitions followed, including a gold medal at the California State Agricultural Society fair in 1870, but competition from eastern makers forced him out of business in the 1870s, although on 4 April 1876 he patented (no.175,813) an improved double-bearing agraffe plate; later that same year he was in Reno, Nevada, seeking orders. He was later accused of transferring assets to his brother-in-law in order to defraud creditors. A seven-octave square of his, serial no.587, was donated to the Society of California Pioneers in 2011.

Jacob's brother, Frederick Zech Sr (1837–1905), was also a piano maker, who went to San Francisco from Philadelphia to work for his brother. Between 1862 and 1864 he ran his own manufactory but was later employed at other piano companies, including his brother's; he specialized in tuning and repairs. See *Daily*

Evening Bulletin (San Francisco, CA, 25 March 1857), 3 only; (7 April 1860), 1 only; (30 June 1863), 3 only; (16 July 1870), 4 only.

Zegari. Rare musical bow of western Mauritania.

Zei. Whistle of the Mamvu people in the Uele region, Democratic Republic of the Congo. The wooden body, typically about 16 cm long, has a slender conical bore. See J.-S. Laurenty: *Systématique des aérophones de l'Afrique centrale* (Tervuren, 1974), 156.

FERDINAND J. DE HEN

Zell [Zelle], Christian (*b* ?1683; bur. Hamburg, Germany, 13 April 1763). German harpsichord maker. The year of his birth is conjectured from an entry in the register of deaths and burials at the Jacobikirche in Hamburg stating that he was 79 and a half when he died. He was probably a pupil of Michael Mietke. He is first mentioned in 1722 in the register of citizens of Hamburg. On 1 Sept of that year he married the widow of the instrument maker Carl Conrad(t) Fleischer (1680–1721/2), whose workshop near the old Gänsemarkt opera house he took over. There were three children of the marriage, all with godparents from Hamburg families of musicians. Three surviving Zell harpsichords are known: an elaborate 1728 double-manual (at *D.H.km*; 8′8′4′, harp stop, *F′–d‴*); a 1737 single-manual (at *E.B.mi*; 8′8′4′, *C/E–c‴*); and a 1741 single-manual (8′8′4′, *C–d‴*) owned by the Ostfriesische Landschaft in Aurich, Germany. The height of the original stand of the last indicates it was played by a standing player. A harpsichord lid acquired in 1992 by a private collector in Hamburg and showing scenes from Ovid's *Metamorphoses* is, from its pictorial composition and choice of subject, as likely to have come from the Hamburg workshops of Hieronymus Albrecht Hass and his son Johann Adolph as from that of Zell.

Zell harpsichords were prized for their rich decoration, with lacquered chinoiserie in the typical Hamburg style, and above all for their matchless tone. The 1728 harpsichord has been copied by modern builders including Alberto Colzani, Robert Goble, John Lyon, Jack Peters, and Craig Tomlinson.

BIBLIOGRAPHY
M. Skowroneck: 'Das Cembalo von Christian Zell, Hamburg 1728, und seine Restaurierung', *Organ Yearbook*, vol.5 (1974), 79–87
H. Vogel: 'Das Cembalo von Christian Zell aus dem Besitz der Ostfriesischen Landschaft', *Ostfriesland: Zeitschrift für Kultur, Wirtschaft und Verkehr* (1978), no.2, pp.27–9 [with illustration]
D. Krickeberg and H. Rase: 'Beiträge zur Kenntnis des mittel– und norddeutschen Cembalobaus um 1700', *Studia organologica: Festschrift für John Henry van der Meer*, ed. F. Hellwig (Tutzing, 1987), 285–310
C. Brink and W. Hornbostel, eds.: *Pegasus und die Künste*, Museum für Kunst und Gewerbe, Hamburg, 8 April–31 May 1993 (Munich, 1993), 228 only [exhibition catalogue]

ALEXANDER PILIPCZUK/R

Zenidaiko. Name of various Japanese percussion instruments whose sound is partly or wholly generated by coins strung on a wire (*zeni*: 'coin'; *daiko/taiko*: generic term for drums). The coins, of a traditional type with a hole in the centre (metal washers can also be used), rattle together when the instrument is shaken or struck. Despite the derivation of the name the two best-known examples of zenidaiko are not drums: one is a small wooden ring, with two wires stretched at right angles across its diameter and coins strung on these wires, shaken as a pair by dancers; the other is a bamboo tube about 4 cm across and 25 to 30 cm long, with similar wires inside and also played in pairs.

DAVID W. HUGHES

Zenti, Girolamo [Zentis, Hieronymus de] (*b* Viterbo, Italy, ?1609–11; *d* Paris, France, 1666/7). Italian maker of harpsichords, spinets, and organs. His first recorded commission is from 1635, and in 1641 he was appointed to maintain Pope Urban VIII's keyboard instrument collection. Zenti was perhaps the best-known Italian keyboard maker of his day. His craftsmanship is neat, although not elaborate, but his extensive employment at the royal courts in Stockholm (1652–6), Paris (1660–*c*1662), and England (1664) testifies to the regard of his contemporaries for his instruments. He was in Paris again in 1666 and died there sometime before Easter the following year. It seems that during Zenti's periods abroad his wife oversaw his workshop in Rome, with various assistants.

No organ by Zenti survives. In 1660 he was commissioned by Camillo Pamphili to build the new organ of S Agnese in Navona, Rome, but he never executed the work, having taken up the appointment to the French court. The inventory of instruments belonging to Ferdinando de' Medici in Florence in 1700 lists six harpsichords and spinets by Zenti, dating three of them: 1653 (made in Stockholm), 1656, and 1658 (both made in Rome). A harpsichord (now in *D.M.dm*) bearing a faked Cristofori inscription has been attributed to Zenti and is probably identical with the instrument of 1658 in the Medici inventory. Only five of the surviving signed instruments are thought to be authentic: a bentside spinet (in *B.B.mim*, 1631), an undated trapezoidal octave spinet in ebony (in *US. NY.mma*), and three harpsichords made in 1656 (in *B.B.mim*), 1666 (in *US.NY.mma*), and 1668 (in *F.P.cm*). The last of these was apparently finished in Paris by Zenti's workshop after his death, and is in most respects a French rather than an Italian harpsichord. A harpsichord formerly attributed to Zenti (in *D.LE.u*), originally with split sharps, was made by Querci. It is probable that Zenti was the first to build bentside spinets, the whereabouts of a possible earlier example by the French maker Montazeau, reportedly dated 1632, being unknown.

BIBLIOGRAPHY
E. Ripin: 'The Surviving Oeuvre of Girolamo Zenti', *Metropolitan Museum Journal*, vol.7 (1973), 71–87
D. Wraight: *The Stringing of Italian Keyboard Instruments, c1500–c1650* (diss., Queen's U. of Belfast, 1997), pt 2, 317–21
L. Purchiaroni: 'Girolamo Zenti and Giovanni Battista Boni da Cortona: an unsuspected relationship', *GSJ*, vol.60 (2007), 63–9

EDWIN M. RIPIN/DENZIL WRAIGHT

Zeze [zenze, nzenze, dzendze, lunzenze, sese, etc.]. Stick zither widely distributed throughout the Democratic Republic of the Congo. The stick is a solid bar of wood 55 to 65 cm long and 2 to 3 cm wide throughout most of its length. Both ends of the bar terminate in a small knob to which the strings, of plant fibre, are attached. Three cylindrical 'frets' protrude on both sides of the stick. The U-shaped bridge is usually made of a feather quill. One or more drone strings pass beside the frets. A resonator made of two superposed calabash halves, or seldom a single half-calabash shell, is attached near one end; it is affixed to the underside of the bar by means of a small part-calabash collar and a cord. The zither produces four notes (open string and one note from each of the three frets) together with the drone(s). Accounts of the method of performance vary. Among the Shi the zither is held to the left so that the frets can be stopped with the fingers of the left hand while the thumb activates the drone string and the fingers of the right hand stroke the melody string. The half-calabash is usually placed on the player's chest and opened or closed in the same way as the resonator of a musical bow. Other accounts give the position as inverted with the calabash opposite the player's mouth so that he appears to sing into it. The zither accompanies songs and dances; among the Ngombe it is used only on the same occasions as the lamellaphone. While the name *zeze* or a variant is generally used in the northern and eastern DRC, the zither is known by many different local names elsewhere, for example *isusu*, *djedji* (*idjendje*), *bongele* (*bonguele*, *bongwele* among the Ngando and Mongo), *ifata*, *ikole*, *keke*, *akende*, *oda*, *djinge*, *mongele*, and *kinanda*.

The name *zeze* also denotes a double-headed cylindro-conical drum (34 cm long) with laced heads, of the Bati people of the DRC.

BIBLIOGRAPHY

G. Knosp: *Enquête sur la vie musicale au Congo belge, 1934–1935* (Tervuren, 1968)

J.-S. Laurenty: *L'Organologie du Zaïre*, vol.4 (Tervuren, 1997), 29–33

K.A. GOURLAY/FERDINAND J. DE HEN

Zhaleyka [rozhok]. Generic term for folk clarinets or hornpipes found throughout Belarus and Russia under several specific names (e.g. *pishchik*, *charotka*, and *dudka*). Each name reflects certain essential characteristics of the instrument—acoustical, structural, functional, etc. The word *zhaleyka* is derived from Slavonic *zhal* ('sad, sorrowful, mournful'), also the root of *zhalnik* ('a grave'). Inhabitants of northern Belarus remember that the *zhaleyka* could be heard during burial ceremonies in the 1930s. The term *golos* ('voice') as applied to Belarusian instruments is related to the belief that some instruments arose from trees growing on the graves of murdered children. The soul and voice of the child were thought to move first into a sacred tree, then into the instruments made from its wood. Thus, an instrument with an extraordinary and distinctive voice is an integral feature of ancient Belarusian burial rituals. The types of zhaleyka differ in shape, size (typically 10 to 36 cm long), material (e.g. wood, straw, goose quill, reed,

horn), construction, and the presence or absence of fingerholes (normally four to 12) and a bell (often of birch bark, horn, or wood). Generally it has an idioglot reed and a loud, shrill sound with a distinct nasal undertone. Typically it plays a diatonic scale spanning a 6th or 7th beginning from g'.

The Russian instrument, also known as *bryolka*, can be made of willow or elder, 15 cm long, with a bell (*rastrub*) of cow horn or birch bark. It has three to seven fingerholes. Zhaleyki with one pipe are found in the north, double ones in southern regions. The Yaroslav zhaleyka has only two fingerholes, producing a scale of four whole tones.

The repertory of folk clarinettists playing solo mainly for their own amusement was mostly limited to imitations of bird songs, improvisations, and melodies of ritual and secular songs. When played in ensembles with bagpipe, violin, dulcimer, and accordion, the zhalejka's repertory included dance music; it was also played for children's games. During the 20th century Belarusian folk clarinets were largely replaced by standard modern clarinets, influenced tonally by the traditional instruments.

INNA D. NAZINA

Zheng. Zither of China. It is one of the principal Chinese zithers, and the parent instrument of the East Asian long zither family. The zheng has a flat bottom and a convex soundbox over which the strings are stretched. Sizes vary from 120 to 170 cm long and 20 to 35 cm wide. The soundboard is made of *wutong* wood (*Firmiana platanifolia*), with hardwood sides and bottom, usually of red sandalwood, rosewood, or sometimes boxwood. The strings were traditionally made of silk but nowadays commonly of steel wound with nylon. Each string is secured on a pin at one end of the instrument and runs over a movable bridge to a tuning peg at the other end. The bridges are usually made of wood, although occasionally of bone or synthetic materials. Placed in a diagonal row, the bridges divide the strings into two sections, plucked to the (player's) right and ornamented with pitch modifications to the left.

The zheng has a history dating back more than 2500 years. The Chinese character for zheng has two portions: *zhu*, the radical for 'bamboo', above, and zheng, the icon for 'fight', below. The 2nd-century CE dictionary *Shuowen jiezi* states: 'The zheng has plucked strings and a bamboo body. [Its music onomatopoeically] sounds "zheng"'. This suggests that the name is a phonetic complex: the bamboo radical refers to the material used to construct the instrument during its early development, while zheng, the lower portion, is a representation of its sound when played. However, the lower portion 'zheng', kindled legends of a fight between two people over a 25-string *se* zither that led to splitting the instrument in half, thus creating both a 12-string and 13-string zheng.

The *Fengsu Tongyi*, another 2nd-century CE document, indicates that the *zheng* had five strings, whereas a 3rd-century CE poetic essay *Zhengfu xu* describes it

Zheng, South China, probably 19th century. (Edinburgh University Collection of Historic Musical Instruments (447))

as follows: 'Its upper part is convex like the vault of heaven; its bottom flat like the earth; its inside is hollow to accommodate the six points of the compass, and its 12 strings with their bridges symbolize the 12 months of the year'. Thus by this period, the number of strings had already increased to 12.

Traditional Chinese scholarship proposed that the zheng was invented by Meng Tian, a Qin general, in the north-central state of Qin about the 3rd century BCE. In the 1970s, however, several 12- and 13-string zithers, possibly zheng, dating to the 6th century BCE were unearthed in Guangxi and Jiangxi provinces in the south, thus challenging traditional theories. Conceivably, the Southeast Asian half-tube bamboo zither was the prototype of the zheng.

Zheng performance was first documented in the *Shiji* ('Records of the Historian', *c*109 BCE): '[People of the Qin state, now Shaanxi province] beat clay drums [and] earthen jars, play zheng [and] slap their thighs to accompany songs. This is the true music of [the state of] Qin'.

During the Han dynasty, the zheng was part of a small string and wind ensemble that performed *xianghe daqu* ('great harmonious suite'), a popular entertainment genre, while conversely, solo performances on the *zheng* became a tool for self-cultivation among literati. In the Sui, Tang, and Song dynasties (581–1279), sophisticated performance techniques and compositions for solo zheng were further developed. Concurrently, it was utilized in professional court ensembles performing *yanyue*, music for banquets and other non-ritual court activities. The 12-string zheng was included in the *qingshang yue* (pure music) ensemble, which performed older Han Chinese music, including the *xianghe daqu*, while the more popular 13-string version was used in non-Han genres. The image of the zheng played by young women from this period became a symbol of beauty in poetry, literature, and visual art.

From the 17th to 19th centuries the number of strings increased to 16. By the mid-20th century, the 21-string *zheng* had become standard. Earlier types are still used by some traditional musicians, especially in rural regions, along the southeastern coast of mainland China, and in Taiwan.

The open strings are traditionally tuned to an anhemitonic pentatonic scale, usually in either the key of D or G, with the lowest string tuned to D. By moving specific bridges the key can be transposed. Since the 1950s, various types of the zheng have been constructed to

accommodate diatonic and chromatic tunings, as well as key-changes, notably a 44-string diatonic pedal *zheng* (1972), a 49-string chromatic 'butterfly zheng' (1978), and a 'multi-scale' zheng (2007) that includes a separate set of 16 strings and bridges added on the left side of the elongated soundboard of a 21-string zheng to allow for two separate tunings simultaneously.

Historically, the right end of the zheng was placed on the performer's knees, whereas it is now played on a table or a pair of stands. The technique used in playing is twofold. Traditionally the right hand plucks the strings with fingernails (either real or simulated), producing single notes or octaves. The left hand depresses and releases the strings for ornamentation, such as vibrato, portamento, and pitch alterations. In modern practice the right-hand technique has greatly expanded to include chords, tremolo on single or multiple notes, and rapid plucking with the thumb and three fingers, known as *kuaisu zhixu* ('fast finger patterns'). The left hand can also join in plucking on the right side of the bridges to create accompaniment and counterpoint.

The earliest known zheng notation is preserved in the 12th-century Japanese manuscript *Jinchi yoroku*, which, together with signs for fingering movements, employs 13 Chinese characters and numbers to represent the 13 strings of the instrument. This is believed to be Chinese zheng notation used in the Tang dynasty. At least from the Qing dynasty, the *gongche* system of notation, which uses Chinese characters to denote a kind of *solfeggio*, was widely used for zheng music. Chaozhou music also utilizes *ersi pu* ('2–4 notation'), distinguished by its employment of seven numbers and metrical symbols. Since the early 20th century, cipher notation has become the standard, although Western staff notation is also used by some conservatory-trained musicians.

BIBLIOGRAPHY

R.H. van Gulik: 'A Brief Note on the Cheng, the Chinese Small Cither', *Tōyō ongaku kenkyū*, vol.9 (1951), 10–25

Hayashi Kenzō: *Dongya yue qi kao* [Study of East Asian musical instruments] (Beijing, 1962/*R*), 165–93

Cao Zheng: 'A Discussion of the History of the Gu Zheng', *AsM*, vol.9/2 (1983), 1–16

L. Rault-Leyrat: *Comme un vol d'oies sauvages: la cithare chinoise* (Paris, 1987)

Cheng Te-yuan: *Zheng, Tradition and Change* (diss., U. of Maryland, 1991)

Liu Dongsheng and others, eds.: *Zhongguo yueqi tujian* [Pictorial guide to Chinese instruments] (Ji'nan, 1992), 200–9

HAN MEI

Zhong. Bronze bell of the Han Chinese, used mainly in ritual music. Bells found in Zhou dynasty sites (*c*11th–3rd centuries BCE) are of many sub-types, differentiated by shape of the cross-section (leaf-shaped, elliptical, or circular), curve of the 'mouth' (concave or flat), lateral profile (elongated or broad), method and angle of suspension (vertical, oblique, or hand-held upright), and method of striking (internal clapper or external beater). The term zhong (pronounced 'jung') refers generically to all clapperless bells (including *bo*, *nao*, and *zheng*) and specifically to one sub-type—clapperless bells built in tuned sets, known as *bianzhong* ('arranged bells'). Bells with internal clappers are generally called *ling*. Chinese bells are cast from bronze, an alloy known as *qingtong* ('green copper'), or *xiangtong* ('resonant copper'), consisting of three or more parts of copper to one part of tin. Maintaining a 3000-year tradition, zhong and *bo* types are still used in Confucian rituals. The remaining Chinese bell types, such as *zheng*, *ling*, *duo*, *chunyu*, and *luanling*, are mostly historic relics traditionally used for other occasions. For large Buddhist bells, *see* FANZHONG.

1. Structures and types. 2. History and usage.

1. STRUCTURES AND TYPES.

(i) Zhong. The bell specifically identified as zhong has a leaf-shaped cross-section (oblate ellipsoid) and a slightly expanding profile (narrowly trapezoidal) from the crown outward. The mouth (or rim) of the bell is concave, with pointed corners left and right. Suspension methods are of two types. Most common among ancient bells is the elongated handle or shank (*yong*) extending up from the crown, with a small attached ring at its base from which the bell is suspended at an oblique angle. The second suspension method is by a loop (*niu*), from which the bell hangs vertically. Both types are suspended in a frame, together with other bells in a graduated set (*bianzhong*), and struck externally with large T-shaped mallets. While most zhong measure between 15 and 40 cm in overall height (bell and shank), some are as tall as approximately 150 cm and struck with long hand-held poles. Outer surfaces are typically decorated with raised rectangular ribs and protruding knobs or 'nipples'—typically four clusters (two on each side of the bell) containing nine knobs each. The early sets were tuned by maintaining uniform thickness while varying the size (smaller bells producing a higher pitch).

The most distinctive acoustical feature of bells in this shape is their ability to produce two pitches: the main pitch sounded when the centre of the bell is struck (several centimetres above the rim), and a higher secondary pitch sounded near the lower left or right corner. The famous Zeng Hou Yi set bears pitch names cast into the bells. The interval between these pitches is most commonly a minor 3rd, though some bells sound major 3rds, and very occasionally 2nds or 4ths. A few sets show evidence that fine tuning was attempted by scraping or filing the inside walls.

Zhong, China, possibly Eastern Zhou Dynasty (475–221 BCE). (Aurelia W. Hartenberger, EdD)

(ii) Bo. The *bo* is large, typically with an elliptical or circular cross-section (although some are leaf-shaped), a flat mouth, and an oversized suspension loop on its crown. Unlike the zhong, the *bo* sounds one pitch only. While normally cast as single bells, several small coordinated sets have been found. The oldest Zhou *bo* are more elaborately decorated than zhong of the same period, with abstract zoomorphic designs and loops in the shape of dragons or other auspicious animals. *Bo* average about 40 cm in overall height, though some are as tall as 1 metre. When zhong were cast following the 10th century CE, *bo* construction became the ideal, and entire sets (also called *bianzhong*) were made of uniform size but of varying thickness (bells with thicker metal producing a higher pitch).

(iii) Nao/Yong. Bells cast during the late Shang and very early Zhou periods (*c*13th–11th centuries BCE)—the most ancient of Chinese clapperless bronze bells—established the basic pattern for zhong bells, with a leaf-shaped cross-section and concave mouth. The Shang

bells differ from Zhou dynasty zhong in that their shanks are short and hollow, designed to be mounted on poles or pegs, with the mouth facing upward. Their bodies are also short and moderately trapezoidal in profile. Two regional types are differentiated: large, mostly single bells found in Hunan and neighbouring southern provinces; and sets of three or more small bells found on the Central Plain of North China, especially in Henan province. Both large and small bells were mistakenly called *nao* in late Zhou texts. Recent scholarship has demonstrated that large mouth-upward bells were called *yong*, an onomatopoeic name. That small bells in sets might have been called *geng* is speculative.

Large *yong* bells (*c*40 cm to 1 metre in overall height) were mounted on poles inserted into their hollow shanks and struck externally with unpadded mallets. Since most of these bells were not cast in sets, decoration varies considerably, including claw-like and horn-like motifs, images of circling clouds, and occasionally animal profiles. Small bells, usually cast in sets of three (average overall heights *c*18, 15, and 12 cm) resemble the large bells in construction, but their decorative patterns are coordinated within each set, commonly with variations of the *taotie* emblem (stylized animal face) on both sides—though some sets are undecorated. Small bells were designed to be either hand-held or mounted in a frame on short pegs inserted into their hollow shanks. They were struck externally with an unpadded beater.

(iv) Other bells. The *zheng* (pronounced 'jeng') has the appearance of a thin, elongated *yong*-type zhong (typically between 20 and 40 cm), though more tubular and with either a flat or concave mouth. Decorative patterns are diverse, some having protruding knobs like zhong, some with inscribed geometric or other designs, but most without any design. These bells were hand-held by long shanks (*yong*) and struck with external beaters. Zheng were historically used as military instruments, to accompany marching soldiers and possibly for other functions.

The *ling*, which generally resembles the *niu*-type of zhong, with its suspension ring or loop mounted on the crown, has a leaf-shaped cross section and concave (sometimes flat) mouth. Unlike other Chinese bells, it has an internal clapper of metal or wood and is sounded by shaking. Sizes and shapes differ widely. Large bells (*c*20 to 25 cm tall) resemble *niuzhong* in size, shape of the suspension ring, and concave mouth. Small bells (*c*8 to 12 cm) have very broad suspension loops and usually flat mouths. While small bells were used as amulets and decorations on animals, the specific usage of large *ling* is not clear. Related to the *ling* is the *duo* (or *duoling*), a small bell (*c*8 cm high) with internal clapper, but hand-held rather than hung by a ring. Minimally decorated, the *duo* is cited in Zhou texts as a military instrument used in signalling.

Many small bells are called *ling* types. Miniature leaf-shaped *ling* with clappers (as short as *c*3 cm) are broadly trapezoidal in profile, with wide concave or straight mouths. They were made in large numbers for animal decoration and other functions. Cup-shaped bells known as *fengling* ('wind bells') are hung from the outer eaves of Buddhist temples. With clappers extending below their mouths, tipped with thin metal vanes, *fengling* are sounded by the wind. For small pellet bells hung on horses and around dancers' waists, *see* Pailing; for small cup-shaped brass bells, *see* Pengling.

The *chunyu*, a name of unknown etymology, is a large bronze bell of varying sizes (*c*35 to 55 cm tall), with circular cross-section, a crown resembling a flat platform (*c*45 to 55 cm in diameter), and bulbous shoulders curving downward to a narrower rim. The bell is suspended by a loop-type hanger, typically in the shape of a crouching tiger, though some have a plain *niu*-type loop. Decorative patterns on the sides include geometric and zoomorphic designs, though most are plain. *Chunyu* have been found in large numbers in Hunan province and neighbouring regions of South China. Most were cast singly, though sets of four and five bells have been found in Hunan and Guizhou provinces. Zhou texts state that the *chunyu* was used on the battlefield, though iconographic evidence shows that it was used together with the bronze drum in ritual performances among southern minority peoples.

The *luanling* ('chariot bell') is a globular bell (*c*5 cm in diameter) with pellets enclosed. The globe is surrounded by a large decorative vertical ring, both attached to a hollow trapezoidal bronze column (bell and column *c*16 cm tall). This assembly was mounted on spikes attached to chariots and shaken during travel. *Luanling*, dating from the early Zhou dynasty, have been found in small numbers.

Representative examples of most bell types can be found at the Palace Museum (Beijing), Hubei Provincial Museum (Wuhan), Hunan Provincial Museum (Changsha), National Palace Museum (Taipei), Academia Sinica (Taipei), British Museum (London), and the Metropolitan Museum of Art (New York).

2. History and usage. The earliest clapperless bells found in China, uncovered in Shaanxi province sites (north-central China) and dating to about 2100 bce, are made entirely of clay. Nothing is known about their usage. Bells constructed of bronze, notably *nao/yong* and *zheng*, first appeared during the late Shang dynasty (13th–11th centuries bce). Numerous small *nao* have been found in Henan province and elsewhere on the Central Plain, often in sets of three and five. Large single *nao* have been found in Hunan and neighbouring southern provinces. The *Zhouli* text (*c*3rd century bce) states that 'the metal *nao* is used to stop the drum', implying use by army commanders for signalling—though scholars now believe that early writers confused the *nao* and *zheng*. Since small *nao* were cast in tuned sets, they most probably were used for ceremonial occasions.

The bell known as zhong, with its longer body, distinctive decorative features and mouth-downward oblique suspension, emerged during the Zhou dynasty (*c*11th–3rd centuries bce), the earliest bells dating from about 1000 bce. Zhong were normally constructed in tuned sets (*bianzhong*) for melodic performance. During the 20th century, uncountable numbers of these sets were broken up and sold piece by piece to art dealers outside China. Of the sets still intact, most noteworthy are those found at Changtaiguan Tomb no.1 and the tomb site of the Marquis Yi of the Zeng state. The 13-bell Changtaiguan set, found in a mid-Zhou site in Henan province, is now kept at the Chinese Historical Museum in Beijing. The bells are of graduated sizes, each producing two pitches distributed within a two-octave range (allowing limited chromatic capability), and suspended by *niu* loops mouth downward from an elaborately decorated frame. More spectacular in size, decoration, and diversity is the 65-piece *bianzhong* found at the tomb of Marquis Yi of the Zeng state, a 5th-century BCE site in Hubei province, now kept at the Hubei Provincial Museum. The bells in this set are of three different types, suspended from a three-tiered frame: 45 very large *yong*-type zhong on the lower two tiers, 19 *niu*-type zhong on the upper tier, and a single *bo* in the middle of the bottom tier. The pitch range spans five octaves, with full chromatic capability in the middle three octaves.

Bell founding continued into the Han dynasty (206 BCE–220 CE) but, with the introduction of music and instruments from India and Central Asia, this technology was abandoned for most of the next thousand years. When bell casting was revived during the Song dynasty (960–1279), construction details had changed. As seen in 12th-century Chinese sources and instruments preserved in Korea (*p'yonjong*), sets of bells usually totalled 16, suspended in a two-tiered frame. Most *bianzhong* sets from this period onward are of the *bo* construction, with same-sized barrel-shaped or related profiles, *niu* hangers, and flat mouths. These single-pitched bells were tuned chromatically over a range of one octave and a minor 3rd (for a 16-bell set). Two *bianzhong* sets dating from the Qing dynasty (1644–1911), with 16 *bo*-type bells tuned in this manner, are preserved at the Palace Museum and Confucian shrine in Beijing. The prevailing bell types of the Qing period are still employed in Confucian ritual ceremonies in Taiwan, though occasionally the ancient Zhou-style *yong* bells are used.

BIBLIOGRAPHY

A.C. Moule: 'A List of the Musical and Other Sound-Producing Instruments of the Chinese', *Journal of the Royal Asiatic Society, North China Branch*, vol.39 (1908), 1–160; repr. separately (Buren, 1989), 35–46

N. Spear: *A Treasury of Archaeological Bells* (New York, 1978), 27–46

Tong Kin-woon: *Shang Musical Instruments* (diss., Wesleyan U., 1983); repr. in *AsM*, vol.15/1 (1983), 103–51

Shen Sin-yan: 'The Acoustics of the Bian–Zhong Bell Chimes of China', *Chinese Music*, vol.4/3 (1986), 53–7; vol.4/4, 73–8; vol.10/1 (1987), 10–19

Liu Dongsheng and Yuan Quanyou, eds.: *Zhongguo yinyue shi tujian* [Pictorial guide to the history of Chinese music] (Beijing, 1988/R2008), 17–49

Liu Dongsheng and others, eds.: *Zhongguo yueqi tujian* [Pictorial guide to Chinese instruments] (Ji'nan, 1992), 62–93

L. von Falkenhausen: *Suspended Music: Chime-Bells in the Culture of Bronze Age China* (Berkeley, 1993)

Li Chunyi: *Zhongguo shanggu chutu yueqi zonglun* [Survey of ancient excavated musical instruments in China] (Beijing, 1996), 65–353

Wang Zichu and others, eds.: *Zhongguo yinyue wenwu daxi, Hubei juan* [Compendium of Chinese musical artefacts, Hubei volume] (Zhengzhou, 1996), 5–98, 187–247

R. Bagley: 'Percussion', in *Music in the Age of Confucius*, ed. Jenny So (Washington, DC, 2000), 35–63

ALAN R. THRASHER

Zhu (i). Percussion idiophone of the Han Chinese, used in imperial court rituals. Made of softwood, it is shaped like a grain measure, with outward-sloping sides, closed at the bottom, open at the top, and a circular hole in one side. 19th-century instruments measure approximately 60 cm square at the top by 45 cm deep, though historic sources cite different measurements. It is beaten on the inside wall with an unpadded wooden mallet, which was formerly attached to the bottom on a hinge and swung alternately left and right against both sides. Nowadays the mallet is held in the player's hand and struck from above, but scholars says that the hand should be inserted through the side hole.

While ancient instruments have not been found, the 7th-century BCE *Shijing* ('Classic of Poetry') mentions the *zhu* (along with the related *yu* idiophone) among ritual instruments, and the *Shujing* ('Classic of History') identifies its function in signalling the beginning of a piece of music. The zhu was part of the court ritual ensemble throughout most of the imperial period. Regularly scheduled performances, which fell from favour in China during the 20th century, have been marginally preserved in the annual Confucian ritual. The player strikes the instrument three times to signal the beginning of a ritual hymn. The Korean *ch'uk* and Vietnamese *chúc* are related surviving instruments.

BIBLIOGRAPHY

A.C. Moule: 'A List of the Musical and Other Sound–Producing Instruments of the Chinese', *Journal of the Royal Asiatic Society, North China Branch*, vol.39 (1908), 1–160

Liu Dongsheng and others, eds.: *Zhongguo yueqi tujian* [Pictorial guide to Chinese instruments] (Ji'nan, 1992), 104–5

A. Thrasher: 'The Changing Musical Tradition of the Taipei Confucian Ritual', *CHIME Journal*, vol.16–17 (2005), 7–33

ALAN R. THRASHER

Zhu (ii) [chu]. Obsolete struck zither of the Han Chinese, popular between the 4th century BCE and the 3rd century CE. It was used especially in performing *xianghe ge* ('harmonious songs'), a popular genre. Early texts give disparate descriptions and numbers of strings. The 2nd-century CE dictionary *Shuowen Jiezi* states, 'The zhu is an instrument with five strings [and] struck with bamboo. [The Chinese character] is composed of a bamboo radical on top, and a graph for *gong*, denoting an object held by hand'. *Shiming*, another dictionary from the same period, says 'The zhu is similar to the *zheng* with a slim neck and 13 strings', and the *Han Shu*, dynastic record of the Han (206 BCE–220 CE), describes the zhu as 'similar to the *qin*, with strings secured at the larger end. [It is] struck by a bamboo stick, therefore named zhu'. These early texts were repeatedly quoted throughout the Chinese imperial era.

A non-functional zhu intended for burial, dating to the Western Han dynasty (206 BCE–8 CE) and found in the Mawangdui Tomb (Hunan province), and three zhu from a nearby royal tomb, have elicited extensive organological study and correction of historical inaccuracies. Based on these finds, the zhu had a long slim rectangular soundbox narrowing into a thin three-sided neck. The excavated instruments vary in length from 93 to 145 cm. Five silk strings attached at the top of the neck ran the length of the instrument over movable bridges to a single hitch peg. A separate stick of bamboo or wood was used to strike the strings. Two depictions of the zhu, one from Mawangdui, another from a Western Han tomb from Jiangsu province, illustrate a player holding the neck with the left hand, the soundbox pointing away from his body and resting on the floor. The player uses the left thumb and first finger to press the strings on either side of the neck, while striking the strings with the stick held in the right hand.

The zhu is known in Chinese legend from accounts of the 3rd-century BCE musician Gao Jianli playing the zhu for his friend Jin Ke, a famous assassin, as well as of his own attempt to kill the infamous emperor of the Qin dynasty (221–207 BCE) by throwing a zhu filled with lead at him.

BIBLIOGRAPHY

Huang Xiangpeng: 'Qinhan Xianghe Yueqi "Zhu" de Shouci Faxian Jiqi Yiyi' [The initial discovery of Qin and Han dynasties Xianghe instrument 'Zhu' and its significance], Kaogu, vol.8 (1994), 722–6

B. Lawergren: 'Strings', Music in the Age of Confucius, ed. Jenny So (Washington, DC, 2000), 65–85

HAN MEI

Ziegler. Austrian firm of woodwind instrument makers. Its founder, Johann Joseph Ziegler (b Komorn [now Komárom], Hungary, 1795; d Vienna, Austria, 10 March 1858), was granted a privilege to trade in Vienna in 1821. He made all kinds of high-quality orchestral woodwinds, as well as the *csakan*, which enjoyed great regional popularity during the early 19th century. Ziegler worked on improvements to instrument design, for example introducing metal clarinet mouthpieces. In 1837 he sold six clarinets (two in A, two in B♭, and two in C) and two bassoons to the Vienna Hofmusikkapelle. His efficient and prolific firm met extremely large orders: in 1845 Ziegler apparently supplied instruments to 30 Austrian regimental bands, and he had a flourishing export business. After Ziegler's death the firm was continued by his son Johann Baptist (b 19 April 1823; d 10 Jan 1878), who maintained high quality. His instruments were awarded a gold medal at the 1867 Paris Exposition. The firm continued until the early 20th century, trading under the name 'Johann Ziegler Nachfolger'. Ziegler instruments bear the mark of the double eagle and the wording 'I: ZIEGLER/WIEN' (to 1847 and after 1858) or 'I: ZIEGLER & SOHN/WIEN' (1847–58).

In the Austrian territories in particular, the Ziegler flute with its full, soft tone and its extended range (lowest note b, and g when made with an extension) remained the orchestral instrument of choice until the 20th century, when it was superseded by the stronger tone of the Boehm flute. Unlike its rival, the Ziegler flute had an inverted conical bore. Ziegler's key system represented a further development of the Classical and early Romantic design, with several doubled keys.

BIBLIOGRAPHY

R. Hopfner: Wiener Musikinstrumentenmacher: 1766–1900 (Tutzing, 1999)

A. Rice: From the Clarinet d'Amour to the Contra Bass: a History of Large Size Clarinets, 1740–1860 (Oxford and New York, 2009), 157 only

RUDOLF HOPFNER/R

Ziernicki, Ignacy (b 1752; d 1829). Polish organ builder. Active in Kraków and its environs, he seems to have specialized in large structures, building organs in conservative style for Wawel Cathedral (1785), St Mary (1800), and the Franciscan and Dominican churches. The Dominican church organ perished in the great fire of 1850. The organ built for St Mary was of high quality and served the congregation for more than a century before falling victim to the Romantic trend in organ building. Ziernicki's last, equally prestigious assignment was a reconditioning of the main organ of the Marian sanctuary at Jasna Góra (Częstochowa) started in about 1828 and cut short by his death the following year. See J. Gołos: *Polskie organy i muzyka organowa* (Warsaw, 1972; Eng. trans., 1992, as *The Polish Organ*, vol.1: *The Instrument and its History*).

JERZY GOŁOS

Zildjian. Cymbal makers, comprising the Avedis Zildjian Co. of Norwell, Massachusetts, and Sabian, Ltd, of Meductic, New Brunswick, Canada. The family traces its lineage back to Avedis Zildjian I, an alchemist in Constantinople (now Istanbul) who in 1623 discovered a process for treating alloys. He applied this process to the making of cymbals, an already flourishing craft in Turkey. The details of his secret were closely guarded and have been passed down through the family. From 1623 until 1983 (with the exception of a short period of political exile for Aram Zildjian) Zildjian cymbals were manufactured in Turkey, ending when the American company, established in 1929, acquired all international trademarks.

In 1928 Aram (b c1863; d c1930), living again in Constantinople, contemplated retirement, and (being childless) passed the family secret to his nephew Avedis Zildjian III (b Dec 1889; d 8 Feb 1979) who had emigrated to the USA in 1908 and was operating a confectionary firm in Boston. In 1929 Avedis established a foundry in North Quincy, later moving to Norwell. Soon after World War II, Avedis initiated his sons Armand (b 18 Feb 1921; d 26 Dec 2002) and Robert (b 14 July 1923) into the craft. In 1968 a second factory was established in Meductic, New Brunswick, under the name Azco Ltd, and in 1977 Avedis appointed his elder son, Armand, president of the company. In 1981 the company split; Armand retained the Norwell facility and the trade name Zildjian, and Robert established a new company, Sabian Ltd, at the Azco facility. In 1996, Armand's daughter Craigie (b 4 Jan 1948) became CEO of Zildjian. Robert's sons, Andy and Bill, in the early 2010s were president and chairman, respectively, of Sabian. The two firms have become great competitors in the lucrative cymbal industry.

The brilliant and unique 'Zildjian sound' continues to be heard in the world's top orchestras, rock, and jazz bands, and wherever cymbals are used. The metallurgical formula of Zildjian cymbals is known to be 80% copper and about 20% tin with the addition of a small amount of silver. The methods of casting, rolling, tempering, and hammering are also no secret. What is not known outside the family, however, is the ingenious method of treating alloys in the cymbal casting process that was discovered in 1623. Into the early 21st century, Zildjian and Sabian make cymbals of all types, two octaves of crotales, hand-hammered gongs, and a wide range of mallets. They also provide significant philanthropic support for the arts.

BIBLIOGRAPHY

T.R. Navin: 'World's Leading Cymbal Maker: Avedis Zildjian Company', *Percussive Notes*, vol.4/5 (Sept 1965), 3–5; repr. from *Bulletin of the Business Historical Society*, vol.23/4, (Dec 1949), 196–206

P.J. Reale: 'The Secret of the Cymbals is Yours!', *Yankee* (Feb 1972), 78–125

H. Pinksterboer: *The Cymbal Book*, ed. R. Mattingly (Milwaukee, WI, 1992)

J.A. Strain: 'Avedis Zildjian Company', *The Encyclopedia of New England*, ed. B. Feintuch and D.H. Watters (New Haven, CT, 2005), 1159–60

JAMES BLADES/JAMES HOLLAND/JAMES A. STRAIN

Zilli maşa. Turkish tongs with cymbals attached. A pair of steel tongs, each arm with two or more branches bearing cymbals about 4 cm in diameter, is welded together at the base or formed of one piece of metal folded at the base to form a spring action. The player holds the zilli maşa in one hand and beats it against the palm of the other causing the opposite cymbals to strike one another. The instrument is usually, though not exclusively, played by men. It is found in small ensembles that accompany dance and song. In the Ottoman era it was played by dancing-boys (*köçek*). See L. Picken: *Folk Musical Instruments of Turkey* (London, 1975), 22–4.

Zimmermann, Charles [Carl] (Friedrich) (*b* Morgenroethe, Saxony, Germany, 4 Sept 1817; *d* Philadelphia, PA, 20 Oct 1898). American instrument maker, of German birth. He emigrated to the USA in 1864 and settled in Philadelphia. His work with and improvements to the accordion led him to devise a complex 'tone numbering' system of music notation that used numbers in place of notes; he wrote articles describing this as early as 1871. After years of revising the system he decided to invent a musical instrument that would require its use; he tried at first to adapt the accordion for this purpose but soon turned his attention to the autoharp, a zither with attached chord bars. He first alluded to his plans to manufacture the instrument about 1878 in his book *Zimmermann's Directory of Music in General*; he applied for a patent in 1881 (issued the following year) and began production in 1885. Within three years he had sold 50,000 instruments. His models ranged from one with 21 strings and three bars that could produce only three chords to a concert instrument with 49 strings, six bars, slides, and levers that could produce 72. In 1892 he sold the controlling interest in his company to Alfred Dolge, who moved the manufacturing operations to Dolgeville, New York, where production continued until the company's insolvency in 1898. The autoharp came to be employed widely for teaching rudimentary harmony in schools and was also used by Appalachian folk musicians.

BIBLIOGRAPHY

'Autoharp Progress: How Alfred Dolge & Son have Improved the Autoharp until Zimmerman, its Inventor, Scarcely Knew it', *Music Trade Review* (3 Aug 1895), 15 only

A.D. Moore: 'The Autoharp: its Origin and Development from a Popular to a Folk Instrument', *New York Folklore Quarterly*, vol.19/4 (1963)

B. Blackley: 'C.F. Zimmermann's System of Musical Notation', *The Autoharpaholic* (Winter 1983), 10–13

B. Blackley: *The Autoharp Book* (Brisbane, CA, 1983)

MICHAEL I. HOLMES /R

Zimmermann, Julius Heinrich (*b* Sternberg, Germany, 22 Sept 1851; *d* Berlin, Germany, 25 April 1922). German instrument manufacturer and music publisher. Trained

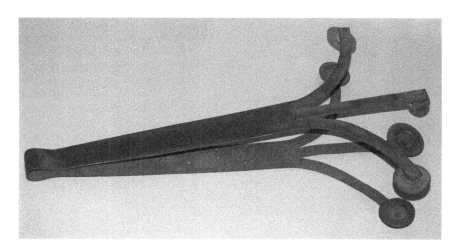

Zilli maşa, tong cymbals, Turkey. (Aurelia W. Hartenberger, EdD)

as a bank clerk in Berlin, he moved to St Petersburg where he opened a music shop in 1876, selling instruments imported from Markneukirchen. He opened his own factory for making brass instruments in 1880 and in 1882 became the exclusive supplier of brass instruments to the Russian army. He also had factories in Moscow (1882) and Riga (1903) and branches in Leipzig (where in 1886 he established the headquarters of his publishing firm, with the printing carried out by Breitkopf & Härtel), London (1897), and Berlin. He supposedly was among the first German saxophone manufacturers. As well as winds, his firm also dealt in string instruments (reportedly produced for Zimmermann by such Markneukirchen makers as Robert Hammig, Reichel, and Roth) and, from 1891, mechanical instruments and gramophones. The firm exhibited in St Petersburg (1876), Moscow (1882), Leipzig (1886), and beginning with the Chicago World's Fair in 1893, won numerous awards at international expositions. About 1904, Zimmermann acquired the piano and harmonium factory of Gustav Fiedler in Leipzig. The Zimmermann company was well known in Russia for balalaikas; it also sold domras, banjos, and 'Japanese fiddles' as well as all conventional instruments and accessories, advertised for example in a 172-page catalogue issued in 1908.

In 1901, czar Nicholas II bestowed the Order of St Stanislaus on Zimmermann, who served as a deputy in the German Reichstag from 1905 until 1918. He suffered financial hardship during World War I, but, although he resumed the publication of music by Russian composers in 1919, he was unable to reopen his former Russian factories and shops, which had been nationalized by the Bolsheviks. At that time Zimmermann's son August (1877–1952), general manager of the St Petersburg operation, left Russia for Germany where he directed the instrument division (woodwind factories in Berlin and Leipzig) until its confiscation in 1933, due largely to the family's part-Jewish heritage. August's younger brother Wilhelm (1891–1946) was imprisoned in Russia but later escaped to Germany, where in 1928 he became the proprietor of the publishing operation, separated in that year from the instrument division. Among the firm's woodwind makers or suppliers were A. Gerl (*fl* St Petersburg, Russia, 1908) and Alois Hörl (*fl* Leipzig, Germany, 1930), who made double flageolets under the name 'Fortuna'.

After World War II, the publishing firm was established in Frankfurt by Wilhelm's widow, Edith Zimmermann (1900–75). The confiscated instrument factory in St Petersburg was continued during the Soviet era and again privatized in 1991 as the St Petersburg Musical Wind Instruments Factory.

BIBLIOGRAPHY

B. Vol'man: *Russkiye notnïye izdaniya: XIX–nachala XX veka* [Russian Editions of Music: 19th Century–Beginning of the 20th] (Leningrad, 1970)

W. Waterhouse: *The New Langwill Index: a Dictionary of Musical Wind-Instrument Makers and Inventors* (London, 1993), 444 only

EDWARD GARDEN/R

Zirbaghali [zerbghali]. Single-headed goblet drum of Afghanistan. It is usually made of pottery, and occasionally from a block of mulberry wood, carved or turned in a wide variety of shapes and sizes. The single goatskin head, usually slightly narrower than the widest part of the body (which curves in at the top), is glued on and can be tuned by heating or wetting it. Sometimes the head bears a patch of black tuning paste. Some modern instruments have the head lapped on a ring with metal tuning rods. The drummer sits cross-legged on the floor with the drum resting on its side on the ground, or in the player's lap. Drummers use a large variety of rhythmic patterns and special techniques such as the *riz*, a fast roll executed with the fingers of the right hand. The zirbaghali is regarded in Afghanistan as a folk instrument and is especially important in the north of the country. It is similar to the Iranian *zarb*. See M. Slobin: *Music in the Culture of Northern Afghanistan* (Tucson, AZ, 1976), 261.

JOHN BAILY/R

Zither. Term having two main senses in modern organology. The first denotes (in both English and German) a large category of string instruments also known as 'simple chordophone' (defined in §1 below); the second—more limited and perhaps more familiar—sense refers to a small group of Alpine folk and popular instruments. From the late 15th century the term 'zither' was used exclusively to denote chordophones with necks, of the cittern type. It was only from the early 19th century that the name began to be used for descendants of the north European *Scheitholt* type of instrument (see §§2 and 3 below), which had no neck, and frets placed directly on the box. From the *Scheitholt* evolved the modern Alpine instrument still known as the zither (Fr. *cithare*; Ger. *Zither*; It. *cetra da tavola*); other types of fretted zither are found elsewhere in Europe and America.

1. The generic term. 2. The modern Alpine zither. 3. Other fretted zithers. 4. East and Southeast Asia.

1. THE GENERIC TERM. According to the classification system of Hornbostel and Sachs, a zither is a 'simple chordophone', consisting solely of a string bearer (and its string or strings) or of a string bearer with a resonator that can be detached without destroying the sound-producing apparatus. Zithers are thus distinguished from 'composite chordophones', such as harps and lutes, in which the string bearer and a resonator are organically united and cannot be separated without destroying the instrument. Whereas the strings of a lute or lyre extend past the face of the instrument along a neck or out to a yoke, and those of a harp extend away from the soundboard, the strings of a zither do not go beyond or away from the body of the instrument.

2. THE MODERN ALPINE ZITHER. The present form of the south German and Austrian instruments that are generally known simply as zithers dates from the 19th and

Concert zither, Washburn, c1898. (©Gregg Miner)

early 20th centuries. Structurally they have the same elements as other fretted zithers (a box, fretted melody strings, and open strings), but their playing technique is distinct. The five chromatically fretted metal melody strings, which are usually tuned by machine screws, are individually finger-stopped with the left hand and plucked with a plectrum attached to the right thumb; the remaining fingers of the right hand select individual notes or chords from the open gut or nylon strings (numbering perhaps 30 or more and tuned by metal wrestpins).

The early forms of the modern zither, known as *Kratzzithern*, were played in the same way as the *Scheitholt* (see §3 below), although they have differently shaped bodies. The crucial innovation was that the frets were no longer anchored directly to the box but placed on a fingerboard stuck to it. These early zithers derived their names from the manner of playing, which was to 'scratch' (*kratzen*) or strum with a horn plectrum, a quill, or the like. One *Kratzzither* type, the *Raffelzither* ('grater zither'), had a fingerboard but no accompanying strings; another had a curved body and octave strings with shorter scalings fitted to a wrestplank of their own, the *Oktävchen* or *Trompeterl*.

The *Schlagzither* (struck zither) differed from the *Scheitholt* and *Kratzzither* types in the abandonment of bourdon tuning and in the technique of striking the strings separately with the fingers and a plectrum on the thumb. The fingerboards of both the *Kratzzither* and the *Schlagzither* have partly diatonic fret patterns,

usually producing a major scale beginning with the lower 4th. To increase the musical possibilities open to the *Kratzzither*, some were made with two or three differently scaled fingerboards on the same body. Sections tuned a 4th or 5th from each other allowed a change to another register. Such double zithers are still used in Switzerland, known as *Schwyzer Zither*.

The body shape of some modern zithers is analogous to that of guitars or citterns (the 'Mittenwald' form); others imitate the structure of keyboard instruments with transverse stringing (such as the spinet and clavichord), with the rounded projection on the side furthest from the player (the 'Salzburg', 'Hallein', or 'Pinzgau' form). The 'Salzburg' has become the more usual. There were many attempts to improve the zither's acoustics and structure. The *Luftresonanzzither* ('air resonance zither'), attributed to Johann Jobst of Graz around 1890, had a second soundhole located above the wrestplank; the special structure of the wrestplank and fingerboard was intended to reduce their vibration-damping effects. The *Harfenzither* ('harp zither') had a pillar (*Baronstange*) between the wrestplank and the middle of the body.

In the modern zither the accompanying strings are tuned in 4ths and 5ths. Initially, many different tunings existed; a few standard tunings were established in the late 19th century. Various efforts were made to devise an arrangement that would be both physiologically practicable for the right hand and based on functional harmony. Nikolaus Weigel (*Theoretisch praktische Zitherschule*, 2/1844) was the first to call for a 28-string zither having a complete chromatic fingerboard, and for the accompanying strings to be tuned in 4ths and 5ths on the basis of the circle of 5ths. Different regional tunings of the melody strings subsequently came into use. 'Stuttgart tuning' (*e″–e″–a′–d′–g–c*), probably developed by the Stuttgart instrument maker Lorenze Kriner, was in use until the early 20th century. For 'Munich tuning' (*a′–a′–d′–g–c*), the accompanying strings are notated up an octave in the treble clef; both this system and 'Vienna tuning' (*a′–d′–g′–g–c*) are still used. The tuning of the 'Perfekta' zither superimposes the third circle of 5ths on the second, thus better accommodating the span of the hand. In the 'Reform' zither the first five strings of the fifth circle of 5ths are placed under the strings of the second circle, passing over a bridge about 2 to 3 mm lower. In the 'Ideal-Reform' zither there are additional strings in the first and second circle of 5ths passing over a second lower bridge. These modifications decreased the distance between the outer strings of the third circle of 5ths and the fingerboard. The transformation of the zither into a concert instrument and the construction of an entire zither family began in the mid-19th century, only a few years after the introduction of the new tuning system. Concert zithers differ from their predecessors in having a fully chromatic fingerboard with 29 frets, and in the enlarged scaling of the fingerboard strings (while the stringing remains unchanged). The modern zither family, whose earliest member is the *Altzither* (1851), is described in Table 1.

Table 1

names	scaling	tuning
Quintzither (Piccolozither)	380	e″–e″–a′–d′–g
Diskantzither (Primzither)	430	a′–a′–d′–g–c
Altzither (Sekundzither, Quartzither)	510/530	e′–e′–a–d–G
Basszither	570	a–a–d–G–C

3. OTHER FRETTED ZITHERS. While iconographical evidence suggests that unfretted box zithers were used in Europe from at least the 12th century, zithers with one or more fretted strings have been used extensively in some form or other in most of Europe except the British Isles, Italy, and the Iberian and Balkan peninsulas. They appear to be of northwest European development, and have not been traced back much further than the 16th century. Since zithers with one or more stopped strings and several bourdons existed previously in eastern Asia, the idea might have been brought to Europe after European merchants had visited the East in the 16th century. The large number of regional variants in Europe and the circumstances in which they have developed provide a striking example of non-evolutionary history. Although a rectangular instrument with few strings seems to have been the earliest, there has been no universal change towards larger and more complex forms. Rather, different forms seem attributable to different situations. Chronology cannot be consistently established, and terminology can be variable, even within small areas.

Among 31 angel musicians in a fresco from 1560 in the church of Rynkeby in Denmark, there is one playing a long, narrow, rectangular zither, stopping one of its strings with two left-hand fingers and striking with the right-hand fingers. The instrument is much longer than the brass-strung *Scheitholt* ('wooden log') depicted in Praetorius's *De organographia* (1619) and called by him a disreputable (*lumpen*) instrument. This instrument had one melody string with 18 frets beneath it, set directly into the box, and two or three bourdon strings—one tuned to the same pitch as the melody string, another hooked down at a third of its length (thus giving a 5th higher), and an optional one an octave above the first. All were tuned by laterally set, hand-turned wooden pegs. The melody string was stopped against the frets by a small rod held in the left hand, and the right-hand thumb struck across all the strings. A Danish schoolmaster, Hans Mikkelsen Ravn, mentioned in his *Heptachordum danicum* (1646) an instrument called 'langeleg', somewhat like a monochord and played by peasants. In Norway in the 17th century, an instrument called 'langspil' was referred to by Anders Arrebo, who described it as being between a crwth and a *Hackbrett* and used for ballad tunes. In 1699 the Friesian organist-pedagogue Claas Douwes described (*Grondig ondersoek van de toonen der musijk*, 1699/R1970) the *noardske Balke* as an instrument some 60 to 90 cm long, with three or four strings and diatonic frets under the melody string, the rest being unison-tuned bourdons; some players used a rod for stopping and a plectrum for striking, others stopped

with the left-hand thumb and sounded the strings with a bow. The earliest known use of this name is in 1660; in Reynvaan's *Muzikalwordenboek* (1795) it was synonymous with *hommel* ('drone'). In Iceland in 1772, a Swedish traveller, Uno van Trojel, noted a bowed *langspil* with six brass strings; presumably these were in three double courses. In 1809 W.J. Hooker was more specific about technique and use:

> ... Danish and Icelandic songs ... which she accompanied with tunes upon the Lang-spil ... It is usually played with a bow of horsehair ... but the Etatstroeds daughter frequently made use only of her fingers, as with a guitar ... she pressed the end of her thumb upon the wires, moving it up and down to produce the different modifications of sound.

Apart from some instruments of conservative styling, such as the epinette de Vosges, most modern fretted zithers have elements of structure and technique derived from sources other than these three- or four-string instruments. In the Norwegian *langeleik* and the Appalachian dulcimer, strings are still generally tuned by lateral wooden pegs. The *langeleik*, however, has up to ten bourdons, three of the short ones sometimes being set in a second pegbox at the opposite end from the main one, and pyramid-shaped individual bridges. Its playing technique includes the use of three fingers on the melody string, enabling the player to produce the elaborate characteristic Norwegian gracing, and stylized rhythmic striking patterns executed with a flexible plectrum. Virtually all other fretted zithers have strings affixed to sagittal iron wrestpins tuned with a key; on some instruments melody strings are tuned by machine heads.

Like the *langeleik*, the *kisfejes citera* (the characteristic Hungarian instrument) has some bourdons set in separate pegboxes, but they are always at the same end as the main pegbox; both rod and finger-stopping are used and plectra range from quills or wood to flexible plastic. Those zoomorphic- or anthropomorphic-headed instruments with many courses are the most spectacular of European zithers. Rectangular instruments resembling the *Scheitholt* are considered by some scholars to be fairly new to Hungary; it is this type that is now sometimes electronically amplified. Terminology in central Europe is shifting: in the Hungarian plains the *kisfejes citera* is often called 'tambura', a term that could also denote a small 'zitherized' lute, while in the Czech Republic and Slovakia the zither name is 'kobza', which in Romania denotes a true lute.

Not all zithers are plucked. Bowing has been an occasional alternative sounding method for fretted zithers that were generally plucked or struck. A few true bowed zithers have also been known in Europe. The *Streichmelodion* and *Schossgeige* were four-string instruments invented in the late 19th century in south German and Austrian regions, where they are still used to a small extent; they might well be described as zitherized fiddles and guitars. Baltic fretted monochords are also classified as a kind of zither. They consisted of a single string over a long, tapering box with 28 or 30 chromatic frets, generally with the note names painted in. Such an instrument was known as *psalmodikon* in Sweden, *versikannel* in Karelia, *mollpill* in Estonia, and *diga* in Latvia; it was popular in the 19th century as an aid in teaching singing and for playing regional and religious songs. Unfretted bowed zithers have included the *Trumscheit* and the Icelandic *fidhla*, both now extinct. A two-string bowed zither was formerly played by some of the indigenous peoples of Mexico: this might have been imported in the early Colonial period for teaching purposes.

4. EAST AND SOUTHEAST ASIA. It is clear from Chinese archaeological finds and historic citations that zithers were already major instrument types in China by the mid-Zhou dynasty (*c*7th–5th centuries BCE). That they were known many centuries earlier is apparent from the pictographic character of about the 12th century BCE for *yue* (meaning 'music'), a graph depicting silk strings over wood. Other string instrument types were not known in China until later periods. Several early zither types are still in use, all of which have been found in Zhou burial sites and cited in texts from the ancient *Shijing* onward. Of these, the bridgeless *qin* (pronounced 'chin') is unquestionably the most highly venerated. Having emerged from earlier (generally smaller) models, the *qin* of today, with a soundbox of irregular shape (*c*120 cm long) and seven silk strings, was in recognizable form by about the 3rd century CE. Perhaps because of its close association with Confucian ideology and the values of the literati class, the *qin* was not widely known outside of China.

The zither *se* is a generally larger instrument, with rectangular soundbox, 25 strings and a bridge under each string. Early *se* zithers found in Zhou and Han sites are short (*c*100–20 cm) and broad (*c*40 cm), their length increasing to nearly double this by the 18th century. The primary function of the *se* throughout history has been mostly restricted to the ritual tradition of the imperial courts.

Third among the major Chinese zithers is the *zheng*, an instrument shorter and thinner than the present-day *se*, with variable string numbers (12 or 13 during the 8th century) and a bridge under each string. The early 20th-century Chaozhou style of *zheng* (South China) is close in size to the *qin* (*c*110–20 cm), though with highly arched soundboard and 16 metal strings; the late 20th-century style is considerably longer (*c*160 cm), with a more gently arched soundboard and 18 or 21 metal strings. The *zheng* is a 'popular' (i.e. non-ritual) instrument with a large solo and chamber repertory. Its influence upon other East Asian zither traditions has been considerable. Less significant of the Chinese zithers are the ancient five-string *zhu* (for which specimens have been found in Zhou sites) and the medieval multistring bowed *yazheng* (still marginally preserved in Hebei province).

Numerous related zithers subsequently emerged among other Asian cultures, most being adaptations of Chinese types. The Japanese *koto* and Korean *kayagum* were among the earliest, both appearing by the 8th century CE, possibly earlier. The 13-string *koto* (*c*180 cm) with movable bridges under each string is a clear adaptation of the 13-string Tang-style *zheng*. While the word *koto* is Japanese, it is written with the same Chinese graph for *zheng*, and it shares significant repertory characteristics as well. The Korean 12-string *kayagŭm* is shorter (*c*145 cm for the *sanjo kayagŭm*), with tall wooden bridges and stylized carvings of 'rams horns' at the lower end of the instrument. Distantly related to the *koto* is the Japanese *wagon* (*c*190 cm), a six-string zither with movable bridges. The *wagon* is documented from the 2nd century CE onwards and is believed to be indigenous to Japan. Two other Korean zithers, the *komungo* and *ajaeng*, are more idiosyncratic. The six-string *komungo* (*c*150–60 cm) has 16 broad, fixed frets glued to the soundboard, and three movable bridges. Appearing in 7th-century CE tomb paintings, it was possibly derived from the Chinese 'horizontal' *konghou* (a zither in appearance if not in name). The seven-string *ajaeng* (*c*160 cm) with movable bridges is unusual in that it is bowed with a rosined stick rather than plucked. Appearing between the 10th and 14th centuries, the *ajaeng* was clearly derived from the Chinese *yazheng*.

To the north and south of China, other related zither traditions emerged from about the 14th century onwards. Among Mongolian people the *yatga* (*c*160 cm), with between ten and 13 strings, has been in use since this period. In Thailand the three-string, fretted *chakhē* (literally 'crocodile', *c*130 cm), used in the traditional *mahōrī* ensemble, appears to reflect both Indian and Chinese influences. The 16-string Vietnamese *Đàn tranh* (90–110 cm), however, is identical in all essential features to the Chaozhou-style *zheng* of south China, from where it was introduced.

Other Asian zithers are less clearly related to the above types. The most ancient are probably the various tube zithers marginally preserved among peoples of the Pacific islands. Constructed from tubular sections of stout bamboo, their multiple strings are usually raised from the bamboo surface itself (i.e. idiochordal) and plucked with the fingers of both hands or struck with a stick. Examples include the *kolitong* (or *kulibit* and known by many other names) in the Philippines (*c*60 cm), the rare *celempung bambu* in West Java (*c*80 cm), and the *zharong* (Chinese: *zhuqin*, 'bamboo *qin*') among the Yao and other groups of southwest China. Zither types possibly similar to these were reported in the 2nd-century CE Chinese dictionary *Shuowen jiezi* as being constructed from a bamboo tube and possessing five strings.

Finally, the peoples of Southeast Asia have very unusual single-string zithers. The Thai *phīn* is a short stick zither (*c*80 cm) with one or two metal strings and an attached half-gourd resonator. It bears close similarities to Indian zithers, notably the early *bin* (or *vīṇā*) from which its name derives. Another is the *dàn bầu* (*c*100 cm) of minority peoples of northern Vietnam and southwest China, a box zither with a single metal string attached to a flexible neck (for pitch control), sounding the harmonic series.

BIBLIOGRAPHY

J.E. Bennert: *Illustrierte Geschichte der Zither* (Luxembourg, 1881)

A.V. Nikl: *Die Zither: ihre historische Entwicklung bis zur Gegenwart* (Vienna, 1927)

T. Norlind, ed.: *Systematik der Saiteninstrumente*, vol.1: *Geschichte der Zither* (Stockholm, 1936)

J.L. de Jong: *De noordske balke* (Assen, 1942)

A. Edelmann: 'Die Toggenburger Halszither', *Internationale Zeitschrift für Literatur, bildende Kunst, Musik und Wissenschaft*, vol.2 (1952)

T. Alexandru: *Instrumentele muzicale ale poporului romîn* (Bucharest, 1956) [incl. Fr. and Russ. summaries]

J. Grossier: 'L'épinette dans la vallée des lacs', *Au pays des lacs: arts et traditions des Hautes-Vosges* (Gérardmer, 1960)

J.F. Putnam: *The Plucked Dulcimer and How to Play it* (Berea, KY, 1961, rev. 2/1964)

J. Brandlmeier: *Handbuch der Zither* (Munich, 1963)

K. Vertkov: 'Beiträge zur Geschichte der russischen Guslitypen', *Studia instrumentorum musicae popularis 1: Study Group on Folk Musical Instruments of the International Folk Music Council: Brno 1967*, ed. E. Stockmann (Stockholm, 1969), 134–41

J. Manga: *Magyar népdalok, népi hangszerek* (Budapest, 1969; Eng. trans., rev., 1969, 3/1988)

F. Stradner: 'Vom Scheitholz zur Kratz-Zither', *Jb des österreichischen Volksliedwerkes*, vol.18 (1969), 66–80

J. Hickerson, ed.: *A Bibliography of Hammered and Plucked (Appalachian or Mountain) Dulcimers and Related Instruments* (Washington, DC, 1973)

H. Boone: 'De hommel in de Lage Landen', *Brussels Museum of Musical Instruments Bulletin*, vol.5 (1975), 9–151 [incl. important bibliography]

L. Kunz: 'Scheitholt—Kobza: ein Beitrag zur Kenntnis der volkstümlichen Zitherinstrumente in den böhmischen Ländern', *Casopis moravsleho muzea*, vol.63 (1978), 227–55

Y. Mitani: *Higashi Ajia koto no kenkyū* [A Study of Long-zithers and their Music in the Far East] (Tokyo, 1980)

B. Bachmann-Geiser: *Die Volksmusikinstrumente der Schweiz* (Leipzig, 1981)

K. Junger: 'Die Zither: Entwicklung eines Instruments und seiner Besaitung', *Das Musikinstrument*, vol.37 (1987), 68–75

W. Breckle: 'Die Entwicklung der Zither als Volksinstrument', *Gut Klang: 100 Jahre Zitherklub Dachau*, eds. W. Breckle, H. Müller and H. Heres (Dachau, 1991)

L. Mühlemann: *Die Grosse Familie der Zithern* (Oberthal, 1993)

J. Folprecht: *Citera maj Nastroj: Citera v Cechách, na Morave a ve Sleszku* (Brno, 1995)

V.D. Laturell, ed.: *'Die Zither is a Zauberin … ': Zwei Jahrhunderte Zither in München* (Munich, 1995)

A. Michel: *Zithern: Musikinstrumente zwischen Volkskultur und Bürgerlichkeit: Katalog: Musikinstrumenten-Museum der Universität Leipzig* (Leipzig, 1995)

B. Wackernagel: *Europäische Zupf- und Streichinstrumente, Hackbretter und Äolsharfen: Deutsches Museum München, Musikinstrumentensammlung Katalog* (Frankfurt, 1997)

A. Thrasher: *Chinese Musical Instruments* (Hong Kong, 2000)

MARK LINDLEY (1); ANDREAS MICHEL (2–3);
ALAN R. THRASHER (4)

Zither, fretless. Popular term for an American or European zither that has only non-fretted (open) strings, as opposed to a concert or 'Alpine' zither, which utilizes a fretted fingerboard. Fretless zithers were commercially developed and widely distributed in many forms from the late 19th century, especially in the USA. The earliest such invention is the autoharp, patented in 1882 by the German immigrant Charles F. Zimmermann in Philadelphia. Its strings are strummed by one hand while the other hand operates a series of damper bars, which mute those strings that do not sound notes of the desired chord. It was followed by the Guitar-Zither patented in 1894 by Friederich Menzenhauer (1858–1937) in Jersey City, New Jersey. Its 15 unfretted, diatonic melody strings are accompanied by four groups of four open strings, each group sounding a chord (tonic, 3rd, 5th, sometimes dominant 7th or octave). Variant types were produced in great numbers by several dozen manufacturers, from the late 1890s onward. Many types (e.g. the Marxophone) include mechanical attachments that strike or pluck the strings. The Ukelin and related types have bowed melody strings. Other types have only melody strings or strings configured into chord groups, sometimes with a melody playable from the chords. The most prominent American manufacturers were Menzenhauer (later Menzenhauer & Schmidt); The Phonoharp Co. (Boston); Oscar Schmidt (Jersey City); and H.C. Marx/Marxochime Colony (Boston, Chicago, and elsewhere).

Ornamentation and body designs of German products are typically more elaborate than their American-made counterparts, and often include many more strings. Nearly all German models were designed to be played flat on a table top. Generally, fretless zithers were mass-produced, relatively inexpensive, and intended for amateurs or non-musicians. A chart with staff notation or names of the strings was often attached as a decal to the soundboard. Paper song sheets, with notation or diagrams of notes to be played, could be placed under the strings as a guide. Thousands of pieces were published for these 'numerical instruments' from their first appearance to about 1935. A mainstay of American mail-order catalogues from the 1890s, and later peddled door-to-door, these instruments were used to accompany singing, in small instrumental ensembles and as solo instruments. They were played in concert by Pete Seeger and other folk-style musicians during the 1960s. Development and production of German fretless zithers has continued to the present day.

BIBLIOGRAPHY

B. Blackley: *The Autoharp Book* (Brisbane, CA, 1983)

A. Michel: *Zithern: Musikinstrumentenmuseum der Universität Leipzig* (Lepzig, 1995)

L. Mühlemann: *Die Zither in der Schweiz* (Bern, 1999)

GREGG MINER

Zither, fretted. Zither of various forms in which the melody strings pass over a fretboard against which they are pressed to produce different pitches. The fretted zither was widely introduced to the American public by Joseph Hauser of the Hauser Family, a group of Tyrolean singers, in the late 1840s. Numerous songs performed by the family were published by Oliver Ditson in Boston, Massachusetts. Sheet music selections published by the company feature a lithograph of the performers, with Joseph Hauser holding a zither. With German emigration to the USA, the number of zither players in the country increased. The zither was played by soldiers of German descent in the Civil War. In Washington, Missouri, Franz Schwarzer—originally from Olmütz, Austria (now Olomouc, Czech Republic)—began manufacturing the instrument to fulfil a growing demand. In the coming decades, Germans were the principal architects for the zither's advancement in the USA.

Since the 1870s zither players established clubs in cities throughout the USA. Maurice Jacobi wrote of his early experiences with a zither club in Philadelphia, Pennsylvania. In May 1877 the Detroit Zither Club was founded. The trend to form zither clubs continued until the years preceding World War I. In Washington, DC, in 1879 Franz Waldecker published *The Zitherplayer*, the first zither newsletter in America. It promoted the art of zither playing and kept players abreast of current events in America and Europe.

In the 1880s Franz Schwarzer continued to expand his business in Missouri. Numerous other American companies also sold branded zithers. These included Franz Waldecker & Co., Washington, DC; Carl Fisher, New York City; Hartmann Bros. & Reinhard, New York City; Lyon & Healy, Chicago; and Wm. Teubner, Baltimore. In 1911 A.W. Schepp wrote to several colleagues and proposed the establishment of a national association of zither players. His idea took hold and in September 1912 the first congress of the American Zither Verband (AZV) was held in Washington, Missouri. But in 1915 the AZV ceased its activities due to the outbreak of World War I and rising anti-German sentiment. Production at the Schwarzer factory, which had peaked in 1893, declined dramatically.

The American Zither Verband reconstituted in 1919, and met again in Washington, Missouri. During this congress, the name of the organization was changed to the United Zither Players of America (UZPA). In 1920 Henry Wormsbacher was elected president. In total, the UZPA held ten zither congresses. The final congress was held in Rochester, New York, in 1937. Although interest in the zither continued to wane, the zither music of Anton Karas, used to score the movie *The Third Man* (1949) created a sensation. The movie popularized the zither and provided a boost to the careers of American zither players.

The last remaining worker at the Schwarzer factory, Albert Hesse, died in the early 1950s and the factory closed. A zither periodical, *The Zither Newsletter*, was published in 1962 in Philadelphia, Pennsylvania, but the effort was short-lived. In 1987 *Zither Newsletter USA* (ZNUSA) was first published in Chicago. ZNUSA is America's longest-running zither periodical and remains in publication. Interest in the zither at the national level was expressed at the National Zither Gathering in April 2008 in Davenport, Iowa. The event marked the largest assemblage of zither players in Davenport since the Second Congress of the American Zither Verband in 1913.

BIBLIOGRAPHY

J. Brandlmeier: *Handbuch der Zither*. T. 1. *Die Geschichte des Instruments und der Kunst des Zitherspiels* (Munich, 1963)

T.M. Davis and F.R. Beinke: 'Franz Schwarzer: Missouri Zither Maker', *Missouri Historical Review*, vol.40/1 (Oct 1965)

A.A.T. Pesavento: *The Concert Zither in America* (diss., Kent State U., 1994)

DAVID J. KYGER/R

Zither harp. Colloquial term for a simple German table-top or lap zither commonly plucked by the thumbs. One group of strings, for the right hand, is tuned to a diatonic scale and used for the melody; a second group, for the left hand, is tuned in several chords and is used for accompaniment. Many varieties were mass-produced in Markneukirchen and elsewhere from the late 19th century to the mid-20th under such brand names as Jubel Töne. They were widely played by children, and the cheapest kind were distributed as premiums by American retailers of other goods.

The term is also used loosely for many other types of zither, including Asian ones.

It is not to be confused with the harp zither.

Zitter (Ger.). Zither or cittern. In Pennsylvania German the term often denotes a *Scheitholt* or related type of few-stringed, fretted, or partly fretted box zither of elongated shape, resembling an Appalachian dulcimer or *hommel*. The type was probably introduced by German and Swiss colonists in the 18th century. Alternatively, *zitter* could denote the common cittern or English guitar, played by women from the late 18th century into the 19th.

Zitzmann, Johannes (*b* Töpfenmühle bei Gersfeld, Germany, *c*1754; *d* Kassel, Germany, 2 March 1814). German organ and harpsichord builder. Son of a master joiner and carver in Gersfeld, he was trained in that craft, and then as an instrument maker by, among others, one Kliem in Kassel, whose business Zitzmann eventually took over. In 1782 he repaired and installed an organ in Habel, near Tann (Hesse). The following year he was licensed as a harpsichord maker in Kassel, but no harpsichord or clavichord by him is known. In 1784 Zitzmann became a citizen of Kassel and married. In 1788 he repaired and enlarged the organ in Niedergrenzebach bei Ziegenhain (now Schwalmbach, Hesse). In 1790 he built a new organ for Weißenborn, and in 1791 he built another in Lendorf bei Borken. In 1792 Zitzmann completed an organ in Spangenberg that had been begun by Johannes Schlottmann (*b* Heringen (Werra), 30 May 1726; *d* Landau bei Arolsen, 24 April 1795). In 1795 Zitzmann built a new instrument for Welferode, near Homberg (Efze), and in 1796 he moved an organ from Lohne to Heßlar. In 1798 he built a new organ for Wollrode, near Guxhagen, and in 1800 he repaired the organ of the Oberneustädter church in Kassel. Johann Heinrich Völler (1768–1834), one of Zitzmann's pupils, reportedly worked with him from 1789 to about 1799 and in 1800 introduced his Apollonion, a hybrid piano-organ. Zitzmann's son Nikolaus, first of his seven children, seems also to have become an instrument maker; his relationship to the composer of the same name (1813–74), also from Gersfeld, is uncertain.

BIBLIOGRAPHY

H. Fischer and T. Wohnhaas: *Lexikon süddeutscher Orgelbauer* (Wilhelmshaven, 1994)

U. Pape, ed.: *Lexikon norddeutscher Orgelbauer. Band 1, Thüringen und Umgebung* (Berlin, 2009)

LAURENCE LIBIN

Złóbcoki [gęśliki, oktawki]. Small fiddle, usually of the kit type, played in the Tatra Mountains of Poland. It is 50 to 60 cm long, of varying shape, and carved from one piece of wood, apart from the soundtable. It has three or four strings, tuned in 5ths and attached to a tailpiece and to pegs in a normal violin pegbox. The złóbcoki is played solo or with the *basy* (bass fiddle). Its popularity waned in the early 20th century with the increasing dominance of the ordinary violin, but late in the century attempts were made to revive it.

JAN STĘSZEWSKI

Zoebisch, C.A. & Sons. American importer, wholesale and retail dealer, and manufacturer, mainly of brass instruments. Carl August Zoebisch Sr (*c*1800–79), a German immigrant from Neukirchen (born in Meinengen), was a partner of C.F. Martin in Nazareth, Pennsylvania, in the early 1840s and by 1847 was making instruments in New York, where he was joined in business by his sons Carl August Jr (1824–1911), Hermann Ernst (1833–1881), and Bernhard L. (*b* 1836). The family firm won an award for brasses at the 1847 American Institute Fair and displayed brasses and guitars at the 1853 New York Crystal Palace exhibition. In the 1860s Carl Zoebisch Sr and Bernhard reportedly returned to Neukirchen (Markneukirchen after 1858) to operate a family-owned factory, then headed by Carl Jr (Charles), that provided instruments for the New York company. To meet demand from military and civic bands about the time of the Civil War, Zoebisch imported brasses from Markneukirchen and other European sources, and also assembled instruments from imported components. Along with most kinds of band and orchestral instruments the company sold Martin's guitars, zithers, and a range of accessories. The company remained in business at least until 1904. Charles was noted both for his commercial success (he became vice-president of a bank) and for his prominence in the Moravian Church in North America, for which he served as treasurer.

LAURENCE LIBIN

Zogozogo. Tube fiddle of the Sandawe people of central Tanzania; it is probably of Indian origin. It has an open tubular resonator with a pegged-on skin soundtable. Such instruments are found widely under a variety of names throughout East Africa and into the Democratic Republic of the Congo. All have from one to three strings often made of sisal, frontal tuning pegs, and a short, light bow often also strung with sisal. See R. Blench: 'The Morphology and Distribution of Sub-Saharan Musical Instruments of North African, Middle Eastern, and Asian Origin', *Musica Asiatica*, vol.4 (1984), 155–91, esp. 172.

Zokra. Bagpipe of Libya. It has two melody pipes affixed together like those of the double clarinet *magruna*, differing in that each pipe of the zokra has only four fingerholes instead of five. Consequently the entire repertory of the zokra can be performed on the *magruna*, but the reverse is not true. The reeds of the zokra are about twice as long as those of the *magruna*. The bag, which acts as an air reservoir, is made of a whole kidskin with the feet tied. In general, the Libyan zokra resembles the Tunisian *mezwid* bagpipe, although the latter has pipes with five fingerholes rather than four and therefore has features in common with both the Libyan zokra and the *magruna*. (In Tunisia the name *zokra* designates an oboe.)

MONIQUE BRANDILY/R

Žolinė. Oscillating ribbon reed of Lithuania analogous to the Latvian *spiegana*. It is a cylinder of wood, 10 cm long and 1.5 to 2 cm in diameter, with a small lengthwise slit in the upper part. A blade of grass is inserted into the slit and covered with a cut-out wooden strip. When placed horizontally to the lips and blown, a piercing sound is produced. A simpler type of žolinė is a blade of grass or a leaf (of sweet-flag, linden, or birch) pressed between the thumbs and palms of both hands and blown. The žolinė has long been popular, especially among children, who use it to imitate a cock's crow and other bird calls, and also to play simple tunes. The žolinė could be used in ensemble with the accordion and other instruments. It is a seasonal instrument played in spring and summer; in winter the žolinė is replaced by the *tošelė*, an idiophonic interruptive reed made of birch bark.

ARVYDAS KARAŠKA

Zongoră. Romanian term for a kind of guitar in northern Transylvania. At the time of Béla Bartók's research in Maramureş in 1913, this instrument, also called *cobză* or *chitară* in some areas, had only two strings (tuned *d–a*). The strings, unfingered, were struck simultaneously with a plectrum to provide a steady rhythmic pedal irrespective of the nature of the melody played by the violin. Nowadays, the local zongoră has three strings, tuned for example *d–d'–a*, *B–b–f♯*, or *e–c♯'–a*, and the *zongoraş* (guitar player) changes the tuning in order to fit the melody being accompanied. See T. Alexandru: *Instrumentele Muzicale ale Poporului Romín* (Bucharest, 1956), 121 only.

Zoomorphism. Imitation or representation of animal forms in instrument design. Included under this heading is anthropomorphism, referring to human body forms. Zoomorphism appears in all areas of material culture, but sound adds an important dimension to the practice. Musical instruments of many kinds can be made to resemble animals or humans, or parts of them. These forms serve decorative, symbolic, magical, acoustical, structural, and other purposes. Worldwide since prehistory, many instruments, especially those used in rituals, have been constructed of animal parts or whole animals, or made in the shapes of animals, deities, or monsters whose 'voices' and powers the instruments evoke. Animal components such as hollowed horns, bones, and shells lend themselves readily to instrument fabrication, so it is not surprising that recognizable cattle and goat horns (the latter for the *shofar*), sea-shells (in the *sankh*), armadillo bodies (in the *charango*), turtle and tortoise carapaces (in Iroquois rattles, some North African lutes, and the ancient *chelys*), ostrich egg shells (in some late 19th-century sitars), and many other animal elements have been employed to produce sound or as resonators, often conferring such attributes as physical prowess and fertility. The *Bock* (Ger.: 'goat') traditionally has a hairy skin bag mounted with a carved goat head, emphasizing this bagpipe's lusty, rustic associations. In Tibet, human crania (joined to form the *thod-rnga* drum) and leg bones (forming the *rkang-gling* trumpet) have served as lamaistic noisemakers.

Mimicry occurs when wood, metal, ceramic, and other non-zoogenic materials are crafted into representational instruments, either as substitutes for unavailable animal parts or to improve upon them by being more durable, more efficacious, or more easily shaped to produce desired sounds. These forms can be somewhat lifelike (e.g. Moche and Khmer ceramic conch horns; ubiquitous ceramic whistles in the shapes of birds and other animals; the peacock-inspired *mayuri vina* or *ta'us* associated with the Hindu goddess Sarasvati; the crocodilian *mi-gyaung*; and the fish-shaped *cavaco* produced by the 19th-century luthier Augusto M. da Costa of Funchal, Madeira) or highly abstract (African whistles of humanoid form with arms akimbo; standing slit drums of Malekula which represent giant penises; and the North African *rebab*, which viewed from the back recalls a dolphin but is also associated with the hare, sometimes with a fluffy bunny-tail affixed). Many African cult drums incorporate prominent human features such as breasts or are supported by carved human figures that reinforce the drums' social messages. The *mampongui-nguembo* of the Bembe people in the Democratic Republic of the Congo is the 'father' of a family of anthropoid trumpets that also includes the mother, daughter, and son. Colourfully painted Northwest Coast (USA) shaman rattles commonly embody the forms of sacred beings or totems. The mythical phoenix lent its form in flight to the ancient *paixiao*, and nesting, to the *sheng*, whose sound was likened to the phoenix's cry. Flutes in many cultures are considered phallic, and bells considered womb-like, by virtue of their shapes and, sometimes, the connotations of their sounds.

Significant animal forms can appear on instruments as good-luck or apotropaic tokens (e.g. the bat typically carved atop the pegbox of the *yueqin* and its relatives; the elephant head of Ganesh, Hindu patron of performing arts, on the *vīṇā*; and the bull's head on Sumerian lyres), though this protective function is often forgotten. The original meanings of carved human- or animal-head finials found on many instruments from African and New Guinean slit drums and side-blown horns to European viols (recalling figureheads on sailing ships), can be obscure and might have changed over time. More obvious is the visual appeal of bird calls and other sounding lures or toys that resemble the animals they are meant to attract or imitate. Some Baroque recorders have a face carved on the mouthpiece, and ivory horns known as oliphants often bear decorative carvings of human and animal figures. European 19th-century brasses with fanciful dragon-head bells, some incorporating wagging tongues, were appropriate for festive parade bands. A unique 16th-century set of dragon-like *Tartölten* (in *A.W.km*) might have been played in a theatre; other zoomorphic musical props, almost all lost, appear in depictions of Renaissance entertainments.

Sometimes an instrument's zoomorphism has become so disguised that only nomenclature discloses the animal source. For example, the violin's neck, waist, bouts, belly, back, tail, saddle, and other terms collectively point to ancient equine symbolism, explicit in the Mongolian *morin khuur* and related folk fiddles that bear a carved horse head or entire miniature steed atop the neck; these bowed instruments evidently originated among Asiatic nomads to whom horses were sacred. Gut or horsehair strings, horsehair bows, and skin soundtables underscore this animal connection. However, nomenclature can deceive: the toe, foot, mouth, lips, ears, and body of an organ pipe do not indicate anthropomorphic design, even though human or grotesque faces sometimes decorate the mouth area of Spanish and Mexican Baroque organ pipes. Resemblances that give rise to descriptive names such as *Flügel* (Ger.: 'wing') for a grand piano and 'serpent' for the eponymous aerophone are likewise coincidental, as is the poetic likeness of a lute's vaulted back to a woman's pregnant belly. But reference to the human body is explicit in the carved faces and nipples embellishing a *lira da braccio* by Giovanni d'Andrea (1511; in *A.W.km*). Irish Bronze Age *lurs* resemble certain cattle horns (*Bos longifrons* or *brachyceros*, *Bos primigenius*), but no definite connection has been proven. Still, the propensity to view instruments as living beings remains strong especially among performers, who often assign gender and other biological qualities to their instruments.

The sounds of instruments are also often linked to animal, human, or spirit voices. For example, the Belarusian *zhalejka* was once thought to preserve the voice and spirit of a murdered child when it was made of wood from a tree that grew from the child's grave.

BIBLIOGRAPHY

J. Coles: 'Irish Bronze Age Horns and their relations with Northern Europe', *Proceedings of the Prehistoric Society*, vol.29 (1963), 326–56

E. Winternitz: *Musical Instruments and their Symbolism in Western Art* (New York, 1967, 2/1979)

J.-S. Laurenty: 'Anthropomorphism, zoomorphism, and abstraction in the musical instruments of Central Africa', *Sounding Forms: African Musical Instruments*, ed. M.-T. Brincard (New York, 1989), 47–51

P.K. Marsh: *The Horse-Head Fiddle and the Cosmopolitan Reimagination of Tradition in Mongolia* (New York, 2009)

LAURENCE LIBIN

Zorzi, Valentino de (*b* 1837; *d* Florence, Italy, 1916). Italian violin maker. As a youth he enlisted in Garibaldi's army and in 1861 was making army wagons in Bologna. In 1880 he was working as a blacksmith and cabinet maker in Pistoia, where the instrument collector and connoisseur Count Vieri Ganucci Cancellieri encouraged him to take up violin making full-time, relatively late in life. He opened a workshop in Florence on Via del Corso in 1885. His work was awarded medals in Milan (1881), Bologna (1888), Pistoia, Tolone, and Marseilles (1889), and Paris (1890). Zorzi reportedly collaborated with Ferdinando Ferroni but was succeeded after his death by Silvio Vezio Paoletti. One of his followers was Alfeo Battelli.

Zorzi is noted for having invented the 'Contraviolino', a large instrument tuned an octave lower than the violin and played upright in the manner of a cello. He also copied Stradivari's *tenore*. Like other contemporary experimenters, Zorzi was evidently intrigued by the possibility of rationalizing the violin family by introducing new members to fill gaps in range and tone. Some eccentric violins also bear his label. His selection of maple is often highly figured, and he branded his instruments 'V.D.Z.' in various places and signed them often on the belly under the fingerboard.

Zournas. Greek term for the *zūrna* (oboe) played in Macedonia, Thrace, western Roumeli, and Mytilene. As with the *zurna*, the reed is made from river reed (probably *Phragmites australis*), placed on a brass staple with a disc pirouette, and set into a wooden fork inserted into the top of the instrument. The zournas is traditionally played in pairs in some parts of Greece, most commonly in the north, and into Macedonia, with the tenor instrument sustaining a tonic drone while the treble plays the melodic line. The treble is 30 to 40 cm long and the tenor up to 60 cm. The zournas is often accompanied by the *daouli*. In central and southern mainland Greece other names for the zournas are *karamouza* and *pipiza*. In western Roumeli smaller versions are found called *psilá zournádhia*, as short as 22 cm. See F. Anoyanakis: *Greek Popular Musical Instruments* (Athens, 1979, 2/1991), 163–8.

Zuca-truca [bonecos da festada, macacos]. Idiophone of Portugal. It is a set of castanets attached to or disguised as little dolls dressed in traditional costume from northwestern Portugal (Minho). The castanets are placed in pairs along a central tube more than 1 metre long. The tube is held in one hand while the other pulls an internal wire that shakes the castanets. It is mainly used in street performances. In the *brinquinho* of Madeira, the dolls are arranged in three rows on a circular wire frame, with a male and female couple on the top, two couples on the second row, and three on the third row. The *brinquinho* sets the rhythm of traditional street (*brinco*) music, and is compulsory at the regional dance called *bailinho da Madeira*.

PATRÍCIA LOPES BASTOS

Zuchowicz, Dominik James (*b* Winnipeg, MB, 26 March 1949; *d* Ottawa, ON, 8 Feb 2011). Canadian luthier. The son of a Polish-Canadian cabinet maker, Zuchowicz apprenticed as a luthier with James Croft & Son in Winnipeg (1970–74), moving in 1974 to the Winnipeg Folklore Centre, and in 1976 founding the repair shop of the Ottawa Folklore Centre. After a sojourn in Boston (1981–3), where making instruments became a major part of his work alongside restoration, and a period of research supported by the Canada Council, he returned to Ottawa. In 2000 Zuchowicz discontinued restoration except for a few private clients, and instead focused on building new instruments. Working alone, he produced approximately 400 instruments over 40 years: mainly viols, but also historical and modern violins, violas, cellos (often four- to five-string convertibles), a few historical keyboard instruments, guitars, one arpeggione, one lirone, and, early in his career, various folk instruments (hurdy-gurdies, dulcimers, and bodhrans).

Zuchowicz specialized in violones, which attracted his interest due to their wide variety of form, function, and tone quality. He chose his models for their richness and roundness of tone rather than penetrating volume, for example preferring the large, broad (uncut) cellos of Mateo Goffriller and Domenico Montagnana and the smaller cellos of Andrea Castagnieri to the more commonly used forms of Stradivari. All his viol models followed the principles of national historical styles; he abjured strictly copying any maker's work, rather extrapolating principles to his own application. Not a player of bowed strings, he depended on his wife, Barbara, a gambist and cellist, to evaluate the playing qualities of his instruments. Together they developed a keen interest in the social context of historical instruments and how this context influenced their forms.

In 1975 he sold his first bowed string instrument, a treble viol, to York University (Toronto). Since then his instruments have been played and owned by professional musicians in major early music ensembles across North America and Europe, and are in the collections of the Canadian Museum of Civilization, The Juilliard School, and numerous universities. In the USA, these include the University of Connecticut, Harvard University, Johns Hopkins University, Texas Christian University, and Grinnell College; in Canada, they include Carleton University, McGill University, Université de Montréal, and the University of Western Ontario.

Barbara Zuchowicz collaborated professionally with her husband throughout his career, in 2011 initiating an online database of Zuchowicz's oeuvre. After his death, his final instrument (labelled 18 Dec 2010) was completed under the supervision of Peter Tourin.

BIBLIOGRAPHY
C. Bégin: *Opus: The Making of Musical Instruments in Canada*, Canadian Museum of Civilization (Hull, Quebec, 1992) [exhibition catalogue]
K. James: 'Dominik Zuchowicz', *The Encyclopedia of Music in Canada* (Ottawa, 2001–) <http://www.thecanadianencyclopedia.com/articles/emc/dominik-zuchowicz>

BARBARA ZUCHOWICZ

Zuckermann, Wolfgang Joachim [Wallace] (*b* Berlin, Germany, 11 Oct 1922). American harpsichord maker and developer of the kit harpsichord, of German birth. He came to the USA in 1938, studied psychology at Queens College, New York (BA 1949), and continued with postgraduate work. But his musical interests led him to study piano technology. He was never apprenticed to a harpsichord builder, but, having to deal with harpsichords in the course of his work as a piano technician, he determined in 1954 to build one for use in amateur chamber music playing, in which he participated as a cellist. It was a simplified one-manual model with straight slanted side and no claim to historical authenticity. He continued to produce similar harpsichords, which found a ready market; the keyboards were made by a piano action factory but he made the jacks himself. His workshop on 14th Street in Manhattan was destroyed by fire in 1958 but he soon opened another, on Christopher Street in Greenwich Village, where he employed a cabinetmaker as assistant. In 1960 he introduced a kit version in response to the evident demand for a basic inexpensive harpsichord. The pre-packaged kit, with plywood soundboard, one set of strings, and a range of A'–f''', was manufactured mainly by a factory in Philadelphia, and by the end of 1969 some 10,000 units had been sold (including about 210 finished instruments). At that time Zuckermann's staff of ten included his younger brother as manager of kit supplies. A clavichord and a spinet, both in kit form, were also developed and marketed, but were not nearly as successful as the slant-side harpsichord.

In 1969, as a result of an extensive European trip, Zuckermann produced a book, *The Modern Harpsichord: Twentieth-Century Instruments and Their Makers*, that was a shopping guide strongly biased towards the more historically orientated instruments just coming into favour. He subsequently sold his New York enterprise, Zuckermann Harpsichords, to David Jacques Way (who had published his book) and moved to England, where until the late 1970s he continued to produce kits both independently and as a consultant to his former company. He wrote a column, 'Sympathetic Vibrations', that appeared regularly in *Harpsichord* magazine from 1968 to 1973. Later he moved to France; in 1994 he founded an English-language bookstore in Avignon, and later assisted Marc Ducornet in establishing The Paris Workshop, a harpsichord-making firm.

Beginning in the 1960s, Zuckermann became known for his political activism. In 1967, he served as chairman of the music committee of the Angry Arts, a group based in New York's Lower East Side that staged shows and exhibits protesting against the Vietnam War. He later became an advocate for environmental causes, themes of which informed two additional books: *End of the Road: the World Car Crisis and How We Can Solve It* (Post Mills, VT, 1991) and *Alice in Underland* (Avignon, 2000).

HOWARD SCHOTT /EDWARD L. KOTTICK /JESSICA L. WOOD

Zuffolo [chiufolo, ciufolo] (It.). In Italy a name for any small duct flute or whistle. It was first described in the 14th century as having two fingerholes and a thumbhole (it thus falls into the normal pattern for three-hole pipes). It was traditionally carved from boxwood and had a conical bore. The narrow compass obtainable from the three fingerholes could be extended to more than two octaves by stopping and half-stopping the bell with the palm of the hand, and by overblowing. In Sicily the term applies to a larger duct flute with a wide-beak mouthpiece and six fingerholes.

A larger, much improved zuffolo (lowest note c') appeared during the early 17th century. This was also called *flautino* and *flauto piccolo* in works by Monteverdi, Praetorius, Schütz, Schein, and Telemann; only Keiser used the original name. The Germanisches Nationalmuseum in Nuremberg houses a few three-hole duct flutes, some with f' as the lowest note; instruments such as these were also referred to as *flautino*, *flauto piccolo*, and even *flautino piccolo* by Schein, Telemann, and Schürmann, although Keiser again retained the term zuffolo. The existence of similarly constructed instruments at different pitches might explain the varied ranges found in Keiser's opera scores: *Croesus* (1711 and 1730) and *Jodelet* (1726) both have solo passages for zuffolo (both occurring in pastoral scenes) with parts extending from a' to d'''; *Tomyris* (1717), however, calls for *traverso* [flute] *o zuffolo*, and the part has a range of g' to e'''.

A zuffolo about 8 cm long was mentioned by Grassineau (*A Musical Dictionary*, 1740/*R*) as being used to teach birds to sing. This instrument was popularized in London by the blind musician Picco in 1856 and, having become known as the Picco pipe, was manufactured as a toy into the 20th century.

There has been much confusion about the 18th-century zuffolo. Bonanni (*Gabinetto armonico*, 1722) described the *ciufolo del villano* as that small shawm (*ciaramella*) which is used in conjunction with the bagpipe (*zampognari*) in the Abruzzi for dancing. This is no reason for concluding, as some have done, that Keiser's zuffolo was a small shawm; indeed he actually imitated the *zampognari* in *Croesus*, using oboes and bassoons. Kleefeld claimed that this zuffolo was neither flageolet nor shawm, but panpipes, basing his view on another item in Bonanni's list (*ciufolo*: panpipes), on Walther's conjecture that *ciufolo pastorale* meant panpipes, and on V.-C. Mahillon's observation that panpipes were sometimes called *zoffolo pastorale* in Lombardy.

BIBLIOGRAPHY

J.G. Walther: *Musicalisches Lexicon, oder Musicalische Bibliothec: Studienausgabe im Neusatz des Textes und der Noten*, ed. Fr. von Ramm (Leipzig, 1732/*R*2001)

V.-C. Mahillon: *Catalogue descriptif & analytique du Musée instrumental du Conservatoire royal de musique de Bruxelles* (Ghent and Brussels, 1880/*R*; vol.1, 2/1893/*R*; vol.2, 2/1909/*R*)

W. Kleefeld: 'Das Orchester der Hamburger Oper 1678–1738', *SIMG*, vol.1/2 (Feb 1900), 219–89

J.H. van der Meer: *Germanisches Nationalmuseum Nürnberg: Wegweiser durch die Sammlung historischer Musikinstrumente* (Nuremberg, 1971)

J.A. FULLER MAITLAND /ANTHONY C. BAINES
/MARY TÉREY-SMITH /R

Zug (Ger.: 'pull'). (1) Slide, as in *Zugposaune* (slide trombone) and *Zugtrompete* (slide trumpet).

(2) A draw-stop on an organ or harpsichord. A *Zugärmchen* is a roller arm; and a *Zugdraht* or *Zugrute* is a pull-down.

Zuleger, Hermann (*b* Graslitz (Kraslice), Bohemia [now Czech Republic], 23 March 1885; *d* Vienna, Austria, 28 Jan 1949). Bohemian woodwind instrument maker, active in Vienna. Zuleger received his professional training in Graslitz and settled in Vienna in 1912. Until 1924 he lived at Albertgasse 12 and Pfeilgasse 26. From 1925 to 1949 he was registered at Phorusgasse 3. In the 1920s he specialized in oboe making and continued the tradition of making Viennese oboes established by Josef Hajek and Karl Stecher in cooperation with the oboist Richard Baumgärtel. He also made english horns in the same style. In the 1920s and 1940s Zuleger intensively studied the design of double-reed instruments by Otto Mönnig. In the early 1940s he restored several historic woodwind from the Kunsthistorisches Museum, Vienna. After Zuleger's death his estate was estimated to be worth 8463 schillings. His widow, Maria (née Kohlert, *b* 25 April 1888; *d* 2nd half of the 20th century), sold the business to Wenzel Schreiber & Söhne of Nauheim, Gross-Gerau. Under the name Zuleger & Co. the workshop was continued by Zuleger's former apprentice Walter Kirchberger until 1999.

Zuleger is noted for adapting the Viennese oboe to the pitch standard defined in 1939, $a'' = 890$ Hz. One such oboe (in *A.W.km*) was formerly played by Hans Kamesch. During Zuleger's lifetime, almost all renowned Austrian oboists as well as musicians in Munich, Sibiu, Riga, and Budapest preferred his oboes.

BIBLIOGRAPHY

M. Nagy: 'Zur Geschichte und Entwicklung der Wiener Holzbläserschule', *Klang und Komponist. Ein Symposion der Wiener Philharmoniker*, ed. O. Biba and W. Schuster (Tutzing, 1992), 263–82

W. Waterhouse: *The New Langwill Index: A Dictionary of Musical Wind-Instrument Makers and Inventors* (London, 1993), 445 only

BEATRIX DARMSTÄDTER

Zumali [nzumari]. Oboe of Arab origin played by Swahili people in the Malindi District, Kenya. The double reed is made of palm leaf and set on a conical staple with a coconut-shell or gourd disc as a pirouette. The staple is placed into a bamboo body about 7.5 cm long with five fingerholes, in turn inserted into a conical bell made from the neck of a gourd. The overall length is about 18 cm. The scale produced is anhemitonic pentatonic: $g\sharp'-b-c\sharp'-d\sharp'-f\sharp'$. See G. Hyslop: 'More Kenyan Musical Instruments', *AfM*, vol.2/2 (1959), 24–8.

Zumare. Double clarinet of northwest Albania and of Albanians in the region of Malësi in Montenegro. The two pipes, with an idioglot cane reed inserted into each, are normally about 13 to 20 cm long, and made from cane, bird bones, or (more recently) metal; they are bound together with wool and wax, and have five parallel fingerholes. A bell of goat or ram's horn is affixed to the ends of the pipes. The zumare is blown using circular breathing. It is primarily a pastoral instrument. See R. Sokoli and P. Miso: 'Zumarja', *Veglat muzikore të popullit shqiptar* [The musical instruments of the Albanian folk] (Tiranë, 1991), 117–20.

ARDIAN AHMEDAJA

Zumbara. Obliquely held end-blown rim-flute of Sudan. Played by nomads, it has two fingerholes and a perforated metal disc that partly closes the distal end. It is about 90 cm long and was originally made from a dried tree root hollowed with a thin piece of hot iron.

Zumbul. Seven-string bow harp of the Kilba (Huba) people of northeastern Nigeria. It has a wooden boat-shaped resonator covered with gazelle skin. The strings are tuned by pegs in the neck and affixed at the other end to a bamboo string-carrier beneath the skin. Although traditionally associated with blacksmiths and formerly played only for death ceremonies or the ritual forging of a heavy iron hammer, the zumbul is nowadays used for general song accompaniment.

Zummāra. Double clarinet of Iraq and Egypt. It has two parallel cane pipes bound together with tarred twine. The idioglot reeds, usually upcut, are each inserted into a short middle piece, which is then inserted into the body. Egyptian instruments are about 30 cm long with six knife-cut or burned fingerholes. The term *zummāra mufrad* refers to an Iraqi clarinet made of reed; it is 16 to 25 cm long, with four or six fingerholes. Both the number of fingerholes and whether they are cut or burned varies in different areas, and in some places the reeds are downcut. With almost all such instruments either one of the two body joints or one of the middle pieces is 2 or 3 mm shorter than the other so as to produce an acoustic beat between their pitches. Normally a pair of spare reeds is attached with twine in case one breaks. The instrument is used by amateurs, mostly children and adolescents. For the Libyan *zummara*, see GHAYṬA. See J. Montagu: *Reed Instruments: an Annotated Catalogue* (Lanham, MD, 2001), 88 only.

JEREMY MONTAGU

Zumpe, Johannes [Johann Christoph] (*b* Fürth, nr Nuremberg, Germany, 14 June 1726; bur. London, England, 5 Dec 1790). English harpsichord and piano maker of German origin. Trained as a cabinet maker, Zumpe arrived in London about 1760. He worked briefly for Burkat Shudi, and married Elizabeth Beeston on 3 Dec 1760 before setting up his own shop 'at the sign of the Golden Guittar' in Princes Street, Hanover Square, in 1761. There he seems to have concentrated on producing English guitars and related fretted instruments (several survive, including a mandora, 1764; now in *GB.G.mag*) before commencing his successful square piano business. Fétis (1851) wrote that his first lessons were on a Zumpe piano of 1762, a questionable date.

Zummāra, probably 19th century. (Edinburgh University Collection of Historic Musical Instruments (377))

Zumpe's pianos were compact, plain in appearance, and of standardized design from about 1767, though they incorporated advances in scaling and construction that distinguish his model from German predecessors. An early Zumpe square, dated 1766 (in *D.S.lw*) has a compass *G'* to *f'''* (lacking *G♯'*) with accidentals divided for enharmonic tuning. Its action is a simplified version of Cristofori's (possibly via Frederick Neubauer, a German piano builder active in London from the late 1750s), and came to be called the 'English single action' because it was principally used in England. This first action had no escapement, but in the 1780s Zumpe developed his 'double action', which included Cristofori's intermediate lever, but still no escapement; this second action was never widely adopted. The 1766 instrument resembles a clavichord, with the wrestpins, for example, located at the right-hand side of the soundboard. On a typical Zumpe square, the soundboard is small, the scaling of the tenor and bass strings restricted, and the bottom G♯ is a dummy key. The hammers are light and small, and the dynamic range not great; tonally also it rather resembles the large 18th-century clavichord, with the same rich harmonic development. Except in his earliest pianos, two hand stops inside the case at the left-hand side of the keyboard raised the dampers in the treble and the bass (the 1766 pianos have only one damper lever). From about 1769, a third stop operated the 'lute': a strip of wood covered with soft leather or cloth raised to press on the strings from below, at a point immediately in front of the nut, damping the upper partials of the vibrating string. Thomas Gray, writing to William Mason in 1767, observed that 'the base is not quite of a piece with the treble, and the higher notes are somewhat dry and sticky: the rest discourse very eloquent musick'. (*See* PIANO for details of Zumpe's action and a fuller discussion of his place among English piano makers.)

Zumpe attracted a distinguished clientele, including the royal family. J.C. Bach evidently acted as an agent in some sales of Zumpe's pianos, which in 1771 cost 18 guineas each. His workshop is said to have been the first in the world devoted exclusively to piano manufacture; output averaged about 50 pianos per year. From 1768 to 24 Sept 1778 Zumpe was in partnership with Gabriel Buntebart (*b* Mecklenburg-Strelitz, 1726); an exceptionally ornate piano of theirs was designed for Catherine the Great by Robert Adam (in *RUS.PA.p*). In 1778 Meincke Meyer joined Zumpe and a square of this year by them is now at the Museo degli Strumenti Musicali, Castello Sforzesco, Milan. In 1782 Frederick and Christian Schoene (also natives of Fürth), who advertised their piano-making firm as 'Successors to Johannes Zumpe', took over the business. Zumpe's will, dated 1784, states that his address was in Queen Charlotte Row in the parish of St Mary-le-Bone, although he seems to have lived in another house that he owned; he had invested in real estate and died a wealthy man, as did Buntebart. Zumpe's design, never patented, was widely copied by builders such as Frederick Beck and Johann Pohlman and thus played a central role in the democratization of the piano.

BIBLIOGRAPHY
W.H. Cole: 'The Early Piano in Britain Reconsidered', *EMc*, vol.14/4 (1986), 563–6
R. Maunder: 'The Earliest English Square Piano?', *GSJ*, vol.42 (Aug 1989), 77–84
M.N. Clinkscale: *Makers of the Piano* (Oxford, 1993–9)
M. Cole: *The Pianoforte in the Classical Era* (Oxford, 1998)
MARGARET CRANMER /R

Zumzuk. End-blown stopped bamboo pipe of the Kagoro people of Nigeria. The one-note pipes are played in consort using hocket technique. The group may comprise eight players with single pipes of different sizes, or eight players each with five pipes of different length. These are held in the left hand and are not fastened together. Encircled by dancers the players move in an inner circle around one or two *bin* cylindrical drums, pausing at intervals to break into song.

Zuoqing ('sitting chime') [qing]. Bowl-shaped resting bell of the Han Chinese. The bell is hammered out of bronze and constructed in various sizes, medium-sized instruments ranging from 10 to 15 cm in diameter. The zuoqing rests on a cushion and is struck at the rim with a padded beater. A 9th-century Buddhist bell (24 cm in diameter, 19 cm deep) found in a Tang dynasty site is one of earliest of this type reported. The scholar Chen Yang, in his treatise *Yueshu* (*c*1100), called this type a bronze bowl (*tongbo*) but the name *zuoqing* (or *qing*) is now most common. Used in Buddhist temples, the bell is usually paired with a *muyu* ('wooden fish') of a similar size, and struck to punctuate the chanting of monks and nuns. See Liu Dongsheng and others, eds.: *Zhongguo yueqi tujian* [Pictorial guide to Chinese instruments] (Ji'nan, 1992), 85 only.

ALAN R. THRASHER

Zupfgeige (Ger.: 'plucked fiddle'). Colloquial term formerly applied indiscriminately to various plucked string instruments, including the guitar and (as *grosse Zupfgeige*) the harp. The term is seldom used nowadays.

Zupu. End-blown gourd horn of the Sere people in the Uele region, Democratic Republic of the Congo. It is bulbous and about 35 cm long. See J.-S. Laurenty: *Systématique des aérophones de l'Afrique centrale* (Tervuren, 1974), 11.

FERDINAND J. DE HEN

Zurla. Oboe of Macedonia and south Serbia, related to the Arab *zūrnā*. It is made in two sizes, the smaller up to 35 cm long, and the larger up to 60 cm. The body of the instrument is made in one piece of maple, ash, or plum wood. The reed, made of cane, is affixed onto a short metal staple, which is attached to a short, wooden forked pipe inserted into the main bore. The fork forms a stepped cone, which renders the cylindrically bored body effectively an expanding bore. Thus it overblows octaves, instead of 12ths, without the necessity of reaming a conical bore. Both sizes have six fingerholes and a thumbhole. The smaller zurla has two vents on the bell at the front and one on each side, the larger has three in front and two at one side. The reed requires considerable air pressure but produces a loud sound. Circular breathing is normally used. Zurle are usually played in pairs, either two small or two large, never one of each size; one plays the melody and the other accompanies with a drone. A large drum (*tapan* or *goc*) provides rhythmic accompaniment. Such trios are popular at village celebrations, fairs, or weddings among both Serbian and Albanian populations. Small zurle are more common in Kosovo and northern Macedonia, and large in central Macedonia.

BIBLIOGRAPHY

B. Širola: *Sopile i zurle* [Sopile and zurle] (Zagreb, 1932)
J. Montagu: 'The Forked Shawm: an Ingenious Invention', *YTM*, vol.29 (1997), 74–9

RADMILA PETROVIĆ /ZDRAVKO BLAŽEKOVIĆ

Zūrnā. Folk oboe (shawm) of the Arab world, West and Central Asia, Turkey, southeastern Europe, and parts of North Africa. It takes many forms but is most commonly a conical wooden tube 30 to 45 cm long or occasionally up to 60 cm, played with a double reed, usually with a pirouette.

1. Term and distribution. 2. History. 3. Structure. 4. Performance.

1. TERM AND DISTRIBUTION. The instrument is widely distributed under various closely related names: in Iraq, Syria, Turkey, Armenia, Dagestan, Azerbaijan, and to a lesser extent Georgia (zūrnā, with or without diacriticals); in northern Greece and Bulgaria (*zournas*); in Macedonia and former southern Yugoslavia (*zurla*); in Albania (*surle*) and Romania (*surla*); in Uzbekistan, Tajikistan, and Kyrgyzstan (*surnāy*); in Kuwait and the United Arab Emirates (*ṣurnāy*); in Kashmir and Rajasthan (*surnāī*); in Iran and Afghanistan (*sornā*); and in Pakistan (*sūrnā*, but more usually *śahnāī*). The instrument is also found in North Africa, although terminology is more varied: Tunisia (*zukra*) and Algeria (sometimes zūrnā, but more generally *raita*). The *ghayṭa/raita* of Morocco, Algeria,

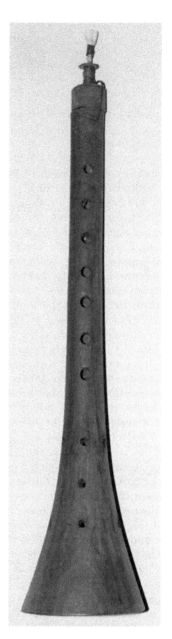

Zūrnā, shawm, Turkey. (Aurelia W. Hartenberger, EdD)

and Libya and the *mizmār* of Egypt are essentially the same instrument. Different but related forms of shawm are widely distributed in India (*śahnāī*), Ladakh (*sur-na*), Sumatra and West Malaysia (*sarunai*), China (*suona*, often popularly called *laba*) and Inner Asia (Tibetan *rgya-gling*; Mongolian *bishgüür*), and eastern Algeria. Sizes vary by region: in Uzbekistan the Khorezm type is larger than that of Tashkent.

2. HISTORY. The instrument now known by these names became established after the advent of Islam (7th century). Its wide diffusion relates to the expansion of Islamic culture. During the pre-Islamic period, types of aerophone with a reed existed in Mesopotamia, North Africa, and Arabia; the *ṣūr* is mentioned in the Qur'an as an aerophone and in the *ḥadīth* (traditions of the

Prophet Muhammad). In classical Arabic texts the names are *surnā* and *surnāy*; the later use of 'z' is due to Ottoman influence. The instrument was probably a synthesis of types from Iran, Mesopotamia, Syria, and Asia Minor, introduced into military bands and spread into newly conquered areas. During the Ottoman period the zurna spread westwards into Europe in the *mehter* janissary bands. A related type of ensemble known as *naqqārakhāna* was used for royal, ceremonial, civic, or military music in West and Central Asia, the Indian subcontinent, Malaysia, and Sumatra. The *suona* arrived in China probably during the 14th century, perhaps from Central Asia.

Nowadays, the zūrnā (apart from the Moroccan *ghayṭa*) survives only in very small ensembles consisting of a double-headed drum called *ṭabl* (Arab), *dohol* (Iranian), or *davul* (Turkish) and a zūrnā; of a *ṭabl*, *dohol*, or *davul* and two zūrnās playing either in unison or with one zūrnā maintaining the drone; or of one or more drums and three zūrnās (Kashmir, Egypt), two of the latter acting as drones. In Algeria (the Aures Mountains), the zūrnā may be accompanied by a *darabukka* (goblet drum) and *bendīr* (frame drum). There are also three different sizes: large, whence *kaba zurna* in Turkey or *ghalīz* (the thick or strong one) in Morocco; normal, zūrnā, or *orta zurna* in Turkey; and small, *cura zurna* in Turkey, *narwija* in Iraq, and *pipiza* in Greece. Generally the large size acts as a drone, but the reverse may be the case, as in Macedonia, where the drone falls to the *cura zurna*.

3. STRUCTURE. The zūrnā has four parts: the reed, the staple, the pirouette, and the flared body; in many areas there is a fifth part, the fork (*nâzik* in Turkey). The reed, made by the performer, is of a flattened stalk of vegetable matter, a trimmed piece of reed pipe, a straw, maize, or barley stalk, or in Turkey and neighbouring areas from an aquatic grass. It looks like a tiny double hand-fan nearly 2 cm long, drawn together to form a waist by a string or wire binding so that the circular distal end will fit on to a short metal tube (the staple); the performer changes the reed frequently.

The whole reed and the upper part of the staple, down to the pirouette, are held in the musician's mouth, and his lips press on the staple and against the pirouette. Over the former Ottoman Empire, through to Morocco and into Central Asia, all such shawms have the staple set into the top of a wooden fork, from 5 to 12 cm long, which extends into the top of the body. The fork has a short cylindrical bore, followed by a wider section opposite the uppermost fingerhole, another section still wider opposite the thumbhole, and finally a short cone into the body, thus forming a stepped cone, which makes the cylindrically bored body in effect an expanding bore. Thus it overblows octaves, instead of 12ths, without the necessity of reaming a conical bore.

The pirouette is a small disc of metal (often a coin), wood, ivory, mother-of-pearl, or other material, which lies against the player's lips and facilitates breath control. It is usually about halfway between the reed and the body of the instrument. Models without pirouette are found in Iraq, Tunisia, and Turkey (especially in the janissary band), but the zūrnā usually has one, and this distinguishes it from the *śahnāī*, which does not. Some players say that a pirouette is needed only by those who have false teeth; others, that it prevents the instrument being knocked down the throat of a dancing player if he collides with someone. It is difficult to pinpoint the appearance of the pirouette historically, but in Europe the first evidence of its use comes from illustrations in the 13th-century *Cantigas de Santa Maria*.

The body of the instrument is made of a single conical piece of wood widening towards the end, which is bell-shaped or flared and 6 to 12 cm in diameter. Although many different kinds of wood are used, including woods of the jujube tree, cherry, ebony, walnut, olive, and plum, apricot has become the most common in some areas. The body has seven fingerholes and a thumbhole. An eighth hole, if present, is a vent; there are also extra vents in the bell, never closed, which have been called 'devil's holes' or 'clarity' or 'timbre' holes, which reduce the intensity of higher partials. The body is often covered or ornamented with metal plates, usually made of finely engraved silver, and in Turkey especially may be further ornamented. Azerbaijani instruments are often enamelled and ornamented with lazurite and metal or silver rings.

4. PERFORMANCE. The compass of the zūrnā is about one and a half to two octaves, depending on the model; the upper register tends to be shrill. The player rarely uses the instrument's full compass. Chromatic notes can be obtained by partly opening the fingerholes. Players in all areas use circular breathing, which calls for the player to blow while breathing continuously. The instrument is physically strenuous to play.

The zūrnā is an outdoor instrument, bright, powerful, and brilliant in tone. It has sometimes been considered strident and unpleasant. It has been used for a variety of functions: in military bands; for funeral music (a use surviving in Armenia and Sri Lanka); at the reception of a notable person; at the beginning of a pilgrimage; on sentry duty; in the *naubat* band (a survival recorded in Meshed, Iran, and in the Indies); at the annual celebrations of the flooding of the Nile and for the ceremonial opening of the Cairo canal; at circumcisions; for escorting a cadi, pasha, or sultan to Friday prayers; on a foreigner's conversion to Islam; and at animal fights. In most areas the instrument is now confined to festive outdoor music, usually played in small ensembles (often two shawms and one or more drums) or simply as a duo of shawm and drum. The accompanying drum is usually the double-headed cylindrical *dohol* (Iran and Central Asia), *davul* (Turkey and southeastern Europe), or *ṭabl* (Arab world). Sometimes there are two or three shawms in an ensemble (as in Kashmir and Egypt). Two may play in unison, or one may maintain a drone. Within an ensemble there may be different sizes, for example in Turkey the *kaba zurna*, the *orta zurna*, and the *cura zurna*.

Nowadays the shawm and drum ensemble provides music for such open-air festivities as weddings, dances,

games, competitions, national independence celebrations, festivals, demonstrations, and marches, and it en-
livens communal work such as ditch-digging. At Edirne,
Turkey, it is played during the wrestling festival; each
team has its *davul* and zurna ensemble, which uses
a rhythmic code to comment on the various stages of
a bout. When the zurna plays in 3/8 time, the fight is
undecided; when the instrument moves into quadruple time one wrestler is about to lose the match. In
Khorezm, Uzbekistan, the *surnāy* is the main instrument for women musicians as well as men; elsewhere
male players are the norm.

In many regions this instrument is played by members of the lowest social classes. In Turkey (including
southeastern Kurdish areas), Greece, and the Balkans
players are Roma. In Afghanistan barber-musicians play
the *sornā*. Arabs seem to have shown some disinclina-
tion, even aversion, towards playing the instrument. In
Syria it is played by various groups of non-Arabs including Ghorbats, and in the Gulf States the *surnāy* is
the prerogative of Baluchis and Africans.

The Central Asian *sornā/surnāy* reveals connections with the *maqām* system of art music. In western
Afghanistan some pieces bear the names of 'Persian
maqāms' (*maqām-e fārsī*), for example *Now Rūz Sabā*,
Now Rūz 'Arab, *Shur*, *Chahārgāh*, *Zāoul*, *Dūgāh Ol-
ang*, and *Shahnāz-e Jām*. In Uzbekistan some *mukom*
pieces might have originated from *surnāy* instrumental
versions, for instance *Surnāy Manosy*, *Surnāy Dugohi*,
Surnāy Munojāty, and *Surnāy Iroki*. Uzbekistan has
three different regional schools of playing: Khorezm,
Ferghana, and Tashkent.

BIBLIOGRAPHY

GENERAL

H.G. Farmer: *Historical Facts for the Arabian Musical Influence* (Lon-
don, 1930/*R*1970)
M. Hāfiz: *Tārīkh al-musiqā wal-ghinā' al-'arabī* [History of Arab mu-
sic and song] (Cairo, 1971)
L. Faruqi: *An Annotated Glossary of Arabic Musical Terms* (Westport,
CT, 1981)
J. Montagu: 'The Forked Shawm: an Ingenious Invention', *YTM*, vol.29
(1997), 74–79

REGIONAL STUDIES

K. Vertkov, G. Blagodatov, and E.Yazovitskaya: *Atlas muzykal'nykh
instrumentov narodov SSSR* [Atlas of musical instruments of the
peoples inhabiting the USSR] (Moscow, 1963, 2/1975 with Eng.
summary)
F. Hoerburger: *Volksmusik in Afghanistan* (Regensburg, 1969), 59
L. Picken: *Folk Musical Instruments of Turkey* (London, 1975)
F. Anoyanakis: *Greek Popular Musical Instruments* (Athens, 1979),
103ff
S. Qassim Hassan: *Les instruments de musique en Irak* (Paris, 1980)
T. Rice: 'The Surla and Tapan Tradition in Yugoslav Macedonia', *GSJ*,
vol.35 (1982), 122–37
V. Atanassov: *Die bulgarischen Volksmusikinstrumente* (Munich,
1983), 195

CHRISTIAN POCHÉ, RAZIA SULTANOVA /JEREMY MONTAGU

Žvangutis (pl. žvangučiai). Pellet bell or crotal of Lithuania. It is spherical or drop-shaped and made of brass
or bronze. A cross-shaped slot is made in one end and
the bell is suspended by a small integral loop at the
other. Most bells found by archaeologists in Lithuania
date from the 11th to the 13th centuries. Several bells,

2 to 6 cm in diameter, were hung on the bridles of soldiers' or noblemen's horses. Smaller ones were worn
as ornaments on women's dresses. Žvangučiai are still
attached to horses' bridles, particularly during various
winter festivals or weddings; a dozen or so bells are
attached to a leather strip and tuned in 2nds or 3rds. It
is nowadays also used by folklore groups. The Latvian
equivalent is *zvārgulis*.

ARVYDAS KARAŠKA/R

Zvans [govju zvans, pulkstens]. Cast and forged metal
bells of Latvia. Small cast bronze bells are known from
the 7th century, found by archaeologists attached to
shawls, belts, and other parts of female costume, usually grouped in threes. The diameter of the opening is
15 to 30 mm, and the clapper in a form of a lamella is
attached inside. Cast church bells are known in Latvia
from the 12th century. The bell was hung in a church
tower or a separate bell tower and rung for ecclesiastic
rites, for special events such as weddings and funerals, and also to sound alarms. The church bells were
thought to offer protection from evil influences.

Forged bells, *govju zvans*, were made of thin folded
brass plates, with riveted edges. A wire with an iron
weight—screw-nuts or similar—was fastened inside.
Such bells were hung around the necks of farm animals
while grazing, especially at night. See Ī. Priedīte: *Ko
spēlēja sendienās* [What they played in the olden days]
(Riga, 1983).

VALDIS MUKTUPĀVELS

Zvārgulis [kaukala, treikuls]. Small crotal or pellet bell
of Latvia. It was hollow sphere of iron about 2 to 4 cm
in diameter, with a slot cut down the side and a loose
iron ball placed inside. Such bells were mostly attached
to a leather strap fastened to a harness bracket above a
horse's collar. Called *zvārguļu josta*, they were used on
horse-drawn vehicles to announce the arrival of suitors,
to signal the wedding procession, and to warn drivers
that another vehicle was approaching. Pellet bells were
sometimes worn on a belt by girls of marriageable age.
See Ī. Priedīte: *Ko spēlēja sendienās* [What they played
in the olden days] (Riga, 1983).

VALDIS MUKTUPĀVELS

Žvegla [haloška žvegla]. Transverse flute of Slovenia. It
is made of plum heartwood, unpolished, in nine sizes from about 20 to 52 cm long, with the two longest
flutes made in two parts. Žvegle are pitched at g'', f'',
db'', $c\sharp''$, b', a', g', f', and eb' respectively and each
encompasses two octaves. The cylindrical tube widens
at each end; the upper end is closed. The highest of
the six equidistant fingerholes lies at the centre of the
tube's length. Žvegle are played alone or in pairs or trios of the same size, and with the *trstenke* (panpipe) or
frajtonerca (accordion). From the 18th century to the
second half of the 20th, žvegle were made principally
by the Merc family from Haloze, in Slovenian Styria.
The folk tradition of the Merc family continues in the
same area. See D. Hasl: 'Haloška žvegla', *Tradiciones*

acta institute ethnographiae Slovenorum, vol.4/1975 (Ljubljana, 1977), 89–116.

DARJA KOTER

Žvejų lenta ('fisherman's board'). Percussion beam of Lithuania. It is made of a well-seasoned wooden board 4 to 5 metres long, with no knot-holes or splits (essential for the quality of sound). A block of wood (*kliugis*) is affixed to one end of the board and struck with wooden sticks. When fishing through the ice, fishermen lower the other end of the žvejų lenta through a hole, with the nets fastened to a long pole. They strike the *kliugis* in a characteristic rhythm and sing to lure the fish into the nets.

ARVYDAS KARAŠKA

Zvonce. Bells of Slovakia. There are many forms: *zvonce drevené* (wooden bells), *zvonce liate* (cast metal bells), *plechové zvonce* or *spiežovce* (bells of folded sheet metal), and *zvonce hlinené* (ceramic bells). Herders hang differently tuned bells on their animals so that in rough terrain they can locate them and know which animals are in front, behind, or in the middle of the group. Herders also pay attention to the harmony of the bells and sometimes say that they are 'making a symphony.'

IVAN MAČAK

Zwerchpfeiff (Ger.). Term used broadly for the transverse flute in 16th-century Germany, derived from the Middle High German *twerch* ('cross' or 'transverse'). It occurs in Sebastian Virdung's *Musica getutscht* (1511) with the earliest-known depiction of a cylindrical flute with six fingerholes. A 1578 woodcut attributed to Tobias Stimmer depicts Minerva playing a *Zwerchpfeiff*. In 16th-century sources, the term is synonymous with *Querpfeife* and *Schweizerpfeife*. In the 17th century *Zwerchpfeife* is largely replaced by *Querpfeife* or *traversa*, while *Schweizerpfeife* is reserved for the fife, a narrow-bore variant. See A. Smith: 'Die Renaissance-querflöte und ihre Musik. Ein Beitrag zur Interpretation der Quellen', *Basler Jahrbuch für Historische Musikpraxis*, vol.2 (1978), 9–76.

PETER THALHEIMER

Zygmuntowicz, Samuel (*b* Philadelphia, PA, 1956). American violin maker. He is a son of Polish concentration camp survivors who settled in Philadelphia in 1952. Interested in art and music since boyhood, at age 18 he enrolled in the Violin Making School of America in Salt Lake City, spending one summer working with Carl Becker of Chicago. After graduation Zygmuntowicz worked for five years in the restoration shop of René Morel in New York, then began copying fine old violins on his own, since 1985 in Brooklyn, New York. His copies soon attracted an elite clientele of performers such as Isaac Stern. Gradually Zygmuntowicz introduced elements of his own design into his instruments, mainly copies of Stradivari and Guarneri violins but others as well. Working usually with two assistants, he makes instruments to custom order, normally between six and eight violins a year and sometimes also a cello, with a several-year waiting list. His instruments have won prestigious awards, including double gold medals for tone and workmanship from the Violin Society of America (1980), and two have sold at auction for record-breaking prices. In recent years Zygmuntowicz has experimented with altering the acoustical properties of violins, using a test instrument of his own devising. This work led him to direct the 'Strad3D' project, a collaborative effort involving scientific testing, advanced 3D imaging, and traditional documentation. Zygmuntowicz judges competitions, occasionally lectures about his art, and has written numerous articles, especially for *The Strad*. In 2000 he selected Pierre Lindström as his apprentice. See J. Marchese: *The Violin Maker: Finding a Centuries-Old Tradition in a Brooklyn Workshop* (New York, NY, 2007).

Index

Page numbers in boldface refer to the main entry of a subject. Page numbers in italics refer to illustrations, figures, tables, and examples.

Each musical instrument that is the subject of an article is indexed under its name and its country of origin, as well as under its instrument type. Instrument makers are indexed under their names as well as under the names of the instruments they make. Companies are indexed under the family names, for example, Adler, Oscar, & Co.

roll-playing apparatus of
McTammany for use in, **3**:426
automatic pianos. *See* Pianino
automatic theatre orchestra, **3**:433
Automatic Virtuosa, **3**:474
Automatic Virtuoso, **5**:245
automatophones. *See* mechanical
instruments
Autonomous Scientific-Technical Sector
(ANTES), **4**:506
autopanphones, **1**:153
Autophone, **1**:153, 509
Autophone Co., **1**:153; **3**:752
autophons, **1**:153
of Dawson, **3**:431
of Seytre, **3**:431
Autopianograph, **4**:506
Auto Pneumatic Action Co., **1**:90; **4**:137;
5:304
Auto-Tune, **3**:113
Autotuner, **2**:75
auxeto (auxetophone), **1**:153; **2**:161
Auxiliis, Francesco de, **2**:568
āvaj (āvaja), **1**:153
avallé. See scordatura
avanaddha, **1**:153
AvantGrand, **2**:541
Avatar guitar synthesizer, **1**:93, 131;
2:182; **3**:650
Avery, John, **1**:153, 499
Avid Technology, **1**:95
Ávila, Gabriel de, **1**:101
Avila, Mateo de, **5**:80
Avilés, David Espejo, **3**:464
avim, **1**:324
aviraré (havirare) (panpipe), **1**:154;
5:146
Avnet acquisition of Guild, **2**:490
Avraamov (Krasnokutsky), Arseny
Mikhaylovich, **1**:104, **154–5**;
2:167, 463, 465
on graphic sound, **4**:506
in Leonardo da Vinci Society, **4**:505
sirens used by, **4**:525
sound effects used by, **4**:583
AWB organ, **1**:155; **2**:160; **5**:181
awiraré, **5**:146
awunene. See sekitulege
'Awwād, Ḥannā Ḥajjī al-, **4**:726;
5:130
ax (axe), **1**:155
axatse, **1**:155, *155*. *See also chocalho*
Axelson, Olof, **3**:400
AxHuwiler, Br. Kurt, **3**:400
Axxe, **1**:131
ayacachtli, **1**:156, *156*
ayamegoto, **3**:209
ayání ´agháát´, **1**:53
ayarichi, **1**:156
ayíguí (págugu), **1**:156
Aymara ensemble, **3**:50
Aymard, **3**:75
áyotl, **1**:156, *156*
Ayoyama, **2**:583

azangi (tonglu), **1**:156
Azari, Fedele, **4**:583
aze, **1**:156
Azerbaijan, collections in, **1**:613
Azerbaijan, instruments from
bagpipes (*See ney-e anbān; tulum*)
chordophones (*See rud*)
drums (*See nagara; tebil*)
frame (*See diaff*)
kettledrums (*See gosha nagara*)
fiddles (*See kamāncheh*)
flutes
duct (*See tutek*)
rim-blown (*See ney*)
lutes (*See chogur; saz*)
medieval *erganun*, **2**:238
oboes (*See bālābān*)
rattles (*See kiaman*)
trumpets (*See sheypur*)
āži. See aje
azongo. See akya
āžrags (āža rags, buka rags), **1**:156–7;
5:82
Aztec people, instruments of
bells (*See coyolli*)
bone scrapers (*See omichicahuaztli*)
conch horns (*See atecocoli*)
drums
cylindrical drums (*See huehuetl*)
slit drums, **4**:543 (*See teponaztli*)
horns (*See tepuzquiquiztli*)
percussion idiophones (*See áyotl*)
percussion plaques (*See tetzilácatl*)
rattles (*See ayacachtli; cacalachtli*)
vessel flutes (*See huilacapitztli*)
azuma-ryū nigenkin, **3**:599
azuma-zawari, **4**:488
azusa. See azusayumi
azusayumi, **1**:157
azzarinu. See acciarino
Azzi, P. De, **1**:564

B

baan. See bala (i)
baarpijp, **3**:757
*baba (go weto, go beto, bemu
nggringgo, tinding)*, **2**:514
babakungbu. See babakungu
babakungu (babakungbu), **1**:159
babandal. See canang
babandil, **1**:454
Babar Layar, **2**:385–6
babatoni, **1**:159
Babb, G., **1**:270
babbar garaya. See komo
Babcock, Alpheus, **1**:84, **159–60**; **2**:454;
3:457; **4**:87
at Chickering, **1**:513
Crehore trained by, **1**:712
financial backing from Mackay family,
3:357
at Klemm, **3**:182
Lotz and, **3**:312
Osborne and, **3**:774

overspun string used by, **3**:778
square pianos, **4**:88, 604
Babcock, Appleton & Babcock, **1**:159
Babcock, Lewis, **1**:159, 712; **3**:774
Babcock, William R., **1**:160
babender, **3**:224f
babendil, **3**:224f
Babitz, Sol, **2**:297, *297e*
B.A.B. Organ Company, **1**:218–19
babu
played with
koṃcạkhīm, **3**:195
pāytā, **4**:182
babulá. See bambulá
baby grand, introduction of term, **5**:295
Babylonian drum, **1**:160
baby scratch, **4**:454
Baby-Z, **4**:610
BAC (Bradford Ahlborn Computer
organ), **1**:58
Bacanos, Yorgo, **3**:266
bacchetta. See baton; bow; drumstick
bacchias. See bachas
Bacchylides, **4**:68
Bach (firm), **1**:91
Bach, Carl Philipp Emanuel, **3**:715;
5:203
on *Bebung*, **1**:286
on clavichords, **1**:591
equal temperament, **4**:742
on fingering, **2**:288, *288e*, 289
on playing the piano, **4**:94
on tuning, **5**:300
Bach, Johann Christian
in London, **4**:77
use of Backers piano, **4**:78
Bach, Johann Christoph, **4**:623
Bach, Johann Nikolaus, **1**:43
lute-harpsichord, **3**:339
Stertzing work with, **4**:623
Bach, Johann Sebastian
19th-century revival around, **3**:723
cellos music, **1**:480–1
collection, **1**:609
on Contius' organs, **1**:683
on *corno da tirarsi*, **1**:697–8
Eichentopf and, **2**:137
harpsichord of, **1**:160–1; **4**:288, 291
hautboy music, **3**:627, 629
J.C. Hoffmann and, **2**:680
instruments used by
english horn, **3**:640
oboe da caccia, **3**:639
oboes, **3**:637
organs, **3**:715–17
taille de hautbois, **3**:638
lute-harpsichords in estate of, **3**:339
Michael Mietke (i) recommended by,
3:470
orchestrations of, **3**:23
organ music, **5**:303
on *organo pleno*, **3**:755
organ reform and, **3**:769, 770
organ registration, **4**:281

Beisbarth, Klaus, **1:**58
Béjard, Elie, **1:**493
bekuru, **1:**293; **4:**657
bel, **1:**293
bela, **5:**238. *See* violin
Belar, Herbert, **4:**232
Belarus, instruments from
  accordions (*See* bayan)
  bagpipes (*See* duda)
  bass fiddle (*See* basetlya)
  clarinets (*See* charotka; *pishchik;*
    zhaleyka)
  drums (*See* baraban)
    frame (*See* buben)
  duct flutes (*See* dudka; parnyaty)
  dulcimers (*See* cymbaly)
  fiddles (*See* gudok; skripka)
  hornpipes (*See* zhaleyka)
  hurdy-gurdies (*See* lira (hurdy-
    gurdy))
  piano accordions (*See* garmonik)
  trumpets (*See* truba)
  violins, **5:**237
Belcke, F.A., **5:**73
bele, **1:**293
belebaotuyan. See belembaotuyan
belémban-bátchot. See belembaopachot
belémban-túyan. See belembaotuyan
belembaopachot (belémban-bátchot),
    1:293
belembaotuyan (belémban-túyan,
    belenbaotuyan), **1:**293;
    187
belembaupachot, **3:**78
belembau tuyan. See belembaotuyan
belembautuyan (belémban-túyan,
    belenbaotuyan), **1:**293
Beleton-Elektric-Musik, **4:**103
Belfast Harp Society, **2:**134, 582
Belgium
  collections in, **1:**613–14
  military bands, **1:**201
  patent law, **4:**34
  Romero clarinets in, **4:**333
  violin technique in, **5:**233
Belgium, instruments from
  bagpipes, **1:**172 (*See* chabrette;
    moezelzak (ii))
  board zithers (*See* huibe)
  clappers (*See* Hanske Knap)
  clarinets (*See* moezelzak (i))
  zithers (*See* vlier)
Belgrano, Giovanni, **3:**512
belikan, **1:**293
bell (i). *See* bells
bell (ii) (part of a wind instrument),
    1:306; **5:**86f
  of horns, **2:**695
  pavillon, **4:**40
  timbre and, **1:**404
Bell, Alexander Graham, **2:**163; **4:**246,
    575
Bellarosa, Vittorio, **1:306–7; 5:**231
bell casting. *See also* bellfounders

De diversis artibus on, **4:**762
bell cittern. *See* cithrinchen
bell diapason stop, **3:**757
Bellefoiere, **4:**237
bellesonorereal (bellsonore), **1:307**
bellfounders
  English (*See* Gillett & Johnston; Lewis,
    Thomas Christopher; Taylor &
    Co., John; Whitechapel Bell
    Foundry)
  Flemish (*See* Vanden Gheyn family)
  Russian (*See* Ganusov, Kashpir)
Bell Foundry Museum, **4:**726
bell gamba stop, **3:**757
bell guitterne, **2:**220
bell harp, **1:307**
Belli, Remo D., **4:**295
Bellini, Gentile, **4:**236
Bellini, Luiz, **1:307; 2:**350; **5:**231
Bellini, Vincenzo, **3:**639
bell-lyra (bell-lyre, lyra-glockenspiel),
    1:307–8; 3:315, 343
bell-lyre. *See* bell-lyra
Bellman, C.M., **2:**221
Bellon, J.F.V., **5:**231
Bellon, Wilhelm, **2:**135
Belloneon, **1:**528
belloneon (bellonion), **1:308; 3:**120
Bellori, Giovan Pietro, **1:**370
Bellosio, Anselmo, **1:308,** 490
Bellot, Louis, **2:**528y
bellows, **1:308.** *See also* concussion
    bellows
  in accordion, **1:**5, 8
  box, **3:**685
  in Greek and Roman antiquity,
    3:690
  in Iberian organs, **3:**712–13
  invented by Van Oeckelen, Petrus,
    5:164
  organ
    medieval, **3:**684
    reservoir and feeder, **3:**684, *685f*
    wedge, **3:**684
  soufflet à lanterne, **3:**685
  suction bellows system, **1:**458
bells, **1:293–306.** *See also* cascabel;
    change ringing; clapper;
    cloche; clopot; cowbells; *gara;*
    ghaṇṭā; gobo (i); handbells;
    kengele; kōdōn; malepe;
    mangenengene; mungiri;
    ndualala; ndwala; ôgane;
    pailing; sistro; tubular bells
  acoustics and, in wind instruments,
    1:27
  ancient Egypt, **1:**116
  animal (*See* cencerro)
  ankle (*See* amagedemsi; icirin;
    tindeche; yolum)
  in art music, **1:**303–5
  bellfounding, **1:**301–3
  bell tree (*See* gentorag)
  Biblical instruments, **1:**329

bronze (*See* chong; *t'ŭkchong*)
cast by A. Hildebrandt, **2:**664
church adoption of, **3:**692
clapper (*See* ájá; atang; enkaniká;
    gbessi; gbwini; gshang; gwarje;
    gyengreeng; ikpo; irna; kendo;
    ketelessi; nkanika; okokan;
    umudende; varpelis)
  acoustics, **1:**32–3
  double (*See* ekput; uyara)
clapperless (*See* agogo; alo; atoke;
    banká; binza (ii) (bell); *bongo*
    (ii); *chiningini mongo; cocowa;*
    dawuro; denkenkelen; elondja;
    fanzhong; inkin; konga; kuge;
    kur; kwen; longa; lubembo;
    makembe; m'balah; *njagba-*
    ogene; nkpane; nkwong;
    ogene; pachchalanse; pengling;
    t'ak; ugbom)
  double (*See* arekwa; elolom;
    ganvikpan; gonga; oyara)
clappers as replacements for,
    1:550
closed (*See* crotal)
čuqlajta used instead of, **1:**731
double (*See* gakókwé; kakwumm';
    kpaliga; kpolo; nenbongbo;
    nzoro)
double clapperless (*See* molu)
East African (*See* bilbilla)
Eastern *versus* Western, **1:***296f, 304f*
electric, **3:**40
European techniques and traditions,
    1:303–4
with external beater (*See* ogán;
    okuelé)
forms and methods of sounding,
    1:294
glass bottle (*See* kpandu)
hip (*See* kororai)
history, **1:**298–301
inverted (*See* sun)
iron rods (or bell-staffs) (*See* ijachi)
Japan (*See* bonshō; kin)
Latin American (*See* chilchil;
    chorromón)
leg (*See* kipkurkur; kisengele;
    mangala; shicheyere)
let (*See* tsindeche)
long (*See* mmanga)
mallets for playing instruments in
    (*See* mallet)
in mechanical instruments, **3:**432
medieval (*See also* cymbalum)
metal pellet (*See* badyerereng)
Native American (*See* k'olálk'olál)
occupation hazards with, **3:**646
ove as term for, **3:**777
pellet (*See* coyolli; mbilit; muyang;
    rāmjhol; sokocandu)
priests' bells (*See* jejeneng)
quint tone, **4:**201
resting, **4:**301

buki, **1:430**
bukka, **4:**605
bukkā, **3:**564
buklo. See dudy (i)
Bukovšek, Marijan, **3:**75
buku. See punu
bulá (boula, bébé), **1:430**; **3:**391
bulaktob. See lantoy
bulbing, **1:430**
bul'-bul', **1:430**
bulbultala. See bulbultarang
bulbultarang (bulbultala), **1:430**;
    3:220; **4:**688
buleador, **4:**296
bulgari, **4:**417
Bulgaria
   brass bands, **1:**208
   collections in, **1:**614
Bulgaria, instruments from
   bagpipes, **1:**173–4
   drums
      double-headed (See tapan)
      goblet (See tarabuka)
   fiddles (See gadulka)
   flutes (See kaval; šupelka)
      duct (See duduk (ii); dvoyanka;
         svirka)
   lutes (See tambura (i))
bulgarija, **4:**701
bulgariya. See tambura (i)
bulgarı, **1:**430
buli, **1:**321. See also kalali
Bulitschek, Joseph Ferdinand, **4:**712
Bull, Joannes Petrus, **1:**109, 430–1;
    2:205, 616
Bull, John, **4:**733, 734e
   equal temperament, **4:**737
Bull, Ole, **1:**313; **4:**353; **5:**233
Bull, William, **1:**431
   on bassons, **1:**261
   J. Harris (trumpet maker) apprenticed
      to, **2:**627
   trumpets, **5:**86
Bulletin du Cercle archéologique,
      littéraire & artistique de
      Malines, **3:**550
büllhäfen, **1:**431
bullhorns, **1:**710. See also cow horns
bull lyres, **3:**345
bullroarers, **1:**431, 431–2; **3:**574
   abume, **1:**4; **3:**56
   atuamba, **1:1:**40
   balum, **1:**190
   baranga, **1:**228
   bimbi, **1:**337
   bora, **1:**376
   brūklys, **1:**418
   bui, **1:**429
   buro, **1:**435
   burubush, **1:**436
   burunga, **1:**436
   compared to whizzers, **5:**311
   goingoing, **2:**445
   guēv, **2:**489

gueyoumo, **2:**489
hevehe, **2:**659
húkadlo, **2:**724
imillutaq, **3:**14–15
jata, **3:**69–70; **5:**312
kabara, **3:**93
kani, **3:**109
khabulubulu, **3:**152
kode, **3:**188
kwese, **3:**237
liahan, **3:**282
luvuvu, **3:**340
madúbu, **3:**359
Native American, **3:**577
ngetundo, **3:**592
ngosa, **3:**594
oeoe, **3:**650
oldest surviving, **1:**118
oro, **3:**771
ower-ower, **3:**70, 781; **5:**312
padok, **4:**3
peer boor egah, **4:**48
pūrorohū, **4:**179
rhombos, **4:**306
rofla, **4:**326
sevuvu, **4:**481
sosom, **4:**561
tăngalōp, **4:**709
tarabilla, **4:**716
tiparu, **5:**23
tsinidi'ni', **5:**96–7
umbubu, **5:**140
wuwu, **5:**337
bul me jok, **1:**432
bulo, **1:**432
bulog tangbut, **1:**432
buloh meurindu, **1:**432
buloh peurindu, **2:**420
bulo surik, **1:**432
Bülow, Hans von, **3:**728; **5:**324
Bultitude, Arthur, **4:**725
Bultitude, Arthur Richard, **1:**432–3;
    5:232, 293
bul tyang' apena, **1:**433
bulu, **1:**436; **5:**295
bulumbata. See bolon
bulungudyung, **1:**433; **5:**27
bulu n'ohi. See feta
bulu pārinda, **2:**323
Bulyowsky, Michael, **2:**227; **4:**371
Bumbass, **1:**433; **2:**85, 99; **3:**780. See
      also boembas
bumbol. See zabumba
bumbumbu, **1:**433
bumbung. See serbung
bummädiya (bummändiya), **1:**433
bummändiya. See bummädiya
bumpa, **1:**551, 564
bumpachu, **1:**433
buna. See sac de gemecs
bunanga ensemble, **3:**533; **4:**500
bunchundo. See buchundo
Bund, **1:**433
bunde, **1:**433–4

Bundes Deutscher Orgelbaumeister,
    4:296
bundfrei, **1:**433
Bundy, George M., **2:**203; **4:**464
bundziņas (baubens, bubyns, sietiņš),
    1:434, 536
bunga, **1:**381
bungas (celma bungas) (Latvia), **1:**434
bungas (Cuba), **1:**454
bungkau (turiding), **1:**434; **2:**414
bung'o, **3:**618
Buni, V., **3:**571
Bunting, Christopher, **1:**484
Bunting, Edward, **2:**582; **3:**51, 52–3
Buonanni, Filippo. See Bonanni
    (Buonanni), Filippo
Buonaventura, Juan, **1:**303
Buonaventura, Simon, **1:**303
būq, **1:**434–5; **5:**84, 128. See also ṭūaṭa
būq al-nafīr, **5:**84
burari. See bidi
buray dipay, **1:**435
burburi, **1:**435
Burchell, W.J., **2:**455
Burckhardt, John Lewis, **4:**707
burczybas (mrěczk, mruczek), **1:**435
Burdett, Riley, **4:**271
burdinbarra, **1:**435
büree, **1:**435
Burelli, Gino, **2:**2
Burge, Kenneth, **5:**337
Burgess, David, **4:**56; **5:**231
Burgess, Geoffrey, **4:**322
Burgess, Richard James, **4:**520
Burgett, Gary, **3:**184, 411
Burgett, Kirk, **3:**184, 411
Burgett Brothers, Inc., **3:**414
Burgett Inc., **4:**92
Burghley, R., **3:**151
burgmote horn, **1:**435
Bürgy, Johann Ludwig Wilhelm, **5:**266
Burhardt, Johann Leopold, **4:**610
Burkart Phelan, **2:**336
Burke, Gary, **2:**187
Burke, Father Thomas, **2:**582
Burkhart-Phelan, **4:**156
Burkina Faso, collections in, **1:**614
Burkina Faso, instruments from
   bells (See kur)
   clappers (See zare)
   drums
      cylindrical (See bambam)
      hourglass (See luinsse)
      kettledrums (See bara (i); bendre;
         bwi)
      tubular (See dialle)
      variable-tension hourglass drum
         (See tama)
   harp-lutes (See konchuhun)
   harps (See salan)
   lamellaphones (See kone)
   lutes (See kologo; konde)
   mouth bows (See kankarma)

chakchaga. See shkashek
čhakchē, **3:**470
čhakhē. See jakhē
chak purdang, **1:495**
chakwana, **1:495**
chalemie, **4:**493
chālghī baghdādī ensemble, **3:**85;
    4:379
Challen, **1:495–6**
Challen, Charles, **1:**495
Challen, Charles Hollis, **1:**495
Challen, Frank, **1:**495; **2:**693
Challen, John Duff, **1:**495
Challen, William, **1:**495
Challis, John, **1:**92, **495–6**
    apprentices, **2:**619
        Marcuse, **3:**395
        F. Rutkowski, **4:**358–9
    employer of Dowd, **2:**82
    harpsichords, **2:**619
    historical instruments, **2:**673
    pedal harpsichords, **4:**44
chalumeau, **1:496–8**, 550; **3:**8, 101.
        See also drček; mock trumpet
    clarinets distinguished from, **1:**554
chalumeau register, **1:**553, 555, 558
chalumeau stop, **3:**758
chalybssonans, **1:498**
chamada do carnaval, **1:**551
chambar, **4:**706
chambelona ensemble, **1:**453; **2:**75
chamber flute-orum, **1:498**
Chamberlain, David, **1:**335
Chamberlain, Robert, **5:**310
Chamberlin, **1:498**, 499; **2:**157, 174
Chamberlin, Hal, **3:**163
Chamberlin, Harry, **1:**498
Chamberlin Rhythmate, **2:**466
chamber music
    vibraphones in, **5:**176
    violas in, **5:**210
chamber orchestras, **3:**29, 672, 673
chamber organs (cabinet organ),
        1:498–500
    compared to rumorarmonio, **4:**354
    machine stops on, **3:**356
    as positive, **4:**151
    by Smith, **4:**544
    by Snetzler, **4:**547–8
Chambers, Wendy, **4:**593
Chambille, E., **3:**310
Chambille, G.P., **3:**310
Chambonnières, **2:**601
Chambonnières, J.C., **2:**33
Chamkis, Jerry, **3:**206
Champlain, Eliza Way, **4:**313
chamutanda, **3:**593
chancega. See čháɲčheǧa
Chancenotte, **2:**175
čháɲčheǧa (chancega, cancega), **1:500**
chanchiki. See atarigane
chande, **1:**511
chandi, **1:500**
Chandonuśāsana, **4:**230

chanfona. See zanfona
chang (i) (harp), **1:500**, 511. See also
        jank
chang (ii) (hammered dulcimer), **1:500**
changa, **1:**436
Changdi fu (poem), **5:**341
change ringing, **1:501–2**, 501f
    chimes and, **1:**516
    occupation hazards in, **3:**646
changgo, **1:**502, 502–3; **2:**88, 714
    played with
        chwago, **1:**534
        kyobanggo, **3:**238
        nabal, **3:**559
    similar to kalgo, **3:**103
    technique, **5:**99
changgu. See changgo
changhao, **1:503**; **3:**241
changi, **1:503**; **2:**562
    played with chianuri, **1:**513
    related to cheng, **1:**511
changiri. See atarigane; fusegane
changko'uz, **1:503**
changuri. See chonguri
Chanin, Sara, **2:**739
chanmera. See charumera
channel messages, **3:**467
Chanot family, **1:503–4**; **2:**656
Chanot, Adolphe, **1:**504
Chanot, François, **1:503–4**
    criticized by J.-P. Thibout, **4:**764
    violin, **5:**230
    violin without corners by, **1:**385
    Vuillaume working for, **5:**270
Chanot, Frederick, **5:**267
Chanot, Frederick William, **3:**648
Chanot, Georges, **1:**504; **3:**369; **5:**230
Chanot, Georges-Adolphe, **1:**504
Chanot, Jean-Paul, **1:**504
Chanot, Joseph, **1:**503
Chanot, Joseph-Anthony, **1:**504
chanson de geste
    accompanied by hurdy-gurdy, **2:**729–
        30
    mention of nakers in, **3:**568
Chanson de Roland
    on buisines, **1:**429
    mention of nakers in, **3:**568
    mention of oliphant, **3:**655
Chansons musicales (Attaingnant),
        2:330
chant biphonique (diphonique). See
        overtone-singing
Chant du Monde, Le, **4:**248
chanter. See also bagpipe chanter
    similar to cornamusa, **1:**691
chanterelle, **1:504**
chanters. See chalumeau
Chants d'Auvergne (Canteloube),
        3:641
chanza, **1:**436
chao, **4:**498
chập, **1:504–5**; **2:**6
chapareke, **1:**505; **4:**213

chapay dang veng, **1:505**
chapay tauch, **1:**505
chập choā, **4:**64
chap lek
    in piphat ensemble, **4:**118
    played in mahōrī ensemble, **3:**368
    in thoet thoeng ensemble, **4:**769
Chaplin, Victoria, **1:**701–2
Chapman family, **5:**310
Chapman, Emmett, **1:**505; **2:**587; **3:**38
Chapman stick, **1:**505; **2:**587; **4:**610
Chapman & Symmes, **2:**529
chappa, **1:**278, 354
Chappell, **1:505–6**; **4:**90
    acquisition of Collard & Collard,
        1:606
    Pianino 'glassichord,' **2:**434; **4:**70
Chappell, Arthur, **2:**669
Chappell, Emily, **1:**505
Chappell, Frank, **3:**455
Chappell, Samuel, **1:**505, 710
Chappell, Samuel Arthur, **1:505–6**
Chappell, Thomas Patey, **1:505–6**
Chappell, William, **1:**505, 710
Chappington family, **1:506**
Chappington, Hugh, **1:**506
Chappington, John, **1:**506
Chappington, Ralph, **1:**506
Chappington, Richard, **1:**506
Chappuy, Augustin, **4:**202
chapuo, **3:**425
chap yai, **3:**368; **4:**118
chara (kwacha), **1:506**
charamela, **4:**495. See also charumera
charango, **1:**507, 507; **2:**505
    by C. Pensiamento, **4:**52
    similar to sachaguitarra, **4:**362
Chardon, André, **1:**504, **507**; **5:**232
Chardon, Antoinette, **1:**504
Chardon, Joséphine, **1:**504
Chardon, Marie-Joseph, **1:**504
Chardon, Marie-Joseph Georges, **1:**507
charha. See cāṟā
charka, **1:507–8**, 534
Charlemagne, **3:**691
Charles, Jacques-Alexandre-Céesar,
        3:450
Charleston, Elizabeth, **1:**730
Charlton, Lee, **5:**293
charotka, **1:508**
chārpāra. See chahār pare
Charpentier, Marc-Antoine, **4:**582
charrango, **1:508**
charrasca, **2:**481; **4:**454. See also
        cacharaina
charrasco, **1:508**
chartar, **1:508**; **4:**17
charu. See kuizi
charumera (chanmera, nanbanbue,
        shinabue), **1:508**; **3:**623
Chase, Bill, **5:**90
Chasey Collins, **5:**288
chastigre, **1:508**
chata, **1:508**

as free-reed idiophone, **2:**351
idoglots for (*See* idioglot)
International Jew's Harp Society, **3:**45
organon, **3:**755
overtone-singing and, **3:**778
palm leaf (*See* saga-saga)
played with the triangle, **1:**4
by Scheibler, **4:**422
scores for, **3:**77
use for talking, **4:**692
virtuosi of, **3:**77
jhālā, **5:**189
jhalar. See ghaṛī
jhallarī, **2:**18; **3:**78
jhamalikā (jamidikā), **5:**166
similar to *ānandalaharī,* **1:**98
jhāni, **4:**690
jhanjh (jhani, jhanj, jhan-jhan), **4:**690.
See also tal
jhān-jhān, **4:**690
jhiṅ (ching), **3:**78
jhumjhumī, **2:**426
similar to *jhumrā,* **3:**78
jhumrā, **2:**426; **3:**78
jhyāli (jhyāmṭa, jhurmā), **3:**78–9
played with
khī, **3:**155
kvakhī, **3:**235
jhyāmṭa. See jhyāli
jiaduo, **1:**415
jiagban, **4:**371
jiajian sheng. See sheng
jiangu, **1:**117; **2:**480; **3:**79
similar to *kŏn'go,* **3:**198
jianzipu notation, **4:**193–4, *194,* 195,
196
jiao (chiao), **1:**191. *See also ban*
jiaoluo, **3:**320. *See also luo*
jicara, **4:**200
jícara de agua, **5:**290
jícara de joba (jícara de moyuba, igbá),
3:79; **5:**290
jicarita, **3:**79–80
quinto and, **4:**201
jicotea, **3:**80
jidiga, **3:**80
jidur, **3:**80
jiegu, **5:**342
bangu based on, **1:**222
compared to *kalgo,* **3:**103
Jieshi Diao Youlan (Solitary Orchid
in Stone Tablet Mode) (Qiu
Ming), **4:**194
jifti, **3:**80; **4:**197
jigijigi. See sekitulege
jilawiri (kilawiri), **1:**521; **4:**20
jilel (djillil, dschilil), **3:**80
jimba, **3:**80. *See also dimba; madimba*
Jiménez, Gabriel, **4:**26
Jimi Hendrix Experience (ensemble),
1:211
jimōkṃōk (dimuggemuck), **3:**80
jin, **3:**320
jina. See suona

jindaiko. See ōdaiko
jing erhu, **2:**240
jinghu (ching-hu), **2:**240, 728; **3:**80;
5:35
jingle-ring, **4:**699
jingles, **3:**80–1. *See also greo; jreo
(greo); kanhang; nūpur; paiá;
pantēruva; sonaja*
jingling Johnny. *See* Turkish crescent
jingluo (shouluo), **3:**320
jingo. See dunun
jingon. See junggotan
jingu, **2:**451; **3:**79, 320. *See also dagu*
related to *chin'go,* **1:**518
jingu (drum), **3:**79
jinjeram (ginyeli), **3:**81
jinjimba, **3:**81
jinkoujiao. See suona
Jinyu qinkan ('Journal of the *Qin*
Society of the Contemporary
Yu Region'), **4:**196
jirba. See qirba
jirukiam. See hirukiam
jitterbug. *See* diddley bow
Jiu Tangshu (Old History of the Tang
Dynasty), **2:**484; **5:**360
on *paiban,* **4:**5
jö, **3:**81; **4:**165
Joachim, Christian, **1:**683
Joachim, Joseph
student of David, **5:**233
on vibrato, **5:**235
on violin fingering, **2:**296
Violinschule, **5:**233
Jobin, Emile, **5:**42
Clarke work with, **1:**567
Jobs, Steve, **1:**114
Jobson, Richard, **1:**180
Jocquet, Florent, **4:**480
Jofer, Josepha, **4:**558
joged gamelan, **1:**184
*joget gamelan (gamelan Terengganu,
gamelan Pahang),* **2:**383–4
jogiyā sārangī, **4:**383–4
Johannes de Garlandia
on *giga* and *viella,* **2:**429
on second-mode phonation, **2:**259
Johannes de Grocheio, **2:**277
on gittern, **2:**432
Johannus organ, **2:**160, 171, 195; **3:**81,
372
Johannus Orgelbouw, **3:**81
Johansson, John, **1:**62
Johansson, Nils Petter, **5:**277
John of Trevisa, **3:**679; **4:**731
Johnson family, **3:**247
Johnson, David, **2:**186
Johnson, Eldridge R., **4:**247
Johnson, Frank, **1:**202
Johnson, Janine, **4:**65
Johnson, J.J., **5:**74
Johnson, John, **3:**81, 306
Johnson, Michael, **3:**82
Johnson, Robert A., **1:**182

Johnson, William Allen, **1:**86; **3:**82
employer of
Steere, **4:**615
Stein, **4:**616
Treat, **5:**55
Howard trained by, **2:**715
Johnson, William H., **3:**82
Johnson & Son, **3:**82
John Spencer & Co. *See* Spencer (John
Spencer & Co.)
Johnston, Ben, **3:**464, 466, 467; **4:**29
Johnston, Thomas, **1:**83; **3:**82, 721
Johnston, William, **2:**667
Johnston, William Grieve, **5:**293
Johnstone, Rick, **5:**288
John Taylor & Co., **1:**296; **3:**40
bells by, **1:**303
jointed, **3:**83
joints, **3:**83
Joinville, Jean Sire de, **3:**568
Joly, Nicholas Pierre, **4:**471
joma. See kwashi
jombarde. See eunuch-flute
Jones (organ builder), **3:**741
Jones, Arthur M.
on *antara,* **1:**106
on lamellaphones, **3:**250
on *lira da braccio* playing technique,
3:292
on xylophone, **5:**344
Jones, A.T., **1:**297
Jones, Bassett, **2:**569
Jones, Cameron, **1:**669; **2:**20
Synclavier by, **4:**668
Jones, Christopher, **5:**42
Jones, Eddie "One String," **2:**45
Jones, Edward
on *pib-braich* ('arm pipes'), **4:**104
on pibcorn, **4:**105
on the sturmant, **4:**646
Jones, Howard, **4:**591
Jones, James, **2:**204; **4:**548
Jones, Joe, **1:**701; **2:**96; **3:**83–4
sound sculptures, **4:**591
Jones, John Paul, **1:**211
user of Fairlight CMI, **2:**255
Jones, Lewis, **1:**280
Jones, Nelson, **3:**400
Jones, Ralph, **5:**109
Jones, Richard, **4:**168
Jones, Samuel H., **4:**271
Jones, Spike, **4:**425, 584
Jones, Thomas, **5:**200
Jones, Timothy, **4:**40
Jones W.C., **2:**632
jongar, **3:**84
jongon. See junggotan
jong tiqin, **5:**23
jonkamentótzi, **3:**84
jonkari, **5:**146
jook organ. *See* jukebox
jor, **5:**189
jora, **4:**706
Jordà, Sergi, **4:**233

played with *ḍamaru,* **2:**10

R. Lee Bailey Co., **2:**203

r'liêt, **4:320**

RMI (Rocky Mount Instruments), **1:**72; **4:320**

Electra-Piano, **2:**174

Keyboard Computer KC-I, **2:**179

Keyboard Computer KC-II, **2:**178, 179

Rocksichord, **2:**174

Rock-Si-Chord, **2:**620

rnga, **2:**89, 349; **4:***320,* **320–1**. *See also rebn-gor*

played with

gsbang, **2:**479

rol-mo, **4:**331

rnga-chen, **4:**320

robab (rubab), **4:321**

Robb, **2:**157

Robb, Morse, **2:**167; **5:**293

Robb Wave Organ Co., **5:**293

robe (genggo, ego), **2:**413; **4:321**

robeka, **4:321**

robeko. See robeka

Robert Manning of Brunne, **2:**272

Robert Morley & Co. *See* Morley, Robert, & Co.

Roberts, John, **2:**128, 569

Roberts, Richard, **2:**569

Robertsbridge Codex, **3:**142; **4:**185

Robertson, Hugh, **4:321–2**

Robertson, James, **1:**171

Robertsons of Lude, **3:**53

Robert-Venn School of Luthiery, **2:**128

Robert Wornum & Sons, **5:**332

Robinette, Robert Allan, **4:**359

Robinson, Joel, **1:**562; **3:**280; **4:**339

Bosworth and Hammer and, **1:**380

shawms by, **4:**494

Robinson, Joel Clime, **3:**636; **4:322**

Robinson, Michael, **1:**701

Robinson, Peter, **2:**663

Robinson, Thomas, **3:**335; **4:**674; **5:**199

Robinstein, Anton, **1:**288

Robison, John, **1:**487; **4:**524

Robjohn, Thomas, **2:**310; **3:**648

Robjohn, William, **3:**648

robotic instruments, **4:322–3**

Robson, Charles, **4:**323

Robson, E. & C., **4:**323

Robson, Edmund, **4:**323

Robson, Joseph, **2:**319; **4:**323

Robson, Thomas Joseph F., **2:**319; **4:323**

Robson & Sons, **4:**323

Robustelly (Robostel), Guillaume

pupil of Philippe Le Picard (ii), **3:**275

rocar. See chocalho

Rocca, Angelo, **1:**370

Rocca, Enrico, **3:**436; **4:**324

Rocca, Giuseppe, **4:323–4**

cellos, **1:**481

employed by Pressenda, **4:**163, 164

violins reproduced by Fagnola, **2:**253

Roccatagliata, Tommaso, I, **2:**657

Rochat, **1:**341

Rochberg, George, **4:**322

Rochefoucauld, Maxime de la, **4:**591

Rochette, Jacquelin, **1:**465

rock bands, **1:**193, 210–12

use of Pianet, **4:**70

rockcong music, **3:**218

Rockets, Les, **3:**246

rocking melodeon. *See* lap organ

Rockmore, Clara (Reisenberg), **4:**763–4

rock music

double basses in, **2:**79–80

drum sets in, **2:**96–7

electronic percussion in, **2:**196

historical instruments and recordings of, **2:**674

rockcong, **3:**218

saxophones in, **4:**415

synthesizers and, **2:**183

use of acoustic feedback, **2:**186

Rockobauer, **1:**564

Rock-Si-Chord, **1:**72; **2:**620

Rockstro, Richard Shepherd, **2:**335, 457

experimental keywork, **3:**151

flute designs, **2:**335

used by Rudall, Carte & Co., **4:**353

Rocky Mount Instruments. *See* RMI (Rocky Mount Instruments)

Rocques, Léon, **3:**452

Roda, Joseph, **3:**282

RodBaschet, **2:**2

Rode, Pierre

Méthode de violon, **5:**233

on violin fingering, **2:**296

Rodensteen (Rottenstein-Pock) family, **4:324**

Rodensteen, Gabriel, **4:**324

Rodensteen, Hermann, **4:**324

Rodensteen, Israel, **4:**324

Rodensteen, Raphael, **4:**324

Röder, Johann Michael, **4:324–5**

Roderich Paesold GbR, **4:326**

Rodgers, **2:**171

acquired by

CBS Musical Instruments, **1:**476

Roland, **4:**328

electronic harpsichords, **2:**174

electronic organs, **1:**92

reproduction of authentic organ sound, **2:**171

Rodgers, Jimmie, **5:**361

Rodgers, Joseph, **1:**85

Rodgers, Prent, **3:**462

Rodgers organ, **2:**160; **4:325**

Rodgers Organ Co.

hybrid organs, **2:**172

Rogers organ, **4:**325

Rodgers Organ Instruments LLC, **4:**325

röding, **4:325**

similar to *ata,* **1:**138

rô dinh, **4:325**

Rodriguez family, **4:326**

Rodríguez, Arsenio, **1:**678

Rodríguez, Baltasar, **1:**259; **4:**493

Rodríguez, Francisco, **1:**378

Rodriguez, Luis Emilio, **5:**205, 232

Rodriguez, Melchor, **1:**259; **4:**493

Rodriguez, Miguel, **4:**304

Rodriguez, Rafael, **4:**326

Rodríguez, Santos Hernández, **2:**453

Rodriguez Alamo, José (Pepe), **4:**326

Rodriguez Beneyto, Miguel, **4:**326

Rodriguez Serrano, Miguel (Jr), **4:**326

Rodríquez, Melchor, **1:**178

Roehm, Fred W., **2:**156

roekua, **4:326**

Roelf, Jacob A., **2:**669

Roentgen, David, **3:**167

Roeser, Valentin, **2:**701

Roethinger, **1:**363; **4:326**

Roethinger, André, **4:**326

Roethinger, Edmond-Alexandre, **3:**189; **4:**326

Roethinger, Max, **4:**326

rofla, **4:326**

rog, **4:326**. *See also borija*

Rogeri, Giovanni Battista, **4:326–7**

bass violins, **1:**479

cellos, **1:**481

working for N. Amati, **1:**80

working for Nicolò Amati, **1:**81

Rogeri, Pietro Giacomo, **1:**437; **4:**327

Roger Linn Design, **3:**290

Rogers, **4:327**

acquired by CBS Musical Instruments, **1:**476

production of pianos by, **2:**693

Rogers, Cleveland, **4:**327

Rogers, George, **4:**327

Rogers, George, & Sons, **4:**327; **5:**307

factory shared with Broadwood, **1:**411

Rogers, John, **4:**40

Rogers, Joseph, **4:**327

Rogers, Keith, **4:**474

Rogers, Troy, **4:**323

Rogers Drum Company, **4:327;** **5:**295

Latin Percussion and, **3:**262

Rogers Engblut, **3:**130

Rogertone, **2:**155

rogetten. See racket

Roggendorf, Bernd, **1:**3

Roggero, Orazio, **2:**253

Roggiero, Carlo de, **2:**251

Rognoni, Francesco, **1:**393; **5:**213

on bowing, **1:**395

Rognoni, Riccardo, **1:**392

on tonguing, **5:**33

Rohé & Leavitt, **2:**343

Rohlfs, Thomas, **4:**725

Rohn, Jan Karel, **1:**555

Rohner, Felix, **2:**539

Rohrflöte. *See* chimney flute stop

Rojas, Juan de, **4:**380

rojeh, **4:327**

rojèh, **2:**380

rökel, **3:**424